The Edinburgh Companion to Virginia Woolf and the Arts

INTERNATIONAL ADVISORY GROUP

THE EDINBURGH COMPANION TO VIRGINIA WOOLF AND THE ARTS

EDITED BY MAGGIE HUMM

EDINBURGH UNIVERSITY PRESS

For Alejandro and Isabella

© in this edition, Edinburgh University Press, 2010
© in the individual contributions is retained by the authors

Edinburgh University Press Ltd
22 George Square, Edinburgh

Typeset in 10.5/12.5 Miller Text
by Servis Filmsetting Ltd, Stockport, Cheshire, and
printed and bound in Great Britain by
CPI Antony Rowe, Chippenham and Eastbourne

A CIP record for this book is available from the British Library

ISBN 978 0 7486 3552 8 (hardback)

CONTENTS

CITED EDITIONS OF VIRGINIA WOOLF

Chapters follow the Harcourt Brace editions of Woolf, unless otherwise specified in each chapter's 'Works Cited' or 'Further Reading'.

AROO	*A Room of One's Own*
BA	Leonard Woolf, *Beginning Again: An Autobiography of the Years 1911–1918*
BP	Virginia Woolf, *Books and Portraits*
BTA	*Between the Acts*
CDB	Virginia Woolf, *The Captain's Death Bed and Other Essays*
CE1–4	Virginia Woolf, *Collected Essays*, 1–4 vols
CH	*Virginia Woolf: The Critical Heritage*, ed. Robin Majumdar and Allen McLaurin
CHN 1–24	*Charleston Newsletter*, vols 1–24
CM	*The Charleston Magazine*
CR1	Virginia Woolf, *The Common Reader*
CR2	Virginia Woolf, *The Common Reader, Second Series*
CS	Virginia Woolf, *Congenial Spirits: The Selected Letters of Virginia Woolf*
CW	Virginia Woolf, *Contemporary Writers*
D1–5	Virginia Woolf, *The Diary of Virginia Woolf*, 1–5 vols
DAW	Leonard Woolf, *Downhill All the Way: An Autobiography of the Years 1919–1939*
DM	Virginia Woolf, *The Death of the Moth and Other Essays*
E1–5	Virginia Woolf, *The Essays of Virginia Woolf*, vols 1–5
F	Virginia Woolf, *Flush*
FW	Virginia Woolf, *Freshwater. A Comedy*
G	Leonard Woolf, *Growing: An Autobiography of the Years 1904 to 1911*
GR	Virginia Woolf, *Granite and Rainbow*
HH	Virginia Woolf, *A Haunted House and Other Short Stories*

JNAM	Leonard Woolf, *The Journey not the Arrival Matters: An Autobiography of the Years 1939–1969*
JR	Virginia Woolf, *Jacob's Room*
L1–6	Virginia Woolf, *The Letters of Virginia Woolf*, 1–6 vols
LWL	Leonard Woolf, *The Letters of Leonard Woolf*
M	Virginia Woolf, *The Moment and Other Essays*
MD	Virginia Woolf, *Mrs Dalloway*
MDP	Virginia Woolf, *Mrs Dalloway's Party*
MELYM	Virginia Woolf, *Melymbrosia: An Early Version of the Voyage Out*
MOB	Virginia Woolf, *Moments of Being*
ND	Virginia Woolf, *Night and Day*
O	Virginia Woolf, *Orlando*
P	Virginia Woolf, *The Pargiters*
PA	Virginia Woolf, *A Passionate Apprentice*
PH	Virginia Woolf, *Pointz Hall: The Earlier and Later Typescripts of Between the Acts*
QB1/2	Quentin Bell, *Virginia Woolf: A Biography* (2 vols)
RF	Virginia Woolf, *Roger Fry*
RN	Brenda Silver (ed.), *Virginia Woolf's Reading Notebooks*
S	Leonard Woolf, *Sowing: An Autobiography of the Years 1880–1904*
SF	Virginia Woolf, *The Complete Shorter Fiction of Virginia Woolf*
TG	Virginia Woolf, *Three Guineas*
TTL	Virginia Woolf, *To the Lighthouse*
VO	Virginia Woolf, *The Voyage Out*
VWB	*Virginia Woolf Bulletin* (Virginia Woolf Society of Great Britain)
VWM	*Virginia Woolf Miscellany*
W	Virginia Woolf, *The Waves*
WF	Virginia Woolf, *Women and Fiction*
Y	Virginia Woolf, *The Years*

LIST OF FIGURES AND PLATES

Figures

Plates

Between pages 180 and 181

VIRGINIA WOOLF AND THE ARTS

Maggie Humm

ALTHOUGH VIRGINIA WOOLF famously refused to be painted for the National Portrait Gallery, she believed that art was essential to life.

> From this I reach what I might call a philosophy; at any rate it is a constant idea of mine; that behind the cotton wool is hidden a pattern; that we – I mean all human beings – are connected with this; that the whole world is a work of art; that we are parts of the work of art. (*MOB*: 72)

Art is everywhere and rooted in human values that transcend periods and genres. Woolf says that she felt this 'intuition . . . ever since I saw the flower in the bed by the front door at St Ives' and that art gives her 'the shock-receiving capacity [that] makes me a writer.' Art shapes her writing and creativity. Virginia Woolf's responses to modern artistic cultures are what make her a modernist writer.

Yet if this 'intuition' was a constant feeling from her childhood, the art world itself was rapidly changing. From 1904, when Woolf and her sister Vanessa moved to Bloomsbury, the arts experienced huge cultural shifts, becoming more international, more commercial, and more diverse. While the reasons for such shifts are complex, involving economic, class and gender issues, as well as political events including the First World War, nevertheless Bloomsbury artists and writers made a major contribution. The Bloomsbury group introduced the British public to modern French painting; influenced gallery acquisitions; shaped art publishing and journals; and were themselves pioneering modernist and domestic artists. The pervasive influence on Woolf's artistic ideas was her immediate circle of Bloomsbury painters: Vanessa Bell and friends Duncan Grant and Roger Fry, as well as a visual inheritance from her great-aunt, the Victorian photographer Julia Margaret Cameron. But this important creative ambience interacts with that wider artistic world into which Woolf evolved. In any case, 'Bloomsbury' was never a manifesto-centric movement. While often modest about her artistic knowledge, Woolf was involved in many artistic issues: the tensions between literature and the other arts; the new arts of

1

cinema and photography; cultural debates and events of her period; exhibitions and artistic friendships; the role of gender in art; tensions of high and low cultures, and domestic and high modernisms; and, above all, the significance of ethical and personal experience in art. All these issues are also the artistic themes of her time and of the *Edinburgh Companion*.

Growing into art

In *Three Guineas* Woolf deplores a historic lack of artistic training for women, but her own family provided a stimulating artistic education. Throughout her childhood and adolescence there were frequent family visits to the National Gallery, the Royal Academy exhibitions, as well as to artists. Woolf's childhood home at 22 Hyde Park Gate, was, Woolf noted, painted red and black like a Titian painting and her parents' portraits, by Edward Burne-Jones, G. F. Watts and William Rothenstein, hung on the walls. Vanessa had art lessons with Sir Arthur Cope, at the Royal Academy and the Slade. Although the word 'art' appears only three times in the novel, *To the Lighthouse* captures much of this artistic atmosphere and is an accomplished portrait of an artist – the character Lily Briscoe. 'It strikes me that it [*To the Lighthouse*] might all end with a picture', Woolf thought.[1]

Born into a world of imperial expansion, Woolf also visited exhibitions devoted to European and colonial display. 'We go once a year to Earls Court . . . without any stretch of the imagination one can think oneself in Venice . . . or Constantinople' (*PA*: 179–80). As a married woman, together with Leonard, Woolf continued to visit exhibitions, in particular the 1924–25 British Empire Wembley Exhibition, with 27 million other visitors. Such imagined artistic geographies inform much of Woolf's fiction from *The Voyage Out*. Woolf's diaries and letters contain impressionistic sketches of landscape, weather, architecture, people and exhibitions. 'We bussed to St Pauls, and saw the mosaics . . . and paid a visit to Burlington House – as it is the last day of the Leighton exhibition. They were mostly very ugly' (ibid.: 53). The lack of a Stephen family carriage necessitated frequent journeys by omnibus, and so from childhood, Woolf also acquired a sense of urban space and architecture.

Although in 1903, Woolf abjured 'I am a person of no discrimination in matters of art – I dont even know what I like', she already knew that 'the Watts show is *atrocious*', and a year later, in Venice, thought that 'till you have seen Tintoretto you don't know what paint can do' (*PA*: 196, *L*1: 174, 138). By 1908 Woolf could technically analyse Perugino's frescoes. 'A group stands without relation to the figure of God. They have come together then because their lines & colours are related', and in 1909 in Dresden, Woolf was well aware that a restored Titian was 'scraped . . . to the bone' (*PA*: 392; *L*1: 410). During these years, Woolf acquired a critical eye from perspicacious viewings, and acquired a critical vocabulary from group discussions. In 1905 Vanessa founded the Friday Club to encourage new art and aesthetics. 'We have begun our Bohemian dissipations: tonight Thoby is reading a paper to the Friday Club upon the Decadence of Modern Art' (*L1*: 224–5). Woolf's letters to Vanessa often contain lengthy descriptions of artists and exhibitions. In one letter, in 1918, Woolf described in detail the work of seventeen artists and, in her diaries, tries to analyse what she can learn from art 'only pictures that appeal to my plastic sense of words make me want to have them for still life in my novel' (*D1*: 168).

There are few art books remaining in the Woolfs' personal library, but Woolf certainly read many biographies of artists, including the lives of William Morris, Delacroix and Cézanne, and art critiques such as Ezra Pound's *Gaudier-Brzeska: A Memoir*. Simon Watney suggests that Woolf's initial choice of a tall writing desk, before she began to write on a board on her knees, enabled Woolf to adopt a stance like those of Walter Sickert's figures, and to mimic her painter sister. Of only eight guests at her wedding to Leonard on 10 August 1912, four were artists (Vanessa, Duncan Grant, Roger Fry and Frederick Etchells). Throughout her life, Woolf shared aesthetic ideas with Vanessa and consistently praised Vanessa's art, commissioning from her and from Duncan Grant, textiles, ceramics, paintings, book jackets and painted furniture. In a review of Vanessa's 1930 Cooling Gallery exhibition, Woolf worried about 'this strange painters' world, in which mortality does not enter, and psychology is held at bay', but Vanessa's work was a central stimulus throughout Woolf's life.[2] In 1938 Woolf wrote ecstatically about Vanessa's painting. 'The picture [unidentified] has just been nailed up – its perfectly lovely – What a great artist you are! Everything complete and entire, firm as marble and ravishing as a rainbow. How I wish I were a painter!' (*L6*: 235–6).

The sisters' mutual artistic enthusiasms, and Woolf's own artistic knowledge, are particularly evident in their joint designs for the Woolfs' Hogarth Press dust-jackets. For example, Woolf selected and captioned the illustrations for her novel *Flush* herself, carefully transferring the end-paper illustrations from the first issue to interspaced illustrations for the second issue. Writing to Vanessa in June 1933, Virginia described the exact visual designs needed for *Flush*. 'We should like if possible to have them [Vanessa's four line drawings] bound in on separate pages in the large sized edition . . . you would have to redraw the designs.'[3] Vanessa requested new colours with endpaper 'printed in brown even if the cover is green', and to achieve a fully orchestrated pictorial schema, the Woolfs agreed more illustrations. The Hogarth Press taught Woolf the practicalities of design as well as aesthetics. This one example of the sisters' careful designing, in often minute detail, illustrates how important aesthetics were to both. The collaborations often brought Woolf unforeseen and original ideas for writing. In February 1937 Woolf 'discussed a book of illustrated incidents with Nessa yesterday; we are going to produce 12 lithographs for Xmas, printed by ourselves' and 'I've written this morning 3 descriptions for Nessa's pictures . . . Clearly I have here in the egg a new method of writing criticism' (*D5*: 57–8). Woolf's contemporaneous short fictions 'Portraits' became those new modernist imagistic texts.

Early twentieth-century art

But the British art world, into which the sisters emerged after the move to
Bloomsbury, was much less harmonious. Early twentieth-century art was being
propelled by a new cosmopolitanism, by new mobility, and by capitalist developments in the art trade with burgeoning publications, dealerships, collectors
and galleries: for example, Agnew's, the Courtauld and the New England Club.
There was a proliferation of new artistic 'isms': Post-Impressionism, Futurism,
Vorticism and Cubism. Cinema and photography offered a new, publicly
embraced aesthetics. Connoisseurship was giving way to Roger Fry's more 'scientific' art historical methods, inspired by Giovanni Morelli's scientific positiv-
ism, marking a transition in art history from an anecdotal nineteenth-century
approach to a more methodological history.[4]

The introduction of modern art to the public was not always welcome. While
dealers, such as Paul Durand-Ruel, exhibited French art at the Grafton Gallery
in 1905, following on from Walter Sickert's work with Degas in Dieppe in 1895,
the focus on Cézanne in Roger Fry's Post-Impressionist Exhibition of 1910 startled the art world as much as it startled London society. Woolf was delighted by
Fry's 'intoxication' with Cézanne, agreeing that Cézanne's paintings have 'some
very mysterious quality of potation [sic]. Woolf adopted Cézanne's phrases in
her diary, and revelled in a Bloomsbury analysis of '6 apples in the Cézanne picture. What can 6 apples *not* be'[5] (*D*1: 140–1). Along with Fry's book on Cézanne,
which Woolf thought 'solid in structure and bathed in light', Woolf owned
Ambroise Vollard's un-translated *Paul Cézanne* (1919) and the Wildenstein
catalogue *Homage to Paul Cézanne* (1939) (*RF*: 236). Bloomsbury was instrumental in introducing Cézanne and French art to a sceptical public. In Fry's
studio Duncan Grant seized the catalogue of the 1918 sale of Degas' collection
and persuaded John Maynard Keynes to win a Treasury grant of £20,000 and,
together with Charles Holmes, Director of the National Gallery, to attend the
sale and acquire French art (although Holmes baulked at Cézanne).

Translations added to this burgeoning art scene. In 1910 Fry translated
the painter-theorist Maurice Denis's 'Cézanne' for the *Burlington Magazine*.[6]
Gerald Duckworth, Woolf's half-brother, published translated and illustrated
monographs. Heinemann's pocket-sized books – for example, *Great Engravers*
(1911) – led *The Studio* art journal to claim that modernism, like Bloomsbury
houses, engaged 'architecture, furniture, textiles, pottery, wood-work, metal-
work, fine books, stage designs which will most appropriately benefit from
modernist experimentation'.[7] The *künstlerroman*, or artist-novel, was hugely
popular from du Maurier's *Trilby* (1894), which sold 100,000 copies in the
first three months, through to Woolf's *To the Lighthouse*. Fry continued to
champion French art in the Contemporary Arts Society and, with Clive Bell and
Duncan Grant, through the Allied Arts Association. Fry's summative account of
these unprecedented decades, 'What France Has Given to Art'[8] was broadcast
on the BBC.

British art also enjoyed a renaissance. Stemming in part from Constable's high status in France, there was renewed interest in Constable's work following the donation of *The Haywain* to the National Gallery by Constable's daughter in 1886. Woolf fictionally recreates Constable's landscapes in her first novel *The Voyage Out*, together with a Rousseau-like landscape, and she wrote enthusiastically to Vanessa 'The English I think are far best at landscape; they have a feeling for that; I like Cox and Constable' (*L2*: 260). This mixture of artistically valued English and French art shared a more diverse hinterland early in the twentieth century. Van Dyck's 'swagger' portraits were celebrated in the Royal Academy's 1900 van Dyck exhibition, shaping John Singer Sargent's *Earl of Dalhousie* (1900); and in 1913 a painting by Edward Burne-Jones sold for a record £5,040 (Dunlop 1972). Woolf was wary of retrospective canonisations. Writing to her friend Violet Dickinson in 1904, Woolf claimed 'he [Burne-Jones] seems rather a backboneless charming creature . . . he was *not* a great painter but only a glorified kind of decorator' (*L1*: 169). In spite of her family ties to Burne-Jones, Woolf already has an incipient understanding of what became a systematic modernism in Bloomsbury's publications including Clive Bell's *Art* (1914) and Roger Fry's *Vision and Design* (1920).

Gender and art

If the first decades of the twentieth century reveal disequilibrium between a popular resurgence of interest in the Pre-Raphaelites and a critical turn to continental art there were further imbalances in representation. Women artists were infrequently grouped in 'high art'. Although the Women's International Art Club (1900) had more than 100 members, and the 1901 census listed 3,699 women artists, Roger Fry included no work by women in the first Post-Impressionist Exhibition, although works by Vanessa Bell and six other women were exhibited in the second in 1912 (Tickner 1992). Yet the New Woman was a central figure in turn-of-the-twentieth-century debates about the progress of modernity. Changes in gender relations from 1882, the year of Woolf's birth, to the 1920s, parallel and shape the development of art and modernism. Women were central players in new deployments of city space as participants in suffrage campaigns and in Woolf's urban modernities, for example, *Mrs Dalloway*. Women's urban experiences included the public spheres of art galleries and exhibitions which offered, in tandem with cinema spaces, new modes of collective seeing. Women artists and art critics were also highly visible in art journals, exhibitions and art schools. For example, Duncan Grant took classes with Louise Jopling, who founded an art school. Press Day at the Royal Academy for the annual summer exhibition was modified to enable women to conveniently visit in safer daylight hours, and exhibitions there included more women artists. By 1914 government ministries organising the war effort commissioned several women war artists.

The growing market for art criticism paralleled women's entry into professional journalism and women writers were prominent in both the popular press *Illustrated London News*, and in specialist publications like the *Art Journal* (Clarke 2005). By the turn of the twentieth century there were over thirty women art critics contributing signed articles, with some earning over £400 a year. Established artists, for example, G. F. Watts, cultivated professional relationships with women art critics, and the writers Vernon Lee, Alice Meynell and others joined Woolf's tutor Jane Harrison in regular networking at the Sesame Club. Although Vernon Lee's books, for example, *Studies of the Eighteenth Century in Italy* (1880), are in the Woolfs' library, Woolf declared herself disenchanted with Lee's writing. 'I am sobbing with misery over Vernon Lee, who really turns all good writing to vapour' (*L*1: 320). Yet Woolf places Lee's books, together with Jane Harrison's, on the book shelves of *A Room of One's Own* and calls for greater public prominence for women. Art writing enabled women 'to record a visual engagement with the city', as well as greater professional status (Clarke 2005: 7). Woolf also denigrated Alice Meynell, another successful art critic. '[T]he lady who wore Jaeger, didn't you say, in her bath . . . I'm so delighted to be relieved of the Mrs Meynell claustrophobia' (*L*4: 300, 361). Yet Meynell had defended Mary Wollstonecraft's writings, encouraged the Royal Academy to include more women artists, and bravely praised Degas's *L'Absinthe*, as early as 1882, as well as being as voluminous a writer as Woolf (Clarke 2005). But by 1919, in 'Pictures and Portraits', Woolf was castigating the National Portrait Gallery for not owning a portrait of Harriet Taylor Mill and Woolf always looks at art through a gender lens as this *Companion* reveals.

The representation of women was part of a wider debate, throughout the arts, about public and private patronage, and the role of art institutions, as well as what Roger Fry, mirroring Woolf's common reader, called a 'lay man's aesthetic', in his reference to the generosity of Samuel Courtauld, in the *Burlington Magazine*.[9] At the turn of the century the National Gallery was barred from collecting the work of living artists and the National Gallery Millbank (now Tate Britain), founded in 1897, could not purchase non-British art. It was left to private patrons, like Samuel Courtauld, and commercial dealers to acquire and display international art, for example, the Sackville Gallery's 1912 exhibition of Marinetti's Futurism. The critic Frank Rutter launched the French Impressionists Fund for public acquisitions, and in 1910 Roger Fry, D. S. MacColl, Keeper at the Tate and the Wallace Collection, and Clive Bell founded the Contemporary Arts Society with a similar aim. Bloomsbury artists and writers were never only Francophile avant-gardists. For example, the Omega Workshops owed much to Fry's friendship with C. R. Ashbee, the founder of the Guild of Handicraft. And Bloomsbury saw modern artistic cultures as a more complex continuum including art education (with Roger Fry's championing of the art teacher Marion Richardson and the Omega Workshops), the performance arts of ballet and theatre, and aesthetics.

Early twentieth-century aesthetics

Art theorists offered sophisticated new aesthetic critiques and Woolf learned from these writings as her reviews make clear. For example, Woolf mentions Julius Meier-Graefe, translated by Roger Fry, and his influential work on modern art in her *Nation and Athenaeum* review of Piérard's biography of van Gogh.[10] T. E. Hulme's 1913–14 lectures introduced the philosopher Wilhelm Worringer to London critics including Bloomsbury (Froula 2005). Kandinsky and the Vorticists had drawn on Worringer's idea that contemporary art was turning to abstraction, and Worringer's important belief that art from differing periods and cultures could be similarly evaluated, 'the urge to abstraction stands at the beginning of every art', resembles Roger Fry's analysis of 'primitivism' in Fry's essays on sculpture in *Vision and Design*.[11] Although Woolf at first felt ambivalent about 'Negro carvings at the book club' in 1920, her brother Adrian Stephen collected African sculpture, and Roger Fry gave 'Negro' art a prominent space in the 1910 Post-Impressionist Exhibition, and curated *Negro Sculpture* in 1919 (*L2*: 429). Clive Bell coined the term 'significant form' sharing Worringer's belief in a contemplative viewer, although Worringer, unlike Fry and Bell, dismissed Byzantine art in favour of the 'exalted hysteria' of Gothic architecture.[12]

Woolf's concern with these artistic ideas is a constant theme in her writing including her authorial self-insertion of a 'prolonged dumb gaze' in 'Pictures and Portraits', *Three Guineas*' descriptions of women watching the world of men below them like modernist photographers, and *To the Lighthouse*'s abstract aesthetics (*E3*: 164). In addition there are similarities between what Jane Goldman has called Woolf's 'doorstep model' of aesthetic experience, and other key contemporary theories, for example, Henri Bergson's notion of 'reflective perception'.[13] Although Woolf famously claimed in 1932 'I may say that I have never read Bergson', Bergson was a bestselling philosopher in Britain by 1910, and a framework of Bergsonian thought shapes Duncan Grant's *Abstract Kinetic Collage Painting with Sound* (*L5*: 91). Bergson's view of the mental processes involved in aesthetic sensibility not only informed Woolf's circle, but shaped art practice at the Slade School (attended by Vanessa). Bergson's idea that interactions of past and present could be envisaged spatially and photographically, is realised in Woolf's photographic practice (Humm 2002).

There are profound associations between the aesthetics of philosophers who were significant figures in the early decades of the twentieth century and Woolf's writings. Woolf inhabited an artistic milieu of friends, art historians and philosophers all focused on issues of perception and consciousness, for example, Bertrand Russell's ideas of the Platonic dualism of appearance and reality. The philosopher at the heart of Bloomsbury G. E. Moore, also held that being and perception are distinct categories and that common sense 'reality' should not be favoured over 'diaphanous' sensations'.[14] These ideas provided Woolf with a vocabulary and creative impetus. In Woolf's first novel, *The*

Voyage Out, Helen Ambrose reads G. E. Moore. In Moore's highly influential 'Refutation of Idealism' he argued that 'we can and must conceive that blue might exist and yet the sensation of blue not exist' (Moore 1903: 451). Woolf adopts Moore's ideas in her short story 'Blue and Green'. 'It's night; the needles drip blots of blue. The green's out' (Woolf 2001: 33). Woolf uses colour terms, like Moore, to show the instabilities of perception. While Woolf was writing *The Waves*, Ludwig Wittgenstein responded to Moore by offering a wider conception of perception and ethics in a lecture at the Heretics Society, where Woolf read 'Mr Bennett and Mrs Brown' in 1924.[15]

This twentieth-century conjuncture of art and philosophy drew on earlier art – Moore's brother the artist Sturge Moore was involved in Arts and Crafts printing – as well as earlier aesthetic concepts, in particular from Kant and Walter Pater. G. E. Moore's PhD dissertation was on Kant, and Kant's notion of the free play of aesthetic contemplation informed both the 1910 Post-Impressionist Exhibition and Virginia Woolf's *The Voyage Out*. The Woolfs' library contains four books by Pater, and Woolf thought Pater 'the writer who from words made blue and gold and green' (*E3*: 172–3). Roger Fry was also impressed by Pater's *Miscellaneous Studies*, which the Woolfs owned. But it was Fry himself who was one of Woolf's major aesthetic influences for over two decades.[16] Originally intending to dedicate *To the Lighthouse* to Fry, Woolf knew that 'you have I think kept me on the right path, so far as writing goes, more than anyone' (*L3*: 385).

Woolf's admiration was shared by the general public, 2,500 of whom flocked to hear Fry lecture in the Queen's Hall (Falkenheim 1980). Woolf enjoyed Fry's expertise during their trip to Greece in 1932, following shared discussions about art and literature during the formative years of her visual writings. The art work by Carrington for Woolf's 'The Mark on the Wall' was designed at Fry's Omega Workshop. Woolf sketched Fry's ideas in two unpublished impressionistic essays 'Incongruous Memories' in her June 1930 notebook, and in 'Roger Fry: a Series of Impressions' written while Woolf completed *Walter Sickert* (Bartkevicius 1992). Woolf's high admiration for Fry culminated in her agreeing (with much persuasion by Fry's sisters) to write Fry's biography after his death in 1934. The biography is very revealing of Woolf's own aesthetic values. Rather than extensively analysing Fry's published works (most of which Woolf owned and knew well), Woolf describes attributes of Fry's life and work identical to her own. Fry's room was a muddle of 'old newspaper cuttings' a congenial environment for Woolf who also collected newspaper and other cuttings in scrapbooks (*RF*: 92). Fry writes books, Woolf quoted, by 'dumping old articles into a basket and shaking them up', a phrase recalling Woolf's own idea of throwing papers into a desk while writing (ibid.: 182).

Fry's holistic aesthetic, which included the domestic arts, is shared by Woolf. Above all, Woolf's Fry is a theorist/practitioner, like Woolf herself, creating art for a common viewer. '[H]e was in touch with every kind of idea, and emotion and human being' (*L6*: 305). Woolf admires Fry's preference for 'exhibitions of serious interest' at the New English Art Club over Royal Academy exhibitions, but also that he 'was always discovering . . . someone in some out-of-the-way place who "is really keen about art"' (*RF*: 87, 71–2). Woolf shared Fry's love of landscape as well as his love of natural colour watching 'the sun go down like a red hot ball into the blue sea of the Campagna' (ibid.: 54). Fry wrote to Virginia in November 1928 as if to a fellow artist. 'There's no doubt about your genius . . . I've never doubted its existence. No doubt genius doesn't ensure one against doing a bad work of art, but, all the same there must be a curious security about it' (Fry 1972: 631).

Artistic ethics

Woolf's long involvement with the arts over many decades is striking in its wide range of formal means, subject matter and genres from ballet to cinema as this *Companion* demonstrates. These share key themes: the importance of a common viewer, and of gender differences, and anti-institutionalism, all coalescing in a commitment to an artistic ethics. Many of Woolf's most perceptive comments on art and ethics are in her letters and diaries. Disliking D. H. Lawrence's preaching, Woolf (who hated manifestos), argued for the aesthetic value of everyday writing. 'Art is being rid of all preaching: things in themselves: the sentence in itself beautiful' (*D4*: 126). The gendered conservatism of the artistic establishment was one of Woolf's continuous targets. In 1928 she argued that 'It is probable, however, that both in life and in art the values of a woman are not the values of a man' (*GR*: 81). Part of Woolf's initial attraction to formalism stemmed from a wish to break with the view that women were artistically inferior, and her desire 'to alter the established values' (ibid.).

Woolf's writings contain differing, but specific, ideas about artistic ethics. While a statement like 'beauty is only two fingers'-breadth from goodness' might be misread as a Hegelian notion of spiritual nature, Woolf's artistic ethics is crucially embodied in modernist forms (*E4*: 77). Rhoda, in *The Waves*, might be describing paintings by Vanessa Bell. 'I find faces rid of features, robed in beauty' (*TW*: 107). Like Bell's depiction of the beautiful, maternal, phantasmagoric spaces of Charleston, Woolf also depicts imaginary connections between aesthetics and the domestic arts, for example, Mrs Ramsay's work in *To the Lighthouse*.

'[T]he understanding of art, the enjoyment of art, are among the most profound and enduring pleasures that life has to give' (*M*: 105). This aestheticisation of life is a constant theme in Woolf's writings, while later in life, Woolf's artistic ethics took a more strategic focus. In *Three Guineas*, and in contemporary essays such as 'The Artist and Politics', Woolf aims to save artistic values from the political exigencies that war demands, giving her writings a radical edge. 'The Artist and Politics' argues that the artist is 'forced to take part in politics' for 'his own survival' as well as for 'the survival of his art' (ibid.: 228). Yet Woolf was also hugely optimistic in *Three Guineas* that if we knew 'the truth

. . . about art we should not believe in war, and we should believe in art' (*TG*: 148). *Three Guineas* clarifies Woolf's belief in a democratic art, a 'poor college' for teaching women 'the art of understanding other people's lives . . . and the little arts of talk, of dress, of cookery' to 'People who love learning for itself' with 'directorships of art galleries . . . beyond their reach' (ibid.: 50–1, 152).

This issue of a gendered artistic ethics was closely associated in Woolf's mind with the importance of the domestic arts. Parties, the design of meals, and sewing are all events in which Woolf's characters have crucial epiphanies. It was a quality she had learnt as a child at home watching Vanessa 'meet Thoby in argument, and press on to the very centre of the matter, whether it were question of art or morality' (*MOB*: 54). In *The Voyage Out* men are blind to these aesthetic values. As Helen points out 'You've all been sitting here', she said, 'for almost an hour, and you haven't noticed my figs, or my flowers, or the way the light comes through' (*VO*: 310). In the Omega Workshops Vanessa designed new dress styles, and Virginia herself embroidered Duncan Grant's and his mother's designs for chair covers and wool-working. While the decorative arts are often constructed as modernism's 'Other' by contemporary art historians, Bloomsbury refused to separate the domestic from the avant-garde (Gronberg 1992).

Virginia and Vanessa also belonged to the first generation of women to be active photographers and cinema-goers from childhood. The sisters took, developed, and mounted in albums hundreds of photographs throughout their lives and these photographs display a range of artistic styles (Humm 2002). In *To the Lighthouse*, Lily describes Mrs Ramsay as a life photograph. The technological aesthetics of sound and film were as crucial to Woolf as they were to her cultural moment. In her diaries Woolf enthuses about Picture Palaces and saw the premier of *Wuthering Heights*, the gramophone plays a central role in *Between the Acts*, and Woolf's essay 'The Cinema' was the first British essay on avant-garde cinema. Where Clive Bell praised *The Cabinet of Dr. Caligari*'s 'aesthetic intention', Woolf makes a knowledgeable analysis of film's technical features including close-up and montage.[17] Woolf's narrative techniques, particularly in *Orlando*, mimic cinematic processes of editing and shot-reaction-shot but, more radically, Woolf understands how cinema, for the first time in the arts, offered modernism a sense of constitutive absence (Trotter 2007). 'We behold them [people and objects] as they are when we are not there' (*E4*: 349).

Further intellectual and artistic influences

That sense of the permeability of cultural hierarchies and of a useful aesthetics, Woolf undoubtedly learned from her tutor Jane Harrison the cultural anthropologist. There is a strong intellectual continuity between Harrison's belief in the social and ethical importance of art, her re-vitalisation of female figures, and address to the common reader, and Woolf's aesthetics. The ties between Harrison, Woolf, Fry and D. S. MacColl, Tate Keeper, and close friend of Harrison and Fry, are crucial threads in Bloomsbury's artistic tissue. MacColl, who accompanied Harrison on anthropological trips to Greece in 1888, believed that 'art means simply a way of making and doing things' and that the arts could range from 'swimming to writing an epic'. Woolf owned MacColl's *Confessions of a Keeper* and a letter sketches one of Woolf's apocryphal London Library encounters with Mrs MacColl.[18] Woolf was taught by Harrison, owned Harrison's books, and *A Room of One's Own* draws on Harrison's Cambridge memoirs. *The Years* recreates Harrison's ideas of matriarchy and myth. Harrison's writings about the lost moments of Greek drama inform *Between the Acts*, which shares Harrison's belief in the centrality of the female principle. Roger Fry's move to art history, away from his undergraduate scientific training, was stimulated by attending Harrison's lectures. That intimate connection between art, collective drama and everyday life was a continual theme in Woolf's life, including the Bell children's theatricals, Woolf's play *Freshwater*, and visits to theatre and ballet, for example, *Pomona* (1933) for which Vanessa designed costumes.

Artists, other than Vanessa, also played an important role in Woolf's responses to art, in particular her discussions with Walter Sickert. Although Woolf sometimes details her aesthetic ideas indirectly, as in her construction of Roger Fry as a self-surrogate in *Roger Fry*, in *Walter Sickert* Woolf analyses Sickert's colours explicitly. Sickert is the most frequently mentioned artist in Woolf's correspondence and diaries, just as he also dominated modern English art at the turn of the twentieth century. As early as 1919 Woolf knew that Sickert is 'now my ideal painter' a view she held throughout her life (*L*2: 331). At a party in 1923, Woolf happily 'sat by Sickert, & liked him ... something indescribably congenial to me in this easy artists talk; the values the same as my own & therefore right' (*D*2: 223–4). The values that Woolf saw in Sickert's paintings, and shared, were of how objects and space in art could create atmosphere and emotions.[19]

Sickert had asked Woolf to review his 1933 exhibition because he thought of himself as a 'literary painter', but, more interestingly, Woolf opens *Walter Sickert* with a dinner-party discussion about the 'new system of coloured [traffic] lights' which quickly transmogrifies into a modernist analysis of colour and spectatorship (Woolf 1930: 5) The placing of a discussion about painting techniques with a conversation about everyday topics is a juxtaposition that often occurs in Woolf's aesthetics. *Walter Sickert*'s dinner-party conversation does however, as Sickert wished, go on to position Sickert's painting (*Ennui*) against the work of nineteenth-century novelists Dickens and Balzac and reflections about literature and the visual arts. Sickert was delighted with Woolf's essay 'said I had written the only criticism worth having in all his life' (*L*5: 282).

These overlapping, and sometimes tense relationships, of literature and art was an overriding theme in Woolf's writings. Throughout her career Woolf sought for ways in which to demarcate literature from art for example, in 'The Cinema', but simultaneously Woolf associated art and literature in terms of creativity. She wrote passionately and knowledgeably about issues of perception and representation in all the arts. Worried in 'Pictures' that 'we [writers] are under the domain of painting' and she was 'extremely doubtful whether he [the writer] learns anything directly from painting' (*E*4: 243–4), yet Woolf did learn a great deal from painting, for example, Fry's 'emotional design' which provided a ground-plan for the two Post-Impressionist exhibitions and for Bloomsbury's aesthetics (Fry 1992: 78). Woolf's *The Voyage Out* explores these ideas in Terence's 'novel about silence' as do Woolf's short stories 'Blue or Green' and 'The Mark on the Wall' (*VO*: 204).

In many ways these new perceptions became the common currency of English art and culture in the early decades of the twentieth century. For example, the artist Mary Lowndes, designer of suffrage banners, thought the Post-Impressionist exhibition was a revelation, Fry's *Vision and Design* had four printings in five years, and Fry's aesthetic language was liberating, as Vanessa Bell claimed, because it 'was as if one might say things one had always felt instead of trying to say things that other people told one to feel'.[20] Other Bloomsbury figures took up these ideas. The novelist E. M. Forster described Woolf's fiction in terms of the visual arts, arguing that two centuries of English fiction had been a collection of 'portraits' and a 'still life' and that Woolf's writing would 'destroy the gallery'.[21] The Woolfs published Charles Mauron's *The Nature of Beauty in Art and Literature*, translated by Fry, and Mauron clarified for Woolf how spatial design in art might parallel psychological depth in literature.[22] In *Walter Sickert* Woolf had touched on that theme and deplored boundaries between the arts: 'nowadays we are all so specialized', arguing that her favourite writers 'Dryden, Lamb, Hazlitt were acutely aware of the mixture of elements and wrote of literature with music and painting in their minds' (Woolf 1930: 24). In *The Waves* Bernard's soliloquies are similarly structured by visual patterns. In 'Incongruous Memories' Woolf noted how 'scenes have a peculiar power to go on living', offering a complex sense of modernist presence and absence.[23] Descriptions of art, particularly paintings, often allow Woolf to marry artistic with social themes, for example, as with her use of a Gainsborough portrait in *The Years* to highlight issues of gender and class.[24] Art is part of characters' everyday lives and memories and will also outlive individual perceptions. John's 'lump of glass' in Woolf's story 'Solid Objects' and Crosby's Indian elephants in *The Years* stand for a memorialised past, but in a more complex manner than simply as metaphoric images. The objects reveal characters' aesthetics but also puncture the reality of time. Art is as much a manifestation of modernity's fear of forgetting, as artistic emblems.

Conclusion

Throughout her life, Virginia Woolf challenged traditional art boundaries by signifying modernity in a wider range of aesthetics than avant-garde painting and sculpture. In her writings, art and the conditions of creativity, are interwoven with social history, ethics and philosophy. The elaborate and hybrid roles that art plays in Woolf's writings confuse the traditional temporality of material life and history, as well as its period bifurcations, in favour of a modernist aesthetic. Woolf's significant motifs are a fundamental artistic challenge to traditional understandings of culture. As an adolescent, Woolf found visiting the National Portrait Gallery with her father 'rather dull, and we spent our time in yawning', but by the time of *To the Lighthouse* she could capture Mrs Ramsay in a Post-Impressionist brush-stroke, and, at the end of her life, art was again for Woolf 'an intuition' (*PA*: 16). The arts gave Woolf a vocabulary and aesthetics to echo the development from Victorian culture to modernity.

The Edinburgh Companion to Virginia Woolf and the Arts

Given space limits, this chapter has focused on aesthetics and visual cultures, but the *Companion*'s twenty-six chapters examine the totality of Virginia Woolf's relation to the arts, from childhood through her writings and career. It is over a decade since Diane Gillespie, Leslie Hankins and other critics began 'the turn to the visual' in Woolf studies. Modernist scholarship also now focuses on the significance of visual technologies, on the porous boundaries between high and low cultures, and the relation of art and politics. *The Edinburgh Companion*'s originality lies in its combination of fresh historical, archival and genetic research with innovative literary analysis. Such an all-encompassing examination of the significance of the arts to Woolf has not been attempted. Indeed, this is the first time that a twentieth-century woman writer's aesthetics have been addressed in such depth.

The arts are always indicators of changes in the *zeitgeist* and the *Companion* recreates that lived feeling and aesthetics of Woolf's time while offering new ways of assessing art, literature and modernity. Each chapter attends to a different genre, feature or area in Woolf and the arts, but what the chapters share is a set of concerns that cross disciplines. The book proposes a much wider definition of literary and artistic forces, for example, by demonstrating the intellectual significance of entertaining (Minow-Pinkney, Chapter 13) and gardening (Hancock, Chapter 14). Aesthetics are everywhere in Woolf's life, milieu and in these chapters – in interactions with political imagery (Goldman, Chapter 2), in city walks and systems of commerce (Neverow, Chapter 5), and in houses as laboratories of culture (Rosner, Chapter 10). The interconnectedness of the arts is another significant theme – in gramophones and modernism (Caughie, Chapter 19, Kelly, Chapter 23), in Woolf's choreographic mind (Haller, Chapter 25), and in her translations between the arts (Uhlmann, Chapter 3). For the first time genetic criticism reveals a treasure trove of pre-texts (Hankins, Chapter 20) impacting on Woolf's writing.

The roles of gender and performance are much more significant in Woolf's life than hitherto thought, as this volume shows. Bloomsbury's freedom from gender constraints in artistic groups (Brooker, Chapter 12), in sartorial performances (Garrity, Chapter 11), accompanies its performances of Britishness and race (Gerzina, Chapter 4), and the use of theatre as a self-reflective gaze (Putzel, Chapter 24). And of course Woolf herself is a polysemic icon (Silver,

Chapter 22). All the chapters describe complex new constructions of modernity present in art objects (Peach, Chapter 6), in portraits as fictive identities (Hirsh, Chapter 9), in the dialogue between journalism and fiction (Collier, Chapter 18), even in the political patterns of scrapbooks (Pawlowski, Chapter 17).

Woolf's family and Victorian inheritance (Flint, Chapter 1) still gives significant shape to Woolf's arts. Vanessa Bell's artistic influence (Gillespie, Chapter 7) is more dominant than previously shown, as is Woolf's matrilineal inheritance and synaesthetic recall of childhood whether photographically (Dickey, Chapter 21) or in art. The curatorial character of Woolf's writing is marked by these inheritances as well as by her active gallery visits (Harvey, Chapter 8, Humm this chapter). And Virginia Woolf is revealed as a professional 'artist' in her own right as book designer and publisher (Bradshaw, Chapter 16, Marcus, Chapter 15).

All these detailed historic and aesthetic formations are gathered here for the first time. The *Companion* itself mirrors a Bloomsbury artistic community by sharing genuine trans-disciplinary conversations, enabling readers to have their own innovatory encounters with Virginia Woolf and the arts.

Notes

1. Woolf, 'Notes for Writing'. Holograph notebook, unsigned, dated March 1922–March 1925, p. 10. Berg Collection New York Public Library.
2. 'Foreword. Recent Paintings by Vanessa Bell', in *The Bloomsbury Group*, ed. S. P. Rosenbaum, Toronto: University of Toronto Press, 1995. See Gillespie 1988 and Chapter 7 in this volume.
3. A signed one-page letter to Vanessa Bell headed 'WOOLF:FLUSH' in the Hogarth Press Archive, University of Reading, June 1933.
4. Bernard Berenson's publications are a good example of this transition in art history with their detailed catalogues of European collections matched by a wide knowledge of European philosophy (see *The Italian Painters of the Renaissance*, Oxford: Phaidon 1986). Roger Fry owed a great deal to Berenson's expertise, noted by Woolf in *Roger Fry*, ed. D. F. Gillespie, Oxford: Blackwell, 1995. By 1927, the critic R. F. Wilenski in his influential *The Modern Movement in Art* was confidently specifying the methods of Cubism with great precision (London: Faber & Gwyer, 1927).
5. Cézanne's *Still-life with Apples* (1877–78), acquired by John Maynard Keynes at the Degas sale in March 1918, actually has seven apples.
6. Maurice Denis and Roger Fry, 'Cézanne-I', *Burlington Magazine*, January 1910, 16.82: 207–9.
7. Editorial 'Art in the Machine Age II', *The Studio*, 96:425, August 1925: 79. Leonard had reviewed *The Studio* in the *Nation & Athenaeum*, 26 April 1924.
8. Published in *The Listener*, 30 December 1931, pp. 1121–3, to coincide with the Royal Academy's French Art exhibition of 1932. Fry was Executive Committee member.
9. See House (1994) for a discussion of these issues. Roger Fry 'The Courtauld Institute of Art', *Burlington Magazine*, December 1930, 57.333: 13–14.
10. 'Since the standard life of van Gogh by Meier-Graefe is beyond most pockets, the present translation of M. Piérard's more modest biography is welcome' (*E4*: 249). Meier-Graefe's *Modern Art*'s theory of the structural significance of colour influenced Fry's Post-Impressionism. See Goldman (1988).

11. See Wilhelm Worringer (1998) 'Abstraction and Empathy', in *Modernism: An Anthology of Sources and Documents*, ed. V. Kolocotroni, J. Goldman and O. Taxidou, Edinburgh: Edinburgh University Press.

12. Worringer. (1964) *Form in Gothic*, London: Alec Tiranti, pp. 32 and 79. Interestingly Worringer's aesthetic concept of 'exalted hysteria' appeared in the same year as Freud's *Studies on Hysteria*.

13. Goldman (1998) and Henri Bergson (1991) *Matter and Memory*. New York: Zone Books, p. 104.

14. G. E. Moore (1903) 'Refutation of Idealism', *Mind*, 12. 48: 433–53.

15. Ludwig Wittgenstein (1965) 'Lecture on Ethics', *The Philosophical Review*, 74:4.

16. Among the numerous critical writings about Woolf and Fry, see Diane F. Gillespie and L. K. Hankins (eds) (1997) *Virginia Woolf and the Arts*, New York: Pace University Press; and S. P. Rosenbaum (2003) *Georgian Bloomsbury: The Early History of the Bloomsbury Group 1910–1914 Volume 3*, London: Macmillan, and (1998) *Aspects of Bloomsbury: Studies in Modern English Literary and Intellectual History*, London: Macmillan. Jocelyn Bartkevicius (1992) 'A Form of One's Own: Virginia Woolf's Art of the Portrait Essay', *Iowa Review*, Winter, 22. 1: 123–34, Lorraine Janzen Kooistra's 'Virginia Woolf's *Roger Fry*: A Bloomsbury Memorial', *Woolf Studies Annual*, Volume 2, 1996, pp. 26–38. Christopher Reed's many publications on Fry, and D. F. Gillespie's immaculate editorial matter in *Roger Fry* are insightful critiques.

17. C. Bell, 'Art and Cinema', *Vanity Fair*, November 1922, pp. 39–40. See Hankins, Chapter 20, for an expert discussion of Bell and cinema.

18. See D. S. MacColl (1931) *Confessions of a Keeper*, London: Alexander Maclehose & Co.; the quotation is from p. 30. See also Woolf *L2*: 303; Jane Harrison (1978) *Ancient Art and Ritual*, Bradford-on-Avon: Moonraker Press (first published 1913). On the Woolf/Fry/Harrison/MacColl nexus, see Martha C. Carpentier (1998) *Ritual, Myth and the Modernist Text: The Influence of Jane Harrison on Joyce, Eliot and Woolf*, Amsterdam: Gordon and Breach, Falkenheim 1980, and Stephanie Callan (2006), 'Exploring the Confluence of Primitive Ritual and Modern Longing in *Between the Acts*', in *Woolf and the Art of Exploration*, ed. Helen Southworth and Elisa Kay Sparks, Clemson South Carolina: Clemson University Press among others.

19. Hermione Lee suggests that *The Years* evokes Sickert. See also Ruth Hoberman, 'Aesthetic Taste, Kitsch, and *The Years*', *Woolf Studies Annual*, vol. 11, 2005, 77–98.

20. See Dunlop 1972: 72 and Tickner 1992: 102–3; V. Bell in Spalding 1983: 92.

21. E. M. Forster (1967) 'The Early Novels of Virginia Woolf', *Abinger Harvest*, Harmondsworth: Penguin pp. 119–29.

22. C. Mauron (1927) *The Nature of Beauty in Art and Literature*, trans. R. Fry, London: Hogarth Press.

23. Woolf, 'Incongruous Memories', in 'A Form of One's Own', ed. J. Bartkevicius, *Iowa Review*, Winter, 22.1, 1992: 127.

24. See Ruth Hoberman 'Aesthetic Taste, Kitsch and *The Years*', *Woolf Studies Annual*, 2005, volume 11, pp. 77–98.

Works Cited and Further Reading

Ardis, Ann L. (2004) 'The Gender of Modernity', in *The Cambridge History of Twentieth-century English Literature*, ed. Laura Marcus and Peter Nicholls, Cambridge: Cambridge University Press, pp. 61–79.

Bartkevicius, J. (ed.) (1972) 'A Form of One's Own', *Iowa Review*, Winter 22.1, 1992: 27.

Brown, Karen E. (ed.) (2008) *Women's Contribution to Visual Culture 1918–1939*, Aldershot: Ashgate.

Clarke, Meaghan (2005) *Critical Voices: Women and Art Criticism in Britain 1880–1905*, Aldershot: Ashgate.

Corbett, David Peters (1997) *The Modernity of English Art*, Manchester: Manchester University Press.

Dunlop, Ian (1972) *The Shock of the New*, London: Weidenfeld and Nicolson.

Falkenheim, Jacqueline (1980) *Roger Fry and the Beginnings of Formalist Art Criticism*, Ann Arbor, MI: UMI Research Press, especially chapter 1.

Froula, Christine (2005) *Virginia Woolf and the Bloomsbury Avant-Garde: War, Civilization, Modernity*, New York: Columbia University Press.

Fry, Roger (1972) *Selected Essays Volume 2*, ed. Denys Sutton, London: Chatto and Windus.

Gillespie, Diane F. (1988) *The Sisters' Arts: the Writings and Painting of Virginia Woolf and Vanessa Bell*, New York: Syracuse University Press.

Goldman, Jane (1998) *The Feminist Aesthetics of Virginia Woolf: Modernism, Post-Impressionism and the Politics of the Visual*, Cambridge: Cambridge University Press.

Gronberg, Tag (1992) 'Decoration: Modernisms' Other', *Art History*, 15:4 (December), pp. 547–52.

Hirsh, Elizabeth (2008) '*Roger Fry* and Bloomsbury Historiography', *Back to Bloomsbury: Selected Papers from the Fourteenth International Conference on Virginia Woolf*, ed. Gina Potts and Lisa Shahriari, Bakersfield: Center for Virginia Woolf Studies, California State University.

House, John (1994) *Impressionism for England*, New Haven, CT: Yale University Press.

Humm, Maggie (2002) *Modernist Women and Visual Cultures*, Edinburgh: Edinburgh University Press.

Lee, Hermione (1996) *Virginia Woolf*, London: Chatto and Windus.

McConkey, Kenneth (2002) *Memory and Desire: Painting in Britain and Ireland at the Turn of the Twentieth-Century*, Aldershot: Ashgate.

Spalding, Frances (1983) *Vanessa Bell*, London: Macmillan.

Tickner, Lisa (1992) '"Men's Work": Masculinity and Modernism', *differences*, 4:3, pp. 1–37.

Trotter, David (2007) *Cinema and Modernism*, Oxford: Blackwell.

Watney, Simon (1980) *English Post-Impressionism*, London: Studio Vista.

Woolf, Virginia (1930) *Walter Sickert: a Conversation*, London: Hogarth Press.

——. (2001) 'Blue and Green', in *The Mark on the Wall and Other Short Fiction*, ed. D. Bradshaw, Oxford: Oxford University Press.

Part I   Aesthetics

1

VIRGINIA WOOLF AND VICTORIAN AESTHETICS

Kate Flint

In 1924, Virginia Woolf posed for the fashionable studio photographers Maurice Beck and Helen Macgregor. Her image appeared in the 'Hall of Fame' in London's *Vogue* magazine: this fame, according to the accompanying caption, rested on her role as a publisher, on her writing as a critic, on her fiction – 'in the opinion of some of the best judges she is the most brilliant novelist of the younger generation', and on her family ties: 'she is a daughter of the late Sir Leslie Stephen and a sister of Vanessa Bell' (*Vogue*, May 1924: 40). Woolf is positioned, in other words, in relation to the new generation and the old.[1] This message is emphatically reinforced by her costume. Seated at a polished table, her hands demurely folded in front of her, looking pensively to one side, Woolf wears a dress that had belonged to her mother, Julia Stephen. With lace at the collar and cuffs, and a clump of jewellery at the neck fastening, Woolf has on the clothing of the Victorian past.

The relationship of Virginia Woolf to Victorian aesthetics is a great deal more complicated than some of her more outspoken pronouncements would lead one to believe. In her 1927 essay, 'How It Strikes a Contemporary', she wrote:

> We are sharply cut off from our predecessors. A shift in the scale – the sudden slip of masses held in position for ages – has shaken the fabric from top to bottom, alienated us from the past and made us perhaps too vividly conscious of the present . . .. No age can have been more rich than ours in writers determined to give expression to the differences which separate them from the past and not to the resemblances which connect them with it. (*CE2*: 157–8)

This is a rupture that may be traced in her critical meditations with which she surrounded her fiction in the postwar decade, stressing the jettisoning of old habits of plot, old conventions of melodrama and love interest, old ways of imposing artificial structures on the mobility of consciousness and one's overlapping impressions of the world – and in her visual environment. Gone were the dark and cluttered Victorian interiors. The desire for severance from

19

Figure 1.1 Virginia Woolf, photographed for *Vogue* by Maurice Beck and Helen
Macgregor, May 1924

the Victorian past was similarly recollected by Leonard Woolf in 1960, writing
in the first volume of his autobiography that he and his contemporaries, when
they arrived as undergraduates in Cambridge, 'found ourselves living in the
springtime of a conscious revolt against the social, political, religious, moral,
intellectual, and artistic institutions, beliefs, and standards of our fathers
and grandfathers.' They were, as he sees it, in the vanguard of a movement, a
revolution, against 'what for short one may call Victorianism' (*S*: 160). In artistic terms, the first Post-Impressionist Exhibition at the Grafton Galleries in
December 1910 could be seen as symbolising a decisive shift, since, as Vanessa
Bell put it, 'English painters were on the whole still under the Victorian cloud,
either conscientiously painting effects of light, or trying to be poets or neo-Pre-
Raphaelites' (Bell 1998: 128). All of these retrospective assessments, in which
the members of Bloomsbury's inner aesthetic circles energetically proclaim the
freshness of their vision and their severance with the past, have fed into the

common view of these writers and artists as being a group that, to quote S. P. Rosenbaum, 'divested itself of the restraints that the Victorians had maintained on religious, ethical, political, and artistic ideas' (Rosenbaum 1987: 23).

And yet, as Woolf's anachronistic dress suggests, her Victorian inheritance was not something that she could, in fact, readily – or, I shall argue, willingly – shrug off. In 'A Sketch of the Past', one of the last pieces of autobiography that she penned, she wrote with a much more internalised sense of conflict than Leonard was to do about the double consciousness that she experienced growing up in two worlds. 'Two different ages confronted each other in the drawing room at Hyde Park Gate: the Victorian age; and the Edwardian age.' More like grandchildren than children to Leslie Stephen, she explained, they 'lived under the sway of a society that was about fifty years too old for us.' Stephen himself was 'a typical Victorian', as were her two half-brothers. While – and she describes the situation of Vanessa and herself – 'we looked into the future, we were completely under the power of the past . . . . We were living say in 1910: they were living in 1860' (*MOB*: 147). Ostensibly, Woolf is here describing the weight of male authority, and of social convention, that was upheld by her father, and George and Gerald Duckworth, respectively. But for her, description of the moral and material environments are intertwined, and in her creative fiction, just as much as in her memoir writing, the heavy, crowded, over-ornamented, busy, pompous Victorian interior – illuminated by occasional touches of beauty that can suddenly shine brightly in the cluttered gloom – acts as a synecdoche for a familial atmosphere that gently, but perniciously, constricted the lives of those who inhabited it. This was especially true for the women who felt, as the Stephen sisters did, strong ties of obligation and tradition that moored them, at least up to a point, to these domestic settings.

So far as the interior decoration of 22 Hyde Park Gate had a guiding hand behind it, that hand belonged to Julia Stephen. Leslie Stephen was notoriously uninterested in the visual ('I have always been shy with artistic people, who inhabit a world very unfamiliar to me', (Stephen 1977: 30) he confessed in the *Mausoleum Book* that he put together for his children). Woolf wrote, critically, that he was 'spartan, ascetic, puritanical. He had I think no feeling for pictures; no ear for music; no sense of the sounds of words' (*MOB*: 68) – although, to be fair to him, one should point out that he enjoyed learning poetry and reciting it in sonorous tones; that he not only recognised Vanessa's talent as an artist when she was quite young, but saw that she took drawing lessons from Ebenezer Cooke, a leading reformer in art education, and that he drew amusing sketches, of admittedly rather depressed-looking animals, in letters and in the margins of books. But Virginia Woolf's mother – whom she (and many others) always remembered and associated with an intangible personal beauty – had brought to the home of her second marriage many of the tastes she had developed in Little Holland House, her childhood home, and – as Caroline Dakers has comprehensively described – the centre of a notable mid-Victorian artistic circle. (The house was demolished in 1875, seven years before Woolf was born.)

Although contemporaries remembered greens and blues of this house's decor as fresh and harmonious, by the time the Venetian influence transferred both to Hyde Park Gate and to the colours that lodged in Woolf's memory, it had become dark, heavy and oppressive. When she spoke to the Memoir Club in 1920 or 1921 about the social spaces in the house in which she grew up, the very first impression that she delivers is of one of the weight of the past enhancing a claustrophobic darkness. The drawing room, she recalls,

> was divided by black folding doors picked out with thin lines of raspberry red. We were still much under the influence of Titian. Mounds of plush, Watts' portraits, busts shrined in crimson velvet, enriched the gloom of a room naturally dark and thickly shaded in summer by showers of Virginia Creeper. (*MOB*: 164)

The most extensive picture that Woolf paints of the decor of 22 Hyde Park Gate is in one of the drafts of 'A Sketch of the Past'. Here, she elaborates on the gloomy lighting, and the red velvet-covered furniture; the green baize of the dining room table where she and Vanessa did their lessons; the heavily carved sideboard, on which stood a blue china dumb waiter and a biscuit tin shaped like a barrel, the engravings by Sir Joshua Reynolds round the walls. 'It was a very Victorian dining room; with a complete set of chairs carved in oak; high backed; with red plush panels' (*MOB*: 117). She recollects, too, the slight but pervasive smell of wine and cigars and food that lingered in this room: alert as Woolf is, in her memorialising, to material objects, to light and to colour, hers is always a synaesthetic recall. The hall facing the front door contained a cabinet with blue china and a gold-faced clock, a three-cornered chair, a chest in which rugs were kept, and on the chest a silver salver deep in visiting cards. In writing about Talland House in St Ives, where the Stephen family spent their summer holidays, Woolf stressed its view – complete with lighthouse – and the leafiness and airiness of outside spaces, but an 1892 photograph showing her parents reading (her ten-year-old self is just visible in the background) gives a vivid impression of the fussiness of late Victorian domestic decoration: flowery, William Morris-style paper on the walls and on the panels on the back of the door; painted screens; and dark oil paintings in heavy gilt frames.

In her fiction, Woolf invokes sepulchral interiors and cluttered rooms as a kind of shorthand for the Victorian period – not just to sum up the taste of an era, but to convey, through it, something of the weight of the conventional that pressed down upon those who were cocooned by these over-stuffed spaces and the attitudes they represented. At her most parodic, in *Orlando*, she portrays the Victorian world as a cloudy, damp presence, saturating and swathing every-thing: 'furniture was muffled; walls and tables were covered too' (*O* 228). One thing led to another – the drinking of coffee to

> a drawing-room in which to drink it, and a drawing-room to glass cases, and glass cases to artificial flowers, and artificial flowers to mantelpieces,

and mantelpieces to pianofortes, and pianofortes to drawing-room ballads, and drawing-room ballads (skipping a stage or two) to innumerable little dogs, mats, and antimacassars. (*O*: 228)

Consequently, 'the home – which had become extremely important – was completely altered' (*O*: 228). Outside, ivy grew in profusion, filtering out the light that in any case had problems in penetrating the 'curtains of brown and purple plush' (ibid.: 229). This effect of accumulation and literal obfuscation is quickly tied in by the narrator to Victorian habits of thought and writing: to an efflorescence of literary output, and an inability to write or talk directly about elementary subjects ('how much that we talk of openly was . . . hidden away behind plush curtains', Woolf was to write in 1930) (Woolf 1930: 32). On a rare occasion, when sunlight penetrates this environment, Orlando is shocked by the Victorian aesthetic excrescences that are revealed. It as though the whole contents of the Illustrated Catalogue to the 1851 Great Exhibition had been piled together in one place, as Woolf's own baroque prose imitates the grotesque decorative 'pyramid, hecatomb, or trophy' that is revealed in all its hideous monumentality:

> Draped about a vast cross of fretted and floriated gold were widow's weeds and bridal veils; hooked on to other excrescences were crystal palaces, bassinettes, military helmets, memorial wreaths, trousers, whiskers, wedding cakes, cannon, Christmas trees, telescopes, extinct monsters, globes, maps, elephants, and mathematical-instruments – the whole supported like a gigantic coat of arms on the right side by a female figure clothed in flowing white; on the left by a portly gentleman wearing a frock-coat and sponge-bag trousers. (*O*: 232)

But even when she is not piling object upon object, incongruously setting one over-ornamented piece of furniture against another in gleeful parodic excess, Woolf establishes her Victorian settings through the same accrual of furniture, knick-knack and pattern. As we see in *The Years*, these crowded interiors were found across social classes. The lodging house where Colonel Pargiter visits his mistress, Mira, is a social world away from the stuffy propriety of Abercorn Terrace

> He looked round the room with distaste. There were too many little objects about. He felt out of place, and altogether too large as he stood upright before the draped fireplace in front of a screen upon which was painted a kingfisher in the act of alighting on some bulrushes. (*Y*: 7)

But the difference is one of taste rather than decorative ethos: one of the first things that we learn about his home in the 1880 section of *The Years* is that '[t]he room was full of furniture'(*Y*: 10). With its Dutch cabinet containing blue china, its carved chairs, its oil paintings, its solid sideboard, this interior is remarkably similar to that of 22 Hyde Park Gate. In Oxford, the same day, the young Kitty Lasswade goes to visit the much poorer, yet more intellectual Robson family – where the main room somehow manages to be 'bare yet crowded' (ibid.: 68). Entering a smaller parlour, the 'awful . . . taste' is just as apparent. Again it is 'crowded with objects. There were bamboo tables; velvet books with brass hinges; marble gladiators askew on the mantelpiece and innumerable pictures' (ibid.: 71). In a further evocation of Victorian interiors, describing Elizabeth Barrett's home in Wimpole Street in *Flush*, albeit back in 1842, the effect is once again very similar:

> the chest of drawers was surmounted by a bookcase; the bookcase was pasted over with crimson merino; the washing-table had a coronal of shelves upon it; on top of the shelves that were on top of the washing-table stood two more busts. Nothing in the room was itself; everything was something else. (*F*: 20)

This 'cushioned and fire-lit cave' (*F*: 33) has its light filtered out by the ivy that hangs down past the windows, like that of Woolf's childhood home. Even if the fact that the patriarchally oppressive environment is viewed at table-leg height through a dog's eyes; even if Flush's ears and nose are more active than his eyes, hearing the sounds of the household at work and the organ-player in the street, sniffing out eau de cologne and roasting joints and the smells of food and wine and cigars, this odiferous detail once again confirms that the heavy aura of 22 Hyde Park Gate, especially in the years after her mother's death in 1895, intimately and reliably informs Woolf's depiction of Victorian interiors.

Woolf did not, however, compose such set-pieces with the reluctance that she inhabited such rooms: indeed, she relished in the opportunities for description, satiric or otherwise, that they offered. 'I see I shall have to write a novel entirely about carpets, old silver, cut glass and furniture', she wrote to Vanessa in 1918 after a visit to the Victoria and Albert Museum. 'The desire to describe becomes almost a torment' (*L3*: 284). Nor was it just the furniture and general atmosphere of Hyde Park Gate that provided material for her writing, but the pictures that hung on the walls, and the artists responsible for them: pictures that, as family heirlooms, helped establish continuity, rather than a break, with the Victorian period. In *Night and Day*, Katharine Hilbery looks up, at one point, to her grandfather's portrait, and, 'for the thousandth time, fell into a pleasant dreamy state in which she seemed to be the companion of those giant men, of their own lineage, at any rate, and the insignificant present moment was put to shame' (*ND*: 16).[2] The eyes of Leslie and Julia Stephen, and of some of their contemporaries, continued to gaze out over their daughters after their deaths. G. F. Watts's 1878 portrait of Leslie Stephen had hung in the front drawing room of 22 Hyde Park Gate, facing the door: 'a flattered, an idealized picture', Woolf rather bluntly called it, 'up to which father would lead admiring ladies; and pause and contemplate it, with some complacency' (*MOB*: 117). It was very visible at 45 Gordon Square, when Vanessa orchestrated the move there after their father's death; it subsequently moved with Virginia and Adrian to 29 Fitzroy Square. Julia Stephen's portrait by Watts, painted around 1875, hung in the main bedroom of 22, and later in Vanessa and Clive Bell's country house at Charleston. The puffed sleeves and lace collar of her dark dress suggest a garment that at the very least is highly similar to that in which Woolf was to be photographed by Bell and Macgregor. (A further Watts portrait, of Minny Thackeray, Stephen's first wife – 'a charming shy face – nestling away, not noble, not heroic, but shy and sweet, hung over the fireplace' in his study) (ibid.: 119).

If Leslie Stephen brought little aesthetic influence into his household, Julia Stephen provided numerous links with the mid-Victorian High Art world. Born Julia Jackson, she married first Herbert Duckworth in 1867 (he died in 1870) – and then, in 1878, Leslie Stephen. As part of the artistic circle that revolved around Little Holland House, she was in frequent contact not just with Watts, who lived there for over twenty years with her uncle and aunt, Sara and Henry Thoby Prinsep, but with other painters – she sat to Edward Burne-Jones, and was the model for the serene, elongated, yet solid Virgin Mary of his *The Annunciation* (1876–9), bathed in the golden glow of angelic revelation. In the 1870s, too, she posed in front of the camera operated by another aunt (and Sara Prinsep's sister) and godmother, the pioneering photographer Julia Margaret Cameron (as, also, Minny Thackeray had done, most notably in *The Whisper of the Muse*, 1865, which shows her and her sister Anny nuzzling up to Watts as he played the violin). These photographs of their mother were to be hung on one side of the entrance hall in Gordon Square, while others of Cameron's portraits – of Herschel, Lowell, Darwin, Tennyson, Browning and Meredith – were on the opposite wall.

George Frederick Watts was a familiar figure in person in Woolf's childhood, part of the general social circle – a notably elderly social circle – in which her father and half-brothers moved. He held a central position in her thinking about Victorian painting – for her, he was a talismanic figure who invited iconoclasm. A rhyming alphabet in the Stephen children's home newspaper, the *Hyde Park Gate News*, in 1891, offers 'W for Watts/a painter is he' (Woolf, Bell and Stephen 2005: 8). Like Burne-Jones and Millais, Watts visited Talland House when the family were there on vacation, and Vanessa, Virginia and Adrian Stephen stayed at Watts's house, Limnerslease, in 1893, when Walter Crane also visited. From Woolf's reminiscences, one gets occasional, vivid glimpses of this artistic milieu: one that is very much on its way out. In 1922, for example, she looked back to one particular evening in 1903, when her half-brother George Duckworth took her 'to the Holman Hunts, where "The Light of the World" had just come back from its mission to the chief cities of the British Empire', where the Burne-Jones, the Morrises, the painters Marie Spartali Stillman and her husband William Stillman, the art critic Mrs Russell Barrington and numerous others were present:

I know not what distinguished old gentlemen with black ribbons attached to their eyeglasses and elderly ladies with curious vertebrae showing through their real but rather ragged old lace had talked in hushed voices of the master's art while the master himself sat in a skull cap drinking, in spite of the June night, hot cocoa from a mug. (*MOB*: 181–2)

Watts himself was to die in July 1904: and, as Veronica Franklin Gould notes in her comprehensive biography of the artist, 'newspapers throughout the world mourned the passing of the "Grand Old Man of English Art", "The English Titian", "England's Michael Angelo", "The Great Symbolist", "The Last of Our Great Victorians"' (Gould 2004: 355).

For Virginia Stephen, visiting the big Watts memorial exhibition, that opened on 2 January 1905 and ran for two months, was a deflating experience. She wrote to her friend Madge Vaughan; 'By the way, the Watts show is *atrocious*: my last illusion is gone. Nessa and I walked through the rooms, almost in tears. Some of his work indeed most of it–is quite childlike' (*L1* 174). The same month, the *Saturday Review* rejected an article that Vanessa composed about Watts: although, in fact, his reputation was about to collapse, it was presumably considered not sufficiently reverential. For as Virginia told Violet Dickinson in February, she had been at a dreary dinner party where 'every person I talked to spoke almost with tears of the greatness and beauty of Watts–and wouldn't admit the possibility of criticism, and this, I suppose, is the sample British Public' (*L1* 179). Yet for Woolf, Watts's potential was to lie precisely in the fact of his ridiculousness, his ability to stand for the most preposterous features of Victorian aesthetics. In her diary entry on 30 January, 1919 she recorded that she had been reading the two-volume 1912 biography of her late husband by Mary Fraser Watts, and was contemplating the rich comic potential of Freshwater–the village on the Isle of White where both Julia Margaret Cameron and Tennyson had homes, and where Watts stayed during his brief, disastrous marriage to the actress Ellen Terry, thirty years younger than himself, in 1864. Woolf drafted her first version of her Victorian burlesque in 1923, and the longer, two-act version of *Freshwater* was privately performed in 1935.

Watts does not come off well in the play, whether as husband or as artist. He is characterised by pretentious rhetoric–constantly repeating his mantra of 'The Utmost for the Highest'–the motto that in real life he was to choose for his seal in 1888; by self-important proclamations about the way in which he has devoted his long life to 'the service of art' (*FW*: 11), and by overblown allegorical subject matter: he is working on painting called *Modesty at the Feet of Mammon*. This is not an actual Watts canvas, but strongly reminiscent of such ambitious, densely textured, and opaque works as *The All-Pervading* (1887–90), *She Shall Be Called Woman* (c.1875–92) and, indeed, *Mammon (Dedicated to His Worshippers)* of 1885. Woolf mocks his search for symbols. He wants to convey the idea that Modesty is always veiled–and that Modesty is always naked. He hits on a solution–to wrap her 'in a fine white substance that has the appearance of a veil' (ibid. 17)–but that is composed of innumerable stars–that is, indeed, the Milky Way. He fervently consults a book to find the import of this celestial trail to the ancients–and is horrified to find that it

> was the universal token of fertility. It symbolized the spawn of fish, the innumerable progeny of the sea, and the fertility of the marriage bed. Horror! Oh Horror! I who have always lived for the Utmost for the Highest have made Modesty symbolise the fertility of fish! (*FW*: 18).

Victorian prudery, pomposity, and over-intellectualised painting practices are simultaneously debunked.

In her portrayal of Watts, Woolf mocks, too, what she sees as his absurd attention to detail: he has spent six months drawing Mammon's great toe. To some extent, this can be read as a tribute to the view that Vanessa came to hold on the painter–formed, not least, through her 1903 meeting with him as he worked on a painting of an ivy-covered tree trunk to send to the Royal Academy '"as a protest against Impressionism. You see every leaf is clearly painted", he explained', according to Vanessa's account (Gillespie 1988: 65–6). Woolf's reservations about Watts's detailism parallel those that she held about Pre-Raphaelite painting. In a 1917 article, she favourably contrasted Keats's evocative descriptions–at their best when least accurate, as though he is describing a landscape with his eyes shut–with those of Tennyson, whose

> method of sifting words until the exact shade and shape of the flower or the cloud had its equivalent phrase has produced many wonderful examples of minute skill, much like the birds' nests and blades of grass of the pre-Raphaelite painters. (*E2*: 162–3)

giving the detail, but missing the mood. In 1921, she wrote with mannered incredulity to Vanessa Bell from Manchester about the morning that she had spent in the art gallery, with its Pre-Raphaelite collection, including Holman Hunt's *The Hireling Shepherd*.

> I assure you the number of incidents one can pick out is amazing. If Leonard hadn't got impatient I could have found grasshoppers copulating in the very background . . . . The shepherds hair is done one by one. Then there's a lamb with 8 separate whiskers. (*L2*: 458)

Furthermore, Woolf disliked the type of sententious moralising about art that she associated with Watts, and that she wove into his lines in the first draft of *Freshwater*: 'It shall never be said that George Frederick Watts painted a single hair that did not tend directly – or indirectly – to the spiritual and moral elevation of the British Public' (*FW*: 65). This aesthetic tenet owes its direct lineage to the mid-century writings of John Ruskin, with his belief that art must reflect the morality both of its producer, and of the society of its time. Woolf had little sympathy with 'the arrogant scolding and preaching of the big books' written by the critic, even as she admired the clarity, simplicity and evocative prose of *Praeterita* (*E4*: 504). Despite having used his *Elements of Drawing*

when first studying art, Vanessa, too, distanced herself from Ruskin's moralising and fondness for allegory, writing in 1904 to her art school friend Marjorie
Snowden that 'He never cares for anything unless it is a symbol or has several
deep meanings which doesn't seem to me to be what one wants' (quoted in
Gillespie 1988: 85). But Woolf's praise of his autobiography, plus the fact that
the cloud that hangs dank and pall-like over the Victorian pages of *Orlando*
seems derived from Ruskin's own environmentally doom-laden 'storm-cloud
of the nineteenth-century' (as Gillian Beer shows in her assessment of Ruskin's
influence on Woolf), points to a more equivocal relationship with someone
whose hyperaesthetic sensibility spoke to her in a way that his didacticism did
not (Beer 1988: 220–4).

According their younger son, Vanessa told Clive Bell 'that she had succeeded
in persuading Virginia that "there was nothing to be said" for that family idol,
G. F. Watts' (Bell 1972: I: 95). The fact that her sister was a talented artist, and
had exhibited this talent since she was very young, cannot be separated from
Woolf's understanding and interpretation of Victorian aesthetics. It was not
that Woolf had no artistic talent – sketches after William Blake and Dante
Gabriel Rossetti that she executed in 1904 show her to have been an able, if
slightly timid copier – but there was an understanding between the sisters that
Vanessa was the artist, Virginia the writer. Woolf was very well aware of the
barriers that Vanessa had to face in becoming accepted as a serious painter.
But she had more opportunities than her immediate predecessors: threaded
through Woolf's writing are acknowledgements of Victorian women painters'
suppressed talents. In her 1930 Introduction to an exhibition catalogue of her
sister's work, Woolf wrote about the difficulties that a young woman could have
in getting her family to accept the kind of training that was required in the first
place, since attending art school involved drawing from the nude. Hence the
fact that 'every Victorian family has in its cupboard the skeleton of an aunt' who
turned to philanthropy

> because her father would have died rather than let her look upon a naked
> man. And so she went to the Church; and so she went to China; and so she
> died unwed; and so there drop out of the cupboard with her bones half a
> dozen flower pieces done under the shade of a white umbrella in a Surrey
> garden when Queen Victoria was on the throne. (Quoted in Rosenbaum
> 1995: 202)

In *The Pargiters* – the experimental novel-essay that ended up splitting into
The Years and *Three Guineas* – the young Milly Pargiter wants to paint, but her
father is unwilling to let her study, since 'painting at the Slade meant painting
from the nude'. So she 'joined a sketching club which went for expeditions in the
summer – and painted flowers in her bedroom. Her most successful sketch – of
a cottage in Surrey – was hung in the dining room over the mantelpiece under
the dagger' (Woolf 1977: 29–30) – her talent virtually impaled, in an exaggerated image, by the militarist emblem of masculine self-assertion. There is even

something of suppressed passion, both personal and artistic, in the water-colour paintings of 'orchids (startling blossoms, never beheld before)' executed in India by the once young Miss Helena Parry in *Mrs Dalloway* (*MD*: 178).

Yet Woolf acknowledged the public success of one Victorian woman artist – albeit one who worked in a less traditional medium. Her great-aunt, the photographer Julia Margaret Cameron, was indeed lampooned in *Freshwater* for her fanatical devotion to chasing down and dressing up subjects for her photographs. She wrote more sympathetically of her indefatigable, perfection-ist pursuit of her art in one of the two Introductions that prefaced the 1926 volume, *Victorian Photographs of Famous Men and Fair Women* – a volume containing several likenesses of her mother, as well as of those luminaries whose Cameron portraits moved from Hyde Park Gate to Fitzroy Square. But there is, nonetheless, again something rather arch about Woolf's writing, here, finding comedy in an excess that she locates not just in Cameron's own energy, but in her exemplification of Victorian aesthetic idealism – as we see in Woolf's tragi-comic scene of her death in Ceylon (Sri Lanka) in 1879: 'The birds were fluttering in and out of the open door; the photographs were tumbling over the tables; and, lying before a large open window Mrs Cameron saw the stars shin-ing, breathed the one word "Beautiful", and so died' (Woolf and Fry 1973: 19). Woolf, although an able leisure photographer since 1896, does not seem to have had much appreciation for it as a form of high art – however much, as *Orlando* and *Three Guineas* testify, she understood its interpretive or polemical value as part of a text. But the other introduction to this volume, by Roger Fry, takes the question of photography's status as an independent art very seriously. To be sure, he writes with self-conscious retrospection about the gulf of time between the 1860s and the mid-1920s: of the way in which Cameron, and her sitters, infused with a Pre-Raphaelite inspired worship of beauty, manifest something 'touching and heroic' in their poses, 'so unconscious of the abyss of ridicule which they skirt' (Woolf and Fry 1973: 24). But Fry also knowledgeably consid-ers the technical demands facing Cameron, her powers of composition, and her 'wonderful perception of character as it is expressed in form, and of form as it is revealed or hidden by the incidence of light' (ibid.: 26).

Roger Fry, together with Clive Bell, was extremely influential to Woolf's aesthetic education. They helped to provide the concepts and vocabulary – the concern with form, with colour and space, with light and shade – that informed the break with Victorian art that the artistic tastes and productions of the Bloomsbury group represented. In the preface to *Orlando* – not, admit-tedly, a document always to be taken entirely at face value – Woolf claims that 'to the unrivalled sympathy and imagination of Mr Roger Fry I owe whatever understanding of the art of painting I may possess' (*O*: 5). In her posthumous biography of Fry, written in 1940, she celebrates his influence, not just on her personally (indeed, in many ways, this is an awkwardly impersonal book), but more broadly. 'He changed the taste of his time by his writing, altered the cur-rent of English painting by his championship of the Post-Impressionists, and increased immeasurably the love of art by his lectures' (*RF*: 294). But although the 1910 Grafton Gallery exhibition, 'Manet and the Post-Impressionists', has often been cited as a rupturing moment (following Woolf's cue about the epoch-changing nature of December 1910), Fry's own way of introducing and explaining this unfamiliar art did not emphasise the idea of a break with the past. Quite the reverse: as Woolf noted, 'he would explain that it was quite easy to make the transition from Watts to Picasso; there was no break, only a continuation. They were only pushing things a little further' (ibid.: 152). In taking this line, Fry built on the ground that had been laid by two prominent Victorian art critics, D. A. S. MacColl and R. A. M. Stevenson, introducing the Impressionists to a sceptical British public through stressing a continuity with earlier artists when it came to a preoccupation with colour and tonality, and through demonstrating their technical ability as draughtsmen. Moreover, the language used about painting by these earlier critics anticipates terms that Woolf herself, contemplating the nature of fiction, was to employ. For example, praising Monet's *The Coast of Belle-Isle, Bretagne*, exhibited at the Royal Society of British Artists late in 1887, Stevenson lauded its 'wonderful luminousness', and described how all its elements 'fall into a harmonious whole, without holes or breaks in the continuity of the aerial envelope' (quoted in Flint 1984: 88) – giving it a visual completion that prefigures Woolf's encapsulation of life as 'a luminous halo, a semi-transparent envelope' (*E*4: 160). Clive Bell, one might note, remarked that Woolf's 'vision, and superficially her style, may remind anyone, as it reminded the French critic, M. Abel Chevalley, of the French Impressionists' (Bell 1956: 114).

Whereas Clive Bell (born 1881) was younger than Fry (born 1866), his aesthetic tenets had, likewise, been formed by the late Victorians. From the philosopher G. E. Moore, he and others of his Cambridge – and later Bloomsbury – contemporaries absorbed the tenets of the so-called 'philosophical Realism'. In terms of aesthetics, his ideas especially fed into Woolf's interest in the nature of knowledge and our means of obtaining by it – including the place of sense-impressions – even if, as Ann Banfield argues in her magisterial study (2000) of the philosophical influences at work on Woolf, Moore's ideas did not play as central a role on her thought as has often been argued.[3] Moving back into the Victorian period a little further, one can certainly detect the influence of Walter Pater on her: she studied Latin and Greek with his sister Clara during 1898–1905 (remembering her particular domestic interiors as 'all blue china, Persian cats, and Morris wallpapers' *L*4: 411) and bought a copy of his *Collected Works* during this time. As Perry Meisel has comprehensively explored, Woolf's concern with 'moments of vision' owes a good deal to Pater (although she herself credits her awareness of the concept to Thomas Hardy and Joseph Conrad); moreover, Meisel writes,

[i]f we look for the organizing principle at work in Woolf's criticism, it is, like Pater's based upon a criterion of expressiveness in art, and generates a

search for the temperament or personality of the artist behind what he has made. (Meisel 1980: 40).[4]

When one considers these influences on Woolf's aesthetics, then, one comes up against two factors that destabilise the very term 'Victorian'. As Woolf herself used the epithet, it connotes a style, rather than an accurate dating: one associated by her, time and again, with red plush, over-stuffed interiors, and 'Victorian gloom' (*E3*: 399), as well as with sentimentalism, and with over-attention to detail, whether Pre-Raphaelite, or located in the works of those narrative realists whom Bell wrote off as 'Victorian illusionists – the photographers without cameras' – exemplifying the Victorian art that he would happily pitch onto 'one large bonfire in the corner by the pig-sty and have done with . . . for ever' (Bell 1927: 17, 8). Certainly, later nineteenth-century artists in general, and the Impressionists and earlier Post-Impressionists in particular, share Woolf's interest in the moment, in evanescent qualities, in the expressive play of shadows, in the translucent and semi-transparent, in the juxtaposition of colours, and in shifting effects of light and shifting perspectives. But can continental artists, albeit of the nineteenth century, legitimately be thought of as 'Victorian'? The same question may be asked of theorists and critics. Fry, for example, was early influenced by Hermann Helmholtz's 1860s research into physiological optics and perception, especially his theory of binocular vision, which supported the idea that seeing involves framing and flattening (Robins 1999: 50–1). Vanessa, although she had studied at the Royal Academy under artists who had come under the sway of the French (George Clausen changed his style after meeting Bastien-Lepage; John Singer Sargent was a friend of Monet's) and had seen Impressionist art in London, was fully converted to the importance of these painters by Camille Mauclair's *The French Impressionists*, published in translation in 1903, about which she wrote that it opened her eyes to the fact that these living artists might offer 'something fundamental and permanent and as discoverable now as in any other age' (Bell 1998: 129).

Indeed, it may be the fact that European artists and thinkers could not strictly speaking be counted as 'Victorian' that accounted in part for their appeal, and led to an under-recognition, at the time and since, of certain late nineteenth British influences. Wyndham Lewis noted back in 1934 that there is 'a very much closer connection than people suppose between the aesthetic movement presided over by Oscar Wilde, and that presided over in the first post-war decade by Mrs. Woolf and Miss Sitwell' (Lewis 1934: 170). Chistopher Reed has drawn our attention to Roger Fry's perhaps surprising quasi-dismissal of J. A. McN. Whistler's importance (Fry ranks his aesthetic thinking way below that of Leo Tolstoy), and attributes this in large part to the way in which what Fry saw as Whistler's cultivated isolationism did not mesh with the Bloomsbury artists' emphasis on 'the formation of aesthetic identity in a social context' (Reed 1994: 190). But Whistler is, I would suggest, an understated influence on Woolf's writing. In *The Voyage Out*, when Mrs Dalloway boards the *Euphrosyne*, she looks out at the Portuguese coast: '"It's so like Whistler!" she exclaimed, with a wave towards the shore', barely giving the slightly startled Rachel 'time to look at the grey hills on one side of her' (*VO*: 40–1). Even if the new traveller is a tad pretentious here, Woolf's general love of twilight, mist, haze and the sudden pinpricks of light that momentarily irradiate a portion of a scene have much in common with the artist, whose work she certainly knew. The painter Arthur H. Studd, who occasionally entertained the Stephens in his Cheyne Walk rooms, owned a number of Whistler's works, including *Nocturne: Blue and Silver – Cremorne Lights*, and *Chelsea Fruit Shop* – both of them thoroughly crepuscular – and *Symphony in White, No. 2: The Little White Girl*, in which the subject leans languidly on the mantelpiece, staring at her reflection. There is a definite echo of this painting in the 1925 short story 'The New Dress', when Mabel hopes to be able to look chic enough for a party of Clarissa Dalloway's – while knowing all too well that she will never appear fashionable, or anything other than her faded age. None the less, as she glances quickly, wistfully in the dressmaker's mirror, for a second 'there looked at her, framed in the scrolloping mahogany, a grey-white, mysteriously smiling, charming girl, the core of herself, the soul of herself' (*SF*: 172).

This ghost of a reference to Whistler is just part of the evidence that shows that Woolf did not share Clive Bell's incendiary fantasies about the Victorian period. Certainly, in 'The Mark on the Wall' (1917), she expressly desires to jettison the nineteenth century and its social protocols into 'the dustbin where the phantoms go, the mahogany sideboards and the Landseer prints' (*SF*: 86). But for all her willingness to call on 'Victorian' as a quick term of approbation, and for all her detestation of some of the attitudes – particularly those of smug and repressive patriarchy – that she saw reflected directly or indirectly in its decor and artistic products, Woolf's prose repeatedly reveals the influence of the arts and of the aesthetic criticism of the previous century. Indeed, Bell himself located in her 'a sort, a very odd sort, of Victorianism. Sometimes it seemed to me that Virginia had inherited from her immediate ancestors more than their beauty and intelligence' (Bell 1956: 100–1). Although we should not lose sight of her quarrels with the age, the reclamation of Woolf's connections with the Victorian past is already underway, part of a broader questioning of the degree to which it is possible to assign neat boundaries to the Victorian period – a scepticism about periodisation very much in accord with Woolf's own. Steve Ellis's excellent study, *Virginia Woolf and the Victorians*, reads these connections in the light of 'her characteristic search for continuity and conciliation' (Ellis 2007: 9), and, indeed, running through Ellis's book, like a chorus, is the phrase in which Woolf expressed her affection for 'the mellow light which swims over the past' (*E2*: 168). Victorian aesthetics served a symbolic function for Woolf, in that they could be invoked to stand for values with which she had absolutely no sympathy. Yet nonetheless, with her belief that the present was richer when one recognised the layers of the past that sustained it, they continued to underpin her perception. One might, after all, recollect that when Woolf praised the way in which 'the light and the air [in 46 Gordon Square] after the rich red gloom of Hyde Park Gate were a revelation', this did not just serve to symbolise the end of an era, but served to illuminate the past: 'Things one had never seen in the darkness there – Watts pictures, Dutch cabinets, blue china – shone out for the first time in the drawing room at Gordon Square' (*MOB*: 184).

Notes

My thanks go to the Huntington Library, San Marino, California, whose award of an Andrew W. Mellon Fellowship allowed me to write this in the most beautiful of surroundings, and to Alice Echols, who brought her sharp mind and eye to the piece.

1. Woolf's relationship with *Vogue* was a good deal more complicated than this brief summary would suggest, and, in the years 1924–6, she appeared in its columns more often than not in the context of cultural modernity.
2. None the less, Woolf had decreasing confidence in the consolatory visual presence of one's forebears: Peggy, in the 'Present Day' section of *The Years*, looks at her grandmother's picture 'as if to ask her opinion. But she had assumed the immunity of a work of art; she seemed as she sat there, smiling at her roses, to be indifferent to our right and wrong' (*Y*: 327).
3. In particular, Banfield argues for the importance of Bernard Russell to the development of Woolf's (and Roger Fry's) aesthetic thinking.
4. Meisel's persuasive demonstration of the connections between Woolf's and Pater's writing is, however, somewhat skewed, to my mind, by his determination to account for the relatively slight direct attention that she pays Pater through a Freudian argument that positions him as a figure of masculine authority analogous to Leslie Stephen, whose influence must, at least overtly, be suppressed.

Works Cited

Banfield, Ann (2000) *The Phantom Table. Woolf, Fry, Russell and the Epistemology of Modernism*, Cambridge: Cambridge University Press.

Beer, Gillian (1988) 'The Victorians in Virginia Woolf: 1832–1941', in Joanne Shattuck (ed.) *Dickens and Other Victorians. Essays in Honour of Philip Collins*, Basingstoke: Macmillan, pp. 214–35.

Bell, Clive (1927) *Landmarks in Nineteenth-Century Painting*, London: Chatto and Windus.

—— (1956) *Old Friends. Personal Recollections*, London: Chatto and Windus.

Bell, Quentin (1972) *Virginia Woolf. A Biography*, 2 vols, London: Hogarth Press.

Bell, Vanessa (1998) 'Memories of Roger Fry', in Lia Giachero (ed.), *Sketches in Pen and Ink*, London: Pimlico, 1998, pp. 117–47.

Dakers, Caroline (1999) *The Holland Park Circle. Artists and Victorian Society*, New Haven, CT and London: Yale University Press.

Ellis, Steve (2007) *Virginia Woolf and the Victorians*, Cambridge: Cambridge University Press.

Flint, Kate (1984) *Impressionists in England. The Critical Reception*, London: Routledge.

Gillespie, Diane Filby (1988) *The Sisters' Arts. The Writing and Painting of Virginia Woolf and Vanessa Bell*, Syracuse, NY: Syracuse University Press.

Gould, Veronica Franklin (2004) *G. F. Watts. The Last Great Victorian*, New Haven, CT and London: Yale University Press.

Lewis, Wyndham (1934) *Men without Art*, London: Cassell.

Meisel, Perry (1980) *The Absent Father: Virginia Woolf and Walter Pater*, New Haven, CT and London: Yale University Press.

Reed, Christopher (1994) 'Making History: The Bloomsbury Group's Construction of Aesthetic and Sexual Identity,' *Journal of Homosexuality*, 27: 189–224.

Robins, Anna Greutzner (1999) 'Fathers and Sons. Walter Sickert and Roger Fry', in Christopher Green (ed.), *Art Made Modern. Roger Fry's Vision of Art*, London: Merrell Holberton, pp. 45–56.

Rosenbaum, S. P. (1987) *Victorian Bloomsbury*, London: Macmillan.

—— (1995) *The Bloomsbury Group. A Collection of Memoirs and Commentary*, London: Croom Helm.

Stephen, Leslie (1977) *Mausoleum Book*, Oxford: Clarendon Press.

Vogue (1924) Unsigned article, 'Hall of Fame', late May: 40.

Woolf, Virginia (1930) 'The Essays of Augustine Birrell', *Life and Letters*, 5: 29–38.

—— (1977) *The Pargiters*, ed. Mitchell Leaska, New York: New York Public Library.

Woolf, Virginia, Vanessa Bell with Thoby Stephen (2005) *Hyde Park Gate News. The Stephen Family Newspaper*, ed. Gill Lowe, London: Hesperus Press.

Woolf, Virginia and Roger Fry (1973) *Victorian Photographs of Famous Men and Fair Women*, ed., Tristram Powell Boston, MA: David R. Godine (originally published 1926).

Further Reading

Aleksiuk, Natasha (2000) ' "A thousand angles": Photographic Irony in the Work of Julia Margaret Cameron and Virginia Woolf', *Mosaic*, 33: 125–42.

Boyd, Elizabeth French (1976) *Bloomsbury Heritage: Their Mothers and Their Aunts*, London: Hamish Hamilton.

Joyce, Simon (2007) 'On or About 1901: The Bloomsbury Group Looks Back', in *The Victorians in the Rearview Mirror*, Athens: Ohio University Press, pp. 17–40.

Prettejohn, Elizabeth (1999) 'Out of the Nineteenth Century. Roger Fry's Early Art Criticism, 1900–1906', in Christopher Green (ed.), *Art Made Modern. Roger Fry's Vision of Art*, London: Morrall Holberton, pp. 31–44.

Reed, Christopher (2004) *Bloomsbury Rooms: Modernism, Subculture, and Domesticity*, New Haven, CT: Yale University Press.

Rosner, Victoria (2004) *Modernism and the Architecture of Private Life*, New York: Columbia University Press.

Spalding, Frances (1983) *Vanessa Bell*, New Haven, CT: Ticknor & Fields.

VIRGINIA WOOLF AND MODERNIST AESTHETICS

Jane Goldman

WOOLF'S FAMOUS ASSERTION in 1924, in 'Character in Fiction' (the essay also known in variant forms as 'Mr Bennett and Mrs Brown'), that 'on or about December 1910 human character changed' (Woolf 1988: 421), remains for modernism one of her most important, most disputed interventions. It has become a critical slogan for the inception of modernity and modernist aesthetics, themselves terms of equally fierce critical dispute. But any attempt to define Woolf's modernist aesthetics, or modernity and modernist aesthetics more broadly (all irreducible to one defining quality), might well attend to her analogy for the similar impossibility of empirically or substantively confirming her chosen historical moment of change itself: 'I am not saying that one went out, as one might into a garden, and there saw that a rose had flowered, or that a hen had laid an egg' (ibid.). This qualification, hard on the heels of her essay's main proposition, should alert us to its quixotic and argumentative mode. To reflect on modernity, and on modernism aesthetics, then, is to enter into unresolved argument, even with oneself.

Woolf's reworking of the essay, including one version she read to the Cambridge Heretics in 1924, and her re-titling of its published drafts and variants, also evidence her dialogical mode, and enhance the sense present (in every version) that we, as readers, are entering into a continuing argument rather than passively receiving a polished set-piece. But this virtuoso manifesto of modernism did not evolve entirely from – or as – Woolf's arguments with herself; it was borne of a fierce and radical critical disagreement between herself and Arnold Bennett over the status of 'character' in modern fiction, not least her own:

> People, like Arnold Bennett, say I cant create [. . .] characters that survive. My answer is – [. . .] only the old argument that character is dissipated into shreds now: the old post-Dostoevksy argument. I daresay its true, however, that I haven't that 'reality' gift. I insubstantise, wilfully to some extent, distrusting reality-its cheapness. But to get further. Have I the power of conveying the true reality? Or do I write essays about myself?

Answer these questions as I may, in the uncomplimentary sense, & still
there remains this excitement. (*D2* 248)

Woolf's view of character in modern fiction here as 'dissipated' suggests a
modern concept of subjectivity in process rather than unified and complete;
while her concern over her own possible lack of objectivity in her essays suggest
an equally modern acknowledgement of the inevitable subjectivity of all utter-
ances, which, if not quite a recognition of a stable ego behind them, does imply
the mustering of a more coherent and unified one. Woolf opens up a new sense
of self somewhere between these contradictory models of subjectivity, while still
keeping both in play. Significantly, her doubt over her status as realist, shared
by generations of critics after her, is situated in this quandary over subjectivity. Her partisan readiness to enter into fierce critical debate with her literary
opponent is also in keeping with the dialectical energies of modernist and
avant-garde writing which continue in today's modernist studies. The present
reflection on Woolf and modernist aesthetics, then, will not attempt to hand
over a rose or an egg, as if there were some objective, substantive version of
either, but it will plunge with open partisanship into the continuing arguments
over modernist aesthetics and Woolf's writing that her essay has generated.

In typical contradictory fashion, having offered such a singular, definite and
momentous historic point when 'human character changed', Woolf, in the very
next sentence, undercuts with her rose and egg analogies all such exactitude,
continuing: 'The change was not sudden and definite like that' (Woolf 1988:
421–2). Yet the clarification, in its use of natural analogies, may also alert us to
a sense of change that is not some natural (cyclical or evolutionary), change but
change by social and political means.

> The first signs of it are recorded in the books of Samuel Butler [...]; the
> plays of Bernard Shaw continue to record it. In life one can see the change,
> if I may use a homely illustration, in the character of one's cook. The
> Victorian cook lived like a leviathan in the lower depths, formidable, silent,
> obscure, inscrutable; the Georgian cook is a creature of sunshine and fresh
> air; in and out of the drawing room, now to borrow the *Daily Herald*,
> now to ask advice about a hat. Do you ask for more solemn instances of
> the power of the human race to change? Read the *Agamemnon*, and see
> whether, in process of time, your sympathies are not almost entirely with
> Clytemnestra. Or consider the married life of the Carlyles, and bewail the
> waste, the futility, for him and for her, of the horrible domestic tradition
> which made it seemly for a woman of genius to spend her time chasing
> beetles, scouring saucepans, instead of writing books. All human rela-
> tions have shifted – those between masters and servants, husbands and
> wives, parents and children. And when human relations change there is
> at the same time a change in religion, conduct, politics, and literature. Let
> us agree to place one of these changes about the year 1910. (Woolf 1988:
> 422)

Woolf posits an abrupt historical change in modernity in tandem with a rupture in the aesthetic order, a concatenation that produces both modernism and new, modernist subjectivities. In modernist representations of 'character' a new discursive and performative model of subjectivity emerges with the recognition that there is no unified identity prior to representation or performance. Aesthetic representation of 'character' is therefore understood not as the (realist) reflection of an already formed subject, but as the very site of the production of subjectivities in process. Woolf's 'character' may be read both as the human characters who have changed and who initiate change, then, but also as a changed and changing model of the concept of subjectivity itself. The example of 'the character of one's cook' suggests, furthermore, the stake here is political access to the status of subject itself. Woolf's cook constitutes a modernist allegory of the emergence of modern women into the public sphere and her essay explores the aesthetic and political ramifications of that event. Woolf presses the constitution of modern subjectivities in terms of class, gender and even race, as I will explore below. Here, in this passage where Woolf offers an account of changing human character on and off stage and page, in public and domestic spheres, the boundaries between life and art are blurred; fiction interpenetrates with fact, myth with reality; and aesthetic form becomes less a question of the representation of the political, or an escape from it, and more a matter of its very production.

Woolf's aesthetics, and modernist aesthetics more broadly, cannot meaningfully be summarised in a checklist of formalist features, but perhaps they may be understood, in all their various and often conflicting manifestations, in terms of the impetus to test the political and discursive limits of modern concepts of subjectivity. Contemporary critics' reactions to Woolf's much cited and frequently anthologised essay, furthermore, often betray the faultlines that open up as the historical turn in literary studies meets with modernism's literary theoretical legacies and its inherent resistance to easy historicism and simple periodisation. They also evidence the significance of Woolf's work in the resultant rich developments in current modernist studies. In *Virginia Woolf and the Victorians*, his sustained attempt to claim Woolf as a 'post-Victorian', Steve Ellis, however, goes so far as to question the 'political modernity' (Ellis 2007: 104) many feminist critics of Woolf (myself included) have found in the essay's famous passage about 'one's cook'.

Woolf's clear caesura between Victorian and Georgian cooks seems to have escaped Ellis who finds 'problems' in critical appraisals of this passage and Woolf's work more generally that find 'ideas of a radical project in Woolf relating to social class'. Switching to my reading of the eclipse essay, 'The Sun and the Fish' (1928), which occupies the first half of my book (and to which this essay will briefly return at its close), he complains that my work 'betrays an exaggerated belief in Woolf's consistent and thoroughgoing radicalism, in her hopes for a new socio-political order, for a "luminously colourful and shadowless" world, so to speak.' (Ellis 2007: 105) Woolf's undeniable 'radical feminism,' Ellis asserts, and her Post-Impressionist colourism 'coexist with conservative elements which, while weakening in the 1930s [. . .] by no means disappear entirely' (ibid.). Nor am I alone in my naïve identification of a '"prismatic" optimism' in Woolf's writing, particularly regarding the 1910 declaration. Ann Banfield too, 'in the space of two pages' of *The Phantom Table: Woolf, Fry, Russell and the Epistemology of Modernism* (2000),

> brings together what have become practically the three clichés of Woolfian criticism in positing her identification with modernity: the December 1910 comment, the words on the 'Georgian cook' [. . .] compared with the Victorian cook [etc. . . .] and the 'revelation' of the light and air of [. . .] Gordon Square after the 'rich red gloom' of [. . .] Hyde Park Gate [. . .] in Woolf's 'Old Bloomsbury' memoir.

Banfield does not go as far as 'some critics' who have claimed this 'as key evidence for Woolf's Labourite affiliation', but she errs in using 'such statements as foundational support for a general Woolfian positioning where "sunshine and fresh air are also a new ethos, one which substitutes free exchange for the 'prison' – 'the cage' – of the old social relations"' (Ellis 2007: 104; Banfield 2000: 15).

Below, I examine Woolf's great modernist manifesto, 'Mr Bennett and Mrs Brown', referring to 'Modern Fiction', *A Room of One's Own, To the Lighthouse*, and her memoir, and building on my reading of 'The Sun and the Fish', partially in response to Ellis's sustained critique of my work, in order to explore current critical debates on Woolf's contributions to modernist aesthetics. I have already demonstrated, in *The Feminist Aesthetics of Virginia Woolf: Modernism, Post-Impressionism and the Politics of the Visual* (1998), links beween the colourism and solarism of Post-Impressionist art and the colourism and solarism of suffragist and suffragette art and propaganda, and the significance of both for Woolf's designated moment of change in December 1910. Ellis's intervention is part of a recent critical impetus in modernist and Woolf studies to reconsider the ways our periodising definitions of modernist aesthetics tend to rely on constructed notions of the Victorian 'other' of modernism. These notions are of course in part supplied by Woolf herself in contrasting Victorian and Georgian cooks and marking a conscious political and cultural rejection of the dominant values of the Victorian era. Ellis's argument for Woolf's 'own Post-Victorianism' (Ellis 2007: 74) is more subtle than Donald Child's case for Woolf the 'eugenical' and 'prudish Victorian' (Childs 2001: 35, 71), but both push for her radical re-categorisation as conservative, Victorian. This recent critical pressure to make a Victorian of her cannot be ignored in exploring Woolf's current status in the field of modernist aesthetics.

The first exhibition of Post-Impressionism was mounted in London in the winter of 1910, the second in 1912, by Woolf's Bloomsbury colleagues, Roger Fry, Desmond MacCarthy and Clive Bell, the proponents of aesthetic formalism and of 'significant form', theories which have become enormously influential in critical definitions of modernist aesthetics. These art shows coincided with a heightened period of political turbulence on the streets. Woolf's reflections in 1924 on the significance of December 1910 resonate both with the formalism of Fry's and Bell's formulations on modern European art glossing the exhibitions, and with the formulations and practices of British suffragist artists, evident in the mass suffragist demonstrations agitating for political change in London that coincided with the opening of the first exhibition. Woolf's own verbal colourism, as my book demonstrates in detail, draws, then, on the shocking colourism of both Post-Impressionist and suffragist art. The politics and aesthetics of both are caught up in the staging and reception of the notorious Post-Impressionist exhibitions.

Any attempt to define the emergence of a modernist aesthetics from these origins must attend to both the politics of the art on the gallery walls and to the art of the politics on the streets. *Blast* magazine famously reprimanded suffragettes for their headline grabbing campaign of violence against famous works of art in public collections: 'LEAVE WORKS OF ART ALONE./ YOU MIGHT SOME DAY DESTROY A GOOD PICTURE BY ACCIDENT [. . .] LEAVE ART ALONE, BRAVE COMRADES' (*Blast* 1 1914: 151–2). But their reputation for vandalism and for the destruction of art should not detract from the suffragettes' constructive achievements as artists of considerable talent themselves who mounted in mass demonstrations spectacular pageants of orchestrated colourism (dominated by purple, white and green) and who produced powerful visual images in support of their campaign, in banners, posters, cartoons, clothing and jewellery as well as the more traditional genres of painting and drawing. Their work exemplifies modernist dissolution of the great divide between 'high' and 'low' art, and the role of the aesthetic in representing and militating for political change.

Returning to the passage under scrutiny, Woolf's figurative attempt to calibrate change is complex. Her use of the figures of women from fiction and history as allegorical harbingers of change echoes the suffragist pageant masquerades representing numerous mythical and historic women. It also anticipates discussion, in *A Room of One's Own*, of the discrepancies between the lived historical lives of real women and their representation in art and literature, and of the use of 'woman' as a sign co-opted to signify anything but real women themselves. In recognising that 'she pervades poetry from cover to cover' but is 'all but absent from history', the narrator of the manifesto uses a series of figures herself to explore how the feminine is always and already caught up in the conventions of figuration and representation itself: 'It was certainly an odd monster that one made up by reading the historians first and the poets afterwards – a worm winged like an eagle; the spirit of life and beauty in a kitchen chopping up suet' (Woolf 1929: 56). Recognising the impossibility of total rejection of figuration itself, Woolf seeks to turn such gendered figuration to the advantage of real women by converting the patriarchal monster into a positive emblem for a feminist aesthetics:

What one must do to bring her to life was to think poetically and prosaically at one and the same moment, thus keeping in touch with fact – that
she is Mrs. Martin, aged thirty-six, dressed in blue, wearing a black hat and
brown shoes; but not losing sight of fiction either – that she is a vessel in
which all sorts of spirits and forces are coursing and flashing perpetually.
(Woolf 1929: 56–7)

Feminine subjectivity is caught up in a process of signification and the way all
identities are in part discursively formed, where the prosaic dimension of language communicates historical fact and lived experience, and the poetic subjective and lyric potential. As a 'vessel' Mrs Martin is always and already allegorical,
vehicular. Woolf's argument, in 'Mr Bennett and Mrs Brown', for a change in
human character on or about December 1910, then, does not entail the destruction or burial of all former figurations but their radical modification. The burial
of the dead is no easy matter for modernism where everything tends to surface
at once, suspended by a syntax sinuous enough to connect or juxtapose such
diverse elements as beetles and saucepans, the Carlyles and Clytemnestra, or by
a narrative design flexible enough to shift from the antics of cooks in drawing
rooms of different eras to famous authors stalking mysterious railway carriage
passengers on 'a journey from Richmond to Waterloo' (Woolf 1988: 422).

   Calibration of change involves the identification of some sense of continuity too, as those keen to foreground Victorian elements in Woolf's work have
noticed. Without some sense of continuity, how else is change discernible?
Aristotle argues as much in the *Metaphysics*. Aristotle's *Poetics* is also relevant
to Woolf's essay, given its detailed interest in plot and character. (We know
Woolf read Aristotle's *Poetics*, in the spring of 1905.)[1] It is possible to understand in his terms Woolf's revelatory 'signs' of a universal change in 1910, where
his 'Reversal of the Situation', and 'Recognition', as well as 'Scenes of Suffering'
(Aristotle 1902: 21, 49), are discernible or implicit in Woolf's own examples,
her 'homely illustration' of 'one's cook' and her 'more solemn instances' of
Clytemnestra and Jane Carlyle, which invite the reader to participate in the
reading of both art and life as performance. Our reception of these performances in turn becomes evidence of change.

   Woolf's account of our reception of these performances, then, elicits an
Aristotelian moment of recognition: she puts before the reader evidence for a
universal potential for radical revision, 'the power of the human race to change'.
The evidence lies not with the cook *per se* or Clytemnestra *per se* or Jane
Carlyle *per se* but with our invited or alleged revised interpretation of them:
our approval, as spectators, of the cook's emergence, reversing servile relations;
our total shift of sympathy, implicitly from the matricidal Orestes to the husband murderer Clytemnestra (revising the judgement of Athena herself); our
bemoaning of the Carlyles' sorry marriage and recognition of Jane Carlyle as a
'woman of genius' in her own right rather than mere wife of genius. Revisionary
feminist politics, then, are caught up in the very formulation of the modernist

impetus for aesthetic change, making it new. These self-conscious interpretative scenes, pointing up the act of reading itself, engage the reader in a process of constructing as much as interpreting new characters, new subjectivities.

Woolf's reference to the public reputation of the Carlyle marriage and Thomas Carlyle's notorious ill-treatment of his wife can hardly be innocent of the highly publicised suffragette assault on John Millais's unfinished portrait of him as it hung on public display in the National Portrait Gallery, London, in July of 1914 (see Figure 2.1) The National Portrait Gallery, like the *Dictionary of National Biography*, edited by Woolf's father, is, of course, a cultural site for the exhibition of exemplary national 'character'. The portrait of the great Victorian patriarch and champion of history as the biography of great men, is an unsurprising target for feminist anger. The press reports of this assault on Carlyle's likeness, including the choice of weapon, are as blood-curdling as any Greek tragedy. *The Suffragette* (18 July 1914) quoted the *Morning Chronicle*'s report of the 'outrage':

> A young woman of refined appearance and very respectably dressed attacked Millais's unfinished portrait of Carlyle with a butcher's cleaver which she carried concealed beneath her blouse, and before she could be restrained made three large cuts on the face and head of the portrait [...] The blows were delivered with lightning-like rapidity, and then an attendant sprang forward, and, grasping her round the waist, swung her away from the picture. (Atkinson 1996: 163)

The attack on Carlyle's portrait occurred four years after Woolf's date of December 1910, but it was a continuation of the suffragette campaign of violence initiated in 1910 when suffragettes turned to window-smashing and picture-slashing in response to the police brutality meted out to peaceful suffrage demonstrators on the notorious 'Black Friday' rally of November 1910, itself coinciding with the opening of the Post-Impressionist Exhibition mounted by Woolf's impresario Bloomsbury friends (Goldman 1998: 117). So the inception of British formalist theories associated with the opening of the Post-Impressionist exhibition is also rooted in the aesthetics of political events on the streets that attended it. It is impossible to understand the formalist aspects of modernist aesthetics as occurring in a political vacuum. Woolf's modernist manifesto makes this clear.

Aristotle frequently refers to the tragic renditions of the House of Thebes, and in likewise citing Clytemnestra in Aeschylus's *Agamemnon*, Woolf invites reinterpretation of her legend but not total departure from it, just as Aristotle recommends the poet 'may not indeed destroy the framework of the received legends – the fact, for instance, that Clytemnestra was slain by Orestes' (Aristotle 1902: 27) Whereas T. S. Eliot's delineation of the 'mythical method', as he understands it to be exemplified in James Joyce's *Ulysses* and implicitly in his own poem, *The Waste Land*, has led to an understanding of modernist aesthetics as the seeking in the mystical and apparently unifying order of classical myth a refuge from the

Figure 2.1 John Millais's unfinished *Portrait of Thomas Carlyle*, 1877, damaged
by a suffragette in 1914 © Museum of London

'chaos' and 'anarchy' of the real, political world (Eliot 1997b: 371, 373), Woolf's adaptation of the Aristotelian notion of transforming without destroying legend, allows for an alternative, politically engaged mythic dimension to modernist aesthetics, where life and art interpenetrate. The suffragist masquerade of mythic women is a publicly visible and historical example of this.

In Woolf's narrative the hierarchies of class and gender are dissolving as 'human relations have shifted [. . .] between masters and servants, husbands and wives, parents and children' (Woolf 1988: 422). In presenting our reception of the character of one's cook as her primary example of change, Woolf subverts Aristotle's dicta on 'good' character relative to class and gender as well as punning on the employer's professional character reference (Aristotle 1902: 29). Aristotle's advice is aimed at the author, but Woolf's at the audience, yet the distinction between the two is also dissolving in her account of change. She slips quickly from the artistic record of the novelist, Butler, and the dramatist, Shaw, to the record of 'life', which is the locus of the spectator or reader who observes in a new light the cook in the drawing room, and Clytemnestra and the Carlyles on the page. The audience is (co-)author of the changes mooted. Life reframes art. Woolf's correctives to Aristotle not only contribute to a modernist aesthetics that ties life to art but one that understands life, as it is embodied in 'human character', to be remade through art. This version of modernist aesthetics is at odds with that of Eliotic escapism where myth is a Platonic formalism, art the measure of an ideal against which life always fails.

Later in the essay the elusive Mrs Brown comes to embody 'life itself', and the heat is off the apocalyptic cook. But where precisely is the 'human character' whose changes Woolf evidences in this apocalyptic passage? There is no Aristotelean consistent type. Whereas his account of 'character' offers a fixed hierarchical model of the human subject which allows for women ('inferior being[s]') and slaves ('quite worthless') as lesser forms of subjectivity (Aristotle 1902: 29), Woolf's fluid model of 'human character' foregrounds women – wives and servants – as the primary examples of a new subjectivity. She depicts them as emergent from the shadows of the previously dominant, patriarchal subjectivity (Aristotle's primary character 'type'), understood to be present in the person of the cook's employer (whether 'one' is a man or a woman), or figured as Thomas Carlyle, or implicit in the elided figures of Clytemnestra's husband, Agamemnon, and her son, Orestes. Here modernist aesthetics is caught up in a gender war over the constitution and representation of subjectivity.

In the essay as a whole, it is the figure of Mrs Brown who comes to personify an elusive new *feminine* subjectivity, bringing with her 'a tingling, Brownian zone of encounter' (Doyle 2004: 1), in which the very concept of subjectivity is on trial. But at its beginning Woolf's figure of human character is androgynous and universal. She introduces 'character-creating' as the 'foundation of good fiction' with the help of a 'demon' who whispers in the ear '– the figure of a man, or of a woman, who said, "My name is Brown. Catch me if you can"' (Woolf 1988: 420). If the figure's gender is unstable, so too is its name: 'Some Brown,

Smith, or Jones comes before [novelists] and says [. . .] "Come and catch me
if you can'" (ibid.:). Yet Woolf soon begins to favour the feminine as the gender
of this "'will-o'-the-wisp'", this "phantom" of whom most novelists 'have to be
content with a scrap of her dress or a wisp of her hair' (ibid.: 420–1). The figure's feminine gender communicated in this reference to material remnants of
her clothing and body may suggest, too, that the outer, material representation
or signifier itself of subjectivity (or anything else for that matter) is always and
already feminine, as much as it may also signal Woolf's implicit assertion of
feminine subjectivity emergent over masculine. Compare Woolf's figure of the
woman languishing in the shadow of the letter 'I', suggesting the signified of
inner subjectivity is always and already masculine: 'In the shadow of the letter
"I" all is shapeless as mist. Is that a tree? No it is a woman' (Woolf 1929: 130).
Here the male subject of writing (in Mr A's novel) is invisible, or only a sketchily
constructed shadow over the object, material world of Nature, itself identified
with or as the excluded woman – an outer remnant of the male subject.

By the time 'Brown' returns in the essay, shortly after the passage about the
emergent cook, she is a woman who is accompanied in Woolf's famous railway
carriage by a man, Mr Smith, 'a man of business I imagined' with 'unpleasant
business to settle with Mrs Brown; a secret, perhaps sinister business, which
they did not intend to discuss in my presence' (Woolf 1988: 423). The witnessed
conversation reprises and renders into self-reflexive dialogue Woolf's earlier
narrative on servants and change in the domestic sphere: "'Yes, the Crofts have
had very bad luck with their servants." [. . .] My grandmother had a maid who
came when she was fifteen and stayed till she was eighty." [. . .] "One doesn't
often come across that sort of thing nowadays." [. . .] "What changes they're
making in this part of the world"'. (ibid.: 423–4)

The carriage scene plays out various permutations of the master/slave model
of subjectivity introduced in the 1910 passage where new modernist aesthetics
are seen to undo the traditional hierarchized binaries. There has been a splitting-
off in the model of subjectivity represented by 'Brown' whereby Brown is now a
woman, not a man. And Mrs Brown persists as a woman even when, towards the
close of the essay she masquerades under other names too, regardless of gender:
'Ulysses, Queen Victoria, Mr Prufrock – to give Mrs Brown some of the names
she has made famous lately – is a little pale and dishevelled by the time her
rescuers reach her' (Woolf 1988: 435). The male residue of Brown has perhaps
become Mr Smith. On the other hand, her designated married status renders
Mrs Brown subordinate to her absent husband, 'Mr Brown', who is never mentioned by name yet whose marriage to her has given her the name and title by
which she is known. In one version, Woolf's narrator imagines her perhaps to be
a war widow: 'I thought of her in a seaside house [. . .]. Her husband's medals
were on the mantelpiece. [. . .] And then, into this fantastic and secluded life, in
broke Mr Smith' (ibid.: 425). We are left to speculate on the whereabouts of Mrs
Brown's husband in ways that may remind us of Clytemnestra's predicament
during her husband Agamemnon's long absence in the Trojan war. Is he still at

war? Is he dead? Is he an adulterer or a bigamist? Is she? Has he absconded? Meanwhile Mr Smith ushers in an Aristotelian scene of Recognition:

> They sat closeted together.
> And then Mrs Brown faced the dreadful revelation. She took her heroic decision. Early, before dawn, she packed her bag and carried it herself to the station. She would not let Smith touch it. She was wounded in her pride, unmoored from her anchorage; she came of gentlefolks who kept servants – but details could wait. The important thing was to realize her character, to steep oneself in her atmosphere. (Woolf 1988: 425)

Whatever the details of the plot or of the 'dreadful revelation', then, the status of Mrs Brown's character as 'unmoored' is the most important point to establish. The undoing of subjectivity here may compare to Eliot's rejection of poetic 'personality' (Eliot 1997a: 369) in his modernist manifesto, 'Tradition and the Individual Talent', but if his male poetic subjects, for example Prufrock, flirt with the possibility of dissolution into the object world ('I should have been a pair of ragged claws'), Woolf's women characters are already struggling with this object status.

'Unmoored' suggests the loosening of patriarchal ties and of self-definition via relation to others, but it also puns on the notion of supplement ('more') – Mrs Brown has lost her status as the object that supplements and defines her husband; or she has lost that which supplements herself as a (subordinated) subject. 'Unmoored' also puns on the notion of negritude ('Moor'), suggesting that her name marks her as racially subordinate in imperial patriarchy, thereby rendering Mrs Brown brown-skinned too. Has Mrs Brown (or Mr Brown) been passing for white, we might wonder. Is that Smith's 'dreadful revelation'? But '*un*moored' suggest the opposite: Mrs Brown's apparent negritude has been undone: she is no longer designated a Moor, or the status of a Moor. She has become unothered as well as untethered from 'her anchorage'. But just as her marriage to Mr Brown anchors her, so it anchors him. If 'her anchorage' suggests her subordination to him as a supplement that gives him definition as master to her slave, then its loss signifies the loosening of the paternalistic imperial model of relations between 'masters and servants, husbands and wives, parents and children'.

Woolf alludes to the notion of supplement in traditional gendered, hierarchized models of subjectivity when she talks of the reading 'public', who, when informed 'with sufficient conviction' that

> 'All women have tails, and all men humps' [. . .] will actually learn to see women with tails and men with humps, and will think it very revolutionary and probably improper if you say: 'Nonsense. Monkeys have tails and camels humps. But men and women have brains, and they have hearts; they think and they feel' – that will seem to it a bad joke, and an improper one into the bargain. (Woolf 1988: 432–3)

The bodily appendages of tails and humps in this somewhat Darwinian account may be understood to supplement animal bodies just as the body of the human animal may be understood to be appended by genitalia and breasts. But in outlining the priorities of modern fiction writers, Woolf chooses not to define humans by the anatomy that marks the differently sexed bodies of humans as male or female; she refers instead to the internal organs common to both men and women – 'brains' and 'hearts'. She also acknowledges and predicts the great violence done to traditional character by modernist authors: 'And so the smashing and the crashing began' (Woolf 1988: 433). Woolf posits a revolution in both aesthetic and political orders, but she is simultaneously rewriting orthodox somatic orders (which gender the material body feminine and elevate masculine subjectivity as beyond the somatic). As well as reclaiming subjectivity for the feminine she restores common somatic experience to the masculine. Evolutionary discourse emphasises the idea of the progressive modernity of these new models of the subjective and somatic and Woolf is positing a modernist aesthetics borne out of the attempt to both represent and produce these models.

In describing the shocking new treatment of Mrs Brown, Woolf again points up Mrs Brown's bodily features that are common to both women and men, and their common capacity for action and speech: 'But the things she says and the things she does and her eyes and her nose and her speech and her silence have an overwhelming fascination' (Woolf 1988: 436). But Woolf significantly defers any sense of 'a complete and satisfactory presentment' of Mrs Brown. She is incomplete. The reader is buttonholed in the final lines of the essay, to

> Tolerate the spasmodic, the obscure, the fragmentary, the failure. Your help is invoked in a good cause. For I will make one final and surpassingly rash prediction – we are trembling on the verge of one of the great ages of English literature. But it can only be reached if we are determined never, never to desert Mrs Brown. (Woolf 1988: 436)

The 'unmoored' Mrs Brown, then, has in the course of the essay become split off from husband (dead or alive), from home, and from Mr Smith – until, that is, he reappears on the train. But even Smith abandons her to the narrator's sole company: 'He [. . .] jumped out of the train before it had stopped at Clapham Junction. He had got what he wanted, but he was ashamed of himself; he was glad to get out of the old lady's sight' (Woolf 1988: 424). Mr Smith's final, and silent, exit from the carriage and the essay, along with his apparent theft of something from Mrs Brown's person (verbal or concrete), marks another moment of Mrs Brown's 'unmooring' from patriarchy. She and the narrator, whose gender is never determined, are 'left alone together', here, and at the close of the essay. Mrs Brown's character emerges in the process of narrating varying constellations of personnel, Mrs Brown, Mr Smith, a number of novelists, the narrator, and the reader – whose proxy is both Mrs Brown and the narrator: 'A writer is never alone. There is always the public with him – if not on the same seat, at least in the compartment next door' (Woolf 1988: 432). In tandem with this narrative of Mrs Brown's emergence, emerges a modernist model of incomplete, 'unmoored', subjectivity-in-process – or intersubjectivity – by which we realise that to identify Mrs Brown, or the universal individual subject, she will always and already be caught up in a nexus of other subjects-in-process and, along with them, will always and already be dislocated, damaged, robbed of certain elements, incomplete and 'unmoored'. Hurtling towards Waterloo station, the model of character in fiction is already meeting its own Waterloo in the scene between Mrs Brown, Mr Smith and the narrator. The self-conscious narration of the story of 'human character' as a parable of new writing means that we are obliged to understand this story as an allegory of modernist aesthetics itself, and an allegory of the politics of aesthetic production and representation of subjectivity.

Woolf's narrator is early aroused by Mrs Brown to the Arisotelian response to tragedy: 'I was beginning to feel a great deal of pity for her' (Woolf 1988: 424). She finds Mrs Brown 'somewhat tragic, heroic, yet with a dash of the flighty, and fantastic' and the cause of 'myriads of irrelevant and incongruous ideas crowd[ing] into one's head' (ibid.: 425). Woolf, then, has identified an Aristotelian 'framework of [. . .] received legends' (Aristotle 1902: 27) in the figure of Mrs Brown who becomes the dramatic agency by which 'someone begin[s] almost automatically to write a novel about her'; and she imagines her generating numerous other narratorial possibilities:

> old Mrs Brown's character will strike you very differently according to the age and country in which you happen to be born. It would be easy enough to write three different versions of that incident in the train, an English, a French, and a Russian. (Woolf 1988: 425–6)

Woolf's other great modernist manifesto, 'Modern Fiction' (1925), a companion piece to 'Mr Bennett and Mrs Brown', explicitly rejects conventional plot in its libertarian declaration: 'if a writer were a free man and not a slave [. . .] there would be no plot, no comedy, no tragedy, no love interest or catastrophe in the accepted style' (Woolf 1994: 160). But this is not an out-and-out rejection of plot so much as a call for plot to be completely restyled. Modernist fiction, as Woolf represents it, compresses its myriad, fragmentary plots into dense imagery, complex figures and tropes, and into its endlessly mutable representations of character. This imagistic turn is famously exemplified by Woolf's own amplification of her call to restyle plot in her ensuing declaration that 'Life is not a series of gig lamps symmetrically arranged; life is a luminous halo, a semi-transparent envelope surrounding us from the beginning of consciousness to the end' (ibid.: 160). In the space of one sentence life has become a lamp, a halo and an envelope; and it soon becomes, under the pen of James Joyce, 'a bright yet narrow room', which is apparently too confining for Woolf's tastes, 'centred' as it is 'in a self which, in spite of its tremor of susceptibility, never embraces or creates what is outside itself and beyond' (ibid.: 162). If 'self' here is understood as Joyce's representation of his characters' subjectivity through stream-of-consciousness technique, then Woolf seems to be dissatisfied by the sense of the self's completeness, its confinedness, and its disappointing 'tremor', which suggests she is looking for a more radical and seismic, undermining, destabilising, and decentring of subjectivity than her reading of *Ulysses* has identified.

Character, contra Edna Rosenthal, is not 'inflated' over plot by Woolf (Rosenthal 2008: 83), so much as undone. Rosenthal's Aristotelian reading of Woolf is untroubled by the gender politics of Aristotle's terms that so clearly trouble Woolf herself, not least his founding binary opposition of Nature and Art. Rosenthal does not acknowledge Woolf's sustained undermining of the unified model of patriarchal subjectivity constructed from this binary. For example, Aristotle's proposition that Art completes Nature is turned on its head and exposed as a primary metaphor of gender in the famous passage of pseudo-philosophical speculation in 'Time Passes', the central section of *To the Lighthouse* that bridges the pre-1910 Victorian-Edwardian era of first section to the post-1918 era of the third section, and might be understood as Woolf's attempt to inscribe the political process of human character eclipsing and changing after 1910: 'Did Nature supplement what man advanced? Did she complete what he began? [. . .] That dream, of sharing, completing, of finding in solitude on the beach an answer, was then but a reflection in a mirror [. . .] the mirror was broken' (Woolf 1927: 207–8). Anticipating Woolf's acerbic observation, in *A Room of One's Own*, that 'women have served all these centuries as looking-glasses' to patriarchs, as 'mirrors' complicit in war and Empire given that they are 'essential to all violent and heroic action' (Woolf 1929: 34–5), this passage is a restatement of Mr Ramsay's loss of Mrs Ramsay, the servile feminine object's supplementary reflection of the patriarchal, imperial subject. Woolf's modernist aesthetics may be understood, then, as rewriting the gender politics of subject and object.

Woolf's broken mirror seems to trump Joyce's 'cracked lookingglass of a servant', Stephen's symbol of Irish art, at the opening of *Ulysses*, but both are emblems for 'non serviam!' (Joyce 1922: 11, 536). December 1910 endures as an emblematic year in British history when not only did a King die and a government topple, but when the refusal to serve was a radical gesture publically and forcibly made not only by suffragettes, and by many others, including striking miners and those agitating for an Irish Free State. 'And so the smashing and the crashing began', Woolf says of the Georgian age, in 'Mr Bennett and Mrs Brown' (Woolf 1988: 433). 'It is an age [. . .] littered with fragments', she remarks in 'How It Strikes a Contemporary' (1925; Woolf 1994: 237); and towards the close of 'Mr Bennett and Mrs Brown', she counsels that 'we must reconcile ourselves to a season of failures and fragments [. . .] the truth itself is bound to reach us in rather an exhausted and chaotic condition' (Woolf 1988: 435). We must learn to read such writing in its splinters and fractures.

Representation of present change, in any era, necessitates misrepresentation of the past. Modernism is no different – except perhaps in the openness and advocacy of its misrepresentation. Woolf's frequently cited passage on the changes in 1910 endures precisely because it is so helpful in thinking through the relationship between political and aesthetic changes, between ruptures in modernity and its interpenetration with the inception of modernism. The reader is invited by the unfinished, provisional, and playful qualities of the 1910 passage (and the essay it is taken from) continually to supplement what is there. This dialogism contributes to its longevity as a literary, political and cultural theoretical tool.

In 'Old Bloomsbury' (c.1922) Woolf again seeks to calibrate change with reference to the photological and chromatic politics of the domestic interior when she makes the much-cited claim that, on leaving the Victorian household of her parents for the modern domestic enterprise of Gordon Square, the 'light and the air after the rich red gloom of Hyde Park Gate were a revelation' (Woolf 1989: 184). But that first interior was not entirely abandoned. Rather, some of its transported details and qualities became visible for the first time: 'Things one had never seen in the darkness there – Watts pictures, Dutch cabinets, blue china – shone out for the first time in the drawing room at Gordon Square' (ibid.: 184). It is as if Woolf's memory, recorded earlier in the memoir, of the 'gloom' of Hyde Park Gate depends upon the retrospective light shone here from the contrasting remembered experience of Gordon Square's bright interior (ibid.: 184). Woolf dialectically reprises details of the outmoded Victorian interior in describing the new 'exhilarating' spacious context of Gordon Square where 'Watts pictures' survive without the obscuring Watts-inspired interior decorative scheme:

> the Watts–Venetian tradition of red plush and black paint had been reversed; we had entered the Sargent–Furse era; white and green chintzes were everywhere; and instead of Morris wall-papers with their intricate patterns we decorated our walls with washes of plain distemper. (Woolf 1989: 185)

The light and colourism of the new era owes something, then, to the old, since it arises from the appropriation and recontextualising of the art of the past. 'We were full of experiments and reforms', Woolf continues. 'Everything was on trial' (Woolf 1989: 185). In this experimental context, it becomes difficult to read the retention of 'Watts pictures, Dutch cabinets, blue china' as the retention and approval of 'conservative elements' (Ellis 2007: 105). Given that Woolf explicitly states that they 'shone out for the first time', it would seem more appropriate to understand these objects as having undergone a radical transformation and re-evaluation simply by virtue of being recontextualised.

Woolf's account of her new domestic interiors, so significant an example in modernist aesthetics of recontextualising the old as a means of making it new, is for Ellis a cliché (Ellis 2007: 104). But it is nevertheless worth recalling in returning to his argument for a post-Victorian Woolf where he focuses on the political significance of her colour and light tropes. Prismatic colourism is

often depicted in Woolf's writing alongside traditional chiaroscuro. Whereas
the latter is read off by Ellis as evidence of Woolf's 'Post-Victorianism' and as
undermining feminist readings of her colourism, I suggest that the doubling of
chiaroscuro and colourism marks Woolf's 'engagement with the aesthetics and
(gender) politics of light and colour tropes,' which, when 'understood in historical and political contexts' may find chiaroscuro 'reclaim[ed . . .] for feminism'
(Goldman 1998: 22). Chiaroscuro, in Woolf's design has feminist capacity; and
I read Woolf's deployment of colourism and chiaroscuro dialectically through a
feminist theoretical frame (ibid.: 13–24).

Woolf's careful engagement with chiaroscuro needs to be read with attention to the formal properties of Woolf's writing: the precisions of its syntax,
free indirect discourse, its shifting point of view, shifting voice, its highly
complicated extended troping, allegorical play, slippage between simile and
metaphor, its playfully sliding signifiers, its shimmering mosaic of fragmentary
allusions and citations, its intertextuality. It would be foolish to make a case for
the recategorisation of Woolf as Victorian simply by plucking out the carefully
recontextualised and fragmentary allusions to Victorian things and concepts
from the shifting epistemological orderings and ontological loosenings of
Woolf's modernist writing. In his counter-reading of Woolf's eclipse writings,
Ellis disputes my 'prismatic' Woolf, and not least her references to the overturn-
ing of patriarchy in the persons of the squire and his dogs attending the eclipse
scene. Ellis's case for unmasking the modernist Woolf as 'Post-Victorian' Woolf
rests on his insistence on her reverence for class hierarchy. I ignore Woolf's
alleged 'applauding and upholding of aristocratic tradition', he contends, and
her next diary entry, exemplifying her pro-aristocratic stance, on her 'visit to the
Nicolsons at Long Barn':

> 'Vita very opulent, in her brown velvet coat with the baggy pockets, pearl
> necklace . . . I mean, certain gifts & qualities & good fortunes are here
> miraculously combined . . .' [Woolf 1980: 144]. Admittedly, unlike the
> Yorkshire squire Vita was not on this occasion attended by her dogs, as she
> often was when Woolf saw her at Knole ('a sort of covey of noble English
> life' [*D3*: 125]), and as she tends to be throughout *Orlando*. Discounting
> the shadows in Woolf, in the far-reaching symbolism of Woolf's attitude
> towards the past, particularly the Victorian past, and disregarding its
> complexity, its mixed nature of rejection and recuperation; it also betrays
> an exaggerated belief in Woolf's consistent and thoroughgoing radicalism
> [. . .]. (Ellis 2007: 104–5)

In fact this diary entry (for 4 July) *does* mention Sackville-West's dogs in attendance: 'Such opulence & freedom, flowers all out, butler, silver, dogs, biscuits,
wine, hot water, log fires, Italian cabinets, Persian rugs, books' (Woolf 1980:
144); and the sentence that Ellis partially quotes on the opulence of her lover's
garbs actually ends by describing Sackville-West herself in almost canine terms:
'very opulent, in her brown velvet coat with the baggy pockets, pearl necklace,

& slightly furred cheeks'. A few lines later Lord Sackville-West is 'smooth & ambling as a blood horse, [. . .] his great Sackville eyes drooping, & his face all clouded with red & brown' (ibid.:). Woolf also records here arguing with her lover's husband, Harold Nicolson, about the Empire, and Nicolson's own lover Raymond Mortimer siding with her:

> 'The point is, Raymond, our English genius is for government.' 'The governed don't seem to enjoy it' said Raymond. [. . .] So on to the system of bribery; to the great age of England being the age of colonial expansion. [. . .] 'But why not grow, change?' I said. Also, I said [. . .] 'can't you see that nationality is over? All divisions are now rubbed out, or about to be.' Raymond vehemently assented. [. . .] I was sitting on a carved Italian stool over the log fire; he & Raymond bedded in the soft green sofa. Leonard's injustice to the aristocracy was discussed. (Woolf 1980: 145)

Ellis makes no reference to this conversation where Woolf is clearly arguing with her aristocratic hosts over imperialism and class.

To ascertain how far the historical person, Virginia Woolf, could be said to countenance 'Labourite' or other political 'affiliation', I would turn to various sources, including (with a wary eye) to her own diary records of how she voted, to her various and contradictory writings on her involvement in labour and women's movements; and to David Bradshaw's painstaking account of the complicated history of her formal political affiliations. Attempting to think through 'Woolf in suffrage and suffrage in Woolf', I turn to Sowon S. Park's excellent analysis of Woolf's changing and often contradictory feminist and suffragist stances in her life and her writing. But there is more interest for me in what kind of politics and political subjectivities are inscribed and produced in the writing, as she shaped and reshaped it for publication; how relevant autobiography, the material facts of her formal politics, are framed, reorganised and interpenetrate in the writing itself. Ellis retreats from the artistry of Woolf's essay into the apparently empirically more secure factual life realm of the diary; counters my reading of the essay with his of the diary.

The 'Post-Victorian' depiction of Woolf's languishing in the shades ignores the formal methods by which she frames and re-inscribes patriarchal chiaroscuro. Ellis puts Woolf in the mould of her 'Victorian forebears numerous and eminent' who comprised a 'consolidated network that effected Woolf's "heredity position" [T. S. Eliot's phrase], and that she would spend the lengthy Post-Victorian portion of her life continually remaking' (Ellis 2007: 11). 'Remaking' suggests here a punishing regime of Victorian cud-chewing and regurgitation, rather than the transformational modernist force of Ezra Pound's slogan, 'Make it New', or that of Woolf's own splintering and fragmentary eclipse and prismatics imagery. Ellis has her merely reheating Victorian leftovers. Woolf has become a postmodernist pasticheuse of the Victorian.

Returning to 'The Sun and the Fish', and noting my neglect of the contiguous diary entry, Ellis himself neglects altogether the essay's second half. Rectifying both our omissions proves productive. Is the second half of the essay a reworking of this diary entry on the home life of the Nicolsons? 'The Sun' half is juxtaposed with 'the Fish' half: bang after the eclipse scene comes something completely different: the illuminated aquarium at London's Zoological Gardens. If 'the Fish' section is read as a counterpart to Woolf's diary observations on the Nicolsons, they may be read as the targets of Woolf's satirical description of the fish inhabiting the tank, 'lined with red electric light [. . .] undulating like white pancakes on a frying pan [. . .] armoured in blue mail [. . .] some given prodigious claws, some outrageously fringed with huge whiskers' (Woolf 1994: 523). We may also read Woolf's description of Vita's opulent clothes into the essay's final salvo on the ephemeral nature of sartorial indices of rank in contrast to the levelling democracy of common human nakedness:

> Under our tweed and silk is nothing but a monotony of pink nakedness. Poets are not transparent to the backbone as these fish are. Bankers have no claws. Kings and Queens themselves have neither ruffs nor frills. In short, if we were to be turned naked, into an Aquarium – but enough. The eye shuts now. It has shown us a dead world and an immortal fish. (Woolf 1994: 524)

Revisiting this passage now, in the light of Proust (whom Woolf was reading throughout the 1920s), I would suggest her aquarium scene also echoes (in its imagery and its narrative mobility over the glass wall of the tank), the class-inflected chiaroscuro deployed in the following passage, describing how the hotel dining-room at Balbec, flooding with light, became

> an immense and wonderful aquarium against whose wall of glass the working population of Balbec, the fishermen and also the tradesmen's families, clustering invisibly in the outer darkness, pressed their faces to watch, gently floating upon the golden eddies within, the luxurious life of its occupants, a thing as extraordinary to the poor as the life of strange fishes or molluscs (an important social question, this: whether the wall of glass will always protect the wonderful creatures at their feasting, whether the obscure folk who watch them hungrily out of the night will not break in some day to gather them from their aquarium and devour them). (Proust 1924: 363)

As well as the class politics of high modernist Proustian aesthetics, Woolf's eclipse essay also draws on the gender politics of suffragist aesthetics. The art-work of Sylvia Pankhurst, who was born into the Victorian era like Woolf herself in 1882, makes me more convinced of the significance of suffragist and prismatic feminist aesthetics in Woolf's writing, which never entirely banishes patriarchal chiaroscuro. Woolf subverts the normative gendered terms of traditional chiaroscuro and patriarchal subjectivity in her image of the shadow 'across the page', mentioned above, blocking the woman reader of Mr A's novel, and 'the shadow of Alan [. . .] obliterat[ing] Phoebe'(Woolf 1929: 105). In 'Professions for Women' (1931), the woman writer's page is overshadowed

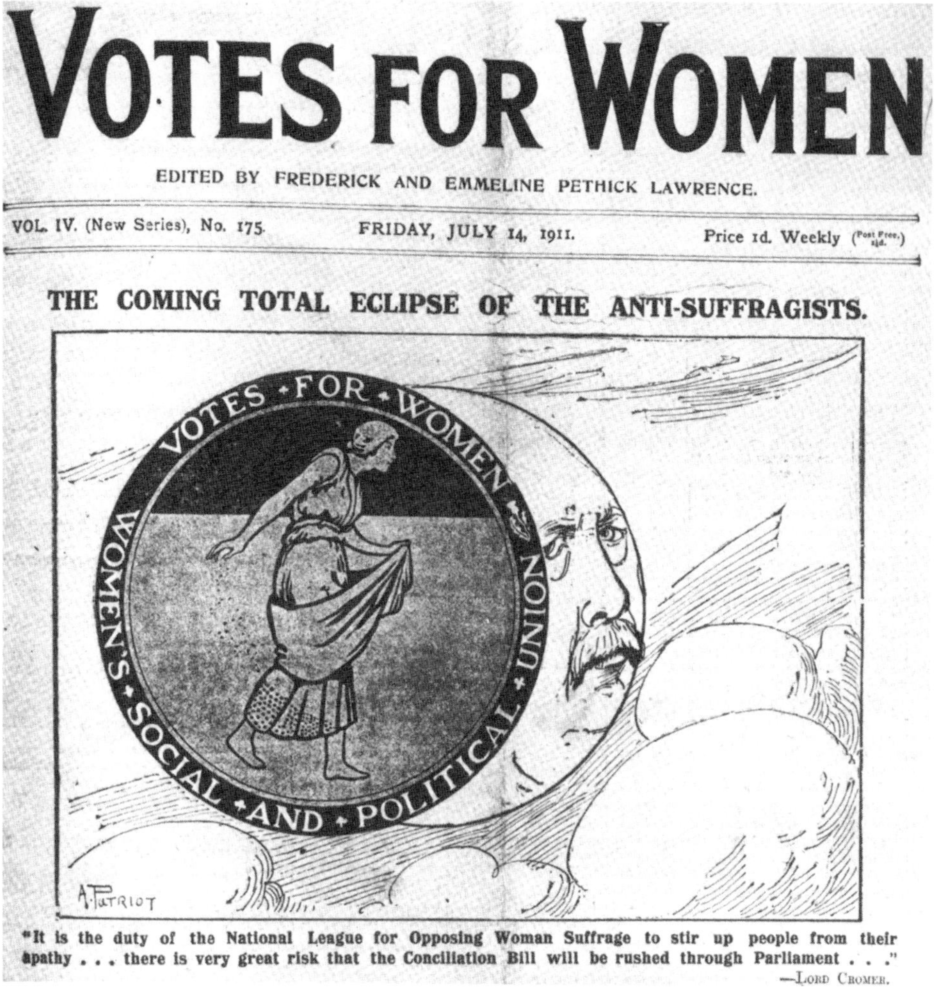

VOTES FOR WOMEN

EDITED BY FREDERICK AND EMMELINE PETHICK LAWRENCE.

VOL. IV. (New Series), No. 175.   FRIDAY, JULY 14, 1911.   Price 1d. Weekly (Post Free. 1½d.)

THE COMING TOTAL ECLIPSE OF THE ANTI-SUFFRAGISTS.

*It is the duty of the National League for Opposing Woman Suffrage to stir up people from their apathy . . . there is very great risk that the Conciliation Bill will be rushed through Parliament . . ."
—LORD CROMER.

Figure 2.2 Contemporary cartoon by 'A Patriot', 1911 © Museum of London

by something feminine: the self-hating, self-effacing Victorian 'Angel in the House' (the female draught excluder, skirt rustler, and chicken-leg bin): 'She sacrificed herself daily. If there was a chicken, she took the leg; if there was a draught, she sat in it [. . .]The shadow of her wings fell on my page [. . .] I turned upon her and caught her by the throat. [. . .] Had I not killed her she would have killed me. She would have plucked the heart out of my writing' (Woolf 1942: 150, 151).

This repeated feminist eclipsing of patriarchal eclipsers, is one already performed visually in suffragist aesthetics, as evidenced by the 1911 cartoon by 'A Patriot' (see Figure 2.2) in *Votes for Women*, the feminist organ edited by Frederick and Emmeline Pethick Lawrence, which enjoyed mass circulation.

Entitled 'THE COMING TOTAL ECLIPSE OF THE ANTI-SUFFRAGISTS', it depicts the sun with the face of Lord Cromer being eclipsed by the circular emblem of the Women's Social and Political Union, with the figure of a maiden sowing seeds at its centre (itself subversively regendering the image of solar dissemination, and solar subjectivity), and sporting the name of the union and its slogan 'VOTES FOR WOMEN'. A sample of Lord Cromer's antifeminist cant is cited below the image: 'It is the duty of the National League for Opposing Woman Suffrage to stir up people from their apathy . . . there is a very great risk that the Conciliation Bill will be rushed through Parliament'.

The cartoon is in black and white, but its circular WSPU image resembles the highly coloured mass-produced tin badge designed by Sylvia Pankhurst for the suffragette campaign, so much so that one suspects she may be the anonymous 'Patriot' who authored the cartoon. 'Incorporating the purple, white and green colour-scheme of the [WSPU]', the motif in this particular example (see Plate 2) from the Museum of London

> depicts a woman breaking free: stepping through a gate with iron bars and over heavy chains, carrying a 'Votes for Women' streamer. By 1909 the [WSPU] was commissioning a wide range of badges, brooches, pendants, pins and hatpins. These raised funds for the campaign and helped to promote the Votes for Women cause. (Museum of London)

Even in the cartoon's black and white, it is difficult not to read the colourism of the WSPU's tricolour as present in the eclipsing suffragist disc. Woolf herself was clearly aware of the wealth of commodity-based suffragist propaganda flooding the culture. She makes direct reference to such wares in *The Voyage Out* (1915), where Miss Allan pins onto herself 'the parti-coloured button of a suffrage society' (Woolf 1915: 243), and in *The Waves*, as I have discussed elsewhere, Miss Hudson wears 'purple buttons on her bodice', Miss Lambert a purple ring (Woolf 1931: 19, 48; Goldman 194).

Woolf's account of the eclipse in 'The Sun and the Fish', composed as it was for publication in the feminist magazine *Time and Tide*, also re-inscribes such iconography. The colours of the union jack turning to the colours of the suffragist tricolour in Woolf's essay account of the defeat of the sun are clearly feminist. 'The blue turned to purple; the white became livid as at the approach of a violent but windless storm. Pink faces went green, and it became colder than ever' (Woolf 1994: 522). But Woolf's 'eye has not done with us yet' (ibid.: 523). After light capsizing, comes the rejuvenating power of returning light. This time it is a 'rainbow-like in a hoop of colour', which moves beyond the narrow allegorical possibilities of the purple, white and green (ibid.: 522).

Woolf's diary on Saturday 9 March 1918 records her attendance at a 'Suffrage Rally' (celebrating the partial enfranchisement of women), and her sight of Pethick Lawrence 'rising & falling on her toes, as if half her legs were made of rubber, throwing out her arms, opening her hands, & thought very badly of this form of art (Woolf 1977: 125). Woolf also had links with Lord Cromer.

She knew (and frequently mentions in her diaries and letters) his second wife, Lady Cromer, née Katherine Thynne (1865–1933). Evelyn Baring, first Earl of Cromer (1841–1917), was a diplomatist and proconsul who became the Consul-General in Egypt. Woolf records a number of conversations in the 1920s with the widow concerning her marriage to Lord Cromer and her experience, as his consort, of colonial life. His published works are counted as classics of Victorian imperialist writing: *Modern Egypt* (1908), *Ancient and Modern Imperialism* (1910); *Political and Literary Essays* (1913–16). Lady Cromer was still complaining to Woolf in 1925: 'And why did I marry Cromer? I loathed Egypt' (Woolf 1980: 51). Perhaps some of the many references to Egypt in *The Waves* may be sourced in these exchanges.

Certainly these fragmentary allusions need to be understood in relation to the solar imagery structuring this novel, and to Bernard's account of the solar eclipse (Woolf 1931: 313), which itself reprises and re-inflects Woolf's diary and essay accounts of the eclipse (significantly *sans* feminist colours). It is clear that Woolf's solar eclipse imagery is deployed as an emblem of subjectivity in eclipse in all these accounts. There is a trace of the feminist anti-Cromer cartoon too, which offers further evidence of the wider cultural currency of solar and eclipse imagery in suffragist aesthetics and of Woolf's engagement of these aesthetics in her writing. Like the cartoon, Woolf's stylised redesign of the solar eclipse also provides us with a Venn diagram in which there is a merging and interpenetration of feminist and modernist aesthetics, in a new zone of avant-garde aesthetics. In both designs, there is clearly too an eclipsing of Victorian imperialism.

Returning to Woolf's modernist manifesto, 'Mr Bennett and Mrs Brown', which offers a series of broken and fragmentary narratives about the historical changes undergone by human character in recent and contemporary writings, it becomes clear that Woolf's figurative designs on Mrs Brown trace a similar process of eclipse and refiguring. In warning us against the expectation of 'a complete and satisfactory presentment of her' (Woolf 1988: 436), Woolf is pointing up a model of modernist and feminist aesthetics as self-consciously incomplete and arising from the impetus to always undo unifying and fixed models of subjectivity. Her assertion that 'on or about December 1910 human character changed' ushers in the realisation that human character continues to change. In this sense, the work of modernist aesthetics is never done.

Note

1. 'Really excellent bit of literary criticism!' she reports 22 February 1905, 'laying down so simply & surely the rudiments both of literature & of criticism. I always feel surprised by subtlety in the ancients – but Aristotle said the first & the last words on this subject'; and a few days later she finds him 'singularly interesting & not at all abstruse' (Woolf 1990: 240–1, 242). S. H. Butcher's 1902 edition is in her library.

Works Cited

Aristotle (1902) *Poetics*, trans. S. H. Butcher, 3rd edn, London: Macmillan.

Atkinson, Diane (1996) *The Suffragettes in Pictures*, Stroud: Sutton Publishing.

Banfield, Ann (2000) *The Phantom Table: Woolf, Fry, Russell and the Epistemology of Modernism*, Cambridge: Cambridge University Press.

Blast 1 (1914), ed. Bradford Morrow, Santa Rosa, CA: Black Sparrow Press, 1993.

Bradshaw, David (1997) 'British Writers and Anti-Fascism in the 1930s, Part I: The Bray and Drone of Tortured Voices', *Woolf Studies Annual*, 3: 3–27.

—— (1998) 'British Writers and Anti-Fascism in the 1930s, Part II: Under the Hawk's Wing', *Woolf Studies Annual*, 4: 41–66.

Childs, Donald J. (2001) *Modernism and Eugenics: Woolf, Eliot, Yeats, and the Culture of Degeneration*, Cambridge: Cambridge University Press.

Doyle, Laura (2004) 'Introduction: What's Between Us?', *Modern Fiction Studies*, 50.1: 1–7.

Eliot, T. S. (1997a) 'Tradition and the Individual Talent', in *Modernism: An Anthology of Sources and Documents*, ed. Vassiliki Kolocotroni et al., Edinburgh: Edinburgh University Press (originally published 1919).

—— (1997b) '*Ulysses*, Order and Myth', in *Modernism: An Anthology of Sources and Documents*, ed. Vassiliki Kolocotroni et al., Edinburgh: Edinburgh University Press (originally published 1923).

Ellis, Steve (2007) *Virginia Woolf and the Victorians*, Cambridge: Cambridge University Press.

Goldman, Jane (1998) *The Feminist Aesthetics of Virginia Woolf: Modernism, Post-Impressionism and the Politics of the Visual*, Cambridge: Cambridge University Press.

Joyce, James (1922) *Ulysses*, New York: BiblioLife, 2007.

Park, Sowan S. (2005) 'Suffrage and Virginia Woolf: "The Mass Behind the Single Voice"', *Review of English Studies*, 56: 119–34.

Proust, Marcel (1924) *Remembrance of Things Past*, vol. 3: *Within a Budding Grove, Part One*, trans. C. K. Scott Moncrieff, London: Chatto & Windus, 1966.

Rosenthal, Edna (2008) *Aristotle and Modernism: Aesthetic Affinities of T. S. Eliot, Wallace Stevens, and Virginia Woolf*, Eastbourne: Sussex Academic Press.

Virginia Woolf (1915) *The Voyage Out*, London: Duckworth.

—— (1927) *To the Lighthouse*, London: Hogarth Press.

—— (1929) *A Room of One's Own*, London: Hogarth Press.

—— (1931) *The Waves*, London: Hogarth Press.

—— (1942) *The Death of the Moth*, London: Hogarth Press.

—— (1977) *The Diary of Virginia Woolf*, vol. 1, ed. Anne Olivier Bell and Andrew McNeillie, London: Hogarth Press.

—— (1978) *The Diary of Virginia Woolf*, vol. 2, ed. Anne Olivier Bell and Andrew McNeillie, London: Hogarth Press.

—— (1980) *The Diary of Virginia Woolf*, vol. 3, ed. Anne Olivier Bell and Andrew McNeillie, London: Hogarth Press.

—— (1988) *The Essays of Virginia Woolf*, vol. 3, ed. Andrew McNeillie, London: Hogarth Press.

—— (1994) *The Essays of Virginia Woolf*, vol. 4, ed. Andrew McNeillie, London: Hogarth Press.

—— (1989) *Moments of Being*, ed. Jeanne Schulkind, 2nd edn, London: Grafton.

—— (1990) *A Passionate Apprentice: The Early Journals*, ed. Mitchell E. Leaska, London: Hogarth Press.

Further Reading

Banfield, Ann (2000) *The Phantom Table: Woolf, Fry, Russell and the Epistemology of Modernism*, Cambridge: Cambridge University Press.

Bahun, Sanja (2008) 'The Burden of the Past, the Dialectics of the Present: Notes on Virginia Woolf's and Walter Benjamin's Philosophies of History', *Modernist Cultures*, 3.2, Summer, http://www.js-modcult.bham.ac.uk/articles/issue6_bahun.pdf

Brown, Bill (1999) 'The Secret Life of Things (Virginia Woolf and the Matter of Modernism)', *Modernism/Modernity*, 6.2, April: 1–28.

Carpentier, Martha C. (1998) *Ritual, Myth, and the Modernist Text: The Influence of Jane Ellen Harrison on Joyce, Eliot and Woolf*, London: Taylor & Francis.

Daugherty, Beth Rigel (1983) 'The Whole Contention between Mr. Bennett and Mrs. Woolf, Revisited', in *Virginia Woolf: Centennial Essays*, ed. Elaine Ginsberg and Laura Gottlieb, Troy, NY: Whitston.

Doyle, Laura (2004) 'Introduction: What's Between Us?', *Modern Fiction Studies*, 50.1: 1–7.

Fernald, Anne E. (2007) 'Modernism and Tradition', in *Modernism*, ed. Astradur Eysteinsson and Vivian Liska, Amsterdam and Philadelphia, PA: John Benjamins.

Goldman, Jane (2007) 'Modernist Studies', in *Palgrave Advances in Virginia Woolf Studies*, ed. Anna Snaith, Basingstoke: Palgrave.

Cuddy-Keane, Melba (2003) *Virginia Woolf, the Intellectual, and the Public Sphere* Cambridge: Cambridge University Press.

Luftig, Victor and Reese, Steven (1986) 'Woolf and "The Leaflet Touch": A Political Context for "Mr. Bennett and Mrs. Brown"', *Virginia Woolf Miscellany*, 27: 1–2.

Miller, Andrew John (2007) *Modernism and the Crisis of Sovereignty*, London: Routledge.

Pankhurst, Richard K. (1979) *Sylvia Pankurst: Artist and Crusader*, London: Paddington.

Ross, Stephen (ed.) (2008) *Modernism and Theory: A Critical Debate*, London: Routledge.

Sorum, Eve (2007) 'Taking Note: Text and Context in Virginia Woolf's "Mr. Bennett and Mrs. Brown"', *Woolf Studies Annual*, 13: 137–58.

Seshagiri, Urmila (2004) 'Orienting Virginia Woolf: Race, Aesthetics, and Politics in *To the Lighthouse*', *Modern Fiction Studies*, 50.1: 58–84.

Whitworth, Michael (2000) 'Virginia Woolf and Modernism', in *The Cambridge Companion to Virginia Woolf*, ed. Sue Roe and Susan Sellers, Cambridge: Cambridge University Press.

—— (2005) 'Philosophical Questions', in *Virginia Woolf in Context*, Oxford: Oxford World's Classics.

Winkiel, Laura (2008) *Modernism, Race, and Manifestos*, Cambridge: Cambridge University Press.

3

VIRGINIA WOOLF AND BLOOMSBURY AESTHETICS

Anthony Uhlmann

THIS CHAPTER WILL focus on passages from *To the Lighthouse* which relate to Lily Briscoe and her process of creation. In a way this novel might be understood as an attempt by Virginia Woolf to enter into conversation with those visual artists and visual arts critics who were at the very centre of Bloomsbury aesthetics: Vanessa Bell, Clive Bell, Duncan Grant and Roger Fry. Virginia Woolf's interest in painting, and her anxiety as to how her descriptions of painting in *To the Lighthouse* would be received by painters, and in particular her sister Vanessa Bell and her friend Roger Fry, is well known. I want to roughly sketch three things in this chapter. First, how the understanding of the interlinked ideas of 'sensation' and 'rhythm' which she develops might be drawn into relation with aesthetic ideas explored by the great French painter Paul Cézanne and described by Roger Fry in his critical writings. Second, by considering her 1934 essay *Walter Sickert: A Conversation*, I want to draw these ideas into relation with Woolf's anxiety about entering into dialogue with the visual artists and aesthetic theorists in the Bloomsbury group.

Sensation and Aesthetics: Banfield and Bloomsbury

In *The Phantom Table*, Ann Banfield argues convincingly that Woolf moves towards an aesthetic theory that was 'discovered by Fry in Cézanne' (Banfield 2000: 293). Yet like Allen McLaurin, who has also written an important study linking Cézanne, Fry and Woolf, Banfield does not move very far back from Fry's reading towards the ideas of Paul Cézanne. Rather, her thesis requires that she find a way of identifying Fry's thought with that of British Analytic Philosophy of the early twentieth century. While Banfield establishes that this tradition was an important point of reference for both Fry and Woolf, at times she goes too far in the process of identification, glossing over the real differences between the kinds of thinking which take place on the one hand in a work of analytical philosophy and on the other in a work of art or art criticism. Yet a 'logic of sensations' cannot be identified with analytic logic. As Fry states in

Cézanne, 'What is here called intellect is not, of course, a purely logical function' (Fry 1927: 71).

Banfield states: 'Artistic form . . . is subject to logic, like scientific laws' and proceeds to quote Fry from *Cézanne*, describing the artist's 'sensual intelligence'. She then concludes that 'The logical form discovered has the status of a scientific law which approximates to some fact' (Banfield 2000: 279). The problem here is that of turning an analogy into an identification. While Fry indeed, borrowing his terms from Cézanne, talks of a 'logic of sensations' (ibid.: 276), this is not to suggest that this logic is identical with an analytical or mathematical logic. The idea that there were differences between kinds of logic and forms of expression is something Cézanne insisted upon. He told Joachim Gasquet, 'There's a logic of colour, damn it all! The painter owes allegiance to that alone' (Gasquet 1991: 161).

While it is true that the artist needs to refine or develop the logic of sensation she or he puts to use in making a painting or writing a novel, the process of refinement does not necessarily follow the same steps or tend towards the same end as the 'process of simplification' through which, according to Banfield via Russell, the analytical philosopher develops a scientific language. In buttressing her argument Banfield makes use of the following quotation from Russell: 'Ordinary language is totally unsuited for expressing what physics really asserts, since the words of everyday life are not sufficiently abstract. Only mathematics and mathematical logic can say as little as the physicist means to say' (cited in Banfield 2000: 283). While this may be true in relation to Russell's idea of scientific language, it by no means squares with the manner in which Woolf makes use of language, or Cézanne makes use of visual motifs and colour.

As will be drawn out below in a reading of Woolf's essay on Walter Sickert, for Woolf 'conversation', or everyday language itself, is capable of accomplishing things which a more overtly rational form would be unable to accomplish, and it does this through its very capacity to be *imprecise*. That is, while conversational language might not be proper to scientific enquiry, it does not follow that a logic of sensations, drawing upon colour and visual material, or even such apparently mathematical material as the motifs of geometrical forms, can be identified with a scientific language. The forms created in Cézanne's art are never pure geometrical forms. Banfield herself recognises this in citing a passage from Fry's *Cézanne* where this point is explicitly made as Fry insists that, 'the apparent continuity of the contour is illusory' and that there is a movement from an extreme simplicity of form to extreme complexity (Banfield 2000: 284).

That is, Cézanne's expression, the 'logic of sensations' involves an insistence upon a specificity of thought to painting, one that can be translated, but only by making use of materials proper to the medium into which it is translated. This is a point which Woolf herself insists upon in *Walter Sickert: A Conversation* (Woolf 1934: 23–4).

In short, then, there are types of thinking. Banfield cites the famous dinner party conversation between Virginia Woolf and Bertrand Russell where Russell told Woolf that if she had his mind she would see the world mathematically, as colourless matter. While Banfield notes that Woolf disagreed with much of this, she still manages to conclude that Woolf must have, through the influence of Fry, perhaps, moved closer to Russell's position (Banfield 2000: 262). It might, on the contrary, be argued that these different ways of seeing do nothing but confirm the novelist's intuition that there are different ways of thinking, that there are different minds with different dispositions, different lives with different rhythms, and that these differing dispositions allow or require different types of engagement with the matter of being.

The question of disposition is one which occurs throughout Woolf's works: *The Waves* might be understood to picture how 'types', or people attracted to particular capacities of the human organism (which are not infinite in number, for Woolf, but break rather, into a reasonably small number of types), understand similar sets of experience in differing ways. So too, as will be discussed below, she understands there to be various types of artists: the 'literary' painter, and the painterly writer, being examples of possible types. In this way one might recognise something of a difference between Fry and Woolf. Whereas Fry considers that there is a proper way to do things: a *genuine* logic of sensations for example, which allows him to consider Van Gogh an inferior artist because he does not develop the same conception of form as Cézanne (Fry 1927), Woolf contends, more generously, that there are types of art. The literary painter is not worse than the pure painter: rather, he or she is a different type of painter, one who thinks in a different way, and who, therefore, is capable of different things (see Woolf 1934).

Style, Rhythm and Sensation

The importance of 'rhythm' to an understanding of Virginia Woolf's aesthetic practice has long been known, with a passage from a letter to Vita Sackville-West of 16 March 1926 having often been cited by critics. Yet it is worth quoting again from this letter, which was written while Woolf was working on *To the Lighthouse* (*TTL*), to begin to get our bearings:

> As for the *mot juste*, you are quite wrong. Style is a very simple matter; it is all rhythm. Once you get that, you can't use the wrong words. But on the other hand here am I sitting after half the morning, crammed with ideas, and visions, and so on, and can't dislodge them, for lack of the right rhythm. Now this is very profound, what rhythm is, and goes far deeper than words. A sight, an emotion, creates this wave in the mind, long before it makes words to fit it; and in writing (such is my present belief) one has to recapture this, and set this working (which has nothing apparently to do with words) and then, as it breaks and tumbles in the mind, it makes words to fit it: But no doubt I shall think differently next year. (*L3*: 247)

There are two processes at work here. First, rhythm is created by external sensation, and second, writing seeks to recapture this sensation. The word 'rhythm' is not one that occurs in Cézanne's letters or in the reported conversations with him in which he described his aesthetic methods (see Gasquet 1991; Kendall 1988; Cézanne 1976). A related term, 'harmony' does occur in these sources, however, and in a manner quite similar to that seen in Woolf's description of rhythm, Cézanne discusses the problem of reproducing the harmony of a sensation encountered in the world.

> [Borély] 'Isn't painting a matter of producing a harmonious impression? And what if I want to celebrate light like this?'
> [Cézanne] 'I know what you mean; there is a languid glow which I will not be able to emulate on canvas; but what if I could create this impression by means of another, corresponding one, even if it meant using bitumen [i.e., the darkest available pigment]!' (Cited in Kendall 1988: 296)

In his important study of Woolf, Allen McLaurin considers the nature of sensation in literature and painting. While he suggests that literature and art must distinguish themselves from sensation (McLaurin 1973: 189), he concedes, following Roger Fry, that there is a purely physiological process (which Fry disparages) at play in painting, such as the direct sensation of colour, for example (ibid.: 193). For McLaurin, this immediate physiological process cannot be conveyed in literature, yet he argues that literature is nevertheless able to create, through the development of formal relations, an analogous sensation, similar to the process that Cézanne describes to Borély. McLaurin argues that Woolf attempts to develop a kind of painting in literature in order to better convey the 'jar on the nerves' of immediate sensation that Lily Briscoe describes in *To the Lighthouse* (ibid.: 189).

While I am in broad agreement with many of the points McLaurin makes in his fine study I would also wish to underline the manner in which rhythm itself, as Woolf insists in her letter to Vita Sackville-West, both comes from sensation and immediately conveys sensation. That is, first, for Woolf, rhythm comes from sensation as 'A sight, an emotion, creates [a] wave in the mind'. Second, the rhythm of a sentence, whether silently sounded in the head or read aloud, has a physical presence. That is, unlike the meaning of the words which are attributed to sounds, the sounds themselves and the patterns they form in being linked together are purely material, corporeal, bodies which pass as sound waves through the air, or are silently sounded as verbal images by the neurons within the brain.

'Rhythm' is an important term in Roger Fry's critical writings, and is discussed by Woolf in her biography of Fry. In Fry rhythm is a difficult concept that also seems to be understood to correspond with the personal style of an artist. It must be found if the work is to cohere, but it presents certain dangers: one has to be attuned to the correct rhythm (the rhythm proper to the work), and one cannot allow the rhythm to harden into an habitual form. In *Roger Fry: A Biography*, Woolf discusses Fry's use of the word in his essay 'Art and Life':

> Art and Life are two rhythms [Fry says] – the word 'rhythm' was hence-
> forth to occur frequently in his writing – [Woolf quotes Fry:] 'and in the
> main the two rhythms are distinct, and as often as not play against each
> other. . . under certain conditions the rhythms of life and of art may coin-
> cide with great effect on both; but in the main the two rhythms are distinct,
> and as often as not play against each other.' (*RF*: 214)

Later in her biography Woolf praises Fry both for his power to stimulate and his
power to suggest. She offers two examples of passages she considers to 'break
off heavy with meaning' and 'go behind the picture' being discussed. The first of
these concerns rhythm, Fry states: 'There is great danger in a strong personal
rhythm . . . unless [the artist] constantly strains it by the effort to make it take
in new and refractory material it becomes stereotyped'. The second quotation
from Fry also concerns the development of an aesthetic method: 'You cannot
imitate the final results of mastery without going through the preliminaries'
(*RF*: 228). Passages such as these are elusive, yet certain of their implications
can be clarified through consideration of some of the key ideas of Paul Cézanne,
the painter with whom Roger Fry's career as a critic is most closely associated.

In short, the first idea 'rhythm' can be illuminated by a related term, drawn
from Cézanne, the 'sensation'; while the second idea, of 'going through the preliminaries', corresponds with Cézanne's assertions that the painter is comprised
of two parts, the eye and the mind. While it is possible to work without the
mind, in the manner of the best Impressionists, such as Monet whom Cézanne
says had 'the most prodigious eye since painting began' (Gasquet 1991: 164), the
kind of art Cézanne is seeking to develop involves the processes of organising
and understanding what the eye has perceived. Émile Bernard quotes Cézanne
as follows:

> There are two things in the painter: the eye and the mind; each of them
> should aid the other. It is necessary to work at their mutual development,
> in the eye by looking at nature, in the mind by the logic of organized sen-
> sations which provides the means of expression. (Cited in Kendall 1988:
> 299)

In her biography of Fry, Woolf describes Fry's development as a critic and a
painter. His first passion was for the art of the Renaissance, and this, in effect,
made his own art appear somehow old fashioned. Rather than this being due to
a failure to remain up to date, it reflected Fry's feeling that something important was missing from the art of his time that seemed, as he wrote in 1902,
'paralysed by the fear of failure' (*RF*: 160). What was missing, in part, was a full
understanding of the classical heritage, which, for Fry, was being ignored in line
with:

> a sophistical theory of aesthetics, which denies them the full use of the
> pictorial convention. The arbitrary rule that they have formulated is that
> they may leave out anything they like in a given scene, but that they must

not introduce forms which do not happen to be there, however much these might increase the harmony or intensify the idea. (*RF*: 110)

Although Fry is here discussing English painting in 1902, the arbitrary rules he describes no doubt owe a great deal to French Impressionism. A review of the 1876 Impressionist exhibition described the painter's goal as follows: 'to render which absolute sincerity the impression that features of reality have made rise within them, avoiding compositional adjustment or any attenuation' (cited in Shiff 1998: 14). All of this helps to explain the powerful effect Cézanne's work had upon Fry, both when he first saw it in 1906, and then when he began to look at it in much greater detail while preparing the first Post-Impressionist exhibition at the Grafton Gallery in 1910. While he had exhibited as an Impressionist and had been influenced and taught elements of technique by Claude Pissaro, as Fry outlines in his study (Fry 1927: 35), Cézanne was not satisfied with certain of the tenants of Impressionism. He wanted to bring Classicism to Impressionism; that is, he wanted to marry the kind of formal quality apparent in the classical schools of painting to the impressionist emphasis on working direct from nature (see Goldman 1998). He wanted to emphasise the structure of an image and to create that structure in the process of painting.

In painting, that structure comes from composition and the system of relations built up within the picture by answering motifs. The compositional relations are echoes and repetitions of form, or balancing elements: as Cézanne told his son, 'the whole thing is to put in as much rapport as possible' (cited in Maloon 1998a: 74). These elements are apparent in the overall design of the painting, but Cézanne also understood the brushstroke itself, the small repeated 'touches' which build up the image as forming part of the motif. This is apparent in the use Cézanne made of the term 'sensation', and it is this idea, which can be seen to be developed in *To the Lighthouse*.

Cézanne's Sensation

The 'sensation' is a many sided concept for Cézanne. He used it to refer to the brushstroke itself and the repetition of brushstrokes, as is apparent through the famous story of his falling out with Paul Gauguin because Gauguin copied his technique of marking. Cézanne was reported as saying: 'Oh, this guy Gauguin! I had a little sensation, just a little, little sensation . . . But, you know, it was mine, this little sensation. Well, one day this guy Gauguin, he took it from me' (cited in Shiff 1998: 26).

Yet Cézanne also spoke of the sensation in much more general terms. Émile Bernard reported the following conversation:

'By a perspective I mean a logical vision; in other words one which has nothing absurd about it.'
'But what will you base your perspective on, Master?'
'On nature.'

'What do you mean by that word? Our human nature or nature herself?'

'Both.'

'So you understand art to be a union of the world and the individual?'

'I understand it as personal apperception. This apperception I locate in sensation and I require of the intellect that it should organise these sensations into a work of art.'

'But what sensations are you referring to? Those of your feelings or of your retina?'

'I don't think you can distinguish between the two; however, as a painter, I believe in the visual sensation above all else.' (Cited in Kendall 1988: 289)

While critics such as John Rewald and Richard Shiff have written on the difficulties which are at times involved in determining the extent to which the reported conversations provided by Bernard and Joachim Gasquet among others have been altered in being dramatised, they also consider that the core ideas, which can be further verified in Cézanne's letters, remain clear (see Rewald in Gasquet 1997, and Rewald in Cézanne 1976; Shiff 1991). Among these, for Shiff, is the idea that the sensation involves the interaction of two natures: internal human nature, or that of the artist, and external nature or that of the world perceived. The exchange between these two natures is ongoing: rather than the mind of the artist seeking to impose classical order on nature by applying some iron-cast intellectual formula to it, the artist brings tentative formulas which are open to ongoing modification in the face of nature itself (ibid.: 20–21). Gasquet, whom Shiff considers close to the mark with regard to this (ibid.: 21), reports Cézanne as follows: 'Yes, we need a system. But once the system is established, work from nature. One has a system all arranged, then one forgets it: one works from nature.' (Gasquet 1991: 169).

Cézanne's 'sensation', then, is a remarkably mobile concept. Whereas the idea of an 'impression' carries the sense of a passive reflection, with nature impressing its image on the artist who then faithfully records the moment, 'sensation' involves a complex process of interaction which is more active than passive. The sensation is projected by an external nature, is registered by an internal nature; that is, the sensation is both in the image received and in the artist's response to that image. Further, a sensation analogous to that received from the world is then reprojected by the artist via a process of mental organisation or composition and the brushstrokes that correspond to and build up the new sensation upon the canvas. The sensations in turn inhere in the canvas where they are able to be received by viewers. In a passage cited by Fry (Fry 1927: 68) in his study of Cézanne, Gasquet reports Cézanne as stating:

The landscape is reflected, humanized, rationalized within me. I objective it, project it, fix it on my canvas [. . .]. It may sound like nonsense, but I would see myself as the subjective consciousness of that landscape, and my canvas as its objective consciousness. (Gasquet 1991: 150)

The world, then, can be drawn into the painting, even in unexpected ways. In a letter to Émile Bernard of 1888, Vincent van Gogh wrote of the apparent clumsiness of some of Cézanne's brushstrokes:

> I thought about Cézanne, especially in regard to his touch, which is so inept in certain studies – skip the word inept, given that he probably executed those studies when the mistral was blowing. Since, half the time, I have to cope with the same difficulty, it dawned on me why Cézanne's touch is sometimes so sure and sometimes appears clumsy: it's his easel shaking. (Cited in Maloon 1998b: 171)

While Allen McLaurin, apparently oversimplifying a point he renders much more complex earlier in his book, states that, 'language and art gain their value by their difference from sensation, by their escape from the tyranny of immediacy' (McLaurin 1973: 189), he nevertheless goes on to show that Woolf develops a form capable of creating this very immediacy; 'the jar on the nerves' of which Lily Briscoe speaks. Like Fry, McLaurin tends to undervalue and disparage purely physiological effects in art (Fry criticises both Vincent van Gogh, and music, for their reliance on the physiological). Yet through his reading of Fry, McLaurin does underline how the sensation can be generated, created, through the formal relation of elements within a work. For Cézanne, as we have seen, there is no attempt to escape from sensation; rather, the process of creation is inexorably entwined with the sensation: the sensation, indeed, is that which is conveyed to the canvas, it *is* the brushstroke, and McLaurin has noted how, for Woolf, the brushstroke is equated with the sentence (ibid.: 197). Further, as we have seen, there is no naïve conception of pure immediacy or lack of thought involved in this concept of sensation; rather, the sensation is 'thought' but not necessarily conscious thought or thought mediated through language. This too is clear in the comments Woolf makes with regard to rhythm, where the process of recapturing the rhythm that has been first sensed through nature ('A sight, an emotion') in writing 'has nothing apparently to do with words'. It is, instead, a felt thought: it is sensation and nothing other than sensation, even though it is conveyed or translated by another medium: be it 'bitumen' for Cézanne, or for Woolf, some thought prior to words which the mind 'makes words to fit'. That is, sensation itself, as cognitive scientists (Damasio 2000) and philosophers (Deleuze 1996; Nussbaum 2001) have come to affirm, deserves to be understood to be thought, as much as language is thought.

Such a reading, of sensation as thought, is, I would contend, consistent with Cézanne's understanding. I would further contend that Cézanne's theories, as a number of critics have noted, are developed by Roger Fry, and further adapted by Virginia Woolf: especially in *To the Lighthouse* and *The Waves*.

Fry's Sensation

Fry begins using the word 'sensation' long before he becomes aware of Cézanne. In an unpublished article of 1894, 'The Philosophy of Impressionism', he outlines the manner in which Impressionism moves away from an attempt to depict things, by instead rendering the flux of sensations, which are understood as appearances (Fry 1996: 13–14). The term 'sensation' here has a different sense to that given to it by Cézanne. Whereas the 'sensation' of the Impressionists relates to the appearance of things, Cézanne, as we have seen, brings the appearances, or sensations offered by external nature, into dialogue with the internal nature of the artist; that is, the painter is no longer all 'eye' as with the Impressionists, but now also mind, an organising mind, which orders these external sensations with recourse to its own internal sensations: a sense of form apparent in the answering motifs and perceived harmony of nature. Writing in his essay 'Post Impressionism' of 1911, Fry ventures that Cézanne took this step, a step away from mere recording to reinstating the kind of expressive form that had been lost to modern art, 'almost unconsciously' (ibid.: 109). In doing this, Fry contends that Cézanne went beyond appearances in creating *the real* in his pictures. In his full length study of Cézanne, Fry moves away from this notion of the unconscious, indicating that Cézanne represents an almost miraculous coming together of a rigorous intellect and a 'sensibility of extreme delicacy' (Fry 1927: 70). He recognises the discomfort with the word 'intellect' and offers a rare footnote in which he justifies the term:

> What is here called intellect is not, of course, a purely logical function. All apprehension of formal relations depends on the special sensibility of the artist. . . an artist's sensibility to form appears as having two almost distinct functions according as it is applied to the correlation of all the separate forms in a design, and as applied to the detailed texture of form, its minor variations and play of surface. In comparing these two one is tempted to use the word intellectual of the former . . . . (Fry 1927: 71)

Fry, then, has separated the terms somewhat, using 'sensation' to apply to the data received from external nature, and an intellectual 'sensibility', for the apprehension and organisation of this that is applied by the internal nature of the artist. The understanding of the process involved, however, is identical with that described above through Cézanne's descriptions of his own endeavours. Elsewhere in this study, indeed, Fry recognises that these two domains might be understood, in Cézanne's terms, to correspond through the sensation: '[Cézanne] alone was sincere enough to rely on his sensations and abandon all efforts at eloquence or emphasis' (Fry 1927: 72).

Woolf's Sensation

In a letter to Roger Fry of April 1923, Virginia Woolf states that she is reading a biography of Cézanne. While she does not indicate whether this is Vollard's 1914 biography, or Gasquet's book, which appeared in 1921, Vollard's biography is held in her and Leonard's library. While Woolf would have known of Cézanne's notion of the sensation through Fry, then, she also clearly knew of his key ideas through her own reading.

In the final section of *To the Lighthouse*, Lily Briscoe is described finally beginning to solve the problem posed by external nature, the image that confronts her, which has been held suspended over the many years since the time recounted in the opening section of the novel. At last she begins:

> With a curious physical sensation, as if she were urged forward and at the same time must hold herself back, she made her first quick decisive stroke. The brush descended. It flickered brown over the white canvas; it left a running mark. A second time she did it – a third time. And so pausing and so flickering, she attained a dancing rhythmical movement, as if the pauses were one part of the rhythm and the strokes another, and all were related; and so, lightly and swiftly pausing, striking, she scored her canvas with brown running nervous lines which had no sooner settled there than they enclosed (she felt it looming out at her) a space. Down in the hollow of one wave she saw the next wave towering higher and higher above her. For what could be more formidable than that space? Here she was again, she thought, stepping back to look at it, drawn out of gossip, out of living, out of community with people into the presence of this formidable ancient enemy of hers – this other thing, this truth, this reality, which suddenly laid hands on her, emerged stark at the back of appearances and commanded her attention. (Woolf 2000: 172–3)

Not only the emphasis on sensation (which begins this passage and infuses it through the rhythm of the brushstrokes) but also on moving from appearance to reality bring Cézanne sharply to mind here. The links are even more fully apparent if one looks at the drafts of *To the Lighthouse*, where the link that Cézanne makes between the sensation that is felt and the sensation that is conveyed by the brushstroke and now comes to life on the canvas is underlined through the repeated use of the words 'sensitive' and 'sensibility':

> Her preparations were made; her palate spread; & now
> With a curious physical sensation of ~~leaping~~, . . . she laid the t made
> The first quick decisive stroke. It flickered brown over the pure
> white canvas . . . attaining by degrees, a
> ~~dancing~~ rhythmical ~~sensitive~~ movement, as if the
> brush itself were a one sensitive ~~proboscis of instrument of some~~
> some sensitive weapon ~~in the inspired~~ with nerves ~~of its own~~
> she ~~scribbled~~ scored her canvas ~~over with~~ with light brown
> ~~sl~~ lines ~~wavering, whose~~ which ~~extreme~~ sensibility froze into
> ~~whose~~ sensibility ~~enclosed described the~~ at once settled into something
> ~~formidable~~ permanent. (Woolf 1983: 256)

As with Cézanne, then, there is a complex interaction around the idea of sensation: sensation is projected by external nature and seen, but then it needs to be organised by the internal nature of the artist (and the process of organisation, the understanding or compositional thinking required of the 'mind' of the artist, has been that which has been in suspension, for Lily, between the first and third parts of the novel). Once it has been organised or understood the sensation is transferred to the touch, with each touch constituting a sensation, laying down sensation in turn on the canvas, which might then be experienced or confronted by a viewer.

The process of ordering sensations, then, is something that concerns the artist, but it also concerns the viewer. Everyone has sensations; what is required, however, both with the creation of the work and with any response to the work, is that those sensations be given solidity in being properly composed within the work. This problem, of how to properly connect the work by drawing the relations between motifs, is the very one which confronts Lily:

> It was a question, she remembered, how to connect this mass on the right hand with that on the left. She might do it by bringing the line of the branch across so; or break the vacancy in the foreground by an object (James perhaps) so. But the danger was that by doing that the unity of the whole might be broken. She stopped; she did not want to bore him. (Woolf 2000: 60; see also Woolf 1983: 93)

The problem of making connections in the work is immediately linked with the problem of making connections in life, connections with other people. Mr Bankes has seriously engaged with her picture, and to Lily, who is used to being patronised, this involves both on the one hand having something which is very important to her taken from her (she hates the violation of her unfinished work being seen) and on the other being exhilarated by being able to share in an almost unimaginable intimacy, one which is not simply sexual but related to the emotional intellect which Fry has seen in the work of Cézanne. Mr Bankes's genuine engagement with her work has opened to her a power of the world, 'which she had not suspected, that one could walk away down that long gallery not alone any more but arm-in-arm with somebody' (Woolf 2000: 60). The metaphor here links the interaction around the work with immediate human intimacy. What allows this as a possibly is a corresponding effort on each side: Lily's effort to relate, and Mr Bankes's effort to understand what is being related.

Again it is a problem of translation between, in this case, the medium proper to art and the medium proper to life. The problem of translation between forms or rhythms was something that greatly occupied Woolf and in some senses structured her relationships with her circle, the Bloomsbury group, which contained so many painters and theorists of artistic practice. It seems as if in some way she wanted to translate for them.

Literature and Painting

In 1934 Woolf published a pamphlet on the English painter Walter Sickert, entitled *Walter Sickert: A Conversation*. This work returns to the question of the relation between the arts of painting and writing. Sickert told Woolf, 'I have always been a literary painter' (Woolf 1934: 26, see Lee 1999: 632). It is apparent, however, that what is at stake in this relation between painting and literature needs to be clarified.

Cézanne, for his part, condemned a certain kind of 'literary' painting (see Gasquet 1991: 16). Yet, the rejection of the literary is not as straightforward as it might appear. Cézanne here equates 'literary' painting with the over-explanatory, the merely illustrative: the kind of painting which directs a viewer's interpretation. Fry's study of Cézanne, however, makes clear that the relations between Cézanne's art and literature are more complex. Fry underlines how Cézanne, in his early work, came to painting with an imagination which was already steeped in poetry, and, rather than seeking to draw upon external nature (as he was to later do), he at first attempted to draw upon his imagination. Fry states:

> He worked . . . to find expression for the agitations of his inner life, and, without making literary pictures in the bad sense of the word, he sought to express himself as much by the choice and implications of his figures as by the plastic exposition of their forms. (Fry 1927: 9)

Hermione Lee outlines in her biography how Woolf came to write *Walter Sickert: A Conversation* (Lee 1999: 632–3). Clearly, the problem of how one might begin to consider positive relations between literature and painting when her visual artist friends where hostile to the very idea of 'literary' painting, is one which preoccupied her. No doubt Woolf was encouraged in this project by Walter Sickert himself, yet the sense of difficulty in establishing this relation would have been exacerbated for her by her attraction to, and sense of distance from, the kind of visual aesthetic intelligence developed by her artist friends, and Vanessa Bell, Duncan Grant, Clive Bell and Roger Fry in particular. Lee, indeed, alludes to the feelings of ridicule she exposed herself to in developing the idea that there might be such a thing as a worthwhile 'literary' reading of a painting.

Some of the anxiety inherent in the process makes itself felt in the form of this piece. While the dialogue form was a well-known technique within art criticism (see Shiff 1991: 16), Woolf chooses to write a 'conversation' rather than a 'dialogue'. The dialogue, with its echoes of Plato and the history of philosophy, is a serious form, one in which questions are dissected and analysed until the truth is at last discovered. Woolf opposes 'the conversation' to this: while it is still a matter of entering into a kind of dialogue, where contrasting positions might be brought into comparison, the conversation is not serious; rather, it is impure, 'it runs hither and thither, seldom sticks to the point, [and] abounds in exaggeration and inaccuracy' (Woolf 1934: 5). Yet while conversation might only 'haunt the borders' of the true silence that is at the core of any art, this borderland is nevertheless 'a region of very strong sensations' (ibid.: 12). Furthermore, towards the end of her essay, Woolf hints that this kind of impurity inheres in any major work of art, so that, in effect, the conversation allows us to see the

kinds of hybrid forms that can emerge in the arts. The apparent lack of seriousness that Woolf develops reveals a deeper seriousness, and an impatience with
forms of criticism that do not countenance the necessarily impure mixtures that
emerge both in life and art.

> Undoubtedly, they agreed, the arts are closely united. What poet sets pen to
> paper without first hearing a tune in his head? . . . The best critics, Dryden,
> Lamb, Hazlitt, were acutely aware of the mixture of elements, and wrote of
> literature with music and painting in their minds. Nowadays we are all so
> specialized that critics keep their brains fixed to the print, which accounts
> for the starved condition of criticism in our time, and the attenuated and
> partial manner in which it deals with its subject. (Woolf 1934: 24)

This quotation brings us back to the question of rhythm and offers more detail
as to how we might understand it. Further, when one reads this essay in the
light of Lee's biography, it becomes strangely apparent that the conversation
described involves not a true dialogue but two parallel dialogues, one of which,
indeed, might well be a monologue. In the set piece of the conversation we are
given a number of heterogeneous elements. We begin with small talk about
traffic lights, which leads to speculative fictions on the invention of the art
gallery in England. From here we are entertained with a fanciful myth, linked
with natural history, of an insect that lives on colour alone. Yet as the conversation progresses, we meet a point at which two 'groups' at the imagined dinner
party diverge (and they are never really reconciled, with each developing their
separate conversations). When one speaker ventures, as Woolf herself does in
the piece as a whole, that Sickert's paintings could be read to involve stories –
biographical stories in that each of the characters portrayed have, folded within
them but somehow visible on their faces, all of their life story presented to us
in the pictures; or fictional or novelistic stories, as the characters seem to be
set in action, and cause the viewer to want to make up stories about them – the
experts in painting laugh, and turn to one another, discussing the pure forms
within the paintings, the kinds of relations between geometrical and chromatic
motifs described by Cézanne, and in Fry's criticism, for example. This group
then proceed to 'talk' among themselves, but without words, as words are not
adequate to fully convey this level of meaning, which Woolf's narrator concedes
is at a deeper and truer level. A second group, however, cannot follow these
experts. This second group are privileged Englishmen and women, who are
habituated to talk and cannot escape from the implications of words.

As we have noted, Lee shows how Woolf was dismissed as naïve for wanting
to make a link between literature and painting. With this in mind, then, one
tends to read the 'groups' as involving Virginia's painter friends as the experts
on the one hand, and herself, more or less alone, on the other. The conversation
between the talkers, who consider that painting, and Sickert's in particular, can
be biographical and novelistic, seems really to involve a dramatisation of a monologue within Woolf's own head. The 'real' conversation, then, that between

different people, involves the complete failure to communicate that is witnessed between the experts and the talkers. Yet the form itself works upon us, putting us in a scene that we picture and sense: the scene of an interesting dinner party among intelligent and amusing friends. It disarms us: we are urged to leave our weapons at the door for the evening, and, in the course of the evening, we imbibe substances that, if our nature is favourable to such processes, might work upon us and change our minds.

At the heart of this are a few ideas concerning the relation between literature and art. While it is recognised that the two forms part ways at a given point and that painting is not writing, it is asserted that they indeed have much in common: the painter writing, the writer painting. What is important, however, is that neither compromise her or his art in looking to the other for guidance: the writer cannot succeed in 'painting' by pure description; rather, metaphors hidden at the heart of individual words are brought into contact to suggest rather than describe visual affects (Woolf 1934: 23–4). So too, the painter is not literary in the sense that the images are explained by some story or life history; rather, the painted image includes such stories and histories in virtual form, curled within even while visible on the surface. The stories have to be unravelled, unfurled; what is given is the immediate truth of a moment, a moment that reveals elements towards a meaning of an entire life (ibid.: 10–19). Here Woolf makes us think of Cézanne, who admitted the possibility of the revelation of the truth about a life in painting, in the work of Velásquez, if not in his own work.

> Ah! Velasquez, that's another story. He took his revenge [...]. He painted the king and his buffoons the way Flaubert presented his Homais and Bournisien . . . . Velasquez bears no resemblance to his portraits, but look how Rembrandt and Rubens are always there, you can recognize them under all the faces. (Gasquet 1991: 215)

While Woolf, then, argues for the possibility of an art like that of Velásquez, one might suggest that she herself paints more like a Rubens or Rembrandt: recognisable under the surface of her characters and the situations they encounter. Yet she insists on the idea that there are *kinds* of artists: that artists have different gifts and different ways of working. If one sees Cézanne as a kind of poet, as Fry does, one might read Velásquez here as that rare thing: the true, objective biographer, a species which Woolf considers more likely to emerge in painting than in writing, given the various compromises the writer of biography is required to make (Woolf 1934: 12–13). Yet the painter as novelist is a somewhat different beast (ibid.: 13–14).

It is possible, however, to link all this with well-known insights Woolf expressed elsewhere: the idea of 'moments of being', which allows us to see something in common between portrait painting, at least, and fiction. The moment of being Woolf describes is a moment of pure intensity. It is intense because it involves the folding within of pure potential. All life, or at least a clue to its meaning, is condensed into a moment, is held within that moment.

In writing one seeks to recapture such a moment or to approximate the intense sensations it produces, by other means. Such a moment, however, because it is folded in, might in turn be unfolded, teased out, either in interpretation, or in the stories which surround that moment, leading up to and away from it. This is the kind of 'story' Woolf, or her avatars, find in Sickert, stories which are implicit within a captured moment, which carry a power to make a viewer want to enter into it and tease out its implications. Lily Briscoe is striving to capture such a moment, to fold relationships within a canvas. *To the Lighthouse*, of course, is also structured around such moments: James's failure to reach the Lighthouse in 'The Window' and his finally achieving it in 'The Lighthouse' provide motifs which are echoed throughout in the stories of the parents. So too Lily Briscoe's attempts to finish her painting echoes Woolf's complex relationships with Bloomsbury painting and painters.

Works Cited

Damasio, Antonio (2000) *Descartes' Error: Emotion, Reason, and the Human Brain*, New York: Quill.

Deleuze, Gilles (1996) *Francis Bacon: logique de la sensation*. Paris: Éditions de la différence.

Maloon, Terence (1998a) 'Classic Cézanne: Exhibition Notes', in *Classic Cézanne*, Sydney: Art Gallery of NSW.

Maloon, Terence (ed.) (1998b) *Classic Cézanne*, Sydney: Art Gallery of NSW.

Nussbaum, Martha (2001) *Upheavals of Thought: The Intelligence of Emotions*, Cambridge: Cambridge University Press.

Shiff, Richard (1991) 'Introduction' to *Cézanne: A Memoir with Conversations*, by Joachim Gasquet, trans. Christopher Pemberton; preface by John Rewald, London: Thames and Hudson.

Shiff, Richard (1998) 'Sensation, Movement, Cézanne' in *Classic Cézanne*, ed. Terence Maloon, Sydney: Art Gallery of NSW.

Vollard, Ambroise (1937) *Cézanne*, New York: Crown.

Further Reading

Banfield, Ann, (2000) *The Phantom Table*, Cambridge: Cambridge University Press,

Cézanne, Paul, (1976) *Paul Cézanne, Letters*, ed. John Rewald, New York: Da Capo Press.

Fry, Roger (1927) *Cézanne: A Study of His Development*, London: Hogarth Press.

Fry, Roger (1996) *A Roger Fry Reader*, ed. with Introductory Essays by Christopher Reed, Chicago: University of Chicago Press.

Gasquet, Joachim (1991) *Cézanne: A Memoir with Conversations*, trans. Christopher Pemberton; preface by John Rewald; introduction by Richard Shiff, London: Thames and Hudson.

Goldman, Jane (1998) *The Feminist Aesthetics of Virginia Woolf: Modernism, Post-Impressionism, and the Politics of the Visual*, Cambridge: Cambridge University Press.

Kendall, Richard (ed.) (1988) *Cézanne by Himself: Drawings, Paintings, Writings*, London: Macdonald Orbis.

Lee, Hermione (1999) *Virginia Woolf,* London: Vintage.

McLaurin, Allen (1973) *Virginia Woolf: The Echoes Enslaved,* Cambridge: Cambridge University Press.

Woolf, Virginia (1934) *Walter Sickert: A Conversation,* London: Hogarth Press.

Woolf, Virginia (1976) *Roger Fry: A Biography,* New York: Harcourt Brace Jovanovich.

Woolf, Virginia (1983) *To the Lighthouse. The original holography draft.* Transcribed and edited by Susan Dick. London: Hogarth Press.

Woolf, Virginia (2000) *To the Lighthouse,* ed. Stella McNichol with an Introduction by Hermione Lee, London: Penguin.

VIRGINIA WOOLF, PERFORMING RACE

Gretchen Holbrook Gerzina

B LOOMSBURY CAME OF age with a climate of popular and high culture that had much to do with race. While my previous work specifically addresses exhibitions of Africanism and Bloomsbury's response to it, this chapter looks more specifically at Virginia Woolf and the ways in which race in her first and last novels takes on particular aspects of performativity: as minstrelsy, plays, tableaux, staged performances, even when not set before an audience. The often discussed Dreadnought Hoax at the beginning of her writing career, the novels *The Voyage Out* and *Between the Acts*, as well as the 1924 Empire Exhibition at Wembley, which she attended as an established writer, all are based in part on the performativity of race and empire. I wish to analyse how theatricality and role-playing allowed her to both participate in and stand outside the confluence of race and empire, both of them perceived as spectacle.

In order to understand the context for these assertions, we need to go back to earlier centuries, when the stage for such performances was quite literally set. As I wrote in *Black England*, black people were a familiar sight on the streets of eighteenth-century London, where the servants of returned colonialists, and even of anti-slavery advocates like Samuel Johnson, rubbed shoulders with the Black Poor, those often indigent former soldiers from the American Revolution who were promised freedom and brought to England for fighting on the Loyalist side, and arrived in London at the end of the war. They attended the theatres on their own or with their masters and mistresses; they performed, like Billy Waters and others, on street corners and in fairs; they wrote, as the 'Sons of Africa' and others to newspapers, and produced narratives like that of Olaudah Equiano. Their images appeared on street signs, in the works of Hogarth and in other 'comic' drawings, and in paintings. Some also appeared in plays; in one noted episode, two newly freed African princes brought an audience to tears when they were observed weeping in their seats at a performance of Thomas Southerne's play *Oroonoko*, based rather loosely upon Aphra Behn's 'novel' of the same title.[1]

Heidi J. Holder, in her chapter 'Other Londoners: Race and Class in Plays of

Nineteenth-Century London Life', and Hazel Waters, in her book *Racism on the Victorian Stage*, have shown that long after the slave trade's end in 1807, black people were not only presented as beggars, servants and dancers in the hugely popular adaptations of Pierce Egan's *Tom and Jerry* novel, but continued on into the Victorian era where an 'essentialist reading of black characters would lead to a very specific kind of racial "comedy" of city life by the 1830s'.[2] On the stages of the Adelphi, Covent Garden, Victoria, Olympic, Surrey and other theatres in and near London, black and Indian characters, generally white actors in blackface, were used to illustrate the class pretensions of characters, both black and white, throughout the nineteenth century. As Holder suggests, 'for the West End theater audiences, the sense of strangeness and the thrill of the classes' mingling were intensified by the presence of other races'.[3] Audrey Fisch has similarly shown in her work on *Uncle Tom's Cabin* the enormous popularity of black characters on Victorian British popular culture.[4]

These depictions eventually gave way to music hall minstrelsy, sparked by the introduction of American 'Ethiopian' performers singing and dancing on English stages as well as on those of their own country. 'Men in masks', Michael Pickering writes,

> were central to the theatrical purpose and appeal of blackface minstrelsy, one of the most pervasive forms of popular entertainment in England and in Britain during the Victorian period. It was associated most of all with the minstrel show and music hall, but it was taken up in all sorts of other performance venues, from street corners to seaside piers, circuses, and amateur concerts.[5]

This continued well into the twentieth century, throughout Woolf's lifetime, in stage and radio minstrelsy shows. By the time Woolf was in the last decade of her career, radio minstrelsy had replaced music halls as an entertainment staple, with shows like Harry S. Pepper's *White Coon's Minstrel Party* (1932–39) and the BBC's *Kentucky Minstrels* (1933–50), although live minstrel shows still could be seen all over Britain.[6]

These were primarily lowbrow productions, designed to appeal to the masses in a very different way from the consciously created performances of race and empire that thrived in the second half of the nineteenth century, beginning with the Great Exhibition of 1851, which featured people and products, along with technologies, from around the world. The Crystal Palace paid tribute not only to British ingenuity, but also to the reach and successes of the empire. Thirty-five years, and a number of exhibitions later, the Colonial and Indian Exhibition of 1886 had displays that ran the gamut from ostrich farming to diamond washing, from silks to grains. In that exhibition, each colonial area was arranged by a different colonial administrator, just the sort of man whom Woolf would deplore in *Three Guineas*. The West African colonies exhibition, for example, was headed by Executive Commissioner Sir James Marshall, late Chief Justice of the Gold Coast Colony. The catalogue gave grudging praise to the people who created these products, saying that, 'Among all the rude and barbarous exhibits in this section there are many articles which show a high standard of native skill and industry.'[7] As in the much later Wembley exhibition, one 'travelled' the regions of the empire without venturing far from home, and could see heaped the riches of the world – from Australasia, Africa, the Indian subcontinent, and the West Indies – brought under British control and into its coffers, during the heyday of the exhibition movement.

In March 1890, when Woolf was nine, the Stanley and African Exhibition opened at the Victoria Gallery in Regent Street, London. Henry Morton Stanley, the British-born, workhouse-bred, New Orleans transplant, famously set off on assignment for the *New York Herald*, after several years spent covering the American Civil War, to locate the explorer David Livingstone, missing since he had left in 1866 to search for the source of the Nile. Successful in that endeavour, Stanley went on to explore Africa and later joined King Leopold II of Belgium to build roads through the Congo, using forced labour that some have described as 'brutal',[8] in order to promote European commerce. After the exhibition opened, Stanley also launched a successful British lecture tour. When he married in London that same year, Queen Victoria, in honour of his contributions to the empire, gave him a wedding gift of an image of herself, 'painted on enamel, set with diamonds and pearls'.[9]

This facilely negative view of Stanley, however, has been revised in recent years. Tim Jeal now writes that Stanley's strong opposition to the slave trade led him to promote the development of commerce on the continent, and that for Stanley,

> the prospect of ending the suffering of the slave trade made the colonial development of East Africa urgently necessary. He was one of the very few Europeans to have seen with his own eyes the extent of the mass murder in central Africa.[10]

Although Jeal describes him as a 'paternalist', he is quick to add that 'this did not make [him a] hypocrite'.[11] Furthermore, Stanley was in Cairo when the Stanley and African Exhibition 'was drawing crowds in London's Regent Street', and it was named after the explorer, but not by him, even though it featured items from his collection.[12]

Pre-dating the Wembley Exhibition that Woolf famously visited in 1924, the Stanley exhibition set the standard for public performances of race and empire. While Wembley celebrated all of the nations and products of the British Empire, the Stanley concentrated on African people, domestic life and geographies – complete with trees, skulls, gorillas and simulated villages. In these villages, 'Africans' – often black Londoners portraying villagers – acted out the daily work of cooking, weaving, playing sports as they would have in Africa, and similar villages were set up to simulate other colonial locations. Minus the technologies of production that Wembley flaunted, the Stanley purported to offer a visual representation of the continent that the celebrated Stanley had explored.

Writing of the many exhibitions that took place between 1890 and 1913,

Annie E. Coombes observes that the promoters were only too keenly aware of the amusement value of these racialised exhibits and their potential as massive crowd pleasers, a potential lacking in most other exhibits at these events. Ironically, this appeal relied on precisely those qualities which the literature about the exhibits, emphasising authenticity, went to such lengths to negate.[13] While the authenticity of African art was celebrated in Roger Fry's work, the far more widely disseminated popular images of the performance of race became the recognised representations of people of colour themselves. On stage and screen the preponderant image was of white actors and musicians pretending to be non-white; this image was so prevalent that even if one had visited the exhibition villages and seen actual people of colour, they likely did not see the falseness of the more familiar imitations. Even the exhibition villages themselves presented layers of performativity: black British people pretending to be Africans; Londoners pretending to be villagers; simulated tableaux and work scenes pretending to be of daily life in the colonies.

By the time Woolf was developing as a writer, England had been steeped in performances of race and empire for nearly two centuries. Small wonder, then, not only that in February 1910 – just months before the First Post-Impressionist Exhibition during which 'human character changed'[14] – Woolf felt comfortable in disguising herself as a black man in the Dreadnought Hoax, and reciting lines in a false language as though she were on stage, but that the naval officers that she and her friends deceived did not detect what was an obvious charade. Following her friends and relatives Horace de Vere Cole, Duncan Grant, Adrian Stephen and others, the young Virginia Stephen literally came onto the public stage in a racialised guise when the group, dressed as 'Abyssinian' dignitaries were given a tour of the warship, the HMS *Dreadnought*. Protected by the disguise, she was as much audience as performer, watching the captain and crew performing the rituals of a state visit.

For Woolf, therefore, the performing of race was a 'natural' and pervasive part of the London scene. Surrounded by old venues of performance, such as theatres, music halls and exhibitions, and new technologies of racialised performance such as radio and film, it is unsurprising that Woolf participated in it. The real question is how she participated, what use she made of it in her writing, and what meaning we can draw from that.

In *A Room of One's Own*, written five years after the Wembley exhibition, Woolf wrote that 'all women together ought to let flowers fall upon the tomb of Aphra Behn . . . for it was she who earned them the right to speak their minds'.[15] Accused of plagiarism in her own lifetime, and doubted for centuries afterward in her claim that her book *Oroonoko* was based upon her own experiences, Behn gives a remarkable rendition of the performance of race in the account. Most readings of the book concentrate on the melodrama and description of its African characters in the book, but it is a longer scene of encounter between native villagers and whites that perhaps forms the basis for an important scene in Woolf's own first novel, *The Voyage Out*.

Here is the scene in Behn's 1688 book, set in Surinam:

About Eighteen of us resolv'd, and took Barge: and after eight days, arriv'd near an *Indian* Town: But approaching it, the Hearts of some of our Company fail'd, and they would not venture on Shore; so we poll'd, who would, and would not. For my part, I said, if *Caesar* would, I would go. He resolv'd; so did my Brother, and my Woman, a Maid of good Courage . . . . A little distant from the Houses, or Huts, we saw some dancing, other busy'd in fetching and carrying of Water from the River. They had no sooner spy'd us, but they set up a loud Cry, that frighted us at first; we thought it had been for those that should kill us, but it seems it was of Wonder and Amazement. They were all naked; and we were dress'd, so as is most commode for the hot Countries, very glittering and rich; so that we appear'd extremely fine: my own Hair was cut short, and I had a tafety Cap, with black Feathers on my Head; my Brother was in a Stuff-Suit, with silver Loops and Buttons, and abundance of green Ribbon. This was all infinitely surprizing to them . . . .[16]

In this seventeenth-century encounter, the white colonials, led by the intrepid African prince, venture by boat for the purpose of viewing an authentic South American village of native people in their own environment. The villagers, engaged in their daily routines, are astonished by the sudden appearance of bizarrely dressed Europeans. Much in the same way that the actors in Miss La Trobe's play in *Between the Acts* turn the mirrors upon the audience, the villagers become the spectators of the European display of visitors, with their strange ideas of being dressed 'commode' for the hot climate in their 'glittering and rich' attire, who come to look at them. The European spectators thereby themselves become the spectacle, dressed deliberately to perform their colonial status, and the two groups are brought together by their African guide.

Knowing of Woolf's admiration for Behn makes it impossible not to see the similarity between this scene and that of the Britons' visit to the village in *The Voyage Out*. As in Behn's account, the visitors arrive at the Indian village after several days' journey by boat.

Stepping cautiously, they observed the women, who were squatting on the ground in triangular shapes, moving their hands, either plaiting straw or in kneading something in bowls. But when they had looked for a moment undiscovered, they were seen, and Mr. Flushing, advancing into the centre of the clearing, was engaged in talk with a lean majestic man, whose bones and hollows at once made the shapes of the Englishman's body appear ugly and unnatural. The women took no notice of the strangers, except that their hands paused for a moment and their long narrow eyes slid round and fixed upon them with the motionless inexpressive gaze of those removed from each other far, far beyond the plunge of speech. Their hands moved again, but the stare continued. It followed them as they walked, as they peered into the huts where they could distinguish guns leaning in the corner, and bowls upon the floor, and stacks of rushes; in the dusk the solemn eyes of babies regarded them, and old women stared out too. As they sauntered about, the stare followed them, passing over their legs, their bodies, their heads, curiously, not without hostility, like the crawl of a winter fly. As she drew apart her shawl and uncovered her breast to the lips of her baby, the eyes of a woman never left their faces, although they moved uneasily under her stare, and finally turned away, rather than stand there looking at her any longer. When sweetmeats were offered them, they put out great red hands to take them, and felt themselves treading cumbrously like tight-coated soldiers among these soft instinctive people. But soon the life of the village took no notice of them; they had become absorbed into it. The women's hands became busy again with the straw; their eyes dropped. If they moved, it was to fetch something from the hut, or to catch a straying child, or to cross the space with a jar balanced on their heads; if they spoke, it was to cry some harsh unintelligible cry. Voices rose when a child was beaten, and fell again; voices rose in song, which slid up a little way and down a little way, and settled again upon the same low and melancholy note. Seeking each other, Terence and Rachel drew together under a tree. Peaceful, and even beautiful at first, the sight of the women, who had given up looking at them, made them now feel very cold and melancholy.

'Well', Terence sighed at length, 'it makes us seem insignificant, doesn't it?'[17]

There are obvious correlations: the naturalness of the villagers and the over-dressed, stiff unnaturalness of the English interlopers; the way the English become the display as they are watched by the villagers; the setting in an Indian village in South America, arrived at only by several days' journey by boat. Instead of the African guide, this trip is instigated by Winifred Flushing, the Ottoline Morrell-like artistic wife of a man who owns a magnificent house, but who spent her childhood in Ireland and has a certain exotic wildness to her character.[18]

Woolf's village also owes a great deal to the London exhibitions which often included simulated villages, where the English visitors could observe what passed for daily life in other countries. Coombes, referring to photographs taken of these villages, describes one which 'villagers' are shown 'cooking in the kraal' but where the 'three black men [are] huddled together by an open fire, wearing blankets or, in one instance, an old army greatcoat against the cold and drizzle of a London winter' in the 'Briton, Boer and Black in Savage South Africa' held at Olympia in 1899–1900.[19] They are observed, or watched over, by British military officers, much in the way that the villagers in Behn's and Woolf's books are observed, but nowhere in this particular photograph appear the crowds of visitors who watched them as though they were aliens or, as in David Garnett's disturbing novella *Man in the Zoo*, caged animals.

Even more disturbing was the case of the 'Somali Village', in which the supposed villagers were portrayed by black London actors. When fire broke out the actors attempted to escape; guards tried to stop them; they had to make their way to safety by climbing a fence.[20] Londoners all, they were hired to portray outsiders and to trick them, through costume, setting and performance, into believing they were genuine Somalis. Not only did the disguise seem real, but they were unable at first to convince the guards through language or emergency to see through the disguise. As with Woolf and her friends on the HMS *Dreadnought*, the authorities – accustomed to representations of Africans – were unable to see beyond the false presentations. Where in the London renditions of indigenous villages the people of colour were deemed the outsiders, in Woolf's and Behn's renditions, it is the Europeans who are visibly the aliens and interlopers in foreign lands.

Aware of the insider/outsider dichotomy, Woolf, in *The Voyage Out*, is careful to present the English at the hotel as continually performing their Britishness. Viewed first by Rachel Vinrace and Helen Ambrose at night, they are watched by the two women who move from lighted window to lighted window, as though observing a series of tableaux:

> A row of long windows opened almost to the ground. They were all of them uncurtained, and all brilliantly lighted, so that they could see everything inside. Each window revealed a different section of the life of the hotel.[21]

With the rooms presented as a series of stages with the curtains open, the audience to actors who cannot see them: 'Mr. Hewet . . . came straight towards them, but his eyes were fixed not upon the eavesdroppers but upon a spot where the curtain hung in folds'.[22] Rachel and Helen themselves turn out to have an audience, and 'started to think that some one had been sitting near to them unobserved all the time'. Unlike the puzzled audience in La Trobe's play in *Between the Acts* when mirrors are turned back on the audience, the two women flee and 'did not stop running until they felt certain that no eye could penetrate the darkness'.[23] Rachel once more becomes an observer when she later stumbles into the courtyard where the Spanish woman kills a chicken, and once again recognises that some things are not meant to be viewed. Finally, at the end of the novel, Rachel herself becomes the 'play' as the visitors come one by one to watch her dying.

How then to put this all together in terms of Woolf's use of race and empire? We see that Woolf's most famous early public performance took place within the disguise of an African man; that foreign men and women were frequently represented by white performers in Britain; that native Londoners of colour sometimes portrayed foreigners as part of British exhibitions. Woolf turns the tables on these familiar performances and, like her predecessor Behn, imagines the actual villages where indigenous peoples lived and makes them the audience to white outsiders who themselves become the performance, showing themselves off as 'genuine' Europeans. In *The Voyage Out*, the villagers – two-

and-a-half centuries removed from Behn's encounter – have become bored by the familiar performance. Recognising that the whites have come to view them, they go about their business, but with a recognition of the price of admission. The visitors, caught in this transformation from audience to interloping performer, are humbled by the double complicity, wonder if they've paid too much for the trinkets they purchase – trinkets which now stand in for the embarrassment of the experience. As they leave, Helen realises that they have 'ventured too far and exposed themselves'.[24]

Throughout the novel, Rachel's world expands, with Richard's outrageous kiss and then, beginning with this chapter, contracts, as she becomes ill and moves within herself. As Mark Wollaeger puts it,

> Although Rachel feels 'her small world becoming wonderfully enlarged' under Richard's influence, her subsequent encounter with the indigenous women suggests that her world actually remains quite small: as if transplanted from the pitch at Wembley, this scene of ethnographic exhibition reproduces the complex dynamics of spectatorship that obtains when one's only real knowledge of the other comes from looking at picture postcards or people on display.[25]

The novel takes place in an imagined country, on a continent that Woolf never visited; like Candide or Rasselas, she has travelled a metonymic world in order to make her attack on empire and nation.

These dynamics of spectatorship apply to the author herself. Wollaeger suggests that

> Woolf's struggle with racial difference in her first novel's culminating scene of exhibition brings her to the brink of acknowledging the imperial grounding of her own whiteness, and the depth of her affective engagement makes race a crucial feature of her work, for the first and last time.[26]

While there is no doubt that Woolf, as an English woman, is implicated in the whiteness of empire, her criticism of it pervades, and to many, forms the foundation of, the novel. Yet of course, this was not the last time that race became 'a crucial feature of her work'.

Much has been written about the use of race and colonialism in *Orlando*, which opens with the boy Orlando 'slicing at the head of a Moor which swung from the rafters', and which later conflates desire, exoticism and gender in the conversation between Orlando and Shelmerdine about a 'black woman' and 'kissing a negress in the dark', in which the 'negress' stands for illicit sexual behaviour and the couple's own bisexuality in what Jaime Hovey calls 'their triangulation of desire [reconfiguring] the violent image of the Moor's head, domesticating the dynamics of imperialism and conquest into a primitivist, orientalist style'.[27]

Taking *Orlando* as a love letter to Vita Sackville-West and another indictment of imperialism has allowed critics to elide Woolf's problematic use of race, however, particularly for those who made their interventions into her work in the 1970s and 1980s. Writers of colour, often great admirers of her writing, raise the more difficult questions about the conflation of anti-empire opinions and views about race. Jamaican Creole writer Michelle Cliff, herself steeped in British literature and culture through her colonial education, asks after re-reading *Orlando*,

> is Woolf, the daughter of the Victorian tea table, who learned the racial attitudes of her time and class, able to *see* the African? To have tears in her eyes? What is captured in her mind's eye, she who has imagined him?[28]

The same Woolf who opposed the militaristic and colonial attitudes of empire, also wrote in her journal on 15 April 1920 of being 'unhappy all day long' the day after viewing an exhibition of African art: 'The day before I went to the Niggers' show in Chelsea; very sad impressive figures; obscene; somehow monumental'.[29] Cliff points out that on the same day as the diary entry, Woolf wrote to her sister Vanessa Bell that she had gone to see 'a show of Negro carvings at the book club . . . . I went to see the carvings and I found them dismal and impressive', using in the place of the obscenity a more accepted word than she used for her private ruminations.[30] Yet we know from the work of Clive Bell and others that the word 'nigger' was used comfortably and freely among the members of Bloomsbury, especially in the discussion of art. Urmila Seshagiri reminds us that 'ideas about race shape Woolf's writing across many genres: her letters, essays, and novels allude frequently to racial difference, flirt with cultural crossovers, and draw on images of the racially marked exotic and primitive'.[31] Seshagiri is quick to point out that just 'because her anti-imperialism does not manifest itself through claims about racial or cultural equality, Woolf's novels often reproduce a wide range of assumptions about non-white otherness as well as inscribe tropes of racial difference onto white English identity'.[32]

White British identity is literally on display in Woolf's last novel, *Between the Acts*, in which Isa's father-in-law Bart Oliver 'of the Indian Civil Service' represents the colonial Britain of his past and dreams of 'savages' ('Many old men had only their India – old men in clubs, old men in rooms off Jermyn Street'): her husband Giles the new Britain of the City and finance in the waning years of empire; and her small son a new and uncertain kind of manhood ('"Your little boy's a cry-baby," he said scornfully').[33] Lucy Swithin understands neither the older civil servants nor the modern men like her nephew, who

> 'take a job in the city . . . at men who spent their lives, buying and selling – ploughs? glass beads was it? or stocks and shares? – to savages who wished most oddly – for were they not beautiful naked? – to dress and live like the English?'[34]

Their roles in the novel are established early, and the rest of the novel circulates in part around the idea of performance.

The London that Giles Oliver occupies during the week can be seen as an imperial space, and Felix Driver and David Gilbert state that it is important to view empire 'as shaping the identity and spaces of the colonisers as much as the colonised'.[35] In their view, the urban landscape offered an imperial experience to all who occupied and consumed it, through landmarks, monuments, advertising and exhibitions, and they argue that neither the metropolis nor the colony can be fully understood without each other.[36] In *Between the Acts*, this urban imperial space is mirrored by the rural or village space, where the pageant of imperial and literary history takes place in Miss La Trobe's play.

The novel is replete with racialised references, all against the backdrop of the play. Giles refers to the homosexual William Dodge as a 'half-breed';[37] La Trobe 'worked like a nigger'.[38] As others have noted, Budge the publican, in his guise as the London policeman, is the gatekeeper of the empire:

> *Fog or fine weather, I does my duty* (Budge continued). *At Piccadilly Circus; at 'Yde Park Corner, directing the traffic of 'Er Majesty's Empire. The Shah of Persia; Sultan of Morocco; or it may be 'Er Majesty in person; or Cook's tourists; black men; white men; sailor, soldiers; crossing the ocean; to proclaim her Empire; all of 'em Obey the Rule of my truncheon.*[39]

A page later he declaims that '*It's a Christian country, our Empire; under the White Queen Victoria.*'[40] And the job of the policeman, he declares, '*is a white man's job*'.[41] The Victorian characters Edgar and Eleanor get engaged while pledging to convert the heathens in Africa and the scene ends with the singing of 'Rule Britannia';[42] shortly after pledging in the song to never be slaves, the League of Nations, which Leonard Woolf so strongly supported, is represented by a 'black man in fuzzy wig; coffee-coloured ditto in silver turban,' which is a 'flattering tribute to ourselves. Crude of course'.[43]

The pageant's audience, comfortably familiar with the white man's burden, easily accepts Budge performing his, and the nation's, whiteness. Yet Woolf brings a new urgency to the discussion of how one performs race. It is, after all, set in 1939, the year the Second World War began, although published in 1941. Isabella too is thirty-nine years old, the age of the century at this moment of change and fear. A sense of geography and change permeate the pageant through the images of flight, migration and invasion. The world has become smaller, and as the play presents English history as a long, but finite, literary panorama during the waning years of the empire.

The frivolousness of Restoration drama, parodied in the play, of the bombastic sense of superiority of the Englishman directing the world's traffic, are set against what is taking place in the sky. Throughout the novel Lucy Swithin notices swallows and is intrigued by the way they come so far from Africa in a timeless and miraculous cycle of nature that belittles the exhibition of empire on the ground. Yet, ominously, another flight of empire-building is taking place above them, and only a page after their last appearance, 'Twelve aeroplanes in perfect formation like a flight of wild ducks came overhead. *That* was the music. The audience gaped; the audience gazed. Then zoom became drone. The planes had passed'.[44] But as Woolf knows well, they have not passed forever and the world is about to be plunged again into war. As the players silently turn the looking glasses back onto the audience, the viewers slowly understand with indignation that they are part of the changing world performance. At that moment they realise that the play, like the empire, is over.

Fifteen years earlier, long before Woolf was working on her final novel, the British Empire Exhibition opened at Wembley on 23 April 1924, to much fanfare. Like earlier exhibitions, this one had commerce at its heart, showing the goods, arts and technologies gathered from around the colonies, but also to 'illustrate the Wembley theme of empire as family'.[45] There visitors, according to Woolf, 'stand in queues to have their spectacles rectified gratis; to have their fountain-pens filled gratis; they gaze respectfully into sacks of grain; glance reverently at mowing machines from Canada'.[46] In addition to these more pragmatic exhibits, there was a Palace of Arts, whose neo-classical structure held painters and sculptors from Australia, New Zealand, Canada, South Africa, India, Burma – works primarily that suited 'all that was refine[d] and cultivated about Britannia at home and overseas'. Whatever failed to suit that standard was displayed elsewhere, and it was

> in the individual territorial pavilions of the imperial section where one could find the art of the Maoris, black South Africans and the populations of the dependent empire. Here, the emphasis was not art but rather artefact, housed within an appropriately exotic architecture that entertained the crowds and invoked images of traditional societies in the historical period 'BC' – before colonialism.[47]

Despite her depressed response to the African art on display in the Chelsea exhibit four years earlier, Woolf's negative response to Wembley may have rested on this false dichotomy between art and artefact, art and entertainment 'for the crowds'. Looking first at the visitors she asks, 'Can it be that one is seeing human beings for the first time?' On the streets they are ordinary; here at Wembley they are part of the display:

> Here against the enormous background of ferro-concrete Britain, of rosy Burma, at large, unoccupied, they reveal themselves simply as human beings, creatures of leisure, civilization, and dignity; a little languid, perhaps, a little attenuated, but a product to be proud of. Indeed they are the ruin of the Exhibition.[48]

Against the false backdrop that will soon melt and blow away in the rainstorm, the visitors become like the visitors to the villages in the novels, somehow falsified, but also somehow above the places they visit.

Appalled by the display of empire, Woolf is at first unable to tell whether the 'rushing sound' is that of the natural world and the weather, or whether it emanates from the falseness of the British Empire Exhibition. Like the swallows and the airplanes she will later write into the end of *Between the Acts*, she sees the dual existence of nature and imperialism. At Wembley she concludes that the natural world trumps the constructed colonial world, for 'The Empire is perishing; the bands are playing; the Exhibition is in ruins. For that is what comes of letting in the sky.[49] By the time of her last novel, and nearly the end of her life, she is not so sure.

Throughout all these representations there has been a constant back and forth between actors and audiences, between observers and the observed. As author Woolf stands apart from these exhibitions; as a British woman she is necessarily implicated in them. As Miss La Trobe says shortly before she is fin-ishes her job and sits down to her lonely drink in the pub, '"Curse 'em!" She felt everything they felt. Audiences were the devil'.[50]

Notes

1. Gerzina 1995: 11.
2. Holder 2002: 34.
3. Holder 2002: 32.
4. Audrey Fisch, (2000) '"Exhibiting Uncle Tom in Some Shape or Other": The Commercialization and Reception of *Uncle Tom's Cabin* in England', in Audrey Fisch, *American Slaves in Victorian England. Abolitionist Politics in Popular Literature and Culture*, Cambridge: Cambridge University Press, pp. 11–32.
5. Michael Pickering, 'The Blackface Clown', in Gerzina 2003: 159.
6. For more information, see Gerzina 2006: 46–64.
7. Cundall 1886: 91.
8. www.bbc.co.uk/history/historic_figures/stanley_sir_henry_morton.shtml
9. *New York Times*, 27 July 1890: 14.
10. Jeal 2007: 387.
11. Jeal 2007: 387.
12. Jeal 2007: 388.
13. Coombes, 1994: 85.
14. Virginia Woolf, 'Mr Bennett and Mrs Brown', in *CDB*: 96.
15. Virginia Woolf, (1959) *A Room of One's Own*, London: Hogarth Press, p. 98.
16. Aphra Behn, (1975) *Oroonoko: or, The Royal Slave*, New York: W. W. Norton, pp. 54–5.
17. Virginia Woolf (1920), *The Voyage Out*, New York and London: Harvest, pp. 284–5.
18. There are many conscious nods to *Heart of Darkness* as well. In the previous chapter, as they set out for the village and board the boat, 'They seemed to be driving into the heart of the night, for the trees closed in front of them, and they could hear all round them the rustling of leaves. The great darkness had the usual effect . . .' (Woolf 1920: 265).
19. Coombes 1994: 94.
20. Coombes 1994: 102.
21. Woolf 1920: 100.
22. ibid.: 102.
23. ibid.: 102.
24. ibid.: 286.
25. Wollaeger 2001: 43.
26. ibid.: 44.
27. *O*: 258 Hovey 1997: 402.
28. Cliff 1994: 98.

29. *D2*: 30. Quoted in Cliff 1994: 99.
30. *L2*: 429. Quoted in Cliff 1994: 100. A number of years ago, when I first began speaking in public about Bloomsbury and race, a fellow speaker, from England, informed me that 'nigger was never considered a bad word'. The other Americans at the table were appalled.
31. Seshagiri 2004: 59.
32. Ibid.: 61.
33. Virginia Woolf, (1960) *Between the Acts*, London: Hogarth Press, pp. 24–5.
34. Ibid.: 59.
35. Driver and Gilbert 1998: 13.
36. Ibid.: 14.
37. Woolf 1960: 61.
38. Ibid.: 176.
39. Ibid.: 189.
40. Ibid.: 190.
41. Ibid.: 191.
42. Ibid.: 194 and 199.
43. Ibid.: 212.
44. Ibid.: 225.
45. August 1993: 38.
46. Woolf 'Thunder at Wembley', in *CDB*: 224.
47. August 1993: 43.
48. 'Thunder at Wembley', in *CDB*: 225.
49. Ibid.: 227.
50. Woolf 1960: 209–10.

Works Cited and Further Reading

Abravanel, Genevieve (2001) 'Woolf in Blackface: Identification across *The Waves*', in *Virginia Woolf Out of Bounds. Selected Papers from the Tenth Annual Conference on Virginia Woolf*, ed. Jessica Berman and Jane Goldman, New York: Pace University Press, 113–19.

August, Tom (1993) 'Art and Empire – Wembley, 1924', in *History Today*, 23, October: 38–44.

Cliff, Michelle (1994) 'Virginia Woolf and the Imperial Gaze: A Glance Askance', in Mark Hussey and Vara Neverow (eds), *Virginia Woolf: Emerging Perspectives. Selected Papers from the Third Annual Conference on Virginia Woolf*, New York: Pace University Press, pp. 91–102.

Cohen, Scott (2004) 'The Empire from the Street: Virginia Woolf, Wembley, and Imperial Monuments', in *Modern Fiction Studies*, 50.1, Spring: 85–109.

Coombes, Annie E. (1994) *Reinventing Africa: Museums, Material Culture and Popular Imagination*, New Haven, CT: Yale University Press, p. 85.

Cundall, Frank (ed.) (1886) *Reminiscences of the Colonial and Indian Exhibition*, London: William Clowes & Sons.

Driver, Felix and David Gilbert (1998) 'Heart of Empire? Landscape, Space and Performance in Imperial London', in *Environment and Planning D: Society and Space*, 16: 11–28.

Garrity, Jane (1999) 'Selling Culture to the "Civilized": Bloomsbury, British *Vogue*, and the Marketing of National Identity', in *Modernism/Modernity* 6.2: 29–58.

Gerzina, Gretchen Holbrook (1995) *Black England: Life before Emancipation*, London: John Murray.

—— (2006) 'Bushmen and Blackface: Bloomsbury and Race', in *The South Carolina Review*, 38.2, Spring: 46–64.

—— (ed.) (2003) *Black Victorians/Black Victoriana*, New Brunswick, NJ: Rutgers University Press.

Heady, Chene (2001) '"Accidents of Political Life": Satire and Edwardian Anti-Colonial Politics in *The Voyage Out*', in *Virginia Woolf Out of Bounds. Selected Papers from the Tenth Annual Conference on Virginia Woolf*, ed. Jessica Berman and Jane Goldman, New York: Pace University Press, pp. 97–104.

Holder, Heidi J. (2002) 'Other Londoners: Race and Class in Plays of Nineteenth-Century London Life', in Pamela Gilbert (ed.), *Imagined Londons*, Albany: State University of New York Press.

Hovey, Jaime (1997) '"Kissing a Negress in the Dark": Englishness as a Masquerade in Woolf's *Orlando*, in *PMLA*, 112.3, May: 393–404.

Hughes, Deborah L. (2006) 'Kenya, India and the British Empire Exhibition of 1924', in *Race and Class* 47.4: 66–85.

Jeal, Tim (2007) *Stanley: The Impossible Life of Africa's Greatest Explorer*, New Haven, CT: Yale University Press. First published in the UK by Faber and Faber.

Phillips, Kathy J. (1994) *Virginia Woolf against Empire*, Knoxville: University of Tennessee.

Seshagiri, Urmila (2004) 'Orienting Virginia Woolf: Race, Aesthetics, and Politics in *To the Lighthouse*', in *Modern Fiction Studies*, 50.1, Spring: 58–84.

Waters, Hazel (2007) *Racism on the Victorian Stage. Representation of Slavery and the Black Character*, Cambridge: Cambridge University Press.

West, Shearer (ed.) (1996) *The Victorians and Race*, Aldershot: Ashgate.

Wollaeger, Mark (2001) 'Woolf, Postcards, and the Elision of Race: Colonizing Women in *The Voyage Out*', in *Modernism/Modernity*, 8.1: 43–75.

Woodham, Jonathan (1989) 'Images of Africa and Design at the British Empire Exhibitions between the Wars', in *Journal of Design History*, 2.1: 15–33.

5

VIRGINIA WOOLF AND CITY AESTHETICS

Vara S. Neverow

L ONDON THOU ART a jewel of jewels, & jasper of jocunditie – music, talk, friendship, city views, books, publishing, something central & inexplicable. (*D2*: 283)

Virginia Woolf was a Londoner from birth, and London, for her, was magical, intoxicating and unparalleled by any other metropolis – but also fraught with dangers and divided by class and gender. In her descriptions of her beloved London, Woolf balances the hustle and bustle of industry and traffic and crowds, the façades of buildings and the stony pavements, the vagrants and the street vendors, the glow of street lights and the shimmering displays of goods in stores, the filth and the elegance, against the diurnal rhythms of dawn and twilight, the seasonal changes, the sunlight, wind and rain, the inevitability of death and decay and the unfurling of new life. For Woolf, London's allure is its contradictions– multiplicity and permutation paralleled by stability. Her recurrent references to specific places (Piccadilly Circus, the Serpentine, the British Museum) and phenomena (traffic, seasons, rhythms of the day) show her love of enduring patterns and her fascination with change. She is also very conscious of the porous membranes between exteriors and interiors, the public and the private spheres, the modern and the historical, as well as the ever-shifting prismatics of perception.

As she writes enthusiastically in her diary on 5 May 1924:

> London is enchanting. I step out upon a tawny coloured magic carpet, it seems, & get carried into beauty without raising a finger. The nights are amazing, with all the white porticoes & broad silent avenues. And people pop in & out, lightly, divertingly like rabbits; & I look down Southampton Row, wet as a seal's back or red & yellow with sunshine, & watch the omnibus going & coming, & hear the old crazy organs. One of these days I will write about London, & how it takes up the private life & carries it on, without any effort. (*D2*: 301)

The passage is typical of Woolf's sense of the cityscape and reveals much about her perception of London's urban aesthetics. She delights in the pure excitement and seeming immediacy of access to an almost iridescent urban space as it shifts from night to day, from rainfall to sunshine. In her phrasing she elides the distinction between human and animal, between pavement and creature. She also mentions many of the major attributes of a metropolis – its architecture, streets and vehicles, the random spontaneity of human activity; the osmotic city life that pulses between the outer, often anonymous world of the street and the inner, more intimate zones of the metropolis, including the mind itself.

In a particularly ecstatic passage from *The Waves* (1931), Woolf bestows on her character Bernard her own integral love of the splendid London skyline, contrasting London's extraordinary beauty with its distinctively industrial grittiness and its random jumble of buildings, all factors which are intensified by the excitement of entering the metropolis by train:

> 'How fair, how strange', said Bernard, 'glittering, many-pointed and many-domed London lies before me under mist. Guarded by gasometers, by factory chimneys, she lies sleeping as we approach. . . . Not Rome herself looks more majestic. . . . Factories, cathedrals, glass domes, institutions and theatres erect themselves. (*W*: 111)

Woolf identifies London as a living being, not just as a destination, but the metropolis is also, strangely, a target, Bernard's incoming train being depicted as an almost sexualised weapon: 'this missile. . . . We are about to explode . . . like a shell in the side of some ponderous, maternal, majestic animal. She hums and murmurs; she awaits us' (*W*: 111).

There is certainly a grim side to London as well. Consider Delia in *The Years* (1937) observing from the shelter of a cab 'the vice, the obscenity, the reality of London . . . lurid in the mixed evening light' (*Y*: 114) or Flush's horrible experience of being just a dog held for ransom in a Rookery where 'poverty and vice and misery had bred and seethed and propagated their kind for centuries without interference' (*F*: 88). Consider, too, the narrator's description of sleazy, dismal streets in *Jacob's Room* (1922) where 'The lamps of Soho made large greasy spots of light upon the pavement' and 'The by-streets were dark enough to shelter man or woman leaning against the doorways' (*JR*: 81).

Woolf routinely infuses her descriptions of London with techniques from the visual arts as well as elements from popular culture. As Jennie-Rebecca Falcetta argues, London is depicted in a distinctively cubist style in *Mrs Dalloway* (1925). Woolf's narrator in *Jacob's Room* (1922) satirically transforms the daily departure of workers from the City of London into a multimedia word collage, combining futurist motion with the flickering cinematic frames of film and the mechanical motion of wind-up toys:

> Innumerable overcoats of the quality prescribed hung empty all day in the corridors, but as the clock struck six each was exactly filled, and the little figures, split apart into trousers or moulded into a single thickness, jerked rapidly with angular forward motion along the pavement. (*JR*: 66–7)

Always, Woolf is aware of the layered history of London. In *Orlando* (1928), she creates a palimpsest of medieval, Renaissance and contemporary London, describing the layered urban silhouette in a passage is rife with historical significance:

> the sun sank, all the domes, spires, turrets, and pinnacles of London rose in inky blackness against the furious red sunset clouds. Here was the fretted cross at Charing; there the dome of St Paul's; there the massy square of the Tower buildings; there . . . were the heads on the pikes at Temple Bar. (*O*: 53)

Contrasting the ever-accelerating modernity of London with the ancient past, Woolf depicts Jinny in *The Waves* admiring the contemporary metropolis with its 'superb omnibuses, red and yellow, stopping and starting, punctually in order', but then transforms Jinny's perception of the traffic flow into a 'triumphant procession', an 'army of victory with banners and brass eagles and heads crowned with laurel-leaves won in battle', invoking the Roman occupation of Britain and the founding of London in AD 43 (*W*: 194). Jinny, a very fashionable twentieth-century woman, thinks with revulsion about early populations of the region, opining that modern pedestrians 'are better than savages in loin-cloths, and women whose hair is dank, whose long breasts sag' (ibid.: 194). Bernard also muses about London's deep past, but his thoughts are more philosophical and are organised in a specifically cinematic fashion: 'The growl of traffic might be any uproar – forest trees or the roar of wild beasts. Time has whizzed back an inch or two on its reel; our short progress has been cancelled' (ibid.: 113). Fast-forwarding, Woolf wonders about the future of the metropolis itself and writes in *Mrs Dalloway* of

> sifting the ruins of time, when London is a grass-grown path and all those hurrying along the pavement this Wednesday morning are but bones with a few wedding rings mixed up in their dust and the gold stoppings of innumerable decayed teeth. (*MD*: 16)

Julian Wolfreys, in *Writing London: The Trace of the Urban Text from Blake to Dickens*, quotes a passage from nineteenth-century writer Richard Jefferies' 'The Lions of Trafalgar' that coincides precisely with Woolf's own sense of the metropolis: 'The heart of the world is in London, and the cities with the simulacrum of man in them are empty. They are moving images only; stand here and you are real' (quoted in Wolfreys 1998: 7–8).

Woolf's observations about cities other than London can be enthusiastic – or not. Of Venice she says in 1904: 'there never was such an amusing and beautiful place' (*L1*: 137); in 1909, she describes Florence as a rather rural 'happy place', where 'the poorest mother might let her children play among long grass' and thinks highly of the Duomo and the palaces lit up at night (*PA*: 396). A dog's-eye view of Florence shows a city that is old and labyrinthine with statues and stone fountains, markets with awnings and flowers in jars. In *Jacob's Room*, relying on her own observations in Athens in 1906, Woolf describes a city that is extremely provincial and 'incongruous', dwarfed by its ancient history. 'Now it is suburban; now immortal'. The roadway is 'pitted' and 'a shepherd . . . very nearly drives his herd of goats between the royal wheels' of the monarch's landau', but above the city looms the breathtaking Acropolis (*JR*: 147–8).

Although some of Woolf's characters love London as much as she herself does, some recoil from it, whether they are failing to see its majesty and its beauty – or just feeling irritable. Urban ugliness comes through strongly in a passage from *The Voyage Out* as Helen Ambrose filters the cityscape through her own ill-tempered sensibility: 'A fine rain now made her still more dismal; vans with the odd names of those engaged in odd industries – Sprules, Manufacturer of Saw-dust; Grabb, to whom no piece of waste paper comes amiss – fell flat as a bad joke' (Woolf 1990: 12).

Rezia in *Mrs Dalloway*, already depressed by Septimus's mental instability, is further disheartened by London itself. Even at the peak of the Season, London seems to her drab and dismal in comparison to the beauty and vitality of her own city, Milan (see Falcetta 2007: 117). Peter Walsh, of course, sees the same metropolis through a different lens and thinks with astonishment and delight that 'Never had he seen London look so enchanting' (*MD*: 71).

Like the brightly coloured London omnibuses, the London Underground is a ubiquitous element in Woolf's experience of London, a constant and distinguishing feature of the metropolis. In *The Waves*, Jinny's observations of the Underground vaguely suggest Hades, the ancient Greek abode of the dead:

> Millions have died . . . [T] the soundless flight of upright bodies down the moving stairs [is] like the pinioned and terrible descent of some army of the dead downwards and the churning of the great engines remorselessly forwarding us, all of us, onwards. (*W*: 193–4).

But in *Jacob's Room*, Woolf explicitly equates the Underground with the underworld, possibly alluding to the slaughter in the trenches of the First World War:

> Beneath the pavement, sunk in the earth, hollow drains lined with yellow light for ever conveyed them this way and that, and large letters upon enamel plates represented in the underworld the parks, squares, and circuses of the upper. 'Marble Arch – Shepherd's Bush'. (*JR*: 67)

As Paul Fussell observes in *The Great War and Modern Memory*, for British military personnel an informal way 'of identifying sections of trench was by place or street names with a distinctively London flavor' (Fussell 2000: 42). He notes that:

> *Piccadilly* was a favorite; popular also were *Regent Street* and *Strand*; junctions were *Hyde Park Corner* and *Marble Arch*. . . . Directional and traffic control signs were everywhere in the trenches, giving the whole system the

air of a parody modern city, although one literally 'underground'. (Fussell
2000: 42–3; his emphasis)

Deeply scored into Woolf's sense of London is the perpetually changing river,
the Thames, with its bridges and barges, its ships and warehouses. In her essay,
'The Docks of London', one of six (1931–2) written for *Good Housekeeping* (see
Squier 1985: 52–79), Woolf describes not just the vast scale of riverfront commerce with a thousand ships arriving weekly but the almost mathematical art of
unloading the cargo, how 'Barrels . . . rhythmically, dexterously, with an order
that has some aesthetic delight in it' are 'laid one beside another in endless
array'. She admires the aptness of the cranes and warehouses, appreciating their
functional elegance. In addition to predictable raw materials and commodities
such as 'Timber, iron, grain, wine, sugar, paper, tallow, fruit', there are also the
intriguing surprises. The aesthetics of stowaways (snakes in sacks of cinnamon,
scurrying scorpions) are complemented by 'Oddities, beauties, rarities', such as
'the tusks of mammoths that have lain frozen in Siberian ice for fifty thousand
years' which, unlike ivory from elephants, are unworthy to become billiards
balls and will be made into 'umbrella handles' (Woolf 1975: 11–12).

Woolf links the exchange system and the flow of products to consumers'
whims – a topic thoroughly appropriate for a article in a women's magazine! –
driven not just by practical demand, but by spectral desire. Yet, as great liners
arrive from ports unknown and depart for India or other exotic outposts of
the Empire, with their precious cargoes, they sail past the ugly secrets of the
metropolis: 'rubbish barges, and sewage barges' (Woolf 1975: 10) headed to
rat-infested dumps heaped along the banks of the river, the slimy underbelly
of commerce and trade, urban life and its waste. Woolf makes little mention of
the dock labourers, but as Sonita Sarker points out, many of them 'would have
been Africans and Asians' (Sarker 2001: 25 n.20), markers of the global nature
of trade as well as the hierarchies of race and class.

As 'The Docks of London' suggests, Woolf sees an aesthetic element in all the
systems of commerce and labyrinths of transactions that riddle the metropolis,
and she follows the thread to Oxford Street in the second essay: 'The Oxford
Street Tide'. The raw materials, now transformed, are being rapidly consumed
at a deep discount in a shopping area very different from Mrs Dalloway's Bond
Street. Here, on Oxford Street, among the swarming crowds, all of which are
seeking the impossible ('unending beauty, ever fresh, ever new, very cheap and
within the reach of everybody' [Woolf 1975: 20]), Woolf compares the aesthetics of Oxford Street's architecture to that of previous centuries, noting the durable is no longer fashionable, or as she humorously puts it: 'The charm of modern
London is that it is not built to last; it is built to pass' (ibid.: 19).

This casual phrasing – 'built to pass' – subtly recalls the motif of death that
casts a faint shadow over the glories of the metropolitan scene. In *Jacob's Room*,
Fanny Elmer indulges in window-shopping as an antidote to her lovelorn
yearning for Jacob, a clear instance of what would now be considered a form

of retail therapy. Momentarily entranced by lovely clothing exhibited in a shop window, Fanny sees 'the *parts* of a woman . . . shown *separate*. In the left hand was her skirt. . . . [L]ike the *heads of malefactors* on Temple Bar were hats. . . . And on the carpet were her feet – pointed gold, or patent leather *slashed with scarlet*' (*JR*: 121; my emphases). The display disturbingly suggests mutilation and murder, 'the violence of the desiring female gaze . . . link[ing] the woman for sale to the woman in search of sales' (Attewell 2004: 11–12)

Jinny, in *The Waves*, is fascinated by the sheer spectacle of London's shopping temptations located in an illuminated underground arcade at Piccadilly Circus (such areas beneath Leicester Square, Hyde Park Corner and Piccadilly Circus were developed in the 1930s to alleviate pedestrian traffic on the street level [see 'London Pedestrian . . .' 1930]). The narrator's description of the merchandise is alluring, yet is delicately infused with images of death and decay:

> Look how they show off clothes here even under ground in a perpetual radiance. *They will not let the earth even lie wormy and sodden.* There are gauzes and silks illumined in glass cases. . . . Crimson, green, violet, they are dyed all colours. (*W*: 194–5; my emphasis)

Not all of Woolf's characters regard commodities in the same fashion, some recoiling, some dully buying necessities without pleasure. Countering Jinny's extravagant pleasure is Rhoda's profound revulsion which mingles images of seduction and violation: 'faces . . . coarse, greedy, casual; looking in at shop-windows with pendent parcels; ogling, brushing, destroying everything, leaving even our love impure, now touched by their dirty fingers' (*W*: 160). Bernard, too, is aware of some impending and dire fate for 'these starers and trippers; these errand-boys and furtive and fugitive girls who, ignoring their doom, look in at shop-windows' (ibid.: 114).

Urban economies rely almost entirely upon the steady delivery of resources whether from surrounding rural areas, from factories in other regional cities, or from the far-flung Empire to support the cosmopolitan consumer culture of the metropolis. Further, the exchange of products and services also requires systems of transportation and communication. Whether accomplished on foot or by vehicle or by vessel, motion is the driving force of the exchange system and a compelling city aesthetic. The traffic, the trains and the Tube, the vendors crying their wares, the varied pedestrians – shoppers, workers trudging to and from their places of employment – or even 'a little thief' (*JR*: 67; see also 'Oxford Street Tide', Woolf 1975: 21), all emphasise the constant flow of commodities (whether legitimate or otherwise) and all appear in Woolf's descriptions of the metropolis in motion. And then there are the stationary figures as well – the beggars, the men playing barrel organs, 'a girl . . . for sale' (*JR*: 81). Further, just as robbery and prostitution are threats to an orderly society, so too are accidents. The turmoil of traffic in the metropolis constitutes a potential, indeed inevitable hazard. Young Virginia Stephen, a witness to several street calamities, writes in her diary:

Luckily neither horse nor driver suffered though the hansom was broken –
Then again, I managed to discover a man in the course of being squashed
by an omnibus, but, as we were in the midst of Piccadilly Circus, the details
of the accident could not be seen. (*PA*: 83; see Woolf 1990: 13 for an
averted incident)

In addition to pure chance bringing traffic to a halt, there is always a possibility
of deliberate political action, like the 2 million workers of the General Strike of
1926. The strike began on 3 May, lasted ten days and brought most of London
to a standstill. As Woolf wrote to her sister Vanessa on Wednesday, 12 May
1926,

there are no tubes and no buses and no taxis – except those run by special
constables often with fatal results. . . . [A]fter going to Westminster by
bus, with a policeman on the box, and boards up to protect us from stone
throwers . . . walking seems preferable. (*L3*: 260)

Communication supplements transportation but also has its own independent
exchange systems, connecting the diffuse and disparate elements of the metropolitan to each other and to the outer world. These vehicles of communication
include the writing of letters, delivery of the post, telephone calls, calling cards,
telegrams, radio, newspapers, gossip, quarrels, gatherings, speeches and social
events – all are transactions and negotiations, whether calculated or casual; all
are entangled in the machinery of the 'unseizable force' mentioned in *Jacob's
Room* (*JR*: 156) that drives culture into war and catastrophe. Advertising, too,
is a component of this elaborate exchange system. It does not necessarily function as a lucid means of communication or succeed in achieving its purported
goals. The aeroplane, sky-writing a puzzling advertisement in *Mrs Dalloway*,
is aesthetically pleasing – the letters forming a puzzle before dissolving into
wisps – even though entirely ineffective, suggesting that such advertising can
readily transcend its function and become a kind of public artwork, a part of
visual culture.

In 'Present Day' in *The Years*, Woolf describes another advertisement – a
mechanised billboard: 'Here was a bottle of beer: it poured: then stopped: then
poured again' (*Y*: 336) – that would intrigue passers-by initially but potentially
become exasperating. Woolf aligns the beer advertisement with the memorial
statue of Edith Cavell, the British nurse who was executed by the Germans in
the First World War for assisting Allied troops to escape from Belgium. The sce-
nario places Eleanor and Peggy in a taxi caught in heavy traffic. Peggy, glancing
out the window, notices the unidentified memorial – described as the 'figure of
a woman in nurse's uniform holding out her hand', and remarks curtly: 'Always
reminds me of an advertisement of sanitary towels' (*Y*: 336). The juxtaposition
effectively reduces militaristic propaganda in the form of monuments to the
level of advertising, selling patriotism rather than alcoholic beverages, while
also referring by association to the bodily shame and embarrassment related

to the marketing of sanitary products (see *L3*: 76). The reference to sanitary towels blurs women's cyclical menstrual blood with the beer pouring from the bottle and men's bloodshed in a war, and also calls up images of women who devoted themselves to nursing wounded soldiers or rolling bandages to support the war effort.

While public advertisements – or for that matter, the exteriors of monuments and buildings – blur class distinctions because they are available for everyone to see, appreciate or ignore, the social divide in London nonetheless remains intact. *Mrs Dalloway*, of course, is very much about social hierarchy, and a fleeting snapshot of Richard Dalloway's mind reveals his class attitudes. Richard, returning to his privileged home and his pampered wife after his well-appointed luncheon with Lady Bruton, walks through Green Park carrying an enormous and extraneous bunch of roses. As a politician, 'having championed the downtrodden and followed his instincts in the House of Commons' (*MD*: 115), Richard is inclined to aestheticise the plight of the poor, indulging in utopian ideas while also fantasising about the moment when he will (not!) tell his wife he loves her. He sees with pleasure 'how in the shade of the trees whole families, poor families, were sprawling; children kicking up their legs; sucking milk; paper bags thrown about' and makes eye-contact with a female vagrant who 'laughed at the sight of him' while 'he smiled good-humouredly' (ibid.: 116), an accidental frisson of connectedness that offsets his distant relationship with Clarissa.

Richard's strange and fleeting sense of intimacy with a total stranger is not just a persistent attribute of Woolf's city aesthetic, but, in this instance, an occluded allusion to the ever-present undercurrent of sex trafficking in the metropolis. While Woolf despises what she calls 'street love' in the excised passages of *The Years*, published as *The Pargiters: The Novel-Essay Portion of* The Years (see Woolf 1978 and Squier 1985: 142–53), her depictions of the women and girls who must sell themselves to survive or are sold in brothels for a profit are often compassionate, even affectionate. Orlando's semi-sororal/semi-Sapphic relationship with the eighteenth-century prostitutes during her phase of walking the streets in male drag is exceptionally intimate and relaxed. Nell, Prue, Kitty and Rose, the prostitutes with whom she consorts, even have 'a society of their own of which they now elected her a member' (*O*: 219). And there is the curious description of the City of London as 'hoary, . . . old, sinful, and majestic', a City who 'loves her prostitutes' (*JR*: 67).

Woolf admired the political work of Josephine Butler (1828–1906) and other activists such as Millicent G. Fawcett (1847–1927) who sought to repeal the discriminatory and humiliating Contagious Diseases Acts and end human trafficking. But, as with the suffrage effort, Woolf did not participate directly in the ongoing struggle to end the sexual exploitation of women and children, a political effort which continues today. Nevertheless, in asserting that all women are potentially prostitutes in a patriarchal culture, Woolf emphasises a degree of likeness between prostitutes and female upper- and middle-class captives of patriarchy. As she provocatively states in *Three Guineas*: 'If such is the real nature of our influence . . . many of us would prefer to call ourselves prostitutes simply and to take our stand under the lamps of Piccadilly Circus rather than use it' (*TG*: 15).

The very titles of *A Room of One's Own* (1929) and *Jacob's Room* (1922) are clearly gendered references to the possession and control of personal space. Women writers in *A Room of One's Own* are, of course, desperately in need both of financial resources and privacy but are thwarted by a patriarchy that denies them gender equity. Even though the gossips say 'he hadn't a penny' (*JR*: 155) Jacob – who is a dilettante writer, among other things – has tolerable London lodgings: the sitting room and separate bedroom with their raspberry-coloured walls and eighteenth-century roses or ram's heads carved into the door lintels are not just private but also comparatively spacious if sparsely furnished. By contrast, Florinda's bedroom is a multi-purpose space described as 'cheap, mustard-coloured, half attic, half studio', although it is 'curiously ornamented with silver paper stars, Welshwomen's hats, and rosaries', decor choices highlighting her bohemian creativity (ibid.: 77). Florinda has very limited financial resources (she even accuses a waitress of poisoning her so that she will not have to pay for her tea [ibid.: 78]), and all her income seems to come from her admirers. Fanny Elmer seems to have even less money than Florinda, living in 'a room that she shared with a school teacher' (ibid.: 122). Fanny's financial situation perhaps explains why she is so entranced with Jacob's pocket change (ibid.: 117). Apparently, women of limited means living on their own in London during the 1910s just could not afford the aesthetic pleasures of decent lodgings and privacy.

Deborah L. Parsons points out that 'Rooms in *Night and Day* are highly symbolic and suggestive of the ideas and position of Edwardian men and women in relation to the city and to each other' and observes that Mary Datchet, who 'has a private income', lives in a flat that is 'largely modelled on the rooms of the traditional male bachelor', an indicator of her independence, while Katharine Hilbery, dependent on her parents, has no privacy whatsoever in her family home (Parsons 2000: 117). Mary has sufficient means to be able to work as a volunteer for a suffrage organisation rather than draw a salary, can afford lunch at 'a gaudy establishment, upholstered in red plush, near by, where . . . you could buy steak, two inches thick, or a roast section of fowl, swimming in a pewter dish' (*ND*: 81) and, as noted, have a flat of her own. However, her private space actually makes her feels guilty: 'She was robbing no one of anything, and yet, to get so much pleasure from simple things, such as eating one's breakfast alone in a room which had nice colours in it' (ibid.: 77) was rather disconcerting. The aesthetic of privacy is enhanced for Mary by pleasing light and colour:

> High in the air as her flat was, some beams from the morning sun reached her even in November, striking straight at curtain, chair, and carpet, and painting there three bright, true spaces of green, blue, and purple, upon

which the eye rested with a pleasure which gave physical warmth to the body. (*ND*: 77)

These clean bright colours are an implicit contrast with the gloom of Victorian decor – and the new-found urban independence of a young woman.

Woolf's formative years were defined by the very Victorian urban aesthetics of 22 Hyde Park Gate, the tall, narrow, dreary building in a cul-de-sac of the well-to-do enclave of South Kensington in central London where she grew up. The house was inhabited by too many people sharing just one bath and three water closets (amenities that were nevertheless markers of the family's relative wealth), and the cramped living area for the family was positively luxurious by contrast with the servants' quarters and workspace. Morag Shiach observes that these spaces have 'psychological meanings' for Woolf:

> They are small and uncomfortable, and generate unwelcome intimacies. Family life depends on boundaries that are always in fact permeable; those folding doors were clearly far from soundproof. There is a stifling sense of isolation, of being cut off from the energy of the modern city and encased in a constraining Victorian shell. But there is also a saturation of emotion through which space becomes history, so that Woolf insists she could 'write a history of every mark and scratch in my room'. (Shiach 2005: 257; see also Froula 2005: 559, 575)

While awaiting Leslie Stephen's death, Virginia and her siblings planned their escape from South Kensington to the unfashionable and seedy district of Bloomsbury, located about four-and-a-half miles north-east of Hyde Park Gate. However, Virginia was not entirely convinced of the merits of the idea probably because of an aesthetic aversion both to the houses for let and the location. Thus, on Thursday night 31 December 1903, Virginia wrote to her friend Violet Dickinson:

> We have been tramping Bloomsbury this afternoon with Beatrice, and staring up at dingy houses. There are lots to be had – but Lord how dreary! It seems so far away, and so cold and gloomy . . . . Really we shall never get a house we like so well as this, but it is better to go. (*L*1: 119)

However, in October 1904, seven months after Leslie's death, the daring move to Bloomsbury was made and the Stephen siblings took possession of their new residence, deeply relieved that their half-brother, George Duckworth, who had originally planned to accompany them, was instead getting married (see Froula 2005: 571).

The house Vanessa chose – 46 Gordon Square – was not just the incubator for the Bloomsbury Group and the Friday Club, but also a site of liberation for the Stephen sisters. Both Virginia and Vanessa were able to claim possession of private inviolable space, and they were active agents in the first of many Bloomsbury experiments in interior decor, a declaration of their independence from Victorian aesthetics. Christopher Reed notes that 'the extraordinary look of the house betokened an iconoclastic life within', and that, 'Although it has been disparaged as incompetent by adherents of high-finish modernist aesthetics . . . Bloomsbury's domestic aesthetic makes its own claims to modernity' (Reed 2004: 23).

Even before the escape to Bloomsbury, Woolf was rebelling against an entrenched definition of home (see Sennett 1990: 26–9) epitomised by John Ruskin's *Sesame and Lilies* (1864–5), his Victorian paean of praise for a woman's 'true wifely subjection' and proper space 'within [a man's] house', where she holds an 'office, and place' that shelters her 'from all danger and temptation'. As Ruskin contends, 'the true nature of home . . . is the place of Peace; . . . it is a sacred place, a vestal temple' (Ruskin 2002: 77–8)

In 'Great Men's Houses', one of the six essays Woolf wrote for *Good Housekeeping*, Woolf counters Ruskin's utopian vision. Her essay is almost a journalistic exposé of a crime committed at 5 Cheyne Row, where historian Thomas Carlyle and his wife Jane and their one maidservant lived. As Woolf declares, the house was 'not so much a dwelling-place as a battlefield – the scene of labour, effort and perpetual struggle' and utter misery for Jane (Woolf 1975: 25). While Thomas focused on his writing, Jane focused on the household challenges which included the lack of 'bath, h. and c., gas fires in the bedrooms and indoor sanitation' (ibid.: 26) – a far cry from Ruskin's 'vestal temple' indeed.

Woolf saw the Victorian home as a virtual prison, but she also saw gender discrimination outside in the workplace. At the time Woolf wrote *Three Guineas* (1938), women of the urban professional classes who had won the privilege of salaried employment after great struggle still had to fight a private war against patriarchy both in their office spaces and the public sphere, especially against the looming threat of Mussolini and Hitler and their surrogates in the British culture. As Woolf asks with urgency: 'And is not the woman who has to breathe that poison and to fight that insect, secretly and without arms, in her office, fighting the Fascist or the Nazi as surely as those who fight him with arms in the limelight of publicity?' (*TG*: 81).

Woolf's vision of women's independence and also resonates with the concept of *flânerie* as articulated by Walter Benjamin. Leslie Kathleen Hankins recognises cogent similarities between Benjamin and Woolf seeing them both as thinkers who:

> held in dialectical tension the conflicted roles of cultural inheritor and outsider, combining tempered nostalgia for the very institutions they critiqued (the Bloomsbury squares, the bourgeois interior, rooms of one's own, the capitalist city, the Academy) with radical commitment to outsider status and to revolutionary change. Acknowledging their complicity with class privilege as inheritors, they manipulated nostalgia to interrogate urban and class spaces in radical ways. (Hankins 2000: 9)

To Woolf, the streets of London are the connective tissue of the metropolis. Woolf seems to be intrigued by every aspect of street life ranging from prostitution to parades and protests; from high society gatherings to the peregrinations and performances of vagrants; from the pleasures of window-shopping to the pleasures of voyeurism. Truly appreciating such archetypal urban elements requires some form of *flânerie*. Yet, Janet Wolff claims in her landmark article 'The Invisible *Flâneuse*', that '[t]here is no question of inventing the *flâneuse*: the essential point is that such a character was rendered impossible by the sexual divisions of the nineteenth century' (Wolff 1985: 45).

Rachel Bowlby, in 'Walking, Women and Writing', identifies several instances of the twentieth-century *flâneuse* in Woolf's work, expands the definition of *flânerie* to include Elizabeth Dalloway's adventure on an omnibus and analyses the peregrinations of the narrator in 'Street Haunting' (Bowlby 1997: 204–19). Parsons, continuing the discussion, argues that 'the concept of the *flâneur* itself contains gender ambiguities that suggest the figure to be a site for the contestation of male authority, rather than the epitome of it' (Parsons 2000: 5–6). Referencing Charles Baudelaire's categories of 'urban spectators', Parsons notes that 'male and female, authoritative and marginal, they all have in common a detached bohemian existence, a lack of place in bourgeois society and an aura of isolation' (ibid.: 19–20). Attewell, moving beyond the *flâneuse*, suggests that 'street-wandering' 'signals the possibility of gaining a more generalised freedom; freedom perhaps from gender itself' (Attewell 2004: 13).

Given these evolving viewpoints, one is tempted to re-examine the *flânerie* in Woolf's city aesthetic. While Deborah Epstein Nord (1995) interprets the narrator(s) in 'Street Haunting' as projecting 'into the roles of washerwoman, publican, dwarf and street singer . . . without fully relinquishing her middle-class, male-identified stance' (Nord 1995: 192), Sara Gerend makes a case for a multiplicity of protagonists (Gerend 2006: 238). Applying Attewell's argument, the collective viewpoint of an anonymous first-person plural obscures the narrator(s) gender. One might also want to ruminate about the ratio between the narrator in 'The Mark on the Wall' (1917), who displays a kind of mental *flânerie* via random thinking and obsessively scopic fascination regarding a small mysterious spot (*HH*: 37–46), and the narrator in 'Street Haunting'. One remains protected by the snail-shell of the home itself while the other sheds the protective 'shell-like covering' and becomes 'an enormous eye' (*DM*: 21–2) as does, perhaps, the housemate in 'Mark' who decides to go out and get a newspaper (a mission not that different from the purchase of a lead pencil [*HHs*: 46]).

Based on Parsons' position, one can also readily imagine the female vagrants, prostitutes and beggars in Woolf's cityscape evidencing 'a detached bohemian existence, a lack of place in bourgeois society and an aura of isolation'. Examples include the vagrant in Green Park and 'the battered woman – for she wore a skirt – with her right hand exposed', singing 'ee um fah um so' for a coin (*MD*: 81) in *Mrs Dalloway* and the street woman clutching her dog to her chest while 'singing out loud, not for coppers, no, from the depths of her gay wild heart – her sinful, tanned heart' (*JR*: 67) in *Jacob's Room*.

Jennifer Poulos Nesbitt points out that 'unlike male characters in Woolf's novels, who feel themselves to be "ideal residents in the geographical city"', women characters have a 'sense of anomalousness' because of the 'historical discomfort with the idea of women on the city streets' (Nesbitt 2005: 28). Possibly Woolf attempts to redress this incongruity since one might legitimately expand the definition of *flânerie* to include another category of female street nomads: the pair of girls mentioned in *Jacob's Room* who are 'striding hand in hand, shouting out a song, seem[ing] to feel neither cold nor shame. They are hatless. They triumph' (*JR*: 113). They are filled with exhilaration, energy and derring-do defiance, demanding that they be seen and heard but not objectified. This possible doubling of *flâneuses* who bond with each other in their adventures might be another way to challenge the patriarchal guidelines for female behaviour.

David Macauley, building on the work of Michel Certeau, suggests that, 'by understanding the aesthetic, dynamic and democratic dimensions of walking, we can . . . begin to interrogate and critically contest the opaque and authoritarian features of urban architecture, private property and public space' (Macauley 2007: 100). Woolf makes a similar suggestion in 'The Leaning Tower', telling her readers to take 'a piece of advice that an eminent Victorian who was also an eminent pedestrian once gave to walkers. Whenever you see a board with the words "'Trespassers will be prosecuted", trespass at once' ('Leaning Tower', *CE2*: 181). Purportedly, Woolf's recommendation is intended to encourage 'commoners and outsiders' to challenge the establishment literary viewpoint, but she also implicitly advocates questioning all authority. Whether Woolf analyses the politics of city aesthetics (see also Evans 2008 regarding the political cityscape in *The Years*) or expands her critique of empire to include suburban displays of imperial power, Woolf resists the status quo. Scott Cohen sees Woolf's 1924 essay (*E3*: 410–14), 'Thunder at Wembley', as her 'earliest and arguably most vivid critique of empire', a vision of 'an imperial apocalypse . . . as serious as it is humorous' (Cohen 2004: 86) and contrasts 'Wembley rigidly monumentalized' with the 'strikingly antimonumental' perspective of 'geographical imagination' in *Mrs Dalloway*' (Cohen 2004: 98).

Woolf uses the motif of memorial architecture to launch a transgressive attack on conventionality, trespassing gleefully on Victorian values by imagining a monument made entirely of the detritus of the era:

a pyramid, . . . a conglomeration . . . of the most heterogeneous and ill-assorted objects, [was] piled higgledy-piggledy in a vast mound where the statue of Queen Victoria now stands! Draped about a vast cross of fretted and floriated gold were widow's weeds and bridal veils; hooked on to other excrescences were crystal palaces, bassinettes, military helmets, memorial wreaths, trousers, whiskers, wedding cakes, cannon, Christmas trees, telescopes, extinct monsters, globes, maps, elephants, and mathematical instruments. (*O*: 232)

This overdetermined heap of Victorian artifacts combines all the societal elements Woolf most despised. The fictitious structure is an iconic representation of the excesses perpetrated by patriarchy, Empire, capitalism and consumerism. For Woolf, it represents the familial and cultural forces that curbed and constrained her generation. It symbolises the captivity of 22 Hyde Park Gate. Satire cleanses the palate and Woolf is able to affirm her own city aesthetic by ridiculing her immediate predecessors, and – ironically – appreciating the urban aesthetics of every other era in London's history.

Note

I would like to thank Maggie Humm, Jackie Jones, Camille Serchuk, Kathryn Simpson, Hilary Clark, Elizabeth F. Evans and Jennie-Rebecca Falcetta for their support and excellent suggestions regarding this article.

Works Cited

Attewell, Nadine (2004) 'Risky Business: Going Out in the Fiction of Virginia Woolf and Dorothy Richardson', in *The Swarming Streets: Twentieth Century Representations of London*, Amsterdam: Rodopi, pp. 7–18.

Bowlby, Rachel (1997) 'Walking, Women and Writing', in *Feminist Destinations and Further Essays on Virginia Woolf*, Edinburgh: Edinburgh University Press, pp. 191–219.

Cohen, Scott (2004) 'The Empire from the Street: Virginia Woolf, Wembley, and Imperial Monuments', *MFS Modern Fiction Studies*, 50: 85–109.

Evans, Elizabeth F. (2008) 'Art, Propaganda, and Virginia Woolf's Search for an Anti-Tyranny Aesthetic', unpublished article.

Falcetta, Jennie-Rebecca (2007) 'Geometries of Space and Time: The Cubist London of Mrs Dalloway' *Woolf Studies Annual*, 13: 111–36.

Froula, Christine (2005) 'On French and British Freedoms: Early Bloomsbury and the Brothels of Modernism', *Modernism/Modernity*, 12.4: 553–80.

Fussell, Paul (2000) *The Great War and Modern Memory*, New York: Oxford University Press.

Gerend, Sara (2006) '"Street Haunting": Phantasmagorias of the Modern Imperial Metropolis'. *Literature Compass*, 4.1: 235–42.

Hankins, Leslie Kathleen (2000) 'Virginia Woolf and Walter Benjamin Selling Out(siders), in *Virginia Woolf in the Age of Mechanical Reproduction*', ed. Pamela Caughie, New York: Garland Publishing, pp. 3–35.

'London Pedestrian Driven Under Ground; Shops Follow – New Trend Here Is Toward Overhead Rather than Tunneled Streets' (1930) *New York Times*, 12 June.

Macauley, David (2007) 'Walking the City', in *The Aesthetics of Human Environments*, ed. Arnold Berleant and Allen Carlson, Buffalo, NY: Broadview Press, pp. 100–18.

Nesbitt, Jennifer Poulos (2005) 'The Act of Passing By', in *Narrative Settlements: Geographies of British Women's Fiction Between the Wars*. Toronto: University of Toronto Press, pp. 27–45.

Nord, Deborah Epstein (1995) '"Neither Pairs Nor Odd": Women, Urban Community, and

Writing in the 1880s', in *Walking the Victorian Streets: Women, Representation, and the City*, Ithaca, NY: Cornell University Press, pp. 181–206.

Parsons, Deborah L. (2000) *Streetwalking the Metropolis: Women, the City and Modernity*, New York: Oxford University Press.

Reed, Christopher (2004) *Bloomsbury Rooms: Modernism. Subculture, and Domesticity*, New Haven, CT: Yale University Press.

Ruskin, John (2002) *Sesame and Lilies*, ed. Deborah Epstein Nord, New Haven, CT: Yale University Press.

Sarker, Sonita (2001) 'Locating a Native Englishness in Virginia Woolf's *The London Scene*', *NWSA Journal*, 13.2: 1–30.

Sennett, Richard (1990) *The Conscience of the Eye: The Design and Social Life of Cities*, New York: Alfred A. Knopf.

Shiach, Morag (2005) 'Modernism, the City and the "Domestic Interior"', *Home Cultures*, 2: 251–67.

Squier, Susan Merrill (1985) *Virginia Woolf and London: Sexual Politics of the City*, Chapel Hill: University of North Carolina Press.

Wolff, Janet (1985) 'The Invisible *Flâneuse*: Women and the Literature of Modernity', *Theory, Culture & Society*, 2.3: 37–46.

Wolfreys, Julian (1998) *Writing London: The Trace of the Urban Text from Blake to Dickens*, New York: Palgrave.

Woolf, Virginia (1990) *The Voyage Out*, Definitive Collected Edition, London: Hogarth Press.

—— (1975) *The London Scene*, New York: Random House.

—— (1978) *The Pargiters: The Novel-Essay Portion of* The Years, ed. Mitchell A. Leaska, London: Hogarth Press.

Further Reading

Beker, Miroslav (1972) 'London as a Principle of Structure in Mrs. Dalloway', *MFS Modern Fiction Studies*, 18: 375–85.

Brewster, Dorothy (1960) *Virginia Woolf's London*, New York: New York University Press.

Caughie, Pamela (1989) 'Purpose and Play in Virginia Woolf's *London Scene* Essays', *Women's Studies* 16: 389–408.

Clark, Hilary (2004) 'The Traveling Self', *Virginia Woolf Miscellany*, 66: 6–8.

Espley, Richard (2007), 'Courting Danger: Virginia Woolf, Sylvia Plath and Wooing at London Zoo', *Virginia Woolf Miscellany*, 71: 23–4.

Jacobs, Karen (2001) *The Eye's Mind: Literary Modernism and Visual Culture*, Ithaca, NY: Cornell University Press.

Johnson, Jeri (2000) 'Literary Geography: Joyce, Woolf, and the City', *City* 4.2: 199–214.

Lord, Catherine (1999) 'FRAMES OF SEPTIMUS SMITH: Through Twenty Four Hours in the City of *Mrs Dalloway*, 1923, and of Millennial London: ART IS A SHOCKING EXPERIENCE', *Parallax*, 5.3: 36–46.

McCue, Megan M. (1997) 'Confronting Modernity: Virginia Woolf and Walter Benjamin', in *Virginia Woolf and the Arts: Selected Papers from the Sixth Annual Conference on Virginia Woolf*, ed. Diane F. Gillespie and Leslie K. Hankins, New York: Pace University Press, pp. 310–19.

McVicker, Jeanette (2004) 'Six Essays on London Life': A History of Dispersal Part II', *Woolf Studies Annual*, 10: 141–72.

Nicolson, Juliet (2006) *The Perfect Summer: England 1911, Just Before the Storm*, New York: Grove Press.

Sparks, Elisa (2003) '*Mrs Dalloway* as a Geo/Graphic Novel', *Virginia Woolf Miscellany*, 62: 6–7.

Tambling, Jeremy (1989) 'Repression in Mrs Dalloway's London', *Essays in Criticism: A Quarterly Journal of Literary Criticism (EIC)*, 39.2: 137–55.

Thacker, Andrew (2003) 'Virginia Woolf: Literary Geography and the Kaleidescope of Travel', in *Moving through Modernity: Space and Geography in Modernism*, Manchester: Manchester University Press, pp. 152–91.

Wilson, Jean Moorcroft (1988) *Virginia Woolf, Life and London: A Biography of Place*, New York: W. W. Norton.

Wood, Andelys (2003) 'Walking the Web in the Lost London of Mrs Dalloway' *Mosaic*, 36.2: 19–32.

Zemgulys, Andrea P. (2000) '"Night and Day Is Dead": Virginia Woolf in London "Literary and Historic"', *Twentieth Century Literature*, 46.1: 56–77.

6

VIRGINIA WOOLF AND REALIST AESTHETICS

Linden Peach

WOOLF'S MODERNIST NOVELS of the 1920s have generally been seen as a rejection of the nineteenth-century realism which her second novel, *Night and Day* (1919), which was written at a time of postwar suffragist triumphs for women in the Parliamentary Qualifications of Women Act (1918) and the Sex Disqualifications (Removal) Act (1919), appeared to mimic. At the time she was working on her non-realist modernist texts of the 1920s, Woolf's critical writings were concerned with the extent to which realist aesthetics brought the reader close to 'reality'. In her essay 'Modern Fiction' (1919), which she revised for inclusion in *The Common Reader* (1925), Woolf appears reluctant to use the term 'realist', referring to Hardy, Conrad, Wells and Bennett, without making distinctions between them, as 'materialists', and seems to be reaching after something which she is unable to define: 'whether we call it life or spirit, truth or reality' (*CR*1: 147, 149). Despite the fact that Hardy, Conrad, Wells and Bennett are very different writers, each is criticised for his 'simplicity' (ibid.: 146). By 'simplicity', Woolf appears to mean what we might call 'naïve realism', based on the assumption of 'close resemblance', which Woolf believed underpinned realist fiction. In her essay 'Mr Bennett and Mrs Brown' (1924), Woolf maintains that the Edwardian novelists provided readers with 'a vast sense of things in general' and of institutions such as industry, factories, prisons and workhouses. But she argues that it is insufficiently concerned with particulars to create 'characters who are real, true, and convincing' (*CE*1: 319).

In a letter to David Garnett on 20 October 1922, following the publication of *Jacob's Room*, Woolf asks: 'But how far can one convey character without realism? That is my problem – one of them at least. You're quite right that I can't do the realism, though I admire those who can' (Woolf 1976: 571). Six years earlier, she had complained that Arnold Bennett 'depresses me with his very astute realism' and that Miss Viola Meynell 'depresses me with her lack of realism' (ibid.: 81). These two admissions betray the extent to which realism preoccupied her when she was working on her first novels. From what she says about Joyce in 'Modern Fiction', Woolf appeared to be particularly interested in how the modernists 'attempt to come closer to life, and to preserve more sincerely and exactly what interests and moves them, even if to do so they must discard most of the conventions which are commonly observed by the novelist' (*CR1*: 150).

Whereas criticism has tended to see *Night and Day* as mimicking nineteenth-century and Edwardian realist aesthetics, it can be seen more accurately through what Woolf said of the work of Bennett and Meynell in 1916. It is a novel which avoids Bennett's 'astute realism' but also Meynell's 'lack of realism'. At one level, the novel is a somewhat convoluted romance: Katharine Hilbery, the daughter of a middle-class London family, is courted by an aspiring poet, William Rodney, while being involved with a lawyer Ralph Denham, who is in turn courted by a young suffragist-cum-socialist, who is also attracted to Katharine. However, it would be misleading to interpret the novel in terms of a romance and realism binary. Woolf employs her principal characters as vehicles for exploring not so much the 'real' as proximity to the 'real'. Indeed, 'real' is a word used in this novel more often and more consciously than in any of her other works. Susan Sontag, in her study of photography, suggests that realism is a 'reductive approach to reality which is considered realistic' and maintains: 'The "realistic" view of the world compatible with bureaucracy redefines knowledge – as techniques and information' (Sontag 1977: 21, 22). *Night and Day* encourages the reader to address the complexities of the 'real' as a concept through phrases such as 'real world' (*ND*: 141), the 'real body' (234), 'real people' (153), 'real feelings' (140, 244)), 'real life' (108, 127, 184), 'real country' (186), 'real existence' (430) and 'real person' (330). Within the novel, 'real' proves a slippery concept. Through references to Rodney's poetry and other texts, such as Henry Fielding's work which Katharine chooses to read when her mother asks for something 'real' (ibid.: 104), it examines the relationship between literary genre and techniques and the legitimacy of common place assumptions in even everyday language about what is called 'real'.

At the heart of *Night and Day* is the concept of 'feelings' freed from the constraint of the 'real' (*ND*: 141). The notion of the 'constraint' of the real suggests that for Woolf 'realism' was not simply an aesthetic concept but was locked into a socio-symbolic network or Order that oppresses and constrains. This is evident in the 'relics' room which Katharine shows guests to the house:

> As Katharine touched different spots, lights sprang here and there, and revealed a square mass of red-and-gold books, and then a long skirt in blue-and-white paint lustrous behind glass, and then a mahogany writing-table, with its orderly equipment, and, finally, a picture above the table to which special illumination was accorded. (*ND*: 15)

The picture which is illuminated is a portrait of the poet Richard Alardyce, whose biography is being written by his granddaughter, Katharine, and her mother. In other words, a male ancestry is potentially being rewritten by a female voice, and because of the involvement of women from different generations, not necessarily a single female voice. What is significant here is that Alardyce's portrait, and the mahogany writing table associated with him, dominates the room. At one level, Woolf's text addresses detail, but, at another level, it invites us to interrogate the verisimilitude with which it presents us. It brings us close to the 'realism' of the room but makes us aware of how we are distanced from it. These two objects, the portrait and the writing table, are in a relationship to each other which up to a point reflects the masculinist, symbolic Order of which they are a part.

I say 'up to a point' because they also have a role in constructing that symbolic Order. In Woolf's work, the objects that constitute 'reality' are active elements in a context defined by shifting and dialectical discourses. As the exhibits are gradually lit, building up to the 'special illumination' above Alardyce's portrait, there is a sense of a narrative of a kind which soon proved fundamental to Woolf's realist aesthetics. Before Alardyce's portrait is revealed, we see a skirt behind glass which signifies the relative status of women but also makes a statement about the way in which women are represented. The female is synonymous with her body and the female body is signified by the skirt which dresses it. The glass distances her, and keeps her separated from the mahogany writing table which, through its links with Alardyce, suggests that ideas which shape society and intellectual culture are basically male.

Thus, the realistic aesthetic here reflects Woolf's cryptic reading of 'reality' and the way she was increasingly to see reality in the modernist texts of the 1920s as a sum of discourses which her texts identify and analyse. Reflecting the influence of Roger Fry, the Post-Impressionists and others to which we will return later, Woolf is interested in the social perspective within 'realism'. Her work invariably exposes the perspectives responsible for the occlusion and suppression of women. In *Mrs Dalloway*, Clarissa's daughter, Elizabeth, takes an omnibus ride past Somerset House, the public records office representing the symbolic Order that prevented women such as her mother from entering the professions and condemned many women from the poorer classes to a life of domestic drudgery.

Like the modernist novels of the 1920s, *Night and Day* suggests that Woolf engaged with 'realism' on two fronts that I want to examine in more detail: the liberation of 'human consciousness' from the so-called 'real'; and the 'real' as a symbolic Order in which particular prejudices, assumptions and discourses were legitimised. The importance to Woolf of realism's alleged failure to grasp the nature of human consciousness is evident in 'Mr Bennett and Mrs Brown', in which Woolf makes a number of attempts to construct a fictional character using the methods of Edwardian writers in order to expose the deficiencies in their approach. She implies that the main problem is that the Edwardians take 'realism' for granted: they 'have laid an enormous stress upon the fabric of things. They have given us a house in the hope that we may be able to deduce the human beings who live there' (*E*1: 332). In furthering her argument, she urges the reader to 'examine for a moment an ordinary mind on an ordinary day' (*CR*1: 149). In attempting to represent how the mind at any given moment 'receives a myriad of impressions' and 'an incessant shower of innumerable atoms' (ibid.: 150), Woolf sought to develop a realist aesthetic which is close to 'real life'. In 'Modern Fiction', Joyce's so-called 'scene in the cemetery' in *Ulysses*, the Hades episode in the sixth section of the novel that Woolf read as a serial in September 1918, is singled out to show that Joyce 'does undoubtedly come so close to the quick of the mind' (ibid.: 151).

There is no denying that the extent to which Woolf's early modernist novels, *Jacob's Room*, *Mrs Dalloway* and *To the Lighthouse*, examine an ordinary mind distinguishes them from *Night and Day*. However, *Night and Day*, too, betrays her conviction that the representation of human consciousness was a problem, as she explained in her letter to David Garnett, for realist aesthetics generally. This is clear, at the outset of the novel, in the description of Ralph Denham entering Mrs Hilbery's drawing-room. While the drawing-room and the street from which he has come are 'real', they are indistinguishable from Denham's mental, and even physiological, being:

> A fine mist, the etherealized essence of the fog, hung visibly in the wide and rather empty space of the drawing-room, all silver where the candles were grouped on the tea-table, and ruddy again in the firelight. With the omnibuses and cabs still running in his head, and his body still tingling with his quick walk along the streets and in and out of traffic and foot-passengers, this drawing room seemed very remote and still. (*ND*: 10)

While the realist aesthetic as developed by Bennett demanded some account of the street from which Denham has stepped, in Woolf's passage one part of Denham's consciousness and indeed his body – 'still tingling with his walk' – are still in the street. Although the room is a kind of refuge from the busyness of the street, Denham, his thoughts full of omnibuses, cabs and traffic, is alert to the movement of light and shadow within the room.

Despite her criticism of Edwardian writers in 'Mr Bennett and Mrs Brown', Woolf always retained an interest in real detail. In 1933, she complained to David Garnett about his review of *Flush*, the spoof biography of Elizabeth Barrett Browning's spaniel, because he overlooked a slip that she had made: 'But how could you let slip the horrid anachronism which stares at you, bright red, on page I don't know what? There were no pillar boxes in the year 1846' (Woolf 1979: 232). Woolf is right of course; red pillar boxes were not erected in London until 1874. But what generally vexes her is not so much authenticity as far as the detail of external objects is concerned as the convergence of human consciousness and the constraints of the 'real' when viewed as a symbolic Order.

Bill Brown points out, quoting Alex Woloch, that even as a novelist concerned with 'redirecting the genre away from realistic poetics, "away from the observed object toward the observing subject, away from exterior description toward inner apprehension"', Woolf was 'mesmerized by Defoe's reality effects' (Brown 2006: 91). But he points out that her account of Robinson Crusoe's pot-making amounts to more than the material representation of his world: 'The realist commitment, the belief in things, grants him his organizational authority, the power of the novelistic art' (ibid.: 92).

In Woolf's mind, as *Night and Day* demonstrates, realism is a particular organisational view of the world, suggested in the account of the 'orderly equipment' on the writing table in the relics room. This perspective meant that she could explore the relationship between the mind and the material world in ways that distinguished her fiction from that of the 'materialists' whom she criticised in 'Modern Fiction'. Brown argues that Woolf helped 'mark a proliferation of the discourse on objects in the 1920s, a new effort to think about things, to think with them, to think through them' (Brown 2006: 92). We have seen the truth of this in our discussion of the relics room. However, the 'new effort to think about things, to think with them' that we saw there is also developed in Woolf's work in the representation of figures in interiors. This is a trope that, once again, can be traced back to some degree to Roger Fry's exhibition, 'Manet and the Post-Impressionists', the first major showing of the work of avant-garde European art including the work of Van Gogh, Gauguin and Cézanne. However, it is an aspect of her work that was developed under two additional influences in the 1930s: the correspondence of the Victorian poet Elizabeth Barrett Browning and the work of the nineteenth-century British realist painter and friend of Woolf's, Walter Sickert. Her re-engagement with the realist aesthetic at this time is worth consideration because in the 1930s, as Chris Hopkins points out, largely because of the depression, the rise of fascism in Europe and fears about a forthcoming war, modernist ideas about 'the self as largely subjective and self-creating' were being replaced by social realism (Hopkins 1995: 279).

The influence of Elizabeth Barrett Browning's correspondence upon Woolf's engagement with realist aesthetics was the product of one of Woolf's digressions after working on a particularly difficult text. In this case, she took to reading Elizabeth Barrett Brownings's letters to Robert Browning as a relief from working on *The Waves*. Also she saw Besier's play *The Barretts of Wimpole Street* in London and it inspired her to write a mock biography of Flush. *Flush* remains a relatively neglected text, but it is important to an understanding of Woolf's engagement with realism. I use the word 'engagement' deliberately, for although Woolf frequently quotes Elizabeth Barrett Browning's letters verbatim, she also rewrites many of them, too. This is evident in the way in which Woolf adapted Elizabeth Barrett Browning's description of her bedroom in a letter to Mrs Martin which was actually quoted verbatim in Besier's play:

> The bed, like a sofa and no bed; the large table placed out in the room, towards the wardrobe end of it; the sofa rolled where a sofa should be rolled – opposite the arm-chair: the drawers crowned with a coronal of shelves fashioned by Settle and Co. (of papered deal and crimson merino) to carry my books; the washing table opposite turned into a cabinet with another coronal of shelves; and Chaucer's and Homer's busts in guard over

these two departments of English and Greek poetry; three more busts con-
secrating the wardrobe which there was no annihilating . . .! (EBB to Mrs
Martin, 26 May 1843, Kenyon 1897: I, 143–4).

Elizabeth Barrett Browning was an invalid in her father's house for much of
her early adult life; her illness, which was never precisely diagnosed, seemed to
have started as early as 1821. Her description of her back bedroom is rendered
differently in *Flush* although there is a great deal of reliance upon Browning's
account. Woolf's emphasis is upon the way in which the room emerges in
Flush's consciousness:

> Very slowly, very dimly, with much sniffing and pawing, Flush by degrees
> distinguished the outlines of several articles of furniture. That huge object
> by the window was perhaps a wardrobe. Next to it stood, conceivably, a
> chest of drawers. In the middle of the room swam up to the surface what
> seemed to be a table with a ring round it; and then the vague amorphous
> shapes of armchair and table emerged. But everything was disguised. On
> top of the wardrobe stood three white busts; the chest of drawers was
> surmounted by a bookcase; the bookcase was pasted over with crimson
> merino; the washing-table had a coronal of shelves upon it; on top of
> the shelves that were on top of the washing-table stood two more busts.
> Nothing in the room was itself; everything was something else. (*F*: 23–4)

Unsurprisingly, Woolf leaves out details that Flush could not have known –
the purpose of the shelves, the name of the furniture company, the reference
to Chaucer and Homer – and focuses upon the way in which objects achieve
their solidity when their outlines become distinct. The objects are the same
as in Browning's letter – the wardrobe, the chest of drawers, table, armchair
and coronal of shelves. But Woolf develops what Elizabeth Barrett Browning
suggests when she says 'the bed, like a sofa and no bed': 'Nothing in the room
was itself; everything was something else.' The key element in Woolf's account
of Elizabeth Barrett Browning's bedroom is that the spatial intimacy between
Elizabeth Barrett Browning and the objects in her room can be interpreted
in more than one way. From one point of view, the room is a prison in which
Elizabeth Barrett Browning, dominated by her father, lives the kind of life
which Woolf herself might have lived if her father had not died. But there is also
a strong sense that Elizabeth Barrett Browning's room, reflects how, like Woolf,
she had educated herself and, in her back bedroom, achieved a degree of intellectual freedom from the constraints of the 'real'.

What has been clear up until now – in the account of Mrs Hilbery's drawing-
room, the relics room and Elizabeth Barrett Browning's bedroom – is that
Woolf's realist aesthetic is a visual aesthetic, rooted in Bloomsbury, in her introduction to the Post-Impressionists through Roger Fry, the work of Vanessa
Bell and Walter Sickert, to which I will return in a moment, and the increasing
importance of photography and film in the first half of the twentieth century.

There are significant references to photographs in many of her works, including *Night and Day*. Indeed, it is important to an understanding of realist aesthetics as a recurring trope in her work to appreciate that through the references to photographs Woolf often questions our reliance upon them. Thus, in *Night and Day*, a wall has 'photographs of bridges and cathedrals and large, unprepossessing groups of insufficiently clothed young men', Katharine has a photograph of her grandfather's tomb in Poet's Corner and there are portfolios of old photographs (*ND*: 26, 38, 115). Woolf suggested that photographs offer something 'more real, or real with a different reality from that which we perceive in daily life' (*L2*: 496). This idea anticipates Sontag's more detailed analysis of what photographs offer:

> Through photographs, the world becomes a series of unrelated, freestanding particles; and history, past and present, a set of anecdotes and *faits divers*. The camera makes reality atomic, manageable, and opaque. It is a view of the world which denies interconnectedness, continuity, but which confers on each moment the character of a mystery. (Sontag 1977: 22–3)

Woolf's realist aesthetic recognises the mystery of the moment but is interested in what weaves the apparently 'freestanding particles' together.

Sontag has also argued:

> Photography is the paradigm of an inherently equivocal connection between self and world – its version of the ideology of realism sometimes dictating an effacement of the self in relation to the world, sometimes authorizing an aggressive relation to the world which celebrates the self. One side or the other of the connection is always being rediscovered and championed. (Sontag 1977: 123)

This serves as an introduction to the first British edition of *Flush*, which contained a number of photographs as well as illustrations by Vanessa Bell. In a cream dust jacket, printed in brown with an illustration of a cocker spaniel on a stool, *Flush* was eventually published as the 'Large Paper Edition' on 5 October 1933. In addition to the frontspiece of Woolf's own family dog, Pinka, it contained ten illustrations: six pictures and drawings listed together on the contents page, and four drawings by Vanessa Bell listed together, even though all the pictures and drawings, including those of Vanessa Bell, are interwoven through the text. The first group of pictures and drawings are from the nineteenth century: a lithograph of Flush's birthplace from a sketch by Edmund Havell, with the caption in capital letters, 'FLUSH'S BIRTHPLACE', facing p. 14; a picture of Miss Mitford, Flush's first owner, by John Lucas, facing p. 16; a drawing of Elizabeth Barrett Browning facing p. 28 and of Robert Browning, facing p. 48, each by Field Talfourd; and a painting of Elizabeth Barrett Browning by Michèle Gordigiani, facing p. 80. The pictures and drawings of Miss Mitford and the Brownings are acknowledged in the text as having been reproduced with permission from the National Portrait Gallery. The second group of drawings, by Vanessa Bell, are contemporary to the biography rather than to its subject: of Miss Mitford, with the caption 'Miss Mitford takes Flush for a walk', facing p. 20; of Elizabeth Barrett Browning sitting up in her bed against the pillows, with the caption 'The back bedroom', facing p. 32; of a back view of Elizabeth Barrett Browning, now a married woman living with Robert Browning in Italy, reading opposite a view of the city, with the caption 'At Casa Guidi'; and, opposite p. 145, with a caption 'So she knitted and he dozed', a drawing illustrating how on hot days Flush sought the shade next to women like his 'friend' Catterina.

These illustrations immediately draw attention to the dialectic within *Flush* between the verbal and the visual arts. This is the case when Woolf's account of Flush seeing Elizabeth Barrett Browning for the first time draws on the similarities between Barrett's portrait and the face of her spaniel:

> Each was surprised. Heavy curls hung down on either side of Miss Barrett's face; large bright eyes shone out; a large mouth smiled. Heavy ears hung down on either side of Flush's face; his eyes too, were large and bright: his mouth was wide. There was a likeness between them. As they gazed at each other each felt: Here am I – and then each felt: But how different! Hers was the pale worn face of an invalid, cut off from the air, light, freedom. His was the warm ruddy face of a young animal; instinct with health and energy. Broken asunder, yet made in the same mould, could it be that each completed what was dormant in the other? (*F*: 26–7)

Woolf's suggestion in *Flush* that Elizabeth Barrett Browning and her spaniel, to judge from the portraits, are visually alike encourages the reader to look more closely at the 'realism' here. In a sense, portraits and, more so, photographs imply, as Sontag says about photographs, that 'we know about the world' (Sontag 1977: 23). However, she points out: 'But this is the opposite of understanding, which starts from *not* accepting the world as it looks. All possibility of understanding is rooted in the ability to say no' (ibid.: 23). Sontag distinguishes between portraits and photographs:

> The point of the standard portraits in the bourgeois household of the eighteenth and nineteenth centuries was to confirm an ideal of the sitter (proclaiming social standing, embellishing personal appearance); given this purpose, it is clear why their owners did not feel the need to have more than one. What the photograph-record confirms is, more modestly, simply that the subject exists; therefore, one can never have too many. (Sontag 1977: 165)

In her work, Woolf accepts that there is such a distinction between portraits and photographs, but frequently suggests that both portraits and photographs bring what is known up against what is not known. In *Night and Day* this concept is developed through the relationship between Katharine and the portrait of her grandfather. It is an aspect of the viewer's experience of which Katharine becomes aware in being so used to showing the portrait of her grandfather to visitors that she has 'ceased to see anything but a glow of faintly pleasing pink and brown tints' (*ND*: 319).

In *Night and Day*, Katharine talks about being 'at my ease' but also 'bewildered' (*ND*: 421). It is at this kind of boundary that Woolf appears to be at her most stimulated as a writer. When Katharine talks about the 'unreality – the dark – waiting outside in the wind' (ibid.: 421), she draws attention to an important aspect of Woolf's engagement with realist aesthetics in Elizabeth Barrett Browning's correspondence and Walter Sickert's paintings. Although Woolf focuses in *Flush* upon Elizabeth Barrett Browning as an example of an independently-minded, intellectual woman struggling with the challenges posed by a male-oriented society, she sees in her portrait solitude, grief over the sudden death of her brother, the tyrannical dominance of her father, her fairly desperate reliance upon her spaniel and, prior to her meeting with Robert Browning, the possibility that there would be no end to this kind of life. Indeed, with the arrival of autumn and winter, the 'unreality' of which Katharine speaks in *Night and Day*, is literally and metaphorically outside the window in Wimpole Street.

In Woolf's realist aesthetics, there are the two dimensions which Sontag identifies in discussing realistic aesthetics in relation to photographs: mystery but also interconnectedness. Although, as noted earlier, Woolf retained a fidelity to accuracy of detail in writing *Flush*, her primary interest always remained in the way in which 'details' could be used deliberately and often cryptically in a text. *Flush* pursues parallels between Elizabeth Barrett Browning's spaniel, who is referred to many times in relation to his collar and chain, and women and slavery. This linking of confined women and collared dogs is one that she makes in *Night and Day* when Katharine thinks of a woman being led 'about, as one leads an eager dog on a chain, past rows of clamorous butchers' shops, poor dear creature' (*ND*: 12). In the course of *Flush*, this detail acquires important connotations. In her poem 'Hiram Powers' "Greek Slave"', Elizabeth Barrett Browning compares the way in which women and slaves are both in their different ways chained. The poem is about a sculpture in Florence of a naked, female Greek slave in chains by the American sculptor Hiram Powers, who became a close friend of the Brownings and who is invoked in quotation from her correspondence in the text. At the time, parallels were drawn between the enchained Greek slave and the slaves on American plantations in Virginia, Powers' home state. Thus, the 'real' in *Flush*, is part of a network of details which are meant, like the repetition of the word 'real' in *Night and Day*, to stimulate the reader into thinking about the 'real'. The references to collars and chains not only invoke Elizabeth Barrett's poem, slaves and the way women are 'collared', but Elizabeth Barrett Browning's family's own slave plantations in Jamaica, which Woolf mistakenly calls the East Indies.

In many respects, the dialectic between the verbal and the visual, which Woolf establishes by including photographs and illustrations in the first British edition of *Flush*, anticipates her re-engagement with Walter Sickert's paintings less than a year after the novel was published. Although in regard to realist aesthetics Walter Sickert influenced Woolf most directly and most extensively in the mid-1930s, she had long known him and his work. When Woolf and her sister Vanessa set up home together in Gordon Square, Bloomsbury, after the death of their father in 1904, Sickert lived nearby, at work on many of the paintings that eventually constituted the 1933 exhibition of his paintings and the subject of Woolf's essay on him. It was at that time, too, that Sickert formed the Fitzroy Street Group (1907), consisting of William and Albert Rothenstein, Walter Russell, Spencer Gore, and, later, Ethel Sands, Nan Hudson and Lucien Pissarro, and the Camden Town Group (1911). Vanessa Bell and Duncan Grant were strong admirers of Sickert's work, and, with Paul Nash, they eventually took over Sickert's Fitzroy Street studio.

I have argued elsewhere that integrating human subjects and objects was central to Sickert's work (Peach 2007: 66). This aspect of his painting was influenced by Lautrec, whose *Femme nue devant une glace* (1897) famously included a tousled bed and clothes thrown over a chair; Degas, whom Sickert met when he visited Manet's studio; and Vuillard and Bonnard, whose absence from Roger Fry's 'Manet and the Post-Impressionists' exhibition at the Grafton Gallery Sickert criticised. Others, too, in the Sickert circle – Spencer Gore, Harold Gilman, and Charles Ginner – soon became known for their treatment of figures in interiors.

Notwithstanding the fact that masculinity in Woolf's work is a subject about which more can and needs to be said, her friendship with a painter who excluded women from the painting groups that he established may seem unusual. However, there are profound similarities between them in their engagement with realist aesthetics. Despite the apparent emphasis upon outward physical appearance in Sickert's early twentieth-century paintings, they explore a range of expressions, moods and gestures on the part of the individual in relation to the rooms they occupy and the objects in them. Sickert, like Woolf, pushed at the boundaries of what constitutes the 'external' when the concept is applied to physical surroundings, objects, memories and individual consciousness. What is interesting about Sickert's pictures in the style of Degas and Vuillard, as Woolf herself observed over twenty years later in *Walter Sickert: A Conversation* (1934), is the level of intimacy between the models and the spaces which they occupy (Peach 2007: 67). *Le Lit de Fer* (1905), painted in one of the rooms at Fitzroy Street, achieves an effect whereby the female nude, lying on a bed aligned diagonally to the picture frame, seems identifiable with the bed. The viewer is made to feel that this is the woman's room.

Sickert's 'Camden Town' paintings which he began around 1908, and which combine Impressionist-influenced nudes in interiors with North London subject matter, give the viewer a more strongly realised social context than his earlier pictures. They include some of his more infamous work based on the murder of the prostitute Emily Dimmock in September 1907 which includes

The Camden Town Murder, or What Shall We Do for the Rent? (1908) which
I have discussed in a previously published essay and to which I wish to return
now in regard to realist aesthetics (Peach 2007: 69–70). This painting demonstrates Woolf and Sickert's shared concern with a type of realist aesthetic in
which the known meets the unknown. This particular painting by Sickert is very
much located at this boundary.

First, there is what is known. This painting depicts a clothed, middle-aged
man in waistcoat and shirt sleeves seated on the edge of an iron bedstead.
Behind, but close to him, with her hand on his knee, lies a naked female companion visible from the abdomen upwards. Her face is turned away from us; he
wrings his hands and his head is bowed. The painting conveys the consciousnesses of the two figures and in this regard I want to return to the details which
I highlighted in my previous essay on it (Peach 2007: 70) The intimacy between
them is conveyed through the detail that her hand is on his leg and is mirrored
in the way they are integrated with the room, the blankets and the pillow that
supports her head. The despair evident in his agonised posture is underlined by
the contrast between her hand on his leg and her turned head. The proximity
of the bed to the wallpaper, which gives the crisis a specific material moment,
is echoed in the way the two lives are physically, sexually and psychologically
entwined with each other. In this painting, the 'real' is a symbolic, discursive
and material Order. His upper arm is thickened by the loose cut of his sleeve,
suggesting the manly power which is rendered futile by the circumstances in
which they find themselves while the bedrail suggests the way she is imprisoned
with the only option left them being for her to prostitute herself. They may be
discussing this option or perhaps she has just met with a punter. In any event,
Sickert's interior is inseparable from the consciousnesses of the two individuals.
The constraint of the room is a manifestation of the restrictions of the symbolic
and material Order in which they find themselves and the extent to which it
determines their being.

Woolf's engagement with the 'realism' in Elizabeth Barrett Browning's letters
about her back bedroom might have prepared her to revisit the dialectical relationship between figures and their interiors in Sickert's early twentieth-century
paintings in the year in which *Flush* was published. The most sustained account
of her interest in his work is her essay on it. It was an essay for which she was
well prepared, having been making notes on his paintings in the summer and
autumn of that year and, in November, she had attended the major loan exhibition of his work at Agnew's. The influence of Sickert's paintings, as I have
argued in my previous essay on the subject, evident in *The Years* (1937) (Peach
2007: 74–80). It includes Woolf's clearest attempt at reproducing in words
what Sickert achieved in his paintings. The intimacy between an individual and
their rooms that she found in Sickert's paintings is conveyed with Sickert's con-
scientious use of detail and objects in the luncheon in Maggie's rooms at Hyams
Place, attended by Sara and Rose.

One of the reasons why Woolf may have chosen to develop a scene so closely based on her reading of Sickert's Camden Town paintings at the centre of the novel is that it serves to anchor the Sickert-inspired realism of the text as a whole. The cultural material reality of the lives of women who inhabit rooms in districts such as Camden Town and Hyams Place dominated the paintings at the Agnew's exhibition that Woolf attended. The prospect from the rooms at Hyams Place is very much the combination of boarding houses and businesses that Sickert would have encountered in Camden Town in 1905. Their interiors in his paintings are rendered in ways that suggest that, like Woolf, he was interested in the 'real' as a symbolic Order. What Woolf has done in the luncheon episode at Hyams Place is not simply to transfer Sickert's Camden Town, but the symbolic Order, which for Sickert constituted the Camden Town Group's realist aesthetics, to the south of the river. As in Sickert's paintings, the interiority is based on a fusion of the physical and the psychological.

As is the case with Sickert's Camden Town paintings, the nature of the rooms in *The Years* is a product of real socio-economic forces. Although, or perhaps because, previously she had lived round the corner from Hyams Place, Rose is uncomfortable in Sara and Maggie's lodgings. As I have suggested previously, this aspect of the luncheon might well have been inspired by Sickert's painting *The New Home* (1908) which depicts a young woman ill at ease in what appears to be a second-rate lodging house (Peach 2007: 75). Rose is equally uncomfortable in Sara and Maggie's room as Sickert's young woman is in hers. She notices that the carpet does not entirely cover the room and seems embarrassed that they appeared to have fallen on hard times: Maggie now cooks her own food and makes her own clothes. As in Sickert's paintings, the scene is constructed around key objects: a sewing machine, to which a single sentence is devoted; an armchair by a fireplace with springs like hoops; an old Italian glass blurred with spots that used to hang in their mother's bedroom; and a crimson and gilt chair from the hall in Abercorn Terrace. As in Sickert's paintings, the dialectic between inner subjectivity and the material is in the detail, the silk cotton in the sewing machine, the little carvings on the doorposts, and the visible chair springs.

However, the 'realism' in *The Years* is not located simply in the interiors. The representation of the environment in, for example, the views from Sara and Maggie's windows, bring to mind an entry in Woolf's diary as she thought about *Flush*: 'I mean in the city today I was thinking of another book – about shopkeepers, & publicans, with low life scenes' (Woolf 1983: 53). The most obvious 'low life scenes' in *Flush* are the descriptions of Whitechapel. In Elizabeth Barrett Browning's day, Whitechapel was a cosmopolitan but also notorious district adjacent to the City known for poverty, prostitution and crime. Woolf's descriptions of the area are not first-hand but drawn from Thomas Beames's *The Rookeries of London*, particularly his quotations from the report of the medical practitioner Anselbrook to the inhabitants of the parish of St James Westminster.

Like photographs, as Sontag sees them, Sickert's paintings do not give us 'reality' but 'images' (Sontag 1977: 165). In her use of *The Rookeries* in *Flush*, Woolf appears to look at the visual accounts of Whitechapel through the eyes of one interested in photographic images and how they can make the 'real' immediately accessible. She selects details from Beames as if they are images, but addresses the ambiguity of the visual image: that it is both accessible and distant. What Woolf takes from Beames are images, which unlike many visual images, provide what Sontag calls 'the texture and essence of things' (Sontag 1977: 164). In doing so, Woolf edits Beames's 'realist' writing in a way which is reminiscent of Pound's editing of T. S. Eliot's *The Waste Land*, delivering up the image which is the nub. Thus, Woolf's description of how Beames 'saw a child dipping a can into a bright-green stream and asked if they drank that water' (*F*: 74) substitutes the painstaking empiricism and materialism of Beames's account, the qualities which Woolf found in nineteenth-century realist fiction, into a provocative, imagistic type of realist writing. Woolf highlights the images of the child drinking and of the bright-green stream which are products of editing the following sentences from Beames and engaging with his type of 'realism': 'As we stood, we saw a little child, from one of the galleries opposite, lower a tin can with a rope, to fill a large bucket that stood beside her' (Beames 1850: 95–6) and 'In the bright light [The sewer] appeared the colour of strong green tea . . . yet we were assured this was the only water the wretched inhabitants had to drink' (ibid.: 95). While Beames is at pains to make what he sees known, Woolf chooses an image that is at the boundary of what is known and unknown, that conveys so much detail but withholds enough for the image to work provocatively on our imaginations.

An essay of this length cannot hope to do justice to Woolf's engagement with realist aesthetics. But when *Night and Day*, *Flush* and *The Years* are juxtaposed, the extent of that engagement and the way Woolf developed a distinctive realist aesthetic begins to emerge. *Night and Day*, which employs the word 'real' more times and in more diverse contexts than any of her other novels, is an important text in Woolf's initial interrogation of the concept of 'real'. In that novel, two approaches to 'realism' are evident in embryonic form: 'reality' perceived as a symbolic Order which privileged men and the masculine over women and the way a more 'real' depiction of consciousness brings the writer closer to what Woolf saw as 'the quick of the mind'.

In *Night and Day*, Woolf shows a determination to think with and through objects in new ways that separates her fiction from that of her nineteenth-century predecessors. Shifting the emphasis from 'observed objects' to 'observing subjects' is an important element in Woolf's 'realist' perspective and, once again, it is an aspect of her writing which can be traced back to *Night and Day*. In *Night and Day*, Woolf not only thinks through objects but through figures in their relationships with interiors. This is a trope to which she returned forcefully in the 1930s, under the influence of Barrett Browning's correspondence, in *Flush* and, under the influence of Walter Sickert's paintings, in *The Years*. In *Flush*, Woolf's ambition to depict scenes of what she calls 'low life' suggests that she wished to embark upon a more sustained engagement with 'realism' than we find in many of her works. The 'realism' of her writing in *Flush* is dependent upon secondary sources, particularly Thomas Beames's depiction of London, but Woolf's creative editing of Beames's material suggests that she was interested in developing an 'imagistic' type of realist writing. Perhaps among the important influences upon Woolf's realist aesthetics was photography, for photographs are mentioned in many of her novels, including *Night and Day*, and, in the first British edition of *Flush*, she sets up a deliberate dialectic between verbal and visual texts. In her texts, photographs and portraits juxtapose the known with the unknown, emphasising the way in which they bring the viewer close to them while also distancing them. At its heart, Woolf's realist aesthetic is based at the boundary between the known and the unknown, on cryptic readings of the discourses that constitute 'reality' as a symbolic Order, and the way in which objects and figures in interiors provide the basis for an active and speculative engagement with the 'real'.

Works Cited

Beames, Thomas (1850) *The Rookeries of London*, London: Thomas Bosworth.

Brown, Bill (2006) 'Object Relations in an Expanded Field', *Differences: A Journal of Feminist Cultural Studies*, 17.3: 88–106.

Hopkins, Chris (1995) 'Elizabeth Bowen, Modernism and Gendered Identity', *Journal of Gender Studies*, 4: 271–80.

Kenyon, F. G. (1897) *Elizabeth Barrett Browning, Letters*, 12 vols, London: Smith, Elder.

Peach, Linden (2007) '"Re-reading Sickert's Interiors": Woolf, English Art and the Representation of Domestic Space', in Anna Snaith and Michael H. Whitworth (eds), *Locating Woolf: The Politics of Space and Place*, Basingstoke: Palgrave Macmillan.

Sontag, Susan (1977) *On Photography*, Harmondsworth: Penguin.

Woolf Virginia (1976) *The Letters of Virginia Woolf*, vol. 2, ed. Nigel Nicolson and Joanne Trautmann, London: Hogarth Press.

—— (1979) *The Letters of Virginia Woolf*, vol. 5, ed. Nigel Nicolson and Joanne Trautmann, London: Hogarth Press.

—— (1983) *The Diary of Virginia Woolf*, vol. 4, ed. Anne Olivier Bell and Andrew McNeillie, London: Penguin.

Further Reading

Goldman, Jane (2006) *The Cambridge Introduction to Virginia Woolf*, Cambridge: Cambridge University Press.

Goldman, Jane (1998) *The Feminist Aesthetics of Virginia Woolf: Modernism, Post-Impressionism and the Politics of the Visual*, Cambridge: Cambridge University Press.

Merli, Carol (ed.) (2004) *Illuminations: New Readings of Virginia Woolf*, New Delhi: Macmillan.

Peach, Linden (2000) *Virginia Woolf: Critical Issues*, Basingstoke: Palgrave Macmillan.

Snaith, Anna (2007) *Palgrave Advances in Virginia Woolf Studies*, Basingstoke: Palgrave Macmillan.

Whitworth, Michael (2005) *Authors in Context: Virginia Woolf*, Authors in Context Series, Oxford: Oxford University Press.

Part II   Paintings

7

VIRGINIA WOOLF, VANESSA BELL AND PAINTING[1]

Diane F. Gillespie

Reviewing *Jacob's Room*, Rebecca West observes that Virginia Woolf 'can write supremely well only of what can be painted, best of all, perhaps, of what has been painted' (1922: 142). In 1925, however, Woolf distinguishes between 'partial and incomplete writers', who try to produce descriptions that rival paintings, and 'great writers' – such as 'Proust, Hardy, Flaubert, or Conrad' – whose eyes have 'fertilized' thought, emotion and other senses, and who go to paintings for fresh perspectives, a sharpened colour sense, and small details to pocket for future use (Woolf 1994: 243–6). Always playfully representing herself as a somewhat ingenuous amateur, Virginia Woolf admired, criticised, and raided painting for contributions to what she considered her more inclusive medium. It is easy to imagine her mind, not only as teeming with whole and partial memories of books – what she calls 'ghosts' in an incomplete story of that name (Woolf 1989: 335) – but also as haunted by colours and images culled from paintings. Art works seen with, and created by Vanessa Bell would be well represented for, as Nigel Nicolson concludes, 'Virginia learned to understand painting through her [sister's] eyes' (*L2*: xxi). Looking back over their creative careers in 1935, Virginia asked Vanessa, 'Do you think we have the same pair of eyes, only different spectacles?' (*L6*: 158).

Growing out of feminist criticism, the emphasis on Vanessa Bell's influence on Virginia Woolf's writing corrects and augments a past and continuing tendency to credit Roger Fry (or other male contemporaries) for her understanding and use of the visual arts, especially modern painting.[2] Certainly both sisters enjoyed talking with Fry about relations between visual and verbal art forms. Virginia especially appreciated his encouragement of common viewers like herself to 'live with, and laugh at, love and discuss' paintings ('Roger Fry' 1947: 84). She experimented with applications of his theories, and acknowledged his influence (Reid/Broughton 1993: 36–57; Briggs 2005: 96–112), but on an everyday level both sisters also declared independence. Virginia resented, for example, the implication that literature was aesthetically impure; she also combined feminism with her early interest in formalism (Reed 1993: 34), and declared

Fry's *Vision and Design* (1920) 'rudimentary compared with Coleridge' (*D2:* 81). Vanessa quoted Fry's theories but, beyond his teaching her 'to paint much more solidly', insisted that 'in detail of practice', she went her own way.[3]

After Fry's death and near the end of her own life, Virginia envisioned writing a history of literature for painters like Vanessa and her companion Duncan Grant. Keeping 'the writer in the foreground', Virginia's 'common angle' would be 'the desire to create', including the impact of social and other forces on those with a 'twin gift' of 'seeing & writing' (Woolf 1979: 375–7). This need to create, combined with the sisters' mutual curiosity about each other's creative processes and medium, enabled them to identify with each other. Sibling and media rivalry notwithstanding, Virginia and Vanessa were women artists who had to negotiate expectations for, as Woolf called them in *Three Guineas* (1938), 'daughters of educated men' (*TG:* 4).

Sisters and artists

Still proliferating biographies of Virginia Woolf, from Quentin Bell's (1972) to Julia Briggs's (2006), as well as Frances Spalding's biography of Vanessa Bell (1983) and Angelica Garnett's memoirs of her mother (1984), all naturally acknowledge the importance of the sisters to each other. The emphasis remains, however, on one sister's life and works. In 1985, Marianna Torgovnick laid groundwork for a joint study of the sisters as artists in a portion of *The Visual Arts, Pictorialism, and the Novel: James, Lawrence, and Woolf.* My book-length investigation of Woolf's and Bell's mutual creativity, *The Sisters' Arts,* appeared in 1988. With eighty-two visual images, among them Vanessa's illustrations and dust-jacket designs for the Woolfs' Hogarth Press publications of Virginia's books, it stresses the need to look beyond the classical pairing of writing and painting as sister arts (*ut pictura poesis*), to the professional and aesthetic interactions of two sister artists, especially as a context for certain characteristics of Virginia Woolf's writing.

In the 1990s and beyond, more writers on Virginia Woolf and Bloomsbury treated aspects of the sisters' mutual creativity in book-length studies, book chapters and journal articles. Among them is Jane Dunn, whose *A Very Close Conspiracy* (1990) covers some of the same territory as *The Sisters' Arts* but, with chapter titles like 'Marriage and Betrayal' and 'Husbands and Sisters', is more a thematic dual biography. In the same year, Mary Ann Caws in *Women of Bloomsbury* includes Carrington and examines how three creative women struggle to balance the needs of others with their own need to work (1990: 21). Then, in a chapter of their book on modernist *Women Artists and Writers,* Bridget Elliott and Jo-Ann Wallace usefully investigate Virginia's and Vanessa's wariness, as they negotiated feminine traditions and genre hierarchies, of professionalism and fame and of identification with various groups and movements (1994: 61, 75).

Hermione Lee, in a biography of Virginia Woolf that assimilates feminist assumptions, nevertheless concludes that 'feminism has romanticised and heroinised' the sisters' relationship (1997: 116). There is some truth to Lee's remark. Those who focus on Virginia's and Vanessa's creative work and on times when they inspired, admired, constructively criticised, collaborated, or even competed with each other often do downplay dissonances in domestic situations, sexual preferences and involvements with other people; jealousies and periods of 'estrangement and hostility'; and sometimes hurtful inequalities in their feelings for each other, Virginia being 'in love with her sister' (ibid.: 116–17). Lesbian feminist Woolf criticism of the 1990s includes Virginia's love for Vanessa (Bellamy 1997: 31–3; Hankins 1997: 195–8; Cramer 1997: 230),[4] while Panthea Reid's 1996 biography of Woolf highlights the traditional rivalry between literature and art (*paragone*) as embodied in her relationships with important figures in her life, including Vanessa Bell. Acknowledging moments of harmony, Reid emphasises the sisters' bickerings and inadequacies, and implicates instances of Vanessa's distance and criticism as partial causes of Virginia's periods of illness, even of her suicide.[5]

The century ends, however, with the sisters' mutual creativity in the foreground. In a portion of *The Feminist Aesthetics of Virginia Woolf*, Jane Goldman looks at examples of suffrage art and colours, as well as Vanessa's use of colour in specific paintings, to posit for Virginia's writing a feminist 'prismatic aesthetics' separate from Roger Fry's and Clive Bell's 'significant form' (1998: 115, 123, 141).[6] Lisa Tickner, comparing Vanessa's *Studland Beach* (1912) to Virginia's *To the Lighthouse* (1927), concludes that, whatever the current aesthetic theory, both sisters 'embraced the consciousness of everyday life as something to be caught and held in new forms of expression' as inevitably emotional experiences impressed themselves upon their art (Tickner 1999: 76, 80). Just as Vanessa realised when she read *The Voyage Out* how much Virginia drew from such experiences, however disguised (Bell 1993: 173), so Quentin Bell noted how much his mother's paintings 'seem to be replete with psychological interest', even when she was 'firmly denying that the story of a picture had any importance whatsoever' (Bell 1986: 116).[7]

Dialogues and flirtations

For decades, Virginia and Vanessa – formally as well as informally in letters and diaries – compared writing and painting. Following a discussion of colour, for instance, Vanessa wrote to Virginia in 1919, 'Perhaps you don't really describe the looks but only the impression the looks made upon you' (Bell 1993: 87). The sisters' comparisons continue to intrigue writers on Woolf and painting (Gillespie 1988: 63–103; Goldman 1998: 113–16; Matz 2001: 239–49; Louvel 2005: 57–66; Surry 2007: 157–63). For our purposes, Vanessa's 'Lecture Given at Leighton Park School' (1925; see Bell 1997) and Virginia's *Walter Sickert: A Conversation* (1934; see *CE2*) provide a useful foundation for selected instances in which the sisters reflect such dialogues in their creative work.

The topic of Vanessa's entertaining, illustrated lecture for teenaged school-boys was how a painter's 'rather mad' perspective of the world 'as form and colour' (Bell 1997: 150–1) differs from a writer's, specifically as her sister describes it in 'Mr Bennett and Mrs Brown'. Writers may differ from each other, Vanessa concludes, but they are alike in that their interest is not 'a purely visual one' (ibid.: 153). When painters look at grey hair, for example, they see 'a grey as different from other greys as one chord in music is different from others' (ibid.: 156), whereas writers see human or social significance.

A painter's colours, Virginia wrote in 'Pictures', in the same year as Vanessa's lecture, may entice a literary nation of writers 'starved' on diets of 'thin black print', but the muteness of paintings repels as well as attracts; frustrates as well as tempts narration, description, morality and emotion; obliterates language but, by freshening the senses, reinvigorates it (Woolf 1994: 244–6). Almost ten years later, she wrote for a larger audience than Vanessa's schoolboys, a differ-ent response. Virginia had teased her sister in 1919 by telling her that Walter Sickert was her 'ideal painter', his works perfect for 'describing' (L2: 331). Still it was Vanessa's encouragement, after a 1933 retrospective exhibition of his paint-ings, that prompted Virginia's complimentary letter to him followed in 1934 by her pamphlet (L5: 253–4).

Virginia Woolf defends Sickert as a literary painter, a heresy she did not need his encouragement to commit but, complicating her sister's simpler painter–writer opposition, she looks for common ground. *Walter Sickert* playfully describes an associational dinner-table conversation among people, some inter-ested in the purely visual aspects of a painting and others in its human interest. If one diner becomes 'all eye' and responds only to Sickert's colour, another defines him as 'a great biographer' (CE2: 235). When painters use their fingers to define relationships among colours and shapes, others use words to discuss Sickert as 'a novelist' (ibid.: 237). Even they admit, however, that he transcends suggested human dilemmas in his paintings by creating tensions and pleasing harmonies among shapes and colours. 'For though they must part in the end', the diners agree, 'painting and writing have much to tell each other: they have much in common. The novelist after all wants to make us see', and sensitive critics realise that 'all great writers are great colourists' (ibid.: 241–2). Woolf is clearly comfortable at 'the sunny margin where the arts flirt and joke and pay each other compliments', and with Sickert who, like her, is 'among the hybrids, the raiders', who plunder the other arts to feed their own (ibid.: 243–4).

Vanessa Bell's cover design 'flirt[s] and joke[s]' with a hybrid writer's essay about a hybrid painter (Figure 7.1). If colour is an important topic in *Walter Sickert*, Vanessa's drawing of a round dining table is loops, spirals and cross-hatchings in black ink. If Virginia includes people's verbal dialogues and paintings' human interest, Vanessa's design asserts the visual supremacy of inanimate objects. Those in the foreground (plate, knife, spoon, napkin) direct the eye inward to a composition of wine bottle, glasses and centrepiece arrange-ment on a pedestal plate. Is Vanessa's table setting also a commentary on some

Figure 7.1 Vanessa Bell's cover jacket design for *Walter Sickert: A Conversation* by Virginia Woolf © Estate of Vanessa Bell, courtesy Henrietta Garnett

of Virginia's recent poetic treatments of solid objects? In the omniscient interludes of *The Waves* (1931), a novel that Vanessa admired (Bell 1993: 367–8), the
morning sun transforms a plate into 'a white lake' and a knife into 'a dagger of
ice'; the evening sun makes 'knife, fork and glass' appear 'lengthened, swollen,
and [...] portentous' (*W*: 110, 208). Or did Vanessa take a cue from Bernard,
who blurs the barrier between voluble people and silent objects? 'Let me sit here
for ever with bare things, this coffee-cup, this knife, this fork, things in themselves', he says, 'myself being myself' (ibid.: 295, cf.290). Sensing and enjoying
the subtleties of sisterly dialogue, Virginia pronounced the cover design 'very
lovely' (*L5*: 327).

Portraits: self and other

There are far too many similarities and differences between the sisters' experiments with genre and media boundaries to include here. One way to suggest
what we might call the sisters' ongoing visual–verbal flirtation – part identification, part competition; part a similar sensitivity to everyday life, part the lenses
of different mediums – is to look first at several works that show them working out their own and each other's identities, then at selected instances where
they transform sometimes painful experiences into less personal works of art.
The following examples come not just from the 1910s, the period supposed to
be Vanessa's most innovative, but also from the 1920s and 1930s. Virginia,
without the contemporary art historian's background or a retrospective view,
neither downplayed her sister's later paintings as domestic realism, nor dwelt
on her retreat, after a dalliance with abstraction, from newer movements like
surrealism (c.f. Shone 1999: 50, 205, 223). On the contrary, Virginia wrote in
1927 that she and Vanessa were 'both mistresses of our medium as never before'
(*L3*: 341).

   Although Vanessa painted bold modifications of feminine subjects like
Nursery Tea (1912) (Spalding 1983: 105, 126), an equally early *Self-Portrait at
the Easel* (1912) is a confident rendition of herself as an artist (see Plate 3).[8] She
depicts herself holding a palette and extending her right arm to reach an invisible canvas on a tall easel, its brown edge slanting along the left of the painting.
When Virginia Woolf wrote in 1931 that women painters, unlike women writers, required 'models, studios, north lights, masters and mistresses', and travel,
she did not mention that painters like her sister had managed to meet some of
those needs in domestic settings (*P*: xxviii). Although working at home was not
without conflict, here Vanessa's professional role visually trumps a more traditional 'domestic fragility' (Reed 2004: 85). She paints herself in a grey-blue
dress outlined in black against a well-known symbol of women's role – a hearth
with a pale-grey mantelpiece so tall that, rivalling the easel, it extends off the top
of the canvas. She sits, however, with her back towards it. Her sensitive painting
hand, positioned in front of a black unlit firebox, is the source of vitality.

   Draped over the chair arm in the foreground is geometrically patterned fabric, evidence of increasing interest in the decorative arts. 'Manufactured by Foxton's of Manchester for the African market', it had been purchased by Roger Fry soon 'to be sold at the Omega'.[9] No wonder, especially after helping to found the Omega Workshops in 1913 and after moving to Charleston farmhouse in 1916, Vanessa Bell and Duncan Grant increasingly co-opted tops of mantelpieces for still-life arrangements and used the sides of them as spaces for exuberant painted panels and tile work. This creative energy spilled over onto domestic surfaces at the Woolfs' Monk's House and even their London flats. Both sisters increasingly lived and worked amid paintings and decorative art, much of it by Bell and Grant (see, e.g., Reed 2004: 223–5).

Vanessa merely suggests her own facial features, privileging overall composition over professional self-definition. Still, the large 'V' of her light collar may be more than a structural element (Reed 2004: 85). Consciously or not, Vanessa paints her identifying initial. It anticipates a later in-joke, what Virginia interpreted as the 'stir'-causing 'V' of both sisters' names (*L4*: 81) formed by clock hands in Vanessa's jacket design for Virginia's *A Room of One's Own* (1929). That shared 'V' asserts the need for an income and privacy for women artists in both their mediums.

Although also in the background of this early self-portrait is a shelf filled with books, Vanessa did not yet associate her younger sister with the literary and intellectual traditions of England, at least not in several well-known portraits painted at Asheham during this same year, 1912.[10] Although Virginia was busy with reviews and stories and working on what became *The Voyage Out* (1915), she had not yet produced her first novel. Vanessa's portraits reflect the period when Virginia was still recovering from a breakdown. There is, in one portrait, a 'gentleness that reflects the protective care and affection' of Vanessa for her sister at this time (Tranter 1998: 14). With soft greens and blues, she catches her with open eyes and parted lips, as if speaking. A second portrait with a brighter palette shows Virginia in a domestic pose, facial features barely suggested. Wearing a greenish sweater, she leans back between the wings of a brilliantly orange armchair boldly outlined in black, a piece of rose-coloured needlework in her hands.

Another portrait from 1912, *Virginia Woolf in a Deckchair*, has Vanessa's dark outlining, now combined with a featureless face characteristic of several paintings from this period (see Plate 4). Although quite capable of capturing a likeness, Vanessa challenged the representational tradition of portrait painting by subordinating individualising details to larger visual patterns. In *To the Lighthouse* (1927), Virginia's painter Lily Briscoe similarly concludes that 'one way of knowing people' is by 'the outline, not the detail' (*TTL*: 195). When Virginia experiments further in *The Waves* (1931) with this borrowed image to render characters' inner lives, Rhoda's 'I have no face' (*W*: 223) reflects her psychological fragility, alienation and fear, although similar featureless experiences connect Bernard with the stream of 'omnipresent, general life' and death in ways that interest and calm him (ibid.: 112–13, 224).

Virginia may be even less animated in this portrait than in the other two, but Vanessa's colours, shapes, and overall composition are powerful and dynamic. Virginia's reclining figure creates a strong diagonal that fills most of the canvas. Strategically spaced spots of colour – red flower, tie and stocking; angular yellow deck-chair and sun-drenched lawn – suggest nascent vitality. Beneath the ovals of a large hat brim and Virginia's face is another rounded form, her knee; covered by a dark-grey dress, it is prominent in the foreground. Below a white collar, the white page of a book or paper forms a wide 'V' on her lap, but she neither reads nor writes.

Soon, however, Virginia was writing fictional sketches based on Vanessa, if not as an artist *per se*, then with some of her creative personality traits. Helen Ambrose, in *The Voyage Out*, who sits observing, embroidering, or reading while everyone else goes for walks, has some of Vanessa's watchful outward calm. Virginia was teasingly more candid about Katharine Hilbery's resemblance to Vanessa in *Night and Day* (1919; *L*2: 109, 232, 400). At the same time, she encoded their artistic rivalry by disguising her sister's love of painting as a desire to substitute the impersonality of mathematics for her forced immersion in the realm of letters – the endless ambiguities of helping to write a life of her ancestor, a famous poet. Later, some of Vanessa's maternal characteristics animate Mrs Ramsay in *To the Lighthouse*, but mostly contribute to the characterisation of Lily Briscoe, a woman whose feelings of inferiority, determination and validation of the creative process are similar to Vanessa's. Among other partial portraits is Susan in *The Waves* who has much of Vanessa's domestic and rural artistry, along with maternal preoccupations, to which I will return.

Elliott and Wallace conclude that, if women artists exist at all in the sisters' portraits and novels, they either are not professionals or are undercut as such. True, Vanessa's portraits of women, like the writer Iris Tree, do not hint at their artistic careers. Also true, her women painters do sit and paint while their supposedly stronger, masculine counterparts stand, as in *Frederick and Jessie Etchells Painting* (1912) (Elliott and Wallace 1994: 61, 76, 82). The conclusion that Vanessa did not do a painting like the 1912 *Self Portrait at the Easel* until 1952 (ibid.: 175 n 27), however, we now know is inaccurate. Women artists were slowly getting more training and chances to exhibit (Gillespie 2007: 767–8) but, in England of the 1910s, perhaps painting one's self or another woman at her easel at all was daring enough.

Disliking thinly veiled autobiography in fiction (*D*2: 14), Virginia Woolf mainly recorded her own creative commitment, processes and conflicts as a writer in her diaries. Yet her fictional portrayals of a range of women, creative in many aspects of art and life, affirm women's artistic career potential, still a subject of debate during her lifetime. True, among her women artist characters – like Lily Briscoe, the painter in *To the Lighthouse* – most are amateurs, however committed. Yet Lily's creative process is important, and she structures her painting in a way similar to the three parts of the novel itself. The much-revised poem in *Orlando* mainly reflects style changes over the centuries but, as a fanciful portrait of prolific writer Vita Sackville-West, *Orlando* has many characteristics of a professional, among them self-criticism and awareness of critics, other writers and the marketplace. Miss La Trobe, the writer/director of a village pageant in *Between the Acts* (1941), has limited public identity, but her creative struggles and awareness of her audience are central. These women characters, however indirectly, also reflect, explore and define Virginia's own evolving aesthetics – and sometimes Vanessa's – one that, in general, is 'a matter of *relations*' (Caughie 1991: 33).

Parties: visual and verbal

One traditional outlet for women's creativity that alternately repelled and fascinated both sisters was what Virginia Woolf dubbed the 'party consciousness' (*D3*: 12). In the 1920s they found ways to transform some of its variations into art. After their mother's death, as biographers note, first Vanessa and then Virginia were forced by George Duckworth to try to dress and speak appropriately at society events where they felt alienated and miserable. In later years, Virginia combined misery with a complex mix of curiosity, envy, enjoyment, amusement and satire. Among the results were *Mrs Dalloway* (1925) and seven short stories (1922–27) introduced by Stella McNichol in 1973 as *Mrs Dalloway's Party*. The Dalloways appear already in *The Voyage Out* (1915), and Woolf knew by late 1922 that her further exploration of their lives in a story called 'Mrs Dalloway in Bond Street' was the beginning of a book (*D2*: 207), possibly called 'The Party' (Woolf 1989: 302).

There is also a little-known painting by Vanessa Bell called *Mrs Dalloway's Party* (Figure 7.2). Dated 1920, it pre-dates her sister's emphasis on Clarissa's party-giving gift. Since Virginia apparently owned the painting at one time, however, she or a dealer may have named it in retrospect.[11] Just as Vanessa's 'Three Women' (*L3*: 498), or *The Conversation* (1917–18), contributed to Virginia's story 'A Society' (*c.*1920), so Vanessa's *Mrs Dalloway's Party* may well have been one link in the complex evolution of *Mrs Dalloway* and a visual impetus for the party scene that closes the novel.

Like Virginia, Vanessa as an adult enjoyed 'plays, parties, charades' and, for all her interest in 'formal values', she could also 'be witty, caricatural, sharply observant' (Shone 1980: 5). Vanessa's *Mrs Dalloway's Party* depicts several guests crowding a fashionable, formal event. Created around the time when she was admiring Matisse's and Picasso's large female nudes (Bell 1993: 238, 244), the plump woman in the centre foreground of her painting stands – stemmed glass in hand, pale flower below one breast – almost bursting out of the décolletage of her elegant black dress. She exchanges glances with a seated, round-faced woman holding a red rose and wearing a dull green, off-the-shoulder gown. Behind them are glimpses of women's aqua and black evening dresses; men dressed formally in shades of black; red and deep-blue cushions; and reddish-brown floor, white walls and mustard-yellow curtain.[12] Although Vanessa has

Figure 7.2 Vanessa Bell's painting *Mrs Dalloway's Party*, 1920 © Estate of
Vanessa Bell, courtesy Henrietta Garnett. Private collection

blurred facial features in the background and suggested potential movement
among her temporarily frozen party-goers by arranging them so they are partly
obscured by each other or edges of the canvas, she has orchestrated shoulders
and gestures to draw our eyes back to the woman dominating the center.

Virginia later wrote of another painting, in her brief one-page 'Foreword'
to Vanessa's 1934 exhibition, 'not a word sounds and yet the room is full of

conversations'. Virginia juxtaposes to Vanessa's *Mrs Dalloway's Party*, however, a scene in *Mrs Dalloway* less about conversations or external appearances
than about thoughts and feelings of Clarissa Dalloway and her guests. Virginia
does include visual glimpses, but only as they periodically flit by. Through her
characters' eyes, we get colours and images that, as Vanessa charges in her lecture, suggest age, economic status, taste, or personality: young women's chill-
inducing 'naked shoulders', Ellie Henderson's self-abnegating 'old black dress',
Jim Hutton's only clean socks, red ones, budding Elizabeth's 'pink frock' or,
more poetically, Clarissa's 'silver-green mermaid's dress' and 'an apricot bloom
of powder and paint' on Nancy Blow (*MD*: 168, 169, 176, 194, 174, 177). In contrast to the substantial volumes of the woman anchoring Vanessa's painting,
Clarissa contemplates her own and her guests' feelings of unreality – results of
evening clothes, a rupture in 'their ordinary ways', and a formal setting (ibid.:
171). Ironically she remembers how young Sally Seton, now looking so different,
once ran 'down the passage to fetch her sponge bag, without a stitch of clothing
on her' or wore, as Peter Walsh remembers, 'rags and tatters' (ibid.: 181, 188).
Opposing images, events and tensions from the past underlie the harmonious
but ephemeral experience Clarissa creates among disparate people. Ultimately,
news of Septimus Smith's suicide renders the occasion superficial and reminds
Clarissa of the war and of medical malfeasance, the latter represented at her
party by Sir William Bradshaw. Yet, when death also prompts Clarissa to 'feel
the beauty . . . feel the fun' more intensely (ibid.: 186), Virginia returns to the
simpler moment of Vanessa's painting. Although we imagine a different physical type from her sister's dominant female, *Mrs Dalloway* achieves a similar
aesthetic closure when Peter Walsh freezes and centres Clarissa: 'For there she
was' (ibid.: 194).

Bodies: art and convention

By the early 1930s, the sisters were aware of themselves and each other as
productive and respected women artists, both 'very much a part of the London
"scene"' (Spalding 1983: 240). The decade was also tragic, with its escalation of
international hostilities and deaths of Lytton Strachey, Roger Fry and, worst
of all for Vanessa, her son Julian. Although Virginia had voiced her concerns
before, against this background of destruction and loss, women's creativity took
on increased importance. By the 1930s traditional restrictions on women painters became, for Virginia, a motif, one related to patriarchal hypocrisy embedded
in her culture as a whole and expressed in her catalogue 'Foreword' to Vanessa's
1930 one-artist exhibition, *Recent Paintings by Vanessa Bell*. Virginia now
focused on the genre of the nude and thought about women violating traditional taboos by daring to paint from live, undraped models for public exhibitions. This concern found its way into *The Pargiters*, the novel/essay portion of
The Years (1937), as well as into *Three Guineas* (1938).

Although it is tempting to dismiss Virginia Woolf's 1930 'Foreword' as merely wry and amusing, it is also serious. Goldman says it reveals 'the complexities and ambiguities of Woolf's position as a woman observing another woman's art in a man's world', that of reputable Bond Street galleries where women, accustomed to nudity as mothers, wives or mistresses, have been denied the ability to look upon it with '"the eye of an artist"' (Goldman 1998: 151). Virginia mocks this double standard. More recently, I have looked at her 1930 'Foreword' in the context of actual paintings by Vanessa Bell and some of her female contemporaries who, in defiance of tradition, painted and exhibited nudes (Gillespie 2006: 11–16). Virginia's 'Foreword' anticipates contemporary discussions among feminist art historians of what happens when women, socialised to define themselves in 'the "feminine position"' as passive and decorative 'object[s] of the look', assume in front of their easels, 'the "masculine position" as subject[s] of the look'. They learn to occupy, Mary Kelly suggests, a dual-gendered position, both colluding with and challenging simple voyeuristic reductions of women to nature, emotion, sex and biology (Kelly 1984: 98).[13]

Vanessa deflects moral criticism when she names the only nude painting I could locate from her 1930 exhibition *Study for a Composition* (see Plate 5) (Gillespie 2006: 15). This painting of nude women was neither her first, her last, nor arguably her best, but it is one that caught Virginia's eye.[14] By describing it, not generically as a 'nude', but rather as 'naked girls couched on crimson cushions', Virginia calls attention to the boldness of the subject, if not of the actual painting which domesticates potentially erotic material (Woolf 1975: 171). Forming an open half-circle are four relaxed women, two partially towel-wrapped, whose meditative gazes engage neither each others' nor a viewer's. A woman on one side, comfortable with her nudity, leans her back against a large crimson cushion. Unlike two women farther back and in the middle, her raised arms expose her breasts. A woman on the opposite side, with her back towards the viewer, leans against a second crimson cushion. Bell wrote to Grant, once the painting was hung, 'I am going to paint my large nudes all over again . . . as I came to the conclusion I could never get the composition right with the old poses' (Bell 1993: 349).

Virginia implies in her 1930 'Foreword' that a painter can avoid violating moral precepts more easily than a writer by asserting the irrelevance of the subject: 'children are no more important to her than rocks, and clothing no more than "stark nakedness"' (Woolf 1975: 171). Yet a writer, she soon says in 'Professions for Women' (1931), 'cannot review even a novel without . . . expressing what you think to be the truth about human relations, morality, sex' (*DM*: 238). Still, if Vanessa can defy a restricting taboo and look 'on nakedness with a brush in her hand' (Woolf 1975: 170), why can't Virginia also risk shocking conventional people by using her pen to write 'about the body, about the passions which it was unfitting for her as a woman to say'? (*DM*: 240).

In *The Waves*, where the sisters' mutual influence is especially strong, Virginia tries her hand with bodily feelings of all three women characters. Aware of her sisters' nude paintings, however, Virginia especially uses her characterisation of Jinny to collude with, challenge and even reverse the kind of traditional gaze that, in both the visual and verbal arts, often objectifies women. Like Vanessa in her painting, Virginia is well aware of the overall composition of which Jinny is a part, but her verbal medium enables multiple perspectives and temporal development. If Jinny exists in the eyes of others, she also sees others seeing her, gazes back at them, and sees herself. Fully aware and empowered, she consciously raises attracting men to an art form, even possibly to a profession. She flaunts the sensuality she knows Victorian puritans denounce. On a train, conscious of a man's gaze, her 'body instantly . . . puts forth a frill'. Equally aware of 'a sour woman['s]' disapproval, Jinny's 'body shuts in her face, impertinently, like a parasol' (*W*: 63). Enjoying her own role-playing ability, she has costumed herself in different colours to attract a variety of men, as unnamed and objectified as women traditionally have been. Ironically, Virginia adapts for a female voice erotic imagery from the secular poetry of John Donne which she was reading for an essay ('Donne After Three Centuries', 1932) (Gillespie 1999: 233). Thus Jinny, more poetically than graphically, recalls how her body has easily become 'fluid . . . forming even at the touch of a finger into one full drop, which fills itself, which quivers, which flashes, which falls in ecstasy'. The sexual act that follows is 'a furious conflagration,' after which 'we have sunk to ashes, leaving no relics, no unburnt bones, no wisps of hair to be kept in lockets' (*W*: 221–2). Jinny sees the sensual pleasures she has offered and experienced as gifts, antidotes for 'the torments, the divisions' she sees in her friend's lives (ibid.: 221).

On social occasions, scrutiny is mutual. In her prime, Jinny joins other party guests, 'exposed to their gaze, as they are to mine'. '[M]y silk legs rub smoothly together. The stones of a necklace lie cold on my throat', she thinks (*W*: 101). Again Jinny describes herself and Rhoda as 'exposed', and again wearing 'a few precious stones nestling on a cold ring round our throats' (*W*: 126). Just as she later called one of Virginia's stories 'too full of suggestions for pictures almost' (Bell 1993: 454), Vanessa may have had such passages in mind when in 1932 she painted *The Green Necklace* (see Plate 6).

Around the time Vanessa was rethinking *Studies for a Composition*, she wrote to Duncan Grant about another nude painting. 'I defy anyone to look at her without thinking of volumes', she wrote somewhat defensively. In her studio, she had curtains hung to 'completely shut off the back part of the room' to keep Grace Higgns, her servant, from being offended, presumably by a nude painting or by any woman willing to pose naked (Bell 1993: 351–2). The painting about 'volumes' is unidentified, but it must have been one like *The Green Necklace*, with its model's round face; the curves of her back, buttock and belly; and her full limbs. The deep-red curtain hanging in thick gathers may well be the 'background' described in the letter.

Virginia in *The Waves* combines cold stones with party dresses but, painting in the nude genre, Vanessa removes all but the stones. A brilliantly green, beaded necklace is her focal point, a single adornment that calls attention to the nudity of the woman wearing it. Did Vanessa both allude to and defuse Manet's

scandal-causing *Olympia* (1865), an unlikely reclining odalisque whose nakedness is emphasised by a neck ribbon, bracelet and single shoe? Vanessa has
posed her seated model to draw the viewer's eye towards the necklace. Head
tilted to the side, she gazes boldly and directly out of the picture space. More
discreet than seductive, however, her legs and shoulders are turned so that
one arm and thigh obscure breasts and crotch. Vanessa does not use the dark
outlining of her earlier style, but achieves a strong contrast to the model's skin
tones with a dark shadow behind her. As the title suggests, the painting also is
a study in shades of green, complemented by shades of crimson. As Fry wrote
of Vanessa in the early 1930s, 'Her colour gets better and better' (quoted in Bell
1993: 370).

With her temporal medium, however, Virginia Woolf could portray more
than lush young models frozen in time. She can render such a woman's feelings
about her ageing body. Jinny looks in the mirror and notes loss of seductive
power: 'How solitary, how shrunk, how aged! . . . I shall look into faces, and
I shall see them seek some other face' (*W*: 193–4). She allies herself, however,
with a society that has given her opportunities, like an artist, to colour and outline herself: 'I too, with my little patent-leather shoes . . . my reddened lips and
my finely pencilled eyebrows march to victory with the band' (ibid.: 194). Again,
grey to a writer means age, and the attitude not the shade is important: 'Now I
turn grey; now I turn gaunt', Jinny says. 'But I am not afraid' (*W*: 222).

Creativity and procreativity

Another long-standing preoccupation of the sisters that culminated in *The
Waves* was artistic creativity versus physical procreativity. Already in 1909,
Vanessa had lamented her inability to paint with a small child in the house
and expressed her envy of her childless sister's uninterrupted time: 'You would
turn it to account though', Vanessa added, imagining how a writer would treat
maternity.[15] Then, in 1919, she wrote that Virginia still had 'several notes to
take' of her, now as 'mother of a daughter'.[16] 'What a lot I could say about the
maternal instinct', she repeated in 1927, this time encouraging her sister to
do a better job than men 'with birth'. Admitting the truth of one of Virginia's
repeated charges, that the maternal instinct 'is one of the worst of the passions',
Vanessa hoped that once her young reached their teens, she would become
'more rational' (Bell 1993: 315).

Why is Vanessa repeatedly encouraging Virginia to write about an experience
she sometimes mocks but, in darker moods, sorely laments never having had?
Is Vanessa cruelly underscoring Virginia's childlessness, or is she consoling her
by agreeing about the maternal instinct and by emphasising Virginia's advantages? Caws thinks Vanessa is being 'generous. The very fact that mothering
can be shared, birth discussed and maternal feelings expressed goes to confirm
the power of the network *à deux* set up with such an intensity between the two'
(Caws 1990: 57).

That Virginia Woolf put her sister's suggestions to artistic use, at least in part, supports Caws' conclusion. In the context of a cosmology Virginia figures as feminine in the interludes of *The Waves*, the first holograph draft shows that she planned to handle birth poetically, identifying pervasive wave imagery with childbirth (Woolf 1976: 7). In the published version, Woolf retains only nine sections and interludes that echo nine months from conception to birth as the cycles of days, years and lives repeat themselves like waves.

The Waves depicts not so much birth as the maternal instinct. Having observed and listened to Vanessa, Virginia created Susan who predicts she will be 'debased and hide-bound by the bestial and beautiful passion of maternity. I shall push the fortunes of my children unscrupulously' (*W*: 132). When Susan's children are born, she lives close to the cycles of the earth and is 'glutted with natural happiness' (ibid.: 173). As her children grow, however, she is impatient, 'sick of the body . . . of the unscrupulous ways of the mother who protects' (ibid.: 191). Virginia limits Susan's creativity primarily to nurturing children and crops. She hints at her model's painterly side, however, when the elderly Susan thinks that, although her body 'has been used daily, rightly, like a tool by a good workman, all over', her more cerebral, verbal friends cannot envision her life. 'I have seen life in blocks, substantial, huge', she thinks, 'I sit among you abrading your softness with my hardness, quenching the silver-grey flickering moth-wing quiver of words with the green spurt of my clear eyes' (*W*: 215). An artist's tactile description of life as 'blocks', along with the hard purity and exquisite colours of a visual life, oppose insubstantial words. Although fleeting, the 'moth-wing' image may allude to the odd story Vanessa had related to Virginia in 1927. Vanessa wrote that her 'maternal instinct', so 'deplore[d]' by Virginia, had prompted her to let in, then chloroform for a specimen, one of the 'huge moth[s]' tapping at a lighted window at Cassis (Bell 1993: 314). Given *The Waves'* early title ('The Moths'), the passage suggests Virginia's awareness that she, like her sister, is a collector of specimens, and that Susan's perceptions are among those captured in a 'quiver of words' that is less death-dealing than life-giving.

Virginia Woolf had thought, as she wrote *The Waves*, that perhaps it was 'too abstract', due to her desire to please her sister and other painters (*D3*: 203). At the same time, this 'mosaic' of lives has enabled her to say what she wanted to such a degree that she 'had a day of intoxication' when she realised, 'Children are nothing to this' (ibid.: 298). She was especially pleased, therefore, when Vanessa wrote to her about being 'completely submerged in The Waves', in beautiful writing that moved her in a way 'quite as real . . . as having a baby or anything else' but also that 'made one's human feelings into something less personal' (Bell 1993: 367). Vanessa characteristically emphasized, less her sister's real-life sources less than the overall design. She added that Virginia had done in *The Waves* what she had been attempting in a large painting, again one with a maternal subject. In describing *The Nursery* ([1930–2] Spalding 1983: 250–2), Vanessa emphasised her composition – trying to control light and to keep figures and toys on a floor 'in relation to each other' (Bell 1993: 368).

The sisters did not always see eye-to-eye, and their lives diverged in many ways. At their best, however, they could ponder and tease each other, as Virginia did Vanessa, about their 'same pair of eyes only different spectacles'. In relation to each other's verbal or visual medium, each could understand her similar desire to create art out of the intense experiences of everyday life, and each could better define her own methods of doing so. The sisters, in many more instances than mentioned here, responded artistically to each other's work. Virginia especially, who considered her verbal medium all-encompassing, looked at paintings by or with Vanessa to inspire her writing, to find images, metaphors, relations, and potential stories that could help her break the moulds of traditional novels without sacrificing aesthetic wholeness. Vanessa – committed painter as well as doting mother, creative colleague and competitor – was not the only important influence and touchstone in Virginia's career as a hybrid writer who raided the other arts, but she was central. In response to her sister's praise of *The Waves*, Virginia Woolf wrote, 'I always feel I'm writing more for you than for anybody' (*L*4: 390).

Notes

1. My thanks for invaluable assistance to Henrietta Garnett and the Estate of Vanessa Bell, Tony Bradshaw (the Bloomsbury Workshop), Celia Coke-Steele (Ivor Braka Limited), Claire Harries (Kings College, Cambridge), Christopher Reed, Sandra Lummis and Leslie Hankins, as well as Charles Samuel Stevens and other private collectors.
2. Clive Bell popularised similar theories, and Banfield (2000) adds Bertrand Russell's contributions to Bloomsbury philosophy and aesthetics.
3. Vanessa Bell to Roger Fry, 22 June 1916, Kings College Library, Cambridge.
4. Bellamy, artist as well as scholar, has created a dual portrait of the sisters, part of 'A Virginia Woolf Print Series' (1997). Using screen printing and etching techniques to adapt two photos, Bellamy puts Vanessa's image on a book cover and Virginia's on an easel. An early example of interest in the sisters' intimacy is McNaron (1985).
5. Recently (2008), Sellars has adapted biographical material in a novel that tells the story of the sisters' rivalry from Vanessa's point of view.
6. Ellis challenges Goldman's rejection of chiaroscuro in describing Virginia's work, implicating my work as well (2007: 95–102). Certainly Virginia's dialogical bent and verbal medium enabled her to combine experiments that paralleled Vanessa's (Goldman's and my focus) with more conservative traditions (Ellis's emphasis).
7. Humm reads the sisters' interest in photography, and their albums of 'domestic, family, and cultural' snapshots (2006: 21), as overtly autobiographical.
8. This painting was first reproduced and discussed, so far as I know, in 2004 (Reed 2004: 86). It is in addition to the 'six extant self-portraits', all 'resolute and withdrawn', tallied by Shone (1999: 236).
9. Sandra Lummis (formerly of Sandra Lummis Fine Art), email (16 February 2008).
10. In 1934 Vanessa did paint Virginia seated among books, but also surrounded by Bell and Grant murals, fabrics and rugs (Gillespie 1988: 186 figure 4.11).
11. Leslie Hankins (email 30 June 2008) acquired a photo (Anthony d'Offay Gallery) labelled: 'Vanessa BELL (1879–1961) / Mrs Dalloway's Party / 1920 / Oil on canvas / 28 × 23½ inches / Signed and dated / Provenance: Virginia Woolf.' Tony Bradshaw (email 13 August 2008) thinks d'Offay would have 'got it through Davis and Langdale'.

12. The current owner of the painting kindly described the colours for me.
13. Virginia's 'Foreword' and Vanessa's paintings of nude women also anticipate the daring spirit that risks self-exposure to scrutinise patriarchal tyrannies and gender hierarchies as causes of war in *Three Guineas* (Gillespie 2006). See also my discussion of Vanessa Bell in the context of five women artists who were her contemporaries (Gillespie 2007).
14. *The Bedroom, Gordon Square* (1912), versions of *The Tub* (1917, 1918), and *Nude* (1922–3) are most reproduced and discussed. Several examples survive from the 1930s and a number of Vanessa's decorative designs include female nudes. Unlike Duncan Grant, she rarely painted adult male nudes.
15. Vanessa Bell to Virginia Woolf, 11 March and 27 August 1909, New York Public Library.
16. Vanessa Bell to Virginia Woolf, 19 March 1919, Kings College Library, Cambridge.

Works Cited

Banfield, Ann (2000) *The Phantom Table: Woolf, Fry, Russell and the Epistemology of Modernism*, Cambridge: Cambridge University Press.

Bell, Quentin (1986) *Bloomsbury*, London: Weidenfeld and Nicolson.

Bell, Vanessa (1993) *Selected Letters of Vanessa Bell*, ed. Regina Marler, New York: Pantheon Books.

—— (1997) 'Lecture given at Leighton Park School', in *Sketches in Pen and Ink: A Bloomsbury Notebook*, ed. Lia Giachero, London: Hogarth Press.

Bellamy, Suzanne (1997) 'The Pattern Behind the Words', in *Virginia Woolf: Lesbian Readings*, ed. Eileen Barrett and Patricia Cramer New York: New York University Press.

Briggs, Julia (2006) *Reading Virginia Woolf*, Edinburgh: Edinburgh University Press.

Caughie, Pamela L. (1991) *Virginia Woolf and Postmodernism: Literature in Quest and Question of Itself*, Urbana: University of Illinois Press.

Caws, Mary Ann (1990) *Women of Bloomsbury: Virginia, Vanessa and Carrington*, New York: Routledge.

Cramer, Patricia (1997) '"Pearls and the Porpoise": *The Years* – A Lesbian Memoir', in *Virginia Woolf: Lesbian Readings*, ed. Eileen Barrett and Patricia Cramer New York: New York University Press.

Dunn, Jane (1990) *A Very Close Conspiracy: Vanessa Bell and Virginia Woolf*, Boston, MA: Little, Brown, and Company.

Elliott, Bridget and Jo-Ann Wallace (1994) *Women Artists and Writers: Modernist (Im)positionings*. London: Routledge.

Ellis, Steve (2007) *Virginia Woolf and the Victorians*, Cambridge: Cambridge University Press.

Garnett, Angelica (1984) *Deceived with Kindness: A Bloomsbury Childhood*, London: Chatto and Windus/Hogarth Press.

Gillespie, Diane Filby (1988) *The Sisters' Arts: The Writing and Painting of Virginia Woolf and Vanessa Bell*, Syracuse, NY: Syracuse University Press.

Gillespie, Diane F. (1999) 'Through Woolf's "I"s: Donne and *The Waves*', in *Woolf: Reading the Renaissance*, ed. Sally Greene Athens: Ohio University Press.

—— (2006) 'Godiva Still Rides: Virginia Woolf, Divestiture, and *Three Guineas* in *Woolf and the Art of Exploration: Selected Papers from the Fifteenth International Conference on Virginia Woolf*, ed. Helen Southworth and Elisa Kay Sparks, Clemson, SC: Clemson University Digital Press.

—— (2007) 'The Gender of Modern/ist Painting', in *Gender in Modernism: New Geographies, Complex Intersections*, ed. Bonnie Kime Scott, Urbana: University of Illinois Press.

Goldman, Jane (1998) *The Feminist Aesthetics of Virginia Woolf: Modernism, Post-Impressionism and the Politics of the Visual*, Cambridge: Cambridge University Press.

Hankins, Leslie (1997) '*Orlando*: 'A Precipice Marked V' between 'A Miracle of Discretion' and 'Lovemaking Unbelievable: Indiscretions Incredible', in *Virginia Woolf: Lesbian Readings*, ed. Eileen Barrett and Patricia Cramer, New York: New York University Press.

Humm, Maggie (2006) *Snapshots of Bloomsbury: The Private Lives of Virginia Woolf and Vanessa Bell*, New Brunswick, NJ: Rutgers University Press.

Kelly, Mary (1984) 'Re-viewing Modernist Criticism' in *Art After Modernism: Rethinking Representation*, ed. Brian Wallis, New York: The New Museum of Contemporary Art/ Boston, MA: David R. Godine.

Lee, Hermione (1997) *Virginia Woolf*, New York: Alfred A. Knopf.

Louvel, Liliane (2005) 'Vanessa Bell and Virginia Woolf: An Artist and a Critic?', *Cahiers Victoriens et Edouardiens*, 62: 53–68.

Matz, Jesse (2001) *Literary Impressionism and Modernist Aesthetics*, Cambridge: Cambridge University Press.

McNaron, Toni A. H. (1985) 'Billy Goat to Dolphin: Letters of Virginia Woolf to Her Sister, Vanessa Bell', in *The Sister Bond: A Feminist View of a Timeless Connection*, ed. Toni A. H. McNaron, New York: Pergamon.

Reed, Christopher (1993) 'Through Formalism: Feminism and Virginia Woolf's Relation to Bloomsbury Aesthetics', in *The Multiple Muses of Virginia Woolf*, ed. Diane Gillespie, Columbia: University of Missouri Press.

—— (2004) *Bloomsbury Rooms: Modernism, Subculture, and Domesticity*, New Haven, CT: Yale University Press.

Reid, Panthea (1993) 'The Blasphemy of Art: Fry's Aesthetics and Woolf's Non-"Literary" Stories', in *The Multiple Muses of Virginia Woolf*, ed. Diane Gillespie, Columbia: University of Missouri Press.

—— (1996) *Art and Affection: A Life of Virginia Woolf*, New York: Oxford University Press.

Sellers, Susan (2008) *Virginia and Vanessa*, London: Two Ravens Press.

Shone, Richard (1980) *Vanessa Bell: 1879–1961 A Retrospective Exhibition*, New York: Davis and Long.

—— (1999) *The Art of Bloomsbury: Roger Fry, Vanessa Bell and Duncan Grant*, London: Tate Gallery Publishing.

Spalding, Frances (1983) *Vanessa Bell*, London: Weidenfeld and Nicolson.

Surry, Tara (2007) '"Over the Boundary": Virginia Woolf as Common Seer' in *Woolfian Boundaries: Selected Papers from the Sixteenth Annual International Conference on Virginia Woolf*, ed. Anna Burrells, Steve Ellis, Deborah Parsons, and Kathryn Simpson, Clemson, SC: Clemson University Digital Press.

Tickner, Lisa (1999) 'Vanessa Bell: *Studland Beach*, Domesticity, and "Significant Form"', *Representations*, 65: 63–92.

Torgovnick, Marianna (1985) *The Visual Arts, Pictorialism, and the Novel: James, Lawrence, and Woolf*, Princeton, NJ: Princeton University Press.

Tranter, Rachel (1998) *Vanessa Bell: A Life of Painting*, London: Cecil Woolf.

West, Rebecca (1922) 'Review', *New Statesman*, 4 November: 142. Reprinted in Robin Majumdar and Allen McLaurin (eds) (1975) *Virginia Woolf: The Critical Heritage*, London: Routledge and Kegan Paul.

Woolf, Virginia (1930; 1975) 'Foreword' to *Recent Paintings by Vanessa Bell*, in *The Bloomsbury Group* ed. S. P. Rosenbaum, Toronto: University of Toronto Press. Orginally published by The London Artists' Association, for exhibition 4 February to 8 March.
—— (1934) 'Foreword' *Catalogue of Recent Paintings by Vanessa Bell*, London: Lefevre Galleries.
—— (1935; 1947) 'Roger Fry', in *The Moment and Other Essays*, London: Hogarth Press (speech delivered and printed for private circulation, 1935).
—— (1979) 'Notes for Reading at Random' Brenda Silver (ed.) *Twentieth Century Literature* 25, 3/4, 369–79.
—— (1976) *Virginia Woolf, The Waves: The Two Holograph Drafts* (ed.) J. W. Graham, Toronto: University of Toronto Press.
—— (1989) *The Complete Shorter Fiction of Virginia Woolf*, ed. Susan Dick, 2nd edn, San Diego CA: Harcourt Brace Jovanovich.
—— (1994) *The Essays of Virginia Woolf*, vol. 4, ed. Andrew McNeillie, London: Hogarth Press.

Further Reading

Caws, Mary Ann (1990) *Women of Bloomsbury: Virginia, Vanessa and Carrington*, New York: Routledge.
Dunn, Jane (1990) *A Very Close Conspiracy: Vanessa Bell and Virginia Woolf*, Boston, MA: Little, Brown, and Company.
Elliott, Bridget and Jo-Ann Wallace (1994) *Women Artists and Writers: Modernist (Im)positionings*, London: Routledge.
Gillespie, Diane Filby (1988) *The Sisters' Arts: The Writing and Painting of Virginia Woolf and Vanessa Bell*, Syracuse, NY: Syracuse University Press.
Gillespie, Diane F. (ed.) (1993) *The Multiple Muses of Virginia Woolf*, Columbia: University of Missouri Press.
Goldman, Jane (1998) *The Feminist Aesthetics of Virginia Woolf: Modernism, Post-Impressionism and the Politics of the Visual*, Cambridge: Cambridge University Press.
Louvel, Liliane (2005) 'Vanessa Bell and Virginia Woolf: An Artist and a Critic?', *Cahiers Victoriens et Edouardiens*, 62: 53–68.
Torgovnick, Marianna (1985) *The Visual Arts, Pictorialism, and the Novel: James, Lawrence, and Woolf*, Princeton, NJ: Princeton University Press.

8

VIRGINIA WOOLF, ART GALLERIES AND MUSEUMS

Benjamin Harvey

For Woolf, the physical and psychological threshold to be crossed 'on first entering a picture gallery' (Woolf 1992: 14) was always a complicated matter. But there is a good reason why, after 1933, entering the National Gallery (NG) might have felt a little harder than it had before. That summer, Boris Anrep, the Russian-born mosaicist, unveiled the latest portion of the mosaic pavements he had been making for this august institution's entrance hall. Here, on the halfway landing of its stairway, could now be seen a mosaic representing *The Awakening of the Muses* (see Plate 7). Humorously updating *The Parnassus* fresco from Raphael's *Stanza della Segnatura* (1509–11), Anrep had skilfully arranged his tesserae to depict eleven figures occupying a rocky landscape. Bacchus and Apollo are placed at its centre and surrounded by the nine muses, each helpfully identified by a label. The mosaicist also followed Raphael's conceit, as seen in *The School of Athens*, of conflating ancient figures with their modern counterparts, and the work includes several major figures associated with the Bloomsbury Group: Clive Bell (the *bon vivant*) serves as Bacchus and Lydia Keynes (the dancer) is appropriately cast as Terpsichore. Another figure – Clio, the muse of history – is dressed in robes and wears her silvery hair tied up in a loose bun; holding a quill in her left hand, she rests her right on the side of the neighbouring muse (Thalia, or comedy). Looking as though she is speaking, or on the verge of speech, she is pictured in profile and bears the distinctive features of Virginia Woolf. Still *in situ* today, there is perhaps no more complete, no more programmatic image of Woolf and the arts.

The installation of the mosaic was probably the first time Woolf's likeness had entered a major gallery on a permanent basis, if not exactly into its permanent collection. Woolf had long been a regular visitor both to the NG and to many of London's other museums and galleries. Indeed, the combination of an art gallery and an image of Woolf, writing implement in hand, prompts one to consider how her own writing might be used to reconstruct her museum- and gallery-going habits.

In *Walter Sickert: A Conversation*, Woolf gives her reader a sense of the

140

kind of artistic fare on view in the capital in late 1933, just a few months after the mosaic had been unveiled. 'Many pictures were being shown in London at that time', she writes. 'There was the famous Holbein; there were pictures by Picasso and Matisse; young English painters were holding an exhibition in Burlington Gardens, and there was a show of Sickert's pictures at Agnews' (Woolf 1992: 14–15). Woolf's seemingly casual list of attractions indicates how she divided the London art world into three or four different categories. The 'famous Holbein' must almost certainly refer to *The Ambassadors*, in the NG; Woolf's phrase evokes London's wealth of old masters and, by extension, the venerable institutions housing them. Next, she shifts her focus from permanent collections to temporary exhibitions. 'Picasso and Matisse' brings to mind recent French art, and especially those associated with Post-Impressionism (in Fry's original, open-ended sense of the term). No longer so controversial, each artist had had solo exhibitions in London by this time. In November 1933, illustrations by both artists could be found at the Zwemmer Gallery, Charing Cross Road. This show featured Matisse's etchings for Mallarmé's *Poésies* and Picasso's for Ovid's *Metamorphoses*; appearing just below a favourable review of the Sickert show, the critic for *The Times* noted that the occasion allowed 'a more direct comparison [of Matisse and Picasso] than is often afforded' (*The Times*, 2 November 1933, p. 10).

Woolf also mentions several generations of English artists, the 'young English Painters' standing in contrast to the more senior Sickert, then in his seventies. Some of these painters were, in November 1933, young only euphemistically. Woolf is referring to the London Group show at the New Burlington Galleries 'in Burlington Gardens'. Among the group's members were a number of Woolf's friends and intimates: Duncan Grant, Roger Fry, Gwen Raverat, Vanessa Bell and Walter Sickert. Woolf's list evokes a final institution that is never directly named in it: the Royal Academy (RA). The mention of 'Burlington Gardens' is inevitably a reminder of Burlington House, the impressive structure just around the corner and home to the RA. Even though the London Group was established as an alternative to the RA, Sickert exhibited with both. He had been an associate of the RA since 1924, but by referring to him as 'Richard Sickert R.A.' (Woolf 1992: 38), Woolf discreetly indicates that he had just become a full-blown Academician.

London's permanent collections, the Royal Academy, and the capital's steady fare of modern English and French art – these categories account for most but certainly not all of Woolf's experiences in galleries and museums. They do not, for example, include those institutions Woolf saw during her trips around Britain and on the Continent. Focusing on them makes sense, however, because they had the most direct impact on Woolf's criticism and fiction, and this interaction is my chapter's chief concern.

London's great permanent collections played a crucial role in the home schooling of Virginia Stephen. If the year 1897 was at all typical, then we can conclude that, as a teenager, Woolf spent many afternoons in these institutions, accompanied by her siblings and sometimes her father, too. Her journal of that year records regular trips to the 'SKM' – the South Kensington Museum (now the Victoria and Albert Museum). So numerous were these that, in an entry for March, she mentions going there to look at, for 'the 20th time the picture gallery' (*PA*: 55). Her weary tone is perhaps explained by the fact that she was accompanying her older sister, whose interests (and need for a chaperone) probably drove these repeat visits. Around the same time, a trip to the Dulwich Picture Gallery in South London illustrates what would be an important characteristic of Woolf's responses to museums and galleries – namely, that she would seldom restrict her comments to the art on display, often preferring to expand her observational framework to include institutional and social details. 'We saw the gallery', she wrote in her diary, 'which I did not think very beautiful – There are some nice pictures, and a Sir Josh[ua Reynolds] – Mrs Siddons. In the middle of the gallery there is a door leading to the Mausoleum of the founders' (ibid.: 49). The observations are seemingly casual, but relate to two recurring issues in Woolf's writing: the representation of prominent women and the origins of cultural institutions, when legacies become, so to speak, visible as bricks and mortar. But rather than seeing these as distinct issues, Woolf's tendency is to make connections between the institution and the objects within.

In 1897, the NG stood in its familiar location at the north end of Trafalgar Square, where, the year before, it had been joined by the NPG (National Portrait Gallery). It is, of course, natural to treat these galleries as a pair. They are, as Woolf put it, 'two buildings on the same promontory of pavement, washed by the same incessant tides' (*E3*: 163). Woolf's father, Sir Leslie Stephen, served as a trustee at the NPG: it was, after all, the obvious visual analogue to his great biographical enterprise. Nevertheless, in January 1897, Virginia Stephen's remarks about it are less than entirely respectful: 'It was rather dull, and we spent our time in yawning. Father left us, and we went on to the National Gallery, which neither Thoby or A[drian]. has ever seen' (*PA*: 16). Still, not everything at the NPG was simply dismissed out of hand. 'We went on the top of a bus to Trafalgar Square', she writes a few months later, 'and saw all the Watts and George Eliot and Mrs [Elizabeth Barrett] Browning – skilfully missing the proper [i.e. Royal] portraits upstairs' (ibid.: 52).

Despite Woolf's interest in Britain's history and in portraiture (particularly images of creative women), the larger NG seems to have exerted an even greater attraction. Aided by Vanessa, Woolf took her class of working class women to the NG in 1905, guiding them 'laboriously through the Early Italians' (*PA*: 246). She visited the NG alone and with friends (Roger Fry and Clive Bell). She visited during the Great War, when she was depressed that:

> the glory of war has to be taught by a life size portrait of Lord Kitchener, & almost life size battle scenes; though as the battles are 18th century battles,

one can only look upon them as scenes in a gymnasium on rather a large scale. (*D1*: 168)

And she visited it as late as January 1940, when the gallery's works had been transported, like tender evacuees, to a secure location in Wales. This time she was there not to look at art at all, but to enjoy a new use to which the emptied-out galleries had been put: she was attending a concert (*D5*: 257).

The physical proximity of the two galleries encouraged Woolf to write about the NG and the NPG together. Ostensibly a review of Edmond X. Kapp's book of caricatures, *Personalities* (1919), Woolf's 'Pictures and Portraits' (1920) uses the device of the peripatetic narrator to connect the two galleries. At the beginning of the piece, Woolf contemplates the prospect of entering the gallery, but finds herself caught '[i]n the current of the crowd, so swift and deep' (*E3*: 163). Surrounded by the hustle and bustle of modern London, Woolf wittily exaggerates the task before her: 'As easily might a pilchard leap from the shoal and join the free sport of dolphins as a single individual ascend those steps and enter those doors' (ibid.). The toll to be paid, in other words, is more psychological than physical or monetary: the intimidating 'elevation' in question more a matter of culture, and of cultural capital, than of a physical change in gradient. Once in the NG, and attending to the impressive pictures there, the narrator's problem becomes a writerly dilemma. The pictures, she finds, do evoke words but, alas, only:

> sluggish, slow-dropping words that would, if they could, stain the page with colour; not writers' words. But it is not here our business to define what sort of words they are; we are only concerned to prove our unfitness to review the caricatures of Mr Kapp. (*E3*: 164)

And so Woolf moves from the NG's *pictures* to the NPG's *portraits* – the title of the piece alludes both to the two institutions Woolf visits and to the order of these visits.

The NPG has a clear relationship to the book of caricatures at hand, and a lower threshold than the NG. This lower threshold is partly aesthetic and a consequence of its distinctive agenda which, in the institution's own language, was 'to look to the celebrity of the person represented rather than to the merit of the artist' (Holmes 1914: x); but, since the main entrance is only just a few steps above street level, the lower threshold is also literal and physical. 'It needs an effort,' Woolf continues, 'but scarcely a great one, to enter the National Portrait Gallery' (*E3*: 164). Woolf now divulges an additional reason for her trip to the NPG – to find a likeness of Harriet Taylor Mill, 'a paragon among women' (ibid.). Despite the institution's inviting entrance, Woolf finds herself turned away from it: 'But the National Portrait Gallery, interrogated, wished to be satisfied that the inquirer was dependent upon a soldier; pensions they provided, not portraits' (ibid.). Accordingly, Woolf is 'set adrift in Trafalgar Square once more' (ibid.).

The explanation for her failure is fairly simple: during the war and in its immediate aftermath, the NPG had been taken over by the Separation Allowance Department of the War Office and was closed for normal business. As compensation, from early 1919 a selection of some forty portraits had been relocated to the NG, where, it was argued, dominion and other troops might benefit from them. Curiously, Woolf encourages us to read the episode at the NPG's door not as a failure to see all the portraits displayed in the gallery, so much as a failure to see a particular portrait, that of Harriet Taylor Mill. Her choice of subjects was surely calculated. Woolf chooses an important nineteenth-century woman, but not one as immediately familiar as, say, 'George Eliot and Mrs Browning' (*PA*: 52). Indeed her previous visits to the NPG, as well as the gallery's catalogue, would have informed Woolf that there was as yet no portrait of Harriet Taylor Mill in the national collection. Woolf was drawing attention to this worrying absence at an apt moment. Harriet Taylor Mill had been one of the key Victorian advocates for 'The Enfranchisement of Women' (to use the title of her 1851 essay) and Woolf was writing just shortly after British women had voted for the first time. Representation in both the aesthetic and political senses is at stake here. In her essay, Woolf pointedly notes an asymmetry in the caricaturist' choice of subjects: 'we turn eagerly . . . to see what faces Mr Kapp provides for the twenty-three gentlemen and the one old lady whom he calls *Personalities*' (*E3*: 164). That ratio of male to female subjects, we should note, was even worse than the unimpressive ratio in the NPG itself.

The NPG was failing both to represent women adequately and, furthermore, failing to provide a visual history of the nation's suffrage movement. Immediately after the war, the NPG's trustees were, in fact, making a case to expand the institution, but they were doing so chiefly on the grounds that they should include portraits of 'persons distinguished for their service to the Empire during the war' (*The Times*, 8 August 1919, p. 13). That this rationale would not have pleased Woolf is evident in her reaction (quoted above) to the increasing visibility of military-themed paintings in the NG; she had even made these comments during the same 1918 excursion to the NG and NPG that would later provide much of the material for 'Pictures and Portraits' (*D1*: 168). Her essay, then, is a timely intervention in a public debate, and functions as a reminder that their might be other compelling reasons for rethinking the contents, size and function of the NPG. Woolf's interest in the NPG's acquisition policy continued in the 1930s, when she supported a failed attempt to place a portrait of Katherine Mansfield in the institution. 'I should have thought', she told Theodora Bosanquet in a letter of December 1932, 'that there could be no doubt that the National Portrait Gallery ought to have a picture of Katherine Mansfield' (*L5*: 135). Having been dead for almost ten years, Mansfield would in a month be eligible for inclusion in the collection. When, in 1934, the NPG approached Woolf about her own willingness to pose, her familiarity with this policy informed her decision to decline the overture:

they keep the drawing in a cellar, and when I've been dead ten years they have it out and say Does anyone want to know what Mrs Woolf looked like? No, say all the others. Then its torn up. So why should I defile a whole day by sitting? (*L5*: 277)

Here, Woolf imagines herself as the subject of deliberation for the NPG's trustees, those people who, like her father, had been charged with assessing 'the celebrity of the person represented'. 'They' were also, of course, all men. Woolf reminds us of this in *Three Guineas* (1938), when she is discussing women's exclusion from the process of deciding how the state spends money on culture.

> Not a single educated man's daughter, Whitaker['s Almanac] says, is thought capable of teaching the literature of her own language at either university. Nor is her opinion worth asking, Whitaker informs us, when it comes to buying a picture for the National Gallery, a portrait for the Portrait Gallery, or a mummy for the British Museum. (*TG*: 104–5)

'Pictures and Portraits' indicates that Woolf had been thinking about these issues long before she wrote *Three Guineas*.

'Pictures and Portraits' contains two comparative tactics Woolf frequently uses in her writings about cultural institutions. Linking interior and exterior spaces, the first and more common approach involves the stark contrast between the calm and controlled atmosphere of the building and the clamorous flux of the surrounding streets. Often embedded in the first form of comparison, the second pits one institution against another (or *others*) in quick succession, so that the peculiar quality or aura of each might be better apprehended. Woolf typically used this approach in her writings about established institutions: St Mary-le-Bow, St Paul's, Westminster Abbey and St Clement Danes ('Abbeys and Cathedrals'); the House of Commons Chamber and Westminster Hall ('This is the House of Commons'); and The United Services Museum and Westminster Abbey ('Waxworks at the Abbey'). In all examples, the comparison extends beyond architecture to include objects within each building – respectively, tombs, statues and a morganatic marriage of unlikely objects.[1]

In 'Waxworks at the Abbey' (1928), Woolf combines these two forms of comparison in a brief, virtuosic essay. Woolf starts by asserting a 'connexion between the waxworks in the Abbey and the Duke of Wellington's top hat' (*E4*: 540). The waxworks have, we are told, their 'their hours of audience like other potentates' (ibid.). While waiting for these hours to arrive, we might, Woolf suggests, usefully fill our time at the nearby Royal United Services Museum, where we will find the top hat. One of the issues Woolf explores here is that of aesthetic differentiation and its lack. While the top hat and the waxworks are pleasingly different, 'there is not as much contrast as one would wish, perhaps, between the Museum at one end of Whitehall and the Abbey at the other' (ibid.). The precise problem is the Abbey itself, which, with its milling tourists and guides, its objects demanding attention and explication, fails to distinguish itself both from the Museum and from the thoroughfare of Whitehall: 'too many sightse-ers shuffle and stare for the past and the dead and the mystic nature of the place to have full sway. Solitude is impossible' (ibid.). It is only when Woolf manages to 'slip aside' and furtively looks at the waxworks that the desired contrast is felt. For now she is 'in a very small chamber alone with Queen Elizabeth' (ibid.). 'The Queen', Woolf continues, 'dominates the room as she once dominated England. Leaning a little forward she seems to beckon you to come to her, she stands, holding her sceptre in one hand, her orb in the other' (ibid.: 540–1). Woolf proceeds to describe many of the other effigies in the room, but at the very end of the essay returns to her initial montage of objects which she now states more forcefully. Running back into the main space of the Abbey, we 'enter that strange muddle and miscellany of objects both hallowed and ridiculous. Yet now the impression is less tumultuous than before. Two presences seem to control its incoherence, as sometimes a chattering group of people is ordered and quieted by the entry of someone before whom, they know not why, they fall silent. One is Elizabeth, beckoning; the other is an old top-hat' (ibid.: 542).

Woolf uses the essay as a means to exercise a kind of curatorial impulse. Two objects that will presumably never be placed by one another together can, nev-ertheless, be forcibly brought together in her prose – *juxtaposed*, if you prefer. Despite their obvious commonality, their association with great figures from British history, the wax queen and the top hat make a compellingly odd com-bination, akin to a surrealistic coupling of unlikely objects (sewing machine and umbrella, stool and bicycle wheel, iron and tacks). The rhetorical contrast between Woolf's disparate objects is pleasing. One uncannily duplicates a Queen; the other evokes a male figure metonymically (through contact and absence). One is dressed lavishly and surrounded by a 'garish bright assembly' (*E4*: 542); the other is associated with uniform and uniformity, and stands 'as tall as a chimney, as straight as a ramrod, as black as a rock' (ibid.: 540). Gender differentiation obviously plays a role here. The top hat is a familiar phallic symbol, and neither comparing it to a ramrod, nor placing it in front of the Virgin Queen, will lessen this association.[2] The union can only be consum-mated in prose, in the very last sentence of the essay, where Woolf recapitulates more forcefully the morganatic marriage she had outlined at the beginning of the piece.

   In 'Waxworks at the Abbey', the sexual is also given a spatial and social dimension, and it is this that ultimately determines the essay's logic. As we have seen, like a charismatic person entering a room, the objects seem to control the 'chattering' city around them. Each object is associated with a distinctive mode of address. Wellington's top hat could have been seen, Woolf speculates, 'a mile off advancing indomitably down the street. It must have been to this emblem of incorruptible dignity that the Duke raised his two fingers when passers-by respectfully saluted him. One is almost tempted to salute it now' (*E4*: 540).[3] While the hat seems to project outwards into the (public) space around it; the effigy of the Queen intimately draws, or beckons, people towards it. Might the reader even travesty the logic of Woolf's essay by pushing the conflation of the two objects further – by imagining the orphaned item of apparel resting on the Queen's head? The thought experiment has, at least, the benefit of reminding us that, in 1928, Woolf was in the middle of writing *Orlando*, a novel preoccupied with questions of gender, dress and the historical imagination. For the first chapter of the book, Woolf needed to describe her eponymous character's meeting with Queen Elizabeth and her language repeats some of the elements she had rehearsed in 'Waxworks at the Abbey' – the Queen's air of fear and paranoia, the emphasis on her hands, and the symbols of power associated with them (orb and sceptre). Orlando and the Queen experience each other in fragments: Orlando only sees the Queen's hands, who in turn only sees, not his hat, but his head. She looks down on this with eyes that are 'always, if the waxworks at the Abbey are to be trusted, wide open' (*O*: 18). The layers of meaning contained in this aside hardly bolster our trust in the narrator. Not only are the waxworks obviously not to be trusted on this issue, but we are suddenly made aware that the narrator's description of the scene is probably entirely based on this (rather obvious) source. The narrative spell is broken, the curtain pulled aside, and Orlando's biographer no long fully inhabits the past and becomes just another tourist at the Abbey, extrapolating from the fragmentary historical record. As Woolf pointed out in her essay 'Pictures' (1925), writers have their own peculiar motives for visiting such places. Objects will be pilfered for the sake of prose. 'From a portrait, too,' she writes, 'we get almost always something worth having – somebody's room, nose, or hands, some little effect of character or circumstance, some knick-knack to put in our pockets and take away' (*E*4: 245–6).

The RA, Woolf discovered, could also be plundered by an enterprising writer. As an institution it had several functions: art school (Vanessa Stephen trained there), prestigious professional organisation, and venue for temporary exhibitions. The annual Summer Exhibition, a large juried show, was a crucial event towards the end of the London Season. Judging from her responses to the Summer Exhibition, the RA's social role both fascinated and alarmed Woolf. One of her former suitors, Walter Lamb, became Secretary to the RA in 1913 and on occasions provided Woolf with an insider's perspective. Her diary entry of 10 January 1915 vividly records Lamb's account of a royal visit to the Academy, noting that the King talked about false teeth in front of the paintings and now treated Lamb, 'as Leonard says, like a superior footman' (*D*1: 14). Woolf visited at least five of the RA's Summer Exhibitions and presumably more. Her fundamental response to the show was unvarying. She went in 1897 (finding it 'terrible' [*PA*: 108]), in 1903 ('the light & space are not becoming' [ibid.: 176]), and several times in 1905 (a 'painted desert' [ibid.: 270]). Her most prolonged response can be found in 'The Royal Academy', an essay she wrote for *The Athenaeum* about the 1919 Summer Exhibition. The exhibition was exceptional this year for the simple reason that, following the end of the war, it represented a return to business as usual. The glittering Royal Academy banquet took place for the first time since 1914 and was attended by prominent members of the royal family and aristocracy, the armed forces, the government, and the artistic elite (Thomas Hardy and Rudyard Kipling among them). It 'was marked', *The Times* noted, 'by all its old brilliancy from a social point of view' (*The Times*, 5 May 1919, p. 17).

Woolf's 1919 essay does not claim to be a review of the show in the usual sense; she amusingly invokes Roger Fry at the end of the essay, as a kind of critical higher power who might 'decide whether the emotions here recorded are the proper result of one thousand six hundred and seventy-four works of art' (*E3*: 93). Indeed Woolf's essay appeared in August, towards the end of the exhibition's run, and a full three months earlier it had been reviewed (in two parts) by Jan Gordon, *The Athenaeum*'s regular critic. An unsigned editorial in the journal had also scathingly commented upon Winston Churchill's speech at the exhibition's opening banquet. Writing about an exhibition in a journal that had already amply covered it, Woolf would presumably have read these earlier pieces, if only to avoid unnecessary duplication and to position her essay in relationship to them. In a letter to Vanessa Bell, Woolf mentions working on her essay and spending 'a good deal of my time at the Royal Academy' (*L2*: 377). Despite paying repeated visits to the show, her essay is structured around the more economical and shapely conceit of a single visit with a premature end.

Woolf's essay is concerned with two connected issues. One is stated explicitly: what makes a 'good Academy picture' (*E3*: 91)? The other concerns the RA's role and how this relates to the pictures within it. The first question is easily answered through her discussion of Alfred Priest's *Cocaine* and John Reid's *The Wonders of the Deep*. Woolf ventures that a successful Academy picture, like *Cocaine*, allows you to search it 'for ten minutes or so and still be doubtful whether you have extracted the whole meaning' (ibid.). (Reid's work, by contrast, is 'rather obvious'; once the tell-tale detail has been identified the story 'reels itself out like a line with a salmon on the end of it' [ibid.].) This definition, along with her choice of paintings, suggests that by 'Academy picture' Woolf means something fairly specific – a descendent of the Victorian 'problem picture'.[4] The other major work Woolf discusses at some length is John Singer Sargent's *Gassed* (see plate 8) and this is the painting that finally pricks 'some nerve of protest' in her narrator, causing her to flee the exhibition (ibid.: 92).

Her selection of this work as her 'last straw' can hardly be accidental. No painting received more press attention that year, and none so starkly divided viewers and reviewers. Lent by the Imperial War Museum, it was, for *The Times*, the 'picture of the year' (*The Times*, 3 May 1919, p. 15) and the only work singled out in the speeches at the RA Banquet, where Churchill praised its 'brilliant genius and painful significance' (*The Times*, 5 May 1919, p. 17). Devoting a lengthy paragraph of his review to the painting, Jan Gordon took a dissenting view:

> This picture is a descriptive work; it recounts the result of a gas attack in very much the language that an English schoolboy of the self-conscious age might use . . . It seems as though after much preliminary the schoolboy had mounted to the top of the Trafalgar Monument and thence shouted his simple message through a megaphone. (Gordon 1919: 306)

In her discussion of the work, Woolf hones in on a telling detail, a crucial 'piece of over-emphasis'. 'In order', she writes:

> to emphasize his point that the soldiers wearing bandages round their eyes cannot see, and therefore claim our compassion, he makes one of them raise his leg to the level of his elbow in order to mount a step an inch or two above the ground. (*E3*: 92–3)

Woolf might herself be guilty of a little exaggeration here, since the soldier's leg, though undoubtedly high, is still well beneath elbow level. Woolf's general point, however, echoes Gordon's. She, too, casts *Gassed* as a rhetorical and 'noisy' work and, further, as the painting that makes audible the general clamour of the exhibition:

> From first to last each canvas had rubbed in some emotion, and what the paint failed to say the catalogue had enforced in words. But Mr Sargent was the last straw. Suddenly the great rooms rang like a parrot-house with the intolerable vociferations of gaudy and brainless birds. How they shrieked and gibbered! How they danced and sidled! Honour, patriotism, chastity, wealth, success, importance, position, patronage, power – their cries rang and echoed from all quarters. (*E3*: 93)

In 'The Royal Academy', Woolf situates her titular institution in the streets. Her narrator begins by leaving the 'indiscriminate variety of Piccadilly' and ends by escaping into the 'comparative sobriety of Piccadilly'. She thus inverts our expectations: Piccadilly should be noisy and chaotic, and the 'mute poetry' of painting should be, well, mute and orderly. The noise she discovers in the exhibition relates to the issue of the RA's function. The paintings in the Summer Exhibition, Woolf suggests, serve to clarify, underline, and perpetuate the dominant ideology of the British Empire. The paintings contribute, Woolf writes, to:

> a very powerful atmosphere; so charged with manliness and womanliness, pathos and purity, sunsets and Union Jacks, that the shabbiest and most suburban catch a reflection of the rosy glow. 'This is England! these are the English!' one might exclaim if a foreigner were at hand. (*E3*: 92)

Gassed, then, is not simply a painting but a confirmation of the belief that the suffering and sacrifice of soldiers is a necessary price to pay for the greater good of the Empire. In Churchill's speech, immediately after his appreciative words about *Gassed*, he claimed that art 'would emerge from this war . . . not merely to the position in which it entered the struggle, but vivified and purified as it always had been by trial and tribulation. (Cheers)' (*The Times*, 5 May 1919, p. 17). In Woolf's essay, the relationship between the question of the Academy picture and the Academy's function is perhaps not as straightforward as it might initially seem. For if the former depends upon narrative complexity and ambiguity, the latter seems to require a clear, unequivocal, and amplified message. Like the architecture of the RA itself, such a work of art 'radiates back the significance of everything fourfold' (*E3*: 89). And so it is that Woolf has trouble finding a 'good Academy picture' in the Academy.

Woolf would repeat the main lines of her argument against the RA in two other pieces. In the short story 'A Society', the character Helen sets out to investigate the RA but, when asked to deliver her report, can only repeat lines of well-known poetry – lines that, when placed together, presumably repeat the well-worn sentiments expressed in the works of art she has seen: 'O! to be in England now that April's there. Men must work and women must weep. The path of duty is the way to glory –' (*SF*: 127). Helen, coming to her senses, resolves to '"roll on the carpet and see if I can't brush off what remains of the Union Jack. Then perhaps –" here she rolled energetically' (ibid.). In 1924, Woolf attended the private view of the 1924 Summer Exhibition accompanied by Walter Lamb; the paragraph she wrote about the experience for the *Nation & Athenaeum* repeats the main lines of her 1919 essay. But the shorter space forces Woolf to be, if anything, more brutal in her assessment of the show. The works on display, she writes:

> inevitably recall the glories of our blood and State rather than suggest reflections upon form in the abstract. At the Private View one tends to glance at pictures as one turns the pages of an amplified and highly coloured illustrated newspaper devoted to the celebration of the British Empire . . . . (*E3*: 405–6)

That the 1919 essay can so readily be retooled to treat the later exhibition is itself revealing. One begins to sense that, for Woolf, she is always attending the same Summer Exhibition – that the general character of the show is always more striking than the particularities of any work included within it.

As though to compensate for the diminishing relevance of the Summer Exhibition, the RA became increasing important as a venue for large single-artist retrospectives and for what we now call 'blockbuster exhibitions'. These tended to take place over the winter months and Woolf went to many. In March 1897, she recorded paying 'a visit to Burlington House – as it is the last day of the [Frederic Lord] Leighton exhibition. They were mostly very ugly' (*PA*: 53). Woolf also had an antipathetic, though more expansive, response to the 1904–5 G. F. Watts exhibition at the RA,: 'Today, I think N[essa] & I went to the Academy Watts exhibition which is weak & worthless – almost incredibly so, considering his reputation. Not a single first rate picture there, & many 5th rate. His "ideas" here swamped his art' (ibid.: 218). The last sentence might serve as a neat summary of Woolf's own Watts – that is, the character she later included in *Freshwater*.

For Woolf, the RA offered more pleasure when it did manage to 'brush off' the Union Jack. Later in her life, between 1927 and 1936, she attended a number of shows devoted to the art of various national schools – loan exhibitions of Flemish and Belgian, Persian, French, and Chinese art. Beyond just the objects on display, these exhibitions presented Woolf with opportunities to forge connections and conversations with her friends and family. She mentions seeing the Flemish and Belgian exhibition (1927) in a letter to Vanessa Bell, where she also responds to some of her sister's paintings on display elsewhere in London; to prove that her 'susceptibilities are freakish and wayward' (and thus should not be taken altogether seriously) she writes that she 'liked the two Breugels (Icarus: and a storm: I'm not sure of the man's name) far better than anything' (*L3*: 341). The next month, she reported to Bell that she'd seen two other Brueghels in Naples, but 'didn't care for them so much as the London one – Too melodramatic' (ibid.: 365). (The painting, incidentally, is an obvious source for Sargent's unsteady soldiers.) Woolf probably saw the display of Persian art (1931) with the author of *Passenger to Tehran*, Vita Sackville-West (*L4*: 282). She went to see Roger Fry lecture in conjunction with the exhibition of French Art (1932); these talks provided both the basis of his book *Characteristics of French Art* and fodder for her later biography, where she memorably describes his skills as a lecturer (*RF*: 261–3). Lastly, for the exhibition of Chinese art (1935–6), Woolf read up on the subject in "some letters of Rogers" (*L4*: 3). The show allowed her to experience objects from a culture her nephew was then experiencing first hand. 'We have just been to the Chinese show', she informed Julian Bell in a letter to China, 'about which I dont expect you want information' (*L5*: 450).

Woolf gallery-going habits regularly took her to London's many commercial galleries. In 1933, Sickert's exhibition at Agnew's ('a neat set of rooms in Bond Street' [Woolf 1992: 12]), the Matisse and Picasso show at Zwemmers, and the London Group's exhibition at the New Burlington Galleries, all fall into this category. The venues for such shows included, aside from those already mentioned, the Chelsea Book Club, the Cooling Galleries, the Grafton Gallery, the Independent Gallery, the Leicester Galleries, the Lefevre Gallery, the Mansard Gallery, the New Gallery and (between 1913 and 1919) Fry's Omega Workshops. With some notable exceptions – for example, the 1920 show of African Art at the Chelsea Book Club – Woolf's general preference was for contemporary French and British art. Her demand was matched by what London could supply. She especially favoured shows featuring the work of friends and acquaintances, often attending their opening receptions. Predictably, exhibitions featuring the art of her sister, Vanessa Bell, and her close friends, Duncan Grant and Roger Fry, were the most numerous; but Woolf also went to solo displays of art by Jacques Raverat (1917), Walter Sickert (1919 and 1933), Max Beerbohm (1925),

Will Arnold-Foster (1928), Ethel Sands (1931) and her nephew Quentin Bell (1935).

These exhibitions elicited further publications from Woolf (as well as a speech), which vary in the ways they relate to their origins. In terms of their temporal nature of these relationships, one might summarise them simply as before, during, and after. The two prefaces to Vanessa Bell's work appeared as catalogue prefaces and so were written in advance and with the expectation that they might well be read in front of the pictures. They orient the viewer to Bell's visual world, suggest ways of approaching the work, and indicate her broader achievement. The speech Woolf gave at the opening of a show of Roger Fry's paintings at the Bristol Museum and Art Gallery served a similar function, but since it was a posthumous exhibition, Woolf is more direct in talking about her subject's varied achievements. Tactfully side-stepping the perennially awkward issue of Fry's artistic achievement – an issue made more awkward still by the presence of family members at the opening – Woolf instead called for her audience to look at the works with 'open eyes and open minds in the spirit of enjoyment' (*M*: 105). Woolf made at least one other speech on the subject of the visual arts, to a meeting of the London Group at Pinoli's restaurant in March 1924. The text of this speech (assuming there was one) has not survived, but later that year Woolf penned a paragraph about the group's twenty-first exhibition for the *Nation & Athenaeum*. Woolf finds the show 'curiously unequal', but the piece is notable for containing brief comments about two of Woolf's future subjects (Vanessa Bell and Walter Sickert) and for including some of her few published comments on the art of Duncan Grant and Mark Gertler (*E3*: 448).

This was neither the first nor the last time Woolf would record her appreciation for examples of Sickert's 'very fine' art (*E3*: 448). In 1919, after seeing a show of his work, she had declared him 'my ideal painter; I should like to possess his works, for the purpose of describing them' (*L2*: 331). Over a decade later, in her essay on Sickert, Woolf did just this. The premise of the piece is that the 'seven or eight people' are discussing an exhibition that is still running (Woolf 1992: 11); but knowing that the piece would not be published until long after the show had closed, Woolf established some distance between her narrator and the art. Instead of the first person, she uses free indirect discourse; instead of placing herself in the exhibition and in front of the art (her more usual tactic), she describes a modest symposium, an evening dinner party. This reason for gathering, along with the setting (a private residence), separates the conversation from the show. To argue their points, the debaters rely on their memories of the show and, at one point, produce a 'book of photographs from Sickert's paintings' (ibid.: 17). Even Vanessa Bell's cover design, a still-life of a table-setting, draws attention to the framing device in Woolf's essay rather than simply to Sickert, who seldom worked in that genre.

Sickert's years in Paris and Dieppe, and his associations with Degas and Whistler, meant that he provided an important link back to an earlier generation of artists, the French Impressionists. As though to stress his role as a mediator between Britain and continental Europe, Woolf leaves us with an image of Sickert on a boat, painting 'a divinely lovely picture of Dieppe, Harwich, or the cliffs of Dover' (Woolf 1992: 38). Around the turn of the century, French Impressionism – and its followers in the New English Art Club (NEAC) – had offered an obvious alternative to the mainstream of Victorian art. Woolf would have been familiar with these debates through her sister, whose Friday Club divided along these lines. '[O]ne half of the committee', Woolf noted in 1905, 'shriek Whistler and French impressionists, and the other are stalwart British' (*L1*: 201). That year was, in fact, crucial in exposing Woolf to these very artists. Her diaries record that, in early February, she attended a lecture by the critic Frank Rutter given in junction with a large exhibition of Impressionist painting at the Grafton Gallery; she found the talk 'pompous & dull' but presumably also took the opportunity to look at the paintings (*PA*: 233). Drawn from the exceptional collection of Durand-Ruel, the Impressionists' most important dealer, these included examples of the school's major artists, as well as Manets and Cézannes. Just a week after attending the lecture, Woolf was looking at Whistler and Legros engravings at 'an interesting shop in a back street' and thinking about buying them (ibid.: 237). Then, a few weeks after that, she went to the large Whistler Memorial Exhibition at the New Gallery. This elicited from Woolf what is perhaps her most enthusiastic written response to any exhibition, and one that contrasts starkly with her assessment of the Watts show she had recently attended:

> He is a perfect artist – uses his gifts to the utmost & with the finest discretion, so that all his pictures are perfect in their way – & sometimes it is a very noble way. Oh Lord, the lucid colour – the harmony – the perfect scheme. This is what matters in life. (*PA*: 241–2)

Woolf also, of course, attended Roger Fry's famous Post-Impressionist shows of 1910–11 and 1912–13. In the first of these – *'Manet and the Post-Impressionists'* – Fry drove a theoretical wedge between the Impressionists and his so-called 'Post-Impressionists,' who included Cézanne, Van Gogh and Gauguin. Woolf, whose husband served as secretary of the second exhibition, focused on the brouhaha surrounding the exhibitions in her letters, but she also clearly grasped the larger significance of the events. The first show has been one of the events associated with her famous quote that 'on or about December 1910 human character changed' (*E3*: 421). As early as 1911, in a notice for Lewis Hind's *The Post-Impressionists*, she referred to the 'now historic exhibition at the Grafton Gallery' and in a 1921 review of Fry's *Vision and Design*, she expressed it in more personal terms, saying that:

> It was due to Mr Fry that these spheres of jelly began painfully to concentrate, about the autumn of 1912, upon the canvases of Cézanne. It was not merely that he caused the pictures to be brought across the Channel. . . . He liberated a stream of pleasure of an entirely unknown kind. (Woolf 1995: 382)

Her chronology is a little shaky here and Woolf probably means the more significant 1910 exhibition.[5] It is a lapse she would not have made later, when writing her biography of Roger Fry forced her to take a more scholarly approach to these exhibitions. The 'appallingly difficult PIP [Post-Impressionism] chapter' (*D5*: 220) was researched in conversations with Bell, Grant and other art-world friends (including Simon Bussy, Max Beerbohm and Sir William Rothenstein); more formally, it was investigated in the London Library, where, in September 1937, Woolf consulted *The Times*'s coverage of the exhibitions. In her biography, Woolf uses a comparison between exhibitions as a way of measuring a temporal and cultural distance. 'It is difficult in 1939,' she wrote,

> when a great hospital is benefiting from a centenary exhibition of Cézanne's works, and the gallery [Wildenstein & Co.] is daily crowded with devout and submissive worshippers, to realize what violent emotions those pictures excited less than thirty years ago. (Woolf 1995: 122)

But if the public was now enthusiastic, Woolf was also aware that a large number of artists still disliked Post-Impressionism, partly because they perceived that its critical success may have taken away from their own. Artists such as Sickert thought that Fry had stressed the wrong part of the modern French tradition and disliked, as Woolf put it 'his criticism of the New English Art Club shows (he had resigned his place on the Jury of the New English Art Club in 1908)' (Woolf 1995: 127). Others criticised him for promoting *any* sort of Franco-centric model. Thus in 1936 Woolf had felt irritated when 'Nevinson, the [Vorticist] painter, gave 50 centimes to the Fund to buy a Cézanne, in Roger's memory. Now that sort of meanness makes me angry' (*D5*: 16). The fund had been established in 1934 and Woolf's name appears in the letter to *The Times* that announced the appeal. By paying in centimes, Nevinson was obviously making a symbolic point as well as an economic one. The scheme's anticlimactic outcome might have amused Sickert and Nevinson: having failed to raise enough money to buy the desired Cézanne, a Sisley was purchased instead.

Post-Impressionism, of course, also provided Woolf with a compelling aesthetic model. In her biography of Fry, she used the chapter on 'The Post-Impressionists' as a hinge for the book's divided structure. Since she also met Fry in 1910 she could, after this point in her biography, draw on her own memories and impressions of him. As Woolf wrote in her diary: 'So to the Post I[mpressionists]. & ourselves. That will make the break in the book. A change of method' (*D5*: 160). But Woolf's experiments with literary form were shaped not merely by Post-Impressionism, but by the broader 'stream of pleasure' in the visual arts it had unleashed; and a large part of this pleasure could only be found by attending museums and galleries.

Discussions of Woolf's Post-Impressionist aesthetics have tended to focus on *To the Lighthouse* and to align the novel's tripartite form with that of the painting Lily completes at its end. But it is also worth noting that Woolf had a tendency to connect different portions of fictional texts with different artworks;

in these cases, her role as a writer takes on an almost curatorial character, and she composes as one might position objects in relationship to one another on a wall or a surface. Sections of texts, in such cases, become analogous to objects, the 'breaks' between them to the spaces separating objects. Negotiating these transitions is akin to those moments when, as viewers, we transfer our attention from one object to the next – when, having acclimatised to one aesthetic atmosphere, we readjust to another.

This type of structure is evident in several pieces of Woolf's shorter fiction. 'Blue & Green', for example, presents the reader with an imagistic diptych or pendant images, a resemblance that was particularly evident in the original context of *Monday or Tuesday* (1921), where each paragraph filled its own page and faced its partner opposite. In 'Three Pictures', which was probably written in the late 1920s, Woolf's story is given the form of a paradoxical trio of images: two picturesque landscapes bracketing something that tests the limits of visual representation. An untimely death in 'The Second Picture' is signalled by a single cry: 'It had been merely a voice. There was nothing to connect it with. No picture of any sort came to interpret it, to make it intelligible to the mind' (*SF*: 229). With an ABA pattern, and death at its centre, the three pictures recall the format of *To the Lighthouse*. It is worth recalling that, in the last section of the novel, Lily is explicitly working on a *different* painting than she was during the first, even though both belong to the same larger project. The tripartite structure of the painting, that is, might echo what we imagine Lily's final painting looks like, but (less obviously) might also suggest a sequence of three pictures. As in 'Three Pictures', the central portion, with its theme of death and loss, addresses the limits of representation. (It is relatively easy to imagine a painting with the title 'The Window' or 'The Lighthouse', much harder to visualise one called 'Time Passes.') The last section of the novel presents Lily as a more isolated figure than the first, but there are perhaps also reasons for being more optimistic about the fate of her paintings. If one recalls the novel's approximate timeframe, it is perhaps significant that 'The Window' seems to be set just before the first Post-Impressionist exhibition occurs; in the final section, Lily still fears that her work is a failure, that it might be hung in an attic, rather than, say, a museum or a gallery, but the aesthetic climate has also changed. Thanks to Fry's exhibitions, it can be assumed that an educated figure, someone like William Bankes, would now be at least somewhat familiar with the premises of Lily's approach. There is, that is, no reason for believing that Lily has compromised her art, but at least some cause for hoping that the world might now be more open to receiving it.

'Faces and Voices', a collaborative project that Woolf and Vanessa Bell undertook, would have also evoked a gallery hang had it been completed. It was to be a 'book of illustrated incidents', featuring Woolf's prose and '12 lithographs' by Bell (*D5*: 58). What survives of Woolf's contribution to the project – a series of short sketches – has been reconstructed by Susan Dick. The intention was probably to pair Woolf's character sketches, her 'voices', with Bell's illustrations, or 'faces'. In a diary entry dating from February 1937, Woolf mentions writing '3 descriptions for Nessa's pictures' (*D5*: 57) and these would have mobilised text-and-image relationships to suggest a series of portraits and (perhaps) figure studies, a gallery of images 'animated' in various ways by Woolf's prose. The portrait gallery returns us to Woolf's longer fiction, and to *Orlando*, a work that also reproduces a series of portraits in its pages. Woolf makes no attempt to align these images with the structure of the novel in any systematic way, but nevertheless the sense of an updated ancestral portrait gallery permeates the work. Writing about visiting Knole, Woolf's descriptions of Vita Sackville-West's sense of the past might double as a description of walking along the Brown Gallery at Knole: 'but a crowd of people stood behind, not dead at all; not remarkable; fair faced, long limbed; affable; & so we reach the days of Elizabeth quite easily' (*D3*: 125). The ancestral portrait gallery presents (makes visible) those common elements that produce a sense of family character and become evident through their repeated appearance in specific portraits. They appear in both sexes, and (crucially) survive by being passed on from generation to generation. Thus many of the innovative aspects of Woolf's novel can be found in the more conservative form of the ancestral portrait gallery: the assertion of a connection between face and place, the idea of temporal persistence and simultaneity, and the creation of an identity that exceeds binary gender categories. The reader is left uncertain as to the nature of the relationship between text and image. Do the images illustrate the text, as their placement within it might indicate? Or, since this is notionally a 'history' of Orlando, and most of the images clearly predate the book, is the narrator playing the role of tour guide and giving us the story behind this odd portrait gallery?

This returns us to the NG's mosaic, *The Awakening of the Muses*. Boris Anrep may, after all, have drawn his ideas not merely from Raphael but also from the anachronistic and witty spirit of *Orlando*, which was the most recently published of Woolf's novels when Anrep began planning the work. As the daughter of the editor of the *DNB*, as someone concerned with literary history, and as the creator and biographer of Orlando, Woolf makes a credible candidate for Clio. She had, moreover, also used similar types of doubling devices in *Orlando*, where the same figure could take on multiple identities; Orlando's chief double identities are as a man/woman and, for those in the know, as an alter ego for an actual person, Vita Sackville-West. The queer erotics of Woolf's writing (nowhere more conspicuous than in *Orlando*) might also shape how we choose to read Clio's body language in the mosaics – specifically, the way she touches Thalia, the muse of comedy (bearing the features of Lesley Jowitt[6]). This chimes nicely with the mood of Orlando, where history and comedy certainly meet. Of all the nine muses in the mosaic, only these two are in unambiguous contact with one another: Thalia, shaking off stiffness, stretches her arms out above her head. The pose serves to underline the idea of waking up, while also visually stressing the figure's breasts, which fall, so to speak, just above Clio's helping hand.

Woolf strongly disliked the work – or at least, took exception to her appearance within it. Although she had agreed to her inclusion in the mosaic in 1930 (*L4*: 170) and must have known that Anrep had reasons for selecting her likeness, she still seems to have been surprised by how recognisable she was in the final work. As her fame grew, she had been attempting to assert control over the production and circulation of her own image. 'I preach anonymity to you', she told Ethel Smyth:

> and then have my portrait in mosaics in the Nat. Gall. Yes: but my stipulation was that I was to be Clio: not V.W. Its not my fault if Anrep from motives of his own gives all the names to the papers. (*L5*: 200)

But perhaps Woolf was also uneasy about the Anrep's use of allegorical and literal levels of meaning, which refuse to stay entirely separate and compete with one another in potentially awkward ways. It was one thing to read this part of the image as merely Clio touching Thalia, or history reaching for comedy, but quite another to encounter a potentially 'Sapphic' allusion to oneself in such a prominent location. To make matters worse, Woolf knew that she could scarcely avoid encountering the work on her visits to the NG.

Woolf's relationship to art galleries and museums was, then, remarkably rich, varied, and layered. She visited these spaces as someone interested in art, as a writer of criticism and fiction, as a friend and relative of artists, and as someone who could even expect, every now and then, to find her own likeness before her. These various roles often overlapped and once coalesced almost completely. In early March 1934, Woolf attended an exhibition, 'Recent Paintings by Vanessa Bell', at the Lefevre Gallery; it was, she told Quentin Bell, 'a great occasion – Nessa's private view' (*L5*: 281). While there, Woolf would have socialised with friends, probably congratulated her sister, and possibly looked at the printed copy of the exhibition catalogue, for which she had written the brief foreword. As she occupied the gallery space, one of the paintings may have exerted an especially strong presence in her consciousness – perhaps causing her to look at it more closely, to avoid it altogether, or even (if she was in the mood to entertain) to pose before it.

Another Virginia Woolf, a painted version, was already occupying the space when the real one entered. For forty-five guineas, a visitor could have laid claim to this portrait, a rather formal image of Woolf sitting in an armchair, smoking, and surrounded by books – books on shelves and, as though to accommodate the overflow, piles of books stacked on a pair of side tables. Through her foreword, Woolf now supplied a voice to accompany the face she had provided when posing for the work just a few months earlier.

> [W]ith an infinitude of varied touches [the voice says] the finished picture came into being. For us the experience has its excitement too. A meaning is given to familiar things that makes them strange. Not a word sounds and yet the room is full of conversations (Woolf 1934).

And then, eventually, Woolf's own words near their conclusion. The foreword's penultimate sentence provides us with a final glimpse at Bell's 'world of glowing serenity and sober truth'. But this is not enough and at the end we must also grasp what the gallery is not: 'Compare it, for example, with Piccadilly Circus or St. James's Square' (Woolf 1934).

Notes

1. On Woolf and the morganatic marriage, see Goldman (2001: 41–4). Typically in a morganatic marriage, the male is of higher status than the female – a pattern inverted in the unlikely combination of Queen Elizabeth and the Duke of Wellington.
2. In a 1938 letter to Vita Sackville-West, Woolf wrote: 'But what does it mean? autograph collecting? Something sexual, like the dukes Hat I expect' (*L6*: 231).
3. Woolf is perhaps recalling Tennyson's 'Ode to Wellington': 'No more in soldier fashion will he greet / With lifted hand the gazer in the street.'
4. 'Of the regular Academy subject-pictures', wrote the reviewer for *The Times*, 'the kind of picture that asks a question or gives a moment in a drama which the spectator can complete as he will, there are very few' (*The Times*, 5 May 1919: 18).
5. The 1910 show had also included Cézannes, as indeed had the Durand-Ruel's 1905 show (though few paid them much attention to them then).
6. The wife of Sir William Jowitt, Lesley Jowitt was a prominent society figure, an acquaintance of the Woolfs, and a patron of the arts; in 1922, the Jowitts had commissioned Anrep to make a floor mosaic for their Mayfair residence.

Works Cited

Goldman, Jane (2001) *The Feminist Aesthetics of Virginia Woolf: Modernism, Post-Impressionism and the Politics of the Visual*, Cambridge: Cambridge University Press.

Gordon, Jan (1919) 'The Royal Academy. I', *The Athenaeum*, 9 May: 306–7.

Holmes, Charles (1914) *National Portrait Gallery, Historical and Descriptive Catalogue, 15th Edition*, London: Darling and Son.

The Athenaeum (1919) 'A Modern Prophet', 9 May: 293–4.

The Times (1919) 'The Royal Academy. A First Notice' 3 May: 15d.

The Times (1919) 'Royal Academy Banquet', 5 May: 17b.

The Times (1919) 'The Royal Academy. II. – Types of Subject Pictures', 5 May: 18b.

The Times (1919) 'Gift of National War Portraits', 8 August: 13c.

The Times (1933) 'Matisse and Picasso', 2 November: 10b.

The Times (1933) 'The London Group at the New Burlington Galleries', 14 November: 12d.

Woolf, Virginia (1934) *Catalogue of Recent Paintings by Vanessa Bell*, London: The Lefevre Gallery (unpaginated).

—— (1992) *Walter Sickert: A Conversation*, London: The Bloomsbury Workshop.

—— (1995) 'A Review by Virginia Woolf of Roger Fry's *Vision and Design*', in Diane Gillespie (ed.), *Roger Fry. A Biography*, Oxford: Blackwell Publishing, pp. 81–3.

Further Reading

Fletcher, Pamela M. (2003) *Narrating Modernity: The British Problem Picture, 1895–1914*, Aldershot: Ashgate Publishing.

Fry, Roger (1920) *Vision and Design*, London: Chatto and Windus.

Gillespie, Diane Filby (1988) *The Sisters' Arts: The Writing and Painting of Virginia Woolf and Vanessa Bell*, Syracuse, NY: Syracuse University Press.

Harvey, Benjamin (2007) 'Borderline Personalities: Woolf Reviews Kapp', in Anna Burrells, Steve Ellis, Deborah Parsons and Kathryn Simpson (eds), *Woolfian Boundaries: Selected Papers from the Sixteenth Annual Conference*, Clemson, SC: Clemson University Digital Press, pp. 127–37.

Humm, Maggie (2003) *Modernist Women and Visual Cultures: Virginia Woolf, Vanessa Bell, Photography and Cinema*, New Brunswick, NJ: Rutgers University Press.

Oliver, Lois (2004) *The National Gallery Mosaics*, New Haven, CT: Yale University Press.

Reed, Christopher (2004) *Bloomsbury Rooms: Modernism, Subculture, and Domesticity*, New Haven, CT: Yale University Press

Roe, Sue (2000) 'The Impact of Post-Impressionism', in Sue Roe and Susan Sellers (eds), *The Cambridge Companion to Virginia Woolf*, Cambridge: Cambridge University Press, pp. 164–90.

Saumarez Smith, Charles (1995) 'A Question of Fame: Virginia Woolf and the National Portrait Gallery', in *The Charleston Magazine: Charleston, Bloomsbury and the Arts*, 12: 5–9.

9

VIRGINIA WOOLF AND PORTRAITURE

Elizabeth Hirsh

WOOLF GREW UP in a world filled with portraits, and her engagement with the practices of visual portraiture continued throughout life and even after death: Brenda Silver documents how the production of the original Historical Products, Inc. Virginia Woolf T-shirt in 1973, more than thirty years after Woolf's appearance on the cover of *Time* magazine, helped initiate a boom in the dissemination of her image that sealed her status as cultural icon and made her one of the most famous portrait subjects ever. During her lifetime, Jane Garrity argues, Woolf was implicated in the culture of celebrity and the logic of commodity exchange through the images of her that appeared in British *Vogue* as well as her literary contributions to the magazine. Shaped in childhood by the ancestral gaze emanating from portraits at Hyde Park Gate, Woolf was, too, an inveterate domestic photographer who snapped more than 1,000 informal portraits and, as Maggie Humm notes, belonged to 'the first generation of women to be active photographers and cinema goers from childhood' (Humm 2003: 28).

As a student and critic of portraiture Woolf's affinities sometimes align with 'high modernism', as in Diane Filby Gillespie's analogy between Vanessa Bell's featureless portraits and Woolf's fictional efforts to capture an unchanging essence of individuals or human communities. Lily Briscoe's avant-garde portrait of Mrs Ramsay as a purple triangle – making 'no attempt at likeness' (*TTL*: 52) as Lily must explain to a bemused Mr Bankes in *To the Lighthouse* (1927) – might stand as an emblem of this affinity. But in *Orlando* (1928) and *Three Guineas* (1938) Woolf's deployment of the conventions of portraiture seems to have more in common with Cindy Sherman than Vanessa Bell, exploiting the resources of mechanical reproduction not to fix identities but to expose their fictive nature. Nonetheless, Woolf valued the documentary function of portraits. In 1929 she thanked William Rothenstein for drawings of her parents he'd sent, writing, 'I have the ordinary persons [sic] love of a likeness and desire to be reminded by portraits of real people . . . . I am very glad to have these records of them' (*L4*: 6–7). The Victorian persistence in Woolf, examined in recent studies by Steve Ellis and Jane de Gay, sometimes emerges in this context. In 1920 she was stricken with remorse at having sold a painting of her great, 'Uncle Thoby' [Prinsep] done by the arch patriarch of Victorian portraiture, G. F. Watts (RA) – the epitome of everything 'Bloomsbury' supposedly despised. '[D]irectly I got the cheque I regretted it', Woolf confesses (*D2*: 21).

Regarding portraits, then, as in other ways, Woolf may seem modernist, postmodern, or late Victorian depending upon one's point of entry. Gillespie's 1988 study of Woolf and Vanessa Bell explored connections between the visual and verbal portraits created by the sisters. Concerning the analogy between portraiture and biography, Gillespie notes that both preferred to be free from the mimetic obligations imposed by commissioned portraits and authorised biographies (such as Woolf's biography of Roger Fry) in order to experiment with various strategies of representation. As portraitists, they shared an interest in everyday subjects and ordinary experience. The play of speech, silence and image is important to both and acts to maintain a strategic distance between subject and audience in their portraits: Bell paints conversations we can't hear, while Woolf tries to write silence into her novels, and insists in her 1925 essay 'Pictures' that painted portraits 'must not attempt to speak' (*E4*: 246). Gillespie shows how the frequent use of portraits as signifiers in the text of Woolf's fiction serves to evoke the cultural environment within which character unfolds, while Bell's several portraits of her sister parallel Woolf's brief 1908 life of Bell as well as the fictional figures she inspired, notably Helen Ambrose and Katharine Hilbery (but apparently not Lily Briscoe).

Recent developments in Cultural Studies, Postcolonial Studies and Queer Studies direct attention to the public function of portraiture, its status as a site for the (re)production of national and imperial as well as personal and familial identities. More accurately, such perspectives foreground Woolf's character-istic interest in the ways that portraiture, as a cultural practice intimately linked to biography and history writing, both produced and traversed the distinction between public and private. This double effect proceeds from the interface of portrait painting and portrait photography as well as the chang-ing aesthetics of portraiture during Woolf's lifetime, but also from the various practices of display and consumption associated with portraiture, including the mass production and marketing of portraits, the practice of keeping family photo albums, the development of a museum culture within which historical portraiture flourished, and the emergence of a contested heritage movement that fostered public access to the portrait galleries in the country homes of the landed elite.

Modernising Portraits

Woolf spins her version of 'Bloomsbury', a myth of modernisation as liberation, by invoking the names of portraitists. All three memoirs we have by Woolf register the prominence of Watts's portraits in what Woolf calls 'the cage' at Hyde Park Gate (*MOB*: 116). 'A Sketch of the Past' mentions portraits of

Julia Duckworth Stephen, Leslie Stephen and Minny Thackeray, recalling Julia's reverential view of 'the great painter' and the way Leslie would 'lead admiring ladies' up to the portrait of himself by Watts in the front drawing room – despite the fact he'd once been told 'it makes me look like a weasel' (ibid.: 117–18). 'Old Bloomsbury' recounts how at 46 Gordon Square, in a first stage of Bloomsbury's self-modernisation, 'the Sargent-Furse era' cast out 'the Watts-Venetian tradition of red plush and black paint' (ibid.: 185), suggesting a familiar narrative of modernisation as movement away from the public and ceremonial toward more fluid, informal styles such as Sargent's impressionism. Full modernisation, following Vanessa's marriage to Clive Bell, is signalled by the neo-heroic style of Augustus John's portrait of his young son, Pyramus. Woolf writes,

> The drawing room had greatly changed its character since 1904. The Sargent-Furse age was over. The age of Augustus John was dawning. His 'Pyramus' filled one entire wall. The Watts' portraits of my father and my mother were hung downstairs if they were hung at all. (*MOB*: 195)

That in 1908 the name of Watts should stand for all things benighted, out-moded and *past* is a kind of family joke, for of course Watts had close ties to Julia Stephen's family and his childlike grandiosity is cheerfully travestied in *Freshwater*. In their youth Virginia and Vanessa held it a point of honour to have outgrown Watts: thus in 1897 Virginia's teenage diary respectfully records visits with 'Mr.Watts' and with 'Mr and Mrs Watts' (*PA*: 50, 49), as well as a trip to 'the New Gallery where Mr Watts is exhibiting his pictures' (ibid.: 16), but by January 1905, less than a year after Watts's death, the tone shifts to one of unalloyed disdain:

> Today, I think N[essa] & I went to the Academy Watts exhibition which is weak & worthless – almost incredibly so, considering his reputation. Not a single first rate picture there, & many 5th rate. His 'ideas' here swamped his art. (*PA*: 218)

Such post-Victorian posturing is itself ironized in 'Old Bloomsbury', however, and still later, when Woolf writes her life of Roger Fry, she repeatedly regis-ters Fry's respect for Watts. '[F]or the work of one living Academician at least he expressed again and again the highest admiration', she observes. 'Watts's portraits of Joachim, Garibaldi and the Countess Somers he said "take rank with the finest achievements of English art for all times"' (*RF*: 107). Fry placed Watts within the same anti-naturalist tradition as Picasso, and 'would explain that it was quite easy to make the transition from Watts to Picasso; there was no break, only a continuation' (ibid.: 152). Woolf quotes a commentary by Fry in which the modernising trajectory that in 'Old Bloomsbury' moves from Watts through Sargent to John is instead construed as a later generation's return to draughtsmanship and formalist values. '[T]he younger men, really going back to an earlier tradition, carry the analysis [of appearances] further, penetrating through values to their causes in actual form and structure', Fry wrote. 'Mr. John . . . has arrived already at a control of his medium which astonishes . . . . One must go back to Alfred Stevens or Etty or the youthful Watts to find its like (ibid.: 114). Similarly, Fry's Introduction to *Victorian Photographs of Famous Men and Fair Women* (1926), the Hogarth Press volume of portraits by Julia Margaret Cameron, finds Cameron's work inferior to that of her mentor Watts even while embracing photography's claims as art. In the Fry biography Woolf takes care to distinguish her perspective from that of her subject, but Fry's respect for Watts was clearly something she weighed.

Woolf registered Watts's impact in part through Cameron, whose efforts to elevate 'photographic portraiture' to the status of an art were inspired, as Fry observed, by Watts and the pre-Raphaelites. Woolf's own introduction to *Famous Men and Fair Women* quotes Mary Watts's biography of her husband to describe Cameron's approach: "'her object [was] to overcome realism by diminishing just in the least degree the precision of the focus'" (*E4*: 382). Watts famously insisted that a portrait 'should have in it something of the monumental; it is a summary of the life of a person, not the record of accidental position or arrangement of light and shadow' (quoted in Piper 1992: 227); Cameron's laboriously posed photographs accordingly sought to suppress the casual and 'accidental' qualities of photography. Indeed Woolf notes with amusement,

> She cared nothing for the miseries of her sitters nor for their rank. The carpenter and the Crown Prince of Prussia alike must sit as still as stones in the attitudes she chose, in the draperies she arranged, for as long as she wished. (*E4*: 382)

In *Freshwater* Cameron's devotion to art and indifference to her sitters' pain parallels Watts's obtuseness vis-à-vis his child bride and model Ellen Terry. ('Stiff, Ellen? Why you've only kept that pose for four hours this morning' [*FW*: 10]). In the Victorian marketplace the accidental effects attendant on photographic process could be compounded by the randomness associated with the display of mass produced portraits. Cameron's practice of placing her camera 'out of focus' derived from her photographic mentor David Wilkie Wynfield, and Joanne Lukitsh shows that during the 1860s Wynfield and Cameron were both widely praised for elevating photographic portraiture above what one reviewer termed the 'vulgar, leveling and literal' practices of commercial photography, especially as embodied in the mid-century craze for the *carte de visite* portrait (Lukitsh 1992: 215). *Cartes* were mass-produced and marketed in the shop windows of urban streets with other commodities, often in 'purely casual' arrangements where, to the distress of some commentators, aristocrats and cardinals were juxtaposed willy-nilly with prizefighters and fashion plates (ibid.). Cameron's compositions instead implied the artist's mastery of received aesthetic and social codes as well as her personal proximity to eminent subjects, advertising their status as non-commissioned works of art outside the market-place. Woolf's emphasis on her great aunt's uncompromising attitude toward her sitters, both 'high' and 'low', underscores Cameron's artistic autonomy as well as her commanding personality.

Before the invention of photography, royals and aristocrats made up the majority of portrait subjects, and while portraitists might be sullied by their association with trade, they could also assume some of their sitters' prestige. Portraiture implies a certain intimacy of subject and artist but, in many senses, this relation is mediated by the social field as such. Following Hans-Georg Gadamer, Richard Brilliant situates portraiture's specificity in the artist's intention to portray someone, 'an individual human being, actually existing outside the work', whether or not the viewer recognises that intention. The relationship between the portrait and its object of representation 'directly reflects the social dimension of human life as a field of action among persons', Brilliant writes. Because portraiture entails 'the representation of the structuring of human relationships going back to the earliest stages of life', it depends ultimately on 'the primary experience of the infant . . . gazing up at its mother' (Brilliant 1991: 8–9) and the dialectic of recognition that founds the child's psycho-social development. (Lacan's Mirror Stage theory, in which subjectivity initially takes shape in the infant's misidentification with the reflection or image of the (M) other, seems to be implied.)

Maggie Humm's post-Lacanian study of the 'unconscious optics' at work in the photo albums created by Virginia and Leonard Woolf and by Vanessa Bell interprets their psychodynamics with reference to domestic photography and Stephen family history. Humm reads the albums as culturally marginal, distinctively modernist sites for the psychic and aesthetic reconstruction of fragmentary maternal memories. Photography was central to modernity's destruction of 'classical vision'; snapshot photography especially tended to defy pictorial conventions and encourage 'active participation in the construction of memory' (Humm 2003: 23). The Woolfs assembled their albums into sequences marked by repetition, the over-representation of certain domestic elements, and a preference for contiguity over chronology, suggesting overall 'a past which haunts the present rather than a past which precedes the present' (ibid.: 57). Collectively the albums constitute a 'contrary cultural formation' in which a female Imaginary achieves a kind of borderline visibility in the symbolic. Humm finds that Woolf's eight miniature fictions, 'Portraits', probably part of an unrealised collaboration with Vanessa Bell, stage an array of 'gendered gazes shaped by a photographic syntax' (ibid.: 28). Humm's reading of *Three Guineas* foregrounds the tension between the photographic portraits that Woolf includes in her text and the Spanish Civil War propaganda photos she refers to but does not reproduce: silently contesting the heroicised public history of the former, the 'implied' war photos evoke an alternative form of history comparable to Pierre Nora's idea of memory inherent in bodily reflexes and affectively charged images.

Portraiture, Biography, History

The 'search for diversity in history writing is a constant theme' of Woolf's career, as is the centrality of family memories in our histories and identities (Humm 2003: 207). Woolf's recourse to the names of portraitists in her history of Bloomsbury reflects an awareness of portraiture's capacity to articulate the public space of history and the intimate space of home – a capacity much apparent during Victoria's long reign, whose final decades overlap Woolf's youth. During this period family photo albums were proliferating in middle-class homes across Europe, creating what Roger Hargreaves terms a 'new visual genealogy' associated with the image of the royal family. 'The established tradition of recording the births, deaths and marriages of successive generations on the fly leaf of the family Bible evolved into the family photographic album', Hargreaves writes.

> This new visual genealogy was designed for posterity and functioned as a cherished heirloom to be handed down through the generations. In Britain at least the royal family found their way into the opening pages as the model for an idealised family structure that embodied tradition and continuity, those twin virtues of ancestry. (Hargreaves 2001: 46)

Avoided by Bell and the Woolfs, this Victorian visual genealogy pervades Leslie Stephen's photo album, whose images inform his sentimental memoir of Julia Stephen, the *Mausoleum Book*, as well as the memories encoded in *To the Lighthouse* (Kukil 2003). The Victorian nationalisation of British culture through state subsidies, meanwhile, underwrote the creation of institutions like the National Portrait Gallery (NPG), founded in 1856 and sometimes called 'the national album'. In mid-Victorian society, as Lara Perry writes, 'The royal family as a family, and not just a dynasty, was central to the conception of its role at the heart or centre of the nation' (Perry 2006: 35).

Woolf's dealings with the NPG began early. She visited the Gallery at age fifteen, finding the experience 'rather dull', according to her diary. 'We spent our time in yawning', she writes, referring presumably to her siblings Stella, Vanessa, Thoby and Adrian, and not to Leslie Stephen, all of whom were included in the party (*PA*: 16). The visit was probably occasioned by the Gallery's recent move from working class Bethnal Green to its new and improved venue in the heart of the imperial capital, Trafalgar Square. More than thirty years later, Woolf still found the NPG tiresome: she reports to Vanessa Bell in June of 1929 that she has been to see 'cadavers in the National Portrait Gallery' after finding the Leicester Gallery closed and the National Gallery spoiled by the intrusive presence of Clive Bell (*L4*: 69). Still later, in February of 1934, the 52-year-old Woolf refuses the NPG's offer to draw her, complaining to Quentin Bell that 'they keep the drawing in a cellar, and when I've been dead ten years they have it out and say Does anyone want to know what Mrs Woolf looked like? No, say all the others. Then its [sic] torn up. So why should I defile a whole day by sitting?' (*L5*: 277).

Woolf had been asked to sit in connection with a scheme for a Contemporary Portraits Collection. Under the Gallery's so-called ten-year rule (which ended in 1969) subjects could only be admitted to the collection ten years after their death, a policy designed, Charles Saumarez Smith indicates, to ensure that they were really famous and not just notorious. A portrait so commissioned was thus to be 'kept in a cellar' until ten years after the sitter's death and only then considered for acceptance. The Trustees agreed that a woman – one woman – should be included but were hard-pressed to identify a candidate. '[A]mong writers, nobody I fancy could survive our ten year rule', Lord Crawford wrote, 'unless it be Elinor Glyn' (quoted in Saumarez Smith 1995: 6). The historian G. M. Trevelyan reluctantly suggested half a dozen women ('all the real ones seem to have departed with the enfranchisement of their sex', he opined), and so Woolf's name emerged. In declining the Gallery's offer she wrote to the chairman of the Trustees, 'I feel that a drawing done by a stranger in one or two sittings would be far less satisfactory as a likeness, if one were wanted, than the photographs which are already in existence' (quoted ibid.: 7).[1] At the time of Woolf's death in 1941 Francis Dodd offered the NPG his Medusaesque drawing of Virginia Stephen, but this was refused: 'I think in the case of this lady her portrait might wait ten years', the trustee Dean Inge wrote (ibid.: 7) – a comment that may reflect contemporaneous sentiment that Woolf's suicide during wartime was somehow unpatriotic as much as the decline in her literary reputation. However, the Dodd drawing was acquired in 1951, and in 1953 a cast of Stephen Tomlin's portrait bust, whose unfinished state, according to David Garnett, resulted from Woolf's having left during the sitting on account of her 'morbidly sensitive, or vain' dislike to sitting (ibid.: 7).

Though refusing to serve the NPG as token, Woolf recognised the potential portraiture held to animate the past as well as embalm it. She composed a miniature biography for a 1931 postcard depicting George Eliot as part of a series the Gallery sponsored engaging contemporary writers (Saumarez Smith 1995: 5). And her 1920 review of a book of caricatures by Edmund X. Kapp recalls an abortive visit to the NPG during the War at a time when – as she reported to Vanessa Bell in July 1918 – she found the Gallery shut 'save to the widows of officers' (L2: 259, 951). Apparently she'd gone in search of a portrait of Harriet Taylor, for she writes:

> It needs an effort, but scarcely a great one, to enter the National Portrait Gallery. Sometimes indeed an urgent desire to identify one among the dead sends us post haste to its portals. The case we have in mind is of Mrs John Stuart Mill. Never was there such a paragon among women. Noble, magnanimous, inspired, thinker, reformer, saint, she possessed every gift and every virtue. One thing alone she lacked, and that, no doubt, the National Portrait Gallery could supply. She had no face. But the National Portrait Gallery, interrogated, wished to be satisfied that the inquirer was dependent upon a soldier; pensions they provided, not portraits; and thus

set adrift in Trafalgar Square once more the student might reflect upon the paramount importance of faces. Without a face Mrs John Stuart Mill was without a soul. Had her husband spared three lines of eulogy to describe her personal appearance we should hold her in memory. Without eyes or hair, cheeks or lips, her stupendous genius, her consummate virtue, availed her nothing. She is a mist, a wraith, a miasma of anonymous merit. The face is the thing. (*E2*: 164)

The sentiment here isn't far from those that inspired the founding of the NPG, a wedding of portraiture, biography and history. Since antiquity portraiture and biography had been linked; in eighteenth- and-nineteenth century England they were linked both by learned analogy, as Richard Wendorf shows, and in popular practices like the circulation of portraits with brief biographies in the illustrated London press (Barlow 1997: 222) and the 'Grangerising' of books, in which the cut-out heads of eminent subjects were pasted into biographical works – so called after Rev. James Granger, compiler of a well-known biographical dictionary (Pointon 1993: 228). Both arts were considered particularly English. Benjamin Robert Haydon (who preferred history painting) commented in 1817 that 'Portraiture is . . . one of the staple manufactures of the empire. Wherever the British settle, wherever they colonise, they carry and will ever carry trial by jury, horseracing, and portrait-painting' (quoted in Nuding 1992: 238). Another reluctant portraitist, William Hogarth, lamented that 'Portrait-painting ever has, and ever will, succeed better in this country than any other' (quoted in Vaughan 1999: 38). It was largely through the huge success of portraitists like Hogarth, Romney, Gainsborough, and especially Reynolds, that a 'British School' of painting finally emerged in the eighteenth century, fuelling and fuelled by the national stereotype of a pragmatic race with a special aptitude for the arts of observation. Throughout the nineteenth century, 'the affinity for portraits was interpreted as a British (or English) preference for empirical exactness over what was construed as a continental propensity for idealization or ornamentation' (Perry 2006: 22). Harold Nicolson invoked essentially the same stereotype when he claimed in *The Development of English Biography* (1928) that 'the Anglo-Saxon mind is best when proceeding inductively' (Nicolson 1959: 110).

In mid-Victorian days the celebrity historian Thomas Carlyle did more than anyone to identify portraiture with biography and biography with history, providing a brief for the NPG. Carlyle's lectures on 'Heroes and Hero Worship' expounded the view that the biographies of Great Men epitomised the spirit of an age. Commending portraiture as a complement to historical biography, Carlyle announced with characteristic reticence, 'Painting is worthless, except portrait painting' (quoted in Piper 1992: 218). When in 1856 the historian Lord Stanhope made his proposal for a 'British Historical Portrait Gallery' to the House of Lords, he quoted a letter written by Carlyle:

[I]n all my poor Historical investigations it has been, and always is, one of the most primary wants to procure a bodily likeness of the personage inquired after; a good *Portrait* if such exists; failing that, even an indifferent if sincere one. In short, *any* representation, made by a faithful human creature, of that Face and Figure, which *he* saw with his eyes, and which I can never see with mine, is now valuable to me . . . every student and reader of History, who strives earnestly to conceive for himself what manner of Fact and *Man* this or the other vague Historical *Name* can have been, as the first and directest indication of all, search eagerly for a Portrait . . . . Often have I found a Portrait superior in real instruction to half-a-dozen written 'Biographies', as Biographies are written; or rather, let me say I have found that the portrait was a small lighted *candle* by which Biographies could for the first time be *read*. (quoted in Saumarez Smith 1997: 11–12).

We know how completely Woolf rejected the Great Man view of history, but that rejection doesn't exhaust her relation to Carlyle, whom she devoured in adolescence and reread in adulthood. Her assertion in 1920 that 'the face is the thing' that allows us to encounter Harriet Taylor and 'hold her in memory' as a historical subject echoes Carlyle's precept that serious students of history must seek out portraits. Informing Woolf's continued interest in Carlyle was her awareness of the encounter between belletristic and 'scientific,' and between amateur and professional, styles of history writing, which preoccupied English historians for the first thirty years of her life. Leslie Stephen defended biography's claims as a species of historiography, which he knew were being damaged by the importation of 'scientific' history from Germany. In his capacity as the first editor of the *Dictionary of National Biography* (*DNB*) – another monument of Victorian national culture – Stephen served the NPG as trustee. But, unlike the older Carlyle, he neither embraced Great Man history nor repudiated the new professional ideal. His daughter's historiographical allegiances were still more complex. Woolf's fascination with biography, and her recognition of the DNB's inadequacies, are well known. I argue elsewhere that she explored biography specifically as a form of experimental *historiography*, one that could resist the increasing prestige of professional history without either rejecting science as such or reverting to belletristic complacencies. Woolf's interest in portraiture, like her interest in biography, was integral to an evolving awareness of the problematics of history writing in general and of British history in particular.

As the letter quoted by Stanhope indicates, for Carlyle historical portraiture went beyond illustration, positing what Paul Barlow calls a 'direct material contact' between the moment of the sitter and that of the viewer, made possible by the kind of eye-witness registration that could be captured only by the 'faithful' or 'sincere' portraitist. In the tradition of romantic historiography, the theory of authentic portraiture privileged empathy above knowledge: 'it was not "scientific" history but an attempt to restore a lost form of experience – to make the past present' (Barlow 1997: 226). As a principle informing the NPG, 'authenticity' mandated that the selection committee couldn't commission copies of known portraits but had to rely primarily on existing originals – although portrait copies created during the lifetime of the sitter were allowed (Perry 2006: 163). Closely allied to Carlyle's vision were Watts's efforts to reinvent portraiture as a modern form of history painting that could preserve 'the character of a nation as a people of great deeds', as Watts wrote to *The Times* in 1887 (*Victorian Portraits* 1996: 4). Stanhope claimed that a National Portrait Gallery would be an improvement on the historical galleries of Versailles, which he said were full of 'tawdry battle scenes' and 'court pageants' (quoted in Perry 2006: 23); thus between 1850 and his death in 1904 Watts dutifully crafted an ambitious series of portraits depicting his most eminent contemporaries, which he christened 'the Hall of Fame' and bequeathed to the NPG.

Compared to many van Dyck-style portraits of the eighteenth century, Watts's approach was intimate even in its monumentality, eschewing accessories, antique dress and stylish studio poses in order to focus attention sharply on the subject's head and face, usually outlined against a sombre, unspecified background; J. E. Millais and other Victorians cultivated a similar portrait style. Joanna Woodall argues that nineteenth-century portraiture apotheosised a non-noble elite by reconciling 'a convincing characterisation of the sitter's socio-political position with depiction of the essential inner quality which was considered to justify his privileged place' (Woodall 1997: 5). For Woodall the emphasis on inner merits constitutes not a radical break with the past but a new kind of nobility reliant, like the old aristocracy of 'blood', on 'notions of exemplary virtue'. She observes, '[f]rom their beginning in the later [fifteenth] century, collections of exemplary portraits included both members of the heredity nobility and the non-noble elites which ultimately became identified as bourgeois' (ibid.: 15). This context helps to explain why in late Victorian England a Watts portrait could seem equally 'at home' hanging in the NPG and in the front drawing room at Hyde Park Gate.

Carlyle's modest house in Cheyne Row was (and is) chock-a-block with portraits, as shown in 'The Back Drawing Room', a watercolour made by Helen Allingham soon after his death (Figure 9.1). Depicted on the right side of Allingham's picture is a moveable screen covered with portraits that was decorated by Jane Welsh Carlyle in 1849 (*Carlyle's House* 1979: 27) and that the irascible biographer carried with him like a kind of fetish when he moved his study from room to room in search of quiet. Virginia Stephen visited Cheyne Row in 1909, about a month before reviewing a new edition of the Carlyles' letters, and closely scrutinised the portraits of Jane Welsh Carlyle she found there. Her brief sketch describing the visit comments at length on Mrs Carlyle's face, discerning evidence of her famously unhappy marriage and thwarted intellect:

> Her eyes droop in the pictures, and have a peculiar expression, of humour and melancholy lying dormant, which produces this quizzical look that I speak of; at any moment they might flash with passion, or kindle into tenderness. I think that in her life the expression must have been one of

Figure 9.1 *The Back Dining Room* (Thomas Carlyle's house) by Helen Allingham, 1881 © NTPL/John Hammond

mockery for the most part, with a background of pathos; an unhappy face in spite of the brilliant eyes; the late photographs, which exaggerate the hollow of the cheeks, and the length of the upper lip, are horrid. The eyes are the only parts with warmth or depth in them: the rest is granulated skin tight stretched over a skull. (Woolf 2003: 3–4)

If at the time of this visit she was unhappily preoccupied with the question of marriage, as David Bradshaw suggests, her response to Mrs Carlyle's face may reflect that anxiety. In fact, she may have glimpsed her own mother's face in Mrs Carlyle's: an identification encouraged by the *Mausoleum Book*, where her father worries that his treatment of Julia Stephen, like Carlyle's bad behaviour toward Jane Welsh Carlyle, may have hastened her death. The emphasis on Mrs Carlyle's eyes, and the arresting contrast between eyes and skull in the last sentence above, register traces of the absent maternal gaze. Equally striking, Virginia Stephen's extraordinary account of her experience seems to correspond to Carlyle's idea of an *authentic* historical encounter, and may suggest the sort of insight Woolf 'urgently desired' to find in the face of Harriet Taylor – another maternal forebear – when visiting the NPG nine years later. Woolf's struggle to locate the female face in and of history was also always a coming-to-terms with her own familial past.

Portrait Galleries and Country Houses: Reading *Orlando*

Of the book-length works Woolf published in her lifetime, every one makes reference to portraits, usually in a way that bears thematic weight. Four included reproductions of portraits: *Orlando*, *Flush* (1933) (originally with illustrations by Vanessa Bell), *Three Guineas* and *Roger Fry* (1940).[2] Woolf's most sophisticated use of portraits occurs in *Orlando* and *Three Guineas*. Jane Marcus's 2006 introduction to her edition of *Three Guineas* summarises recent work on its five photographs, including Alice Staveley's identification of the subjects as real people Woolf's contemporaries would've recognised. Through effects closely tied to the history of portrait display, *Orlando* insinuates an alternative – that is, a queer – history of England, and by way of conclusion I briefly consider these effects. Far from 'domesticat[ing] . . . an imperialist national history into an individual sexual history' (Hovey 1997: 402), *Orlando* disrupts the canny construction of imperial national history *as* (heteronormative) family history by de-privatising Vita Sackville-West's sex life. Harold Nicolson told his wife the book had 'identified you and Knole forever' (quoted in Glendinning 1983: 205), and a critical commonplace holds that *Orlando* symbolically restores the rightful inheritance that Sackville-West was denied by the patriarchal law of entail. But *Orlando* also forever identifies Knole with Virginia Woolf, installing her as a kind of permanent interloper in the family line whose imaginary integrity Sackville-West took pains to preserve.

Like Woolf – though on a grander scale – Sackville-West grew up surrounded by portraits. Knole's famous Brown Gallery (see Plate 9) houses one of the greatest of the collections of family portraits that began to be assembled in country mansions after Van Dyck's arrival at the court of Charles II in 1632. Such galleries documented a family's rise to power through royal ties and alliances with other powerful families. 'In no other nation have portrait galleries been so pervasive and possessed such historical continuity as in Britain', Gertrude Prescott Nuding writes (Nuding 1992: 238). In the elaboration of Victorian national culture country house galleries furnished the model for the NPG which, unlike the National Gallery, was designed as an intimate space; its first site was in a private home in Westminster (Perry 2000: 148). Country houses were often described as historical palimpsests, and the NPG was similarly conceived as a visible *history* of the nation, arranged in an immediately legible chronological order and inscribed in a common public space. Funded through Parliament, it aggrandised the political institutions of the imperial centre while encouraging a newly enfranchised middle class to identify with the national self-image it projected. Moreover, donations from country-house portrait collections helped to supply the 'authentic' portraits required by the NPG. Thus a real and imaginary traffic between public and private spaces enabled the production of national culture: family portrait galleries held in private houses helped to furnish the nation's portrait gallery, while the latter mimicked the family portrait gallery of a country house, producing the nation as a kind of family, and its history as a family history within which portraits, like children, linked the generations in 'a naturalized hierarchy of likeness' (Woodall 1997: 5). Meanwhile, as the franchise grew, country houses themselves were marketed as the imaginative possession of the public (Mandler 1997: 37), as in Sackville-West's *Knole and the Sackvilles* (1922). Sites like Knole became accessible to middle-class tourists with the spread of railway travel, and in the popular press their images were widely disseminated.

But toward the end of the century the heritage system comprised of private ownership, voluntary beneficence and tax concessions to land owners began to show strain. An incident at Knole in 1884 was symptomatic. When Sackville-West's great-uncle Mortimer inherited Knole in 1876 he closed its doors to tourists, whom he found rowdy and uncouth. Seven years later he barred access to Knole Park even to the residents of the surrounding town of Sevenoaks, who regarded it as a public amenity. The ensuing outcry was widely reported in the London press.

> On the night of 18 June 1884, a crowd of people from Sevenoaks broke down the posts across the entrance and, singing 'Rule Britannia,' marched on the house where they deposited the posts at the main door. The next evening they entered the park again, surrounded the house, smashed a few windows, and shouted abuse at Mortimer before proceeding to the Fawke Gate, at the far end of the park. There they forced the gate open and ceremonially rode back and forth through the entrance. (*Knole* 1998: 87)

Conflicts over rights of access to country houses could focus specifically on their portrait galleries. In 1894 MP Joseph Pease 'objected that his constituents should be taxed extra in order that somebody else might see a collection of pictures which was only to be seen in a private house' (quoted in Mandler 1997: 166). When in 1895, following pressure from Vita Sackville-West's mother, among others, new exemptions were proposed for death duties on heirlooms of 'national or historic interest', MP David Lloyd George tried unsuccessfully to limit the exemption to collections that 'have been accessible during the lifetime of their late possessor to public view and inspection' (quoted ibid.: 168–9). But as Chancellor of the Exchequer under Henry Asquith, England's first non-landed Prime Minister, Lloyd George inaugurated a Land Campaign in 1908 that defined the enclosures of the sixteenth to the nineteenth centuries (through which the great estates were created) as confiscatory. 'Heritage' was now invoked to support not the *preservation* of an imagined cultural inheritance but the *redistribution* of material benefits expropriated from the labouring class. Meanwhile Lady Sackville negotiated the sale of selected Knole heirlooms to J. P. Morgan, using the proceeds to make Knole, as she said privately, 'the most comfortable large house in England, combining the beauties of Hampton Court with the comforts of the Ritz' (quoted ibid.: 169).

Woolf first visited Knole in July 1924 to lunch with Baron Sackville, and her diary records a sense of incongruity surrounding the visit. Remarking upon Knole's enormity and the extravagance of its collections alongside the 'perfection' of Sackville-West's body, Woolf boarded the train back to Bloomsbury 'carrying her & Knole in my eye as I travelled with the lower middle classes, through slums. There is Knole, capable of housing all the desperate poor of Judd Street, & with only that one solitary earl in the kernel' (*D2*: 306, 307). Knole's rightful ownership had been legally contested among the Sackvilles for decades before and during Sackville-West's youth, as Woolf knew. In a lawsuit that attracted 'massive press coverage on both sides of the Atlantic' (*Knole* 1998: 92), Lady Sackville herself – in order to disqualify her brother's claim at the time of their father's death – had been required in 1908 'to avow, openly and emphatically, that she and her siblings were bastards' (Nicolson 1973: 65). While family scandals and secrets had long been part of Knole's history, the publication of *Orlando* provoked a new kind of disquiet among the Sackvilles. Lady Sackville even Grangerised her copy of the book, gluing a newspaper photograph of Woolf on the flyleaf and writing: 'The awful face of a madwoman . . . . I loathe this woman for having changed my Vita and taken her away from me' (quoted in Glendinning 1983: 206). Her sense of dispossession was extreme but not unique. Vita's cousin Eddy felt his *name* had been expropriated in that readers would identify him as the 'Mr S.W.' referred to in Chapter 2. More ominously, his father Charles, who'd just succeeded to ownership of Knole, complained that he had never authorised *Orlando*'s use of portraits from the Knole collection. Woolf wrote letters of apology to both men and showed them to Vita, who replied:

> Yes, of course I mentioned the pictures to Uncle Charlie. I didn't tell him the exact purpose for which they were wanted, because Orlando was then a secret. I just said 'for her new book.' He said 'Of course – naturally – delighted,' and all those things . . .
>
> As for Eddy's own private grievance, it just shows what his egoism is, to think that everybody would immediately associate the initials S.W. with him . . . (DeSalvo and Leaska 1985: 295)

Apparently 'Uncle Charlie' changed his mind about Woolf's use of the portraits when he saw the context in which they were displayed. Their publication in *Orlando* might be read as a kind of family imprimatur, a public endorsement of something he wished, in retrospect, to keep private. Suzanne Raitt observes that 'Sackville-West's lesbianism was exactly the "open secret" of which Eve Kosovsky Sedgwick and others speak' (Raitt 1993: 79). The force of the 'open secret' is 'not to conceal knowledge, so much as to conceal the knowledge of the knowledge', D. A. Miller writes; it doesn't collapse, but rather protects the opposition private/public, preserving 'the sanctity of [the] first term' inviolate

(Miller 1988: 206–7). A lifelong student of biography and memoir, Woolf was well acquainted with the epistemological structure of the open secret and the codes required to protect it. In *Orlando* the encoding of same-sex desire has been taken to reflect the atmosphere of censorship surrounding the 1928 trial of Radclyffe Hall's *The Well of Loneliness*. But the collective discomfort of the Sackvilles suggests that *Orlando*'s deployment of the conventions of biography and portraiture actually roils the structure of the open secret, along with the property interests and heteronormative historiography it served to perpetuate.

Orlando doesn't only publish family portraits from Knole; it also sets these portraits in a sequence with recent photographs of Sackville-West in a way that seems designed – through and despite the effects of masquerade – to underscore Vita's physical resemblance to her ancestors.

Woolf visited Knole to select portraits for *Orlando*, and years later Sackville-West wrote to Woolf that she'd recently discovered 'a portrait of an ancestor of mine who is far more like me than any which we found for *Orlando*!' (DeSalvo and Leaska 1985: 399). The comment indicates that Woolf's selections had been made specifically to capture family likeness. Moreover, by its nature, portrait photography, even more than portrait painting, furnishes the 'real material contact' between sitter, artist and audience that was the hallmark of Carlyle's 'authentic' historical portrait. 'The viewer of [a] photograph is oddly aware of both the photographer's artistry and the subject's reality,' Talia Schaffer notes vis-à-vis *Orlando* (Schaffer 1994: 46). The active participation of Sackville-West required to produce the photographs not only advertises her consent; it also means her face functions in context as a historical document of a particularly compelling kind. 'Biographies and portraits not only record facts and include documents', Wendorf observes, 'they function *as* documents themselves' (Wendorf 1990: 9). 'The face is the thing,' Woolf had written. *What* Vita's face documents, in effect, is at once her place in the Sackville line *and* her love affair with Virginia Woolf.

Orlando makes good Woolf's threat to Sackville-West in a letter concerning her affair with Mary Campbell: 'If you've given yourself to Campbell, I'll have no more to do with you, and so it shall be written, plainly, for all the world to read in *Orlando*' (DeSalvo and Leaska 1985: 241). The offset word, 'plainly', rebuffs Sackville-West's repeated appeals to Woolf for 'discretion' in the conduct of their affair. Vita, the mother of sons, took pains to preserve the open secret, and in consenting to sit for *Orlando*'s portraits actually had no more information than her Uncle Charles about how the images would be used, since Woolf kept the text secret from her until the day of its publication 'for all the world to read' – a gesture that abruptly situates Sackville-West as a member of Woolf's public. Of course, the text of *Orlando* isn't so much plainly written as conspicuously cryptic; in the final chapters, its densely coded quality becomes so exorbitant that – like the strategically deployed portraits – it serves to advertise the machinery of the open secret, not protect it. What the open secret conceals is not knowledge but 'the knowledge of the knowledge'; what *Orlando* reveals is not Sackville-West's lesbianism (which everybody knew about), but the knowledge of this lesbianism – that is, the disavowal of this knowledge. If, as Jaime Hovey argues, Woolf participates in the racism of Orlando and Shelmerdine's coded sexual language about 'kissing a negress in the dark', it's also true that, as a secret love language, *Orlando*'s own codes are strangely dysfunctional. Sackville-West wrote to Nicolson,

> The more I think about it, the weaker I think the end is . . . I simply cannot make out what was in her mind. What does the wild goose stand for? Fame? Love? Death? Marriage? Obviously a person of V[irginia]'s intellect has had *some* object in view, but what was it? (Quoted in Glendinning 1983: 204)

What, indeed? A secret code that remains unintelligible to its primary addressee is functioning as something other than a secret code.

Orlando is a book about history, but also a book that *made* and continues to make history, while exposing the machinery through which history is made. Pitting Woolf's right of access as a historian – and her wrath as a lover betrayed – against the property rights of the Sackvilles, it deploys the conventions of portraiture to inscribe a queer presence in the very heart of 'England'. In a strangely Carlylean connection between past and present, Woolf's holograph of *Orlando*, in violet ink, is today displayed (in facsimile) as the property of the National Trust at the focal point of Knole's Great Hall, just beneath a portrait of Thomas Sackville, first Earl of Dorset.

Notes

The Humanities Institute at the University of South Florida generously supported research for this chapter.

1. Included among the photographs in existence as of February 1934 were the now famous Beresford portrait in profile take when Woolf was twenty, the portrait of a forty-one year old Woolf in her mother's Victorian dress taken by Maurice Beck and Helen Macgregor that had appeared in *Vogue* in 1924, and the well known Lenare studio portraits taken in 1929 at the request of Vita Sackville-West. Not yet in existence were the portraits Man Ray took in late 1934, one of which appeared on the cover of *Time* in 1937, and the Gisèle Freund photographs engineered, to Woolf's annoyance, by Victoria Ocampo in 1939. Saumarez Smith (1995) provides a brief history of the NPG's acquisition of Woolf portraits.
2. In several past editions of *Orlando* and *Three Guineas* the pictures were omitted. See Hussey and Marcus.

Works Cited and Further Reading

Barlow, Paul (1994) 'The Imagined Hero as Incarnate Sign: Thomas Carlyle and the Mythology of the "national portrait" in Victorian Britain', *Art History*, 17.4: 517–45.

—— (1997) 'Facing the past and present: the National Portrait Gallery and the search for 'authentic' portraiture', in Woodall 1997.

Brilliant, Richard (1991) *Portraiture*, Cambridge, MA: Harvard University Press.

de Gay, Jane (2006) *Virginia Woolf's Novels and the Literary Past*, Edinburgh: Edinburgh University Press.

Carlyle's House (1979) The National Trust.

DeSalvo, Louise and Mitchell A. Leaska (eds) (1985) *The Letters of Vita Sackville-West to Virginia Woolf*, New York: William Morrow and Co.

Ellis, Steve (2007) *Virginia Woolf and the Victorians*, Cambridge: Cambridge University Press.

Fry, Roger (1973) 'Mrs. Cameron's Photographs', in *Victorian Photographs of Famous Men and Fair Women by Julia Margaret Cameron*, ed. Tristram Powell, Boston, MA: David R. Godine.

Garrity, Jane (1999) 'Selling Culture to the "Civilized": Bloomsbury, British *Vogue*, and the Marketing of National Identity', *Modernism/Modernity*, 6.2: 29–58.

Gillespie, Diane Filby (1988) *The Sisters' Arts: The Writing and Painting of Virgina Woolf and Vanessa Bell*, Syracuse, NY: Syracuse University Press.

Glendinning, Victoria (1983) *Vita: The Life of V. Sackville-West*, New York: Knopf.

Hargreaves, Roger (2001) 'Putting Faces to the Names: Social and Celebrity Portrait Photography', in *The Beautiful and the Damned: The Creation of Identity in Nineteenth Century Photography*, ed. Peter Hamilton and Roger Hargreaves, Aldershot, Hants: Lund Humphries.

Hirsh, Elizabeth (2003) 'Biography as Spatial Historiography: Virginia Woolf's *Roger Fry* and the National Identity', in *Mapping the Self: Space, Identity, Discourse in British Auto/biography*, ed. Frédéric Regard, Saint-Etienne: Publications de l'Université de Saint-Etienne.

Hovey, Jamie (1997) '"Kissing a Negress in the Dark": Englishness as Masquerade in Woolf's *Orlando*', *PMLA*, 112.3: 393–404.

Humm, Maggie (2003) *Modernist Women and Visual Cultures: Virginia Woolf, Vanessa Bell, Photography and Cinema*, New Brunswick, NJ: Rutgers University Press.

—— (2006) *Snapshots of Bloomsbury: The Private Lives of Virginia Woolf and Vanessa Bell*, New Brunswick, NJ: Rutgers University Press.

Hussey, Mark (1995) *Virginia Woolf A to Z: A Comprehensive Reference for Students, Teachers and Common Readers to Her Life, Work and Critical Reception*, New York and Oxford: Oxford University Press.

Knole (1998) The National Trust.

Kukil, Karen (ed.) (2003) *Leslie Stephen's Photograph Album*. Online at www.smith.edu/libraries/libs/rarebook/exhibitions/stephen/

Lukitsh, Joanne (1992) 'Julia Margaret Cameron and the 'Ennoblement' of Photographic Portraiture', in *Victorian Scandals: Representations of Gender and Class*, Athens, ed. Kristine Ottesen Garrigan, Ohio: Ohio University Press.

Mandler, Peter (1997) *The Fall and Rise of the Stately Home*, New Haven, CI: Yale University Press.

Marcus, Jane (2006) 'Introduction' in Virginia Woolf, *Three Guineas*, Orlando, FL: Harcourt, Inc.

Miller, D. A. (1988) *The Novel and the Police*, Berkeley: University of California Press.

Nicolson, Harold (1959) *The Development of English Biography*, London: Hogarth Press.

Nicolson, Nigel (1973) *Portrait of a Marriage*, New York: Athenaeum.

Nuding, Gertrude Prescott (1992) 'Britishness and Portraiture' in *Myths of the English*, ed. Roy Porter, Cambridge: Polity Press.

Perry, Lara (2000) 'The National Potrait Gallery and its constituencies, 1858–96', in

Governing Cultures: Art Institutions in Victorian London, ed. Paul Barlow and Colin Trodd, Burlington, VT: Ashgate.

—— (2006) *History's Beauties: Women and the National Portrait Gallery 1856–1900*, Aldershot, Hants; Burlington, VT: Ashgate.

Piper, David (1992) *The English Face*, London: National Portrait Gallery.

Pointon, Marcia (1993) *Hanging the Head: Portraiture and Social Formation in Eighteenth Century England*, New Haven, CT: Yale University Press.

Raitt, Suzanne (1993) *Vita and Virginia: The Work and Friendship of V. Sackville-West and Virginia Woolf*, Oxford: Clarendon Press.

Saumarez Smith, Charles (1995) 'A Question of Fame: Virginia Woolf and the National Portrait Gallery', *Charleston Magazine*, Autumn/Winter: 5–9.

—— (1997) *The National Portrait Gallery*, London: National Portrait Gallery.

Schaffer, Talia (1994) 'Posing *Orlando*', *Genders*, 19: 26–63.

Silver, Brenda (1999) *Virginia Woolf Icon*, Chicago: University of Chicago Press.

Vaughan, William (1999) *British Painting: The Golden Age*, London: Thames and Hudson.

Wendorf, Richard (1990) *The Elements of Life: Biography and Portrait-Painting in Stuart and Georgian England*, Oxford: Clarendon Press.

Victorian Portraits (1996) London: National Portrait Gallery.

Woodall, Joanna (ed.) (1997) 'Introduction: facing the subject', in *Portraiture: Facing the Subject*, Manchester: Manchester University Press, pp. 1–25.

Woolf, Virginia (2003) *Carlyle's House and Other Sketches*, ed. David Bradshaw, London: Hesperus Press.

Part III   Domestic Arts

Part II · Domestic Art

Plate 1 *Sir Leslie Stephen*, by George Frederic Watts, 1878 (oil on canvas)
© National Portrait Gallery, London

Plate 2 Women's Socialist and Political Union suffragist badge, 1908–14

Plate 3 *Self-Portrait at the Easel*, by Vanessa Bell, 1912
© Estate of Vanessa Bell, courtesy Henrietta Garnett. Private collection, England

Plate 4 *Virginia Woolf in a Deckchair*, by Vanessa Bell, 1912
© Estate of Vanessa Bell, courtesy Henrietta Garnett. Private collection

Plate 5 *Study for a Composition*, by Vanessa Bell, 1930
© Estate of Vanessa Bell, courtesy Henrietta Garnett. King's College, Cambridge

Plate 6 *The Green Necklace*, by Vanessa Bell, 1932 © Estate of Vanessa Bell, courtesy Henrietta Garnett. Collection Charles Samuel Stevens

Plate 7 *Gassed* by John Singer Sargent, 1919
© The Art Archive/Imperial War Museum

Plate 8 Anrep mosaics at the National Gallery, London
© The National Gallery, London. By courtesy of the Anrep Estate

10

VIRGINIA WOOLF AND MONK'S HOUSE

Victoria Rosner

W HY ARE WE drawn to the homes of great writers after their deaths? If the writer is one whom we admire or love deeply, we travel to the house like pilgrims, lingering with devotion over relics like a chair or a desk that the writer once used. We associate certain writers with the places where they dwelt: the Brontës with Haworth Parsonage; Faulkner with Rowan Oak; Freud with Berggasse 19. All three of these houses – and they are far from unique among the homes and haunts of celebrated writers – now operate as museums open to the public year-round and even accessible via virtual tour on the internet. They seem to hold out the promise of special access or a unique window into the books we cherish.

Monk's House, the Sussex country home that the Woolfs owned and occupied together for over twenty years, is a bit more shy about itself. Though it is now a National Trust property, it is open to the public only a few months a year and during those months for only seven hours a week divided between two days. It does not mount exhibitions and most of its rooms are not available for viewing. The house has also not attracted much interest thus far from scholars of the Bloomsbury Group; most critics, like Jean Moorcroft Wilson (1987) and Susan Squier (1985), focus on Virginia Woolf in London.[1] In discussions of Bloomsbury's domestic spaces, Virginia and Leonard Woolf have received the least attention. Although they were patrons of the Omega Workshops, the design collective founded by Duncan Grant, Roger Fry, and Vanessa Bell, they were not themselves contributors. In the public eye, Monk's House places a distant second to Charleston, Bell and Grant's Sussex home a few miles away.

Is this benign neglect justified? If we look more carefully into the history of Monk's House during the Woolfs' tenure, we may find it has an important perspective to offer on Virginia Woolf's life and work, one belied not only by its critical neglect but also by the house's own modest self-presentation. The guidebook issued by the Trust describes the house as a 'welcome country retreat' (National Trust 1998: 3) a description supported by the house's location in the village of Rodmell, which, though only 47 miles from London, possesses but a single street and in 1931, when the Woolfs were in residence, numbered 244 inhabitants (Salzman 1940: 69). The house itself is long and plain and seems almost to be set into the earth. 'One stepped into it', recalled Angelica Garnett, Virginia Woolf's niece, 'rather as though one steps into a boat' (Garnett 1995: 251). The garden behind, Leonard Woolf's special passion, is large and lovely, but the house itself is the farthest thing from grand (see Plate 10). Its low ceilings and naked wood beams give it a rural character; and its characterisation as 'old fashioned' at the 1919 auction where the Woolfs bid successfully for it seems fully justified: at purchase the house had no electricity, no bathrooms and only an oil stove for cooking. Water had to be drawn up from a well. So in its locality, setting, equipment and even in its name, Monk's House apparently seems to fit the definition of a retreat, a place for withdrawal, contemplation and stasis.

Yet initial appearances are deceptive in this case. Even the name of the house is misleading, since it never housed any monks. According to the 1987 edition of the National Trust guidebook for the house, 'its name is almost certainly the product of an imaginative estate agent's mind. Until 1877 it was called after the families who owned it' (National Trust 1987: 4). Despite its location far from the whirl of London, Monk's House was a place Virginia Woolf associated with action, involvement and change, a place where she worked on all her major books and where Leonard held meetings of the Labour Party in the sitting room. This purposeful activity was only the most obvious work taking place at the house. More subtly, the house itself also became a means of putting into practice some of Virginia Woolf's central ideas: about feminism, writing as a profession for women, the importance of the physical spaces of authorship, the gendering of space, the elements and condition of modernity, and the violence lurking in everyday life. This unprepossessing house was not simply the place where these ideas were formulated, it was the original site of their practice. The Woolfs famously upended the division between public and private spheres in their London residences, running their own publishing house, the Hogarth Press, from their basement (Cucullu 1997). In a different but related vein, Monk's House was the place Virginia Woolf worked to make a physical place for herself as a woman writer, to explore how the autonomy of the intellectual was shaped both by gender and by space. It was not a retreat but a place very much dedicated to creative and activist work, a place, despite its apparent remoteness, that was fully connected to the outside world. The neglect of Monk's House in the universe of writer's residences has led us to misunderstand a place that is crucial to Virginia Woolf's ideas about women writers' often conflicting responsibilities to the private life of the home and the public life of the author.

It is fair to say that the Bloomsbury Group has a history of going to the country to work rather than to relax. Charleston was a laboratory for aesthetics, a place where nearly every wall, or piece of furniture came, over the years, to be covered in Bell and Grant's art. Roger Fry was similarly ambitious in the design and décor at Durbins, his home in Guildford. Though Monk's House displayed some decorative flourishes (like the bright green that Virginia Woolf painted the sitting room), it was a writer's rather than a painter's house (see Plate 11). Charleston and Durbins are showplaces, while the achievements of Monk's House are woven into the fabric of the house rather than painted on its surfaces.

The unprepossessing appearance of Monk's House conceals the time, money and attention that the Woolfs poured into it, modernising, renovating and expanding the structure time and again. Incredibly, between the years 1919 and 1940, records show that the Woolfs undertook more than sixteen substantial enlargements or modernisations of the house and its grounds. As this number suggests, the Woolfs were in an almost constant state of planning and executing renovations at Monk's House. Why? Most families renovate as their family expands; the Woolfs did not have this as an excuse. Then as now, such projects tend to be messy, unsettling and much more involving and expensive than originally thought. Yet no sooner had the Woolfs completed one project than they were on to the next. The records of these renovations, including correspondence with builders and floor plans, were preserved by Leonard Woolf and now are archived with his papers at the University of Sussex. They offer a special perspective on both the lives and work of the Woolfs, revealing their domestic priorities and desires and forming a counterpoint to the works that were written as the house grew.

It was Leonard Woolf who carried on most of the correspondence related to the house, but his wife's influence is a steady presence. In 1929, for instance, he wrote to Philcox Brothers, the local builders,

> If convenient to you, Mrs. Woolf will come down and meet you at your office in Lewes on Thursday morning next in order to choose colours of paint for the two new rooms and to settle about bricks for fireplace. Would you have the samples of bricks for her to see? And would you, if necessary, be able to take her out to Monk's House? (Woolf 1929)

'Mrs. Woolf' also wrote frequently and enthusiastically about the current projects at Monk's House in her letters and diaries. Given Virginia Woolf's reliance on architectural imagery throughout her work, examining the architecture she helped create is a useful way to discern the connection between matter and metaphor in her work, between, as it were, *A Room of One's Own* (1929) and the actual rooms that were her own (Henley 1990). By doing so, I think we can derive some real insights about what Virginia Woolf was searching for as she built and rebuilt her home over the years, about the significance of renovation for the work of a woman writer who told us that her rooms, as she wrote in her memoirs, 'explain a great deal' (*MOB*: 124).

At least half of the renovations at Monk's House were directed at modernization. The Woolfs rebuilt the kitchen soon after moving in. In 1925–6 they installed the first bathroom and the first lavatory at the house and a few years after that acquired a hot water boiler and a range. In the sketch plan for this renovation prepared by Philcox Brothers there is a seemingly odd juxtaposition between the practicalities of the WC and the new cesspool and the study located on the other side of a thin matchboard partition. Perhaps it is not surprising that these might go together, since Virginia Woolf argued in her writing that without the practicalities of everyday life in place, intellection and creativity could not prosper.

In 1931 the house was electrified and acquired lights, electric fires in the bedrooms and a Frigidaire in the kitchen. In 1932 the Woolfs got a telephone and in 1934 they went on the mains water system. Virginia Woolf delighted in these additions and wrote to her friends about the joys of central heating, flush toilets and her expanding experiments in cooking. In a 1931 diary entry she noted,

> When the electric light fused, we could hardly tolerate Aladdin lamps, so soon is the soul corrupted by comfort. Yesterday men were in the house all day boring holes for electric fires. What more comfort can we acquire? And, though the moralists say, when one has a thing one at once finds it hollow, I dont at all agree. I enjoy my luxuries at every turn, & think them wholly good for what I am pleased to call the soul (*D4*: 27–8).

Woolf's new comforts symbolised a modernity that she was eager to embrace. In novels including *To The Lighthouse* (1927), *Orlando* (1928) and *The Years* (1937), she explored how war, expanded opportunities for women and changing social mores all put pressure on the home and compelled it to change in accordance with the times, changes that, in the main, meant less drudgery for women. Her 'luxuries' of light and heat went on pleasing her because they eliminated labour and allowed for an increased dedication to creative rather than custodial activity.

Virginia Woolf also saw these improvements as freeing her from dependence on live-in household help, always a vexing issue for her (Light 2007). As she wrote with exasperation, 'the fault lies in the system. How can an uneducated woman let herself in, alone, into our lives?' (*D3*: 220). She dreamed of a future in which 'our domestic establishment is entirely controlled by one woman, a vacuum cleaner, & electric stoves' (*D2*: 281). Writing in 1924, she could not imagine a future where domestic help could be eliminated completely; to reduce, through the aid of modern machines, to a single servant was the best to be hoped for. This sentiment was very much in keeping with the changing times; the servant population in England had been declining steadily since the 1890s as working women acquired other, more palatable career options than living in an employer's home and doing demeaning work for long hours and little money (Light 2007: 179).

Woolf's musings focused on her own domestic needs rather than on the pinched and difficult lives led by domestic workers. For her, technology was a means to her own more independent living, not that of others. Her diary entry for September 25, 1929 begins:

> But what interests me is of course my oil stove. . . . At this moment it is cooking my dinner in the glass dishes perfectly I hope, without smell,

waste, or confusion: one turns handles, there is a thermometer. And so I see myself freer, more independent – & all one's life is a struggle for freedom – able to come down here with a chop in a bag & live on my own (*D3*: 257).

Woolf's hope that the mechanisation of the home might transport her into a hygienic and orderly existence is connected to the value she placed on independence: independence of income, independence of space, independence from cumbersome social conventions and independence from the special constraints placed on women. The fantasy she expresses in this passage is one of perfect freedom, though it is only her own freedom she considers and not that of the women who have worked for years for her domestic comforts. This oversight is repeated in Woolf's famous claim about the rupture of modernity: 'On or about December 1910', she writes, 'human character changed.' 'One can see the change', she continues, 'in the character of one's cook' (*CE1*: 320). Despite modernity's celebrated arrival, certain verities went unquestioned – that her readers would continue to have cooks, and that none of them could possibly *be* cooks. Woolf's fantasy is also one of solitude; her diary entry depersonalises food preparation to the point of eliminating the cook altogether. We can hear the frustrated author in these lines, just pleading to be left alone.

Another reason that Woolf enjoyed her modern conveniences so much was that she was able to pay for them herself, with money she earned from her writing. She had already paid for the first sanitary facilities in the house from the profits of *Mrs Dalloway* and *The Common Reader*, both published in 1925. But it was in 1929, with the publication of *Orlando*, that she began to earn substantial sums from her work. She immediately poured the money into the house. In March of that year she wrote with evident pride,

After all, I say, I made £1000 all from willing it early one morning. No more poverty I said; & poverty has ceased. I am summoning Philcox next week to plan a room – I have money to build it, money to furnish it. (*D3*: 219–20)

Surely it was no coincidence that she had just finished drafting the long essay 'Women and Fiction' that would be published as *A Room of One's Own*. In that essay she argued with great conviction that women must have money and rooms of their own if they are to write fiction, that in the long course of history women, however wealthy their families might have been, were themselves impoverished and had none of the privacy so essential to creative concentration. Magically, the assertion of that claim seem to bring about its own fulfilment, although Woolf did not stop at a single room in this renovation; she added at the same time a two-storey extension, an additional bathroom and a greenhouse, among other alterations. The imperious tone of the diary entry conveys her new sense of herself as an increasingly grand individual who can will her desires into being. Money buys her autonomy; money buys her privacy.

Woolf herself mapped out the original plan for this addition. On the reverse

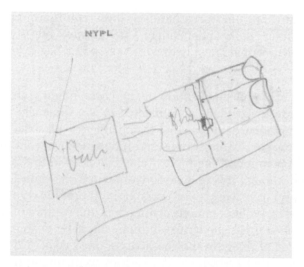

Figure 10.1 Virginia Woolf's sketch of a study and bath from the *Reading
Notebooks*. The Berg Collection of English and American Literature, New York
Public Library, Astor, Lenox and Tilden Foundations and the Society of Authors as
the Literary Representative of the Estate of Virginia Woolf

side of a page in her reading notebooks, she sketched this drawing for a study
and a bath at the top of Monk's House[2] (see Figure 10.1). Despite the spontaneous character of the sketch, it might be said to have a history that dates back to
1886. It was in that year that Woolf's parents, Leslie and Julia Stephen, undertook a major renovation of their London home at 22 Hyde Park Gate in order
to accommodate their growing family. They also added, among other items, a
bath and a study at the top of the house. And Woolf remembers: 'My mother, I
believe, sketched what she wanted on a sheet of notepaper to save the architect's
fees' (*MOB*: 182). Here we have an intriguing connection between mother and
daughter, both usurping the architect's role to plot their own spaces. But there
are significant differences as well: the study Julia Stephen planned was for her
husband's use, while Virginia Woolf designed rooms for both herself and her
husband, affording them each their privacy.

Julia Stephen's sketch affirmed her role as devoted wife and mother, protecting her husband's privacy and the family's resources.[3] She had no room of
her own at Hyde Park Gate. If the architecture of that house upheld the male
writer's authority and authorship, Monk's House, where two writers dwelt,
took a more egalitarian approach to renovation where gender was concerned.
Woolf's sketch claimed the right to privacy for herself and used her own money
to provide for her husband.[4] Moreover, the placement of this sketch in her reading notebooks invokes the analogous relations she saw among reading, writing
and building. As she wrote in 'How Should One Read a Book?' in 1926, 'The
thirty-two chapters of a novel . . . are an attempt to make something as formed

and controlled as a building: but words are more impalpable than bricks; reading is a longer and more complicated process than seeing' (*CR2*: 259). If books could be buildings, Woolf was their literary architect; if buildings could be texts, Woolf made herself both their author and their interpreter.

Throughout her life Virginia Woolf was deeply interested in how people both imprinted themselves on their living spaces and were shaped, in turn, by their environments. She was influenced in part by the decorative experiments of other members of the Bloomsbury Group. Domestic interiors designed by the Omega had a spontaneous, playful and colourful appearance, the furthest thing from the serious, heavy and dark spaces of the artists' Victorian childhoods. In fact, many of the furnishings at Monk's House were created by Bell and Grant in the style of the Omega, giving the house an eclectic and casual disposition. By designing her own living spaces, Woolf was trying to create a home that was designed around its owners' identities and ambitions. Monk's House still contained hierarchy, but it was a different hierarchy than the one she had known as a child, one centred around hers and Leonard's needs, not Leslie Stephen's.

Living spaces were vitally important to Woolf and none more so than the places where she wrote. Unlike her father, who spent a good part of his life in his study at the top of the house, Woolf shifted her place of writing many times during her years at Monk's House. At the time of the 1929 renovation Woolf was doing most of her writing outside of the house altogether, in a one-room outbuilding that had been converted from a tool shed and outfitted for her use in 1921, shortly after the Woolfs bought the house. This writing lodge, off by itself in the garden, was perhaps the ideal type of a room of one's own. Underfurnished to the point of bareness and rustic in construction, it was visibly a place for one person and with one purpose. Woolf wrote there every morning that she was in Rodmell; in the afternoons she went out and walked on the Sussex Downs that were visible out of the room's window. Because the room had no heat, when the weather was cold she shifted to writing in her bedroom with a lap desk across her knees.

For a woman writer, more likely than her male counterpart to be called upon for any domestic crisis, writing outside the house was as a way to isolate herself from interruption. The domestic sphere, as Woolf points out, is invariably characterised as female: 'one has only to go into any room in any street for the whole of that extremely complex force of femininity to fly in one's face' (*AROO*: 87). Writing outside the house, even as near as the backyard, was a way to step outside that web of encumbering associations. Woolf's attention to the physical spaces of authorship and in particular her choice to isolate herself resonates with the outrage she expressed in *A Room of One's Own* about the way in which Jane Austen, compelled to write in the family sitting room, had to whisk her work out of sight if anyone else entered the room. Florence Nightingale too, Woolf recorded, expressed frustration that '"women never have an half hour . . . that they can call their own"' (*AROO*: 66). Woolf's novels offer portraits of women's pleasure when they can claim their own private spaces. Clarissa Dalloway has a room at the top of her London home where she goes to remember her happy youth. In *Night and Day* (1919) Mary Datchet uses her room to host meetings and debates. In Woolf's first novel, *The Voyage Out* (1915), the 24-year-old Rachel Vinrace is delighted when her aunt provides her with 'a room cut off from the rest of the house, large, private – a room in which she could play, read, think, defy the world, a fortress as well as a sanctuary' (Woolf 1923: 123). In all three of these novels, women derive far more pleasure from their architectural privacy than they do from the men in their lives.

A Room of One's Own constitutes Virginia Woolf's most developed proof of the need for women writers to have private spaces. For Woolf, women's new legal rights to vote, to receive an education, and to own property after marriage made a new concept of female authorship possible. *A Room* was published in 1929 and quickly sold 22,000 copies in six months, earning her more money with which to build. Though the previous renovation was not a year past, in November she started another new project, the addition of a new room for herself in the attic of Monk's House. Six months earlier she had complained that in cold weather she had no place to write when in Rodmell: 'until I have a room, I cannot go there meaning to work' (*D3*: 220). Again the imagined room seemed to represent for Woolf a perfected space of privacy for writing. 'The bedroom will be a lovely wonderful room', she fantasised, 'what I've always hoped for' (*D3*: 267). In this context we should note that Leonard and Virginia, like many married couples at the time, did not share a bedroom. Virginia Woolf's new room had a single point of access from the garden and was labelled in the plans as 'detached', an apt invocation of her desired state of mind as a writer.

Woolf frequently shifted the spaces where she worked at Monk's House, building new rooms, moving between bedroom and outdoors, and even composing in the bathtub. In 1934 the Woolfs knocked down Virginia's existing outdoor lodge and built another one (still extant, though enlarged since her death) in a different location in the garden (see Figure 10.2). Her writerly wanderlust is noteworthy since many writers prefer to settle into a single space and stay. Leslie Stephen, for example, is depicted by Woolf as rooted in a single spot in his Hyde Park Gate study: 'he had written all his books lying sunk in that deep rocking chair' (*MOB*: 119). As Diana Fuss has recently argued, writers are often closely identified with a particular space of composition (Fuss 2004). Woolf's numerous changes in location suggest that her quest for that room of her own sprang from a desire that could never be fully satisfied. It also suggests a refusal to become too comfortable or settled, to insist, as it were, on shifting her perspective with frequency. Indeed, in planning the second lodge, her concern was to capture the broadest view of the Downs allowable. When Leonard wrote to the builder to accept his estimate (naturally, it was exceeded) he requested certain changes in the proposed design:

The alterations which I have in view are as follows: the window on the south side would be as planned but on the north side there should be two

Figure 10.2 Virginia Woolf's writing lodge in the back garden at Monk's House, Rodmell. Photograph © Victoria Rosner

windows with a double door in the centre, the doors to have glass in their upper halves. (Woolf 1934)

A great deal of glass was employed in the final construction, opening up the lodge's view of the Downs.

For Woolf, spatial flexibility was necessary to the cultivation of flexibility of mind. This idea emerges in her diaries as early as 1903, when Woolf (then Virginia Stephen) was twenty-one years old. Stephen women, she writes, 'are equally at home everywhere (not at all, that is to say)' (*PA*: 167). While living at Hyde Park Gate she tried to imagine a way of living that would allow one to move around continually and avoid the mental limits imposed by fixed dwelling. In another early diary entry she writes:

I never see a gipsy cart without longing to be inside it. A house that is rooted to no one spot but can travel as quickly as you change your mind, & is complete in itself is surely the most desirable of houses. Our modern house with its cumbersome walls & its foundations planted deep in the ground is nothing better than a prison; [. . .] & more & more prison like does it become the longer we live there & wear fetters of association & sentiment, painful to wear – still more painful to break. (*PA*: 208)

These sentiments seem directly at odds with those expressed in *A Room of One's Own*. Is the writer's study a palace or a prison? In Woolf's spatial wanderlust we see her two ideals, of secure spatial privacy on the one hand and a freedom to roam on the other. Shifting her spaces of writing was a way to combine them. It also, she argued, inculcated a desirable mental flexibility, the opposite of her father's fixity. Instead, she sought to feel always a little uncomfortable, a little challenged by newness. She converted this preference into a political practice in *Three Guineas* (1938), the sequel to *A Room of One's Own*, where she rhetorically proposed the creation of an activist group of women to be dubbed the Outsider's Society. 'Broadly speaking', she wrote to her imaginary male interlocutor in the book,

> the main distinction between us who are outside society and you who are inside society must be that whereas you will make use of the means provided by your position . . . we, remaining outside, will experiment not with public means in public but with private means in private. (*TG*: 113)

Again, Woolf has recourse to a true social 'outsider' – a gypsy this time, rather than a servant – to articulate her own idea of personal freedom. Feminists of the next generation would rally around the idea that 'the personal is political', in a sequel to Woolf's formulation.

Virginia Woolf's belief that the private sphere could be a space of political engagement took on a different meaning in the late 1930s. Settled in her new writing lodge at Rodmell she received the news in 1935 that Mussolini had invaded Ethiopia, the first stirrings of the larger conflict to come. While travelling in Germany later that year, the Woolfs found themselves driving down a road in Bonn with crowds of uniformed Nazis and flag-waving children lined up along both sides to greet the arriving Goering. The Woolfs' car was open on top and the crowds were charmed by the sight of their pet marmoset Mitz reclining on Leonard's shoulders. Driving slowly along the road they were offered innumerable Nazi salutes and shouts of 'Heil Hitler!' (*DAW*: 191). Back at home, they found the war closing in on them. In 1937 Woolf's nephew Julian Bell was killed fighting the Spanish Civil War, personalising the violence in an acute way.

Leonard had always been more directly involved in politics than Virginia. In 1935 he published an antiwar polemic *Quack, Quack!*, followed in 1939 by *Barbarians at the Gate* and in 1940 by *The War for Peace*. Virginia's *Three Guineas* treated the prevention of war and patriotism in terms of gender. As the possibility of British involvement in the war grew, Leonard gave speeches and participated in committees and pressure groups. By 1937 Labour Party meetings were being held in the Monk's House drawing room (*L6*: 107). When England entered the war, both the Woolfs became increasingly involved in local community organising: Leonard joined the local fire brigade and donated their pots and pans for scrap metal, while Virginia spoke to the Women's Institute about 'Women and the War' and later became its treasurer (Glendinning 2006: 319).

Alongside this political activity, Virginia Woolf continued to plan alterations at Monk's House. In March of 1938 she recorded in her diary that 'we have asked Mr Wicks to estimate for a library at MH. in spite of Hitler' (*D5*: 130). This new project was to convert existing loft space into a library with a new staircase built beneath for access. The incongruous reference to Hitler in this context can be taken in at least two ways: the first and perhaps more obvious is that with the war looming, the conditions for building were not ideal. It might also be argued that for Virginia Woolf, the building of the library was a gesture of resistance on several levels: an insistence on not letting the threat of Hitler undermine normal life, a celebration of liberal intellectual values in the face of a regime that was trying to stamp them out, and an affirmation of belief in the durability and permanence of their home in the face of threats.

France fell to Hitler in June of 1940 and in August the Blitz came to Monk's House. The Woolfs were eating lunch when they heard a deafening roar; they rushed outside to see planes with swastikas painted on their sides diving down over the village church spire and bombing local cottages. Air battles over Rodmell became a common occurrence as Hitler prepared to invade from across the Channel. When German warplanes flew over their backyard the Woolfs would, according to instruction, lie face down on the ground under a tree, with their hands clasped behind their heads. The violence that lurks in everyday life was a theme of Virginia Woolf's work from the earliest days, but it took on an entirely new valence now. Like many of their friends, they made plans for suicide in the case of invasion, suspecting (correctly) that they were on the Third Reich's list of wanted persons.

Against the optimistic and constructive work of renovation, the Woolfs saw homes destroyed on a daily basis. London too was under attack and bombed nightly; this was considered an immediate precursor to invasion. In September 1940 the Woolfs learned that their home in Mecklenburgh Square had been damaged, with windows broken and ceilings collapsed. Woolf asked in her diary, 'Why did we ever leave Tavistock?' their longtime London home from which they had moved only recently (*D5*: 322). But a month later Tavistock Square was reduced to rubble. The Woolfs went to London and picked through the remains of both houses. At Tavistock Square: 'I cd just see a piece of my studio wall standing: otherwise rubble where I wrote so many books' (ibid.: 331). At Mecklenburgh, she wrote 'In my sitting room glass all over Mrs Hunter's cabinet – & so on. Only the drawing room with windows almost whole. A wind blowing through. I began to hunt out diaries. What cd we salvage . . . ?' (ibid.: 331). The Woolfs were hard pressed to build studies as quickly as the Germans could destroy them. The image of the ruined house, of domesticity destroyed, was tragic, but for Virginia Woolf it was also liberating, another version of freedom: 'But its odd – the relief at losing possessions. I shd like to start life, in peace, almost bare – free to go anywhere" (ibid.: 332). As in the gypsy fantasy of her younger days, she found a certain relief in the idea of shrugging off possessions, responsibilities and social hierarchies. Yet two days later the Woolfs were visiting an estate agent in Sussex, seeking another house.

Virginia Woolf's belief in the importance of domestic life and its values, of privacy and space for writing and of women's rights and aptitudes might seem to be more suited to peacetime, but she believed that in wartime they were more important than ever. In her August 1940 essay, 'Thoughts on Peace in an Air Raid', she emphasised that private life had a role to play in ending war. Men, with their focus on politics, economics and armaments, overlooked the fact that the domestic was at the back of it all. 'Are we not leaving the young Englishman without a weapon that might be of value to him', she asked, 'if we give up private thinking, tea-table thinking, because it seems useless?' (*DM*: 244). Her work at this time was not limited to political topics; she also produced a biography of her friend, the art critic Roger Fry and a final novel, B*etween the Acts* (1941) that is in many ways a celebration of English village life

Looking at the ways the Woolfs inhabited Monk's House for those twenty-odd years, we see Virginia Woolf's fantasy of freedom breaking out repeatedly, expressed in two divergent forms. Freedom could mean being alone in a room of your own, seeing yourself mirrored in the familiar objects all around you, with endless time at your disposal. This is the freedom enjoyed by the fictional female narrator of *A Room of One's Own*, whose personal library contains all books written by women. But freedom could also mean being unhoused, without possessions and totally unencumbered; we see a version of it in the abandoned house in the central chapter of *To the Lighthouse*, as the deteriorating house stands in for a family that has fallen apart and with it many limiting social conventions. One is a vision of security and solitude, and the other is of possibility, of the anticipation of having everything still before you.

For Virginia Woolf, both would seem to be views of the condition of middle-class women in her time, with their feet anchored in the domestic and the new winds of education, financial independence and sexual freedom blowing through the air. And both were built into Monk's House. Virginia Woolf believed the home, as an institution, still had much to offer women, once it had been reshaped so that its benefits were equally distributed among family members. But she also believed in getting out of the house altogether, in the value of seeing as an outsider. Her idea of 'building to spite Hitler' may have been a form of whistling in the dark, of trying to ward off her increasingly overpowering sense that the forces of darkness were overtaking her domestic peace. But the gesture expressed her conviction that having a quiet room of one's own could change everything.

The continual reshaping of Monk's House suggests a project that could never have been completed. The Woolfs' domestic space was permanently provisional, ever-adapting to the needs of its owners. Flexibility, not static perfection, was the goal. Modernisation, too, was a project that could never be fully realised but had to be continually sought nonetheless. It was Virginia Woolf's yearning for an ideal room of one's own, a fantasised temple of authorship, that kept her sketching plans and hiring builders, but that yearning could never find satisfaction in a single space, since the room had to change to reflect the times and the writer's needs. Monk's House was no retreat: it was a place for taking work seriously, whether that work was house cleaning, writing or politics. Monk's House was always a work in progress, an architectural palimpsest through which we can read the history of the forging of rooms of one's own.

Notes

This chapter first took shape as a talk I gave at Duke University and I wish to thank Ranjana Khanna and Ara Wilson for their invitation. I am grateful to Georgia Johnston, Jane Marcus and Brenda Silver for their advice on the Woolfian world. Linda Dowdeswell generously gave permission to reprint Woolf's drawing and Isaac Gewirtz at the Berg Collection helped me to find it. The staff at the University of Sussex archives helped me to piece together the history of Monk's House during Virginia Woolf's lifetime; I am especially grateful to Fiona Courage and Donna Hetherington. Maggie Humm was a careful, knowing, and supportive editor. Finally, I wish to thank Laura Frost and Nancy K. Miller, who read this essay in draft and offered their insights.

1. Katherine C. Hill-Miller is one of the few critics to investigate the influence of Monk's House on Virginia Woolf's work, though she too casts the house as a retreat, arguing that its appeal lay in the 'quiet' and 'seclusion' it offered (Hill-Miller 2001: 244). For Anna Snaith, Monk's House was a place where Woolf 'attempted to carve out a private space' (Snaith 2003: 132). Also see Nuala Hancock's *Gardens and the Work of Virginia Woolf* (2005).
2. The reading notes on the reverse side refer to Geraldine Endsor Jewsbury's *Zoe. The History of Two Lives*, vols. 1–2 (of 3), London: Chapman & Hall, 1845.
3. The Married Women's Property Act had been passed only four years before Julia Stephen made her sketch; it gave married women the same rights to buy, sell and own property as unmarried women.
4. Leonard paid £80 for outdoor work and Virginia paid £454 for indoor alterations.

Works Cited and Further Reading

Cucullu, Lois (1997) 'Retailing the Female Intellectual', *differences*, 9.2: 25–68.

Fuss, Diana (2004) *The Sense of an Interior: Four Writers and the Rooms that Shaped Them*, New York: Routledge.

Garnett, Angelica (1995) 'Virginia and Leonard Woolf', in S. P. Rosenbaum (ed.). *The Bloomsbury Group: A Collection of Memoirs and Commentary*, rev. edn Toronto: University of Toronto Press.

Glendinning, Victoria (2006) *Leonard Woolf: A Biography*, New York: Free Press.

Hancock, Nuala (2005) *Gardens and the Work of Virginia Woolf*, London: Cecil Woolf.

Henley, Ann (1990) '*The whole building of a book*': Architectural Analogy in Virginia Woolf's Essays and Novels, Ann Arbor, MI: UMI.

Hill-Miller, Katherine C. (2001) *From the Lighthouse to Monk's House: A Guide to Virginia Woolf's Literary Landscapes*, London: Duckworth.

Light, Alison (2007) *Mrs Woolf and the Servants: The Hidden Heart of Domestic Service*, London: Penguin/Fig Tree.

National Trust (1998) *Virginia Woolf and Monk's House*, Swindon, Wilts: National Trust (originally published 1987).

Rich, Adrienne (1986) 'Notes toward a Politics of Location', in *Blood, Bread and Poetry*, New York: Norton.

Salzman, L. F. (ed.) (1940) 'Parishes: Rodmell', in *The Victoria History of the County of Sussex: Volume 7, The Rape of Lewes*, London: Oxford University Press for the University of London, Institute of Historical Research.

Snaith, Anna (2003) *Virginia Woolf: Public and Private Negotiations*, London: Palgrave Macmillan.

Squier, Susan Merrill (1985) *Virginia Woolf and London: The Sexual Politics of a City*, Chapel Hill: University of North Carolina Press.

Wilson, Jean Moorcroft (1987) *Virginia Woolf, Life, and London: A Biography of Place*, London: Cecil Woolf.

Woolf, Leonard (1929) Letter to Philcox Bros, 8 December, unpub. MS Monk's House Papers, University of Sussex.

Woolf, Leonard (1934) Letter to P. R. Wicks, 23 October, unpub. MS Monk's House Papers, University of Sussex.

11

VIRGINIA WOOLF AND FASHION

Jane Garrity

V IRGINIA WOOLF'S DIARY and letters are replete with references to the pleasures of getting dressed: 'My love of clothes interests me profoundly, only it is not love; & what it is I must discover' (*D3*, 21). Although not known for her sense of fashion, Woolf is preoccupied with 'the eternal, & insoluble question of clothes' (*D* I, 226) precisely because they are objects of perpetual invention; to the extent that clothing makes explicit the notion of personal identity as a malleable entity, it functions for Woolf as a sign, however ambivalent, of modernity. In this way Woolf builds upon the long-standing association of women with fashion, but she moves away from the typical condemnatory association of femininity and dress (or femininity and shopping). Woolf loathes the frankly commercial, but relishes distinctive style, luxury clothing, and the aesthetic aura of beautiful objects. The question of what clothing means to Woolf, then, is also what this essay seeks to discover, and toward that end it begins with an examination of the complex associations between clothing, shame, and rapture in 'A Sketch of the Past'. This is where we see the origins of Woolf's fundamentally ambivalent relation to dress, for, while she loves clothes, she dislikes being seen – a phenomenon that informs the way she writes about the clothed body in modernity. I am not attempting to argue that Woolf's ambivalence toward fashion is a psychological symptom, but rather, that a reading of 'A Sketch' can help us to understand why modernity is often staged as a crisis of sartorial representation in her fiction. This essay juxtaposes a variety of examples drawn from Woolf's essays, fiction and diaries in order to show how fashion and sartorial discourse, although at times saturated with the values of conformity, are ultimately a means of exploring the perpetual re-making of an invented subjectivity. While fashion is not a stable or monolithic category in Woolf, clothing and fashionability function by turns as signs of contemporaneity, vehicles for self-construction, signifiers of cultural resistance, and figures for the contemplation of the boundary between self and other. By juxtaposing fictional and autobiographical writings, this essay will explore Woolf's perception: that fashion is a social, situated practice; that one's relation to dress is class-inflected; that the public purchase of commodities produces a level of anxiety that private consumption does not; that the imaginative grasp of clothes can facilitate moments of aesthetic transcendence; and that fashion often functions as a metonym for modernity.

I. Sartorial Self-Mortification

Woolf's memoir, 'A Sketch of the Past', forges a confluence between the body, rapture, shame, and clothing that underscores the fundamentally ambivalent position that clothing occupies in her autobiographical writings and her fiction. Yet her first memory, that of sitting on her mother's lap while gazing at a pattern of 'purple and red and blue flowers' against the black background of her 'mother's dress' (*MOB*: 65), is associated with unmediated pleasure. This pre-linguistic memory of vivid colour on maternal fabric is linked to a second sensory moment in which Woolf recalls 'hearing the waves breaking . . . behind a yellow blind' (ibid.: 64) as she lies in her bed at St Ives. Both of these 'highly sensual' memories bleed together in 'A Sketch' and are associated with 'rapture' (ibid.: 66) – what Woolf calls 'the purest ecstasy I can conceive' (ibid.: 65). Such pre-individualized moments, in which she is 'hardly aware of [her]self' (ibid.: 67) as a separate being, are linked not only with bodily integrity – feeling 'whole' (ibid.: 66) – but with unmistakable eroticism. Woolf uses words such as 'warm', 'ripe', 'buzz', 'croon', and 'smell' to capture these early inchoate memories that 'press voluptuously' (*MOB* 66) upon her being yet elude verbal expression. Sidonie Smith remarked that Woolf's earliest memories exemplify the 'semiotic pleasure[s] of pure sensation and experiential wholeness', and this reading is still persuasive to the extent that Woolf's depiction of these pre-linguistic moments of sensual pleasure and receptivity constitutes a kind of textbook example of 'preoedipal bondedness and boundlessness' (Smith 1993: 87–8). But what's curious about Woolf's representation of this succession of memories is the degree to which they are associated less with maternal flesh *per se* and more with maternal *clothing* – not only that inaugural memory of her mother's flowery dress, but an image of her mother in 'her white dressing gown' standing on a balcony, 'the scratch of some beads on her [mother's] dress . . . as [the young Virginia] pressed her cheek against it', the 'button on her [mother's] nightgown' after she has died, and a vision of her mother 'wearing [a] striped silk dress buttoned at the throat with a flowing skirt that appears in [a] photograph' that the author either fondly remembers or imagines (*MOB*: 81, 92, 87).

These early memories of maternal centrality, beauty and dress – what Woolf calls the 'complete rapture of pleasure' – stand in stark contrast to the acute discomfort she experiences when she contemplates clothing herself as an adult: 'Everything to do with dress – to be fitted, to come into a room wearing a new dress – still frightens me. . .makes me shy, self-conscious, uncomfortable' (*MOB*: 66, 68). Whereas the tactile beads on her mother's dress suggest a pleasurable confluence between the corporeal and clothing, subsequent memories

– those associated with a post-individualised and socially regulated subjectivity – highlight a violent disjunction between the body and dress. One such salient memory is when Woolf gazes into the looking-glass at Talland House as a young child of six or seven and feels 'ashamed' (ibid.: 68). She initially attributes this shame to her 'tomboy phase' – the period in which she and Vanessa climbed trees, scrambled over rocks, and 'were said not to care for clothes' – shorthand for her defiance of the culture's investment in gendered clothing (ibid.). Mirror-gazing, Woolf tells us, was strictly 'against [her] tomboy code,' but this explanation does not adequately account for why 'feeling[s] of shame' and 'guilt' (*MOB* 68) persist long after the so-called tomboy phase is over: 'the looking-glass shame has lasted all my life' (ibid.). Despite the intractability of these feelings of debasement, her solitary practice of self-reflection gives rise to thoughts about her own attractiveness – 'femininity was very strong in our family. We were famous for our beauty' (ibid.). Yet at the same moment that Woolf introduces the concept of female beauty and its links to the familial, she immediately dissociates herself from any claim to this maternal legacy. '[M]y natural love for beauty', she confesses, 'was checked by some ancestral dread' (ibid.) – that is to say, her father's puritanical and ascetic streak. The text is slippery on whether the 'looking-glass shame' is an ancestral predisposition or the result of social conditioning, but Woolf does insist that this self-loathing 'did not prevent [her] from feeling ecstasies and raptures spontaneously and intensely without any shame or the least sense of guilt', as long as those pleasurable sensations remained 'disconnected [from her] own body' (ibid.). Pleasure is accessible, in other words, as long as it is displaced. An example of such displacement in relation to clothing occurs when she remembers the daughter of Ottoline and Philip Morrell joyfully putting on a new dress: 'Oh to be able to run, like Julian Morrell, all over the garden in a new dress' (ibid.). Here clothing is a specific source of bodily pleasure, but only in mediated form. Without this mediation, sartorial shame results.

Is Woolf's identification with shame an impulse of modesty, or is it more of what Kathryn Bond Stockton, in writing about clothing and shame within a queer context, calls a 'psychic wound' (Stockton 2006: 34)? Stockton analyses the self-loathing which adheres in key situations where clothing and skin 'touch upon each other's meanings' because 'each is a surface – with intense, complex, and variable codings attached to it – that may be the object of prejudice, violence, attraction, and invective' (ibid.: 40). Both, in other words, elicit strong emotions such as vanity or modesty, and both invite a contradictory range of responses that include sexual attraction, aesthetic delight, or violent repulsion. She further argues that clothing and skin can be physically marked with a wound (such as torn garments, or torn skin), and each can elicit psychic wounds (such as self-denigration) because of the shame that can attach to it. This analysis is particularly useful for a reading of Woolf's preoccupation with shame because of the complex ways that clothing and the body lend associations to each other in the memoir. Critics have read Woolf's identification with shame in terms of her half-brother Gerald Duckworth's sexual abuse – Woolf 'remember[s] the feel of his hand going under [her] clothes. . .explor[ing] [her] private parts' (*MOB*: 69) – and indeed in 'A Sketch' her revelation of sexual violation is conflated with the 'looking-glass shame' (ibid.: 68), which is in turn associated with the cultural imperatives of getting and being dressed. Both clothing and the body elicit 'strong feeling[s] of guilt' (ibid.) in Woolf, though the episode of sexual violation gives rise to an injunction against touch that does not fully extend to clothing. Without attempting here to explain the origins of Woolf's feelings of debasement, it is arguably safe to say that 'A Sketch' suggests that the pre-linguistic, sensate body is painfully at odds with the socially regulated body, and that clothing is one large component in this regulation – or, as Woolf succinctly puts it: 'I feel that strong emotion must leave its trace' (ibid.: 67). The memoir contains several examples of how this 'trace' operates, of how clothing – both literally and figuratively – functions, to borrow Stockton's language, as a 'surface to which shame attaches'. When Woolf writes, 'I cannot now powder my nose in public' (ibid.: 68), she economically conveys the total paralysis that can accompany such repression.

A salient example of how clothing functions as a repressive vehicle of female enculturation and containment occurs when Woolf recounts the 'rules of the game of Victorian society' (*MOB*: 150) around 1900, when her family was living at Hyde Park Gate. Woolf recognises how effectively clothes, external signs of sexual difference, produce a certain kind of homogenised, commodified femininity – 'young ladies possessed of a certain manner' (ibid.: 149). She writes:

> About seven thirty the pressure of the machine became emphatic. At seven thirty we went upstairs to dress. However cold or foggy, we slipped off our day clothes and stood shivering in front of washing basins . . . . Neck and arms had to be scrubbed, for we had to enter the drawing room at eight with bare arms, low neck, in evening dress. (*MOB*: 150)

Here the social life of the household becomes synonymous with female bodily display. Earlier, Woolf had lamented the demand for such compliance when she wrote about how her half-brother, George, had given her a long mirror for the expressed purpose of encouraging her to learn to style her hair and 'take general care [of her] appearance' (*MOB*: 122). Both half-brothers then are implicated in 'the looking-glass shame' (ibid.: 68) that contributes to Woolf's feelings of psychic debasement. That she literally identifies herself as an object of the male gaze is evident when she recounts how George 'always inspected [her] clothes' with 'extraordinarily observant scrutiny . . . look[ing] . . . up and down . . . as if [she] were a horse brought into the show ring' (ibid.: 151). Where Gerald literally violated her body, George's behaviour here produces a kind of psychic wounding that adheres to the gender prescriptions of women's clothing. This memory of sartorial distress is compounded when Woolf recounts the extreme discomfort she feels when George seeks to induct her and Vanessa into 'the London season'; she refers to her social failure as 'my intense shame' (ibid.:

154, 181). Woolf's account of this dark period of her life, when several times a week after dinner she and her sister would be forced to go upstairs and change into 'long satin dresses . . . long white gloves . . . satin shoes' and party jewellery (ibid.: 154), captures the degree to which clothes – even beautiful, expensive ones – can be bound to the concept of psychic wounding.

Woolf writes not only about how George's social aspirations required the sisters' complicity in high society, but how his desire for obedience was a kind of perverse sexual pleasure. She explains this sadistic 'insistence that [they] should . . . do as he wished' in terms of some 'crude wish to dominate . . . some sexual urge . . . [or] sexual jealousy that fermented in his depths' (*MOB*: 154–6). Woolf collapses the distinctions between the 'ruthless machine' (ibid.: 157) that is society and the malignancy that is George Duckworth, for in both cases the female body is territorialised in accordance with rules which are beyond its conscious control. Woolf's sacrificial lament – 'A girl had no chance against its fangs' (ibid.: 157) – speaks both to the wrenching physical pain of social convention and the psychic lacerations which result when one is objectified. The monstrous image of 'fangs' recalls her earlier depiction of 'minutely-teethed saws' and 'innumerable sharp teeth' (ibid.: 152) which are invoked to characterise the commodification of the female body and George's 'brainless' insertion of herself and Vanessa into the mechanics of heterosexual convention. When Woolf records that these teeth ruthlessly 'bit into us' (ibid.) she overtly alludes to the regulative force of Victorian manners, but the image of biting also conjures gashes and puncture wounds that remind us of how fangs can violate skin as well as clothing.

We see an example of this eroticized dynamic in '22 Hyde Park Gate', which Woolf wrote almost twenty years before 'A Sketch' but which takes up the same narrative of George Duckworth's ruthless 'lesson[s] in the art of behaviour' (*MOB*: 176). In this memoir Woolf writes about an evening out with George to an 'indecent French play' (ibid.: 181) and a series of parties at the height of the season in 1903, after which she arrives home, goes up to her bedroom, and describes the process of undressing:

> I . . . took off my beautiful white satin dress . . . I stood slipping off my petticoats, withdrew my long white gloves, and hung my white silk stockings over the back of a chair . . . how pleasant it would be to stretch out in bed, [and] fall asleep. (*MOB*: 177).

The narrative then reveals how, as she was falling asleep, George stealthily entered the room, called her 'beloved', and then 'flung himself on [her] bed and took [her] in his arms' (*MOB*: 177).

Woolf is mute on the details of George's advances but she draws attention to the dress and undergarments that she removes, casting those white, feminine clothes that accumulate in her bedroom as sacrificial garments – the social holding of her humiliation. The essay ends with this scandalous revelation: 'Yes, the old ladies of Kensington and Belgravia never knew that George Duckworth was not only father and mother, brother and sister to those poor Stephen girls; he was their lover also' (*MOB*: 177). There is a profound sense of how Woolf metaphorically reveals her degradation by displacing it onto the virginal pile of garments which are implicitly soiled by George Duckworth. Although Woolf momentarily acknowledges that there is a 'thrill in that unreality' of being encased in 'white [satin] and gloves' (ibid.: 156) at a party, the text undercuts this pleasure by showing more forcefully how visual attraction, being dressed up and put on display, functions as a form of male violence which results in 'humiliation' (ibid.: 155) for women.

And yet, Woolf's account of just how fraught clothes are also contains evidence of sartorial resistance: her representation of what I'm calling the dress of modernity functions as an effective and stylish tool of rebellion against the rules and observances that governed taste in the Victorian age. Near the end of 'A Sketch of the Past' Woolf apprehensively enters the drawing room wearing what she refers to as her 'home dress', a cheaply made garment constructed out of 'green fabric, bought at Story's, the furniture shop' (*MOB*: 150) and sewn by a dressmaker named Jane Bride (rather than Sally Young, the designer of Vanessa and Virginia's expensive evening dresses). Woolf describes the unexceptional fabric of her 'home dress' as 'not velvet; nor plush', but 'something betwixt and between', upholstery material intended for 'chairs, presumably, not dresses' (ibid.: 151). Woolf knows that her 'home dress' will incite a violent response from George, the fossilised arbiter of Victorian style, but she is still 'elated' when she enters the drawing room and contemplates how her unconventional 'green dress [will] set ringing in him a thousand alarm bells' (ibid.: 151, 152). Immediately George – dressed in black tie – responds with 'not simply aesthetic disapproval' but moral indignation, 'as if he scented some kind of insurrection, [in] defiance of his accepted standards' (ibid.: 151). If clothes are components in the regulation of the body, then Woolf's 'home dress' clearly emblematises her rebellion against the appalling rigours of Victorian convention. While we have no specific information as to the style or hue of this home dress, we learn that it is 'extreme . . . artistic . . . [and] not what nice people thought nice' – in other words, it is a marker of modernity, a cultural artifact that is an infringement upon the suffocatingly rigid standards of George Duckworth's 'Victorian code' (ibid.: 151, 152).

Woolf's language – extreme, artistic, not nice – brings to mind the rhetoric both of the Rational Dress Society, which sought during this time to protect the anatomy of the female body from aggressive fashion practices such as tight-lacing, and the proponents of Artistic Dress, a category which evolved initially from the art world through the influence of people like William Morris and John Ruskin, who decreed that garments should be simple, flowing and reflect the personality of the wearer (Nicholson 2002: 138, 105–6). Woolf's language also reminds us of how certain bold colours were inassimilable to the Victorians because they were considered an infraction of the rules governing good taste. For example the *Etiquette of Good Society*, written by Lady Colin Campbell in

1898, is adamant that bright colour must be treated with caution because it had explosive potential, aesthetically and socially speaking (ibid.: 132). Woolf refers directly to none of these things, but her association of the 'home dress' with 'insurrection' and 'defiance' (*MOB*: 151) illustrates that the garment is an affront to English notions of propriety; in this way it represents resistance to cultural authority, even though Woolf confesses to feeling 'fear . . . shame . . . [and] . . . anguish' when George orders her to tear it up (ibid.).

This psychologically complex territory of sartorial shame and rebellion can be seen in Woolf's short story, 'The New Dress', which was written in 1925 (as she was completing *Mrs Dalloway*) and was published in *The Forum: A Magazine of Controversy* in May 1927. Composed during the period that Woolf was publishing articles in *Vogue* and going on shopping trips with the magazine's editor, Dorothy Todd, 'The New Dress' contains evidence of the tension between clothing, uninhibited rapture and shame that we saw in 'A Sketch of the Past'. Primarily, it explores the psychic and bodily shame that adheres to certain clothes as it showcases Woolf's interest in the permutations of what she called 'frock consciousness' (*D3*: 12) – her private code for the interrelationship between subjectivity and clothing. The story's protagonist is the aptly named Mabel Waring, a lower-middle-class woman who arrives at Clarissa Dalloway's party wearing a new dress that was 'not quite right' because she cannot afford to 'be fashionable' (*SF*: 164). Although Mabel had spent hours on the design with her dressmaker, Miss Milan, her yellow frock now 'seemed sordid, repulsive', and a sign of her 'appalling inadequacy' (ibid.: 164) beside the Dalloways', with their affluent lives. Mabel based her dress upon a nineteenth-century Parisian design that she found in 'an old fashion book of her mother's', thinking that the dresses represented there looked 'much prettier, more dignified, and more womanly' than the fashion of her own era – which in the 1920s meant a severe silhouette which emphasised a slender, flat-chested, and narrow-hipped female body (ibid.: 164, 165). In contrast to this boyish frame, the pale yellow silk dress that Mabel wears emphasises a passé, rounded figure; the dress itself is 'modest and old-fashioned', with a 'long skirt', 'high sleeves', and 'looked so charming in the fashion book' (ibid.: 165) but in reality makes her feel 'foolish,' 'self-conscious' (ibid.: 167), and like a 'dressmaker's dummy' (ibid.: 165). Yet when she tries on the finished dress in Miss Milan's cramped workroom before a mirror, Mabel momentarily feels like 'a beautiful woman', rapturously happy, and full of 'extraordinary bliss' – as though she had miraculously 'rid [herself] of cares and wrinkles' (ibid.: 166).

This euphoric experience, when the reflection of herself in the new dress enables Mabel to see 'the core of herself, the soul of herself' and is accompanied by a spontaneous rush of love for her dressmaker (*SF*: 166), is a classic Woolfian 'moment of being' (*MOB*: 78) – one of those epiphanic moments of rapture and transcendence – but this 'divine moment' (*SF*: 169) is undermined by the mirror scene at the party. There, Mabel captures fleeting images of 'little bits of her yellow dress' in a visually distorting 'looking-glass' that makes her feel such acute 'humiliation and agony' that her dress shrinks to the size of a 'yellow dot' that renders her 'solitary' and 'disconnected' (ibid.: 168). The two mirror scenes – one reflecting wholeness, the other, fragmentation – draw attention to the way that clothes can produce both feelings of transcendence and debilitating isolation. The logic of sartorial wounding, Woolf suggests, furthermore affects the body, which has direct contact with the fabric that covers and purports to protect it. When Mabel feels a painful 'peck[ing]' at her left shoulder . . . as if spears were [being] thrown at her yellow dress from all sides' (ibid.: 66), we see how clothes can debase the body that they allegedly adorn. Mabel's objective is to dress in 'the height of fashion' and be 'original', but in attempting to replicate the fashion of a previous era and another country she makes a fatal mistake that sends her into a depressive spiral (ibid.: 164, 165).

As Jessica Burstein reminds us, the concept of timeless fashionability is a standard upheld by the fashion industry but, Mabel misreads the code by attempting to replicate the past, rather than transcending it; in doing so, she fails to secure a place within the radically hierarchical fashion system and instead merely relegates herself to the position of an 'absurdly dressed' fashion outcast (*SF*: 169). This imaginative failure, which Mabel calls the 'horror' of remaining 'idiotically old-fashioned' (ibid.: 165), can be read as a class marker, exposing the degree to which the desire for certain garments represents the promise, however elusive, of class mobility. She suffers social ostracism so profound that she identifies her 'creeping, crawling life' with the non-human – she is a 'beaten mongrel' one moment, 'some dowdy, decrepit, horribly dingy old fly' the next – abject images that underscore her deep-seated shame, insoluble loneliness and acute 'self-loathing' (ibid.: 170, 167, 165, 168).

Yet despite all of this she still clings tenaciously to the impossible notion that if only she had the perfect party dress instead of her 'hideous new dress' she would be saved 'from shame, from humiliation' (*SF*: 164, 167). Mabel couches this belief in the language of martyrdom, maintaining that her 'yellow dress was a penance which she had deserved' because she was a 'feeble, vacillating creature', and if she had only 'been dressed like Rose Shaw, in lovely, clinging green with a ruffle of swansdown, [then] she would have deserved that' (ibid.: 169). Kathryn Stockton's query – 'What can it mean to be martyred for clothes – to believe in your clothes as you suffer from clothes . . . ?' (Stockton 2006: 42) – reminds us of Mabel's faith in the salvational effects of clothing and her willingness to suffer the pain that is inseparable from their wearing. Mabel seeks to make an image of perfection of herself through dress, but by the end of the story she imagines taking refuge in a 'uniform' so that 'she would never give a thought to clothes again' (*SF*: 170). Woolf here seems to anticipate the psychoanalyst J. C. Flügel, whose famous treatise, *The Psychology of Clothes* (1930), argued for the abolition of fashion in favour of some kind of uniform dress which would level individual differences, but this short story does not dwell on that fantasy. Instead, in 'The New Dress' Woolf demonstrates the largely antagonistic relationship between women and clothing, how one is damaged by clothes even as one is seduced by their social promise.

II. Woolf in *Vogue*

Woolf's attraction to the seductiveness of clothing can perhaps best be seen in her relationship with *Vogue* magazine during the 1920s. Madge Garland, the stylish fashion editor during this period, recollects the first time that she saw Woolf, several years earlier, sitting in the audience of an art lecture given by Roger Fry in London. Garland's account highlights the author's 'madonna-like' beauty – her 'angular face, high cheek-bones, deep-set eyes' – and also makes note of Woolf's sartorial *faux pas*: 'she appeared to be wearing an upturned wastepaper basket on her head. There sat this beautiful and distinguished woman wearing what could only be described as a wastepaper basket' (Noble 1972: 171). Published photographs of Woolf during this period do not reveal an obvious corollary for this unconventional millinery, but it is safe to say that Woolf's selection is at odds with the close-fitting cloche hat that was fashionable for women during this period. Some years later, Garland, who made it 'her business to be flawlessly put together' (Cohen 2005: 374), had the opportunity to select an outfit for Woolf when the author approached her in early 1925 and invited her to choose clothes that would be suitable for her to wear to special dinner parties and to the theatre. Although Woolf exhibited a lack of attention to clothes – several of her contemporaries comment upon her 'rather nondescript', 'long . . . [and] shapeless' garments that 'hung . . . loosely' (Noble 1972: 56, 74, 169) from her body – we know that she was deeply invested in her appearance. Yet Woolf's moments of sartorial gratification and curiosity are always counterbalanced by what she calls 'my profound trepidation about my clothes' (*D4*: 104). Much of this anxiety stems from the terror of shopping in public for appropriate clothes to wear. Woolf conveys her emotional turmoil in terms of a fear of disgrace: 'Unhappiness, horror: The irrational pain: the sense of failure . . . [of] buying a new dress' (*D3*: 110). It is arguably this misery that compelled Woolf to seek the expert fashion advice of Marge Garland, a woman who was not only always impeccably dressed but was known as a fashion educator, an 'intellectual devotee of haute couture' (Cohen 2005: 372).

Although Woolf consulted both Garland and Dorothy Todd – the editor-in-chief of *Vogue* and Garland's lover during this period – about clothes, her diary and letters notably make no reference to the incident in which she acquired a couture dress. It was during a luncheon at Boulestin's restaurant in Southampton Row that Woolf admired Garland's elegant outfit, which was designed by the fashion editor's friend, Nicole Groult, the Parisian couturier and younger sister of Paul Poiret (the well-known designer). Garland's couture dress and coat were made of 'flowered silk by Bianchini [the leading French silk manufacturer] in a pattern of rose-pink and black on a white background . . . [with] a wide-brimmed hat to match . . . edged with a plain scallop of matching pink' (Mellown 1996: 228). While this confectionary, hyperfeminine ensemble seems at odds with Woolf's more understated, signature look – a cardigan-jacket, dark skirt, oxford-style shoes, and plain straw hat – her admiration of these garments compelled Garland to commission Groult to make a copy for her in blue. Imitation is fundamental to the workings of the fashion industry, and here Woolf's desire to procure a copy can arguably be read as both a tribute to Garland's taste and as evidence of her interest in appearing fashionable despite observations to the contrary. Garland was delighted to orchestrate a new look for Woolf via Groult in order to 'put all that beauty into its right setting' (Noble 1972: 171). Groult's distinguished clientèle comprised an 'international "who's who",' including Dorothy Parker, the Comtesse Marie Laure de Noailles – a society hostess, arts patron, and perennially best-dressed Frenchwoman – and Garland herself (Hay 2000: 141). Groult, known for her 'artistic' fashions (ibid.: 140), had the garments made in her Parisian *salon*, and later, when she travelled to London to show a new collection she brought a fitter with her so that last-minute adjustments could be made on Woolf's body. Garland vividly remembers the 'absolutely beautiful' dress and coat and recounts not only how 'supremely elegant' Woolf looked in her couture clothing, but how 'pleased and happy' Woolf was 'because its creation had not taken a moment of her time' (Noble 1972: 172). Garland's memory of Woolf's fitting with Groult ends with an allusion to the author's lifelong preoccupation with the fraught relationship between clothing and authorship: 'At this fitting Virginia said to me, "If only you would always dress me I should have time to write an extra book which I would dedicate to you!"' (ibid.). This dedication never happened, and Woolf makes no mention of the incident.

   Garland's snapshot captures what we might call Woolf's official posture, that only if one occupies a disinterested position in relation to fashion can one produce literature, but we know two important things that complicate this view: a preoccupation with the materiality of things – in particular, clothing – runs throughout Woolf's fiction and autobiographical writings; and one of Woolf's favoured metonyms for modernity is clothing. Garland conveys both Woolf's disengagement from the labour of becoming fashionable, and her investment in a certain kind of connoisseurship: exquisitely attuned to the pleasures (and miseries) of dressing oneself; attracted to the appearance of effortless elegance; happy to defer to the authoritative discourse of the fashion expert. Again, Woolf says nothing about this couture experience in her diary or letters, and instead highlights her distance from '[t]he fashion world . . . [of] Mrs. Garland . . . where people secrete an envelope which connects them & protects them from others, like myself, who am outside the envelope, foreign bodies' (*D*3: 12–13). Woolf professes estrangement from the fashion world, but these remarks, albeit painful, are made within the context of her photo-shoot for *Vogue* magazine at the studios of Maurice Beck and Helen Macgregor, the magazine's chief photographers during this time. As Woolf poses for Beck and Macgregor and observes that 'Mrs Garland was there superintending a display', she thinks about how the fashion industry is the province of an insulated elite (ibid.: 12). Of course, there is a certain irony to this juxtaposition since those who circulate 'outside the [fashion] envelope' (ibid.: 13) are not normally photographed for *Vogue*, nor do they purchase clothes from a Parisian couturier. Yet Woolf's besieged and joyless language – 'outside . . . foreign' – casts her in opposition to the magazine, even though she was featured there on several occasions as both a contributor and a celebrity. Instead of recounting Garland's heady role as fashion consultant in her diary or letters, Woolf elides this fact and is characteristically dismissive. She describes Garland as overdone, 'pear[l]hung & silken', and too ingratiating – possessing 'excessive charm' (ibid.: 184).

Garland's lover, Dorothy Todd, with whom Woolf also socialised during this period, is described in even more contemptuous terms. Todd is 'like a slug with a bleeding gash for a mouth' (an allusion to her lipstick), a 'primeval animal emerging from the swamp, muddy, hirsute' (*D3*: 175–6) This antipathy is consistent not only with prevailing sexological perceptions of the lesbian as atavistic during this period, but of Woolf's pathologisation and linkage of the lesbian body with degeneracy elsewhere in her writings (Garrity 2003: 64–5). We know that Todd was considered 'alarmingly butch' (Pender 2007: 522) in contrast to Garland's hyperfemininity, yet this alone cannot account for the virulence of Woolf's derision. It is arguably the overlap between lesbianism and the taint of commercialism that fuels Woolf's contempt and impels her to denounce Todd, however disingenuously, as an aberration: 'a woman who is commercial – rather an exception in my world' (*D3*: 176). Woolf repudiates the 'open and shameless' (*L3*: 158) vulgarity of Todd's magazine, but she luxuriates in the thought of 'sweeping guineas off the Vogue counter' (*D* 3: 33) and acknowledges that she 'lets you write what you like, and its your own fault if you conform to the stays and the petticoats' (*L* 3: 158). This allusion to women's constricting undergarments reminds us of the fact that, despite Woolf's antipathy for the *Vogue* editor, she still valued Todd's 'shimmer of dash & "chic"' and sought her advice about clothing and fashion (*D3*: 176). A visceral 1926 diary entry illustrates this combination of repudiation and allure:

> I am involved in dress buying with Todd; I tremble & shiver all over at the appalling magnitude of the task I have undertaken – to go to a dressmaker recommended by Todd, even, she suggested, but here my blood ran cold, with Todd. (*D3*: 78)

Woolf confesses to harbouring 'a great lust for lovely stuffs, & shapes', but she loathes the public aspect of shopping, 'parad[ing] Oxford Street' with the masses, and feels tormented by 'the fret of clothes' (*D3*: 86). It is therefore understandable why, despite Woolf's characterisation of Todd's and Garland's fashionable circle as 'incredibly louche' (*L3*: 501) she would agree to a shopping consultation and trip with the *Vogue* editor. Yet this excursion does not resolve what Woolf calls 'my clothes complex' (*D3*: 81). Instead of fashion triumph, the experience results in fashion humiliation:

> [I am] in black despair because Clive laughed at my new hat, Vita pitied me, & I sank to the depths of gloom . . . .I was wearing the hat without

thinking whether it was good or bad ... & we were all sitting round talking [and] Clive suddenly said ... what an astonishing hat you're wearing!
Then he asked where I got it. I pretended a mystery, tried to change the
talk, was not allowed .... I never felt more humiliated. Clive said did Mary
choose it? No. Todd said Vita. And the dress? Todd of course: after that I
was forced to go as if nothing terrible had happened; but it was very forced
& queer & humiliating. (*D3*: 90–91)

Lisa Cohen remarks that 'the queer Dorothy Todd' is 'at least partly responsible
for this "forced and queer" fashion humiliation' (Cohen 1999: 162), and indeed
we might speculate what role Todd's 'flamboyantly lesbian' (Luckhurst 1998: 9)
taste played in the construction of Woolf's ensemble. But what is most strongly
conveyed is Woolf's humiliation and a ferocious sense of fashion run amok.

Surprisingly, the next day, Woolf wears the exact same dress and hat to lunch
with Maynard Keynes. What possessed her to do this, given the 'black despair'
and 'depths of gloom' that these allegedly fashionable – yet ridiculed – clothes
had evoked earlier? Is Woolf motivated by the seductive allure of haute couture,
the aesthetic dictates of Dorothy Todd, or simply her own belief in the indefin-
able power of dress? When she meets Clive and Mary Hutchinson (his lover)
while wearing Todd's garments, the response is quite different: 'dress praised to
the skies, hat passed. So that's over ... the cloud began to lift' (*D3*: 91) And a few
weeks later to Vita Sackville-West, she again refers to Todd's dress:

Vanity compels me to admit that I should cut a very fine figure, in Todds
dress (Thank God, I'm sitting in an old silk petticoat at the moment with a
hole in it, and the top part of another dress with a hole in it, and the wind
is blowing through me). (*L3*: 281)

Here the previously shunned dress is embraced, but what Woolf draws attention to are the conspicuous holes in her old garments, a credentialising move
that announces her 'bohemian artist' status and betrays her ambivalence about
vanity. This rendering of the repudiation-reception of Todd's dress highlights
the perennially unstable and performative nature of clothing, how the meaning
of fashion shifts depending upon the social context and the receptivity (or not)
of the audience.

III. Materiality, Modernity and Aesthetic Consumption

Woolf's ambivalence toward clothing reveals her belief in the dangers inherent
in an unqualified embrace of fashion. One of the clearest examples of this occurs
in 'Modern Fiction' (1925), where Woolf uses clothing metaphors to express her
grievance against the 'materialists' – Wells, Bennett, and Galsworthy – whose
novels, she argues, are constrained by the 'ill-fitting vestments' (Woolf 1994:
160) of realist narrative conventions. Here, Woolf uses the language of dress to
critique those writers who 'are concerned not with the spirit but with the body'

(ibid.: 158). References to clothing acquire a complex resonance throughout the essay as Woolf invokes the rhetoric of contemporaneity – 'the form of fiction most in vogue' (ibid.: 160) – but links it to the materialists' adherence to accepted conventions. Wells 'takes too much delight in the solidity of his fabric', while Bennett's characters are 'dressed down to the last button of their coats in the fashion of the hour' yet are the antithesis of lifelike (ibid.: 159, 160). It is a paradox that in Bennett's desire to capture the details and verisimilitude of the story – 'the solidity, the likeness to life' – he succeeds only in 'embalming the whole' (ibid.: 160). His novels feature characters who appear *au courante*, but here fashionability is synonymous not with modernity but with cultural regression. In 'Modern Fiction' Woolf does not explicitly link the transgressive new styles of 'spiritual' modernists such as Joyce to the language of fashion; instead, she maintains that 'if a writer . . . could write what he chose . . . there would be . . . perhaps not a single button sewn on as the Bond Street tailors would have it' (ibid.: 161, 160). Those who follow fashion slavishly are at odds with writers who seek to characterise that ineffable quality, 'reality' – 'the essential thing' (ibid.: 160).

It is worth noting that Woolf's lament, 'we are sick of our own materialism' (Woolf 1994: 163), has an implicitly gendered component that links the implicitly masculinised 'unscrupulous tyrant' (ibid.: 160) of narrative conventions to the dictates of elite male 'Bond Street tailors'. Just as the tyrant has writers such as Bennett 'in thrall, to provide a plot, to provide comedy, tragedy, love interest', fashion compels the tailors of Bond Street to function as conservative connoisseurs of dominant masculine taste. Implicit in this critique is Woolf's understanding that fashion has the ability to signify rank and social distinctions and is a powerful force for regularisation, uniformity and the reproduction of rigid formal structures. Yet this strategic attack on fashion as conservative and formulaic is at odds with what Woolf says elsewhere about clothing, and is even inconsistent with what she says at the end of 'Modern Fiction' when she invokes an image of fabric in order to argue that 'the proper stuff of fiction is a little other than custom would have us believe' (ibid.: 161). The word 'stuff' would be vague but for reminding us of the rejected images of materialism earlier in the essay and suggests that a new form of sartorial expressiveness is needed.

In other words, 'Modern Fiction' pursues a discourse of fashionability ultimately in order to point toward the transformative potential of modernist innovation. When Woolf states, as she contemplates the problems facing the modern novelist, that 'a different outline of form becomes necessary' (Woolf 1994: 162), one hears the powerful sway of fashion discourse and imagines the outlines of a dressed body. At the start of 'Modern Fiction' Woolf berates the materialists for focusing too intently upon the body, but by the end she invokes 'the splendour of the body' as she considers the 'delight[s]' (ibid.: 163) of English literature and leaves us with a feminised and embodied image of 'the art of fiction come alive and standing in our midst' (ibid.: 164). The essay critiques fashion under a masculine rubric only to recuperate it under a feminised one. If 'everything is the proper stuff of fiction', and if 'no experiment, even the wildest – is forbidden' (ibid.: 164) then one wonders: what experimental 'stuff' is 'she' (ibid.: 164), the art of fiction, wearing? The answer remains unarticulated but the ending is important for two reasons: it re-frames the images of materiality and corporeality that were invoked and rejected earlier, and it implicitly draws upon the idea that the purpose of fashion is endless variation and innovation.

Woolf acknowledges fashion's frankly commercial function, but she also judiciously observes the profound importance of sartorial expressiveness for women and upholds fashion as a feminine signifier of value. In *A Room of One's Own* she critiques the cultural inequities between the sexes in terms that privilege the feminised character of fashion: 'Speaking crudely, football and sport are "important"; the worship of fashion, the buying of clothes "trivial"' (*AROO*: 74). Woolf's interest in exploring the 'unrecorded life' (ibid.: 89) of women focuses at one point upon the fictional writer, Mary Carmichael, whom she imagines within the context of a department store, surrounded by the profusion of feminine goods displayed for mass consumption. Woolf's preoccupation with the materiality of things – clothing – serves an attempt to introduce an entirely different valuation to 'stuff', that is synonymous with capitalist consumption but here appears more like a shrine to the collective fantasies of women:

> Above all, you must illuminate your own soul with its profundities and its shallows, and its vanities and its generosities, and say what your beauty means to you or your plainness, and what is your relation to the everchanging and turning world of gloves and shoes and stuffs swaying up and down among the faint scents that come through chemists' bottles down arcades of dress material over a floor of pseudo-marble. For in imagination I had gone into a shop; it was laid with black and white paving; it was hung, astonishingly beautifully, with coloured ribbons. Mary Carmichael might well have a look at that in passing, I thought, for it is a sight that would lend itself to the pen as fittingly as any snowy peak or rocky gorge in the Andes. And there is the girl behind the counter too – I would as soon have her true history as the hundred and fiftieth life of Napoleon or seventieth study of Keats. (*AROO*: 90)

This is a noteworthy passage for several reasons, not the least of which is Woolf's representation of the department store as a kind of surreal Benjaminean space in which the 'everchanging' labyrinth of merchandise – women's gloves, shoes, perfumes, ribbons, dress material – seem to hold out the potential for insight ('illuminate your own soul') and eventual transformation. We can see in Woolf's rendering of the self's relation to the magical properties of fashion evidence of Benjamin's belief that capitalism endows objects with the means to express collective dreams.

Woolf's entreaty to Mary Carmichael to discern the idea of beauty in her own person – 'you must . . . say what your beauty means to you or your plainness' – and her desire that the writer focus upon the phenomena of everyday life and record the seemingly incidental 'world of gloves and shoes and stuffs' (*AROO*: 90) is arguably an attempt to give value to the unarticulated preoccupations and desires of all women.

What's interesting here, too, is Woolf's delight in material culture, despite her acknowledgement of its superficiality (the floor is 'pseudo-marble'), and her use of the objects of women's consumer desire as imaginative vehicles to probe the 'profundities', 'shallows', 'vanities' and 'generosities' (*AROO*: 90) of the female soul. Woolf's claim that the documentation of women's relation to mass culture is as important as historical accounts of masculine achievement makes clear her desire to recuperate that which has earlier been perceived as trivial and frivolous. She observes that the store is 'a sight that would lend itself to the pen as fittingly as any snowy peak or rocky gorge in the Andes' (ibid.). The value here results not in accumulation but in aesthetic absorption, what Bill Brown calls 'an alternative economy . . . a noninstrumental passion for things' (Brown 1999: 17). Woolf is interested in 'the girl behind the counter' not because she wants to buy something, but because she is intrigued by the singularity of her 'true history' (*AROO*: 90). Moreover, her assertion that the shop girl's private narrative is as desirable as the life history of Keats or Napoleon can be read as a vision of how an understanding of women's relation to the objects of modernity can create a potential for democratisation and, perhaps, a social transformation of the relations between the sexes.

In Woolf's writing, we see evidence of both the false consciousness of women's relation to mass cultural forms and the belief that new spaces of consumption can actually create opportunities for liberation and transformation. Her work explores the material object's capacity to facilitate an intensely private kind of aesthetic transcendence while simultaneously demonstrating an awareness of the dangers inherent in the commodification of women. Woolf acknowledges the constitutive paradox of modernity for women: that the freedom to shop for fashionable clothes and wear make-up is not an inevitable sign of their equality, but often serves only to coerce them into proscribed social roles. This however is not to suggest that Woolf retreats altogether from the desirability of fashion, or represents sartorial shifts as merely oppressive or markers of corporeal discipline. On the contrary, as we have already seen, clothes function in Woolf as vehicles for self-fashioning, metonyms for modernity and signifiers of nonconformity. Sartorial discourse figures prominently in Woolf's playful meditations on the performative nature of gender and sexuality (one need think only of the extended satirical treatment of dress in *Orlando*), but it is also a vehicle for serious reflections on the boundary between self and other and perform a mediating function. In *To the Lighthouse*, as elsewhere in Woolf's work, garments are poignant markers of physical absence and function as archival traces of loss. Fashion, Woolf suggests, is a sartorial reminder of how garments and things can be brought to life through memory, but because women's cultural value is often linked to their status as objects of desire, it is also an ambivalent marker of modernity.

Works Cited and Further Reading

Abbott, Reginal (1992) 'What Miss Kilman's Petticoat Means: Virginia Woolf, Shopping, and Spectacle', *Modern Fiction Studies*, 38.1: 193–216.

Abbs, Carolyn (2006) 'Writing the Subject: Virginia Woolf and Clothes', *Colloquy: text, theory, critique*, 11: 209–25.

Brown, Bill (1999) 'The Secret Life of Things (Virginia Woolf and the Matter of Modernism)', *Modernism/Modernity*, 6.2: 1–28.

Burstein, Jessica (2010) *Cold Modernism*, University Park, PA: Penn State University Press.

Cervetti, Nancy (1996) 'In the Breeches, Petticoats, and Pleasures of *Orlando*', *Journal of Modern Literature*, 20.2: 165–75.

Cohen, Lisa (1999) '"Frock Consciousness": Virginia Woolf, the Open Secret, and the Language of Fashion', *Fashion Theory*, 3.2: 149–94.

—— (2005) 'Madge Garland and the Work of Fashion', *GLQ*, 11.3: 371–90.

DiGregorio, Jennifer-Ann Kightlinger (2003) 'Sex Costumes: Signifying Sex and Gender in Woolf's "The Introduction" and *The Years*', in *Woolf in the Real World: Selected Papers from the Thirteenth Annual International Conference on Virginia Woolf*, ed. Karen V. Kukil, Clemson, SC: Clemson University Digital Press, pp. 117–22.

Edson, Laura Gwyn (1997) 'Kicking off Her Knickers: Virginia Woolf's Rejection of Clothing as Realistic Detail', in *Virginia Woolf and the Arts: Selected Papers from the Sixth Annual Conference on Virginia Woolf*, ed. Diane F. Gillespie and Leslie K. Hankins, New York: Pace University Press, pp. 119–24.

Flynn, Deirdre (1999), 'Virginia Woolf's Women and the Fashionable Elite: On Not Fitting In', in *Virginia Woolf and Communities: Selected Papers from the Eighth Annual Conference on Virginia Woolf*, ed. Jeanette McVicker and Laura Davis, New York: Pace University Press, pp. 167–73.

Flügel, J. C. (1940) *The Psychology of Clothes*, London: Hogarth Press (Orginally published 1930).

Garrity, Jane (1999) 'Selling Culture to the "Civilized": Bloomsbury, British *Vogue*, and the Marketing of National Identity.' *Modernism/Modernity*, 6.2, April: 29–58.

—— (2000) 'Virginia Woolf, Intellectual Harlotry, and 1920s British *Vogue*', in *Virginia Woolf in the Age of Mechanical Reproduction*, ed. Pamela L. Caughie, New York & London: Garland Publishing, pp. 185–218.

—— (2003) *Step-Daughters of England: British Women Modernists and the National Imaginary*, Manchester and New York: Manchester University Press.

Hay, Susan (2000) 'Paris to Providence: French Couture and the Tirocchi Shop', in *From Paris to Providence, Fashion, Art and the Tirocchi Dressmakers' Shop, 1915–1947*, Providence: Rhode Island School of Design, pp. 133–71.

Holmes, Rachael (2000) 'Clothing and the Body: Motifs of Female Distress in Virginia Woolf and Katherine Mansfield', *Virginia Woolf Bulletin*, 3, January 9–14.

Koppen, R. S. (2006) 'Sartorial Adventures: Woolf and the (Other)Worldliness of Dress', in *Virginia Woolf and the Art of Exploration: Selected Papers from the Fifteenth International Conference on Virginia Woolf*, ed. Helen Southworth and Elisa Kay Sparks, Clemson, SC: Clemson University Press, pp. 212–19.

—— (2007) 'Real Bodies and the Psychology of Clothes: *Three Guineas* and the Limits of Sartorial Reasoning', in *Woolfian Boundaries: Selected Papers from the Sixteenth Annual International Conference on Virginia Woolf*, ed. Anna Burrells, Steve Ellis, Deborah Parsons and Kathryn Simpson, Clemson, SC: Clemson University Digital Press, pp. 72–9.

—— (2009), *Virginia Woolf, Fashion and Literary Modernity*, Edinburgh: Edinburgh University Press.

Laing, Kathryn S. (1997) 'Addressing Femininity in the Twenties: Virginia Woolf and Rebecca West on Money, Mirrors and Masquerade', in *Virginia Woolf and the Arts: Selected Papers from the Sixth Annual Conference on Virginia Woolf*, ed. Diane F. Gillespie and Leslie K. Hankins, New York: Pace University Press, pp. 66–75.

Luckhurst, Nicola (1998) *Bloomsbury in Vogue*, London: Cecil Woolf Publishers.

—— (1997) 'Vogue [. . .] is going to take up Mrs Woolf; to boom her . . .', in *Virginia Woolf and the Arts: Selected Papers from the Sixth Annual Conference on Virginia Woolf*, ed. Diane F. Gillespie and Leslie K. Hankins, New York: Pace University Press, pp. 75–84.

Marsaleix, Nadège (2003), 'Politics of the Sartorial Sign: Power and Representation', *Virginia Woolf Bulletin*, 14, September 7–11.

Mellown, Elgin W. (1996) 'An Annotated Checklist of Contributions by Bloomsbury and Other British Avant-Garde Writers (and of Articles Relating to Them) in *Vogue* Magazine during the Editorship of Dorothy Todd, 1923–1927', *Bulletin of Bibliography*, 53.3: 227–34.

Nicholson, Virginia (2002) *Among the Bohemians: Experiments in Living 1900-1939*, New York: Harper Collins.

Noble, Joan Russell (ed.) (1972) *Recollections of Virginia Woolf*, New York: William Morrow & Company.

Outka, Elizabeth (2000) '"The Shop Windows Were Full of Sparkling Chains": Consumer Desire and Woolf's *Night and Day*', in *Virginia Woolf: Out of Bounds Selected Papers from the Tenth Annual Conference on Virginia Woolf*, ed. Jessica Berman and Jane Goldman, New York: Pace University Press, pp. 229–35.

Pender, Anne (2007) '"Modernist Madonnas": Dorothy Todd, Madge Garland and Virginia Woolf', *Women's History Review*, 6.4: 519–33.

Reed, Christopher (2006) 'A *Vogue* that Dare Not Speak Its Name: Sexual Subculture during the Editorship of Dorothy Todd, 1922–26', *Fashion Theory*, 10.1–2: 39–72.

Sheehan, Elizabeth M. (2009) 'Dressmaking at the Omega Workshops: Experiments in Art and Fashion', *Beyond Bloomsbury: Designs of the Omega Workshops*, Exhibition catalogue. London: Courtauld Gallery, pp. 51–9.

Silver, Brenda (1999) *Virginia Woolf Icon*, Chicago: University of Chicago Press.

Smith, Sidonie (1993) *Subjectivity, Identity, and the Body: Women's Autobiographical Practices in the Twentieth Century*, Bloomington and Indianapolis: Indiana University Press.

Stockton, Kathryn Bond (2006) *Beautiful Bottom, Beautiful Shame: Where 'Black' Meets 'Queer'*, Durham, NC and London: Duke University Press.

Wicke, Jennifer (2001) 'Frock Consciousness: Virginia Woolf's Dialectical Materialism', *Virginia Woolf Out of Bounds*, ed. Jessica Berman and Jane Goldman, New York: Pace University Press, pp. 221–35.

—— (1994) '*Mrs. Dalloway* Goes to Market: Woolf, Keynes, and Modern Markets', *Novel: A Forum on Fiction*, 28.2: 5–23.

Woolf, Virginia (1977–84) *The Diary of Virginia Woolf*, 5 vols, ed. Anne Olivier Bell, London: Hogarth Press.

—— (1977) *A Change of Perspective: The Letters of Virginia Woolf, Vol. III: 1923-1928*, ed. Nigel Nicolson, London: Hogarth Press.

—— (1994) 'Modern Fiction', *The Essays of Virginia Woolf, Vol. IV, 1925-1928*, ed. Andrew McNeillie, London: Hogarth Press.

12

VIRGINIA WOOLF AND BOHEMIAN LIFESTYLES

Liz and Peter Brooker

Anyhow, I like Bohemians. (*D2*: 175)

A T ITS MOST straightforward, the idea of the bohemian conveys the combination of a conspicuously unconventional personal style, exhibited in clothing and conduct, along with an associated social scene and urban enclave which fosters a culture of artistic endeavour. In truth, however, both the bohemian and bohemia are marked by a persistent ambivalence, for bohemia is both a mythological and actual place while the bohemian is as much poseur as serious talent; 'both a genius and a phoney, a debauchee and a puritan' the bohemian's identity, as Elizabeth Wilson points out, is 'always dependent on its opposite' (Wilson 2000: 1, 3; Brooker 2007: viii–ix, 1–10). Nor is this figure confined to one place, one style, one class or one period.

Two features however, account for this divided image: the unstable relation between 'art' and what might be termed 'the art of life', and the opposition, in particular, between the bohemian and his or her more conventional bourgeois other. These combined ambiguities derived from the changing perception and role of art in the increasingly complex circumstances of technologised modernity and mass society in the nineteenth and early twentieth centuries. The figure of the bohemian emerged therefore as an uneasy, protesting outcome of bourgeois modernity, opposed to the domestic mores and business ethic of a capitalist middle-class and a debased popular taste. In Henri Murger's already romanticised stories in *La Vie de la Bohème* (1845–9), the bohemian was the young would-be artist who, with his 'grisette', gathered with like-minded companions in the cheap student-populated Latin quarter; a life 'only possible', said Murger, 'in Paris' (Murger 45). But Murger also distinguished between the pseudo-bohemian dreamer and the amateur and the real bohemian 'called by art' and emphasised the poverty and ruin which darkened the romance (ibid.: 49). The bohemian's prospects and likely grim destiny, as sketched by Murger, of the French Academy, the hospital of the Hôtel de Dieu or the morgue was played out in earnest across nineteenth-century European artistic culture. By the turn of the century, however, aided by such works as Puccini's *La Bohème* and Du Maurier's *Trilby*, the image of the carefree bohemian had entered popular currency as a familiar stereotype. This, in turn, gave rise through the 1900s and into the 1920s to new provocative variations on the type, to the open challenge of sexual dissidence, and to the appearance, in an added complexity, of the female bohemian, caught in new ways in a tension between artistic integrity, looking the part of the artist, and the demands of bourgeois life upon women, including the sexist assumptions of their male bohemian companions.

By 1904 a version of the stereotype had been absorbed by the Stephen sisters. On an evening spent with Clive Bell on a visit to Paris, Virginia reported 'talking of Art, Sculpture and Music till 11.30' at what felt like 'a real Bohemian party' (*L*1: 140). Bloomsbury, to which the sisters moved in this same year, was an initially dilapidated area of the city neighbouring the better-known bohemian quarter of artists' studios in Fitzrovia and the emerging café society of Soho. As a group, Bloomsbury was of course to produce its own iconoclasts and innovators. Its core members, however, did not circulate in London's bohemian café society. Unlike other modernists associated with the world of little magazines and manifestoes, early Bloomsbury made little collective public showing. They met, rather, over time, for different purposes and with changing personnel at, for example, the Friday Club, at meetings of the 1917 Club in Gerrard Street, in the Memoir Club from 1920, and, often, initially at Gordon Square, in private houses, in a version of the more traditional salon or 'at home'. As a select company, in a marked innovation, of both men and women, they gathered in such settings to develop a social milieu and discourse that sought to redefine abstract principles, but was, above all, a way of going on talking about such matters among friends. Its guiding topic, as is often said, was personal relations, of which they themselves were, in truth, the principal evidence.

Bloomsbury's 'bohemianism' rests on this unique social experiment: a concern with the interior life and relationships prompted by its radical break with Victorian social and sexual mores. As Woolf commented in the early 1920s in response to a wild scheme by Maynard Keynes to build a hotel south of Charleston – 'No doubt we have re-arranged life almost completely. Our parents were mere triflers at the game . . . we have all mastered the art of life, & very fascinating it is' (*D*2: 199). At the same time its unconventionality was differently expressed in the varied lives of its members and qualified, we might think, by class privilege. Any claim to Woolf's own bohemian credentials is discounted, we might think, by the fact that she employed servants – though neither class, wealth nor servants would seem to rule out figures as different as Nancy Cunard or Ottoline Morrell. And, as Alison Light comments, though 'The Stephen siblings were not Bohemians glorying in slumming or in eating scratch meals . . . many a Bohemian kept a maid or manservant as soon as they could afford it' (Light 2007: 53).

In Woolf's case, commentators tend to cite the bohemian exploit of the 'Dreadnought Hoax' of February 1910 (see Stansky 1996: 17–46; and Brooker

2007: 175). In this incident a party of six friends, including Virginia, who was the only woman, Duncan Grant and Adrian Stephen, dressed as Abyssinian royalty and embarrassed the British navy by tricking them into accepting them as *bona fide* visiting dignitaries. The escapade had more the air of an undergraduate prank than a bohemian provocation. At the same time it signalled the younger Stephens' wilful flouting of Victorian proprieties and establishment protocols. Woolf certainly never regretted it (Woolf 2008; Barkway 2006). What it also signified in the youthful Virginia was a penchant for dressing up – as an Abyssinian prince and, along with Vanessa, as a Gauguinesque maiden at the celebration of the first Post-Impressionist Exhibition in 1910–11 when Vanessa apparently danced naked to the waist (Bell 1997: 133–4; Hall 2007: 128). Later this materialised in a flair for amateur dramatics. More broadly, however, these dramas, public and private, expressed an instinct for impersonation. Woolf sensed that her personality was multiple and that her books presented 'a variety of styles and subjects: for after all that is my temperament' (quoted in Lehmann 1975: 60). This brought by turns the risk of disintegration and the adventure of a rush of impressions and the meandering rhythms of consciousness in life and in fiction. The character of Bernard in *The Waves* (1931) was to give notable expression to the implications of this perception for an understanding of personal identity and relationships. As he notes, 'To be myself . . . I need the illumination of other people's eyes, and therefore cannot be entirely sure what is my self', and again, 'I am not one person; I am many people . . . . For this is not one life; nor do I always know if I am man or woman' (*W*: 83, 196, 199). *The Waves* and, more directly, *Orlando* (1928) and *A Room of One's Own* (1929), explore in particular the implications of the doubled, androgynous self; in *Orlando,* of course, in a fantasised extrapolation of the bisexuality of Vita Sackville-West. These examples and the understanding of a mobile, liminal subjectivity bring us closer to a way of viewing Woolf and bohemianism and this we attempt below in a discussion of Woolf's fluent, exploratory relationships in particular with unconventional women. Woolf's own remarks, also, on 'mastering the art of life', above, inform what follows.

In her study of *Virginia Woolf's Women*, Vanessa Curtis describes how each of the women she discusses was 'able to extract different strands of Woolf's personality from the complex, multifarious web that was Virginia's mind' (Curtis 2002: 16). In a similar but more focused way we view Woolf's relationship to bohemianism through her relationships with four women who have been more readily identified as bohemian: her sister Vanessa Bell, the transgressive aristocrats of high bohemia, Ottoline Morrell and Vita Sackville-West, and the writer Katherine Mansfield. Angela Smith draws on Julia Kristeva's concept of 'liminality' to describe how in this last relationship Woolf and Mansfield encounter both the familiar and the foreign in each other and by turns acknowledge, internalise and expel the latter (Smith 1999). Smith's analysis applies most acutely to Woolf and Mansfield, but helps too to understand these other relationships.

The bohemian figure, we remember, is 'always dependent on its opposite' (Wilson 2000: 3) and as much fraud and poseur as genuine artist. Even the clichéd type betrays a strong performative aspect in making a staged appearance on the public scene. However, an emphasis on the outward traits by which the bohemian of this period is known – soft, wide-brimmed hat, velvet jacket or corduroy suit for men; bobbed hair, coloured stockings, pumps, for young women – fails to acknowledge both the different styles and degrees of commitment to experiment in art and life and the differentiated social positioning by class, sexuality and talent which marked the general type.

All of these factors are at play in what follows. Much too is revealed in Woolf's tone, especially in her letters and diary entries which are in some cases strikingly, and by turn, admiring, loving, waspish, mocking and jealous. This may be accounted for by changes in these women themselves or by differences between them, but it is just as clear that Woolf was herself capable of seeing them differently, to the point of self-contradiction. As Andrew McNeillie points out, Woolf's correspondence could itself be 'intensely performative and recipient-specific' and that as a consequence 'we can't always take it that she "means" what she says' (McNeillie 2000: 13). Her diaries similarly frequently show a self-conscious awareness of audience. The result was that Woolf acted the part of observer, story-teller and satirist as much as participant in these, as in other relationships. Her instincts and priorities, we come to perceive, placed her 'elsewhere': as, above all, the writer who is here but there at the same time; who, in experiencing the 'splitting off of consciousness' as she describes it in *A Room of One's Own* (1929), was aware in London, for example, of being 'the natural inheritor of that civilisation' but also 'outside of it, alien and critical' (*AROO*: 146). How we describe this perspective upon the internally divided figure of the bohemian woman is the subject of this chapter.

Virginia and Vanessa

Woolf's relationship with her sister Vanessa Bell has been described as the most important of her life, after that with Leonard Woolf. As Jane Dunn documents in her *Virginia Woolf and Vanessa Bell. A Very Close Conspiracy*, Virginia's 'conspiracy' with Vanessa began at birth, and lasted until her death. The relationship between the sisters could be both close and confidential or distant and discordant, but it remained important to both, and their letters and diaries both implicitly and explicitly debate issues of bohemianism.

History has viewed Vanessa as the more bohemian of the sisters. She is known for her early awakening to bohemian society in Paris, and her later adoption of France as an artistic refuge; for her transformation by marriage and motherhood into a sexually liberated mother-figure; for her creation of a domestic ménage, at Charleston and Cassis, which defied the conventions of Edwardian households by including her husband Clive Bell, her lover Duncan Grant, his lover David Garnett, and their combined children, as well as offering a home to long-term (also homosexual) intellectual friends. Her experiments in life, in other words, which began with her decision to move the family to Bloomsbury after their father's death, matched her experiments in art, coalescing in her innovative decoration of her house in Gordon Square and the farmhouse at Charleston.

Long before Bloomsbury, the sisters had identified themselves, reports Dunn, as 'secret revolutionaries' (Dunn 2000: 57). Their revolt was against almost every aspect of the life they had been brought up to in Hyde Park Gate: the afternoon tea ceremonies, the calling cards, the domestic patriarchy, and above all the social scene to which their half-brother George introduced them, and where they felt such failures: 'Really, we can't shine in Society. I don't know how it's done. We aint popular – we sit in corners and look like mutes who are longing for a funeral', said Virginia (*L1*: 43). They dreamed of a future life free of these constraints and embarrassments, and had already begun to build it in the early years of their shared existence in Gordon Square and the distinctly unconventional co-habitation, shocking to relatives, of Virginia and male friends at Brunswick Square. They meant 'to try all kinds of experiments' wrote Virginia (*L1*: 480); 'we were in the van of the builders of a new society', thought Leonard Woolf (Woolf 1960: 161). And of course they talked freely about sex, it 'permeated our conversation', said Virginia. (*MOB*: 173–4). 'We did not hesitate to talk of anything' said Vanessa, 'about art, sex or religion' as freely as 'about the ordinary doings of daily life' (Bell 1997: 105). In the event, they were more liberal than libertine, 'only spiritual bohemians' in Leon Edel's description (Edel 1979: 172). But their revolt against the conformism of the Victorian household was real enough. To choose an artistic vocation and new personal and domestic arrangements promised independence after oppression, and success after failure, so that when Clive Bell first proposed marriage to Vanessa, he was rejected on the grounds that, as she wrote to Margery Snowden 'I get all the fun and none of the bother of married life as it is' (CP, 11 August 1906).

Vanessa cherished the memory of pre-war 'old' Bloomsbury when it was '"very heaven" to be alive' (Bell 1997: 111). Virginia had a more flexible sense of when and where Bloomsbury was and a more intensely imagined, if more strenuous, picture of an alternative life: of 'a colony where there shall be no marrying'; of 'somewhere . . . a world where people did not go to parties' but 'discussed pictures – books – philosophy –'; and of another life, as in *To the Lighthouse*, for 'daughters who could sport with infidel ideas' (*L1*: 41; *MOB*: 135; *TTL*: 16).

The marriages – Vanessa's to Clive Bell in 1907, and Virginia's to Leonard Woolf in 1912 – marked the beginning of a lifelong tension between aspects of the sisters' lifestyles and attitudes. On the one hand, Vanessa is characterised (and characterises herself) as the more bohemian of the two, a charge which Virginia finds hurtful and wounding: thus, on leaving for France in 1922, Vanessa '[t]old me I shouldn't enjoy café life in Paris', that 'I liked my own fireside & books . . .that I was settled & unadventurous' (*D2*: 159). Dunn agrees that 'Virginia was never to be as enamoured of the bohemian way of life' (Dunn

2000: 139) but there is an undertow to this exchange between the sisters. For Vanessa's remarks were a response to Virginia's frequently-voiced view of her sister as the 'normal' one: 'I set out to prove that being childless I was less normal than she. She took offence', wrote Woolf (*D*2: 159). The Charleston ménage which is taken to represent a bohemian lifestyle – sexual irregularity, naked children – was construed by Virginia as the touchstone of normality. She was to confess later to 'a desire for children, I suppose; for Nessa's life', determined she must 'never pretend that the things you haven't got are not worth having' (*D*2: 221), but here she reverses the comparison so as to make herself the more unconventional and exceptional sister.

Virginia's comments express together a defiant self-affirmation and her own sense of lack, and reflect too upon the real nature of her sister's existence, less, as time went on, a life of sexual liberation and fulfilment, than of decades of unreciprocated devotion to Duncan Grant which obliged her to repress her passionate feelings, or transfer them to her children. In the end, it was Vanessa's marvellous stoicism that impressed Virginia, who describes her as having 'that queer antique simplicity of surface' of a Greek statue, a reflection prompted by Vanessa's 'perfectly open, unresentful, philosophic' acceptance of Clive Bell's behaviour with Mary Hutchinson (*D*2: 156–7). As Dunn has shown, Vanessa's tendency to depression, though less dramatic in its consequences, was not unlike Virginia's own, and her lifelong submission to Grant's whims and wishes was much closer to the Victorian model of wifely devotion, which both sisters had consciously rejected, than Virginia's relationship with Leonard. This narrowing of horizons, and a frequent sense that her own work as an artist, despite its impressive range, was crowded out by family life, or unappreciated, may help to explain why Vanessa looked back on early Bloomsbury as the real Bloomsbury at its most utopian and bohemian. Virginia too remembered this time, before Vanessa's marriage, as a time of uncomplicated experiment and liberation ('the most beautiful, the most exciting, the most romantic') but was able also to ask 'Who was I then?' (*MOB*: 162, 65) and had a sense of herself as altered and alterable over time, so that in recollecting the past she was defining her present difference both from Vanessa and from her own earlier self, attempting 'to make the two people, I now, I then, come out in contrast' (ibid.: 75).

But there is an additional factor or, rather, personality here: the figure of the male bohemian, Duncan Grant. The sisters' descriptions of him on his arrival on the Bloomsbury scene are strikingly similar – and distinguish him too from the others directly from Cambridge who formed the early group, and who Virginia came to see as 'dingy', 'lacking in physical splendour' (*MOB*: 169), and who deprived them as women of 'one of the chief necessities of life' – since '[t]he society of buggers has many advantages' but 'with buggers one can't . . . show off' (ibid.: 172). Grant was the painter who with Fry helped define the public character of 'old Bloomsbury', and gave Vanessa a distinctive role. He was the unmistakeable bohemian type: no money, borrowed clothes, a studio he shared in Fitzrovia, but he could 'charm' even their cook and 'always alighted exactly where he wanted to' (*MOB*: 176). Vanessa portrays him as an art student who though penniless 'seemed unaware of the fact'. He borrowed money ('the exact sum' only) and found that food was provided: 'So he solved the problem of living on air with satisfaction to everyone' (Bell 1997: 107). As such, Grant characterised the carefree, liberated air and tolerance of the 'old Bloomsbury' which both sisters subsequently recalled as a time of unqualified hope and pleasure. In particular, said Woolf, 'the old sentimental views of marriage . . . were revolutionised'; there was 'nothing shocking in a man's having a mistress, or a woman's being one' (*MOB*: 174). Human character and human relations changed; marriage was no longer sentimental, there was nothing shocking about adultery, less about homosexuality. But there was still to be marriage and complex questions of motherhood and sexuality for both women, neither of whom can be said to have 'alighted exactly' where they wanted to be, or to have 'solved the problem of living on air'. Vanessa and Virginia remained mutually defining in their sameness and difference, by turns 'normal', stay-at-home, adventurous and experimental, but it is clear too how gendered the conditions and relative advantages of Bloomsbury's bohemia, old and new, remained.

Ottoline and Vita

Ottoline Morrell and Vita Sackville-West had wealth, aristocratic status and bearing and, of course, servants. Both dressed conspicuously, even flamboyantly in an overt show of unconventionality. In their public lives, Morrell entertained and cultivated artists, while Sackville-West wrote bestselling verse, essays and fiction; in their private lives, both had what were strictly adulterous affairs. They appear therefore to conform more obviously to type, though of 'high' and not simply middling bourgeois bohemia. Woolf's relationships with them were of different intensities, as we shall see, but she was evidently attracted to their aristocratic breeding and social ease – Morrell, as Miranda Seymour records, had, she said, 'An element of the superb' (Seymour 1992: 300). But both women were also at times the objects of her mockery. As ever, Woolf explored her own identity through her relationships with both women, finding, measuring and affirming herself against their difference.

Did Bloomsbury, asked Virginia Woolf of the Memoir Club in the early 1920s, include Ottoline Morrell and Bedford Square? 'Before the war', she says, 'I think we should most of us have said "Yes"' (*MOB*: 177). In a way, this simply confirms Bloomsbury's heyday as belonging to the 1910s, but it is a curious question and answer, nonetheless, in relation to Morrell, whose Thursday gatherings at 44 Bedford Square included not only figures from the Bloomsbury group but also other writers, artists and politicians, including Augustus John, Charles Masterman, and Max Beerbohm. Invitations to Morrell's country home, Garsington Manor, from 1915 into the early 1920s were a source of amusement, luxury and free board for a wide range of guests who included the inner and outer circles of Bloomsbury as well as, among many others, Bertrand Russell, the Lawrences, Mansfield and Murry, T. S. Eliot, Aldous Huxley, Diaghilev, Siegfried Sassoon, Yeats and the Prime Minister Herbert Asquith, Morrell's personal friend. Her reign as a society hostess and *salonière* extended into the 1920s when she moved to Gower Street, London. Her social domain extended beyond the Bloomsbury group, therefore. Hers resembled a more traditional role, of course, and one of the marks of Bloomsbury is that Vanessa and Virginia helped to bring the combination of a new informality, frankness, intellectual intensity and more intimate scale to this kind of socialising. Bedford Square was formal and Garsington grand, frivolous and gossipy, and this difference may be one reason why Strachey and Virginia, especially, took delight in ridiculing Ottoline Morrell while praising her lavishly to her person. Virginia's hypocrisy is revealed in her letters and diaries. Thus, from the first, she wrote to Morrell of her 'great joy' at the prospect of their friendship and of how 'delightful' it is 'to know you and like you as I do' (*L1*: 381) only shortly after to describe her as having 'the head of a Medusa' (ibid.: 395) and later as 'brilliantly painted, as garish as a strumpet' (*D1*: 201).

Why did she attend these gatherings when Vanessa more readily dismissed Morrell as simply talking 'waffle', and Leonard was reluctant to accompany her? Perhaps the aristocrat Morrell was fair game to someone who had left the world of social pretension behind, but perhaps too she posed a specific challenge to Woolf herself: less a matter simply of her status than of her outré manner and assumptions: her extravagantly feminine dress, her excessive use of powder and scent, her conspicuous affairs and her emotional vapourings about art and the soul. All those things, in short, that made Ottoline Morrell a queen of high bohemia, were, we might surmise, traits of a kind of unconventional Edwardian woman 'discontented with her own class' (*MOB*: 177) which Woolf had no interest in herself adopting, but which she had nonetheless to contend with in establishing how she herself was to be unconventional in another way.

Garsington was a world of gossip, kowtowing and back-biting and perhaps this was part of the fun, but it's clear, all the same, that not all the guests felt as Virginia did. Duncan Grant, Mark Gertler, the MacCarthys and Eliot were consistently affectionate towards Morrell and she must have had some skill at least to hold Russell and Huxley and Murry in intense conversation into the early hours. In David Cecil's telling description she was 'a creative artist of the private life' (Seymour 1992: 324). She was fervent in her support of pacifism and Home Rule for Ireland and she was also free of the homophobia of many of her guests – hence her role as confidante to Lytton Strachey. Her taste in painting and writing was consistently contemporary and genuine – she helped Fry select the paintings for the First Post-Impressionist Exhibition, she found Lewis's work 'superlatively good', admired Eliot and Lawrence's verse, and had 'loved' Joyce's Anna Livia Plurabelle (ibid.: 411, 361, 390). Her clothes too, pale pink Turkish trousers, full Cossack and Oriental outfits, shawls, scarves and flowing gowns of bold design and colours, including those of the Sinn Fein, along with her abundant red hair and sing-song voice, surely made her a remarkable figure.

For all the whiplash sarcasm, Woolf had early on acknowledged Morrell's 'vitality', 'bursts of shrewdness' and generosity, embodied, as she saw, in the grand gesture of Garsington (*D*1: 79). And in time Woolf's spitefulness diminished as Morrell moved back to London, her eccentricity now on unselfconscious display against the humbler setting of Gower Street. She acknowledged that Morrell's physical ailments were real and admired her uncomplaining suffering from severe headaches and deafness, from cancer of the jaw and encroaching decrepitude. They shared the grief of Mansfield's and Strachey's deaths, Carrington's suicide, and then the death of Roger Fry, but, most importantly, Woolf had encouraged Morrell to write her memoirs, even to take revenge. Morrell could not follow the advice to 'Pick us all to pieces. Throw us to the dogs' (HRC, quoted in Seymour 1992: 346) but for Woolf to encourage her to write, and write candidly, was the one important gesture by which she could express her friendship and give something of herself – to the point of allowing her own earlier duplicity to be exposed.

The bohemian is both fraud and serious artist, the failed amateur and the genius. Morrell and Woolf seem at first, in Woolf's eyes, to take these respective parts across class lines and as opposite types of the feminine. Woolf came, however, to see that what she had derided in Morrell's bohemian dress and manner were the unforced signs of her independent spirit, that the surface expressed a genuine depth. As Seymour comments, whereas Woolf had seen Morrell at Bedford Square and Garsington as simply 'grand and artificial', on Morrell's return to Gower Street she realised that she 'continued to be as vivid, as idiosyncratic and as unselfconsciously bizarre' wherever she was, 'whether you put her in a Lyons Corner Shop or in Windsor Castle' (Seymour 1992:392). With this change of attitude and in recognising Morrell's courage in the face of physical afflictions, Woolf was able to offer affection and sympathy and to acknowledge a kinship as that same serious artist, but in a now open and supportive spirit as the chief adviser to Morrell's own efforts as an author. The parts were reconciled without compromise.

On first meeting Vita Sackville-West, Woolf drew a similar initial contrast with herself: 'the lovely gifted aristocratic Sackville West' was '[n]ot much to my severer taste – florid, moustached, parakeet coloured, with all the supple ease of the aristocracy, but not the wit of the artist' (*D*2: 216).The artist as puritan judged the exotic aristocrat as at once too much out of the ordinary and not extraordinary enough. But four days later Sackville-West records not only her view that Woolf 'dresses quite atrociously', but the fact that 'She was smarter last night; that is to say, the woollen orange stockings were replaced by yellow silk ones' – an odd image of a 'severer taste' perhaps (in Nicolson, 185). This relationship too however changed over time and functioned similarly for Woolf as a means of self-definition and affirmation.

Vita Sackville-West presented one of the most notorious of the 'experiments in life' of the Bloomsbury group and their associates. She was a larger-than-life figure in every respect: a tall and florid physique, outlandishly dressed; an aristocrat whose innate confidence gave her access to all social milieux; a passionate woman whose affairs and 'elopements' with both men and women continued over decades; a prolific and bestselling author of poetry, fiction, drama and journalism; and yet, equally famously, a devoted wife, mother, home-maker and gardener. Woolf, like others before and after her, was mesmerised.

Their friendship, which lasted until Woolf's death, developed when Virginia was in her early forties. She initially recorded her pleasure that 'Mrs Nicolson' had heard of her and praised her work. Her early comments on Vita, however, such as the above, are far from flattering and ran to disparaging comments on Vita's florid manliness of appearance (including her tendency to 'double chins') and her inferior intellect. Her diary entries were cruel and unfeeling about Vita's appearance and her mind, as well as about her writing. Her letters to Vita, on the other hand, in a familiar but here heightened contradiction, contained such passionate expressions of love and longing that it is hard to imagine the Woolfs' stable working partnership carrying on, as it did, throughout the lengthy 'affair'.

Here too, as in her relationship with Ottoline Morrell, Woolf was drawn to a fervent admiration for the physical grace and social ease of the aristocrat:

> All these ancestors & centuries, & silver & gold, have bred a perfect body. She is stag like, or race horse like, save for the face, which pouts, & has no very sharp brain. But as a body hers is perfection. . . all very free & easy, supple jointed as the aristocrat is; no inhibitions, no false reserves; anything can be said. (*D*2: 306–7)

Unlike Morrell, Vita's determined non-conformism took her into a succession of torrid individual relationships rather than into the exhibitionism and role of hostess in a public social sphere. Her transgressive sexual appetite (in an interesting comparison with the gay male bohemian Duncan Grant) created domestic disruption and scandal but her class-confidence carried her through every mishap and misjudgement with unscathed aplomb. Woolf's sexuality in this case is much debated, but however we interpret her diaries and letters, it appears that her passionate feelings were constrained by a physical reticence which Sackville-West both recognised and respected. In a not dissimilar trajectory to Woolf's relationship with Morrell, a lifelong and valued friendship evolved from the tangled and contradictory aspects of the early years of their relationship, although the tensions persisted. Woolf was stung by Sackville-West's cordial accusation that she looked 'upon everything, human relationships included' as 'copy': as material, that is to say, for writing (DeSalvo and Leaska 1985: 51), though she bravely responded that 'I enjoyed your abuse very much' (ibid.: 52). In both these cases, too, it is when Woolf establishes her control as a writer over the material of her life, one sphere of experimentation administering to the other, that the contradictions if not resolved are transported into another medium, one that confers the hoped-for accolades and title of 'genius' upon herself. Her admiration for Vita's masterful, androgynous personality consequently took its most demonstrable and joyous form – as the affair itself cooled, and Vita took up with another woman – in the novel *Orlando*. That this was a fitting expression of the relationship is suggested perhaps by the fact that Vita took it as a profound tribute and compliment, willingly posing in fancy dress for the period photographs which adorned the book.

'K.M.'

The contrast, with its attendant class and sexualised associations, between the disparaged female bohemian and the admired experimental, modernist writer, emerges most acutely in Woolf's relationships with Katherine Mansfield who was problematically for Woolf both bohemian and rival modernist.

In June 1917, a few months after they had first met, Woolf commented after an 'odd talk' that Mansfield 'seems to have gone every sort of hog since she was 17' (*L*2: 159). Mansfield ('K.M.' in Woolf's diaries) had first come to London in 1903 and returned alone in 1908. Unlike Woolf, she had experienced some formal education, she had had affairs with men and women, she was very briefly married; she had had a still-born child; had written for the *New Age*, and with Middleton Murry, with whom she was now living, had co-edited *Rhythm* and the *Blue Review*, and with D. H Lawrence and Murry contributed to the short-lived *Signature*. Her collection of stories *In a German Pension* had been published in 1911. Her family was wealthy but she had only a small allowance and shifted from one humble rented accommodation to another. She was also increasingly ill, having contracted gonorrhea and grown arthritic. As Woolf remarked again in 1919, 'she's had every sort of experience' (*L*2: 248).

They met through Ottoline Morrell, who had herself been confused by what she described as Mansfield's changes in mood and her 'delicate, exotic vulgarity and sensitively showy bad taste' (Shaw 1984: 118). Incredibly, Morrell failed to recognise the disparity between their circumstances when Mansfield was so patently aware of them: as she wrote from her kitchen, groaning over a bill and her 'ugly makeshift furniture', 'Confound my poverty! . . . I positively lead another life with you there [Garsington]' (ibid.: 123).

When Woolf met Mansfield, she was 'awed by the wildness of both her colonial and her bohemian life' (Smith 1999: 1). In truth, her reaction, like Morrell's, was mixed, particularly, as in Woolf's own relationship with Morrell, she learned of Mansfield's illnesses. Earlier Woolf had been more fiercely judgemental than Morrell, deciding on their first acquaintance that Mansfield was 'unpleasant' and 'utterly unscrupulous' (*L*2: 144). In some respects, Woolf's attitude was simply crude and contemptuous, as in the notorious comment that Mansfield 'stinks like a – well, civet cat that had taken to street walking' (*D*1: 58). There was also her response not only to Mansfield's person but to her writing, of which she was uncontrollably jealous, sometimes almost comically, but at other times triumphantly. On first reading Mansfield's *Bliss*, she exclaimed, 'She's done for!' Mansfield was 'content with superficial smartness', it was 'poor, cheap' and 'I don't see how much faith in her as woman or writer can survive that sort of story' (ibid.: 179). Four years later, meanwhile protesting that she was not jealous of Mansfield 'though every reviewer praises her' (*L2*: 454), she confirmed her distaste: *Bliss* was 'so hard and so shallow and so sentimental that I had to rush to the bookcase for something to drink' (*L2*: 514).Even after her death she confessed to Vita Sackville-West that she was reading Mansfield's journal 'with a mixture of sentiment and horror' (*L3*: 408). But Mansfield was, of course, the one writer Woolf admitted as a serious rival: hers was 'the only writing I have ever been jealous of' (*D2*: 227). They shared the same aims, as both acknowledged. Thus Mansfield found it 'very curious and thrilling' that they 'should both, quite apart from each other, be after so very nearly the same thing' (Murry 1928: 80), while Woolf recognised that 'to no one else can I talk in the same disembodied way about writing' (*D2*: 45).

Woolf's relationship with Mansfield was distinguished by the combination of the strength of her feelings, and the closeness of Mansfield's literary ambition to her own. Vanessa was a rival in another artistic medium and this was a cause of some jealousy, but Woolf expressed no such feeling towards Morrell, nor towards Sackville-West's writing, which was popular rather than serious and an evident money-spinner – useful for the Hogarth Press, but in another league, Woolf could be sure, from her own writing. Her relation with Mansfield, therefore, as, on the one hand, the 'bohemian' woman whom she instinctively associated with 'cheap' dress, scent, make-up and sexual promiscuity, and, on the other hand the 'serious writer', was unique: a medley of the vicious, fearful and admiring.

Biographers and critics have tracked these complex emotions in the lives and writings of both women. Woolf and Mansfield shared a wide concern with female and family identity, with male bullying and egoism, the dissatisfactions of marriage, and an almost interchangeable idiom in descriptive narrative passages (see Curtis 2002: 116–22 and Smith 1999: chapters 4–7). Angela Smith accounts for these combined similarities and differences in terms of their 'liminality'. Mansfield and Woolf, Smith argues, were similarly outsiders in relation to mainstream society, but felt a combined affinity, admiration and strangeness in relation to each other; involving, on Woolf's part, some trepidation at and contempt for Mansfield's foreignness and her imputed vulgarity. They experienced, as Smith underlines, what Woolf termed 'a queer sense of being "like"' (*D2*: 45).

As Smith suggests, this relationship involves both the person and the writer. The more pronounced otherness they sensed, existed less in their writing than in their personal lives – their everyday moods and manners, their pasts, their circumstances, their relative wealth and poverty, their sexual attitudes, their moral and social codes – but all these features are simultaneously inseparable from, though not identical with, Mansfield and Woolf's identities as writers. Woolf's comment on *Bliss* above was a judgement explicitly on Mansfield as both woman and writer. She found its 'whole conception is poor, cheap, not the vision, however imperfect, of an interesting mind'. The effect was 'to give me an impression of her callousness & hardness as a human being' (*D1*: 179).

Woolf's reaction raises, to a degree that her opinions on others do not, the complex question of the relation between a lived and a literary aesthetic, when neither is fixed or stable, but both are realms of imaginative construction, intelligence and struggle. The bohemian life as lived by the writer Mansfield more evidently crossed the dividing line between life and art; hence the challenge she presented as someone who was in both respects self fashioning and experimental, in Ottoline Morrell's description of her as not 'a fraud' but 'more of an adventuress' (KCLC, quoted in Curtis 2002: 125). For Woolf too, Mansfield and her fiction, as evidenced in Woolf's sustained antipathy to *Bliss*, are melded into one. That same judgement however reveals in its very terms the instability of Woolf's perception; for while Mansfield's mind is condemned as 'a very thin soil, laid an inch or two deep upon very barren rock' (*D1*: 79), Woolf had felt earlier that year how, 'As usual', she and Mansfield 'came to an oddly complete understanding' since 'I get down to what is true rock in her, through the numerous vapours & pores which sicken or bewilder most of our friends' (ibid.: 150). Mansfield was as hard as rock: superficial but direct; barren but true.

Bohemians at Home

Woolf, as E. M. Forster averred, was a lady, 'She made no bones about it. She was a lady by birth and upbringing' (Forster 1942: 41). She was neither an aristocrat nor outside the British class system; neither a member of 'high bohemia' nor a rebel like Katherine Mansfield. Nor does Edel's 'spiritual bohemia' describe her. She was first and foremost of course a modernist novelist and free-thinker who, in common with Leonard, was committed to radical progressive ideas of suffrage, the cooperative movement, contraception, pacifism and internationalism: a set of commitments which Christine Froula in *Virginia Woolf and the Bloomsbury Avant-Garde* describes as comprising a 'sociability' – 'conceived as humanity's highest end' (Froula 2005: 2). The Woolfs, and indeed Bloomsbury's shared belief in 'sociability', saw art and ideas as playing a part in framing what Froula terms 'a modernist discourse on civilization' (ibid.: 4). The way of life shaped by such an informing purpose had all the ingredients of a prospective general, more modern, culture; more prosaically, it supplied a point of view upon the world which sought to transfigure that world, and was, given the Woolfs' location in London, at Richmond or at Rodmell, a physically situated perspective. We rarely think of them and what they stood for, that is to say, apart from these dwelling places. This situated culture of art and ideas was also, of course, the place for many years of the actual means of production of Woolf's own and other books at the Hogarth Press.

The houses, Monk's House at Rodmell perhaps especially, displayed the everyday evidence too of Bloomsbury design, in the paintings and decorative work of Grant and Vanessa Bell, as well as, on occasion, in matters of interior decoration, by Woolf herself. Even so, and even as Monk's House gained in amenities of all kinds in house and garden as the Woolfs became more successful, the house, as Alison Light reports, 'remained messy, dusty and smelly' (Light 2007: 232). One significant change was the use of a 'daily' rather than a 'live-in' servant which meant that Woolf herself cooked. She welcomed the particular freedom this brought of 'eating one's dinner off a table anywhere, having cooked it previously' (*D3*: 316). Monk's House consequently conformed, we might say, neither to the conventions of fashionable nor of low-life bohemia. But no more did it conform to the conventions of the regimented bourgeois household. The Woolfs' experiment in living, their art of life, in short, comprising the ideas, achievements and way of living in these houses, expressed the improvised and 'lived' bohemianism of the dedicated artist and intellectual.

Approaching fifty, after her most productive decade, celebrated and confident, and experiencing the simple but significantly liberating effect of living without a 'live–in' servant, Woolf remarked in the late summer of 1930, how she felt nearer Vanessa and Duncan's 'Bohemianism' than ever before: 'My bent that way increases', she decided – she was 'more & more attracted by looseness, freedom' (*D3*: 316). 'This rhythm' as she termed it, in association with the writing of *The Waves*, was 'in harmony with the painters' Vanessa and Duncan. 'Ease & shabbiness & content therefore are all ensured' (ibid.).

Woolf came, in time, to regret her spiteful treatment of Morrell's eccentricities, to understand and value Mansfield better, and to value Vita Sackville-West's difference from herself. 'What odd friends I've had', she commented to Vita, of Vita herself and Mansfield (*L3*: 408). On Ottoline Morrell's death, she found she was 'rather lacerated' and dwelt on 'a queer loveliness departed' (*L6*: 225). But she was herself 'odd' too. Dirk Bogarde, who as a child lived nearby, remembered her at Rodmell 'marching about the water-meadows'; her 'hair wispy caught into a loose sort of knot' wearing 'a droopy cardigan . . . a big floppy straw hat'. Sometimes she sang to herself 'and picked little bunches of wild flowers'. The children 'thought she was a witch' or was 'barmy' and Bogarde comments, looking back across the years, how 'there was a strange décontracté air about her. . .' (Bogarde 1990: 114–15). This was her oddness, carelessly, comfortably adopted with Leonard, an habitual, relaxed ('décontracté') estranging perspective on the world which drew her to the oddness of the extra-ordinary, which we term bohemian, in others, acknowledged in time as like but unlike herself.

Works Cited and Further Reading

CP: Charleston Papers, University of Sussex, Special Collections.

HRC: The Harry Ransom Humanities Research Center, University of Texas at Austin.

KCLC: King's College Library, Cambridge.

Barkway, Stephen (2006) 'The "Dreadnought" Hoax: The Aftermath for "Prince Sanganya" and "His" Cousins', *The Virginia Woolf Bulletin*, 21, January 2006: 20-7.

Bell, Vanessa (1997) *Sketches in Pen and Ink. A Bloomsbury Book*, ed. Lia Giachero London: Hogarth Press.

Bogarde, Dirk (1990) *A Particular Friendship*, London: Penguin.

Brooker, Peter (2007) *Bohemia in London*, London: Palgrave.

Curtis, Vanessa (2002) *Virginia Woolf's Women*, Madison: University of Wisconsin Press.

DeSalvo Louise and Mitchell Leaska (eds) (1985) *The Letters of Vita Sackville-West and Virginia Woolf*, San Francisco: Cleis Press Inc.

Dunn, Jane (2000) *Virginia Woolf and Vanessa Bell. A Very Close Conspiracy*, London: Virago Press.

Edel, Leon (1979) *Bloomsbury. A House of Lions*, London: Penguin.

Forster. E. M. (1942) *Virgina Woolf – The Rede Lecture, 1941*, Cambridge: Cambridge University Press.

Froula, Christine (2005) *Virginia Woolf and the Bloomsbury Avant-Garde. War, Civilisation, Modernity*, New York: Columbia University Press.

Hall, Sarah M. (2007) The *Bedside, Bathtub & Armchair Companion to Virginia Woolf and Bloomsbury*, London: Continuum.

Lehmann, John (1975) *Virginia Woolf*, London: Thames and Hudson.

Light, Alison (2007) *Mrs Woolf and the Servants*, London: Penguin/Fig Tree.

McNeillie, Andrew (2000) 'Bloomsbury', in Sue Roe and Susan Sellers (eds), *The Cambridge Companion to Virginia Woolf*, Cambridge: Cambridge University Press.

Murger, Henri (1990) 'The Bohemians of the Latin Quarter: Original Preface 1850', in César Graña and Marigay Graña (eds), *On Bohemia. The Code of the Self-Exiled*, New Brunswick, NJ: Transaction Publishers.

Murry, John Middleton (ed.) (1928) *The Letters of Katherine Mansfield*, 2 vols, London: Constable.

Nicolson, Nigel (1983) *Portrait of a Marriage*, London: Weidenfeld and Nicolson.

Seymour, Miranda (1992) *Ottoline Morrell. Life on the Grand Scale*, London: Hodder and Stoughton.

Shaw, Helen (ed.) (1984) *Dear Lady Ginger, an Exchange of Letters between Lady Ottoline Morrell and D'Arcy Cresswell together with Ottoline Morrell's Essay on Katherine Mansfield*, London: Century Publishing.

Smith, Angela (1999) *Katherine Mansfield & Virginia Woolf. A Public of Two*, Oxford: Clarendon Press.

Stansky, Peter (1996) *On or about December 1910*, Cambridge, MA: Harvard University Press.

Wilson, Elizabeth (2000) *Bohemians the Glamorous Outcasts*, London: I. B. Tauris.

Woolf, Leonard (1960) *Sowing: An Autobiography of the Years 1880–1904.* London: Hogarth Press; New York: Harcourt, Brace, Jovanovich.

Woolf, Virginia (2008) '*Dreadnought* Hoax Talk', in S. P. Rosenbaum (ed.), *The Platform of Time: Memoirs of Family and Friends*, 2nd edn, London: Hesperus Press.

13

VIRGINIA WOOLF AND ENTERTAINING

Makiko Minow-Pinkney

IN 'MR BENNETT and Mrs Brown' Virginia Woolf uses an analogy between the hostess and the writer: in order to achieve 'intimacy' as the final goal, both hostess and writer have to bridge a gulf, between the hostess and the unknown guest, or between the writer and the unknown reader, by establishing common ground through the use of conventions. In this essay, which is now well known as a modernist literary manifesto, her point is that the old conventions no longer work for the moderns, hence the necessity of new conventions, of a modernist aesthetics. This analogy between hostess and writer is not surprising if we note that Woolf was writing *Mrs Dalloway*, a novel about a society hostess, at the time. But her use of 'entertaining' is not limited to a literary trope in her attempt to adumbrate a modernist aesthetics: famously, a scene of entertaining is structurally and thematically central to several of her major novels. After establishing a biographical context of Woolf's own experience of diverse cultures of entertainment, I shall study these issues in relation to the two novels, *Mrs Dalloway* and *To the Lighthouse*, which feature her most memorable hostesses, Clarissa Dalloway and Mrs Ramsay.

The popular image of Woolf, influenced by our knowledge of her repeated mental breakdowns and eventual suicide, is that of a delicate invalid, ethereally existing in seclusion with her selected and socially privileged intimates. But to the reader who is more acquainted with the 'real' Woolf, it is well known that she had an extremely active social life: she loved parties, loved the excitement of sparkling champagne, silk clothes and jewellery, of opportunities for social jousting and adventurous new encounters. Leonard Woolf writes: 'Virginia loved "Society", its functions and parties, the bigger the better; but she also liked – at any rate in prospect – any party' (L. Woolf 1967: 98). Her own powers of entertainment, the mesmerising flair of her witty and imaginative talk, remained vividly in the memories of her friends and family. As we shall see, Woolf identified this social side of herself as her matrilineal inheritance. After her marriage and her ensuing severe mental breakdowns, the Woolfs settled in Richmond, which was far enough out in the London suburbs to avoid, on health grounds, too much family contact and 'brilliant and hectic parties' like Lady Ottoline Morrell's (Bell 1972, 2: 22), but was also close enough to be in touch with London friends. After living there for more than eight years, however, Woolf became increasingly frustrated by the limitations this suburban residence imposed and pined to be back in the hub of things in the capital as, with *The Voyage Out, Night and Day* and *Jacob's Room* behind her, she started to be known as a rising new writer and to receive invitations from a wider society; 'I get my wages partly in invitations' (*D2*: 251). In her diary she complains that Leonard resists the idea of their returning to Bloomsbury, of his being 'too much of a Puritan, of a disciplinarian'. Against Leonard's 'intellectual side' she asserts her own 'social side' and defends it as 'genuine', as not 'reprehensible' but valuable and even necessary for her work, 'a piece of jewellery I inherited from my mother' (ibid.: 250).

Sociability and social life are inherently associated with the mother in Woolf. Her own mother, Julia Jackson, a daughter of one of the beautiful and famous Pattle sisters, was part of two legendary Victorian salons presided over by her aunts. Julia's beautiful facial structure made her a favourite subject for her aunt Julia Margaret Cameron, the photographer; she was also a favourite at Little Holland House, the home of her other aunt, Sara, and her husband Thoby Prinsep. These salons were unique cultural worlds where many literary, artistic and political figures of the age were entertained by the Pattle sisters, who were original and creative, perhaps even eccentric, but at the same time 'worldly in the thoroughgoing Victorian way' (*MOB*: 88). Little Holland House, which Virginia Woolf images as 'a summer afternoon world' where tea, strawberries and cream were served to distinguished men, great painters and poets, was in effect Julia's education; 'the training of life at Little Holland House' (ibid.: 86) taught her Victorian manners of entertaining founded on feminine deference, sympathy and unselfishness. It is from people's talk and memories, Woolf writes, that she gathers this image of her mother as a girl entertaining the eminent men of Victorian society in a 'summer afternoon world'. In her own memory too, her mother appears always surrounded by family and visitors, as 'the creator of that crowded merry world' (ibid.: 84), presiding over a dinner party or dashing off in white summer clothes in a hansom to a private view or a party. Woolf writes that even her father, in spite of all his brusque unconventionality, appears in her memory of those days not merely 'a Cambridge steel engraving intellectual', but as part of 'that well to do sociable late Victorian world' (ibid.: 113, 114).

Because Woolf was still a child and not yet allowed to be part of formal dinner parties,[1] in her memories of Victorian family life 'the tea table rather than the dinner table was the centre' (*MOB*: 118). From this heart of the family Julia Stephen commanded life around her, attracting people 'of the most diverse kinds' (ibid.: 35). Woolf's fantastical description of the scenes of Sunday afternoon tea in her paper for the Memoir Club, with eccentric old gentlemen and ravishing female beauties (ibid.: 164–5), gives us a picture of these family entertainments, 'very merry, very stirring, crowded with people' (ibid.: 84). After

Figure 13.1 The Stephen family and their guests. Virginia Woolf is the child in the middle. St Ives, *c.* 1892. From the Monk's House Photograph Albums of Virginia and Leonard Woolf, Gift of Frederick R. Koch, the Harvard Theatre Collection, Houghton Library

her mother's and then Stella's death, however, this tea-party ritual, the heart of her Victorian family life, became a perfectly preserved 'fossil of the Victorian age' in the early years of the new century (ibid.: 151). A powerful machine with 'the framework of 1860', preserved by her father and 'with all kinds of minutely teethed saws' (ibid.: 152) added by her half-brother George, held Virginia and Vanessa tightly in its grip. What made this anachronism at 22 Hyde Park Gate in the early twentieth century the more unbearable was the division of life: 'Downstairs there was pure convention [George]: upstairs pure intellect [her father]. But there was no connection between them' (ibid.: 157). The diverse realms used to be held together in a 'merry various world' by her mother (93), who inherited 'Pattledom' by nature and by education. Whether such qualities had been innate in Julia Stephen or not, this complexity of character – 'the mixture of simplicity and scepticism . . . extremely practical but with a depth in her' (ibid.: 90) – certainly developed through the tragic sudden death of her first husband, 'the perfect type of public school boy and English gentleman' according to Leslie Stephen. She lost 'all her gaiety, all her sociability' and through 'solitary and independent thinking' (ibid.:) she reached agnosticism, which led to her acquaintance and then eventually her marriage with Leslie Stephen.

When her mother, the centre of sociality, died, the world split asunder. George played the part her mother would have played, and brought the young Stephen sisters out in society, which was convinced 'that girls must be changed into married women' (ibid.: 135). The parties which George forced upon Virginia and Vanessa became 'wrangles,' 'often humiliations' (ibid.:), far from the occasions of gaiety and romantic beauty that Woolf had anticipated. Her life during the period '1897–1904 – the seven unhappy years' (ibid.: 136) – was bafflingly divided between downstairs – the 'pure convention' of George Duckworth's sociality – and upstairs – the 'pure intellect' of her father (*MOB*: 157). Woolf's ambition was to write, and this meant a struggle to be freed from the downstairs drawing room and to have 'a room of one's own' upstairs, both literally and metaphorically. But if this was clearly the wish of an emergent modernist-feminist self in Woolf, the problem seems more complex than just the division between George's conventionalism and her father's intellectuality, or between the Victorianism of her father and half-brothers and the new modern age to which Vanessa and Virginia wished to belong. Woolf had a deep affinity with her father's intellectualism, but Leslie Stephen was also a typical Victorian, an embodiment of the past which in her view was blocking the progress of life. Particularly for Vanessa, who by contrast did not have any intellectual affinity with him, he was nothing but an oppressive tyrant. On the other hand, though the 'unspeakably conventional' Duckworth brothers might be philistines who cared only about social respectability and success, their world was also Julia's. The ghosts of their mother and half-sister, Stella, were often both deliberately and involuntarily evoked in such contexts. And above all Woolf had in her, as she claimed, 'a piece of jewellery', that 'social side' inherited from her mother (*D2*: 250). The origin of Woolf's romantic fascination with Society and its parties inheres in her memory of her mother, 'so soothing, and yet exciting when one ran down to dinner arm in arm with mother; or chose the jewels she was to wear' (*MOB*: 95). Therefore the gaping division in the household between upstairs/pure intellect and downstairs/pure convention presented tangled issues for Woolf to negotiate if she were to become a modernist and feminist writer, and are a source of her lasting emotional ambivalence towards the social world and entertaining.

In spite of the many humiliations she suffered in the parties of her coming-out years under George's tutelage – such as standing unasked against a wall, of being unable to dance or get young men to talk – Woolf could still write of 'some moments of elation: some moments of lyrical ecstasy', 'the excitement of clothes, of lights, of society, in short' (Woolf 1976: 134). There are three short pieces (1903) on social parties that the young Woolf as an aspirant author sent to Violet Dickinson: 'A Dance in Queens Gate' describes a dance party in the neighbourhood, 'A Garden Dance' evokes one of the parties she has just been to, and 'Thoughts upon Social Success' generalises upon these issues. These brief essays record her fascination with society parties, which, since she lacked the 'social gift', she was forced to observe from an outsider's position, with a cool detachment but at the same time riveted to their gaiety: 'this incongruity – the artificial lights, the music – the talk – & then the quiet tree standing out there, is fantastic & attracts me considerably' (*PA*: 166). When she writes that 'To be socially great, I believe, is a really noble ambition' (ibid.: 168), we cannot be sure if she means to be ironic or not. Even if she does, such irony coexists with a genuine fascination. 'Thoughts upon Social Success' reverses the moralist's criticism of the socialite as hollow and heartless and celebrates him instead as 'a brave man' and 'a Stoic', who sets aside 'sorrows & worries at home' to please and amuse others; this has more the air of a genuine argument than a mere witty reversal (ibid.:). Woolf even acknowledges the merits of fine dresses, which make one 'artificial – ready for lights & music – ready to accept that arti-ficial view of life which is presented to one in a ballroom – life seen by electric light & washed down by champagne' (ibid.: 169–70). This fascination with the gilded world of parties stayed with her, and after two decades what she termed 'party consciousness' would become a major subject for her writing to explore, resulting in *Mrs Dalloway* and several related short stories.

Leslie Stephen's death in 1904 finally liberated the young Stephens geograph-ically and psychologically from 22 Hyde Park Gate and made it possible for them to start a new, experimental 'extremely social' life in Bloomsbury (*MOB*: 185). Thoby's Thursday Evenings, whose members were to become known as the Bloomsbury group, were a radical antidote to the tea rituals and parties of Victorian society and of their anachronistic after-life in the Stephens family. The lack of physical splendour, the shabbiness of men in a smoke-filled room with 'buns, coffee and whisky strewn about', as well as the extreme abstractness of their conversations were in her eyes 'a proof of their superiority' (ibid.: 192). All this reassured her 'in some obscure way' that there would be no reverting to the mores at Hyde Park Gate, where nothing mattered except young women's 'appearance and behaviour' and 'love and marriage' (ibid.: 191). No self-denying feminine skills from tea-table training were required in discussions about the nature of beauty, goodness or reality. However, Woolf was soon to discover that she was wrong. In the wake of Thoby's death Vanessa and Clive Bell married, and the 'abstractness' of Thursday evenings turned out to be the deadening bar-renness (for women) of the society of homosexuals, mistaken as refreshingly revolutionary. Woolf realised that she was missing the showing-off between the sexes, 'the delightful effervescence of soda water or champagne through which one sees the world tinged with all colours of the rainbow' (ibid.: 194). So other kinds of parties had to come into play to satisfy her desire, such as Lady Ottoline Morrell's at Bedford Square, whose 'lustre and illusion' sent her into rhapsodic exhilaration (ibid.: 195, 200). In turn such lustre and illusion started to tinge Bloomsbury too and ultimately transformed it; 'parties of a very different sort' – fancy dress parties, performance parties, 'bawdy' parties – soon broke out, scandalising their old family friends and giving the group a reputation as the

Figure 13.2 Virginia Woolf takes centre-stage at Lady Ottoline Morrell's party at Garsington Manor, Oxfordshire, 1923. National Portrait Gallery, London

Figure 13.3 'Alice in Wonderland' birthday party for Angelica, age 11, 8 Fitzroy Street, London, January 1930. Virginia Woolf dressed herself as the March Hare
© Tate, London 2009

cultural and aesthetic centre of anti-conventionalism. Such was Bloomsbury before the First World War. Lady Ottoline became part of the Bloomsbury circle after the group got to know her in 1908/9, according to Woolf; and her parties at Bedford Square and at Garsington in Oxfordshire provided the high points and continuity of social life during the war when the Bloomsbury group was dispersed.

The 1920s was the age of swinging jazz and dance, of cocktails and costume parties – the time of modernism. Personally too Woolf's social life acceler-ated decisively; her diary records her extraordinarily crowded social schedule. Bloomsbury as a whole grew in reputation and became famous in fashionable sections of society. Now, with an even younger avant-gardist generation like the Sitwells or the Bright Young People scandalising the public, Bloomsbury became the 'Establishment' of anti-conventionalism in the new cultural ethos of modern-ism, and was sought after by sympathetic social hostesses: 'As Nessa says, we are becoming fashionable' (D2: 239). By the early 1920s, with three novels as well as essays and critical reviews published, Woolf was known as a rising new writer. One of the famous social hostesses of the day, Sibyl Colefax, was quick to culti-vate her after the publication of *Night and Day*. According to Leonard Woolf, there were three great London hostesses in the 1920s, Lady Ottoline Morrell, Lady Colefax and Lady Cunard. Woolf and Bloomsbury had already been close to Ottoline, though the Bloomsbury group were not always grateful for her generous hospitality. Woolf was invited by Lady Cunard too, but did not develop any close relationship with her. It is with Sibyl Colefax, the most professional of the three, that Woolf developed over many years a close yet ambivalent friendship, which she analysed in 'Am I a Snob?' She was wary in the beginning when this famous society hostess, who was regarded by many as a predatory collector of celebrities, approached her. A few years later, on 3 July 1924, Woolf wrote about her:

> the enamelled Lady Colefax, . . . like a cheap bunch of artificial cherries, yet, loyal, hard, living on a burnished plate of facts . . . in fear, inquisitive, not at all able to sink to the depths; but a superb skimmer of the surface; which is bright, I suppose, & foam tipped. I can't bring myself to despise this gull as I ought. But aristocrats, worldlings, for all their surface polish, are empty, slippery, coat the mind with sugar & butter, & make it slippery too. (D2: 305)

There is a tension here which always troubled Woolf about the gleaming shal-lowness of Society, which she 'ought' to despise, but which part of her cannot help being attracted to. In the early 1920s as her desire for Society was gratified by the increasing invitations she started to earn by her writing – 'One of the perquisities [*sic*] of Jacob seems to be society' (D2: 210) – her old interest in the psychology of the society party re-emerged as a subject for literary explo-ration. A short story, 'Mrs Dalloway in Bond Street', which is first mentioned in her diary in June 1922, developed into an idea for a book, initially with the possible title of 'At Home' or 'The Party' before becoming *The Hours* and finally

Mrs Dalloway.[2] To develop the character of Clarissa Dalloway, who had already briefly appeared in her first novel *The Voyage Out*, Woolf now had many models of high society hostesses to draw on such as Kitty Maxse, Lady Ottoline Morrell, Sibyl Colefax as well as her mother, Julia Stephen.

The narrative voice of *Mrs Dalloway* (1925) behaves not unlike a hostess at a party, moving between characters smoothly, bringing them into contact with each other. Asserting her own opinion and judgements is clearly not her role; the narrative voice/hostess exists dispersed among the characters/guests (as Clarissa Dalloway is) as a mere connecter, a facilitator, and yet by thus bringing characters together she creates a charged, coherent atmosphere across the novel/party as a whole. This narrative style and structure did not come quickly or easily for Woolf; it was a year-long struggle for her to find a satisfactory narrative format for the novel.[3] In 'Mr Bennett and Mrs Brown' which was written and revised while she was working on what was to become *Mrs Dalloway*, Woolf likens 'a convention in writing' to 'a convention in manners' which helps the social hostess get in touch with her unknown guest as a prelude to the more exciting intercourse of friendship (*CE*1: 330). But for the writers of her generation, the young Georgians, the Edwardian code of manners is of no use. Hence it is that, in the novel itself, real communication will not follow as the safe traditional 'phatic' topic of the weather dismally fails to spark off conversation between Richard Dalloway and Ellie Henderson: 'many people really felt the heat more than the cold. "Yes, they do," said Richard Dalloway. "Yes." But what more did one say?' (*MD*: 170). Here indeed is the challenge for the modern writers of the early twentieth century, but Woolf, as modernist, is unequivocal about where to find 'a way of telling the truth' (*CE*1: 335). 'Look within' she asserts in 'Modern Fiction', and lets the narrator of 'The Mark on the Wall' (1917, revised in 1919) speculate that 'the novelists in future will realise more and more the importance of [people's] reflections . . . those are the depths they will explore . . . leaving the description of reality more and more out of their stories' (*SF*: 85–6). Her modernist aesthetics asserts that internal depth, rather than the minutiae of the external facts, are 'the proper stuff of fiction' (*CE*2: 106). From the invention of Septimus as a counterpoint to Clarissa, through the invention of Peter Walsh, to Clarissa's final self-identification with Septimus, Woolf is concerned to demonstrate the internal depths of the eponymous heroine. Her concern was that Mrs Dalloway was 'too thin and unreal somehow' (18 June 1923 Berg Collection); her character 'may be too stiff, too glittering & tinsely [sic]. . .' (*D*2: 272), emptily measuring out her life in coffee spoons, to borrow T. S. Eliot's Prufrockian phrase. After a year's literary struggle, her prime discovery was what she calls a 'tunnelling process' (ibid.); 'how I dig out beautiful caves behind my characters; I think that gives exactly what I want; humanity, humour, depth' (ibid.: 263); 'I decided to give it up, because I found Clarissa in some way tinselly. Then I invented her memories.' (*D*3: 32).The idea of creating depth by adding the element of time to character is further elucidated by Woolf in the diary: 'The idea is that the caves shall connect, & each comes to daylight at the present moment' (*D2*: 263). This is made possible by the kind of narrative voice which moves smoothly in and out among characters, weaving them together like the genially dispersed existence of a successful hostess.[4]

In terms of narrative form, *Mrs Dalloway* is thus a significant achievement for Woolf in her struggle for 'finding a way of telling the truth' (*CE1*: 335) by a successful formal combination of the social hostess's artistry in the drawing room and a modernist belief in depth. However, in terms of creating character, there seems to be an inherent contradiction here. Woolf's initial interest in the artificiality of the society hostess's mode of being, for which she later invents the term 'party consciousness', does not sit well with the authentic internality which modernist writers should pursue. Woolf writes in her diary that she 'should like to investigate the party consciousness':

> people secrete an envelope which connects them & protects them from others, like myself, who am outside the envelope, foreign bodies . . . (obviously I grope for words) but I'm always coming back to it. The party consciousness, for example: Sybil's [*sic*] consciousness. You must not break it. It is something real. You must keep it up; conspire together. (*D3*: 12–13)

Party consciousness is thus artificial and false in one sense but true and even realer-than-real in another – or in Clarissa's own words, 'this feeling of being something not herself, and that every one was unreal in one way; much more real in another' (*MD*: 171). This paradox mesmerised Woolf in her early years as a debutante in society: 'A more unreal relationship cannot be imagined; but there was a thrill in the unreality' (*MOB*: 134). Woolf's fascination with this realm of tinselly illusion is so strong that after finishing *Mrs Dalloway*, still feeling that her interest in party consciousness was not exhausted, she wrote several short stories as spin-offs of the novel. However, as a modernist Woolf was also committed to explore the authentic depths, in antithesis to the artificial surface of being. The narrator of the short story 'The Lady in the Looking Glass: A Reflection' (1929) expresses her wish to find out 'the truth about Isabella', the vital essence of her being, and refuses to be put off by the sayings and doings which dinners, visits and polite conversations bring forth: 'It was her profounder state of being that one wanted to catch and turn to words, the state that is to the mind what breathing is to the body.' However, the narrator then tries to 'penetrate a little farther into her being' and traumatically discovers that 'there was nothing. Isabella was perfectly empty' (*SF*: 224–5).

Clarissa Dalloway at her worst can be insincere, as Peter Walsh criticises her for being, but the heroine of the novel must not be empty like Isabella; she has to be filled with thoughts and meaning. The innate discrepancy between certain characteristics which come with perfect hostess-ship – worldliness, insincerity, a certain hardness, in short, what Peter condemns as 'the death of the soul' (*MD*: 58, 59) and on the other hand her profound side – her inner existential angst and perceptive sensibility – could thus be a problem for the convincing reality of the character. Such characterological ambivalence no doubt articulates Woolf's critical contempt towards Society and its glittering inhabitants such as her old family friend, Kitty Maxse, who is regarded as the main model of Clarissa Dalloway, or towards many of her newer Society friends: 'I want to bring in the despicableness of people like Ott: I want to give the slipperiness of the soul . . . . The truth is people scarcely care for each other' (D2: 244). Woolf's fascination with the duality of the social hostess, as someone who amalgamates opposite traits – an ability to create a brilliant appearance by pleasurably skimming on the surface with her well-honed social skills *and* the possession of profundity of experience and understanding of life – goes back, as I have shown, to her memory of her mother whose nihilistic despair, she remembers, made Julia Stephen all the more keen to make the most of the joys of life.[5] For if Woolf admires the artistry of hostess-ship, as Peter does Clarissa's courage and 'power of carrying things through' (*MD*: 62), or the heroic bravery of the socially successful, this admiration comes only if they are deliberately maintaining the polished surface over serious tensions beneath. If they are ultimately empty like Isabella in 'Lady in the Looking Glass', there is no stoic heroism to admire in the party world, which would become no different from the merely philistine cultural realm of her half-brothers. So Woolf frequently finds herself repulsed by her Society lady friends like Morrell and Colefax when she found them to be vacuous indeed, 'aristocrats, worldlings, for all their surface polish, are empty' (D2: 305). But this troubled interest in the psychology of society hostesses seems to explain Woolf's long and intimate, albeit qualified, friendship with Sibyl Colefax which lasted for nearly two decades from the early days when a glimpse of her made Woolf liken her 'to hard red cherries on a cheap black hat' (ibid.: 181), through innumerable dinner parties and lunches or informal, intimate tête-à-tête teas at Woolf's home. Woolf had other more glamorous aristocratic female friends such as Vita Sackville-West and Christabel Aberconway whom she was less complicatedly fond of, but the more middle-class Sibyl Colefax seems to have intrigued as well as repelled Woolf by her indomitable role as social hostess. What intrigued Woolf, apart from the obvious social pleasures offered by Sibyl, were the repressed depths beneath her polished surface, glimpsed only at rare moments. On one occasion, for example, Woolf gathered that Sibyl was saying, with her eyes looking 'very tragic', that what she wanted was, she realised belatedly, 'intimacy, simplicity & friendship' (D3: 265). However, Colefax is after all too armour-plated to let herself talk and sink into the depths: 'No, I cant talk to anyone. I go on.' (D5: 27),[6] rather like the lady in T. S. Eliot's 'Portrait of a Lady'. For Woolf, Society may well involve a kind of steely heroism: 'I have been reflecting about society again, & think one of its merits is that it needs courage' (D2: 239), and she often talks of society in terms such as 'taking one's fence', 'jumping', 'whipping oneself to dine'.[7]

Woolf upheld the plan of her novel *Mrs Dalloway* 'to criticise the social system, & to show it at work, at its most intense' (D2: 248), but Clarissa is crucially not on the side of the social system in her heart, even if she is part of it socio-economically; by her intense dislike of Sir William Bradshaw and her empathetic identification with Septimus at the end she is shown to be on the side of the victim. It is true that the novel presents reservations about Clarissa, but criticisms from the other characters, all of whom have their own shortcomings, are never powerful enough to discredit her defence of herself. Her implicit self-defence against Miss Kilman's overzealous commitment to political causes – 'but she loved her roses (didn't that help the Armenians?)' (*MD*: 120) – may sound too frivolous to be taken seriously, but the novel's presentation of Kilman as odious and aggressive hardly endears her to the reader either. Against Richard's and Peter's criticisms of Clarissa's parties as foolish and snobbish, her defence is that she gives parties simply for the love of life. They are an offering:

> Here was So-and-so in South Kensington; some one up in Bayswater; and somebody else, say, in Mayfair. And she felt quite continuously a sense of their existence; and she felt what a waste; and she felt what a pity; and she felt if only they could be brought together; so she did it. And it was an offering; to combine, to create; but to whom?
> An offering for the sake of offering, perhaps. (*MD*: 122)

If the answer to Peter's question, 'Why does she give these parties' (*ibid*.: 54), is that they serve to bring people together and thus reassemble the scattered parts of the human jigsaw, we should recall here that Woolf writes in *Moments of Being* that 'to put the severed parts together' is 'the strongest pleasure' known to her: 'It is the rapture I get when in writing I seem to be discovering what belongs to what' (*MOB*: 72). We could therefore see a connection between Clarissa's need to connect people by giving parties and Woolf's own to connect words by writing. Indeed, in the holograph draft of the novel, *The Hours*, Woolf makes Clarissa defend her party by saying: 'Life meant bringing together. An artist did the same sort of thing presumably'. Later Woolf reworked this as: 'And she did it because it was an offering. Just as somebody writes a book after all'.[8] If Peter and Richard both 'criticised her unfairly, laughed at her very unjustly', then at least one guest at her party understands, albeit outside the novel itself. In the short story 'A Summing Up', Sasha, a guest at Mrs Dalloway's party, pays a tribute to Clarissa: 'This, she thought, is the greatest of marvels; the supreme achievement of the human race' (*SF*: 209). Sasha applauds the party, 'humming with people coming close to each other, going away from each other, exchanging their views, stimulating each other' as a supreme scene of 'the society of humanity' (ibid.: 209). Like laying 'paving stones over the bog', it is a contribution to civilisation. But this glittering world created in the wastes of the night turns out to be an illusion after all, as she realises when she finds in the end the prosaic cityscape of drab London life just behind the wall of Mrs Dalloway's garden. So Sasha's tribute to Clarissa is to her creation of a glorious illusion, just like the writer creating a fictional world through her/his imagination – a supreme human activity which has made civilisation possible. The conventional social skills of the middle-class woman in the drawing room are not only likened to the aesthetic practice of the artist, but are regarded as an equally significant human contribution in this

short story written as a spin-off of the novel. The domestic art of social entertaining can be equated to an aesthetic practice, because both combine people,
things, words, shapes, colours together to create an illusion which alleviates the
devastating possibility (from which Septimus so traumatically suffers) 'that the
world itself is without meaning' (*MD*: 88).

   In a state of being characteristic of this novel, withdrawn into the depths of
reflection, Clarissa defines herself: 'She sliced like a knife through everything; at
the same time was outside, looking on' (*MD*: 8). This inside/outside double positioning is what Woolf used to notice about herself, socially speaking. She writes
that she had this feeling in her wrangles with George about Society parties: 'the
outsider's feeling,' 'a spectator' in her who 'remained cool, critical, observant'
while none the less experiencing all the nervous flurry which the situation put
her through (*MOB*: 132–3). Such a dual perspective is perhaps a necessity for
any novel writing, but the narrative voice of *Mrs Dalloway* explores this double
positioning most dexterously by using free indirect speech to create the uniquely
Woolfian narrative voice, a narrative voice existing outside character and yet at
the same time inextricably interfused with the character. This double positioning is not only essential to Woolf's narrative voice, but also to her character creation. Sasha in 'A Summing Up', in spite of her enthusiastic appreciation of Mrs
Dalloway's party, is 'condemned to be herself and could only in this silent enthusiastic way, sitting outside in the garden, applaud the society of humanity from
which she was excluded' (*SF*: 209). The ultimate outsider is Septimus in *Mrs
Dalloway* itself, unlike Clarissa in almost all points – gender, age, social position,
mental state. But after being finally pushed out of society, he is brought into
Mrs Dalloway's party by (of all people) William Bradshaw. If to include as many
perspectives as possible is the narrative voice's role, so too is it the hostess's. By
identifying herself with him through empathetic imagination, Clarissa includes
even this outsider, the total stranger or scapegoat who is now dead.

   In most of Woolf's novels there exist such outsider characters who need to
be brought into the circle, at the very scene of social gathering which naturally exposes their outsider-ness. This seems to point to Woolf's own fears and
yearnings as an outsider. Such a perspective is always ambivalent, consisting of
both disdainful distancing and desire for belonging at the same time. The artis-
tic/intellectual self, which could well be the source of Woolf's fear of exclusion
from the fecund circle of life her mother created, feels to her like a contradiction
to the womanhood her mother so richly embodied, which in its turn is a source
of anxiety in Woolf's sexual identity. Her fascination with the stimulating surface world of beauty and pleasure, and her intellectual ambition to pursue the
authentic depths of being as a modernist writer, are decidedly non-compatible
interests which are held precariously together in *Mrs Dalloway*. Woolf herself
felt unsure of the degree of her success in bringing them together; for after the
publication of the novel she admits of Clarissa that 'I think some distaste for
her persisted' (*D3*: 32). More aesthetic work needs to be done, then, to resolve
the innate tension in Woolf which is, I take it, the source of her difficulty with

the book; for, as she herself had suspected, 'The doubtful point is I think the character of Mrs Dalloway' (*D2*: 272).

The question of the gleaming surface and what lies beneath it, nothingness or truth, becomes a more conscious theme in *To the Lighthouse* (1927). It has various manifestations in the novel, but is beyond all else the question Mrs Ramsay arouses: 'But was it nothing but looks, people said? What was there behind it – her beauty and splendour? . . . Or was there nothing? nothing but an incomparable beauty which she lived behind . . . ?' (*TTL*: 28). She 'never spoke. She was silent always' (ibid.), and whether or not some earlier lover had died the week before she was married remains a mystery. Her past is closed to the other characters in the book and to the reader. It is Lily who does 'tunnelling' into the past later as Clarissa Dalloway did in her novel, but not Mrs Ramsay. Whether there is some momentous experience behind her physiognomy or not, however, there is no question about the profundity of Mrs Ramsay's knowledge and understanding. Proving its credentials as a truly modernist text, the narrative makes sure that 'depth' is heavily vested in her. She therefore has 'eyes of unparalleled depth' (ibid.: 50) and her sad expression prompts the narrator to imagine that: 'Bitter and black, half-way down, in the darkness, in the shaft which ran from the sunlight to the depths, perhaps a tear formed; a tear fell . . . . Never did anybody look so sad' (ibid.: 28). There may be a faint lingering suspicion that this is the 'deceptiveness of beauty', but Lily believes that 'knowledge and wisdom were stored up in Mrs Ramsay's heart' (ibid.: 51) and yearns to gain access to them by becoming one with her.

In a rare solitary moment in the afternoon, Mrs Ramsay sinks deep into her self, shedding attachments, 'all the being and doing, expansive, glittering, vocal', and shrinks to 'a wedge-shaped core of darkness' (*TTL*: 62). This self, however shrunken, is paradoxically limitless and free because beneath the meagre personality 'it is all dark, it is all spreading, it is unfathomably deep' (ibid.:). This typically modernist discourse of authentic depths prepares the revelatory moment for Mrs Ramsay: 'Losing personality, one lost the fret, the hurry, the stir; and there rose to her lips always some exclamation of triumph over life when things came together in this peace, this rest, this eternity' (ibid.: 63). She re-experiences this sense of 'a summoning together' in the midst of the dinner party later, dissociating herself from the moment and sensing a 'coherence in things', 'something . . . immune from change' (ibid.: 105). When she is peering into the depths of the earthenware pot, even 'a specially tender piece of meat' from that Boeuf en Daube to which she is helping William Bankes, for a brief moment seems to have acquired some symbolic resonance of eternity; as indeed after dinner does the Shakespeare poem which she reads intently, 'the essence sucked out of life and held rounded here – the sonnet' (ibid.: 121). When she involuntarily exclaims 'We are in the hands of the Lord', she is annoyed at insincerity slipping in among the truths. Her austerity is such that she searches 'into her mind and her heart, purifying out of existence . . . any lie' and will not let herself be diverted from her belief that 'there is no reason, order, justice:

but suffering; death; the poor' (ibid.: 60). So there seems to be no doubt of her sincerity and authenticity.

But the question of her sincerity is not so easily settled perhaps. As a consummate hostess, Mrs Ramsay would not refrain from making use of her adroit social manners to impose some order upon the guests around the table who are as yet without any warm mutual rapport. As Peter Walsh winces at Clarissa's insincerity in her role as hostess, so Charles Tansley and Lily Briscoe critically watch Mrs Ramsay's insincere (as they see it) manners. Tansley who is not familiar with such social codes immediately suspects insincerity in the exchange between Mrs Ramsay and William Bankes, and he condemns the Ramsays, and the whole social class they represent, as redundant human existences. But fundamentally it is, in his view, 'the women's fault. Women made civilisation impossible with all their "charm," all their silliness' (*TTL*: 85). On the other hand, Lily, who herself critically notes Tansley's 'meagre fixity' (ibid.:), knows such codes of behaviour all too well, particularly as they impinge upon women, and she is forced to renounce her thought-experiment – 'what happens if one is not nice to that young man there' (ibid.: 92) and remains true to oneself instead – after pressure from Mrs. Ramsay. Mr Ramsay, too, is outraged by his wife's willingness to flout facts and raise their children's hopes without any objective basis in fact. But this accusation involves his repressing the fact that he himself depends constantly on her exaggerations to pacify his assorted anxieties, while Mrs Ramsay for her part is often uncomfortably conscious of the untruthfulness of her words. From her viewpoint, however, 'to pursue truth with such astonishing lack of consideration for other people's feelings' amounts to rending the thin veils of civilisation wantonly (ibid.: 32).

Here the opposing views of civilisation are divided along gender lines. Mr Ramsay (and Tansley) and Mrs Ramsay (and Lily) regard themselves as protectors of civilisation and the other pair as wrecking it. Mrs Ramsay is happy to trust herself to the 'admirable fabric of the masculine intelligence . . . like iron girders spanning the swaying fabric, upholding the world' (*TTL*: 106), but she regards it as her job to protect the deeper essence of civilisation. The traditional female sphere of human relationships and feelings is not auxiliary or ornamental but, on this showing, the fundamental fabric of civilisation. Feminine occupations in the drawing room and dining room, far from being 'silly, superficial, flimsy' (ibid.: 85), require rigorous discipline, courage, flair and artistry. In 'A Summing Up' Sasha had imaged Mrs Dalloway's party as a dry, well-built house, stored with valuables and humming with people, which has been erected where there was once a swamp with 'osier beds and coracles', as 'paving stones over the bog' (*SF*: 209). *To the Lighthouse* also images the Ramsays' candle-lit dining room as a 'dry land' where order reigns, protected from the waters outside, a 'common cause against that fluidity out there' (*TTL*: 97). The significance and purpose of the act of entertaining is thus more explicitly expressed in this novel than in the case of Clarissa's party in *Mrs Dalloway*. As Mrs Dalloway's party serves to bring disparate individuals together, so Mrs Ramsay's dinner party aims first of all to assemble people, to create 'community of feeling with other people' as if they are 'all one stream' (ibid.: 113–14). After the initial excruciating difficulty of bringing the truculent sentiments of the diners into some workable mutual rapport, Mrs Ramsay triumphs, achieving a fleeting but sure sense of the 'eternity' of the moment. In the novel's famous formulation, 'Of such moments, she thought, the thing is made that endures. This would remain' (ibid.: 105).

The disintegration which sets in as soon as Mrs Ramsay steps out of the room foretells what is to follow. The 'Time Passes' section unravels all that she achieved, as if the ugly truth, or non-existence of any truth, behind the enticing surface appearance of the world erupts, and in the narrative which depicts the chaos of a rampant nature mere human affairs are relegated into parentheses. Hence it is that when Lily returns to the Ramsays' summer house after ten years, what she experiences is a sense of profound disorder, 'as if the link that usually bound things together had been cut' (*TTL*: 146). Thus the novel poignantly emphasises the death of Mrs Ramsay, that centripetal force of integration. In this place which was once for Lily so emotionally charged, she sees the words becoming 'symbols', writing themselves all over the grey-green walls, but is unable to connect them: 'If only she could put them together, she felt, write them out in some sentence, then she would have got at the truth of things . . . how bring them [the parts] together?' (ibid.: 147). As an artist, it is of course not by writing but painting that Lily tries to 'bring them together', connecting not words but sensuous shapes and colours. The problem of her picture ten years ago was, she remembers, how to connect the mass on the right with the mass on the left. In her aesthetic struggle to complete her painting, the process which Lily pursues is very similar to that meditative discipline whereby Mrs Ramsay reached 'a wedge-shaped core of darkness' and her own ensuing epiphanic revelations (ibid.: 62–3). 'Drawn out of gossip, out of living, out of community with people', Lily must open herself to a tentative reality emerging 'at the back of appearances' (ibid.: 158). The word 'tunnelling', that key technical term in relation to *Mrs Dalloway*, is used also of Lily: 'She went on tunnelling her way . . . into the past' (ibid.: 173). Lily too, then, has her epiphany, not the definitive revelation but one of those ' little daily miracles, illuminations' that 'In the midst of chaos there was shape', a moment of being which she feels she owes to Mrs Ramsay (ibid.: 161). Lily realises that what the older woman achieved in her conventionally feminine middle-class domestic life in drawing-room, nursery and dining-room, survives in its bricolating of social fragments into some kind of completion 'like a work of art' (ibid.: 160). As I have shown above, both *Mrs Dalloway* and *The Hours* provide evidence of Woolf's intention to liken Clarissa's desire for giving parties to the aesthetic desires of an artist or a writer. *To the Lighthouse* explores and elaborates this analogy further; it compels its own artist figure to recognise the underlying identity between the practices in different spheres, domestic and artistic.

To acknowledge that Mrs Ramsay's domestic practice of bringing people together and thereby making something whole and permanent is equivalent to what her own art aspires to is vital for Lily in order to resolve her 'anxiety of authorship'. In the dinner party ten years ago, Lily had protested against Mrs Ramsay's feminine pity for men as 'one of those misjudgements of hers': 'he [Mr Bankes] has his work' (*TTL*: 84) and she also asserted the value of her own work to denounce the older woman's model of womanhood. But this refusal of Mrs Ramsay's paradigm of femininity by asserting her professional work and pleading exemption from the creed of marriage runs the risk of de-sexing Lily. Unable to respond to Mr Ramsay's demand for sympathy, she accuses herself of being 'not a woman, but a peevish, ill-tempered, dried-up old maid presumably' (ibid.: 151). For Lily to emerge fully as a woman and a modernist painter, she needs to be able to meet the older woman she desperately wishes to be fused with in an impersonal realm, in that 'wedge of dark core' which has shed all personal trappings, as proleptically suggested perhaps by the 'purple shadow' her modernist painting had reduced Mrs Ramsay to ten years ago. She could then without anxiety and guilt 'over-ride her wishes, improve away her limited, old-fashioned ideas' (ibid.: 174). The biographical parallels are strong here, as has often been remarked. Woolf writes in 'A Sketch of the Past' that until she was in her forties and wrote *To the Lighthouse*, 'the presence of my mother obsessed me' (*MOB*: 80). Through the artist Lily Briscoe, Woolf resolves the long-standing dilemma she had struggled with since her days under her half-brother George's regime at Hyde Park Gate: the conflict between upstairs and downstairs, between her father's unworldly intellectualism and George's worldly conventionality, but which was, as I have suggested, related to a more complex, internal conflict about the legacy of her mother. If she was to emerge as a modernist writer, with a literary room of her own, these compounded tensions needed to be resolved. In a now famous formulation, Woolf claimed that in writing *To the Lighthouse* 'I did for myself what psycho-analysts do for their patients. I expressed some very long felt and deeply felt emotion. And in expressing it I explained it and then laid it to rest' (ibid.: 81). Only then could she assert her feminism more explicitly in speech and print. *A Room of One's Own*, which is based on a paper read at Cambridge, was published in 1929; she could even in 'Professions for Women', originally a speech given in 1931, recommend killing 'the Angel in the House' as a mode of self-defence necessary for a woman to become a writer.

The equation of conventionally female domestic practices of entertaining and the aesthetic practices of painting or writing, which is first hinted at in *Mrs Dalloway*, is thus fully established in *To the Lighthouse*, thereby freeing Woolf from the anxiety and guilt of rejecting her maternal legacy. Also if these two activities are fundamentally the same effort to achieve stability in the face of constant change as 'all that is solid melts into air' (Marx, *The Communist Manifesto*), then social life and serious professional life would no longer need to be opposed to each other in the ways that Woolf often in her own life felt they were. Her diary records much annoyance over visitors or invitations disrupting her professional solitude and concentration; on the other hand, she also covets stimulating social life on those occasions when she is for whatever reason prevented from participating. The opposition is now not serious work versus

Figure 13.4 The Woolfs' sitting room at 52 Tavistock Square, London, 1924,
decorated by Duncan Grant and Vanessa Bell.
Vogue © Condé Nast Publications Ltd

enjoyable but frivolous social life, but between human activities, whether social,
intellectual or aesthetic, and a radical disorder or flux which nullifies any such
human achievements. This polarity which ultimately emerges as the new focus
of the novel's consciousness in *To the Lighthouse* is at the very centre of *The
Waves*, which is written from a perspective which views *all* human activities
from the outside; this later novel is therefore beyond the remit of this essay,
which focuses on tensions *within* the human, between Woolf's enduring but
ultimately reconciled ambivalences about the worth, or otherwise, of the culture
of domestic entertainment. If the culture of modernist experimentation can be
flexibly understood not as the opposite to, but rather as some kind of sublimated
version of, middle-class entertaining, then Virginia Woolf has at last closed the
gap between herself and her mother. Which is hostess and which is guest in this
dyad, it thenceforth becomes impossible to say.

Notes

1. For Woolf's mention of 'the grown-ups' dinner' at St Ives, see *MOB*: 132.
2. See the introduction by Elaine Showalter in *Mrs Dalloway* (Showalter 1992: xxxvi) and
   *D*2: 189, 190 and 207.

3. See *D2*: 249, 262 and 272.
4. Emily Blair relates the 'dispersed' subjectivity of Clarissa and Mrs Ramsay to the nine-teenth-century middle-class ideology of ideal womanhood, particularly as articulated by John Ruskin. See chapter 6 of *Virginia Woolf and the Nineteenth-Century Domestic Novel* (Blair 2007) in which Blair devotes insightful and well-researched attention to the dimension of entertainment in *Mrs Dalloway* and *To the Lighthouse*.
5. See *MOB*: 36.
6. Also see *MOB*: 218.
7. For example, see *D2*: 210; *D3*: 42, 337.
8. Woolf 1996: 194–5.

Works Cited

Bell, Quentin (1972), *Virginia Woolf: A Biography* (2 vols), London: Hogarth Press.
Blair, Emily (2007) *Virginia Woolf and the Nineteenth-Century Domestic Novel*, Albany, NY: State University of New York Press.
Showalter, Elaine (1992) 'Introduction', *Mrs Dalloway*, Harmondsworth: Penguin Books Ltd, pp. xi–xlviii.
Woolf, Leonard (1967), *Downhill All the Way: An Autobiography of the Years 1919–1939*, London: Hogarth Press.
Woolf, Virginia (1976) *Moments of Being*, ed. Jeanne Schulkind, London: Chatto & Windus for Sussex University Press.
—— (1996) *Virginia Woolf 'The Hours': The British Museum Manuscript of 'Mrs. Dalloway'*, transcribed and ed. by Helen M. Wussow, New York: Pace University Press.

Further Reading

Bell, Quentin (1995) *Bloomsbury Recollected*, New York: Columbia University Press.
Briggs, Julia (2005) *Virginia Woolf: An Inner Life*, London: Allen Lane.
Curtis, Anthony (2006) *Virginia Woolf: Bloomsbury and Beyond*, London: House Publishing Limited.
DiBattista, Maria (2009) *Imagining Virginia Woolf: An Experiment in Critical Biography*, Princeton and Oxford: Princeton University Press.
Dunn, Jane ([1999] 2000) *Virginia Woolf and Vanessa Bell: A Very Close Conspiracy*, London: Virago Press.
Dwan, David (2008) 'Woolf, Scepticism and Manners', *Textual Practice*, 2: 249–68.
Garnett, Angelica (1984) *Deceived with Kindness: A Bloomsbury Childhood*, London: Chatto & Windus/Hogarth Press.
Lee, Hermione (1996) *Virginia Woolf*, London: Chatto & Windus.
Light, Alison (2007) *Mrs Woolf and the Servants*, London: Penguin Books/Fig Tree.
Marder: Herbert (2000) *The Measure of Life: Virginia Woolf's Last Years*, Ithaca, NY and London, Cornell University Press.
McLeod, Kirsty (1991) *A Passion for Friendship: Sibyl Colefax and Her Circle*, Harmondsworth: Michael Joseph Ltd.
Reed, Christopher (2004) *Bloomsbury Rooms: Modernism, Subculture, and Domesticity*, New Haven, and London: Yale University Press.
Sellers, Susan (2008) *Vanessa and Virginia*, Ullapool, Ross-shire: Two Ravens Press.
Virginia Woolf Bulletin, January 15 2004, (special issue on Woolf's relationship with Christabel McLaren, later Lady Aberconway, including previously unpublished Woolf's letters to her).

14

VIRGINIA WOOLF AND GARDENS

Nuala Hancock

L[eonard] pruned, which needed heroic courage. My heroism was purely literary. (*D3*: 4)

Virginia Woolf was not a garden-maker. Certainly, there were times when, through a pure lust for living, she plunged her hands into the soil; envisaged aesthetic effects by reading appetitive seed catalogues; created exhilarating views through the radical clearing of obscuring shrubs. Her passion for practical garden-making was breathless – and unsustained. Surrendering to the prowess of the garden-makers around her – Vanessa Bell, Leonard Woolf and, most notably, Vita Sackville-West – Woolf's relationship with gardens was immersive rather than directive; interpretive rather than pragmatic.

It is not in the making of gardens, then, but in their sensate experience and their literary interpretation that Virginia Woolf's interest lies. Gardens, both private and public, occur frequently as designed landscapes in her work, both fictional and autobiographical. She represents them as highly significant contexts, both in her creative process and in her personal, emotional topography. From the formal arenas of the Victorian park to the intimate spaces of her garden at Monk's House, gardens are richly resonant in her work; highly charged. Woolf walked in gardens, 'rehearsed phrases' in gardens, 'made up' books in gardens. Many of her illuminating 'moments of being' were realised in the context of gardens. Further, the gardens of her experience are artistically transcribed into literary contexts in her novels. This chapter explores Woolf's many-layered relationship with gardens – formative, sensate, creative, literary – and proposes the idea of a Woolfian 'garden aesthetic' whose poetics reverberate across the spaces of her work.

Formative gardens

As she embarks on her 'Sketch of the Past' in 1939, Virginia Woolf adopts a topographical approach, identifying those salient spaces and places of her childhood at the core of her self-configuration. Childhood gardens, she reveals, in both London and Cornwall, are the context for some of her most potent emplaced memories. Her very first memory is of a 'floral' immersion: of lying in her mother's lap on the way to St Ives, absorbing at close range the red and purple anemones on the fabric of her mother's dress (Woolf 2002: 78). From the beginning, Woolf identifies her mother with flowers; clothes her in floral imagery. As the memories accumulate, so this association intensifies. The nursery at Talland House, that cradle of plenitude where Woolf lay as a child hearing the waves splashing and the blind blowing, had a balcony attached to her parent's bedroom. Here, Woolf witnessed her mother emerging, surrounded by the passion flowers that hung loosely from the wall. (ibid.: 79) Her next memory is of the garden itself – of being physically immersed in an encircling sensorium of warmth and fecundity. 'The buzz, the croon, the smell', she recalls, 'all seemed to press voluptuously against some membrane; not to burst it; but to hum round one such a complete rapture of pleasure . . .' (ibid.: 80) In this mellifluous space, this warm and fertile garden, Woolf memorialises her mother. 'I have a vision of her now', she writes later, 'as she came up the path by the lawn at St Ives' (ibid.: 93) (See Figure 14.1).

The garden at Talland House takes on the attributes, in Woolf's memoir, of an elegiac garden – a lost world of rapturous childhood summers, from which she was forever excluded following her mother's death: 'the ending of society; of gaiety; the giving up of St Ives' (Woolf 2002: 130). Her father, Leslie Stephen, in his *Mausoleum Book*, equally locates his wife in the spaces of this commemorative garden.

> I can see my Julia strolling among her beloved flowers: sitting in the 'loo corner', a sheltered seat behind the grape-house, or the so-called 'coffee garden', where on hot days she would be shaded by the great escallonia hedge . . . .(Stephen 1977: 62)

Gardens in Victorian culture, were viewed as feminised domains – as natural extensions of the domestic sphere. An affinity with nature was associated with a sense of purity, of moral uprightness; indifference deemed unwomanly (Brevis 2004). Woolf constructs an idealised image of her mother, later on in her memoir, in the style of a Victorian genre painting, as Hermione Lee suggests (Lee 1997: 86), as a young woman in a garden, presiding over tea. 'I make up pictures of a summer's afternoon' (Woolf 2002: 98). But where women were historically associated with flowers – frail and passively decorative – as the nineteenth century progressed, Rozsika Parker points out, the notion of femininity that once signified 'too frail to garden' began to indicate, on the contrary, a 'natural proclivity for gardening' (Parker 2005: 91). The 'angel in the house' emerged into the spaces of the garden, where she might 'demonstrate her moral goodness and her worth as a wife by the neatness, orderliness and health of her flower- beds'. In Leslie Stephen's text, Julia Stephen is portrayed as having not only a natural affinity with flowers but a facility (albeit that its expression

Figure 14.1 'Family Group outside the Dining Room window, Talland House
c.1894'. From the Leslie Stephen Photograph Album, 37f, Mortimer Rare Book
Room, Smith College, Northampton, MA 01063

was limited by the seasonal nature of this Cornish villa garden) to extend the
domestic sanctuary of the interior out into the spaces of the garden. 'Julia loved
flowers and delighted in such gardening as was compatible with the shortness
of our residences' (Stephen 1997: 62).

In Woolf's re-enactment of this garden in *To the Lighthouse* (1927), it becomes
an inter-subjective arena for the painful acting out of gendered difference – of
conflicting intellectual and aesthetic sensibilities – and the playing out of
memory. While the literary setting is the Isle of Skye, the imaginary garden

resembles the actual in many instances. The thick separating hedges, the tennis lawn, the look-out place, the purple passion flowers recur as leitmotifs from novel to memoir. (Woolf 2002: 134; *TTL*: 33) Mrs Ramsay, presiding over her household and her guests, orchestrates her garden with equal élan. She directs the gardener, sends bulbs down from London, plans next season's flowers (*TTL*: 101). She expresses an attunement to the natural world: 'if one was alone, one leant to inanimate things; trees, streams, flowers; felt they expressed one; felt they became one; felt they knew one, in a sense were one; felt an irrational tenderness thus' (ibid.: 97/98). Such susceptibilities are outside the domain of her husband. Mr Ramsay did not see flowers. He 'pretended to admire' them, but sees only 'something red, something brown' (ibid.: 108, 102). Perhaps he was 'made differently from other people', Mrs Ramsay considered. 'His understanding often astonished her. But did he notice the flowers? No.' (*TTL*: 107) When Mrs Ramsay dies in this novel, both house and garden communicate her loss: 'the trees plunge and bend and their leaves fly helter skelter until the lawn is plastered with them'; violets and daffodils in windblown urns are 'eyeless' and behold nothing (ibid.: 193, 203). In both novel and memoir, the garden at Talland House is an emotionally charged terrain; dense with the memory of Julia Stephen; impregnated with associations of plenitude and loss.

If Virginia Woolf 'finds' her mother in the sensorily, the memorially drenched spaces of the elegiac garden at Talland House, she 'finds' her father striding across the extended spaces of London's Kensington Gardens. This historic, royal terrain with its decorous walks and avenues of trees offered spectacle and recreation to Victorian London. Once the private grounds of the Royal Palace, and open freely to the public from around 1820, the original formal Gardens were laid out anew in the eighteenth century in grandiloquent style, with expansive lawns and open views.[1] Moments away from their London home in Hyde Park Gate, the Stephen family made regular excursions here – as Leslie Stephen had done as a child,[2] – to walk, to play, to sail boats on the Round Pond, to skate in cold winters as the contemporary *Hyde Park Gate News* and Woolf's retrospective 'Sketch' record. Now intensely joyous, now languorously dull, the Gardens were an integral tract in the Stephen children's formative geographies. But this pleasure ground, too, was blighted with sorrow. Here, following their mother's death in 1895, the Stephen children emerged from Hyde Park Gate to process, hand in hand, in solemn *marche funèbre* into Kensington Gardens – 'and how golden the laburnum shone' (Woolf 2002: 104). The insensitivity of nature is a recurrent motif in Woolf's work; a taste of bitter-sweetness forever accompanies her accounts of summer inflorescence.

Recovering in 1897, Woolf was prescribed a recuperative regime of 'No lessons, no excitement: open air, simple life' (Lee 1997: 178). She was to take the air in the Gardens, accompanied by her father (Woolf 1992: xvi) 'Walked in the gardens with father', she relates repeatedly in her journal; 'round the pond' and 'by Kensington Palace' (ibid.: 22, 24, 27). Such references in this journal from 1897 become so familiar, so quotidian, that they take on an incantatory role.

Leslie Stephen, Woolf recalls in her commemorative essay from 1904, recited poetry – 'shouted' poetry – as he walked, 'at the top of his voice as he went about the house or walked in Kensington Gardens' (*CE*1: 129). He developed, she recalls in her later retrospective from 1932, a 'strange rhythmical chant' for 'verse of all kinds', and that 'the act of walking' (or climbing) generated this idiosyncratic flow (*CDB*: 70). There are no references to such outpourings in these journal reports (and Leslie Stephen, like his daughter, was much altered by grief), yet there is a sense of rhythm, of something litanised in Woolf's text, suggestive of some internal incantation, however muted. 'Walked in the morning with father. Went round the Pond as usual' (Woolf 1992: 24) And what of plants, on these garden walks? Did Leslie Stephen 'see' flowers? Plant development in the Gardens is much in evidence in this journal: 'the almond trees out, the crocusses going over, squills at their best, the other trees just beginning to seed' (ibid.: 55) – but intriguingly, such observations in Woolf's journal are made with reference to female companions. Yet later that summer, in Painswick, Woolf reports that she 'botanised with Father', and went with him 'hunting for plants' (ibid.: 118). If Mr Ramsay is blind to the aesthetic qualities of flowers – only 'something red, something brown' – Leslie Stephen's relationship with flowers, according to his contemporaries, is significantly more nuanced. His mother declared that as a child he had 'a remarkable love for lovely things' and 'a passion for flowers'; his biographer that he was an understated authority on flowers, and had become 'a very fair British field botanist' whose conversations with fellow walkers in Cornwall might be interrupted by his discovery of 'a rare little plant upon a wall' (Maitland 1906: 24, 4). Herbert Fisher in his memoir offers a contemporary account of Leslie Stephen 'striding over the Cornish cliffs, botanizing as he went, repeating poetry' (Fisher 1940: 20). Stephen's predilection may well have been for wild rather than cultivated plants, but surely sensibility to flowers can hardly be in question? Might we imagine him, then, as Woolf did, 'Taking his hat and his stick, calling for his dog and his daughter', to 'stride off into Kensington Gardens' (*CDB*: 73) – 'botanizing as he went', perhaps, as Fisher witnessed, and 'repeating poetry'? Woolf's rhythmic listing of plants in her journal suggests a learnt chanting of names and observation of cyclical performance, enunciated to the cadences of walking: 'the almond trees out, the crocusses going over, squills at their best, the other trees just beginning to seed' (Woolf 1992: 55) Both botany and poetry are audible here.

These two childhood gardens – one private and rural, one public and urban – one saturated with memories of her mother, the other pulsing with the energy of her father – deeply informed, I think, Woolf's idea of garden. On the one hand, gardens in her experience are richly associative theatres of memory – emotionally textured, psychically weighted; on the other, they are iterative green spaces where the free movement of the body elicits the rhythmic articulation of language. Both of these constructs are at play in her literary rendering of gardens, and often simultaneously. In both fiction and non-fiction, gardens in Woolf's work are arenas of emotional intensification whose physical passage promotes a releasing flow of words.

Compositional gardens

Woolf's diaries are rich in the celebration of walking – the 'trance like, swimming, flying through the air; the current of sensations & ideas' (*D4*: 246). Walking and creativity are closely related in her work. She adventures on her imagination, tossing her 'brain into the air', as she walks (*D3*: 141). In London, the city's parks and squares offered contexts for such refreshment, and she incorporated them, as she had since her childhood, as an instinctive rhythm in the pattern of her day. 'Just in from a walk in the Park on this incredibly lovely autumn day' (*D1*: 211). Walking in London's gardens released her expressivity – generated her flow of words.

> There is no doubt that the greatest happiness in the world is walking through Regents Park on a green, but wet – green but red pink & blue evening – the flower beds I mean emerging from the general misty rain – & making up phrases. (*D4*: 319)

Even in the face of great sadness, walking in the park elicited a quickening, a restoration of her imaginative flow. 'A vast sorrow at the back of life this winter', she writes in 1935, following the death of Roger Fry: 'And then my blood rises & I create – yesterday walking by the lake in Regents Park, going to Hugo's' (*D4*: 277). London's green spaces provided a rich seam of writing material, and the opportunity of rehearsing compositional effects, both visual and spatial: 'We got out of the car last night & began walking down to the Serpentine. A summer evening. Chestnuts in their crinolines, bearing tapers: grey green water & so on' (*D4*: 152). In Spring 1935, Woolf visited Hyde Park while composing *The Years*: 'Spring triumphant. Crocuses going over. Daffodils & hyacinths out. [. . .] I want to make vegetable notes for my book' (ibid.: 292).

The Bloomsbury Squares, those intimate gardens at the heart of the city, so inextricably woven into her biography, were particularly propitious to her process. Gordon Square, Fitzroy Square, Brunswick Square, Tavistock Square – for much of her life in London, Woolf overlooked these redolent square gardens, and moved through their spaces with quotidian ease. Living in such vegetal proximity – trees gesturing outside drawing room windows, expansive lawns unfurling underfoot – Woolf gives a sense of an organic immersion, a close-up encounter, even in the city, with the processes and vibrations of plants. Arriving in Gordon Square in 1904, Woolf recalls looking 'into all those trees': the tree which releases its branches to 'fall in a shower'; the tree which 'glistens after rain like the body of a seal' (Woolf 2002: 46). Through their expressiveness, their animation, these live organic elements enact, in her account, the exhilaration of this move. Letters and diaries from Tavistock Square express a heightened attunement to signs of quickening in the gardens – 'trees shaking green'

(*L3*: 254); leaves 'pushing' (*D4*: 17); 'leaves visibly drawing out of the bud' (*D3*: 18). The stirring of nature's rhythms paralleled her own expressive potential: she 'made up' *To the Lighthouse*, she reports 'in a great, apparently involuntary, rush' – an organic emergence – 'one thing' bursting 'into another' (Woolf 2002: 92) as she walked around Tavistock Square.

In Woolf's re-enactment of London's parks and gardens in her novels, the cadences of walking are audible in her texts. In *Night and Day* (1919) she revisits Kew Gardens, a landscape made familiar to Woolf while she lived in Richmond. The topography of the terrain is articulated through the phrasing of language: 'the lake, the broad green space, the vista of trees . . . the Ducal castle standing in its meadows' (Woolf 1990b: 316). In *Mrs Dalloway* (1925) 'the swing, tramp and trudge' and 'the silence; the mist; the hum' give the sensations of moving from clamorous terrain to the distilled atmosphere of the park, treading on soft ground (Woolf 1990a: 2, 3). The ease of this inter-modality parallels Woolf's own daily rhythms, and mirrors the ebb and flow of interiorised thought in her text. In *The Years* (1937) Woolf revisits Hyde Park and Kensington Gardens, the formative geographies of her childhood – by 1937, instinctive body-ballets. She takes pleasure in the laying out of her familiar landscape, choreographing its fluent modulations: 'The urbanity of the Park, the gleam of the water, the sweep and curve and composition of the scene' (Woolf 1990d: 211).

But these recontextualised city parks in Woolf's novels are neither merely recreational pleasure grounds nor topographic contrasts with the city's streets: they are emotionally freighted arenas; psychically toned. In *Mrs Dalloway* London's parks are contexts for internalised reviewing of the past; for contemplating the impossibility of reaching the other; for witnessing the commonality of humanity and the ultimate solitude of the individual. Natural beauty may abound in Regent's Park, but private pain is everywhere in this public place. Maisie Johnson is horrified to find herself estranged in this unfamiliar city; Peter Walsh cries out at the memory of being rejected by Clarissa; Lucrezia Septimus Smith is tortured by the loneliness of her separation from Septimus, locked in his private world (Woolf 1990a: 22, 56, 57).[3] Intimate lives are played out on these public stages to the rhythms of nature's cycles that progress inexorably, indifferent to human impermanence. Woolf brings to her representation of gardens the emotional texture of her own lost gardens – a mellifluence tainted with sorrow. 'Doesn't one always think of the past, in a garden with men and women lying under the trees? Eleanor proposes in *Kew Gardens*. 'Aren't they one's past, all that remains of it . . . ?' (Woolf 1985: 91). Woolf rewrites London's gardens as arenas of heightened existentiality, for apprehending 'the infinite oddity of the human position' (*D3*: 62), the relationship between 'the I and the 'not I', between the self and the cosmos.

Garden-making

If gardens are significant in the literary art of Virginia Woolf, what is her relationship with the art of the garden? Virginia Woolf was not a garden-maker, but
for her sister Vanessa Bell, garden-making was a significant expressive medium.
In Woolf's journal from 1897 there is an account of an early artistic collaboration between the two sisters – the transformation of the unpromising dust patch
behind their house in Hyde Park Gate into a garden. Woolf was commissioned
by her father, as part of her doctor's recuperative regime that 'as a lover of
nature' she should be 'health-fully employed out of doors' (Woolf 1992: 84) – a
directive reflecting late Victorian notions of gardening as both recreational and
ameliorative (Brevis 2004: 104). But Bell appears to take the lead in the project,
demonstrating both a modernity of attack and an already assured assertive-
ness in the handling of materials and the manipulation of space. 'Nessa was
valiant, & created another flower bed by the garden wall, but I basely deserted
her, when the worms & stones became too numerous, & the heat was too great'
(Woolf 1992: 86). Woolf becomes caught up in the transformative process of
this shared creative enterprise – 'This desert place is under our hands, becoming
a quite beautiful spot' – and gives an account of the lay-out of the new flower
beds, 'liberally' planted up with 'half grown pansies, lobelia, & sweet peas', very
much in the Victorian bedding-plant tradition. (ibid.: 89) Collaborative garden-
making was taken up anew in 1912 at Asheham, Woolf's and Bell's first house
in Sussex, and correspondence at the time shows a developing exchange on the
subject. (*L*2: 22, 24) Bell's energy and focus for garden-making become increasingly evident: 'I am today having a large square flower bed dug and manured . . .
I shall have flowers sent from Seend', (Marler 1998: 127) and while Virginia and
Leonard Woolf take on significant projects – creating a path ('Great fun to do'),
and planting 'wall flowers, daisies, foxgloves' (*D1*: 54, 55), Woolf continues to
defer to her sister's authority; 'Nessa, Mabel, & children came to tea. Our pink
flower she says is phlox: not stocks' (*D1*: 42); 'Bicycled to Charleston. Roger
there. Fine border of flowers. Monkbrettia(?) is the name of the orange lily' (*D1*:
53). This diffidence, on Woolf's part, in the expressive medium of garden-making is reminiscent of her deference to her sister in all matters visual – painting,
interior decorating, dress.

The artist's garden

Vanessa Bell was an intuitive garden-maker, at ease with organic materials
(and plant nomenclature); flairful in the handling of space. Through Bell,
Woolf was in touch with garden-making as an expressive art among others
at the beginning of the twentieth century. She watched closely as her sister
took on the development of the house at Charleston in 1916, and extended
the living space out into the garden. How did this ground-breaking artist who
radically reinterpreted the domestic interior, who washed the walls of her house

in idiosyncratic colour, who covered its surfaces in her animated decorative écriture – how did she interpret the garden? How did Vanessa Bell's garden-making aesthetic sit within the context of the work of other garden-artists of the time? At Charleston she began in functional mode and with characteristic zeal, making 'great efforts' to 'get the garden dug' (Bell and Nicholson 1997: 128). But the utilitarian wartime garden soon gave way to a more idiomatic aesthetic. In 1922, Woolf reports: 'Charleston is as usual. [. . .] Nessa emerges from a great variegated quilt of asters & artichokes' (*D2*: 195). This image of billowing full-ness is taken up by Bell in her letters (Tate Gallery Archive), gathering momen-tum as the garden develops. In 1926 it is 'full of dahlias and red admirals'; in 1930, a 'medley of apples, hollyhocks, plums, zinnias, dahlias'; in 1936 'a mass of flowers & as gay as possible'; and reaching its crescendo in 'a dithering blaze'. Such exhilarating layers of growth and colour suggest an organic parallel to the painted surfaces in the house: an immersion in paint translated into a drench-ing in inflorescence in the garden.

Bell's approach to garden-making developed not only in collaboration with Duncan Grant, with whom she shared Charleston – but as part of her aesthetic exchange with Roger Fry. Much of her correspondence about the garden is with Fry, and the overall design of the garden was conceived in collaboration with him after the war. Through Fry, Bell had an indirect connection with Gertrude Jekyll, the artist/plantswoman, and one of the most prominent figures in Edwardian garden-making. Fluent in a range of crafts, trained as a painter, Jekyll was the co-creator, with the architect Edwin Lutyens, of a prodigious repertoire of highly influential twentieth-century English gardens in the Arts and Crafts style. Fry consulted Jekyll on the design and planting of his own garden at Durbins, [4] and there was much in her approach to speak to Fry's and Bell's aesthetic. In a reaction against the rigidity and artifice of formal Victorian bedding, Jekyll created schemes where plants could drift and flow with ease and natural expressiveness. [5] Bell's 'medley' and 'massing', Woolf's 'variegated quilt' recall the rhythm and amplitude that Jekyll sought in her swathes and 'clouds' of planting. Jekyll, both artist and plantswoman, experimented with colour, manipulating space with hot advancing reds and recessive blues and greens. She planned single-colour borders – and so did Vanessa Bell, paint-ing three-dimensionally, creating a scheme in 1930 using plants flowering in a repertoire of reds: 'the garden . . . is incredibly beautiful', she writes to Roger Fry, 'it's full of reds of all kinds, scabious & hollyhocks & mallows & every kind of red from red lead to black' (Tate Archive). Bell and Grant enjoyed grey- and silver-leafed plants – signature subjects in Jekyll's repertoire: *Cynara cardun-culus*, the statuesque ornamental artichoke, (Woolf's 'variegated quilt'), which unfurls deeply-cut metallic leaves, and *Stachys byzantina*, the softly felted lamb's ears, offering subtle textural contrasts and a cool soft grey against which other colours sing. Jekyll pursued 'shocks of eye-pleasure' in her juxtaposition of complementary colours (Jekyll 1908: 103). Bell, a consummate colourist was celebrated by her sister for the 'singing quality of her tone', and her juxtaposition in a garden painting of her 'pigeon breast' grey against 'hot pokers', causing her sister's mind to 'shiver with joy' (*L3*: 271).

But where there is a composed artfulness in the work of Jekyll, there is an idiosyncratic insouciance implicit in contemporary accounts of the garden at Charleston – a provocative sense of freedom that characterises the decorative surfaces of the house. Witnesses remember a simple design aligned to the architecture of the house – but 'richly overlaid', as Sir Peter Shepheard has it, with a 'teeming mass of flowers' (Charleston Archive). Gathering evidence for its restoration in the mid-1980s, Shepheard drew up lists of old, (uncontrived) cottage garden plants – pæonies, poppies, daisies and columbines, lambs' ears and phlomis, with roses and clematis clothing the walls. 'It was a garden filled to overflowing. The plants jostling and blending with one another as in a meadow, not too precise but in a sweet disorder' (ibid.). It is as though the Omega aesthetic of 'a free handling' of paint, an embracing of 'the accidental', a 'play and vivacity' of gesture and effect (Fry 1917) were translated organically into the spaces of the garden. Where the 'angel in the house' was judged on the 'neatness and orderliness' of her flower-beds, in his sensitive restoration of Vanessa Bell's garden, Peter Shepheard strove to 'avoid neatness' as a guiding principle.[6] Charleston garden, for Woolf, represented a further manifestation of her sister's effortless fertility – 'Nessa humming & booming & flourishing over the hill' (*D3*: 111) – and the careless ease with which she created sensuous milieux where artistic expression might kindle and flower: 'yesterday at Charleston . . . We had tea from bright blue cups under the pink light of the giant hollyhock' (*D3*: 190).

Vita

Nowhere is Virginia Woolf's dalliance with the art of garden-making more propitious than in her relationship with Vita Sackville-West. Author of Sissinghurst, one of the most celebrated gardens in England, surely Woolf's affair with Vita Sackville-West would have initiated her into the ways of the long border, engaged her in conversations about floral colour and form? Yet there is nothing in their correspondence to suggest sustained exchanges on the art of the garden. Where organic vocabulary enters their exchange, it is not for the purposes of design or composition, but for the expression of intimacy and eroticism. When Woolf spent three days at Long Barn in December 1925, it was not the garden's latent fecundity that she records in her diary, but Vita's: 'stalking on legs like beech trees, pink glowing, grape clustered, pearl hung' (*D3*: 52). Awaiting Vita's arrival at Monk's House in June 1926 she invokes the lavishness, the fertility of the mid-summer garden: 'the June nights are long and warm; the roses flowering; and the garden full of lust and bees, mingling in the asparagus beds' (*L3*: 275). In September 1929 she notes lasciviously: 'I am just back from Long Barn . . .where L. fetched me; & I have just eaten a pear warm from the sun with the juice running out of it' (*D3*: 251). Vita communicated through flowers and plants, and Woolf responded with sensuous imagery: 'I am lying under a purple and blue forest, the lupins you brought. [. . .] I have walked around the Square, but I much prefer lying on my chair under the blue and purple forest' (*L3*: 388). Gardens, in their relationship, became a shorthand for their intimacy: 'Look here Vita – throw over your man, and we'll go to Hampton Court . . . and walk in the garden in the moonlight' (*L3*: 393). When the intensity of their liaison fades, Woolf constructs it, still, in organic vocabulary – 'as ripe fruit falls'. Vita, she judges, has 'run to seed'; no longer curious about books, she 'kindles' only about 'dogs, flowers, & new buildings' (*D4*: 287).

It was Vita's ripeness that interested Woolf – her relationship with the land, her ancestral sense of place – rather than the detail of her garden-making. Long Barn, the apprentice garden for Sissinghurst, flowed easily from the house in the Arts and Crafts style, lavishly planted with roses and clematis on the walls, herbs and scented flowers around the building (Brown 1987: 99). It is barely recorded by Woolf. Sissinghurst, acquired in 1930, and begun in 1932, was barely visited. 'S[issinghurs]t is to have a new wing; a new garden; a new wall', Woolf reports, unmoved, in 1935. 'Well, its like cutting off a picture' (*D4*: 287). When Vita wrote to Woolf in 1939 asking her to come, the garden was already laid out; the yew hedges of the Rondel in place; roses and clematis burgeoning on walls; the orchard underplanted with fritillaries (Brown 1987: 129). But if Woolf had ever shown interest in her garden-making, it was no longer expected. 'Will you and Leonard ever come here, on your way down to Rodmell? I would so like Leonard to see my garden. You, I know, are no gardener, so I confine this interest to Leonard' (DeSalvo and Leaska 1984: 423). Woolf was never to see the postwar Sissinghurst, developed up until Vita's death in 1962 – and now, under the auspices of the National Trust, one of the most visited of gardens – with its robust walls of yew, its sumptuous planting, cresting and spilling, its sequence of rooms, its 'succession of privacies' (Lane Fox 1986: 11).

Writing the garden

Vita Sackville-West was both garden-maker, and garden writer. She published *Some Flowers* in 1937; *The Garden* in 1946, and for nearly fifteen years, from 1947 until 1961, she wrote a weekly column for the *Observer*. Much of her garden writing was addressed to the amateur gardener, which increased her readership but constrained her style, combining the 'descriptive with the practical', 'petals, in fact, with slugs' (Sackville-West 1937: Foreword). Even outside the generic limitations of the column, there is a reserve in her garden-writing, a resistance, as though, even in the context of poetry, she fears relinquishing the stance of the practical gardener. *The Garden* becomes advice-giving in verse – her horticultural knowledge and botanical observation at all times overriding sensation. She is at her most telling investigating flowers close up (she liked to keep a single cut flower in a vase on her desk), communicating their intricacy, their delicacy: 'Tuscany' (the rose) 'opens flat . . . thus revealing the quivering and dusty gold of its central perfection' (Sackville-West 1937: 40).

When Virginia Woolf investigates flowers, it is sensation that she seeks. In *Kew Gardens* (1919), that high-key Woolfian *tour de force*, we plunge down the throats of flowers, become engorged with their fleshy anatomy, brushed with their pollen. Stalks spread, leaves unfurl, spots of colour are 'raised', a central gold bar 'emerges' from the 'gloom'; we feel its colour – 'rough with gold dust', and hear its shape – 'slightly clubbed at the end' (Woolf 1985: 90). Woolf wrenches garden-writing from the realms of the visual in this daring, experimental text and re-vivifies it as multi-sensory, haptic, enfleshed. Plants take on a life of their own – unconstrained by pictorial composition. Woolf was stimulated, it seems, long before her affair with Sackville-West, by post-Darwinian revelations about the inner workings of plants and regularly visited Kew Gardens – that archive of living plants – especially when living in Richmond. She enjoyed discovering the detail of plants – a facility enabled by Kew's prestigious glass-houses, a nineteenth-century architectural phenomenon that coincided with increased scientific interest in the processes of plants, and the active adventuring of plant-hunters. She visited the Orchid House in 1917, where she observed 'the spotted & streaked flesh' of those 'sinister reptiles', noting: 'They always make me anxious to bring them into a novel' (*D1*: 82). They re-appear in *Night and Day* (1919), 'peering' and 'gaping' at Katharine Hilbery from their 'striped hoods and fleshy throats' (Woolf 1990b: 318) Infinitely more complex than their surface affect, flowers are sinister, lewd – 'living things endowed with sex, and pores, and susceptibilities' (ibid.: 317). Woolf's approach to flowers is more Darwinian than Jekyllesque. She is less interested in cultivating nature, than in inviting nature in, in all its strangeness; its otherness. She enjoys it in its primitive manifestations as in its artifices. Where Vita is alerted by an encroaching snail, Woolf is enthralled. Where Vita Sackville-West invites us to look at flowers, Woolf connects us to their secret parts; suggests their inner promptings.

The writer's garden

The correspondence between the inner rhythms of the natural world and the stirring of the creative impulse is at its most apparent in Woolf's writing in her relationship with the garden at Monk's House. The Woolfs' rural retreat in Sussex from 1919 until Woolf's death in 1941, the spaces of both house and garden became enmeshed over time with the processes of their daily lives, inscribed with their creative rhythms. If Woolf experienced vegetal proximity living in Tavistock Square, in this private Sussex garden, she achieved a veritable vegetal immersion. Where the house is modest – 'long & low' – Woolf expresses in her diary her 'profound pleasure at the size & shape & fertility & wildness of the garden' (*D1*: 286). From the beginning, it exerted an irresistible draw: 'The temptation whispers from the window all the time' (ibid.: 296). Garden-making – 'the first pure joy of the garden I mean' – began immediately

and as an exhilarating shared enterprise. She records the excitement of sowing
seeds, of weeding – 'this is happiness' – the thrill of clearing the view to the
Downs (ibid.: 302; *D2*: 43, 50). But it is Leonard Woolf who takes ownership
in time: 'Our garden is the envy of Sussex', Woolf writes to Janet Case in 1925;
'this is all Leonard's doing [. . .] I offer my admiration, but am seldom allowed
an active part' (*L3*: 202).

Woolf's diary accounts from Monk's House are full of references to Leonard
Woolf's 'heroic' commitment to the garden – pruning, spraying, climbing trees,
installing pools, planning terraces The expense of the garden was a source of
disharmony between them but Woolf's celebration of her husband's work is
frequent and profound. 'Leonards garden has really been a miracle – vast white
lilies, and such a blaze of dahlias that even today one feels lit up' (*L4*: 213). The
significance of this intimate garden, then, for Virginia Woolf was not configu-
rational but contextual; her desire not for intervention, but immersion. Monk's
House itself is set low, sunk within the folds of the garden, giving a sense of
vegetal suspension. Woolf constantly refers in her diary to this sensation of
being wrapped-around in green: of 'flowers & leaves nodding in all round us'
(*D3*: 89).

Such is her desire for organic environs, the individuated spaces that she constructs for herself in this place are set not within the house but within the spaces
of the garden. Her writing room, at first, in 1921, is a converted tool house in the
garden (*L2*: 475) – and later, her garden 'lodge', installed in 1934 beneath the
orchard wall. 'There will be open doors in front; & a view right over to Caburn. I
think I shall sleep there on summer nights' (*D4*: 263). In 1930, she constructed
a bedroom for herself that stretched, as an extended arm, out into the soft
organic spaces of the garden, 'where the rising sun on the apples & asparagus
wakes me, if I leave the curtain open' (ibid.: 174) (see Figure 14.2). From these
satellites of the house, Woolf was garden-surrounded – not as a witness but as
a participant: 'This is our world, lit with crescents and stars of light; and great
petals half transparent block the openings like purple windows' (Woolf 1990b:
12).

In these dreaming and writing spaces at Monk's House, Woolf fine-tunes her
sensate apprehension to the garden's vibrations; responds to quickening; mirrors emergence. The interludes in *The Waves* (1931) record the directness of her
vegetal encounter: buds 'split asunder', shaking out flowers, 'green veined and
quivering'; currants hang 'in ripples and cascades of polished red'; a tree 'shifts'
its mass; 'multitudinous leaves' blow 'up and down' (ibid.:16, 97, 138, 120)
Woolf positions herself in this garden such that she is able not only to see but
to feel nature's rush. Stalks 'rise', flowers 'swim' – such is the commingling that
at times, flesh and vegetable matter enmesh, in her text, in pursuit of organic
connection: 'I am green as a yew tree'; 'my hair is made of leaves'; ' My roots
go down to the depths of the world . . . through veins of lead and silver' (ibid.:
4, 5).

In the writing of *The Waves*, Woolf's own process is articulated in botanical

Figure 14.2 Monk's House, Rodmell, Sussex (back view) © NTPL/Eric Crichton

imagery. This serious, poetic work might be contained, she considers, by the fall of the petals of a flower (*D3*: 118, 131). As the work begins to take form in June 1927 – 'France: near the sea; at night; a garden under the window', she notes that 'it needs ripening' (*D3*: 139). The following year she reports on the progress of the gestation: 'As for my next book, I am going to hold myself from writing till I have it impending in me: grown heavy in my mind like a ripe pear; pendant, gravid, asking to be cut or it will fall' (ibid.: 209). There is an active reciprocity between the fertility of the garden and her own generative surge.

An aesthetic of gardens

Virginia Woolf's garden aesthetic, then, emerges as more performative than pictorial; more visceral than visual. In her modernist project to 'saturate every atom', to 'give the moment whole' (*D3*: 209), Woolf offers an account not of the configuration of gardens, but of their phenomenology. Unenthralled by dialoguing with garden-makers, however celebrated, within her own circle, Woolf attunes directly to organic processes; seeks the primitive origins of plants; pursues source. She takes us inside flowers, plunges us into the interior of plants, roots us to the ground, invites us to study foliage from the underside, to imagine vegetal enfleshment. She dispenses with the viewer in her accounts of gardens: leaves 'push' (*D4*: 17), petals 'flash' (Woolf 1985: 95), the earth 'emerges', 'chastened & sharpened from winter under a veil' (*D4*: 201). In this, her capacity to invoke the quickening of plants, their cyclical vibrations, Woolf suffuses her garden texts with a redolent sense of place. It is not the stylistic elements of parks and gardens that concern her, but their sensations. Where an ineffable sense of atmosphere resists articulation, Woolf's gardens are emotionally textured; psychically toned. They are saturated with pleasure; fretted over with memory; pierced with loss. An acute apprehension of the cyclicity of the natural order penetrates her idea of garden. Flowering is succeeded by evanescence; exaltation by regret. Woolf's gardens are fraught with this tension: transience and perpetuity; 'the incessant rise and fall and fall and rise again' (Woolf 1990c: 199). In an early journal, Woolf noted to herself: 'If you lie on the earth somewhere you hear a sound like a vast breath, as though it were the very inspiration of earth herself, & all the living things on her' (Woolf 1992: 203). In Woolf's work, trees 'shake green', buds 'split asunder', currants 'ripple'; in Virginia Woolf's version of the garden, the earth herself respires.

Notes

1. See Williams 2006.
2. See Annan 1984, 144; Maitland 1906 22–3.
3. For a fuller account of the role of London's parks and gardens in Woolf's novels, see Hancock (2005).
4. See Surrey History Centre, Woking Collection Reference 6950 Michael Tooley (n.d.) 'The Plant Nursery at Munstead Wood': Miss Jekyll 'provided plans and 600 plants from her nursery for Durbins in Guildford, home of Roger Fry, the artist and art critic'.
5. Jekyll worked in association with William Robinson who attacked the artifice of Victorian bedding where plants were 'mutilated', 'stuck up' with sticks: 'It is the *life* we want'. See Robinson, 1883.
6. Related by Annabel Downs, landscape architect and garden designer, and editor of Downs 2004. She worked alongside Shepheard in the restoration of Charleston garden.

Works Cited and Further Reading

Annan, Noel (1984) *Leslie Stephen: The Godless Victorian*, London: Weidenfeld and Nicolson.

Bell, Quentin and Virginia Nicholson (1997) *Charleston: a Bloomsbury House and Garden*, London: Frances Lincoln.

Brevis, Monica (2004) '"The Garden that I love": Middle-class Identity, Gender and the English Domestic Garden 1880–1914' unpublished thesis, University of Brighton.

Brown, Jane (1987) *Vita's Other World*, London: Penguin Books.

Charleston Archive: 'The Charleston Garden: Sir Peter Shepheard's Account of the Restoration of the Garden', January 1987, pp.1–2.

DeSalvo, Louise and Mitchell Leaska (eds) (1984) *The Letters of Vita Sackville West and Virginia Woolf*, San Francisco, CA: Cleis Press Inc.

Downs, Annabel (2004) *Peter Shepheard* London: Landscape Design Trust.

Fisher, H. A. L. (1940) *An Unfinished Biography*, London/New York/Toronto: Oxford University Press.

Fry, Roger (1917) 'The Artist as Decorator', in Reed 1996.

Hancock, Nuala (2005) *Gardens in the Work of Virginia Woolf*, London: Cecil Woolf, pp. 9–19.

Jekyll, Gertrude (1908) *Colour in the Flower Garden*, London: Country Life.

Kingsbury, Noel and Tim Richardson (eds) (2005) *Vista: The Culture and Politics of Gardens*, London: Frances Lincoln pp. 87–99.

Lane Fox, Robin (1986) *The Illustrated Garden Book, Vita Sackville West: A New Anthology*, London: Michael Joseph.

Lee, Hermione (1997) *Virginia Woolf*, London: Vintage.

Maitland, Frederick William (1906) *The Life & Letters of Leslie Stephen*, London: Duckworth & Co.

Marler, Regina (ed.) (1998) *Selected Letters of Vanessa Bell*, Wakefield, RI: and London: Mayor Bell.

Parker, Rozsika (2005) 'Unnatural History: Women, Gardening, and Femininity', in Kingsbury and Richardson 2005.

Reed, Christopher (ed.) (1996) *A Roger Fry Reader*, Chicago: University of Chicago Press, pp.207–11.

Robinson, William (1883) *The Wild Garden*, London: John Murray, p. 103.

Sackville-West, V. (1937) *Some Flowers*, London: Cobden-Sanderson.

Sackville-West, V. (1946) *The Garden*, London: Michael Joseph.

Stephen, Sir Leslie (1977) *Sir Leslie Stephen's Mausoleum Book*, intro by Alan Bell, Oxford: Clarendon Press.

Tate Gallery Archive: The Letters of Vanessa Bell: (1) To Roger Fry: Sept 1926 (8010.8.382 p. 2); 15 Aug. 1930 (8010.8.428 p. 5). (2) To Julian Bell: 15 Aug. 1936 (9311.55 p.2); 29 Aug. 1936 (9311.57 p. 5). (3) To Roger Fry: 6 Aug. 1930 (8010.8.427 p. 3).

Woolf, Virginia (1985) *The Complete Short Fiction of Virginia Woolf*, London: Hogarth Press.

—— (1990a) *Mrs Dalloway*, London: Hogarth Press.

—— (1990b) *Night and Day*, London: Hogarth Press.

—— (1990c) *The Waves*, London: Hogarth Press.

—— (1990d) *The Years*, London: Hogarth Press.

—— (1992) *A Passionate Apprentice*, ed. Mitchell A. Leaska, London: Hogarth Press.

—— (2002) *Moments of Being: Autobiographical Writings* (ed.) Jeanne Schulkind, intro and rev by Hermione Lee, London: Pimlico.

Williams, Sally (2006) '"The Ingenious Mr. Charles Bridgeman" and His Work at Kensington Palace', *The London Gardener*, 11: 19–38.

Part IV   Publishing, Broadcasting and Technology

15

VIRGINIA WOOLF AS PUBLISHER AND EDITOR: THE HOGARTH PRESS

Laura Marcus

Then Virginia described the beginning of the Hogarth Press, and at the age I then was, I listened like a child entranced. Her husband, Leonard Woolf, had won a prize in the Calcutta Sweepstake. With this they had brought a printing press and some type, and in the house where they then lived at Richmond they had printed stories by Virginia herself and by Leonard Woolf, T. S. Eliot's *The Waste Land*, and several other small volumes. She described how they had done this with little thought except to please themselves, and then one book (I think it was her own *Kew Gardens*) had been well reviewed in the *Times Literary Supplement*. She described running downstairs and seeing the door-mat deep in letters bringing orders for more copies. They then had to farm out the printing of a second edition with a local printer: and hence they found that they had become no amateur printers who sold their own work privately, but The Hogarth Press, a small but flourishing firm which even produced a few best-sellers.

(Spender 1951: 153–4)

NANCY CUNARD, IN her memoir of the private press she established in 1928, *These Were the Hours*, calls attention to the flourishing of small presses in the first decades of the twentieth century: in Europe, Britain and the United States (Cunard 1969: 5–6). She notes that 1917 saw the emergence of the Beaumont Press in London and the Woolfs' Hogarth Press; 1919, John Rodker's Ovid Press; 1923, Francis Meynell and David Garnett's Nonesuch Press, with its 'lavish editions of books by classic and modern authors'; 1926 Jack Lindsay's Fanfrolico Press; 1928 Robert Graves's and Laura Riding's Seizin Press. In Paris, Sylvia Beach set up Shakespeare and Company, which would bring out Joyce's *Ulysses*, while 1927 saw the founding of Harry and Caresse Crosby's Black Sun Press and 1928 that of Edward Titus's Black Manikin Press. A number of small presses were also linked to the 'little magazines' that flourished in the same period. The Egoist Press was set up, and incorporated *The Egoist* journal as one of its imprints, in 1916: the Press published numerous modernist works, including those of Joyce and T. S. Eliot. Robert McAlmon's Contact Publishing Company extended his 'little magazine' *Contact*, founded with William Carlos

263

Williams in 1920. The Contact Publishing Company, and its imprint Contact Editions, published many of the most significant works of modernist literature, with writing by Joyce, Mina Loy, H.D., Mary Butts and Gertrude Stein.

Recent histories of modernism have explored the networks of patronage which sponsored the little magazines and the small presses, as well as the creation of niche marketing, the limited edition format and an attendant 'exploitation of notions of cultural distinction' (Armstrong 2005: 54). The circumstances of modernist publishing are now taken to be an essential dimension of our understanding of modernist and avant-garde literature and art. This intellectual context, in addition to the development of 'the history of the book' as a part of literary and cultural studies, has led to a substantial growth of interest in the Hogarth Press, along with the other small presses of the period.

There are, however, a number of aspects of the Hogarth Press which differentiate it strongly from these other presses. For one thing, it survived when so many other small presses established in the same period failed to do so: few of the presses named by Cunard lasted long into the 1930s, the period when the Hogarth Press began to show more substantial profits. Those presses which had committed themselves to 'fine printing' and deluxe editions could not survive the economic climate of the 1930s. The Hogarth Press, which had, as we shall see, rejected 'fine printing' from the outset, and which was run on extremely low overheads under Leonard Woolf's direction, not only survived, but retained total autonomy until its merger with Chatto and Windus in 1946.

The Hogarth Press was also marked out by the heterogeneity of its list, with publications in the fields of poetry, fiction, literary criticism, art criticism, psychoanalysis, history, politics and economics. It was wide-ranging, too, within these categories, publishing, in the literary sphere, not only the works of high modernists such as Gertrude Stein and T. S. Eliot, but the Georgian poets, and, in the 1930s, the work of the new generation of writers, including Henry Green, Edward Upward, Christopher Isherwood, Cecil Day Lewis and John Lehmann, who became a partner in the Press in the late 1930s. While the Press's literature list reflects some of the most significant developments in the literary production of the first part of the twentieth century, publications in the sphere of politics had, by the mid-1930s, outnumbered literary works. Feminist writing was central to the Press's output, and Virginia Woolf made a highly significant contribution here, with *Three Guineas* appearing as one of eleven Hogarth Press publications on women and feminism. The Press's pamphlet series included important interventions into cultural and political debates: aesthetics, feminism, pacifism and disarmament, imperialism and anti-imperialism, communism and the USSR, and the nature of fascism. The Press also became the most significant producer of psychoanalytic literature in Britain, acting as the sole UK publisher of Freud's work from 1924 onwards and, after the Second World War, publishing the twenty-four volumes of the *Standard Edition of the Complete Psychological Works of Sigmund Freud*, under the general editorship of James Strachey, in collaboration with Anna Freud.

The Hogarth Press's reach was thus exceptionally extensive. It was an extraordinary enterprise with an extraordinary history, not least given its beginnings as, in Leonard Woolf's account, a form of therapy for Virginia Woolf in the late 1910s, and one started on a small printing press in their dining room at Hogarth House in Richmond. Its sheer reach creates a difficult task for the press historian and the literary critic. It is not, as I have suggested, easy to situate in the history of publishing: does it take its place, for example, alongside the more mainstream publishers such as Faber and Faber and Jonathan Cape, or with the more experimental, modernist ventures with which I began my discussion? It may be that the story of the Press is not a single one: we could trace its history as one which begins in experimentation and subsequently develops to occupy a central place in British intellectual and cultural life.

In 1992, J. H. Willis's *Leonard and Virginia Woolf as Publishers: The Hogarth Press 1917–1941* appeared, offering the first synoptic history of the Press. Willis's invaluable study is a heroic construction of a narrative history out of the publishers' archives. It discusses the Press in relation to its 'stages' and, following Leonard Woolf's accounts of the Press in his autobiographies, 'turning-points'. It shows, as I have suggested, that the Press had a very different profile in the 1920s from the one it would acquire in the 1930s. In recent years, constructions of the Press's history as a whole, and the broad categories of its wide and diverse list, have been supplemented by an interest in the histories of individual authors and artists who contributed to the Press, moving outwards from the particular work to its broader placing, both within the Press's history and beyond that to the wider cultural sphere. Such instances reveal historical, biographical and cultural relationships and networks, as, for example, in the case of publications by Vita Sackville-West, which were some of the Press's most successful volumes.

The focus of this chapter is primarily on the impact of the Press and its publications on Virginia Woolf as a writer. From her third novel *Jacob's Room* onwards, she published her fiction exclusively, in its UK editions, with the Hogarth Press; some of her most important essays were also Hogarth Press publications. I take the direction of my discussion from an announcement produced in 1922, on the Press's fifth anniversary.[1] In the five years since its founding, the statement notes, the Press had published nineteen volumes, not one of which 'has failed to justify, even in a pecuniary sense, the faith we put in it' (p. 1). 'Pecuniary' considerations, it is emphasised, were very much secondary to the judgement of 'genuine merit', but the books selected had not failed to satisfy at a commercial as well as a literary and artistic level. The appended list of 'previous publications' shows that four of the nineteen publications were out of print: T. S. Eliot's *Poems*, Hope Mirrlees' *Paris: A Poem*, Virginia Woolf's *Kew Gardens* and Leonard and Virginia Woolf's *Two Stories*. The success of the Press's early publications had altered the initial plans:

It had been our original intention to print every book with our hands, but the sales much exceeded our expectation. We found ourselves compelled to issue editions not of two or three hundred but of one or two thousand, and thus in many cases it became necessary to employ the services of professional printers'. (p. 1)

'It is our intention', the pamphlet continues,

> to proceed more boldly in the future, and to publish a greater number of books and books of greater length. But we do not mean to depart in any other respect from the principles which guided us in the beginning. We shall continue to give particular attention to the work of young and unknown writers. We shall proceed with our translations from the Russian. We intend to issue reproductions from the works of living painters. On the other hand, it is none of our purpose to reprint the classics; nor shall we sacrifice time or money to embellish our books beyond what is necessary for ease of reading and decency of appearance. We shall continue to print the smaller editions with our own hands – for the larger editions we shall employ the services of the usual printing presses. Our experience in the past confirms us in our belief that it is essential to keep our prices at the ordinary level, and to aim rather at cheapness and adequacy than at high prices and typographical splendour. (p. 2)

The statement opens up a number of topics: the Press's commitment to new work; its engagement with the visual arts, combined with its differentiation of its task from that of the small presses which were extending late nineteenth-century arts and crafts publishing in the reprinting of classics and in 'fine printing'. There are two further emphases, on which I focus in this chapter: the commitments to hand-printing and to 'translations from the Russian'. Both these aspects open up the ways in which Virginia Woolf's multifarious relationships to the work of the Press and its publications – as reader, editor, translator, printer, publisher – became inseparable from her own creative practices as a writer.

Printing with our own hands

Between 1917 and 1932, the Woolfs hand-printed thirty-four texts for the Press, with Virginia Woolf (aided by various assistants over the years) doing most of the typesetting. The hand-printed books begin with Leonard and Virginia Woolf's 'Two Stories': further texts written and hand-printed by the Woolfs include Virginia's *Kew Gardens* (1919) and *On Being Ill* (1930), and Leonard's *Stories of the East* (1921). Works by other authors, a number of which I discuss in the following section, include Katherine Mansfield's *Prelude* (1918), T. S. Eliot's *Poems* (1919) and *The Waste Land* (1923), Theodora Bosanquet's *Henry James at Work* (1924), Nancy Cunard's *Parallax* (1925), Laura Riding's *Voltaire* (1927), Vita Sackville-West's *Sissinghurst* (1931) and Dorothy Wellesley's *Jupiter and the Nun* (1932). The list also includes Roger Fry's *Twelve Original Woodcuts* (1921), as well as works by John Middleton

Murry, E. M. Forster, Clive Bell, Robert Graves, Herbert Read, John Crowe Ransom and Edwin Muir.

Hand-printing – printing 'with our own hands' – is seen as an activity in which the embodied work of the compositor becomes part of the printing process, thus militating against the idea that printing is pure mechanism. This understanding bears closely on Bloomsbury theories of the visual arts, and in particular those of Roger Fry, whose Omega Workshop (which set out to produce books as well as fabrics, furniture and artefacts) was an undoubted stimulus for the creation of the Hogarth Press. Fry, writing of the position of photography in his preface to the Hogarth Press's edition of Julia Margaret Cameron's photographs, *Victorian Photographs of Famous Men and Fair Women*, revised his long-held view that the hand-made object was superior to the machine-made because, in Francis Spalding's words, 'the tremors of movement visible in the end product betrayed the sensibility of the maker' (Spalding 1998: 136). In earlier writings, Fry had expressed his strongly held belief that manual dexterity equated to artistic power, as well as the view that the nervous control of the hand, which lay at the furthest remove from 'mechanism', was alone capable of transmitting the artist's feeling to us. The Woolfs' emphasis on 'printing with our hands' takes at least some of its meaning from this context. In a letter to Leonard Woolf, the artist William Rothenstein commented of 'Two Stories' that the 'woodcuts were very attractive and [the] hand-printing gave the book a more human quality'.[2] His assertion also suggests an important link between the hand-printed text and the use of woodcuts: both word and image become part of the 'graphic' nature of the text, reinforcing the understanding of writing (including the 'character drawing' on which Woolf's narrator reflects in *Jacob's Room*) as a form of engraving. There are broad and complex issues relating to the perceived relationship between hand-writing, typing, hand-printing and machine-compositing, a relationship which Martin Heidegger, for one, would explore in his writings on the hand and the typewriter, in which he argued:

> The hand is, together with the word, the essential distinction of man. . . . Man does not 'have' hands, but the hand holds the essence of man, because the word as the essential realm of the hand is the ground of the essence of man. . . . The typewriter tears writing from the essential realm of the hand, i.e. the realm of the word. (Heidegger 1992: 80–1)

In a letter to Katherine Cox, written on 19 March 1916, Virginia noted that

> Leonard is as usual writing away at about 6 books, and he has now trained himself to compose straight on to a typewriter, without a mistake in sense or spelling. I feel like the owner of some marvellous dog who does tricks – there's pointing to my husband's gifts.

Their real dog, Max, she continues, had had a fit the previous night, but had now made a full recovery. On the other hand, as she states in rather bald terms, 'Henry James is dead' (James died on 28 February 1916). Woolf writes: 'His last words, according to Sydney [Waterlow], were to his secretary, whom he sent for. "I wish to dictate a few faint and faded words" – after which he was silent and never spoke again'. She concluded the letter by noting that 'Leonard has just come in . . . and says I cant write any more, so I must leave out about our Printing Press' (*L*2: 83–4). The long and playful letter thus brings together the marvels of Leonard's composition onto a typewriter, without the mediation of handwriting, combined with some irony in the allusion to a 'trained' dog, as if composition were now to be perceived as reflex rather than creativity; Henry James's method of dictation, turning voice into typewritten text through the medium of the stenographer's hand; reference (in the mode of default) to the printing press.

These elements curiously anticipate the Hogarth Press's publication in 1924 of Theodora Bosanquet's *Henry James at Work*: the only one of the Hogarth Essays to be hand-printed. Bosanquet had sent a manuscript to the Woolfs, after she had published a number of accounts, following James's death, of her role as his secretary, in journals including the *Fortnightly Review*, the *Little Review* and the *Yale Review*. Bosanquet had been hired by James in 1907 to work his newly acquired Remington typewriter, which she taught herself to do: 'The business of acting as a medium between the spoken and the typewritten word was at first as alarming as it was fascinating' (Bosanquet 2006: 34). James, Bosanquet observes, 'found dictation not only an easier but a more inspiring method of composing than writing with his own hand . . . "It all seems," he once explained, "to be so much more effectively and unceasingly *pulled* out of me in speech than in writing"' (ibid.: 34) 'He had reached a stage', Bosanquet continues,

> at which the click of a Remington machine acted as a positive spur. He found it more difficult to compose to the music of any other make. During a fortnight when the Remington was out of order he dictated to an Oliver typewriter with evident discomfort, and he found it almost impossibly disconcerting to speak to something that makes no responsive sound at all. (ibid.: 35)

The Woolfs at the Hogarth Press were thus setting and printing, 'with our hands', the record of a period, running from 1907 to 1917 when, in Friedrich Kittler's words, 'a typewriter and its female operator produced the modern American novel' (Kittler 1999: 216). The comment opens onto questions of gender and reproduction, and of the new relationship between the hand and the machine in the context of 'writing' in modernity.

It also leads us to the nature of the engagement with the word entailed in the work of compositing. This issue was raised by Nancy Cunard in her memoir of the Hours Press. Cunard came to the Woolfs for advice at the outset. 'Leonard and Virginia Woolf, whose Hogarth Press had steadily grown in importance', Cunard writes, were less than encouraging:

> They too had been hand-setters and worked in the ancient manner. I cannot think that they actually wanted to discourage me, yet I can still

hear their cry: 'Your hands will always be covered in ink!' This seemed no deterrent. And it was with curiosity [that] I looked at my black and greasy hands after the first go with the inking table. (Cunard 1969: 8)

It is the work of the hands – the work of the hands that work – which Cunard emphasises: 'I would so much rather have been the artisan . . . than the "Director"'.

In 1925, the Hogarth Press had hand-printed and published Cunard's poem *Parallax*, with a cover designed by the American painter Eugene MacCown, who became a close friend of Cunard's, along with the Dadaist Tristan Tzara, at this time in Paris. In 1923 MacCown had painted a portrait of Cunard, wearing her father's old top hat, which was said to be one of her favourite self-images. *Parallax* is the poetic bildungsroman, and series of meditations, of a young male poet, journeying from London to France and Italy: it contains, as contemporary reviewers noted, marked echoes of *The Waste Land*, which the Hogarth Press had hand-printed and published two years previously. The resonant title of Cunard's poem, 'parallax', alludes to a concept in geometry, astronomy and optics, referring to the relationship between different angles and perspectives on a distant object: it is a term that resounds throughout *Ulysses*, in which Bloom's pondering of its meanings is a recurrent trope. Cunard's poem thus becomes the nodal point in a network of associations and authorships, including the Parisian avant-garde, Eliot and Joyce: it is hand-printed by Virginia Woolf and 'covered' by MacCown. Like Mirrlees' *Paris*, *Parallax* formed a bridge between Bloomsbury and the different cultural formation (of Anglo-American-European modernism) at its height in the Paris of the 1920s.

Publishing *Parallax* with the Hogarth Press was almost certainly one of the motivating factors in Cunard's decision to start up her own printing press in 1928. She wrote of the 'hard beginning' of the Hours Press:

I do not mean the text. For such is one's absorption – at first especially – that it matters little to the appraising part of one's mind what one is transferring from written or typed pages to what will become the printed page. (Cunard 1969: 11)

Yet, later in the memoir, Cunard comments: 'An intimate communion with a long, intense poem is already there, if one reads it as often as one does, say, *The Waste Land*. How much more so when, letter by letter and line by line, it rises from your fingers around the type' (ibid: 51). There would appear to be two contradictory assertions here. The first suggests the bypassing of reading and critical judgement in the absorption of the work of typesetting 'with the hands' (a reminder that type is set in reverse, so does not readily reveal its created meaning to the compositor). The second argues for the 'intimate communion' with the word 'as it rises from your fingers' in a model in which typesetting becomes both an extension of the body and an extension of reading.

In his autobiography, Leonard Woolf suggested that the 'amateur' printer was more fully aware of the words on the page than the professional:

> Professional compositors, indeed all professional printers, do not attend to the sense of anything which they print (or so I was told by McDermott, who also said one day that of all the millions of lines which he had set in his time he doubted whether more than a few of them were worth reading.) But as an amateur printer and also the publisher of what I was printing, I found it impossible not to attend to the sense, and usually after setting a line and then seeing it appear again and again as I took it off the machine, I got terribly irritated by it. (L.Woolf 1980: 176)

It was only in the case of printing T. S. Eliot's verse, Woolf notes, that he 'never tired and still do not tire of those lines which were a new note in poetry' (L. Woolf 1980: 176): reproduction and repetition thus become associated, as they do in Cunard's remarks on *The Waste Land*, with reading and re-reading, and with the perception of Eliot's inexhaustibility by repetition.

Woolf's comments on the printing process raise further questions as to what happens when the printer is not only the publisher of what he or she is printing, but also the writer. Would Virginia Woolf's awareness of the structure of writing (including the shapes words form on the page, and the ways in which the reader's experience is shaped by the structure of printed words) have been as acute if she had not become a printer and publisher? Cunard certainly emphasised the ways in which printing led her to see the design of a page in a new light:

> I began to learn that letters are one thing, and a mass of type something else to be thought of in relation to the space to be printed and the unprinted space surrounding it . . . . Every bit as important in the total aspect is the non-printed as well as the printed surface. (Chisholm 1979: 114)

Such concerns lead to broader issues of modernist literary production including (to borrow the subtitle of Jerome McGann's 1993 study of modernist composition, *Black Riders*) 'the visible language of modernism'.

It would certainly seem to be the case that Woolf's typesetting of the Hogarth Press texts helped shape her use of white space and fragmentation in *Jacob's Room*, the first of her novels to be printed by the Press, and one in which she also suggested some ambivalence towards the mechanisation of writing, linked in the novel to the war machine and the automatisation and destruction of bodies as machines. There is, furthermore, a recurrent imagery of screens and inscriptions in her work, as in 'The Mark on the Wall' (the first text to be printed by the Press). We see here a significant 'transition', to which Woolf's writing often seems to allude: the shift from writing to typing/printing. Her early short stories take much of their meaning from the fact that she was typesetting them herself for the newly founded Press. The 'Mark on the Wall', the first text that Woolf type-set, is an exploration of consciousness and of the surface/depth relationships that result from observing an inscription or 'mark' upon a surface: a kind of writing on the wall which is revealed, finally, to be a snail. The 'mark' on the wall could be read as a punctuation mark, beginning and ending trains of thought. In the aesthetic of Woolf's early short stories ('The Mark on the Wall', *Kew Gardens*) and in *Jacob's Room*, there is an insistent emphasis on types and typing, imprinting, inscription and engraving (and a reminder that the word 'character' is derived from the Greek 'kharratein', 'to engrave') which draws attention to tactile and graphic surfaces while the narrative voice simultaneously insists upon a hollowing out of the world, the production of meaning as depth.

As Julia Briggs and Anna Fewster have shown, Virginia Woolf's hand-printing of Mirrlees' long poem *Paris* was a particularly significant influence on her 'experiments' in writing in the early 1920s. *Paris* followed the writings of Stéphane Mallarmé and Guillaume Apollinaire in its play with white spaces and, in the case of Apollinaire's *Calligrammes*, the creation of

> pictorial shapes out of the words of his poems . . . . From these examples, and those of Jean Cocteau and Pierre Reverdy, Mirrlees learned that the placing of a line of poetry itself constituted a form of punctuation, and that the spaces of the page form a crucial part of the rhythm of writing. (Briggs 2006: 84)

A 'city poem' (bearing in significant ways not only on Eliot's *The Waste Land*, begun later in 1920, but on the 'city symphonies' that became central to film and fiction in the 1920s), *Paris* uses experiments in typography in its representation of urban sign systems. Its graphic qualities, and its 'cinematicity', inhere in its representation of advertisements, bill-boards, sign-writings: elements of the modern city which the American film theorist Vachel Lindsay was identifying, in 1922, as definitional of modern America's 'hieroglyphic civilization' (Lindsay 2000: 12).

The typesetting of *Paris*, which Woolf described in a letter to Margaret Llewelyn Davies as 'a very obscure, indecent, and brilliant poem which we are going to print', was a significant challenge for Woolf (*L2*: 385). There is a suggestion, in the ways in which she defines the poem here, of a compensatory response to the Woolfs' rejection of Harriet Shaw Weaver's request, made in the Spring of 1918, that the Hogarth Press take on the printing of Joyce's *Ulysses*. The reason given for the Woolfs' refusal was the text's length, but it seems that their decision was more substantially informed by the fact that two printers had told Leonard Woolf that the publication of the novel would lead to prosecution (ibid: 243). Virginia Woolf's description of *Paris* was perhaps intended to suggest that the Press did not fear 'indecency', the term Woolf also applied, in her 1919 essay 'Modern Fiction', to the work of Joyce (*E3*: 34).

Woolf worked on the printing of *Paris* as she was re-writing *The Voyage Out* and as she was beginning to write *Jacob's Room*. It seems indisputable that the printing of Mirrlees' poem was formative in Woolf's construction of *Jacob's Room*, the first of her novels to be printed by the Hogarth Press, and one which she would come to define as an 'experiment'. As Edward Bishop observes, in his preface to the Shakespeare Head Press Edition of *Jacob's Room*: 'What strikes a reader first are the space breaks on the page, making the work look more like a prose poem than a traditional novel' (Bishop 2004: xi). These breaks were not present at the start of composition, but introduced to replace chapter divisions. It could also be suggested that Woolf, in writing this her most sexually explicit novel (an explicitness much more pronounced in draft versions), was reaching out for the 'indecency' which she associated with the 'brilliant' Mirrlees as a representative of a younger and bolder generation of women.

In this regard, Mirrlees became associated for Woolf with Katherine Mansfield, though Mansfield was in fact only six years younger than Woolf. Woolf's and Mansfield's relationship, as friends and fellow writers, was often a difficult one. On 20 March 1922, Woolf wrote to Janet Case:

> Literature still survives. I've not read K. Mansfield [presumably *The Garden Party*, 1922], and don't mean to. I read Bliss, and it was so brilliant; – so hard, and so shallow, and so sentimental that I had to rush to the bookcase for something to drink. Shakespeare, Conrad, even Virginia Woolf. (*L*2: 514–5)

Here 'brilliant' seems to connote the hardness and sharpness (terms Woolf at other times associated with Mansfield herself) of a diamond, or 'brilliant', rather than functioning as a value term. It may also be worth noting that a 'brilliant' is the smallest unit of printing type. Yet there is no doubting the regard in which Woolf and Mansfield held each other as writers, nor their shared sense that, in Mansfield's phrase, they were 'after so very nearly the same thing'. Mansfield wrote this in August 1917, after reading *Kew Gardens*, adding: 'Yes, your Flower Bed is *very* good. There's a still, quivering, changing light over it all and a sense of those couples dissolving in the bright air which fascinates me' (Mansfield 1928: 80).

The intensity of the visual imagery here, coming closest, perhaps, to an Impressionist aesthetic, indicates one significant way in which Mansfield and Woolf were pursuing 'the same thing'. Mansfield frequently defined her 'vision' in relation to painting and the captured 'essence' of things in the world, while Woolf, in the early 1920s in particular, was deeply preoccupied with visuality, writing to Vanessa Bell and Duncan Grant about the paintings which were absorbing her and of her desire to train her visual and aesthetic eye, through an understanding of the qualities of shape and colour. Such concerns are of central relevance to the Press, which represented a version of material creativity and, in its reproductions of woodcuts and its artists' covers, contributed to the ongoing dialogue between writers and artists, word and image. This was powerfully depicted in Vanessa Bell's woodcuts and cover design for the 1919 Hogarth Press version of *Kew Gardens* and, more dramatically, in the edition printed in 1927, in which Bell's drawings of trees and flowers wind around and through the printed text. The collaboration, and the competition, between writer and artist is itself illustrated on the pages of the book. The dialogue is also at work in Bell's covers for Virginia's novels: the cover for *A Room of One's Own*, for example, turning the question of space (the room) into time through its representation of a mantelpiece clock; that for Woolf's *Roger Fry* pointing up the conceptual relationship between biography and portraiture.

'I threw my darling to the Wolves', Mansfield wrote of *Prelude* to Dorothy Brett, 'and they ate it and served me up so much praise in such a golden bowl that I couldn't help feeling gratified' (Mansfield 1928: 83). The printing of *Prelude* took the Woolfs nearly a year. It became too much of a labour to print it on their small press, so, after Virginia (with the help of their assistant Barbara Hiles) had set the type, they took it to the Richmond printer McDermott's machine, which Leonard Woolf operated. The first few copies included lino-cuts, on front and back covers, by the Scottish artist J. D. Fergusson, a friend of Mansfield's, who had produced extensive illustrations, including the cover design, for the 'little magazine' *Rhythm*, edited by Mansfield and her husband John Middleton Murry. Virginia Woolf expressed an extreme distaste for Fergusson's lino-blocks of a woman's head – 'He has done a design for her story [*Prelude*] which makes our gorges rise, to such an extent that we can hardly bring ourselves to print it' (*L2*: 244) – the exaggerated response suggesting some rivalry between Fergusson and the Bloomsbury artists. The rest of the printing run appeared without Fergusson's designs.

Prelude was a reworking, for the Press, of Mansfield's story *The Aloe*. The title of the earlier version refers to the tree that flowers only once in its lifetime, and which Mansfield connected with, as she wrote in her journal (April 1920), our 'flowering for our moment upon the earth . . . . This is the moment which, after all, we live for – the moment of direct feeling when we are most ourselves and least personal' (Mansfield 1977: 173). The structure of *Prelude*, with its distinct but overlapping scenes, finds its echo not only in *Jacob's Room* but in Woolf's later novels, including *Mrs Dalloway*, *To the Lighthouse* and *The Waves* (born out of Woolf's perception of a nameless woman watching 'the flower upright in the centre; a perpetual crumbling and renewal of the plant' (*D3*: 229) and defined by Woolf as an impersonal form of autobiography). So do Mansfield's modes of perception, with their intense evocations of memory, consciousness, the irruptions of the past into the present, and the animation of the inanimate world.

Throughout the early years of the Press, Virginia Woolf referred to the freedom it gave her, both as publisher and as writer. In a letter to Vanessa Bell on 26 July 1917 she wrote:

> We should very much like you and Duncan to do a book of woodcuts – in fact we are getting a machine that is specially good for printing pictures, as we want to do pictures just as much as writing. Of course they would take much less time to do. . . . It is tremendous fun, and it makes all the difference writing anything one likes, and not for an Editor'. (*L2*: 168–9)

As independent publishers, she was suggesting, she and Leonard need not be constrained to and by words. As a writer, she could enjoy an exceptional degree of freedom. This was a constant refrain throughout her discussions of the Press.

To David Garnett, who had admired 'The Mark on the Wall', she wrote: 'its very amusing to try with these short things, and the greatest mercy to be able to do what one likes – no editors, no publishers, and only people to read who more or less like that sort of thing' (*L2*: 167). Here the work of the amateur printer and the experimental writer coalesce as they 'try with these short things'. At a later date, she wrote in her diary: 'I'm the only woman in England free to write what I like. The others must be thinking of series & editors' (*D3*: 43).

In the Press's early years, in particular, the nature of Woolf's 'experiments' with form – 'how I could embody all my deposit of experience in a shape that fitted it', as she wrote to Ethel Smyth in 1930 about the composition of her short story 'An Unwritten Novel' (*L4*: 231) – was inseparable from the freedom represented by the Hogarth Press. The 'unwriting' of the conventional novel seems to have become intimately bound up for Woolf with the work of typesetting: the material and the conceptual labour of compositing and (de)composition. The nature of her experiment cannot be separated, however, from her work – as editor, printer and publisher – with the experiments of her contemporaries, including those of Mirrlees, Mansfield, Eliot and Cunard.

Translations from the Russian

I now want to turn, more briefly, to the importance of Russian literature in the Press's list and for Woolf as a writer. In 1920, the Press published its first work of Russian literature in translation, Maxim Gorky's *Reminiscences of Tolstoy*. This work, Leonard was later to write, marked the moment at which the Press became a small publishing house: 'The success of Gorki's book was really the turning point for the future of the Press and for our future' (L. Woolf 1980: 234). It was also the start of the Hogarth Press's substantial engagement with translations of Russian literature which, as we have seen, the 1922 publicity statement made central to the Press's aims.

The key figure in this history was S. S. Koteliansky, or 'Kot', as he was known, whom the Woolfs first met around 1917 through Katherine Mansfield and John Middleton Murry, and who was responsible for the translation of the Gorky, with Leonard Woolf's collaboration. Kot was a Russian Jew, born in Ostropol, Ukraine, in 1880; he had studied in Odessa and Kiev, though he had been confined to Ostropol between 1900 and 1906 under police surveillance, presumably for his political activities. He travelled to England from Kiev in 1911. Kot, John Carswell has written,

> was overjoyed by the revolution that had brought Kerensky to power, but almost from the first had been appalled by the ascendancy of Lenin, Trotsky and (worst of all) Stalin. As early as 1922 he was sending Leonard Woolf cuttings from *Pravda* to illustrate 'the criminal policy of indiscriminate requisitioning on the part of the government' and 'Soviet guilt for the present state of the famine-stricken provinces'. (Carswell 1978: 260)

Kot's correspondence with Leonard Woolf indicates that their shared interests were as strongly in the political and economic aspects of contemporary Soviet society as in Russian literature, and this would be reflected in a number of Hogarth Press pamphlets and other publications. Between 1924 and the late 1930s, the Hogarth Press published eight pamphlets on Russia, communism and Marxism, developing out of the visits of various writers and commentators to the USSR: these included Maurice Dobb's *Russia To-Day and Tomorrow* (1930), C. M. Lloyd's *Russian Notes* (1932) and Harold J. Laski's *Love and Justice in Soviet Russia* (1935).

The early 1920s were the most intensive period of the literature translations: eight out of the twenty-seven Hogarth Press publications produced in its first years (up to 1923) were translations from the Russian. Koteliansky had, indeed, attempted to persuade the Woolfs that the Press should become exclusively a publisher of Russian literature. The topic of the Hogarth Press's Russian list leads us outwards into the widespread cultural fascination with Russian literature and Russian culture of the period (a Russophilia which included an absorption in the Russian ballet, music, theatre and, increasingly, film), intersecting with the complex question of engagement with the turbulence of Russian history and politics in this period. It leads us inwards to the focus of my discussion here: the question of Woolf's engagement with Russian literature – as reader, translator, editor, publisher – and its impact on her writing.

The period between 1912 and 1925 was one in which Woolf was extensively involved with Russian literature, writing a dozen essays and reviews on nineteenth-century Russian texts, and in her more general essays on literature, using Russian fiction as a standard against which to measure English writers or to explore a modern aesthetic, as in her essays 'On Rereading Meredith' and 'Modern Fiction'. The impact of Russian literature was also manifested in Woolf's fiction in a number of ways: in her engagement with the spheres of the psychological and with unconscious life more generally; in her habitual preoccupation with the relationship between speed and surface on the one hand and depth and immutability on the other; in her representations of the permeable boundaries between selves, echoing as it does Dostoevsky's depictions of the interrelationships between subjects, a topic central to Mikhail Bakhtin's study of the author. The soul for Dostoevsky is, Woolf seems to imply, like the water in a samovar: 'The soul is not restrained by barriers. It overflows, it floods, it mingles with the souls of others. . . . Out it tumbles upon us, hot, scalding, mixed, marvellous, terrible, oppressive – the human soul' (*E4*: 187).

In 1917, Woolf had reviewed Louise and Aylmer Maude's *The Cossacks and Other Tales of the Caucasus* in the *Times Literary Supplement*. She noted that increased interest in Dostoevsky and Chekhov had somewhat obscured the figure and the work of Tolstoy, though, she suggested, he might well be, as the Maudes argued, 'the greatest of Russian writers'. She alighted on the observations of Tolstoy's 'wonderful eye', which let no detail escape – 'every gesture seems to be received by him automatically, and at once referred by his brain to some cause which reveals the most carefully hidden secrets of human nature' – and on the 'continuous vein of thought', focalised in one central, 'rather lonely', consciousness (*E2*: 77–8). She also observed the inconclusiveness and incompletion that marked Tolstoy's short stories, an aspect of Russian literature which was always to absorb her. In 'Modern Fiction' (1925), she wrote of 'the inconclusiveness of the Russian mind . . . the sense that there is no answer' (*E4*: 163). This incompleteness and open-endedness was the dimension of Russian literature that seems to echo most powerfully in Woolf's own fiction, from *Jacob's Room* to *The Years* and *Between the Acts*.

At the start of the 1920s, Kot began to teach Leonard and Virginia Woolf the Russian language, and their work in 'translating' Russian texts with him intensified. Virginia Woolf worked with Kot on three texts: *Tolstoi's Love Letters*, *Talks with Tolstoi* and *Stavrogin's Confession*. The last of these was the omitted portion of Dostoevsky's *The Devils*, recounting Stavrogin's rape of a young girl and her subsequent suicide: it had emerged in the State Archives in 1921. There is no record of Woolf commenting on this text, though she clearly worked closely with the material: the Tolstoy material remained, on the other hand, an important touchstone for her. Koteliansky was also, during the early 1920s, acting as the Woolfs' literary as well as linguistic and cultural guide in Russian: 'I have been cross examining Kot upon the quarrel between Dostoevsky & Turgenev', Woolf wrote in her diary in November 1921, '& find him stuffed with facts, & of course passionate severe & uncompromising. For once in a way I shall have some truth to put in my article' (*D2*: 145).

Throughout her writing on Russian literature – and in particular that of Tolstoy, Chekhov and Dostoevsky – Woolf focused on its 'strangeness' to the English reader. While this was initially represented as its power and attraction, Woolf began to conceive of it as a barrier. This was a question she explored in detail in 'The Russian Point of View', in which she focused on the 'difference of language' and the inadequacy of translation. The essay marks her own growing estrangement from the Russian literature that had so absorbed her: one echoed in the broader cultural climate, as the 'Dostoevsky cult' began to burn itself out. Yet the impact of the Russian writing with which she had worked – as reader, reviewer, editor, translator, publisher – continued to make itself felt in her work of the 1930s and, in particular, in *The Years*, the most 'Russian' of her novels, perhaps, in its epic sweep and its intense, at times estranging, dialogues.

Questions remain about the nineteenth-century focus of Woolf's engagement, and that of the Hogarth Press, with Russian literature. The Russian ballet, the Ballets Russes, which so fully engaged Bloomsbury and its artists, did find its way into *Orlando*. Yet there is no discussion in Woolf's work of the new Soviet literature and theatre. We can assume, however, that she would have had some knowledge of this new writing. In May 1924, Woolf's friend Margaret Llewellyn Davies became Chair of a newly founded society, the Society for Cultural

Relations between the Peoples of the British Commonwealth and the Union of Soviet Socialist Republics – the SCR for short. Its first headquarters were at 23 Tavistock Square. For a brief period, Leonard Woolf was on the executive committee, along with L. T. Hobhouse, Ashley Dukes and the literary critic Madame Z. Vengerova. Virginia Woolf's name appears among the list of the Society's vice-presidents right through to the late 1930s.

The national press reported the Society's activities on its founding, noting that the object of the society was 'to restore the many cultural links [between Britain and the Soviet Union] broken during recent years' (*New Leader*, 18 July 1924). In the Society's first years, there were also press reports of lectures given under the Society's auspices, including talks on contemporary Russian literature and culture: 'interest has already been aroused in the "symbolist". "imagist", "futurist" and proletarian poets, and in the Russian theatre', the *Manchester Guardian* reported in 1924 (11 July 1924). In 1925, the *Daily Herald* advertised a Society literary evening – 'Russian Literature Did Not End with Chekhov' – noting the emergence of a new generation of writers, who 'represent a new age, very much opposed to the old spirit of pessimism'. A lecture by Madame Vengerova would be followed by 'recitations of post-revolutionary poems translated into English verse, and by readings from the latest Russian fiction' (7 December 1925). There were references in the *Daily News* report of this occasion to Blok, Mayakovsky, Yesenin and Gastev –'a singer of machinery and factory life' (10 December 1925).[3]

At the Society's inaugural meeting in July 1924, Madame Vengerova had given an account of the new literature emerging after the Revolution: 'In contrast to our classical writers who were interested in the psychology of the humanity they described, the new Russian writers take man in the midst of the nightmare of revolutionary realities, and study him in a cosmic light as part of nature. They do not indulge in psychological niceties, but they keenly feel the rhythm of life, its beat, and create a very new and complicated verbal system in order to render the throbbing of cosmic life all through the individual adventures of their heroes. One and the same incident is described in several different ways as viewed by different minds, through different emotions. The constant object of their study is the Revolution'.[4] Russian soul, we are told on a number of occasions, has given way to Russian vitality.

Madame Vengerova appears to have returned to the Soviet Union in 1927, along with a great many of the Society's Russian members. There is a larger story here, but I would just point for the present to the intense activity around modern Russian literature in the Society's first years, at meetings which Woolf may well have attended: there are some very brief references in her letters to the 'Russian society' evenings in 1924. So we may pose two questions, both meriting further exploration. First, why did Woolf not seem to engage with the new literature of Russia when she would appear to have gained some access to it? Second, if we looked a little differently, could we in fact trace the shift from Russian 'soul' to Russian 'vitality' in her literature and her aesthetics?

Conclusion

The topic of Virginia Woolf and the Hogarth Press is a deep and a broad one. In this chapter, I have focused on two aspects of the Press which the Woolfs singled out in their 1922 publicity statement – hand-printing and translations from the Russian – which open out into complex questions of creativity and culture. The chapter has been particularly concerned with the significance of the Press for an understanding of Woolf's writing practices and the development of her work and thought. The Hogarth Press, however, also needs to be understood in its role as cultural institution. It was founded in the domestic interior; the Woolfs represented their labour as artisanal; it reached out into the broadest literary, cultural and political arenas. It contributes in the most significant ways to our understanding of the relationship between private and public, which has become central to Woolf criticism in recent years, and to the crucial understanding of Woolf as public intellectual, a Woolf in the world.

Notes

1. Anniversary announcement with list of publications and description of A and B subscriptions 1922. Leonard Woolf Archive, Special Collections, University of Sussex. Q The Hogarth Press, 3 a.
2. Leonard Woolf Archive, Special Collections, University of Sussex. Leonard Woolf Papers, III: General Correspondence, William Rothenstein to Leonard Woolf, n.d. My thanks to Anna Fewster for this reference.
3. Newspaper cuttings relating to the Society for Cultural Relations foundation and activities are held in the archives at the Society for Co-operation in Russian and Soviet Studies, 320 Brixton Road, London SW9 6AB.
4. Minutes of the Inaugural Meeting, held on 9 July 1924, of the Society for Cultural Relations between the Peoples of the British Commonwealth and the Union of Socialist Soviet Republics. (Archives held at the Society for Co-operation in Russian and Soviet Studies, 320 Brixton Road, London SW9 6AB.)

Works Cited

Armstrong, Tim (2005) *Modernism: A Cultural History*, Cambridge: Polity Press.
Bishop, Edward (2004) 'Introduction' to Virginia Woolf, *Jacob's Room*, Oxford: published for the Shakespeare Head Press by Blackwell Publishing.
Bosanquet, Theodora (2006) *Henry James at Work*, ed. Lyall H. Powers, Ann Arbor: University of Michigan Press.
Briggs, Julia (2006) *Reading Virginia Woolf*, Edinburgh: Edinburgh University Press.
Carswell, John (1978) *Lives and Letters*, London: Faber and Faber.
Chisholm, Anne (1979) *Nancy Cunard*, London: Sidgwick and Jackson.
Cunard, Nancy (1969) *These Were the Hours: Memories of My Hours Press, Réanville and Paris, 1928–1931*, Carbondale and Edwardsville: Southern Illinois University Press.
Fewster, Anna (2008) *Bloomsbury Books: Materiality, Domesticity and the Politics of the Marked Page*, thesis submitted for the award of PhD, University of Sussex.

Heidegger, Martin (1992) *Parmenides*, trans. André Schuwer and Richard Rojcewicz, Bloomington: Indiana University Press.

Kittler, Friedrich (1999) *Gramophone, Film, Typewriter*, trans. Geoffrey Winthrop-Young and Michael Wutz, Stanford, CA: Stanford University Press (originally published in German, 1986).

Lindsay, Vachel (2000) *The Art of the Moving Picture*, New York: Modern Library (Originally published 1922).

Mansfield, Katherine (1928) *The Letters of Katherine Mansfield Volume 1*, ed. John Middleton Murry, London: Constable.

Mansfield, Katherine (1977) *Letters and Journals*, ed. C. K. Stead, Harmondsworth: Penguin.

McGann, Jerome (1993) *Black Riders: The Visible Language of Modernism*, Princeton, NJ: Princeton University Press.

Spalding, Francis (1998) *Duncan Grant: a Biography*, London: Pimlico.

Spender, Stephen (1951) *World within World*, London: Hamish Hamilton.

Willis, J. H. Jr (1992) *Leonard and Virginia Woolf as Publishers: The Hogarth Press 1917–41*, Charlottesville: University Press of Virginia.

Woolf, Leonard (1980) *An Autobiography*, vol. II. London: Oxford University Press, 1980.

Further Reading

Cuddy-Keane, Melba (2003) *Virginia Woolf, the Intellectual and the Public Sphere.* Cambridge: Cambridge University Press.

Gillespie, Diane Filby (1998) *The Sisters' Arts: The Writing and Painting of Virginia Woolf and Vanessa Bell*, Syracuse, NY: Syracuse University Press.

Goldman, Jane (2006) '1925, London, New York, Paris: Metropolitan Modernism – Parallax and Palimpest', in Brian McHale and Randall Stevenson (eds), *The Edinburgh Companion to Twentieth-Century Literatures in English*, Edinburgh: Edinburgh University Press, pp. 61–72.

Kennedy, Richard (1979) *A Boy at the Hogarth Press*, Harmondsworth: Penguin.

Lehmann, John (1978) *Thrown to the Woolfs*, London: Weidenfeld and Nicolson.

Marcus, Laura (1996) 'Virginia Woolf and the Hogarth Press', in W. Chernaik, W. Gould and I. Willison (eds), *Modernist Writers and the Marketplace*, London: Macmillan, pp. 124–50.

Marcus, Laura (2002) 'The European Dimensions of the Hogarth Press', in Mary Ann Caws and Nicola Luckhurst (eds), *The Reception of British Writers in Europe: Virginia Woolf*, London: Continuum, pp. 328–56.

Marcus, Laura (2006) 'Introduction', *Translations from the Russian by Virginia Woolf and S. S. Koteliansky*, London: Virginia Woolf Society of Great Britain, pp. vii–xxiv.

Mepham, John (1991), *Virginia Woolf: A Literary Life*. Basingstoke: Macmillan.

Porter, David H. (2008) *The Omega Workshops and the Hogarth Press: An Artful Fugue*, London: Ceil Woolf.

Smith, Angela (1999) *Katherine Mansfield and Virginia Woolf: A Public of Two*. Oxford: Oxford University Press.

Snaith, Anna (2000) *Virginia Woolf: Public and Private Negotiations*, London: Palgrave.

16

VIRGINIA WOOLF AND BOOK DESIGN

Tony Bradshaw

VIRGINIA WOOLF WAS surrounded by books from the time she was born. Her father, Sir Leslie Stephen, was devoted to books, introduced the young Virginia to them and encouraged her from a very tender age to express herself through writing and storytelling. As early as 1888, when Virginia was only six, Leslie Stephen was able to tell his wife 'The babies flourish. Ginia tells me a story every night – it does not change much but she seems to enjoy it. She wrote to Miss Vincent today in a most lovely hand'.[1] Considerable family time was spent together as Leslie read aloud to his children; while doing so he also sustained their interest and encouraged a visual relationship with the text by drawing enchanting sketches into the books they were reading together. This early encouragement was to sustain Virginia's lifelong interest in the appearance of books as well as in their literary content.

Virginia's first real attempt at writing came with the Stephen children's collaborative newspaper the *Hyde Park Gate News*, to which she was a major contributor. As she grew up she began to create a library of her own through gifts of books from family members. On turning fifteen, Virginia received from her father the *Life of Sir Walter Scott* by John Lockhart and wrote excitedly to her brother Thoby

> Gradually all my presents have arrived – Fathers Lockhart came the evening I wrote to you – ten most exquisite little volumes, half bound in purple leather, with gilt scrolls and twirls and thistles everywhere, and a most artistic blue and brown mottling on their other parts. So my blinded eyesight is poring more fervidly than ever over miserable books – only not even you, my dear brother, could give such an epithet to these lovely creatures. (*L*1: 4)

This is a very clear early indication that the outward appearance of books was able to excite Virginia.

The visual appeal of books and their binding led Virginia to explore the technique of bookbinding and as early as 1901, when she was only nineteen, she visited family friend Sylvia Stebbing, then sharing a bindery with Anastasia Power in Museum Street, and asked for lessons in binding old books of sheet music. Anastasia Power (who had acquired her skills from Douglas Cockerell at the Essex House Press) also gave Virginia some lessons and while the bookbinding was perhaps more of a hobby than the serious study that her sister Vanessa was engaged in at Mr Cope's School of Art and later at the Painting School of the Royal Academy, Virginia engaged in her bookbinding with purpose and application, possibly in some sense in competition with Vanessa's art.

Virginia was able to share her enthusiasm for the craft with her older cousin Emma Vaughan. She wrote to Emma in 1902.

> Do come to lunch – then we can begin directly afterwards . . . I have been making endless experiments and almost smelt my room out this afternoon trying to do gold lettering. Tomorrow I shall experiment with gold on cloth. I believe there is an immense field for this kind of thing. There seem ever so many ways of making covers – of leather – linen – silk – parchment – vellum – japanese paper etc. etc. etc. which the ordinary lidders never think of. (*L*1: 56)

There is no doubt that these early experiments with covering materials had significant bearing on the first books which she was to create when she came to start publishing.

Virginia's confidence in her ability grew so much that in writing to Thoby in May 1902 she was able to assert 'I am really rather a good binder' (*L*1: 52). Less than a year later, also to Thoby, she wrote 'my whole existence seems to pass in doing up books. All fathers ladies send him books which have to be returned . . . . I have invented a new way of bookbinding, which takes half the time, is just as strong' (ibid.: 67). She also took pride in their appearance telling her cousin Madge Vaughan that 'I wish you could see my room at this moment, on a dark winter's evening – all my beloved leather backed books standing up so handsome in their shelves' (ibid.: 167).

The main repository of Virginia's bound books is the Woolf Collection at Washington State University in the United States.[2] Here one can appreciate the standard she attained and her choice of materials. Included in the collection is *English Garner*, a seven volume anthology of poetry and prose that belonged to Leslie Stephen. Virginia re-covered volumes 3–7 of the well-used set using paper, cloth and morocco leather, and on the spine of Volume 4 she embossed a monogram heart enclosing the initial 'V'. This is the only sign of flamboyance, her attitude to the covering of books being otherwise essentially practical. To Virginia books were for reading, not just retained as a beautiful adornment or furnishing. Those who have personally handled a number of books that she owned testify that she was without concern to keep her books in pristine condition.[3]

Virginia married Leonard Woolf in 1912 and less than three years later, on 25 January 1915, the two of them celebrated her birthday at Buszard's Tea Rooms in Oxford Street. The event was recorded in her diary.

> Sitting at tea we decided three things: in the first place to take Hogarth, if we can get it; in the second, to buy a Printing press; in the third to buy a Bull dog, probably called John. I am very much excited at the idea of all three – particularly the press. (*D*1: 28)

Over the next couple of years Virginia was plagued with mental instability which prevented her from leading a normal life and pursuing her writing on a regular basis. However, the Woolfs were to buy Hogarth House in Richmond, from which the Press took its name, they did acquire a dog (*not* named John) and two years later they purchased their first hand-press. The impetus for these acquisitions came from Leonard, who recognised that the printing process could be a relaxing occupation and, having had to deal with several bouts of Virginia's mental problems, felt that the activity could prove therapeutic. Ever solicitous, Leonard recognised some classic remedies for depression – a new home, a new hobby and a new pet.

The founding of the Hogarth Press arose from the interest that the Woolfs had in the printing process, and in 1917 they applied to the St Bride's Foundation Institute, headquarters of the London Society of Compositors, to take instruction in the art of printing. The Woolfs were, however, denied tuition by their refusal to join the printers' trade union, which was a necessary pre-requisite. But they were not to be deterred. Walking later in Farringdon Street, they called in at a printing shop, the Excelsior Printing Supply Company, where they bought for just over £19 (some £2,000 today) a small hand-press, some Caslon Old Face type and what Leonard described as 'all the necessary implements and materials' (L. Woolf 1964: 234). Included in the transaction was a pamphlet which the sympathetic Excelsior salesman assured the Woolfs would explain all the requirements of working the hand-press so that their attendance at printing school would be unnecessary.

The equipment was brought to the Woolfs' home at Hogarth House, Paradise Road, Richmond and installed in the dining room. There was an initial mishap with a broken part (Virginia's claim that they 'discovered it was smashed in half!' [*L*2: 150] was certainly a cheerful overstatement) but Excelsior repaired the part while giving the Woolfs time to sort out and place the type in containers. The salesman was correct, however, when he said that the pamphlet would fully explain procedures and Leonard recalled that, with its help, 'we found we could pretty soon set the type, lock it up in the chase, ink the rollers, and machine a fairly legible printed page' (L. Woolf 1964: 234).

Because it proved too heavy for the dining room, the press was later transferred to the pantry. This was the heart of the operation where the machining was done – always by Leonard after Virginia had set the type. The books, sometimes little more than pamphlets, were bound in the dining room and finally wrapped in the sitting room. All in all, it was a most domestic affair.

So it was that in late 1917 Leonard and Virginia Woolf, naming the press after their house, were to produce their first volume, *Two Stories*, with every single

Figure 16.1 Vanessa Bell's dust jacket design for the *Complete Catalogue of the Hogarth Press*. Courtesy of the E. J. Pratt Library, Victoria University, Toronto, Canada

process in the production of the book a collaboration between them. They both wrote a short piece, Virginia set the type, Leonard machined the paper over the inked type and Virginia sewed the thirty-two pages and the cover together in the dining room of Hogarth House.

Two Stories was covered in what Leonard Woolf described as variations of 'rather unusual, gay Japanese paper' (L. Woolf 1964: 236). in blue or a geometric red-and-white pattern, while a few copies were produced in plain white or yellow paper covers. Leonard's contribution was 'Three Jews' while Virginia's essay was 'The Mark on the Wall'. Published in an edition of about 150 copies, it contained four small woodcut illustrations by Dora Carrington, much appreciated by the Woolfs as evidenced by Virginia's letter to the artist:

> Dear Carrington,
> We like the wood cuts immensely. It was very good of you to bring them yourself – We have printed them off, and they make the book much more interesting than it would have been without. The ones I like the best are the servant girl and the plates, and the Snail. (*L2*: 162)

Virginia and Leonard's second publication for the Hogarth Press (briefly interupted by a very restricted printing of *Poems* by C. N. Sidney Woolf) was that of *Prelude* by Katherine Mansfield. This was perhaps a surprising choice of author given Virginia's feelings of professional rivalry towards Mansfield and her ambivalent attitude to her on a personal level. Buoyed by the success of *Two Stories*, the print run was doubled, despite Virginia complaining to Vanessa at the labour involved: 'I can't do anything just now except fold and staple 300 copies of K.M.'s story. It takes a good deal of time by hand' (*L2*: 258). There was debate over a cover design for the book and in a letter to Ottoline Morrell Virginia wrote: 'I wish she [Katherine Mansfield] and Murry didn't think Ferguson a great artist. He has done a design for her story which makes our gorges rise, to such an extent that we can hardly bring ourselves to print it' (*L2*: 243–4). Ultimately the design was placed on the cover of only a very small number of books, the remainder carrying the title only. It is interesting to note that the Woolfs' 'eye' for an artist was certainly lacking in this instance: as one of the 'Scottish Colourists', J. D. Fergusson's paintings and drawings are highly prized today.

The next book from the Woolfs' fledgling Press was to feature a then little-known poet, who later was to make a significant impact. This was T. S. Eliot, described by Virginia after their first meeting as 'a polished, cultivated, elaborate young American' (*D1*: 218), and whose ability she recognised immediately. She and Leonard were to publish his *Poems* in 1919 – the covers of which are described warmly and eloquently by Rick Gekoski, a noted London bookseller, in his *Tolkien's Gown*:

> If this delicate little volume didn't have a printed label on it, you could mistake it for a painting. I suppose that's because it is a painting, and by no less

an artist than Roger Fry, who hand-made the marbled paper in which it's covered. It's an exuberant abstract design in swirling yellows, oranges and browns, all mixed up together, onto which a bright green has been allowed to drip, as in a painting by Jackson Pollock. It's gorgeous, ravishing, my second favourite book of the twentieth century. The printed label though, reveals the object for what it really is. A bound volume of a few pages of *Poems* by T. S. Eliot. It was handprinted and published in 1919 by Virginia and Leonard Woolf at the Hogarth Press.

So attractive is the book that it had a place of honour in a vitrine at the Tate Gallery exhibition 'The Art of Bloomsbury', 1999. The curator of that show, the art historian Richard Shone, is a great admirer of the design. If you run your finger very carefully over it, (you're not allowed to though) you'll feel it's got a texture to it, where the paint has thickened or thinned and I think it's simply a brush or sponge perhaps swept across the paper. I think it is very beautiful. I think it is one of the prettiest books of the early Hogarths. (Gekoski 2004: 205)

Unlike many private presses founded in the aftermath of the Arts and Crafts movement such as the Doves Press, the Ashendene Press and the Golden Cockerel Press, the Hogarth Press had little interest in employing elaborate papers, bindings and covers to enhance their books. The Woolfs were far more concerned with the literary content issued from their publishing house. Nevertheless they certainly took pleasure in the appearance of their publications and made careful choices of artists to decorate or illustrate their books or design book jackets. Naturally their friends in Bloomsbury – Duncan Grant, Vanessa Bell, Roger Fry and Carrington – dominated, particularly in the early stages of the Press, but as their production extended and became more profitable the Woolfs made wider artistic choices. Among designers who worked for the Hogarth Press at various times in the 1920s and 1930s were Edward McKnight Kauffer, John Armstrong, William Nicholson, John Banting, Robert Medley, Enid Marx and Trekkie Ritchie Parsons.

Even before artists were employed to design book jackets for the Hogarth Press, the earliest publications were notable for their distinctive and unusual covers. One that comes to mind is *Paris* by the poet Hope Mirrlees. Another is I. A. Bunin's *The Gentleman from San Francisco and Other Stories*, translated from the Russian by D. H. Lawrence, S. S. Koteliensky and Leonard Woolf. 'For many years', Leonard Woolf wrote in his autobiography,

we gave much time and care to finding beautiful, uncommon and sometimes cheerful paper for binding our books and, as the first publishers to do this, I think we started a fashion which many of the regular, old established publishers followed. We got papers from all over the place, including some brilliantly patterned from Czechoslovakia and we also had some marbled covers made for us by Roger Fry's daughter in Paris. (L. Woolf 1964: 236)

For a period after *Two Stories*, for which Carrington's woodcut illustrations received favourable notice, the Woolfs showed a strong bias towards the utilisation of woodcuts and Carrington was co-opted again to design a cover for Leonard Woolf's *Stories of the East*. Although a book comprising only woodcuts was contemplated, along the lines of the successful 1918 Omega Workshops publication *Original Woodcuts by Various Artists*, the project never came to fruition. The idea largely foundered because Vanessa Bell's determination to have final artistic control was met by Leonard's uncompromising insistence that he and nobody else would make the ultimate decisions. In the face of Leonard's determination to have the final say Vanessa withdrew, observing to Roger Fry dismissively 'knowing what his taste in those ways is'.[4]

Following *Two Stories*, however, the Woolfs were quick to accept Vanessa Bell's offer to make woodcut illustrations for Virginia's *Kew Gardens*, but when the hand-printed story was published Vanessa was furious at the uneven printing where her blocks had been over-inked in places. Vanessa conveyed to the Woolfs her extreme unhappiness at the outcome, even expressing the view that any ordinary printer could have done better and going so far as 'to doubt the value of the Hogarth Press altogether' (*D*1: 279). This sharp criticism hurt Virginia deeply and the second impression of the rapidly selling *Kew Gardens* was put out to commercial printers. However, this led to even worse mistakes, the labels on the covers being applied so crookedly that Virginia tried to pare them down by hand with a knife. The quarrel between the sisters over technical aspects of their collaboration inevitably resolved over time, but it might well have erupted again when Vanessa's four woodcut illustrations for Virginia's 1921 book of short stories, *Monday or Tuesday*, hand-set by Virginia but printed commercially, again were so heavily inked on poor-quality paper that they 'bled' into the opposite page. Leonard Woolf regarded this as technically the worst issue from his publishing house, but enthusiasts of the Hogarth Press today regard this book (with a woodcut cover also by Bell; see Figure 16.2) as one of the most charming, if idiosyncratic, issues from the Press.

The last foray in woodcut illustration by the Hogarth Press came with Roger Fry's *Twelve Original Woodcuts*, the birth of which is recorded in a memorable passage in Virginia Woolf's diary in 1921 'Roger again last night, scraping at his woodcuts while I sewed; the sound like that of a large pertinacious rat' (*D*2: 109). Hand-printed by the Woolfs, the publication was a great triumph, with the print-run of 150 copies being 'gulped down' (ibid.: 144), as Virginia recorded, in only two days. This huge success led to two further hand-printed editions where the last plate, *Iris and Vase* (arguably the least effective image of the twelve), was reproduced additionally to form the front panel of the book in place of the coloured papers of the first edition.

Fry's woodcut book remains one of the most satisfying of the many publications from the Hogarth Press with stiff, hand-decorated paper covers in imitation of the covering for *Kew Gardens*. The *Twelve Original Woodcuts* were produced in covers predominantly red, brown or green and have real texture to

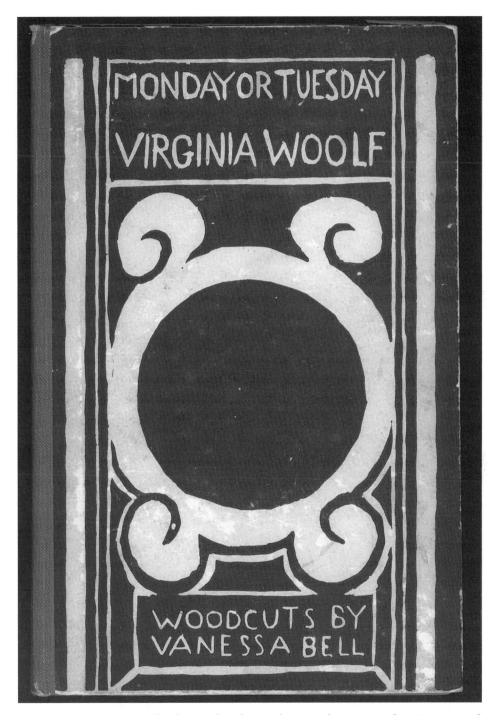

Figure 16.2 Vanessa Bell's dust jacket design for *Monday or Tuesday*. Courtesy of the E. J. Pratt Library, Victoria University, Toronto, Canada

them caused by brush strokes across the heavy paper. The edges of the paper overlap the body of the book as if enclosing it for protection. The novelist Jeanette Winterson has said that the book provides her with 'immediate bodily delight'. She asks whether this is due to 'the hand-decorated coloured paper wrappers, or the thick cream insides or the fact that [Virginia Woolf] stitched this book I have before me now?' The answer, she concludes, lies in its 'association, intrinsic worth, beauty, a commitment to beautiful things, and the deep passage of the woodcuts themselves' (Winterson 1995: 123).

Despite the very considerable commercial success of Fry's book, woodcuts were never again to feature in any way with the Hogarth Press. In hindsight this appears strange but it seems that the limited interest Duncan Grant and Vanessa Bell had in the technique had evaporated – they were never again to produce work in that medium – while Fry, the main protagonist of the woodcut, had also characteristically moved on to other challenges.

The Woolfs, too, were exploring new avenues and in 1922 they were to produce their first dust-jacket to one of their publications. This was to cover the first of Virginia Woolf's novels to be published by the Hogarth Press, *Jacob's Room*. Naturally enough they turned to Vanessa Bell for the design, this proving to be the forerunner of many charming and distinctive covers to Virginia's books. *Jacob's Room* was in fact a true collaboration between the three, Vanessa making the drawing, Virginia selecting the colour employed and Leonard advising changes to the lettering to be used. Vanessa Bell's dust-jacket for *Jacob's Room* is a gentle assembly of different shapes in a warm tone of terracotta showing flowers in a vase on a corner of a table enclosed by a pair of draped curtains. Today it is widely regarded as one of the loveliest images for her sister's books that Vanessa ever devised but at the time the image was mocked by both buyers and booksellers accustomed to linear designs or functionally illustrative jackets. The motif 'did not represent a desirable female or even Jacob or his room', stated Leonard Woolf in his autobiography, and 'it was what in 1923 many people would have called reproachfully post-impressionist' (L. Woolf 1967: 76).

It is not widely appreciated today that the dust-jacket, which we now associate with virtually every hardback publication, only came into general usage in the 1920s with improvements in printing techniques facilitating this development. Nowadays few people would destroy the dust-jacket on a new book but earlier jackets were widely regarded as just a fancy bit of advertising and were often discarded. Nigel Nicolson recalled seeing his mother Vita Sackville-West taking jackets off new publications even when it was a book written by Virginia with a cover designed by Vanessa Bell.[5]

The second jacket collaboration between Virginia and Vanessa (where, for the first and only time in their association, the jacket image was also replicated on the hard cover of the book) invited further ridicule and even a critical newspaper review. This was *The Common Reader*, where Vanessa's design in green and brown of two flowers in a slender vase set amid some simple decorative

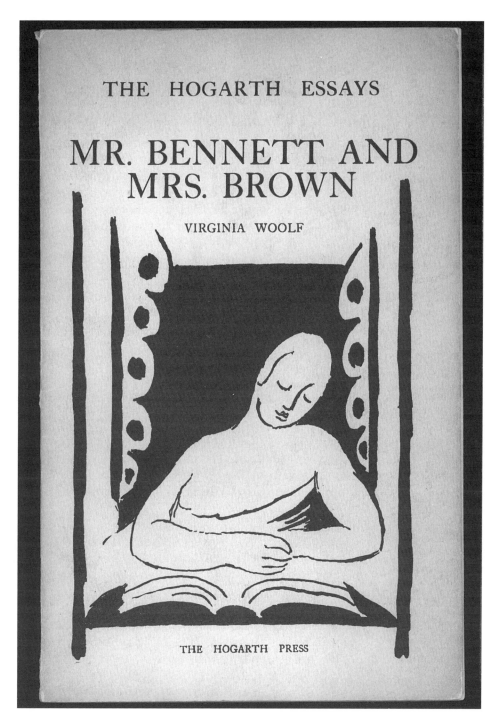

Figure 16.3 Vanessa Bell's dust jacket design for *Mr. Bennett and Mrs. Brown*. Courtesy of the E. J. Pratt Library, Victoria University, Toronto, Canada

motifs received the damning notice from *The Star* that 'only a conscious artist could have done it so badly' (*D3*: 16). Virginia was to make light of this attack and, writing to Vanessa, reported to her that 'The Star has a whole column about your decorations of the Common R: and says I try to live up to them by being as revolutionary and nonsensical – a very good advertisement' (*L3*: 182).

Despite the criticism, which may well have strengthened the collaborative bond, Virginia Woolf was from this point never to abandon the partnership forged with her sister and, with only four exceptions, Vanessa Bell had a lifelong involvement with the covers for every one of Virginia's Hogarth Press books, including those published after Virginia's death. The four books written by Virginia Woolf and published by the Hogarth Press that do not have a Bell image on the cover are *Orlando, Flush, A Letter to a Young Poet* and *Reviewing*.

On the first of these, *Orlando* (1928), a black-and-white photograph of a Tudor portrait from the Worthing Art Gallery is reproduced. This appears a somewhat curious choice for a novel of transsexual escapades described by J. H. Willis as 'a valentine to Vita Sackville West and her beloved Knole' (Willis 1992: 132). Vanessa Bell could certainly have devised an attractive jacket and Duncan Grant, with his love of ancient mythology and capacity for fantasy, would have been even more suited to provide an arresting cover.

The book jacket of *Flush* features a photograph of an anonymous cocker spaniel on what appears to be a Victorian stool. Although Vanessa did a number of preparatory dog sketches, these were not used for the jacket, but ultimately she executed four delightful line drawings relevant to the text that appear as full page illustrations in the book. The short *Letter to a Young Poet* was part of the Hogarth Letter series, for which John Banting's cover design was used throughout, but in different colours for each issue. The last of the four covers that did not have a Bell image on the cover was *Reviewing*. This was a small pamphlet written in 1939 and appropriately carried only the title and author's name on its plain cover.

It is worth noting that *Orlando* and *Flush* achieved commercial success notwithstanding the absence of Vanessa Bell jackets. Eleven thousand copies of *Orlando* in three editions sold rapidly in 1928/9, while *Flush* sold more than 14,000 copies in its first six months. *Orlando*, in fact, was for Virginia Woolf and the Hogarth Press a pivotal work, firmly establishing for both their commercial credibility.

Virginia recorded in her diary early in 1921 that Clive Bell had proposed that the Hogarth Press 'bring out his private poems' (*D2*: 96) and this led to a publishing collaboration of two books of poetry with her brother-in-law. The first was simply called *Poems*; hand-printed by the Woolfs, it was a slim volume of thirteen poems encased in stiff white paper covers with a modest but attractive red clover-leaf design. The second production was altogether a more elaborate and indeed handsome issue of twenty-one hand-printed pages in the largest format (10¼ × 7 inches) of any of the hand-printed publications. The work was

Figure 16.4 Vanessa Bell's dust jacket design for *The Legend of Monte della Sibilla*. Courtesy of the E. J. Pratt Library, Victoria University, Toronto, Canada

a single long poem entitled *The Legend of Monte Della Sibilla* (1923) for which Vanessa created the figurative design on the hard cover (see Figure 16.4; the jacket itself was simply fairly flimsy plain white paper, carrying the title and other information). In addition Vanessa contributed one illustration within to this cheerful tale of wine, women and song while Duncan Grant also had a hand with two further illustrations (all described as 'decorations' on the dust jacket). Printed on Basingwerk parchment paper from Basingwerk Abbey in Wales, the Woolfs took particular care with this publication which evidenced the printing and designing ability they had acquired over some six years of publishing. It remains one of the most beautiful books to have been produced at the Hogarth Press.

The Legend of Monte Della Sibilla marked one of the most significant working collaborations in the history of the Bloomsbury Group with no less than five of the group closely involved in the same project – Clive Bell writing the poem, Vanessa Bell and Duncan Grant bringing to bear their artistic talent and Leonard and Virginia Woolf being responsible for the physical printing as well as the publishing. Certainly no other book production was ever to involve so many of the Bloomsbury Group working together. *The Legend* may not be a masterful poem, but the final outcome was a visual treat of which the five participants must have been proud.[6]

Most of Clive Bell's books, including his most important *Art* as well as *Civilization*, were published by Chatto and Windus. However, in 1928 the Hogarth Press was to publish his *Proust*, one of the earliest critiques in English of the French writer's work. Running to two editions and, unlike the two earlier productions of Bell's poems, which could be regarded as a sop to his vanity, *Proust* was an intelligent commentary, conforming directly to the Woolfs' objective of bringing out serious literary works.

While Leonard and Virginia naturally depended heavily on Vanessa Bell for Hogarth Press covers they also employed designs created by their friends within the Bloomsbury circle. The earliest, and in fact pre-Vanessa, was Carrington whose woodcut design of a tiger striding out between two palm trees (printed in red on buff covers) was used for Leonard's own *Stories of the East* (1921). Two years later Roger Fry designed the jacket for his own *Sampler of Castile*, the image being replicated on the hard cover. An entertaining record of a journey through Spain, Fry recorded discerningly and sometimes amusingly his impressions of the local people and their culture; a number of the author's landscape illustrations are grouped together at the back of the book but, as his biographer has observed, 'lack the same verve and energy that animates his prose' (Spalding 1980: 242). Fry's other jacket designs were for *Paper Houses*, William Plomer's collection of stories about Japan, and his own *Cézanne: A Study of His Development* (1927).

Duncan Grant, rather surprisingly, contributed only two designs to the Hogarth Press during Virginia's lifetime, the first being for Roger Fry's monograph *Living Painters: Duncan Grant* (1924). This was a semi-abstract

Figure 16.5 *The Striped Dress*, woodcut by Roger Fry. Courtesy of the E. J. Pratt
Library, Victoria University, Toronto, Canada

Figure 16.6 *The Servant Girl*, woodcut by Carrington. Courtesy of the E. J. Pratt Library, Victoria University, Toronto, Canada

decorative design for the jacket and replicated on the hard cover; a second edition, published in 1930, used the same design on a soft cover. Grant also produced a fluent image of a head of a young woman for Julia Strachey's *Cheerful Weather for the Wedding*. It had been intended that Carrington, a good friend of the author's, would prepare this particular jacket, but following Carrington's suicide earlier in the year (1932), Grant was asked to step into the breach. Although initially he had some misgivings, he produced, after several preparatory sketches, a most attractive design.

In 1927 the Woolfs decided on a reissue of the successful *Kew Gardens* and Virginia invited Vanessa to design the cover and to decorate each page of the short text. This can be regarded as their closest and most complete collaborative enterprise, described by John Lehmann as 'the perfect sisterly accord of writer and artist sharing the same vision' (Lehmann 1978: 26). The large-format 1927 *Kew Gardens*, effectively the third edition, had a simple but delightful yellow-and-brown cover by Vanessa and each of the twenty-one pages contains her swirling decorative motifs which allude to the movement of the story, complementing what has been called the 'flickering' (Bradshaw 1999: 18) quality of Virginia's piece. Virginia underlined the depth of their collaboration with her sister in two short sentences: 'God made our brains upon the same lines, only leaving out 2 or 3 pieces in mine' (*L2*: 289), she wrote to Vanessa after receiving the first batch of illustrations for *Kew Gardens*; later she asked, 'Do you think we have the same pair of eyes, only different spectacles?' (*L6*: 158).

In the late 1920s Virginia Woolf wrote two of her most important and best-remembered novels, *Mrs Dalloway* and *To the Lighthouse*, with Vanessa Bell naturally designing the jackets for both. The dust jacket for *Mrs Dalloway* shows a bridge with several arches in the centre with decorative motifs at the base and to the side in yellow and black. It is an attractive cover although the image of the bridge reflected in the water is not instantly recognisable as such and has been irreverently described as a submarine with dark portholes. In contrast the blue-and-black jacket of *To the Lighthouse* unambiguously shows a bold image of a lighthouse. Vanessa's dust jackets, however, rarely allude to the title or contents of her sister's books and that attitude is clearly explained in a letter she once wrote to John Lehmann:

> I've not read a word of the book – I have only the vaguest description of it and what she wants me to do from Virginia – but that has always been the case with the jackets I have done for her. (Lehmann 1978: 27)

The predominantly lime-green jacket for *The Waves*, showing two shadowy figures in the foreground with waves behind them, has relation to the title but another major novel, *The Years*, reveals only a single dominant rose in the midst of interlocking circles. It would be incorrect, however, to assume there was little forethought in Vanessa's designs for her sister's books. As already noted, she produced a number of preparatory drawings for *Flush* and she filled a complete sketchbook with concepts for *A Room of One's Own* before deciding on a simple clock on a mantelpiece. Other memorable designs included *On Being Ill*, a geometric combination of cross-hatching, circles and lines; *Walter Sickert: A Conversation*, a still-life line drawing of fruit and drink on a table (Virginia liked the cover so much that she increased the price of the essay because of it); and *Three Guineas*, a mauve design of three bank cheques with a quill pen and an ink bottle in the foreground, considered by Leonard Woolf as the most beautiful of her book-jacket designs. Virginia was also delighted with it, writing to Vanessa 'Many thanks for the jacket. I think it is one of the best you ever did – quite lovely, and also practical' (*L6*: 251).

The essential element of the sisters' interdependence was the reliance and trust that Virginia placed in Vanessa's professional ability. In turn Vanessa admired Virginia's novels, especially their visual eloquence. Virginia was always encouragingly responsive, writing of the jacket for *To the Lighthouse*; 'Your style is unique: because so truthful; and therefore it upsets one completely' (*L3*: 391). Together they forged a long-lasting and effective partnership and Vanessa, as the most prolific artist to work for the Hogarth Press, created what was to become almost its house style. Apart from Virginia's books, she devised several designs for the various series of pamphlets issued by the Press in 1920s and 1930s which greatly enhanced the Woolfs' growing list of authors and made a significant contribution to the standing of the Press. In addition to these publications, she designed book jackets for such authors as Susan Buchan (wife of the better-known author of *The Thirty-Nine Steps*), Edward Upward and Henry Green.

Vanessa's book jackets use many of the distinctive motifs recognisable from her work in other media, such as circles, loops, curtains and flowers, images radiating a sense of calm well-being. Her designs, which can merge into the semi-abstract, often include panels or other perpendiculars (as in *To the*

Lighthouse), a device which can be regarded as almost a signature in her work. Probably the single most-recognised Bloomsbury print is Vanessa's wolf's head colophon which (apart from a brief period in the 1930s when an Edward McKnight Kauffer design supplanted it) was used by the Hogarth Press from 1925 onwards.

When it came to a choice of jacket for Virginia's biography of *Roger Fry* (1940) a reproduction of an earlier portrait of Fry by Vanessa was employed. This, of course, was unsurprising. What does seem surprising is that the portrait was reproduced not in colour but in black and white and one wonders why Virginia and Leonard decided on this rather dull exterior to the book. Had Virginia lost heart at the end of a book she found difficult to write? Perhaps so. In any case it was the last of her books to be published in her lifetime.

After Virginia's death Leonard continued to publish her writing. *Between the Acts*, her last novel, concluded just a month before her suicide in 1941, was issued after revision by Leonard, towards the end of the same year and carried a black-and-white jacket by Vanessa showing theatre curtains. This is, of course, allusive to the title but one can surmise it might have the valedictory aspect of closing the curtains on Virginia's life. Thereafter Leonard was to husband his late wife's essays and stories, releasing them for publication every two or three years. While Leonard was alive, the Hogarth Press published eight posthumous collections of Virginia's work which included a selection from her diaries entitled *A Writer's Diary* as well as *Virginia Woolf and Lytton Strachey Letters*. All of these books carried Vanessa Bell jackets and while those in the 1940s, hampered by wartime restrictions, were all in black and white, those from the 1950s glowed with colour, and jackets such as *Granite and Rainbow, The Captain's Death Bed* and *A Writer's Diary* reveal Vanessa at her best. The penultimate Vanessa jacket was for *Virginia Woolf and Lytton Strachey Letters* (1956), which carried a profile portrait of Virginia. It was a fitting testimony to an illustrious collaboration between the two sisters.

Vanessa Bell's book jackets for her sister Virginia's novels remain among the best-known and most celebrated pieces of art that the Bloomsbury Group produced. It is these jackets for Virginia's books that the American critic Hilton Kramer, no friend of Bloomsbury art, has ranked 'among the loveliest works of their kind produced in this [the twentieth] century' (Marler 1997: 60).

Virginia Woolf has achieved great fame as an innovative writer of fiction, has received deserved notice as an essayist and critic and has been acclaimed as an icon of feminism. However, outside the coterie of Woolf and Bloomsbury scholarship she has received scant acknowledgement as a publisher of distinction. True, she had a partner in the running of the Hogarth Press; true, too, she was not the main editor. However, her aesthetic, her influence and her decisions relating to the design and content of the books issued by the Hogarth Press, from its inception until her death, made a massive contribution to the success of the Press and had significance in the publishing world outside. This contribution remains a little acknowledged but most important part of Virginia Woolf's legacy, an aspect of her professional life that deserves adequate recognition.

Notes

1. Leslie Stephen to Julia Stephen, 15/4/88 (HPG), Berg Collection, New York Public Library.
2. The Library of Leonard and Virginia Woolf, Washington State University, Pullman, USA. See www.wsulibs.wsu.edu/holland/masc/woolflibrary
3. The author has personally handled a number of books owned by Virginia Woolf.
4. Vanessa Bell to Roger Fry, September 1917, Tate Britain.
5. Recounted by Nigel Nicolson to the author in 1989 while visiting Vita Sackville-West's library at Sissinghurst.
6. The E. J. Pratt Library, Victoria University, Toronto holds a copy of *The Legend of Monte Della Sibilla* signed by all five participants.

Works Cited and Further Reading

Bradshaw, Tony (1999) *The Bloomsbury Artists: Prints and Book Design*, Aldershot: Scolar Press.

Gekoski, Rick (2004) *Tolkien's Gown*, London: Constable.

Lehmann, John (1978) *Thrown to the Woolves*, London: Weidenfeld and Nicolson.

Marler, Regina (1997) *Bloomsbury Pie*, New York: Henry Holt.

Spalding, Frances (1980) *Roger Fry*, Berkeley and Los Angeles: University of California Press.

Willis, J. H. (1992) *Leonard and Virginia Woolf as Publishers/The Hogarth Press* 1917–1941, Charlottesville: University Press of Virginia.

Winterson, Jeanette (1995) *Art Objects*, London: Jonathan Cape.

Woolf, Leonard (1964) *Beginning Again*, London: Hogarth Press.

Woolf, Leonard (1967) *Downhill all the Way*, London: Hogarth Press.

17

VIRGINIA WOOLF AND SCRAPBOOKING

Merry M. Pawlowski

ON 13 AUGUST 1938, Virginia Woolf wrote to Vera Douie, the librarian of the Women's Service Library: 'Dear Miss Douie, I wonder if you could very kindly help with a quotation . . . . The note books in which my cuttings are kept are in London, & I cannot get at them' (Woolf 2002: 32). Coming two months after *Three Guineas* (1938) appeared in print, Woolf's request indicates that even though the book had been finished, the critical arguments she had brought to the forefront with its publication were still very much alive in a public conversation. The cuttings 'note books' Woolf refers to in her letter are her *Reading Notes for Three Guineas*, catalogued in the Sussex University Library manuscript collection as Monk's House Papers B16f, volumes 1, 2 and 3.[1] The letter to Vera Douie is significant for several reasons: first, it is one of the few direct references anywhere in Woolf's papers, other than in her footnotes to *Three Guineas*, to this collection of notebooks; and, second, it clearly indicates Woolf's reliance on those notebooks as a foundation of facts to sustain a political argument. Just as important as these hints of their importance by Woolf herself is the function of the 'note books' as a collection of 'cuttings', marking them as containing a unique collection of documents which, in these three volumes, outnumber Woolf's own handwritten and typed reading notes.

Virginia Woolf kept volumes of reading notes for years, filling them with salient quotes and observations, working in the early years to develop and refine her ideas for reviews and articles that she planned. But the *Reading Notes for Three Guineas* represented a departure from Woolf's usual practice of maintaining reading notes. For the first time, Woolf inserted 139 documents – newspaper cuttings, letters, pamphlets, and manifestos – into these volumes, selecting a particular order, sequence and arrangement for each page, even holding newspaper cuttings out of order chronologically and inserting them with other cuttings of different dates, either later or earlier, to create a thematic construct. The volumes continue as well Woolf's usual practice of note-taking from books that she was reading to build research and support for the arguments she planned to feature in *Three Guineas*. Yet, even this usual practice seems modified as the 96 pages which contain reading notes are not written directly on the page but rather are typed onto cards or ruled paper and then pasted or attached with gummed labels onto the pages of the notebook volumes. The catalogue index for the University of Sussex Library manuscript collection includes the following terse description for MH/B16f: 'Press cuttings and extracts collected or copied by Virginia Woolf relating to *Three Guineas*. Three bound volumes.' How, then, do such extraordinary volumes fit within the framework of a section in the present work entitled 'Domestic Arts'; and, in assigning their place in such a discussion, how do we more fully describe their form or genre and recognise their impact on the making of Woolf's most blatantly feminist, anti-fascist work?

The volumes are positioned within two rich traditions, one readily acknowledged and the other not much noticed in relationship to these volumes before now, the traditions of the scrapbook and the commonplace book. Both traditions have enjoyed a long, intertwined history, dating back as early as Graeco-Roman times. Their differences lie in the tendency to place cut material, illustrations, objects and photographs more into scrapbooks and to 'journal' or keep notes and cogent quotations culled from readings in a commonplace book; however, in practice, individual use of these forms has tended to overlap.

Woolf was well aware of both traditions, given the history of her family's engagement with the photograph album as a scrapbook collection, and her acknowledged awareness of the more scholarly practice of 'commonplacing'. Woolf, herself, as Maggie Humm has admirably demonstrated, kept photograph albums filled with portraits that 'memorialise family and friends' (Humm 2003: 54). As I intend to show, Woolf carries forward from the more private world of family photograph albums a practice of selection, combination, and arrangement which she deploys in organising the public documents, both text and illustration, in the three 'scrapbook' volumes of *The Reading Notes for Three Guineas*.

The practice of keeping a 'commonplace book' reaches back at least into the 1600s where, at universities such as Oxford, commonplacing was formally taught. John Locke even formalised his own method of commonplacing, publishing his *A New Method of Making Common-Place-Books* (1706) in Latin, French and English translations. Locke's method sought to facilitate the storage and retrieval of information by organising material in indexes to make the most efficient possible use of space. The commonplace book provided a vehicle for compiling knowledge in a way unique to each individual and acted as a journal containing pithy fragments, phrases, and quotations culled by the writer as he/she read. The practice was especially attractive to writers, George Eliot, John Milton and Thomas Jefferson are but a few examples, for developing a suggestively rich compendium of such nuggets of knowledge.

Woolf seems to have particularly embraced the tradition of the commonplace book from her earliest reading notebooks, using these as receptacles for knowledge to which she could return as needed when it was time to write for publication. Her awareness of the tradition is evident in several locations in her published works; I'll offer one example. In her essay 'The Strange Elizabethans' (1932), Woolf remarked:

> But happily Harvey left behind him a commonplace book; he had the habit of making notes in the margins of books as he read. Looking from one to the other, from his public self to his private, we see his face lit from both sides, and the expression changes as it changes so seldom upon the face of the Elizabethans. (*CR2*: 15–16).

The quote is suggestive for the work at hand, for in examining her *Reading Notes*, we see Woolf's face lit from both sides.

In short, by loosely referring to the *Reading Notes* as scrapbooks as many of us have, myself included, we acknowledge their commonality with a more domestic, private practice. But the volumes are not only private albums, nor are they only commonplace books filled with nuggets of information to remember but nowhere to go. Rather, they are both; out of the union of the two traditions, a new form is born. Within this new form, Woolf crosses domestic place and workplace, private space with public space, to construct a gendered map of her contemporary society. And while they are utterly fascinating in and of themselves, the *Reading Notes* are not only valuable for what they are but also for what they point to, the publication of *Three Guineas* as their culmination. Woolf's *Reading Notes for Three Guineas* are one woman's record of the climate and temperament of her time – apparently meant for her eyes only but clearly pieced together with an eye to posterity out of the 'orts, scraps, and fragments' (*BA*: 189) she found – they are her feminist history of the 1930s.

Physically, *The Reading Notes for Three Guineas* consist of three crumbling ring-bound notebooks whose covers vary from a marbled design on the first to cloth covers on the second and third, which Woolf must have taped on herself. All three covers bear brief handwritten indexes to the contents pasted onto the top-left corner, in the spirit of Locke's method of commonplacing but not in his manner. For Volume 1, Woolf has entitled the cover 'Notes & Cuttings', decorating this typed label with a typewritten border of '4's. Above this larger label, she's pasted a small rectangular white label bearing the Roman numeral I. Volume 2 is labelled with the handwritten Arabic number 2 pasted onto a small circular label. If Volume 3 had a numeric label, it is now gone.

I pay attention to these details to underscore the care with which Woolf assembled the volumes, the way in which she marked them with her own decorative touch, but, most importantly, the way she organised the volumes as commonplace compendia of information. Indeed, it appears that the brief handwritten indexes on each cover were pasted on when the volume was complete, probably, in the case of Volume 1, just before Woolf began to write *The Pargiters*, and, in the case of Volumes 2 and 3, just before she began to write *Three Guineas*. These cover indexes may have been quick references to those items she intended to cite when she began to write. A look at the fuller, typed index to Volume 1, for example, shows that Woolf has marked, either by an ink 'x' or a green pencil circle, several of the items which appear on the cover.

My main focus in what follows will be to explore Woolf's organisational strategies for the *Reading Notes* in an effort to illuminate the construction, content, and thematic matrices which emerge. With that in mind, I intend to begin by describing items on Woolf's cover indexes which appear to be 'shortlisted' for their value as indications of broader themes within the volume as well as pointers to the deployment and support of those themes in *Three Guineas* itself.

The cover index for Volume 1 of the *Reading Notes* lists thirteen items, among them: 'Joad. w. not to dine 2', and 'Lady Lovelace 29'. These items with page numbers locating them in the volume are intriguing for the very fact that all of them centre, in one way or another, on the central theme of gender and society. Why Woolf chose these thirteen items from the sixty-seven pages of Volume 1 is anybody's guess, but all of these items except two appear in *Three Guineas*, and Woolf reached beyond this list to include ten more items from the volume throughout the chapters of *Three Guineas*. The list here divides into two broad areas of concern for Woolf: first, a masculine backlash against women's increasing freedom coupled with outworn clichés about female vanity and second, evidence to refute masculine perceptions of female inferiority coupled with first-hand reports of women who have suffered from patriarchal oppression.

Perhaps the most virulent expression of masculine backlash appears in the very first item, Woolf's quotation from C. E. M Joad. 'Women', Joad writes and Woolf quotes, 'ought not to sit down to table with men; their presence ruins conversation, tending to make it trivial and genteel or at best merely clever' (*RN*: 1.2). Using the full sentence in a footnote to *Three Guineas*, Woolf glosses it to comment: 'This is an admirably outspoken opinion, and if all who share Mr. Joad's sentiments were to express them as openly, the hostess's dilemma – whom to ask, whom not to ask – would be lightened and her labour saved' (*TG*: 159). Woolf's wonderfully malicious and subtle humour strikes right at the heart of Joad's open misogyny.

Surely Woolf remembered that in November 1922, Joad and his mistress at the time, Marjorie Thomson, took tea in Woolf's home. Woolf left us this record in the second volume of her *Diary* of the occasion:

> Joad . . . a philosopher; a sturdy short man, with very bright round eyes, hair touched with grey, cocksure, reposing much weight upon the sterling quality of his intellect, & thus dispensing with the graces & amenities, as usual with sterling young men. He tipped one of my chairs on two legs, & ate a large tea. (*D2*: 213)

We are left to wonder, but not for long, if Woolf's presence ruined the conversation.

To return to Joad's comment about not dining with women, I note that the section of Joad's autobiography containing this quote, all of which, presumably, Woolf would have read, goes on for fifteen pages, affording him ample space to express many more views on women that are shocking at best. Styling himself a 'feminist' in his youth, Joad describes the change in his attitude toward women; he's angry that middle-class women are largely unhappy, despite the 'wide opportunities which the modern world offers [them] for a fuller and more varied life' (Joad 1932: 50). Joad acknowledges the debate swirling in the popular press about the need for women to return to the home, one which Woolf herself chronicles in her *Reading Notes*, but he insists that the middle-class woman has no home to go back to – in other words, given modern appliances, there is little left for women to do. Then, Joad continues, when women become bored at home, they seek a life in the professional world which remains essentially closed to them. However, Joad suggests, women aren't really suited to professional life either, 'Put them in positions of power and authority and they are intolerable' (Joad 1932: 53). Joad's reason for such behaviour in women 'manageresses' is interesting – sex starvation. 'In my view', comments Joad, 'nobody should be put in a position of authority over his or her fellows who does not lead a normal and satisfied sex life.' Joad's great admission follows these observations: 'the root of the trouble lies, I suspect, in the commonplace fact that I don't like women's company' (ibid.). Indeed, Woolf's evidence clearly suggests that Joad's sentiments indicate only the tip of the iceberg, and the remaining indexed items on this theme from Walter Bagehot, Judge MacCardie and Winston Churchill echo them.

To the weight of this majority male view, Woolf opposes real women's experiences. I take as examples two of the shortlisted items: one on Mary Kingsley and the other on Mary, Countess of Lovelace. In reading Gwynne on Mary Kingsley, for example, Woolf's attention was caught by Kingsley's comment in a letter to her friend and publisher in the last year of her life, 'I don't know if I ever revealed to you the fact that being allowed to learn German was *all* the paid-for education I ever had. £2000 was spent on my brother's, I still hope no [*sic*] not in vain' (*RN*: 1.33). Woolf takes Mary Kingsley as emblematic of the many 'daughters of educated men' whose own educations were sacrificed for their brothers (*TG*: 4).[2] Kingsley, however, was a determined woman who entered a profession without professional training, travelled to Africa to collect and identify rare species of fish, and brought back samples to the British Museum which were previously unidentified by science. Through her bravery and extraordinary writing, she not only added to our scientific knowledge but also to our understanding of African culture and religious customs. One wonders if her brother, with his educational advantages, gave so much back to his society.

Woolf's use of the newspaper clipping from the 'Fifty Years Hence' feature in *The Times* by Mary, Countess of Lovelace displays the view of a Victorian woman, here an aristocrat, trapped in the private house. Into Lovelace's memoir creeps a clear measure of dissatisfaction as she writes about female confinement, 'How many a long dull summer afternoon have I passed immured indoors because there was no room for me in the family carriage and no lady's maid who had time to walk out with me' (*RN*: 1.29).

Lovelace's sentiments accumulated such resonance in Woolf's argument that she uses her words without acknowledgment, lifting the phrase about the shortage of unattached males as 'the price we pay for our splendid Empire, and the price is paid mainly by the women' to write of Woman in the abstract: 'Thus consciously she desired "our splendid Empire"; unconsciously she desired our splendid war' (*TG*: 39). Woolf dissects Lovelace's phrase to reveal how the gendering of public and private space in Victorian society encouraged, even insisted upon, women's complicity with war – a remarkably striking and prescient observation and sharp response to the initiatory question posed by a man to the daughters of educated men in *Three Guineas*: 'How in your opinion are we to prevent war?' (ibid.: 3).

Equal in importance to these broad thematic concerns revealed in Woolf's choices of materials to collect in her *Reading Notes*, Volume 1, is the care in selection and arrangement that went into their organisation. What might initially appear as a slip, for example, is the confusion in page numbers for Woolf's entry 'Young Women and the Church'. Woolf identifies this shortlisted item on the cover of Volume 1 as appearing on page 62, she also lists its page in a handwritten entry to the fuller index of the volume as appearing on page 62; the item does not, however, appear there. This brief newspaper cutting appears alone on the next page, 63, instead of 'GBS. definition of A Lady' as Woolf indicates in her full index. The George Bernard Shaw note was then pushed to the next page to appear together with Woolf's note from *The Doctor's Second Thoughts* (*RN*: 1.64). I would argue that the rearrangement was deliberate, that Woolf chose not to paste the cutting on the same page with her notes from Shaw, which she probably felt fit better thematically with the note on doctors' wives. Furthermore, the cutting stands alone as a signpost to a much larger argument regarding the institutionalisation of patriarchy in religion and its impact upon women. Titled and subtitled 'Young Women and the Church: "A Suspicion That They are Not Wanted"', the article reports that, in contrast to the past, when women constituted 75 per cent of the attendance at church services, young women are staying away from churches because they feel excluded. Woolf came back to this cutting for the third chapter of *Three Guineas* where she virtually quotes the brief article in its entirety (*TG*: 117–18).

A second shortlisted item, 'C[ivil].S[ervice]. on male rule', points to another fascinating feature of Woolf's organisational strategies. The page contains two newspaper cuttings, 'Whitehall Storm Over a Woman' and 'Woman Appointed Librarian' (*RN*: 15). Woolf apparently intended to use the first, an article which details male backlash against a woman appointed to management of the Shoreditch Labour Exchange. And though Woolf does refer to Civil Service issues in *Three Guineas*, she does not directly quote this article. The page, however, contains two articles on the same theme. In 'Whitehall', despite the competence of the woman selected to enter management, the men protesting her advancement argue against it purely on the grounds that a woman should not supervise men. In 'Librarian', eleven members of the Wolverhampton Public

Library Committee resign rather than accept the appointment of a fully qualified female librarian. Since the two articles do not appear on the same date,
we learn something about Woolf's management of her cuttings. 'Whitehall'
appeared in the *Evening Standard* on 8 April 1932 – Woolf has penciled in the
date at the top of the clipping, which is fortunate since the identifying information has been cut away. On 'Librarian', Woolf has written the date, 'Feb.
12 1932', but not the name of the newspaper. The key fact here is that the two
clippings appeared in their respective newspapers almost two months apart,
which suggests that Woolf not only held clippings for use at the appropriate
moment in her *Reading Notes*, but that she also linked them thematically as she
pasted them on the page. Such organisational strategies, as we shall see, operate
throughout the three volumes of the *Reading Notes*.

The cover of Volume 2 of the *Reading Notes* includes twenty-one shortlisted
items (technically twenty-two, but 'Pommer' appears twice), seventeen of which
are used in *Three Guineas*. Additionally, Woolf went beyond those items she
must initially have thought she would use and included reference to another
thirteen items from this volume in *Three Guineas*.

The twenty-one items on the cover, like those of Volume 1, group themselves
into a related set of themes linked to the overarching argument regarding the
separation and gendering of space. 'Joad on peace. w. +food', for example, acts
as a centrepiece for items surrounding the concept of masculine ideology. A
new idea enters here, though certainly implied in Volume 1, and that is the
evidence of male vanity to counterpoint a masculine ideology of female vanity
– 'Honours in 1937' and 'decorations for desk' serve as examples. Woolf adds
evidence to support the growing importance of her theme regarding education – both for men and women – in 'Miss Weeton', 'Pendennis AEF [Arthur's
Education Fund]', 'Knight on artists', and 'Alington on Eton 50th'.

A second new, insidious theme which slips into Volume 2 relates to war, as
evidenced in the shortlisted item, 'Church on War'. The absence of this important theme in Volume 1 points to that volume's dates. Most likely begun sometime in 1929 or early 1930 with clippings that date back to 1927, the latest dated
item in Volume 1 is from January 1933, most of the newspaper cuttings (those
which are identified by date) appeared in 1932, and the majority of book titles
from which Woolf took notes were published in 1932 (some were published
before, but none after that year). I would also argue that Woolf stopped inserting material in Volume 2 once she separated materials in *The Pargiters* and
began to write *The Years*, for she has clearly used items from Volume 1 in the
'Essay' portions of *The Pargiters*.

There are a number of items in this volume which are extremely significant
and which provide further evidence of Woolf's conscious crafting of feminist
history in *Three Guineas*. One of the most compelling among these is a reference
to a woman jailed for insulting the Nazis, which widens out to enhance the map
of misogyny traced throughout the volumes of the *Reading Notes*. The figure of
Antigone, an important icon for Woolf of women's exclusion from 'Culture', was

herself an outsider by choice; and the first link between the *Reading Notes* and *Three Guineas* through Antigone is in the reference to Frau Pommer, arrested by the Nazis for 'slandering the State and the Nazi movement' (*RN*: 2.20). Dated 12 August 1935, the *Times* article '"The Thorn of Hatred"' reports that when her usual confectioner's shop was out of her favourite brand of chocolate, Frau Pommer reportedly claimed that she intended to go to another shop to buy it, a shop that the shopgirl identified as 'pure Jewish'. Frau Pommer's reply was:

> I and my husband are and remain German nationalists; but as long as one does not cohabit with a Jew one may safely buy from him. The thorn of hatred has been driven deep enough into the people by the religious conflicts and it is high time that the men of to-day disappeared.

These words were all it took for Pommer to be arrested on a charge of 'slandering the State and the Nazi movement.' Woolf's use of Frau Pommer in *Three Guineas* appears in a footnote where Woolf argues that Frau Pommer could be Antigone transformed (*TG*: 169).

If Frau Pommer serves as an Antigone figure, Cyril Joad, whom we've already met in Volume 1, continues to serve as a lightning rod for the theme of misogyny. Shortlisted again on the cover index for Volume 2 and included twice in the fuller index to the volume, Joad's presence eliminates any doubt that many English men harboured sentiments similar to those of European dictators. In this volume, Woolf included an entire article by Joad, entitled 'Women of To-day and To-morrow – by a Man – C. E. M. Joad', evidence that brings him further into the nexus of a cultural conversation juxtaposing women and war (*RN*: 2.17). Sporting an illustration of a woman stirring her pot, the article begins with three epigraphs quoted from figures Joad considers to be exemplary men:

> The woman's task is to be beautiful and to bring children into the world.
> – Herr Goebbels
> Woman – her place is in the home, her duty the recreation of the tired warrior.
> – General Goering
> Women's duty is limited to the three k's – Kinder, Küche, und Kirche . . .
> Motherhood is undeniably the aim of feminine education.
> – Hitler
> (Quoted in *RN*: 2.17)

The illustration shown in Figure 17.1 – a housewife in her apron stirring her cooking pot – visually anchors the sentiments expressed by Joad's German models, sentiments which Joad intends to support and reinforce in his conclusion. Joad begins by questioning the seemingly reactionary postures of these pronouncements, but quickly moves to counter that position by reflecting upon the 'modernity' and success of the young Nazi movement. He also mentions

Figure 17.1 Illustration from 'Women of To-Day and To-Morrow, By a Man –
C. E. M. Joad'. With permission of the Society of Authors as literary representative
of the estate of Virginia Woolf

the apparent lowering of all the barriers to women's equality, but recognises
the reality of lack of access to the professions for women. It is a shame, Joad
opines, that well-educated and intelligent women are reduced to accepting
unfulfilling jobs at low wages. His conclusion, therefore, is that women should
continue to be free and independent, by being the boss in their homes, 'better
to look after a man's comforts than to look after his correspondence, better to
attend to children than to a card-index'. Joad fails to explain how looking after
a man's comforts and attending to children equates with being the boss in the
home; but he does manage to echo a core element of fascist doctrine – that a
militarising nation needs subservient women who agree to their domination,

accept their confinement to private space, and provide the nation with the next generation of soldiers.

But Woolf is not finished with Joad. While the item discussed above does appear in the full index to Volume 2, it is not shortlisted. The item Woolf shortlisted consists of two pages of typed notes from *The Testament of Joad* (1937). The sentiments expressed in the notes are appalling. 'I doubt wteher [*sic*]', Woolf quotes Joad, 'at any time during the past fifty years young women have been more politically apathetic, more socially indifferent than at the present time' (*RN*: 2.58). Apparently a subsequent passage caught Woolf's eye, though, in which Joad claims that organisers in the Labour movement have told him that they 'regard with bewildered despair the present generation of young people who, surfeited with cinemas and dances, dog-racing and the wireless, ice-cream and peanuts, cannot be induced to take any serious interest in politics.' Woolf turns this into a deliciously witty reversal of Joad's concerns, telling her readers, the daughters of educated men:

> According to Mr. Joad you are not only extremely rich; you are also extremely idle; and so given over to the eating of peanuts and ice cream that you have not learnt to cook him a dinner before he destroys himself, let alone how to prevent that fatal act. (*TG*: 42–3)

Let Joad stand as the 'testament' to numerous inclusions in this volume's documents that express sentiments so very similar to his. He is not, however, the epitome of the face of the 'dictator' as Woolf will paint it. That honour is reserved for St Paul. Regardless of the fact that the inclusion of notes detailing Woolf's visit to St Paul's Cathedral or from St Paul's letter to the Corinthians are not shortlisted, Woolf spares no space in featuring his attitudes on women's chastity, shame and inferiority in a lengthy footnote to *Three Guineas*. 'Having thus invoked the familiar but always suspect trinity of accomplices, Angels, nature and law, to support his personal opinion', Woolf writes, 'St. Paul reaches the conclusion which has been looming unmistakably ahead of us: "And if they would learn anything, let them ask their own husbands at home: for it is shameful for a woman to speak in the church"' (*TG*: 167). Paul, Woolf concludes, 'was of the virile or dominant type, so familiar at present in Germany, for whose gratification a subject race or sex is essential' (ibid.). Paul's image fits in with the many faces of a single type: the Dictator.

Woolf placed, in my view, an illustration in her *Reading Notes* that reflects the image of all dictatorial men combined into one; it is the face of Count Galeazzo Ciardi. Ciardi's illustration is not shortlisted nor does it even appear on the longer index to the volume. But his image is important not only because it serves as an icon but also because it appears on a page which clearly emblematises Woolf's method of assembly for her notebook pages. The page contains three items: the article on Frau Pommer, the image of Count Ciardi with only the caption 'Count Ciano in flying kit' to identify it, and a news clipping entitled '"A Nation of Men"', which reports on a Hitler speech to his Old Guard outlining just the sentiments we've already seen repeatedly in the Joad materials (*RN*: 2.20). The two articles are pasted side by side, both annotated in Woolf's hand with the date '12th Aug 1935'. Both clippings were taken from *The Times* on that date, '"The Thorn of Hatred"' from page ten and '"A Nation of Men"' from page nine. So far, nothing too unusual to note here – both articles relay information about occurrences in Nazi Germany, both come from the same paper on the same date, so it would seem logical that they appear together. Even more reason why they should appear so joined is the fact that they act as reverse mirrors – '"Thorn"' works to counter Nazi ideology while '"Nation"' underlines Hitler's increasing imperialist agenda, quoting him, '"He who wishes to disturb our peace will no longer fight a nation of pacifists but against a nation of men."'

However, Ciano's image, which appears in the bottom left of the page bears no accompanying text or annotation to indicate its source. It was through sheer luck that we found the image as my colleague Vara Neverow and I pored through pages of microfilm of the newspapers from which Woolf clipped. Ciano's picture, included in the column 'London Day by Day', emerges on the bottom half of page 12 of the 9 September 1936, edition of the *Daily Telegraph* – a paper dated more than a year after the two clippings which appear above it on Woolf's notebook page. This evidence of Woolf's intentional thematic construction of her pages is, in my view, inescapable. Furthermore, we have to inquire why Woolf would have included only the image and not the column surrounding it, a light-hearted and gossipy account of the doings of 'notables' in London and abroad. The account of Ciano, written by an anonymous columnist, cheerfully reports that Ciano would represent Italy at the upcoming League of Nations meeting in Geneva, where he and Anthony Eden, England's Foreign Secretary, would share the common bond of being the two youngest ministers, thirty-three and thirty-nine respectively. But, the gossipy columnist goes on to say, Ciano, unlike Eden, has had chickenpox – the thrust of the joke being, of course, that they're just mere boys playing at being men. Such a breezy portrait of Ciano belies what Woolf undoubtedly saw as his menace. Ciano was Mussolini's son-in-law, a bomber pilot in the Abyssinian war who later negotiated the Axis agreements with Germany and helped further Italian expansion into the Balkans. The ironic contrast to the rather enthusiastic account in the newspaper clipping is that Ciano was noted for bombing civilians indiscriminately in Ethiopia, writing in 1935, 'We have carried out a slaughter.'[3] His image on Woolf's notebook page appears youthful, handsome and smiling; his jacket sports the skull and crossed bones emblem of his bomber squadron, 'La Disperata'.

The cover for Volume 3 reveals an index bearing twenty-five shortlisted items; seventeen will appear in *Three Guineas*. A quick glance at the list confirms that the overarching themes are just as important in this final volume as they were in the other two: a prevailing masculine ideology which trivialises women's efforts at equality, women's concerns with their status in public space, and a continued concern with the growing threat of global war, this time represented by inclusions on the civil war in Spain.

One of the shortlisted clippings combines a number of these concerns into one: 'Seule la culture désintéressée', it reads, 'peut garder le Monde de sa ruine' (Only disinterested culture can save the world from its ruin) (*RN*: 3.24). Woolf clipped this headline from an unidentified French newspaper, most likely sometime during 1937; it suggests that in culture there is hope for the future, while at the same time it intimates the grave seriousness with which the world was facing its next world war.[4]

In *Three Guineas*, Woolf cites 'Seule la culture' directly, proposing,

> you say that war is imminent; and you go on to say, in more languages than one – here is the French version: *Seule la culture désintéressée peut garder le monde de sa ruine* – you go on to say that by protecting intellectual liberty and our inheritance of culture we can help you to prevent war. (*TG*: 87)

But, Woolf insists, 'disinterested culture' has not been 'disinterested' in excluding women: 'culture for the great majority of educated men's daughters must still be that which is acquired outside the sacred gates, in public libraries or in private libraries, whose doors by some unaccountable oversight have been left unlocked' (*TG*: 89). Since women have been largely segregated from the public space of culture, from access to higher learning, from access to the professions, why, then, Woolf asks, should women concern themselves with saving anything?

The organisation of the page on which 'Seule la culture' is found is another example of Woolf's construction of thematic matrices. Beneath it, Woolf has pasted a one-page, folded pamphlet entitled 'International Peace Campaign', which announces the formation of a peace campaign whose function will be to enable all of the 'peace movements throughout the world to speak with one voice' (*RN*: 3.24). Undated by Woolf, the pamphlet can be generally attributed to sometime in 1937 since it refers to the 1936 Brussels World Peace Congress as having happened 'last September'. The underlying message of the pamphlet, signed by the Viscount Cecil, president of the League of Nations Union and co-founder of the International Peace Campaign, is to ask donors to contribute to the cause of peace. Though not referred to directly in *Three Guineas*, the pamphlet serves obliquely as a model for those letters to which Woolf refers in *Three Guineas* asking for donations and asking how to prevent war.[5] However, as a part of the notebook page where it appears, the pamphlet resonates in complicated ways. The Woolfs knew Robert Cecil and were familiar with his tireless work on behalf of peace – he was awarded the Nobel Prize for Peace in 1937 – yet if we fit this pamphlet in as part of the puzzle of meaning on the notebook page, we must acknowledge that Woolf takes an unusual spin on the headline and so may also, silently, have asked the same question of the pamphlet – 'why ... should women concern themselves with saving anything?' (*TG*: 89).

The lengthiest document Woolf includes in her *Reading Notes* is a pamphlet entitled *The Martyrdom of Madrid*. Consisting of more than fifty pages, it contains an unpublished eyewitness account by journalist Louis Delaprée of the civil war raging in Madrid during the month of November 1936 (*RN:* 3.20). The pamphlet appears by itself on the page, and its contents reveal an impassioned narrative about the fall of Madrid. What Delaprée describes parallels Woolf's description of the 'ruined houses and dead bodies' in *Three Guineas* but there are no illustrations in the pamphlet. There is no way of knowing when the pamphlet came into Woolf's possession – possibly while her nephew, Julian Bell, was volunteering with the Republican Army in Spain, or not until after she had learned of his death on 18 July 1937. Given that the 'Seule la culture' headline is dated 31 July 1937, and it appears four pages later in the *Reading Notes,* my guess would be that Woolf pasted in the *Martyrdom of Madrid* right around the time of Julian's death.

The pamphlet is extraordinary reading. At the time of his dispatches in November 1936, Delaprée suspected that his reports were being censored and only partial accounts were appearing in *Paris Soir.* The pamphlet, privately published by friends in 1937 after Delaprée's death, identifies all material not previously published in the newspaper by printing it in italics (more than half the pamplet is italicised) and further identifies and prints language suppressed by Spanish censors. As a final word, Delaprée wrote an angry message to his editor at *Paris Soir,* fatefully predicting his own death the next day and closing with these bitter words: 'Till then I shall send you nothing. It is not worth while. The massacre of a hundred Spanish children is less interesting than a Mrs. Simpson's sigh' (*RN:* 3.20, p. 47).

Delaprée's sad observation that the newsworthiness and sensationalism of the furore over Edward VIII's determination to marry Wallis Simpson, a divorced American, far outweighed the tragedy in Spain was quite true. Delaprée's plane was shot down just after he sent his final message, a self-fulfilling prophecy, but his eyewitness account lives on and details such scenes of death and destruction that photographs are hardly needed to add to the graphic horror. Descriptions like this abound in Delaprée's account:

> Three hundred thousand persons run in the streets, seeking a shelter. Mothers go back towards the barrio that burns, towards the collapsed house to look for a child who now, though they do no [*sic*] not know it, is no more than a little heap of ashes, children, mad with terror, call a mamma who has just been carbonized under the ruins. A whole people seeks a refuge against heaven's wrath and do not find it. (*RN:* 3.20, p. 27)

Woolf's use of this pamphlet in *Three Guineas* echoes the use she makes of the headline 'Seule la culture'. Writing about the patriotic fervour that men believe women should feel, Woolf claims that the 'Educated man's daughter . . . will ask herself, "What does 'our country' mean to me an outsider?"' (*TG:* 107). In the footnote to this passage, Woolf quotes Delaprée. But it is not his account of dead bodies and ruined houses or of the rising tide of blood that Woolf uses, but rather it is his description of a Spanish 'amazon', Amalia Bonilla, who has killed five, perhaps six men in the fighting; for Woolf intends to show that if the fighting instinct is sanctioned, it can be developed in women (*TG*: 177–8). Bonilla, age thirty-six, tells Delaprée that her two daughters were militiawomen and the younger has been killed: "'I thought I had to supersede her and to avenge her'" (*RN*: 3.20, pp. 34–5). "'This woman'", Delaprée writes and Woolf quotes, "'was for the envoys of the House of Commons an excellent introducer to the Spanish War'" (*TG*: 178).

There is a later addition to the *Reading Notes* that counterbalances Woolf's concern that more women could become warriors, a 20 December 1937 article from the *Evening Standard* – 'Mayoress Would Not Darn Socks for War' – appears near the end of the last volume of the *Reading Notes* and Woolf has cut it out in cruciform shape to capture the full width of the headline centred over the narrow, vertical column (*RN*: 3.63). It is one of the seventeen items not shortlisted on the volume cover which Woolf chose to use in *Three Guineas*. According to the clipping, Rance asserts that:

> So far as my husband and I are concerned, we shall do all we can for peace during our year of office. We are both members of the Peace Pledge Union, and neither of us would take part in a war. I myself would not even do as much as darn a sock to help in a war.

As she read this article, Woolf must have remembered Frau Pommer and heard the linguistic echoes in her quoted speech: "'I and my husband are and remain German nationalists; but as long as one does not cohabit with a Jew one may safely buy from him'" (*RN*: 2.20). Two women, one a German private citizen and the other an English mayoress, interviewed more than two years apart, spoke out against militarism and on behalf of peace and Woolf has preserved their memory.

Rance's expressed sentiments, like Pommer's, were those of Woolf herself, who uses Rance as an example of her 'Outsiders' Society' in *Three Guineas*. Woolf quotes Rance's assertion that she "'would not even do as much as darn a sock to help in a war'", as well as the correspondent's comment that the remarks 'were resented by the majority of the Woolwich public, who hold that the Mayoress was, to say the least, rather tactless.' 'There is no need', Woolf continues,

> to comment upon the tactlessness of such a statement made publicly, in such circumstances; but the courage can scarcely fail to command our admiration, and the value of the experiment, from a practical point of view, should other mayoresses in other towns and other countries where the electors are employed in armament making follow suit, may well be immeasurable. (*TG*: 116)

The spirit of Antigone hovers over the closing pages of *Three Guineas* and Woolf's notes on the play appear near the end of the third volume of the *Reading Notes*. Antigone is Woolf's icon for female courage, linked to her own contemporaries Mrs Pankhurst and Frau Pommer, and, by extension, to Kathleen Rance, Mayoress of Woolwich. Each of these women, and many others whose stories populate the pages of the *Reading Notes* and *Three Guineas* live as 'outsiders,' expressing through their words and actions the courage to refuse complicity with their own oppression or with the oppression of one nation over another.

Blending the tradition of scrapbooking and commonplacing to create a new form as eyewitness to history, Woolf knowingly used newspaper clippings and other documentary evidence contained in her *Reading Notes for Three Guineas* as a cultural map, revealing the existence of an 'Outsiders' Society' of women through, as Woolf cogently observed in *Three Guineas*, 'history and biography in the raw – by the newspapers that is – sometimes openly in the lines, sometimes covertly between them. There, anyone who wishes to verify the existence of such a body, can find innumerable proofs' (*TG*: 115). The *Reading Notes for Three Guineas* expose the stink of misogyny when read with the grain, and, when read against the grain and between the lines, the story of female heroics in the face of overwhelming oppression in the 1930s.

Notes

1. These 'scrapbooks' or reading notebooks are published online as *The Reading Notes for Three Guineas: An Archival Edition* at the Center for Virginia Woolf Studies, www.csub.edu/woolf. I will refer to them mostly as the *Reading Notes,* as the web-published edition is a digital facsimile of the originals, and will reference them in parenthetical citation through the abbreviation *RN* followed by the volume and page number. However, the actual physical volumes are entitled Monk's House Papers B16f, and where necessary, will be referred to as MHP B16f.
2. Woolf also refers to Mary Kingsley in the context of the lack in women's education in *AROO*: 68.
3. Quoted in Ray Moseley 1999: 18.
4. Stuart N. Clarke reports in an email dated 2 August 2008, that he has located the source of the headline; it appears in *Les Nouvelles Litteraires*, 31 July 1937.
5. See Black 2003: 77, for more on Viscount Cecil, the Woolfs' relationship with him and his inappropriateness as the addressee of *Three Guineas*.

Works Cited and Further Reading

Black, Naomi (2003) *Virginia Woolf as Feminist*, Ithaca, NY: Cornell University Press.

Clarke, Stuart (2008) 'Seule la culture désintéressée . . . ' Email to Merry Pawlowski, 2 August.

Humm, Maggie (2003) *Modernist Women and Visual Cultures: Virginia Woolf, Vanessa Bell, Photography and Cinema*, New Brunswick, NJ: Rutgers University Press.

Joad, C. E. M. (1932) *Under the Fifth Rib: A Belligerent Autobiography*, London: Faber and Faber.

—— (1937) *The Testament of Joad*, London: Faber and Faber.

Locke, John (1706) 'A New Method of a Common-Place-Book', trans. from vol. 2 of

Bibliothèque universelle, in *Posthumous Works of Mr John Locke*, London: printed by W. B. for A. and J. Churchill, pp. 311–36.

Moseley, Ray (1999) *Mussolini's Shadow: The Double Life of Count Galeazzo Ciano*, New Haven, CT: Yale University Press.

Pawlowski, Merry and Vara Neverow (eds) (2000) *The Reading Notes for Three Guineas: An Archival Edition*, www.csub.edu/woolf

Woolf, Virginia (2002) 'The Virginia Woolf and Vera Douie Letters', ed. Merry Pawlowski, *Woolf Studies Annual*, 8: 3–62.

—— Monk's House Papers B16f, volumes 1, 2 and 3, University of Sussex Manuscript Library, Sussex, England.

18

VIRGINIA WOOLF AND THE ART OF JOURNALISM

Patrick Collier

Hᴇʀᴇ ɪs Vɪʀɢɪɴɪᴀ Woolf in 1931, at the apex of her success, recalling the beginnings of her writing life:

> But to tell you my story – it is a simple one. You have only got to figure to yourselves a girl in a bedroom with a pen in her hand. She had only to move that pen from left to right – from ten o'clock to one. Then it occurred to her to do what is simple and cheap enough after all – to slip a few of those pages into an envelope, fix a penny stamp in the corner, and drop the envelope into the red box at the corner. It was thus that I became a journalist; and my effort was rewarded on the first day of the following month – a very glorious day it was for me – by a letter from an editor containing a cheque for one pound ten shillings and sixpence. ('Professions for Women', *DM*: 236)

Like so many writers in the early twentieth century, Woolf received her first exposure as a contributor to newspapers, so it is not surprising to find her accounting for her career in terms that celebrate a newspaper publication. This sweetly romantic recollection posits an innocent birth into the world of print: the girl is 'moving her pen' at her own pleasure and in what appears to be a room of her own, and it only occurs to her later that her writing might appear in print, earn her money, make her, in the essay's terms, 'professional'. By the time Woolf wrote this anecdote, however, she had been writing at the call of and in (sometimes vexing) negotiation with editors for more than twenty years, and she had considered and written extensively about the costs and benefits, the pleasures and frustrations, of balancing her own desires as a writer with the imperatives of editors, periodicals and audiences.

The anecdote is however a rare positive evocation of journalism for Woolf, who is better known for her critique of newspapers, the masculine authority of the printed word, and the press's complicity with repressive ideologies. In *Three Guineas* (1938) Woolf would characterise journalism – writing as 'at the command of another person what you do not want to write for the sake of money',

– as intellectual prostitution (*TG*: 93). 'Professions for Women' thus offers a rare image of a purely beneficial exchange in the print marketplace. And, by positing the writing in the bedroom as the starting point of her professional life, Woolf implies an organic connection between her early reviewing and her art. Yet neither Woolf nor most of her contemporaries would have seen journalism as an 'art'. Though Woolf was to become one of the most original and durable essayists of her generation – and though most of her essays came into existence as contributions to periodicals – neither Woolf, nor most of her academic supporters, nor many of her contemporaries would view this work as 'journalism', which is instead seen as a hindrance to full artistry or, at best, a necessary evil. Thus as we consider Virginia Woolf and the much-maligned art of journalism, we begin with the paradox of a woman who produced more than 600 pieces of journalism, who served her apprenticeship as a writer by doing scores of book reviews and ultimately became a sought-after contributor to prestigious periodicals, and yet had very little positive to say about journalism.[1]

Plotting Woolf's ever-changing practice of and attitudes towards journalism thus results in anything but the 'simple story' she promises in 'Professions for Women', for in addition to registering the many subtle changes in her orientation, we must contend with the fact that Woolf seldom seems to be of one mind on the topic. Woolf had a profoundly dialogic mind, ever aware of the validity of competing claims, of the costs and benefits of any course of action. Certainly by 1931, when she recalled the story of the girl in her bedroom, in a speech to the National Society for Women's Service (published in 1942 as 'Professions for Women'), any such simple satisfaction with the exchanges of the print marketplace are long gone, and we are deep into conflicted territory.[2] The speech contains Woolf's famous claim that she had to 'kill the Angel in the House' – the proverbial guardian of Victorian gender proprieties – in order to write freely for publication, and this claim specifically invokes the newspaper context. The angel's voice proclaimed:

> You have got yourself into a very queer position. You are young and unmarried. But you are writing for a paper owned by men, edited by men – *whose chief supporters are men*; you are even reviewing a book that has been written by a man – one Mr Arnold Bennett. Therefore whatever you say let it be pleasing to men. (*P*: xxxi)

The 'Angel's' call for flattery, tact, self-censorship must be resisted vigorously; Woolf recalls hurling her inkpot at the angel in the house whenever she felt her shadow on the page. A deeply characteristic moment: Woolf's diaries, letters and essays are replete with instances in which Woolf ponders the competing forces that must be managed when one writes for publication, where she attempts to sort through the claims of editors and readers, to test out which pressures are to be welcomed as stimulants to the writer's art and which are to be resisted as binding, limiting, corrupting. (Years later, Woolf would mark the dawn of print culture as the moment when '[a]t once come into existence some of those innumerable influences that are to tug, to distort, to thwart; as also they are to stimulate and draw out' (Woolf 1979: 390).

While at an earlier stage, Woolf scholarship was preoccupied with questions of whether her writing was essentially 'private' (i.e. domestic, idiosyncratic, apolitical, aimed at a very small audience) or 'public' (meant to be shared, engaged in contemporary questions, political, aimed at having real effects in the world), it is perhaps more useful to conceive of Woolf's attitudes at different times as existing along a continuum between uncompromising devotion to her unique vision (tending towards self-enclosure) and a powerful desire to reach and influence an appropriate (and at times relatively wide) audience.[3] Since she published more total words in periodicals than in novels – and for most of her working life earned more from them – Woolf's journalistic practices, and her attitudes towards journalism, are inseparable from her ever-shifting orientation towards audiences, the literary marketplace and the public sphere, and thus essential to understanding Woolf's various conceptions of the purposes of her work (Lee 1997: 550).[4]

For convenience's sake Woolf's relations with journalism might be divided into three periods: 1904–22, before the publication of Woolf's first mature novel, *Jacob's Room*, and when her writing, and her earnings from writing, consist overwhelmingly of journalism; 1922–31, when Woolf had her first commercial successes as a writer of books, gained the greatest critical reputation of her lifetime, and published a majority of her finest essays in periodicals; and 1931–41, when her critical reputation declined somewhat and when she simultaneously wrote the least for periodicals and was most stridently critical of journalism. In the first two periods, while Woolf was always aware that to publish involves a compromise of the writer's wants, she willingly made that compromise, exercising the many subtle calibrations necessary to please, in acceptable proportions, herself, her editors and her readers. In the final period, this balance became more difficult, and Woolf began to imagine ways of circumventing the institutions of the print marketplace rather than working within them. Here I will focus primarily on the second and third periods, before situating Woolf's relations with the press within the wider discourses about journalism in her time.[5] 'Professions for Women' marks a pivot between the two later periods, containing both the critique of the public sphere that was to predominate in Woolf's writing in the 1930s and elements of the balanced optimism on questions of publicity that characterised most of the 1920s.

The 1920s: critique and equilibrium

Between *Jacob's Room* and 'Professions for Women', Woolf achieved the greatest equilibrium between the writer's integrity and the needs and desires of readers and institutions of the print marketplace. The year 1921 had seen scant sales and poor reviews of the story collection *Monday or Tuesday*, pushing Woolf to one edge of the attitude continuum, where she imagined, in her diary, that queer, & very pleasant sense, of something which I want to write; my own point of view. I wonder, though, whether the feeling that I write for half a dozen instead of 1500 will pervert this? – make me eccentric, – no, I think not. (*D2* 107)

Within a few years, however, Woolf would be writing imaginative works for considerably more than 1,500 readers: *Mrs Dalloway* and *To the Lighthouse*, *Orlando* and *A Room of One's Own*, along with extensive and remunerative journalism (Lee 1997: 464). None the less Woolf was neither silent nor sanguine about the media landscape in these years: while her essays contend with the print marketplace's influence upon the serious writer, her books register the daily newspaper as a central artifact of daily life and critique its social function. *Mrs Dalloway* (1925) dramatises Woolf's lasting impression, later developed fully in *Three Guineas*, that newspapers are the province of men, disseminators of male language and purveyors of masculinist understandings of reality. In *Mrs Dalloway*, Lady Bruton's draft letters to *The Times* must be revised into publishable form by the pompous royal functionary Hugh Whitbread; with his phallic fountain pen, whose durability is 'somehow to Hugh's credit', he 'reduce[s] Lady Bruton's tangles to sense, to grammar such as the editor of the *Times* . . .must respect' (*MD*: 110). In *A Room of One's Own* (1928), Woolf's narrator surveys the contents of a daily paper, finding stories about cricket, an axe murder, a woman 'lowered from a peak in California and suspended in mid-air' as a publicity stunt; all demonstrate to Woolf that 'England is under the rule of a patriarchy', underscoring the discursive and epistemological power of *A Room*'s archetypal angry, misogynistic male, Professor von X: 'He was the cricketer . . . . His was the power and the money and the influence . . . . He suspended the actress in mid-air. . .he it is who will acquit or convict the murderer' (33–34). As Karin Westman notes, Woolf here asserts that the newspaper offers 'a direct link to current events even as it prescribes the reader's experience of those events' (Westman 2006: 2). Throughout *Orlando*, Woolf uses the poet/critic/professor Nick Greene to parody the functioning of publicity in various historical marketplaces. By and large, Woolf's books of the 1920s display her particular spin on widely available critiques of early twentieth-century journalism and the wider print marketplace.

A more hybrid text illustrates the dynamic equilibrium that characterised the mid-to-late twenties: *The Common Reader* (1925), a volume of essays about literature, most of them reprinted or revised from initial appearances in periodicals. The book marks a temporary *rapprochement* with journalism and publicity in several ways. In it, she recovers, often reworks, and thus revalues a number of fugitive journalistic pieces; articulates her understanding of the 'common reader' – her attempt to bridge (or navigate around) class differences and imagine a progressive but classless 'republic of readers', a sort of Utopian public sphere (*CR*1: 232); and includes numerous essays that elucidate this equilibrium, acknowledging both the compromises exacted by publicity and the necessity of a successful negotiation between the artist's vision and the needs of mediators and readers.[6]

'The Patron and the Crocus' best illustrates this dynamic. The essay begins with an extended meditation on the perplexity writers face, given the segmented audience and the vast array of publishing outlets through which one might reach it. Woolf embeds both elements – audience and mediating outlet – in the figure of the 'patron', and asks her readers to imagine an artist, inspired to write by 'the sight of the first crocus in Kensington Gardens' (*CR*1: 207). Newspapers, she suggests, offer easy access to an audience but require extreme brevity and a flashy style, one guaranteed to 'give two million eyes something bright and brisk and amusing to look at'. But if reaching for the newspapers' mass audience is undesirable, so is a disregard for audience or despair at finding the appropriate conduit to it. '[A] book is always written for somebody to read', Woolf writes; 'the crocus is an imperfect crocus until it has been shared . . . . To know whom to write for is to know how to write' (ibid.: 206, 208). Indeed, Woolf herself describes the dynamic pull between the writer's vision and the audience's desires as a continuum, and specifically faults Henry James, George Meredith and Samuel Butler for veering too far towards self-indulgence:

> Each despised the public; each desired a public; each failed to attain a public; and each wreaked his failure upon the public by a succession . . . of angularities, obscurities, and affectations which no writer whose patron was his equal and friend would have thought it necessary to inflict. (*CR*1: 207)

If this extreme is unfruitful, producing the 'tortured plants' of James, Meredith and Butler, Woolf asks, 'Shall we then rush to the opposite extreme . . .', and produce the brilliant but ephemeral crocuses of the daily newspaper, accepting the editor's offer of 'Twenty pounds down for your crocus in precisely fifteen hundred words?' (*CR*1: 207). Woolf characteristically offers no clear answers – the essay concludes, 'But how to choose rightly? How to write well? Those are the questions' (ibid.: 210). But the balance clearly favours meeting the reader halfway.

The 1930s: Critiquing and reimagining the Public Sphere

Woolf pivots away from this balance in the 1931 speech that would become 'Professions for Women' and toward the critique embedded in *Three Guineas* (1938) and *Between the Acts* (composed between 1938 and 1941), books preoccupied with questions of journalism and the public sphere.[7] By noting the *a priori* influence the 'Angel in the House' exerts upon composition, and by linking the Angel's censorship with a newspaper controlled by men, Woolf both enfolds the masculinist newspapers from *Mrs Dalloway* and anticipates her anatomy of the chilling effect of journalistic militarism in *Three Guineas*.[8] At the same time, 'Professions for Women' partakes of the optimism of the 1920s even as it marks

the beginning of a newly sophisticated (and ultimately pessimistic) understanding of the public sphere. To be sure, the optimism is restrained: Woolf
hypothesises that in 'fifty years' attitudes will have changed enough for women
novelists to tell the truth 'about womens bodies' (P: xxxix). And she issues a call
to action, geared precisely at broadening the boundaries of the public sphere
and increasing women's access, thus enriching the conversation. 'The future of
fiction', Woolf writes, 'depends very much upon what extent men can be educated to stand free speech in women', and she places the responsibility in her
listeners' hands: it lies 'not upon the laps of the Gods, but upon your laps, upon
the laps of professional women' (P: xl). The emphasis upon free speech, the
view of the public sphere as an ecosystem whose health must be maintained, the
history of women in the professions – all point towards *Three Guineas*, whose
dire diagnosis of the public sphere would require a radical re-thinking of how
to exercise one's free speech. As Alex Zwerdling has noted, Woolf's writing in
these years partakes of a wider darkening of the political landscape in response
to the global depression, the rise of fascism and the increasing inevitability of
world war (1986: 326).

   In *Three Guineas*, Woolf explores how much influence women at her moment
in history can have on public events. How, given women's partial access to the
political and professional spheres, *can* they exercise their (still limited) public
voice, and how *should* they do so? Woolf places this exploration in the fictional frame of a narrator who has been asked to donate three guineas to three
separate progressive causes. Responding to these requests leads her to several
substantive discussions of newspapers and journalism, and Woolf is characteristically double-voiced. Laying before her fictive interlocutor evidence culled
from various daily newspapers, she documents the continued oppression of
women throughout Europe, and argues that male domination in the domestic
sphere is inseparable from political tyranny in the public sphere.[9] But while
newspapers offer 'history in the raw' (*TG*: 7) their data have partial and tenuous
truth-value: one must buy 'three dailies . . .and three weeklies' and lay them side
by side in order to divine the truth about any issue (ibid.: 95). Because newspaper writers work for editors and boards with vested interests in militarist forces
that dominate Europe, Woolf asserts, their work is 'adulterated' by the 'money
motive, power motive, advertisement motive, publicity motive, vanity motive'
(ibid.: 97). She thus urges women writers of her class to forego her society's
dominant media channels and write instead for individual readers. '[S]ingle
[the public] into separate people instead of massing it into one monster, gross
in body, feeble in mind', Woolf writes, and urges her readers to use such anachronistic means of production and distribution as the private printing press and
the hand-distributed leaflet (ibid.: 98). This solution has seemed to some commentators a retreat from the public sphere, to others a critique and subversion
of it. Combined with the book's pacifism in the face of fascist aggression – a
position that has not fared well historically – Woolf's pessimism about public
debate has made *Three Guineas* one of her most controversial texts. Recently,

Christine Froula has defended the text as offering 'a historically muted alternative to the dominant voices of public authority', one that, rather than constituting a sort of retreat from publicity, circumvents the current media structures in order to channel the differences between men and women into 'a vision of a shared world' (Froula 2005: 283).[10]

In *Between the Acts* (1941), which was virtually complete at the time of her death, Woolf similarly critiques newspapers and expresses scepticism towards print culture as a whole. As Westman has pointed out, *The Times* of London functions as a *leitmotif* in the novel, and is first linked to the ageing imperialist Bart Oliver; he crafts the morning paper into a beak, menaces his toddler grandson with it, then, asserting retrograde gender codes, labels him a 'crybaby' (*BA*: 13). The novel also evokes a hierarchy of print forms, with its heroine, Isa, noting that '[f]or her generation the newspaper was a book' (ibid.: 20). But for Isa, the now-dominant print form offers no relief, no escape, no useful framework for narrating experience: in the morning's *Times* she finds the horrifying account of a woman sexually assaulted by soldiers – an episode that foregrounds the novel's linkage, continued from *Three Guineas*, between the personal tyranny of sexual relationships and the public violence of war. Finally, as the village in which the novel is set gathers for its annual pageant, a newspaper reporter roams the grounds, constructing in his notebook a reductive interpretation of the play by Miss La Trobe, the novel's artist-figure. But neither the newspaper reporter nor the village parson – markers of masculine discursive authority – is allowed to fix the play's meaning; as the pageant concludes, a heteroglossic village voice mulls the play's meaning, inconclusively. If Miss La Trobe's artistic intentions emerge somewhat muddled in the process, the villagers are empowered 'readers' of the play, which inspires them to unmediated discussion.[11] Woolf thus offers as an alternative to the repressive, monologic authority of the priest and the press the dialogic, communal voice of the village; and, to the private, mediated experience of reading the communal, traditional experience of the village pageant. Westman, indeed, argues that Woolf's narrative technique in *Between the Acts* is geared to evoke 'a critical evaluation of the ways in which a newspaper's and a novel's seeming transparency can naturalize ideology' (Westman 2006: 2).

Based on Woolf's self-creation myth about the girl writing in her bedroom, then, Virginia Stephen/Woolf developed from a *naïf* delighted to have her words appear in a newspaper, and to receive a cheque for them, to an increasingly sophisticated and strident critic of the press and the print marketplace. This trajectory shows in its particulars Woolf's individuality, but it is also typical of serious writers of the late-nineteenth and early-twentieth centuries, who had to contend with these dual facts: writing for the press was virtually inescapable, and journalism was the subject of widespread, anxious cultural discussion. The 1880s to the 1940s were marked by a series of expansions of print culture in Britain, which included a dramatic growth in the markets for 'low-brow' reading material, whether it took the form of cheap or serialised novels or sensationalistic daily newspapers. Modernist literature and the study of English as an academic subject both emerged in relation to these developments. Woolf's attitudes towards these changes and her efforts to envision for herself a place in this landscape were characteristic of her social and historical location and deeply embedded in her own upbringing.

The Victorians and the 'higher journalism'

Part of Leslie Stephen's ambiguous intellectual legacy to his daughter was a sense of the mid-nineteenth century as a golden age of journalism. In Bloomsbury's copious output of opinion it would be hard to find a statement about the Victorians more respectful, more gently mocking, than Woolf's nostalgic reference to Victorian readers in 'The Modern Essay', a review of a 1921 essay anthology, first published in the *TLS* and reprinted, largely intact, in *The Common Reader*:

> But, however much they differ individually, the Victorian essayists yet had something in common. They wrote at greater length than is now usual, and they wrote for a public which had not only time to sit down to its magazine seriously, but a high, if peculiarly Victorian, standard of culture by which to judge it. It was worth while to speak out upon serious matters in an essay; and there was nothing absurd in writing as well as one possibly could when, in a month or two, the same public which had welcomed the essay in a magazine would carefully read it once more in a book. But a change came from a small audience of cultivated people to a larger audience of people who were not quite so cultivated. The change was not altogether for the worse. (*CR*1: 215–16)

Here is the dialogic Woolf, qualifying her arguments, ceding bits of ground all the way, yet with that 'altogether' archly implying that the change to 'a large audience . . . not quite so cultivated' is, if not entirely, then *substantially* a change 'for the worse'. Woolf reiterates a narrative of journalistic achievement and decline that developed late in her father's generation and was in her own time reiterated, with changes, more often and more urgently as the press continued to expand. As Joanne Shattock (2008) has argued, mid-Victorian essayists 'wrote for the press without fear of the loss of social standing'. G. H. Lewes wrote in the 1860s that literature had 'become a profession', largely because of 'the excellence and quality of periodical literature'.[12] By the 1880s, however, anxiety becomes visible in commentaries on the press, provoked by the number of new periodicals cropping up, many with accelerated schedules and shorter articles, all seeming to pose a threat to the 'critical impulse' that had flowered under the 'higher journalism'. Essentially, for Woolf's father 'journalist' was not (or at least was not always) a bad word; in Woolf's time, it would increasingly become one, forcing intellectuals who earned substantial real or cultural capital via periodicals into a wide range of defensive positions.[13] Even within Leslie

Stephen's generation, the expansion of the press in the 1870s and 1880s and the dawn of the politically radical and aesthetically populist 'New Journalism' gave rise to anxieties about journalism as a profession, anxieties visible, according to Shattock, in the titles Stephen gave to essay collections such as *Hours in a Library* and *Studies of a Biographer* – the one gesturing towards a refined leisure, the other to scholarly expertise.

By Woolf's time, the late-Victorian journalistic trends of expansion and popularisation had accelerated. In a trend typically identified at the time with Alfred Harmsworth, Lord Northcliffe, the innovations of earlier editor/publishers George Newnes (editor of the largely apolitical, entertainment-driven *Tit-Bits*) and W. T. Stead (the radical editor of the *Pall Mall Gazette* and, later, the *Review of Reviews*) had largely taken hold – innovations such as short (even single paragraph) articles, written in short and punchy sentences, large-print headlines, personal interviews, and gossip items. In the late 1910s and 1920s, Woolf's carefully wrought essays, including 5,000-word review leaders in the *TLS* and equally lengthy stand-alone essays in the *Nation and Athenaeum*, coexisted in the universe of print with breezy, 500-word essays in the daily newspapers on such subjects as 'If I Had My Life to Live Again'.[14] The genre in which Woolf was working, though common, was a retro-Victorian holdover. Her *TLS* leaders, often rich and exploratory pieces like the aptly named 'Rambling Round Evelyn', ostensibly a review of John Evelyn's diary, neatly match Walter Bagehot's 1855 delineation of the journalistic genre of the 'review-like essay or the essay-like review', even if Woolf had 5,000 words to work with where her father might have enjoyed 10,000.[15] By the late 1910s, Woolf's mastery of this form had secured her relationships with weekly and monthly periodicals whose format allowed space to accommodate the mix of detail, thought, allusiveness and suggestive development that came to characterise her essays. Still, Woolf continued to produce short notices, reviews and reflective 'paragraphs' in the 1920s – more than sixty of them between 1923 and 1928 – beginning when Leonard Woolf became literary editor of the *Nation and Athenaeum*.[16] She did so from a range of motives – to help Leonard secure sufficient copy for the paper's literary columns, to spur her catholic and voracious reading, and to earn the small increments of money they provided. This wide range of journalistic practice informs Woolf's analyses of the two journalistic genres so central to her career, the essay and the review.

The hierarchy of literary forms

If the *Common Reader* marks the point of balance for Woolf between the claims of the audience, the marketplace, and the writer, that book itself, as a print artefact, is poised perilously amid these forces, straddling the highly contested symbolic and material border between journalism and literature. It fit into a popular genre, the volume of collected essays, that has since the mid-Victorian years served writers, publishers and audiences well. As Lee Erickson has pointed out, genres are the product of interactions between writers, readers and the marketplace, 'historical, aesthetic products of market forces reaching a momentary equilibrium between the aspirations of writers and the desires of their audiences' (Erickson 1996: 8). As we have seen, Woolf's *Common Reader* reprint 'The Modern Essay' praises the Victorian marketplace's accommodation of book reprints of lengthy periodical essays (*CR*1: 216). Such volumes of collected journalism, however, were at least as common in her own age: Wilfred Whitten ('John O'London'), T. S. Eliot, Rebecca West, Rose Macaulay, Robert Lynd, J. C. Squire and Arnold Bennett were just a few of the writers to publish collected journalism within a few years of the *Common Reader*. Woolf in fact goes to some length to posit the *Common Reader* as something other than collected journalism – indeed, to *make* it something other: she heavily revised a number of essays, wrote four new essays for the volume and carefully arranged them to create a sort of chronological survey of key English writers, punctuated by meditations upon criticism ('How It Strikes a Contemporary') and publication ('The Patron and the Crocus'). All to turn the *Common Reader* into a 'book' rather than a 'collection of articles', the latter denoting for her an 'inartistic method' (*D*2: 261).

Historically the movement of a text from a periodical setting into a cloth-bound volume marks an increase in its status, what Margaret Beetham calls the 'rescue of the text', not only from physical decay but 'into a recognizable genre – i.e. fiction or poetry or essay' (Beetham 1990: 25). As Laurel Brake, Erickson and others have shown, the establishment of English as an academic discipline in England necessitated drawing clear boundaries around its subject matter, boundaries that resulted in the 'subjugation' of periodicals, the construction of a qualitative distinction between journalism and literature, and the establishment of the book as the privileged object of study (Brake 1994: 2, Erickson 1996: 12). This process, well underway in Woolf's lifetime, produced what Erickson calls a 'hierarchy of written formats' with books at the top, magazines in the middle and newspapers at the bottom (Erickson 1996: 13). The essay volume was ambiguously situated, its hard covers demarking greater permanence but its contents culled from the devalued sphere of journalism. And, like so many print genres in the early twentieth century, it was overproduced, which also tended to devalue it. Woolf's disregard for the essay volume is evident in 'The Patron and the Crocus', where she argues that 'the most brilliant of articles when removed from its element is dust and sand and the husks of straw. Journalism embalmed in a book is unreadable' (*CR*1: 208). An odd statement in a book consisting primarily of texts that had appeared in periodicals, it speaks to the power of the journalism/literature distinction in Woolf's time, and to the resultant, ambiguous status of the essay volume.

Considering how attuned she was to the material conditions that facilitate or thwart creativity, including the limitations of time and space embodied in periodical form, Woolf's generic evasion within *The Common Reader* must be strategic. When Woolf examines post-Victorian essays in 'The Modern Essay', she attributes their shortcomings to the material conditions under which they are produced: for every one essay Charles Lamb wrote, Woolf reckons (with hyperbole), Hilaire Belloc writes 365. While she admires the dexterity with which the modern essayist gets his meaning into his shorter space allotment, Woolf writes that his personality 'comes to us not with the natural richness of the speaking voice, but strained and thin and full of mannerisms and affectations, like the voice of a man shouting through a megaphone to a crowd on a windy day' (*CR1*: 218–19). The megaphone and the crowd neatly encode the determining, formal properties of the mass periodical and the mass audience to which it appeals, deforming forces that get redrawn in the next paragraph:

> To write weekly, to write daily, to write shortly, to write for busy people catching trains in the morning or for tired people coming home in the evening, is a heart-breaking task for men who know good writing from bad. They do it, but instinctively draw out of harm's way anything precious that might be damaged by contact with the public, or anything sharp that might irritate its skin. (*CR1*: 219–20)

In the later essay, 'Reviewing', Woolf similarly emphasises such material aspects of journalistic practice as article length, deadline, pay rates and imagined audience as reasons for the poor quality of book reviews. A 'man who is in a hurry; who is pressed for space; who is expected to cater in that little space for many different interests' produces the review; under such conditions, even the most well-intentioned reviewer is 'incapable of taking a fresh impression or of making a dispassionate statement as an old piece of blotting paper on a post office counter' (*CDB*: 133, 137). Many of Woolf's contemporaries, however, were making or augmenting their livings doing this sort of journalism – journalism written 'weekly . . . daily . . . shortly' for the diversion of tired commuters – including such writers as Rebecca West, Rose Macaulay and Winifred Holtby.[17] Woolf's determined and successful apprenticeship of short and frequent book reviewing, combined with her inheritance and Bloomsbury connections, secured her access to prestigious and commodious periodicals. This access freed her from the more offhand piece-work of light newspaper columns, those illegitimate cousins to the *belles-lettres* essays and 'essay-like reviews and review-like essays' Woolf produced from the late 1910s onwards.

Modernism and journalism, little magazines and 'quality' outlets

Woolf's critiques of the press none the less place her in step with fellow modernists, and many other cultural commentators, in reproducing the cultural narrative of journalistic decline. Such neo-Arnoldian commentaries typically see mass journalism as contributing to intellectual decline, threatening British traditions of rational self-governance, and imperiling the future of literature, whether by upholding lowbrow or bourgeois aesthetic standards or by disseminating a truncated, imprecise language of catch-words and stock phrases. Mass journalism was thus a useful rhetorical enemy for various modernist projects (estrangement, revitalisation of the language and others). Woolf's particular insight in these discussions lies in her emphasis on material conditions: the lack of time and space facing the journalist in Woolf's 'The Modern Essay' and 'Reviewing' are analogous to the lack of private space and uninterrupted time decried so famously in *A Room of One's Own*. But if Woolf's critiques are broadly in step with her modernist contemporaries, modernist interactions with journalism varied widely. As Karen Leick (2008) has shown, as modernism became an identifiable cultural phenomenon, it was very much 'covered' by the mainstream press on both sides of the Atlantic. Modernists, in their own publication and self-promotion strategies, largely avoided mass periodicals of the *Daily Mail* or *Tit-Bits* variety.[18] As scholars have been making increasingly clear in recent years, however, just as no monolithic 'modernism' existed in these years, so there was no easily generalised 'modernist' attitude towards the *fin-de-siécle* revolutions in print. Mark Morrisson, for instance, has traced an early optimism towards the innovations in periodical publishing and advertising in the 1910s, and describes such celebrated modernist 'little magazines' as the *Egoist*, *Little Review*, *Blast* and *The Masses* as varying responses to, and practices of, modern publicity (Morrisson 2000). A journal such as *Blast* thus becomes for Morrisson, despite its pugnacious opposition to the mainstream, an artefact reliant on the visual and technical innovations of modern print culture. Modernist little magazines were simultaneously rejections *of* mass and bourgeois journalism and radical experiments *in journalism*.

Woolf's success in gaining access to prestigious and relatively high-circulation (if decidedly not *mass*) periodicals largely kept her on the sidelines of these experiments in radical publicity. While the *Egoist* was publishing early chapters of *Ulysses* and declaring its hostility to the public taste, Woolf was publishing almost exclusively in the *Times Literary Supplement*, whose 1918 circulation was 29,106 (May 2001: 123). She published few articles in 'little' or identifiably 'modernist' magazines, according to Kirkpatrick and Clarke's bibliography, which identifies four publications in T. S. Eliot's *Criterion* (one of them the lengthy and important 'Character in Fiction') and seventeen in the *Athenaeum* while it was being edited by J. Middleton Murray, which was modernist in content but Edwardian in appearance. Likewise, the *Criterion* was worthy of the monicker 'little' in its circulation (ranging between 600 and 1,000) and its opposition to bourgeois aesthetics, but rather quasi-Edwardian in its muted visual style and *ex cathedra* tone, to say nothing of its establishment financial backing, by the wife of *Daily Mail* magnate Harold Harmsworth, Viscount Rothermere (Harding 2002: 17, 21). By contrast Woolf published at least thirty articles in the *Nation* or (its later incarnation) *Nation and Athenaeum* and twenty-seven in the American *New Republic* – both political, intellectual and prestigious (or, in the contemporary parlance, 'quality') weekly journals – in short, neither mass nor coterie publications, far removed from the quirky insurgence of the little magazines. As Leila Brosnan notes, Woolf largely produced a journalism that she 'characterized as low, but which in the main was written for a cultured audience' (Brosnan 1997: 71). In the *Nation*, *Nation and Athenaeum* and *New Republic*, Woolf appeared in periodicals whose primary *raison d'être* was political rather than commercial – to quote Margaret Beetham, publications more committed to 'making their meanings stick' than to making money (Beetham 1990: 20). The *Nation/Nation and Athenaeum* and the *New Republic* were also subsidised in these years by companies or individuals devoted to their politics – the *Nation* by the Rowntree chocolate company, the *Nation and Athenaeum* by Rowntree's and later by Bloomsbury economist Maynard Keynes, and the *New Republic* by progressivist Dorothy Whitney Straight, wife of industrialist Willard Straight.

By far the leading host to Woolf's journalism, however – from early short notices to ambitious essays – was the *Times Literary Supplement*, where Woolf's intermittent, thirty-six-year, somewhat fractious relationship with editor Bruce Richmond produced no fewer than 289 contributions. A large majority of these appeared in what Jeanne Dubino and Beth Daugherty have separately referred to as Woolf's period of apprenticeship: 113 were published before 1916, and another 140 by 1920, according to Kirkpatrick and Clarke's bibliography. The *TLS* was of course a property of the London *Times*, held in these years by the Northcliffe/Harmsworth combine, built on the colossal success of the downmarket *Daily Mail*. Despite these lowbrow associations it was widely perceived as the leading literary periodical in Britain (Kaufmann 138). T.S. Eliot, upon securing a commitment from Richmond in 1919 to accept his articles regularly, and to give him the leading article occasionally, wrote to his mother that, 'This is the highest honour possible in the critical world of literature, and we are pleased' (Eliot 1990: 337). One cannot overestimate the importance of Woolf's relationship with this prestigious, financially sound organ. Dubino traces Woolf's development from 'book reviewer to literary critic' in her writing at the *TLS* from 1904 to 1916, and Daugherty suggests that Richmond gave Woolf the space to develop her aesthetic principles and, once he was confident in her abilities, the freedom to write on canonical authors, which from 1909 on she often did in front-page, leading articles.[19]

More than half of Woolf's journalism thus appeared in the 'quality' *Nation/Nation and Athenaeum*, *New Republic* and *Times Literary Supplement*: well-established, intellectual periodicals that were more culturally central and on firmer financial ground – whether via healthy circulations, strong financial backing or a combination of these – than the little magazines. While her contributions to more commercial magazines such as *Vogue* and *Good Housekeeping* have garnered attention recently, they represent exceptions to Woolf's fairly consistent practice of publishing for a relatively small number of journals of recognised quality. By contrast, her contemporaries West and Macaulay published in a much wider range of outlets, West ranging from *Blast* to the six-figure-circulation *Evening Standard*, Macaulay from the feminist *Time and Tide* to the *Daily Mail*. Woolf's reliance on this fairly narrow range of periodicals, where she could count on relatively copious space and highly educated, intellectual editors (Leonard Woolf among them) created the material conditions that enabled the art of Woolf's journalism, though most literary critics have had as much difficulty yoking the words 'art' and 'journalism' as Woolf herself did.

The art of journalism?

In 'How It Strikes a Contemporary', the closing essay of *The Common Reader*, Woolf suggests that her generation is replete with 'reviewers' but lacking in a 'critic' (*CR1*: 233). In making this distinction, Woolf reiterates a contemporary binary (critic/reviewer) that aligns with related binaries (literature/journalism, essay/review). These binaries are subsets of the larger distinction between art and commerce and, as Brake as shown, products of the *fin-de-siécle* establishment of English studies.[20] Literary scholars reliably reproduced these binaries for decades, even as they called attention to Woolf's essays. Brosnan's *Reading Virginia Woolf's Essays and Journalism* reproduces the distinction in its title even as it usefully historicises and theorises the relationship between the terms 'essay' and 'journalism'. Brosnan refigures the terms to denote not a qualitative distinction between two 'types of non-fiction' but rather to signify Brosnan's own 'difference in approach to the one body of [Woolf's] non-fiction' (Brosnan 1997: 5). Viewing Woolf's periodical writings as essays, Brosnan writes, allows a focus on their deep linguistic structure, enabling a post-structural, feminist analysis sensitive to 'the internal operations of language and genre' (ibid.: 9). Viewing the contributions as journalism, on the other hand, sees them as 'intimately linked to the public domain' and allows us to resituate Woolf 'in relation to the culture of her time' (ibid.: 10). What remains to be done, perhaps, is analysis that synthesises these two approaches, looking at the mutually determining relations between the material conditions of journalism and the linguistic artefacts it both hosts and creates. Such an analysis would recognise that the 'essay' as a genre is no more independent of its periodical history than the Victorian novel is of the three-decker form, and it would probe that relationship. Differences do exist between Woolf's early notices and reviews and her mature essays, but they are all also journalism.

In the introduction to their splendid *Virginia Woolf and the Essay*, Beth Carole Rosenberg and Jeanne Dubino discuss the decades of critical neglect of Woolf's essays, which they attribute in part to the relative ascendancy of T. S. Eliot's essays. But this neglect may owe more to the literary-historical neglect of periodical writing; one might press further and ask why Eliot's essays have garnered more scholarly support not only than Woolf's but than *anyone else's* in the period. Perhaps Eliot was more effective than anyone else at distancing his essays from their periodical births and figuring himself as a cultural guardian in opposition to the degradations of print. Rosenberg and Dubino note, too, that the essay has proven elusive as a genre, 'polyphonic and difficult to describe in absolute terms' (1996: 11). This fact may also stem primarily from the essay's journalistic nature – its reliance on the contingencies of column space, editorial interference (or non-interference) and periodicals' varied constructions of their audiences – all conditions that vary over time and from individual case to case. That Woolf's essays received very little scholarly attention until the mid-1990s speaks volumes about the historical neglect of journalistic writing by the academic field of English, about what Erickson calls the 'hierarchy of written formats' (Erickson 1996: 12) Brake the 'subjugation' of periodical literature to Literature (Brake 1994: 2) – a hierarchy and a subjugation that Woolf, like so many of her contemporaries, helped to construct.

Notes

Heartfelt thanks to Beth Rigel Daugherty and Deborah M. Mix for their careful commentary on drafts of this chapter.

1. Kirkpatrick and Clarke's bibliography lists more than 500 contributions to periodicals, and remains an essential guide to scholars, who have continued to discover essays since its publication in 1997. Andrew McNeillie's projected six-volume edition of the complete essays, for the Hogarth Press and Harcourt Brace, is to be completed by Stuart Clarke (vols 5 and 6).

2. I will henceforth be quoting from the manuscript of the speech, reprinted by Mitchell Leaska in his edition of *The Pargiters*.

3. See Collier 2002; Zwerdling 1992; Snaith 2000.

4. Brosnan offers the most complete analysis of Woolf's attitudes towards journalism; see especially ch.3. For work specifically on book reviewing, see Lee 1989; Collier 2006: ch.3.

5. Woolf's years of apprenticeship are certainly the least studied of her career, and much work remains to be done on them. Early writings are available in *A Passionate Apprentice* and *Essays of Virginia Woolf*, vols 1 and 2; Dubino (1996) tracks Woolf's development 'from reviewer to critic'. Beth Rigel Daugherty is nearing completion of a book-length study of the apprenticeship years.

6. The 'common reader' has been the focus of a great deal of discussion, raising as it does the complex question of Woolf's class politics. For the most nuanced recent defence of Woolf's politics via the 'common reader', See Cuddy-Keane 2003, especially ch.3, and, for another view, McManus 2008. For a summary of previous criticism that deals with the concept, see Collier 2006: 217–18 n.24.

7. I use the term in the sense derived from Habermas' 1989 and the body of theory that has been generated in response to it. In simplified form, his 'public sphere' denotes the cultural space in which rational deliberation takes place through the exercise of free speech. In Habermas's influential account, an idealised bourgeois public sphere existed in the English eighteenth-century setting, located in the coffee houses, clubs, and newspapers in which 'private citizens' debated matters of public import in a disinterested search for truth. These disinterested citizens could then 'speak truth to power' and influence governance. Habermas identifies a decline from this idealised moment to a twentieth-century pseudo-public sphere marked by manufactured consensus, distraction, hyper-mediation and competition between distinct interests. While many critics have qualified Habermas's model, a sense of the public sphere in decline was widespread in Woolf's time, even if the term itself was not available. For Woolf criticism that deals specifically

with the concept, see Froula 2005, Cuddy-Keane 2003, Snaith 2000 and McManus 2008.

8. Mitchell Leaska noted the link between 'Professions for Women', *Three Guineas* and *The Years* when he published the manuscript of the 'Professions for Women' speech in his edition of *The Pargiters* (Woolf 1977). That volume contains the essay-chapters that Woolf envisioned as alternating with fiction chapters in a novel to be called *The Pargiters*. Woolf ultimately split the novel into the essay *Three Guineas* and the novel *The Years*. See also McVicker 2003–4, who similarly sees 'Professions for Women' as a turning point.

9. See Pawlowski 2003 on Woolf's scrapbooking of news articles for *Three Guineas*.

10. Hussey 1996 offers an excellent summary of opposed responses to *Three Guineas*. See Snaith 2000 on questions of publicity and privacy, and ch.5 specifically on *Three Guineas*.

11. See Beer 1996, Snaith 2000, Dick and Millar 2006 and Westman 2006, all of whom see *Between the Acts* as engaged in questions of authorial control and readerly agency.

12. Quoted in Shattock 2008.

13. Laurel Brake writes that despite Stephen's short stint as a professor at Cambridge and his work on the *Dictionary of National Biography*, Stephen's articles demonstrate decisively that he 'considered himself a journalist' (1994: 3).

14. Rose Macaulay was one of several writers to contribute on this topic to the *Daily Mail* (25 August 1928: 10).

15. Bagehot quoted in Brake 1994: 4. 'Rambling Round Evelyn' is reprinted in *CR*1: 78–86.

16. Thanks to Beth Rigel Daugherty for pointing these out to me.

17. Macaulay and West's practice of this sort of journalism did not mean that they were sanguine about the media landscape. It did inflect their criticisms differently. See Collier 2006.

18. The youthful Virginia Stephen and the youthful James Joyce both submitted material, unsuccessfully, to *Tit-Bits*.

19. Rosenberg and Dubino 1996: 25–39; Daugherty 2008.

20. See Wexler 1997, especially 'Introduction: Art v. Money'.

Works Cited and Further Reading

Beer, Gillian (1996) *Virginia Woolf: The Common Ground*, Ann Arbor: University of Michigan Press.

Beetham, Margaret (1990) 'Towards a Theory of the Periodical as Publishing Genre'. *Investigating Victorian Journalism*, ed. Laurel Brake, Aled Jones and Lionel Madden, New York: Palgrave, pp. 19–32.

Brake, Laurel (1994) *Subjugated Knowledges: Journalism, Gender, and Literature*, New York: New York University Press.

Brosnan, Leila (1997) *Reading Virginia Woolf's Essays and Journalism*, Edinburgh: Edinburgh University Press.

Collier, Patrick (2002) 'Virginia Woolf in the Pay of Booksellers: Privacy, Publicity, Professionalism, *Orlando*', *Twentieth Century Literature*, 48.4 (Winter): 363–92.

—— (2006) *Modernism on Fleet Street*, Burlington, VT and Aldershot Hants: Ashgate.

Cuddy-Keane (2003) *Virginia Woolf, the Intellectual, and the Public Sphere*, Cambridge: Cambridge University Press.

Daugherty, Beth Rigel (2008) 'Virginia Woolf: Book Reviewer,' unpublished conference paper, Eighteenth Annual International Conference on Virginia Woolf, Denver.

Dick, Susan and Mary S. Millar (2006) 'Introduction' in *Between the Acts*, Oxford: Blackwell, pp. xi–liii.

Dubino, Jeanne (1996) 'Virginia Woolf: From Book Reviewer to Literary Critic', in Rosenberg and Dubino 1996: 25–40.

Eliot, T. S (1990) *The Letters of T. S. Eliot* ed. Valerie Eliot, New York, San Diego and London: Harcourt Brace.

Erickson, Lee (1996) *The Economy of Literary Form: English Literature and the Industrialization of Publishing*, Baltimore, MD: Johns Hopkins University Press.

Froula, Christine (2005) *Virginia Woolf and the Bloomsbury Avant-Garde: War, Civilization, Modernity*, New York: Columbia University Press.

Habermas, Jürgen (1989) *Structural Transformation of the Public Sphere: An Inquiry into a Category of Bourgeois Society*, trans Thomas Burger, Cambridge, MA: MIT Press.

Harding, Jason (2002) *The Criterion: Cultural Politics and Periodical Networks in Inter-War Britain*, Oxford: Oxford University Press.

Hussey, Mark (1996) *Virginia Woolf A to Z*, Oxford and New York: Oxford University Press.

Kaufmann, Michael (1996) 'A Modernism of One's Own: Virginia Woolf's *TLS* reviews and Eliotic Modernism', in Rosenberg and Dubino 1996: 137–55.

Kirkpatrick, B. J. and Stuart N. Clarke (1997) *A Bibliography of Virginia Woolf*, Oxford: Clarendon Press.

Lee, Hermione (1989) 'Crimes of Criticism: Virginia Woolf and Literary Journalism' *Grub Street and the Ivory Tower: Literary Journalism and Literary Scholarship from Fielding to the Internet*, ed. and introd. Jeremy Treglown and Bridget Bennet, Oxford: Clarendon Press, pp. 112–34.

—— (1997) *Virginia Woolf*, New York: Knopf.

Leick, Karen (2008) 'Popular Modernism: Little Magazines and the American Daily Press', *PMLA*, 123.1 (January): 125–39.

May, Derwent (2001) *Critical Times: The History of the Times Literary Supplement*, London: HarperCollins.

McManus, Patricia (2008) 'The "Offensiveness" of Virginia Woolf: From a Moral to a Political Reading', *Woolf Studies Annual*, 14: 92–138.

McVicker, Jeanette (2003–4) 'Six Essays on London Life: A History of Dispersal', *Woolf Studies Annual*, 9 (2003): 143–65 and 10 (2004): 141–72.

Morrisson, Mark (2000) *The Public Face of Modernism*, Madison: University of Wisconsin Press.

Pawlowski, Merry (2003) 'Exposing Masculine Spectacle: Virginia Woolf's Press Clippings for *Three Guineas* as Contemporary Cultural History', *Woolf Studies Annual*, 9: 117–41.

Rosenberg, Beth Carole and Jeanne Dubino (eds) (1996) *Virginia Woolf and the Essay*, New York: St Martin's Press.

Shattock, Joanne (2008) 'The Press and Nineteenth-century Literary Culture', unpublished paper from Nineteenth-century Serials Edition conference, 13 May. British Library.

Snaith, Anna (2000) *Virginia Woolf: Public and Private Negotiations*, Basingstoke: Palgrave Macmillan.

Westman, Karin (2006) '"For Her Generation the Newspaper Was a Book": Media, Mediation, and Oscillation in Virginia Woolf's *Between the Acts*', *Journal of Modern Literature*, 29.2 (Winter): 1–18.

Wexler, Joyce Piell (1997) *Who Paid for Modernism?*, Fayetteville: University of Arkansas Press.

Williams, Kevin (1998) *Get Me a Murder a Day! A History of Mass Communication in Britain*, London: Arnold.

Woolf, Virginia (1979) 'Anon', ed. Brenda Silver, *Twentieth Century Literature*, 25.3–4 (Fall/Winter): 382–98.

Zwerdling, Alex (1986) *Virginia Woolf and the Real World*, Berkeley: University of California Press.

—— (1992) 'The Common Reader, the Coterie, and the Audience of One', *Virginia Woolf Miscellanies. Proceedings of the First Annual Conference on Virginia Woolf*, ed. Mark Hussey and Vara Neverow-Turk, New York: Pace University Press, pp. 7–9.

19

VIRGINIA WOOLF: RADIO, GRAMOPHONE, BROADCASTING

Pamela L. Caughie

'H ow do you start thinking in terms of sound?' This question, asked about broadcast drama by reviewer Grace Wyndham Goldie in a 1938 issue of *The Listener*, the journal of the BBC, articulates the challenge of this chapter. Long accustomed to and trained in methodologies of close reading, and given the predominance of visually oriented language in our critical discourse, how indeed do we, as scholars, begin thinking about modernist writing in terms of sound? Typically modernity and modernist literature have been conceived in terms of *looking on*, not *listening in*. In his classic treatise on modernity and *flânerie*, for example, Walter Benjamin writes that interpersonal relationships in modern urban life 'are characterised by a markedly greater emphasis on the use of the eyes than on that of the ears' (Benjamin 1968: 191). Woolf's *flâneuse* in 'Street Haunting' (1930) becomes, upon entering the street, 'a central oyster of perceptiveness, an enormous eye' (*DM*: 22). And yet, rarely noticed alongside those fashionable public personae of the modern era, the *flâneur* and the spectator – at once created by and figures for the ocular modality of modernity – emerged their aural counterpart, the self-effacing and private listener, a new cultural identity in the 1920s and 1930s. The emblematic date for literary modernism, 1922, marks not just the publication of *Jacob's Room*, *Ulysses* and *The Waste Land* but also the first BBC broadcast. How, then, can we think about *sound* in relation to the *writings* of Virginia Woolf, especially when, as Melba Cuddy-Keane writes in the most comprehensive treatment of Woolf and sound technologies to date, '[modernist] technology has indeed *produced* our current understanding of sound' (Cuddy-Keane 2000: 70)? The sensory experience of hearing and the cultural practice of listening are themselves historical. The challenge, then, is not only writing about sound in a critical vocabulary that has privileged sight, but trying to represent in writing a phenomenon (sound) that is inseparable from the very technologies that produce it. Modernist scholarship and Woolf criticism have recently begun to face this challenge.

In their 2008 essay, 'The New Modernist Studies', Douglas Mao and Rebecca L. Walkowitz describe current transformations in modernist studies in terms of its expansion in 'temporal, spatial, and vertical directions', the latter referring to the erosion of boundaries between high art and mass culture (Mao and Walkowitz 2008: 737–8). 'Recent studies', they assert, 'locate literary modernism in a rhetorical arena transformed by media's capacity to disseminate words and images in less time, across bigger distances, and to greater numbers of people than ever before' (ibid.: 743). As the authors go on to point out, it is not that modernist scholarship has hitherto neglected mass culture as an important historical development in the early twentieth century, but recent studies in particular attend to 'how modernist writers absorbed and remade forms of mass culture rather than merely disparaging them' (ibid.: 743–4). New scholarship focuses less on what modernists have to say about technology and mass culture than on the mutually shaping relations among technologies, mass culture and modernist writing. Sound technologies, as Lisa Gitelman writes in her important study of phonography, 'had to make sense within an ambient climate of textual and other representational practices' (Gitelman 1999: 1), and modernist literature within an ambient climate of sound technologies. Two of the four books that Mao and Walkowitz cite as examples of this new 'vertical' expansion, Todd Avery's *Radio Modernism* (2006) and Timothy Campbell's *Wireless Writing in the Age of Marconi* (2006), take as their subject what Tim Armstrong terms 'sonic modernity', attesting to the ascendancy of aurality in the new modernist studies (ibid.: 743; Armstrong 2007: 1). This scholarship, including my essay here, is anchored by the important historical work of cultural critics such as Paddy Scannell and David Cardiff (1991), David Laing (1991), Douglas Kahn and Gregory Whitehead (1992), Lisa Gitelman (1999) and Jonathan Sterne (2003).

As I write in the introduction to *Virginia Woolf in the Age of Mechanical Reproduction*, an analysis of the relations among technology, mass culture and literary modernism proves particularly fruitful for Woolf studies (Caughie 2000: xx). Woolf wrote about sound technologies – such as the telephone, the gramophone and the radio – in her novels, essays and personal writings; she gave three broadcasts at the BBC and wrote about those she listened to in her diaries and letters; she explored in her critical essays and broadcasts the social and aesthetic implications of emerging mass culture and the increasing literacy and democracy fostered by mass communications, especially broadcasting; and, she experimented with narrative techniques that were responsive to new technologies. Her modernist experimental prose, as I will demonstrate here, helped to make readers receptive to the sound technologies that also inspired those techniques. But just what were modernists listening to, and what kind of listeners were they?

A Brief History of Sound Technology

At the 2008 conference of the Association for Recorded Sound Collections, audio historian David Giovannoni played what he and fellow researchers claim is the first recording of the human voice, a presumably female voice singing *'Au clair de la lune, Pierrot répondit'*, though the distorted quality of the ten-second recording renders the words no more decipherable than the gender to the untutored ear. The recording was made in April 1860 in Paris on a 'pho-nautograph' invented by Édouard-Léon Scott de Martinville (aka Leon Scott) in 1857, twenty years before Thomas Edison patented the phonograph (1877). Sound waves captured by a horn attached to a diaphragm vibrated a stiff brush that inscribed the pattern of waves on smoked glass or blackened paper. Scott wanted to produce a *visual* inscription of human speech but had not yet conceptualised sound as something that could be *audibly* reproduced; that would be Edison's contribution when he replaced Scott's paper with a more pliable and durable substance. Yet the recovery of that early inscription foregrounds the historicity of listening itself. Now that researchers have discovered a technique for playing those etchings, we can literally hear a text sing.

Edison also initially conceived the phonograph as a textual device, intended to record voices for the purposes of dictation. 'Phonograph' and 'gramophone' (the latter catching on in Britain as the generic name) derive from the Greek for 'sound-writing'. Yet the wavy lines etched on tinfoil (and by 1887, on wax cylinders) rivalled the stenographer or the typewriter in that the phonograph could capture accent and intonation. The audio threatened to usurp the textual as people began to imagine sending voice recordings in place of letters. Given the challenge of writing about sound that we face today, it is ironic that in its inception, sound technology was seen as a form of writing, setting the stage for a decades-long debate, waged in the pages of *The Listener* through the 1930s, over whether recording and listening would replace writing and reading, a possibility fictionalised in Aldous Huxley's *Brave New World* (1932) where the wireless takes the place of literature. The very newness of sound (odd as that may sound) is evidenced by the fact that conceptually as well as linguistically the textual and the visual imagination prevailed in the development of sound technology.[1]

Not until 1887 when Edison replaced tinfoil with waxed cylinders and Emil Berliner patented his gramophone (which differed from the phonograph in using lateral grooves and hard discs rather than vertical grooves and wax cylinders) did sound become a form of mass communication as the new technology became available to the general public and, over the next two decades, increasingly affordable. From the turn of the century, record sales began to exceed sales of sheet music for the piano, hitherto the dominant medium for listening in the home, as the talking machine evolved into a musical device (Laing 1991). 'In the decades that coincided with the rise of modernism (1910–1920)', writes Bonnie Kime Scott, 'records became a mass medium' (Scott 2000: 97). Hardly anyone has remarked that the first mention of the gramophone in Woolf's diaries dates from 1922 and associates the machine with a middle-class lifestyle, suggesting it had become a commonplace: 'Poor young man! [Ralph Partridge] For really he was never meant for intellectual whirlpools. No: he was meant for punts in backwaters, gramophones, ices, flirtations, a pretty wife, large family, & interests in the City' (*D2*: 185). By 1922 sound had been commodified, 'as much an article of commerce as a barrel of sugar' (Meadowcroft 1922: 699), and the ubiquitous symbol of sound recording, the dog with his ear to the horn of a gramophone, first acquired by the London Gramophone Company in 1898 and used as a trademark by Berliner from 1900, 'assail[ed] the eye in all the shopping centers of the world', as Claude McKay writes in his 1929 novel, *Banjo*. Sound technology, like modernist writing, disrupted notions of temporality and spatiality. Voices conveyed instantaneously across vast distances by telephone and later radio waves now penetrated domestic space through the gramophone and the wireless, making listening at once a private activity and a (mass) cultural practice.

It was Theodor Adorno, curiously enough, the cultural critic most strongly identified with an anti-technology stance, who saw early on the cultural significance of sound reproduction. As Thomas Levin writes, Adorno, in his early essay on the gramophone, 'The Curves of the Needle' (1928), reflects on a range of responses to gramophone recordings – psychological (the kind of pleasure it provides), auditory (its effect on hearing), social (its form of reception), and commercial (its reification of music as a commodity) – but most crucially on the ways in which 'the mechanical mediation of the gramophone transforms in various and subtle ways the events it records' (Adorno, quoted in Levin 1990: 30). Significantly in terms of the history of this technology, sound, initially understood as materialised by technology, is, forty years later, transfigured by it. Adorno attends to 'the very meaning of mechanization', not just to the gramophone as a medium (Levin 1990: 29). Writing in 1929 on what he terms '*Mechanische Musik*' ('mechanical music'), Adorno declares:

> the mechanical presentation of music today is of contemporary relevance in a deeper sense than merely being currently available as a new technological means. To put it another way, this position arises out of the conviction that the availability of means corresponds to an availability of consciousness and that the current historical state of the [art] works themselves to a large extent requires them to be presented mechanically. (Adorno, quoted in Levin 1990: 29)

Aural receptivity, or auscultation, is organised differently by sound technology so that *how* we hear, not just *what* we hear, changes. Hearing becomes historical, not just physiological; listening becomes technique. Listening can now be repeated, interrupted, slowed down, speeded up and experienced apart from the spatio-temporal performance itself.

A new form of listening entails a change in the concept of sound itself. 'Phonautograph' means, literally, sound writing *itself* (the subtitle of Scott's 1878 book); thus the term serves to undercut or de-emphasise the very machine that is (re)producing the voice. 'Phonautograph' suggests that the sound is literally *there*, textually inscribed on the blackened paper, and thus, technically, is not a reproduction. Embedded in Scott's nomenclature is the germ of the debates that sound technology aroused over the relative value of – and the very distinction between – original and copy, live and recorded, authentic and mechanically produced, sincerity and fakery, reproduction and representation. The concept of 'sound writing itself' animates sound, eliminating the human agent, an understanding graphically presented in the image of the dog listening to 'his master's voice' as well as anecdotes, cartoons, photographs and advertisements in which people mistake the talking machine for a person talking, the mimetic representation for the real thing.[2] As I see it, that slippage is precisely the achievement of sound technology; it is not a mistake but what makes it work. In that slippage lies the key to a new, modernist understanding of music, poetry, realism, indeed, of art itself.

Adorno understood the gramophone record as an allegory for art itself. A passage from Levin's article on Adorno is worth quoting at length:

> The record eliminates the subject (and the concomitant economy of intentionality) from the musical inscription. [...] Along with the subjectivity of the interpreter(s), the record also eradicates the spatio-temporal uniqueness of the performance. It becomes a citation or, one might say, an allegory of a phenomenal moment [...], that is, a present marker of a past event which is radically past: determinate yet irrevocable. [...] The curves of the needle are [...] materializations (gramme) of phenomenal events (phone-) which allegorise them in the process. The gramophone record may in fact be [...] an allegory of art itself: [...] artworks only become 'true,' fragments of the true language, once life has left them; perhaps even only through their decline and that of art itself. (Levin 1990: 41–2)

Far from being nostalgic for the 'real thing', Adorno understood acoustic mediation as a thing itself, a materialisation with its own form that needed to be exploited and which was 'even *superior* to the live performance' (Levin 1990: 39, 44). 'The technologically mediated [sound]', writes Adorno, 'gains a corporeal proximity which the immediacy of the live performance often denies to those whose goal is a concentrated reception' (Adorno, quoted ibid.: 44). Such 'corporeal proximity' comes, paradoxically, with the removal of the listener from other bodies as the listening experience moves into the privacy of domestic space. With the gramophone as with radio, listening, and listening in, allow for greater intimacy than looking on.

Mrs Dalloway, begun in 1922, figures in its very narrative form this kind of intimacy-in-isolation. Sounds in this novel connect characters, even those unknown to one another, even when they are unconscious of 'the invincible thread of sound' that binds them to others (*MD*: 82, 102, 127, 128), as the 'tick tick tick of the gramophone' binds the audience together in *Between the Acts* (*BTA*: 154). Throughout *Mrs Dalloway*, narrative transitions from one character to another are effected through sounds.

Big Ben struck the half-hour.

How extraordinary it was, strange, yes, touching, to see the old lady (they had been neighbours ever so many years) move away from the window, as if she were attached to that sound, that string. Gigantic as it was, it had something to do with her. Down, down, into the midst of ordinary things the finger fell making the moment solemn. She was forced, so Clarissa imagined, by that sound, to move, to go – but where? (*MD*: 127)

The words 'Big Ben struck' narrate sound; the phrase 'the leaden circles dissolved in the air' (*MD*: 94) materialises it. Sounds do not just connect people but envelop them. Riding an omnibus up Fleet Street, Elizabeth becomes immersed in the soundscape:

She liked the geniality, sisterhood, motherhood, brotherhood of this uproar. It seemed to her good. The noise was tremendous [. . .].

[T]his voice, pouring endlessly, year in year out, would take whatever it might be; this vow; this van; this life; this procession, would wrap them all about and carry them on [. . .]. (*MD*: 138)

Kate Flint cites an earlier scene in which Clarissa attentively listens to household sounds – 'the swish of a mop; . . . a loudness when the front door opened; a voice repeating a message in the basement' (*MD*: 38) – separating herself from the 'acoustic environment' to assemble 'that diamond shape, that single person' (ibid.: 38), that is, 'her own sense of individuation' (Flint 2003: 191). That listening enables connection (as with Elizabeth) and individuation (as with Clarissa) itself denotes the new form of listening shaped by sound technologies. Aeroplanes, motor cars, clocks, street singers, gramophones – the resonant world of *Mrs Dalloway* creates a sonic experience that mimes the aural sensitivity of the newly auscultated culture it dramatises. The mutual influence of 'sonic modernity' (particularly, the gramophone) and modernist writing is captured by Harold Nicolson in a 1931 broadcast when, in discussing how modernist writing changes reading practices, he credits modernism with 'driving new grooves through the brain' (*Listener*, 6.144, 14 October 1931).

A New Cultural Persona, the 'Listener'

After 1922, that 'voice, pouring endlessly, year in and year out' might well be the voice of radio. Broadcasting, the wireless transmission of sound and voice to multiple receivers through regularised programming, began in 1920 in the US and two years later in Britain as a means of connecting dispersed populations and isolated individuals to one another and to the cultural life of the nation. As with the gramophone, broadcasting has a long history, beginning with James Clerk Maxwell's theory of electromagnetic waves (1860s) and its realisation by Heinrich Rudolf Hertz, who produced radio waves in the 1880s, and Sir Oliver Lodge, who used those waves to send Morse code messages in the 1890s.

Guglielmo Marconi, however, is credited with inventing radio. Although voices had been transmitted across distances since 1902, Marconi's company produced the first wireless broadcast on 15 June 1920 when the Australian opera singer, Dame Nellie Melba, was heard across Europe and North America (Marconi, 'How the Wireless Began', *Listener*, 6.142, 30 September 1931). Building on the technology of the telephone and telegraphy, wireless broadcasting was less a technological revolution, like the phonograph, than a social revolution. A modern mass public dates from the inception of broadcasting (*Listener*, 16.392, 15 July 1936).

That mass public coalesces in that singular construction 'the listener', a figure associated with the radio more than the gramophone. 'The ontological fact of radio's existence', writes Todd Avery, 'brought into being a new kind of audience, the listener, whose emergence coincided with the moment of modernism's heyday in the 1920s and 1930s' (Avery 2006: 8). Phrases such as 'listening in', 'tuning out', and 'wirelessing on' came into use to reference this new experience of mass communication that was at once collective (by definition broadcasts have multiple receivers) and individual (broadcasts are typically experienced in private spaces, often alone). 'The great pleasure of the Broadcasting to me', writes Woolf, 'is that I can sit at home & conduct The Meistersinger myself' (*D*4: 107). 'Listening in' was proclaimed, especially in the pages of *The Listener*, as an *active* form of listening: highly attentive to technique; sensitive to nuances of voice; selective in tuning in certain kinds of programmes and tuning out distractions, including the sound of the technology itself. Listening became a skill, producing a heightened critical awareness and independence of thought. Indeed, the listener would seem to be a manifestation of Woolf's common reader, the collective persona of a changing demographics produced, in part, by mass communication. Radio 'gave voice to the previously voiceless', as Avery, drawing on Scannell, puts it (Avery 2006: 27), creating a new sense of both the private citizen and the public sphere. Indeed, one might oppose the 'wireless class' to what Woolf calls the 'tower class' in her essay, 'The Leaning Tower', insofar as broadcasting was credited with bringing about a 'classless and towerless world' (*M*: 151).

From Leon Scott to Thomas Edison to the BBC, sound technology has been perceived as a social levelling and cultural unifying phenomenon that crosses class, regional and national boundaries. Scott conceived hearing and speaking as a new form of literacy; Edison promoted the phonograph for its ability to bring opera to remote and poor populations; the BBC saw the formation of a national identity not just as the promise of wireless technology but as its moral mission (Levin 1990: 36; Gitelman 1999: 137; Avery 2006: 7). John Reith, Director General of the BBC from 1922 to 1938, discerned in the radio audience a new kind of public, not mass culture as one unified and mechanised body thinking alike, but a collective sense of a shared national identity and moral purpose. To foster a common and culturally literate public, the BBC produced programmes that involved and addressed diverse social groups: workers, politicians, artists, scientists, clergymen, women, the young and the unemployed all took their turn at the microphone, were published in *The Listener*, and listened in from home. A 1929 series, for example, 'My Day's Work', featured broadcasts by miners, dock workers, sewer workers and telephone operators; a 1933 series broadcast the 'Memoirs of the Unemployed'; a 1935 series featured younger broadcasters ('Youth Looks Ahead'); and in a 1937 broadcast a taxi driver gave advice on his favourite books (*Listener*, 18.455, 29 September 1937). Woolf's advice in *Three Guineas* to the daughters of educated men might well have been modelled on the BBC's policy: 'Find out new ways of approaching "the public"; single it into separate people instead of massing it into one monster, gross in body, feeble in mind' (*TG*: 98). For all her disparaging remarks about the BBC, Woolf too valued the kind of independence of thought that Reith said listening in fostered, and used her broadcasts as one way to forge 'bonds of sympathetic and coopera-tive union' with 'the "common" culture of readers' (Avery 2006: 41).

What Woolf has to say *on* the BBC (on the air) suggests their shared desire to form a common culture and to shape the tastes and values of the listen-ing public; what she says *about* the BBC suggests that their tastes and values differed markedly. In her broadcasts as in her essays, Woolf urged people to read widely and indiscriminately, in borrowed books and cheap editions, and to write for themselves: 'Write daily; write freely; but let us always compare what we have written with what the great writers have written', she advises in 'The Leaning Tower'; for 'Literature [like the airwaves] is no one's private ground; literature is common ground' (*M*: 153–4). Sounds like the BBC. Yet for Woolf, such independence of mind, conceived as trespassing (ibid.: 154), serves to elude the control of the very class that ran the BBC: the professional middle class. Many intellectuals, such as George Orwell, felt that the wireless did more than cross boundaries through diverse programming; it erased them. The increasing accessibility of radio, through better transmission and decreas-ing cost, meant that the item itself and the luxury of listening were no longer class markers. Even if the wireless did not produce that mythic monster Woolf spurns, a public with the same tastes and desires that thinks alike, a form of social levelling did produce, in Orwell's words, 'people of indiscriminate social class' (quoted in Scannell and Cardiff 1991: 367). Like Orwell, Woolf associates this new class with the wireless and the suburbs, but unlike him she identifies this social group with the producers, not the consumers, of broadcasting. The listener Woolf addresses retains its lowbrow identity, with all the vitality that term connotes for her.

Woolf's criticism of the BBC is not that it erodes class distinctions, but that it breeds a new monster, the middlebrow. She characterises Hilda Matheson, Director of Talks from 1926 to 1931, as 'the earnest middle-class intellectual' (*D3*: 239), the kind Woolf satirised in the Cambridge professors (*JR*: 40) and Sir William Bradshaw (*MD*: 94–5). In her 1932 essay 'Middlebrow', she nick-names the BBC 'the Betwixt and Between Company', her phrase for the middle-brow who is 'neither one thing nor the other' (*DM*: 184, 179). Listening and speaking became skills propagated through broadcasting schools, radio discussion groups, and how-to manuals advertised in *The Listener*, just as reading and writing were taught by middlebrow professors, practices that Woolf deplored. Why, Woolf wonders, do lowbrows buy middlebrow books, attend middlebrow lectures, or let middlebrows teach them how to write: 'Why, I ask (not of course on the wireless), are you [lowbrows] so damnably modest?' (*DM*: 182). And why, I ask, 'not . . . on the wireless'? Clearly Woolf blamed middlebrows, especially the BBC, for creating strife between highbrows and lowbrows (the BBC had staged such a debate in a broadcast aired on 15 April 1930), and she looked to lowbrows themselves to 'trespass' on literary culture (*M*: 153). More to the point, however, the aside reveals the ideological dilemma of broadcasting. In this essay Woolf professes to speak to lowbrows as 'friends', privately over muffins not over the mass medium of radio. And yet she used that very medium to form an intimate connection with the common listener and, particularly in her 1927 broadcast with Leonard, to embrace a more diverse population of cultural producers and consumers. Bloomsbury's broadcasts, Avery claims, show how 'highbrows challenged the ideological foundations of an emergent mass communications medium while embracing the medium itself in order to shape the mass culture of which radio was quickly becoming an integral part' (Avery 2006: 36). Thus, the self-styled highbrow, Virginia Woolf, found herself, we might say, betwixt and between. Using that medium ran the risk of colluding with middlebrows, as she slyly acknowledges in her 1937 BBC talk, 'Craftsmanship', when she says that words, the subject of her broadcast, 'hate making money' and 'being lectured about in public' (*DM*: 206). Not to use the medium, however, risked relinquishing to the middle-class professionals 'the most potent engine for expression and communication [. . .]' in the history of civilization', at least according to the BBC (*Listener*, 6.137, 26 August 1931). If it would be an exaggeration to say, as this *Listener* editorial does, that through broadcasting, 'the ear has returned to power', certainly a new public was being formed through the ear. Woolf wanted to connect with that public, not en masse – 'the same sort of people living the same sort of lives', as she describes the middle class in her broadcast debate with Leonard ('Are Too Many Books Written and Published?', 15 July 1927, BBC National Archives) – but as individuals. Sensitive to the ways in which listening in can create a 'communal BBC dictated feeling' (*D5*: 306), Woolf nonetheless reaches out to the new cultural persona produced by it, the isolated, independent, self-educated listener.

The 'Common Listener'

Impersonal, cosmopolitan, sensitised to the minutiae of everyday life and sensitive to any form of insincerity or trickery, the listener – at least as constructed by the BBC – would also seem to be the ideal audience for the new realism of modernism. Radio immersed the listener in a sonic world so that reality, 'life itself' (Woolf's phrase), was experienced *as experience*, not as image or picture;

reality as metonymic not metaphoric. An example of this new realism is the crab in the bucket at the end of the first chapter of *Jacob's Room*:

> Outside the rain poured down more directly and powerfully as the wind fell in the early hours of the morning. [. . .] The child's bucket was half-full of rain-water; and the opal-shelled crab slowly circled round the bottom, trying with hits weakly legs to climb the steep side; trying again and falling back, and trying again and again. (*JR*: 14)

This detail cries out for an allegorical reading that the narrative denies us. It is what it is: a crab in a bucket.

Similarly, everything in a broadcast carries effects, including the background sounds and the humming of the machinery itself, but not everything *means* something. Woolf infuses her 1922 novel with random sounds – the tick of a clock, the creak of an armchair, snatches of conversation, the boom of the waves – creating the effect of an actuality programme, as does Miss La Trobe in her use of environmental sounds in *Between the Acts*.[3] Although this aurality thickens in her later novels, and narrated sound ('she may hear the cheap clock on the mantelpiece tick, tick, tick' [*JR*: 52]), combines with vitalised sound ('the leaden circles dissolved in the air' [*MD*: 94], 'Chuf, chuf, chuf' [*BTA*: 151]), *Jacob's Room* already prepares the reader to become the listener, especially in its use of 'spatial silence' (Bishop 2004: 31). The blank spaces between passages shape the reading experience much as the silences used within and between broadcasts structure the listening experience. Throughout *The Listener* commentators discuss the strategic use of silence in broadcasting. For Reith, silence between programmes made listeners more discriminate, guarding against a kind of aural numbness that can come from continual broadcasting. But it also serves a functional purpose insofar as silence enables us to discriminate sounds, affects what we hear not just what we think. 'The spaces between [sounds] were as significant as the sounds' (*MD*: 22). Whereas environmental sounds immerse us in a sonic world, spatial silence in *Jacob's Room* as in *Between the Acts* fosters attentive listening, associated in *Mrs Dalloway* with the most acute characters: 'He [Septimus] listened'; 'She [Clarissa] heard'; but Rezia 'heard nothing' and Doris Kilman 'had no ear' (ibid.: 24, 40, 140, 124).

That *Jacob's Room* was published in October 1922, a few weeks before the BBC went on the air, should be enough to caution us against talking about influence as literary scholars have traditionally understood that relationship. Bizarre as it might sound to say that the BBC imitated modernist writers like Woolf, that would be as accurate as claiming that modernists imitated the BBC (though Woolf's 1932 essay, 'A Letter to a Young Poet,' supposedly inspired the BBC series 'To an Unknown Listener' [*L5*: 83]). The fact that the BBC signed off each night with the sound of Big Ben may have led Woolf to sound those chimes throughout her 1925 novel, but we might also speculate that her use of a female voice to animate the lagging chimes of St Margaret's timepiece (*MD*: 49) may have predisposed the Post Office to select a woman (Miss Ethel Cain) as the voice of the first talking clock (*Listener*, 13.326, 10 April 1935). And the BBC's increasing interest in audience surveys in the later 1930s to determine who is listening to what (a practice that Reith had earlier disparaged in his effort to educate listeners not pander to their tastes) may give broader meaning to Woolf's comment in 1940 that she was writing without a 'public to echo back' (*D5*: 304). However much the war distracted readers, as this comment implies, it engrossed listeners, including the Woolfs. The public may not echo back because it is oversaturated, not distracted. In the waning days of modernism, when the new is now familiar, Woolf shares with the BBC an anxiousness that the public may be tuning out.

The sonic experience of modernity affects – or should affect, according to Adorno – the kind of art produced. 'Changes in life are necessarily accompanied by changes in art', writes a contributor to *The Listener*; 'Motor-cars, aeroplanes and radio have speeded up not only our physical but our mental motions, and art changes have been just as revolutionary. [. . .] the new music is causing the listener to listen differently – horizontally rather than perpendicularly' (*Listener*, 20.512, 3 November 1938). While I have no idea what it means to listen perpendicularly, the idea expressed here that technology changes art and our experience of art, producing a new listener and a new reader, is itself modern. To grasp this insight, however, we had to learn to read modernism, well, vertically.

Listening to Writing

Sound technologies emerged with modernism in the 1920s and 30s, but what does that historical convergence mean for how we read, or hear, a book? Scholarship on Woolf has tended to focus on representations of the gramophone or the wireless in Woolf's works, some arguing that Woolf was resistant to such technology, others that it was a formal influence on her writing, but all illustrating Woolf's acute sensitivity to her sonic environment and its effect – formally, conceptually, politically – on her writing. The challenge, however, in learning to listen to a book is how to treat 'sound as sound and not as something else' (Cuddy-Keane 2000: 70), a challenge best addressed by the vertical dimension of the new modernist studies where modernist writing and new technologies are understood as reciprocal cultural forms. Melba Cuddy-Keane has been most influential in this regard. Not only does she offer an 'interactive rather than deterministic' model for cultural studies, arguing against any notion that Woolf's treatment of sound in her writing was '"produced" by an emerging technological culture' and focusing instead on 'the way broad currents of thinking circulate' (ibid.: 73); but most importantly, she provides scholars with a critical vocabulary to analyse sound in narrative, distinguishing between 'the linguistic representation of sound and the linguistic conceptualization of it' (ibid.: 70). The 'leaden circles' represents a pattern of sound ('sonicity') not its meaning ('semantics') in contrast to a statement like the one in *Three Guineas* comparing human nature to 'a gramophone whose needle has stuck' (*TG*: 59), where the gramophone functions as a trope (Cuddy-Keane 2000: 70, 75). To describe sonicity, Cuddy-Keane distinguishes between 'diffusion', the emission of sound from its source, and 'auscultation', the act of listening. The 'leaden circles' are diffused from Big Ben, but they are auscultised from various characters' positions (physical and social) and various spatial locations throughout London, miming the kind of 'expanded listening' actualised by broadcasting (ibid.: 71). 'Auscultation' complements 'focalization' in narrative theory, giving us a term for analysing 'the reception of sound in literary texts' (ibid.: 71), and in turn helping to produce a new generation of ear-sensitive readers. Although Big Ben is hardly a new technology in 1925, the way Woolf auscultates that sound 'reflects the new aural sensitivity coincident with the emergence of the gramophone and the wireless' (ibid.: 71). If not literally at least narratologically, scholars can now, with the metalanguage Cuddy-Keane provides, *listen to* a text.

Nowhere was the need for a metalanguage of sound more apparent to me than at the BBC Sound Archives. Forbidden to make copies of the recordings I listened to, I was forced to rely on my woefully inadequate critical vocabulary to capture the texture, tone, accent and resonance of the voices I heard in broadcasts from Guglielmo Marconi in 1901 to Vita Sackville-West in 1954. When I returned home I found that my description of Lloyd George could have been Stanley Baldwin, Ethel Smyth's voice was indistinguishable from Lady Astor's, at least on the pages of my notebook. The only voice I am certain I could identify again was Sigmund Freud's from 1938 because the prosthetic device he was wearing slurred his speech. I found some consolation, however, in recalling that Virginia Woolf and Rebecca West were no more able to transcribe the voices they heard on the wireless than I was. Writing on Woolf's broadcast on Beau Brummell (20 November 1929), West says a talk records personality more than does the written word, a justification, perhaps, for the description of Woolf's voice that follows:

> From the tones of her voice one realised her fineness, her fastidiousness, her inheritance of a great cultural tradition, and, over and above everything else, the light grace with which she can run on ahead of the ordinary person's understanding.[4]

Woolf similarly describes Vita's voice as 'subtle, profound, humorous, arch, coy' (*L4*: 160), terms used for character, not sound itself. So adept at conveying audible experience in her fiction, Woolf nevertheless faced the same difficulty scholars do of 'mediating sound through language', resulting in the 'inevitable translation of sound into a conceptual category' (Cuddy-Keane 2000: 70).

Even before literary scholars began to create a vocabulary for sound, Gillian Beer (1996) and Michele Pridmore-Brown (1998) had aroused our sensitivity to the acoustics of Woolf's writing by tracing the influence of the new physics and sound technology in her works. Beer was the first to realise the importance of physicists James Jeans and Arthur Eddington, whom Woolf read and listened to on the wireless, to Woolf's fiction, drawing connections between the new 'wave' theory and Woolf's ideas about writing and community. Building on Beer's work, Pridmore-Brown details how Woolf, like Miss La Trobe, 'engages her audience's participation by exploiting the concept of noise inherent in communications technology' to counter its totalitarian use: Woolf 'short-circuit[s] the herd impulse by privileging [. . .] the act of listening' (Pridmore-Brown 1998: 408, 415). Pridmore-Brown focuses explicitly on a politics of listening in Woolf's last novel in which the noise of the gramophone in La Trobe's pageant works against Fascism's efforts to organise the new masses into one receptive listener. Just as Woolf's concept of the listener as a lowbrow functions to undercut the authority of the middlebrow institution at Savoy Hill, as I have suggested, so the concept of noise in *Between the Acts* serves to employ the very technology used for fascist ends against them: 'By increasing the noise in the communication channel', Pridmore-Brown writes, 'La Trobe deliberately draws attention to the channel itself [. . .] even Giles is aware of being manipulated' (ibid.: 414). Woolf's novel, she continues, may 'compel the reader to acts of listening' – a verb that conjures up menacing images of people being forced to listen to broadcasts against their will, as they were in Nazi Germany as a form of punishment for indiscriminate listening (*The Listener*, 15.385, 27 May 1936) – but her concept of the common listener and her immersion of the individual listener/reader in an 'acoustic field' that links him or her 'somatically' to others (Pridmore-Brown 1998: 418–19) undermine the more ominous use of sound technology by both the BBC and the Nazis.

That comparison, unconsciously exposed in BBC editorials, only strengthens the connection Woolf draws in *Three Guineas* between fascism abroad and nationalism at home. An editorial in *The Listener* (28 August 1935) on the opening of the Berlin Radio Exhibition, for example, cites Dr Goebbels' claim that as a result of Hitler's seizing the airwaves in January 1933, broadcasting in Germany is now political and not a matter of money or the reputation of broadcasters (something the BBC had also complained about in American broadcasting). Revenues from broadcasting, Goebbels says, are now 'subsidising the cultural life of Germany' and broadcasting itself is becoming a form of 'cultural production'. Although the editor of *The Listener* says Goebbels's remarks 'throw an illuminating light on the development of nationalistic propaganda in Germany,' the BBC was also accused of promoting a nationalist agenda. In the May 1936 editorial cited above, the BBC warns its listeners that while 'no one can be compelled to read, [. . .] he can be compelled to listen'; because we cannot shut our ears, 'we are physiologically much more at the mercy of audible than of visual impressions', a warning Woolf responds to in her last novel. As Woolf listened to the BBC in the years leading up to war, her notion of listening became increasingly politicised: 'every BBC [broadcast] rises to that dreary false cheery hero-making strain' (*D5*: 292). If, however, we keep in mind that many of Woolf's most brutal comments on the patriotism of the BBC, the ones that critics often cite to argue that Woolf associates radio with forces of oppression, came from her listening to broadcasts on the General Strike (1926) and the pending war, we can better appreciate Woolf's complex response to broadcasting. On the one hand, her sensitivity to aural culture had aesthetic implications, providing a way out of the impasse of Edwardian realism, as Beer has argued; on the other hand, Woolf understood the political implications of the aurally saturated atmosphere of her day, making *active* listening all the more imperative.

It is arguably *The Waves* (1931) – a novel that reads like a radio drama and was eventually broadcast, in an abridged version, on the BBC (1955) – that most effectively conveys an aurally saturated environment, compelling its readers to be attentive listeners. Precisely because *The Waves* is Woolf's most abstract writing – like the 'Time Passes' section of *To the Lighthouse* (1927) in which we hear the sound of time passing without being auscultised through any '*personal* ear' (Cuddy-Keane 2000: 85) – sound is not a topic or theme but infuses the very form of the novel. Woolf called *The Waves*, initially conceived as a new kind of play, her 'eyeless book' (*D3*: 128, 203); she said she was writing it to a rhythm not a plot (*L4*: 204), and that she was reading it aloud while writing, trying to master the speaking voice (*D3*: 298). 'Suppose I could run all the scenes together more? – by rhythm, chiefly. [. . .] I want to avoid chapters; that indeed is my achievement, if any here: a saturated, unchopped, completeness' (ibid.: 343). The novel is replete with sounds, most obviously the sound of the waves heard throughout the book: 'the concussion of the waves breaking fell with muffled thuds, like logs falling, on the shore' (*W*: 29). But more than any other, this novel is *conceptualised* in terms of sound. The six characters speak in soliloquies to an unseen listener (Bernard uses 'you' to address no one in particular) using the pure present tense of a broadcast: 'Now . . . the time has come. . . . The cab is at the door' (ibid.: 30).[5] Indeed, 'speakers' may be more appropriate than 'characters' in that the six are not located in any specific social setting or geographical space; nor are they shown interacting with others, such as parents, teachers or passers-by. They are individuated not by physical details but through their talk, by the recurring motifs of their speeches. We literally *hear* the difference between the characters rather than visualise them. Like 'the listener', then, the characters form a universal, collective body and yet are individuated without materialising as distinct individuals. On every level – e.g., idiom, characterisation, diegesis – the listening experience in *and to* the novel resembles that of the wireless.

This is not to suggest that the BBC was a greater influence on the novel than Shelley. But as Beer points out, after the 1920s, the question of what an author heard becomes as crucial to literary criticism as the question of whom she read (Beer 1996: 150). Insofar as the conceptual challenge posed by sound technology serves to figure the newness of modernist art itself, understanding this technology and the new form of listening it produced can make us, as modernist scholars, more attentive listeners to texts.

Notes

I am deeply indebted to my students, Erin Holliday-Karre and Kathleen Schaag, for their invaluable research on this project.

1. In addition to Scott's and Edison's conceptions of phonography as stenography, the primacy of the visual is evident in advertisements for the phonograph and the radio that show people watching the machine, as well as in the language used to discuss sound. An article in *The Listener* states, 'At first *sight*, it seems strange that the ear has not become tuned . . . to the voice' (Dr J. H. Shaxby (1931) 'When Does a Sound Become a Noise', *Listener*, 5.116: 56.; my emphasis); an editorial in another issue of that journal argues that though the British may not like the spread of American English 'we gain little by shutting our eyes to it' (*Listener*, 1.15, July 1936); and Woolf refers to the BBC as the 'eyes of the whole world' (*D5*: 251). In the early days of the BBC, broadcasters dressed in formal attire, actors in radio dramas wore costumes, and dance numbers were performed on air. Lydia Lopokova Keynes proposed setting *Orlando* to music and dancing to it 'behind a micro-phone at Savoy Hill' [the BBC headquarters] (*L4*: 279).

2. A corollary phenomenon is turning people into talking machines, as in the December 1928 'Gabfest' in New York City, modelled on the dance marathon, in which ordinary citizens competing for the title of 'Champion Talker' talked non-stop for over four days, a testament if anything is to the ascendancy of aural culture (*Listener*, 1.15, 24 April 1929).

3. The 1931 invention of the Blattnerphone, a machine that records on erasable magnetised steel tape rather than gramophone records, led to a new genre, the actuality programme, a kind of sound documentary, or 'sound pictures.' The first such broadcasts date from 1934 (*Listener*, 5.127, 17 June 1931; 12.310, 19 December 1934).

4. Rebecca West Papers, McFarlin Library, Series II, Box 36, Folder 28; my thanks to Debra Rae Cohen for this quotation.

5. A Christmas Day broadcast in 1933, 'Absent Friends', for example, begins with: 'We give you the toast, absent friends', addressing, as the characters do, the unseen audience. Then the narrator, Howard Marshall, takes us on a tour of London's holiday scenes, using the same language the characters use: 'I can see it now', he tells us in describing a family party or church gathering. In both cases, however, we hear and see not so much a specific event or location but a general sense of the kind of acoustical event or scene we might experience.

Works Cited and Further Reading

Armstrong, Tim (2007) 'Player Piano: Poetry and Sonic Modernity', *Modernism/Modernity*, 14.1, 1–20.

Avery, Todd (2006) *Radio Modernism: Literature, Ethics, and the BBC, 1922–1938*, Aldershot, Hants: Ashgate.

Beer, Gillian. (1995) '"Wireless": Popular Physics, Radio and Modernism', in *Cultural Babbage: Technology, Time and Invention*, ed. Francis Spufford and Jenny Uglow London: Faber and Faber.

Benjamin, Walter (1968) 'On Some Motifs in Baudelaire', in *Illuminations*, ed. Hannah Arendt, trans. Harry Zohn, New York: Schocken Books.

Bishop, Edward L. (2004) 'Mind the Gap: The Spaces in *Jacob's Room*', *Woolf Studies Annual*, 10: 31–49.

Campbell, Timothy (2006) *Wireless Writing in the Age of Marconi*, Minneapolis: University of Minnesota Press.

Caughie, Pamela L. (2000) Introduction, in *Virginia Woolf in the Age of Mechanical Reproduction*, ed. Pamela L. Caughie, New York: Garland Publishing.

Cuddy-Keane, Melba (2000) 'Virginia Woolf, Sound Technologies, and the New Aurality', in *Virginia Woolf in the Age of Mechanical Reproduction*, ed. Pamela L. Caughie, New York: Garland Publishing.

Gitelman, Lisa (1999) *Scripts, Grooves, and Writing Machines: Representing Technology in the Edison Era*, Stanford, CA: Stanford University Press.

Flint, Kate (2003) 'Sounds of the City: Virginia Woolf and Modern Noise', in *Literature, Science, Psychoanalysis, 1830-1970: Essays in Honour of Gillian Beer*, ed. Helen Small and Trudier Tate, Oxford: Oxford University Press.

Kahn, Douglas and Gregory Whitehead (eds) (1992) *Wireless Imagination: Sound, Radio, and the Avant-Garde*, Cambridge, MA: MIT Press.

Laing, David (1991) 'A Voice without a Face: Popular Music and the Phonograph in the 1890s', *Popular Music*, 10.1: 1–9.

Levin, Thomas (1990) 'For the Record: Adorno on Music in the Age of Technological Reproducibility', *October*, 55: 23–47.

The Listener (1929–present) London: British Broadcasting Company.

Mao, Douglas and Rebecca L. Walkowitz (2008) 'The New Modernist Studies', *PMLA*, 123.3: 737–48.

Meadowcroft, William H. (1922) 'The Story of the Phonograph', *St. Nicholas*, 49: 692–9.

Pridmore-Brown, Michele (1998) '1939–40: Of Virginia Woolf, Gramophones, and Fascism', *PMLA*, 133.3: 408–21.

Scannell, Paddy and David Cardiff (1991) *A Social History of British Broadcasting, Vol. 1: 1922-1939 Serving the Nation*, London: Basil Blackwell.

Scott, Bonnie Kime (2000) 'The Subversive Mechanics of Woolf's Gramophone', in *Virginia Woolf in the Age of Mechanical Reproduction*, ed. Pamela L. Caughie, New York: Garland Publishing.

Sterne, Jonathan (2003) *The Audible Past: The Cultural Origins of Sound Reproduction*, Durham, NC: Duke University Press.

Part V Visual Media

20

VIRGINIA WOOLF AND FILM

Leslie Kathleen Hankins

Bᴜᴛ, ʏᴏᴜ ᴍᴀʏ say, we asked you to write about Virginia Woolf and film – what has that got to do with an extremely well-appointed library? And who is Judith Chaplin? I will try to explain. When you asked me to write about Woolf and film, I sat down at the computer and began to wonder what the words meant. They might mean simply a few remarks about Woolf's essay 'The Cinema', a few more about Vanessa Bell's love of Tarzan flicks; a tribute to the cinematic narrative in *Mrs Dalloway*; some witticisms if possible about Nicole Kidman's nose in *The Hours*, and one would have done. But at second sight the words seemed not so simple. The title 'Virginia Woolf and Film' might mean, and you may have wished it to mean, an exploration of Woolf's engagement with film aesthetics and theory, or it might mean Woolf and the films she screened; or it might mean a survey of scholarship on Woolf and film, or it might mean that somehow all these are inextricably mixed together and you want me to consider them in that light. But when I came to consider the subject in this last way, which seemed the most interesting, I soon saw that it had one fatal drawback. I should never be able to come to a conclusion.

But, perhaps it is delightful that no conclusion is in sight, as scholars and critics have continued to find the relationship between Woolf and the cinema intriguing since the first reviewers and Winifred Holtby noted the cinematic in Woolf's experimental novels. Decades afterwards, scholars began to consider Woolf's essay on cinema (Tiessen, Kellman) and in 1993, my own chapter on cinema in *The Multiple Muses of Virginia Woolf*, Diane Gillespie's pioneering collection of essays on Woolf and the arts, helped to inaugurate studies of her writing within the film culture of her time; such studies continued in the next decades, exploring her film connections from the London Film Society to the little magazines, *Vogue* and popular magazines (Hankins, Humm, Marcus, Trotter, Shail). Attention to the topic of Bloomsbury and film has been a staple of conferences such as the international annual Virginia Woolf conferences 1991–2009, Modern Language Association Conferences and Modernist Studies Association Conferences; publications draw on those presentations.[1] Maggie

Humm's *Modernist Women and Visual Cultures* brought considerable attention to the topic of Woolf and cinema in 2003. Recent books on cinema and
modernism include David Trotter's slender but provocative study, *Cinema and
Modernism*, and the hefty and impressive *The Tenth Muse* by Laura Marcus.

Pre-Texts: Holographs in the Berg Collection

> One way of thinking about the subject opens up if the stages of the textual
> genesis are followed: from the first jottings in a notebook to the final man-
> uscript, we are following a process of socialization of the writing, leading
> from the most brusquely individual notations to interference by cultural
> codes and the regulated contours of the text. (Hay 1996: 207)

A timely archival turn is to 'an extremely well-appointed library', the Henry W.
and Albert A. Berg Collection of English and American Literature at the New
York Public Library, to examine with care the holograph pre-texts of Woolf's
'The Cinema'.

'The Cinema' was first published in June 1926 in *The Arts* in New York,
and republished with significant changes in the *Nation and Athenaeum* on 3
July 1926 in London, as well as reprinted as 'The Movies and Reality' without
Woolf's permission on 4 August 1926 in the *New Republic*. Though scholars
have written about the published versions of 'The Cinema' (Hankins, Humm,
Trotter, Marcus), we have only recently begun to explore the rich drafts
(Hankins).[3] Twenty-first-century scholars will find Woolf's holographs and
revisions a treasure trove, providing theoretical and conceptual clarity for
her shifting arguments, as well as missing links and vital details, and bringing to life her complex and conflicted thoughts on film. A solid grounding in
the pre-texts will enhance our speculations about Woolf's cinema aesthetics.
In addition to the pre-texts, the two published versions of the essay, with
telling variations, reward investigation.[4] Exploring the pre-texts, attending
to the convoluted traces of the process of writing and thinking, provides
for dynamic, multi-directional and interactive scholarship. Tracing Woolf's
changes, tracking her contradictory sentiments about cinema, and probing
tensions within the pre-texts and among the drafts and published versions
invite revelations.

Woolf's holograph working papers on the cinema include two fragmentary
sheets of early jottings and two later drafts of 'The Movies' (manuscripts of nine
pages and eight pages respectively) leading to the published versions of 'The
Cinema'. These nineteen holograph pages of pre-texts, demonstrating repetitions and rewritings, exposing sites of contested ideas, and revealing surprise
alterations, intrigue us just as the thought of studying the manuscripts of Milton
appealed to Woolf's inquisitive narrator in *A Room of One's Own*. Changes in
the pre-texts on film reveal a significant shift in Woolf's take on cinema from
the positive to the qualified. Her first rough pages are full of curiosity and

gratitude, as she writes, 'we remain happy, greedy, & indiscriminate' (Berg 1).[5] She wonders about the popularity of film, trying to understand why 'moving picture versions of famous novels and imaginary adventures are so popular' (ibid.). She is most grateful for the 'photographs of ordinary sights', particularly for the opportunity to see things on film that she has never been able to see with the unaided eye, such as a flower transformed from bud to bloom, or a chrysalis tearing open to 'let forth a deaths head moth with crumpled wings' (ibid.: 2).

Later, in the first of the holograph drafts entitled 'The Movies', Woolf considers at length what type of raw material is available for film; though she acknowledges how much we owe to literature, music and painting (personifying those arts through Shakespeare, Beethoven and Titian), she finds 'at the same time things happen, sensations occur' that suggest that 'we are not completely represented even by these great masters' (Berg 2: 135). She is intrigued by this untamed area that has not yet been captured by the other arts. Overall, nonetheless, in Draft 1 her responses are less 'indiscriminate' than in the initial fragments; she is more critical, especially as she writes about film adaptation. She notes that real sights are more exciting than film adaptations of *Oliver Twist* or *Lorna Doone*, and calls for someone to invent conventions for the filmmaker, such as the scale in music. Draft 2 raises intriguing questions about the materials and choices for the poet and the filmmaker, and recommends further studies of sight and motion and their effects on spectators.

The holograph drafts contain buried treasure. One curious find is that in both drafts she describes the suffragettes marching in the newsreels of yesteryear, though she eliminates them from the published versions' list of patriarchal public moments.[6] As Woolf speculates in *A Room of One's Own*, the revisions in a manuscript may help to solve riddles a published text presents. For example, Draft 1 informs us that the image of a threatening shadow, a pivotal image that Woolf projects onto a screening of *The Cabinet of Dr Caligari* in the later pages, did not originate in a film screening at all. Another gem, within the second draft's pages 181 and 183, is the startling revision that shows that Woolf originally penned her blast against film adaptation about the character of Becky Sharp from *Vanity Fair*, not Anna Karenina at all, and that only within the draft did she change the reference to a film of *Anna Karenina*. These findings are thought-provoking, because the prototypes of the threatening shadow and Becky Sharp remind us that Woolf was not at heart a *cinéaste*, focusing on actual films and learning from them, but an imaginative writer, projecting her own hypothetical films and spinning from them her theories.

Studying the pre-texts with their plethora of literary allusions demonstrates how thoroughly Woolf's reflections about the cinema were grounded in literature. For her, literature trumped. The holographs refer to many literary models, including *Oliver Twist*, *Vanity Fair*, *Lorna Doone*, *Tess of the d'Urbervilles*, 'or any other novel with a sufficiently melodramatic plot' (Berg 2: 143), though

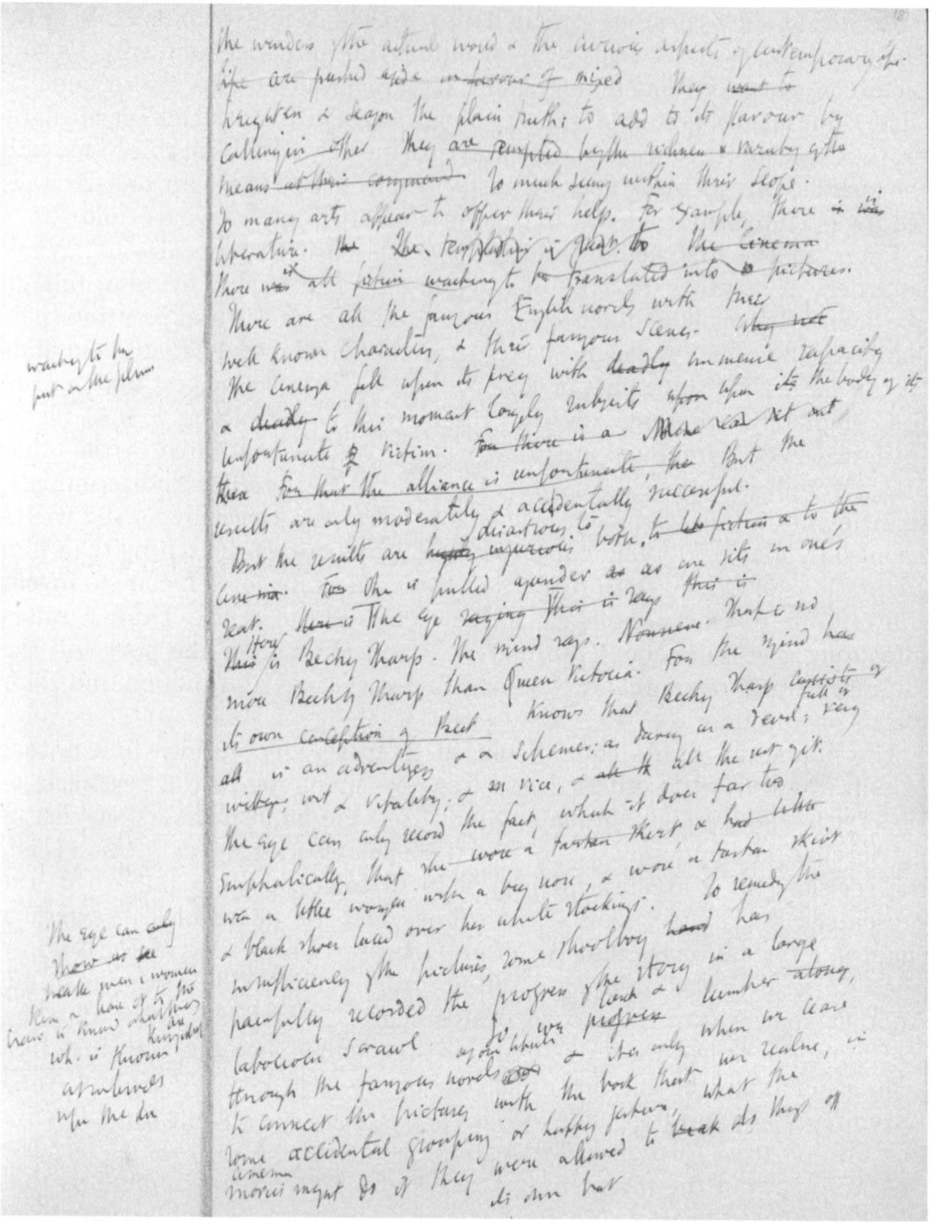

Figure 20.1 Page 181 of Woolf's second holograph draft of 'The Movies'. Courtesy of the Henry W. and Albert A. Berg Collection of English and American Literature, the New York Public Library, Astor, Lenox and Tilden Foundations. © 2009 The Estate of Virginia Woolf. By permission of the Society of Authors, as the literary representative of the Estate of Virginia Woolf

those references were omitted from the published version. Our recognition of Woolf's take on film is deepened by the investigation of the pre-text fragments and holograph drafts that trace Woolf's complex and conflicted responses, particularly when the cinema threatened to encroach upon her field of literature. These compelling sneak previews in the archives make it clear that the pre-texts warrant further investigation; scholars have far from exhausted Woolf's thoughts on cinema.

Conversations and Contexts: Bloomsbury and Cinema: Lydia Lopokova, *Vogue*, Clive Bell, Vita Sackville-West and Berlin

As enticing as it is to explore Woolf's own pre-texts for 'The Cinema', she cautions us that 'masterpieces are not single and solitary births; they are the outcome of many years of thinking in common' (*AROO*: 65) so we must consider how others – through conversations and publications – may also have shaped her thoughts on film. And that, of course, leads us to Bloomsbury. A letter from Woolf to Vita Sackville-West dated 13 April 1926 demonstrates that cinema played a role in Bloomsbury conversations:

> My mind is all awash with various thoughts; my novel; you; shall you take me for a drive to the sea?; the cinema; and so on; when the door opens and Dadie comes in. [. . .] Eddy comes. Telephone rings. Duncan is coming. We all have tea together. [. . .] very interesting: we compare movies and operas: I'm writing that for Todd: rather brilliant. (*L3*: 253–4)

Among the cast of characters in this conversation, Angus Davidson, Duncan Grant and Eddy Sackville-West were actively involved with the London Film Society. Duncan Grant attended many London Film Society programmes as well as Russian films with Angus Davidson, who also encouraged Hogarth Press to publish Eric Walter White's film studies and to advertise those publications in the London Film Society Programmes and with a special slide made for The Academy screenings.[7]

1922: Lydia Lopokova's *Pas de deux* with Cinema[8]

[H]ow curiously the sister arts might illustrate each other if they chose. (Woolf, 'Plays and Pictures', *E4*: 564)

Bloomsbury did more than chatter hard about film; members were spectators, too, and, in one case, on the other side of the camera, one danced. In 1922, Pathé's theatre and fashion series, *Eve's Film Review*, included *Dancing Grace – Novel Studies of Madame Lopokova*, a short experimental film. *Dancing Grace* choreographs the relationship between cinema and the arts: the film stars the high culture icon of the revolutionary ballet dancer, inserts its moving picture in an ornate picture frame, and uses calligraphic title cards. Through slow motion, doubling, superimposition and other camera techniques, as well as the commentary in the title cards, the filmmaker breaks the dancer free from time and space (by slow motion), defies the laws of gravity (suspending the dancer in mid-leap) and challenges identity (crafting multiple images of the dancer). The title cards also interrupt the dance and participate in the film, directing the viewer how to read/view the filmcraft of the dance. Dramatically reinventing dance, the film shifts the creative role from the dancer or the choreographer to the camera and the film editor. The film is a *pas de deux* between the filmmaker and the dancer, as the filmmaker takes on the role of re-choreographer, using the actual dance footage as raw material for a dance crafted at the editing table. *Dancing Grace* claims by association a relationship for cinema with the other arts. However, the film also suggests that cinema is an advance beyond the other arts, by showing how film can take the established forms and create an art distinctly cinematic. Four years before Woolf was to write in her essay that film could take the 'exactitude of reality' and 'flesh' and that 'if into this reality [the filmmaker] could breathe emotion, could animate the perfect form with thought, then his booty could be hauled in hand over hand', *Dancing Grace* was doing just that and 'improving, altering, making an art of their own' (Woolf 1926: 382–3).

Contexts: Woolf's 'The Cinema' and 1920s British *Vogue*[9]

[W]e compare movies and operas: I'm writing that for Todd: rather brilliant. (*L3*: 253–4)
[T]he cinema proved the most adequate purveyor of the truly modern thrill. (Anon, 'Paris Screens and Footlights', *Vogue* (London), Early January 1925: 37)

The wave of cinema crested over literary London during 1924–26 and Virginia Woolf rode that wave with her article on film published in three journals in 1926, and a year later she considered publishing it in *Close-Up*.[10] Surprisingly, however, the initial impetus for the article was not one of these journals; it was rather British *Vogue*. Dorothy Todd was the editor of *Vogue* from 1922 to 1926; when Woolf notes, 'we compare movies and operas: I'm writing that for Todd', it is clear she wrote 'The Cinema' with *Vogue* in mind. Woolf was immersed in that culture – as a reader of *Vogue*, as well as a writer for the publication.[11] Though Woolf's essay was not finally published there, *Vogue* remains a fascinating companion piece for her essay; its cinema articles from 1924 to 1926 shaped her discussion of film.

Film is an integral part of *Vogue* during the editorial reign of Todd; chic cinema is touted as a modernist fashion statement. *Vogue* reviews the London Film Society programmes starting in 1925, thus linking two cultural institutions so influential for fashioning film culture for London. An overview of *Vogue*'s film contributions reveals a tension between mainstream and avant-garde film, with

Iris Barry[12] writing five signed articles as the advocate for all film (mainstream as well as avant-garde), while various other authors (mainly anonymous) take a more exclusive approach, celebrating the avant-garde as the ultra-modern, and scorning mainstream film. The Early February 1925 feature, 'Paris Screens and Footlights', through its lengthy subtitle, leaves no doubt about the rising status of avant-garde cinema: 'Two of the Latest Plays Follow the Old Traditions of the Paris Stage while an Extraordinary Film is the Newest Achievement of the Ultra-Modern School' (Anon 1925b: 63). Celebrating the innovative kinetic quality of the ultra-modern film (*Ballet mécanique* by Fernand Léger and Dudley Murphy), the anonymous author writes,

> Of course the picture is as 'Dada' as you please, but somehow the screen lends itself beautifully to 'Dada' treatment, and we are willing to stand all sorts of delightful nonsense from it because it is an art still in its infancy, and its unreasonableness seems charming. Its elder sister arts, painting and literature, have, perhaps, to be judged by more adult standards. (Anon 1925b: 83)

The Early March 1926 *Vogue* is of note for Woolf and film studies because it contains an unsigned feature article,[13] 'The Future of the Cinema' (Anon 1926: 69), which anticipates Woolf's thoughts published four months later. The *Vogue* article begins, 'The Film Society has now given enough performances for one to be able to judge the present state of the Art of the Cinema' (ibid.), and points out that 'the Film Society is gradually giving us all the most admired high-brow films' (ibid.). Unlike Iris Barry, this writer does not find artistic merit in most films; rather, the author insists, 'the ordinary film to be seen at any cinema has usually very little pretension to be a work of art' (ibid.). The essay does find certain significant advantages in cinema:

> It can move the action from one end of the world to another in an instant, it can achieve good ironical effects by showing what is occurring simultaneously in two places, it can emphasise by a 'close-up' the significant movement of a hand or a window, it can show the smallness of man in the vastness of nature, it can reproduce the feeling of speed, it can muster enormous crowds, it can use natural cataclysms, fires and earthquakes and tempests, it can show the world as it appears to a person fainting or drunk or delirious. (Anon 1926: 69)

A few months later, Woolf echoes similar thoughts:

> The most fantastic contrasts would be flashed before us with a speed which the writer can only toil after in vain; the dream architecture of arches and battlements, of cascades falling and fountains rising, which sometimes visits us in sleep or shapes itself in half-darkened rooms, could be realized before our waking eyes. No fantasy could be too far-fetched or insubstantial. The past could be unrolled, distances annihilated, and the gulfs which

dislocate novels (when, for instance, Tolstoy has to pass from Levin to Anna, and in so doing jars his story and wrenches and arrests our sympathies) could, by the sameness of the background, by the repetition of some scene, be smoothed away. (Woolf 1926: 383)

After detailing its impressive potential, both authors then deflate cinema. The anonymous *Vogue* author asserts, 'But even so it is doubtful whether it can be used for any subtle psychological purpose' (Anon 1926: 69), and finds that film is inadequate to express emotions 'more delicate and complicated' than the primary ones. Woolf squelches film with a parallel debunking strategy, claiming 'It can say everything before it has anything to say' (Woolf 1926: 383). Ultimately, the cinema articles in *Vogue* suggest that if Woolf's 'The Cinema' did not end up in *Vogue*, *Vogue* ended up in Woolf's 'The Cinema'.

1922–9: Clive Bell: Conversations, Cribbing, Woolf's drafts, and Surrealist films[14]

[I]t has become a joke almost – Clive's cribbing –
(*L3*: 132)

Though he held out for a long time against the cinema – referring to it as the one vice he withstood – Clive Bell is essential to Virginia Woolf's take on cinema. Certainly, Bell could hardly be mistaken for an ardent *cinéaste*, but his attitude toward cinema underwent a subtle but marked transformation during the years 1922 to 1929. His hostility, ambivalence and evolving but qualified appreciation for that medium – as he responded to the German Expressionist art film, *The Cabinet of Dr Caligari*; the Dada film, *Entr'acte*; a sneak preview of the cubist film, *Ballet mécanique*, and unnamed Surrealist films – are noteworthy. It is intriguing to imagine conversations Bell and Woolf may have had about cinema, and to find traces of such in their writings on film. Bell wrote of *The Cabinet of Dr Caligari* in 1922 in *Vanity Fair*; his essay forms a provocative backdrop for Woolf's article, 'The Cinema', published four years later. Both writers hinge their arguments about cinema on insights they gleaned from screening the *Caligari* film, as did many writers on cinema. Both suggest that their insights are rather in spite of the film than because of it. Woolf's argument shares some elements with Bell's: she, too, is scathing about popular movies. However, Woolf creates a space for elite cinema as art, as she envisions crafting abstract film art from the leftovers of poetry and music.

Woolf's arguments for elite cinema may have encouraged Bell to rethink his wholesale condemnation of film. At any rate, it would be a mistake to limit Bell's take on cinema to his early rant. Film culture changed dramatically in the years after 1922 when this first essay was penned, and, as a frequent visitor to Paris, Clive Bell witnessed the cinematic avant-garde in that revolutionary centre. In 1924, in Paris, Fernand Léger showed him what Bell termed a rehearsal of Léger's cubist cinema, *Ballet mécanique*; though not impressed

Figure 20.2 Still from *The Cabinet of Dr. Caligari*, directed by Robert Wiene.
Courtesy of the Museum of Modern Art Film Stills Archive, New York

by the film itself, Bell thought there were possibilities.[15] This sneak preview is
significant because *Ballet mécanique* was shortly to become the darling film of
the highbrow and high-fashion scene, praised in the pages of such publications
as *The Little Review* and *Vogue*, and screened on one of the first programmes
of the trendy London Film Society, Programme 6 of 14 March 1926, which also
presented a revival of *The Cabinet of Dr Caligari*. Clive Bell himself starred at
another performance of the Film Society, the screening of *Entr'acte* by the Film
Society on 17 January 1926 when, according to Ivor Montagu, Clive leapt up to
defend the film.[16]

Performance art aside, one article best demonstrates Clive Bell's awareness of
cinema as an art: 'Cinema Aesthetics: A Critic of the Arts Assesses the Movies',
published in 1929 in the American journal, *Theatre Guild Magazine*. Bell was
writing the article for the Americans in October 1928 and according to a letter
from Paris he was quite pleased with it. The 'Contributors' Notes' for the magazine indicate the status that Bell enjoyed in that cultural moment: 'Clive Bell
is regarded by many as the foremost living writer on aesthetics. At the request
of the *Theatre Guild Magazine* he consented to test the application of his own
critical standards to the cinema' (*Theatre Guild Magazine* 1929: 65). The article

is prefaced by a full-page still of an experimental film, *Waxworks*, with the editor's caption:

> The regard for the values of 'pure cinema' urged by Clive Bell in the accompanying article, has been exemplified in a series of experimental films, mostly of foreign origin. One of the most striking of these, indeed, one which may be said to have inaugurated the little cinema movement in America, was 'The Three Wax Works,' produced by Paul Leni, and sponsored at its initial showing here by the Film Guild under the direction of Symon Gould in 1926. Emil Jannings, Werner Krauss and Conrad Veidt were the distinguished actors in this cinematographic fantasy. (*Theatre Guild Magazine* 1929: 38)

The film still and caption, extolling pure cinema, respond to Bell's article, rather than simply supporting it.

Reading Clive Bell's articles is often complicated by the recognition of his 'cribbing' in the diaries and letters of Roger Fry and Virginia Woolf. For our purposes, Bell's tendency to borrow the thoughts of others is of interest because it allows us to posit that he either read or talked with Virginia Woolf about her drafts and the published versions of 'The Cinema'. In 'Cinema Aesthetics', what saves the new medium for Bell is its emerging potential to become an abstract, elite art, potential that Woolf sketched in 'The Cinema'. Bell urges,

> If you want an art of the 'cinema' you must make possible the existence of 'cinema' artists; they cannot exist till you who could appreciate their art support studios where it can be created and theatres where it can be shown. (Bell 1929: 63)

Traces of Woolf's drafts that did not end up in her published essay also surface in Bell's article. Bell reframes her suggestion from holograph draft 1 of 'The Movies' that there are sensations and emotions outside of the existing arts that may await the cinema. In Woolf's first draft, seeking aesthetic scope for film, she writes that despite

> how much we owe to Shakespeare, ~~how much~~ to Beethoven, ~~how much~~ to Titian & the rest. At the same time things happen, sensations occur, which intimate ~~that even so~~ /that we are not completely represented even by these great masters. (Berg 2: 135)

Bell in his essay ponders,

> There is no reason *a priori* why the film should not express some purely aesthetic experience; on the contrary, it would seem reasonable to suppose that there are phases of modern experience which the film and the film alone can express. (Bell 1929: 39)

Echoing Woolf's thoughts, he asserts, 'It would be strange if this modern instrument of expression could find no modern experience to work on' (Bell 1929: 39).

Bell may well have borrowed from Woolf. On the other hand, what Bell no doubt contributed to Woolf's understanding of the elite role for film as an art would have been through his provocative discussions of Surrealist film, probably in conversations from 1924 on, and finally published in 'Cinema Aesthetics'. Bell was the main conduit through which Virginia Woolf received information about Surrealism and Surrealist films. The self-proclaimed English expert on the movement, in 1924 Bell prided himself on being the first in England to understand Surrealism. His delight in the Surrealists' ability to make us laugh (expressed in his 1926 *Vogue* pieces) continues in his 1929 assessment of '*surréalistes*' films:

> But so far the only serious attempts, of which I am aware, to provide the new instrument [film] with appropriate material are certain '*surréalistes* films' [. . .] In speaking of films I use the word '*surréaliste*' very freely to describe those which depend for their effect on the super-or contranatural – on making alarum-clocks waltz, for instance, or the traffic go backwards'. (Bell 1929: 39)

Bell gives what is for him rather a rave review:

> Certain films that I have seen at the *studio des Ursulines* and in other 'advanced' picture-palaces exploit, rather better I think than most *surréalistes* paintings, the aesthetic possibilities of surprise; and surprise is the emotion with which the post-war generation has dealt most effectively so far. (Bell 1929: 39)

Bell cites surprise as the one case where film is better than the other arts: 'It [surprise] has been exploited before, by seventeenth century draughtsmen and others; but unless I mistake, the cinema makes possible an exploitation of this curious emotion undreamed of by any former age' (Bell 1929: 39). It is worth noting what Bell claims for film:

> The supernatural (I had rather say the contranatural) is the one wholly appropriate element which has been brought into the film business so far; the one thing that neither plays, stories, pictures nor illustrated papers even can give as convincingly as the movies. (Bell 1929: 39, 62)

Finally, however, Bell finds that surprise has limited appeal: 'if cinematography is to become a means of artistic expression, producers, I think, must discover material as appropriate but more permanently significant than these pretty April foolings and decorative practical jokes' (Bell 1929: 39), and he urges further development: 'It is something well worth having; but if the cinema is to give us works of art it must further enrich its content' (ibid.: 62). He asks: 'With what? That is for some modern-minded and creative genius to discover' (ibid.).

Bell's reference to 'some modern-minded and creative genius' leads us back to hypothetical conversations about film between Bell and Woolf. Did

Figure 20.3 Still from *Entr'acte*, directed by René Clair. Courtesy of the Museum of Modern Art Film Stills Archive, New York

Bell describe to Woolf the films he saw in Paris at 'advanced' picture palaces? Did they chat about the sneak preview of *Ballet mécanique* or the riot over *Entr'acte*? At any rate, in the years from 1924 on, Bell's interest in Surrealist film and his assertion that it could do some things better than any other art form seem to be exactly the kind of dare that would have inspired Virginia Woolf to plunder those possibilities for her writing. Or, perhaps, as Bell was writing his article in October 1928, and Woolf's *Orlando* was published on 11 October, his ideas may have been shaped by her cinematic tricks in that novel. Certainly, if Clive Bell in his article is unable to imagine the 'with what?' that could 'enrich the content' of film, Virginia Woolf not only gestures towards the 'with what' in her 1926 essay, but, one might argue, in her *'surréaliste'* novel, *Orlando*, which plays with the 'contranatural' and projects mini-films onto the natural landscapes throughout. Surely, if waltzing alarm-clocks and reversals in traffic are 'contranatural' so would be a character switching from male to female and living across many centuries. For scholars, considering with more care Clive Bell's engagement with cinema, and tracking possible conversations and cribbing provide a nuanced way to re-examine the connections between Virginia Woolf and film.

Viewing with Vita: 'remember when I dragged you to see the film called 'Grass'?'

For a whole fortnight I shan't be able to write to you or to anybody, while we are camping. You remember when I dragged you to see the film called 'Grass'? (Letter from Vita to Virginia, Teheran, 19 February 1927)

In 1926 Vita took Virginia to see *Grass*, Cooper, Schoedsack and Harrison's 1925 travelogue-adventure-documentary film of the migration of a nomadic tribe across the Bakhtiari Mountains in south-western Persia. Imagine these two women in love sitting together in the dark watching the screen, viewing *Grass*, witnessing the drought, the ice, the agony, the extremity of that Other culture while warmed by the heat of infatuation in a comfy English cinema. The screening led them in markedly different directions, however; Vita left for Persia herself where she participated in embassy culture and then took off for a twelve-day journey across the Bakhtiari Mountains; that adventure Vita turned back into literature in a travel book, *Twelve Days*, published by the Hogarth Press in 1928. Woolf composed the fantasy-biography-novel *Orlando* which portrays, among other things, the title character's life with a gypsy tribe in the mountains. The elemental struggles in *Grass* form a backdrop for the conflicts about Nature in the gypsy sections of *Orlando* and may have inspired Vita's attempts to re-live the film trek on foot. We may read chapter 3 of *Orlando* as Woolf's response to *Grass*; the segment of Orlando among the gypsies projects a critique of the imperialist position of *Grass* and *Twelve Days*. Woolf's subtly critical portrait of Orlando in the East depicts a character so deeply dyed British that he/she can more readily change gender than alter his/her Englishness. Exploration of the different after-life of the screening of *Grass* in the lives and works of Woolf and Sackville-West provides one example of how to approach Woolf's documented film screening.

Spectator Sport: 1929 Bloomsbury in Berlin screens *Storm over Asia*[17]

If Clive Bell and Vita Sackville-West are spectators to watch more closely, what possibilities await us in the astonishing opportunity to examine Bloomsbury as a group of spectators? Re-viewing Bloomsbury's screening of the Soviet propaganda film *Storm over Asia* places Virginia Woolf's film screening in a broader cultural context. In mid-January 1929, Virginia and Leonard Woolf, Vanessa Bell and Duncan Grant, Eddy Sackville-West, Vita Sackville-West, and Harold Nicolson together in Berlin saw a highly con-troversial Soviet film, *Storm over Asia*. All that is missing is Clive Bell – or perhaps Walter Benjamin passing by as a *flâneur* taking notes. The film was drawing such crowds that special police had to be called in to contain them; because it was banned in England, the film was not shown there until 1930, and only then at one of the London Film Society screenings; seeing the film in Berlin a year before, Woolf was on the cutting edge of a cultural storm. The peculiar, complex screening moment in Berlin enables us to see connections between Pudovkin's 1928 film and Woolf's essays, *A Room of One's Own* in 1929, and *Three Guineas* in 1938.

In letters to Roger Fry and to her son Julian, Vanessa Bell describes in hilarious detail the 'thundery evening' in which this anti-imperial masterpiece was screened:

> We spent one of the most edgy & badly arranged evenings I can remember with them. [...] we went to see a Russian film called *Storm over Asia*. [...] The film seemed to me extraordinary – there were the most lovely pictures of odd Chinese types, very well done. I enjoyed it immensely & was under the impression that everyone else did too until we got out into the street when it appeared that feeling was running very high on the question whether it was anti-British propaganda! No doubt it was – at least the feeblest part of it consisted of the flight of soldiers in British uniforms flying from Asiatics. Vita again enraged Leonard by asking him 6 times whether he thought they were meant for Englishmen – she and Harold both thought they weren't but managed to quarrel with each other all the same. This discussion went on & on, all standing in the melting snow, & the general rage & uneasiness was increased by Eddy who was also of the party [...]. Never have I spent such a thundery evening. As I was quite uninvolved however I got a good deal of amusement out of it. (Quoted in Bell 1972: 374–6)

Her letter to Julian of 22 January 1929 adds:

> Then the film (which I thought very good) was Russian propaganda against the English in Asia. At least some thought it was and some thought it wasn't (I didn't notice particularly) and Harold's feelings ran high on the subject [...]. Altogether tempers waxed so hot that they hardly felt the bitter cold as we stood helplessly in the slush afterwards. (Bell 1993: 341–2)

The vignette Vanessa Bell portrays is not only amusing; the Berlin episode is a microcosm of cultural responses to revolutionary Soviet film. Harold Nicolson was a career diplomat on the British Embassy staff; his 'feelings ran high on the subject'. And what would be the odd position of Leonard Woolf, a socialist who had also been a colonial administrator in Ceylon? Clueless, Vita Sackville-West appears almost a caricature of imperial obtuseness. Eddy Sackville-West, as an active member of the London Film Society, would have been familiar with the strong advocacy of Soviet film by the Film Society and the *Close Up* group, the *cinéastes* Kenneth Macpherson, Bryher, H. D. and others who published the cinema journal *Close Up* (1927–33) which advocated strongly for film art, and was a champion of international film. Vanessa Bell, as a visual artist, passed over the propaganda, admired the lovely visuals – and documented the spectator sport.

Soviet films – proudly political propaganda – troubled the authorities in England and elsewhere; as the London Film Society programme notes about the film demonstrate:

It was imported into England by Pro Patria Films, by whom it was submitted to the British Board of Film Censors. It was rejected by this body on the grounds that the conduct of the troops shown wearing British uniforms made it unsuitable for exhibition in this country. (Amberg 1972: 146)

The energy and outrage generated by the film and/or its censorship poured into print from various sides – from the hostile London *Times* to the celebratory *Close Up* and the programmes of the London Film Society. Certainly, Woolf would have been aware of the public discussion about *Storm over Asia* before she saw the film – *The Times* was attacking the film already on 12 January before she left for Berlin.

The Times presented concerns about Soviet film as early as 1927. Bryher and H.D. saved a clipping file of the press response to *Storm over Asia*, a file which demonstrates that the film was a cultural battleground, one in which the radical intellectuals and the patriotic reactionaries met head on.[18] The Berlin correspondents of the *Morning Post* and *The Times* articulate arguments no doubt akin to Harold's 'high' feelings: 'It would require a trained pathologist rather than a film critic to do justice to the latest specimen of Muscovite film-craft which has reached Berlin and is entitled, "Storm over Asia"' ('From our Own Correspondent', 22 January 1929) and

The praise accorded to *Storm over Asia* was so remarkable that one was prepared resolutely to close one's eyes to the propaganda and see something really notable. But the impression remaining after the Asiatic storm has swept the Imperialist troops out of Asia is that it is one of the silliest of films. (*The Times*, 12 January 1929: 10)

The Times, the *Morning Post* and Harold Nicolson did not speak for all viewers. Ivor Montagu, a founder of the London Film Society, and *Close Up* figures such as Bryher and H.D. lauded the film. In January, February and March 1929, *Close Up* ran articles in favour of *Storm over Asia*; Kenneth Macpherson excoriated *The Times* for its knee-jerk hostility to the film:

It is anti-British, they told me. [. . .] Pudovkin has been no harsher than that class deserves. The film is by no means anti-British. It is certainly and definitely anti-militaristic, and therefore not particularly kind to the classes that seem to go on caring nothing about war and living their lives in readiness for it. In this, at bottom, it is entirely pro-British, and any Briton worthy of the name might well have been proud to have made it. Naturally, it will be forbidden here. Even more so than *Potemkin*. But what would happen if it were shown would certainly be far less impartial than my comments. (Macpherson 1929: 46)

Though Vanessa Bell remarks that she didn't really notice the politics, one can be certain that Virginia Woolf would have. When she saw *Storm over Asia*, Woolf had already written *Mrs Dalloway*, in which she hoped to criticise the social system and to show it operating at its most intense, and was writing her polemical essay, *A Room of One's Own*. What an adventure the film – and the responses to it – must have provided her, ever gathering material for her ongoing indictment of the patriarchal, imperial system. Ideas Woolf was penning at the time suggest her likely response to the patriotic hysteria directed towards the film; in *A Room of One's Own*, which she was revising into a book between the October 1928 lectures and the May 1929 publication date, she writes:

> Again if one is a woman one is often surprised by a sudden splitting off of consciousness, say in walking down Whitehall, when from being the natural inheritor of that civilisation, she becomes, on the contrary, outside of it, alien and critical. Clearly the mind is always altering its focus, and bringing the world into different perspectives. (*AROO*: 97)

How much sympathy would Virginia Woolf have had for Harold Nicolson's defensive outrage as a representative of the British diplomatic corps? In *Three Guineas*, after quoting an Englishman's patriotic claims, including 'Englishmen are proud of England', Woolf debunks that passage: 'But the educated man's sister – what does "patriotism" mean to her? Has she the same reasons for being proud of England, for loving England, for defending England?' (*TG*: 12).

In *Storm over Asia*, Pudovkin effectively uses the artistic and emotional power of cinema to make its ideological points; cinematography and editing capture the sheer ugliness of the greedy imperialists and bloated ruthless generals and link the avarice of Buddhist Lamas with that of the colonial authority. The film deftly portrays connections between political, economic and religious exploitation, displaying rituals and uniforms as props of imperial power and using collision-montage to undercut iconic visual images. In one example from the film, the editing composes (without words) a stinging social critique as it cross-cuts between the preparations at the Buddhist temple and the elaborate dressing of the British general and his wife as they prepare for an ornate ceremony as representatives of the imperial government. Pudovkin's cinematic combination of political content and breathtaking art must have been a timely model for the writer Virginia Woolf inventing ways to craft radical argument and art. Several years later, when she wished to compose a comparable critique in *Three Guineas*, Woolf edited into her text photographs of elaborately attired priests, professors and generals to undercut their authority in a way that recalls the scene – and others – from *Storm over Asia*:

> Your clothes in the first place make us gape with astonishment. How many, how splendid, how extremely ornate they are – the clothes worn by the educated man in his public capacity! [. . .] Tabards embroidered with lions and unicorns swing from your shoulders; metal objects cut in star shapes or in circles glitter and twinkle upon your breasts. Ribbons of all colours – blue, purple, crimson – cross from shoulder to shoulder. (*TG*: 23–4)

Figure 20.4 Still from *Storm over Asia*, directed by Pudovkin. Courtesy of the
Museum of Modern Art Film Stills Archive, New York

The wide-ranging responses that Woolf's eclectic group registered to *Storm over Asia* anticipate the question Woolf would articulate nine years later in *Three Guineas*: 'Let us see then whether when we look at the same photographs we feel the same things' (*TG*: 14); if we substitute 'movies' for 'photographs' scholars have a strategic way to approach Woolf's film-going. We may mine vaults for more films (what we might term *ciné*-texts) to view alongside Woolf's written texts. The light from the projection booth allows us to read Woolf's writings in radically new ways in relation to such films. As we explore more fully Woolf's actual film viewing, what will emerge? What will scholars find about the writer of *The Waves* (1931) seeing *Le Million* (1931) by René Clair?[19] Or from her seeing the *Bengal Lancers* (1935) and Chaplin in *Modern Times* (1936) while working on *Three Guineas* (1938)?

Watching the Pictures: Woolf, 'The Savages of the Twentieth Century' and Judith Chaplin

Projects to investigate films seen by Woolf beckon; yet, as appealing it may be to explore the connections between Woolf's writings and the films she saw, we are somewhat limited in our research by her unfortunate disregard of future scholars; she tells us precious little about her film viewing and we should soon come to a halt for want of facts. All is not lost, however; the opening lines from 'The Cinema' may inspire and advise scholars:

> PEOPLE say that the savage no longer exists in us, that we are at the fag-end of civilization, that everything has been said already, and that it is too late to be ambitious. But these philosophers have presumably forgotten the movies. They have never seen the savages of the twentieth century watching the pictures. They have never sat themselves in front of the screen and thought how, for all the clothes on their backs and the carpets at their feet, no great distance separates them from those bright-eyed, naked men who knocked two bars of iron together and heard in that clangour a foretaste of the music of Mozart. (Woolf 1926: 381)

We must look – and look carefully – at common spectators (including philosophers and 'savages') watching the pictures, as one promising suggestion for expanding the horizons for future scholarship. Rather than seeing films solely from a Woolf's-eye view, we might explore how the common reader and the common spectator encountered Woolf's novels and various films at the same time. For example, we might consider readers in 1925 reading *Mrs Dalloway* and viewing war films, such as King Vidor's *The Big Parade*, which was a huge success advertised in the *Nation and Athenaeum* throughout the time Woolf drafted 'The Cinema'. Would readers of *Mrs Dalloway* in 1925 recall the momentous screenings of Abel Gance's *J'accuse* from London of 1920?[20] What of a variety of travel films seen alongside Woolf's essays on travel, or her novel, *Orlando*? The possibilities are endless. And, one may imagine, if we are daring enough and willing to follow Woolf's own inventive bent, we may even bring into being a hypothetical reel reader – a Judith Chaplin perhaps – to read Woolf's novels and essays by the light of the silver screen – gaining fresh fanciful insights through those myriad juxtapositions. What might Judith Chaplin make of placing Adrian Brunel's burlesques of travel, censorship and others alongside Woolf's larks, *Flush* and *Freshwater*? With the freedom of her fictitious nature, what light could she cast on the topic of Woolf and the cinema?

Meanwhile back 'In an Extremely Well-Appointed Library': The End

Then 'Anna falls in love with Vronsky' – that is to say, the lady in black velvet falls into the arms of a gentleman in uniform, and they kiss with enormous succulence, great deliberation, and infinite gesticulation on a sofa *in an extremely well-appointed library*, while a gardener incidentally mows the lawn. (Woolf 1926: 382 my emphasis)

Archival teases such as Duncan Grant's note to Vanessa that Virginia was dying to go to a cinema, and records in diaries and letters of her responsive spectator moments (shedding a tear at *The Bengal Lancers*, writing of her enchantment watching a barge float past Baghdad in a travel film, expressing disappointment at missing the war films) indicate how much Woolf delighted in and exploited film, but there remains a marked difference between her final tamed and tentative take on cinema and that of a *cinéaste* with a loyalty to the medium and a desire to push the envelope for film. Because evidence from the holographs shows us that Woolf worked from literature and from hypothetical films more than from observations as a spectator of actual films, it is sublimely appropriate that she chose to stage her scene critiquing film adaptation in 'an extremely well-appointed library' (Woolf 1926: 382), looking out of the window at the mower, not, certainly, at a movie screen.

So we return to the extremely well-appointed libraries and famous archives, where treasures are yet to be discovered through the archival turn to Woolf's pre-texts and to the many *ciné-texts* that await screening. Certainly, everything has not been said already; for scholars of Woolf and film, it is not too late to be ambitious. We have much to gain. How all this is to be attempted, much less achieved, no one at the moment can tell us. We get intimations only in the chaos of conferences, perhaps, when some momentary assembly of colour, sound, movement suggests that here is a scene awaiting a new scholarship to be transfixed.

Notes

I am very grateful to Anne Garner, Librarian, and Dr Isaac Gewirtz, Curator, at the Henry W. and Albert A. Berg Collection, New York Public Library, who proved generous and patient in their efforts to aid me and locate archival materials in the Virginia Woolf Collection of Papers. Jeremy Crow of the Society of Authors was gracious and prompt as he gave permission to publish the illustration of the holograph draft, as well as to quote from the essay. My eyes thank Mark Hussey, who rescued me from some of the most daunting tangles when deciphering Woolf's handwriting. Any errors are my own. Quotations from Virginia Woolf's works are copyright © 2010 The Estate of Virginia Woolf. By permission of the Society of Authors, as the literary representative of the Estate.

1. Scholars and common readers are encouraged to attend the annual June conference on Virginia Woolf. Scholars are fortunate to have this conference and the publication of the selected papers (as well as the conference programme listing all the papers given) so students and scholars can access cutting-edge research in a timely way. See the annual volumes of selected papers, published by Pace University Press or Clemson Digital Press. Programmes of the conference are posted and archived at the International Virginia Woolf Society website: www.utoronto.ca/IVWS which also offers the Annual Bibliography of Virginia Woolf Studies. Other sources for Woolf and film studies include the *Woolf Studies Annual*, edited by Mark Hussey, and the Virginia Woolf Society of Great Britain's *Virginia Woolf Bulletin* published three times a year. Also, see the programmes for the Modernist Studies Association Conferences: http://msa.press.jhu.edu/conference.html and their publication, *Modernism/Modernity*. In 2008, Andrew Shail in November 2008 hosted at Oxford University a conference on Modernism and Visual Culture, which included several papers on Woolf and cinema.

2. See *Guide to the Virginia Woolf Collection of Papers*, Henry W. and Albert A. Berg Collection of English and American Literature, New York Public Library, Astor, Lenox and Tilden Foundations: www.nypl.org/research/manuscripts/berg/brgwoolf.xml

3. See Hankins 2009d (including some transcripts and illustrations of holographs). The section here offers highlights from that study.

4. This chapter relies upon the *Nation and Athenaeum* version of Woolf's essay (3 July 1926). Some versions, including the one designated as the *Nation and Athenaeum* version in *The Essays of Virginia Woolf*, Volume IV, differ somewhat from that original text. Readers are encouraged to go back to the *N&A* version.

5. The originals of two holograph pages, (hereafter as Berg 1 and 2), Draft 1 of 'The Movies', pp. 135–51 and Draft 2 of 'The Movies', pp. 175–89 (hereafter identified by page number) are in the Henry W. and Albert A. Berg Collection of English and American Literature, The New York Public Library, Astor, Lenox and Tilden Foundations. The Berg Finding Aid describes the pre-texts as follows:

> At back of her: The voyage out. Holograph draft. Vol. 2 [Captain's death bed and other essays?, The. The cinema] Class distinctions. Holograph fragment. One loose page n.d. ms. 5p. and In her: [Articles, essays, fiction and reviews] vol. 2, May 22, 1925 (Part II of 1925), p. 135–151; 175–189 [Captain's death bed and other essays, The. The cinema] The movies. Holograph n.d. ms. 9 p; 8 pg.

> The Berg 1 loose sheet has a torn left upper corner and is a bit rumpled. The paper is ruled with pale blue lines and the large CANSELL watermark fills the left vertical margin. Woolf has not added a vertical blue margin line here as she often does. This loose page (Berg 1) is blank on the back, but the other sheet (Berg 2) is written upside down on the verso of the (unnumbered) 85th leaf of the holograph draft of *The Voyage Out*, which begins 'there was any truth in the story . . .'.

6. I delivered a paper entitled 'Newsreels of the Suffragettes and "Moving Picture Versions of Famous Novels": Holographs of Virginia Woolf's "The Movies" in the Berg Collection

& Archival Films from the Museum of Modern Art Film Studies Center and the British Film Institute', at the Nineteenth Annual Virginia Woolf Conference, New York City, 6 June 2009.

7. See Humm 2003; Hankins 2009b.
8. See Hankins 2000, which includes a still from the film.
9. This section refers to findings from my presentations on Virginia Woolf and *Vogue* at the Modern Language Association and Virginia Woolf conferences 2003 and 2005, as well as Hankins 2004.
10. See Donald, Friedberg and Marcus 1998: 325 fn 47, which includes the text of the Woolf postcard. Though Woolf initiated the correspondence with the journal, hoping to reprint her essay, when she thought it was a foreign publication, once she realised there was a conflict with the *Nation*, she withdrew the offer. *Close Up* was evidently willing to wait for her to write something new, but she states that she was too busy to write anything fresh.
11. See Luckhurst 1997, 1999; Garrity 1999, 2000; Reed, 200 for more on *Vogue*.
12. See Hankins 2004; Marcus 2007.
13. In *The Tenth Muse* Laura Marcus mistakenly identifies this article and two others ('Paris Screens and Footlights') as by Iris Barry. We do not have explicit evidence about the authors, and internal evidence argues against Barry as the author.
14. This captures some highlights of 'Tracking Clive Bell's Takes on the Cinema in the 1920s', given at the Sixteenth Annual International Conference on Virginia Woolf at the University of Birmingham, UK in 2006 (see also Marcus 2007).
15. Many thanks to James Beechey, generous biographer of Clive Bell, who drew my attention to this letter.
16. I discuss the riot more thoroughly in Hankins 1993a: 152–5.
17. This contains insights from the paper "Never have I spent such a thundery evening" Bloomsbury in Berlin screens *Storm over Asia*', presented in June 2004 at 'Back to Bloomsbury' Fourteenth Annual Conference on Virginia Woolf held at the University of London.
18. This file is in the Beinecke Archives at Yale University.
19. Laura Marcus offers a promising example of this approach as she reads *The Years* through the lens of *Le Million*, in Marcus 2007: 160–71.
20. I gave a presentation on *The Big Parade* and *Mrs Dalloway* : 'Adapting Cinema to Novel: Abel Gance's 1918-19 anti-war epic film, *J'accuse* and Virginia Woolf's anti-war novel, *Mrs. Dalloway*, special session at the Eighteenth Annual Virginia Woolf Conference, Denver, 19 June 2008; also see Hankins 2008.

Works Cited and Further Reading
(those with asterisks are especially recommended)

*Amberg, George (1972), *The Film Society Programmes 1925–1939*, New York: Arno Press.

Anon, (1925a) 'Paris Screens and Footlights: The Ballet 'Relâche' and an Exciting Film at the Champs Elysées: Mme. Georgette Leblanc in "L'Inhumaine", *Vogue* (London), Early January: 37, 70.

Anon, (1925b), 'Paris Screens and Footlights: Two of the Latest Plays Follow the Old Traditions of the Paris Stage, While an Extraordinary Film Is the Newest Achievement of the Ultra-Modern School', *Vogue* (London), 65.3, Early February: 63, 82–3.

Anon (1926), 'The Future of the Cinema', *Vogue* (London), Early March: 69.

Barry, Iris (1924) 'The Scope of Cinema', *Vogue* (London), Late August, 64.4: 65, 76.

—— (1924a) 'The Autumn Cinema', *Vogue* (London), Late September, 64.6: 78.

—— (1924b) 'The Cinema in Three Moods', *Vogue* (London), Early October, 64.7: 104.

—— (1925) 'The Cinema Continues to Improve', *Vogue* (London), Late February, 65.4: 78.

—— (1926a) 'The Cinema', *Vogue* (London), Early February, 67.3: 52–3.

—— (1926b) *Let's Go to the Pictures*, London: Chatto & Windus.

The Beinecke Rare Book and Manuscript Library of Yale University.

Bell, Clive (1922) 'Art and the Cinema: A Prophecy that the Motion Pictures, in Exploiting Imitation Art, will Leave Real Art to the Artists', *Vanity Fair*, November, pp. 39–40.

—— (1929) 'Cinema Aesthetics: A Critic of the Arts Assesses the Movies', *Theatre Guild Magazine* October, 39, 62–3.

Bell, Quentin (1972), *Virginia Woolf: A Biography*, New York: Harcourt Brace Jovanovich.

Bell, Vanessa (1993) *Selected Letters of Vanessa Bell*, ed. Regina Marler, London: Pantheon.

Berg 1 Two pages holograph fragments. The Cinema. At back of her: The voyage out. Holograph draft. Vol. 2. Virginia Woolf Collection of Papers, The Henry W. and Albert A. Berg Collection of English and American Literature. The New York Public Library.

Berg 2 Holograph. The cinema The movies. Holograph. n.d. ms. 9p; 8p. In her: [Articles, essays, fiction and reviews] vol. 2, May 22, 1925 (Part II of 1925), p. 135–51; 175–89. Virginia Woolf Collection of Papers. The Henry W. and Albert A. Berg Collection of English and American Literature, The New York Public Library.

Bryher (1929), *Film Problems of Soviet Russia*, Territet, Switzerland: Pool Publishing.

Close Up: A Magazine Devoted to the Art of Films (1927–33) (1971) ed. Kenneth Macpherson and Bryher, Volumes 1–10, Arno Series of Contemporary Art, New York: Arno Press.

*Donald, James, Anne Friedberg and Laura Marcus (eds) (1998), *Close Up 1927–1933: Cinema and Modernism*, Princeton, NJ: Princeton University Press.

'From Our Own Correspondent, Berlin' (1929) *Morning Post*, 22 January.

Garrity, Jane (1999) 'Selling Culture to the "Civilized": Bloomsbury, British *Vogue*, and the Marketing of National Identity', *Modernism/Modernity*, 6.2: 29–58.

—— (2000) 'Virginia Woolf, Intellectual Harlotry and 1920s British *Vogue*', *Virginia Woolf in the Age of Mechanical Reproduction*, ed. Pamela L. Caughie, New York: Garland Press, pp. 185–218.

Hankins, Leslie K. (1993a) '"Across the Screen of My Brain": Virginia Woolf's "The Cinema" and Film Forums of the Twenties', in *The Multiple Muses of Virginia Woolf*, ed. Diane F. Gillespie, Columbia: University of Missouri Press, pp. 148–79.

—— (1993b) 'The Doctor and the Woolf: *Reel* Challenges of *The Cabinet of Dr. Caligari* and *Mrs. Dalloway*', in *Themes and Variations: Proceedings of the Second Annual Conference on Virginia Woolf*, ed. Mark Hussey and Vara Neverow-Turk, New York: Pace University Press, pp. 40–51.

—— (1993c) 'A Splice of Reel Life in Virginia Woolf's 'Time Passes': Censorship, Cinema and 'the Usual Battlefield of Emotions"', *Criticism*, Winter: 91–114.

—— (2000) 'Tracking Shots through Film History: Virginia Woolf, Film Archives and Future Technologies', in *Virginia Woolf Turning the Centuries: Selected Papers from the Ninth Annual Virginia Woolf Conference*, ed. Bonnie Kime Scott and Ann Ardis, New York: Pace University Press, pp. 266–75.

—— (2004) 'Iris Barry, Writer and *Cinéaste* in *The Adelphi*, *The Spectator*, the Film Society and the British *Vogue*: Forming Film Culture in London of the 1920s', *Modernism/Modernity*, September: 488–515.

—— (2005) 'Switching Sex and Redirecting Desire: The Surrealist Film, *Entr'acte* and Woolf's *Orlando*', *Virginia Woolf Miscellany*, Summer: 25–6.

*—— (2006) 'Cinéastes and Modernists: Writing about Film in 1920s London', in *Gender in Modernism: New Geographies, Complex Intersections*, ed. Bonnie Kime Scott, Urbana: Illinois University Press, pp. 808–58.

—— (2008) 'Abel Gance's *J'accuse* and Virginia Woolf's *Mrs. Dalloway*: Re-reading a Modernist Novel by the Light of the Silver Screen', *J'accuse: A Film by Abel Gance: The Newly Restored Original 1919 Version*, [DVD and booklet], The Flicker Alley Collection, pp. 14–17.

—— (2009a) 'Complicating Adaptation: Virginia Woolf's 1925 novel, *Mrs. Dalloway* and Abel Gance's 1918–9 film, *J'accuse, Selected Papers from the Eighteenth Annual Conference on Virginia Woolf*, eds. Eleanor McNees and Sara Veglahn, Clemson, SC: Clemson University Digital Press, pp. 129–37.

—— (2009b), 'Reel Publishing: Virginia Woolf and the Hogarth Essays of Film Pamphlets', in *Selected Papers of the Eleventh Annual Conference on Virginia Woolf*, ed. Jane de Gay and Marion Dell, Clemson, SC: Clemson University Digital Press.

—— (2009c) 'Teaching *Mrs. Dalloway* and Film: from the Historical Avant-Garde Cinema to Current Film Adaptations', in *Approaches to Teaching Virginia Woolf's* Mrs. Dalloway, ed. Eileen Barrett and Ruth Saxton, New York: Modern Language Association Publications.

—— (2009d) 'Virginia Woolf's "The Cinema" Essay: Sneak Previews of the Holograph Pre-Texts through Post-Publication Revisions', *Woolf Studies Annual*, 15: 135–75.

Hay, Louis (1996) 'History or Genesis?', trans. Ingrid Wassenaar, in *Drafts*, special issue of *Yale French Studies*, 89, 191–207, Originally 'Histoire ou genèse?', in *Les Leçons du manuscript. Études Françaises*, 28.1 (1992): 11–27.

Holtby, Winifred (1932) *Virginia Woolf*, London: Wishart.

Hotchkiss, Lia M. (1996), 'Writing the Jump Cut: *Mrs. Dalloway* in the Context of Cinema', in *Virginia Woolf: Texts and Contexts: Selected Papers from the Fifth Annual Conference on Virginia Woolf*, eds Beth Rigel Daugherty and Eileen Barrett, New York: Pace University Press, pp. 134–9.

*Humm, Maggie (2003), *Modernist Women and Visual Cultures: Virginia Woolf, Vanessa Bell, Photography and Cinema*, New Brunswick, NJ: Rutgers University Press.

*Hussey, Mark (ed.) (1997) *Virginia Woolf: Major Authors on CD-ROM*, Woodbridge, CT and Reading, Berkshire: Primary Source Media.

Kellman, Steven (1987) 'The Cinematic Novel: Tracking a Concept', *Modern Fiction Studies*, 33.3, Autumn: 467–77.

Luckhurst, Nicola (1997) '*Vogue* . . . is going to take up Mrs Woolf . . . to boom her', in *Virginia Woolf and the Arts: Selected Papers from the Sixth Annual Virginia Woolf Conference*, ed. Diane F. Gillespie and Leslie K. Hankins, New York: Pace University Press, pp. 75–84.

—— (1998) *Bloomsbury in Vogue*, Bloomsbury Heritage Series, London: Cecil Woolf.

Macpherson, Kenneth (1929) 'Storm over Asia – and Berlin!', *Close Up*, 4.1, January: 37–46.

Marcus, Laura (2005) 'The Great War in Twentieth-century Cinema', in *The Cambridge Companion to the Literature of the First World War*, ed. Vincent Sherry, Cambridge: Cambridge University Press, pp. 280–301.

—— (2006) '"A new form of true beauty": Aesthetics and Early Film Criticism', *Modernism/Modernity*, 13.2, April: 267–89.

*—— (2007) *The Tenth Muse: Writing about Cinema in the Modernist Period*, Oxford: Oxford University Press.

Reed, Christopher (2006) 'Design for (Queer) Living: Sexual Identity, Performance, and

Decor in British *Vogue*, 1922–1926', *GLQ: A Journal of Lesbian and Gay Studies*, 12.3:377–403.

Rubenstein, Roberta (2008) 'Reading over Her Shoulder: Virginia Woolf Reads *Anna Karenina*', *Selected Papers from the Eighteenth Annual Conference on Virginia Woolf*, ed. Eleanor McNees and Sara Veglahn, Clemson, SC: Clemson University Digital Press, pp. 76–83.

Sackville-West, Vita (1985) *The Letters of Vita Sackville-West to Virginia Woolf*, ed. Louise DeSalvo and Mitchell Leaska, New York: Morrow.

Seed, David (2005), 'British Modernists Encounter the Cinema', in *Literature and the Visual Media. Essays and Studies*, ed. David Seed, Woodbridge, Suffolk: D. S. Brewer, pp. 48–73.

*Shail, Andrew (2006) 'She Looks Just Like One of We-All: British Cinema Culture and the Origins of Woolf's *Orlando*', *The Critical Quarterly*, 48: 45–76.

—— (2008) 'The Motion Picture Story Magazine and the Origins of Popular British Film Culture', *Film History: An International Journal*, 20.2: 181–197.

'STORM OVER ASIA: New Russian Film in Berlin (from our Berlin Correspondent)' (1929) *The Times*, 12 January: 10.

Tiessen, Paul (1986–7) 'The Shadow in Caligari: Virginia Woolf and the "Materialists" Responses to Film', *Film Criticism*, 11.1–2 (Fall–Winter): 75–83.

Trotter, David (2005) 'Virginia Woolf and Cinema', *Film Studies* 6 (Summer): 3–18.

*—— (2007) *Cinema and Modernism*, Oxford: Blackwell Publishing, pp. 159–79.

White, Eric Walter (1928) *Parnassus to Let: An Essay about Rhythm in the Films*, Hogarth Essays, Second Series, No. XIV, London: Hogarth Press

—— (1931) *Walking Shadows: an Essay on Lotte Reiniger's Silhouette Films*, based on a paper read to the Newport Film Society on 16 December 1930, London: Hogarth Press.

*Woolf, Virginia (1926) 'The Cinema', *Nation and Athenaeum*. 3 July: 381–3.

—— (1994) *The Essays of Virginia Woolf*: 1925-1928. ed. Andrew McNeillie. London: Hogarth Press: 1994. Vol. IV.

21

VIRGINIA WOOLF AND PHOTOGRAPHY

Colin Dickey

IN A LETTER to her sister Vanessa Bell dated 8 October 1938 Virginia Woolf wrote of the difficulties she was having writing her biography of Roger Fry, in particular his relationship to her: 'What am I to say about you?' she wrote to Vanessa. 'It is rather as if you had to paint a portrait using dozens of snapshots in the paint' (*L6*: 285). Throughout her writing, Woolf uses the words 'picture' and 'portrait' to refer to both painting and photography (usually the former, as in her letter to Vanessa), but regardless of the medium, Woolf always uses 'portrait' to mean something complete, unified, a 'whole picture'. 'Snapshot', by contrast, always means something quick, haphazard, fragmented. To write in 'snapshots' is to miss the big picture, fail to capture the whole subject, to provide only gestures, fragments; Woolf herself would later describe her own articles as being 'always like snapshots, too black, too white, too elementary altogether' (ibid.: 282).

In her letter to Vanessa, a painter herself, Woolf implies that painting – an art requiring great precision and unity of form – is inherently superior to the casual snapshot, and Woolf's attitude would seem at first glance to mirror much of high modernism: painting is exalted as a true art, whereas photography is restricted to popular culture. Writers and artists were noticeably uncomfortable with the mechanical aspect of photography as a replacement for the painter's hand, and saw photography as a less pure form of expression.

But Woolf's attitude towards photography was more complex than many of her contemporaries. Woolf herself took and shared photographs with friends and family throughout her life. 'So now I have assembled my facts', she notes in her diary for 22 August 1922, 'to which I now add my spending 10/6 on photographs, which we developed in my dress cupboard last night; & they are all failures. Compliments, clothes, building, photography – it is for these reasons that I cannot write Mrs Dalloway' (*D2*: 190). More than just a hobby or a distraction, Woolf collected these photographs in albums which reveal a rich tapestry of Bloomsbury life. As Maggie Humm writes, for Woolf and her family photography, 'even if improvised and provisional, was another way of telling their life stories in which the albums become a fully expressive "heterotopic" third space – a thick, dense "imagined community'" (Humm 2006: 38).

This intense, lifelong relationship to photography in turn helped to inform Woolf's fiction. Throughout her work, characters respond to photographs in ways that reveal their complicated relationships to the past and their own self-perception. In addition, the style and structure of her novels often borrow from a photographic lexicon, particularly in her treatment of new modes of subjectivity and experience. This exploration of the relationship between photography and writing ultimately culminates in works like *Orlando* (1928) and *Three Guineas* (1938), where Woolf introduces actual photographs into her works alongside her writing. These books engage in a long-standing discussion of the relationship of text and image, a relationship that Woolf complicates through her own use of photography's distinct qualities.

Looking at Photographs

Photographs in Woolf's early fiction fall roughly into three groups. There are the photographic portraits of dead loved ones and historical figures, hovering on mantelpieces and in albums, haunting the lives of Woolf's protagonists. In addition, there are the photographic prints of Greek and Roman ruins kept by young men like Jacob Flanders, who see themselves as the inheritors of England's great Empire. Finally, there are the casual snapshots taken by women like Clarissa Dalloway, seemingly superficial tokens which Woolf uses to signal more fundamental changes in gender roles and modern culture.

Throughout Woolf's novels, characters find themselves confronting photographic portraits of ancestors and other historical figures from the Victorian era. These 'Victorian Photographs of Famous Men and Fair Women' (to use the title of Julia Margaret Cameron's book of portraits, published by Woolf's Hogarth Press) represent the legacies of the previous generation, with its strict gender roles, patriarchal assumptions and colonial exploits – a culture that Woolf repeatedly critiques. As such, the pull they exert on Woolf's characters is not just familial but cultural; as Woolf later explained in the unpublished essay, 'A Sketch of the Past', later collected in *Moments of Being* (1976),

> while we looked into the future, we were completely under the power of the past. Explorers and revolutionists, as we both were by nature, we lived under the sway of a society that was about fifty years too old for us (*MOB*: 147).

Beset by these ghosts of the past, Woolf's characters are forced to contend with the memories and legacies of these spectral figures, often embodied in photographs. In *The Voyage Out* (1915), Rachel's father consults the photograph of his dead wife in his decision to allow her to accompany Helen Ambrose; he gestures to the photo as he beseeches Helen to help make his daughter into 'the kind of woman her mother would have liked her to be' (*VO*: 86). Throughout the novel

Rachel's actions – culminating ultimately in her engagement to Terence Hewet – are determined by this ghostly presence of her mother and her generation, and she struggles throughout the book to cope with this burden. Later Rachel finds herself in a heated debate with her friend Evelyn Murgatroyd, who, flabbergasted at Rachel's obstinacy, asks her, 'Do you *believe* in anything?' 'In everything!,' she replies. 'I believe in the bed, in the photographs, in the pot, in the balcony, in the sun, in Mrs. Flushing . . .'. But she quickly goes on to qualify this statement:

> 'But I don't believe in God, I don't believe in Mr Bax, I don't believe in the hospital nurse. I don't believe –' She took up a photograph and, looking at it, did not finish her sentence.
>
> 'That's my mother,' said Evelyn, who remained sitting on the floor binding her knees together with her arms, and watching Rachel curiously.
>
> Rachel considered the portrait. 'Well, I don't much believe in her,' she remarked after a time in a low tone of voice. (*VO*: 250)

Like Rachel's mother, Evelyn's mother exemplifies that figure of domestic perfection that Woolf later termed the 'Angel in the House'. Women like Rachel in *The Voyage Out* and Katharine Hilbery in *Night and Day* (1919) are constantly reminded of these women who came before them, and shown their photographs as if these portraits of passive perfection offer objective proof of their own shortcomings. In the course of their own lives, then, they struggle to reject their mother's generation.

But not all of Woolf's characters are as quick to repudiate these ghosts. In general, the men in her novels embrace the past, as evidenced by the way they respond to these photographic portraits. In *Mrs Dalloway* (1925), the Dalloways' house contains a photo prominently displayed in their hallway of General Sir Talbot Moore, 'now deceased, who had written there (one evening in the eighties) in Lady Bruton's presence . . . a telegram ordering the British troops to advance upon a historical occasion' (*MD*: 106). Unlike Rachel, who refuses to 'believe' in her Victorian forebear, Richard Dalloway is captivated by the General's photo; after lunch with Lady Bruton, the narrator tells us, he 'strolled off as usual to have a look at the General's portrait, because he meant, whenever he had a moment of leisure, to write a history of Lady Bruton's family' (ibid.: 110–11) . Comfortable with the past in a way that Rachel can never be, Richard approaches the portrait with a scholarly fascination and reverence. As with Rachel's mother, the General's portrait represents an archetype of a Victorian figure, the military man stalwartly defending the Empire, not unlike the photograph of Evelyn Murgatroyd's father: 'a handsome soldier with high regular features and a heavy black moustache; his hand rested on the hilt of his sword' (*VO*: 250). While these are images against which the men in Woolf's novels compare themselves, they do not provoke the same kind of crisis.

Which is not to say that Woolf's men – particularly the young men like Jacob Flanders, or Katharine Hilbery's two suitors, Ralph Denham and William

Rodney – have an uncomplicated relationship to the past or its photographs. These younger men tend to fetishise the past, seeing themselves as inheritors of a grand tradition that includes more than just the Victorian age and its vast empire, stretching all the way back to the ancient civilisations of Greece and Rome; upon first arriving at college, Neville in *The Waves* (1931) describes how 'a noble Roman air hangs over these austere quadrangles' (*W*: 31). As a result, they tend to collect photographs which reflect this obsession with an archaic past, and are particularly drawn to photographic prints of ruins and classical art. In *Night and Day* Ralph Denham and William Rodney both decorate their rooms with photographs of 'bridges and cathedrals' and 'statues and pictures' (*ND*: 26, 73). And in *Jacob's Room* (1922), the narrator tells us that in the eponymous room are 'photographs from the Greeks, and a mezzotint from Sir Joshua – all very English' (*JR*: 28–9). It is a historical tradition which becomes increasingly distant to Woolf's young men, and as the Britain's global importance wanes, it becomes clear that photographs may be the only connection to the past that these men have.

Surrounded by images which keep them obsessed with the past, these Georgian men in turn judge their contemporaries in light of these classical ideas, as when Ralph tries vainly to quell his feelings towards Katharine:

> No doubt her beauty itself would not stand examination. He had the means of settling this point at least. He possessed a book of photographs from the Greek statues; the head of a goddess, if the lower part were concealed, had often given him the ecstasy of being in Katharine's presence. He took it down from the shelf and found the picture. (*ND*: 385)

As Ralph gazes at the photo of the statue, gradually his memories of Katharine come alive:

> In a second he could see her, with the sun slanting across her dress, coming towards him down the green walk at Kew . . . . He could see her faults, and analyze her virtues. His pulse became quieter and his brain increased in clarity. (*ND*: 385–6)

It is a central moment in the novel, when Ralph finally affirms to himself that he does indeed love Katharine. But this love remains complicated, since he cannot keep himself from seeing her in light of some classical statue, an idealised and objectified image of a woman that only superficially corresponds to Katharine.

Katharine, by contrast, does not think this way; she finds her mother's comparison of Ralph to a portrait of Mr Ruskin unfair, 'for a young man paying a call in a tailcoat is in a different element altogether from a head seized at its climax of expressiveness, gazing immutably behind a sheet of glass' (*ND*: 16). Katharine and Ralph's different ways of looking at these idealised portraits suggest a gendered difference in the way one approaches the past, and, by extension, photography. For alongside these fetishised images of the past is another kind of photographic presence, far more modern and disconnected from the past, one which offers a critique of this male nostalgia for a Victorian and Imperial past. This other photographic presence can best be summed up by the word 'snapshot': casual and ubiquitous photographs, taken with cheap cameras, which are the antithesis of framed Victorian portraits. In *The Voyage Out*, Clarissa Dalloway is described collecting snapshots of her travels: 'while Clarissa inspected the royal stables, and took several snapshots showing men now exiled and windows now broken. Among other things she photographed Fielding's grave' (*VO*: 39). With few exceptions, snapshots in Woolf's fiction are women's work, which reflects the cultural trends of the time: with the advent of Kodak's 'Brownie' camera, photography was promoted as an 'appropriate' activity and proper artistic expression for women. This feminine snapshot culture stands in contrast to the hard and classical world of great men, something Neville excoriates in *The Waves*: 'Let me at least be honest. Let me denounce this piffling, trifling, self-satisfied world; these horse-hair seats; these coloured photographs of peers and parades' (*W*: 70). Neville, a member of the last generation of colonial men, regards London as being spoiled by this influx of superficiality and crass commercialism, which make it impossible 'to read Catullus in a third-class railway carriage' (ibid.: 71).

Like Neville, Jacob Flanders rejects the modern world in favour of a classical purity, making a pilgrimage to Rome and Greece at the end of *Jacob's Room*. Even there, though, in the heart of this ancient civilisation, he is unable to escape the ubiquitous female photographer: '[he] turned, and there was Madame Lucien Gravé perched on a block of marble with her Kodak pointed at his head .... "Damn these women – damn these women!" he thought' (*JR*: 151). Madame Lucien Gravé's intrusive act spoils the profound meditation of Jacob, but this is precisely Woolf's point. These 'damn women' with their snapshots offer a critique of the self-satisfied seriousness of men like Jacob and Neville, and a corrective to men like Ralph Denham who judge their mates according to classical statues. As William R. Handley writes, 'One project of Woolf's modernism was to dissociate the aesthetic from social elitism, to free culture from its stony objectified entrapment in order to include and emancipate the marginalized within a more democratic cultural discourse'. In this, Handley argues, the sudden emergence of Madame Lucien Gravé in Jacob's maudlin meditations offers just such an eruption of the marginalised: 'She turns her "Kodak" with its contemporaneity at Jacob: photography, like the novel, frames the ordinary, mortal individual, not the sculpted epic or heroic type' (Handley 1991: 117). Just as Woolf saw in the novel the possibility of presenting a new kind of subjectivity, her female characters' use of disposable and candid snapshots deflates the narcissistic nostalgia of these 'heroic' men, laying the groundwork for a new kind of subject. Thus Woolf's fiction, especially her early novels, marks a conflict between an older culture exemplified by the staged portrait, and a younger generation represented by cheap prints and disposable Kodaks – a generation whose men long nostalgically for that past (with their prints of classical statues), even as its women break with the past through a more modern form of photography.

For someone like Jacob, obsessed with the great works of the past, this intrusion of Kodak women disrupts not just his concentration, but – more significantly – the very possibility of what he recognises as art. As the portable camera democratises picture taking, the notion of an elite art belonging exclusively to educated men comes under assault, and women go from being the objects of art to the artists themselves. *Mrs Dalloway*'s Sir William Bradshaw seems to suggest this as he is treating Septimus Smith (the kind of man, one can presume, that Jacob Flanders might well have become had he survived the war), and his mind wanders to his wife's photographic talents: 'if there was a church building, or a church decaying, she bribed the sexton, got the key and took photographs, which were scarcely to be distinguished from the work of professionals' (*MD*: 95). If modernity has severed these men's connections to their colonial and classical past, then cheap and widely available cameras further threaten to destroy a male dominated narrative of art. Anticipating Walter Benjamin's 1938 essay 'The Work of Art in the Age of Its Technological Reproducibility', Woolf's fiction suggests the way in which the camera can diffuse the 'aura' that lies at the heart of an entire tradition of art. Unlike Benjamin, however, Woolf sees this tradition as laden with patriarchal assumptions, and thus the camera's assault of art is inherently gendered.

This new snapshot culture's critique of a Victorian portrait culture can be seen, finally, as a larger comment on the changing nature of the British Empire. Gone are the General Sir Talbot Moores, acting decisively to wage and win battles; in their place are men like Jacob Flanders, who brood sullenly before being sacrificed senselessly in trench warfare. Gone are the charming and pure Mrs Ramsays, replaced by the human and flawed Clarissa Dalloways, captured not in staged portraits but in fleeting and at times unflattering snapshots. This theme ran through all of Woolf's writings, of course, but it is especially present in her treatment of photography, and can be seen clearly in the final scenes of Woolf's last novel, *Between the Acts* (1941). After depicting the entire history of England with a troupe of local children, Miss La Trobe ends her play with 'the present day'; Miss La Trobe's innovation, however, is not to simply stage this final act, but to have the actors bring out mirrors trained on the audience:

> Out they leapt, jerked, skipped. Flashing, dazzling, dancing, jumping. Now old Bart . . . he was caught. Now Manresa. Here a nose . . . There a skirt . . . Then trousers only . . . Now perhaps a face . . . Ourselves? But that's cruel. To snap us as we are, before we've had time to assume . . . And only, too, in parts . . .. That's what's so distorting and upsetting and utterly unfair. (*BTA*: 184)

As Gillespie notes, the children act 'in lieu of photographers', 'snapping' the audience before they've had time to 'assume' a pose as they would before a portrait sitting (Gillespie 1993: 145). This camera-like 'snapping', which offers only fragments and body parts (a nose, a skirt, perhaps a face) comes then to stand in for the disintegration of the Empire, as the play's narrator (a disembodied voice from an off-stage gramophone) proclaims,

> *Look at ourselves, ladies and gentlemen! Then at the wall; and ask how's this wall, the great wall, which we call, perhaps miscall, civilization, to be built by* (and here the mirrors flicked and flashed) *orts, scraps and fragments like ourselves?* (*BTA*: 188)

In her final novel, Woolf had marshalled the fragmentary nature of the photographic to critique an equally fragmenting British Empire; Miss La Trobe's closing jeremiad hearkens back to a classical unity of the past that Woolf herself found neither possible nor interesting. The future lay, for Woolf, not in rebuilding the great wall called civilisation, but precisely in these scraps and fragments that make up real life.

Seeing Photographically

Like many of her fellow modernists, Woolf broke from the Victorian tradition of realism and excessive visual description in favour of descriptions of interior consciousness, and complained that her forebears, for all their fidelity to detailed physical description, too often missed 'human nature', something far more ineffable and subjective. At first glance, this turn away from physical description to some intangible human character would seem to indicate a rejection of a photographic way of seeing. Indeed, as Diane F. Gillespie points out, Woolf often used the adjective 'photographic' to mean 'superficial, representational, whether in paintings or in novels' (Gillespie 1993: 115), as in a 1940 letter in which she derisively describes the novelist Winifred Holtby as having 'a photographic mind, a Royal Academicians mind. Its as bright as paint, but how obvious, how little she's got beneath the skin' (*L6*: 382). Her own fiction, one can thus presume, would be far from 'photographic', focusing on invisible subjectivity rather than external objective description. But as Michael North has stressed in his book *Camera Works*, 'to disdain the conventionally photographic is not at all the same as disdaining photography' (North 2005: 24), and following North's distinction, we can see in Woolf's most innovative novels a use of a photographic idiom to describe different modes of consciousness, even as she rejects the 'conventionally photographic' technique of surface objectivity.

In order for Woolf to effect her innovative turn to interior consciousness, she focused increasingly on the nature of seeing itself, and set about describing a new kind of vision that allowed for a focus on interiority and subjectivity. Differentiating herself from naturalism's tradition of excessive exterior description, Woolf's language turns to the 'invisible': her most sympathetic characters are those whose vision extends beyond the immediately evident, such as Clarissa Dalloway ('She had the oddest sense of being herself invisible, unseen' [*MD*: 10–11]) and Septimus Smith ('Look the unseen bade him' [ibid.: 25]). As paradoxical as this may initially seem, many critics have traced this kind of 'invisible sight' to the camera itself. Beginning with Eadweard Muybridge's 1880s images of horses in full gallop, the camera came to be recognised for its ability to exceed the normal limits of human sight, and capture what Walter Benjamin has called the 'optical unconscious':

> Whereas it is a commonplace that, for example, we have some idea what is involved in the act of walking (if only in general terms), we have no idea at all what happens during the fraction of a second when a person actually takes a step. Photography, with its devices of slow motion and enlargement, reveals the secret. It is through photography that we first discover the existence of this optical unconscious, just as we discover the instinctual unconscious through psychoanalysis. (Benjamin 1999: 510–12)

The camera for many thus becomes aligned not with the plainly visible but with the invisible, precisely in its ability to reveal to us some hidden facet of the world which might otherwise slip by unnoticed. As Michael North notes, for many artists 'the peculiar power of photography lay precisely in its differences from ordinary vision, which gave it the ability to expose the irrational underside of what had come to be accepted as reality' (North 2005: 10).

Few artists or writers saw this more clearly than Woolf, and often the moments in Woolf's fiction that reflect this invisible seeing also borrow from a photographic lexicon – as in *To the Lighthouse* (1927), when Lily Briscoe suddenly comes to an understanding of Mr Tansley during Mrs Ramsay's dinner party:

> Sitting opposite him, could she not see, as in an X-ray photograph, the ribs and thigh bones of the young man's desire to impress himself, lying dark in the mist of his flesh – that thin mist which convention had laid over his burning desire to break into the conversation? (*TTL*: 90–1)

Even more striking is a passage from 'A Sketch of the Past':

> While I write this the light glows; an apple becomes a vivid green; I respond all through me: but how? Then a little owl chatters under my window. Again, I respond. Figuratively, I could snapshot what I mean by some image; I am a porous vessel afloat on sensation; a sensitive plate exposed to invisible rays; and so on. (*MOB*: 133)

Her tone is playful perhaps, but the fact remains that there is a close kinship between photography and Woolf's own assessment of her writing as a photographic plate onto which invisible rays are traced. As Woolf's writing turned from external descriptions to the invisible light of human nature, she found in the 'optical unconscious' of the photograph a particularly apt analogy.

Woolf seems to have found that a photographic way of seeing could allow her access to those 'moments of being' that make up real life in her fiction. Just as certain photographic techniques allow one to see beyond the visible, the camera's frame also cuts up the visible into discrete segments; as Rosalind Krauss writes, 'Photographic cropping is *always* experienced as a rupture in the continuous fabric of reality' (Krauss 1986: 115). Describing the lightning storm near the end of *The Voyage Out*, the narrator describes how 'The flashes now came frequently, lighting up faces as if they were going to be photographed, surprising them in intense and unnatural expressions' (*VO*: 368). Photography's ability to cut out a segment of continuous time and freeze it both 'intensely' and 'unnaturally' is reflected in the number of Woolf's characters who fixate not just on the past, but on a particular frozen image of the past. Peter Walsh, for example, remembering an afternoon with Clarissa Dalloway years earlier, exclaims to himself: 'How sights fix themselves upon the mind! For example, the vivid green moss' (*MD*: 64). It is a trait that many of Woolf's most richly drawn and sympathetic characters share; the past exists for them as a series of frozen images that they can return to with uncanny precision, and it is these frozen images of one's memory which invest the present with meaning. As Bernard in *The Waves* says, calling to mind his friends in a series of images in anticipation of their reunion, 'These are fantastic pictures – these are figments, these visions of friends in absence, grotesque, dropsical, vanishing at the first touch of the toe of a real boot. Yet they drum me alive' (*W*: 117).

Structurally as well, Woolf came to see her art as analogous to photography. In 'A Sketch of the Past' Woolf describes her own aesthetic practice as 'scene making':

> A scene always comes to the top; arranged; representative. This confirms me in my instinctive notion – it is irrational; it will not stand argument – that we are sealed vessels afloat upon what it is convenient to call reality; at some moments, without a reason, without an effort, the sealing matter cracks; in floods reality; that is a scene. (*MOB*: 142)

With these scenes, discrete and self-contained, Woolf does not aim for a unified whole; rather, the sharp breaks and disjunctions from one scene to the next are her way of shocking the reader out of a complacent view of reality. In piecing together these disparate fragments, the reader starts to see a pattern that lies behind the fragments, as the 'sealing matter cracks' and 'floods reality in'.

This scene-making finds its analogue not in painting, with its unity and harmony of form, painstakingly created by an artist suffused with vision, but with photography, as a series of momentary snapshots that arrest moments in the past, as in her elegiac description of her parents' bedroom as a camera which records the past:

> It was not a large room; but its walls must be soaked, if walls take pictures and hoard up what is done and said with all that was most intense, of all that makes the most private being, of family life. In the bed four children were begotten; there they were born; there first mother died; then father died, with a picture of mother hanging in front of him. (*MOB*: 118)

This metaphor of the walls as a camera, taking pictures of the 'most private being' of family life, reflects how Woolf structured her mature novels, starting with *Jacob's Room*. Whereas *The Voyage Out* and *Night and Day* had been perfectly plotted narratives building, respectively, towards a death and a marriage, *Jacob's Room* was an intentional cacophony of moments, with scraps of conversation and disconnected events forming a loose impression of its protagonist, rather than a finely detailed portrait – what Edward L. Bishop has described as a 'freeze frame effect', where 'the sections are like individual photographs; the book as a whole is like an album of snapshots' (Bishop 2007: 314–15), though it is, in Vara Neverow's words, 'a rather disorganized photo album', in which 'snapshots' of Jacob's life are 'jumbled together' (Neverow 1999: 78).

Woolf would use various versions of this format throughout her fiction, culminating in *The Years* (1937), in which a sixty-year history of the Pargiter family is told through a series of seemingly random and insignificant events, the narrative alighting at irregular intervals through the generations. Despite this somewhat haphazard structure, though, the book is driven by this same belief in a reality that lies behind a surface appearance; as Eleanor Pargiter wonders, 'is there a pattern; a theme, recurring, like music; half-remembered, half-foreseen? . . . a gigantic pattern, momentarily perceptible?' (*Y*: 369). But Woolf's goal was never to simply present such a pattern through laborious description or discursive explanations, but rather to let its presence be felt through scene making, by pointing to the cracks which might reveal the pattern beneath the surface. These individual scenes, even if all added together, do not form a complete and unified image; as Eleanor's nephew North says, 'These little snapshot pictures of people left much to be desired, these little surface pictures that one made, like a fly crawling over a face, and feeling, here's the nose, here's the brow' (*Y*: 317). Woolf's point was precisely in eschewing the whole portrait in favour of snapshot pictures that 'left much to be desired'; her method of working was to assemble enough of 'these little snapshot pictures' until their inadequacy could no longer be denied, and they cracked and gave way to something else beneath.

Woolf's 'Image/Texts': *Orlando, Three Guineas* and *Flush*

On 5 October 1927 Woolf wrote in her diary an idea for a book: 'a biography beginning in the year 1500 & continuing to the present day, called Orlando: Vita; only with a change about from one sex to another' (*D3*: 161). The concept of a 'mock-biography', a book that was both a biography of her friend and lover Vita Sackville-West while at the same time clearly a novel, seemed to give Woolf licence to do what none of her contemporaries – even those who, like James Joyce, were radically re-conceiving the limits of the novel – had yet done: break the hegemony of the text of the novel by introducing photographs. Disregarding the whole tradition of Victorian illustration, in which images are merely optional supplements to the prose, with *Orlando* Woolf created a work in which the images function integrally in the novel as a whole, as she would do again with *Three Guineas,* and, to a lesser extent, her mock-biography of Elizabeth

Barrett Browning's spaniel, *Flush*. As Maggie Humm has noted (Humm 2003: 213), these books use photographs in conjunction with the text itself to produce what W. J. T. Mitchell calls 'image/texts': 'composite, synthetic works' that act as 'a site of dialectical tension, slippage, and transformation' (Mitchell 1994: 89, 106). In both *Orlando* and *Three Guineas*, the subject of this tension and transformation is mortality itself.

Many of Woolf's major works revolve around a central death, and with such a fascination with the way death impacts the inner lives of those left behind, Woolf's interest in photography makes sense, since, as Susan Sontag writes, 'Photography is an elegiac art, a twilight art . . . . All photographs are *memento mori*. To take a photograph is to participate in another person's (or thing's) mortality, vulnerability, mutability' (Sontag 1977: 15). Sontag's use of the phrase *memento mori* (remember that you must die) is an evocative one when applied to Woolf, because in *Orlando*, a work that stages the relationship of photography to consciousness, includes its own a literal *memento mori*: early in the novel, Orlando (still a young man at that point) descends into his family's crypt to contemplate the bones of his ancestors:

> 'Nothing remains of all these Princes,' Orlando would say, indulging in some pardonable exaggeration of their rank, 'except one digit,' and he would take a skeleton hand in his and bend the joints this way and that. 'Whose hand was that?' he went on to ask. (*O*: 71)

Echoing Hamlet, Orlando contrasts the mortal works of these long-dead men and women with the immortal word of literature, which solidifies his desire to be a writer: 'what remained? A skull; a finger', he muses, turning to the writings of Sir Thomas Browne, 'and Orlando, comparing that achievement with those of his ancestors, cried out that they and their deeds were dust and ashes, but this man and his words were immortal' (*O*: 81). Thus Woolf casts Orlando in the role of St Jerome as he was popularly depicted: writing the immortal word in the presence of a skull that indicates one's mortal life. The moment is ironic, of course, in the sense that, of all of Woolf's characters, the one who need least remember the fact of death is Orlando, who ages a scant twenty years over the course of four centuries, and lives (we presume) well beyond the end of the novel.

But if Sontag is accurate in asserting that the photograph by its nature highlights its subject's mortality, then the scene in the crypt needs to be contrasted with the photographs which punctuate the novel, primarily those of 'Orlando herself' – Vita Sackville-West, the subject of Woolf's mock-biography and the model for the photographs of Orlando. For the photographs in *Orlando* age differently than the rest of the novel. Like Orlando's un-ageing nature, the prose of Woolf's novel is eternally in the present, as is the nature of fictional prose (as opposed to traditional biography). But *Orlando*'s photographs operate differently. Unlike the text of the novel, they acquire an aura that is as much a function of their ageing technology as anything else. While Woolf's prose exists in an eternal literary present, the photographs seem to us now from a different era. 'Photography is the inventory of mortality', Sontag writes. 'A touch of the finger now suffices to invest a moment with posthumous irony. Photographs show people being so irrefutably *there* and at a specific age in their lives' (Sontag 1977: 70). As Orlando's life continues into the present day, her image is rooted in the past. By juxtaposing a prose portrait of a forever un-ageing Orlando with the temporally specific images of Sackville-West, Woolf's novel stages this tension between what the book's narrator calls the 'time of the mind' and the 'time on the clock' (*O*: 98) as a divide between the text and its illustration, between prose and photography. In a work which offers such an elastic vision of temporality, where past and present are blurred, and which contrasts the 'time of the mind' with the 'time on the clock' alongside the time of the novel and the time of the photograph, the caption under the last photograph is notably ambiguous. Labelled simply 'Orlando at the Present Time', the caption invites us to ask, 'Which time?'

The problem of temporality is only one way in which Woolf uses these photographs. In Woolf's image/texts, much of the force comes from the tension between what is shown and what is described. Woolf's work thus offers a surprising contribution to the history of ekphrasis, the literary technique of verbally describing a visual image. Rather than duplicating a photograph with a verbal description, the ekphrastic moments in Woolf's texts are in sharp relief to the actual images presented. In *Orlando,* for example, the narrator uses two contrasting images – one of Orlando as a male and one as a female – to highlight gender differences:

> If we compare the picture of Orlando as a man with that of Orlando as a woman we shall see that though both are undoubtedly one and the same person, there are certain changes. The man has his hand free to seize his sword; the woman must use hers to keep the satins from slipping from her shoulders. The man looks the world full in the face, as if it were made for his uses and fashioned to his liking. The woman takes a sidelong glance at it, full of subtlety, even of suspicion. Had they both worn the same clothes, it is possible that their outlook might have been the same too. (*O*: 188)

But the actual photographs included in the novel, including the paintings showing Orlando as a boy and as ambassador, contain none of these signifiers. Instead the illustrations reveal a figure who transcends these distinctions altogether: the enigmatic pose and at times androgynous features of Sackville-West present an altogether different image than the more rigid gender binary that the ekphrastic description offers (see Figure 21.1). The figure depicted in the photos is, in many ways, absent from the prose itself; Orlando changes from a definitive male to a definitive female, whereas Sackville-West more ambiguously straddles the line, presenting a blurred composite of the two halves of Orlando's self. The full portrait of Orlando lies somewhere between the two, between the prose and the images.

Figure 21.1 'Orlando at the Present Time' from *Orlando*, photographed by Leonard Woolf. Courtesy of the Society of Authors

This is echoed in *Flush*, Woolf's 'biography' of Elizabeth Barrett Browning's spaniel. We are told early on that 'It is to poetry, alas, that we are to trust for our most detailed description of Flush himself as a young dog' (*F*: 10), a line that indicates not only that any verbal description is inherently lacking, but also that it is all that is available to us. Yet *Flush* contains a photographic frontispiece of a spaniel (actually, Woolf's spaniel Pinka), creating an acute tension between the narrator's description and the photograph. The frontispiece would seem to offer all that a poetic description, alas, would be lacking, but this wealth of additional visual information is immediately nullified, since only in poetry is an image of

Flush available. The photograph stands in a curious state of limbo, simultaneously more *and* less than the verbal description in the text.

Later in *Orlando*, Woolf's protagonist returns once more to the crypt, having travelled to Turkey as ambassador and returned, miraculously, a woman. The scene is notable for the shift in awareness that these experiences have left on Orlando, who is now far more aware of issues of class, race, imperialism and gender: 'But even the bones of her ancestors, Sir Miles, Sir Gervase, and the rest, had lost something of their sanctity' (*O*: 174), the narrator tells us, a shift in emphasis in *Orlando*'s *memento mori* scene that suggests a woman might respond to this traditional tableau far differently than one not accustomed to peering beyond surfaces. And indeed, this perspective will anchor Woolf's other major image/text, *Three Guineas*. Much of that essay is staged as an extended meditation on a photograph of death – a contemporary *memento mori* – and the radically different ways in which a woman approaches such an image.

Responding to the question of war and its relationship to patriarchy, *Three Guineas* revolves around a photograph Woolf describes of the Spanish Civil War, which depicts

> what might be a man's body, or a woman's; it is so mutilated that it might, on the other hand, be the body of a pig. But those certainly are dead children, and that undoubtedly is the section of a house. (*TG*: 10–11)

This image is not reproduced in the essay, though she refers to it repeatedly. Woolf instead includes five photos of elaborately dressed men – a general, heralds, a university procession, a judge and an archbishop – which act as parodic counterpoints to the Spanish Civil War image (see Figure 21.2). She does not comment on these images directly, allowing them to interrupt the text at seemingly random moments. Many writers have commented on the tension between these two photographic elements. Writing of Woolf's decision not to publish the Spanish Civil War photograph, Emily Dalgarno points out that in

> the encounter with images of the victims of war Woolf seeks to resist the conventions of the text that accompanies photographs of the wounded, the suffering or the dead. Acting for the moment like Lily Briscoe, Woolf rejects the vocabulary of mastery on the grounds that it would disable her as an artist. (Dalgarno 2001: 165)

This 'vocabulary of mastery' is exactly what is to be found in the images of the general, the archbishop, the judge or the university procession, all of whom display their mastery through elaborate dress, like so many plumed birds. 'As a result', Dalgarno concludes, 'the Spanish photographs become disturbances in the text rather than unproblematic illustrations of human suffering' (Dalgarno 2001: 165).

Because of this, both Maggie Humm and Diane F. Gillespie see the disturbance caused by the photographs in gendered terms, and connect the use of photography to the book's larger critique of patriarchy: 'Woolf counters a

Figure 21.2 'A General' from *Three Guineas*, photographer unknown. Courtesy of the Society of Authors

masculine, patriarchal world represented by the five published newspaper photographs', Humm writes, 'with a feminine "affect" of the narrator's visual memories of photographs of fascist atrocities' (Humm 2003: 196). And, as Gillespie argues, 'What the Spanish Civil War photographs have done to the dead and wounded, so the real photos she includes in *Three Guineas* ironically "feminize" rather than glorify those in power' (Gillespie 1993: 141). As Woolf had done in her earlier fiction, she here once again uses photography as a means of critiquing a masculinist and misogynist worldview.

In her discussion of the Spanish Civil War photograph, Woolf refers repeatedly to its 'truth', the undeniable fact of its indexical status: 'Photographs', she writes early on, 'of course, are not arguments addressed to the reason; they are simply statements of fact addressed to the eye' (*TG*: 10). It would seem that with *Three Guineas* there is no ambivalence towards the medium's objectivity: 'Let us then leave it to the poets to tell us what the dream is; and fix our eyes upon the photograph again: the fact' (ibid.: 143). Yet almost as frequently, Woolf uses photography for a different rhetorical purpose: as a simulacrum of reality, particularly in regards to women's experience. 'And if it is true that the daughters of educated men', she writes, 'have no direct knowledge, still through fathers and uncles, cousins and brothers they may claim some indirect knowledge of professional life – it is a photograph that they have often looked upon' (ibid.: 49). And it is indeed these 'photographs', of empty ritual and pomp, that the reader is looking upon, since Woolf punctuates her book with photographs of the professional life that women have as of yet very little direct access to. Thus the actual reproduced images are meant to be read as simulacra, at the same time that the nonrepresented photo is the truth, the real.

In order, then, to make sense of how the unrepresented photograph functions as 'truth', it is important that the dead body in the image is so mutilated that its sex cannot be identified. In a work that so forcefully articulates a binary between men and women, arguing for radically different experiences and belief-systems between the two genders, it is significant that the central 'truth' of the work is a corpse that has been rendered sexless by war's destruction. The image seems to be telling us that patriarchy's investment in war, if carried through to its utmost level of violence, will ultimately destroy the gender binary that grounds patriarchy in the first place. This photograph, then, is indeed Sontag's *memento mori*, but what it suggests is not only must you remember that one day you'll be dead, but also without a sex. As a young man in his ancestor's tomb, Orlando had had a similar realisation: 'Whose hand was it? . . . The right or the left? The hand of man or woman, of age or youth? Had it urged the war horse, or plied the needle? Had it plucked the rose, or grasped cold steel?' (*O*: 71). By 1938, with war nearly a foregone conclusion, Orlando's unanswerable question became the basis for Woolf's most forceful polemic against war and patriarchy – embodied in a photograph of the dismembered and fragmented body.

Works Cited

Benjamin, Walter (1999) 'Little History of Photography', trans. E. Jephcott and K. Shorter, in *Selected Writings, Vol. 2*, ed. Michael W. Jennings, Howard Eiland and Gary Smith, Cambridge, MA: Belknap Press.

—— (2003) 'The Work of Art in the Age of Its Technological Reproducibility', trans. H. Zohn and E. Jephcott, in *Selected Writings, Vol. 4*, ed. Michael W. Jennings and Howard Eiland, Cambridge, MA: Belknap Press.

Bishop, Edward L (2007) 'Mind the Gap: The Spaces in *Jacob's Room*', in *Jacob's Room*, ed. Suzanne Raitt, New York: Norton.

Cameron, Julia Margaret (1973) *Victorian Photographs of Famous Men and Fair Women*, Boston, MA: A & W Visual Library.

Dalgarno, Emily (2001) *Virginia Woolf and the Visible World*, Cambridge: Cambridge University Press.

Gillespie, Diane F. (1993) '"Her Kodak Pointed at His Head": Virginia Woolf and Photography', in *The Multiple Muses of Virginia Woolf*, ed. Diane F. Gillespie, Columbia: University of Missouri Press.

Handley, William R. (1991) 'War and the Politics of Narration in *Jacob's Room*', in *Virginia Woolf and War: Fiction, Reality, and Myth*, ed. Mark Hussey, Syracuse, NY: Syracuse University Press.

Humm, Maggie (2003) *Modernist Women and Visual Cultures: Virginia Woolf, Vanessa Bell, Photography and Cinema*, New Brunswick, NJ: Rutgers University Press.

—— (2006) *Snapshots of Bloomsbury: The Private Lives of Virginia Woolf and Vanessa Bell*, New Brunswick, NJ: Rutgers University Press.

Krauss, Rosalind (1986) *The Originality of the Avant-Garde and Other Modernist Myths*, Cambridge: MIT Press.

Mitchell, W. J. T (1994) *Picture Theory*, Chicago: University of Chicago Press.

Neverow, Vara (1999) 'Thinking Back through Our Mothers, Thinking in Common: Virginia Woolf's Photographic Imagination and the Community of Narrators in *Jacob's Room, A Room of One's Own*, and *Three Guineas*', in *Virginia Woolf and Communities*, ed. Jeanette McVicker and Laura Davis, New York: Pace University Press.

North, Michael (2005) *Camera Works: Photography and the Twentieth-Century Word*, Oxford: Oxford University Press.

Sontag, Susan (1977) *On Photography*, New York: Picador.

Further Reading

Flesher, Erika (1997) 'Picturing the Truth in Fiction: Re-visionary Biography and the Illustrative Portraits for *Orlando*', in *Virginia Woolf and the Arts*, ed. Diane F. Gillespie and Leslie K. Hankins, New York: Pace University Press.

Knowles, Nancy (1999) 'A Community of Women Looking at Men: The Photographs in *Three Guineas*', in *Virginia Woolf and Communities*, ed. Jeanette McVicker and Laura Davis, New York: Pace University Press.

Luckhurst, Nicola (2001) 'Photoportraits: Gisèle Freund and Virginia Woolf', in *Virginia Woolf Out of Bounds*, ed. Jessica Berman and Jane Goldman, New York: Pace University Press.

Schaffer, Talia (1994) 'Posing Orlando', in *Sexual Artifice: Persons, Images, Politics*, ed. Anne Kidden, Kayann Short and Abouali Farmanfarmaian, New York: New York University Press.

Sontag, Susan (2003) *Regarding the Pain of Others*, New York: Picador.

Stearns, Thaine (ed.) (2008) *Virginia Woolf Miscellany: 'Woolf, the Photograph, and Photography'*, 74, Fall.

Wussow, Helen (1994) 'Virginia Woolf and the Problematic Nature of the Photographic Image', *Twentieth Century Literature*, 40.1: 1–14.

—— (1997) 'Travesties of Excellence: Julia Margaret Cameron, Lytton Strachey, Virginia Woolf and the Photographic Image', in *Virginia Woolf and the Arts*, ed. Diane F. Gillespie and Leslie K. Hankins, New York: Pace University Press.

22

VIRGINIA WOOLF ICON

Brenda R. Silver

Introduction

IT IS SUMMER 2008, and once again Virginia Woolf is everywhere, criss-crossing the cultural field. Not the writer herself, of course, but the 'Virginia Woolf' whose name and face and words have appeared so often in popular and literary culture as to make her a well-established cultural icon, as ubiquitous as Shakespeare albeit, for many, still more controversial. The National Theatre in London announces it is reprising its production of *Waves*, described as 'a work devised by Katie Mitchell and the Company from the text of Virginia Woolf's novel, *The Waves*' (National Theatre 2006). In the spring Patti Smith, poet, photographer, rock singer, included a photograph of Virginia Woolf's bed and a stone from the river Ouse, where Woolf drowned herself, in the one-woman exhibition of her art, 'Land 250', at the Fondation Cartier in Paris; she also gave a live performance billed as a reading of Virginia Woolf's works. The July issue of *Vanity Fair* features a picture of Angelina Jolie with Woolf's words from *Three Guineas* – 'As a woman I have no country. My country is the whole world' – superimposed on Jolie's arm, at first glance suggesting a tattoo. A source at the magazine tells me the quotation probably came from Bartlett's quotations, but was chosen for its appropriateness to the article, which highlights her internationalism. Meanwhile, the image sets off a discussion in the blogosphere as to whether Jolie actually has Woolf's words tattooed on her body. And, not surprising to anyone who follows politics in the United States, an article on Salon.com critiquing the so-called 'image problem' associated with Michelle Obama, the wife of the first African-American candidate for President of the United States, is called 'Who's afraid of Michelle Obama?' The subtitle for the article reads, 'The flap about the potential first lady's "image problem" proves how uncomfortable the country feels about a shift in racial dynamics' (Kaplan 2008), one that should have begun to erase the image of all black women as angry and scary, but has not yet.

These appearances are not a new phenomenon. For almost fifty years now a continuing stream of verbal and visual representations of Virginia Woolf have circulated in Anglo-American culture, endowing her with a visibility and an immediacy, a celebrity, that is still unusual for writers, the living as well as the dead. Occurring across the cultural terrain, whether in academic discourses, the intellectual media, or mass/popular culture, the proliferation of Virginia Woolfs has transformed the writer into a powerful and powerfully contested cultural icon, whose name, face and authority are persistently claimed or disclaimed in debates about art, politics, sexuality, gender, class, the 'canon', fashion, feminism, race and anger. The debates themselves have varied, and they have generated radically conflicting versions of 'Virginia Woolf', who must be understood in this context to be an image or representation, under erasure, between quotation marks.[1] The result has been to transform Virginia Woolf into an emblematic, deconstructive, postmodern phenomenon, multifaceted and border-defying, who undermines or puts into play any fixed, authoritative meaning associated with her image.

But however various or contradictory the representations may be, some clear patterns have emerged. One is the dominance of her association with fear: both the fears she is said to have experienced in her own life, including those linked to her madness and even more her suicide, and the fears she evokes in others. The second, a corollary, is the inseparability of these representations from the historical/cultural moments and locations in which they occur, making them vivid markers of cultural tensions and desires. During the past fifty years, these tensions have all too often been generated by women's entrance into the academic, intellectual, artistic and public realms. As a result, while feminists constructed a vibrant, creative, laughing Virginia Woolf who could be used as a talisman and model, others saw her as the embodiment of a monstrous feminine and very frightening indeed.

In this essay I will outline some of the broader themes suggested by the history of Virginia Woolf's iconicity and provide examples of both the representations that helped construct her extraordinary visibility and those that currently contribute to it. Today, a number of sites monitor her appearances and share them with others. The *Virginia Woolf Bulletin*, issued by the Virginia Woolf Society of Great Britain, for example, publishes a column called 'Virginia Woolf Today' that includes sightings sent in by readers; the column ends with the call, 'Please send me any relevant material that comments on Woolf's current standing and reputation'. Online, Paula Maggio's *Blogging Woolf* both records Virginia Woolf's appearances across literary and cultural venues and provides an extensive list of links to other Virginia Woolf sites; and Anne Fernald's *Fernham* blog charts sightings as part of its focus on 'Books, Food, Friends, and Virginia Woolf'. Meanwhile, posters to the VWOOLF email list both note and debate her iconic appearances; and, if all this is not enough, one can sign up for Google Alerts that will send you weekly updates of her presence on the web. Her status as *the* literary icon in the popular realm is so much a given these days that one journalist, describing the recent Jane Austen trend in novels, film and media coverage, declared, 'Austen is the Virginia Woolf of 2007' (Gates 2007: 70).

Background

This has not always been the case. For almost twenty years after her death Virginia Woolf's reputation and representation suffered an eclipse, acquiring a renewed public vitality only in the early 1960s, due in large part to the phenomenal success of Edward Albee's *Who's Afraid of Virginia Woolf?* (1962). By the time that the film version, starring Richard Burton and Elizabeth Taylor, had been nominated for fourteen academy awards, the media buzz alone ensured that most people, even those had never heard of the writer or her works, recognised the name. The result was to transform Virginia Woolf into a 'celebrity', known, in Daniel Boorstin's phrase, for her 'well-knownness' (Boorstin 1962); she had become a household name. By the end of the 1960s, the decade known for its sexual and political revolutions, including the rise of feminist movements and gay rights, Bloomsbury, and with it Virginia Woolf, were distinctly back in fashion. One impetus was Michael Holroyd's explicit discussion of Bloomsbury's complex sexual relations – its homosexuality, its bisexuality – in his biography of Lytton Stratchey, evoking responses of both pleasure and fear. Meanwhile, the women's movement was beginning to make its mark, both in the academic world and in the wider society. During the 1970s Woolf's words – 'a room of one's own', for instance – became a public slogan and her face, emblazoned on T-shirts, a public sight. By the middle of the decade, feminist literary critics in the academy were drawing upon the publication and interpretation of previously unpublished writings to construct 'Another Version of Virginia Woolf', the title of both a conference panel and a special journal issue (Moore 1977) that foregrounded her political, social and feminist writings and concerns.

Keenly aware of the politics of representation and cultural authority, American feminists in the 1970s, both in and out of the academy, subversively laid claim to Virginia Woolf's image and writings, articulating a new social and cultural text. In many ways they were wildly successful, making Virginia Woolf and her association with feminist agendas a potent cultural force. But as so often happens, success transformed subversiveness into respectability, producing both her elevation to canonical status and the iconoclastic desire to overthrow it. As Virginia Woolf's value increased, so too did the struggles over who would define her cultural standing and meaning, struggles intensified by those who wanted to reclaim her for more traditional sites of cultural power. By 1982, the year of her centenary, her iconicity in the United States had already produced this reaction, evoking denunciations of a Virginia Woolf 'cult' in both academia and popular culture and provoking self-declared 'intellectuals' to call for her return to a more appropriate – i.e., intellectual – sphere. It was during this period that the *New York Review of Books* elevated Virginia Woolf to an icon of western civilisation on a par with Shakespeare, offering its readers the choice of a David Levine T-shirt, featuring either Shakesphere or Woolf (see Figure 22.1), even as it persistently ignored the popular manifestations and feminist scholarship

Figure 22.1 Advertisement, *New York Review of Books*

that had made her so iconic a figure or found non-feminist writers to savage it. But by the early 1990s there was no turning back; Virginia Woolf had achieved an iconicity, however contested, however negative some of her instantiations are, that continues to flourish at all levels of culture and across national borders. This is true even in Britain, where her image and reputation have long faced a critique grounded as much in social class as cultural class and gender, a configuration that often tropes her as an upper-class, highbrow, denizen of Bloomsbury, whose novels are distinctly overrated.

Critical Frameworks

Before turning to specific examples of Virginia Woolf's iconic appearances, I want to introduce a number of critical concepts, all of them premised on her status as text, that help us read her postmodern undecidability and why it is perceived as both subversive and scary. Perhaps the most basic is versioning, a concept with ties to both the academic and popular realms. In literary studies, versioning evokes the practice of publishing all the different versions of an individual work, including prepublication texts (holographs, typescripts, etc.), a practice that challenged and substantially undermined the authority of any one version of the work. While the local effect is to provide 'enough different *primary* textual documents and states of major texts' for readers to explore their 'distinct ideologies, aesthetic perspectives, or rhetorical strategies' (Reiman 1987: 169), the broader impact has been to subvert the power of the single 'authorised' text, privileging instead the unstable, unfixed, postmodern work whose meanings are derived by readings of the differences among the multiple versions: a process of 'democratic pluralism' (Greetham 1992: 341–2). Virginia Woolf's feminist critics in the 1970s understood this clearly when they used her then unpublished works to establish 'Another Version of Virginia Woolf'.

In the popular realm this pluralism has been linked to 'black linguistic and musical practices that accent variance, variability – what reggae musicians call "versioning"' (Hebdige 1987: 12). For Dick Hebdige, the British cultural critic associated with the study of oppositional subcultures, versioning is distinctly subversive, opening up a space for multiple voices and fluid, evolving texts and inscribing a distinctly democratic principle. But in practice, as critics have pointed out, versioning is never distinct from the imbrications of social and cultural hierarchies and power. To this extent versioning intersects with Stuart Hall's useful definition of popular culture as 'the play in cultural relations', a realm in which 'what matters is *not* the intrinsic or historically fixed objects of culture, but . . . the class struggle in and over culture' itself. This definition 'treats the domain of cultural forms', including icons, as 'a constantly changing field' in which 'the meaning of a cultural form' is not only unfixed and very much of its moment, but often follows a trajectory from 'radical symbol' to a more neutral 'fashion' before becoming 'the object of a profound cultural nostalgia' (Hall 1981: 235, 228).

This is particularly true when the cultural form can also be understood as a star and read through the critical framework of star theory, an extremely fruitful method for exploring Virginia Woolf's iconicity. Here, Richard Dyer's characterisation of the star as a 'star image' situated at the intersections of semiology and sociology comes to the fore. To see Virginia Woolf as a star is to approach her as an image that is simultaneously textual (realised in a media text), social fact and ideological (grounded in and expressive of the contradictory sets of 'ideas and representations in which people collectively make sense of the world and the society in which they live'). The concept Dyer uses to explore the complexity of the star image and its necessarily ideological existence, 'structured polysemy', captures both the multiple, contradictory representations of Virginia Woolf and their necessary limitations: limitations of available texts and ideological/ institutional constructs at any particular cultural moment. In Dyer's words, structured polysemy suggests 'the finite multiplicity of meanings and affects they embody and the attempt so to structure them that some meanings and affects are foregrounded and others are masked or displaced' (Dyer 1990: 1–3). This process plays a significant role in representations of Virginia Woolf.

While Dyer's analysis focuses on Hollywood film, the concepts, he notes, are applicable to 'stars' in other realms as well, and several of his concepts are central to Virginia Woolf's status as icon/star. Note, for example, his insistence on the textuality of the star image: the interplay of the various and numerous media texts that constitute the image, including the 'vehicle' developed to feature a star and the responses to it by critics and commentators (Dyer 1990: 72). As Dyer notes, the star image incorporates

> what people say or write about him or her, as critics or commentators, the way the image is used in other contexts such as advertisements, novels, pop songs, and finally the way the star can become part of the coinage of everyday speech. (Dyer 1986: 3)

Who's Afraid of Virginia Woolf? comes immediately to mind. The result is a star image that is both intertextual and constantly changing; any reading of a star's 'meaning' needs to take into account the particular historical moment and the specific group that is responding.

The Importance of the Visual

Readings of Virginia Woolf also have to consider the star image's 'complex configuration of visual, verbal, and aural signs' (Dyer 1990: 38), with an emphasis here distinctly on the *visual*. There is no doubt that the visual aspects of Virginia Woolf icon are crucial to her visibility and her resonance. Virginia Woolf, as we know, was an extraordinary-looking woman, and we know this from the many extraordinary photographs of her that have circulated in our culture, creating by the contexts in which they appear and by their recurrence both the expectation and confirmation of particular sets of meaning. In this sense they fulfil the function of what Richard Brilliant describes as the image-sign and links to the symbolic and mythic. Repetition, he argues, is crucial to this 'consolidated portrait image', an image so familiar that often no label is necessary to evoke the desired response (Brilliant 1991: 47–8, 68). This is particularly true of G. C. Beresford's 1902 portrait of the twenty-year-old Virginia Stephen, seen in profile, looking into the distance, the image most widely reproduced on items ranging from Quentin Bell's 1972 biography of his aunt to T-shirts, posters and mugs; for years at a time it has been the bestselling postcard at the National Portrait Gallery in London. The widespread reproduction of this portrait, Hermione Lee argues, has contributed to one of the most persistent images of Virginia Woolf: ethereal, refined, asexual, vulnerable (Lee 1996: 246).

But other photographic portraits have also contributed to her image, portraits that portray a more powerful woman gazing more directly at the camera and evoke powerful responses from viewers: those taken by the Lenare studio in 1929, and those taken by the photographer Man Ray in 1934. In the Lenare portraits, Virginia Woolf appears either full-face or almost full-face, looking just past the camera; while one of them pictures her down to her waist, this is usually cropped, pulling our eyes once again to her face. These images appear in a number of films that draw upon and reproduce her scariness, including Alan Bennett's *Me, I'm Afraid of Virginia Woolf* (1978) and Stephen Frears' and Hanif Kureishi's *Sammy and Rosie Get Laid* (1987); in both of these, close-ups of her face and/or her eyes dominate the screen, invoking the figure of Medusa. In contrast, when the publicists for the Everywoman's Center at UMass, Amherst, chose the Lenare photograph in which she looks most directly at the audience for a 1972 poster, they paired it with Woolf's description in *Three Guineas* of the daughters dancing around the new house they have created, while their mothers 'laugh from their graves' (Woolf 2006: 100). In this way they anticipated Hélène Cixous's call to women in 'The Laugh of the Medusa' to confront their fears and see Medusa as beautiful, not deadly: as 'laughing,' scary, and strong (Cixous 1980: 255).

The most widely reproduced Man Ray portraits are equally striking and perceived to be just as frightening, particularly the one where, elbow propped on a table, arm raised and fingers spread, she stares off to the side with seeming intensity. This is the photograph that appears on the 12 April 1937 cover of *Time* magazine, bearing the caption 'Virginia Woolf. "It is fatal to be man or woman pure and simple"', the appearance, one could say, that turned Virginia Woolf into an American star. But while the cover marked the publication of *The Years*, which soon became a bestseller in the US, the article inside spends a great deal of time explaining why Americans should not be scared of her ('How Times Passes' 1937: 93–6). This is also the photograph that appears alongside Diana Trilling's 1948 attack on the writer in the *New York Times Book Review*, which includes a verbal portrait of Virginia Woolf's

> long tense face at once so suffering and so impervious . . . . Unmistakably it
> is the portrait of an extreme feminine sensibility, of a spirit so finely drawn

that we can scarcely bear to follow its tracings. But just as unmistakably it is the portrait of a pride of mind a thousand times more imposing than an army of suffragettes with banners! (Trilling 1948: 28–9)

In another of the Man Ray portraits, arms crossed over the back of a chair, Virginia Woolf stares directly at the camera; and a third, a half-length profile against a dark background, head tilted slightly back and the light falling on her hair and face, has a starkness and beauty that takes the breath away. That may well have been what L. Fritz Gruber thought when he chose this photograph, cropped and blown up so that her head and face fill the entire page, to include in his 1965 book *Beauty: Variations on the Theme* WOMAN *by Masters of the Camera – Past and Present*, where it evokes a different sort of fear: 'Here, too, foreshadowed in her haunted face is Virginia Woolf's eventual suicide by drowning' (Gruber 1965: 133).

Sammy and Rosie Get Laid: Why Virginia Woolf Is so Scary

What is it about Virginia Woolf that makes her such a star attraction: what makes her a figure so amenable to postmodern versioning, to 'structured polysemy', to 'the play in cultural relations' that both constructs her as transgressive cultural icon and evokes vehement power plays to contain this transgressiveness? One answer, born out by her representations, resides in the multiple, contradictory sites she occupies in our cultural discourses: British intellectual aristocrat, high modernist, canonical author, writer of bestsellers, Bloomsbury liberal, Labour Party socialist, feminist, sapphist, acknowledged beauty, suicide and woman. This multiplicity not only gives her the ability to cross the boundaries between such categories as high culture and popular culture, art and politics, masculinity and femininity, head and body, intellect and sexuality, heterosexuality and homosexuality, word and picture, beauty and horror, to name a few, but to undo or deconstruct the norms they name and contain. Situated on the borders, she becomes one with the monsters whom culture and cultural critics have always placed on the boundaries of what is acceptable, policing them by their very presence. 'A construct and a projection', Jeffrey Cohen writes, 'the monster exists only to be read: the *monstrum* is etymologically "that which reveals," "that which warns"'; it signifies both the place of social/cultural disruption and the space for change (J. Cohen 1996: 4). 'It is no accident', Slavoj Žižek notes, 'that "monsters" appear at every break which announces a new epoch', threatening to '[dissolve] all traditional symbolic links and [marking] the entire social edifice with an irreducible structural imbalance.' One of his examples is Virginia Woolf (Žižek 1992: 139–40).

At this point I want to turn to the text that was the starting point of my study of Virginia Woolf icon, the 1987 film *Sammy and Rosie Get Laid*, a text that graphically inscribes both the multifaceted, indeterminate, border-crossing Virginia Woolf and her inseparability from fear. Virginia Woolf performs this

role by the appearance of a poster-size reproduction of one of the Lenare portraits in many of the film's most telling scenes; she stares silently out at the
actors and towards the viewers, instilling fear even when she is not on the screen.
When I first wrote about the film I posed a number of questions that still serve
as an introduction to both the undecidability of Virginia Woolf's role in the film
and the multiple cultural discourses signified by her presence: What is Virginia
Woolf doing in this self-consciously postmodern depiction of London in the late
1980s, and why is she presiding over a race riot and the burning of the inner
city? The poster of Woolf hangs in the study of Rosie, social worker, feminist,
sometime political activist; Woolf's writings, in their distinctive Hogarth Press
covers, figure prominently in the centre of her bookshelves. Rafi, Rosie's father-
in-law, the Pakistani politician returned to the 'Home Country' to escape death
threats occasioned by his brutal persecution of his enemies, sees the flames
from the riot superimposed on Woolf's image and experiences her gaze with
horror. In a film where the text of T. S. Eliot's *Waste Land* covers the outside of
a caravan parked on a waste ground reclaimed by a counter-cultural multiracial
community, the status of 'high' modernism in the world of postmodern, postcolonial, metropolitan London is very much at stake, and Virginia Woolf seems to
have become an icon representative of modernism itself. Yet has she? And if so,
what do she and her gaze represent? Aloofness? A life and a writing style out of
touch with the political realities of her own day, let alone those of the present?
Or is her presence more contemporary, and perhaps more sympathetic? Does
it evoke her feminism, including her insistence on the interconnections of the
public and private spheres, and her elevation by modern-day feminists such as
Rosie (whose political commitments within the film are highly ambiguous) to
the position of 'matron saint' (Zwerdling 1986: 33)? Given the history of the
British perception of Woolf as the elite, snobbish Queen of Bloomsbury and, oh
yes, minor experimental writer, what does her centrality in this distinctly political film suggest? Does she preside over it as modernist, as feminist, as pacifist,
as highbrow, as sapphist, as suicide, as failed liberal anti-imperialist? And how
do we begin to decipher the film's construction of her enigmatic, silent, Mona
Lisa-like stare? (Silver 1991: 193–4).

My answer now would be, all of the above. Here, I want to concentrate on
that aspect of the film's construction of Virginia Woolf that associates her with
the mythic female monsters Medusa and the Sphinx and links her to fear. My
starting point is the scene in Rosie's study, where the newly arrived Rafi has
been put to bed under the poster of Virginia Woolf. In the script,

> *Rafi lies in bed in the half-lit room. He's asleep, having a nightmare. He
> cries out, then awakes. He lies there being stared at by Virginia Woolf,
> which becomes more horrible the more she looks at him. The noise from out-
> side rises around him. It could be in his head or for real: he doesn't know.
> He sits up. On the edge of the bed he pulls cottonwool out of his ears. He
> covers his face with his hands.* (Kureishi 1988: 12–13)

Figure 22.2 Still from *Sammy and Rosie Get Laid*, directed by Stephen Frears

In the film, the camera shifts back and forth from Rafi's startled stare to the photograph of Virginia Woolf, moving closer and closer until her eyes fill the screen (see Figure 22.2) What looks like lace curtains cover the portrait; flames burn at the bottom of the frame. Virginia Woolf might be presiding over sacrificial rites, or she might be the sacrifice. At any rate, Rafi's reaction is terror; still wearing his nightclothes, he runs from the room and the house.

What complicates any reading of this scene and Virginia Woolf's extended 'meaning' in the film is the crossover between the film's declared political agenda – its critique of British politics, especially under Margaret Thatcher – and its ambiguous gender politics. When approached through the film's inscription of British politics, Virginia Woolf's role is decidedly mixed. From one perspective she can be read as signalling moral outrage at Rafi's brutal treatment of his compatriots (he is haunted by one of his victims during much of the film), evoking, as in the scene of Rafi's nightmare, a moral terror as well as a fear of revenge. From another, she can be read as the failure of the liberal British intelligentsia, including those associated with Bloomsbury, to understand the complexity of the colonial and postcolonial situation; this latter is suggested by the appearance of the poster in a scene where Rosie defends Rafi to the women who want to confront him about his crimes. 'This is liberalism gone mad!', one of them declares. In the first case, Rafi's fear of Virginia Woolf would be justified, and we are meant to share it; in the latter, it is unclear how we are to read her, since we are not meant to reject Rosie's view. The same

ambiguity complicates our reading of the end of film when Rafi hangs himself
in Rosie's study while Virginia Woolf, we know, looks on.

Critics responded to Virginia Woolf's appearance in the film, when they
commented on it, with an aside that her meaning was obvious, but few explain
what it is and those that do contradict each other. The one thing that is clear is
that Virginia Woolf, capturing and controlling the gaze that has traditionally
belonged to men, is very scary indeed; looks, we could say, kill. It is at this point
that the monstrous female figure Medusa enters the film. In Stephen Heath's
formulation, 'If the woman looks, the spectacle provokes, castration is in the air,
the Medusa's head is not far off' (Heath 1978: 92). Or, as Jean-Pierre Vernant
puts it, 'Whoever sees the head of Medusa', where 'the strange beauty of the
feminine countenance . . . and the horrible fascination of death, meet and cross',
'is changed in the mirror of its pupils, . . . into a face of horror'; functioning as a
mirror, Medusa reflects back to you your own image and your own impending
death (Vernant 1991: 144, 150).

'On looks alone, I'd go for Virginia', Sammy responds when asked who
he'd rather sleep with, Virginia Woolf or George Eliot, projecting her into the
film's sexual/gender discourse. Here the fears associated with Virginia Woolf
read somewhat differently, albeit more clearly, and evoke another monstrous
female, the Sphinx. Virginia Woolf may mirror Rafi's worst nightmares, but as
the film progresses his nightmares have as much to do with his expectations of
'the family' and 'home' and wanting grandchildren as they do with his political
past. In this context Virginia Woolf can readily be read as embodying a threat to
manhood, heterosexuality, marriage, reproduction and the patriarchy: a threat
to the family that Rafi had abandoned earlier but wants Sammy and Rosie to
restore by having children. Rafi is explicit on the subject, asking Rosie, 'What
about the sound of little footsteps; isn't it about time? . . . I know you're a kind
of feminist, but you're not a lesbian too, are you?' As Virginia Woolf's avatar in
the film, Rosie proves scary to Sammy as well, who, despite their open marriage
and his sexual affairs, clearly wants more from her than she is willing to give.
Reviewers readily picked up on this, evincing their own fears in their description of Rosie as 'the Free Woman with the Gioconda smile', who is 'sphinx-like,
self-assured' (Andrews 1988: 13).

Who's Afraid of Virginia Woolf? Me, I'm Afraid of Virginia Woolf: The Monstrous Feminine

While Virginia Woolf's instantiations of both Medusa and the Sphinx are visually powerful and terrifyingly effective in *Sammy and Rosie Get Laid*, they are
not new, which might be the most frightening thing of all. By the time Kureishi
and Frears made their film, there was a long history of representing Virginia
Woolf as an embodiment of an uncanny, monstrous, feminine, associated with
psychic destruction and death. When Hopkins, the English teacher protagonist of Alan Bennett's television film *Me, I'm Afraid of Virginia Woolf*, is asked

whether Virginia Woolf is funny, he replies, 'Killing' (Bennett 1985: 38). The fears evoked by Virginia Woolf in these representations, as in *Sammy and Rosie Get Laid*, inscribe a complicated mixture of gender and sexual politics, including those associated with homosexuality and with childlessness, and a class politics that crosses between social class and cultural class and varies with the specific historical and cultural moment.

Viewed from this perspective, *Who's Afraid of Virginia Woolf?*, both the play itself and the reactions to it, becomes a case study of the fears evoked by the early stirrings of both the women's movement and an openly gay culture, manifested in part by the availability of the birth-control pill, women's increasing entrance into universities and the public sphere, and what conservative commentators perceived as the feminisation of culture. Both couples in the play, the older George and Martha and the younger Nick and Honey, are childless; both the individual figures and the couples were read from the beginning as enacting the behaviour of homosexual men, even as Martha was understood to be emblematic of the destructive dominant woman. The result is a crossing of misogyny and homophobia that is still difficult to unravel, although they both reveal fears that became inseparable from the understanding of Virginia Woolf. To the extent, then, that the moment of Albee's play marked 'a new epoch' that threatened to '[dissolve] all traditional symbolic links' (Žižek 1992: 139–40), Virginia Woolf became one of its warning monsters.

The title, *Who's Afraid of Virginia Woolf?*, and with it Virginia Woolf herself, enters the play initially as an example of academic humour: the play takes place in a small college town; both men are professors. Several commentators at the time described the title as a high-brow elitist joke, aligning Virginia Woolf with high culture in the cultural class wars. It returns at the very end, sung softly by George and answered by a broken Martha, 'I . . . am . . . George. . . . I . . . am . . . ' (Albee 1963: 242). By this time, though, it has taken on the intersecting cluster of meanings associated with sexuality, homosexuality, the fear of strong women, and childlessness that signified a feminisation of culture. For the American critic Leslie Fiedler, the 'new mutants' that populated Albee's play were endemic to the times:

> If in *Who's Afraid of Virginia Woolf?* Albee can portray the relationship of two homosexuals (one in drag) as the model of contemporary marriage, this must be because contemporary marriage has in fact turned into something much like that parody. (Fiedler 1971: 394)

It is a short step from Fiedler to the critics who read the play as a closet drama and the characters as 'saber-toothed humans', as one put it, 'who cannot reproduce, and who need to draw buckets of blood before they can feel compassion for each other' ('Who's Afraid . . . ' 1966: 84).

The childlessness associated with homosexuality becomes even more frightening when read through the women. If Martha, the older woman, represents a woman made monstrous and psychologically destructive of her husband by her failure to conceive, Honey, the younger woman, we learn, is actively intervening in the process. In this way she evokes the dangers attributed to the invention of the birth control pill, which was approved for sale in the United States in 1960 and used by 1,187,000 women by the end of 1962 (Halberstam 1993: 605–6). Fiedler was clear about what this meant: women were out of control; whereas 'the invention of the condom had at least left the decision to inhibit fatherhood in the power of the male, its replacement by the "loop" and the "pill" has placed paternity at the mercy of the whims of women' (Fiedler 1971: 391). As George puts it, evoking abortion as well as the Pill, 'How do you do it? Hunh? How do you make your secret little murders . . . Pills? PILLS?' (Albee 1963: 177). Both women, we could say, become the embodiment of everything that Robert Brustein, in an article headed 'Albee and the Medusa-Head', argues Albee and we fear in contemporary life: 'For if Albee can confront the Medusa-head . . . , he may yet turn us all to stone' (Brustein 1962: 29–30).

At one point in the play Martha yells at George, 'I'm loud, and I'm vulgar, and I wear the pants in this family because somebody's got to, but I am *not* a monster. I am *not*' (Albee 1963: 157), a claim undercut by one of the scripts for the film version that describes Martha 'seated at her dressing table' using 'an eyebrow pencil to apply a mustache and connect her eyebrows; she becomes at once a man and a monster' (Leff 1981: 454).[2] It is also undercut by the question mark in the title, which evokes another female monster, the Sphinx, whose riddle we must answer correctly or be destroyed. The result of Albee's representations of the women was to link Virginia Woolf to a monstrous feminine that brought with her the threat of annihilation.

However witty Alan Bennett's 1978 response, *Me, I'm Afraid of Virginia Woolf*, may be (and it is), and despite the ending in which Hopkins, the English professor who is teaching Virginia Woolf on the day the play occurs, recognises his homosexuality, an acknowledgement of the changed times, the role played by Virginia Woolf reprises her association with both Medusa and the Sphinx. As in *Sammy and Rosie Get Laid* (and Frears also directed Bennett's play), Virginia Woolf enters the play as a visual image, a poster of one of the Lenare portraits that Hopkins brings into his class at the Mechanics Institute. There, she evokes fears that are explicitly linked to her social class ('she'd have really looked down her snitch at me' [Bennett 1985: 60]), her cultural class (high art), her relationship with Vita Sackville-West and hence her homosexuality, and her childlessness: all of which signify her distance from 'life'. The students themselves alternate between sarcasm and dismissiveness, an attitude that would seem to be supported by one of the most significant aspects of her visual presence: her portrait has been defaced. When the poster is unrolled in the class, that is, someone has drawn on it a white moustache and what one reviewer called 'pumpkin breasts', indicative of the 'sexuality which an anonymous graphic critic held [her] to lack' (Barnes 1978: 796–7). This, one would think, would undermine the power of her gaze, but that is not the case. In the process of trying to erase the graffiti, one of the women students erases instead

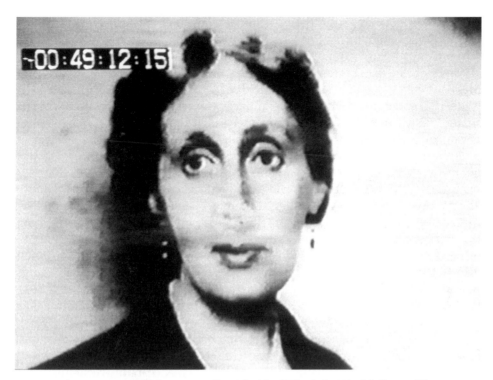

Figure 22.3 Still from *Me, I'm Afraid of Virginia Woolf*, directed by
Stephen Frears

her nose, producing a lack that is very scary indeed. For here Virginia Woolf's
nose, as Bennett and his audience would know, signifies more than class; it
signifies as well a far more frightening power, the phallic power attributed to
strong women. She might appear, in one student's words, a 'gormless-looking
cow' (Bennett 1985: 54) once the nose is gone, but the visible lack of the nose,
foregrounded in a scene when a close-up of her face dominates the screen (see
Figure 22.3), remains a vivid marker of the uncanny threat posed by Virginia
Woolf that no amount of erasing can undo. Instead her noselessness aligns her
the Egyptian Sphinx, whose lack of nose evoked responses that, in one commentator's words, invite us 'to discuss the Sphinx' as 'a new Medusa's Head, the
sign of an absence which can petrify' (Barrell 1991: 103).

Virginia Woolf and/as Female Star

Looking back at the moment of Bennett's play, one wonders if Bennett and
Frears were responding to the increasing appropriation of Virginia Woolf's
face during the 1970s by women who revelled in her power: women who hung
her face on their walls or, more publicly, wore it on T-shirts that were themselves a sign of rebelliousness at the time. As one historian noted, second-wave

feminists proudly displayed their historical icons, including Susan B. Anthony and Virginia Woolf, on T-shirts, no longer afraid to make a spectacle of themselves (Mayo 1978: 216ff.). Indeed, the wearing of Virginia Woolf's image on one's chest, like Perseus's or Athena's or the Greek warriors' wearing of Medusa's head on their aegis or shield, can be read as an act of both self-protection and defiance: a claiming of her powers for oneself. But not everyone shared this view, or they wilfully misinterpreted it, trying to regain control of her image by belittling these women as fans. Helen Dudar makes this clear in 'The Virginia Woolf Cult' when she laments that on 'the 100th anniversary of her birth', [Virginia Woolf] has not only become 'a feminist icon and a flourishing industry, with T-shirts and calendars,' but has also been transformed into 'the Marilyn Monroe of American academia' (Dudar 1982: 32). Interpreting this shared stardom for a sceptical British audience, Peter Watson writes, 'both had periods of neurotic madness; both made odd sheltering marriages; both evinced a subtle and sinewy feminism; both took their own lives' (Watson 1982: 22). But if the mantra 'Like Marilyn Monroe' is 'readily applicable to figures of glamour, femininity, fashion and tragic, early death' (McCann 1988: 181), the crossover also carries with it a scariness that makes Marilyn Monroe 'like Virginia Woolf'. Norman Mailer recognised this when he evoked Virginia Woolf in his 1973 biography of Monroe, associating both women with destructiveness, self-destructiveness, feminism and fear (Mailer 1973: 17–18). And the owners of the Hardback Café in Chapel Hill, North Carolina, certainly recognised this when, in the late 1980s, they put Virginia Woolf's head on Marilyn Monroe's body, creating not just a six-foot cardboard photomontage but yet one more scary female monster.

The crossover between Virginia Woolf and Marilyn Monroe anticipates what has become a recurring cultural trope: the crossing of Virginia Woolf with other female icons, including or particularly stars, that has become more frequent and to some extent less frightening over the past two decades, often having as much to do with celebrity *per se* as with any particular attributes. In the 1960s, for example, if you mentioned the name Virginia Woolf, you might get the response, '"Oh, yes, she was the one in that dirty movie!,"' crossing her with Elizabeth Taylor (Haight 1973: 426). With the advent of the internet and search engines, Virginia Woolf's intertextuality has become even more pronounced. Do a Google Image search for 'Virginia Woolf', for example, and you will find pictures not only of Elizabeth Taylor, but of Diana Riggs and Kathleen Turner, both of whom have performed the role of Martha in Albee's play.

You will, of course, also find innumerable images of Nicole Kidman, who played Virginia Woolf in the 2002 film version of Michael Cunningham's novel *The Hours*, itself a versioning of *Mrs Dalloway*, that turned Virginia Woolf, as one commentator put it, 'into this season's It girl' (P. Cohen 2003). In the novel and even more so in the film, our entry into the text is Virginia Woolf's suicide, setting the stage for one of her most recurring iconic representations: the tortured, mad, suffering, woman artist, characterised more by her own fears than by the fears she invokes in others: a role, my research assistant Laura Romain discovered, that still dominates her recent appearances. 'There is something about women who commit suicide, attempt suicide, or die in an untimely fashion', one commentator notes, 'that we find fascinating. It's not just tabloid stars', she continues, adducing the films *Sylvia* (Sylvia Plath), *Tom and Viv* (Vivien Eliot), *Carrington* (Dora Carrington), and *Fur* (Diane Arbus) along with *The Hours* to make her point (Cochrane 2007).

Ironically, though, what comes to the fore in both Cunningham's representation of Virginia Woolf and the reactions to the film are Virginia Woolf's star status and the way it is played off against the star power of the actress who impersonates her in the film. Cunningham, for example, is quoted on the VWOOLF list as saying, 'I suspect Virginia Woolf would love to be played by a tall, beautiful woman' (VWOOLF 2000), suggesting that Kidman increases Virginia Woolf's star power and cultural currency by impersonating her. This perspective is echoed by Erika Spohrer when she argues that 'Nicole Kidman lends star power to the film – and subsequently to Cunningham's book, Woolf's book [*Mrs Dalloway*], and even Virginia Woolf herself' (Spohrer 2005: 114, 117). Indeed, when the film opened in the US, *The Hours*, *Mrs Dalloway*, and even *To the Lighthouse* shot to the top of bestseller lists, including Amazon. com.

Others, though, see the exchange going in the opposite direction. Mary Desjardins, for example, a film theorist, argued at a 2003 round table on *The Hours* that all the women actors – Meryl Streep and Julianne Moore, as well as Kidman – benefited from their association with Virginia Woolf, a gain in cultural capital that compensated for the absence of good roles for women in Hollywood, especially as they get older, and the loss of economic capital that comes with those roles. This was particularly true for Kidman, she added, whose status had slipped in the period previous to the film.[3] Wendy Parkins is even clearer about who gains from this crossover, arguing that

> the significations of Kidman are played off against those of Woolf in a binary of more and less successful femininity. Genius, madness and childlessness (in the form of Woolf) are represented as ugliness, while by implication, on the other side of the feminine binary, beauty is associated with celebrity, success, and motherhood (Kidman). (Parkins 2007: 144)

This debate illustrates once again not only Virginia Woolf's indeterminancy, but how she becomes the site for struggles 'in and over culture itself' (Hall 1981: 235).

The Current Scene

Where are we today? According to Robert Carr-Archer, Head of Trading at the National Portrait Gallery in London, Virginia Woolf lost some ground to Jane Austen in terms of numbers of sales of their postcards during 2006–7, the year

Jane Austen had her popular revival. But while the postcard of the Beresford portrait is no longer their top-seller, the combined sales of the two postcards of Woolf – the photographic portrait by Beresford and a painting by Vanessa Bell – still come out highest 'in unit terms' and have begun to increase once more. 'The Beresford', Carr-Archer notes, 'in my view sells strongly because it a beautiful and romantic image', and not necessarily, as in the case of Austen, because people have read her works (Carr-Archer 2008).

Other contemporary appearances offer us less romantic, more diverse Virginia Woolfs, especially when she escapes the role of tragic suicide. When the editors at *Vanity Fair* magazine chose to put the quotation from *Three Guineas* on Angelina Jolie's arm, they were evoking Virginia Woolf at her most political and powerful, a woman willing to assert herself in the public realm. Although the article begins with Jolie's pregnancy, the focus is on the charity and refugee work that has taken her around the world and led to her 'appearances before the United Nations and the Council on Foreign Relations' (R. Cohen 2008: 132); it has also led to her adopting children from Cambodia, Ethopia and Vietnam. When it comes to what makes the Virginia Woolf-like Michelle Obama frightening, one commentator writes,

> The very qualities that make [Obama] an icon of twenty-first-century womanhood – her strong opinions, her frankness in expressing them, the confidence born of bootstrap triumphs – make her a rich target for those who still believe that *outspoken woman* and *first lady* should never be synonymous. (Brooks 2008: 115)

Meanwhile, Woolf's association with suicide has been reinterpreted in a number of recent artistic works, including several that take *The Waves* as a premise for their own versions of Virginia Woolf. These works tend to reinscribe and/or evoke some of the more negative readings of her death even in the act of challenging and reinterpreting them. In François Ozon's 2000 film *Under the Sand*, for example, it is not the protagonist, Marie, played by Charlotte Rampling, who kills herself, but, possibly, her husband, who disappears while his wife sleeps on the beach. The film is filled with images of water, including the waves at the beach that we are led to believe claimed him; Marie, an English professor, reads to her class a passage from Bernard's final soliloquy in *The Waves* about losing his youth and recites Woolf's suicide note on a date with a new suitor. Many of the reviews I've read construct Virginia Woolf's presence in the film through her madness and her suicide, troping her as Marie's 'spiritual godmother', presiding over her 'denial and hallucination' (Morris 2001), or reading her as an metaphor for Marie's 'emphatic' link to death (Vincendeau 2000). The latter leads the writer to critique the film as 'a male fantasy of a morbid and unhinged femininity', yet one more example of how 'French cinema loves beautiful, tragic women who go crazy' (ibid.). When it comes to *The Waves*, however, the verdict is mixed. For one reviewer, it a 'mournful book by a suicidal writer' that Marie has the 'misfortune' of reading to her students (Heer 2002: PM4);

for another, Marie 'is overcome by the obscure, complex emotion of Woolf's prose, the steady, sad and self-sufficient intelligence of which *Under the Sand*, at that moment and others, comes close to matching' (Scott 2001: E14).

More recently, Katie Mitchell's *Waves*, my second example, characterised by its multimedia audio, video and spoken rendition of Woolf's words, received a number of laudatory reviews that read it as a reflection of Virginia Woolf's experimental methods in the novel. But as Julia Briggs notes in her review, the words of the play, some from the novel, some from Woolf's memoir 'A Sketch of the Past', and some that sound like invented diary entries, tend to fixate on Rhoda, who is equated with Virginia Woolf herself. 'This identification of the neurotic and ultimately suicidal Rhoda with Woolf', she writes, 'was prefigured in the programme by a photograph of Angelica Bell as a drowning Ophelia, looking recognisably like her aunt.' Contrasting the invented passage at the end of the play that portrays a 'Virginia too careless and depressed to clean her nails' to the defiant 'Against you [death] I will fling myself, unvanquished and unyielding' at the end of the novel, Briggs concludes, 'Given Woolf's courage, creativity and optimism, it is a pity that new versions of her work should return so predictably to the sense of defeat that her fiction so eloquently rejects' (Briggs 2007: 64).

But when Patti Smith, a powerful woman icon in her own right, aligns herself with Virginia Woolf, she does not see her as neurotic or tragic. Introducing her concert in Paris on 28 March 2008, the anniversary of Woolf's death, Smith presents the suicide as a conscious decision,

> what she needed to do as a human being, and so I do not think of this as sad. I just think that it's the day that Virginia Woolf decided to say good-bye. So we are not celebrating the day; we're simply acknowledging that this is the day. . . . [I]f I had a title to call tonight I would call it Waves; we are waving to Virginia. (Smith 2008a)

In the performance itself, Smith interweaves passages from *The Waves* with poetic riffs that describe Virginia Woolf as warrior-like, responding to her losses not with retreat but with words. When she ends with Rhoda's desire to escape her demons, it becomes a powerful statement of self-assertion.[4]

This is not the only time that Smith has performed Virginia Woolf. In her 2003 and 2006 concerts at Charleston, the Bloomsbury outpost in Sussex, Smith combined words from Woolf's writings with her own poems, including the highly political 'Birds of Iraq'. One critic has described this poem as speaking 'about the supposed sanity of America's launching a preemptive strike on Iraq, by contrasting it with the madness and hallucinations of Virginia Woolf, whose loss of control over her own life, ultimately resulted in her tragic suicide' (Baesen 2005). But the poem also suggests something else, inscribed in the lines 'ambulance splattered/in Julian's blood' (Smith 2008b); a reference to the horrifying death of her nephew Julian Bell in the Spanish Civil War, these words bring into the poem the Virginia Woolf who wrote the angry, political, pacifist *Three Guineas*. Whether the 'highbrow' Virginia Woolf 'would approve of this new-found artistic affinity' on Smith's part, one typically sceptical British journalist writes, 'is, of course, debatable. . . . Nevertheless, they share certain stylistic similarities'. In the end, he concludes, we are left with 'one of today's great eccentric American bohemians [paying] homage to one of the great bohemian eccentrics of the 30s' (O'Hagan 2003), creating a hybrid more creative than destructive and giving Virginia Woolf still one more vibrant role on the world's cultural stage.[5]

Virginia Woolf icon, it is clear, continues to resist any single meaning, offering us vivid multifaceted images of our own ever-changing faces, cultures and history: our desires and fears.

Notes

1. Parts of this paragraph first appeared first in 'What's Woolf Got to do with It? or, the Perils of Popularity', *Modern Fiction Studies* (Silver 1992). Other parts of this essay originally appeared in *Virginia Woolf Icon* (©1999 by The University of Chicago. All rights reserved; reprinted with permission); and in 'Textual Criticism as Feminist Practice; or, Who's Afraid of Virginia Woolf Part II' in *Representing Modernist Texts*, ed. George Bornstein (© by the University of Michigan 1991. All rights reserved; reprinted with permission).

2. In an essay called 'Who's Afraid of Elizabeth Taylor?', Brenda Maddox noted that '"Who's Afraid of Virginia Woolf?" marked Elizabeth Taylor's debut as Medusa, the monster-woman with snaky hair and raging eyes that can transform mortals to stone' (Maddox 1977: 195).

3. Panel on *The Hours*, Virginia Woolf Conference, Smith College, June 2003.

4. I am grateful to the Fondation Cartier for providing me with a recording of Smith's performance.

5. Despite the fact that Smith had twice been artist-in-residence at Charleston by 2006 and it was 'close to her heart', a place, she noted in an interview, where '"I feel at home. . . . Whenever I'm here, I just want them to give me a bed so I can stay for ever"' (Sturges 2006: 15), no mention of Smith's artistic and emotional relationship to Virginia Woolf appears in Steven Sebring's film *Patti Smith: Dream of Life* (2008). Ten years in the making, the film covered the period of the Charleston visits and the concerts. In the interview Smith describes how going to the river Ouse to take a photograph of the place where Woolf died moved her to tears, an experience undocumented in a film that shows Smith visiting and photographing the burial places of male writers who have influenced her, such as Blake, Rimbaud and Gregory Corso.

Works Cited

Albee, Edward (1963) *Who's Afraid of Virginia Woolf?*, New York: Pocket.

Andrews, Nigel (1988) 'It's the Method that Damns, Not the Matter', *Financial Times*, 22 January: 13.

Baesen, Todd (2005) 'An Interview with Patti Smith on Auguries of Innocence', Patti Smith website, accessed 1 October 2008: www.kaapeli.fi/aiu/ps/auguries.html

Barnes, Julian (1978) 'Look up Life', *New Statesman*, 8 December: 796–7.

Barrell, John (1991) 'Death on the Nile: Fantasy and the Literature of Tourism, 1840–1860', *Essays in Criticism*, 4/12: 97–127.

Bennett, Alan (1978) *Me, I'm Afraid of Virginia Woolf*, dir. Stephen Frears, London Weekend Television, November.

—— (1985) *Me, I'm Afraid of Virginia Woolf: The Writer in Disguise*, London: Faber.

Boorstin, Daniel J. (1962) *The Image; or, What Happened to the American Dream*, New York: Athenaeum.

Briggs, Julia (2007) '*Waves*', *Virginia Woolf Bulletin*, Virginia Woolf Society of Great Britain, 25: 62–4.

Brilliant, Richard (1991) *Portraiture*, Cambridge, MA: Harvard University Press.

Brooks, Geraldine (2008) 'Camelot 2.0?', *More*, October: 113–17, 213–14.

Brustein, Robert (1962) 'Albee and the Medusa-Head', *New Republic*, 3 November: 29–30.

Carr-Archer, Robert (2008), private email to the author. Used with permission.

Cixous, Hélène (1980) 'The Laugh of the Medusa,' in Elaine Marks and Isabelle de Courtivron (eds), *New French Feminism: An Anthology*, Amherst: University of Massachusetts Press, 245–64.

Cochrane, Kira (2007) 'Why Suicide Is a Feminine Issue', *New Statesman*, 12 March, accessed 1 October 2008, www.newstatesman.com/society/2007/03/cochrane-suicide-women-issue

Cohen, Jeffrey Jerome (1996) 'Monster Culture (Seven Theses)', in Jeffrey Jerome Cohen (ed.), *Monster Theory: Reading Culture*, Minneapolis: University of Minnesota Press, pp. 3–25.

Cohen, Patricia (2003) 'The Nose Was the Final Straw', *New York Times*, 15 February, B: 9, accessed 1 October 2008: http://query.nytimes.com/gst/fullpage.html?res=9D07E4D612 3AF936A25751C0A9659C8B63&scp=2&sq=patricia%20cohen%20%22the%20 hours%22&st=cse

Cohen, Rich (2008) 'A Woman in Full', *Vanity Fair*, July: 68–74, 132–4.

Dudar, Helen (1982) 'The Virginia Woolf Cult', *Saturday Review*, February: 32–4.

Dyer, Richard (1986) *Heavenly Bodies: Film Stars and Society*, New York: St Martin's Press.

—— ([1979] 1990) *Stars*, London: BFI.

Fiedler, Leslie (1971) 'The New Mutants', in *The Collected Essays of Leslie Fiedler*, vol. 2, New York: Stein & Day, pp. 379–400.

Gates, David (2007) 'Jane Austen Outsells Alice Walker and Ann Coulter', *Newsweek*, 2/9 July: 70–1.

Greetham, D. C. (1992) *Textual Scholarship: An Introduction*, New York: Garland.

Gruber, L. Fritz (1965) *Beauty: Variations on the Theme WOMAN by Masters of the Camera – Past and Present*, London and New York: Focal Press.

Haight, Gordon S. (1973) 'Virginia Woolf', *Yale Review* 62: 426–31.

Halberstam, David (1993) *The Fifties*, New York: Villard Books.

Hall, Stuart (1981) 'Notes on Deconstructing "The Popular"', in Raphael Samuel (ed.), *People's History and Socialist Theory*, London: Routledge & Kegan Paul, pp. 227–40.

Heath, Stephen (1978) 'Difference', *Screen*, 19/3: 51–112.

Hebdige, Dick (1987) *Cut 'n' Mix: Culture, Identity, and Caribbean Music*, London and New York: Routledge.

Heer, Jeet (2002) 'Between Hope and Despair', *National Post* (Canada), 1 March.

Holroyd, Michael (1967) *Lytton Strachey: A Critical Biography*, London: Heinemann.

'How Times Passes' (1937) *Time*, 12 April: 93–6.

Jaffe, Aaron (2005) *Modernism and the Culture of Celebrity*, Cambridge: Cambridge University Press.

Kaplan, Erin Aubry (2008) 'Who's Afraid of Michelle Obama?' Salon.com, 24 June,
    accessed 1 October 2008: www.salon.com/mwt/feature/2008/06/24/michelle_obama/
    index.html
Kureishi, Hanif (1988) *Sammy and Rosie Get Laid: The Script and the Diary*, London:
    Faber.
Lee, Hermione (1996) *Virginia Woolf*, London: Chatto & Windus.
Leff, Leonard (1981) 'Play into Film: Warner Brothers' *Who's Afraid of Virginia Woolf?*',
    Theatre Journal, 33: 453–66.
Maddox, Brenda (1977) *Who's Afraid of Elizabeth Taylor*, New York: M. Evans.
McCann, Graham (1988) *Marilyn Monroe*, New Brunswick, NJ: Rutgers University Press.
Maggio, Paula, *Blogging Woolf*, accessed 1 October 2008: http://bloggingwoolf.wordpress.
    com/
Mailer, Norman (1973) *Marilyn: A Biography*, New York: Grosset & Dunlap.
Mayo, Edith (1978) 'Ladies and Liberation: Icon and Iconoclast in the Women's Movement',
    in Ray B. Browne and Marshall Fishwick (eds), *Icons of America*, Bowling Green, OH:
    Popular Press: 209–27.
Moore, Madeline (ed.) (1977) *Women's Studies*, 4/2–3. Special issue on Virginia Woolf.
Morris, Gary (2001) 'François Ozon's *Under the Sand*', *Bright Lights Film Journal*, 33:
    accessed 1 October 2008: www.brightlightsfilm.com/33/underthesand.html
National Theatre (2006), *Waves*, accessed 1 October 2008: www.nationaltheatre.org.
    uk/20233/productions/waves-2006.html
O'Hagan, Sean (2003) 'Making Waves', *Observer Magazine*, 15 June, accessed 1 October
    2008: www.guardian.co.uk/theobserver/2003/jun/15/features.magazine37
Parkins, Wendy (2007) '"Whose Face Was It?" Nicole Kidman, Virginia Woolf, and The
    Boundaries of Feminine Celebrity', in Anne Burrells, et al. (eds), *Woolfian Boundaries*,
    Clemson, SC: Clemson University Digital Press, pp. 144–9.
Reiman, Donald (1987) *Romantic Texts and Contexts*, Columbia: University of Missouri
    Press.
Scott, A. O. (2001) 'The Intoxicating Embrace of Grief Holds Both Pleasure and Distress',
    New York Times, 4 May, accessed 1 October 2008: http://movies.nytimes.com/movie/
    review?_r=1&res=9904EED81238F937A35756C0A9679C8B63&scp=1&sq=AO%20
    Scott,%20intoxicating%20Embrace&st=cse
Sebring, Steven, dir. (2008) *Patti Smith: Dream of Life*, Vivendi Visual Enter. DVD.
Silver, Brenda R. (1991) 'Textual Criticism as Feminist Practice; or, Who's Afraid of Virginia
    Woolf Part II', in George Bornstein (ed.), *Representing Modernist Texts: Editing as
    Interpretation*, Ann Arbor: University of Michigan Press, pp. 193–222.
—— (1992) 'What's Woolf Got to Do with It? or, The Perils of Popularity', in Ellen Carol
    Jones (ed.), *Modern Fiction Studies*, 38.1: 21–60.
—— (1999a) *Virginia Woolf Icon*, Chicago: Chicago University Press.
—— (1999b) 'World Wide Woolf', University of Chigago Press, accessed 1 October 2008:
    www.press.uchicago.edu/Misc/Chicago/757463.html
Smith, Patti (2008a) 'A Reading of Virginia Woolf', Fondation Cartier, 28 March, accessed
    1 October 2008: www.youtube.com/watch?v=0UzS0dwuuHg
—— (2008b) *Auguries of Innocence: Poems*, New York: HarperCollins.
Spohrer, Erika (2005) 'Seeing Stars: Commodity Stardom in Michael Cunningham's *The
    Hours* and Virginia Woolf's *Mrs. Dalloway*', *Arizona Quarterly*, 61:2: 113–32.
Sturges, Fiona (2006) 'Camera Obscura', *The Independent* (London), 6 June.
Trilling, Diana (1948) 'Virginia Woolf's Special Realm', *New York Times Book Review*, 21
    March, sec. 7, 1: 28–9.

Vernant, Jean-Pierre (1991) *Mortals and Immortals: Collected Essays*, ed. Froma I. Zeitlin, Princeton, NJ: Princeton University Press.

Vincendeau, Ginette (2000) '*Under the Sand*,' *Sight and Sound*, accessed 1 October 2008: www.bfi.org.uk/sightandsound/review/2138

Virginia Woolf Bulletin, issued by the Virginia Woolf Society of Great Britain, accessed 1 October 2008: www.virginiawoolfsociety.co.uk/vw_bulletin.htm

VWOOLF (2000) post on email list, 1 December.

Watson, Peter (1982) 'Virginia Woolf follows in Monroe's Footsteps', *The Times* (London) 22 February: 22.

'Who's Afraid . . . ' (1966) *Newsweek*, 4 July: 84.

Woolf, Virginia (2006) *Three Guineas* (1938), ed. Jane Marcus, Orlando, FL: Harcourt Inc.

Žižek, Slavoj (1992) *Enjoy Your Symptom! Jacques Lacan in Hollywood and Out*, New York and London: Routledge.

Zwerdling, Alex (1986) *Virginia Woolf and the Real World*, Berkeley: University of California Press.

Further Reading

For a fuller history of Virginia Woolf iconicity, see Silver 1999a. The book also contains sections on Virginia Woolf and the 'intellectual' media, *A Writer's Diary*, Quentin Bell's biography of Virginia Woolf, Virginia Woolf's face, Virginia Woolf and fashion, adaptations of *A Room of One's Own* and *Orlando*.

For a fuller analysis of *Sammy and Rosie Get Laid*, *Me, I'm Afraid of Virginia Woolf* and *Who's Afraid of Virginia Woolf?*, see Silver 1999a.

On the persistent, uncanny crossing of Virginia Woolf and Marilyn Monroe, see Silver 1999a.

For a view of Virginia Woolf's presence on the internet in 1999, see Silver 1999b. In it I talk about the role of the internet in producing an arena for common users to create and communicate their own representations, undercutting more official renderings. A recent Google search for 'Virginia Woolf' brought up over 3,500,000 hits, while a Google Images search netted 250,000.

For a reading of Virginia Woolf's role in *Tom and Viv*, see Silver, 1999a.

For a history of the use of National Portrait Gallery postcards 'as a yardstick of popular esteem for literary worthies', see Jaffe 2005.

Part VI Performance Arts

23

VIRGINIA WOOLF AND MUSIC

Joyce E. Kelley

She was not, in any strict sense, musical. She played no instrument; I do not think
that she could follow a score with any deep comprehension. Music, it is true, delighted
her; she enjoyed the family pianola (when Adrian did not play it for too long), as she
was later to enjoy the gramophone; it formed a background to her musings, a theme
for her pen. (Bell 1972: 149)

I N 1940, VIRGINIA Woolf told Elizabeth Trevelyan, 'I'm not regularly musical, but I always think of my books as music before I write them' (*L6*: 426).
Her remark echoes Clive Bell's comment in *Art* (1914) when, before going on
to 'give an account of my own feelings about music', he confesses, 'I am not
really musical' (Bell 1958: 30). While music was the art professed to be the
least understood by the Bloomsbury group, it nonetheless served as fodder for
the imaginations of these artistic intellectuals, especially Woolf herself. Woolf
might have agreed heartily with Quentin Bell's above comment about her lack
of conventional musical abilities, yet Bell's statement, while nicely expressing
Woolf's 'delight' in music, perhaps also belies the complexity of her relationship to music, including her sensitivity to the art form and her unusual literary
musicality. Woolf's diaries reveal continual enjoyment of and interest in musical performance, although she notes a difference in the way she listens to music
and the way her 'musical' friends do (*D2*: 39). At a concert of Haydn, Mozart,
Bach and Schubert in 1915, Woolf recorded in her diary that music always made
her 'think of other things' – on this particular occasion both the inability of language to describe music and the capacity of music to make people listen and, no
matter how 'ordinary', to render them each extraordinary (*D1*: 33). Fascinated
both by music's social function and its super-linguistic abilities, Woolf went on
to produce essays and fiction infused with musical metaphor and meaning.

If Woolf indeed thought of her works as music before writing them, the kind
of music that inspired her novels seems to have varied greatly. Nonetheless,
though she remains influenced most by Wagner, Bach, Mozart and Beethoven
and even turns to jazz for colouration in *Between the Acts*, she curiously avoids

the avant-garde composers of her generation. While Woolf, born in 1882, came into the world at the same time as several of the main musical modernists – Igor Stravinsky (1882), Anton Von Webern (1883) and Alban Berg (1885) – her works focus instead on the music of their predecessors, the very composers these men strove to break away from. Yet Woolf's use of these artists is far from old-fashioned. Woolf became attracted to the way music could signify in non-verbal ways and saw in its structure new applications for literary narrative. Her literary experiments took her down pathways parallel to the musical moderns, so that critics may find Schoenbergian qualities in her writing or see her antici-pating musical movements which came after her.

In the last fifteen years particularly, interest has grown on the subject of Woolf and music, though, tellingly, the 1997 collection *Virginia Woolf and the Arts* contains, out of more than forty short essays, only two on music, sug-gesting the subject's need for further development.[1] Today, in contrast, several critics seem to be devoting themselves entirely to exploring these connections.[2] I endeavour to provide an overview of some of the scholarship on this subject while suggesting further observations; my goal is to present a general picture of Woolf's musical interests, investigations and techniques, noting resonances between her diary entries, letters, essays, and fiction. Important to future stud-ies of Woolf and music will be a better understanding of the parallels between her musically inspired works and those of other modernists.[3] Woolf's musical interests seem to follow a larger pattern of the modern era: the movement from welcoming Wagner's experiments in artistic union to contemplating music's subjective potential to envisioning music as a structural model for narrative. Nonetheless, Woolf's own thoughts about and experiments with music are par-ticularly innovative, and invite both further investigation and appreciation.

Musical Beginnings

Woolf received only a little musical education as a child, the standard for Victorian girls, but was surrounded by family and friends who enjoyed music. Her early journals detail outings to the Albert or Queen's Hall with her siblings or half-brothers, though these are often recounted with a sense of whimsy or boredom. By age seventeen, however, young Virginia had become enamoured with the idea of music. On holiday at Warboys in August 1899, she relates how, in the still country setting, 'music alone' could express their jubilant emotions (Woolf 1990: 136). A week later, she similarly comments, 'Somehow ink tonight seems to me the least effectual method of all – & music the nearest to truth' (ibid.: 143). She continually lauds music and bestows upon it a power above written language. In an oft-quoted line from a 1901 letter to Emma Vaughan, Woolf asserts, 'The only thing in this world is music – music and books and one or two pictures' (*L*1: 41).

Woolf explores her feelings for music in 'A Dance in Queens Gate' (1903), where she imagines the festivities at a ball from hearing the music through her window.[4] Here she suggests the 'magic' powers of dance music: 'you forget centuries of civilisation in a second, & yield to that strange passion which sends you madly whirling round the room . . . in the eddies & swirls of the violins' (Woolf 1990: 165). By 1905, Virginia was developing a more scholarly approach to the art form. She records getting a 'book about the relations of poetry & music, which may come in useful for my Morley lectures' (ibid.: 221). Woolf was also at work on an essay called 'Street Music' for the *National Review*. She writes in her journal of the piece, 'It is about music! – naturally depends more upon the imagination than upon facts' (ibid.: 230). Woolf mocks her own ability to write about music, but behind this lies excitement at the chance to dabble in a new art. The essay betrays her passion for the issue: similar to 'A Dance in Queens Gate', it speaks of the musician as 'the most dangerous of the whole tribe of artists' since music 'incites within us something that is wild and inhuman like itself' (Woolf 1986c:29).

Woolf also upholds music as an exceptional form of art in her piece for the *Guardian* that June: a review of the fifth volume of *The Oxford History of Music*. Though the review appeared anonymously, its unusual perspective reveals it was not written by the average music critic. Woolf laments,

> It is, perhaps, to be regretted that the history of music is still so largely a history of form. What we should all like to see is a history rather of musical expression, of the sources and conditions which render possible the 'inspiration' of a noble melody or a striking progression. (Woolf 1905: 1020)

What Woolf asks for reaches beyond common interests, demanding the essence of music apart from its formal qualities and historical significance. In championing expression over form, Woolf refigures the organisation of musical history and, perhaps, is thinking of literary history as well.

By 1905, Woolf had become an avid concert-goer, speaking of Sunday afternoon concerts at Queen's Hall as 'my weekly concert' (Woolf 1990: 257). Whether she realised it or not, Woolf was witnessing some very important moments in British musical history. In March alone, she saw Donald Francis Tovey perform a private piano recital, heard Edward Elgar conduct his own compositions, and attended a premier of songs by Arthur Somervell and Ralph Vaughan Williams. Interestingly, Woolf shared a familial tie with Vaughan Williams, who married Woolf's cousin Adeline Fisher in 1897. Of Ralph, Woolf remarked, 'there is a chance that he has genius' (ibid.: 101). Over the years, Woolf got the chance to see that 'genius' develop as he grew to be one of England's most influential composers.

Woolf also was opening her ears to more modern compositions. In February 1905 she heard 'A long Domestic Symphony by R. Strauss, partly beautiful, partly unintelligible – at least to me on a first hearing' (Woolf 1990: 242). Woolf seems impressed by a work that is both 'beautiful' and 'unintelligible'. The new music of the early twentieth century was introducing previously unheard harmonic language and dissonance, innovations which had roots in the nineteenth-century music of Richard Wagner. When Woolf comments in a letter, 'But beautiful writing is like music often, the wrong notes, and discords and barbarities that one hears generally – and makes too' (*L*1: 223), we may wonder if she has modern music in mind.

Woolf and Wagner

Woolf was not left pondering the richness and complexity of modern music alone. By 1908, Woolf was deeply engaged in the opera interests of her brother Adrian and friend Saxon Sydney-Turner. As Quentin Bell suggests, Woolf's liking for Wagnerian opera was largely 'stimulated by Saxon', an ardent enthusiast (Bell 1972: 149).[5] Wagner was an acquired taste for Woolf. His music challenged the ear accustomed to earlier composers; in Woolf's article 'The Opera', written for *The Times* in April 1909, she mentions that Wagner might cause the listener to leave the concert hall proclaiming, 'This is not music' (Woolf 1986b: 270). Perhaps because he posed these challenges, Wagner was lauded by high society and the intellectual elite. While Wagner was not a 'modernist' *per se*, he was a revolutionary figure, elevating the experience of opera to the spiritual and mythic, exploring new realms of tonality and orchestration, unabashedly incorporating sexuality, and giving his audience the 'intellectual challenge' of tracing *leitmotifs* (recurring symbolic musical gestures) through incredibly lengthy performances (Martin 1991: 3). With these elements, it is no wonder that his music appeared so attractive to literary modernists such as Forster, Woolf, and Joyce. Moreover, Wagner's interests in creating a 'total artwork' of music, drama, and poetry inspired writers 'to bring the techniques and expressive power of music to language' (ibid.: 22). Woolf was no exception, and Wagner proved instrumental in helping her develop ideas about the connections between music and literature.

In August 1909, Woolf had the opportunity to experience more fully Wagner's music with Adrian and Saxon at Bayreuth. During Woolf's slightly uncomfortable visit, she wrote long letters to her sister Vanessa that mock the operas' emotionalism and distance her from the rest of the audience:

> We heard Parsifal yesterday – a very mysterious emotional work . . .
> People dress in half mourning, and you are hissed if you try to clap . . .
> However, Saxon and Adrian say that it was not a good performance, and
> that I shant know anything about it until I have heard it 4 times. Between
> the acts, one goes and sits in a field, and watches a man hoeing turnips.
> (*L*1: 404)

As a newcomer to *Parsifal*, Woolf cannot be a critic; she appears simultaneously a novice who does not know the proper performance protocol and an observer too ordinary for the strange rituals of Bayreuth. What one does in the intermissions becomes as interesting as the strange concert-hall behaviour. This is Woolf's first recorded interest in the space 'between the acts', and she uses this term four times in her letters and once in her essay derived from the experience, 'Impressions at Bayreuth'.[6] The phrase seems to have stuck with her thirty years later; her keen observations of human behaviour both inside, within the artificial performance space, and outside, within nature, look ahead to her last novel.

On a second viewing of *Parsifal*, Woolf grows more admiring. She comments, 'I expect it is the most remarkable of the operas; it slides from music to words almost imperceptibly' (*L*1: 406). Her confidence in describing the music continues in 'Impressions at Bayreuth', written for *The Times* later that month. Unlike her letters, the article does not reveal her lack of experience, and she skirts around it by saying that if a writer is 'dissatisfied with the old evasions' he may 'try to give his impressions as an amateur' (Woolf 1986a: 288). The beginning of the essay is Woolf's own 'evasion' and it works well to establish an authoritative voice. Her perspective here changes from outsider to insider: she notes that other audience members come with 'a secret belief that they understand as well as other people' and she repeats Saxon and Adrian's opinion of *Parsifal* that 'it is not until one has heard it many times over that one can begin, as it were, to move it to and fro' (ibid.: 288, 289). Woolf began her letters to Vanessa as a musical novice, but she left Bayreuth more confident in her own abilities to discuss music. In 'Impressions', Woolf not only lauds Wagner's abilities but also envisions music expressing our most 'exalted emotions' and inhabiting a separate realm of consciousness beyond the 'old tools' of language (ibid.: 292).

Woolf alludes to Wagner in many of her works; nonetheless, as Emma Sutton and John DiGaetani note, the appearance of Wagnerian opera in these texts is somewhat satirical.[7] By the 1920s the British passion for Wagner was beginning to wane. Leonard, who ended up disliking Wagner, but fortunately not Virginia, after some excursions to the concert hall before their marriage, may have helped her interests cool even sooner (see L. Woolf 1964). Less than a year after their marriage, she and Leonard went to see Wagner's *Ring* cycle and she complained afterwards of 'the noise and the heat, and the bawling sentimentality, which used once to carry me away, and now leaves me sitting perfectly still' (*L*2: 26). Yet we must not underestimate Wagner's influence on Woolf; like many modernists, Woolf's interests in the connections between music and language were stimulated by Wagner's art. The excitement of a new 'total artwork' brought writers and poets to examine music anew for its unique representational possibility, and to debate whether musical meaning was mimetic (particularly representative of something specific) or immanent (more subjective, in the mind) (Prieto 2002: 8–9). It is a particularly modernist decision that musical powers connect to subjective experience; this is indeed what Woolf comments on in 'Impressions at Bayreuth' when she muses: 'Perhaps music owes something of its astonishing power over us to this lack of definite articulation; its statements have all the majesty of a generalisation, and yet contain our private emotions' (Woolf 1986a: 291).

The Musician as Modern Artist: *The Voyage Out*

References to music appear in all nine of Woolf's novels and many of her short stories; they resound with melody, like the books on the shelf in *Between the Acts* when Mrs Swithin runs her hand over them 'as if they were pan pipes' (*BTA*: 68). In Woolf's first novel, *The Voyage Out* (1915), Woolf extends thoughts about the power of music and the musician that she explored in her early essays. For her main character she chooses a young amateur pianist who, though young and inexperienced, contains the raw, innovative energy of the modern artist. As Rachel Vinrace leaves England for South America, she brings her piano with her.[8] Nonetheless, Rachel is not the traditional lady pianist who plays only to entertain guests in the parlour. While most young women of the age 'were not intent upon mastering the intricacies of Mozart, Haydn, or Beethoven' (Burgan 1986: 56), in stark contrast, Rachel sits 'for hours' practising 'very difficult music' (*VO*: 33). This includes 'Beethoven Op. 111' (ibid.: 37), the C minor piano sonata which, as James Hafley has noted, is 'a famous and demanding piece' (Hafley 1975: 4). Louise DeSalvo observed that Woolf changed Op. 112, a cantata, to Op. 111 in her 1920 edition; this small change reveals Woolf's careful intent to establish Rachel as an unusually talented musician (DeSalvo 1975).

Emma Sutton has argued that Rachel's growing maturity in the novel is connected to her performance of works by Beethoven and, particularly, Bach. While Wagner is among the sheet music that Rachel brings to South America, it is only Clarissa Dalloway who plays it. Sutton writes:

> The shift in Rachel's taste and in the novel's musical allusions indicate her emerging modernism, as she is aligned with an artist associated with formal perfection (Bach) rather than the emotive, high Romantic music and subjects of Wagner's dramatic works. (Sutton 2006: 63)

Rachel's maturity reflects Woolf's own as she began to leave behind the popular Wagner for the older works of Beethoven, Bach and Mozart: though Wagner was musically innovative, Woolf and Rachel seek novelty in music with less marked representative meaning and more subjective resonance.

Woolf, however, seems less interested in musical gesture or form in this novel than in the idea of the musician as artist. In *The Voyage Out*, Woolf extends the ideas she once discussed in 'Street Music' where she admires the musician's powers of absorption in his art and writes that 'music that takes possession of the soul so that nakedness and hunger are forgotten must be divine in its nature' (Woolf 1986c: 28). While Rachel lacks nothing except a well-rounded education, she plays in a similar state of 'possession'. In Chapter 2, Rachel's playing allows her to 'enter into communion . . . with the spirit of the sea' (*VO*: 37). When Terence sees Rachel practicing a late Beethoven sonata, he observes, 'There she was, swaying enthusiastically over her music, quite forgetful of him' (ibid.: 291). Rachel gains solitary pleasure from the artistic process, enjoying practising in her own quarters and stopping when she is interrupted. Indeed,

Rachel anticipates Woolf's later conception of women artists who need 'a room of one's own' to create.

While Rachel's preference for older composers may be construed as particularly sophisticated, even 'modern', she is even more avant-garde in her performance. When she plays at a hotel dance, Rachel changes her classical repertoire in a way that highlights her as an evolving, improvising artist rather than an imitating amateur. As the dancers show 'a complete lack of self-consciousness', swept along by the music like those in 'A Dance in Queens Gate', Rachel changes Mozart into something suitable for modern dancing by altering the rhythms, then passes on to 'old English hunting songs, carols, and hymn tunes' (*VO*: 166). Mark Wollaeger notes of this scene that Rachel is 'breaking up and reassembling older social and aesthetic forms in a virtuoso performance of her independence' (Wollaeger 2003: 42). Certainly this creative pastiche seems modern in mechanism, and anticipates what Woolf would later explore in *Between the Acts*.

Woolf also takes the opportunity in her first novel to investigate the different signifying realms of music and language that she articulated at Bayreuth. In this *künstlerroman*, Rachel's musical artistry moves beyond that of her fiancé, Terence Hewet, a young aspiring novelist. Though Rachel is a quiet, stuttering character, music allows her expression that language cannot.[9] For Rachel, music is a way of communicating without guise or repression: 'It appeared that nobody ever said a thing they meant, or ever talked of a feeling they felt, but that was what music was for' (*VO*: 37). She asks Terence, 'Why do you write novels? You ought to write music. Music, you see . . . goes straight for things. It says all there is to say at once' (ibid.: 212). Thinking back to 'Impressions at Bayreuth', Terence has the 'old tools'; meanwhile Rachel has the ability, like music without language, 'to cut herself adrift from him, and to pass away to unknown places where she had no need of him' (ibid.: 302). Woolf bestows upon her heroine powers that she herself did not possess, but she looks to her for inspiration.

Mozart and *Night and Day*

In *The Voyage Out*, Woolf predominantly explores music as an individual and revelatory artistic experience, though it is one which, as Elizabeth Bishop has explored, 'creates communion' when shared (Bishop 1981: 355). In her next novel, *Night and Day* (1919), Woolf more fully contemplates the social function of music. As Woolf attended concerts during the First World War, especially concerts of Mozart, this social diversion took on special meaning. On 3 December 1917, she remarks, 'Then on to Figaro at the Old Vic. It's perfectly lovely; breaking from one beauty into another, & so romantic as well as witty – the perfection of music, & vindication of opera' (*D*1: 83). This is immediately followed by a bleak statement about Leonard's brothers: 'On Sunday we heard of Cecil's death, & Philip's wounds' (ibid.). Perhaps Mozart's *The Marriage of Figaro* provided for Woolf what was often missing from the interwar years: joy, gaiety and, after some merry mischief and confusion, a happy ending.

The lightheartedness of Mozart seems to have harmonised with Woolf's current work: nineteen days before she attended *Figaro*, on 13 November 1917, Woolf made the first reference in her diary to the novel that was to become *Night and Day* (*D1*: 76). As Woolf wrote, she attended more concerts; *Figaro* seems to mark the beginning of a vested interest in Mozart which Woolf sustained throughout the coming year. Mozart again distracted Woolf from the horrors of war on 7 June when she attended *The Magic Flute* '& thought rather better of humanity for having that in them' (ibid.: 153–4). On 13 June she continued her rapturous absorption in Mozart opera when she 'went to Don Giovanni, to my infinite delight' (ibid.: 157). The 'delight' and 'pleasure' (ibid.: 142) she found in Mozart was the same sort she hoped others would find in her novel. In March 1919 she wrote of her newly finished work, 'if one's own ease & interest promise anything good, I should have hopes that some people, at least, will find it a pleasure' (ibid.: 259).

Night and Day is perhaps the novel of Woolf's that is most influenced by a single musical style, or at least the one most fervently referencing a single composer. Mozart's music works perfectly to capture the playful feel of the Edwardian drawing-room scenes. Jane Marcus, who has written extensively on the connections between *Night and Day* and Mozart's opera *The Magic Flute* in 'Enchanted Organs, Magic Bells: *Night and Day* as Comic Opera', remarks that the novel's 'ill-matched couples are sorted out and mated, blessed, initiated, and brought into society as in Mozart' (Marcus 1980: 107). Marcus's reading of *Night and Day* as a feminist rewriting of *The Magic Flute* suggests that the novel is much more complex and subversive than most critics acknowledge.

Implicit in this recognition is an understanding that Woolf uses music in the novel in an intricate manner. *Night and Day* lightheartedly reverberates with snippets of Mozart, yet the recurring music operates as no simple *leitmotif*. William Rodney, Katharine Hilbery's fiancé, hums or plays tunes from Mozart opera in several scenes when he is annoyed with Katharine, and the music seems to represent a space for him apart from her. Katharine is not musical, and Cassandra's pairing with William is confirmed as she plays Mozart on the piano (*ND*: 416). While late in the novel 'the melody of Mozart' comes to represent to Katharine and Ralph 'the easy and exquisite love' of William and Cassandra (ibid.: 424), the novel's traditional and slightly inane pair, *Night and Day* reaches beyond this easy idea of love (and of music) towards something more unutterable and profound. When Ralph sees Katharine walking, the 'scene in the Strand wore that curious look of order and purpose which is imparted to the most heterogeneous things when music sounds' (ibid.: 130). Here music represents something compelling, unifying, and mysterious. To Katharine, romance is 'a desire, an echo, a sound; she could drape it in colour, see it in form, hear it in music, but not in words; no, never in words' (*ND* 287). Ralph and Katharine have their music, but it cannot be expressed by a simple tune or familiar melody.

Nonetheless, Mozart's music, like Woolf's novel, is hardly simple. Modern critics even locate something modernist about Mozart: that the beauty and introspection of his music connects to the 'interior realm of consciousness' that both the Romantics and the modernists sought to express (Burnham 2005: 40). It is this aspect of Mozart that Woolf would later explore in 'The String Quartet'.

The Concert Hall and 'The String Quartet'

As Woolf continued to attend concerts, both during and after the war, she began to contemplate how one should 'listen' in the concert hall. Should concert-going be a revelatory artistic experience or a social experience? When Woolf muses in her diary, 'Think of the music I could hear, the people I could see' (*D2*: 272), we realise how much the two are intertwined for her. Woolf records whom she saw at concerts more often than the pieces she heard, underscoring the idea of the concert as social event. On 26 January 1920, for instance, Woolf went to Kensington to hear Mozart and Beethoven. She adds, 'I don't think I did hear very much of them, seated as I was between Katie & Elena' (ibid.: 14). While, in such instances, the concert hall seems a place of reunion and gossip, Woolf also expresses her annoyance at others' disruptions. At a Queen's Hall concert she is

> annoyed by a young man & woman next me who took advantage of the music to press each other's hands; & read 'A Shropshire Lad' & look at some vile illustrations. And other people eat chocolates, & crumbled the silver paper into balls. (*D1*: 34)

Woolf makes an interesting distinction between her own reaction to music at concerts and the behaviour of those she terms 'musical': in May 1920 Woolf writes of a Wigmore Hall concert with works by Franck, Dvorak and Ravel, 'Sat between Oliver [Strachey] & Saxon; & these musical people dont listen as I do, but critically, superciliously, without programmes' (*D2*: 39). While those more familiar with musical structure and theory may have listened for these elements, Woolf found pleasure in listening uncritically. Woolf continues to contemplate the idea of 'listening' in her diaries, which she conceptualises as an active, not passive, activity. During a Beethoven Festival Week in 1921, Woolf describes how every afternoon she has 'listened to Beethoven quartets. Do I dare say listened? Well, but if one gets a lot of pleasure, really divine pleasure, & knows the tunes, & only occasionally thinks of other things – surely I may say listened' (ibid.: 114). While Woolf seems to feel guilty that she is thinking 'of other things' during the concert, it is the idea of the listener's wandering imagination that becomes so important in her story 'The String Quartet' (1921), published that year in the collection *Monday or Tuesday*.

Woolf's musings about audience behaviour and her interest in the relationship between language and music come to a point in this story, which explores the thoughts of a listener during an early Mozart quartet. As the musicians' bows touch the strings, 'Flourish, spring, burgeon, burst!' (*HH*: 23), the listener's mind is transported to an imaginative space, filled with rushing waters and leaping fish. Next comes a boat on a moonlit river and, finally, an elaborate fairytale fantasy. The descriptions are impressionistic, wound together with the musicality and rhythm of Woolf's phrases. Between the three fantasy sequences, the audience talks, signalling the breaks between the quartet movements.[10] In the audience interruptions, everyday speech proves contrastingly uninteresting, but the listeners also remark on the transformative properties of music. One notes that music makes one lose one's inhibitions and join in a debauch of revelry, while another adds, 'That's the worst of music – these silly dreams' (ibid.: 25).

Woolf once observed that 'all descriptions of music are quite worthless' (*D1*: 33). In 'The String Quartet' she describes not just 'music' but the rendering of music filtered through consciousness. As Werner Wolf explains, Woolf here introduces 'a new kind of musicalized fiction'; it is not just a 'modernist mimesis' but a rendering of 'an emotional and aesthetic experience' (Wolf 1999: 150, 158). The music makes the listener, like Woolf, think of 'other things', and this narrator indulges these fantasies completely. James Hafley remarks that, in the story, 'Mozart himself has been thoroughly invented' (Hafley 1980: 31); this is reinforced by the fact that Woolf did not actually use Mozart as a model. In March 1920, Woolf wrote in her diary that 'on Sunday I went up to Campden Hill to hear the S[c]hubert quintet . . . to take notes for my story' (*D2*: 24); the inspiration for the story was thus Schubert, not Mozart.[11] The importance of this becomes clear in contemplating the story's ultimate emphasis on subjectivity over imitative form. In the story, Mozart is a catalyst for thought, yet secondary to the power of the imagination. 'The String Quartet' ultimately demonstrates that 'the worst of music' for the realist may be the best of music for the modern writer.

Woolf continued throughout the next two decades to look to music for inspiration. In November 1924, as she was preparing to revise *Mrs Dalloway* (1925), Woolf excitedly anticipated hearing the Portuguese cellist Guilhermina Suggia perform in the Wigmore Hall: 'For its music I want; to stimulate & suggest' (*D2*: 320). Music often had stimulated her imagination early in her career, and 'The String Quartet' reveals her playing in the gap between music's imagistic and structural resonances. By the end of the 1920s she became more interested in music's formal elements, which provided a new possibility for narrative experimentation. This coincided with a new perspective: that of the composer. Woolf had already explored the power of the musician, the conveyer of emotional meaning; now she turned to the structural artist, the weaver of musical language.

Music Comes Home: Ethel Smyth and *The Waves*

Woolf's home life became increasingly filled with music in the mid- to late 1920s. First, a piano arrived from Vita Sackville-West's cousin, Edward, in July

1925. Woolf wrote Vita, 'your cousin [Eddy] has lent me his piano, and I intend to break up the horror of human intercourse with music' (*L3*: 215). During this period music also came home through the help of an Algraphone, a kind of cabinet gramophone.[12] Woolf speaks of the Algraphone as 'a heavenly prospect' (*D3*: 42) and shows the pleasure it gives when she writes on 28 February 1927, 'Coming back last night I thought, owing to civilisation, I, who am now cold, wet, & hungry, can be warm & satisfied & listening to a Mozart 4tet in 15 minutes' (*D3*: 129). The gramophone was a tool that completely altered the experience of listening: musical works could be heard in the home at any hour; they could be interrupted or replayed at the whim of the listener. We can only imagine how 'The String Quartet' might have been different if Woolf had had the gramophone at her disposal in 1920. Perhaps most significantly, we find Woolf working on her new novel *The Waves* (1931) to the music on the gramophone; she writes on 18 June 1927, 'I do a little work on it in the evening when the gramophone is playing late Beethoven sonatas' (ibid.: 139).

Another musical influence arrived in Woolf's domestic realm as she was writing *The Waves*: the composer Ethel Smyth. On 20 February 1930, Smyth, enamoured with Woolf's feminist text *A Room of One's Own* (1929), came to meet Virginia in person. Ethel was seventy-two and well known for her *Mass in D* (1893), her operas and her autobiographical writings.[13] While Ethel's bombastic nature amused Woolf, she also seemed fascinated by her musical profession; she records in her diary:

> I like to hear her talk of music . . . She says writing music is like writing novels. One thinks of the sea – naturally one gets a phrase for it. Orchestration is colouring. And one has to be very careful with one's 'technique. (*D3*: 291–2).

Certainly the images of the sea and the 'colouring' here suggest that Woolf is thinking not only about the composer's art, but also about her own. As Ethel set words to music, Woolf thought increasingly about setting music to words.

The relationship Woolf built with Smyth shaped her thoughts about music as she composed a musically inspired novel. Six months into their friendship, Woolf tells Ethel that her manner of writing *The Waves* is 'opposed to the tradition of fiction', since she finds herself 'writing to a rhythm and not to a plot' (*L4*: 204). Ethel allowed Woolf to see her own work in musical terms and to consider her craft next to that of the composer; for example, in April 1930, Woolf asks Ethel, 'Are you writing? How does one write music?' (ibid.: 159). Similarly contemplating the connections between writing music and writing fiction one year later, she queries, 'What music is beginning to trumpet and whistle – or how does your work begin – mine in phrases – yours in bars, tunes?' (ibid.: 321).

From Ethel, Virginia gained an inside perspective on the struggles of a female composer, though Woolf seems to have admired the idea of the composer more than her compositions. After attending a concert of Ethel's in May 1930, Woolf wrote an elaborate letter envisioning Ethel as a burning rose in the middle of a 'briar hedge', the music: 'I am enthralled that you, the dominant and superb, should have this tremor and vibration of fire round you – violins flickering, flutes purring; . . . that you should be able to create this world from your centre' (*L4*: 171–2). The description holds visionary excitement and envy for the composer/ conductor – a fantasy of a woman creating a world of music from the 'tremor' and 'fire' of the elements. It is an extended fantasy of the musical creator that Woolf had idolised in Rachel Vinrace fifteen years before.

Eventually, though, Woolf would have to describe the 'briar hedge' to an artist very sensitive about the reception of her work. Throughout her life, Woolf was modest about her ability to judge music; as Peter Jacobs also notes, this tendency became even more pronounced as Woolf tried to avoid giving Ethel her opinions of her music, claiming 'ignorance'.[14] Woolf, at best, saw Ethel's music as 'vigorous & even beautiful' (*D4*: 49) and at worst ridiculous and alarming: 'last night, sweating with horror, I listened to the Prison, set to music – if cat calls, early birds and last posts can be called music' (*L4*: 403). Nonetheless, her impact on Woolf as a fellow artist was extremely resonant. It is Woolf's attention to the structural aspects of music that altered most after meeting Ethel. At the close of the first year of their friendship, in December 1930, Woolf envisioned a new technique for the ending of *The Waves*:

> It occurred to me last night while listening to a Beethoven quartet that I would merge all the interjected passages into Bernard's final speech, & end with the words O solitude: thus making him absorb all those scenes, & having no further break. (*D3*: 339)

Thus does Woolf find the idea for the conclusion of her novel in music. While three years before, prior to her relationship with Ethel, Woolf already was listening to Beethoven as she wrote, she now explicitly draws from him structurally.

The Waves, Woolf's most formally experimental novel, gives the soliloquies of six connected 'characters', beginning in childhood; between sections come italicised interludes describing the shore and sea, traced from dawn until dusk. The novel is like the 'six-sided flower', the character Bernard describes (*W*: 229); the six young people are individuals as well as parts of a whole, and no one voice is championed over the others. In the novel's final section, Bernard, the writer-figure, buys a picture of 'Beethoven in a silver frame' (ibid.: 253) and, attempting to find a model with which to explain the relationships of the group, turns to music:

> How impossible to order them rightly; to detach one separately, or to give the effect of the whole – again like music. What a symphony, with its concord and its discord and its tunes on top and its complicated bass beneath. (*W*: 256)

Here Woolf employs music, with its contrapuntal lines and voices, as a design for both relationships and language.

Woolf's experimental form has inspired scholars to correlate Woolf's text with modern musical innovations of her day. Gerald Levin and Robin Gail Schulze both connect Woolf's writing style to the atonal experiments of Arnold Schoenberg, though Woolf never references Schoenberg and may not consciously have been influenced by him. Gyllian Phillips argues that *The Waves* is not Schoenbergian because Woolf does not give up 'conventional structures (like sentences, punctuation and paragraphs)' to create her own (Phillips 1995: 122). Instead, she sees the novel as Wagnerian, with *leitmotifs* centring the 'shifting tonal structure', and compares it to Wagner's *Parsifal* (ibid.: 137). Because Woolf's diary entries explicitly connect her composition of the novel with Beethoven, however, it is most tempting to investigate how Beethoven's music may have functioned as inspiration. Elicia Clements has successfully explored the relationship between *The Waves* and Beethoven's late quartets, drawing parallels between attributes of Woolf's characters and the six movements of Beethoven's quartet in B-flat major (Opus 130). The 'Grösse Fuge', its original final movement, is contrapuntal in nature and may be seen as 'refiguring' Beethoven's earlier movements; Clements thus connects it with Bernard's final speech (Clements 2005a: 174).

The Waves also shows significant connections with Basil de Selincourt's *The Enjoyment of Music* (1928), an essay printed by the Hogarth Press during the years in which Woolf was drafting her novel. De Selincourt writes, for instance, of single sounds having 'a composite nature', like waves composed of 'little waves of the same pattern' (de Selincourt 1928: 16). In discussing 'rhythm', the very word Woolf clings to in describing her new novel's style, he remarks that Nature's 'great effects are given by a fringe of the variable thrown against oceanic immensities which never change.' He continues, 'The genius of rhythm, therefore, is with that musician who feels in each bar, as it passes, its identity with the other bars with which it is in series' (ibid.: 28). In writing to 'a rhythm,' Woolf thus shows, against the ocean's backdrop, the identities of her characters in a relational series. Whether or not Woolf was directly inspired by de Selincourt, these connections reveal that *The Waves* was very much in tune with the musical discussions around her.

Between the Acts' Meta-Music: New Music and New Ways of Listening

As Woolf began new projects, she continued to experiment with musical structures. When working on *The Years* (1937), she wonders if she can access 'different layers by bringing in music & painting together with certain groupings of human beings' (*D4*: 347). In her last years, Woolf confides to Ethel Smyth, 'I want to investigate the influence of music on literature' (*L6*: 450). She experiments with this idea particularly in her consciously created 'themes', 'developments', and 'variations' of *Roger Fry: A Biography* (1940) (ibid.: 426), whose form Peter Jacobs compares to a 'classical threefold sonata structure' (Jacobs 1993: 253).

One of Woolf's most modern, even postmodern, uses of music comes in *Between the Acts* (1941). The novel concerns an outdoor country pageant, written and directed by the Smythian character Miss La Trobe, which presents a pastiche of scenes representing England's history. Here Woolf synthesises ideas she has expressed throughout her life about the role of the audience in the concert space. Indeed, she takes for her title the very words she used at Bayreuth thirty years before, in her letters and essay, to describe what occurred 'between the acts' of the operas. What happened offstage at Bayreuth also became a part of the artistic whole: in seeing the turnip farmers during the interval, one

> combine[s] the simple landscape with the landscape of the stage. When the music is silent the mind insensibly slackens and expands, among happy surroundings: heat and the yellow light, and the intermittent but not unmusical noises of insects and leaves smooth out the folds. (Woolf 1986a: 290)

Nature's 'music' and opera alternate and combine to form a smooth, seamless composition. Similarly, in La Trobe's pageant, voices from nature fill in 'the gap' and 'continued the emotion' when human voices cease (*BTA*: 140–1).

In transcribing both the play and the audience's response to the play throughout her novel, Woolf's work sets up a model of metatextual counterpoint where each entity influences and comments upon the other: the audience responds directly to what they see and hear, and Miss La Trobe directs the play according to the audience's reactions. Woolf here combines her personal experiences as both creator of texts and recipient of others' art forms. *Between the Acts* particularly recalls those instances in Woolf's diaries and letters when she comments on her own behaviour at concerts, her annoyance at others' interruptions, and her inability to 'listen' to music in the concert hall without a programme. In Woolf's novel, audience members arrive late, comment parenthetically on the performance, and try to understand what the performance signifies until the interpretive programmes begin to replace the work of art.

The novel also recalls Woolf's observation that she attended Ethel's opera *The Prison*, 'if cat calls, early birds and last posts can be called music'. Like this quotation, which redefines audience noise and performance anomalies as 'music', *Between the Acts* questions the parameters of a work of art. The play, with its gramophone, actors and chorus of voices, relies on melody, rhythm and even nursery-rhyme, but these elements are echoed in Woolf's characters, who provide a counter-melody by humming, tapping and playing with language. The value of (re)creation from the 'Scraps, orts and fragments' of existence (*BTA*: 189) is stressed in the novel, a resistive and patchwork modern art developing from other forms. Child's language and song tap into a collective consciousness, and the gramophone ties together the building blocks of language in its 'scales' of ABC and CAT (ibid.: 114). Woolf's text suggests that the elements of language and music are fundamentally intertwined and their connections need to be reconsidered and relearned. Miss La Trobe uses her musical primer to 'summon' back her audience members who think, 'Music wakes us. Music makes us see the hidden, join the broken. Look and listen' (ibid.: 120).

Michele Pridmore-Brown likens La Trobe to a controlling dictator as she, with her gramophone, reduces her wartime audience to a herd mentality; nonetheless, she comments that La Trobe's unusual techniques 'adulterate the messages of authority' (Pridmore-Brown 1998: 411). Throughout her life, Woolf was enthralled by the power of music, but characterised it as positive and resistant; only in military and patriotic music, which Woolf disliked and avoided, did Woolf visualise war, patriarchy, and fascism.[15] It is telling that Woolf once wished for a piano to 'break up the horror of human intercourse with music' and, too, that she complained in 1936 of the journalist Kingsley Martin, 'He always interrupts our one resource against politics which is music' (L6: 19). Woolf visualises music as a refuge from and a defence against political strife and war, though ultimately that defence cannot hold: even La Trobe's musical collage, in its remote location, is ultimately interrupted by the Second World War's 'music' of aeroplanes 'in perfect formation' (BTA: 193).

Though La Trobe uses music to control her listener's emotions, she seems more avant-garde composer than führer. Throwing away convention, she represents 'The Present Time. Ourselves' with ambient sounds of the moment. Her performance notes read, 'try ten mins. of present time. Swallows, cows, etc.' (BTA: 179). Miss La Trobe employs silence as an effect, to encourage the audience to listen consciously to the sounds around them. This technique aligns with experimental practices of postmodern twentieth-century music. As several critics, including Patricia Laurence and Melba Cuddy-Keane, have recently noted, Woolf's work anticipates the experimental music of American composer John Cage.[16] Cuddy-Keane explicitly connects this scene with Cage's 1952 piece '4′33' in which the musician sits in silence for 4 minutes and 33 seconds (Cuddy-Keane 2000: 91). The 'music' thus becomes all the noise in the room that is not the sound of the instrument. Though Cage was one of the principle pioneers of this new music, others such as Henry Cowell were experimenting with 'chance music' in the 1930s. While it is unlikely that Woolf had heard of Cowell's experiments, it is most important to note the incredible way Woolf taps into, even anticipates, experimental music movements.[17]

In the music of Between the Acts, Woolf also ventures beyond the classical; in the pageant's last act, 'The tune changed; snapped; broke; jagged. Foxtrot, was it? Jazz?' (BTA: 183). Jazz, with its swung rhythms and improvisation, embodies modernist notions of moving beyond set patterns and traditional forms. Here the narrator takes up the rhythm and rhyme to describe La Trobe's technique: 'And not plain. Very up to date, all the same. What is her game? To disrupt? Jog and trot? Jerk and smirk? Put the finger to the nose? Squint and pry? Peak and spy?' (ibid.: 183). These jazzy dance tunes, rhyming descriptions privileging sound over sense, and, ultimately, the 'megaphonic' voice (ibid.: 186) are reminiscent of Edith Sitwell's Façade, poems set to music by William Walton, which Woolf attended in June 1923.

We began with Wagner, Mozart and Beethoven as influences for Woolf, and we end with Sitwell and Walton. Sitwell's poems, which used language to represent dance rhythms like foxtrot and polka, challenged the boundaries of music and poetry, and sounded to new ears like fantastical nursery-rhyme. Though Woolf claimed she did not 'understand' or 'admire' *Façade* in 1923 (*D2*: 246), Miss La Trobe's art echoes Sitwell's. Like Miss La Trobe, who hides her body in the bushes and 'behind the tree' during the pageant (*BTA*: 120), Sitwell stood behind a curtain to keep her body from affecting the performance space as she recited through a megaphone (Glendinning 1981: 78). In 1926, Sitwell was invited by the BBC to broadcast sections of *Façade* for 'The Wheels of Time', a programme structured similarly to La Trobe's pageant. The broadcast was 'divided into three sections, past, present, and future', with the present represented by jazz and ragtime, 'the future with extracts from *Façade*, and the past represented by Victorian songs' (Elborn 1981: 62). The BBC imagined Sitwell and Walton as 'futuristic'; perhaps, too, Woolf found postmodern possibility in their sound. Like La Trobe's pageant, it is at once very old and very modern: Jack Lindsay writes that Sitwell's verse makes 'a new thing out of speech . . . . Some of the affinities go back to folksong, to our lyric forms in the days when song and music were one' (Lindsay 1950: 16).

In *Listening In: Music, Mind, and the Modernist Narrative* Eric Prieto reminds us that the modernists' idea to unite music and literature never could have come about if 'not for the fact that the traditional relationship between the two arts, in song, had begun to erode' (Prieto 2002: 1). Woolf ended her career returning to these roots in 'Anon', the first chapter of an uncompleted manuscript on English literary history. *Between the Acts* offers the most modern of music; 'Anon' suggests the most primitive: birdsong, early music, the anonymous minstrel. Yet the two are not dissimilar. In the essay, Woolf suggests that language and music were once intricately bound; today, 'We have lost the sound of the spoken word' (Woolf 1979: 432). Perhaps only in the most 'futuristic' of music could it be found again. Woolf began at Bayreuth by embracing Wagner's union of music and language that 'slides from music to words almost imperceptibly' and ended with a fascination for the early poet who was 'not wholly writer, wholly musician or wholly painter' (ibid.: 389). Throughout her life Woolf found beauty and possibility in the interconnections of the arts. Woolf writes in 'Anon' that for the writer, 'distinct from the minstrel', 'there is a limit to what can be put into words. There is a barrier between the sayable and the unsayable.' Ultimately, she writes, 'If he cannot talk, he must sing' (ibid.: 389). By bringing music to fiction, Woolf found a way to do just that.

Notes

1. See Diane F. Gillespie and Leslie K. Hankins (eds) (1997), *Virginia Woolf and the Arts: Selected Papers from the Sixth Annual Conference on Virginia Woolf*, New York: Pace University Press. Many Woolf critics over the years have commented on music in Woolf's

work. Inez Verga's *Virginia Woolf's Novels and their Analogy to Music*, which I have been unable to access, was published in Buenos Aires in 1945. Jane Marcus particularly led the way in the 1970s and 1980s with many interesting pieces on Woolf and Wagner, Mozart and Ethel Smyth. In 1993, Peter Jacobs' article ' "The Second Violin Tuning in the Ante-Room": Virginia Woolf and Music' appeared in Diane Gillespie's *The Multiple Muses of Virginia Woolf* (see Jacobs 1993).

2. Elicia Clements is currently writing a book on Woolf and music and Adriana Varga is editing a collection of essays on this topic. I had the pleasure of speaking on a 'Woolf and Music' panel at the 2006 Woolf conference in Birmingham, England, with Emma Sutton and Emilie Crapoulet, who continue to write on these issues.

3. For recent studies of modernist literature and music, see Prieto (2002), Wolf (1999), Bucknell (2001) and Albright (2000, 2004).

4. Woolf returned to these ideas in the 1907 section of *The Years* where Sally lies awake hearing waltz music coming 'through the open window' (*Y*: 132).

5. Peter Jacobs argues, as I do, that Saxon and Leonard greatly shaped Woolf's Wagnerian tastes. Jacobs also remarks that 'Virginia's feeble admiration for Wagner . . . did not last long' and finds it difficult to see Wagnerian 'thematic and even structural devices' in Woolf's fiction (Jacobs 1993: 235, 236). While I concur that Woolf never seems to have renewed a true passion for Wagner, I disagree that her interest is 'feeble' since she alludes to Wagner frequently in her novels, continues to attend performances of Wagner, and plays Wagner on the gramophone.

6. Woolf uses the phrase in her letters to describe, not only the turnip farmers, but also the 'fashionable women . . . who stare at me between the acts', Saxon who 'reclines on his hip between the acts, and pulls at a weed', and tea 'between the acts' (*L1*: 407, 409). In 'Impressions at Bayreuth' she writes, 'During the intervals between the acts, when [the audience members] come out into the sun, they seem oppressed with a desire to disburden themselves somehow of the impression which they have received' (Woolf 1986a: 289).

7. See Sutton 2006: 51 and DiGaetani 1978: 117.

8. See Kelley 2007 on Woolf's choice of the piano as an instrument for Rachel.

9. Many critics have examined the significance of Rachel's difficulty with language, some investigating Rachel's choice to turn to music for an alternate means of expression. Terri Beth Miller notes how music is used as 'communication' in the novel but asserts that there remains 'an inherent social resistance to that which is intangible and beyond words' (Miller 2005: 5). The article that most extensively discusses Rachel's use of the piano as voice is Suzanne Raitt's 'Finding a voice: Virginia Woolf's Early Novels' (2000).

10. Werner Wolf suggests that it may be one of Mozart's quartets with three movements (1999: 151); in contrast, Hafley (1980: 29) imagines four movements with no break between third and fourth.

11. Emilie Crapoulet called attention to this substitution (Mozart for Schubert) in a paper at the 2006 International Conference on Virginia Woolf; while the quintet Woolf saw at Campden Hill may have been Schubert's string quintet in C, Crapoulet surmised that it may have been his 'Trout' quintet. This might explain the fish and water imagery at the opening of Woolf's story.

12. On the importance of the gramophone in Woolf's work, see Cuddy-Keane (2000), Scott (2000), and Pridmore-Brown (1998).

13. For insights about the relationship between Woolf and Smyth's writings, especially about their approaches to autobiography, see Raitt (1988) and Wiley (2004).

14. See *L4*: 389, 393. See also Jacobs 1993: 257–60.

15. For example, on 3 January 1915, Woolf exclaims that at a concert in Queen's Hall 'the patriotic sentiment was so revolting that I was nearly sick' (*L2*: 57). She also relays with disgust that the Germans 'on the wireless, between the turns, . . . play military music. Horrible horrible!' (*D4*: 153).
16. See Laurence's remarks on Cage and Woolf (1991a and 1991b).
17. Cuddy-Keane points out that it is not 'anachronistic to parallel the works of Virginia Woolf and New Music' because the 'groundwork' had already been laid by the time she was writing *Between the Acts* (2000: 81). Cuddy-Keane cites experiments in sound and radiophonic art from the 1920s and 1930s and suggests we see Woolf working on a 'diagonal' to these artists (ibid.: 94).

Works Cited

Albright, Daniel (2000) *Untwisting the Serpent: Modernism in Music, Literature, and Other Arts*, Chicago and London: University of Chicago Press.

—— (ed.) (2004) *Modernism and Music: An Anthology of Sources*, Chicago and London: University of Chicago Press.

Bell, Clive (1958) *Art*, New York: Capricorn Books.

Bell, Quentin (1972) *Virginia Woolf: A Biography*, New York: Harcourt Brace Jovanovich.

Bishop, E. L. (1981) 'Toward the Far Side of Language: Virginia Woolf's *The Voyage Out*', *Twentieth Century Literature*, 27: 343–61.

Bucknell, Brad (2001) *Literary Modernism and Musical Aesthetics: Pater, Pound, Joyce, and Stein*, Cambridge: Cambridge University Press.

Burgan, Mary (1986) 'Heroines at the Piano: Women and Music in Nineteenth-Century Fiction', *Victorian Studies*, 30.1: 51–76.

Burnham, Scott (2005) 'On the Beautiful in Mozart', in Karol Berger and Anthony Newcomb (eds), *Music and the Aesthetics of Modernity: Essays*, Cambridge, MA: Harvard University Press.

Clements, Elicia (2005a) 'Transforming Musical Sounds into Words: Narrative Method in Virginia Woolf's *The Waves*', *Narrative*, 13.2: 160–181.

Cuddy-Keane, Melba (2000) 'Virginia Woolf, Sound Technologies, and the New Aurality', in Pamela L. Caughie (ed.), *Virginia Woolf in the Age of Mechanical Reproduction*, New York and London: Garland Publishing, Inc.

de Selincourt, Basil (1928) *The Enjoyment of Music*, London: Hogarth Press.

DeSalvo, Louise A. (1975) 'A Textual Variant in *The Voyage Out*', *Virginia Woolf Miscellany*, 3: 9–10.

DiGaetani, John Louis (1978) *Richard Wagner and the Modern British Novel*, Rutherford, CA: Farleigh Dickinson University Press.

Elborn, Geoffrey (1981) *Edith Sitwell: A Biography*, Garden City, NY: Doubleday & Company.

Glendinning, Victoria (1981) *Edith Sitwell: A Unicorn among Lions*, New York: Alfred A. Knopf.

Hafley, James (1975). 'Another Note on Rachel and Beethoven in *The Voyage Out*', *Virginia Woolf Miscellany*, 4: 4.

—— (1980) 'Virginia Woolf's Narrators and the Art of "Life Itself"', in Ralph Freedman (ed.), *Virginia Woolf: Revaluation and Continuity*, Berkeley: University of California Press.

Jacobs, Peter (1993) ' "The Second Violin Tuning in the Ante-Room": Virginia Woolf and Music', in Diane F. Gillespie (ed.), *The Multiple Muses of Virginia Woolf*, Columbia and London: University of Missouri Press.

Kelley, Joyce (2007) '*Excursions into Modernism: Women Writers, Travel, and The Body*', PhD dissertation, University of Iowa.

Laurence, Patricia Ondek (1991a) *The Reading of Silence: Virginia Woolf in the English Tradition*, Stanford, CA: Stanford University Press.

— (1991b) 'The Facts and Fugue of War: From *Three Guineas* to *Between the Acts*', in Mark Hussey (ed.) *Virginia Woolf and War: Fiction, Reality, and Myth*, Syracuse, NY: Syracuse University Press.

Levin, Gerald (1983) 'The Musical Style of *The Waves*', *The Journal of Narrative Technique*, 13.3: 164–71.

Lindsay, Jack (1950) 'Introductory Essay', in Edith Sitwell, *Façade and Other Poems 1920-1935*, London: Gerald Duckworth & Co., Ltd.

Marcus, Jane (1980) 'Enchanted Organs, Magic Bells: *Night and Day* as Comic Opera', in Ralph Freedman (ed.), *Virginia Woolf: Revaluation and Continuity*, Berkeley: University of California Press.

Martin, Timothy (1991) *Joyce and Wagner: A Study of Influence*, Cambridge: Cambridge University Press.

Miller, Terri Beth (2005) 'Teapots and Transcendence: The Search for Language', *Interactions: Aegean Journal of English and American Studies*, 14.1: 183–96.

Phillips, Gyllian (1995) 'Re(De)Composing the Novel: *The Waves*, Wagnerian Opera and Percival / Parsifal', *Genre*, 28.1–2: 119–44.

Pridmore-Brown, Michele (1998) 'Virginia Woolf, Gramophones, and Fascism', *PMLA*, 133.3: 408–21.

Prieto, Eric (2002) *Listening In: Music, Mind, and the Modernist Narrative*, Lincoln and London: University of Nebraska Press.

Raitt, Suzanne (1988) 'The Tide of Ethel: Femininity as Narrative in the Friendship of Ethel Smyth and Virginia Woolf', *Critical Quarterly*, 30.4: 3–21.

— (2000) 'Finding a Voice: Virginia Woolf's Early Novels', in Sue Roe and Susan Sellers (eds), *The Cambridge Companion to Virginia Woolf*, Cambridge: Cambridge University Press.

Schulze, Robin Gail (1992) 'Design in Motion: Words, Music, and the Search for Coherence in the Works of Virginia Woolf and Arnold Schoenberg', *Studies in the Literary Imagination*, 25.2: 5–22.

Scott, Bonnie Kime (2000) 'The Subversive Mechanics of Woolf's Gramophone in *Between the Acts*', in Pamela L. Caughie (ed.), *Virginia Woolf in the Age of Mechanical Reproduction*, New York and London: Garland Publishing, Inc.

Sutton, Emma (2006) ' "Within a Space of Tears": Music, Writing, and the Modern in Virginia Woolf's *The Voyage Out*', in Robert P. McParland (ed.), *Music and Literary Modernism: Critical Essays and Comparative Studies*, Newcastle, UK: Cambridge Scholars Publishing.

Wiley, Christopher (2004) ' "When a Woman Speaks the Truth about Her Body": Ethel Smyth, Virginia Woolf, and the Challenges of Lesbian Auto/Biography', *Music & Letters*, 85.3: 388–414.

Wollaeger, Mark (2003) 'The Woolfs in the Jungle: Intertextuality, Sexuality, and the Emergence of Female Modernism in *The Voyage Out, The Village in the Jungle*, and *Heart of Darkness*', *Modern Language Quarterly*, 64.1: 33–66.

Wolf, Werner (1999) *The Musicalization of Fiction: A Study in the History and Theory of Intermediality*, Amsterdam: Rodopi.

Woolf, Leonard (1964) *Beginning Again: An Autobiography of the Years 1911-1918*, London: Hogarth Press.

Woolf, Virginia (1905) 'Books on Music', *Guardian*, 60.1, 14 June: 1020.

— (1979) '"Anon" and "The Reader": Virginia Woolf's Last Essays', ed. Brenda Silver, *Twentieth Century Literature*, 25: 356–441.

—— (1986a) 'Impressions at Bayreuth', in Andrew McNeillie (ed.), *The Essays of Virginia Woolf. Vol. I: 1904–1912*, London: Hogarth Press.

—— (1986b) 'The Opera', in Andrew McNeillie (ed.), *The Essays of Virginia Woolf. Vol. I: 1904–1912*, London: Hogarth Press.

—— (1986c) 'Street Music', in Andrew McNeillie (ed.), *The Essays of Virginia Woolf. Vol. I: 1904–1912*, London: Hogarth Press.

—— (1990) *A Passionate Apprentice: The Early Journals 1897–1909*, ed. Mitchell A. Leaska, London: Hogarth Press.

Further Reading

Aronson, Alex (1980) *Music and the Novel: A Study in Twentieth-Century Fiction*, Totowa, NJ: Rowman and Littlefield.

Blissett, William (1963) 'Wagnerian Fiction in English', *Criticism*, 5: 239–60.

Burford, Arianne (1999) 'Communities of Silence and Music in Virginia Woolf's *The Waves* and Dorothy Richardson's *Pilgrimage*', in *Virginia Woolf & Communities: Selected Papers from the Eighth Annual Conference on Virginia Woolf*, ed. Jeanette McVicker and Laura Davis, New York: Pace University Press.

Clements, Elicia (2005b) 'Virginia Woolf, Ethel Smyth, and Music: Listening as a Productive Mode of Social Interaction', *College Literature*, 32.3: 51–71.

Crapoulet, Emilie (2007) 'Virginia Woolf and the Music of the Mind', in *Consciousness, Theatre, Literature and the Arts 2007*, ed. Daniel Meyer-Dïnkgrafe, Newcastle, UK: Cambridge Scholars Publishing.

Eisenberg, Nora (1981) 'Virginia Woolf's Last Words on Words: *Between the Acts* and "Anon"', in *New Feminist Essays on Virginia Woolf*, ed. Jane Marcus, Lincoln: University of Nebraska Press.

Fromm, Harold (1968) 'To The Lighthouse: Music and Sympathy', in *English Miscellany: A Symposium of History, Literature, and the Arts*, ed. Mario Praz, Rome: Edizioni Di Storia E Letteratura.

Galstad, Alison Ames (1997) 'Dame Ethel Smyth: Composing Her Life', in *Virginia Woolf and the Arts: Selected Papers from the Sixth Annual Conference on Virginia Woolf*, ed. Diane F. Gillespie and Leslie K. Hankins, New York: Pace University Press.

Hull, Robert H. (1927) *Contemporary Music*, London: Hogarth Press.

Laurence, Patricia (1992) 'Virginia Woolf and Music', *Virginia Woolf Miscellany*, 38 4–5.

Manhire, Vanessa (2000) 'The Lady's Gone A-Roving: Woolf and the English Folk Revival', in *Virginia Woolf Out of Bounds*, ed. Jessica Berman and Jane Goldman, New York: Pace University.

Marcus, Jane (1977) '*The Years* as Greek Drama, Domestic Novel, and Götterdämmerung', *Bulletin of the New York Public Library*, 80, Winter: 276–301.

—— (1984) 'Virginia Woolf and her Violin: Mothering, Madness, and Music', in *Mothering the Mind: Twelve Studies of Writers and Their Silent Partners*, ed. Ruth Perry and Martine Watson Brownley, New York and London: Holmes & Meier.

Sarker, Sonita (1997) 'An Unharmonious Trio? Georg Lukács, Music, and Virginia Woolf's *Between the Acts*', in *Virginia Woolf and the Arts: Selected Papers from the Sixth Annual Conference on Virginia Woolf*, ed. Diane F. Gillespie and Leslie K. Hankins, New York: Pace University Press.

Vandivere, Julie (1996) 'Waves and Fragments: Linguistic Construction as Subject Formation in Virginia Woolf', *Twentieth Century Literature*, 42.2: 221–33.

Plate 9 The Brown Gallery at Knole, Vita Sackville-West's family home, Kent © NTPL/Andreas von Einsiedel

Plate 10 The seventeenth-century Monk's House in Rodmell, former home of Virginia and Leonard Woolf
© NTPL/Eric Crichton

Plate 11 The sitting room at Monk's House © NTPL/Eric Crichton

Plate 12 Vanessa Bell's dust jacket designs for *To the Lighthouse*, *Kew Gardens* and *Mrs Dalloway*. Courtesy of the E. J. Pratt Library, Victoria University, Toronto, Canada

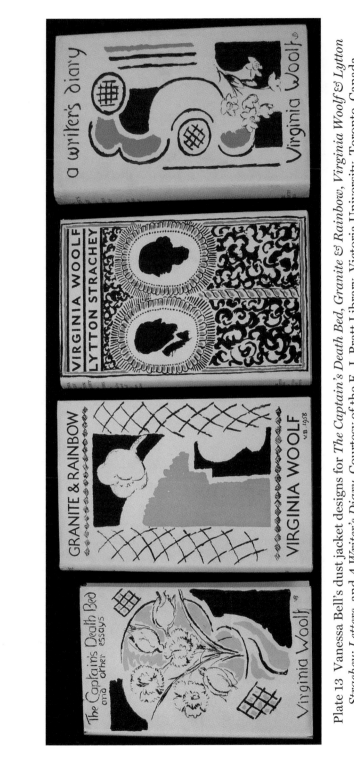

Plate 13 Vanessa Bell's dust jacket designs for *The Captain's Death Bed*, *Granite & Rainbow*, *Virginia Woolf & Lytton Strachey: Letters*, and *A Writer's Diary*. Courtesy of the E. J. Pratt Library, Victoria University, Toronto, Canada

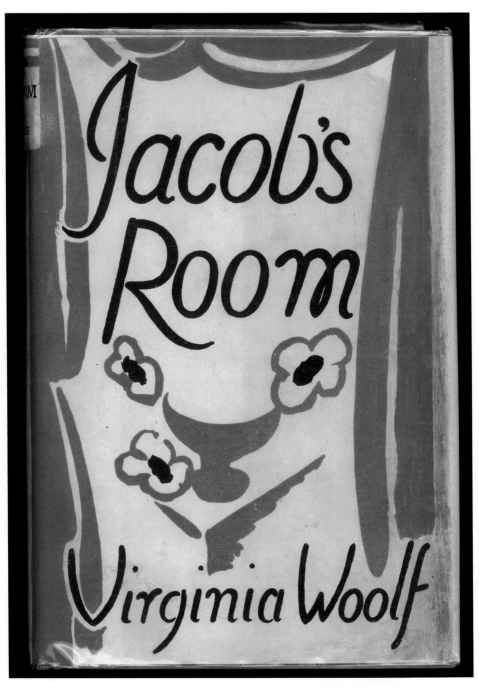

Plate 14 Vanessa Bell's dust jacket design for *Jacob's Room*. Courtesy of the
E. J. Pratt Library, Victoria University, Toronto, Canada

Plate 15 *The Gentleman from San Francisco and Other Stories*, by I. A. Bunin and *Paris*, by Hope Mirrlees. Courtesy of the E. J. Pratt Library, Victoria University, Toronto, Canada

Plate 16 Vanessa Bell's dust jacket designs for *The Common Reader*, *The Years* and *Three Guineas*. Courtesy of the E. J. Pratt Library, Victoria University, Toronto, Canada

24

VIRGINIA WOOLF AND THEATRE

Steven Putzel

Herbert Blau begins his groundbreaking study *The Audience* with a quote from Woolf's diary, 'No audience. No echo. That's part of one's death', and with a reference to the audience's self-reflective 'gaze' in *Between the Acts*, recognising that Woolf had developed an almost postmodern understanding of the complexities of the 'theatrical relationship'. Late in life Woolf was fascinated with the interrelationship among author, play, actor, subject, staging techniques and audience, but what she saw on stage, from the late Victorian period through most of the first half of the twentieth century, placed in the context of the broader audience of which she was a part, allows us a unique, first-hand view of the theatre scene as well as an insight into the genesis of Woolf's ideas about performance and audience. Though she professed a preference for reading over seeing plays, her experience as a spectator is an important though often overlooked part of her aesthetics and her theories about performance.

Among the productions Virginia Stephen saw during the last decade of the nineteenth century were the pantomimes *Aladdin* and *Santa Claus*, the musical farces *The French Maid* and *The White Silk Dress*, the French comic opera *La Poupée*, illusionists John Nevel Meskelyne and George Cook, a black-face minstrel show, and Imre Kiralfy's extravaganza *Venice: The Bride of the Sea*. Much later in life pantomimes would affect her own *Orlando* while the influence of the music hall would be felt in playful Bloomsbury skits, in the two versions of her own play *Freshwater*, in transformations of *Orlando*, and even in the pageants of *Between the Acts*. Comic banter, slapstick action, silly mock-romantic songs, and choruses all find their way into Woolf's work.

Because she saw Kiralfy's spectacle twice, because Virginia and her siblings wrote about it extensively in the *Hyde Park Gate News*, because real and fictitious depictions of Venice would fascinate Woolf throughout her life, and because of Woolf's abiding interest in Shakespeare's plays, Kiralfy's *Venice* and the children's response are worth detailing. Fortune-tellers, glass-blowing demonstrations, and a flooded area for gondola rides filled the Olympia, one of the few Victorian stages large enough to accommodate an entire circus.

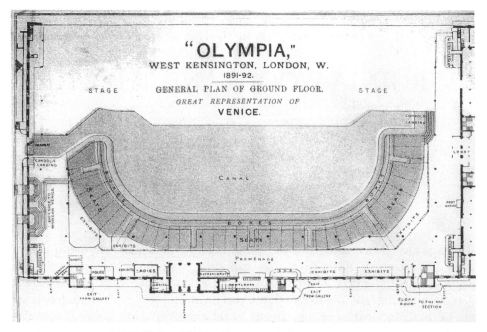

Figure 24.1 Ground-plan drawings from the programme for Imre Kiraly's *Venice: The Bride of the Sea. A grand historic and romantic spectacle and aquatic pageant exhibiting in London*, London: G. Newnes, 1891

Although the children had no trouble seeing beyond the stage illusion, the sheer scale of the production, a two-tiered reproduction of modern and fourteenth-century Venice (see Figure 24.1), captured their imaginations. Kiralfy borrows from and openly bowdlerises Shakespeare, lifting the plot from *The Merchant of Venice*, interspersed with choruses, 'Eccentric Dances', processions and 'Musical Gems'.

Here, then, is one of Woolf's first encounters with Shakespeare on stage, but ironically, there is not one mention of Shakespeare's plot-line in the children's report; for them, as for most of the audience, the spectacle was all, and the plot, characters and spoken lines were mere filler. Other encounters with Victorian stagings of Shakespeare would leave her similarly unsatisfied. As the Edwardian age dawned, Virginia Stephen was primarily a solitary reader, who preferred to read Shakespeare and other playwrights in a book, rather than to see and hear the plays as a member of a theatre audience. If we consider the nature of the theatrical experience when Woolf began seeing the plays, we begin to understand her anti-theatrical point of view. For example, a production of *Henry V* that she saw in 1905 was presented in four acts rather than the traditional five, key moments were frozen in artfully contrived tableaux rather than performed, and all action was punctuated by music. A 1909 production of *King Lear* that Woolf attended with Lytton Strachey cut the blinding scene, reduced the number of scenes from Shakespeare's twenty-six to thirteen, transposed many scenes, and inserted mood music throughout. Even when she reviewed 'Twelfth Night at the Old Vic', she spent the entire essay contrasting the theatrical text on stage with the dramatic text in her own mind, asking why 'should we imprison [characters] within the bodies of real men and women?' (DM: 46).

Woolf understood that this contrast between stage and book is not possible in opera where there can be no solitary reader, where the stage, and the 'bodies [and voices] of real men and women' are not optional components. As a result, opera nudged Woolf toward an understanding of what it meant to be part of a theatre audience. Virginia Stephen reacted like any fifteen-year-old to her earliest recorded experience with opera (Gounod's Faust at Covent Garden in 1897): 'It lasted till 11.30 – rather too long, but very nice' (PA: 94). There is little evidence that Woolf developed a passion for opera before Vanessa's wedding and Virginia's subsequent move to Fitzroy Square where she lived with Adrian, who was already an opera fanatic. Woolf's early essay 'The Opera' forms part of the theoretical basis for understanding Woolf's ideas about theatre and can even provide hints that could help writers and directors in adapting her work for the stage. She recognises that many opera aficionados of her time dismissed Wagner's work precisely because they found it too dramatic, noting that many spectators 'find a Wagner opera much the same as a play, but easier to follow, because the emotions are emphasised by the music' (E1: 270).

During her visit to the Bühnenfestspiele Bayreuth in August 1909, Woolf wrote an article for The Times, later included in her Essays as 'Impressions at Bayreuth'. Concentrating on how operas affect the audience, Woolf takes on the role of double audience: she sits with audience members listening to Wagner's music and at the same time she positions herself beyond both stage and auditorium to observe the audience, the exact position that the narrator of Jacob's Room would later assume. In fact, much of the action and interaction that interests Woolf most occurs not on stage but, as she tells Vanessa, 'between the acts'. Just as with her final novel, which takes this phrase as its title, Woolf structures her essay around what happens and what is felt during the two intervals and after the final curtain descends. Woolf observes that when audience members 'come out into the sun, they seem oppressed with a desire to disburden themselves somehow of the impression which they have received' (E1: 289). This will also be true of the interval and post-production talk in Between the Acts. Parsifal, like Miss La Trobe's pageant, raises audience expectations and then abruptly changes the horizon; the audience is left bewildered, out to sea with a shifting horizon and no reliable point of reference.

Woolf's account of Wagner's achievement accurately describes the effect Miss La Trobe seeks, and what Woolf herself would achieve in The Years, The Waves and Between the Acts. During the first interval of Parsifal the bewildered audience sits silently and 'if one thinks at all, it is to combine the simple landscape with the landscape of the stage' (E1: 290). The changing landscape echoes and extends the changing emotions generated by the music and drama of *Parsifal*. The bat that circles Kundry's head and the moths that flicker about the footlights become part of the action of *Parsifal*, just as the deep base of the cows' voices, the melody of birdsong and the on-cue rain come to the aid of Miss La Trobe in *Between the Acts*.

Woolf's reading of Greek drama and her enjoyment of the music hall take note of the power of the chorus to give voice to unspoken emotion, to externalise thought and to fill in narrative gaps, and her comments on *Lohengrin* also pay tribute to the power of the chorus, 'alive in all its parts', that holds the audience, and preserves the 'mood', even when voices are silent. Woolf's own experiments with choruses will become part of her own 'narrow bridge of art', theoretically connecting music, theatre, poetry and fiction in *The Waves*, *The Years* and *Between the Acts*, and the inclusion of a chorus will become one of the conventions that will help writers, directors and actors bridge the genre gap in their adaptations of Woolf's plays for the stage. In fact, Jane Marcus has called Woolf's experience at the Covent Garden Opera House her 'college', arguing that Mozart's *Magic Flute*, and Wagner's *Götterdämmerung* and *Parsifal* provided structural models for *Night and Day*, *The Years* and *The Waves* (Marcus 1987: 51).

During the first two decades of the twentieth century the plays of Ibsen, Chekhov, Shaw, Pinero, Maugham, Galsworthy, Granville-Barker and others began to define what would become modernist theatre. At the same time, theatre societies such as the Irish Literary Theatre, the Actresses' Franchise League, the Workers' Theatre Movement, and Edith Craig's Pioneer Players were giving voice to contemporary political concerns. Though Woolf saw Galsworthy's *Strife* and a few of the other 'modern' plays, and though she certainly read the plays of Ibsen, Chekhov and Shaw, there is no record that she saw many of their plays during the first two decades of the twentieth century.

Elizabeth Robins' *Votes for Women*, first performed in 1907, and *A Pageant of Great Women*, in 1910, led Edith Craig and Christopher St John to form the Pioneer Players, but ten years passed before Woolf would see one of their plays, M. E. M. Young's *The Higher Court*, and this only because she was asked to review it. Woolf makes clear that ten years of Pioneer productions attracted audiences with a set expectation horizon, i.e. they expect a 'modern', 'alienating', discomforting, thought-provoking, socially conscious and topical play (*E3*: 207), but Woolf's expectation that she would experience a modern play was quickly disappointed. Instead, she saw 'not a play of intellect' but 'a play of sentiment' (ibid.: 208). This review of *The Higher Court* is significant here because in it Woolf begins to outline what is for her the difference between reading a dramatic text and seeing theatre performed. Often in her reviews, letters and diary entries Woolf depicts herself as a spectator watching both play and audience. In her review of *The Higher Court*, however, her constant use of 'we' suggests that she sees herself as one with the audience (ibid.: 209). Certainly this is a strategic placement of voice, encouraging the readers of the review to identify with her point of view, but this 'we' also suggests that Woolf sensed that other audience members shared her prejudices as well as her values. A few days later Woolf visited the Kingsway Theatre where Edith Craig was rehearsing three plays for the Playwrights' Theatre, *Washed Ashore* by Dorothy Massingham, and two plays by Woolf's friend Beatrice Mayor: *The Girl and the City: A Fantasy* and *Thirty Minutes in a Street*. Woolf later attended the public performance of these plays, but her diary suggests that Edith Craig, the actors and the dynamics of the play rehearsal were much more memorable than the public performance (*D2*: 174).

Although Woolf showed little interest in the many plays written and produced by women throughout the Edwardian and Georgian periods, she showed some interest in the women actors. Among these was Elizabeth Robins, an American-born actress who had pioneered major roles in Ibsen's plays. In her 1905 review of Robins' novel *A Dark Lantern*, Woolf criticised Robins for writing her novel as though she were acting a play (*E1*: 42–3), and in 1920 Woolf took a similar tack when she reviewed Robins' collection *The Mills of the Gods and Other Stories* for the *TLS*, concluding that she is 'misled largely by her strong dramatic sense' (*E3*: 228). The Woolfs, however, recognised Robins' talent and the Hogarth Press published her long essay, *Ibsen and the Actress*, in 1928.

In a 1911 review of Francis Gribble's biography of the Swiss-born actress, Elisa Felix, *Rachel. Her Stage Life and Her Real Life*, Woolf continues to explore the lives of women actors as a means of exploring the performative nature of all writing. Woolf questions Gribble's claim that 'The real individual is only to be discovered after the curtain has fallen and the applause has ceased' (*E1*: 351). 'Why', she asks, 'should we draw these distinctions between real life and stage life?' Woolf acknowledges 'the transiency of great acting compared with other forms of art', but she realises that 'one does not stop acting or painting or writing just because one happens to be dining or driving in the Park; only trying to combine the two often ends disastrously' (ibid.: 352). Woolf concludes that Rachel's life as an artist *was* her 'real life' (ibid.: 353).

In contrast to Rachel's short, sad life is the long, extraordinarily successful life of Ellen Terry, whose memoirs Woolf reviewed near the end of her own life in 1941. As fascinated as Woolf was with Terry's life and with her association with Julia Cameron's Freshwater estate and her correspondence with Shaw, there is no evidence in her letters or diaries that Woolf actually saw Terry on stage. Yet Woolf claims to 'remember her as Lady Cicely', the lead role in *Captain Brassbound's Conversion*, and begins her review with an evocative eye-witness account of the performance. Terry 'filled the stage and all the other actors were put out, as electric lights are put out in the sun' (*M*: 205). Echoing Prospero, Woolf again notes that in contrast to the work of a writer, the work of the actor is ephemeral. 'Every night when the curtain goes down the beautiful coloured canvas is rubbed out. What remains is at best only a wavering, insubstantial phantom – a verbal life on the lips of the living' (ibid.: 206).

Woolf may not have seen Terry or Robins make theatre history playing the Shaw and Ibsen 'new women', but she would continue to read Ibsen's plays, would employ Ibsen's female protagonists as icons representing the 'New Woman', and would allude to Ibsen's plays to develop her own characters and themes. For example, Rachel Vinrace in *The Voyage Out* provides a vivid portrait of the play reader who has trouble making the transition from Ibsen's 'imaginary world to the real world'. When she speaks, she 'was speaking partly as herself, and partly as the heroine of the play she had just read', and after reading Ibsen, she would act the plays 'for days at a time' (*VO*: 123). Later, in the scandalous letter that so shocks Mrs Milvain in *Night and Day*, Cyril Alardyce defends his unconventional behaviour with a reference to Ibsen (*ND*: 109), and in *To the Lighthouse*, we learn that the 'awful prig' Charles Tansley would have liked to have been able to tell people that he went not to the zoo with the Ramsays, as he did, but to an Ibsen play (*TTL*: 12); the implication, of course, is that going to an Ibsen play places one among the sophisticated intelligentsia. Although Woolf, like Rachel Vinrace, seemed content early on to read rather than see Ibsen's plays, in the 1930s she attended a number of productions, including two productions of *The Master Builder*, as well as *A Doll's House*, *Hedda Gabler* and perhaps *Rosmersholm*.

Woolf also admired Shaw, both in print and on stage. She and Leonard saw *John Bull's Other Island* in 1913, *Doctor's Dilemma* in 1924, and in 1925 *Caesar & Cleopatra*, which she called 'a strange rhetorical romantic early Shaw play' (*D3*: 13). The Shaw play most closely connected to Woolf, however, was *Heartbreak House*, which she saw on 11 December 1921. Shaw's now-famous flirtatious comment connects Woolf directly to the play: 'There is a play of mine called Heartbreak House which I always connect with you because I conceived it in that house somewhere in Sussex where I first met you and, of course, fell in love with you' (Laurence 1985: 556–8).

In her 1925 essay, 'The Russian Point of View', Woolf considered what she called the 'enormous difference between . . . Tchehov [*sic*] and Bernard Shaw' (*E4*: 184–5). Woolf was most interested in Chekhov's prose fiction, but in 1920 she experienced and reviewed the Arts Theatre production of *The Cherry Orchard*. Despite her complaints about the onerousness of writing reviews, her relative inexperience as a play reviewer and the brevity of the review, her comments on this obscure production of *The Cherry Orchard* are among her most revealing testimonies to the power of live theatre to move her. Woolf traces how this production painfully dismantled her 'imaginary stage', i.e. her experience as reader, and then, to her amazement, constructed a new multilayered and revelatory text. Woolf's review carefully shifts between the safely impersonal 'every member', 'large number', 'readers', 'one' and the revelatory 'I' to make clear that she includes herself among this armchair audience (*E3*: 246). Like the other readers who find themselves 'transformed into seers', she felt 'shocked and outraged'. But Woolf employs the word 'seer' advisedly; the review becomes the record, not only of a previously read play now seen, but also of an epiphanic experience. Woolf documents the difficulty she has in relinquishing her own 'imaginary stage' for the stage the director, actors and designers provide. The theatre had worked its alchemy on the audience members, who were drawn into what Woolf calls the 'atmosphere' by the very cross-talk or 'strange dislocated sentences' that had at first only discomfited them. Few theatregoers have described theatrical catharsis as sensually as does Woolf:

> I do not know how better to describe the sensation at the end of *The Cherry Orchard*, than by saying that it sends one into the street feeling like a piano played upon at last, not in the middle only but all over the keyboard and with the lid left open so that the sound goes on. (*E3*: 248)

Having playfully created an analogy between good theatre and good sex, it is not surprising that Woolf concludes that she would like the director 'to give us the chance of seeing play after play, until to sit at home and read plays is an occupation for the afflicted only, and one to be viewed with pity . . .' (*E3*: 249).

By the 1930s Woolf was a highly experienced and sophisticated theatregoer; her taste was becoming more eclectic, ranging from the music hall of her youth (reprised in the Bloomsbury skits), to the social and political drama of Ibsen, Shaw, Chekhov, to her continued interest in Shakespeare, opera and ballet, to the stage experiments of her friend Tom Eliot. Certainly her interest in theatre increased as more of her own intimate friends, including her niece Angelica, wrote plays and pursued acting careers. Her preference for reading drama over seeing theatre would continue, so much so that even when she attended a performance, she saw herself as a double audience; she remained an audience of one reading between the acts, even as the performance unfolded before her.

Woolf admired T. S. Eliot's poetry and she spoke of a real fondness for him, at one point claiming that 'he makes me feel that I want to write a play' (*D4*: 344). So we might well expect Woolf to see Eliot's verse plays – *Sweeney Agonistes* (1934), *Murder in the Cathedral* (1935) and *Family Reunion* (1939) – as fulfilment of her own desire for modern verse plays. Far from it. When influenza kept her from seeing Eliot's *The Rock*, in 1934, she wrote in a letter that

> in reading, without seeing, perhaps one got the horror of that cheap farce and Cockney dialogue and dogmatism too full in the face. Roger Fry, though, went and came out in a rage. But I thought even the choruses tainted. (*L5*: 315)

Later that same year, when Woolf sat next to Eliot at the Group Theatre's *Sweeney*, her reaction is less than enthusiastic: 'The acting made more sense than the reading but I doubt that Tom has enough of a body & brain to bring off a whole play (*D4*: 261).

After Woolf saw the Group Theatre's *Murder in the Cathedral* in 1935, she wrote to Angelica,

> I think what is wanted is for some actress to make plays in which people are like ourselves only heightened; what is so bad is the complete break between the acting, the words and the scenery. Thus you lose all feeling of

harmony. Why dont you make a play all in one? Thus it is much better to read plays than to see them. (*L5*: 444)

Her letter to Julian is less cryptic:

We went to Toms play, the Murder, last week; and I had almost to carry Leonard out, shrieking. What was odd was how much better it reads than acts; the tightness, chillness, deadness and general worship of the decay and skeleton made one near sickness. The truth is when he has live bodies on the stage his words thin out, and no rhetoric will save them. (*L5*: 448)

For Woolf, Eliot's verse drama fails on stage both in form and theme.

In June 1924 Woolf attended a party at Lytton Strachey's country house where she experienced one of the most controversially avant-garde plays of the decade, Arthur Schnitzler's *La Ronde*. She wrote in her diary that 'we went to a disillusioned party last night, after which L. contemplated, seriously, some scientific form of suicide' (*D2*: 304). Vanessa Bell described the play's plot as a copulation scene, but, in fact, the plot includes not one but ten copulation scenes. The censor's disapproval, which had effectively prohibited public performance, would have been enough to encourage the private performance. Schnitzler made theatre history, not only for the boldly salacious content of the play, but for what was seen as gritty naturalism and an honest depiction of modern attitudes toward sex. Woolf may have forgotten her experience with *La Ronde* when she and Leonard saw Schnitzler's *Fräulein Else* in December 1932. She wrote to Virginia Isham, 'We enjoyed it greatly–I dont think its a good play, but it was a very interesting experiment. I dont think you can do thinking as well as speaking on the stage – or not like that' (*L5*: 150). This problem of depicting thought on stage, which Schnitzler does not solve to Woolf's satisfaction, has also proven to be a problem for performers who attempt to adapt Woolf's work to today's stage.

The plays Woolf read and the theatre she experienced contributed to her ever-changing aesthetics and the application of these theories in her novels, but Woolf was a participant in theatre as well as an audience. From childhood family skits, to an intricate, if short-lived, letter-writing game and Play Reading Society, to the Dreadnought Hoax, to experiments in dramatic dialogue in diaries and letters, to two versions of her own play *Freshwater*, to Charleston private performances, Woolf played with languages of the stage, experimenting with both performance and dialogue creation.

The log book for the Play Reading Society kept first by Saxon Sydney-Turner and then by Clive Bell illustrates that the readings were more than mere parlour games. It was not only the choice of plays (Vanbrugh's *The Relapse*, Jonson's *Every Man Out of His Humour*, Shakespeare's *Henry IV, Part I*, Milton's *Samson Agonistes* and *Comus*, Swinburne's *Atalanta in Calydon*, Ibsen's *Rosmersholm*, Browning's *Luria*, Congreve's *The Double-Dealer* and *Love for Love*, and Dryden's *Aureng-Zebe, Marriage à la Mode, Conquest of Granada I* and *II*), but the 'salon' atmosphere of these early Bloomsbury evenings that defined Woolf's own early interaction with drama and theatre. Members were expected to prepare their parts, and when playing multiple roles were expected to differentiate them. This readers' theatre would help to mould the way Woolf and the others read and understood plays. Participating in reading the parts aloud or verbally acting them out often led the recorder to remark that the process changed his understanding of the plays. The secretary's notes suggest that when reading the part of Cordatus in *Every Man Out of His Humour*, Woolf slipped more easily into the role of observer/commentator than into some of the more central roles she would play in the months to come. Although the Play Reading Society had a rather short run, Woolf continued to participate in Gordon Square 'Thursday Evenings'. What Woolf would call the 'Old Bloomsbury' years (1904 until her marriage in 1912) were dominated by conversational role-playing as well as amateur theatrics and fancy dress.

One not-so-private theatrical performance stands out during these Old Bloomsbury years: the 1910 'Dreadnought Hoax'. Even this oft-discussed episode was a direct outgrowth of her brother Adrian's Cambridge exhibitionism. In 1910 Adrian, along with Duncan Grant, Guy Ridley, Anthony Buxton, Horace de Vere Cole, and the last-minute addition to the group – Virginia Stephen – reprised the joke for a larger stage. Woolf's participation is an example of her youthful adventurousness, of the early Bloomsbury camaraderie and iconoclasm, and of her lifelong criticism of British patriarchal imperialism. But the hoax is also an example of her performative, even theatrical interests. Certainly, convincing the British Admiralty that Anthony Buxton was a visiting Abyssinian Emperor travelling with his entourage, finagling a military escort aboard the HMS *Dreadnought* – the most powerful battleship of its day and flagship of the British fleet – touring the ship, inspecting the Honour Guard, and then leaking the whole story to the press made a laughing stock of the British Navy and demonstrated the group's contempt for the imperial war machine and patriarchal authority. But the hoax also illustrates Woolf's awareness of performance as a means of protest and subversion.

Equally intriguing are the numerous dramatic collaborations between Woolf and her Bell nephews and nieces, some of which were 'published' as supplements to the children's newspaper, first titled *The Charleston Bulletin* then by 1924 renamed *The New Bulletin*. The *Charleston Bulletin* folder, among manuscripts recently added to the British Library collection, contains another play featuring Woolf as the major character entitled *Chinoiseries: A Sequel to 'The Conspirators'*.[1] These plays are more than teenaged Quentin's good-humoured satire of his aunt and other members of the Charleston circle. Woolf encouraged Quentin, Julian, and Angelica, often typed the *Bulletin* and the supplements for them, sometimes wrote or co-wrote the stories and plays, and participated in the dramatic readings, often playing herself. For example, a notice in *The New Bulletin*, No. 2, for December 1927, announced that 'The household was entertained in the evening by Angelica and Mrs. Woolf, who gave a performance of a mummers folk-play, amended and brought up to date, with tricks by Clinker, the performing dog. This was greatly appreciated by all present' (ms: Add 83331). Many of these performances were much more than quick skits. Just as the stories and poems that appeared in *The New Bulletin* were often carefully developed, substantial works, many of the plays included three acts, each with multiple scenes.

It is in the context of these private plays and plays written by friends and family that we should read Woolf's own play *Freshwater*. She wrote the first draft of her play at the same time that she was filling her diaries with dramatic dialogue, compiling a full translation of *Antigone*, seeing *The Beggars Opera* three times, watching old Marie Lloyd at the Bedford Music Hall, seeing *Heartbreak House* for the first time, reviewing *The Cherry Orchard*, hearing Lytton Strachey and Eliot's ideas for plays, and attempting to finish the novel which would become *Mrs Dalloway*. She laments, 'I wish I could write The Hours as freely & vigorously as I scribble Freshwater, a Comedy. Its a strange thing how arduous I find my novels; & yet Freshwater is only spirited fun . . .' (*D2*: 251). Although it would be twelve years until Woolf would dig the play from her files and rewrite it for a production before as many as eighty family members, friends and Bloomsbury hangers-on, an autumn 1923 issue of *The Charleston Bulletin* records that 'Aunt Jinna arrived on Thursday and read her play to the assembled household' (Add 83316). Perhaps Woolf's later insistence that 'the play [is] rather tosh' and that she is 'not going to bother about making a good impression as a play wright' (*D4*: 271), explains why, until recently, little critical attention has been lavished on the play since Lucio Ruotolo's edition first made the text available in 1976.

Woolf's experience at the theatre and her experiments with stage dialogue show up as early as *Night and Day* and *The Voyage Out*, while her later novels become increasingly performative with *Orlando*, *The Years*, as well as parts of *The Waves* showing the influence of her growing appreciation for stage dialogue and audience reception. Her interest in writing a serious and experimental play increases in her last years and leads to what began as a play and ended as the hybrid novel *Between the Acts*. In fact, many recent critical studies of the novels, especially the huge volume of work being done on her last novel, investigate the performative nature of her work.

Although Woolf refers to her experience as opera audience member and especially to her changing attitudes towards Wagner many times in her letters, diaries and essays, it is in two of her novels that she provides her most extensive and most intriguing glimpses into the Edwardian opera scene. A comparison of an 'at the opera' scene in her early novel *Jacob's Room* (1922) to one in her late novel *The Years* (1937) reveals how Woolf transformed her experience at the opera into theme, symbol and narrative technique. Whereas Wagner's Bayreuth Bühnenfestspielhaus was, according to Symons, 'for the first time in the modern world, a literal "theatron", or looking-room . . . constructed . . . solely for the purpose of looking, and of looking in one direction only' (Symons 1905: 308),

Woolf's Covent Garden Opera House was a 'looking-room' in which the audience spent almost as much time viewing itself as listening to the opera.

The famous arch of the Opera House façade, in fact, frames the larger 'looking-room' over which Woolf's narrator hovers, providing readers with multiple perspectives, or scenes, of Jacob's peripatetic short adult life in the years between his leaving Cambridge and his death. The narrator hovers first over the arch that divides the wealthy West End from the poverty-stricken East, then over the opera performance itself and audience reaction to it. Woolf conflates actor and character while at the same time demonstrating the seamless symbiosis between libretto and music, the emotion 'emphasised by the music' that she had described in her essay 'The Opera'. The reader, like the narrator, is almost overwhelmed by the multiplicity of responses and must choose where to focus attention. In her anxiety over where to alight, the hovering narrator slips out of the third person to observe 'wherever I seat myself, I die in exile'. If she listens to the responses in one part of the theatre she misses those in another. Though this choice remains a problem, the potential chaos presented by the cacophony from 2,000 spectators is averted by nature and society's 'system of classification' whose 'moulds are filled nightly': 'stalls, boxes, amphitheatre, gallery' (*JR*: 69). Here then, within the arch of the Royal Opera House framing London and before the proscenium arch framing the stage, the classes who rule and benefit from Edward's empire congregate while the prostitutes and the 'little thief' are left out on the street.

In her penultimate novel, *The Years* (1937), Woolf takes readers back under the arch of the Covent Garden Opera House on 6 May 1910, the final afternoon of the reign of Edward VII. The gulf between this opulent world and the world of 'the dingy little clerks' and the 'coarse-looking women' is even wider than it had been in *Jacob's Room*. As soon as Kitty moves under the arch and into the 'yellow and crimson' glow of the lobby she leaves behind her social conscience and feels appropriate and at ease. No longer is there a hovering, spirit-narrator who alights in stalls, boxes, gallery and amphitheatre to provide readers with multiple perspectives of stage and audience. Now the narrator slips inside Kitty to provide another view from above, but this time readers see everything from the vantage point of Lady Lasswade's box. In fact, filtered through Kitty's senses, the Opera House becomes a living impressionist painting, a synaesthetic version of Degas' opera paintings : 'The whole house glowed–red, gold, cream-coloured, and smelt of clothes and flowers, and echoed with the squeaks and trills of the instruments and with the buzz and hum of voices' (181–2). We see and hear Kitty's favourite opera *Siegfried* through her own eyes and ears, with many of the opera's plot elements evoking Kitty's memories. We learn that the music excites her, but it makes her respond not to Wagner but to her own life, her own emotions. Although Marcus playfully sees Siegfried's breaking of the anvil as 'anarchist and anti-intellectual as well as libertarian' (Marcus 1987: 58), Woolf shows Kitty's response to be visceral, even orgasmic:

The music excited her. It was magnificent. Siegfried took the broken pieces of the sword and blew out the fire and hammered, hammered, hammered. . . . Quicker and quicker, more and more rhythmically, more and more triumphantly he hammered, until at last up he swung the sword high above his head and brought it down – crack! The anvil burst asunder. (*Y*: 184–5)

The focus is on Kitty as audience member. On the eve of the Georgian era, that will usher in the Great War, Kitty remains rooted in the Victorian and Edwardian world, always on her way to or from the opera or ballet, the most artificial (as opposed to naturalistic) of theatrical forms, offering rides in her motor car, always the audience and never quite fully engaged in life.

Although Woolf eventually rejected the theatrical dialogue present in some of the many draft versions of *The Years*, theatre, with its choruses and its speaking characters, remained an essential metonymic device in the finished novel. In the beginning of the 1910 section, for example, an autumnal, early-morning London is a stage 'waiting for something to happen; for a curtain to rise' (*Y*: 160). Critics from Grace Radin and Jane Marcus to Julia Briggs have likened the lyrical prologues beginning each section to the overture of an opera or to the chorus of a Greek play. Unlike a theatrical chorus, however, the interludes express the authorial voice and so act as a stand-in for the non-fictional, sociopolitical commentary that Woolf had first envisioned as a novel-essay. In other words, the interludes serve thematically as the chorus that Marcus, Radin and Wheare hear, but the language is lyrical, authorial and no less theatrical than the dialogue found in the early versions of the Elvira/Maggie scenes.

Many of the problems adapters and directors face when they attempt to stage Woolf's work, which is so dramatic yet seemingly so anti-theatrical, are those facing Woolf's own 'Anon', Miss La Trobe, the frustrated writer-director of the pageant between whose acts the real 'dramatic' narrative unfolds in Woolf's last novel, *Between the Acts*. Although this novel has received a great deal of critical attention, only recently has the focus begun to shift to its dramatic and theatrical qualities.

Woolf chose not to model La Trobe's theatrical conventions on those of Ibsen, Shaw, Chekhov, Elizabeth Robins or the many other serious women playwrights of the first third of the twentieth century. Knowing her audience and her purpose, La Trobe does not attempt psychological realism, naturalism or complex characterisations. And her out-of-doors venue, amateur actors and shoestring budget preclude lighting effects, curtains, fly space, or other amenities of the early twentieth-century public stage. Instead, we experience the conventions of the village pageant. Here is the theatrical problem that interests Woolf: what to do with that vacancy – fill it, span it, maintain it? In one sense, it is filled, as for Woolf all stage drama is, with fragments, in this case words and music that waft in and out with the breeze. Isabella wonders, 'Did the plot matter. . . . . The plot was only there to beget emotion. There were only two emotions: love; and hate. There was no need to puzzle out the plot' (*BTA*: 90). Earlier in the performance, when La Trobe worries that the interrelationship of play and audience is not coalescing, she becomes frustrated and longs to do what Woolf achieves in *Between the Acts*: 'O to write a play without an audience – *the* play' (ibid.: 180). Woolf avoided the pain and frustration of *seeing* her work before an assembled audience when she chose to write *Between the Acts* as a novel rather than as a play, but she knew well that audience is essential to both novelist and playwright, and she knew that theatre, like narrative fiction, must provoke multiple meanings, must force the sometimes reluctant audience into complicity if plays and novels are to convey more than mere plot. Theatre, after all, must forge one audience out of many spectators while fiction assumes an isolated audience of one. Miss La Trobe desired a single response from the hydra-headed entity, while Woolf realised that multiple meanings are less problematic with multiple readers.

In his 2005 *Virginia Woolf: Authors in Context*, Michael Whitworth describes three film adaptations of Woolf's work, adding that the

> stage has proved a medium more resistant to Woolf's works: given her concentration on interior life, and lack of interest in conventional action, they are difficult to adapt for the popular theatre. However, there have been three stage adaptations of *Orlando* and one of *The Waves*, as well as an adaptation of *A Room of One's Own*. (Whitworth 2005: 195)

Interiority has, indeed, posed a problem for those attempting to adapt Woolf's novels to the stage, but a list of productions (see Figure 24.2) suggests that many writers and directors have taken up the challenge, some more successfully than others. Reviews of these productions often echo Whitworth's conviction that the stream-of-consciousness novel is unsuited to dramatisation and that they produce, in the words of one critic, 'the worst kind of "literary" theatre, shorn of narrative drive or genuine emotion'. To these critics the problem is twofold: first, there is not enough action or dialogue for the stage, and, second, there is no satisfying method for conveying interiority on stage.

Many recent productions have fared better. The Berkeley Repertory's *To the Lighthouse* overcomes the problem of interiority with digital projections, an innovative score that begins as atmosphere but becomes almost a character, tableaux that make the audience feel as though it were viewing a painting, and dialogue in which characters speak each other's thoughts (see Figure 24.3). This is certainly theatre that has crossed Woolf's 'Narrow Bridge of Art' to produce what one critic calls 'a post-modern chamber opera . . . a multimedia concert that encompasses text, music and video but is bounded by none of them' (D'Souza 2007). Preparing her equally successful radio adaptation of *To the Lighthouse*, Lindsay Bell discovered that radio inherently 'reduces the distance between the audience and the stage, changes the nature of performance, and is perhaps a more suitable medium for stream-of-consciousness narrative' (Bell 2003: 74).

Novel	Director	Adapter	Company	Theatre	City	Date
To the Lighthouse	Andrew Holmes		Empty Space	Lyric Studio	London	Jan. 1995
To the Lighthouse	Ann Hodges	Lindsay Bell	Shaw Festival CBC Radio	Royal George Theatre	Niagara-on-the-Lake	Aug. 2000 April 2001
To the Lighthouse	Les Waters	Adele Edling Shank	Berkeley Repertory	Roda Theater	Berkeley	March 2007
Mrs. Dalloway	Kellie Mecleary	Kellie Mecleary	Goucher College	Carver Theater	Baltimore	Feb. 2008
Night and Day		Tom Clyde		Transparent Theater	Berkeley	June 2003
Orlando				Illusion Theater	Minneapolis	1977
Orlando			The Guildhall School		London	1988
Orlando	Robert Wilson	Robert Wilson		Théâtre Odeon	Paris	1989
Orlando			Red Shift Theatre Co.	Edinburgh Festival	Edinburgh	Aug. 1992
Orlando	Robert Wilson			Royal Lyceum Theatre	Edinburgh	Aug. 1996
Orlando	David Harradine		Fevered Sleep Co.	Tabard Theatre	London	June 1997
Orlando	Kristel Lessmend	Ene-Liis Semper		Vanemuine Theatre	Tartu, Estonia	2001
Orlando	Joyce Priven	Sarah Ruhl		Priven Theatre	Evanston, Il.	2003
Orlando	Ryan Rilette	Sarah Ruhl	A. C. T.	Zeum Theater	San Francisco	Feb. 2008
Orlando	Robert Chuter	Julia Britton	Fly-on-the-Wall		Melbourne, Au.	2008
The Waves	Lisa Peterson	David Buckman	N.Y. Theater Workshop	Perry St. Theater	New York	May 1990
The Waves	Abigail Anderson	Abigail Docherty	Crowd Proud Productions	Tristan Bates Theatre	London	April 1997
The Waves	Alan Kreizenbeck	Marjorie Lightfoot		UMBC Theater	Baltimore	June 2000
The Waves	Katie Mitchell	Katie Mitchell	National Theatre	Cottesloe	London	Jan. 2006
The Waves		Terence Davies	BBC Radio 4			Oct. 2007
The Waves	Katie Mitchell		National Theatre	The Duke, Lincoln Center	New York	Nov. 2008

Figure 24.2 Adaptations of Woolf's novels for the stage © Steven Putzel

Figure 24.3 *To the Lighthouse*, Berkeley Repertory Theater. Photograph by Kevin Berne, www.kevinberne.com

Filmmaker Terence Davies also found radio drama to be an appropriate medium for his 2007 adaptation of *The Waves*. The narrator's voice dominates, but in the background the audience hears fragments of character dialogue, birdsong, the clatter of trains, a ticking clock, the wind, and of course the rush of waves. The 1990 New York Theater Workshop's musical of *The Waves* approximates the author's stream of consciousness with a collage technique in which overlapping monologues become dialogues and speech evolves into song. But perhaps the most acclaimed stage adaptation of any of Woolf's novels is Katie Mitchell's production of *Waves*, which opened at the Cottesloe Theatre, London in November 2008 and at Lincoln Center, NY in November 2008. In her 'Workpack' for the production, assistant director Lucy Kerbel discusses the difficulty of transliterating the novel to the stage. The director 'had to find a new performance language which would make the thoughts of the characters clear to the audience and could also move between their interior thoughts at great speed' (Kerbel 2006: 3). The production works because Mitchell experimented with video and sound effects to spur spectators' imaginations into visualising scenes, thus producing an experience that is as close to that of a reader as it is to that of an audience member. Like the radio-play experiments, this production uses 'live and recorded sound to create a very full aural world' to 'transport the audience from one location or historical period to the next' (ibid.: 4), a technique inspired by the 'Foley artists' who provide the sound for film and TV.

Figure 24.4 *Waves*, National Theatre. Photograph by Stephen Cummiskey

No Woolf novel has been adapted to film, theatre or performance art more often than has *Orlando*. The colourful romp through four centuries, the sex changes, the scenes set around the world, the narrative voice – all present adapters, producers, designers, directors and actors with exciting challenges. Most of the early productions enjoyed limited success, and Woolf herself was convinced that there are 'certain subtleties that the playwright cannot satisfy' (*M*: 32). Productions that rely on the techniques of realism or that render 'subtleties' literally risk unintentional audience laughter. Among the most successful productions were Robert Wilson's staging in French in 1989, his English production in 1993, the 1997 Fevered Sleep Company's *Orlando*, and ACT's 2008 restaging of Sarah Ruhl's adaptation. Wilson gives us what Woolf might desire but could not even imagine. Rather than expanding to fill the distance between audience and play, Wilson creates a minimalist theatre with his simple lighting, suggestive rather than elaborate costuming, Kabuki-like stylisation, and one actor on stage. Unlike the experience of watching artificial realism that so disappointed Woolf, watching Wilson is like viewing a post- expressionist painting. In the Fevered Sleep production, two mute, androgynous figures write on each other's semi-naked bodies, while oversized costumes hang suspended to suggest the other characters. Far from being what Woolf saw as plot-driven, larger-than-life action, this is theatre that dances to Woolf's own enigmatic text. Just as Wilson rendered Woolf's satiric edge, so Fevered Sleep evokes appropriately

Figure 24.5 *Orlando*, American Conservatory Theater. Photograph by David
Wilson, American Conservatory Theater

wry laughter when actors slip behind the costumes, not to wear them, but to
animate, puppeteer-like, an age. The ACT production (see Figure 24.5) fills the
stage with a cast of eleven, but the minimalist set, doubling, simple lighting and
on-stage costume changes create a stage world in which time and gender are
fluid. As in Mitchell's *Waves*, actors sitting behind tables on stage become Foley
artists producing sound effects that encourage audience complicity.

In addition to theatrical productions adapted from Woolf's novels and the
many productions of *Freshwater* are the dozens of plays based on her life,
such as Eileen Atkins' *A Room of One's Own* and *Vita and Virginia*, Maureen
Duffy's *A Nightingale in Bloomsbury Square*, Edna O'Brien's *Virginia*, and
Carol Samson's *After Tea*, a stage adaptation of *A Writer's Diary*. Woolf's work
is performance – her narrative is dialogic, always engaging readers into co-
authorship. Woolf was drawn to drama but she remained distrustful of theatre.
She sensed the possibilities of the stage, but she could never bring herself
to write a play, other than *Freshwater*, though when she began 'Pointz Hall'
(*Between the Acts*) she referred to it as 'my Play', adding parenthetically, 'Pointz
Hall is to become in the end a play' (*D5*: 139). She was certainly right to distrust
the theatre, for the modernist theatre she knew was particularly unsuited to her
dramatic narrative form. Adapters who rely on realism, naïve symbolism, or the
traditional musical still fail in their attempts to bring Woolf to the stage. It takes
the postmodern stage with its use of mime, dance, opera, contrapuntal music,

minimalist sets, and, most of all, its demand of complicity from the audience to produce successful stage performances of Virginia Woolf.

Note

1. In April 2003 the British Library acquired 188 issues of the Bell children's family newsletter (1923–27), *The Charleston Bulletin* (later issues are entitled *The New Bulletin*) from Anne Olivier Bell. The materials are arranged and catalogued in sixteen folders (Add 83316–83332). Although most of the articles are by Quentin Bell and many are typed (some by Woolf herself), there are notes, corrections, and text in Woolf's own hand.

Works Cited and Further Reading

Barker, Clive and Maggie B. Gail (2000) *British Theatre Between the Wars: 1918-1939*, Cambridge: Cambridge University Press.

Bell, Lindsay (2003) 'Transmitting the Voices, Voyages and Visions: Adapting Virginia Woolf's *To the Lighthouse for Radio*', in *Languages of Theatre Shaped by Women*, ed. Jane de Gay and Lizbeth Goodman, Bristol: intellect, pp. 73–88.

Blau, Herbert (1990) *The Audience*, Baltimore, MD: Johns Hopkins University Press.

Briggs, Julia (2007) '*Waves*, devised by Katie Mitchell and the Company, and performed at the National Theatre, London, November 2006–February 2007' (review), *Virginia Woolf Bulletin*, 25, May: 62–4.

Cockin, Katherine (2001) *Women and Theatre in the Age of Suffrage: The Pioneer Players, 1911-1925*, New York: Palgrave.

D'Souza, Karen (2007) 'An Impressionistic Trip "To the Lighthouse" – Risks Pay off in Stage Adaptation' (review), *San Jose Mercury News*, 2 March: 1E.

Farfan, Penny (2004) *Women, Modernism, & Performance*, Cambridge: Cambridge University Press.

Kerbel, Lucy (2006) *Waves Workpack*, London: The Royal National Theatre.

Laurence, Dan H. (ed.) (1985) *Bernard Shaw Collected Letters: 1926-1950*, 4, New York: Viking Penguin.

Lowe, Gill (ed.) (2005) *Hyde Park Gate News: The Stephen Family Newspaper*, London: Hesperus Press.

Marcus, Jane (1987) *Virginia Woolf and the Languages of Patriarchy*, Bloomington: Indiana University Press.

— (ed.) (1988) *Art and Anger: Reading Like a Woman*, Columbus: Ohio State University Press.

Radin, Grace (1981) *Virginia Woolf's The Years: The Evolution of a Novel*, Knoxville: University of Tennessee Press.

Symons, Arthur (1905) 'The Ideas of Richard Wagner', reprinted in *The Theory of the Modern Stage*, ed. Eric Bentley, New York: Penguin Books, 1983, pp. 283–321.

Wheare, Jane (1989) *Virginia Woolf: Dramatic Novelist*, New York: St Martin's Press.

Whitworth, Michael H. (2005) *Virginia Woolf: Authors in Context*, London: Oxford University Press.

25

VIRGINIA WOOLF AND DANCE

Evelyn Haller

VIRGINIA WOOLF LIVED in England during decades of innovation in dance as well as reclamation of folk dance. She recognised how the comedic vitality of music hall variety acts demonstrated an aspect of national character – the individualistically secular – as indigenous to the English as the collectively religious was to the astoundingly integrated productions of the Russian dancers under Diaghilev from their arrival in Western Europe until his death (1909–29). Dance in all its manifestations – publicly spontaneous as in Trafalgar Square at the 1918 Armistice, jazz-influenced in cafés and homes during the 1920s and 1930s as well as professionally performed – was an art she plundered. Some indications are overt as when she names Nijinsky in the text of *The Years* in 1937 (Woolf 1998: 186) and notes the death of Pavlova in her diary in 1931 (*D4*: 8). Others are subtle as her likely encounter with the Noh plays of Ancient Japan through Ezra Pound's edition of Ernest Fenollosa's notes (1916) about the time she was reading his memoir of the sculptor Gaudier-Brzeska (1891–1915) (*D1*: 90). This chapter explores the circumstances of these influences while noting her own experiences with dance and the extent to which she often encountered dance in paintings and designs made by her sister, Vanessa Bell, and Bell's partner, Duncan Grant, among other contemporaries. When the mosaicist Boris Anrep sited Woolf as Clio, the muse of history, not far from Lydia Lopokova, Lady Keynes, as Terpsichore, the muse of dance, on the landings of the National Gallery (1930–33), he realised in tesserae Woolf's presence in the exuberant play of the arts. Being at the centre of a spinning armillary sphere of dance, Woolf took what she needed for her own art and thereby not only enhanced but experimentally formed her writing. Indeed, her invention of the word 'scrolloping' signifies a predisposition to dance, for the rhythmic word is not unlike the unwinding of a scroll that may wantonly spring back (*O*: 103; *SF*: 172; *W*: 282; *D2*: 232).[1]

Although the ballroom was not a welcome factor in the young Virginia's life, her love of dance was long-standing. When she wrote in 1902 that she and her brother Adrian 'had waltzed (to a Polka!)', she did not share his inability to 'conceive how anyone can be idiotic enough to find amusement in dancing.' Virginia, on the other hand, 'would give all my profound Greek to dance really well, and so would Adrian give anything he had' (*L*1: 63). (In his defence, consider that the nineteen-year-old Adrian Stephen may have already attained his height of six feet, six inches and was adjusting to the length of his limbs.) Although Virginia Stephen was writing mockingly about social dancing, she was perhaps metaphorically sacrificing what she had learned of Ancient Greek language to what she had absorbed of Ancient Greek culture through their choral movements and ritual processions to attain an integrated experience of life she imagined her cultural ancestors to have had. She observed arrested movement on Greek vases at the British Museum, led in part by Jane Harrison's imaginative reconstructions in her writings and dramatic lectures. Later she was to see Nijinsky as the Pan-like faun dancing to Debussy's music in his own choreography, similarly based on Ancient Greek artifacts.

Despite a folkloric movement in dance that was a source of pleasure as well as social bonding among educated contemporaries of Woolf, dance was not an integral part of British culture as it was in that of Russia. As an indication of class-based unease with dance, consider the fate of the Reverend Stuart D. Headlam (1847–1924), a founder of the Church and Stage Guild, who was forced to resign his curacy for lecturing on dance to workers' clubs. The 23-year-old Virginia Stephen, on the other hand, taught her working-class students in dressing rooms in The Royal Victoria Coffee and Music Hall which had opened in 1880. An evening institute adjunct to the Old Vic, Morley College enjoyed an atmosphere hospitable to dance; for ballet, which was not as liable to licensing control as 'performances', did not violate its music hall licence. Thanks to the enterprising Lillian Baylis (1874–1937) who built upon the work of her aunt, Emma Cons (1838–1912), working men and women were served aesthetically as well as educationally inside the labyrinthine structure off the Waterloo Road.

Within living memory of Virginia Stephen's contemporaries, professional dance was at best ancillary. In Charles Kean's production of *Henry V* at Princess's Theatre in 1859, for example, an 'Historical Interlude' with wingèd ballet dancers greeted Henry's return to London after the victory at Agincourt. [2] That unhistorical spectacle was decidedly different from the scene-making that Virginia Stephen devised for her lectures to teach English history at Morley College. Meanwhile programmes at the large theatres evolved featuring both traditional romantic ballets and 'ballets divertissement'. The latter was 'driven less by plot than by panoramic approaches to up-to-date topics'. Between the two divergent styles of ballet, however, the expectations of music hall audiences continued to be fulfilled including 'tumbling acrobats and performing dogs'.[3] In less evolved venues chorus lines flourished with displays of more or less coordinated female legs. That women dancers in those venues understood their appearance as providing prime entertainment is suggested by the hazards many accepted when they chose to dance in gauzy dresses that were liable to catch fire from gaslight. How ironic that women – not magical predecessors to Stravinsky's Firebird – sometimes lit up the British stage.

When Virginia Woolf noted the interment of Anna Pavlova's ashes at Golders Green on 26 January 1931 (*D4*: 8), did she think of Pavlova in comparison or contrast to Diaghilev's Russian dancers with whom she had appeared for a short time near the beginning of her career in Western Europe? The Russian ballerina was (1882–1931) Woolf's contemporary, preceding her in death by a decade. While Pavlova and Nijinsky performed in St Petersburg, they were the stars.

On 7 November 1911 Pavlova appeared at Covent Garden with 'The Russian Ballet Organised by M. Serge Diaghilev' in *Le Pavillon d'Armide*, *Les Sylphides*, and *Le Carnaval* dancing with Nijinsky. Virginia Stephen invited Lytton Strachey to that performance, describing the tickets as 'only amphitheatre this time; but when they do the other thing we will go to the stalls' (*L1*:479). The previous year (27 April 1910) Pavlova and Michael Mordkin had appeared as the twelfth attraction among thirteen at The Palace, following variety acts which included The Palace Girls, a club juggler, and a magician. The Russian dancers were followed by 'Kinemacolour' productions of '*Paris the Gay City*' and *Choosing the Wallpaper* as well as 'Urbanora' Bioscope productions of '*Arrival of Lord Kitchener at Southampton*,' '*Mr. Graham White's Great Aeroplane Flight*' and '*Punchestown Races*.'[4]

By way of synchronous social history one sees atop the 1910 Programme: 'The Management politely request that where necessary Ladies will remove their hats in order not to obstruct the view of those sitting behind.' Woolf later cited as symptomatic of the change in human character that was to take place 'on or about December, 1910' the example of 'the Georgian cook . . . in and out of the drawing room . . . now to ask advice about a hat' which was likely to sport feathers and so resemble the feathered headdress of Karsavina as Stravinsky's Firebird or Pavlova's Dying Swan (Woolf 1981: 91–2).

Pavlova broke with Diaghilev and pursued her own solo course rather than appear as a member of his tightly controlled company. Nijinska quotes the ballerina: 'Let the public that comes to see Pavlova see only Pavlova! Vassia has enough of his own public to fill the Theatre to overflowing . . . .'[5] Instead, Pavlova established herself as a performer of divertissements which differed from those performed at the Empire and Alhambra (Haskell 1956: 3). Pavlova's divertissements, Haskell argues, were 'choreographic poems. What singles them out from the divertissement was their completeness as dramatic episodes . . . they exploited an atmosphere'. Pavlova's most memorable idiosyncratic dance was 'The Dying Swan' which she had devised in 1905. 'It was the type of romanticism that lent itself admirably to the very nature of the dance, something essentially ephemeral.' She 'celebrated all the beauty in nature that fades with the coming of Autumn, a mood that she felt deeply and that she expressed in her only choreographic creation, *Autumn Leaves*' (ibid.: 5). Pavlova ventured into sculpture to model a bronze 'by herself' of herself as the dying swan. No stranger to the benefits of publicity if not anticipating contemporary 'branding', Pavlova kept a series of pet swans named Jack with one of which she was photographed in an affectionate pose. Nonetheless, Pavlova may be said to have raised the level of respect paid to women dancers in Britain as Florence Nightingale had previously raised that of nurses. As Haskell noted: '[W]e were not yet so very far away from the 'naughty-nineties' and lurid tales of champagne drunk from ballet girls' slippers. Pavlova immediately convinced the great public that dancing was an art and that the dancer's life was one of dedication'. (ibid.: 4–5)[6]

In 1909 Henri Matisse painted his first version of *Dance*. His circle of female figures is arrested from their implied motion; indeed their bodies resemble those of the nude Vanessa Bell and the nude Molly MacCarthy with mature loosening flesh in a photograph taken by Duncan Grant (1913) (Reed 2004: 151, fig. 107). One can envision by extrapolation the women's enjoyment of free motion in their linked though open dance positions. Moreover, they would have seen performances of Diaghilev's Russian dancers which might well have inspired (paraphrasing Lucy Swithin) their undanced selves. The idea of dance contributed to Woolf's visual milieu as in decorations by Vanessa Bell and Duncan Grant – both realised and unrealised – in her own residences as well as in the apartments and houses of her family, friends, and acquaintances – those of the group identified with Bloomsbury and beyond.

Lady Ottoline Morrell was the source of an anecdote whereby Leon Bakst was heard to exclaim and Nijinsky repeat '*Quel décor!*' as they watched a tennis game in Bedford Square in 1911. The movements of Duncan Grant and his fellow players against a background of trees and enclosing buildings moved the designer and dancer to the iterated exclamation of delight. As Peter Jacobs notes, 'And this revelation would be the germ of the ballet'[7] *Jeux* or *Playtime* (1913, although set in a future 1930). Nijinsky had initially conceived an erotic ballet with three men instead of the tennis players as two women and one man.[8] He had also planned to dance *sur pointe* himself but did not. In 1912 Nijinsky spoke of sports as a source for contemporary choreography:

> By attentively studying polo, golf, tennis, I have become convinced that sports are not only a healthy pastime but also create their own plastic beauty. From studying them I derive the hope that in the future this contemporary style will be considered a characteristic style as we now consider those of the past.[9]

By any measure, Nijinsky was the ultimate athlete himself. In *The Years* (1937) a young woman exclaims in 1914: '"And when he gives that leap!" . . . she raised her hand with a lovely gesture in the air – "and then comes down!" She let her hand fall in her lap' (Woolf 1998: 186). 'That leap', though not preserved on film, is suggested in photographs and less persuasively in paintings and pastels. More provocatively, Nijinska testifies to his extraordinary prowess during their student days at the Maryinsky. She describes, for example, his inability to raise

Figure 25.1 Anna Pavlova with her pet swan Jack at Ivy House, her home in London. Image courtesy of the Dance Collection, the New York Public Library at Lincoln Center

his leg higher than a ninety-degree angle because of his highly developed thigh muscles. Christopher Reed calls attention to the massively thighed male figures in Duncan Grant's various decorative panels and murals which he attributes to Grant's fascination with Nijinsky. Grant's *Adam and Eve* with an upside down Adam may be juxtaposed with Nijinska's account of her brother's ability 'to make a full pirouette standing on his head' (Nijinska 1992: 297). She also writes of how he was able to dance on his toes. Through his instruction and insistence that she wear men's soft leather shoes instead of those for women with boxed toes, she achieved what she had thought impossible and was also able to dance on her toes.

The Russian dancers permanently influenced professional dance in Britain. Although the often galumphing entertainment in the music hall that passed for dance was contradicted by the innovations of the Russian dancers, the satyr element was not alien to its practitioners. Vanessa Bell's poster of 1927 *The Keynes-Keynes* (a variant on the Can-Can) celebrated a play at 46 Gordon Square, *Don't Be Frightened*, or *Pippington Park*, which was enlivened with cross-gendered choruses and a conclusion danced by the hosts, Lydia Lopokova and, her husband, Maynard Keynes. It hung at Tilton, the Keynes' country home.[10] Following the death of Diaghilev, British audiences were prepared to continue their support of aesthetically serious dance. Key figures in the founding of the Camargo Society (1930–3) were the Woolfs' friends, Maynard Keynes, who was treasurer, and his wife, the Russian ballerina Lydia Lopokova, who was choreographic director. Similarly, the Vic-Wells Ballet Company, formed in 1931, soon based ballet performances at Sadler's Wells in Islington where in 1932 Woolf became 'a life member' (*L*5: 94). The theatre closed in 1940 and sustained damage from bombing in the year of her death, 1941.

Among the treasures preserved by the BBC is an interview with Leonard Woolf dated 22 December 1965. Of his wife's work he states: 'Re her writing, she wasn't an experimental writer, the form of her novels came from her expression of things' – his point is demonstrated in her use of dance.[11] For Virginia Woolf dance suggested an exalted state of being as well as a heightened experience of living. As she wrote in her biography of Roger Fry (1940): 'He went to see the Russian dancers, and they, of course, suggested all kinds of fresh possibilities, and new combinations . . .' (*RF*: 198). Woolf was also writing about herself, nor was she alone in the nature of her response. As Joan Acocella observes, the dances of the pre-War Ballets Russes supplied an image of what 'Europeans felt they had lost: innocence, passion, folk 'roots,' and unselfconscious responses to spiritual mysteries' (1984: 241).

To Woolf's critical mind, each performance she saw was in relation to others of its kind and to others profoundly unlike it. Indeed she evolved a theory of how ethnic origins influence dance. Two weeks after the Armistice, 28 November 1918, Virginia and Leonard Woolf saw a ballet framed by twentieth-century equivalents of Shakespeare's Bottom and his rude mechanicals at the Coliseum. In a letter of 14 July 1909 Pavlova had anticipated the circumstances under which the Woolfs were to see the Russian dancers in 1918 when she wrote to an unidentified theatre manager – perhaps George Edwardes – 'that the London public was only prepared to accept ballet as a half-hour divertissement in a variety programme'. This, among other reasons, including the price of theatre tickets, had convinced her that 'a season in London, even with a small company, would not only involve great financial risk but seriously prejudice the reputation she had gained in Berlin and Paris.'[12]

In 1918 the Woolfs would not have seen the Russian dancers' performance preceded by the drop curtain resembling an icon of St George killing the dragon designed by Vladimir Polunin and made at Diaghilev's insistence seven years later in 1925. That evening Diaghilev's company performed one short ballet (twenty to twenty-five minutes), *Le Carnaval* with Lydia Lopokova and Léonide Massine. Woolf observed 'it was incongruous enough to see what they offered the tolerant good tempered public who had been bellowing like bulls over the efforts of a man [the popular comic Will Evans] to nail a carpet down' (*D1*: 222). Evans (1873–1931) had begun his career early as he took part in his father's performances as a pantomime clown. His adult burlesque sketches, such as 'Building a Chicken House', 'Whitewashing the Ceiling' and 'Papering a House', took their substance from the idea that things are against us in the management of everyday life. One thinks of the 'horror of dirt' Woolf would later encounter during the Second World War when their servant situation changed. In 1918 the labour of the kitchen was relatively unknown to her. She added as if uncomfortable with her detachment: 'What a queer fate it is – always to be the spectator of the public, never part of it' (*D1*: 222).

As Woolf later observed in 1924: 'one feels an enormous gulf between the religious dancing & the perfectly individualistic secular art natural to the English'.[13] That is not to say that Woolf disdained the secular art of the music hall, for she had attended such a performance earlier in 1918 on 26 April while London was under threat of bombs. Indeed she had gone by herself:

> to the Hippodrome, to see life; L. seeing a different variety of it at the 17 Club. The incredible, pathetic stupidity of the music hall, (for surely we could have risen higher, & only politeness made us laugh,) almost made me uncomfortable; but the humour of Harry Tate, though a low grade was still the queer English humour; something natural to the race, which makes us all laugh; why I don't know; & you can't help feeling its the real thing, as, in Athens one might have felt that poetry was. (*D1*: 144)

Harry Tate (1872–1940), a master of comic solo sketches, was in a revue called 'Box of Tricks" (*D1*: 144n.1). Ronald MacDonald Hutchinson (Tate's original name) was known for a series of sketches on golfing, motoring, fishing – activities recognised by discernible movements bearing their own choreography. He took his stage name from Henry Tate & Son, Sugar Refiners where he once worked – an appropriate name for an English comic given the national love of sweets and their consumption at theatres.

Le Carnaval was a ballet–pantomime with 'an uncomplicated libretto of masked guests at a masquerade ball, a succession of romantic interludes, fleeting meetings, light intrigues, and the felicitations and celebrations for the betrothal of Harlequin and Columbine' (Nijinska 1992: 287). It was first produced by the

Figure 25.2 Nijinsky as Harlequin and Lopokova as Columbine in *Le Carnaval*,
which they danced together in Europe in 1910. Image courtesy of the Dance
Collection, the New York Public Library at Lincoln Center

journal *Satyricon* at Pavlov Hall, St Petersburg, 20 February 1910 and then had its premiere at Theater des Westerns, Berlin. Choreography was by Michel Fokine to music composed by Robert Schumann piano suite of 1834. Among the original principal dancers were Nijinsky as Harlequin, Karsavina as Columbine; Fokine, Florestan, and Nijinska as Papillon. The performance that the Woolfs saw on 28 November 1918 featured Lydia Lopokova and Léonide Massine.

Nijinska writes that during their Paris season of 1909 'The portrayal of Harlequin and his dance was one of Nijinsky's greatest achievements.' In Paris he had also 'created a masked image on his own face' (Nijinska 1992: 304). Nijinsky demonstrated what he expected his sister to do as Papillon:

> He circled the studio like a weightless butterfly, his arms fluttering, even his hands and fingers joining in the aerial dance of his feet. I knew that I would never match Vaslav's technique – he skimmed the floor; his arms, like the wings of a butterfly, seemed to hold him in the air. (Nijinska 1992: 285)

Woolf's observation of the public that night in 1918: 'They were tolerant, but, as I fancied, a little bit contemptuous of all this posing & springing against a flat blue wall', suggests that Diaghilev's idea for a deep blue backcloth for *Le Carnaval* was deferred to as a practical matter under the circumstances (*D*1:222). The performance in St Petersburg was on a stage surrounded by long curtains (Nijinska 1992: 285) which several dancers used for their entrances and exits.

Although still without Polunin's iconic drop curtain in December 1924, Woolf's response to the Russian dancers' performance of *The Faithful Shepherdess* was likely influenced by Roger Fry's and Duncan Grant's attraction to the art of Byzantium. The ballet was choreographed by Nijinska with music by Michel Pignolet de Montéclair (1667–1737). The curtain, scenery, and costumes were designed by Juan Gris who was inspired by eighteenth-century paintings by Watteau.

> 'The Faithful Shepherdess' was put on last week at the Coliseum, and proves a less popular but more interesting ballet than 'Cimarosiana' and 'Le Train Bleu.' The finest frontispieces of seventeenth-century folios – half-naked gentlemen with feathers on their heads and greaves on their thighs, standing decoratively surrounded by scrolls and flourishes – seemed to come to life in a manner both imposing and agreeable. But however experts may distinguish between one ballet and another, one quality they all have in common – the extreme seriousness of the Russian dancers' art.
>
> One can understand the remark which was made the other night that there is more religious feeling in a ballet than in most church services. All the flounces and furbelows, their periwigs and flesh-coloured tights are based, for both sexes, upon sober, heelless, drab slippers. However airily they float and spring through the air, their movements are mathematically accurate, punctiliously severe. Not a hint of exertion is allowed to

show itself upon the dancers' faces, which wear for the most part an air of effortless serenity, an exalted composure; but their legs and arms are uncompromisingly muscular. The peculiar pleasure of the ballet arises no doubt from this combination of sensual ecstasy with an extreme severity, having its roots presumably in the religious element which lies at the origin of the dance. Sandwiched between Harry Tate and other characteristically British turns, the seriousness, the religious quality of the Russians is all the more apparent. One indeed, serves as relish to the other. Harry Tate accentuates Nijinska and Sokolova.[14]

The comic turns Woolf refers to were likely without words depending on slapstick humour that had choreographic elements from sports and motoring that were instantly recognisable to the English audience as the plots of tragedies were to the Greeks.

She had imagined processions at Eleusis which she had arrived too late to see. When she considered putting together an edition of the *Agamemnon* she would have factored in the movements of the chorus, for she thought of Greek literature in the context of lives passed in the open air of theatrical landscape as she wrote in 'On Not Knowing Greek'. The women's suffrage movement also performed in the open air where Woolf observed their white-, purple-, and green-hued processional statements which coincided with her values. The women's collective energy would have likely outweighed or offset any lack of specifically ordered movement. Doubtless their marching was enhanced by her friend Ethel Smyth's rousing 'March of the Women'.

In 1908 Alexandre Benois, who was among Diaghilev's collaborators, wrote in a seminal essay of how 'interactions of dance and music had the potential to ignite feelings of near-religious ecstasy in the viewer'. Compare Woolf's response to *Le Carnaval* with Benois's statement that ballet

> permits the two most excellent conveyors of thought – music and gesture – to appear in their full expanse and depth unencumbered by words which limit and fetter thought, bring it down from heaven to earth. In ballet one finds that liturgical quality of which we have lately come to dream so strenuously.[15]

It is tempting to assert that Woolf's empathy for Russian literature had enabled her to understand as a Russian. It is as if she had herself absorbed the Russian soul. Recall how she had noted the absence of soul in the Edwardian fiction of Arnold Bennett, John Galsworthy and H. G. Wells (Woolf 1981: 97). In ballet, especially that of the Russians, one finds an analogy to Woolf's obsession with placing emotions in right relations to each other thereby finding a new and appropriate form for each of her novels (*E3*: 340). Words, despite their variety and capacity for inducing wonder, were grounds for struggle and often ancillary to her vision. Her earliest conception of *The Waves* was choreographic; the interludes she later developed were realised through both cyclical and localised movement in nature. Moreover, they have no spoken words.

Consider Woolf's experience of writing as choreography: 'emotion put into the right relations', as she herself insisted (*L*3:133). Diverging from Vita Sackville-West's echo of Flaubert (*le mot juste*), Woolf wrote:

> Style is a very simple matter; it is all rhythm. Once you get that, you can't use the wrong words. . . .Now this is very profound, what rhythm is, and goes far deeper than words. A sight, an emotion, creates this wave in the mind, long before it makes words to fit it; and in writing (such is my present belief) one has to recapture this, and set this working (which has nothing apparently to do with words) and then, as it breaks and tumbles in the mind, it makes words to fit it. (*L*3: 247)

'When I write I'm merely a sensibility' suggests the experience of the dancer becoming one with the music, the inextricability of the dancer from the dance.

> One must get out of life . . . one must become externalised; very, very con-centrated, all at one point, not having to draw upon the scattered parts of one's character, living in the brain. . . . Sometimes I like being Virginia, but only when I'm scattered & various & gregarious. Now . . . I'd like to be only a sensibility. (*D*2:193)

Thus when Woolf wrote she was *sur pointe* (on point).

Within a year of Woolf's description of how she wrote, Lydia Lopokova rec-ognised a parallel phenomenon in her description of 'the new ballet' (*Les Noces* with music by Stravinsky choreographed by Bronislava Nijinska) in a letter written in her Russian-inflected but expressive English to Maynard Keynes dated 15 June 1923:

> blue curtain at the back with a tiny window and black wings, dancers are dressed in black and white, just as the men look when they rehearse and so the women. It is built on groups, human waves doing the same dance, and when they are about 40 the wave becomes an ocean, primitive and Byzantine mixture, music is very intense with words that nobody under-stands, nor is there any need, altogether it is a well balanced madness in black and white. I go to see to-morrow another time.[16]

Woolf wrote of 'an early Mozart': But the tune, like all his tunes, makes one despair – I mean hope. What do I mean? That's the worst of music! I want to dance . . . ' (Woolf 2003: 24). For Woolf the impulse to dance was realised not only in physi-cal movement but was also transposed into the rhythm of literary creation.

Woolf and the god-dance which is Japanese Noh

Another mode of 'religious dancing' may have captured her imagination. Woolf wrote of reading Pound's biography of Gaudier-Brzeska in 1917, wherein an illustration of the sculptor's *Red Stone Dancer* (1913–14) appears. Stanley Casson wrote of *Dancer* (1913): 'No sculptor . . . has ever depicted a figure thus *descending* out of one movement into another. . . . There is no representation of motion here, only its full and direct expression.'[17]

Gaudier-Brzeska, who died in France at the age of twenty-three, declared his allegiance to rhythm as the governing principle of his art as Woolf was to do: '[S]culpture consists in placing planes according to a rhythm' (Ede 1971: 55). His was a spirit akin to Woolf's as he sculpted orts and fragments in the trenches in France: 'a small Maternity statue out of the butt-end of a German rifle, it's magnificent walnut wood and I managed to cut it quite successfully with an ordinary knife' (ibid.: 158). Ede quotes Gaudier's Captain that he 'did three or four bits of sculpture . . . or in soft stone . . . . These works were preserved for a little while and then thrown away to make room for clothing' (ibid.: 158n). A fate analogous to those sculptures Gaudier carved is that of ballets. Ordinarily, hard wood and stone survive, but not in time of war. To embrace the ephemeral art of ballet is to clasp a less stable element than the music accompanying it. Unlike ballet, however, Japanese Noh is scrupulously preserved:

> though it arose one hundred years before Shakespeare, this continuity has never been broken. The same plays are enacted in the same manner as then; even the leading actors of today are blood descendants of the very men who created this drama 450 years ago.[18]

In her embrace of dance as a source of inspiration, Woolf extends their palimpsestic survival through her modernist technique.

Although Woolf and Ezra Pound may seem like an odd couple, they had several interests in common and a connection: William Butler Yeats whom she admired ('our only living poet – perhaps a great poet') and with whom she memorably spoke (*L4*: 250) at the home of Ottoline Morrell on 7 November 1930. 'He said that . . . mythologies are necessary. Ezra Pound writes beautifully when he uses them' (*D3*: 330). Woolf herself uses mythologies that were important to Pound, such as Egyptian, Roman, and Greek. Consider, however, a synchronous if not more direct connection with the god-dance of Noh, which though it is replete with Japanese mythology, was sufficiently universal in its archetypes to suggest 'fresh possibilities and new combinations' to Yeats that transformed his involvement with Celtic myth into his *Four Plays for Dancers*. The winters spent at Stone Cottage (1913–16), when Pound was Yeats's secretary, were mutually beneficial. Indeed, Yeats discovered through Pound's work on the edition of Ernest Fenollosa's notes and translations of Noh plays a new mode for poetic expression.

Pound wrote of Noh:

> One can only trace out the words of the text and say that they are spoken, or half-sung and chanted, to a fitting and traditional accompaniment of movement and colour, and that they are themselves but half shadows. Yet,

Figure 25.3 *Red Stone Dancer*, by Henri Gaudier-Brzeska, 1913–14 (bronze cast of 1969), 426 × 230 × 224mm. Image courtesy of Kettle's Yard, University of Cambridge

Figure 25.4 *Dancer*, by Henri Gaudier-Brzeska, 1913 (bronze cast of 1967), 765 ×
220 × 210mm. Image courtesy of Kettle's Yard, University of Cambridge

despite the difficulties of presentation, I find these words very wonderful, and they become intelligible if, as a friend says, 'you read them all the time as though you were listening to music'. (Fenollosa and Pound 1917: 5)

Since Woolf wrote of reading Pound's memoir of Gaudier-Brzeska in 1917, she might also have read or been familiar with Pound's transcription and commentary on Ernest Fenollosa's 'Noh' or Accomplishment: A Study of the Classical Stage of Japan which was also published in 1916. Pound expresses his 'very deep thanks to Mr. Arthur Waley' who had assisted him 'out of the various impasses' where his own ignorance would have left him' (Fenollosa and Pound 1917: vii). Arthur Waley wrote in the Short Bibliography to his 1920 edition of The Nō Plays of Japan: 'The versions of E. F. seem to have been fragmentary and inaccurate; but wherever Mr. Pound had adequate material to work upon he has used it admirably' (ibid.: 304).Woolf was also acquainted with Waley, naming him among those to be thanked in a preface to Orlando (1928). As she indicates in her review of Waley's translation of the Lady Murasaki's novel, The Tale of Genji, Woolf was cognisant of Japan's high aesthetic culture when Europe was barbarous. Of Murasaki (AD 978?–c.1031) she wrote: 'On she went . . . without hesitation or self-consciousness, effort or agony, to tell the story of the enchanting boy – the Prince who danced 'The Waves of the Blue Sea' so beautifully that all the princes and great gentlemen wept aloud'.[19]

Not only passages but forms (structures) in To the Lighthouse and The Waves suggest that Woolf had fallen under the enchantment of Noh or was at least open to its subtle methods, for the god-dance was compatible with what she was trying to do.[20] The Noh play Suma Genji is among the notes and translations that Fenollosa's widow had given Pound to edit. In the play an 'apparition' or 'place-spirit' of Genji dances 'the blue dance of the sea waves 'in a sort of glory of waves and moonlight.' Pound observes:

Suma Genji, will seem undramatic . . . . The suspense is the suspense of waiting for a supernatural manifestation – which comes. Some will be annoyed at a form of psychology which is, in the West, relegated to spiritistic séances. . . . If the Japanese authors had not combined the psychology of such matters with what is to me a very fine sort of poetry, I would not bother about it.

The reader will miss the feel of suspense if he is unable to put himself in sympathy with the priest eager to see 'even in a vision' the beauty lost in the years, 'the shadow of the past in bright form.' I do not say that this sympathy is easily acquired. It is too unusual a frame of mind for us to fall into it without a conscious effort. But if one can get over the feeling of hostility, if one can once let himself into the world of Noh, there is undoubtedly a new beauty before him. (Fenollosa and Pound 1917: 44–5)

Mrs Ramsay's evanescent appearance is analogous to the manifestation of Genji in Suma Genji in Pound's edition of Noh:

Some wave of white went over the window pane. . . . Mrs. Ramsay – it was part of her perfect goodness to Lily – sat there quite simply, in the chair, flicked her needles to and fro, knitted her reddish-brown stocking, cast her shadow on the step. There she sat'. (Woolf 2006: 14–5)

Lily's vision of Mrs Ramsay, 'a shadow of the past in bright form', is enhanced by delineating the traditional assignment of roles in Noh: the *Shite* (the hero or chief character) as Mrs Ramsay; the *Tsura* (follower of the hero) as Lily who attempts to capture what she has 'seen' ('I have had my vision') into her painting and was hitherto frustrated at its elusiveness; the *Waki* (guest or wandering priest) as Mr Carmichael. When the bereaved Mr Ramsay and his adolescent children arrive at the distant though barely visible lighthouse, Mr Carmichael gives a benediction, a Christian term perhaps, but universal in meaning:

He stood there spreading his hands over all the weakness and suffering of mankind . . . Now he has crowned the occasion . . . when his hand slowly fell, as if she had seen him let fall from his great height, a wreath of violets and asphodels which, fluttering slowly, lay at length upon the earth. (Woolf 2006: 169–70)

Despite Woolf's impatience with Yeats's involvement with the occult and despite her own awareness of the charlatans of Bond Street who took advantage of the grief of war widows, Woolf had her own commerce with the dead, especially her deceased parents in *To the Lighthouse* and her beloved brother Thoby, to whom *The Waves* is dedicated.

The construction of *The Waves* with its cyclic soliloquies of the six friends surrounding the figure of Percival who is at first present then absent resembles a ballet with each of six dancers coming to the foreground. This novel also bears resemblance to 'The arrangement of five or six Noh into one performance' which 'explains, in part, what may seem like a lack of construction in some of the pieces; the plays have, however, a very severe construction of their own, a sort of musical construction' (Fenollosa and Pound 1917: 45). Woolf's modernist impatience with conventional plots is congruent with Pound's declaration that

The Noh holds up a mirror to nature in a manner very different from the Western convention of plot. . . . We do not find, as we find in Hamlet, a certain situation or problem set out and analysed. The Noh service presents, or symbolizes, a complete diagram of life and recurrence. (Fenollosa and Pound 1917: 17)

The opening of *The Waves* resembles the mythological origins of Noh, which date from the time of Chaucer, that is, the fourteenth century. The rules governing the construction of a Noh stage are as stringent as those for a temple. A vital aspect of the Noh stage is the use of five tilted earthen jars beneath the stage 'to make the sound reverberate' when a Noh actor stamps his foot. 'This stamping dates from the time when some mythological person danced on a tub to attract the light-goddess' (Fenollosa and Pound 1917: 58 and n.1). Louis in his early childhood hears 'something stamping . . . A great beast's foot is chained. It stamps, and stamps, and stamps' (Woolf 1992: 5). The female figure, at the opening of *The Waves* and in the subsequent interludes until the sun reaches its zenith at noon, is comparable to a light-goddess. In the first section (dawn): '[T]he sky cleared . . . as if the arm of a woman couched beneath the horizon had raised a lamp' (ibid.: 73). In the third section (mid-morning): 'The girl who had shaken her head and made all the jewels . . . dance, now bared her brows and with wide-opened eyes drove a straight pathway over the waves' (ibid.: 58). In the fourth section (late morning): 'The sun, risen, no longer couched on a green mattress . . . bared its face and looked straight over the waves' (ibid.: 88). Here the sun becomes merged with the girl. In the fifth section (noon): 'The sun had risen to its full height. . . . as if a girl couched on her green-sea mattress tired her brows with water-globed jewels that sent lances of opal-tinted light falling and flashing in the uncertain air'. After the sun has reached its zenith, the woman or girl, the light goddess, no longer appears in the interludes: Percival has died. 'The waves fell; withdrew and fell again, like the thud of a great beast stamping' (ibid.: 121, 123).

'The blue-grey waves and wave pattern' (Fenollosa and Pound 1917: 27) in the Noh play *Suma Genji* also resemble Bernard's final scene at the ending of *The Waves*: the emotion of the final dance; the figure of the warrior/rider. '[A] bright apparition of Genji in supernatural form' declares: 'I sing of the moon in this shadow, here on this sea-marge of Suma. Here I will dance . . . the blue dance of the waves' (Fenollosa and Pound 1917: 41–2). (This was Genji's dance that moves male spectators to tears that Woolf cites in her review of Murasaki's novel, *The Tale of Genji*.) The Chorus chants in conclusion:

> His sleeves were like the grey sea-waves;
> They moved with curious rustling,
> Like the noise of the restless waves, Like a bell of a country town
> Neath the nightfall. (Fenollosa and Pound 1917: 44)

The emotion of the final dance is realised in Unity of Image both in the apparition of the Gleaming Prince Genji and the comparable figure of Bernard as a galloping warrior flinging himself against Death. Noh has 'Unity of Image', Pound argued, 'at least the better plays are all built into the intensification of a single Image' (Fenollosa and Pound 1917: 45–6). Pound cites the red maple leaves of *Nishikigi* which recalls Pavlova's choreography for her divertissement, *Autumn Leaves*. When Pound raises the question whether one 'Could one do a long Imagiste poem, or even a long poem in vers libre?' (ibid.: 45, n.1) Woolf provides an affirmative answer with *The Waves*.

Having read Pound's memoir of Gaudier-Brzeska, Woolf might well have encountered the Vorticist publication *BLAST* in the puce-coloured first of two issues published in 1914; the second and last issue was the tan-coloured war issue of 1915. W. Roberts's painting *Dancers* appears in shades of grey in the

1914 issue. The style is not unrelated to Gaudier-Brzeska's powerfully contorted, simplified and mimetic *Red Dancer* reproduced in Pound's memoir of the sculptor. Roberts also painted Maynard Keynes and Lydia Lopokova as a couple. His pencil sketch, 'Camargo Ballet Backcloth Design', (c. 1931) was realised in watercolour, pen and ink as *Ballet Rehearsal* (aka *Ballet Dancers*). Roberts limns the muscular dancers as workers engaged in stretches evocative of physical labour at the barre and on the floor. An upright piano is in the foreground; a large mirror or doorway into another room reveals more dancers preparing their bodies as some stretch in pairs. All are wearing practical clothes to keep their legs warm, their arms free, and to allow for sweat. Woolf's love of dance took its intellectual origins from the poetry of the Ancient Greeks and enabled her to recognise spirituality in the severe movements of the Russian dancers. But she also recognised that the choreography of slapstick routines in the music halls was genuine as well as fundamental to the English. For her 'life, life, life' (Woolf 2002: 112) was in all modes of dance as in the whizzing, vibrating, starling-pelted tree of her final novel, *Between the Acts* (1941).

Woolf's work has inspired choreographers such as Stephen Pelton who has been making dances in response to her work for over fifteen years. These include *August* (1993, 18 min.) with a text from *The Waves* to music by Ralph Vaughan Williams, 'Fantasia on a Theme of Thomas Tallis'; *A Haunted House* (2002, 15 min.) to music by Gavin Byars, 'The North Shore'; and *The Death of the Moth* (1998, rev. 2009, 12 min.). In 2009 the Stephen Pelton Dance Theater premiered 'it was this: it was this:' (12 min.) a study of Woolf's punctuation, set to the third movement of Schubert's String Quartet No. 15 in G. Following a single passage from *To the Lighthouse*, the company dances their way from the first word to the last, along with every comma, parentheses, and semi-colon in between.

Notes

1. See Stephen Barkway (2006) 'Virginia Woolf's "Scrolloping"', *Virginia Woolf Bulletin*, 22: 30–1.
2. Richard W. Schoch (1998) *Shakespeare's Victorian Stage: Performing History in the Theatre of Charles Kean*, Cambridge: Cambridge University Press, p. 48, fig. 11.
3. Joseph Donohue (2004) 'The Theatre from 1800 to 1895', *Cambridge History of British Theatre*, Vol. 2: 1660–1895, p. 267.
4. Haskell 1956.
5. Nijinska 1992: 283.
6. Lydia Lopokova wrote: 'Anna Pavlova carried the Muse of the Ballet as Holy Saint of Beauty to high and low to everyone in the world' (in 'Pavlova', *Lydia Lopokova*, ed. Milo Keynes, London: Weidenfeld and Nicolson, 1983, p. 206).
7. Peter Jacobs (1992) "Ah, quel décor!' Nijinsky chez Bloomsbury,' *Écrits sur Nijinsky*, La Recherche en Danse, Comité Nijinsky, Paris: Éditions Chiron: pp. 139–44, esp. 139.
8. From Nijinsky's diary, quoted in Lincoln Kirstein, *Nijinsky Dancing*; Reed 2004: 99.
9. Hector Cahusac (1913) *Le Figaro*, 134, 14 May quoted in Nijinska 1992: 467.
10. *Vanessa Bell poster*: No. 38 *Lopokova with J. M. Keynes*, in Richard Shone (1980)

Catalogue: Vanessa Bell: 1879-1961: A Retrospective Exhibition, in association with Anthony d'Offay Ltd, New York: Davis & Long Company, p. 29.

11. With thanks to Trish Hayes, Archives Researcher, BBC Written Archives Centre BBC, Caversham Park, Reading, who found this entry in a BBC programme catalogue: 'New Release: 6 What Exactly Do You Mean?' Commentary by Jonathan Cecil.

12. Letter from Pavlova No. 235, Letters and Documents (Haskell 1956: 4).

13. Unpublished material: Mrs. Dalloway reel, p. 39. With the kind permission of the Society of Authors as the literary representative of the estate of Virginia Woolf. The Berg Collection of English and American Literature, The New York Public Library, Astor, Lenox and Tilden Foundations.

14. Stuart N. Clarke, editor of the forthcoming vol. 6 of *The Essays of Virginia Woolf*, to be published by Hogarth Press in 2010, generously guided me to the anonymously published final version of the draft I found in the Berg Collection. 'From Alpha to Omega', *N&A*, 20 Dec. 1924, 443.

15. Aleksandr Benua [Benois], 'Beseda o balete', quoted in Richard Taruskin, *Stravinsky and the Russian Tradition* (2 vols), Berkeley and Los Angeles: University of California Press, I, pp. 540-1, quoted in Simon Morrison (2005) 'The 'World of Art' and Music,' Catalogue: *Russia's Age of Elegance*, Palace Editions: The State Russian Museum and the Foundation for International Arts and Education, pp. 36–43, esp. p. 40.

16. Polly Hill and Richard Keynes (eds) (1989) *Lydia and Maynard: The Letters of Lydia Lopokova and John Maynard Keynes*, New York: Charles Scribner's Sons, pp. 95–6.

17. Ede, H. S. (1931 and 1971) *Savage Messiah: A Biography of the Sculptor Henri Gaudier-Brzeska*, London: The Gordon Fraser Gallery Ltd, p. 152.

18. Fenollosa and Pound 1917: 104.

19. Review of *The Tale of Genji*, Vol. I, by Lady Murasaki; trans. from the Japanese by Arthur Waley. *Vogue*, late July 1925, 66.2: 53–80, esp. p. 53. (Kirkpatrick C264.)

20. With thanks to Stuart N. Clarke for calling my attention to Elizabeth Steele's superb delineation of 'A Haunted House' as Noh, in addition to her commentary on Woolf's probable exposure to Noh and the appositeness of *Nishikigi* to her life. Steele (1989) '"A Haunted House": Virginia Woolf's Noh Story', *Studies in Short Fiction*, 26: 151-71.

Works Cited

Acocella, Joan Ross (1984) 'The Reception of Diaghilev's Ballets by Artists and Intellectuals in Paris and London, 1909–1914 (France, Russia)' PhD dissertation, New Brunswick, NJ: Rutgers, The State University of New Jersey, Publication Number: AAT 8411550.

Fenollosa, Ernest and Ezra Pound (1917) *'Noh' or Accomplishment: A Study of the Classical Stage of Japan*, New York: Alfred Knopf. (American printing of 1916 British edition.)

Haskell, Arnold (1956) *Anna Pavlova: Catalogue of the Commemorative Exhibition*, London: London Museum.

Nijinska, Bronislava (1992) *Early Memoirs*, trans. and ed. Irina Nijinska and Jean Rawlinson, Durham, NC: Duke University Press.

Reed, Christopher (2004) *Bloomsbury Rooms: Modernism, Subculture, and Domesticity*, New Haven: Yale University Press for The Bard Graduate Center for Studies in the Decorative Arts, Design, and Culture, New York.

Woolf, Virginia (1981) *The Captain's Death Bed and Other Essays*, London: Hogarth Press.

—— (1998) *The Years*, ed. Jeri Johnson (gen. ed. Julia Briggs), London: Penguin (Twentieth-Century Classics).

—— (2002) *Between the Acts*, ed. Susan Dick and Mary S. Millar, Oxford: Wiley-Blackwell, Shakespeare Head Press.

—— (2003) *A Haunted House: The Complete Shorter Fiction*, ed. Susan Dick, London: Vintage.

—— (2006) *To the Lighthouse*, ed. David Bradshaw, Oxford: Oxford World's Classics.

Further Reading

Ballets russes (2005) Geller/Goldfine Productions. A documentary film that chronicles the world of dance following the death of Serge Diaghilev in 1929 with archival footage and interviews with former dancers.

Davis, Tracy C. (2000) *The Economy of the British Stage: 1800–1914*, Cambridge: Cambridge University Press.

Haller, Evelyn (1993) 'Her Quill Drawn from the Firebird: Virginia Woolf and the Russian Dancers', in *The Multiple Muses of Virginia Woolf*, ed. Diane Gillespie, Columbia: University of Missouri Press.

Jones, Susan (2005) 'Virginia Woolf and the Dance', *Dance Chronicle*, 28: 169–200.

Paccaud-Huguet, Josiane (1995) 'The Crowded Dance of Words: Language and Jouissance in *The Waves*', *Q/W/E/R/T/Y*, 5: 227–40.

Pelton, Stephen (1998) 'Dancing *The Death of the Moth*', in *Virginia Woolf and Her Influences: Selected Papers from the Seventh Annual Conference on Virginia Woolf*, ed. Laura Davis, and Jeanette McVicker, New York: Pace University Press. See also his website: stephenpeltondance.org

Rubenstein, Roberta (forthcoming) *Virginia Woolf and the Russian Point of View*, New York: Palgrave Macmillan.

Walker, Cynthia (1978) 'Virginia Woolf's *The Voyage Out*: A Prelude of Images', *Virginia Woolf Quarterly*, 3: 222–29.

Zimring, Rishona (2007) "The Dangerous Art Where One Slip Means Death': Dance and the Literary Imagination in Interwar Britain', *Modernism/Modernity*, 14: 707–27.

NOTES ON CONTRIBUTORS

Tony Bradshaw is the owner of The Bloomsbury Workshop in London which, through its exhibitions over the years, has explored many aspects of Bloomsbury art. He is the author of *The Bloomsbury Artists: Prints and Book Design*, a comprehensive catalogue of work done in this field, and has edited *A Bloomsbury Canvas*, a well-acclaimed collection of essays covering a number of aspects relating to the Bloomsbury Group.

Liz Brooker's postgraduate research was in the early twentieth-century novel, an interest that has been sustained through an alternative career in education. She is now a Senior Lecturer in Early Childhood at the University of London, Institute of Education, where she teaches, researches and publishes on young children's learning in cultural contexts and their transitions through differing ecological environments. She is author of *Young Children Learning Cultures* (2002) and *Supporting Transitions in the Early Years* (2008).

Peter Brooker is Professorial Fellow at the Centre for Modernist Studies, University of Sussex. He has written widely on contemporary writing and theory and is the author of *Bertolt Brecht: Dialectics, Poetry, Politics* (1989), *New York Fictions* (1996), *Modernity and Metropolis* (2004), *Bohemia in London* (2004, 2007) and *A Glossary of Cultural Theory* (1999, 2003).With Andrew Thacker, he is editor of *Geographies of Modernism* (2005) and co-director of the AHRC funded Modernist Magazine Project. The first of three volumes in the series *A Critical and Cultural History of Modernist Magazines* will appear later this year. He is also co-editor of the forthcoming *Oxford Handbook of Modernisms*.

Pamela L. Caughie is Professor and Graduate Program Director in the English Department at Loyola University Chicago where she teaches twentieth-century literature and feminist theory. Her books include *Virginia Woolf and Postmodernism* (1991), *Passing and Pedagogy: The Dynamics of Responsibility*

(1999), *Virginia Woolf in the Age of Mechanical Reproduction* (ed.) (2000), and *Disciplining Modernism* (ed.) (2009). She has contributed to numerous anthologies and collections on modernist writing, including: *Gender in Modernism: New Geographies; Complex Intersections*, gen. ed. Bonnie Kime Scott; *The Blackwell Companion to Modernist Literature and Culture*, ed. David Bradshaw and Kevin Dettmar; *Palgrave Advances in Virginia Woolf Studies*, ed. Anna Snaith; and *Modernism and Theory: A Critical Debate*, ed. Stephen Ross. She is president of the Modernist Studies Association (November 2009–November 2010).

Patrick Collier is Associate Professor of English at Ball State University in Indiana, USA, where he teaches film studies and nineteenth- and twentieth-century British literature. He co-edited *Transatlantic Print Culture 1880–1940: Emerging Media, Emerging Modernism* (2008) with Ann Ardis. He is the author of *Modernism on Fleet Street* (2006) and numerous articles on the relationship between literature and journalism.

Colin Dickey's most recent publication is *Cranioklepty: Grave Robbing and the Search for Genius*.

Kate Flint is Professor of English at Rutgers, The State University of New Jersey. Her most recent publication is *The Transatlantic Indian 1776–1930* (2008).

Jane Garrity is an Associate Professor in the English Department at the University of Colorado at Boulder. She is the author of *Step-Daughters of England: British Women Modernists and the National Imaginary* (2003); the editor of a special issue on "Queer Space", *ELN: English Language Notes* (Spring 2007); and the co-editor, with Laura Doan, of *Sapphic Modernities: Sexuality, Women, and National Culture* (2006). She is currently at work on a book entitled *Material Modernism: Fashioning Bloomsbury*.

Gretchen Holbrook Gerzina is the Kathe Tappe Vernon Professor in Biography at Dartmouth College in New Hampshire, and Honorary Professor at Exeter University. Her books include *Carrington: A Life*; *Black England: Life Before Emancipation*; *Black Victorians/Black Victoriana* (ed.); and *Frances Hodgson Burnett: The Unpredictable Life of the Author of The Secret Garden*. She is the George Eastman Visiting Professor and Fellow at Balliol College, University of Oxford, 2009–2010.

Diane F. Gillespie is Professor Emerita of English at Washington State University. One of her most recent publications is 'The Gender of Modern/ist Painting', in *Gender In Modernism: New Geographies, Complex Intersections*, ed. Bonnie Kime Scott (2007).

Jane Goldman is Reader in English Literature at the University of Glasgow. She is a General Editor of the Cambridge University Press Edition of the Writings of Virginia Woolf and author of *The Feminist Aesthetics of Virginia Woolf: Modernism, Post-Impressionism and the Politics of the Visual* (1998) and co-editor of *Modernism: An Anthology of Sources and Documents* (1998). Her recent publications include *Modernism, 1910–1945: Image to Apocalypse* (2004) and *The Cambridge Introduction to Virginia Woolf* (2006). She is editor of Woolf's *To the Lighthouse* for Cambridge University Press, and is currently writing a book, *Virginia Woolf and the Signifying Dog*.

Evelyn Haller is Professor of English and Chair of the Fine Arts/Humanities Division at Doane College in Crete near Lincoln, Nebraska. Her next publication, 'Her Father's Gifts: Books in English Ezra Pound Gave His Daughter that She Might Learn His Mother Tongue and More', will appear in *Paideuma: A Journal Devoted to Ezra Pound and His Contemporaries*.

Nuala Hancock is formerly a lecturer in garden design and garden history. She has recently completed doctoral research with the Department of English, University of Sussex in collaboration with the Charleston Trust. Her project was a comparative study of the houses and gardens at Charleston and Monk's House, and the ways in which they reflect the intellectual/aesthetic exchanges between Virginia Woolf and Vanessa Bell.

Leslie Kathleen Hankins is Professor of English at Cornell College. Her latest publications on Woolf and cinema are pieces on Abel Gance's *J'accuse* and Woolf's *Mrs Dalloway*, and her article in *Woolf Studies Annual* (2009) on the drafts of Woolf's essay, 'The Cinema', 'Virginia Woolf's "The Cinema": Sneak Previews of the Holograph Pre-Texts through Post-Publication Revisions'.

Benjamin Harvey teaches at Mississippi State University. His most recent publication is 'Lightness Visible: An Appreciation of Bloomsbury's Books and Blocks' in *A Room of Their Own: The Bloomsbury Artists in American Collections* (2008).

Elizabeth Hirsh teaches English and Women's Studies at the University of South Florida. She is currently working on a project that explores Woolf's engagement with historiography.

Maggie Humm is Professor of Cultural Studies at the University of East London and Co-Director of the Centre for Cultural Studies Research. Her writings on Woolf include *Modernist Women and Visual Cultures: Virginia Woolf, Vanessa Bell, Photography and Cinema*, and *Snapshots of Bloomsbury: the Private Lives of Virginia Woolf and Vanessa Bell*. She was an editor of the

Routledge Encyclopaedia of Women, gave the Third Annual Virginia Woolf Birthday Lecture (2002), and is editing a special issue of the *Virginia Woolf Miscellany* on Woolf and intellectual property.

Joyce E. Kelley is an assistant professor at Auburn University Montgomery. She is currently working on a book project on modernist women writers and travel.

Laura Marcus is Goldsmiths' Professor of English Literature at the University of Oxford. She has published widely on modernism, autobiography and biography, Virginia Woolf, the history of psychoanalysis, and literature and cinema. Her publications include *Virginia Woolf: Writers and Their Work* (1997, 2004) and, most recently, *The Tenth Muse: Writing about Cinema in the Modernist Period* (2007).

Makiko Minow-Pinkney teaches at the University of Bolton. Her most recent publication is a chapter on 'Psychoanalytic Approaches', in *Palgrave Advances in Virginia Woolf Studies*, ed. Anna Snaith (2007).

Vara S. Neverow is a Professor of English and Women's Studies at Southern Connecticut State University. She is currently working on a book-length project, *Against Patriarchy:Virginia Woolf's Rhetorics of Resistance*.

Merry M. Pawlowski teaches in the English Department of California State University, Bakersfield. Her most recent publication is "'Where Am I?'": Feminine Space and Time in Virginia Woolf's *The Years*, in *Literary Landscapes from Modernism to Postcolonialism*, ed. Attie de Lange, Gail Fincham, Jeremy Hawthorn and Jakob Lothe (2008).

Linden Peach is Professor of English at Edge Hill University, near Liverpool, a Fellow of the English Association and a Member of the Welsh Academy. He has published extensively on twentieth-century literature, including books and essays on Virginia Woolf, Toni Morrison, Angela Carter, Irish fiction, crime and literature, and Welsh women's writing. He is currently preparing a scholarly edition of Woolf's *Flush* for Cambridge University Press.

Steven Putzel teaches at the Pennsylvania State University, Wilkes-Barre campus. He has published numerous essays on Woolf and is currently completing his book, *Virginia Woolf and the Theatre*.

Victoria Rosner is an associate professor of English at Texas A & M University. She is the author of *Modernism and the Architecture of Private Life* (2005) and numerous articles on modernism, life-writing, and gender. She is currently working on a book about the modernisation of the household and the formation of modernist literary aesthetics.

Brenda R. Silver teaches at Dartmouth College, Hanover, New Hampshire, and Trinity College Dublin. Her most recent publication is 'Editing Mrs. Ramsay; Or, "8 Qualities of Mrs. Ramsay that Could Be Annoying to Others', forthcoming in 2009.

Anthony Uhlmann is Associate Professor in the School of Humanities and Languages at the University of Western Sydney. He is the author of *Samuel Beckett and the Philosophical Image* (2006) and *Beckett and Poststructuralism* (1999). He is the author of numerous articles on literature and philosophy.

INDEX

Abbreviations used in the index: NG (National Gallery), RA (Royal Academy).
Page numbers in italics are for illustrations; page numbers followed by 'n' are for end of chapter notes. Titles of written and visual works are italicized; all titles other than those for written works have the relevant medium in brackets after the author and title, e.g. Allingham, Helen, 'The Back Drawing Room' (watercolour), 169, *170*

OLDUVAI GORGE

VOLUME 3

Aerial view of Olduvai Gorge

OLDUVAI GORGE

VOLUME 3

EXCAVATIONS IN BEDS I AND II, 1960–1963

BY

M. D. LEAKEY

WITH A FOREWORD BY

PROFESSOR J. D. CLARK

CAMBRIDGE
AT THE UNIVERSITY PRESS
1971

Published by the Syndics of the Cambridge University Press
Bentley House, 200 Euston Road, London N.W.1
American Branch: 32 East 57th Street, New York, N.Y.10022

© Cambridge University Press 1971

Library of Congress Catalogue Card Number: 78–108108

ISBN: 0 521 07723 0

Printed in Great Britain
at the University Printing House, Cambridge
(Brooke Crutchley, University Printer)

OLDUVAI

For every day there was something new; small things most of them, but always of surpassing interest.

— A. TINDELL HOPWOOD

CONTENTS

LIST OF FIGURES

ix

LIST OF FIGURES

LIST OF TABLES

LIST OF PLATES

Frontispiece   Aerial view of Olduvai Gorge

Between pp. 300 *and* 301

xiii

FOREWORD

J. DESMOND CLARK, C.B.E., F.B.A.

This is the book that archaeologists and anthropologists the world over have been waiting for—and they will not be disappointed. Here, exactly set out, is the description of the cultural record contained within the lower half of the sequence at Olduvai Gorge—that unique result of the Rift Valley faulting, cut through the game-covered grasslands of the Serengeti Plains in northern Tanzania. Nowhere else in the world have such outstandingly significant finds been made as those that have come from these 350 feet of stratified lacustrine and volcanic sediments. The land surfaces they contain have preserved some of the richest assemblages of fossil fauna from the African continent and some of the most exciting evidence of the activities of early man that has contributed immensely to improved understanding of our own human origins and the evolving record of inventive ability and manual skills that are the sole prerogative of man.

The concentrations of tools, food waste and other indications of hominid activity now being uncovered on the buried surfaces of the occupation sites of Olduvai form the very basis for understanding the way of life and capabilities of the hominids, once we are able to interpret the evidence correctly. And, as if this *embarras de richesse* were not sufficient, the list of finds of the hominids themselves is unique in the number, biological variability and range of time they cover.

The knowledge of these we possess today we owe to Louis and Mary Leakey and others associated with them in their systematic exploration of the Gorge. The thoroughness and the perseverance over many years with which this investigation has been carried out has resulted in the discovery of no less than seventy-two archaeological sites and has rightly earned for the Leakeys the admiration and thanks of scientists and laymen alike. Indeed, there can be very few instances where the dedicated research of some thirty-nine years has been so spectacularly rewarded.

Up to 1960 most of the work carried out at Olduvai was necessarily on a small scale, but in that year, and subsequently, the National Geographic Society provided financial support of an order that gave the Leakeys the opportunity for the larger, more intensive operations that they had always hoped for and which have now been so amply justified.

Some of these specialist results have already appeared in the first two of the new series of volumes devoted to Olduvai which, when complete, will ensure that this is—and rightly—one of the best documented of any of the localities where early man has been found. The present volume, the third in the series, is by Mary Leakey and describes the cultural remains contained within Beds I and II of the sequence and shows the relationship of these to the various human fossils.

I have had the privilege of knowing Mary Leakey and her work for twenty-nine years and it gives me very great satisfaction to pay tribute here to her fine record of meticulous research and reporting. Her earlier excavations at the 'Neolithic' sites of Hyrax Hill and Njoro River Cave set a standard for Africa that has never been surpassed and she has applied these same methods, working backward in time, at sites of Lower Palaeolithic age and so at Olduvai. In doing so she pioneered a new dimension in Palaeolithic research, making possible the study of human behaviour from the distributed remains on *living floors* of this remote period at a time when it was generally believed that such occupation sites had almost all been destroyed by natural agencies.

Today such methods are *de rigueur* for all investigations of Palaeolithic living sites, but in the

1940s when Mary Leakey was digging Olorgesailie and Kariandusi, they were unheard of, and even the very existence of such sites was unsuspected. In the hard, compacted and consolidated sediments of the East African Rift, the uncovering of a living horizon and the fossils upon it is accomplished only by prolonged patience and most careful and tedious work with the smallest and most delicate of tools. When there is added to this the glaring, shadeless heat of a summer's day at Olduvai, it is possible to appreciate just a little of what we owe to Mary Leakey and her team of skilled and dedicated assistants.

Although the stone artefacts from the bottom of the Olduvai sequence are not the oldest known, they provide the only complete and undisturbed evidence of the range of tool forms in use and the kinds of occupation sites with which they are associated from about two million years ago, through the earlier part of the Middle Pleistocene. The sequence is all the more impressive since it is securely placed both in relation to the geological and palaeo-geographical evidence obtained by Dr Richard L. Hay, who has been able to correlate the stratigraphy at the main and side gorges, but also within the chronological framework established by the potassium/argon method of radiometric dating. Indeed, the potassium/argon programme for Bed I is 'one of the most comprehensive ever undertaken for a single stratigraphic unit' and now establishes the rate of human biological and cultural change in the earlier Pleistocene.

The Oldowan Industry has for many become identified with the manufacture of 'pebble choppers', so that the record of forms from the excavations described in this volume will come as a revelation of the greatest significance for taxonomic studies. Here are artefacts that conventional usage associates typologically with much later times (the late Palaeolithic or even later)— diminutive scraper forms, awls, burins (even on truncations), *outils écaillés*, and a grooved and pecked cobble.

The slow but growing complexity of the Oldowan tool-kits and the sudden appearance of the early Acheulian is superbly documented by records of excavations carried out over a period of two and a half years at some ten occupation sites, two kill sites, twenty-seven sites where the material is diffused through clays or tuffs and three sites associated with stream channels.

The precise meaning behind the presence in the middle of Bed II of two parallel-evolving traditions—the Acheulian and the Developed Oldowan—is, perhaps, one of the most important of the many problems facing students of the Lower Palaeolithic today and more than one explanation is possible for the results of the work so far carried out at Olduvai. We may hope that the discovery of more culturally associated hominid fossils at the Gorge will show whether the primary cause of this was due to biological differences or cultural behaviour.

Besides the stone artefacts a number of tools of bone and ivory showing evidence of percussion flaking and usage have also been identified. A study of the chipping on the utilised stone flakes and fragments provides, in addition, fascinating evidence for several different patterns of wear due to use. The book gives the complete composition of all the archaeological horizons and discusses the significance of the differences revealed by the preliminary comparative work. At the same time it provides the basis for further comparative studies in the future.

No less important than the descriptions and analytical tables are the superb illustrations of the stone and bone implements. There are very few illustrators of archaeological material who can approach the standard set by Mary Leakey and in the present instance these drawings are especially valuable because it is not easy for anyone not accustomed to working with quartz and some of the lavas readily to discern the flaking patterns.

If the composition of the tool-kits is likely to give rise to no small measure of surprise, this will be even more the case when the associated evidence is studied and the distribution of all of this on the living floors is taken into account. A study of the plots of some of these occupation areas cannot fail to arouse respect and admiration for the nicety with which everything is precisely located and identified. This is uniquely important material and the most exciting available anywhere to archaeology for understanding the behaviour of the early hominids. The stone circle and smaller associated concentrations on the DK living-floor; or the relationship of the inner concentration to the peripheral scatter on the FLK ('*Zinjanthropus*') floor; the butchery kit associated with the channel and swamp clays with elephant, *Deinotherium*, *Pelorovis* and *Equus* carcases; and the groups of bifaces in pairs at site TK are only *some* of the many intriguing and intensely interesting patterns shown by these plots.

The magnitude of the work involved in the analysis can in part be appreciated by realising that there were often more than 1,000 artefacts associated with each archaeological level—the '*Zinjanthropus*' floor had 2,275 artefacts; there were 3,510 bone specimens from this horizon and FLK North produced over 14,000 rodent remains from levels 1 and 2 alone.

All the bone has been identified down to Order and Family level; the percentages of the various parts of the animals represented have been calculated and these remains are demonstrated to be the food waste of the hominids.

Of equal interest is the description of the stratigraphic and cultural associations of the thirty-four hominid fossils found in the Gorge, many of which have previously received only brief or, as yet, no mention in print. *Homo habilis* is now definitely associated with six occupation sites with stone tools of the Oldowan Industry and it would, indeed, appear that he was the maker of these tools.

The fact that so much hominid material has been collected is again the direct outcome of the energy and patience that Louis and Mary Leakey bring to bear. Few would have thought it worth while to excavate and sieve an area 300 × 40 sq. ft. at the site of the *H. erectus*? fossil eroded from VEK in Bed IV, but by so doing Mary recovered a significant part of the skull. Similarly, few would have had the patience to set about the reconstruction of the Hominid 16 skull lying in over 1,500 fragments down the slope of Maiko Gully.

Mary is a direct descendant of John Frere, whose discovery at Hoxne in 1797 can be said to have begun the study of Palaeolithic archaeology. Whether she derives therefrom some of her interest in archaeology, her eminence in the field today is directly the result of her own painstaking thoroughness, long experience and the significant contributions she has made to the archaeology of Africa. Recognition has been accorded her in many ways and, most fittingly so, in an honorary doctorate from the University of the Witwatersrand.

Here in this book one is made to realise the essential unity of early man and his culture and the reader finds himself face to face with a record of events which, although incomplete, is the clue, once we can read it aright, to the changing patterns of behaviour that made possible the cultural progress that leads up to modern man. So unexpected have been many of the discoveries at Olduvai that we very confidently expect there will be many more. Dr Mary Leakey's subsequent work on Beds III and IV will help to make even more complete this unsurpassed record of humanity's beginnings.

ACKNOWLEDGEMENTS

My husband and I particularly wish to express our thanks to the Government of the United Republic of Tanzania for permission to work at Olduvai, and to the National Geographic Society, Washington D.C. for their continued financial support, not only of the excavations but for building a laboratory at the Centre for Prehistory and Palaeontology in Nairobi, where the Olduvai cultural material has been studied, as well as making a generous subvention towards the cost of publishing this volume. Our thanks are also due to Mr Henry Fosbrooke, former Conservator of the Ngorongoro Conservancy Unit, for his courtesy and assistance in matters connected with Olduvai.

I am deeply indebted to Professor R. L. Hay, not only for his help in the field and in reading through the manuscript of this book, but also for contributing the section on the geology and permitting his correlated sections to be published here, in advance of his own volume on Olduvai. My sons, Jonathan and Richard, and my daughter-in-law, Mollie, have been of invaluable assistance to me in the field. My former daughter-in-law Margaret has also checked the manuscript in detail and has devoted six months to working on the faunal material in the laboratory. She is responsible for preparing the faunal tables in chapters IX and X and the list of faunal comprising Appendix B. I cannot adequately express my gratitude for her patience and invaluable assistance.

The people who have helped the work at Olduvai, either directly or indirectly, are too numerous to name individually but I would like to take this opportunity to thank them all. Particular thanks are due to Mrs S. C. Savage, Dr Maxine Haldemann-Kleindienst, Dr John Waechter and Dr Glynn Isaac, who took charge of the excavations for short periods during my temporary absences from Olduvai, and to Mr Michael Tippett who was my assistant for two seasons. Mr George Ranney proved of invaluable help in measuring

sections. Miss Claire Taylor and Miss Kathleen Lyons also took an active part in the excavations.

The African staff, under the supervision of Mr Heslon Mukiri (who has now completed forty years of fieldwork), deserve our sincere thanks for their consistently high standard of work. A number have shown outstanding ability, not only in excavation but also in recognising fragmentary hominid material and in developing delicate fossils. On the photographic side we are most grateful to Mr Des Bartlett, who filmed the unearthing of the 'Zinjanthropus' skull and who also took stills of living floors; to Mr R. I. M. Campbell, who has photographed many specimens, including the utilised bones; and to Mr Guy Blanchard, lately attached to the National Geographic Society, who took the magnificent aerial view of the Gorge published as a frontispiece to this volume.

Dr and Mrs A. W. Gentry have been responsible for a great deal of preliminary sorting of the faunal remains from the excavated sites. Mrs Gentry has undertaken a detailed study of the Olduvai bovid material and I am indebted to her for many of the identifications published in Appendix B. Mr Martin Pickford, Miss Jane Flatt and Miss Rosemary Owen have also helped in sorting the faunal material, while Dr Bernard Verdcourt has kindly undertaken the identification of the few Mollusca from Olduvai. To all of these I would like to express my thanks.

Professor P. V. Tobias has been good enough to check the chapter on hominid discoveries and augment the bibliography, for which I am most grateful.

Dr J. Walsh of the Kenya Department of Lands and Mines has kindly carried out identifications of rock samples. I am also grateful to the Department itself for supplying the equipment and the skilled services of the late Mr Goate for dynamiting the tuff overlying the deposits at DK I.

I also have to thank Dr Lewis K. Napton of the

ACKNOWLEDGEMENTS

Department of Anthropology, University of California, Berkeley, for his report on the fossil dung from FLK North. Miss Irene Sedgewick has kindly devoted many days to checking the proofs of this book, for which I am most grateful.

It remains for me to place on record my deep appreciation of the co-operation, encouragement and help that I have received from my husband. He most generously made over to me the direction of excavations at the Gorge and has since accepted without demur my re-evaluation of the cultural material, as well as giving me every assistance in the preparation of this volume.

M.D.L.

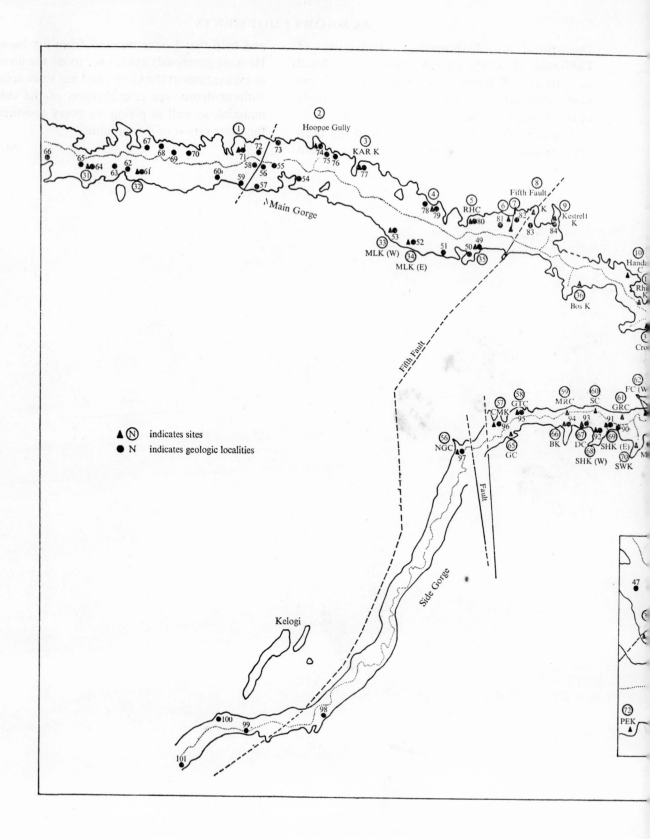

Hoopoe Gully

Main Gorge

KAR K

Fifth Fault

Kestrel K

Bos K

Fifth Fault

MLK (W)

MLK (E)

RHC

Handa

Rhi K

Cro

FC (W)

GTC

MRC

SC

GRC

CMK

BK

DC

SHK (E)

SHK (W)

SWK

NGC

GC

Side Gorge

Kelogi

PEK

▲ Ⓝ indicates sites

● N indicates geologic localities

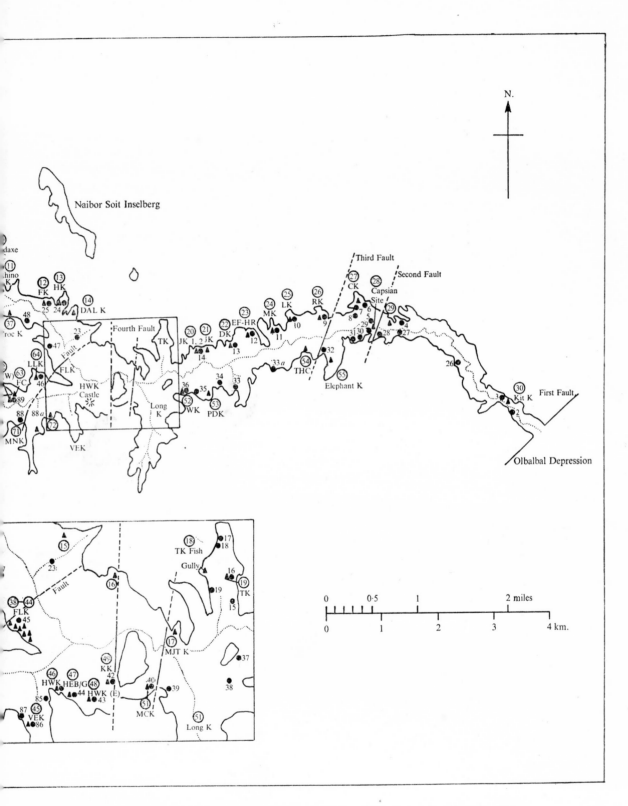

MAP. Sketch map of Olduvai Gorge to show the positions of the sites and geologic localities.

INTRODUCTION

The results of work at Olduvai prior to 1960 have been described in the two volumes by L. S. B. Leakey published in 1951 and 1965 respectively. They will, therefore, not be further discussed here, except in connection with the cultural material obtained from Beds I and II.

Following the discovery of the cranium of *Australopithecus* (*Zinjanthropus*) *boisei* in 1959, funds made available to us by the National Geographic Society, Washington D.C., enabled systematic excavations to be carried out over a period of two and a half years. At the beginning of the first season, in 1960, extensive excavations were undertaken at site FLK, in a search for further parts of '*Zinjanthropus*'. Although largely unsuccessful in this respect, a remarkably clear distribution pattern of an Oldowan living floor was revealed, one that has proved to be the most complete and extensive of any subsequently uncovered. During the same year site FLK NN yielded the remains of *Homo habilis* on part of another Oldowan living floor. FLK North, at the top of Bed I, and DK, at the base of Bed I, were also partly explored.

(Bed I has now been divided into two parts by R. L. Hay, namely an Upper and a Lower Member, separated by the basalt which was formerly considered as the base of Bed I. For the sake of brevity, and since the material discussed in this report was obtained solely from the Upper Member, this will still be referred to as Bed I. When any reference is made to the Lower Member this will be specifically stated.)

At the start of the season in 1962 further excavations were carried out at FLK North and DK where a stone structure had been found. The main objective, however, was a systematic exploration of Bed II. At that time there was still no satisfactory stratigraphic correlation between the important Bed II sites in the Side Gorge, such as BK and SHK, with those in the Main Gorge

(EF–HR, TK, etc.). In fact, it was not until work had closed down and laboratory analysis of various deposits had been completed by R. L. Hay that certain marker tuffs in the Side Gorge could be correlated with tuffs in the eastern part of the Gorge.

Sites in Bed II were selected for excavation as far as possible in stratigraphic sequence, beginning with HWK East, at the base, and working up to BK, the highest known occupation level in the bed. In all, nine sites in Bed II were explored in detail, in addition to the four in Bed I. The relationship of the cultural material from the excavated sites to the sequence published in 1951 is discussed in chapter x, but it may be stated here that no evidence was found to indicate a direct evolution of bifaces from the Oldowan choppers. A different picture has emerged which is still not entirely clear. This is hardly surprising if the time span covered by the Olduvai deposits is considered, as well as the geographic area involved. It has also become evident that the earliest known industry from Olduvai, that from DK, already represents a stage of development in which a multiple tool-kit was in use, indicating the pre-existence of more primitive and less organised stages of tool-making.[1]

The cultural material from Bed I and the base of Bed II can be referred to the Oldowan and remains virtually unchanged from the base of the Upper Member of Bed I to the lowest part of Bed II. It is characterised by choppers of various forms, polyhedrons, discoids, scrapers, occasional sub-spheroids and burins, together with hammerstones, utilised cobbles and light-duty utilised flakes. In Bed II there is evidence for the existence of two industrial complexes whose contemporaneity, in the broad sense, has been confirmed at a number of different sites. One is clearly derived from the Oldowan and has been termed Developed Oldo-

---

[1] Artefacts that can be dated at approximately 2·6 million years have since been found at Koobi Fora, on the east side of Lake Rudolf, in Kenya (Leakey, M.D., 1970*a*).

wan, while the second must be considered as a primitive Acheulean. In the Developed Oldowan A from Lower Bed II Oldowan tool forms persist, but there is a marked increase in spheroids and subspheroids and in the number and variety of light-duty tools. In the upper part of Middle Bed II and in Upper Bed II a few bifaces are also found in Developed Oldowan assemblages, but they form such a negligible proportion of the tools that it has been considered unjustifiable to assign this industry to the Acheulean. It has, therefore, been termed Developed Oldowan B, to distinguish it from the preceding phase (A) which does not include bifaces. Sites where bifaces amount to 40 per cent or more of the tools have been classed as Acheulean. They are known principally from the eastern part of the Gorge, where they occur in the upper part of Middle Bed II. They are, therefore, both contemporary with, and earlier than, Developed Oldowan B sites in Upper and Middle Bed II. The Acheulean appears to be an early form in which the bifaces exhibit minimal flaking and considerable individual variation. They form a high proportion of the tool assemblage, however, and include irregular ovates, oblong picks and a cleaver.

The method of presentation of the material in this volume has posed many problems. A purely stratigraphic approach has finally been considered most satisfactory. The descriptions of the excavated sites and the lithic industries have, therefore, been divided into six groups, based on stratigraphic units demarcated by Marker Tuffs. These are as follows: Lower Bed I, below Tuff I^B; Middle Bed I, between Tuffs I^B and I^D; Upper Bed I and Lower Bed II, between Tuffs I^D and II^A; the lower part of Middle Bed II, between Tuffs II^A and II^B; the upper part of Middle Bed II, between Tuffs II^B and II^C and Upper Bed II above Tuff II^C, as in Table 1.

In previous publications the site names have been followed by the number of the bed in which they occur, i.e. FLK I, BK II, etc. For the present volume the designations of beds have generally been omitted as being needlessly repetitive, since the subdivision of the text on a stratigraphic basis indicates the level at which any particular site occurs.

The material from the different stratigraphic units and from the various sites is described in ascending order, i.e. the earliest is described first. When deposits exposed in sections are listed, however, they are given in the order in which they occur, with the lowest at the bottom. The material from each level has been considered separately when preliminary analysis indicated that this was desirable but, where close similarity was found to exist between assemblages from adjacent levels, they have been pooled and treated as a single series.

Selecting specimens for illustration has also proved difficult. It is clearly impracticable to illustrate on the basis of proportionate representation, although theoretically this would be the ideal method. New elements, as they appear, must necessarily be given prominence and there is a tendency for these to overshadow the familiar tool types which are numerically greater. This applies particularly to the small tools in the Developed Oldowan and to the bifaces in both the early Acheulean and the Developed Oldowan B. In order to overcome this difficulty diagrammatic representations of the more common tools have been included. These, it is hoped, will convey an impression of their relative abundance. Information regarding the proportions of the various elements in the industries is given in the histograms in Fig. 117 and these should be referred to in connection with the illustrations of tools.

In the case of the faunal material from the occupation sites, only a preliminary study has been possible in the time available. This does not include taxonomic identifications or an estimate of the numbers of animals represented. An indication of the proportionate occurrence of the larger mammals and reptiles at different sites has, however, been obtained by counting the number of specimens which can be unquestionably assigned to these taxa. A complete list of all identified faunal material from Beds I and II for which the stratigraphic positions are well authenticated is also given in Appendix B.

Table 1. *The stratigraphic positions of the hominid remains and of the Oldowan, Developed Oldowan and Early Acheulean sites in Beds I and II in relation to the Marker Tuffs*

		Marker tuffs	Hominid remains	Sites	Cultural facies
Bed II	Upper	II^D	H. 3	BK (66)	Developed Oldowan B
			H. 9 (LLK)	TK (19)	Developed Oldowan B
		II^C			
	Middle	II^B	H. 19	SHK (68)	Developed Oldowan B
				MNK Main Site (71)	
				FC West (62)	
				CK (27a)	Probably Early Acheulean
				Elephant K (55)	
				EF–HR (23)	Early Acheulean
			H. 13, 14, 15	MNK Skull Site (71)	Oldowan
				FLK North, Sandy Conglomerate (40)	Developed Oldowan A
				HWK East, Sandy Conglomerate (48)	
		II^A			
	Lower		H. 16 (Maiko Gully)	FLK North, *Deinotherium* Level	Indeterminate
				FLK North, clay with root casts	
				HWK East, Level 2	
		I^F			
Bed I (Upper Member)	Upper	I^D	H. 10	FLK North, Levels 1–6	Oldowan
	Middle			FLK, upper Levels (41)	Indeterminate
			H. 5, 6	FLK, the '*Zinjanthropus*' Floor	Oldowan
			H. 7, 8	FLK NN, Levels 1, 2, 3 (38)	
		I^B			
	Lower		H. 24	DK, Levels 1, 2, 3 (22)	Oldowan
			H. 4 (MK)	FLK NN, Level 4	Indeterminate

DEFINITION OF TERMS

The terminology employed in the preliminary paper on Beds I and II prepared for the symposium on the 'Systematic investigation of the African later Tertiary and Quaternary' held at Burg Wartenstein in 1965 (M. D. Leakey, 1967) has been retained in the present report, with certain minor alterations which became necessary when the entire collection of material had been examined.

The term 'proto' is now omitted when referring to burins, since these tools are, in fact, entirely typical, although some of the Bed I examples are of larger size than is usual in later industries. 'Hand-axe' has been dropped in favour of the more non-committal term 'biface' since this can be applied to specimens of any size, including the diminutive examples found in the later stages of the Developed Oldowan. Among the choppers, the only alteration has been in the series formerly termed 'bilateral'. These are now described as 'two-edged', since in some examples from Bed II the cutting edges are variously placed and are not necessarily situated on either side.

The division of the cultural material into three main groups, i.e. tools, utilised material and *débitage* has been retained. Natural stones introduced to the sites by hominids are termed 'manu-

3

ports', but are not included in the analyses since they lack evidence of modification.

The majority of the tools and utilised material can readily be separated into heavy- and light-duty groups, but, in order to avoid any ambiguity, specimens with a mean diameter exceeding 50 mm. have been termed *heavy-duty*, and those of 50 mm. or less *light-duty*. Except in the case of spheroids and subspheroids, which are almost entirely made from quartz or quartzite, weights have not been recorded since they vary according to the type of raw material and the extent of weathering. In place of weight, the mean diameter $\frac{1}{3}$(length + breadth + thickness) has been recorded for the majority of the heavy-duty tools since this provides a fair indication of overall size. (One series of choppers, in which the average mean diameter is 74 mm. and which is made up of approximately 50 per cent lava and 50 per cent quartz and quartzite, was weighed experimentally and gave an average weight of 1 lb. 6 oz. for each specimen). The ratio of working edge to the circumference has also been noted for side and end choppers, since, if either of these forms eventually gave rise to bifaces, the ratio of the working edge might be expected to be greater in the more evolved assemblages. This has not proved to be the case, and the only significant fact established is that choppers made on blocks of material, such as quartz or quartzite, tend to have a higher edge ratio than those made on cobbles.

The revised terminology used in the present volume for the Oldowan, Developed Oldowan and Acheulean is as follows:—

TOOLS

1. *Choppers*

These are usually made on cobblestones with rounded cortex surface forming the butt ends. When they are made from blocks of quartz or quartzite (particularly in Upper Bed II) the butts are often formed by a flat vertical surface, trimmed and blunted along the upper and lower edges. In the majority the trimming is bifacial, with multi-directional flaking of the working edges. These are essentially jagged and lack secondary trimming, although utilisation has often resulted in the edges having been chipped and blunted. In some examples, particularly in the cobble-choppers from Bed I, the butts have also been used as hammerstones and are extensively pitted and bruised. It is possible to distinguish five types of choppers:

(*a*) *Side*. The maximum diameter is bilateral, exceeding the length from the working edge to the butt; often made on oblong cobbles with the working edge along one lateral edge. Bifacial examples with alternate flaking predominate but there are also a few unifacial specimens and some in which there is multiple flaking on one face of the working edge and a single scar on the obverse. Side choppers are by far the most common type and amount to 64·6 per cent of all the choppers recovered from Beds I and II.

(*b*) *End*. The maximum length is from the working edge to the butt; they are usually made on oblong cobblestones with the working edge at one extremity. Unifacial examples are rare. After side choppers they are the most numerous category and amount to 21·9 per cent of the total number of choppers.

(*c*) *Two-edged*. Two bifacially flaked working edges are present. Specimens from Bed I are generally oblong and blunt-ended, with a working edge on either side, but those from Middle and Upper Bed II include a number in which the working edges are at either end or at one end and on one lateral edge. Two-edged choppers amount to 8·4 per cent of the total number of choppers.

(*d*) *Pointed*. These are usually side choppers. They are characterised by a well-defined median point on the working edge, generally formed by the intersection of a deeply indented flake scar on either side, struck from a flat under-surface. They amount to only 3·7 per cent of the choppers.

(*e*) *Chisel-edged*. The working edge is relatively narrow and lies at right angles to the upper and lower faces of the tools, as in burins. This type of chopper is rare and amounts to only 1·4 per cent.

4

2. 'Proto-bifaces'

These tools are intermediate between a biface and a chopper. They are generally bifacially flaked along both lateral edges as well as at the tip. The butts are thick and are often formed by the cortex surface of a cobblestone. Some specimens are high-backed with a flat under-surface and others are biconvex or lenticular in cross-section. The edges are jagged, as in choppers, and are often utilised. These tools are relatively scarce in all industries but are commonest in Levels 3, 4 and 5 at HWK East, where they amount to 2·4 per cent of the total.

3. Bifaces

The bifaces from sites in Middle and Upper Bed II (apart from the Lower Acheulean site of EF–HR) are generally crude and there is such a degree of individual variation that it has often been necessary to describe each specimen separately. The few cleavers and picks that occur have been described under the broad term of 'biface' in order to avoid further subdivision in a small series of specimens.

(a) *Irregular ovates*. These occur first in the upper part of Middle Bed II. They include elongate and broad specimens as well as those of usual proportions. Some specimens are made on flakes and others on cores. The latter are flaked over both upper and lower faces, whilst in the former the primary flake surface usually shows only a minimum of flaking.

(b) *Trihedral bifaces*. These are generally made on flakes, either end- or side-struck. The lateral edges are steeply trimmed and the tips show a minimum of flaking. They are often formed by two convergent scars which intersect on the dorsal face to form a median ridge which frequently does not extend for the whole length of the tools. Trimming on the primary flake surface is usually restricted to the removal of the bulb.

(c) *Double-pointed*. This is an uncommon form, but one which is represented at several sites. Both extremities are pointed; the tips are generally shaped by means of convergent bilateral flaking and the butts by two intersecting flake scars or natural cleavage planes.

(d) *Flat or square-butted*. This is also an uncommon form. The tools are usually subtriangular and relatively broad at the butt ends, where there is a flat vertical surface. This may be transverse or oblique and consists of either a natural fracture, cortex surface or a negative flake scar.

(e) *Cleavers*. Four sites in Middle and Upper Bed II have yielded single specimens of cleavers. No two are alike. They include a well-made example on a side-struck flake with a parallelogram cross-section (EF–HR), a large, damaged specimen (MNK, Main Occupation Site), a U-shaped specimen, trimmed all round the butt (SHK) and a crude specimen made on a broad side-struck flake with a minimum of trimming (BK). In all examples the cleaver edges are relatively wide and formed in the usual manner, by the intersection of one or more flat flake scars, or natural cleavage planes.

(f) *Picks, oblong*. These are generally trihedral with a more or less flat under-surface from which the dorsal aspect has been steeply trimmed. The cross-sections are generally triangular, but in specimens where the bilateral flaking does not meet along the centre a flat area is present on the dorsal face, resulting in a roughly quadrilateral cross-section. The tips are sometimes pointed, but more often rounded.

(g) *Picks, heavy-duty*. These are massive tools with thick, wide butts tapering rapidly to relatively narrow sharply-pointed tips.

4. Polyhedrons

These are angular tools with three or more working edges, usually intersecting. The edges project considerably when fresh, but, when extensively used, sometimes become so reduced that the specimens resemble subspheroids.

5. *Discoids*

These are often irregular, but a bifacially flaked, jagged working edge is present on the whole or the greater part of the circumference. Specimens made from cobbles are usually plano-convex in cross-section with an area of cortex surface retained in the central part of the convex face.

6. *Spheroids*

These include some stone balls, smoothly rounded over the whole exterior. Faceted specimens in which the projecting ridges remain or have been only partly removed are more numerous.

7. *Subspheroids*

These are similar to the spheroids but less symmetrical and more angular.

8. *Modified battered nodules and blocks*

These are various fragments of no particular form but generally angular, which bear a minimum of flaking and some evidence of utilisation.

(There is no clear demarcation between the above three categories, which grade into one another, although typical specimens of each are quite distinctive.)

9. *Scrapers*

The scrapers have been subdivided into two main groups, namely heavy-duty and light-duty. In Bed II sites the former are often made from pieces of tabular quartzite, steeply trimmed on one or more sides and with the upper and lower faces formed by natural flat cleavage planes. Others are made from parts of cobblestones or on large flakes. Most of the light duty specimens are made from flakes and other small fragments of quartz and quartzite. Many of the heavy-duty scrapers are impossible to assign to any particular type and consist merely of amorphous pieces of lava, quartz or quartzite, with at least one flat surface from which steep trimming has been carried out along one edge. The light-duty specimens from Middle and Upper Bed II, however, fall into a number of recognisable groups to which a proportion of the heavy-duty scrapers can also be allocated. These are end, side, discoidal, perimetal, nosed and hollow. A few combination tools with various types of scraper occur at sites in Upper Bed II.

(*a*) *End.* These are almost exclusively within the light-duty group. They are made on flakes or oblong fragments with a working edge at one extremity (only one double-ended specimen is known). The edges are generally curved, but are sometimes nearly straight and often exhibit small projections at the intersection of the trimming scars, or else a slight spur at one side.

(*b*) *Side.* This is one of the most common forms of scrapers in both the heavy- and light-duty groups. The working edges vary considerably, with either shallow or steep trimming. They are usually curved, but some are nearly straight and there is sometimes a slight median projection, as in nosed scrapers.

(*c*) *Discoidal.* These occur in both the heavy- and light-duty groups. The general form is discoidal although the tools are seldom entirely symmetrical and they are usually trimmed on only part of the circumference.

(*d*) *Perimetal.* This term has been employed for scrapers of various shapes (oblong, triangular or formless) in which there is a trimmed working edge on the entire circumference. They occur in both the heavy and light duty groups, but are more common in the latter.

(*e*) *Nosed.* These are mainly confined to light-duty scrapers. There is a median projection on the working edge, either bluntly pointed, rounded or occasionally spatulate, flanked on either side by a trimmed notch or, more rarely, by straight convergent trimmed edges.

(*f*) *Hollow.* Specimens in which the notch is unquestionably prepared are relatively scarce in both the heavy- and light-duty groups, although light-duty flakes and other fragments with notches apparently caused by utilisation are common. In the few specimens which have been deliberately shaped the notches tend to be wide and shallow rather than deeply indented. They are variable in size.

10. *Burins*

Although not common, burins occur at nearly all Oldowan and Developed Oldowan sites, including the earliest known (DK). Angle burins are the most numerous and are made on transverse broken edges or on trimmed edges, which are usually slightly concave and flaked from the primary surface. Some specimens are double-ended and there are a few with a working edge on either side. Dihedral and polyhedral examples also occur.

11. *Awls*

These first appear in Level 2 at HWK East, at the beginning of the Developed Oldowan. They are characterised by short, rather thick, pointed projections, generally at the distal ends of flakes, but sometimes on a lateral edge. In the majority the points are formed by a trimmed notch, on either one or both sides, but occasionally by straight convergent trimmed edges. The points are often blunted by use and have sometimes been snapped off at the base.

12. *Outils écaillés*

Both single- and double-ended specimens occur. They exhibit the scaled utilisation characteristic of these tools. The edges are blunted and one face is usually slightly concave, whilst the opposite side is straight or slightly convex. They are not known in the Oldowan and occur for the first time at SHK, in the upper part of Middle Bed II (Developed Oldowan B).

13. *Laterally trimmed flakes*

This is a rare tool that, likewise, does not occur in the Oldowan. The flakes are generally elongate and end-struck with one or both lateral edges trimmed for the whole or part of their lengths. The retouch is usually somewhat uneven and the flakes are not entirely symmetrical.

UTILISED MATERIAL

1. *'Anvils'*

These occur at all levels in Beds I and II. In the Oldowan they consist merely of cuboid blocks or broken cobblestones with edges of approximately 90° on which there is battered utilisation, usually including plunging scars. In the Developed Oldowan the anvils have usually been shaped prior to use and are often circular, with flat upper and lower surfaces and vertical flaking on the circumference. Incipient cones of percussion and bruising are sometimes evident on the upper and lower faces, in addition to the utilisation on the edges.

The fact that there is a transition from merely utilised to deliberately shaped specimens has posed a problem in the comparative analyses of the industries, since a distinction has been made between tools and utilised material. It has been considered best, however, to include the anvils as well as the hammerstones among the utilised material, since they represent an aid for tool-making rather than an end-product.

2. *Hammerstones*

The hammerstones consist of water-worn cobblestones (generally lava) with pitting, bruising and slight shattering at the extremities or on other projecting parts.

3. *Cobblestones, nodules and blocks*

These are water-worn cobblestones, weathered nodules and angular fragments that have some evidence of utilisation, either chipping and blunting of the edges or smashing and battering, but no evidence of artificial shaping.

4. *Heavy-duty flakes*

These consist of relatively large flakes with some chipping on the edges. They do not appear in the Oldowan, but occur occasionally in the Developed Oldowan.

5. *Light-duty flakes and other fragments*

Flakes and other small fragments with chipping and blunting on the edges occur in both the Oldowan and Developed Oldowan but are more common in the latter. They fall into three groups: (*a*) with straight edges; (*b*) with concave or notched edges; (*c*) with convex edges. There is also a miscellaneous group with indeterminate chipping. In specimens with straight edges, chipping is usually evident on both sides, while in the notched and convex series it is usually only present on one face.

DEBITAGE

The term *débitage* has been employed in preference to 'waste' for the unmodified flakes and other fragments, since there are indications at certain sites that some, at least, are not merely discarded by-products of tool manufacture but were made expressly, presumably to serve as sharp cutting tools.

The flakes are almost exclusively irregular and the majority are end-struck. They may be sub-divided into three groups, as follows: (*a*) divergent, splayed outwards from the striking platform (the most common type); (*b*) convergent, with the maximum width at the striking platform; (*c*) approximately parallel-sided (rare).

Re-sharpening flakes are uncommon and are often not represented at all, even in large assemblages. Since cores are virtually absent, they are almost certainly derived from re-sharpening the working edges of choppers.

The highest proportion of *débitage* at all sites consists of broken flakes and chips. There are also small angular fragments apparently derived from shattering blocks of raw material. These have been termed core fragments.

MANUPORTS

These consist mostly of lava cobblestones, weathered nodules and blocks of quartz and quartzite, etc., which lack evidence of modification but which appear to have been imported to the sites by hominid agency.

GEOLOGIC BACKGROUND OF BEDS I AND II STRATIGRAPHIC SUMMARY

By R. L. HAY

Olduvai Gorge is a valley in the Serengeti Plains at the western margin of the Eastern Rift Valley in Northern Tanzania. Where cut by the Gorge, the Serengeti Plain has an elevation of 4,000–4,600 ft. The Gorge is generally 150–250 ft. deep in the lower 13 miles of its course. About 5½ miles upstream the Gorge divides into two branches—a smaller, southern branch, or Side Gorge, and a larger, northern branch, or Main Gorge.[1]

The Gorge cuts into Pleistocene beds more than 350 ft. thick which overlie a trachyte welded tuff, here named the Naabi Ignimbrite, and basement rocks of Precambrian age. Schist, gneiss and quartzite form the Precambrian basement that is exposed in the western part of the Gorge and in several inselbergs near the Gorge. The Pleistocene beds were deposited in a broad, shallow basin that lay on a surface of low relief to the east of Ngorongoro and other volcanoes of the Eastern Rift Valley.

The Pleistocene deposits were first studied by Reck and Leakey in 1931 and 1932, and Reck's short report was published in L. S. B. Leakey's first monograph on Olduvai Gorge (1951). This stratigraphy was largely concerned with the eastern part of the Main Gorge, where lava flows were taken as the igneous basement, and overlying sedimentary rocks, termed the *Olduvai Beds*, were subdivided into five mappable units[2] termed Bed I, Bed II, Bed III, Bed IV and Bed V. Between 1956 and 1961 Dr R. Pickering mapped quarter-degree sheets (scale 1:125,000) that include Olduvai Gorge and its environs to the north (Pickering,

1958) and the adjacent areas to the west (1960a) and south (1964).

Beds I–IV*b* are cut by numerous faults but are generally horizontal or nearly so except near a few of the faults. Reck mapped several of the faults, which he numbered as follows from east to west: the First, Second, Third, Fourth and Fifth Faults. Many additional faults are shown by Pickering (1958; in the Press), and a few additional ones were mapped in the course of the present study. Reck's system of numbering is not extended to any other faults. Measured displacements on faults range from about 20 to 120 ft., the maximum figure measured on the Fifth Fault. Several of the faults exposed in the Gorge can be traced for several miles northward across the Serengeti Plain (Pickering, 1958; in the Press), others continue south from the Gorge (Pickering, 1964). Olduvai Gorge drains into Ol'Balbal, a fault graben, the western margin of which may have been dropped down as much as 400 ft. along the First Fault (Pickering, in the Press).

Reck's subdivision into Beds I–IV has generally proved satisfactory and is continued here with some modifications.[3] Bed I is redefined to include all deposits between the Naabi Ignimbrite and Bed II. By this definition the lava flows exposed in the bottom of the Gorge become a member of Bed I and the overlying part of Bed I is termed the Upper Member of Bed I. Bed II as originally defined is continued without modification although a member (the Aeolian Tuff Member) is established within it. Bed III, characterised by reddish-brown claystones and sandstones, interfingers with grey claystones and sandstones similar to those of Bed

---

[1] Columnar sections of the Main Gorge and Side Gorge can be found in the pocket at the end (Figs. 1–3).

[2] In modern stratigraphic practice, Beds I–IV would be considered formations. Each of these Beds or formations comprises many smaller depositional units, or beds.

[3] See note added in proof on p. 18 for subsequent modifications.

IV*a* in the vicinity of JK (Section 14) and FLK (Section 45), and Beds III and IV*a* are not generally separable to the west of the zone of interfingering. Here the equivalent deposits are termed Beds III–IV*a* (undivided).

Deposits now termed Bed IV*a* were previously named Bed IV. A widespread unit generally conformable upon Bed IV*a* is termed Bed IV*b*. It is characterised by aeolian tuffs and in most places is between 5 and 40 ft. thick. The uppermost part of Bed IV*b* contains aeolian tuffs and calcrete over a wide area and is named the Norkilili Member. The Norkilili Member is resistant to erosion and widely forms a cliff along the rim of the Gorge to the west of the Second Fault.

Several of the individual tuff beds in Beds I–IV*a* that were used in correlating are named. These are designated 'Tuff', followed by the formation within which they occur and by a letter designating their position relative to other named tuffs. Tuff I^A for example, is the lowermost marker tuff of Bed I.

Bed V as used by Reck and Leakey comprised deposits of two different stratigraphic units and is abandoned as a stratigraphic term. The older unit, named the Ndutu Beds, comprises conglomerates, sandstones and aeolian tuffs deposited in the Gorge after it had been cut to about three-quarters of its present depth. They are commonly 15–60 ft. thick and contain a Middle Stone Age artefact assemblage. Their sparse mammalian fauna has not been studied. The Ndutu Beds were extensively eroded and the Gorge was cut to its present depth prior to a last widespread series of aeolian tuffs named the Naisiusiu Beds. They generally range from 3 to 20 ft. in thickness and closely resemble some of the aeolian tuffs of the Ndutu Beds. The Naisiusiu Beds contain mammalian bones which gave a C-14 date of 10,400 years (Leakey, Protsch and Berger, 1968). An artefact assemblage termed Upper Kenya Capsian by Leakey (1951) has been collected from the Naisiusiu Beds near the Second Fault.

The faults now exposed in the Gorge were active at various times during the Pleistocene, as indicated by abrupt changes in thickness of stratigraphic units across the faults. A few were active during the deposition of Beds II, III and IV*a*.

Others became active during the deposition of Bed IV*b*, and faulting continued while the Ndutu Beds were being deposited. The Balbal Depression, a fault graben, owes its present configuration to the latest episode of faulting, which displaces the Ndutu Beds. This latest faulting lowered the base level, resulting in erosion of the Gorge to its present depth. The Naisiusiu Beds were nowhere found to be faulted and may post-date the latest faulting in this area.

STRATIGRAPHY OF BED I

Bed I was defined by Reck (1951) as a sequence of tuffs between basalt flows in the bottom of the Gorge and 'lacustrine marls' of Bed II. Bed I by this definition forms only the upper part of a conformable sequence of Beds to the west of the Fifth Fault, where the lava flows of Bed I are absent and the base of Bed I as defined by Reck cannot be recognised. In order to make Bed I a mappable unit where the lava flows are absent, it was redefined (Hay, 1963*a*) to include the entire sequence of tuffs and clays between the Naabi Ignimbrite and Bed II. Where fully exposed in the western part of the Gorge, Bed I is generally 100–140 ft. thick. The type section is taken 4·2 miles west of the Fifth Fault on the south side of the Main Gorge.

Bed I of Reck in the eastern part of the Gorge was redefined as the Upper Member of Bed I, the underlying lava flows comprising the Basalt Member (Hay, 1963*a*). Beds below the Basalt Member at the waterfall upstream from the Third Fault form the Lower Member.

Tuffs provide the principal basis for correlating within Bed I. Six of the tuffs are named as follows, from oldest to youngest: Tuff I^A, Tuff I^B, Tuff I^C, Tuff I^D, Tuff I^E and Tuff I^F. Tuffs I^A, I^C, I^D and I^F are ash-fall tuffs that are reworked to varying degrees. Tuff I^B comprises an agglomeratic tuff (i.e. tuff with pumice bombs), of ash-flow origin (= ignimbrite), and an associated ash-fall tuff, both of which are locally re-worked. Tuff I^E is a massive, unstratified agglomeratic tuff that was emplaced as an ash flow. Tuff I^A crops out only in the western part of the Main Gorge; Tuffs I^C and

I^E are restricted to the eastern part of the Main Gorge. Tuffs I^B and I^F are present in both eastern and western parts of the Main Gorge, and Tuff I^F occurs in the Side Gorge as well. Tuff I^C was earlier termed Marker Bed A; Tuff I^F was termed Marker Bed B (Hay, 1963a).

The tuffs have been correlated on the basis of both field and laboratory work. Crystals and particles of glass were studied in the laboratory to determine their size, shape and optical properties. The content of potassium and sodium was also obtained for many samples of feldspar. Laboratory analysis of the feldspar was particularly useful in correcting a miscorrelation within Bed I between the eastern part of the Gorge and the area west of the Fifth Fault, about 3 miles distant. On the basis of field work alone, Tuff I^F in the eastern part of the Gorge was earlier miscorrelated with Tuff I^A near the Fifth Fault (Hay, 1963a). Subsequent studies of the feldspar showed that the sequence of feldspar types in Tuffs I^B, I^D and I^F in the eastern part of the Gorge could be matched with that in a series of tuffs near the Fifth Fault (Hay, 1967). Moreover, Tuff I^A proved to contain a mixture of basaltic and trachytic volcanic ash, whereas Tuffs I^B–I^F are purely trachytic.

UPPER MEMBER OF BED I

All of the archaeologic materials and nearly all of the faunal remains of Bed I have been found in the Upper Member, within which they are almost exclusively restricted to a sequence of tuffs and claystones forming the western half of the member. The tuffs and claystones interfinger eastward with coarse, unfossiliferous pyroclastic deposits: tuffs, lapilli tuffs, massive agglomeratic tuffs and volcanic conglomerates. Most of the tuffs and lapilli tuffs are water-deposited.

The tuff–claystone sequence has a thickness of 30–50 ft. and extends about 1·5 miles to the west of the coarse pyroclastic deposits. Most of the variation in thickness reflects the uneven basalt surface on which the tuffs and clays were deposited. The tuff–claystone sequence can be subdivided into four major units: (1) a basal claystone unit; (2) a sequence of tuffs; (3) an upper claystone unit; and (4) Tuff I^F, the uppermost layer of Bed I.

The basal claystones are pale olive, greenish grey and yellowish grey. Some are tuffaceous and many are rootmarked. Calcareous concretions occur widely in the claystone and locally they are cemented together to form nodular beds of limestone. A few discontinuous, generally rootmarked, yellowish grey trachytic tuffs are interbedded with the claystone. This basal unit of claystone extends for about 1·5 miles eastward beneath the coarse pyroclastic deposits.

The sequence of tuffs above the basal claystones is generally about 16 ft. thick. Individual tuff beds range from a few inches to about 6 ft. in thickness. Tuffs I^B and I^D can be recognised in this sequence. Claystones are interbedded between several of the tuffs. Some tuffs are extensively water-worked; a few others appear reworked to a very minor extent. Some of the thicker tuffs are massive beds that comprise the products of more than one eruption which have been mixed to form a single bed by organic agencies such as roots and burrowing organisms. The 4 ft. tuff bed above Tuff I^D in Section 45 represents a 'homogenised' tuff of this type. Coarse vertical rootmarkings are common in many of the tuffs and are particularly abundant at FLK in the tuff 10–12 in. thick that overlies the 'Zinjanthropus' horizon and in the 4 ft. massive tuff above Tuff I^D.

The upper claystone unit is generally 5–10 ft. thick. Claystones are generally brownish grey, rootmarked and in outcrop appear massive or crudely bedded. Pumice fragments are disseminated through much of the claystone and become coarser and more abundant in an eastward direction. Nodular and irregular layers and concretions of limestone are locally common, and calcite replacements of coarse gypsum rosettes ('desert roses') are present near FLK a few feet below the top of the claystone.

Tuff I^F ranges from 1·5–7 ft. in thickness. It is evenly laminated in its westernmost exposures and commonly crossbedded towards the east. Characteristically it is yellow and well cemented. Rootmarkings are locally present at one or more horizons within the tuff.

Palaeosols are developed at many horizons over both tuffs and claystones. Where developed on claystones, they are crumbly, rootmarked, discoloured layers generally a few inches thick. On tuffs they are rootmarked layers a few inches to a foot thick that may or may not contain appreciable clay. Pumice is partly weathered in some palaeosols, but the feldspars are unaltered.

STRATIGRAPHY OF BED II

Bed II is a highly variable sequence of sedimentary deposits ranging from 70 to 95 ft. in thickness in the Side Gorge and in the eastern part of the Main Gorge. Following Reck's usage, Bed II is defined as the deposits between the topmost tuff of Bed I (Tuff I^F) and the reddish brown deposits of Bed III. The exposures at HWK (Sect. 42) are proposed as the type section for Bed II. Tuff I^F is widespread and therefore establishes a uniform base for Bed II throughout most of the Olduvai region. The contact between Beds II and III is sharp and locally disconformable in the Side Gorge and in the Main Gorge between the area of the Second Fault (Sect. 27) and FLK (Sect. 45).

North-west of FLK, the upper contact of Bed II is less obvious because of lateral change in both Beds II and III.[1] Here Bed II is divisible into a lower unit consisting of green claystone and an upper unit consisting largely of sandstone. The two units generally have an aggregate thickness of 44–50 ft. between the Fifth Fault and a fault that lies 3 miles further west. The upper, or sandstone, unit thins abruptly from about 40 or more feet to about 7–18 ft. across the westernmost fault. This abrupt change in thickness is attributed to movement along the fault while the upper unit was deposited, with the greater thickness of sediments accumulating on the eastern, downthrown side of the fault.

Several tuffs within Bed II are widespread and hence useful in correlating. An extensive deposit of wind-worked (aeolian) tuff as much as 25 ft. thick is present within Bed II throughout the eastern 5 miles of the Main Gorge and for a distance of about 4 miles north of the Main Gorge (Sect. 1). This unit is defined as the Aeolian Tuff Member of Bed II. Four marker tuffs are designated as

[1] See note added in proof on p. 18.

follows, from oldest to youngest: Tuff II^A, Tuff II^B, Tuff II^C and Tuff II^D. Tuff II^A is dominantly nephelinite, Tuff II^B is andesitic or basaltic, Tuff II^C contains both trachytic and basaltic materials, and Tuff II^D is trachytic. All are reworked and most of them are discontinuous. Tuff II^A is the lowest and most widespread tuff bed of the Aeolian Member and it extends 1·5 miles west of the main body of the member. It occurs in the eastern parts of the Main and Side Gorges. Tuffs II^B and II^D are present in both the Main Gorge and the Side Gorge. Tuff II^C is present only in the Main Gorge. None of these marker tuffs were recognised to the west of the Fifth Fault in the Main Gorge. Probably correlative beds with chert nodules are, however, present in both the Side Gorge and the western part of the Main Gorge. The principal chert horizon is represented in the eastern part of the Main Gorge by abundant chert artefacts.

BED II IN THE EASTERN PART OF THE MAIN GORGE

Bed II in the eastern part of the Main Gorge is a sequence of diverse rock types ranging in thickness from 70 to 95 ft. The western part of Bed II in this area consists largely of claystones and sandstones; the eastern part contains substantial proportions of claystone, reworked tuff and lapilli tuff, sandstone, conglomerate and mudflow deposits. Many of the easternmost beds are reddish brown and resemble Bed III. Both the horizontal and vertical distribution of sediment types is complex and weathered horizons and channelling are visible in many places.

The Aeolian Tuff Member lies 47 ft. above the base of Bed II near the mouth of the Gorge, and it progressively drops in position within Bed II in a westward direction. At HWK (Sect. 43) it lies only 8 ft. above the base of Bed II. According to L. S. B. Leakey (1965a), the mammalian fauna obtained from Bed II below the Aeolian Tuff Member differs considerably from that collected above.[1]

Claystones of Bed II vary considerably. Most of them are brown or grey but those in the lower 20 ft. of Bed II at FLK (Sect. 45) are olive or green, and the upper part of Bed II widely contains reddish brown claystones. Brown and reddish brown claystones commonly contain a dense network of finely textured, branching rootmarkings. Long, coarse vertical rootcasts are abundant in many claystones of the lower 5 ft. of Bed II in the area of FLK and HWK (Fig. 6).

Sandstones in the lower 40–55 ft. of Bed II at FLK (Sect. 45), VEK (Sect. 85) and nearby areas are commonly well sorted, medium grained and rich in pyroxene. Many of them are oolitic. A sheet of medium-grained, well-sorted sandstone 5–10 ft. thick near the middle of Bed II is traceable for 1 mile along the south side of the Main Gorge, from Castle Rock (Sect. 44) to WK (Sect. 36). Sandstones elsewhere in Bed II commonly form lenticular beds and are coarse grained, poorly sorted and consist entirely of volcanic detritus.

Conglomerates are widespread, and they occur at various horizons throughout the thickness of Bed II. They are lenticular, and some of them fill channels, the deepest of which is 15 ft. (Sect. 45). Most of the conglomerates consist of lava pebbles and cobbles.

Individual tuff beds are characteristically reworked, and most of them are discontinuous. Several of them are locally laminated or cross-bedded and elsewhere are massive and intensely rootmarked.

Most of the palaeosols resemble those of Bed I, although some are reddish brown and involve a substantial amount of mineralogic alteration.

BED II IN THE SIDE GORGE

Bed II in the Side Gorge to the west of VEK is 75–85 ft. thick where fully exposed. It consists of about 50 per cent sandstone, 35 per cent clay and 15 per cent tuff and limestone. Limestones and conglomerates are present at several horizons through Bed II, and chert nodules occur at one or more horizons 9–14 ft. above the base of Bed II between MNK and SHK, a distance of about 0·6 miles.

Claystones in the Side Gorge are commonly grey or brown and rootmarked. Sandstones are commonly medium to coarse grained and well

sorted. Some are poorly sorted and may contain almost 50 per cent of clay matrix. Lenticular beds of well-cemented grit several inches to a foot thick are widespread. Conglomerates generally consist of pebbles of limestone and volcanic rock. Most beds are lenticular, and a few fill channels 2–3 ft. deep.

All of the tuffs of Bed II in the Side Gorge are discontinuous and reworked to varying extents. Most of them are massive, poorly sorted, yellow to white, and contain coarse white siliceous rootcasts.

Yellow and white chert nodules with reticulate surface patterns are present at MNK (Hay, 1968). Some of the artefacts at HWK are made of chert strikingly similar to that found 12 ft. above the base of Bed II at MNK, three-quarters of a mile distant. The two chert-bearing horizons are almost certainly correlative.

AGE OF BEDS I AND II

Dating of Bed I by Curtis and Evernden was a pioneer effort in the application of the potassium–argon method to Pleistocene rocks (Leakey, Evernden and Curtis, 1961; Evernden and Curtis, 1965). They published forty-six dates from Bed I, and Curtis has obtained seventeen more dates, not yet published, from Beds I and II which he has generously allowed us to use here.

The dating of Tuff I[B] at 1·75 ± 0·03 m.y. deserves special comment as it is the firmest date from the Olduvai region and shows the high degree of reproducibility attainable on suitable materials. Sixteen age determinations were made, eleven on the ash-flow tuff and five on ash-fall tuff.[1] The dates on ash-flow tuff range from 1·60 to 1·89, average 1·74 m.y., and include four that are 1·75 or 1·76 m.y. Four of the five dates from the ash-fall tuff range from 1·66 to 1·85 m.y., averaging 1·75 m.y. The fifth date, 5·4 m.y., is clearly too old. It was obtained from weathered, root-marked tuff that contains fragments of bone and probably mineral contaminants as well. A fission-track date of 2·03 ± 0·28 was obtained from glass of Tuff I[B]

[1] K-Ar lab numbers of ash-flow tuff dates (Evernden and Curtis, 1965) are as follows: 412, 436, 437, 847, 924, 966, 1043, 1057, 1058, and 1179; ash-fall tuff samples are 848, 1039, 1055, 1079, and 1180.

(Fleischer *et al.* 1965). This result agrees rather well with the K–Ar age of 1·74 m.y., and this is highly significant as the two dating methods are based upon different physical principles.

Other concordant K–Ar dates that seem presently acceptable are 1·85 ± 0·07 m.y. for the Basalt Member of Bed I, 1·87 ± 0·05 for the 8 ft. of tuffs below the Basalt Member, and 2·0 m.y. for the ash-flow tuff of Bed I that lies 8 ft. below the Basalt Member at the waterfall upstream from the Third Fault. The latter date is unpublished (Curtis, lab no. 1983); the others are given in Evernden and Curtis (1965).

Twenty-two dates were obtained from tuffs between Tuff I^B and Tuff I^F. They show greater scatter than those of Tuff I^B but average about the same. Nineteen of these dates have been published by Evernden and Curtis (1965), the other three have not. Most of the tuffs are reworked, but none of them appears to be contaminated with basement detritus. These dates are considered together in view of the geologic evidence that the tuffs accumulated rapidly—possibly over a few tens of thousands of years. Nineteen of the twenty-two dates are between 1·55 and 1·92, averaging 1·77 m.y., and the other three dates are 2·0 m.y. or more and discarded as clearly too old.

Tuff I^F, the topmost layer of Bed I, has given inconsistent results. Curtis has dated seven samples of which two give ages of 1·7 m.y. (lab. nos. 1782, 1787), the other dates ranging from 1·8 to 8·5 m.y. The dates of 1·7 m.y. accord with palaeomagnetic evidence, given below, and they may be close to the true age. None of these samples are contaminated by basement detritus, and the K–Ar dates do not correlate with degree of reworking. Tuff I^F resulted from several eruptions, and the older dates may reflect inherited argon in the materials of one or more eruptions.

Dating of Bed II is far from satisfactory, and the only meaningful dates are from Tuff II^A, the most widespread stratum of the Aeolian Tuff Member. This tuff is everywhere reworked and is commonly contaminated. Curtis has dated the biotite in three samples, each from a different locality. The youngest date, on the least-reworked sample, is 1·7 m.y. (lab. no. 2320), which may be close to the true age.

Other samples gave 1·76 m.y. (no. 1761) and 2·1 m.y. (no. 1863). The date of 1·0–1·1 m.y. given in Evernden and Curtis (1965, nos. 664, 664R) was almost certainly obtained from a sample of the Ndutu Beds[1] where they unconformably overlie Bed II near the Second Fault. The other published date, of 0·50 m.y. (no. 405), cannot be accepted because the sampled bed is not known. Although SHK is given as the sample locality, all of the tuffs there are reworked and contaminated by grains from the metamorphic basement. A sample of Tuff II^D from SHK, dated as an experiment, gave an age of 72 m.y. (Curtis, lab. no. 1762). Potentially the most satisfactory for dating is a welded ash-flow tuff exposed 9 miles north-east of Olduvai Gorge. It underlies the Aeolian Tuff Member and lies 30 ft. above the base of Bed II.

Unfortunately, the duration of Bed II cannot be estimated by using the sedimentation rate of lacustrine claystone in the axis of the basin, which can be established for Bed I on the basis of K–Ar dates. This is because of faulting during the deposition of Bed II which changed the shape and size of the basin, the type of sediment, and almost certainly the rate of sedimentation. I would, however, estimate that the top of Bed II is between 0·7 and 1·0 m.y. old on the basis of the apparent volume of detrital volcanic sediment in Bed II compared to that in Beds III, IV, and the Mesak Beds.

Geomagnetic polarity has proved indispensable in evaluating K–Ar dates and in correlating lavas and ash-flow tuffs of the Olduvai region. This is based on the fact that the earth's magnetic polarity has reversed itself at least several times during the Pleistocene, and volcanic rocks emplaced at high temperatures acquire the polarity of the earth's field in cooling through their Curie temperature. A time scale has now been established, at least roughly for the periods of normal and reversed polarity (Cox, 1969). The episodes pertinent to the Olduvai region are 1·0–1·7 (± 0·05) m.y.— reversed polarity; 1·7–1·85 (± 0·05)—normal polarity; and 1·85–2·4 (± 0·05)—dominantly re-

---

[1] The Ndutu Beds were formerly included within Bed V, which has been abandoned as a stratigraphic unit. The Ndutu Beds are upper Pleistocene.

versed polarity, but with one or more short period of normal polarity; and greater than 2·4 m.y.—normal polarity. The normal polarity episode from 1·7–1·85 m.y., termed the Olduvai event, was based on rocks in Olduvai Gorge. The age limits of this event have been debated extensively, and those given above are taken from Grommé and Hay (in the Press).

Taking first Ngorongoro, which predates Bed I, the polarity changes from normal to reversed going upward in the caldera walls, corresponding to the change at 2·4 m.y., which fits with unpublished K–Ar dates of G. H. Curtis and A. E. Mussett. Within Bed I, the ash-flow below the Basalt Member giving a K–Ar date of 2·0 m.y. has reversed polarity. Normal polarity was found in the Basalt Member, in both ash-flow tuffs of Bed I above the Basalt Member (Tuffs I^B and I^F), and in the ash-flow tuff of Bed II. These rocks of normal polarity fall within the Olduvai event, from 1·85 to 1·7 m.y. ago. A. Brock, of the University College, Nairobi, measured the polarity of the sample from Bed II; for the others I am indebted to C. S. Grommé of the U. S. Geological Survey.

In conclusion, the hominid-bearing deposits of Bed I probably span a period on the order of 50,000–100,000 years. They are very likely Middle Villafranchian using the Villafranchian faunas of the Auvergne region as a standard. The Middle Villafranchian faunas of Coupet (Bout, 1960, p. 139) are overlain by a lava flow giving an age of 1·9 m.y. (Savage and Curtis, in the Press), and dates of 2·5 and 3·4 m.y. were obtained from tuffs associated with Early Villafranchian faunas (Curtis, 1965; Savage and Curtis, in the Press.).

PALAEOGEOGRAPHY AND SEDIMENTATION OF BEDS I AND II

Beds I and II afford rich possibilities for environmental interpretation as they contain a varied fauna and a wide variety of sedimentary structure and rock types, some of which are diagnostic of rather specific environmental conditions. Moreover, the deposits are generally well exposed, and sediments deposited in different environments can be correlated, thus permitting a rather precise palaeogeographic reconstruction for Beds I and II. Some of the main conclusions about the palaeogeography and sedimentation of Beds I and II are given below.

The lower part of Bed I in the western part of the Gorge comprises fluviatile and land-laid deposits. These are succeeded by a rather thick sequence of green claystones deposited in the lake that formed in the Olduvai region about 2·0 million years ago. The lake spread rapidly from east to west and then it remained in approximately the same position for about 400,000 years, until the lake basin was modified by faulting during the deposition of Bed II. Saline, alkaline lake water persisted in the central and western parts of the lake, as indicated by mineralogy of the lake beds (Hay, 1963a, 1966, 1968). The shoreline of the lake fluctuated considerably (Fig. 4), probably because inflow varied and a permanent outlet was lacking.

The fossiliferous tuff–claystone sequence of the Upper Member of Bed I was deposited along the east side of the lake on the marginal terrain that was periodically flooded and exposed to the air. Remains of crocodiles, hippos and *Tilapia* indicate that the eastern part of the lake was fresh, at least periodically. Moreover, fossilised rhizomes similar to those of papyrus are present in claystone at DK (Sect. 13). Fresh water is not surprising along the south-east margin of the saline lake, as stream inlets from the volcanic highlands entered here. Remains of flamingos and mineralogic features at a few horizons indicate, however, that the margin was at times saline. The coarse, unfossiliferous materials deposited to the east of the lake margin represent an alluvial fan of volcanic materials from Olmoti volcano.

The palaeogeography of Bed II was similar to that of Bed I until faulting began in the Olduvai basin shortly after the deposition of the Aeolian Tuff Member. Lake-margin claystones and tuffs are present in both the Main and Side Gorges, and these interfinger eastward, as in Bed I, with coarse tuffs erupted from Olmoti. Then ash from a new source, together with older detritus eroded from the surface, were reworked by wind to form a widespread blanket of aeolian sediment. This sediment reacted with sodium–carbonate solutions

15

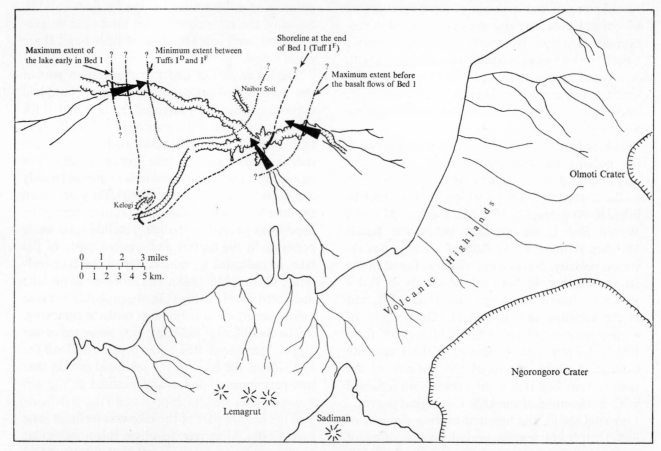

Fig. 4. Map showing the inferred extent of the southern part of the lake and adjacent stream drainage in the Olduvai basin at different times during the deposition of Bed I. Where documented the shorelines are shown solid. Heavy arrows represent directions of streams entering the lake as indicated by the average orientation of stream channel fillings.

at the land surface to form tuffs of unusual mineralogy (Hay, 1963b), which constitute most of the Aeolian Tuff Member. At about the same time, chert nodules formed widely in the lake, which was saline and rich in dissolved sodium carbonate (Hay, 1968).

After faulting began, the perennial lake in the centre of the basin was reduced to perhaps a third of its former size, and the area of grass covered correspondingly increased. This palaeogeographic change, first reflected in the 'sandy conglomerate' above Tuff II^A, explains the faunal change in which remains of swamp-dwelling animals abruptly decrease, and plains animals such as horses increase in abundance. A marginal area to the east of the lake was intermittently flooded over a width of 1–2 miles while the upper part of Bed II ac-

cumulated. Fluviatile and lacustrine sediments alternate in the marginal zone, whereas farther east are fluviatile and mudflow deposits of an alluvial fan that extended to the volcanic highlands.

DISTRIBUTION OF ARCHAEOLOGIC MATERIALS

Occupation sites and stone artefacts in Bed I are only known to occur in the tuff–claystone sequence of the Upper Member, deposited near the southeastern margin of the lake. Most of the occupation sites and artefacts occur within and upon palaeosols (e.g. Sites 22, 38b, 41a). A few artefact concentrations are embedded in claystone beds that may represent dried mudflats, exposed too briefly to develop palaeosols (e.g. Site 40a). Isolated artefacts are present in the 4–6 ft. massive tuff bed with coarse vertical rootcasts that overlies Tuff I^D (Site 41e, 41f).

Artefacts and occupation sites in Bed II are much more widely distributed than in Bed I. Some, as in Bed I, lie in and upon lake-margin palaeosols and in claystones that probably represent marshes and dried mudflats (Sites 40f, 40g, 40h, 46b, 48a, 48b, 62a, 68a, 71a, 71b). Isolated tools are common, as in Bed I, within massive, coarsely root-marked tuffs deposited near the margin of the lake (e.g. Site 68c). A few concentrations of artefacts probably representing occupation sites have been excavated within reworked massive tuffs having the texture of a clayey medium-grained sandstone (Sites 42, 62b, 71c).

Most other artefacts and occupation sites lie in or adjacent to stream-channel deposits at variable distances from the lake (Sites 19a, 23a, 27a, 55, 66, 68b). An unusual stream-channel deposit at SHK (68b) is entirely made up of artefacts and manuports, about 10 per cent of which appear to have been rounded by stream transport. Archaeologic materials at EF–HR (23a), CK (27a) and Elephant K (55) lie on the lower slopes of the alluvial fan rising south-eastward towards the volcanic highlands. Four concentrations of artefacts at TK (19b–e) are in claystones or clayey tuffs whose precise relation to pre-existing stream channels and to the lake margin is unknown.

Chert tools occur over an east-west distance of 2 miles within Bed II at the level of the 'sandy conglomerate' overlying Tuff II^A. They are distributed in deposits of several different environments near the margin of the lake. Tools may be scattered, commonly sparsely, either on a palaeosol (Site 49) or within a thin lacustrine (?) sandstone above a palaeosol (Sites 40h, 44a). They are abundant in a conglomeratic sandstone bed 2–4 ft. thick that fills an east–west series of stream channels (e.g. Site 48c). Finally, they occur together with unworked nodules in the Side Gorge, at MNK and SHK. Here the parent chert, formed in lake deposits, was exposed by erosion and supplied the chert used for tools and probably for some of the tools in the area to the east.

RAW MATERIALS FOR TOOLS

Stone artefacts and manuports are composed of volcanic rock, chert or Precambrian basement rock. Non-vesicular lava is the principal type of volcanic rock used by hominids. A very few artefacts are of tuff, both welded and unwelded, and blocks of vesicular olivine basalt are abundant in the occupation site at DK (22). The lava used most frequently is medium to dark grey, fine-grained and either non-porphyritic or slightly porphyritic. Basalt is the most common type of dark grey lava, but microscopic study shows that some grey lava artefacts are andesite and trachyte. Dark green and greenish grey porphyritic phonolite and nephelinite were widely used for the tools in Beds I and II, but nowhere are they as abundant as the dark grey lava. A moderate proportion of andesite and trachyte lava has oriented feldspar crystals, resulting in a preferred direction of fracture. Most lava is homogeneous, however, and fractures about the same in all directions.

Lava used for tools was probably derived from the volcanic highlands to the south and east. Several streams draining the volcanic highlands were sampled by M. D. Leakey and the writer to compare the natural cobbles in stream channels with the lava used for artefacts in Olduvai Gorge. Both Lemagrut and Ngorongoro are possible sources of dark grey, fine-grained lava, but the assemblage of cobbles from Lemagrut is somewhat more similar than that from Ngorongoro to the lava used for tools in Beds I and II. Sadiman, a volcano between Lemagrut and Ngorongoro, probably supplied the green phonolite and nephelinite used for tools. Blocks of vesicular olivine basalt at DK were clearly obtained from the nearby lava flows of Bed I.

Artefacts of chert are locally abundant in one bed of conglomerate sandstone 8–15 ft. above the base of Bed II (Sites 40h, 44a, 48c, 49). Two flakes of chert were obtained from the lowest occupation level at FLK North, and a very few flakes were found associated with tools in the upper part of Bed II (Sites 23, 62, 68). Chert artefacts in the principal chert-bearing bed were made from irregularly shaped nodules as much as 6 in. long.

The nodules are of dense, homogeneous chert, with a thin coating of porcelainous silica with reticulated surface patterns. Most of the dense chert is milky or pale yellow and translucent; some of it is opaque white.

These chert nodules of Bed II were almost certainly obtained from lacustrine deposits of Bed II that were exposed at the surface during a drop in lake level. Chert nodules are abundant in lacustrine deposits at the same horizon as the chert artefacts in both the Side Gorge and the Main Gorge, to the west of the Fifth Fault (see especially Sections 42, 43, 44, 85, 88). Nodules vary laterally in size, shape, colour and surface texture. However, those in the lower 2 ft. of the 5-ft. thickness of chert-bearing beds at MNK are strikingly similar to some of that used for making artefacts at HWK, three-quarters of a mile distant. Moreover, some of the nodules at MNK are broken, indicating that they were exposed at the surface and reworked before they were finally buried. The beds with chert at MNK may, therefore, have supplied the nodules that were used to make artefacts.

Types of basement rock used by hominids include quartz, quartzite, granite gneiss, pegmatite and pink feldspar. Quartz and quartzite are the principal types of basement rock used for tools. The quartz is colourless or white and it fractures somewhat unevenly, indicating that the quartz is either strained or contains imperfections. Some of the quartzite is micaceous, but most of it is entirely quartz. Nearly all of the quartzite is extremely coarse-grained and fractures about the same as the quartz. A very few tools are of medium-grained quartzite. Hominids utilised two types of gneiss: (1) coarse gneiss with a sugary texture and pale yellow colour, and (2) medium to coarse grained gneiss that is pink to pale grey, and weakly foliated. The fragments of pink feldspar are as much as 5 cm. in diameter and resemble the feldspar of pegmatite dikes.

The quartz and quartzite resemble that of Naibor Soit, an inselberg near the north side of the Gorge. The green quartzite is similar to that of a small outlier near the north end of Naibor Soit. The yellow gneiss contains aegerine and sodic hornblende and is strikingly similar to that of Kelogi, an inselberg 9 miles upstream from the mouth of the Side Gorge. Pink and grey micaceous gneiss are exposed in the western part of the Gorge.

NOTE ADDED IN PROOF

A few changes have been made in the stratigraphic terminology given above. In future publications the Aeolian Tuff Member of Bed II will be termed the Lemuta Member. Beds IVa and IVb warrant formational status, and Bed IVa will be termed Bed IV, as it was originally. Bed IVb is named the Mesak Beds.

Field work in 1970 has shown that the contact between Bed II and Beds III–IV (undivided) is drawn incorrectly in Sects. 24, 25, 47 and 48. The uppermost 16–19 ft. of beds, chiefly sandstone, that are assigned to Bed II should be included within Beds III–IV. The uppermost part of Bed II in this area is green claystone, and the contact between this claystone and the sandstone of Beds III–IV marks the end of a perennial lake in the Olduvai region.

Field work also shows that the 'Kelogi Beds' of the Side Gorge (Sect. 101) represent a northward extension of the Laetolil Beds of the type area, where they are interbedded with the uppermost lavas of Lemagrut on the south-western slopes of the volcano.

REFERENCES

Bout (1960).
Cox (1969).
Curtis (1965).
Curtis and Evernden (1962).
Evernden and Curtis (1965).
Fleischer *et al.* (1965).
Grommé and Hay (1971).
Hay (1963a, 1963b, 1965, 1966, 1967, 1968).
Leakey, L. S. B. (1951), (1965a).
Leakey, Protsch and Berger (1968).
Leakey, Evernden and Curtis (1961).
Pickering (1958, 1960a, 1960b, 1964, in the Press).
Reck (1914b, 1951).
Savage and Curtis (1970).

PART I

PART I

CHAPTER I

LOWER BED I

Site DK and Site FLK NN: Level 4

1. SITE DK (DOUGLAS KORONGO)

Archaeological number (22)   Geologic locality 13

The fossiliferous and tool-bearing deposits at DK, together with those at MK and the lowest level at FLK NN, are among the earliest sites known at Olduvai. They lie above the basalt at the base of the Upper Member of Bed I and are overlain by Tuff I^B, for which a date of 1·75 million years has been obtained.

Equivalent tuffs and clays can be seen upstream of DK at PDK, WK and JK, as well as at many localities downstream in the eastern part of the Gorge. They have yielded faunal remains at a number of sites, notably the only known specimen of a chalicothere (*Ancylotherium hennigi*), found at THC, and parts of two hippopotamus skeletons at PDK. Scattered artefacts and fragmentary fossil bones also occur at other sites, but not in such abundance as at DK and MK.

The clays and tuffs forming this horizon vary considerably in thickness within the DK–MK area, depending on the configuration of the underlying lava. In places where there are depressions they may reach 11 ft. or more, whilst in areas where the basalt rises in hummocks they may be only 3–4 ft. thick. The clay which forms the upper part of this bed was found to be very similar at all the excavated localities, but the lower part, filling depressions in the lava, varied considerably in different trenches. A characteristic feature of the whole bed was the presence of small pebbles of lava, quartz and pink feldspar in otherwise fine-grained sediments.

Trenches were dug in four areas where surface finds indicated that the deposit might be rich in remains (see Fig. 5). The dimensions of the excavations are as follows: the Trial Trench, 20 × 15 ft.; DK I A, 43 × 25 ft.; DK I, Strips 1–111, 54 × 45 ft.; DK IB, 25 × 20 ft. and DK IC, 55 × 18 ft. (Only the plan of finds made at DK I A and DK 1, Strips I–III, is shown in Fig. 7, in pocket.)

The complete sequence of deposits is shown in Fig. 1 and those revealed at the excavated localities in Fig. 6. This was as follows, from the surface downwards:

(*a*) 4–5 ft. of Tuff I^B.

(*b*) Level 1. 1½–2 ft. of brown bentonitic clay with localised lenses of fine-grained white tuff.

(*c*) Level 2. 2–2½ ft. of buff-coloured clayey tuff, merging into Level 3.

(*d*) Level 3. 1–2½ ft. of grey-buff clayey tuff, less clayey than Level 2.

(*e*) Level 4. Silts, clays and tuffs filling depressions in the basalt.

Approximately 75 ft. of Bed I sediments occur above Tuff I^B in the DK area, but in the vicinity of the excavations and elsewhere in the same neighbourhood the soft beds overlying the ignimbrite have been cut back by erosion, leaving it exposed as a low plateau in the floor of the Gorge. The underlying fossiliferous deposits are, therefore, accessible for excavation without removing extensive overburden.

Cultural and faunal remains were found throughout Levels 1, 2 and 3. They become increasingly plentiful in the lower part of Level 3 and it was only at this level that any appreciable concentration of occupation debris occurred at a clearly defined horizon. The material lay on an old land surface, partly on the eroded surface of the Level 4 tuff and partly on the basalt, in places where it rose above the level of the tuff. The surface of this tuff had been deeply eroded prior to hominid occupa-

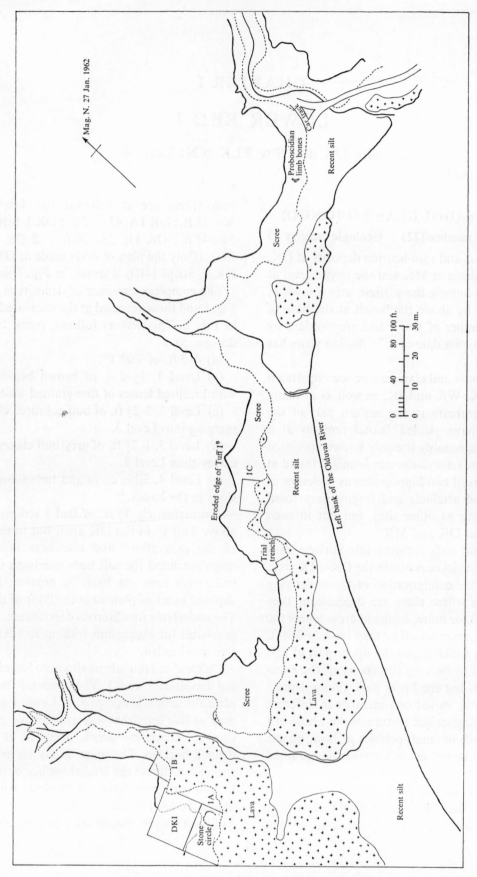

Fig. 5. DK. Sketch map showing the positions of the excavated localities.

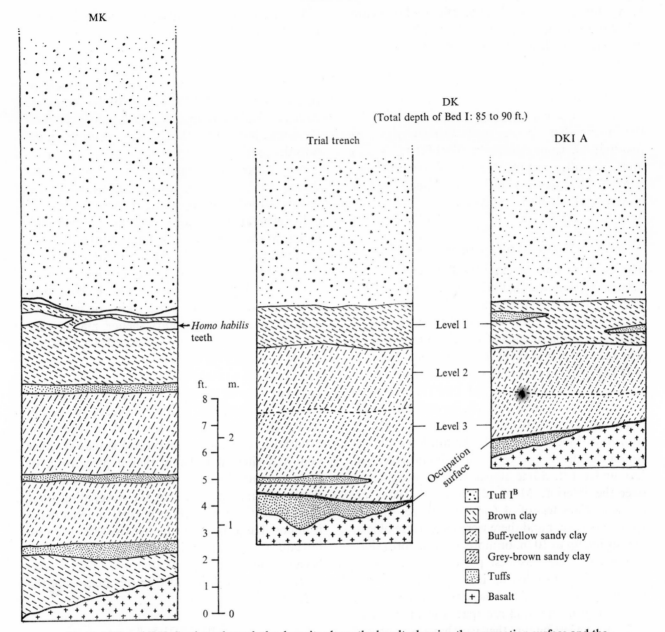

Fig. 6. MK and DK. Sections through the deposits above the basalt, showing the occupation surface and the horizon where the teeth of H. 4 were found.

tion and showed a number of narrow, steep-sided channels 1½–2 ft. deep (Pl. 1). In general appearance these channels strongly resemble the steep-sided game tracks that lead down to the edge of the lake in Ngorongoro and elsewhere.

At DK IA the remains of a loosely-piled circle of stones were found on the occupation floor. The appearance of this circle was so suggestive of an artificial structure that further extensive excavations were carried out during 1963 in an endeavour to find further examples, but none was discovered.

The industry from DK is typical of the Oldowan. Five types of choppers are present, including a number of diminutive examples. There are also polyhedrons and discoids, as well as a few light-duty scrapers and burins and other varieties of heavy-duty tools. The most common tool types are side choppers, polyhedrons and discoids.

A number of fossil rhizomes similar to papyrus and the large quantity of crocodile remains found on the occupation surface suggest that the site was situated close to permanent water. The faunal material is exceedingly fragmentary and most of the mammalian bones were broken prior to fossilisation. Coprolites were plentiful in certain areas, usually occurring in small concentrated patches. They were generally of very small size and closely resemble bird droppings.

THE STONE CIRCLE

The circle of lava blocks was discovered on the occupation floor during 1962, see Pl. 2 and Fig. 7 (in pocket). It lay on the weathered surface of the lowest tuff, which was 9 in. to 1 ft. thick in this area. The southern edge of the circle lay within a few feet of the present erosion slope but the northern part was overlain by 4 ft. of fossiliferous clays and tuffs and by 5 ft. of Tuff I^B. The circle measured approximately 14 ft. in diameter from east to west and 12 ft. from north to south. It was formed by blocks of vesicular basalt, loosely piled round the circumference to a maximum height of just under 1 ft. Some stones were also scattered over the interior. Many of the blocks have an average diameter of 4–6 in. but some smaller stones also occur and there were a few large blocks measuring up to 10 in. or more. On the north side, where the circle was best preserved, there were groups of stones piled up into small heaps. It is possible to identify six of these piles which rise to a height of 6–9 in. and are spaced at intervals of 2–2½ ft., suggesting that they may have been placed as supports for branches or poles stuck into the ground to form a windbreak or rough shelter. The circle lies on a gently sloping surface which rises slightly to the north. The central area is flat and at a slightly lower level than the outside. It will be seen from Fig. 7 that the area immediately outside the circle is relatively clear of loose stones, which become more numerous again at a distance of approximately 2 ft. from the outer circumference.

In the course of excavating the first trench at this site, the stones forming the south-east segment of the circle were removed, before their significance was appreciated. Their positions, however, had been plotted prior to their removal and there is, therefore, a record of the plan of the complete circle. Scattered occupation debris occurred within the circle, but was markedly more plentiful on the outside, particularly to the north-west.

No similar arrangements of stones were found during 1963, when an area 52 ft. by 44 ft. was uncovered to the north of the original circle.

In general appearance the circle resembles temporary structures often made by present-day nomadic peoples who build a low stone wall round their dwellings to serve either as a windbreak or as a base to support upright branches which are bent over and covered with either skins or grass. An example of such a temporary shelter, made by the Okombambi tribe of South West Africa, is reproduced in plate 3 for comparison.

In addition to the stones from which the circle is constructed and those in its vicinity, there were several hundreds of scattered pieces of basalt, particularly on the occupation level. In view of the occurrence of similar unmodified stones at other Oldowan sites, it is likely that a proportion of these was introduced by man. But the proximity of the basalt and the fact that the occupation floor actually rests on its surface in certain areas make it impossible to be sure whether these stones were introduced by hominid agency or whether they became detached by weathering. They have, therefore, not been included in the analysis of the industry.

THE INDUSTRY

The proportion of tools, utilised material and *débitage* made from lava is higher at this site than at any other excavated in Beds I or II. This is particularly evident in the *débitage*, of which 64·0 per cent is of lava, whereas at all other sites, except for the early Acheulean site of EF–HR, the most common materials are always quartz and quartzite.

A few of the artefacts, especially from Level 3, show slight abrasion, but the greater part of the assemblage is in fresh condition.

Level 1 yielded very little material, with a total of only twenty-one specimens, none of which are tools. Level 2 was considerably more prolific, but not to the same extent as Level 3, which included the occupation floor. The proportions of tool types and utilised material from Levels 2 and 3 are very similar, but there is more *débitage* in Level 2. Such minor dissimilarities are not necessarily significant, however, and are no greater than the difference recorded from various localities on a single living floor.

Levels 1, 2 and 3 combined amount to a depth of only 5–6½ ft., with no evidence of any break in the sequence except for the eroded surface at the base of Level 3. It is likely that the period of deposition was relatively short and it is, therefore, proposed to consider the material from the three levels as a single cultural stratigraphic unit in order to make available a larger and more representative series of artefacts for comparison with material from other sites.

TOOLS

With the exception of a single unifacial specimen, the working edges of all the choppers have been bifacially flaked. The flake scars are variable in size and in depth. They are sometimes plunging, but are more often relatively deep and have been removed alternately, giving rise to marked projections on the edges at their points of intersection. The series of choppers is crude and a large proportion of specimens are made from inferior, faulty material; in particular, of vesicular lava. When fine-grained rocks were employed the tools are indistinguishable from those found in the higher levels of Bed I.

In a number of examples the butt ends of choppers are pitted and bruised, showing the type of utilisation characteristic of hammerstones.

(All the tools described below are made from ava unless otherwise stated.)

Side choppers (30 specimens)

Twenty-one are made from cobbles and eight from weathered nodules. There is also one quartzite specimen. The working edges are jagged and any secondary flaking that is present appears to be due to utilisation and not to retouch.

The butt ends are formed by rounded cortex surface and seven specimens show the pitting and bruising typical of hammerstones. Utilisation of the working edges is generally heavy and has often resulted in total blunting as well as the removal of irregular chips and small plunging scars on both faces. One example is rolled and appears to be derived. The length/breadth/thickness measurements range from $86 \times 104 \times 79$ mm. to $30 \times 43 \times 22$ mm., with an average of $65 \times 75 \times 51$ mm. The mean diameters vary from 89 to 31 mm., with an average of 65 mm. The average edge/circumference ratio is 41 per cent.

There are five small specimens in which the mean diameter is under 50 mm., the average figure for the five being 39 mm. The ratio of the working edge to the circumference is 58 per cent, considerably higher than for the larger specimens. (Figs. 8–10.)

End choppers (7 specimens)

Four examples are made from cobblestones and three from weathered nodules. They are entirely similar to the side choppers in technique and in utilisation, the only difference being that the maximum diameter is from the working edge to the butt and not transversely across the width of the tool. Four of the seven specimens show pitting and bruising on the butt ends. The length/breadth/thickness measurements range from $95 \times 80 \times 53$ mm. to $79 \times 65 \times 56$ mm., with an average of $86 \times 68 \times 55$ mm., and the mean diameter varies from 76 to 66 mm., with an average of 70 mm. The average edge/circumference ratio is 33 per cent. (Fig. 10, no. 4.)

Two-edged choppers (4 specimens)

These tools are made on weathered nodules. They are oblong and either roughly quadrilateral or biconvex in cross-section, with blunt, truncated extremities and two parallel longitudinal working edges extending for nearly the whole length of either lateral edge. These are bifacially flaked and are also blunted and chipped by use. One specimen shows additional use as a hammerstone and both extremities are deeply pitted and bruised. The length/breadth/thickness measurements range from $115 \times 79 \times 62$ mm. to $76 \times 63 \times 52$ mm., with an average of $94 \times 72 \times 57$ mm., and the mean diameter varies from 85 to 63 mm., with an average of 75 mm. The working edges vary in length from 95 to 53 mm., with an average of 76 mm. (Fig. 11, no. 1.)

Pointed choppers (5 specimens)

There are three diminutive specimens made on pebbles and two larger examples made on split cobblestones. The working edges are bifacially flaked and there are median points. The butts consist of rounded cortex surface. In the fifth specimen there are two steeply trimmed edges which converge to a point in the centre. The length/breadth/thickness measurements range from $63 \times 53 \times 37$ mm. to $35 \times 41 \times 25$ mm., with an average of $47 \times 44 \times 32$ mm., and the mean diameter varies from 51 to 33 mm., with an average of 41 mm.

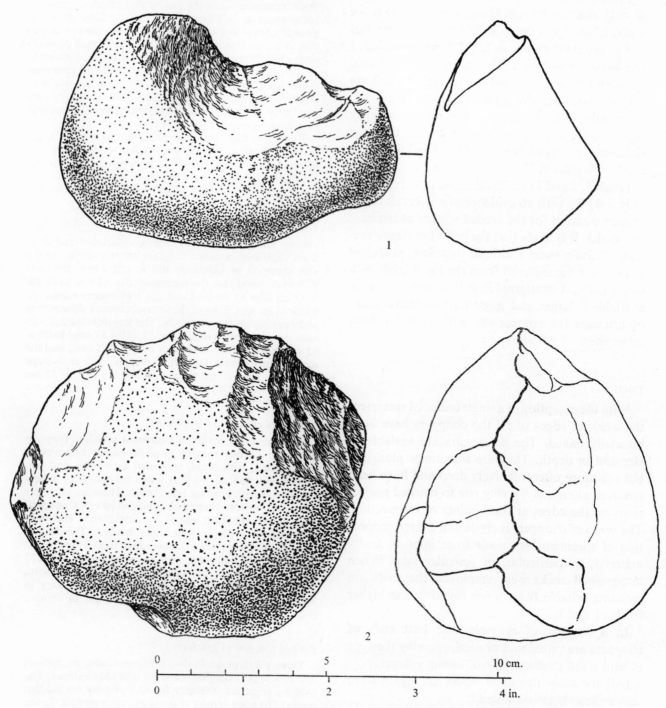

Fig. 8. DK. Side choppers. (1) is the sole example of a unifacial chopper in the DK assemblage. (2) is a massive specimen with multiple bifacial flaking and a jagged, curved working edge. Both examples are made from lava cobbles.

26

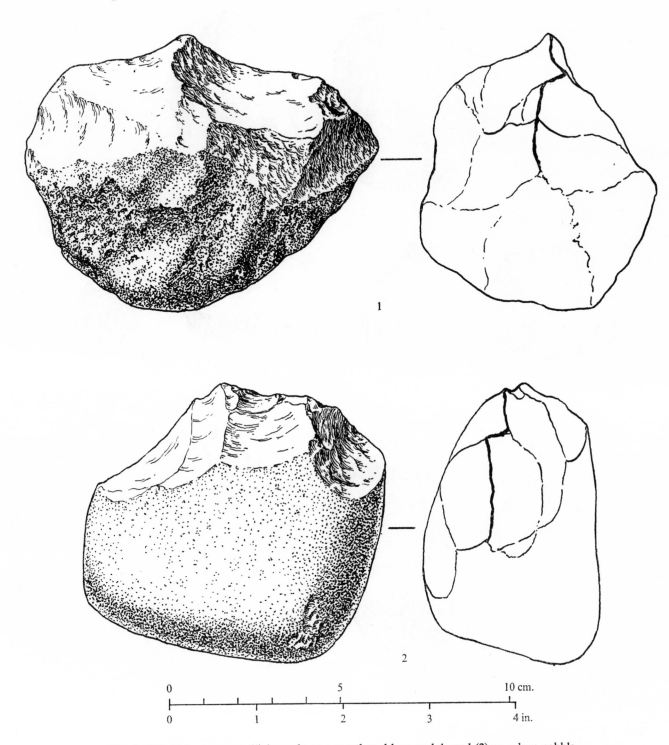

Fig. 9. DK. Side choppers. (1) is made on a weathered lava nodule and (2) on a lava cobble.

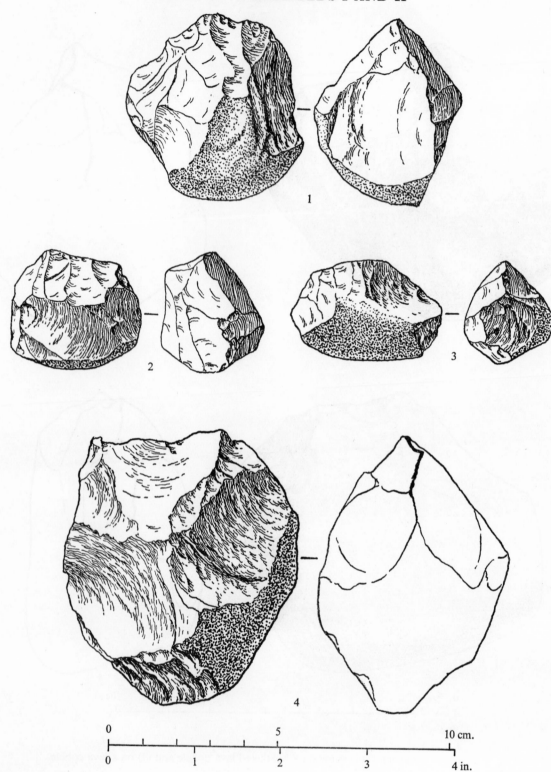

Fig. 10. DK. Three light-duty side choppers and a heavy-duty end chopper. (1) to (3) are bifacial and the butts are formed by cortex surface; (4) is made on a lava cobble. In (1), (2) and (3) the working edge is chipped and blunted, but in (4) it is jagged and particularly sharp.

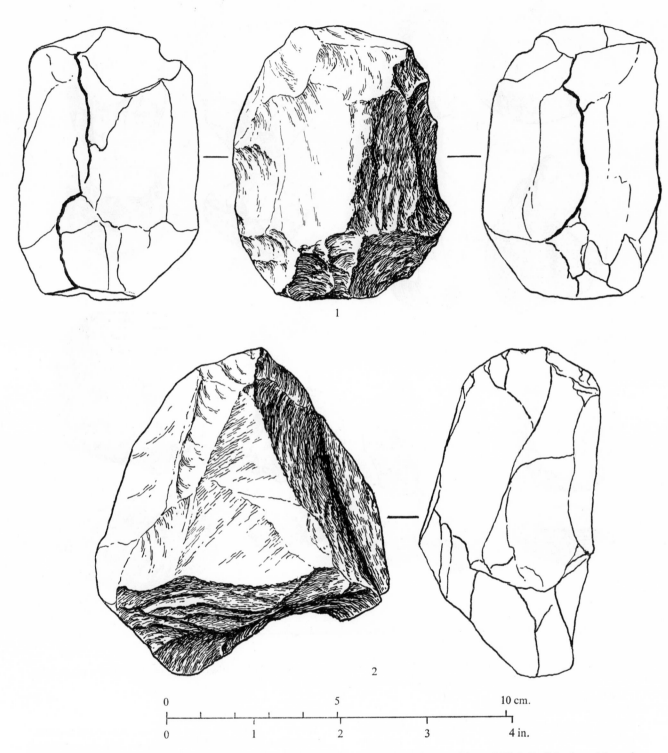

1

2

0   5   10 cm.

0   1   2   3   4 in.

Fig. 11. DK. A two-edged and a chisel-edged chopper. The first is made from lava and has a bifacially flaked working edge on either side. The chisel-edged chopper is made from brown quartzite. The working edge is curved and is at right angles to the upper and lower faces.

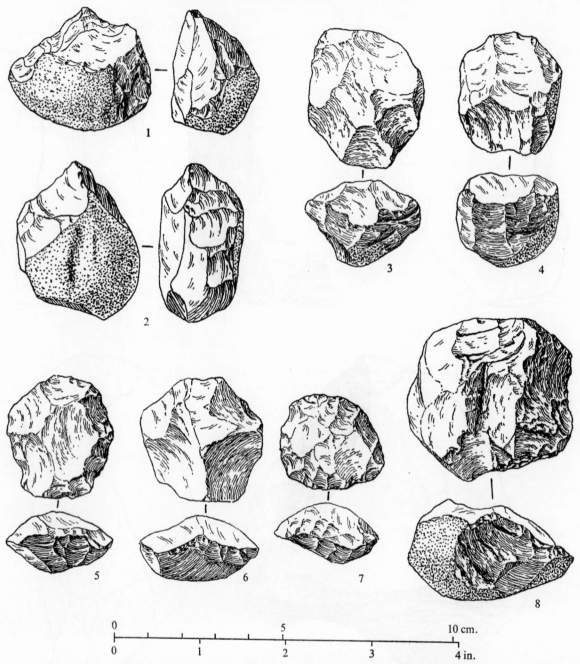

Fig. 12. DK. Light-duty pointed choppers and discoids. Choppers (1) and (2) and discoids (3), (4) and (8) are made from lava; discoids (5), (6) and (7) are of quartz.

Chisel-edged chopper (1 specimen)

This is a particularly well-made tool of brown quartzite. It is triangular in general form, with one apex bifacially trimmed to a slightly convex chisel edge, at right angles to the upper and lower faces. The edge shows unusually fine and even retouch. The specimen measures $86 \times 85 \times 53$ mm. and the length of the working edge is 56 mm. (Fig. 11, no. 2.)

Polyhedrons (32 specimens)

These are one of the most common tools in the assemblage and are only slightly less numerous than the combined side and end choppers. They are characterised by having a minimum of three working edges, usually intersecting. In general form they are angular, the degree of projection of the working edges depending largely on the extent of

30

utilisation; in very heavily utilised specimens the edges may be so blunted and reduced that the general form approaches that of a subspheroid. The surfaces have necessarily been much more extensively flaked than in the choppers or the discoids, but a proportion retains some part of the original cortex and it is evident that irregular-shaped weathered nodules were preferred as raw material, since only four examples are made on cobblestones. There are twelve diminutive specimens which are similar in every respect to the heavy-duty series; they are angular, either subspherical or slightly oblong and have three or more jagged edges, usually intersecting. In some specimens the utilisation is slight, but in others it has been sufficiently heavy to cause complete blunting of the edges. The length/breadth/thickness measurements range from $105 \times 95 \times 93$ mm. to $40 \times 29 \times 28$ mm., with an average of $65 \times 59 \times 49$ mm., and the mean diameter varies between 97 and 32 mm., with an average of 57 mm. (Fig. 13 and pl. 4.)

Discoids (27 specimens)

There are a few symmetrical specimens with regular, radial flaking of the whole circumference but they are mostly crude and only a small number are truly discoidal. The most common variety is made from a split cobblestone with a plano-convex cross-section, the convex face retaining part of the rounded cortex surface, usually in the central area. On this face the flaking may extend round the whole circumference or be only partial, while the flat obverse face is usually flaked over the whole surface and round the entire circumference. The working edges are jagged, as in choppers, with the same degree of blunting and bifacial chipped utilisation.

It seems probable that these tools are, in reality, merely another form of chopper in which the desired working edge was obtained by flaking the fractured edge of a broken cobblestone; the discoidal form is thus primarily due to the shape of the raw material. Pebbles, parts of cobblestones and weathered nodules are almost equally represented and there appears to have been no selection of raw material, such as has been noted for side and end choppers and polyhedrons. In two specimens pitting and bruising of the cortex surface indicates additional use as hammerstones. In eleven specimens the working edge has been bifacially flaked round the entire circumference, while in the remainder it represents an average of 64 per cent of the circumference, even though the whole edge may have been used. Nineteen diminutive specimens are included, four of which are made from quartz. These are remarkable for the refinement of workmanship; the edges are sharp and even, with fine bifacial retouch, whilst the cross-sections are lenticular and symmetrical. All have radial bifacial flaking of the circumference. In common with the larger specimens, those with relatively thick cross-sections are usually made from pebbles or parts of cobblestones in which the convex face retains part of the original surface. The edges are variable and may be jagged, sinuous or nearly even, as in the case of the four quartz specimens. Bifacial chipped utilisation is usually present but is not so pronounced as in other groups of tools. Four small specimens show no trace of utilisation and are clearly unfinished; in two of these the material can

be seen to be faulty, with incipient lines of fracture which have cut across and truncated the flake scars. Twenty-two of the finished specimens are bifacially flaked round the entire circumference or have only negligible areas without trimming. In the remainder the average ratio of the cutting edge to the circumference is 71 per cent. The length/breadth/thickness measurements for the entire series range between $102 \times 93 \times 75$ mm. and $32 \times 28 \times 17$ mm., with an average of $56 \times 45 \times 33$ mm., and the mean diameters vary from 90 to 25 mm., with an average of 54 mm. (Fig. 12, nos. 3–8; Fig. 14.)

Subspheroids (7 specimens)

These tools are irregular in form and are generally slightly oblong. They are made from lava and, in the majority, the entire surface has been flaked and battered. All angularities and ridges are greatly reduced and there is often some additional pitting and bruising of the surface. No smoothly rounded or faceted stone balls occur at this horizon, although there are a few in the uppermost levels of Bed I. The angles of the ridges on the subspheroids tend to be more obtuse than in polyhedrons, due to the greater degree of reduction by battering. Plunging flake scars are usually present. The length/breadth/thickness measurements range from $90 \times 71 \times 56$ mm. to $65 \times 57 \times 46$ mm., with an average of $72 \times 64 \times 55$ mm., and the mean diameters vary from 70 to 56 mm., with an average of 63 mm.

Scrapers, heavy-duty (10 specimens)

With the exception of one specimen made on a large end-struck flake, these tools are all made on cores. They are characterised by steep flaking along the working edge, carried out from a flat or slightly concave under-surface which may consist of a minimum number of flake scars, or a natural cleavage plane. One specimen is of quartz and the remaining examples are made on lava nodules or split cobblestones in which the circumference of the fractured surface has been trimmed to form the working edge; this may be curved or nearly straight, depending largely on the form of the cobblestone or nodule employed. The edges are more obtuse-angled and less jagged than in choppers or discoids, and chipping from utilisation is usually confined to the upper face. The lengths of the working edges range from 155 to 36 mm., with an average of 81 mm. (measured on the curve), and the length/breadth measurements vary from 108×85 mm. to 56×51 mm., with an average of 82×70 mm. (Fig. 15.)

Scrapers, light-duty (20 specimens)

End scrapers (5 specimens). These consist of one quartz and four lava flakes. They are very variable in form. One specimen is square-ended with shallow retouch, the second has a curved and more steeply trimmed 'nosed' working edge; the third is a typical end scraper on a parallel-sided flake. The remaining two are very crude. The average length/breadth measurements are 48×39 mm. (Fig. 16, nos. 1, 2.)

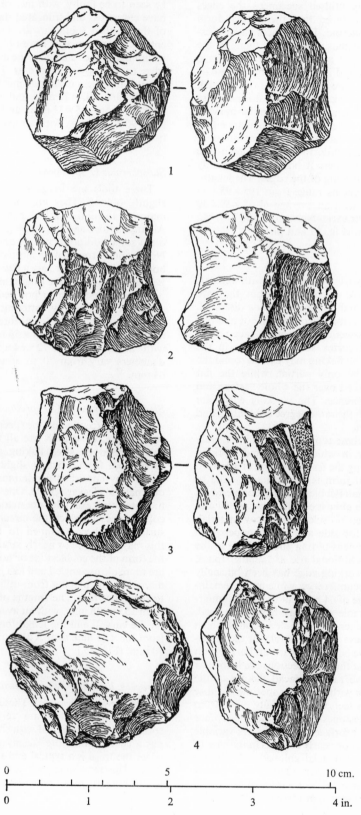

Fig. 13. DK. Light-duty polyhedrons. All the specimens are made from lava and exhibit three or more cutting edges.

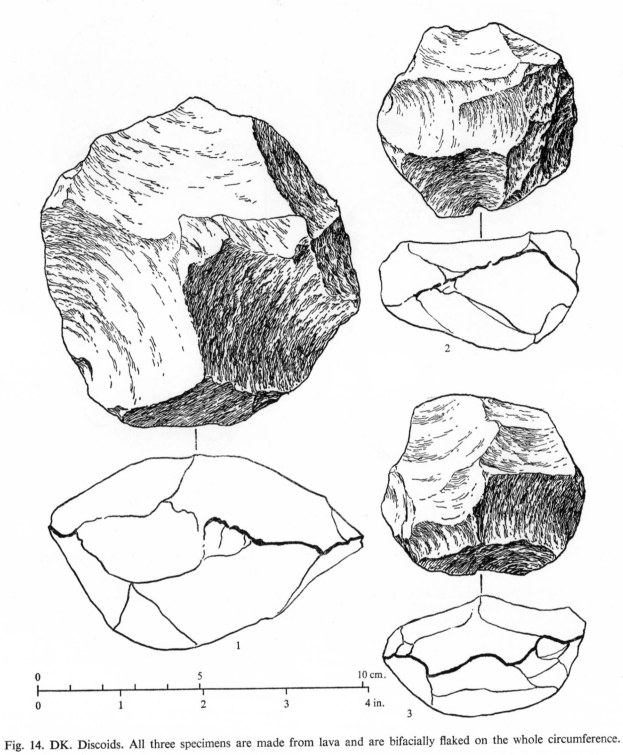

Fig. 14. DK. Discoids. All three specimens are made from lava and are bifacially flaked on the whole circumference.

33

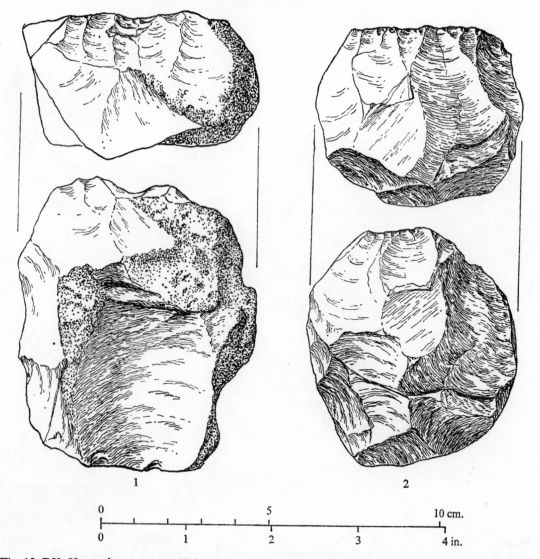

Fig. 15. DK. Heavy-duty scrapers. (1) is made on an end-struck lava flake and (2) on a block of quartzite.

Side scrapers (7 *specimens*). Five specimens are made from lava and two from fragments of tabular quartzite. The working edges are relatively straight and have been trimmed from the lower face by means of shallow, even retouch. Two working edges are present on one example. Lengths of edges range from 76 mm. to 41 mm., with an average of 52 mm. The average length/breadth measurements are 56 × 40 mm. (Fig. 16, nos. 3, 6.)

Hollow scrapers (7 *specimens*). Six of these tools are made on whole or broken flakes and one on a core fragment. Two are of quartz and the remainder of lava. The notches are on relatively thin, sharp edges and are trimmed from either the upper or lower face, but only from one direction. The retouch is fine and regular. The notches range in length from 26 to 11 mm., with an average of 19 mm., and

in depth from 5 to 1·5 mm., with an average of 3·3 mm. The notches on these specimens appear to have been trimmed deliberately rather than being the result of utilisation. (Fig. 16, nos. 4, 5, 7–9.)

There is also one nosed scraper made on a fragment of lava (47 × 37 mm.).

Burins (3 *specimens*)

These tools are made on flat pieces of quartz and lava. A relatively short working edge is present at one pointed end, lying at right angles to the upper and lower faces. The chisel edges are bifacially flaked and.all show fine chipping and blunting. They measure 10, 18 and 27 mm. in length respectively (Measurements: 38 × 20 mm., 42 × 40 mm. and 72 × 75 mm.) (Fig. 17.)

34

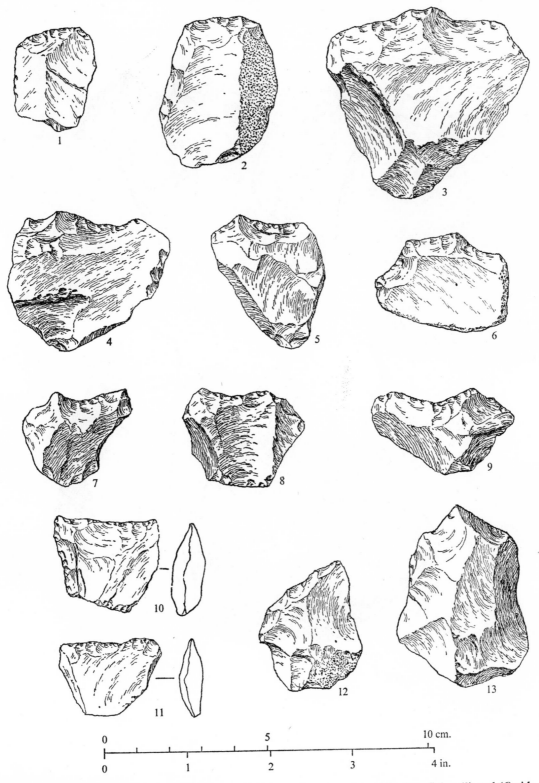

Fig. 16. DK. Light-duty scrapers, etc. (1) and (2) end scrapers made on a quartz and a lava flake; (3) and (6) side scrapers; (4), (7), (8) and (9) hollow scrapers (no. 9 is of quartz, the rest of lava); (10) and (11) knife-like tools, made of quartz; (12) a trimmed point; (13) a beaked point, both made on quartzite flakes.

3-2

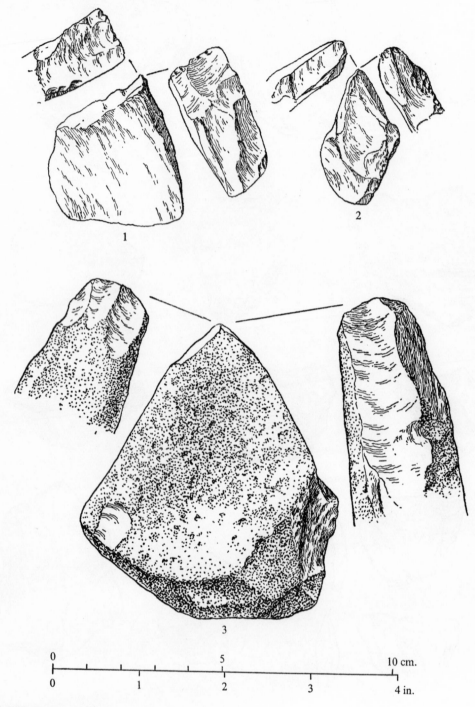

Fig. 17. DK. Burins. (1) and (3) are made from lava and (2) from quartz. (3) is the largest example of a burin known from Olduvai.

Sundry tools (8 specimens)

These consist of two quartz and one lava knife-like tools (Fig. 16, nos. 10, 11), a quartz flake trimmed obliquely across the tip (Fig. 16, no. 12), a steeply trimmed beaked point of quartzite (Fig. 16, no. 13) and three bifacially flaked fragments of lava which may represent small unfinished choppers. The measurements for these are 53 × 39 mm., 48 × 43 mm. and 56 × 48 mm.

UTILISED MATERIAL

'Anvils' (3 specimens)

These are three broken lava cobblestones, two of which are particularly massive, in which edges of approximately 90° have been battered and flaked. One example has been partly shaped and is subspherical in form. (Measurements: 128 × 120 × 97 mm., 99 × 96 × 87 mm. and 87 × 80 × 64 mm.)

Hammerstones (48 specimens)

These consist of thirty-five lava cobblestones, four lava nodules, three quartz cobbles and six small quartz pebbles. The utilisation has occasionally resulted in shattering and the removal of a few flakes, particularly at the extremities, but more often it consists of bruising, pitting and crushing. A proportion of specimens show bruising over the greater part of the surface, but the utilisation is more often only on projecting areas. The mean diameters range from 99 to 50 mm., with an average of 68 mm.

Cobblestones (20 specimens)

A number of whole and broken lava cobblestones show some degree of utilisation. There is a minimum of crude flaking, sometimes combined with battering, which is usually present on broken edges. The mean diameters range from 86 to 69 mm., with an average of 74 mm.

Nodules and blocks (79 specimens)

These consist of weathered nodules or angular blocks on which a minimum of crude flaking and chipping can be seen. In most cases the chipping is from one direction only. More than half the specimens are fragments of local vesicular basalt and presumably represent stones picked up and used for some purely temporary purpose. There are also three fragments of quartz. The mean diameters range from 99 to 29 mm., with an average of 63 mm.

Light-duty flakes and other fragments (37 specimens)

With straight edges (8 specimens). These consist of seven whole or broken flakes, one core fragment and part of a cobblestone. The utilised edges are sharp, with 'nibbled' one-directional flaking which is sometimes present on two of the edges. The length of the edges ranges from 60 to 16 mm., with an average of 30·6 mm. The specimens range from 74 × 53 mm. to 30 × 21 mm., with an average of 46 × 35 mm. (Fig. 18, nos. 1–3.)

With concave edges (16 specimens). These consist mostly of whole or broken flakes but there are also three core fragments. As in the foregoing group, the edges are thin and sharp and would have snapped if used for anything except light work, such as cutting through soft tissues. The notches are formed by regular, one-directional flaking and are relatively small. Double notches are present on two specimens. (It is possible that some of these notched flakes were trimmed deliberately and might be included with the hollow scrapers.) The notches range in length from 26 to 8 mm., with an average of 13 mm., and in depth from 4 to 1·5 mm., with an average of 2·3 mm. The overall length/breadth range is from 58 × 53 mm. to 20 × 19 mm., with an average of 37 × 31 mm. (Fig. 18, nos. 4–10.)

With convex edges (7 specimens). These consist of whole and broken flakes and one core fragment in which a curved edge shows fine chipping, mostly from one direction. It is usually on the lateral edge of a flake, but may be at the tip or at the butt end. The type of flaking is identical to that of the straight-edged utilised flakes and seems to have been caused by the same method of utilisation; it is slightly less regular than in the notched specimens. The length of the edges (measured on the curve) ranges from 43 to 25 mm., with an average of 13 mm. The overall length/breadth range is from 74 × 49 mm. to 28 × 19 mm., with an average of 41 × 33 mm. (Fig. 18, nos. 11–15.)

Miscellaneous (6 specimens). There are also six lava core fragments with some flaking and chipping on the edges. The average measurements are 51 × 43 × 35 mm.

DEBITAGE

Débitage amounts to 857 specimens. It comprises 242 whole flakes, 16 re-sharpening flakes, 481 broken flakes and chips and 118 core fragments. As noted above, lava flakes and other fragments exceed those of quartz or quartzite, with 64 per cent of the total and 82 per cent of the complete flakes. There is also one rolled flake of brown chert.

Whole flakes

All the quartz flakes and 174 of the lava flakes (90 per cent) are divergent; that is, splayed outwards from the striking platform. Only nineteen examples are convergent, with the maximum width at the bulbar end and the entire series is marked irregular. End-struck flakes predominate in both the lava and quartz series and account for 67 per cent of the total.

The length/breadth measurements in millimetres are as follows:

Lava	Range	Average
End-struck	78 × 49 to 16 × 13	37 × 26
Side-struck	57 × 71 to 13 × 18	30 × 36
Quartz/quartzite		
End-struck	64 × 51 to 16 × 12	30 × 23
Side-struck	33 × 36 to 13 × 17	20 × 23

The bulbs of percussion are generally well marked, but, particularly in the quartz flakes, they are sometimes shattered as well as the striking platform. Analysis of the

Fig. 18. DK. Light-duty utilised flakes.

205 specimens in which the bulbs are intact gives the following results:

	Lava	Quartz/quartzite
Marked	56·2 %	55·2 %
Slight	33·0 %	34·4 %
Negative	5·1 %	—
Shattered	5·6 %	10·3 %
Totals	176	29

205

The striking platforms are preserved in only eight of the quartz flakes. The angle can be measured in 132 lava specimens, with the following results:

70–89°	90–109°	110–129°	130°+	Total
4·6 %	47·7 %	46·2 %	1·5 %	132

Re-sharpening flakes (16 specimens)

The majority of these flakes exhibit a longitudinal dorsal ridge, but there are a few examples with transverse ridges and these may be situated either on the body of the flake or at the butt end, forming the striking platform. All the specimens are of lava and appear to have resulted from re-sharpening choppers or other tools with bifacially flaked working edges.

MANUPORTS

It has been noted previously that, owing to the proximity of the basalt, it is impossible to determine whether the numerous lava nodules and other fragments found at this site were artificially imported. With the exception of five broken cobblestones, all of basalt, unmodified cobblestones such as occur in considerable numbers in other Bed I sites are not represented at DK.

Analysis of the Industry from DK

	Nos.	%
Tools	154	12·8
Utilised material	187	15·6
Débitage	857	71·5
	1198	
Tools		
Side choppers	30	19·5
End choppers	7	4·5
Two-edged choppers	4	2·6

	Nos.	%
Tools (*cont.*)		
Pointed choppers	5	3·2
Chisel-edged chopper	1	0·6
Polyhedrons	32	20·8
Discoids	27	17·5
Subspheroids	7	4·5
Scrapers, heavy-duty	10	6·5
Scrapers, light-duty	20	13·0
Burins	3	2·0
Sundry tools	8	5·2
	154	
Utilised material		
'Anvils'	3	1·6
Hammerstones	48	25·7
Cobblestones	20	10·7
Nodules and blocks	79	42·2
Light-duty flakes and other fragments	37	19·8
	187	
Débitage		
Whole flakes	242	28·2
Re-sharpening flakes	16	1·8
Broken flakes and chips	481	56·1
Core fragments	118	13·8
	857	

2. SITE FLK NN. LEVEL 4

The description of this site will be found at the beginning of the next chapter, since the principal bone-bearing and implementiferous levels are stratigraphically within Middle Bed I. However, in the course of digging a trial trench through the lower levels of Bed I in order to ascertain the position of the basalt, some faunal remains and one quartz flake were obtained from the clay beneath Tuff I^B (Level 4).

Considerable numbers of well-preserved bird bones and crocodile teeth were also recovered as well as a few equid and bovid remains. Dr A. Wetmore of the Smithsonian Institution records the presence of flamingos and other aquatic species among the bird bones.

CHAPTER II

MIDDLE BED I

Site FLK NN: Levels 1 to 3. Site FLK: the '*Zinjanthropus*' Level and the Upper Levels

1. SITE FLK NN (FRIDA LEAKEY KORONGO NORTH–NORTH)

Archaeological number (38)

Geologic locality 45

This is the most northerly of the sites within the FLK gullies. It consists of a low ridge running approximately from east to west. Former erosion has removed all of Beds II–IV and in places has cut down even to the level of the occupation surfaces in Bed I. The ridge is now capped by a fawn-coloured tuff resembling Bed V.

The site was discovered on 17 May 1960 by my son, J. H. E. Leakey, when searching for fossils eroding from the Bed I deposits. He first picked up a small piece of a mandible from which all the teeth had been lost but which appeared to be unusual. This was later identified as belonging to a small machairodont or sabre-toothed feline. Since remains of this group of animals are rare among the Olduvai fauna, workmen were set to sieving the soil on the slope where the mandible had been found. Considerable numbers of fossil bones were recovered, but no further pieces of the original specimen. On 25 May, however, an unerupted hominid upper molar was discovered. This was followed on 27 May by the discovery of a terminal phalanx which also appeared to be hominid.[1] Sieving was, therefore, continued and the loose soil on the slope was removed from a strip 15 ft. wide, down to the undisturbed deposits. When this had been completed and the area cleared, it became apparent that fossil bones were eroding from at least two different clay levels, separated

from one another by about 1 ft. of hard, buff-white tuff.

Following the method usually employed at such sites, a trial trench 5 ft. wide was cut into the deposits (Pl. 5). This was subsequently extended downhill in four steps until the basalt was reached. Excavation in the Trial Trench confirmed the preliminary identification of the two clay levels as being the main bone-bearing horizons, but it was also found that the intervening tuff contained a number of fossil bones, including remains of birds, fish and large mammals such as bovids, together with rodents and shrews. On 13 June J. H. E. Leakey discovered a hominid clavicle in the lower clay level and, a few days later, several fragments of a very thin hominid skull. Once the position of the hominid level had been established, work was started on clearing the overburden from a second trench, measuring 40×15 ft., to the east of the Trial Trench. Trenches III and IV were subsequently excavated to the west and a total area of 55×40 ft. was eventually cleared including the hominid level. Trench IV proved to be the last trench which it was possible to dig during the 1960 season, owing to the discovery of the human skull, H. 9, on 2 December, which entailed transferring most of the available labour to the site where it had been found.

The overburden of fawn-coloured tuff attained a maximum thickness of 10–12 ft. in Trench II. The upper part consisted of a wind-blown tuff but the lower part contained pockets and channels filled with gravel and blackish sand (Fig. 19; Pl. 6). A number of derived fossil bones and some artefacts were found in these channels; whereas the few bones obtained from the tuff were completely unmineralised.

---

[1] A descriptive list of the hominid remains from this site, together with a more detailed account of their discovery will be found in chapter VII.

40

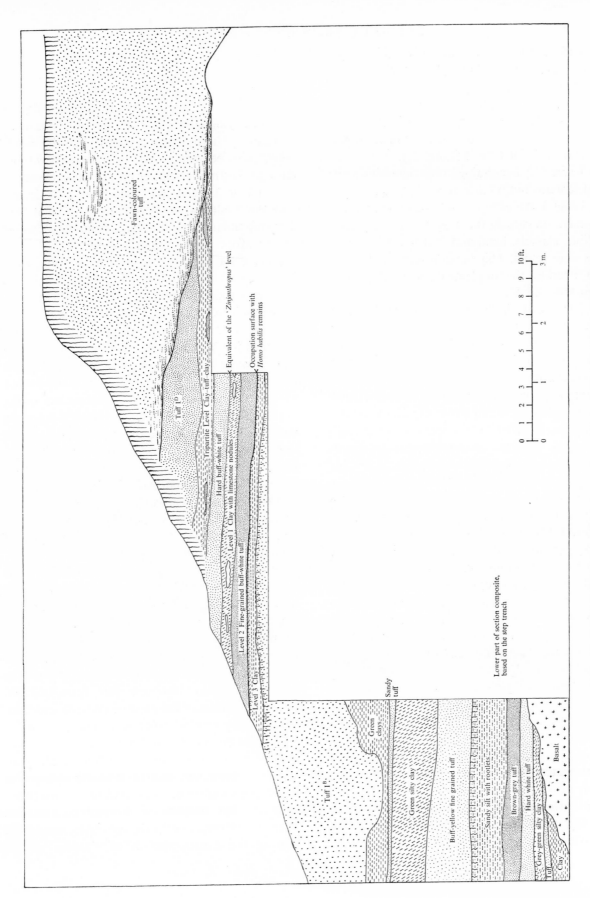

Fawn-coloured tuff

Tuff I D

Equivalent of the 'Zinjanthropus' level

Tripartite Level Clay–tuff–clay

Occupation surface with
Homo habilis remains

Hard buff–white tuff

'Level 1' Clay with limestone nodules

Level 2 Fine-grained buff–white tuff

Level 3 Clay

Tuff I B.

Sandy
tuff

Green
clays

Green silty clay

Buff–yellow fine grained tuff

Sandy silt with rootlets

Brown–grey tuff

Hard white tuff

Grey–green silty clay

Tuff

Clay

Basalt

Lower part of section composite,
based on the step trench

0   1   2   3   4   5   6   7   8   9   10 ft.

0   1   2   3 m.

Fig. 19. FLK NN. Section along the north-east face of the Trial Trench and Trench III.

Four distinct levels with faunal remains and/or artefacts were uncovered in Bed I, as follows, from above downwards:

(a) Level 1. A clay horizon with scattered artefacts and fossil bones on the surface and in the upper part. This can be correlated with the 'Zinjanthropus' occupation level at FLK I (Level 22).

(b) Level 2. A fine-grained tuff containing some faunal remains but no artefacts.

(c) Level 3. An occupation floor on the surface of a clay, on which the fragmentary cranium, mandible, clavicle, hand and foot bones of Homo habilis were found. This horizon rests on Tuff I^B, which overlies the implementiferous clays and tuffs at DK and MK.

(d) Level 4. A clay underlying Tuff I^B. This is the equivalent of the upper levels at DK and MK. It yielded mainly avian remains. (The finds from this level were mentioned briefly at the end of the previous chapter.)

The many rootlet holes and reed casts in Tuff I^B and the occurrence of numerous fish and amphibian remains, together with bones of water fowl, indicate that the site was situated near the shores of the lake or by a swamp.

Among the faunal material associated with the hominid remains in Level 3, hinged tortoises of a variety still living are by far the most numerous remains. Although artefacts are scarce, the series includes typical Oldowan choppers and one of the few utilised bones found in Bed I.

Both cultural and faunal material from Level I was sparsely distributed. Débitage is almost completely absent and the proportions of heavy-duty tools, manuports, etc., are very similar to those found on the marginal areas of the occupation floor at FLK I.

This level also yielded the frontlet and horn cores of an extinct antelope which has been described in volume 1 of this Olduvai series as Strepsiceros maryanus. With very few exceptions, the fossils and artefacts were obtained from the eastern part of the excavations; the western area proving almost barren.

For convenience in excavation and in plotting the finds, the buff-white tuff (Level 2) and the underlying clay, from which the hominid clavicle had been obtained in the Trial Trench, were demarcated in each trench into transverse strips 3 ft. wide. It was found practicable to remove the tuff from only small areas at a time before digging the underlying clay, since this deposit became so exceedingly hard when exposed that the bones could not be uncovered or removed without damage. During the earlier part of the excavations the soil from Levels 2 and 3 was pooled for sieving, with the result that many of the small rodent, bird and amphibian bones recovered from the sieves are listed as from Levels 2 and 3 jointly.

During the second season of excavation, from October 1961 until the beginning of January 1962, Trench IV was extended south for a length of 96 ft., to the limit of the Bed I deposits in that direction (Trench VI). A parallel trench (III) was also extended for 25 ft. and termed Trench V. A small cutting was made to the east of Trench II and a narrow trial trench was dug to the west of Trench IV. These three trenches were excavated in the hope that some extension of the living floor might be found outside the area dug in 1960, but almost the entire existing area of the floor proved to have been uncovered during the previous season, with the exception of a small extension into the northern end of Trench V. This yielded one small piece of hominid skull, lying within 6 in. of the southern end of Trench IV, together with a number of faunal remains and a few tools.

In the extension made to the east of Trench II the greater part of the occupation level had been removed by former erosion, but the small area still remaining proved rich in remains. This would seem to confirm the view, formed at the close of the earlier season, that the area of the most concentrated remains, possibly comparable to the central area of the 'Zinjanthropus' floor, had lain to the north-east of the existing site and had been destroyed by erosion many years ago.

Excavation of the fossiliferous levels was carried out by means of dental probes and small paint brushes, except in those areas where limestone and concretions occurred. These had to be broken up by means of hammers and small cold chisels. Many of the bones were in a very friable condition. During the earlier part of the season diluted

Durofix was used as a preservative but when supplies of Bedacryl became available this was found to be far more satisfactory. In many cases bones which would otherwise have required plaster jackets could be lifted without damage after being treated.

LEVEL 3

This consisted of a silty clay, light grey in colour when dry and greenish brown when wet, containing some tabular and nodular formations of limestone. The clay varied in thickness from 6 in. to 2 ft. and filled pockets in the upper surface of Tuff I^B, which had many root casts and impressions of reed stalks. It was noticeable during excavation that the texture of the clay was not uniform throughout. The upper part was more friable and broke up more readily into small pieces; there were also many small whitish streaks suggesting root marks.

The hominid remains, artefacts and the bones of all the larger mammals, together with many broken-up tortoises and some catfish skulls, were recovered from the surface of the clay or from the topmost few inches (Fig. 20, in pocket). Bones of birds, amphibians and rodents, etc., were also more common in the upper part, but a few also occurred in the lower part. Small concentrations of fish bones were found in certain areas at a depth of 3–4 in. from the top of the clay. These were compressed into very thin localised patches not exceeding 2–3 ft. in diameter. (Conditions giving rise to similar small concentrations of fish remains have been observed on the shores of Lake Jilori, near Malindi on the East African coast, when the lake was in the process of drying up. Shallow pools and even small mud puddles contained hundreds of dead and dying fish which had been cut off from the main waters of the lake as it receded.)

It would seem that the main area of occupation at this site had been partly eroded, or else that it was used for a shorter period (or by fewer individuals) than was the case at FLK I, where a very much greater concentration of occupational debris occurred. Considerable quantities of coprolites, together with tooth marks on some of the bones (including the hominid right parietal and astragalus), indicate that scavengers were active after the site had been abandoned.

LEVEL 2

This consisted of a fine-grained buff-white tuff. In certain areas the base and the central part of the deposit tended to be clayey and it was generally in the clayey patches that the majority of the fossils occurred.

Remains of the larger mammals were noticeably more complete in this deposit than in Levels 1 or 3, although they were often very friable and poorly preserved. Whole bones constitute 38 per cent of the total recovered, as against 14·3 per cent in Level 1 and 16·7 per cent in Level 3. Not only was there a higher proportion of unbroken bones but three partly articulated skeletons were found. Artefacts did not occur and there was no suggestion of hominid occupation. No amphibians or tortoises were found, but bones of rodents, birds and insectivores occurred throughout the deposit and were not confined to the clayey parts. Two skulls of catfish were also found.

LEVEL 1

This level consisted of a greenish grey silty clay. The top was slightly irregular and markedly more friable than the lower part, indicating that it had undergone some degree of weathering before being covered over. The bones and artefacts, however, are in fresh condition and do not appear to have been exposed for any length of time. Many irregular and tabular formations of limestone were present. These became increasingly massive on the western side of the excavations, particularly in Trench III.

Remains of antelopes, suids, one equid femur and parts of an unusually large tortoise were found in this level, together with five tools, some utilised material and a number of manuports. Only two waste flakes were recovered, which is in marked contrast to the contemporary assemblage from the 'Zinjanthropus' floor, where débitage constitutes 92·1 per cent of the artefacts.

With the exception of the frontlet with horn cores of *Strepsiceros maryanus*, the fossil bones were generally very poorly preserved. A startling colour variation was often present, parts of the same bone being black, green or almost white. Greenish-yellow staining was also sometimes evident.

It is clear that if an occupation floor ever existed at this level, then only a small part of the marginal zone has been preserved, comparable to the outskirts of the '*Zinjanthropus*' floor at FLK I.

Apart from one or two isolated finds, all the fossils and cultural material occurred in the Trial Trench, Trench II, the balk, the south-east part of Trench III and Trenches V and VI.

Whereas the cultural material from DK has been considered as a single assemblage, Levels 1 and 3 at FLK NN must be considered separately since there is a clear break in deposition between each of these levels and Level 2.

LEVEL 3

The small series of artefacts from this level is described in some detail in view of its direct association with the remains of *Homo habilis*.

The heavy-duty tools and utilised material are of lava, mostly of basalt, whilst the light-duty utilised flakes and the *débitage* are predominantly of quartz and quartzite. In addition to the tools described below, two choppers and one heavy-duty scraper were obtained from areas where former erosion had cut down to the level of the occupation floor. The two choppers show no trace of Bed I matrix which is present on all other artefacts from this level and also on the heavy-duty scraper. The scraper has therefore been included in the assemblage and the two choppers considered as extraneous, probably derived from the later gravels. In addition to the stone industry, a utilised equid rib was found at this horizon. It is described in chapter VIII.

TOOLS

End choppers (2 specimens)

(*a*) This is made on a lava nodule, with the original surface retained on the greater part of the upper and lower faces. The cutting edge is sharp and broad relative to the width of the specimen; it shows only slight utilisation. Edge length 63 mm. The butt is broken transversely and appears to have been slightly battered on the circumference. ($84 \times 70 \times 58$ mm. Mean diameter 70 mm.) (Fig. 21, no. 1.)

(*b*) This is a narrow-ended specimen made from a lava cobblestone. Cortex is retained on the entire surface, except at the working edge. This is formed by a minimum number of bifacial scars and shows a pronounced median point. ($82 \times 65 \times 52$ mm. Mean diameter 66 mm, edge length 50 mm.) (Fig. 21, no. 2.)

Polyhedron (1 specimen)

This is a large crude specimen made from basalt, boldly flaked over almost the entire surface and retaining only a small area of weathered surface. Five utilised working edges are present, three of which intersect. ($100 \times 88 \times 79$ mm. Mean diameter 89 mm.)

Scraper, heavy-duty (1 specimen)

This is made on a weathered lava nodule. The lower face shows a single, slightly concave negative flake scar or cleavage plane, from which the working edge has been steeply flaked. The specimen is high-backed, with the butt and a large part of the upper face formed by weathered cortex. The working edge is now jagged, showing one-directional utilisation and crushed indentations in certain parts. In other areas, where there is little evidence of utilisation, the edge is relatively even and straight. ($81 \times 91 \times 81$ mm. Mean diameter 84 mm. Length 115 mm.) (Fig. 22, no. 1.)

UTILISED MATERIAL

Hammerstone (1 specimen)

A subtriangular lava cobble has been extensively battered and chipped at one extremity. ($93 \times 70 \times 58$ mm.) (Fig. 22, no. 2.)

Nodules and blocks (5 specimens)

Three quartz or quartzite blocks and two of lava show utilisation or crude flaking on projecting ridges or sharp edges. This appears to be due to utilisation only and not to deliberate flaking. The mean diameters range from 73 to 52 mm., with an average of 64 mm.

Light-duty flakes and other fragments (2 specimens)

There is one fragment of lava with flaking on both faces which also shows slight chipping and blunting on the edges as well as a broken quartz flake with similar utilisation. These measure 48×35 mm. and 47×36 mm. respectively.

DEBITAGE

Whole flakes (7 specimens)

These are irregular flakes and call for no special comment; five are of lava and two of quartz or quartzite. They range in size from 57×61 mm. to 24×19 mm., with an average of 31×36 mm.

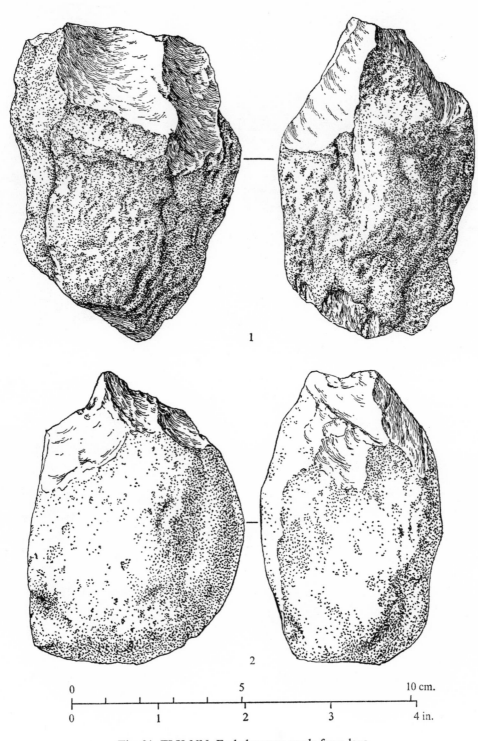

Fig. 21. FLK NN. End choppers made from lava.

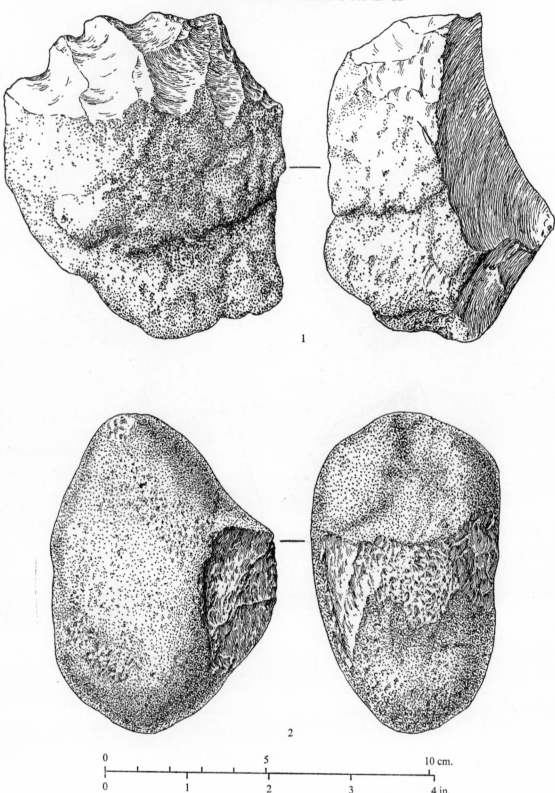

Fig. 22. FLK NN. (1) Heavy-duty scraper made on an irregular lava flake; (2) hammerstone of lava.

Broken flakes and chips (21 specimens)

With the exception of two lava fragments, these are of quartz or quartzite and consist of small chips and broken flakes lacking the bulbar ends.

Core fragments (8 specimens)

All are of quartz or quartzite.

MANUPORTS

Cobblestones (10 specimens)

These consist of natural water-worn lava cobblestones with no evidence of utilisation; the mean diameters range from 72 to 55 mm., with an average of 64 mm.

Nodules and blocks (14 specimens)

These are mainly blocks of the local vesicular basalt, but there is also one block of quartz. The edges are sharp and show no signs of utilisation. The mean diameters range from 91 to 54 mm., with an average of 74 mm.

The proportion of tools, utilised material and *débitage* is as follows:

	Nos.	%
Tools	4	8·5
Utilised material	8	17·0
Débitage	36	74·4
	48	

LEVEL 1

Approximately half the assemblage from this level consists of manuports, either natural fragments of basalt or cobblestones without any evidence of utilisation. All the artefacts are in fresh condition.

TOOLS

Side choppers (3 specimens)

(a) This is made on a quartz or quartzite cobblestone. The flaking is bold, mostly from one direction, and is confined to the working edge. The edge is sharp and generally straight, with only slight evidence of utilisation. (88 × 107 × 82 mm. Mean diameter 92 mm. Edge/circumference ratio 43 per cent.)

(b) This specimen is made on a lava cobblestone with cortex retained on the butt. The cutting edge is curved, bifacially flaked and relatively even. Some secondary trimming is present in addition to utilisation. (77 × 83 × 62 mm. Mean diameter 74 mm. Edge/circumference ratio 40 per cent.)

(c) In some respects this specimen resembles a crude discoid, since the greater part of the circumference has been bifacially flaked. There is one principal working edge which is even and slightly curved, with secondary retouch on one face. The edge is chipped and battered by use. Other parts of the circumference show utilisation. (95 × 85 × 57 mm. Mean diameter 79 mm. Edge/circumference ratio 32 per cent.)

Scrapers, heavy-duty (2 specimens)

(a) This is made on a slab of quartzite 20 mm. thick and is roughly triangular in general form. One lateral edge is steeply trimmed and also utilised. Length 72 mm. A second edge also shows utilisation. (80 × 69 mm.)

(b) This is a crude specimen made on a slab of basalt 46 mm. thick with a natural cleavage plane on the lower face. It is also roughly triangular in general form. One lateral edge is steeply trimmed from the lower face and also shows some flaking which appears to be due to utilisation. Length of working edge 110 mm. (110 × 95 mm.)

UTILISED MATERIAL

Hammerstones (3 specimens)

(a) This is a sub-oval lava cobblestone showing slight chipping on one lateral edge. (79 × 64 × 40 mm. Mean diameter 61 mm.)

(b) This is an irregular-shaped lava cobblestone showing chipping at one end. The opposite end also shows slight pitting. (96 × 66 × 63 mm. Mean diameter 75 mm.)

(c) This is a hexagonal lava cobblestone with slight pitting at one end. (55 × 52 × 43 mm. Mean diameter 50 mm.)

Nodules and blocks (6 specimens)

These consist of nodules or blocks of lava in which some natural edges or sharp projecting ridges show a minimum of crude flaking or chipping. This appears more likely to have resulted from heavy utilisation than to be intentional. All six specimens are of lava, mostly of the local vesicular basalt. The mean diameters range from 78 to 55 mm., with an average of 66 mm.

Light-duty flake

One end-struck quartzite flake shows coarse chipping on one lateral edge and at the tip. (53 × 32 mm.)

DEBITAGE

There are only two broken flakes, one of lava and one of quartz.

MANUPORTS

Cobblestones (8 specimens)

These consist of well-rounded, water-worn lava cobblestones showing no trace of utilisation. The mean diameters range from 82 to 50 mm., with an average of 65 mm.

Nodules and blocks (10 specimens)

These are basalt nodules in every respect similar to the utilised nodules described above, but without trace of utilisation. The mean diameters range from 79 to 40 mm., with an average of 70 mm.

The proportion of tools, utilised material and *débitage* from this level is as follows:

	Nos.	%
Tools	5	29·4
Utilised material	10	58·8
Débitage	2	11·8
	17	

1. SITE FLK

Archaeological number (41)   Geologic locality 45

The site is situated approximately in the centre of the series of gullies known as FLK. The slope on which the cranium of *Australopithecus* ('*Zinjanthropus*') *boisei* was discovered faces north and is opposite the spot where choppers were found *in situ* in Bed I during 1931. Maiko Gully, which yielded the skull of H. 16 in 1963, lies a few hundred yards to the south, with FLK North to the north-east, over the crest of the ridge that is opposite the '*Zinjanthropus*' site.[1]

An account of the discovery of this cranium on 17 July 1959 is given in chapter VII. Since it was found shortly before the close of the season no extensive excavations could be undertaken until the following year. During 1959, however, a small preliminary trench of approximately 280 sq.ft. was dug. A number of stone tools and quartz flakes, together with some broken animal bones were found in the top part of a silty clay, at the same level as the cranium and overlain by a fine-grained tuff, approximately 1 ft. thick. A hominid tibia was unearthed by Mr Des Bartlett at a distance of about 11 ft. from the cranium. Some of the deposit from a small erosion gully immediately below the site was also sieved and yielded a few small fragments of hominid skull as well as the crown of an unerupted upper molar which clearly belonged to another individual since the upper dentition of '*Zinjanthropus*' was complete.

The industry from the FLK occupation floor is clearly Oldowan. When it is compared to the assemblage from DK it is evident that the ratio of tools, utilised material and *débitage* is very similar, as are the proportions of the various forms of heavy-duty utilised material. There are, however, certain dissimilarities in the relative numbers of some tool categories. The proportions of choppers at the two sites are not very different, but polyhedrons and discoids, that are relatively common at DK, are scarce at FLK. Spheroids, which also occur at DK, are entirely missing at FLK, where scrapers are the most common tools.

[1] The name '*Zinjanthropus*' has been retained here in preference to *Australopithecus boisei* for convenience and brevity.

Some examples of the light-duty scrapers are remarkable for the fine and regular retouch of the working edges, but the variety of types is more limited than in later Developed Oldowan assemblages. Diminutive core tools, such as choppers, polyhedrons and discoids are scarce and there are no truly miniature specimens such as were found at DK. Burins occur at both sites. Amongst the light-duty utilised material there are relatively fewer notched or concave-edged specimens and those with straight edges predominate.

Quartz and quartzite tools are more common at this site than at any other excavated in Bed I. At DK nearly all the heavy-duty tools were made of lava, but at FLK the materials were used in almost equal proportions.

A number of scattered artefacts and faunal remains were also found in the higher levels of Bed I, above the '*Zinjanthropus*' occupation floor.

THE EXCAVATIONS

At the beginning of the new season in February 1960 a trial trench, 6 ft. wide was excavated downwards in a series of steps from the marker Tuff I^F to the underlying basalt (Pl. 7). A complete section through the Upper Member of Bed I in this region was thus exposed; it proved to be 40 ft. thick, with the '*Zinjanthropus*' level lying midway, at a depth of approximately 20 ft. from the top (Figs. 2 and 23, in pocket).

While the upper part of the Trial Trench was being excavated the soil remaining in the gully below the skull site was removed and washed. Only a few pieces of the original skull were found, but several fragments of a second and much thinner skull came to light, together with an unworn incisor and the crown of an unerupted premolar. On completion of the Trial Trench, the overburden was removed from a series of large cuttings, A, B, C and D, to the east, and E, F and G, to the west. A balk 3½ ft. wide was left standing until the excavations on either side had been completed. A further cutting, 30 ft. long, was made to the south-west of cuttings E and F, where the overburden was not too excessive, in order to ascertain whether the living floor extended in a westerly direction. The area, however, proved so unproductive that excavation was discontinued. (This cutting is not shown in Fig. 24.) The total area of the 'Zinjanthropus' floor finally exposed was approximately 3,384 sq.ft.

When possible, all finds, including bone fragments and *débitage*, were numbered *in situ* and plotted before being lifted, but in the central area of the excavations there occurred such large numbers of small quartz chips and bone fragments, some no more than a few millimetres in length, that it was impossible to plot or number every chip before removal. Excavation of this level was carried out by means of dental probes and small brushes. As each strip was completed the excavated soil was either washed through $\frac{1}{16}$ in. sieves—when water was available in the Gorge—or else dry-sieved at the site. The method of excavation found to be most satisfactory was as follows: the overburden was removed by unskilled labour, keeping within roughly horizontal spits. When the whitish-yellow tuff overlying the 'Zinjanthropus' level was reached it was left intact and the area was then marked out into strips 4 ft. wide. The tuff within each of these strips was then pared down, with great care, to within a few inches of its contact with the underlying clay. The reduced tuff was then lifted in small slabs. In many cases bones and other objects on the 'Zinjanthropus' floor lay on the actual surface of the clay and even protruded upward into the overlying tuff. Under the very dry conditions normally pertaining at Olduvai it was found that lumps of clay would be found sticking to the base of the slabs when they were lifted. This clearly constituted a great risk of damage to any hominid remains which might occur on the floor and it was found necessary to wet the slabs of tuff some hours before attempting to remove them.

THE 'ZINJANTHROPUS' FLOOR[1]

This level consisted of a grey-green silty clay, approximately 1 ft. thick. The upper surface of the clay was slightly uneven, with the top few inches

[1] The term 'Zinjanthropus' floor is used as a convenient name for the occupation level on which the 'Zinjanthropus' cranium and the two hominid leg bones were found. Whether 'Zinjanthropus' or the co-existent *Homo habilis* was responsible for making the tools and occupying the floor remains an open question, although the balance of evidence favours *Homo habilis*.

noticeably more friable than the lower part, suggesting that it had been weathered into a palaeosol similar to the clay of Levels 1 and 3 at FLK NN. Lenticular slabs of nodular limestone occurred in certain areas, particularly in depressions. All the cultural and faunal remains were found either on the surface of the clay or within the top few inches.

Two minor topographical features connected with the 'Zinjanthropus' level should be mentioned. A small channel was exposed in cross-section during the excavation of the Trial Trench. It measured 1 ft. 9 in. across the top and had been cut down from the surface of the clay to a depth of 1 ft. 2 in. The filling appeared to be a broken-down earthy clay similar to the palaeosol level.

In the southern corner of the excavation there occurred an irregular, oblong hollow in the floor level from which most of the clay had been removed, together with some of the underlying tuff. The hollow measured approximately 5 ft. in length and varied in width from $1\frac{1}{2}$ to 2 ft., being narrower in the middle than at either end. The clay and tuff from the hollow was heaped up on the west side, in a small mound in which a mass of spherical concretions had formed. The most reasonable interpretation of this feature was that put forward by the late Professor C. Arambourg during his vist to the site. He suggested that it might have been caused by the fall and uprooting of a fair-sized tree in which a considerable quantity of earth was caught up among the roots as it fell, thereby giving rise to the pile of soil alongside the cavity.

Both the nature of the clay and the mode of occurrence of the remains on the occupation floor bear a close resemblance to the conditions pertaining in Level 3 at FLK NN. At both sites the clay appears to have been exposed long enough to develop a weak palaeosol, but neither the bones nor the artefacts are weathered or abraded and it is clear that they did not lie for long on the surface before they were buried.

The distribution of remains on the floor is shown in Fig. 24 (in pocket). It will be seen that a very marked concentration of *débitage* and light-duty utilised material, together with many small bone fragments, occurred in an area approximately 21 × 15 ft. lying to the south-east of the spot where the skull was found. Within this area there were over 1,000 broken animal bones, small tools, utilised material, flakes and waste chips large enough to number and enter on the plan (pl. 9). There were also a great many more smaller chips, some measuring only a few millimeters in length, such as may be found on any chipping floor where quartz or quartzite has been worked. Part of this area extended into the 1959 preliminary excavation, where it had been noted that a great deal of debris occurred. Only a small number of heavy-duty artefacts and large bone fragments was found in this area.

It will be seen from the plan that the concentration of material ceases abruptly to the south and east, where there is a marginal zone, 8–9 ft. wide, in which only a few artefacts were found, although some scattered faunal remains were present. Beyond this there is again a marked increase in both cultural and faunal material, forming an irregular outer margin to the more barren intermediate zone.

In this outer area the remains consisted mostly of large tools, heavy-duty utilised material and manuports, together with more complete bones. It has been suggested by Professor J. D. Clark that this gap between the central and the outlying areas may have been caused by the presence of a wind-break surrounding the central part of the camp site, so that debris would either remain inside or be thrown out over the top. The amount of material present in the central area suggests that the occupation may have been of longer duration or by a bigger group of hominids than is the case at other known Bed I sites.

A small secondary concentration of remains occurred in cutting E, to the west, although it is negligible when compared to the concentration in the main area. To the south the finds were dispersed at random and it is not possible to discern any pattern in the distribution, although the scatter resembles that at FLK NN Level 3 and to some extent that at DK, where the proportions of the tool types, utilised material and manuports are also very similar.

With very few exceptions, the faunal remains were so broken and scattered that it was not possible to associate the bones of individual animals, although two halves of an okapi mandible, found 14 ft. apart, could be matched together. On three occasions, however, bones forming the elbow joint of an antelope were found lying together in position, with the shafts smashed and the opposite ends of the bones missing. In all three cases the distal ends of the humeri lay in contact with the proximal ends of the radii and ulnae, the bones having been broken off within a few inches of the extremities. It is thus clear that they were still held together by ligaments when they became fossilised. In another example a bovid thoracic vertebra was found in close association with the heads of the ribs of either side, the shafts having been broken off within 1 or 2 in. of the head. In spite of the large numbers of mammalian bones present, no complete or even partially complete skulls were found. The best preserved specimen is the frontlet and horn cores of *Parmularius altidens* shown in plate 8. It would seem that the skulls were almost invariably smashed in order to remove the brains. In addition to the breaking up of the skulls and limb bones, many of the larger mandibles have had the lower margin broken off. A good example of this type of damage can be seen in the equid mandible shown in Plate 10.

A number of indented tooth marks on some of the bone fragments, such as might be caused by the larger scavenging animals, suggests that the bones on the floor may have been broken by scavengers as well as by the hominids.

THE INDUSTRY

The distribution of the cultural and faunal material is shown in Fig. 24 (in pocket). It will be seen that the proportions of tool types and of utilised and unmodified material from various parts of the occupation floor are strikingly dissimilar, to the extent that separate analysis of the finds from the central and from the different marginal areas would give entirely different pictures of the industry.

The total number of artefacts recovered from

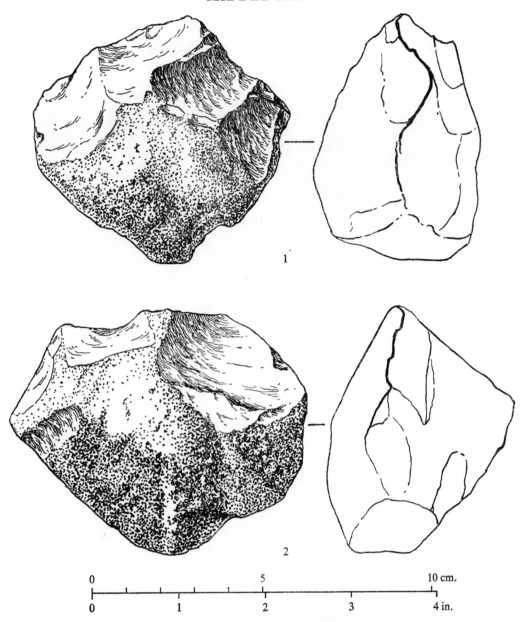

Fig. 25. FLK. Side choppers made on weathered lava nodules, from the '*Zinjanthropus*' level.

this level amounts to 2,470. There are also 96 manuports which mostly consist of weathered nodules and blocks of the local basalt.

TOOLS

Side choppers (*15 specimens*)

Five examples are made from quartz or quartzite and the balance from lava, generally in the form of weathered nodules rather than rounded cobblestones. There is one unifacial specimen. In the remainder the working edges are bifacially flaked and jagged. Five specimens have pitting and bruising on the butt ends and have been used as hammerstones. One example shows clear evidence of re-sharpening by the removal of a single flake from one side. This truncates the previous scars along the edge. The length/breadth/thickness measurements range from $96 \times 121 \times 65$ mm. to $47 \times 50 \times 39$ mm., with an average of $64 \times 82 \times 54$ mm., and the mean diameters range from 94 to 45 mm., with an average of 60 mm. The ratio of the working edge to the circumference ranges from 63 to 30 per cent, with an average of 44 per cent. (Figs. 25, 26.)

51

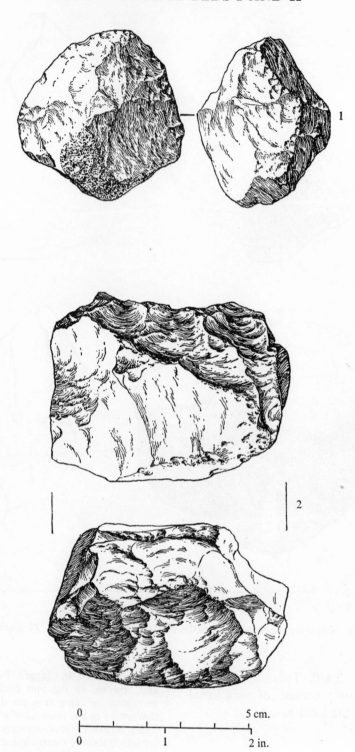

Fig. 26. FLK. A quartz and a lava side chopper from the '*Zinjanthropus*' level.

End choppers (2 specimens)

These two choppers are made from lava. The first is one of the rare end choppers with unifacial flaking of the working edge. The second has been bifacially flaked and also has typical hammerstone type of utilisation on the butt. Only slight utilisation is evident on both specimens. The mean diameters are 63 mm. and 69 mm. respectively and the ratios of the working edge to the circumference are 24 and 32 per cent. (Fig. 27.)

Polyhedrons (9 specimens)

Two examples are made on lava nodules and the remainder are of quartz or quartzite. Typical short, jagged intersecting edges are present. The series ranges from sub-spherical specimens, in which the edges have been greatly reduced by wear, to angular examples with sharp projecting edges. The length/breadth/thickness measurements range from $101 \times 92 \times 68$ mm. to $32 \times 31 \times 26$ mm., with an average of $56 \times 49 \times 41$ mm., and the mean diameters vary from 87 to 29 mm., with an average of 48 mm.

Discoids (3 specimens)

All three specimens are made from quartz or quartzite. One example, found during 1959 near the '*Zinjanthropus*' skull, is particularly well made: the entire circumference is trimmed by means of regular, bifacial flaking. The working edge is sinuous and has become blunted by use (Fig. 28). The remaining two specimens are also bifacially flaked on the whole circumference and utilised. Length/breadth/thickness measurements range from $68 \times 65 \times 45$ mm. to $47 \times 40 \times 19$ mm., with an average of $53 \times 50 \times 31$ mm., and the mean diameters vary from 59 to 35 mm., with an average of 44 mm.

Scrapers, heavy-duty (9 specimens)

Four examples are made of quartz or quartzite, four of lava and one, which is heavily weathered and appears to be derived, is of horneblende gneiss. The whole series is made on cores, usually with a flat natural surface on the lower face, from which the working edges have been steeply trimmed. Three specimens are double-edged and all show considerable blunting of the edges, with most of the chipping on the upper faces. In some cases this appears to be deliberate retouch and not merely due to utilisation. The edges are noticeably more even than those of choppers and may be convex or nearly straight. The specimen made from horneblende gneiss appears to have been imported in its present weathered state and then used, since the edge shows slight fresh chipping. The length/breadth measurements of the nine specimens range from 112×92 mm. to 88×53 mm., with an average of 84×69 mm. (Fig. 29.)

Scrapers, light duty (18 specimens)

End scrapers (9 specimens). Six examples are made on flakes and three on small core fragments. All are of quartz or quartzite. The working edges are either curved or nearly straight and the trimming is generally steep. The length/breadth measurements range from 55×53 mm. to 20×17 mm., with an average of 38×24 mm. (Fig. 30, nos. 1, 2.)

Side scrapers (7 specimens). These are mostly made on broad, side-struck flakes with trimming on one lateral edge, which may be curved or nearly straight and generally shows utilisation. Three specimens have working edges that are unusually wide in relation to the overall size and may represent the tips of end scrapers broken off during use. All are of quartz or quartzite. The length/breadth measurements range from 56×59 mm. to 23×35 mm., with an average of 32×43 mm. (Fig. 30, nos. 4–8.)

Hollow scrapers (2 specimens). These consist of two side-struck quartz flakes with a trimmed notch on one edge. The flakes measure 30×43 mm. and 17×25 mm. respectively and the notches 10×3 mm. and 12×2 mm.

Burins (4 specimens)

These are made either on fragments of tabular quartzite or on parts of broken quartz flakes. In three specimens the working edges are trimmed from two directions and in the fourth on one side only, from a fractured surface. One example, consisting of a broken flake, has two utilised chisel edges, one on either side of the broken edge. The working edges vary from 15 to 10 mm. in length and the length/breadth measurements range from 43×33 mm. to 34×29 mm. (Fig. 30, nos. 11, 12.)

UTILISED MATERIAL

'Anvils' (5 specimens)

Three specimens consist of quartzite blocks and two of broken lava cobblestones in which the circumference of the broken area is shattered and crushed and also shows some plunging flake scars. A similar type of utilisation is present on the ridges of the quartzite specimens. Some pitting and bruising is also evident. The mean diameters range from 75 to 52 mm., with an average of 62 mm.

Hammerstones (13 specimens)

These consist of lava cobblestones with battered, pitted or crushed utilisation, most often at the extremities or, in the discoidal specimens, on the circumference. A few examples have been subjected to particularly heavy blows which have resulted in shattering and the removal of a number of flakes. The mean diameters range from 87 to 60 mm., with an average of 72 mm.

Cobblestones (4 specimens)

There are four cobblestones which are chipped and partly shattered but do not show the form of utilisation typical of hammerstones. The average mean diameter is 65 mm.

Nodules and blocks (40 specimens)

Thirty-two weathered lava nodules, together with eight quartz or quartzite blocks, show some degree of chipping and utilisation on ridges and on natural sharp edges. They are similar in all respects to the series from DK and FLK NN. The degree of utilisation varies from the removal of a few minor chips from one edge to irregular, crude chipping on one, or sometimes both faces of three or more ridges. It

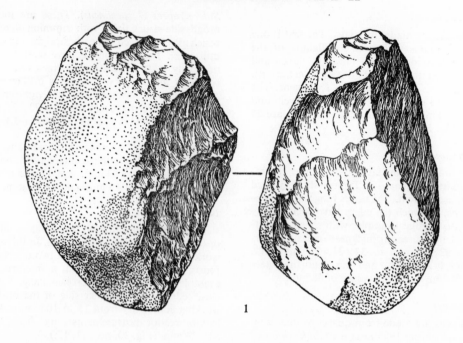

1

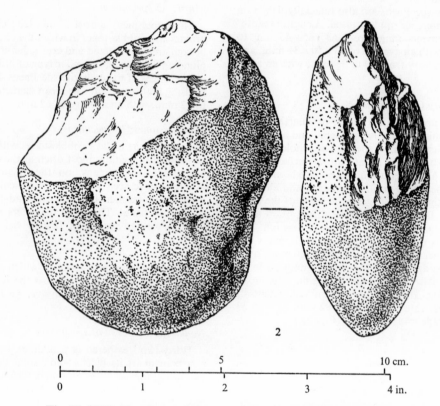

2

Fig. 27. FLK. Two lava end choppers from the '*Zinjanthropus*' level.

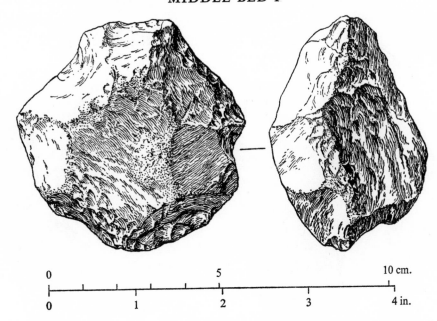

0   5   10 cm.

0   1   2   3   4 in.

Fig. 28. FLK. A quartz discoid, heavily chipped and blunted on the circumference, from the '*Zinjanthropus*' Level.

is possible that in a small number of cases the flaking may have been deliberate and not entirely due to use, but, if so, it is too haphazard for any tool types to be recognized. The mean diameters range from 89 to 44 mm., with an average of 71 mm.

Light-duty flakes and other fragments (*73 specimens*)

These consist of whole or broken flakes or core fragments in which there is shallow chipping along one or more edges. The edges are sharp and even, with no suggestion of the coarse and jagged utilisation often seen in the heavy-duty utilised material. The chipping is usually on one face only and the edges may be straight, concave or convex. (At FLK, straight-edged specimens outnumber the other two categories, whereas at DK, notched specimens are the most numerous.) The whole series is of quartz or quartzite and the majority occurred in the central area of the living floor among the small chips and other waste material. The measurements for the three groups are as follows:

With straight edges (*42 specimens*). The length/breadth measurements range from 46 × 38 mm. to 21 × 18 mm., with an average of 31 × 28 mm. The lengths of the utilised edges range from 37 to 15 mm., with an average of 24 mm.

With concave edges (*20 specimens*). The length/breadth measurements range from 59 × 30 mm. to 27 × 17 mm., with an average of 41 × 29 mm. The notches range in length from 38 to 6 mm., with an average of 16 mm., and in depth from 6 to 1 mm., with an average of 2·6 mm.

With convex edges (*21 specimens*). The length/breadth measurements range from 47 × 32 mm. to 23 × 22 mm., with an average of 36 × 28 mm. The lengths of the utilised edges (measured on the curve) range from 46 to 13 mm., with an average of 27 mm.

DEBITAGE

The total *débitage* amounts to 2,275 specimens. These consist of 258 complete flakes, 1,862 broken flakes and chips and 155 core fragments. Among the whole flakes, 85 per cent are of quartz or quartzite, and the balance of lava. All the lava flakes are divergent, together with the majority of those made from the quartz or quartzite, although twenty-five of the latter are convergent, with the maximum width at the striking platform. Parallel-sided flakes do not occur. Of the complete flakes 68·5 per cent are end-struck. The length/breadth measurements in millimetres are as follows:

Lava	Range	Average
End-struck	110 × 55 to 21 × 14	42 × 32
Side-struck	40 × 50 to 17 × 22	27 × 37
Quartz/quartzite		
End-struck	65 × 44 to 17 × 16	34 × 29
Side-struck	46 × 80 to 16 × 18	24 × 31

Bulbs of percussion

The bulbs of percussion are generally well marked, although in the quartz/quartzite flakes a relatively high

55

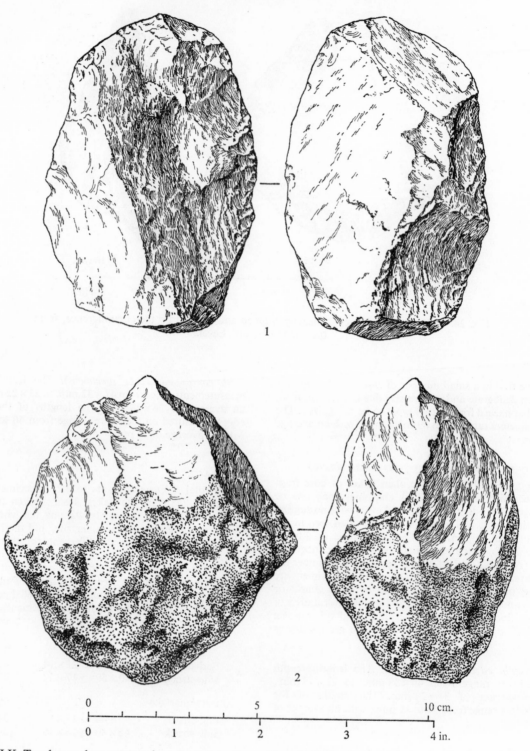

0   5   10 cm.

0   1   2   3   4 in.

Fig. 29. FLK. Two heavy-duty scrapers from the '*Zinjanthropus*' Level. (1) is a double-edged side scraper made from quartz. (2) is made from lava; the edge is crushed and damaged.

56

Fig. 30. FLK. Light-duty quartz and quartzite tools from the '*Zinjanthropus*' level. (1) to (10) scrapers; (11) and (12) burins.

proportion are shattered, together with the striking plat-form. Analysis of the bulbs in the 250 specimens which it is possible to measure gives the following results:

	Lava	Quartz/quartzite
Marked	57·9 %	41·6 %
Slight	18·4 %	25·0 %
Negative	5·2 %	12·0 %
Double	10·5 %	6·4 %
Shattered	7·9 %	15·0 %
Totals	38	212

250

Angles of striking platforms

The angles of the striking platforms can be measured in 135 specimens with the following results:

Angle	Lava	Quartz/quartzite
70–89°	—	10·7 %
90–109°	60·8 %	65·1 %
110–129°	39·1 %	24·1 %
130° +	—	—
Totals	23	112

135

MANUPORTS (96 SPECIMENS)

At DK it was impossible to determine whether the un-modified basalt nodules and blocks found on the occupa-tion surface had been artificially introduced, owing to the proximity of the lava outcrop, but the presence of such stones on the FLK floor is unlikely to be due to natural causes since 20 ft. of sediments overlie the basalt at this locality. Eighty-three nodules or blocks, together with four complete and five broken cobblestones of basalt were found, in which it is impossible to detect any sign of use. In the cobblestones the mean diameters range from 80 to 54 mm., with an average of 58 mm. The majority of the nodules and blocks consists of the local vesicular basalt, but the series also includes one weathered block of quartzite. The mean diameters range from 125 to 44 mm., with an average of 63 mm.

Although a few of these specimens were found among the concentration of *débitage* in the central part of the floor, the majority occurred in the marginal areas, together with the heavy-duty tools and utilised material.

*Analysis of the industry from the
'Zinjanthropus' floor at FLK*

	Nos.	%
Tools	60	2·4
Utilised material	135	5·4
Débitage	2,275	92·1
	2,470	

Tools	Nos.	%
Side choppers	15	25·0
End choppers	2	3·3
Polyhedrons	9	15·0
Discoids (including 1 broken)	3	5·0
Scrapers, heavy-duty	9	15·0
Scrapers, light-duty	18	30·0
Burins	4	6·6
	60	
Utilised material		
'Anvils'	5	3·7
Hammerstones	13	9·6
Cobblestones	4	3·0
Nodules and blocks	40	29·6
Light-duty flakes and other fragments	73	54·0
	135	
Débitage		
Whole flakes	258	11·3
Broken flakes and chips	1,862	81·8
Core fragments	155	6·8
	2,275	

LEVELS IN BED I ABOVE THE 'ZINJANTHROPUS' FLOOR

A number of the levels in Bed I above the '*Zinjan-thropus*' occupation floor (Level 22) yielded a few artefacts and/or fossil bones, as follows:

LEVEL 21

This was a fine-grained tuff that directly overlay the '*Zinjanthropus*' floor. It was approximately 9 in. thick, hard, fine-grained and buff-white in colour, with many rootlet holes in the upper part, some of which penetrated throughout its depth. A bovid right metatarsal and part of a pelvis were found at this level in Cutting F, and the articulated leg and foot bones of a flamingo in Cutting G. (This proved to be one of the very few cases, in any level, where bird bones were found in definite association.)

LEVEL 17

This consisted of a tuff 6–9 in. thick, with uneven upper and lower surfaces. It was cut out in certain places by another tuff which generally overlay it. Five quartz or quartzite artefacts were found in Cutting G, as follows:

Two sub-rectangular fragments of tabular quartzite which are almost identical in appearance and seen to be parts of the same slab. One piece shows 'anvil' type of utilisation on one right-angled edge and has also had one flake removed. (208 × 128 × 76 mm.) The second fragment has been bifacially flaked on the greater part of the circumference and subsequently battered, particularly at one end. It might be described as a large, crude chopper. (189 × 138 × 73 mm.) Two discoidal pieces of quartzite (85 × 78 × 51 mm. and 69 × 68 × 29 mm.) show crude flaking on part of the circumference and some utilisation. There is also one broken flake with slight utilisation on one lateral edge.

LEVEL 16 (a AND b)

This deposit lay 17 ft. below the marker Tuff I^F. In some areas it consisted of two distinct levels (a and b); but, when first observed, it appeared to be a single horizon. The associated radius and ulna of a hyaena were found in this level in Cutting G, together with a few other fragments of poorly preserved bone. Elsewhere the bed yielded no fossils or artefacts.

LEVEL 15

This consisted of a clayey tuff 15 ft. below Tuff I^F. It yielded a number of scattered mammalian bones and nine quartz artefacts in the balk and in cuttings D, F and G. Some of the mammalian limb bones show clear indications of battering and smashing. The artefacts consist of the following:

Two-edged chopper (1 specimen)

Both lateral edges have been bifacially flaked and the flaking also extends in part over the upper and lower faces, resulting in an elliptical cross section. The ends are blunt. (101 × 80 × 43 mm.)

'Anvils' (2 specimens)

Both specimens are high-backed. The first shows flaking and crushed utilisation on the circumference of the base, which is a natural flat cleavage plane. It has also been flaked from two directions along the dorsal crest but shows no utilisation on this edge. (52 × 50 × 35 mm.) The second specimen shows similar utilisation on the circumference of the base and has also been used on the transverse dorsal ridge. (63 × 58 × 41 mm.)

Hammerstones (2 specimens)

There are two quartz nodules with battered utilisation on projecting areas. (66 × 63 × 38 mm. and 83 × 56 × 56 mm.)

Nodules and blocks (2 specimens)

The first is a subtriangular water-worn nodule of quartz with slight flaking and utilisation on one lateral edge. Some chipping is also present on the opposite end. (88 × 78 ×

35 mm.) The second is a triangular quartz fragment in which one edge is slightly concave and shows traces of utilisation. (90 × 76 × 33 mm.)

Débitage

Only one divergent whole flake and one broken flake were found.

LEVEL 13

This horizon was approximately 2 ft. thick and was made up of irregular discontinuous bands of clays and tuffs. In certain areas the tuffs were well defined and evenly bedded but in others they merged into one another and were barely distinguishable. A considerable number of mammalian bones and eleven artefacts were found in Cuttings C, F and G. With the exception of one lava cobblestone, all are of quartz or quartzite. They consist of the following:

Side choppers (2 specimens)

One example is made from a core or possibly part of a thick flake from which the bulb has been removed. It is bifacially flaked along one side to form a jagged edge, 110 mm. long. (74 × 78 × 48 mm.) The second is a crude specimen made on a subdiscoidal fragment. Part of the circumference is bifacially flaked, with flat, plunging scars on the under-surface and almost vertical flaking on the upper face. Length of working edge 92 mm. Utilisation is heavy and has resulted in several small crushed indentations on the working edge and on two short ridges at the butt end. (75 × 86 × 50 mm.)

Polyhedrons (1 specimen)

A slightly oblong specimen, with two main working edges; both partially encircle the tool and are situated at either end. Several longitudinal ridges are also present, abutting on those at the ends. Utilisation has resulted in crushing of the edges, rather than chipping. (70 × 68 × 67 mm.)

'Anvils' (2 specimens)

One is a high-backed example with a flat, circular base, showing crushed and battered utilisation on the greater part of the circumference. The dorsal ridge is bifacially flaked and also shows slight utilisation. (51 × 47 × 43 mm.) The second specimen is very similar, with a flat, circular base and high back, both of which show some battered utilisation. (44 × 41 × 33 mm.)

Utilised cobblestones and nodules

There are one lava cobblestone (66 × 48 × 44 mm.), and three nodules or blocks of quartzite with traces of chipped utilisation on the edges. The average size for the latter is 73 × 66 × 43 mm.

Débitage

This consists of only two quartz core fragments.

LEVEL 12

This was a hard, massive, buff-yellow tuff, often having at its base flattened nodules of limestone. It lays at a depth of $10\frac{1}{2}$–$11\frac{1}{2}$ ft. below the marker Tuff I^F. A few very crushed mammalian bones were found embedded in the limestone nodules. They include an antelope skull and horn cores from Cutting F, and parts of an antelope skeleton from Cutting G.

LEVEL 11

This consisted of a hard, yellow-buff layer of tuff, interbedded between a greenish sandy clay above and a green, well-laminated, silty clay below. The components of this horizon were very variable in thickness. The only fossil remains consisted of the left humerus of a hyaena, found in Cutting G.

LEVEL 10

A consolidated, fairly coarse, grey re-worked tuff, with red rock fragments of sand size. It lay at a depth of approximately 9–10 ft. below the marker Tuff I^F. The upper surface had been eroded and was exceedingly irregular. Fossil bones and some artefacts were recovered from this level in Cuttings D and G.

There are ten quartz or quartzite artefacts, consisting only of utilised material and *débitage*. These comprise four heavy-duty blocks for which the average size is $64 \times 53 \times 36$ mm., with chipped notches on one edge, and one block ($57 \times 53 \times 35$ mm.) with a convex utilised edge, together with three additional miscellaneous utilised fragments and two unmodified core fragments.

The faunal remains consist of three equid phalanges and one incisor, one suid scapula, three hippopotamus molars, several fragments of other teeth and the shaft of a femur, two bovid metapodials, two vertebrae, three scapulae and several other bones.

LEVEL 7

This consisted of an uneven seam of clay interbedded between two layers of yellow-grey tuff. It occurred at a depth of 5–6 ft. below Tuff I^F and was very irregular. No artefacts were recovered from this level and fossil bones occurred only in Cutting D. These are all bovid and consist of the distal end of a left tibia, the proximal end of a right radius and the distal end of a small bovid metapodial.

CHAPTER III

UPPER BED I AND LOWER BED II

Site FLK North: Levels 1 to 6, the Clay with root casts and the Deinotherium Level. Site HWK East: Levels 1 and 2

1. SITE FLK NORTH

Archaelogical number (40)   Geologic locality 45

The depth of deposits revealed in the excavations at this site amounted to 24 ft. There were five implement- and fossil-bearing levels in the upper part of Bed I, extending down to a depth of 5 ft. below the marker Tuff I^F, together with further implementiferous horizons in the lower part of Bed II. (The highest level from which artefacts were recovered was the chert-bearing Sandy Conglomerate which was also excavated at HWK East. This horizon is in the lower part of Middle Bed II and the description of the material is therefore given in chapter IV.)

Four of the levels in Bed I were living floors. The fifth was a butchering site where the skeleton of an elephant was found embedded in clay associated with a number of tools and flakes.

All the levels in Bed I contained large quantities of microfauna, including remains of rodents, insectivores, reptiles, small birds, etc. In Level 5 there also occurred patches of minute bone fragments, consisting entirely of crushed microfaunal bones, which appeared to represent fossil faeces. In Level 4 there were also patches of bone fragments altered by stomach acids. These were in a similar condition to bones that have been regurgitated by large carnivores.

No pattern is discernible in the distribution of the occupation debris in Levels 3, 4 or 5, but in Levels 1/2 there were three areas where remains were particularly concentrated. Two of these were circular, between 8 and 10 ft. in diameter, and lay near to one another. The third area lay to the north-east and was less well defined. Both the circular areas yielded more *débitage*, light-duty tools and utilised material than were found elsewhere on the occupation surfaces.

Among the faunal remains are three frontlets of *Parmularius altidens* with the horn cores and frontlets preserved, which exhibit depressed fractures above the orbits, indicating that the animals were killed by blows, delivered at close quarters.

The industries from all the levels are very similar, although there is some variation in the proportions of the different elements, particularly of tools to utilised material and *débitage*. Choppers, especially side choppers, are the predominant tool type. Polyhedrons are relatively scarce in this context, unlike other Bed I assemblages where they occur in comparable numbers to choppers. If, as has been suggested, they represent an alternative method of obtaining a sharp, jagged, chopper-like working edge when available material consisted mostly of irregular-shaped nodules, their relative scarcity at this site may well be due to the fact that most of the tools were made from rounded cobbles.

The site is situated on the far side of the ridge which lies to the north of FLK (Pl. 11). It was discovered on 15 August 1960 when men of the Geological Survey, Dodoma, were digging a test pit for Dr R. Pickering in order to verify the existence of Marker Tuff I^F in this area, where it had become masked by scree. A level rich in cultural and faunal remains was found beneath Tuff I^F and a trial trench was then cut into the deposits, extending the original pit to the southeast. This yielded a large number of artefacts and fossil bones immediately beneath the Tuff and down to a depth of about 1 ft., the lower part of the deposit being relatively barren. It was subsequently found, however, that further remains occurred at a number of lower levels.

At this site, in common with FLK NN, former erosion has removed Beds III and IV and also the upper part of Bed II. The eroded surface was overlain by a fawn-coloured tuff which rested unconformably on Bed II, within 13 ft. of the I–II contact (Fig. 31; Pl. 12). The sequence of deposits in Bed I and the lower part of Bed II, as revealed in the excavations, is as follows:

Fawn-coloured tuff.

Bed II. (*a*) The highest preserved deposit of Bed II consisted of a grey-brown silty clay with a maximum thickness of $6\frac{1}{2}$ ft. It contained no remains of any kind.

(*b*) A sandy conglomerate, about 1 ft. thick yielded artefacts made from chert, in addition to the usual quartz and lava specimens. (This level corresponds to Levels 3, 4 and 5 at HWK East, where it is richer in tools and where more extensive excavations were carried out.)

(*c*) A horizon of grey-green silty clay, approximately 1 ft. thick, containing a few limestone nodules.

(*d*) A chocolate-brown clay, 1–2 ft. thick, separated from the underlying level by massive blocks of limestone.

(*e*) A second grey-green silty clay, varying in thickness from 6 in. to 2 ft. This level yielded the skeleton of a *Deinotherium* and some associated artefacts.

(*f*) An almost continuous layer of massive nodular limestone measuring up to $1\frac{1}{2}$ ft. in thickness.

(*g*) Another level of grey-green silty clay, approximately 4 ft. thick, containing many rod-shaped and tuber-like concretions which appear to have formed round roots and stems. This level yielded a small number of artefacts and fossil bones.

(*h*) A coarse-grained tuff, generally 6 in. to 1 ft. thick, but attaining a greater thickness where it filled depressions in the underlying Tuff I^F.

Bed I. (*a*) The marker Tuff I^F.

(The following levels all yielded abundant cultural and faunal remains)

(*b*) Levels 1, 2 and 3. These consisted of a single horizon, 2–3 ft. thick, of a grey-brown silty clay. It was arbitrarily subdivided into three levels for convenience in excavation, although the deposit was uniform in composition, with the exception of a slight colour change some 9 in. from the top.

(*c*) Level 4. A dark chocolate-brown silty clay, varying in thickness from $1\frac{1}{2}$ ft. to 3 or 4 in. In certain areas it lensed out entirely, so that Level 3 rested directly on Level 5.

(*d*) Level 5. A greenish-yellow clay. When excavated, this deposit broke with a characteristic conchoidal fracture. One or more ferruginous bands, usually about 1 in. thick, together with several thin horizontal seams of fine-grained white tuff occurred near the base.

(*e*) Level 6. A dark greyish-brown silty clay with white streaks, becoming lighter in colour when dry; approximately $1\frac{1}{2}$ ft. thick.

All these levels were contorted and faulted on a local scale, with displacements of only a few inches.

The excavations were carried out in a series of five trenches, lying parallel to the original Trial Trench and orientated approximately north-west/ south-east. The Trial Trench, as well as Trenches I and II, were excavated during the 1960–1 season and Trenches III–V during the following year. The first two trenches were each 6 ft. wide, but it was later found that there was less chance of damage to the fossil bones if the trenches were wider. Trenches III–V were, therefore, increased in width to $10\frac{1}{2}$ ft. The back wall, or south-east limit of the excavated area, was retained as a single, continuous face and eventually provided a section through the deposits, including the lower part of Bed II. The trenches varied in length, depending on the configuration of the erosion slope to the north-west; the maximum length was 24 ft. in Trench II. Each trench was excavated in sections of convenient length, varying from 6 to 10 ft. Sieves with $\frac{1}{16}$ in. mesh were used throughout the excavations. Experimental washing of the soil, when water was available, proved unsatisfactory, owing to damage to the microfaunal remains. It was found that many of these small bones had incipient cracks, held together by clay which dissolved when wet

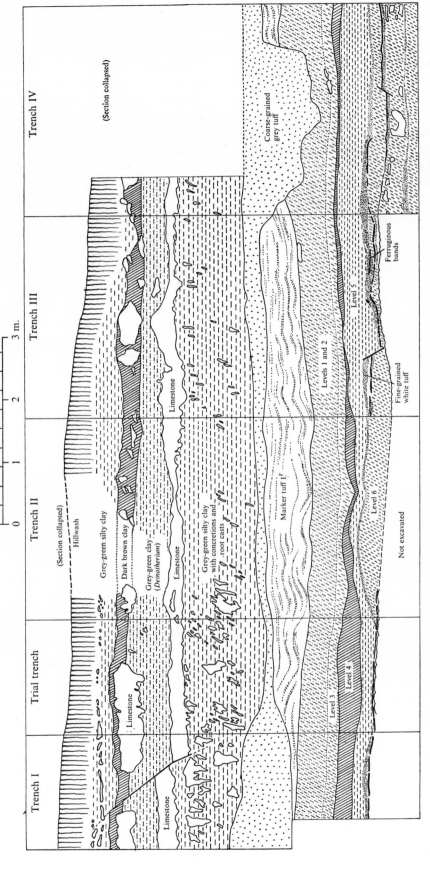

Fig. 31. FLK North. Section exposed on the south-east face of the excavated area, showing the Marker Tuff I^F, the upper part of Bed I with the occupation levels and the lower part of Bed II, overlain unconformably by Bed V.

and left nothing but a number of fragments, too small to be reassembled.

The deposits at this site proved to be some of the most difficult to excavate of any at Olduvai. During the rainy season the clays became water-logged and impossible to work, whilst in the dry weather they contracted on exposure, so that the sides of the trenches collapsed within a few days of their being opened. It was eventually found practicable to work only during the dry season and to shore up the sides of each trench with sandbags as soon as they were exposed.

UPPER BED I

LEVEL 6 (The lowest excavated horizon)

It was only possible to excavate this level in Trenches IV and V and in a small part of Trench II, since it was overlain elsewhere by a massive layer of limestone, several feet thick, which could not be removed by normal methods of excavation. The more important finds consisted of the skeleton of an elephant (cf. *Elephas recki*) associated with a number of artefacts, in Trenches IV and V (Fig. 32, and Pl. 13) and a suid skull in Trench II.

The elephant skeleton was almost complete except for the tusks and skull and was, on the whole, well preserved. It lay with the head to the south-east. The mandible, although crushed, was reasonably intact, but the skull was represented only by some teeth, the occipital condyles (which lay uppermost) and by large numbers of small fragments, cemented into blocks of limestone. Considerable displacement of the bones had occurred, similar to that which takes place when scavengers tug at a carcass, so that it was not possible to determine with certainty the original positions. The fact that the majority of the limb bones belonging to the left side, and particularly the left forefoot, were beneath those of the right side and also beneath many of the ribs and vertebrae suggests that the skeleton probably lay on the left side originally. The epiphyses of the limb bones are mostly unfused, with the exception of the humeri and the distal ends of the tibiae, although

the animal appears to have been fully as large as a present-day adult elephant.

A few heavy-duty tools and utilised pieces, together with a number of flakes, were found near the skeleton, in a similar manner to the tools found with the skeleton of a *Deinotherium* at the base of Bed II (see p. 85). This find clearly does not represent an occupation surface such as occurred in the higher levels at the site. There was no cultural material other than that directly associated with the elephant skeleton, and remains of bovids and other animals whose broken bones are normally found on living sites were scarce. It represents, rather, a butchering site where an elephant was cut up by early man, who may have come upon it accidentally, or deliberately driven it into a swamp to be slaughtered. The tools found nearby would seem to represent those used for cutting the meat off the carcass.

In addition to the nearly complete skeleton, a few bones belonging to a second elephant were found. These consist of a femoral condyle, a magnum and some fragmentary foot bones. It is difficult to account for their presence, since there was no other suggestion of a second skeleton.

THE INDUSTRY

The total number of specimens found in association with the elephant skeleton amounts to 123, of which 7·2 per cent is *débitage*. There are only five tools, all of which are heavy-duty. Heavy-duty utilised material, such as 'anvils', hammerstones, nodules and cobblestones, amounts to a further twenty-nine specimens. Less than half the heavy-duty tools and utilised material are of quartz and quartzite, but 96 per cent of the unmodified flakes are of these materials, once again suggesting that many of the sharp flakes which occur at Oldowan sites are more likely to have been cutting tools than debris from tool-making. In addition to the flakes of quartz, quartzite and lava, there are two flakes of a white-flecked brown chert. Light-duty tools are not present and the average size of both the tools and heavy-duty utilised material is greater than in the other levels at this site, the average mean diameter for the tools being 67 mm. and for the utilised material 78 mm.

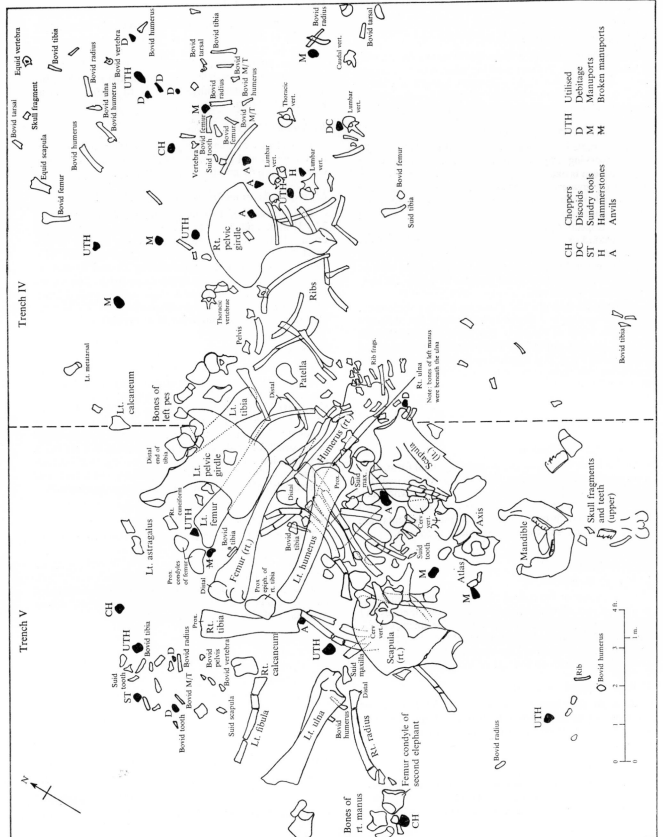

Fig 32 FLK North. Level 6. Plan of the elephant skeleton and associated artefacts

CH	Choppers	UTH		Utilised
DC	Discoids	D		Debitage
ST	Sundry tools	M		Manuports
H	Hammerstones	ꙨM		Broken manuports
A	Anvils			

Trench IV

Trench V

N

TOOLS

Side chopper (1 specimen)

This is made on a lava nodule. It is bifacially flaked, with a relatively short, thickset working edge, which is jagged and sharp, with only slight utilisation. Length of edge 75 mm. Length/breadth/thickness 55 × 86 × 53 mm., mean diameter 68 mm. Edge/circumference ratio 30 per cent.

Two-edged choppers (3 specimens)

One example is made on a fragment of tabular quartzite with a working edge at either end. Part of one lateral edge has been broken away and the breadth must originally have been greater. The flaking is bifacial and shallower than usual, resulting in more even working edges; slight chipped utilisation is present. Lengths of edges 107 and 63 mm., respectively.

The second specimen is of lava. It is oblong and bifacially flaked across both extremities as well as along both lateral edges. In general form it resembles a crude discoid with an unusually thick cross-section. Lengths of edges 120 mm. and 60 mm. respectively.

In the third example, also made on a lava cobblestone, one working edge is at one end and a second lies obliquely across the body of the tool. The edges are jagged, with bifacial chipped utilisation. Their lengths are 56 and 54 mm. respectively. The length/breadth/thickness measurements for the three specimens range from 106 × 82 × 40 mm. to 72 × 53 × 52 mm., with an average of 87 × 68 × 50 mm., and the mean diameters vary from 76 to 59 mm., with an average of 68 mm. The average edge length is 76 mm.

'Proto-biface' (1 specimen)

This is made from lava and is oval in general form, with a plano-convex cross-section. The flaking extends over the entire upper and lower faces and also round the whole circumference. The tip is bluntly pointed and shows chipped utilisation. Length/breadth/thickness measurements are 75 × 61 × 43 mm. and the mean diameter is 59 mm.

UTILISED MATERIAL

'Anvils' (6 specimens)

These consist of five cuboid blocks of quartz or quartzite and one of lava, all of which show battering on the edges and a minimum of flaking. Although all the specimens exhibit evidence of utilisation, it is possible that they were brought to the site as raw material. The mean diameters range from 104 to 70 mm., with an average of 85 mm.

Hammerstones (4 specimens)

There are four lava cobblestones in which the ends or other projecting areas show pitting and bruising. The mean diameters range from 77 to 61 mm., with an average of 69 mm.

Cobblestones (6 specimens)

These consist of cobblestones which appear to have been broken by artificial means but do not show any bruising and pitting on the surface, such as is normally found on hammerstones. They seem to have been used with sufficient violence to cause fracturing of the whole specimen rather than superficial damage to the surface. One specimen resembles an anvil, but is in such a poor state of preservation that it is impossible to determine the original form. The mean diameters range from 81 to 66 mm., with an average of 77 mm.

Nodules or blocks (2 specimens)

Two blocks of quartzite show battering and crushing on the edges and also on parts of the surface. The mean diameters are 67 and 65 mm. respectively.

Light-duty flakes and other fragments (5 specimens)

These consist of two broken quartz flakes measuring 32 × 31 mm. and 31 × 29 mm. respectively, with shallow unifacial chipping on straight edges and of two broken chert flakes with notches on the edges. One specimen (33 × 29 mm.) has two notches measuring 24 and 23 mm. in width and 4 and 2 mm. in depth respectively. The second specimen (27 × 21 mm.) has a single small notch 12 mm. wide and 1·5 mm. deep. A small quartz chip (24 × 20 mm.) also shows a crushed indentation at the tip.

DEBITAGE

The *débitage* consists of eighteen whole flakes, two resharpening flakes, sixty-five broken flakes and chips and ten core fragments. With the exception of two parallel-sided specimens, all the flakes are divergent. As noted previously, only three are of lava and these are cortex flakes struck from cobblestones. The series of whole flakes is too small for analysis but it may be noted that the bulbs of percussion and the angles of the striking platforms are not so variable as in other Oldowan assemblages. End- and side-struck flakes occur in almost equal proportions.

MANUPORTS (7 SPECIMENS)

These consist of four complete and one broken lava cobblestones and two irregular-shaped nodules, in which the mean diameters range from 96 to 70 mm., with an average of 81 mm.

Since this assemblage includes only five tools, no detailed analysis will be given, but the proportions of tools, utilised material and *débitage* is as follows:

	Nos.	%
Tools	5	4·1
Utilised material	23	18·7
Débitage	95	77·2
	123	

LEVEL 5

Artefacts and mammalian bones were noticeably more plentiful at the top of this deposit than in the lower part, although the surface did not appear to have been broken down by weathering to the extent seen on the occupation floors at FLK and FLK NN.

Occupation debris was found scattered over the area excavated, with no marked concentration in any particular part such as occurred in Levels 1 and 2, although both artefacts and fossil bones were rather more plentiful in Trenches IV and V than elsewhere (Fig. 33, in pocket). Minor earth movements had particularly affected this level and had contributed to further fracturing of the faunal remains after they had become fossilised. Among the finds should be mentioned the hominid phalanx of the big toe (H. 10) and one of the three frontlets of *Parmularius altidens* with depressed fractures that are described in chapter VIII.

As noted earlier, there were patches of minute bone fragments, nearly all too broken for identification, but in which it was possible to recognise the bones of rodents, insectivores, birds and chameleons. These patches varied in diameter from 2×3 in. to 9×12 in. and were $\frac{1}{2}$–2 in. thick. They appear to represent the faeces of creatures who subsisted largely on a diet of small mammals, reptiles and birds. The fact that the bone fragments have not been destroyed or even affected by stomach acids indicates that this is unlikely to be carnivore dung. The only alternative appears to be that it is of primate origin and, in view of the fact that it was found on a living floor, a hominid origin cannot be excluded. A sample was sent to Dr R. Heizer of the Department of Anthropology, University of California, Berkeley, where various types of faeces have been studied. Dr Lewis K. Napton has submitted a brief report in which he states, 'A possible approach to establishing the true nature of this specimen would be by detailed analytic identification of the various diminutive bones visible in the matrix. In general, the appearance of the material and the clustered tiny broken bones suggest that the specimen is ancient excrement.'

Since such small vertebrates are consumed whole by some present-day primitive peoples, it may be assumed that they almost certainly formed part of the diet of the early hominids. If such were the case, the crushed small bones would of necessity be found in the faeces, since they would not be dissolved by stomach acids, as in carnivores.

THE INDUSTRY

There are 151 artefacts in this assemblage. It compares closely with those from other levels in respect of tool types, but differs in the almost total absence of light-duty tools and light-duty utilised material. There is the usual imbalance between the materials of the tools and *débitage*, with only 20·6 per cent of tools made from quartz or quartzite, in contrast to 77·2 per cent of the *débitage*. Side choppers are the most common tool type.

TOOLS

Side choppers (14 specimens)

With the exception of one example made on an irregular-shaped block of quartzite, the entire series is made on well-rounded lava cobblestones. A few specimens are crude and may be unfinished, but most consist of classic Oldowan choppers with bifacial multiple flaking of the working edges. Evidence of utilisation is usually present and sometimes includes small crushed indentations. Three specimens show hammerstone type of utilisation on the butt ends. The length/breadth/thickness measurements range from $107 \times 93 \times 61$ mm. to $38 \times 61 \times 33$ mm., with an average of $63 \times 76 \times 46$ mm., and the mean diameters vary from 83 to 44 mm., with an average of 61 mm. The edge/circumference ratios vary from 51 to 21 per cent, with an average of 37 per cent.

End choppers (4 specimens)

All four examples are made on lava cobblestones. One specimen has been utilised as a hammerstone at the butt end, where it is extensively battered and pitted. The working edges are bifacially flaked and jagged. They are less damaged by use than those in most of the side choppers. Length/breadth/thickness measurements range from $93 \times 54 \times 54$ mm. to $72 \times 50 \times 45$ mm., with an average of $77 \times 59 \times 44$ mm., and the mean diameters vary from 67 to 44 mm., with an average of 60 mm. The edge/circumference ratios vary from 41 to 12 per cent, with an average of 24 per cent.

Two-edged choppers (4 specimens)

These tools are made from lava. They are oblong, with blunt, truncated extremities and two longitudinal working edges. In three examples these are situated on either lateral edge: in the fourth they are on the same side; that is, one edge has been vertically flaked and the upper and lower edges subsequently trimmed. The length/breadth/thickness measurements range from $91 \times 73 \times 67$ mm. to $70 \times 61 \times 40$ mm., with an average of $81 \times 68 \times 53$ mm., and the mean diameters range from 77 to 57 mm., with an average of 68 mm. The edges vary in length from 94 to 53 mm., with an average of 74 mm.

There is also one example of an unfinished chopper. It is in particularly fresh condition and shows no trace of utilisation. (A flake found 4 ft. distant can be fitted to it.) (80 × 71 × 45 mm.)

Discoids (3 specimens)

All three are small, light-duty examples; two are of quartz or quartzite and one of lava. They are bifacially flaked round the whole circumference and exhibit sharp, jagged edges, similar to those seen on choppers. The length/breadth/thickness measurements range from 80 × 71 × 45 mm. to 34 × 31 × 24 mm., with an average of 47 × 42 × 28 mm., and the mean diameters vary from 65 to 29 mm., with an average of 36 mm.

Spheroid (1 specimen)

There is a single example of a spheroid, made from lava. It is well-made and symmetrical, with all projecting parts reduced by battering. (74 × 73 × 67 mm.)

Scrapers, heavy-duty (3 specimens)

Two subtriangular fragments of tabular quartzite are steeply trimmed along one edge from flat natural cleavage planes. Length/breadth measurements are 90 × 73 mm. and 74 × 66 mm. respectively. The working edges are curved and measure 79 and 51 mm. (along the curve). The third example is a crude hollow scraper; it consists of a subtriangular lava cobblestone with a steeply trimmed notch 19 mm. wide and 5 mm. deep on one edge. (65 × 64 mm.)

UTILISED MATERIAL

'Anvils' (5 specimens)

These consist of three angular quartzite blocks and two broken lava cobblestones in which there is battered utilisation on one or more edges which approximate to a right angle. One specimen also shows pitting and bruising similar to that which occurs on hammerstones. The mean diameters range from 78 to 59 mm., with an average of 68 mm.

Hammerstones (10 specimens)

Ten lava cobblestones are pitted, bruised and battered, usually at the extremities but sometimes also on other projecting parts. The mean diameters range from 73 to 51 mm., with an average of 63 mm.

Cobblestones, nodules and blocks (14 specimens)

These consist of seven lava cobblestones with some chipping and shattering. The mean diameters range from 73 to 41 mm., with an average of 56 mm. There are also four angular quartzite blocks and three weathered lava nodules which show similar utilisation. The mean diameters range from 76 to 60 mm., with an average of 67 mm.

DEBITAGE

There are fourteen whole flakes, fifty-two broken flakes or chips and twenty-six core fragments. Ten of the whole flakes are divergent, two parallel-sided and two convergent. The majority are end-struck and show great variation in the bulbs of percussion, but the angles of the striking platforms are less variable than usual. They are all between 123° and 100°, with an average of 120°. The flakes range in length from 51 to 18 mm., with an average of 32 mm.

MANUPORTS (29 SPECIMENS)

These consist of fifteen whole and broken lava cobblestones lacking any evidence of utilisation, in which the mean diameters range from 79 to 51 mm., with an average of 64 mm., together with thirteen nodules or blocks of lava and one of quartzite. The mean diameters for the latter range from 84 to 40 mm., with an average of 62 mm.

Analysis of the industry from FLK North, Level 5

	Nos.	%
Tools	30	19·9
Utilised material	29	19·2
Débitage	92	60·9
	151	
Tools		
Side choppers	14	46·7
End choppers	4	13·3
Two-edged choppers	4	13·3
Unfinished chopper	1	3·3
Discoids	3	10·0
Spheroid	1	3·3
Scrapers, heavy-duty	3	10·0
	30	
Utilised material		
'Anvils'	5	17·2
Hammerstones	10	34·5
Cobblestones	7	24·1
Nodules and blocks	7	24·1
	29	
Débitage		
Whole flakes	14	15·3
Broken flakes and chips	52	56·5
Core fragments	26	28·2
	92	

LEVEL 4

Finds in this level were scattered over the area excavated (880 sq.ft.) without any recognisable pattern of distribution (Fig. 34, in pocket). A total of eighty-four artefacts and manuports was recovered, a considerably lower figure than for any other horizon. This is in part due to the sparseness of the finds and in part to the fact that the bed was greatly reduced in thickness in certain areas, so that a smaller volume of deposit was excavated. Faunal remains amounted to 929 specimens, most of which were in particularly fragmentary condition. The patches of what appeared to be a form of carnivore dung or regurgitated material were most common in the Trial Trench and in Trench I. They consisted of part-digested bone fragments, in which the surface of the bone had become corroded by stomach acids. Teeth and broken mandibles of small mammals, such as ground-squirrels and hedgehogs, were often present amongst the bone fragments.[1]

THE INDUSTRY

Side choppers and polyhedrons are the most common tools, with four examples of each.

The amount of *débitage* is unusually low, comprising only 29·8 per cent of the total, whereas the utilised material is proportionately more common than in other levels, with 41·8 per cent. Light-duty tools and utilised flakes are scarce and are represented only by one small end-scraper and one notched flake.

TOOLS

Side choppers (4 specimens)

Two examples are made on lava cobblestones, one on an irregular weathered lava nodule and one on an angular block of quartzite. Hammerstone utilisation is present on the butt end in two specimens. The working edges are bifacially flaked and jagged, with some evidence of utilisation. The length/breadth/thickness measurements range from 79 × 87 × 55 mm., to 69 × 80 × 31 mm., with an average of 73 × 82 × 45 mm., and the mean diameters vary from 77 to 60 mm., with an average of 67 mm. The edge/circumference ratio varies from 49 per cent to 17 per cent, with an average of 33 per cent.

End choppers (2 specimens)

One specimen is made from an oblong lava cobblestone in which one end is bifacially flaked to a sharp, jagged edge. Utilisation is slight. (70 × 61 × 41 mm. Mean diameter 57 mm. Edge/circumference ratio 20 per cent.) The second example is unifacial with the flakes struck from the cortex surface. (79 × 66 × 57 mm. Mean diameter 67 mm. Edge/circumference ratio 20 per cent.)

Two-edged choppers (2 specimens)

Both these tools are made on roughly discoidal lava cobblestones. The trimmed edges are on opposite sides and cortex surface is present on both the upper and lower faces. The flaking is bifacial in one specimen, and from one direction only in the second. The edges show both chipped and crushed utilisation and vary in length from 75 to 40 mm., with an average of 52 mm. The length/breadth/

---

[1] At the present time, patches of material regurgitated by the larger carnivores such as hyaenas or lions can often be seen on the plains in the neighbourhood of Olduvai Gorge. The bone fragments are, on the whole, larger and less rounded than those in the fossil material, and there are usually some perishable substances, such as hooves, hair, pieces of hide and sometimes cloth, in addition to bone fragments and teeth.

thickness measurements are 85 × 84 × 57 mm. (mean diameter 75 mm.) and 81 × 67 × 35 mm. (mean diameter 61 mm.).

Chisel-edged chopper (1 specimen)

This is a unifacial specimen. The working edge, which is at right angles to the upper and lower faces, has been flaked from the cortex surface. The edge is jagged and sharp and appears to have been damaged by use. (77 × 63 × 54 mm.)

'Proto-biface' (1 specimen)

This is made from a lava cobblestone. It is bifacially trimmed round the greater part of the circumference but has an area of cortex surface at the butt end. The flaking is crude, with some plunging scars. A longitudinal ridge is present on both the upper and lower faces, at the intersection of the scars from either edge. The tip has been broken but the specimen appears to have had a sharp point before it became damaged. The edge is jagged and shows chipped utilisation on both sides. Two crushed indentations are also present. The length/breadth/thickness measurements are 75 × 77 × 65 mm., with a mean diameter of 72 mm., and the edge/circumference ratio is 73 per cent. (Fig. 43, no. 1.)

Polyhedrons (3 specimens)

Two examples are made from lava and one from quartzite. All are angular, with short, jagged cutting edges, usually intersecting. The extent of utilisation varies from slight chipping to heavy battering and blunting. The length/breadth/thickness measurements range from 73 × 64 × 60 mm. to 54 × 51 × 50 mm., with an average of 62 × 58 × 56 mm., and the mean diameters vary from 65 to 51 mm., with an average of 62 mm.

Discoid (1 specimen)

This is a small, slightly oblong specimen made from quartz, with bifacial trimming on the greater part of the circumference. The cross-section is biconvex and the edge is sharp, with only slight utilisation. (39 × 35 × 27 mm. Mean diameter 33 mm.)

Subspheroids (3 specimens)

All three examples are made on cobblestones; two are of lava and one of quartz or quartzite. The surfaces are flaked and battered, except for a small area of cortex on each specimen. Length/breadth/thickness measurements range from 85 × 83 × 77 mm. to 60 × 60 × 51 mm., with an average mean diameter of 66 mm.

Scrapers (2 specimens)

These consist of one heavy-duty and one light-duty example. The first is high-backed and made on a wedge-shaped quartzite nodule, with almost vertical trimming and an evenly curved working edge which shows chipped utilisation on the upper face (76 × 58 mm.). The second specimen is of quartz. It is small and stumpy, with trimming on both lateral edges as well as at the tip. (39 × 34 mm.)

UTILISED MATERIAL

Hammerstones (5 specimens)

These consist of one quartz nodule and five lava cobblestones. They are characterized by pitting, bruising and some battering, usually on projecting areas. The mean diameters range from 79 to 47 mm., with an average of 64 mm. (Fig. 43, no. 2.)

Cobblestones (11 specimens)

Eleven lava cobblestones show evidence of utilisation in the form of shattering and fracture of the extremities. The mean diameters range from 71 to 54 mm., with an average of 63 mm.

Nodules and blocks (11 specimens)

Nine quartz or quartzite blocks and two weathered lava nodules show some degree of utilisation, usually in the form of chipping and a minimum amount of flaking on natural sharp edges and ridges. The mean diameters range from 86 to 35 mm., with an average of 60 mm.

Light-duty flake (1 specimen)

A stumpy side-struck flake shows some chipping on the edges and a notch 7 mm. wide and 2 mm. deep.

DEBITAGE

There are only five complete and fifteen broken flakes, four of which are of lava. They are all irregular and range in length/breadth from 49 × 47 mm. to 27 × 25 mm.

MANUPORTS

These consist of twelve lava cobbles and five irregular nodules of vesicular basalt lacking any evidence of utilisation. The mean diameters range from 83 to 46 mm., with an average of 62 mm.

Analysis of the industry from FLK North, Level 4

	Nos.	%
Tools	19	28·3
Utilised material	28	41·8
Débitage	20	29·8
	67	
Tools		
Side choppers	4	21·0
End choppers	2	10·5
Two-edged choppers	2	10·5
Chisel-edged chopper	1	5·3
'Proto-biface'	1	5·3
Polyhedrons	3	15·7
Discoid	1	5·3
Subspheroids	3	15·7
Scraper, heavy-duty	1	5·3
Scraper, light-duty	1	5·3
	19	

Utilised material	Nos.	%
Hammerstones	5	17·8
Cobblestones	11	39·3
Nodules and blocks	11	39·3
Light-duty flake	1	3·5
	28	
Débitage		
Whole flakes	5	25·0
Broken flakes and chips	15	75·0
Core fragments	—	—
	20	

LEVELS 1, 2 AND 3

As mentioned earlier, when the Trial Trench and Trench I were excavated during the first season, the uppermost deposit of brown silty clay, 2–3 ft. thick, which lay directly beneath the marker Tuff I^F, was considered as a single horizon. Later, during the rains, when the clay had become damp, it was possible to distinguish a reddish-brown band a few inches thick at a depth of approximately 9 in. from the top. This was subsequently regarded as the lower limit of Level 1.

Cultural and faunal material occurred throughout the clay, but was markedly more abundant at the top, as far down as the reddened band, and again at approximately 9 in. from the base (Fig. 35, in pocket; Pls. 14, 15). The intervening part of the deposit was relatively poor in remains and they were also scarce in the lowest few inches. The conditions seem to indicate two periods of occupation within this bed, represented by the levels where remains were concentrated, from both of which debris had sunk into the underlying clay. When excavations were resumed during 1961–2, the clay was therefore subdivided, the lowest level being termed Level 3, the intervening relatively barren zone Level 2 and the topmost layer above the red-brown band Level 1. In the description of the industry Levels 1 and 2 have been considered jointly, since the scant material from Level 2 is almost certainly derived from Level 1. The few remains from the lowest part of the bed, below the relatively rich horizon 9 in. from the base, have been assigned to Level 3 for a similar reason.

The three areas in Levels 1 and 2 where occupation debris was particularly concentrated and where remains were as dense as in the central area of the 'Zinjanthropus' floor are shown in Fig. 36 (in pocket). They consisted of two adjacent localities in Trench IV and a third, about 22 ft. distant, partly in the Trial Trench, Trench I and the original test pit. The intervening area also contained artefacts and fossil bones, but these were more sparsely distributed. The two areas of concentrated remains in Trench IV were roughly circular and measured 8 × 9 ft. and 9 × 10 ft. in diameter. In common with the central area of the 'Zinjanthropus' floor, *débitage*, light-duty tools and utilised material were more plentiful within these two areas than elsewhere. There was, however, a higher proportion of heavy-duty tools than at FLK. In the third area, to the north-east, the pattern of distribution and the outer limits were less well defined.

The shafts of the marrow-containing bones of the larger animals were mostly broken, but metacarpals and metatarsals, phalanges, etc., were often found intact (Pl. 15). Very few bones lay in articulated positions. Skulls had also been broken open except for those belonging to the small carnivore *Otocyon*. One of the three antelope frontlets with depressed fractures was obtained from this level (Pl. 41).

LEVEL 3

THE INDUSTRY

The total number of artefacts from this level amounts to 171. There are also thirty-nine manuports. This is a somewhat larger assemblance than from any of the other three lower levels, but not comparable to the series from Levels 1/2. The proportions of the various components are very similar to those from Levels 5 and 6, but differ considerably from Level 4, where there are fewer unmodified flakes and where more of the tools are made from quartz or quartzite.

Choppers are the most common tools, amounting to twenty specimens, of which sixteen are side choppers. They are usually made on lava cobblestones. A few light-duty utilised flakes occur, although only one was found in Levels 4 and 5. Quartz and quartzite predominate in the *débitage*, although most of the tools are made of lava.

TOOLS

Side choppers (16 specimens)

Twelve examples are made on cobblestones and four on irregular-shaped weathered nodules. Two are of quartz or quartzite and the remainder of lava. Bifacial specimens with multiple flake scars on either side and jagged working edges are the most common form. There are, however, three examples which have only been flaked on one face with cortex surface on the obverse. There is also one specimen with a single large scar on one face, opposed to multiple scars on the opposite side. The extent of utilisation varies considerably. In some specimens the edges are sharp and fresh and in others they are blunted by heavy chipping and crushing. The butt ends generally consist of rounded cortex surface. Six examples exhibit pitting and bruising resulting from hammerstone type of utilisation. The length/breadth/thickness measurements range from 87 × 88 × 48 mm. to 38 × 68 × 38 mm., with an average of 66 × 80 × 49 mm., and the mean diameters vary from 74 to 48 mm., with an average of 64 mm. The average edge/circumference ratio is 29 per cent.

End choppers (3 specimens)

All three examples are made on lava cobblestones, with cortex surface retained at the butt ends. The working edges are bifacially flaked and jagged, with multiple scars on either face. In one example the edge is sharp and fresh but in the other two utilisation has resulted in complete blunting of the edges and a number of small crushed indentations. The length/breadth/thickness measurements range from 91 × 76 × 57 mm. to 63 × 53 × 55 mm., with an average of 76 × 64 × 56 mm., and the mean diameters vary from 74 to 57 mm., with an average of 65 mm. The average edge/circumference ratio is 31 per cent.

There is, in addition, one example of a broken lava chopper which may originally have been two-edged.

Polyhedrons (3 specimens)

All three examples are made of lava. In one specimen there are four working edges, all of which are blunted and chipped by use. In the remaining two there are three intersecting edges showing slight chipped utilisation. The length/breadth/thickness measurements range from 86 × 71 × 60 mm. to 59 × 48 × 35 mm., with an average of 71 × 57 × 50 mm., and the mean diameters vary from 72 to 47 mm., with an average of 60 mm.

Discoids (2 specimens)

There is one light-duty example, made from quartz or quartzite. It is elliptical in cross-section and slightly oblong, with bifacial flaking round the whole circumference. The second example is made from part of a lava cobblestone, with cortex surface retained in the central part of one face. The opposite face has been flaked all over and the greater part of the circumference has also been bifacially flaked. The cross-section is plano-convex and the edge jagged with some blunting from utilisation. Length/breadth/thickness measurements are 85 × 82 × 54 mm. and 47 × 43 × 20 mm. respectively, with mean diameters of 73 mm. and 36 mm.

Subspheroids (2 specimens)

These are both made from lava. Nearly all the projecting ridges have been obliterated by battering. Length/breadth/thickness measurements are 54 × 45 × 42 mm. and 78 × 63 × 63 mm., with mean diameters of 47 mm. and 68 mm. (pl. 16.)

Scraper, heavy-duty (1 specimen)

This is an oblong fragment of quartzite with a natural flat surface on one face. One lateral edge has been steeply trimmed to form a side scraper. (81 × 58 × 42 mm. Mean diameter 60 mm.)

UTILISED MATERIAL

'Anvils' (4 specimens)

These consist of three cuboid blocks of quartz or quartzite and one of lava, with crushing and battering on one or more edges. These approximate to a right angle. The mean diameters range from 72 to 63 mm., with an average of 68 mm.

Hammerstones (15 specimens)

This is a series of lava cobblestones with pitting and bruising on the surface, usually at the extremities. The mean diameters range from 84 to 50 mm., with an average of 67 mm.

Cobblestones (5 specimens)

These consist of five lava cobblestones which have been broken by heavy use and do not show the type of utilisation seen on hammerstones. The mean diameters range from 63 to 51 mm., with an average of 60 mm.

Nodules and blocks (14 specimens)

Six examples are of quartz or quartzite and the remainder are of lava. The edges show a minimum amount of wear. The mean diameters range from 89 to 31 mm., with an average of 58 mm.

Light-duty flakes and other fragments (11 specimens)

These consist of whole and broken quartz flakes and one thin fragment of tabular quartzite with utilisation on the edges. The length/breadth measurements range from 48 to 40 mm. to 20 × 18 mm., with an average of 32 × 30 mm.

DEBITAGE

This includes twenty-eight whole flakes, sixty-one broken flakes and chips and five core fragments. The proportions of raw material are 85 per cent quartz or quartzite and 15 per cent lava. Twenty-four of the whole flakes are divergent, two parallel-sided and two convergent; nearly all are end-struck. The bulbs of percussion are variable and the angles of the striking platforms range from 120° to 95°, with an average of 111°. The series ranges in length/breadth from 61 × 42 mm. to 21 × 18 mm., with an average of 35 × 29 mm.

MANUPORTS (39 SPECIMENS)

There are twenty lava cobblestones, six of which are broken, and nineteen nodules and blocks (fifteen of lava and four of quartz or quartzite) in which there is no evidence of utilisation. The cobblestones range in size from 107 × 74 × 66 mm. to 52 × 52 × 33 mm., with an average mean diameter of 60 mm., and the nodules and blocks from 100 × 80 × 63 mm. to 40 × 31 × 22 mm., with an average mean diameter of 60 mm.

Analysis of the industry from FLK North, Level 3

	Nos.	%
Tools	28	16·4
Utilised material	49	28·6
Débitage	94	55·0
	171	
Tools		
Side choppers	16	57·1
End choppers	3	10·7
Broken chopper	1	3·6
Polyhedrons	3	10·7
Discoids	2	7·1
Subspheroids	2	7·1
Scraper, heavy-duty	1	3·6
	28	
Utilised material		
'Anvils'	4	8·2
Hammerstones	15	30·6
Cobblestones	5	10·2
Nodules and blocks	14	28·6
Light-duty flakes and other fragments	11	22·4
	49	
Débitage		
Whole flakes	28	29·8
Broken flakes and chips	61	64·9
Core fragments	5	5·3
	94	

LEVELS 1/2

The series of artefacts available for study from this level is the most comprehensive from the site. Unfortunately, a further 235 specimens obtained from Trench IV, have been lost either in transit from the camp or after arrival in Nairobi. Since only field identifications are now available for this material, it is not included in the analysis of the industry, although a list compiled from the field register is appended below. In the plan of finds (Fig. 36, in pocket), the specimens whose identifications have been checked in the laboratory are shown in large letters and those of the missing series in small letters.

Included among the material from this level are a pecked and grooved stone and two utilised bones. (These are described on pp. 84 and 235, respectively.) Choppers greatly outnumber any other tool type, side choppers alone amounting to 35 per cent of all the tools and end choppers to a further 17·4 per cent. They are generally well made, mostly from finer-grained materials than those from the lower levels of Bed I. The working edges are usually bifacially flaked, sharp and jagged, whilst the butts are formed by the rounded surfaces of cobblestones. Some excellent examples of classic Oldowan choppers are included. Two-edged, pointed and chisel-edged varieties also occur, but are relatively scarce, with a total of only eight specimens, in contrast to seventy-eight side and end choppers. A proportion of all types of choppers show hammerstone utilisation on the butts. Small specimens, such as those that occur at DK, are relatively scarce and none are truly diminutive. There are five 'proto-bifaces'. One example is unusually well made and resembles a small pointed ovate. It is flaked over the greater part of both faces. The cutting edge is relatively even and extends round the whole circumference.

TOOLS

Side choppers (52 specimens)

Forty-five examples are made from rounded cobblestones with cortex surface at the butt ends and the remainder on weathered nodules. Fifty are of lava and two of quartz or quartzite. They are mostly bifacial (81 per cent), with multiple flaking on both faces of the working edges. In 9 per cent there is multiple flaking on one face, opposed to a single scar on the obverse. Only six are unifacial, with one face consisting of cortex surface. Three examples are probably unfinished. The edges are generally jagged, with deeply indented negative scars and projecting points where the scars intersect. The lengths of the cutting edges vary considerably in relation to the circumference of the tools, but in the majority approximately one third of the circumference has been trimmed. The edges are sometimes nearly straight, but are more often slightly curved. Chipping, blunting and crushing is present and in 27 per cent the edges have been battered and entirely blunted. Many show small crushed indentations suggesting a grinding, swivel action against a hard edge. The length/breadth/thickness measurements range from 91 × 96 × 64 mm. to 35 × 32 × 21 mm., with an average of 66 × 77 × 52 mm., and the mean diameters range from 83 to 29 mm., with an average of

65 mm. The edge/circumference ratios vary from 12 to 68 per cent, with an average of 37 per cent. (Figs. 37, 38 and 40, no. 2.)

End choppers (26 specimens)

Twenty-one examples are made on cobblestones and the remainder on weathered nodules or blocks. One specimen is of quartz, one of gneiss and the balance of lava. Most of these tools are also bifacially trimmed, with multiple flaking on either side of the working edges (76 per cent). There are also five examples of unifacial choppers and two in which there is a single negative scar on one face, with multiple flaking on the opposite side. The edges are often jagged, but a higher proportion are sinuous and more even than those of the side choppers. The type and extent of utilisation is very similar; 47 per cent show only light chipping and 33 per cent heavy chipping, blunting and battering. In two examples there is no trace of utilisation whilst in another two crushed indentations are present on the edges. In ten specimens the butt ends have been used as hammerstones. The length/breadth/thickness measurements range from 99 × 91 × 70 mm. to 35 × 32 × 21 mm., with an average of 66 × 77 × 52 mm., and the mean diameters range from 86 to 29 mm., with an average of 61 mm. The edge/circumference ratios vary from 50 to 17 per cent, with an average of 29 per cent. (Fig. 39, nos. 1–8 and Fig. 40, no. 1.)

Two-edged choppers (3 specimens)

Two examples are made on lava cobblestones and one on a quartz nodule. The latter is a light-duty tool and is oblong, with both lateral edges finely chipped, one bifacially and the second unifacially. The edges are blunted by use and the extremities show battering. One of the lava specimens is very similar, except that the extremities consist of cortex surface and are not utilised. The third specimen is deeply weathered and rolled and is clearly not contemporary with the rest of the assemblage, although the utilisation on the edges is fresh. The length/breadth/thickness measurements range from 70 × 55 × 47 mm. to 34 × 33 × 24 mm., with an average of 51 × 45 × 37 mm., and the mean diameters range from 57 to 30 mm., with an average of 44 mm. (Fig. 39, no. 9; Fig. 41, no. 2.)

Pointed choppers (4 specimens)

All four examples are made from lava cobblestones. The lower faces are flat, consisting of one or more shallow, negative flake scars. The upper faces are steeply trimmed, generally with a deeply indented, bold flake scar on either side, forming a median point at the intersection. The length/breadth/thickness measurements range from 75 × 98 × 67 mm. to 54 × 55 × 44 mm., with an average of 67 × 73 × 54 mm., and the mean diameters range from 80 to 51 mm., with an average of 65 mm. The average edge/circumference ratio is 33 per cent. (Fig. 39, nos. 10–12; Fig. 41, no. 1.)

Chisel-edged chopper (1 specimen)

This consists of a triangular slab of quartzite in which all three points have been bifacially flaked, forming three working edges at right angles to the upper and lower faces.

73

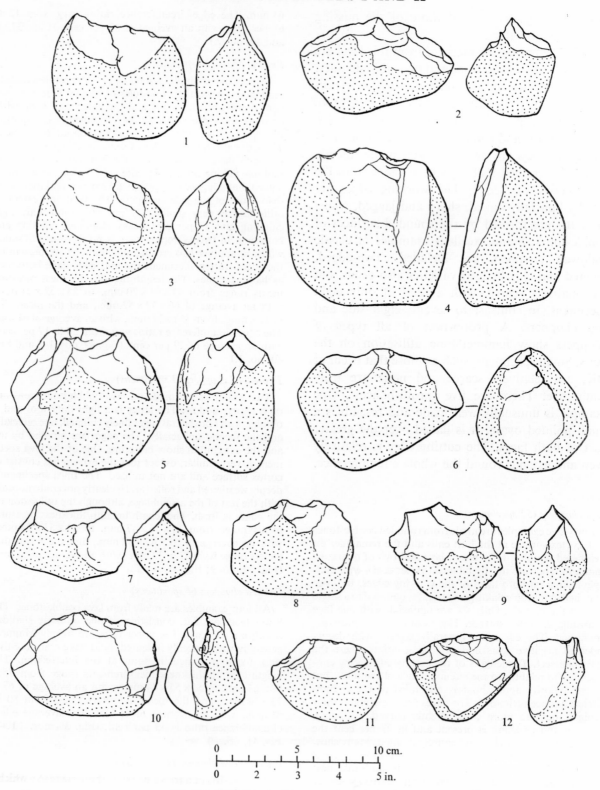

Fig. 37. FLK North. Diagrams of side choppers.

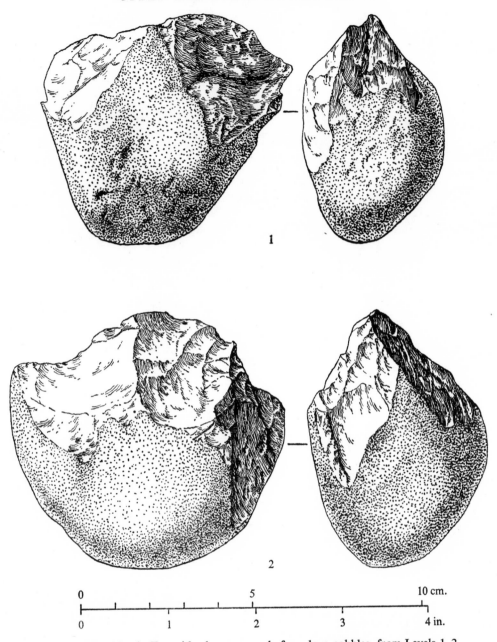

Fig. 38. FLK North. Two side choppers made from lava cobbles, from Levels 1–2.

Heavy utilisation is evident both on the chisel edges and also on the intervening ridges. (65 × 61 × 46 mm. Mean diameter 54 mm.)

There are, in addition to the above, two unfinished and three broken choppers.

'Proto-bifaces' (*5 specimens*)

These five tools exhibit such a degree of variation that it is necessary to describe them individually.

(*a*) Made from a lava cobblestone. It is flaked over both faces and is elliptical in cross-section. The tip is pointed and the base rounded. The edge is relatively even, with chipped, bifacial utilisation. This specimen is better made and more closely approaches a small handaxe than any others in the series. (79 × 61 × 36 mm. Mean diameter 58 mm. Edge/circumference ratio 100 per cent.)

(*b*) A lava cobblestone with three flat flake scars on the under surface. Cortex surface is present at the butt end and

75

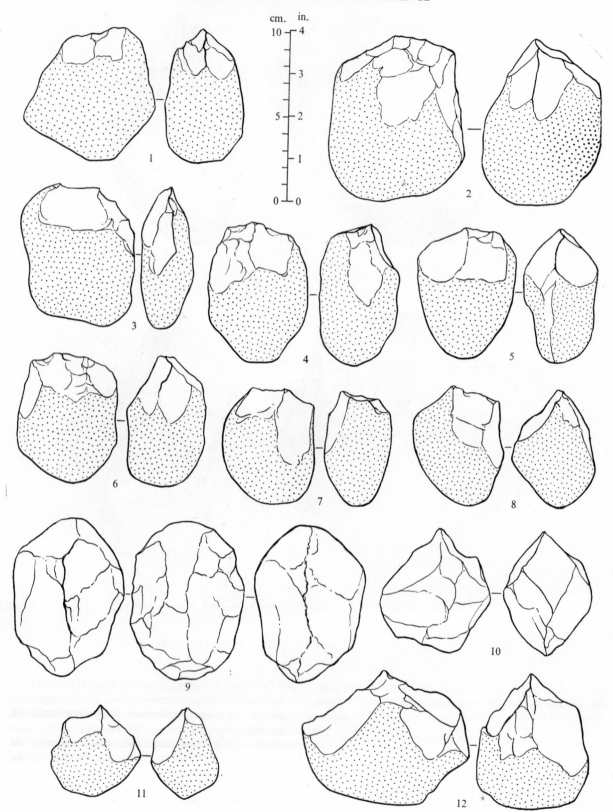

Fig. 39. FLK North. Diagrams of choppers. (1) to (8) end choppers; (9) a two-edged chopper; (10) to (12) pointed choppers.

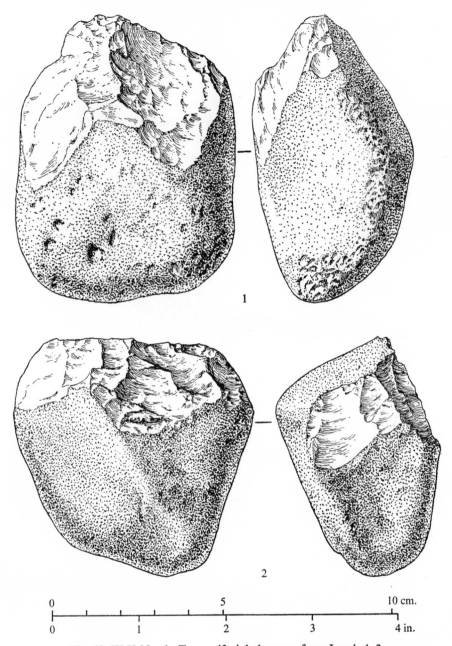

Fig. 40. FLK North. Two unifacial choppers from Levels 1–2.

also on part of one lateral edge. The general form is ovate and the cross-section is plano-convex. The edge is sharp with little evidence of utilisation. (81 × 66 × 45 mm. Mean diameter 64 mm. Edge/circumference ratio 53 per cent.)

(c) A lava cobblestone, plano-convex in cross-section, with three flat flake scars on the under-surface. The edges have been steeply trimmed on the upper face. The tip is sharply pointed and the butt rounded. The edge is somewhat jagged but is more even than in most choppers. Some bifacial, chipped utilisation is evident. (74 × 66 × 47 mm.

Mean diameter 62 mm. Edge/circumference ratio 63 per cent.)

(d) Made from quartz. Both lateral edges and the tip are trimmed by means of relatively shallow flaking. The butt is thick and the tip bluntly pointed. The edge is uneven and extends round more than half the circumference, exhibiting chipped utilisation. The butt has also been damaged by use. (60 × 59 × 52 mm. Mean diameter 57 mm. Edge/circumference ratio 55 per cent.)

(e) Made from lava. The butt is thick and exhibits a

77

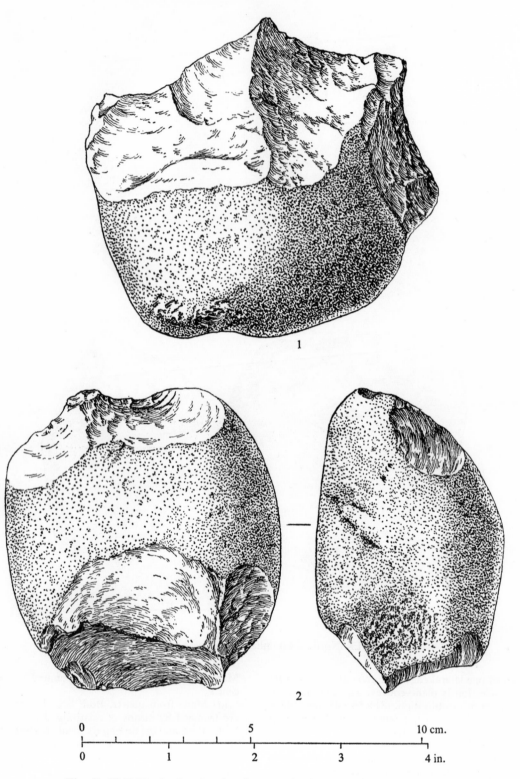

1

2

0   5   10 cm.

0   1   2   3   4 in.

Fig. 41. FLK North. A pointed and a two-edged chopper from Levels 1–2.

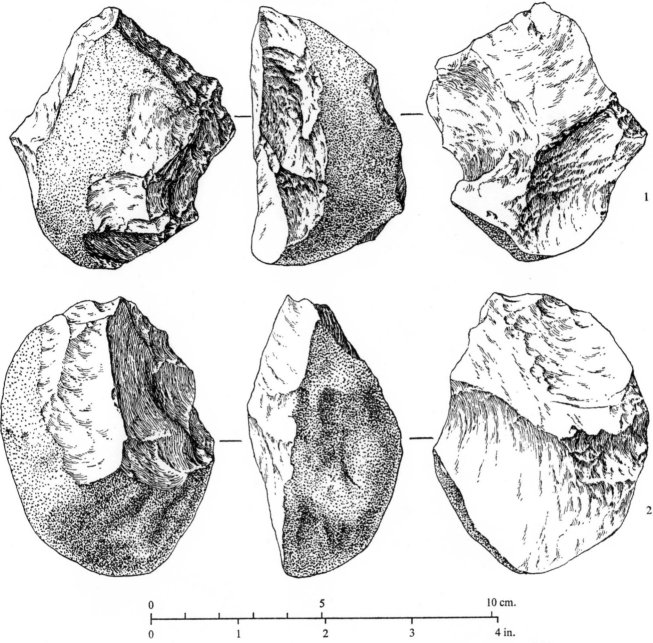

Fig. 42. FLK North. Two 'proto-bifaces' from Levels 1–2. Both are made from lava cobbles.

single transverse flake scar. Both lateral edges are bifacially flaked. One edge and the butt are extensively battered and damaged by use. The tool is elongate and the tip rounded, with a relatively even working edge extending round the greater part of the circumference. (75 × 68 × 57 mm. Mean diameter 66 mm. Edge/circumference ratio 61 per cent.)

The average measurements for the five specimens are: length/breadth/thickness 73 × 64 × 47 mm., mean diameter 61 mm. and edge/circumference ratio 66 per cent. (Figs. 42, 43, no. 1.)

Polyhedrons (5 specimens)

Four examples are made on lava cobblestones and the fifth on an angular block of quartzite. Three specimens are oblong, with four or five intersecting working edges. The remaining two are subspherical and angular, each with three working edges, generally chipped and blunted by use. In one of the specimens made from a cobblestone pitting and bruising is evident on an area of cortex surface. The length/breadth/thickness measurements range from 85 ×

79

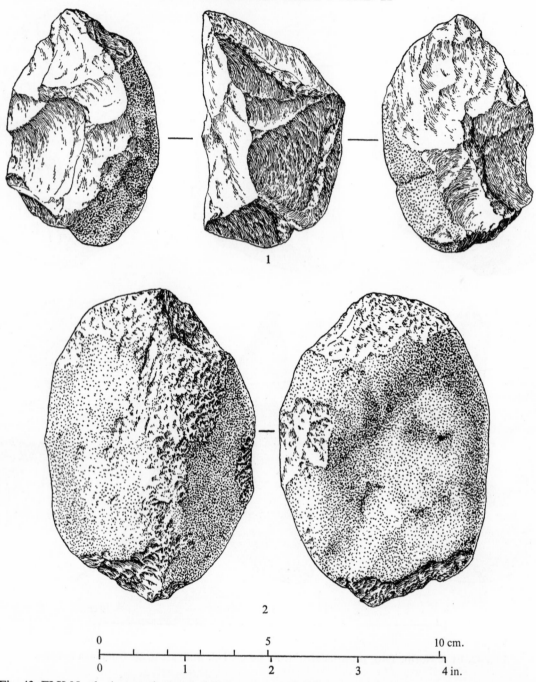

1

2

0				5			10 cm.

0	1	2	3	4 in.

Fig. 43. FLK North. A quartzite 'proto-biface' and a lava hammerstone from Levels 1 and 4 respectively.

65 × 54 mm. to 53 × 47 × 42 mm., with an average of 70 × 59 × 49 mm., and the mean diameters vary from 68 to 47 mm., with an average of 59 mm.

Discoids (8 specimens)

Four examples are made from quartz or quartzite and four from lava cobblestones. With one exception, these tools are bifacially flaked round the entire circumference.

One appears to be unfinished. The quartz/quartzite specimens are smaller, more symmetrical and better finished than those made from lava. They also have more regular, elliptical cross-sections. The edges are usually jagged, chipped and blunted by use, with bifacial trimming. The length/breadth/thickness measurements range from 99 × 81 × 59 mm. to 33 × 32 × 20 mm., with an average of 58 × 52 × 38 mm., and the mean diameters vary from 79 to 28 mm., with an average of 49 mm. (It will be seen that the average size is considerably less than that of the choppers or polyhedrons.)

Spheroids (3 specimens)

Two examples are made from quartz and one from a lava cobblestone. One is a true stone ball, almost entirely symmetrical and smoothly rounded over the whole surface. It is the earliest known example of a stone ball at Olduvai. The remaining two examples are faceted, with imperfectly reduced ridges. The length/breadth/thickness measurements range from $73 \times 72 \times 58$ mm. to $67 \times 66 \times 61$ mm., and the average mean diameter is 65 mm. (Pl. 16.)

Subspheroids (9 specimens)

Two light duty examples are made from quartz and the balance from lava. In several specimens one side is formed by rounded cortex surface. The series is generally spherical, but not so symmetrical as the foregoing category. The measurements range from $86 \times 80 \times 60$ mm. to $23 \times 22 \times 18$ mm., with an average mean diameter of 58 mm. (Pl. 16.)

Scrapers, heavy duty (13 specimens)

The entire series is made on blocks, nodules or parts of cobblestones; eight examples are of quartz or quartzite and five of lava. The majority exhibit steeply trimmed, curved working edges, flaked from a flat under-surface, usually consisting of a natural cleavage plane. Three examples are double edged. Only one specimen is made on a piece of tabular quartzite, a material which was later used extensively for the manufacture of heavy-duty scrapers. The extent of utilisation is variable, but in the majority of specimens there is some chipping and blunting of the edges, predominantly on the upper surface. There is a crushed notch 5 mm. deep and 26 mm. wide on one example. The length/breadth/thickness measurements range from 108×75 mm. to 52×41 mm., with an average of 78×55 mm., and the edge lengths vary from 107 to 30 mm., with an average of 69 mm.

Scrapers, light-duty (12 specimens)

The entire series is made from quartz or quartzite.

End scrapers (8 specimens). These are generally made on whole or broken flakes. The working edges are curved and are often slightly denticulated. The trimming may be either steep or shallow, depending on the thickness of the flake. The length/breadth measurements range from 46×36 mm. to 22×18 mm., with an average of 32×27 mm. (Fig. 44, no. 2.)

Side scrapers (3 specimens). Two are made on side-struck flakes and one is broken. The complete specimens measure 33×44 mm. and 21×33 mm. respectively.

Hollow scraper (1 specimen). This is made on part of a flat, wide flake with fine shallow retouch along one edge. This is on the primary surface and forms a notch 31 mm. wide and 3·5 mm. deep. (45×39 mm.)

Sundry tools (3 specimens)

These consist of: (a) a small blunt point, at the tip of a quartz flake (40×28 mm.), (b) a chisel-shaped point with fine, bifacial retouch (4×35 mm.), (c) part of a flake with retouch and utilisation on both lateral edges and with a point at one end, formed by a notch on either side (53×34 mm.) (Fig. 44.)

UTILISED MATERIAL

'Anvils' (12 specimens)

Nine examples consist of quartzite blocks, mostly of tabular material, with heavy battering and crushing on one or more edges. They vary considerably in form and may be circular, cuboid or subtriangular, but the utilised edges are always approximately 90°. Two further examples consist of broken lava cobblestones in which the edges of the fractured surfaces exhibit a similar type of utilisation. There is also a high-backed conical block of vesicular basalt in which the circumference of the flat base has been steeply flaked and battered. In the centre of the flat surface there is an oblong depression 29×17 mm. in diameter and 9 mm. deep. The interior of the hollow is rough and dark grey in colour and is similar to the flake scars on the circumference, in contrast to the remainder of the surface, which is light brown or buff coloured. ($96 \times 94 \times 91$ mm.) (Pl. 17.) The mean diameters for the whole series range from 93 to 44 mm., with an average of 68 mm.

Hammerstones (62 specimens)

These consist entirely of waterworn cobblestones. The utilisation occasionally includes slight shattering, but is more often in the form of battering, bruising and pitting. This may be present on any part of the exterior, but is usually evident on projecting areas and on the extremities. Four examples are of quartz or quartzite and the balance of lava. The measurements range from $116 \times 85 \times 75$ mm. to $61 \times 53 \times 39$ mm. and the average mean diameter is 66 mm.

Cobblestones (23 specimens)

These are broken or otherwise damaged by use but the type of utilisation seen on hammerstones is not present. Parts of the edges are often shattered and in some specimens a number of flakes has also been removed by particularly heavy blows. One example is of quartz or quartzite and the rest of lava. The series ranges in size from $108 \times 71 \times 61$ mm. to $35 \times 52 \times 40$ mm., with an average mean diameter of 63 mm.

Nodules and blocks (49 specimens)

Quartz or quartzite and lava occur in almost equal proportions in this series. The forms are variable and there is no suggestion of shaping prior to use, although most of the specimens have presumably been fractured by human agency and there are occasional flake scars. The utilisation is on natural sharp edges and is generally in the form of

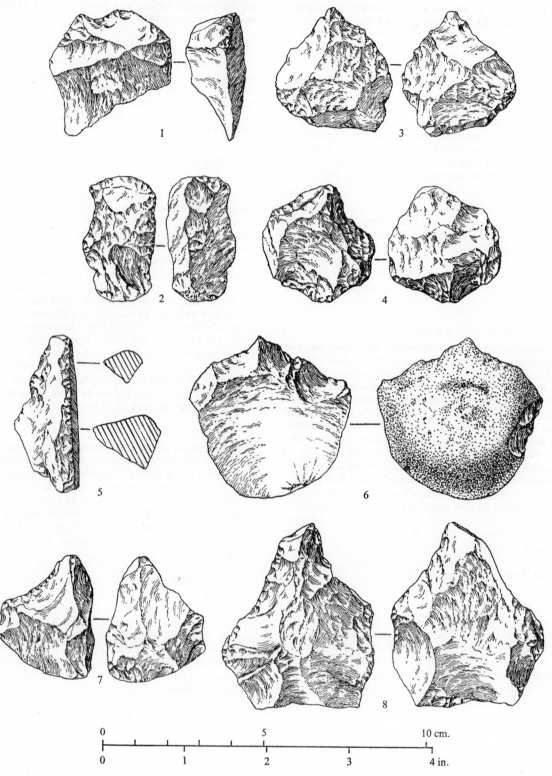

Fig. 44. FLK North. Light-duty tools and utilised pieces. The majority are from Levels 1–2. (1) and (2) scrapers on quartz flakes; (3) and (4) small pointed quartz tools; (5) a triangular fragment of quartz, utilised along one side; (6) a pointed tool made on a flake from a lava cobblestone; (7) and (8) fragments of quartz with chipped utilisation on the edges.

irregular chipping and some blunting. The measurements range from 111 × 102 × 58 mm. to 67 × 50 × 36 mm., with an average mean diameter of 60 mm.

Light-duty flakes and other fragments (68 specimens)

With straight edges (24 specimens). These consist of two lava and twenty-two quartz or quartzite flakes, some of which are broken, with fine chipping on one or more edges. This is usually more pronounced on one face than on the other.

With concave or notched edges (29 specimens). With the exception of one lava flake, all are of quartz or quartzite. There is a higher proportion of whole flakes than in those with straight edges, but several broken flakes and core fragments are also included. In a few specimens there are two notches but more usually a single shallow notch, chipped mostly from one direction. The notches vary in width from 22 to 6 mm.; a few exceed 3 mm. in depth, but the average for the whole series is 2·2 mm. and the average width 11·5 mm. (Fig. 44, nos. 7, 8.)

With convex edges (15 specimens). With the exception of one lava specimen, these are all of quartz or quartzite. The edges are curved as in scrapers and the type of chipping tends to be coarser and more irregular than in the notched specimens. The series comprises whole and broken flakes and two small fragments of tabular quartzite.

The sixty-eight specimens in this series range in length/breadth from 98 × 34 mm. to 28 × 18 mm. with an average of 43 × 30 mm., whilst the lengths of the utilised edges vary from 38 to 21 mm. with an average of 30 mm.

DEBITAGE

The *débitage* amounts to 842 specimens, consisting of 178 complete flakes, 3 re-sharpening flakes, 575 broken flakes and chips and 86 core fragments; 82·6 per cent is of quartz or quartzite and 17·4 per cent of lava. In the complete flakes, however, a higher proportion is of lava (32·9 per cent). Many of these specimens are cortex flakes, struck from cobblestones.

Complete flakes

Twenty-five examples are convergent, with the maximum width at the striking platform. There are no parallel-sided flakes and the remainder are divergent; 62·6 per cent are end-struck. The length/breadth measurements in millimetres are as follows:

Lava	Range	Average
End-struck	69 × 49 to 25 × 17	44 × 33
Side-struck	42 × 57 to 27 × 32	36 × 43
Quartz/quartzite		
End-struck	57 × 64 to 20 × 17	34 × 26
Side-struck	46 × 54 to 13 × 22	26 × 27

Bulbs of percussion. The bulbs of percussion are preserved in 165 specimens and can be sub-divided as follows:

	Lava	Quartz/quartzite
Marked	50·4 %	47·7 %
Slight	30·2 %	34·5 %
Negative	11·3 %	7·1 %
Shattered	8·0 %	10·6 %
Totals	52	113

165

Angles of striking platforms. The angles of the striking platforms can be measured in 116 specimens. They all lie between 70° and 129°.

	Lava	Quartz/quartzite
70– 89°	2·2 %	4·2 %
90–109°	40·0 %	57·7 %
110–129°	57·8 %	38·0 %
Totals	45	71

116

MANUPORTS

Cobblestones (83 complete and 40 broken specimens)

Unmodified cobblestones are particularly common at this level. The entire series is of lava and consists of water-worn stones which must have been brought to the site by man, since there is no suggestion of water action. The range in size is from 107 × 80 × 62 mm. to 41 × 36 × 31 mm., with an average mean diameter of 62 mm.

Nodules and blocks (87 specimens)

Eight examples are of quartz or quartzite and the balance of lava. The majority consists of irregular-shaped, weathered nodules of vesicular basalt, a material from which very few tools were made at this level, although it was used to some extent at DK. This seems to indicate that the nodules and blocks were not brought in to serve as raw material but for some different purpose. There is no indication of utilisation and they may have been kept in readiness for use as missiles against predators or scavenging animals. The size range is from 123 × 101 × 53 mm. to 38 × 32 × 27 mm., with an average mean diameter of 64 mm.

Analysis of the industry from FLK North, Levels 1 and 2

	Nos.	%
Tools	149	12·4
Utilised material	214	17·7
Débitage	842	69·9
	1205	

6-2

Tools	Nos.	%
Side choppers	52	35·0
End choppers	26	17·4
Two-edged choppers	3	2·0
Pointed choppers	4	2·7
Chisel-edged chopper	1	0·7
Unfinished choppers	2	1·3
Broken choppers	3	2·0
'Proto-bifaces'	5	3·4
Polyhedrons	5	3·4
Discoids	8	5·4
Spheroids	3	2·0
Sub-spheroids	9	6·0
Scrapers, heavy-duty	13	8·7
Scrapers, light-duty	12	8·0
Sundry tools	3	2·0
	149	
Utilised material		
'Anvils'	12	5·6
Hammerstones	62	29·0
Cobblestones	23	10·7
Nodules and blocks	49	22·9
Light-duty flakes and other fragments	68	31·8
	214	
Débitage		
Whole flakes	178	21·1
Re-sharpening flakes	3	0·3
Broken flakes and chips	575	68·3
Core fragments	86	10·3
	842	

Additional material from Levels 1 and 2 in Trench IV classified on field identifications and subsequently lost (this is not included in the foregoing analysis)

Choppers, unspecified	32
Polyhedrons	3
Discoids	2
'Proto-biface'	1
Scrapers	5
Tools, various, unspecified	25
Hammerstones	11
Utilised cobblestones and nodules	9
Débitage (probably including a proportion of utilised flakes)	115
Manuports	32
	235

A GROOVED AND PECKED STONE

An unusual stone was found in Level 1 of Trench II (Pl. 18). It consists of a phonolite cobblestone measuring 79 × 54 × 49 mm. in which almost the whole of the original smooth cortex surface has been removed by pecking and battering. It is oblong in form, the base and one side being flat, whilst the upper surface and the opposite side are convex. One end is blunt and the opposite end obliquely pointed. There is a well-marked artificial groove on the upper surface. This is continuous, except for an area 20 mm. wide where the surface has scaled off subsequently, and for a second area, on the opposite side, where part of the cortex surface still remains. This is approximately 9 mm. wide. The groove varies from 18 to 9 mm. in width and from 4·5 to 2 mm. in depth and encircles a raised oval area, measuring 60 × 41 mm., which is pecked over the entire surface. There is no evidence of wear inside the groove, although it is not so coarsely pecked as are other areas of the surface. Experiment has shown that the groove is sufficiently deep to hold a thong or string in position if it is tied round the stone at this point. On the convex side of the stone and at the edge of the cortex area, there is a line of four symmetrical indentations 3–4 mm. in diameter, either circular or oval in shape, and measuring 0·5 mm. in depth, together with two adjacent pitted indentations which are both larger and shallower. Other parts of the surface show additional battering and pitting, with several irregular shallow depressions, apparently caused by wear. No explanation can be offered here, either for the groove or for the line of peck marks; similar artefacts are not known from any other Oldowan assemblage.

LOWER BED II
2. THE CLAY WITH ROOT CASTS

The lowest level from which artefacts and faunal remains were recovered from Bed II at FLK North consisted of a clay horizon 4½ ft. thick, which also contained many root casts. This level can be correlated with Level 2 at HWK East. It yielded twenty-one artefacts as well as a number of isolated fossil bones, many of which occurred as 'cores' in the centre of concretionary nodules. Both the artefacts and the fossil bones were scattered sparsely through the deposit and did not occur at any particular level.

The artefacts consist of the following:

Side choppers	4
Spheroid	1
Scrapers, heavy-duty	2
Utilised nodules	6
Utilised flake	1
Débitage	7
	21

A single unmodified cobblestone of welded tuff was also found.

The side choppers are crude. Two are of lava and two of quartz or quartzite. The latter show hammerstone utilisation on the butt ends. The flaking of the working edges is bifacial and a number of plunging scars are present. Utilisation is evident on all four specimens. The mean diameters range from 71 to 58 mm., with an average of 64 mm., and the length of the working edges varies from 95 to 70 mm., with an average edge/circumference ratio of 33 per cent. The single spheroid is well made and symmetrical. It is considerably larger than any recovered from the Bed I levels and is made from quartz. The whole surface is battered smooth. It measures 95 × 86 × 87 mm., with a mean diameter of 89 mm. Both the scrapers are side scrapers. One is made of a relatively thin slab of quartzite. It is discoidal in general form and has been trimmed on one side to a curved edge 100 mm. long. The edge on the opposite side is blunt and has been battered and used as a hammerstone. The intermediate area has been trimmed from the opposite direction to form a shorter working edge 65 mm. long (106 × 96 mm.). The second specimen, made on a nodule of white quartz, has been steeply trimmed on the greater part of the circumference from the flat natural surface on the lower face. The edge is heavily utilised and blunted. Length of working edge: 195 mm. (82 × 74 mm.).

The utilised material consists of six quartz blocks or nodules showing varying degrees of chipping and blunting on the edges. In two examples some crude flaking is also present. The average mean diameter for the series is 72 mm. There is also an end-struck quartzite flake (56 × 45 mm.) which shows fine, uneven chipping on one lateral edge, mostly on the upper surface.

This small series calls for no special comment, with the exception of the spheroid. This is quite symmetrical, worked over the whole surface and resembles the spheroids from the middle and upper levels of Bed II both in size and general appearance.

3. THE DEINOTHERIUM SKELETON AND ASSOCIATED ARTEFACTS

The skeleton of a *Deinotherium* (cf. *Deinotherium bozasi*) was discovered in a clay horizon 7 ft. above the base of Bed II, when overburden was being removed before extending the excavations in Bed I. Apart from the tusks, which were reasonably well preserved, all the bones were in an extremely friable condition. The skull, which projected into the area being cleared for excavation, had been entirely crushed and reduced to a pinkish powder. It was dug into and partly destroyed by the workmen before they realised that it represented bone.

At the time of the discovery the only preservative available in sufficient quantity was shellac and this proved virtually useless for the massive *Deinotherium* bones. During a visit to the site Professor J. D. Clark suggested that Bedacryl might prove more effective. When supplies of this chemical had been obtained it was possible to remove the more important bones after they had been liberally treated with Bedacryl and reinforced with plaster jackets.

The position of the bones were very similar to those of the elephant skeleton found in Level 6 (described on p. 64). The head lay to the northwest and the limb bones were partly articulated, although one scapula had been displaced, and lay 8 ft. distant from the humerus. The vertebral column and ribs were represented by many small fragments, none of which could be preserved. Remains of the foot bones were found considerably below the rest of the skeleton, suggesting that the animal probably died as a result of sinking into a swamp.

Thirty-nine artefacts and manuports were found scattered among the bones of the *Deinotherium*, one chopper being actually within the pelvic girdle. They consist, for the most part, of manuports and utilised nodules. The average size for the whole series (not counting *débitage*) is noticeably smaller than for the assemblage found with the elephant skeleton in Level 6. In the present series the average mean diameter for the heavy-duty tools is 59 mm., in contrast to 70 mm. in the Level 6 assemblage.

The series consists of the following:

End chopper	1
Chisel-edged chopper	1
Polyhedron	1
Discoid	1
Scrapers, heavy-duty	2
Subspheroid	1
'Anvil'	1
Hammerstones	2
Utilised cobblestones	1
Utilised nodules and blocks	5
Débitage	7
	23

There are also 16 manuports.

The end chopper is made on an oblong lava cobble. The working edge is rounded and flaked on one face only. It is considerably blunted and damaged by use (97 × 72 × 46 mm.). The chisel-edged chopper is made on a weathered triangular fragment of quartzite with a working edge 35 mm. wide at one point. It is in sharp condition with little evidence of wear. (76 × 63 × 54 mm.)

Both the polyhedron and the discoid are made from quartz. The former has a number of short, intersecting edges, most of which show crushing and chipping. (66 × 64 × 49 mm. Mean diameter 59 mm.) The latter is crude, with a relatively thick cross-section, although there is a continuous, bifacially flaked working edge on the whole circumference. (64 × 61 × 42 mm. Mean diameter 55 mm.) Both the scrapers are heavy-duty and both are made of quartzite; one on a tabular fragment. The working edges are curved and have been steeply trimmed from flat undersurfaces. Some chipped utilisation is present. Length of edges 85 mm. and 65 mm. The respective measurements are 71 × 62 mm. and 75 × 61 mm.

The utilised material includes one 'anvil' consisting of a hexagonal block of quartzite, in which the edges approximate 90° and show crushing and

chipping. (93 × 89 × 72 mm.) Mean diameter 84 mm. There are also two hammerstones, one of which is a lava cobblestone and the second a subspherical quartz or quartzite nodule. Both are bruised and pitted on the extremities and other parts of the exterior. The measurements are 76 × 66 × 54 mm. (mean diameter 65 mm.), and 72 × 66 × 66 mm. (mean diameter 64 mm.). Four quartz or quartzite blocks and one nodule of fine-grained tuff together with one cobble, also show indeterminate chipping and blunting of the edges.

The *débitage* consists of three complete and four broken flakes all of quartz or quartzite. There are also eleven lava cobblestones and five quartz or quartzite blocks lacking evidence of utilisation.

4. SITE HWK EAST (HENRIETTA WILFRIDA KORONGO)

Archaeological number (40)   Geologic locality 43

The HWK gullies lie to the south of the confluence of the Main and Side Gorges. They originate mainly from a saddle connecting two pinnacles capped with Beds III and IV which form prominent landmarks in the area and are known as the 'Castle' and the 'Tower'. The HWK East gully begins at the saddle and runs in an easterly direction for the first quarter of a mile. It then turns sharply north to drain into the Main Gorge a short distance below the confluence.

In the whole of the HWK area the Upper Member of Bed I is represented only by the upper series of deposits since the underlying basalt rises in irregular hummocks to within 20 ft. of the marker Tuff I^F. Bed II is normally 85–90 ft. thick. Two implementiferous horizons in the lower part of Bed II had been identified at HWK East during 1930–1 and had yielded a number of tools, then attributed to stages 1 and 2 of the 'Chelles-Acheul' cultural sequence (as defined in 1951). The levels consisted of an occupation surface at the base of Bed II, now termed Level I, and a sandy conglomerate approximately 10 ft. higher in the sequence (Levels 3, 4, 5).

Further exploration of the site was undertaken in 1962 in order to obtain material which would provide a stratigraphic succession to the upper levels of Bed I that had been excavated at FLK North.

(The general description of this site and of the levels within Lower Bed II are included in this chapter. The description of the material from Levels 3, 4 and 5, which are in the lower part of Middle Bed II, will be found in chapter IV.)

The lowest level (Level 1) consisted of a palaeosol on the surface of a clay resting on the marker Tuff I^F. It yielded mainly heavy-duty tools and utilised material of Oldowan type, closely comparable to the material from the outskirts of the 'Zinjanthropus' floor at FLK I.

A horizon of clay 6–7 ft. thick occurred above Level 1. It contained many root and stem casts and can be correlated with the clay with root casts at FLK North. Remains of *Deinotherium*, *Elephas* (cf. *recki*) and a number of artefacts, including some made from chert (which are characteristic of the higher levels) were obtained from the level. The industry appears to represent a stage intermediate between the Oldowan of Bed I and the Developed Oldowan of Bed II. A thin seam of tuff representing Tuff II^A occurred between this horizon and the lowest of the three overlying levels, which contain an industry typical of the Developed Oldowan A.

Three adjacent parallel trenches, each 15 ft. wide, were cut into the deposits on the northern side of the HWK East gully, approximately 150 yards south-east of the 'Castle'. The trenches were dug in a succession of steps 10 ft. wide, which were staggered in order to avoid falls from the higher levels. A total of 1,230 sq.ft. of the lowest occupation level was exposed, but, since the higher levels had been considerably cut back by the erosion slope, the area of these deposits was considerably less. A step trench 5 ft. wide was also dug into the deposit above the implementiferous levels, to a height of 30 ft. above the base of Bed II. It proved to be almost entirely barren.

The overall section of Beds I and II in the HWK East gully is shown in Fig. 3. The detailed sequence of the deposits in Lower Bed II and the lower part of Middle Bed II, as revealed in the trenches (Fig. 45) is as follows:

(*a*) A thick deposit of reddish brown and grey tuffs, with some minor clay horizons. The top was approximately 30 ft. above the base of Bed II, the lower part yielded a few artefacts that appeared to be derived.

(*b*) Level 5.[1] A re-worked tuff varying in thickness from 1 to 2 ft. It included lenses of unconsolidated coarse grey sand that filled hollows in the surface of the underlying Sandy Conglomerate. Level 5 was excavated only in Trench III. It yielded 178 specimens, most of which were artefacts. Faunal remains were scarce and very fragmentary.

(*c*) Level 4. The chert-bearing Sandy Conglomerate referred to at FLK North. This was generally about 2 ft. thick and the lower surface was normally horizontal and even, lying approximately 8 ft. above the base of Bed II. The upper surface was extensively eroded by channels with overhanging walls. The deposit consisted of a cemented, coarse-grained grey sand that contained large numbers of artefacts and unmodified cobblestones as well as a few broken animal bones, many of which are rolled. This level contained the highest number of chert artefacts found at any locality.

(*d*) Level 3. A buff-grey, reworked tuff, varying in thickness from 9 in. to 2 ft. A few artefacts and some bone fragments were scattered throughout this deposit; an unusually dense concentration of artefacts and unmodified stones occurred at the base. Faunal remains were very scarce. A substantial proportion of the artefacts are rolled and it seems likely that the material was water-sorted to some extent. A small proportion of the artefacts in this level are made from chert.

(*e*) The aeolian tuff (II^A). A very attenuated tuff horizon was noted between Levels 2 and 3 during the excavations. This was no more than a few inches thick and occurred in depressions on the surface of Level 2. At the time of excavation this deposit was not regarded as particularly significant. Subsequently, however, it was traced laterally to

---

[1] The various levels at this site are enumerated from the lowest to the highest, since the excavations were begun by L. S. B. Leakey who intended only to explore the lowest level in Bed II (Level 1). When additional implementiferous levels were subsequently found higher in the sequence, it became necessary to refer to them in ascending order—Level 1 is thus the lowest and Level 5 the highest.

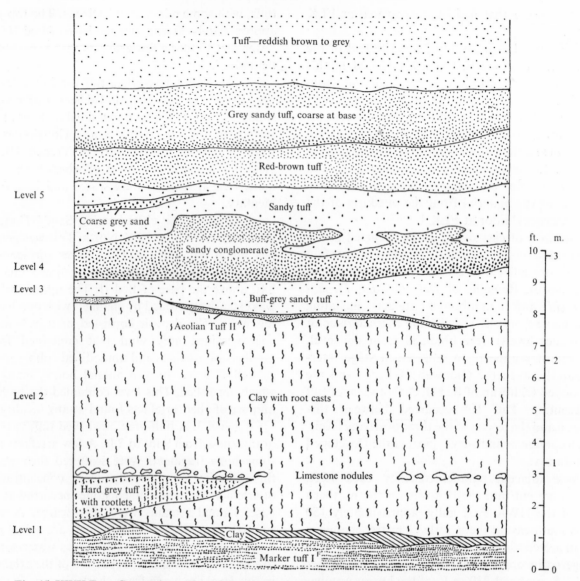

Fig. 45. HWK East. Composite section of the deposits in the lower part of Bed II exposed in Trenches I and II, showing the implementiferous horizons.

nearby exposures, where it became considerably better defined and thicker and was clearly recognisable as the westward equivalent of Tuff II^A.

(*f*) Level 2. Approximately 5½ ft. of light brown or buff-coloured clay. It contained many root casts and also a horizontal band of limestone nodules about 2 ft. from the base. Artefacts and fossil bones were scattered throughout the clay but were more concentrated at two levels, which occurred approximately midway and near the base. A few of the artefacts are made from chert. The faunal remains in this level were more plentiful and better preserved than in any of the other horizons at this site. The fauna from the upper level consisted mostly of rhinoceros ribs, vertebrae and limb bones which appear to have belonged to a single animal. The lower levels yielded a number of artefacts, manuports, etc. and were also particularly rich in avian remains, including several well-preserved skulls. (This level corresponds to the clay with root casts at FLK North.)

(*g*) Coarse-grained grey tuff. In certain parts of

88

the trenches, particularly in Trench I, a hard grey tuff containing rootlets occurred between Levels 1 and 2. This deposit is well represented elsewhere in the HWK gullies and was also found at FLK North.

(h) Level 1. This consisted of an irregular horizon of brown silty clay filling depressions in the surface of Tuff I^F, which had undergone considerable erosion in this area prior to the deposition of the clay.

LEVEL 1

The form of erosion seen at this level was unusual and included a number of shallow meandering channels, 2–6 in. deep and 6 in. to 1 ft. wide. In Trench III there was also a curious raised bank. This was flat-topped, 9–10 in. high and had an average width of 1 ft. 6 in. It was remarkably regular and formed a gentle curve along a length of approximately 20 ft. The top of the bank yielded only a few artefacts and bone fragments but there was a marked concentration of occupation debris below it, on the eastern side (Fig. 46).

Unlike the higher implementiferous levels at this site, Level 1 appears to represent an occupation floor on which the material has not been disturbed by water action or other natural causes. Faunal remains were scarce and most of the bones were in a very fragmentary condition.

There is possibly some significance in the distribution pattern of occupation debris on this surface. The debris exposed in Trench III was concentrated in an irregular ring, approximately 1–1½ ft. wide and 6–7 ft. in overall diameter. A relatively barren area of approximately the same width lay within the ring, and remains became more plentiful again in the central part (Fig. 46). Since the occupation surface in this particular area was almost entirely flat and devoid of the channels and raised banks which occurred elsewhere, the pattern of distribution is unlikely to have been caused by natural means.

The artefacts recovered from this level do not appear to be a typical assemblage of material from an occupation site. Heavy-duty tools, utilised material and manuports are unusually plentiful, whereas light-duty tools, utilised flakes and

débitage are very scarce. The proportions are similar to those on the outskirts of the FLK occupation floor, although the material was not so densely concentrated. One hundred and fifty-four artefacts were recovered, together with 163 unmodified cobble-stones, nodules and blocks. *Débitage* amounts to only 21·4 per cent of the total, whereas tools represent 33·8 per cent and utilised material 44·8 per cent. Choppers are by far the most common tool, with side choppers predominating. They include some simple specimens in which only two flakes have been removed from the working edge, one from either side. Another type of side chopper is made on oblong cobblestones in which one or both ends have been trimmed, as well as the main working edge. In other respects the choppers are of normal Oldowan types. The remaining tools call for no special comment, but it should be mentioned that there are unusually large numbers of manuports, both of cobblestone and nodules. Only one subspheroid is present. On the basis of the material available the industry appears to be typical of the Oldowan from Bed I.

It may be noted that two fair-sized pieces of obsidian were found in this level. They were submitted for dating by the fission track technique, but proved to be too devitrified to date.

TOOLS

Side choppers (23 specimens)

Two examples are made on irregular-shaped weathered nodules and the balance on well-rounded cobblestones, with cortex surface retained on the butt ends. The whole series is made from lava. In three specimens the butts have been pitted and bruised by hammerstone utilisation. Most of the specimens are bifacially flaked with multiple flaking on either face. There are also three examples with a single flake removed from each face; one is unifacial and two have a single scar on one face with multiple flaking on the obverse. One example exhibits two periods of flaking. The degree of utilisation is very variable. In some specimens the edge has been so heavily battered and chipped that it has become entirely blunt; in others it remains fresh and sharp. There is one specimen with a crushed indentation of the working edge. The length/breadth/thickness measurements range from $89 \times 140 \times 70$ mm. to $43 \times 53 \times 46$ mm., with an average of $70 \times 80 \times 51$ mm and the mean diameters vary from 93 to 47 mm., with an average of 68 mm. The edge/circumference ratio varies from 53 to 14 per cent with an average of 36 per cent.

89

OLDUVAI GORGE BEDS I AND II

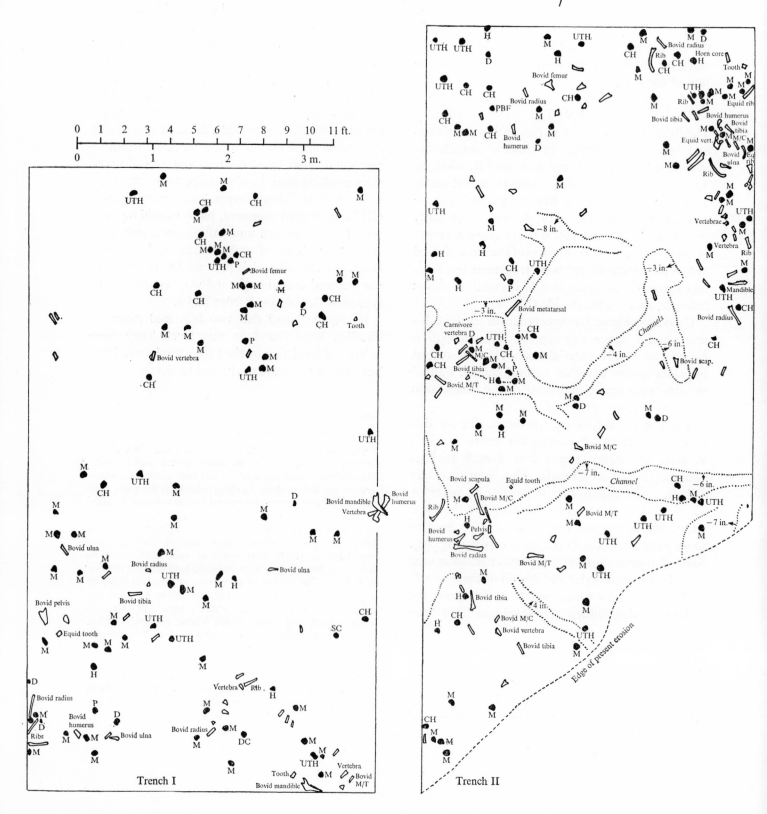

Trench I

Trench II

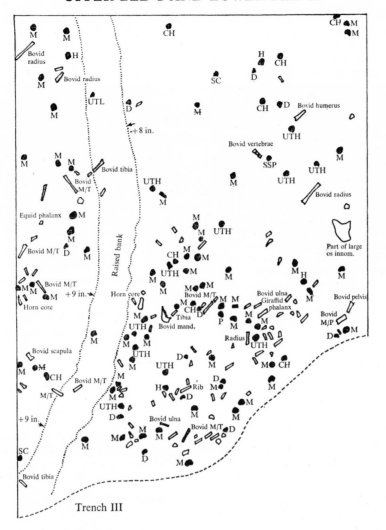

CH Choppers
DC Discoids
P Polyhedrons
SSP Sub-spheroid
SC Scrapers
PBF Proto-biface
ST Sundry tools
UTH Utilised, heavy-duty
UTL Utilised, light-duty
D Debitage
M Manuports
M Broken manuports

Fig. 46. HWK East. Plan of finds in Level 1.

End choppers (*12 specimens*)

The whole series is made on rounded lava cobblestones. Five examples show hammerstone utilisation on the butt ends. There are two unifacial specimens and ten that are bifacial. The working edges vary from jagged to relatively even, depending on the nature of the trimming scars. Utilisation is also variable, but usually takes the form of chipping. The length/breadth/thickness measurements range from $101 \times 80 \times 70$ mm. to $72 \times 50 \times 50$ mm., with an average of $81 \times 61 \times 49$ mm., and the mean diameters vary from 71 to 58 mm., with an average of 63 mm. The edge/circumference ratio varies from 50 to 19 per cent, with an average of 30 per cent.

Two-edged choppers (*3 specimens*)

In two examples the working edges are on either side and in the third at opposite ends but rotated so that they lie at right angles to one another. This last specimen is bifacially trimmed at one end and on one face only at the opposite end, where it shows unusually heavy utilisation, including a deeply indented crushed notch. Otherwise all the edges in these three specimens are sharp and jagged. (Measurements: $104 \times 77 \times 58$ mm., $84 \times 64 \times 50$ mm. and $72 \times 58 \times 53$ mm.)

Pointed chopper (*1 specimen*)

This is a well-made symmetrical specimen made on a lava cobblestone. The working edge is wide, with a small, sharp median point. This is formed mainly by a large negative scar on either side, but has also been slightly retouched. Edge length 125 mm. The butt end is chipped and shattered by use. ($84 \times 101 \times 50$ mm. Mean diameter 78 mm. Edge/circumference ratio 43 per cent.)

There are also two broken choppers.

'Proto-biface' (*1 specimen*)

This is a sharply pointed specimen with cortex butt, made on a lava cobble. It is relatively thick and exhibits many plunging scars on either side. ($82 \times 69 \times 54$ mm.)

Discoids (*3 specimens*)

One example is of quartz and two of lava. One of the latter is high-backed and steeply trimmed round the circumference. It has a particularly jagged and sharp working edge. ($80 \times 75 \times 65$ mm.) The second lava specimen is slightly oblong and plano-convex in cross-section. ($50 \times 47 \times 27$ mm.) The discoid made of quartz is the smallest and the most symmetrical of the three. It is steeply trimmed on the whole circumference. ($32 \times 31 \times 22$ mm.)

Subspheroid (*1 specimen*)

This is made of quartz and is irregular in shape, but has been blunted and battered on all the projecting parts. ($69 \times 63 \times 54$ mm.)

Scrapers, heavy-duty (*4 specimens*)

One example is made on part of a lava cobblestone and the balance on blocks of quartz or quartzite. In three specimens the working edges are rounded and in the fourth they are nearly straight. The trimming is steep and has been carried out from a flat under-surface, which consists of either a natural fracture or negative flake scar. One example is double-edged. The length/breadth measurements range from 86×66 mm. to 68×51 mm., with an average of 77×60 mm.

Burins (*2 specimens*)

Both examples are made from lava. In the first, the working edge has been flaked longitudinally down one side from an oblique fractured surface, and has been damaged by use. It is 30 mm. wide (52×44 mm.). In the second specimen the working edge is particularly thin and sharp. It is flaked on one side only, from a natural fracture surface. Width 13 mm. (55×40 mm.).

UTILISED MATERIAL

Hammerstones (*21 specimens*)

These consist of waterworn lava cobblestones with pitting, bruising and battering on projecting areas. The mean diameters range from 84 to 47 mm., with an average of 66 mm.

Cobblestones (*32 specimens*)

In addition to the hammerstones, there are a further thirty-two lava cobblestones which are broken and chipped by use, but which do not show the pitting and bruising characteristic of hammerstones. The mean diameters range from 81 to 45 mm., with an average of 66 mm.

Nodules and blocks (*14 specimens*)

These consist of irregular-shaped nodules or blocks of quartz or quartzite, of lava and one of horneblende gneiss (cf. Kelogi variety), all of which show some degree of chipping or other form of utilisation. The mean diameters range from 100 to 49 mm., with an average of 73 mm.

Light-duty flakes (*2 specimens*)

There are two broken quartz flakes which show some irregular chipping on the edges.

DEBITAGE

This consists of only thirty-three specimens, comprising eleven complete flakes, eleven broken flakes and eleven core fragments. The complete flakes are all divergent; nine are of lava and two of quartz. They are irregular, with variable bulbs of percussion and angles of striking platforms. Length/breadth measurements range from 53×50 mm. to 31×34 mm., with an average of 43×38 mm.

MANUPORTS (163 SPECIMENS)

Since there is no suggestion of water action at this level the unmodified cobbles and nodules must be regarded as artificially introduced. Whole cobblestones amount to eighty-three specimens, in which the mean diameters range from 95 to 52 mm., with an average of 66 mm. There are also fifty-six weathered nodules in which the mean diameters range from 101 to 47 mm. with an average of 68 mm. They include one fragment of gneiss (cf. Kelogi variety), three of quartz and two of obsidian.

Analysis of the industry from HWK East, Level 1

	Nos.	%
Tools	52	33·8
Utilised material	69	44·8
Débitage	33	21·4
	154	
Tools		
Side choppers	23	44·2
End choppers	12	23·0
Two-edged choppers	3	5·7
Pointed chopper	1	2·0
Broken choppers	2	3·8
'Proto-biface'	1	2·0
Discoids	3	5·7
Subspheroid	1	2·0
Scrapers, heavy-duty	4	7·7
Burins	2	3·8
	52	
Utilised material		
Hammerstones	21	30·4
Cobblestones	32	46·4
Nodules	14	20·3
Light-duty flakes	2	2·9
	69	
Débitage		
Whole flakes	11	33·3
Broken flakes and chips	11	33·3
Core fragments	11	33·3
	33	

LEVEL 2

A total of 313 artefacts was recovered from this level, together with twenty-one manuports. Tools amount to 23·6 per cent of the total, utilised material to 14·0 per cent and *débitage* to 62·3 per cent. Most of the specimens were scattered at random through the deposit, although some were associated with the faunal remains at the two horizons mentioned previously (Fig. 47). A small number of chert artefacts also occurred in the upper part of the level, indicating that this material had already become available. Unmodified cobblestones and nodules were unusually scarce, but those that occur must have been artificially introduced since the deposit consists of a fine-grained clay. The side choppers are of the usual Oldowan types. Spheroids do not occur, although there are a few subspheroids. Modified and battered blocks of quartz, which become such a dominant feature in later phases of the Developed Oldowan, are common here for the first time. 'Proto-bifaces' are represented in approximately the same proportion as in Level 1 and in the overlying Levels 3, 4 and 5. The number of tools is relatively small (seventy-four) but the series differs from the typical Oldowan of Level 1 by the increase of subspheroids and modified battered modules and blocks. Small flake tools, however, have not yet become common.

TOOLS

Side choppers (12 specimens)

Eleven examples are made of lava cobblestones and one of chert. Two specimens bear hammerstone type of utilisation on the butt ends and three are rolled. With the exception of one unifacial specimen, the whole series exhibits multiple bifacial flaking on the working edges. These are jagged and generally curved. Variable degrees of utilisation are present on the edges; some examples are heavily battered and blunted, whilst others are relatively fresh and sharp. The length/breadth/thickness measurements range between 105 × 103 × 96 mm. and 45 × 55 × 34 mm., with an average of 78 × 64 × 53 mm., and the mean diameters vary from 98 to 44 mm., with an average of 66 mm. The edge/circumference ratios vary from 50 to 24 per cent, with an average of 32 per cent.

End choppers (3 specimens)

All three examples are made on lava cobblestones; two are bifacial and one is unifacial. The latter, together with one other example, has been extensively chipped and blunted by use on the working edge. The measurements range from 94 × 74 × 58 mm. to 48 × 40 × 40 mm., with an average of 70 × 56 × 45 mm., and the mean diameters vary from 75 mm. to 42 mm., with an average of 55 mm.

Two-edged chopper (1 specimen)

This is an oblong, blunt-edged specimen made from quartz. Both lateral edges are bifacially flaked and blunted by use. (77 × 53 × 44 mm.)

There are also one broken and one unfinished chopper.

'Proto-bifaces' (3 specimens)

(a) A quartzite specimen. It is bifacially flaked at the tip and on both lateral edges. The tip is rounded and the butt is formed by an oblique vertical fracture plane. It is in sharp, fresh condition with only slight utilisation. (Edge length 160 mm.)

(b) A triangular specimen. It is more sharply pointed and made on a split lava cobblestone with cortex surface retained on one face. The greater part of the circumference shows bold bifacial flaking. (Edge length 130 mm.)

(c) This is very similar to (b) and is also made on a lava cobblestone. The butt is formed by an oblique cortex surface. Bifacial flaking extends round the tip and down both lateral edges. It is slightly rolled. (Edge length 143 mm.)

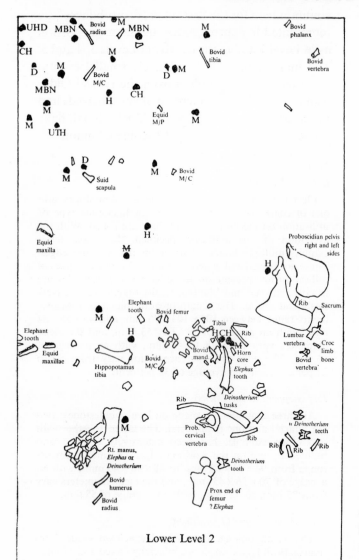

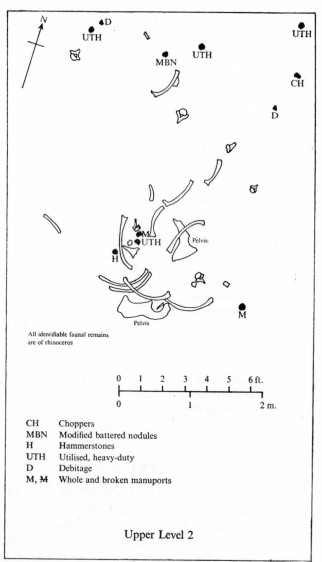

Fig. 47. HWK East. Plan of finds in Level 2.

The length/breadth/thickness measurements range from 72 × 60 × 44 mm. to 66 × 65 × 44 mm., with an average of 70 × 62 × 38 mm., and the mean diameters vary from 58 to 51 mm. The edge/circumference ratio varies from 88 to 60 per cent, with an average of 70 per cent.

Polyhedrons (4 specimens)

These consist of a chert nodule flaked over most of the surface, with four short, sharp edges; a lava cobblestone retaining cortex surface on part of the exterior, but with five intersecting cutting edges, and two angular quartz specimens. All four are in fresh, sharp condition. The measurements range from 105 × 95 × 69 mm. to 42 × 38 × 29 mm., with an average of 61 × 56 × 45 mm., and the mean

diameters vary from 89 to 36 mm., with an average of 55 mm.

Discoids (2 specimens)

Both these tools are made from quartz. They exhibit bifacially flaked cutting edges on the entire circumference. The cross-sections are biconvex and one example has been battered and bruised on one face. (50 × 45 × 40 mm. and 74 × 73 × 56 mm. Mean diameters 45 mm. and 67 mm.)

Subspheroids (11 specimens)

These consist of subspherical quartz or quartzite specimens with extensive battering on the projecting ridges. The mean diameters range from 74 to 31 mm., with an average of 50 mm.

94

Modified battered nodules and blocks (27 specimens)

This series of quartz and quartzite nodules and blocks shows some preparatory flaking in addition to battering and crushing of the edges. The mean diameters range from 84 to 33 mm., with an average of 43 mm.

Scrapers, heavy-duty (2 specimens)

(*a*) One is made on part of a lava cobble in which a fractured surface forms the lower face. The trimming on the upper face is steep and the edge is particularly sharp and fresh, with no evidence of utilisation. (64 × 90 mm. Edge length 95 mm.)

(*b*) The second is a high-backed rolled specimen made from lava, with a steeply trimmed circular working edge. The lower face has three negative scars. Chipped utilisation is evident on the upper face only. (52 × 63 mm. Edge length 155 mm.)

Scrapers, light-duty (3 specimens)

Two examples are made from quartzite and one from chert. The quartzite specimens are rolled and are made on pieces of tabular material. The working edges are steeply trimmed and are somewhat jagged and uneven. The length/breadth measurements range from 55 × 52 mm. to 34 × 50 mm.

Awl (1 specimen)

This consists of an end-struck chert flake with a trimmed point at the tip. (30 × 28 mm.)

Sundry tools (3 specimens)

There are three small core tools with one or more bifacially flaked edges. Two are of chert and one of lava. The measurements range from 63 × 46 × 29 mm. to 45 × 29 × 19 mm.

UTILISED MATERIAL

Hammerstones (6 specimens)

Six lava cobblestones are pitted and bruised at the ends or on other projecting parts. Shattering is also present on some of the specimens. The mean diameters range from 86 to 58 mm., with an average of 75 mm.

Cobblestones (20 specimens)

These consist of lava cobbles similar to those employed for hammerstones, but lacking pitting and bruising. They are often shattered. The mean diameters range from 83 to 43 mm., with an average of 63 mm.

Flake, heavy-duty (1 specimen)

A pointed and roughly triangular quartz flake shows extensive chipping along both lateral edges. (74 × 69 mm.)

Light-duty flakes and other fragments (17 specimens)

Two specimens show utilisation on straight edges, five on concave edges and three on convex edges. There are also seven examples with indeterminate chipping. Twelve are made from quartz or quartzite, one from lava and four from chert. The measurements range from 73 × 68 mm. to 26 × 27 mm.

DEBITAGE

This amounts to 195 specimens, of which twenty-five are complete flakes, 130 broken flakes and chips and forty core fragments. Quartz and quartzite predominate in the raw materials, with 169 specimens. Of the remainder, fourteen are of chert and twelve of lava.

Whole flakes

These are all divergent. The bulbs of percussion and the angles of the striking platforms are very variable. The length/breadth measurements range from 80 × 77 mm. to 15 × 31 mm., with an average for both the end- and side-struck flakes of 41 × 36 mm.

MANUPORTS (21 SPECIMENS)

These consist of ten complete and six broken lava cobbles, two of quartz and one of pegmatite as well as two lava blocks. The average mean diameter is 72 mm.

Analysis of the industry from HWK East, Level 2

	Nos.	%
Tools	74	23·6
Utilised material	44	14·0
Débitage	195	62·3
	313	
Tools		
Side choppers	12	16·2
End choppers	3	4·0
Two-edged chopper	1	1·4
Broken and unfinished		
choppers	2	2·7
'Proto-bifaces'	3	4·0
Polyhedrons	4	5·4
Discoids	2	2·7
Sub-spheroids	11	14·9
Modified battered nodules		
and blocks	27	36·5
Scrapers, heavy-duty	2	2·7
Scrapers, light-duty	3	4·0
Awl	1	1·4
Sundry tools	3	4·0
	74	
Utilised material		
Hammerstones	6	13·6
Cobblestones	20	45·5
Flake, heavy-duty	1	2·3
Light-duty flakes and other		
fragments	17	38·6
	44	
Débitage		
Whole flakes	25	12·8
Broken flakes and chips	130	66·6
Core fragments	40	20·5
	195	

CHAPTER IV

THE LOWER PART OF MIDDLE BED II

Site HWK East: the Sandy Conglomerate: Levels 3, 4 and 5. Site FLK North: the Sandy Conglomerate. The Skull Site at MNK

1. SITE HWK EAST
THE SANDY CONGOLOMERATE

LEVELS 3, 4 AND 5

This horizon lies approximately 10 ft. above the base of Bed II and can be traced from HWK East through the exposures at FLK South and VEK, to FLK North. It consists of a coarse sand or gravel and is normally very rich in artefacts. At HWK East the deposit reaches 2 ft. in thickness and consists of a coarse conglomerate with large numbers of pebbles and cobbles. In some areas it also contains a number of fossil bones. Some of the material is considerably rolled, but the greater part is fresh. Artefacts made from white or yellow chert are a characteristic feature and it is possible that the availability of chert led to the increased variety in small tools that occurs at this time.

A peak period for the use of chert was reached in these levels, particularly in Level 4. It is noticeable that the increased use of chert coincides with a proportionate decrease in the use of quartz and quartzite, particularly for light-duty tools and utilised flakes. Fig. 48 shows that in Level 4 the decrease in the use of quartz and quartzite corresponds almost exactly with the increased use of chert, indicating that these two materials were probably selected for the same purpose, i.e. the manufacture of sharp-edged light-duty tools. It would seem that when chert could be obtained it was preferred to any other material, particularly for this purpose.

The nearest exposed source of chert at present is at MNK, in the southern branch of the Gorge, three-quarters of a mile distant. Here chert nodules can be seen *in situ*. They occur in horizontal bands within a reworked tuff, 12 ft. above the base of Bed II, and are exposed in a small cliff which rises from the present-day river course. At MNK, and elsewhere, the main chert-bearing horizon, containing a greyish-white variety, is underlain by a tuff containing a smaller number of yellow chert nodules.[1]

The industry from Levels 3, 4, and 5, which overlie Tuff II^A, appears to be a direct development from the Oldowan of Bed I and the base of Bed II although certain tools become more common: there are greater numbers of spheroids, subspheroids, battered angular core fragments and also small scrapers of various types. The three levels combined correspond to the Sandy Conglomerate at FLK North, although Levels 3 and 5, which occur above and below the conglomerate at HWK East, are not present at FLK North.

The detailed descriptions of the artefacts from each level are given separately, but since it is evident that there is no appreciable difference either in typology or in the proportions of the various elements in the three assemblages, the material is considered jointly in the final review.

Several of the artefacts are rolled, particularly the heavy-duty tools. Level 3 has the highest proportion, with 17 per cent. In Level 4, 6 per cent is rolled and in Level 5 only a few specimens show slight abrasion.

[1] A chipping floor on the chert bed has since been found at MNK. Many hundreds of broken chert nodules, flakes and chips as well as a few hammerstones and bone fragments occur at the western end of the small cliff referred to above. The site was discovered during July 1968 and a part has since been excavated. It will be the subject of a separate publication.

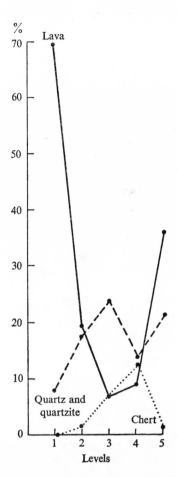

Fig. 48. HWK East. Graph showing the proportions of quartz, lava and chert used for raw materials in Levels 1 to 5.

LEVEL 3

This level was particularly rich in artefacts and also yielded large numbers of unmodified cobblestones, some of which may be of natural origin (Fig. 49). Fossil bones were rare and always in a very fragmentary condition.

TOOLS

Side choppers (57 specimens)

Thirty-seven examples are made of lava, eight of quartz or quartzite and twelve of chert. With the exception of a few quartz specimens and those made on chert nodules, the whole series is made on cobblestones. Bifacial choppers with multiple flaking on either side of the working edges predominate. Seven are unifacial and five exhibit a single scar on one face, opposed to multiple flaking on the obverse. Several specimens resemble those described from

Level 2, in which the working edges extend partly along both lateral edges. In the bifacial series the edges are usually jagged, with deeply indented flake scars, but in a few examples the scars are relatively shallow, giving rise to a more even working edge. The butt ends are formed by cortex or weathered surfaces. Only three examples show hammerstone utilisation on the butt ends. Nineteen specimens are rolled.

The extent of utilisation varies considerably. In 40 per cent of the specimens that show chipping of the working edges it has caused extensive blunting. In 51 per cent there is some chipping and blunting, but not to such a marked extent. The remaining specimens are too abraded to determine the extent of utilisation. The length/breadth/thickness measurements range from 87 × 101 × 76 mm. to 39 × 48 × 36 mm., with an average of 63 × 77 × 45 mm., and the mean diameters vary from 88 to 41 mm., with an average of 62 mm. The edge/circumference ratios vary from 69 to 19 per cent, with an average of 37 per cent.

End choppers (17 specimens)

These are all made on lava cobblestones. Two examples are unifacial, three exhibit steep flaking on one face of the working edge, with only one or two negative scars on the obverse. In two examples only one flake has been removed from either side. The others show multiple flaking on both faces. The butt ends are generally formed by cortex surface. Hammerstone utilisation occurs on two specimens; three are rolled. The degree of utilisation is variable and is similar to that described for the side choppers. The length/breadth/thickness measurements range from 90 × 64 × 67 mm. to 59 × 44 × 32 mm., with an average of 73 × 62 × 49 mm., and the mean diameters vary from 73 to 45 mm., with an average of 65 mm. The edge/circumference ratios vary from 35 to 14 per cent, with an average of 27 per cent.

Two-edged choppers (5 specimens)

One example is made of quartz and four are made on lava cobblestones. The working edges are situated in various positions relative to one another; at either end (one specimen), on either lateral edge (two specimens) and at right angles to one another (two specimens). All the edges are bifacially flaked and exhibit a considerable degree of wear. The length/breadth/thickness measurements range from 109 × 97 × 60 mm. to 84 × 59 × 33 mm., and the average mean diameter is 67 mm.

Pointed choppers (3 specimens)

Two specimens made on lava cobblestones are flaked on one face only, from the cortex surface. The flaking is steep and forms a short, thickset point, approximately in the centre of the working edge. The third specimen is made on a split lava cobblestone. The working edge is steeply trimmed from the fractured surface and has a short, well-defined point in the centre. Two specimens are rolled. The measurements are 88 × 100 × 63 mm., 52 × 64 × 57 mm. and 68 × 86 × 46 mm. respectively, and the average mean diameter is 68 mm.

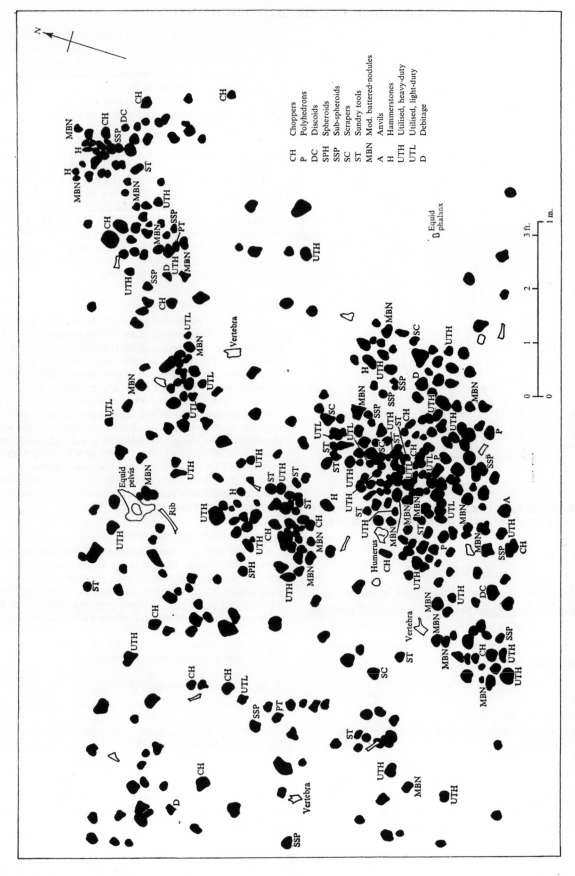

Fig. 49. HWK East. Trench II. Plan of finds at the base of Level 3. Unmarked stones represent natural cobblestones. Bones are shown in outline.

CH   Choppers
P   Polyhedrons
DC   Discoids
SPH   Spheroids
SSP   Sub-spheroids
SC   Scrapers
ST   Sundry tools
MBN   Mod. battered-nodules
A   Anvils
H   Hammerstones
UTH   Utilised, heavy-duty
UTL   Utilised, light-duty
D   Debitage

Chisel-edged choppers (*2 specimens*)

One example is made of a lava cobblestone and one is of quartz. Both are bifacially flaked, with a single scar on one side of the working edge and multiple scars on the opposite side. Some chipped utilisation is evident. The working edges in both specimens lie at right angles to the upper and lower faces; they measure 37 mm. and 33 mm. respectively in width. The length/breadth/thickness measurements are $95 \times 74 \times 73$ mm. and $66 \times 57 \times 50$ mm.

'*Proto-bifaces*' (*12 specimens*)

Three examples are of quartz and eight of lava. Three are rolled. There is great individual variation in these tools and it is necessary to give separate descriptions for each specimen. (Figs. 50–52.)

(*a*) This is made on part of a cobblestone, with the cortex surface retained at the butt end. The lower face shows two flat negative scars, detached from either lateral edge. The upper face is steeply flaked and the trimming extends across the tip and down both edges, with an area of cortex surface retained in the centre. The widest part of the tool is at the butt and it narrows rapidly to the tip. Edge/circumference ratio 58 per cent.

(*b*) This specimen is made on a cobblestone. It is bifacially flaked on almost the entire circumference, but retains cortex surface in the central part of both the upper and lower faces. The edge is jagged and heavily used and the tip is sharply pointed. Edge/circumference ratio 63 per cent.

(*c, d*) These are made on flat cobblestones, flaked over the greater part of both upper and lower faces and with cutting edges on the greater part of the circumference. The edges are unusually even and the tips are trimmed to symmetrical, rounded points. Edge/circumference ratios 61 and 63 per cent.

(*e*) This is a pointed specimen with a cortex butt, made on an oblong cobblestone which has been boldly flaked on both lateral edges and at the tip. Edge/circumference ratio 54 per cent. (Fig. 50, no. 2.)

(*f*) This is made on a large flake, struck from a cobblestone, with cortex surface on the dorsal face. Edge/circumference ratio 82 per cent. (Fig. 51, no. 1.)

(*g*) This is a crude specimen with cortex butt, made from a lava cobblestone, bifacially flaked on both lateral edges. The tip is rounded and the edge is jagged and sharp, with some chipped utilisation. Edge/circumference ratio 80 per cent.

(*h*) This is an oblong quartz specimen, bi-convex in cross-section and bifacially flaked round the circumference, except for a small area at the butt end. Edge/circumference ratio 85 per cent. (Fig. 52.)

(*i*) This is a small stumpy quartz specimen, very heavily used, it is bluntly pointed with a thick, oblique butt end. Edge/circumference ratio 75 per cent.

(*j*) This is an oval, blunt-ended quartz specimen, flaked on the entire circumference and over both faces. The edge is even and considerably blunted by use. Edge/circumference ratio 100 per cent.

(*k*) This is a symmetrical specimen with a thick, wide butt and rounded tip; it is made from a cobblestone. The flaking is bold and bifacial and extends down both lateral edges. The butt end is also flaked, but transversely. Part of the cortex surface is retained on the upper and lower faces. Edge/circumference ratio 63 per cent.

(*l*) A symmetrical specimen with a thick, wide butt and rounded tip. The flaking is bold and bifacial; it extends along both lateral edges and round the butt. Both the upper and lower faces retain areas of cortex surface. Edge/circumference ratio 53 per cent.

The length/breadth/thickness measurements range from $97 \times 101 \times 65$ mm. to $70 \times 60 \times 33$ mm., with an average of $82 \times 69 \times 48$ mm., and the mean diameters vary from 87 to 54 mm., with an average of 61 mm. The edge/circumference ratios vary from 100 to 54 per cent with an average of 70 per cent.

Polyhedrons (*13 specimens*)

Four examples are made from quartz or quartzite, eight from lava and one from a chert nodule. They are angular or subangular, generally flaked over the entire surface and exhibiting three or more bifacially flaked cutting edges, which often intersect. Utilisation is generally present. Three examples are rolled. The length/breadth/thickness measurements vary from $88 \times 83 \times 68$ mm. to $56 \times 54 \times 54$ mm., with an average of $74 \times 66 \times 65$ mm., and the mean diameters vary from 79 to 54 mm., with an average of 65 mm.

Discoids (*4 specimens*)

Two examples are made from lava, one from chert and one from quartzite. The quartzite specimen and one of those made from lava are relatively thick in cross-section with bifacially flaked cutting edges on the circumference. The second lava specimen is elliptical in cross-section and is heavily rolled, while the small chert discoid is in sharp condition, although chipped by use on the circumference. It also exhibits a crushed notch. (Fig. 55, no. 5.) The length/breadth/thickness measurements range from $85 \times 78 \times 60$ mm. to $39 \times 35 \times 25$ mm. The average mean diameter for the four specimens is 55 mm.

Spheroids (*8 specimens*)

Seven examples are of quartz or quartzite and one of lava. These tools are pecked and smoothly rounded over the whole surface. Two are symmetrical stone balls and the remainder are well finished, although not quite so symmetrical. Two appear to be rolled. The mean diameters range from 76 to 31 mm., with an average of 57 mm. (Pl. 19.)

Subspheroids (*75 specimens*)

Seven examples are of lava, one of obsidian, one of gneiss and the balance of quartz or quartzite. They are spherical in general shape but not entirely symmetrical, and the projecting ridges have been only partly reduced. Some examples are faceted and three are rolled. The mean diameters range from 78 to 26 mm., with an average of 53 mm. (Pl. 19.)

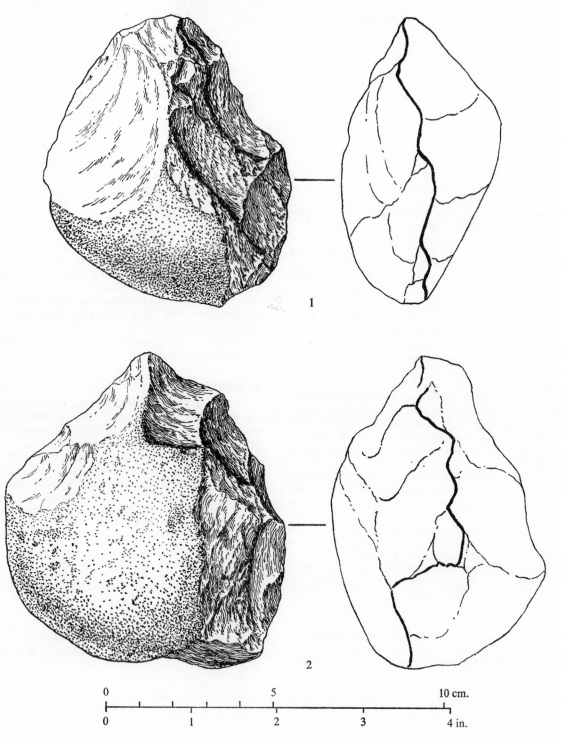

Fig. 50. HWK East. Level 3. Two 'proto-bifaces' made on lava cobbles.

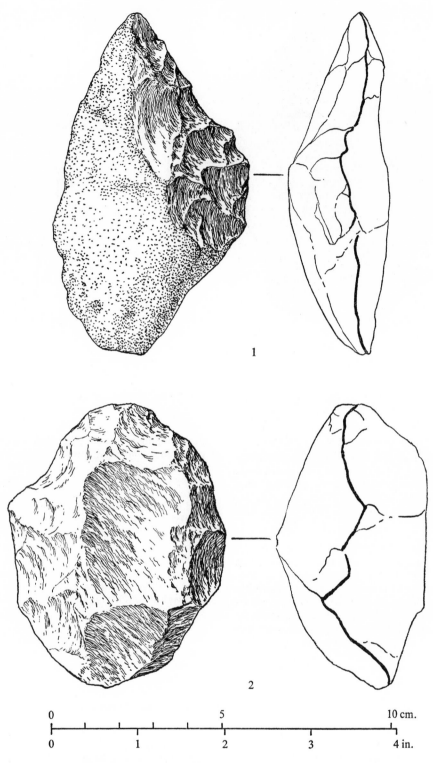

1

2

0   5   10 cm.

0   1   2   3   4 in.

Fig. 51. HWK East. Two 'proto-bifaces' from Levels 3 and 4. (1) is made on a flake struck from a lava cobble and has been trimmed on the primary flake surface as well as the dorsal aspect; (2) is made from quartzite.

101

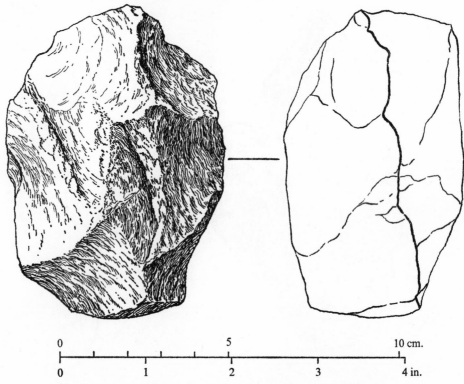

0   5   10 cm.

0   1   2   3   4 in.

Fig. 52. HWK East. Quartz 'proto-biface' from Level 3.

Modified battered nodules and blocks (*61 specimens*)

With the exception of one specimen of horneblende gneiss, the series is made of quartz or quartzite and consists of irregular-shaped subangular fragments, showing some flaking and considerable utilisation. Eight examples are rolled. The mean diameters range from 79 to 38 mm., with an average of 52 mm.

Scrapers, heavy-duty (*12 specimens*)

Five examples are made of quartz, one of horneblende gneiss and six of lava. In the majority the lower face consists of a natural flat surface. In one example there is a dorsal crest. The trimming of the working edges is invariably steep although the edges may be curved or nearly straight. Three examples are rolled. The series also includes two hollow scrapers with chipped, utilised notches on one edge. These measure 50 × 7 mm. and 31 × 4 mm. respectively. The length/breadth measurements for the twelve specimens range from 101 × 82 mm. to 70 × 56 mm., with an average of 84 × 73 mm.

Scrapers, light-duty (*29 specimens*)

Most of the small scrapers are made of chert (nineteen examples). There are ten of quartz or quartzite. The series includes end, side, butt-end and one hollow scraper. End scrapers are the most numerous and the majority are made on chert flakes. The working edges are generally rounded, but a few examples are square-ended. Although the trimming is relatively fine and regular, it is not always continuous and small projections at the intersections of trimming scars often remain, unless they have been broken off by use. There are five butt-end scrapers made on chert flakes. The striking platforms are unusually wide and deep and have been trimmed from the upper or dorsal aspect of the flakes to form a working edge. The trimming also usually extends along one edge. One quartz flake exhibits chipped notches on one edge, flaked from the under-surface. These measure 31 × 3 mm. and 25 × 2 mm. respectively.

The overall length/breadth measurements for the light-duty scrapers range from 65 × 49 mm. to 18 × 15 mm., with an average of 35 × 32 mm. (Fig. 53, nos. 1–12.)

Awls (*10 specimens*)

With the exception of two quartz flakes the series is made of chert. Since these tools constitute a new element, characteristic of the Developed Oldowan, they will be described in detail. (Fig. 53, nos. 13–20.)

(*a*) This is a stumpy flake with a trimmed notch on one side of the tip. The opposite edge is also chipped by use and the extreme tip of the point has been broken and damaged.

(*b*) This is made on a large flake which has been trimmed transversely at the tip to a slightly concave edge, 34 mm. long. Further retouch is present on the right lateral edge; the junction of the two edges forms a point which has snapped at the base.

(*c*) These consist of five small flakes with unifacially

102

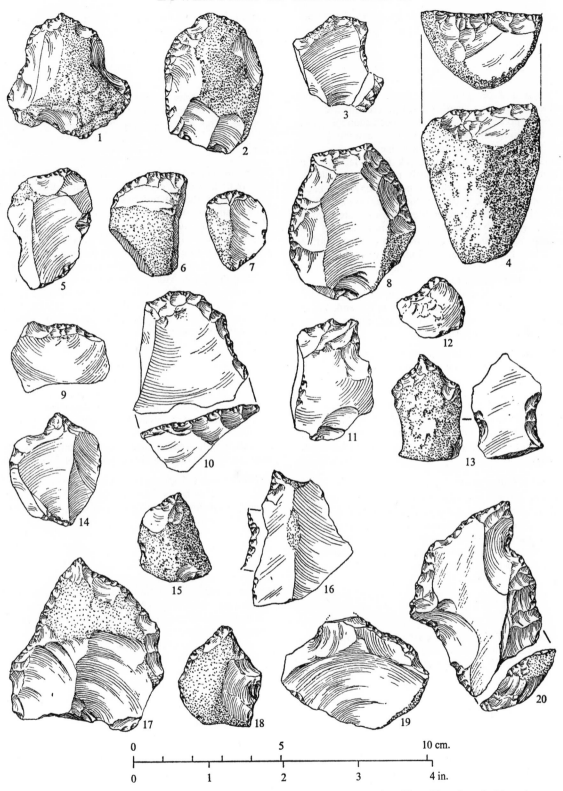

Fig. 53. HWK East. Light-duty chert tools. The majority are from Level 3. (1) to (8) end and side scrapers; (9) to (12) butt-end scrapers; (13) to (20) awls.

trimmed points at the tips. In three examples the points are formed by a notch on either side and in the remaining two by intersections of approximately straight trimmed edges. In one specimen the notch on one side of the point is 17 mm. wide and 2·5 mm. deep and may have served as a hollow scraper. (Fig. 53, nos. 14, 15.)

(*d*) This is a wide, side-struck flake. Both edges are trimmed and converge towards the tip, where only the base of the point is preserved, the tip having been snapped off in use. The trimming on the right-hand edge extends for 27 mm. and forms a curved scraper-like edge.

(*e*) This is made on an end-struck flake, lacking the bulbar end. The extremity is steeply trimmed to a short, sharp point resembling an awl. Two notches have also been trimmed on the under-surface; they are opposite one another and the specimen resembles a strangulated flake. The trimming of the point and of the notches and the fractured surface at the butt end are of a different patina to the primary flake surfaces and indicate re-utilisation of an older flake. Measurements of notches: 15 × 3 mm. and 10 × 1·5 mm. (Fig. 53, no. 13.)

(*f*) This is a double-pointed specimen. It is rolled and consists of a broken flake with a point at either end. These are formed by a trimmed notch on one side and a straight trimmed edge on the opposite side.

The length/breadth measurements for the series of ten specimens range from 56 × 49 mm. to 29 × 31 mm., with an average of 34 × 36 mm.

Laterally trimmed flakes (3 specimens)

Three chert flakes are trimmed along both lateral edges. The flakes are irregular and the tips have not been shaped. Measurements: 43 × 29 mm., 49 × 27 mm. and 35 × 30 mm. respectively.

Sundry tools (24 specimens)

These consist of irregular-shaped chert nodules on which there are one or more bifacially flaked working edges, usually showing utilisation. The form of the raw material is clearly responsible for the varying shapes of the tools, which might perhaps be classed as atypical small choppers. The mean diameters range from 70 to 20 mm., with an average of 36 mm. (Fig. 54.)

UTILISED MATERIALS

'Anvils' (9 specimens)

These consist of seven blocks of quartz or quartzite, one of gneiss and one cobblestone of lava, in which edges of approximately 90° show heavy utilisation. The mean diameters range from 114 to 51 mm., with an average of 76 mm.

Hammerstones (11 specimens)

Eleven lava cobblestones show some pitting and bruising on projecting areas. The mean diameters range from 78 to 51 mm., with an average of 58 mm.

Cobblestones (73 specimens)

These consist of lava cobblestones showing some evidence of utilisation, such as chipping or shattering, but not pitting as in the case of hammerstones. The mean diameters range from 81 to 51 mm., with an average of 60 mm.

Light-duty flakes and other fragments (70 specimens)

With straight edges (11 specimens). These consist of six quartz or quartzite flakes and five of chert in which one or more approximately straight edges are chipped and blunted by use. The length/breadth measurements range from 48 × 29 mm. to 18 × 16 mm., with an average of 35 × 26 mm.

With concave edges (15 specimens). Six examples are of quartz or quartzite, eight of chert and one of lava. There are relatively shallow notches on one or more edges. These do not appear to have been intentionally trimmed, but to have resulted from a particular type of utilisation. They occur on both thickset and thin edges. The chipping is usually from one direction only, but may be from either the upper or lower face. There are also a few examples with bifacial chipping. Most of the quartz and quartzite specimens are on core fragments and those of chert on broken flakes. The length/breadth measurements range from 53 × 51 mm. to 18 × 19 mm., with an average of 37 × 30 mm. The notches vary in width and depth from 18 × 2·5 mm. to 10 × 3 mm., with an average of 15 × 1·7 mm.

With convex edges (28 specimens). Nine examples are of quartz or quartzite and nineteen of chert. This series also consists of whole and broken flakes and core fragments in which chipping or blunting due to utilisation is present on one or more convex edges. It is usually in the form of fine 'nibbling', but is sometimes coarse and irregular. The overall length/breadth measurements range from 58 × 38 mm. to 18 × 20 mm., with an average of 33 × 28 mm.

Miscellaneous (16 specimens). An additional sixteen flakes and other fragments show a degree of chipping on the edges; seven are of quartz or quartzite, two of lava and seven of chert.

DEBITAGE

A total of 785 unmodified flakes and other fragments was recovered from this level, representing 61·2 per cent of the artefacts. Five hundred and seventy-nine broken flakes and chips (73·7 per cent) greatly outnumber both whole flakes (88 specimens) and core fragments (118 specimens). Five complete flakes, nineteen broken flakes and eight core fragments are rolled.

Chert represents 27·1 per cent of the *débitage* as a whole including most of the complete flakes. The proportions for the three groups are as follows:

	Whole flakes	Broken flakes and chips	Core fragments
Lava	9·9 %	2·7 %	0·9 %
Quartz/quartzite	17·3 %	72·2 %	95·4 %
Chert	72·8 %	25·1 %	3·6 %
Totals	88	579	118

785

104

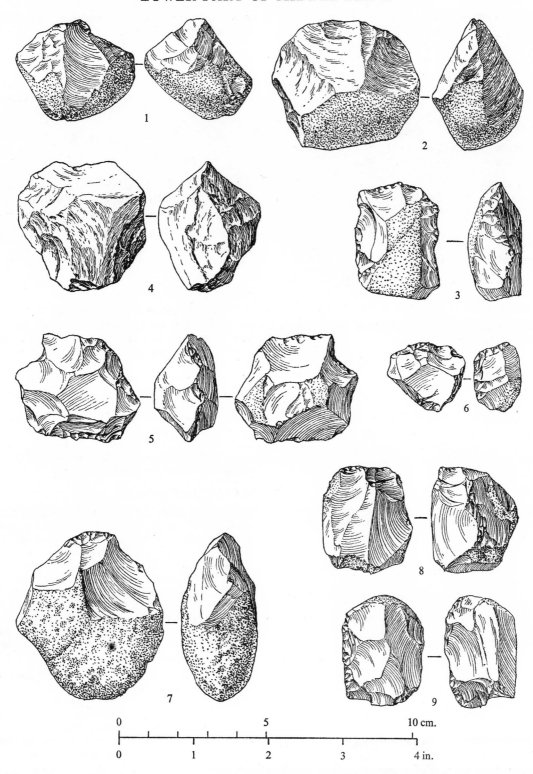

Fig. 54. HWK East. Sundry light-duty tools. (2) is of lava and (4) of quartzite; the balance are made on small chert nodules. (1) and (2) side choppers; (3) and (6) small core tools; (4) and (5) discoids; (7) end chopper. The majority are from Level 3.

Complete flakes (88 specimens)

With few exceptions these are divergent. The average length/breadth measurements vary considerably with the different materials, as the following table demonstrates. It is noticeable that the chert flakes, struck from small, irregular-shaped chert nodules, tend to be smaller than those of other materials.

Lava	Range	Average
End-struck	70 × 53 to 29 × 22	45 × 39
Side-struck	40 × 51 (1 specimen)	—
Quartz/quartzite		
End-struck	48 × 43 to 25 × 19	34 × 24
Side-struck	39 × 45 to 25 × 30	29 × 34
Chert		
End-struck	55 × 43 to 14 × 13	26 × 19
Side-struck	34 × 40 to 16 × 18	24 × 29

(Measurements are in millimetres.)

Bulbs of percussion

The proportions of the various forms of bulbs of percussion are as follows:

	Lava	Quartz/quartzite	Chert
Marked	25·0 %	14·3 %	83·0 %
Slight	50·0 %	35·7 %	6·8 %
Negative	—	28·5 %	—
Double	—	—	1·6 %
Shattered	25·0 %	21·4 %	8·5 %
Totals	8	14	59
		81	

It will be seen that in the chert flakes pronounced bulbs of percussion are more numerous than in other materials.

Angles of striking platforms

The figures for the angles of the striking platforms are as follows:

	Lava	Quartz/quartzite	Chert
70–89°	—	10·0 %	—
90–109°	—	50·0 %	31·0 %
110–129°	100·0 %	40·0 %	68·9 %
Totals	6	10	29
		45	

UNMODIFIED COBBLESTONES, NODULES AND BLOCKS (911 SPECIMENS)

The total number of unmodified lava cobblestones from this level amounts to 689, of which 54 are broken. It seems likely that the occurrence of such large numbers is due to water action rather than human agency. In a sample of thirty specimens the mean diameters range from 86 to 42 mm., with an average of 61 mm.

Nodules and blocks are considerably fewer, amounting to 222 specimens; many of these are of quartz and quartzite.

(The analysis of the industry from this level will be found on p. 109 with those of Levels 4 and 5.)

LEVEL 4

THE SANDY CONGLOMERATE

This level yielded considerably fewer artefacts than Level 3, with 601 specimens in contrast to 1,282. As has been stated, the relative proportions of the various elements are very similar, except for a larger amount of utilised material.

TOOLS

Side choppers (27 specimens)

Four examples are of quartz or quartzite, one of gneiss, six of chert and the balance of lava. Two are rolled. All the choppers in this series are bifacial and there are a number in which the working edges extend round more than half the circumference of the tools. The edges are jagged and exhibit the usual chipping and blunting from utilisation. The chert specimens are made on relatively small, irregular-shaped nodules. The length/breadth/thickness measurements range from 89 × 97 × 72 mm. to 34 × 35 × 28 mm., with an average of 58 × 72 × 47 mm., and the mean diameters vary from 80 to 30 mm., with an average of 60 mm. The edge/circumference ratio varies from 71 to 19 per cent with an average of 38 per cent.

End choppers (7 specimens)

Three are made on lava cobbles, two on small chers nodules and two on quartz blocks. One lava specimen it unifacial, while the remainder exhibit multiple flaking on both faces. There is chipped utilisation on the working edges in all seven examples. The length/breadth/thickness measurements range from 95 × 70 × 62 mm. to 35 × 30 × 20 mm., with an average of 66 × 58 × 39 mm. and the mean diameters vary from 75 to 28 mm., with an average of 54 mm. The average ratio of the working edges to the circumference is 32 per cent.

Two-edged choppers (5 specimens)

With the exception of one example made on an irregular nodule of yellow chert these tools are made on oblong lava cobbles with bifacially flaked working edges on either lateral edge. In the chert specimen there is one relatively short working edge at one extremity and a second along one side. The measurements range from 93 × 83 × 40 mm. to 66 × 61 × 44 mm., and the average mean diameter is 66 mm.

Pointed chopper (1 specimen)

This is made from a lava cobblestone and has a well-defined, sharp point approximately in the centre of the working edge, which is steeply flaked on the upper face from a flat cortex under-surface. The butt shows pitting and bruising resulting from hammerstone type of utilisation. (80 × 82 × 52 mm. Mean diameter 71 mm.)

Chisel-edged choppers (3 specimens)

All three examples are made on relatively flat lava cobblestones, with the working edges at right angles to the upper and lower faces. In two examples the edges are bifacially flaked with multiple scars on both faces; the third has a single large scar on one face, with multiple flaking on the opposite face. One example is rolled. The length/breadth/thickness measurements range from 71 × 74 × 44 mm. to 53 × 52 × 34 mm., with an average mean diameter of 51 mm. The average edge/circumference ratio is 13 per cent.

'Proto-biface' (1 specimen)

This specimen is made from quartz. It has a blunt point at either end and is boldly flaked on both faces round the entire circumference. The edge is jagged to sinuous and is blunted by utilisation, particularly on one side. (81 × 65 × 45 mm.)

Polyhedrons (10 specimens)

Five examples are made of quartz or quartzite, one of lava and four of chert; two are rolled. The whole series is angular, with three or more projecting edges, which are often jagged and usually exhibit chipping and blunting from utilisation. There is a wide variation in size, from the lava specimen in which the mean diameter is 101 mm., to the smallest chert example with a mean diameter of 27 mm. The length/breadth/thickness measurements range from 118 × 95 × 92 mm. to 32 × 30 × 29 mm., with an average of 68 × 58 × 52 mm., and the average mean diameter is 58 mm.

Discoids (3 specimens)

These consist of three small quartz or quartzite specimens which are roughly discoidal and which have a bifacially flaked cutting edge on the whole circumference. In two specimens the edges are sharp, with light chipping and in the third the edge is largely crushed and blunted. The mean diameters range from 40 to 32 mm., with an average of 34 mm.

Spheroids (6 specimens)

The whole series is made from quartz. The surfaces are battered with most of the projecting ridges greatly reduced. Only one is sufficiently symmetrical and well made to be described as a stone ball. The mean diameters range from 68 to 45 mm., with an average of 56 mm.

Subspheroids (17 specimens)

These are all of quartz or quartzite. They are similar to the spheroids but are sub-angular and less symmetrical. The mean diameters range from 79 to 30 mm., with an average of 43 mm.

Modified battered nodules and blocks (21 specimens)

These consist of a series of quartz and quartzite blocks with some flaking and utilisation on the edges. Convex surfaces are also frequently battered. The mean diameters range from 76 to 27 mm., with an average of 44 mm.

Scrapers, heavy-duty (4 specimens)

Three examples are of quartz or quartzite and one of lava. They are steeply trimmed from flat or slightly concave under-surfaces. The working edges are curved and tend to be uneven. Chipped utilisation is present and one example bears a crushed indentation. The length/breadth measurements range from 76 × 83 mm. to 53 × 64 mm., with an average of 65 × 65 mm.

Scrapers, light-duty (15 specimens)

These consist of seven end scrapers, six side scrapers and two butt-end scrapers. One example is made of quartz, one of quartzite and the balance of chert. They closely resemble the light-duty scrapers from Level 3 and will not be described in further detail. The length/breadth measurements range from 53 × 48 mm. to 23 × 17 mm., with an average of 36 × 31 mm.

Awls (4 specimens)

These are four chert flakes with points formed by a trimmed notch on either side. The points are situated at the tips or on one lateral edge. Length/breadth measurements vary from 54 × 55 mm. to 25 × 31 mm., with an average of 42 × 42 mm.

Sundry tools (8 specimens)

These consist of chert nodules flaked and utilised on one or more edges. The mean diameters vary from 31 to 25 mm., with an average of 27 mm.

UTILISED MATERIAL

'Anvils' (6 specimens)

Four lava cobblestones, a discoidal piece of quartz and a hexagonal block of hornblende gneiss (of the type which occurs at the Kelogi inselberg) show battering and crushing on edges which approximate 90°. Two examples are rolled. The mean diameters range from 87 to 53 mm., with an average of 67 mm.

Hammerstones (10 specimens)

These consist of eight cobblestones of lava and two of quartz with pitting and bruising on the extremities and on other projecting areas. The mean diameters range from 77 to 33 mm., with an average of 60 mm.

Cobblestones (24 specimens)

These consist of lava cobblestones that have been broken or otherwise damaged by use, but do not show the type of utilisation found on hammerstones. The mean diameters range from 90 to 51 mm., with an average of 65 mm.

Light-duty flakes and other fragments (84 specimens)

With straight edges (4 specimens). Three flakes of quartz and one of chert show utilisation on one or more approximately straight edges. Two are rolled.

With concave edges (*15 specimens*). Seven quartz and eight chert flakes and other fragments are notched, in addition to having some utilisation on other edges. Chipping in the notches is almost entirely on one face, the notches ranging in width from 20 to 8 mm., and in depth from 4 to 2 mm., with an average of $12 \times 2 \cdot 6$ mm.

With convex edges (*25 specimens*). Twenty-one quartz or quartzite flakes and four of chert show chipped utilisation on curved edges. This is usually in the form of fine 'nibbling', but in some specimens the chipping is coarse and irregular.

Miscellaneous (*40 specimens*). Twenty-eight chert flakes, eleven quartz and one lava exhibit haphazard chipping on the edges, either on one or both faces. There are three flakes in which the upper margins of the striking platforms have been utilised.

The length/breadth measurements for the eighty-four specimens range from 70×40 mm., to 21×15 mm., with an average of 45×32 mm.

DEBITAGE

The total of *débitage* from this level amounts to 345 specimens, consisting of 70 whole flakes, 212 broken flakes and chips and 63 core fragments. The series includes a higher proportion of complete flakes than Level 3 ($20 \cdot 3$ per cent in contrast to $11 \cdot 2$ per cent). The proportions of various raw materials are as follows:

	Whole flakes	Broken flakes and chips	Core fragments
Lava	7·0 %	0·5 %	1·7 %
Quartz/quartzite	27·7 %	82·6 %	84·2 %
Chert	65·2 %	16·8 %	14·1 %
Totals	70	212	63

345

As in Level 3, whole flakes of chert are more common than those of other materials.

Whole flakes

Most of these flakes are divergent, with end-struck specimens predominating. The length/breadth measurements (in millimetres) are as follows:

Lava	Range	Average
End-struck	68 × 63 to 64 × 40	66 × 46
Side-struck	36 × 70 (1 specimen)	
Quartz/quartzite		
End-struck	48 × 20 to 25 × 23	33 × 25
Side-struck	25 × 38 to 21 × 23	24 × 29
Chert		
End-struck	41 × 31 to 18 × 15	25 × 21
Side-struck	26 × 40 to 21 × 25	24 × 31

In this series more of the quartz flakes have marked bulbs of percussion than those of chert, as follows:

	Lava	Quartz/ quartzite	Chert
Marked	60·0 %	82·3 %	69·0 %
Slight	20·0 %	17·6 %	28·5 %
Negative	20·0 %	—	2·4 %
Totals	5	17	42

64

Angles of striking platforms

It is possible to measure the angles of the striking platforms in thirty-four specimens. The figures are as follows:

	Lava	Quartz/ quartzite	Chert
70–89°	—	—	—
90–109°	66·6 %	50·0 %	4·7 %
110–129°	33·3 %	50·0 %	95·2 %
Totals	3	10	21

34

UNMODIFIED COBBLESTONES, NODULES AND BLOCKS (202 SPECIMENS)

192 cobblestones and ten nodules or blocks were recovered from this level. Although some of the lava specimens may be of natural origin, the pieces of basement complex rocks must be regarded as manuports, since the drainage in contemporary stream channels was not from any known basement complex outcrop.

LEVEL 5

Only 106 artefacts were recovered from this level. These include an unusually high percentage of tools ($30 \cdot 2$ per cent), which are more numerous than utilised material ($28 \cdot 3$ per cent). *Débitage* amounts to $41 \cdot 5$ per cent.

TOOLS

Side choppers (*6 specimens*)

All six examples are made on lava cobblestones. There is one specimen in which the working edge is trimmed by means of a single scar on one face, with multiple flaking on the obverse. Another is unifacial. The remainder show multiple flaking on both faces. The edges are jagged and generally chipped by use. The length/breadth/thickness measurements range from $98 \times 96 \times 68$ mm. to $85 \times 46 \times 29$ mm., with an average of $71 \times 79 \times 53$ mm. The average mean diameter is 67 mm. and the average edge/circumference ratio 34 per cent.

End chopper (*1 specimen*)

This is a unifacial specimen made on a lava cobblestone. It is steeply trimmed on one face ($56 \times 52 \times 39$ mm.)

Analysis of the industry from HWK East, Levels 3, 4 and 5

	Level 3		Level 4		Level 5		Totals	
	Nos.	%	Nos.	%	Nos.	%	Nos.	%
Tools	334	26·1	132	22·0	32	30·2	498	25·0
Utilised material	163	12·7	124	20·6	30	28·3	317	16·0
Débitage	785	61·2	345	57·4	44	41·5	1,174	59·0
	1,282		601		106		1,989	
Tools								
Side choppers	57	17·1	27	20·4	6	18·7	90	18·1
End choppers	17	5·1	7	5·3	1	3·1	25	5·0
Two-edged choppers	5	1·5	5	3·8	—	—	10	2·0
Pointed choppers	3	0·9	1	0·7	—	—	4	0·8
Chisel-edged choppers	2	0·6	3	2·3	—	—	5	1·0
'Proto-bifaces'	12	3·3	1	0·7	1	3·1	13	2·6
Polyhedrons	13	3·9	10	7·6	2	6·3	25	5·0
Discoids	4	1·2	3	2·3	2	6·3	9	1·8
Spheroids	8	2·4	6	4·5	3	9·4	17	3·4
Subspheroids	75	22·4	17	12·9	5	15·6	97	19·5
Modified battered nodules and blocks	61	18·2	21	16·0	7	21·9	89	17·9
Scrapers, heavy-duty	12	3·6	4	3·0	—	—	16	3·2
Scrapers, light-duty	29	8·7	15	11·3	4	12·5	48	9·6
Awls	10	3·0	4	3·0	—	—	14	2·8
Laterally trimmed flakes	3	0·9	—	—	—	—	3	0·6
Sundry tools	24	7·2	8	6·1	1	3·1	33	6·6
	335		132		32		498	
Utilised material								
'Anvils'	9	5·5	6	4·8	4	13·3	19	6·0
Hammerstones	11	6·7	10	8·0	6	20·0	27	8·5
Cobblestones	73	44·8	24	19·3	16	53·3	113	35·6
Light duty flakes etc.	70	42·9	84	67·7	4	13·3	158	49·8
	163		124		30		317	
Débitage								
Whole flakes	88	11·2	70	20·3	11	25·0	169	14·4
Broken flakes and chips	579	73·7	212	61·4	27	61·3	818	69·6
Core fragments	118	15·0	63	18·2	6	13·6	187	15·9
	785		345		44		1,174	

'Proto-biface' (1 specimen)

This is a small, slightly asymmetrical quartz specimen, bluntly pointed, with a relatively wide butt. The edge, which extends round the whole circumference, is irregular and is both chipped and crushed by utilisation in certain areas. (71 × 65 × 42 mm. Mean diameter 59 mm.)

Polyhedrons (2 specimens)

Both examples are angular, with a number of short intersecting edges, all of which show utilisation. Made from quartz and quartzite respectively. (43 × 43 × 38 mm. and 40 × 37 × 27 mm. Mean diameters 41 mm. and 24 mm.)

Discoids (2 specimens)

Both specimens are made of quartz. The circumferences are bifacially trimmed and the edges are blunted by use.

(103 × 100 × 62 mm. and 57 × 52 × 33 mm. Mean diameters 88 and 47 mm.)

Spheroids (3 specimens)

These consist of three well-made quartz or quartzite specimens. The mean diameters are 60 mm., 38 mm. and 45 mm.

Subspheroids (5 specimens)

These are all made of quartz. They are battered over the exterior and are similar to the spheroids, but less symmetrical and more angular. The mean diameters range from 56 to 35 mm., with an average of 49 mm.

Modified battered nodules and blocks (7 specimens)

One lava and six quartz fragments show some preparatory flaking in addition to utilisation of the edges. The mean

109

diameters range from 63 to 39 mm., with an average of 52 mm.

Scrapers, light-duty (4 specimens)

These consist of three end-scrapers, two of which are made from quartz and one from chert, as well as one hollow scraper made from lava. Two of the end scrapers are square-ended. The third is stumpy and round-ended. In the hollow scraper the notch is steeply trimmed from one direction only and measures $19 \times 3 \cdot 5$ mm. The length/breadth measurements for the five specimens range from 57×52 mm. to 25×21 mm., with an average of 37×28 mm.

Sundry tool (1 specimen)

One small oblong core tool has a bifacially flaked, jagged working edge, chipped by use. The mean diameter is 27 mm.

UTILISED MATERIAL

'Anvils' (4 specimens)

These consist of two blocks of tabular quartzite and two of lava, in which edges of approximately 90° have been heavily utilised. The mean diameters are 86, 71 and 69 mm.

Hammerstones (6 specimens)

There are six lava cobblestones in which the extremities and other parts of the surface have been pitted and bruised. The mean diameters range from 64 to 56 mm., with an average of 61 mm.

Cobblestones (16 specimens)

A further series of lava cobblestones exhibits some chipping and also battered utilisation. The mean diameters range from 90 to 51 mm., with an average of 65 mm.

Light-duty flakes and other fragments (4 specimens)

These consist of two quartz flakes and two other fragments with utilisation including notches on the edges. The average measurements for the four specimens are 50×45 mm.

DEBITAGE

The *débitage* consists of eleven complete flakes, twenty-seven broken flakes and six core fragments. Of these forty-four specimens, five are of chert and the balance of quartz. The former are extensively weathered with a white chalky texture, and very light in weight.

UNMODIFIED COBBLESTONES, NODULES AND BLOCKS (71 SPECIMENS)

Fifty-seven lava cobblestones, six of which are broken, were recovered as well as fourteen blocks and nodules of lava, some of which may be of natural origin.

THE COMBINED INDUSTRIES FROM LEVELS 3, 4 AND 5

As has been noted, some of the tools from these three levels are rolled. This is more noticeable in the choppers and other heavy-duty tools than in the light-duty tools or utilised material.

Most of the choppers are made from waterworn lava cobblestones but some quartz, quartzite and chert specimens also occur. Side choppers are by far the most numerous type, with 90 specimens out of a total of 134. Hammerstone type of utilisation on the butt ends occurs in only four specimens, although it is found on a large number of the Bed I choppers. Some unifacial examples occur, but they are generally of the normal Oldowan type, with jagged, bifacially flaked working edges. In a number of the side choppers that are made on oblong cobblestones the trimming of the working edge extends partly across one or both ends in addition to that on the main edge. Other types of choppers represented in the series are end, two-edged, pointed and chisel-edged.

'Proto-bifaces' are relatively numerous. They are all bifacially flaked on both lateral edges, with roughly pointed tips. In four specimens the cutting edge extends round the whole circumference, whilst in others the butt is formed by cortex surface. The edges are normally jagged with only occasional slight retouch at the tips. Discoids are poorly represented and are generally crude. The spheroids, subspheroids and modified battered nodules and blocks amount to $40 \cdot 8$ per cent of the tools and include a few stone balls pecked and smoothed on the whole exterior, as well as faceted examples. Apart from the stone balls there is no clear distinction between the three groups, which grade into one another.

The heavy-duty scrapers are made on cores, mostly on split cobblestones or on blocks of tabular quartzite. The lower faces are flat and the upper faces are steeply flaked. The series includes crude specimens with uneven working edges and others in which the edges have been retouched to a regular curve. The edges are generally blunted by use; chipped utilisation is also usually present on the upper faces.

110

The light-duty scrapers include a variety of different types. There are end, side and hollow scrapers, mostly made on flakes, together with seven specimens in which the striking platforms of the flakes have been converted into the scraping edge. The majority are made from chert. End scrapers exceed any other type and include both square- and round-ended specimens; the retouch is fine and regular but small projections at the intersections of the trimming scars often remain, causing the edges to be somewhat uneven. The seven examples in which the scraping edge has been made at the butt end consist of flakes with unusually pronounced striking platforms. These have been trimmed from the dorsal face to form the working edges. Side scrapers and hollow scrapers are relatively scarce and call for no particular comment. The proportions of the various types of scrapers in the total of forty-eight light-duty specimens are as follows:

	Nos.	%
End scrapers	30	62·5
Side scrapers	9	18·7
Butt-end scrapers	7	14·6
Hollow scrapers	2	4·2
	48	

Among the small pointed tools classed as awls there are a number that have been trimmed to curved, scraper-like edges along one or both sides, in addition to the trimming at the points. They may possibly represent convergent scrapers or combined awl-scrapers although no other combination tools are known at this level. In two examples the points at the intersection of the retouched edges have been snapped off at the base and no attempt has been made to re-trim the broken edges.

The appearance of awls and the increase in small scrapers indicates a change of some importance in the tool requirements at this time. This may possibly have been the beginning of leather- or hide-working, although, if this were the case, the edges of the scrapers might be expected to be more even, without the small pointed projections that are evident on many specimens.

The heavy-duty utilised material includes 'an-vils', hammerstones, cobblestones, a few nodules and two flakes. The 'anvils' are of the usual Oldowan type. They consist of blocks or broken cobblestones in which one or more approximately right-angled edges have been battered. Roughly circular, cuboid and flat-based conical specimens are represented. In a few examples there is a minimum of preparatory flaking.

The light-duty utilised material consists of flakes and other fragments of quartz, quartzite and chert, with chipping and occasional blunting on straight, concave or convex edges, together with a miscellaneous group in which the utilisation is more haphazard. These categories are represented among the total of 158 specimens in the following proportions: straight-edged 9·3 per cent, concave-edged or notched 20·5 per cent, convex-edged 30·5 per cent, miscellaneous 39·7 per cent. Only four flakes are of lava. Quartz or quartzite and chert are represented in almost equal proportions.

In the *débitage* only 14·4 per cent is whole flakes. There is considerable variation in the bulbs of percussion and also in the angles of the striking platforms between the lava flakes and those of quartz, quartzite or chert. In the latter a larger percentage have pronounced bulbs and the angles of the striking platforms tend to be higher.

The industries from these levels, as well as that from the Sandy Conglomerate at FLK North, have been termed Developed Oldowan A. The variety of tools is greater than in the Oldowan, although there are, as yet, no true bifaces such as occur in the Developed Oldowan B.

2. SITE FLK NORTH, THE SANDY CONGLOMERATE

(The general description of FLK North has been given in the previous chapter.)

The deposit excavated from this horizon was not sieved, with the result that some of the smaller elements of the industry may not be represented. Side choppers are relatively common, but there are fewer with hammerstone utilisation than in the earlier assemblages. The series includes a number of specimens made on spherical cobblestones in which the thickness is equal to, or exceeds the the length or breadth. An unusually high proportion of the utilised material consists of light-duty flakes and other fragments with fine chipped utilisation on the edges; they are mostly made of chert. *Débitage* is particularly scarce, amounting to only 26·4 per cent of the whole assemblage.

TOOLS

Side choppers (22 specimens)

Ten examples are made on lava cobblestones, one on a chert nodule and the rest on blocks of quartz or quartzite. There are three unifacial choppers and the balance are bifacial, with multiple flaking on either side of the working edges. The flake scars are generally bold and deeply indented, giving rise to sharp, jagged edges, but in one specimen the trimming is fine and even and the edge is relatively straight. In another example there is a single negative scar on one side and multiple scars on the opposite face. The series includes two quartz specimens in which the butt ends are formed by a flat vertical surface and the working edges are evenly curved, extending round the greater part of the circumference. Blunting and chipping of the edges, caused by utilisation, are usually present. Six examples also exhibit hammerstone type of utilisation on the butt ends. The length/breadth/thickness measurements range from 89 × 95 × 103 mm. to 37 × 40 × 46 mm., with an average of 60 × 71 × 55 mm., and the mean diameters vary from 95 to 37 mm., with an average of 61 mm. The edge/circumference ratios vary from 72 to 23 per cent with an average of 42 per cent.

End choppers (3 specimens)

One example is made on an irregular chert nodule and two on lava cobblestones. In two specimens the working edges are trimmed by means of a single scar on one face, opposed to multiple flaking on the opposite side. In the third the trimming is carried out from the cortex surface. The butt ends are formed by cortex surface and the edges are sharp and fresh, with a minimum of utilisation. Length/ breadth/thickness measurements range from 81 × 80 × 58 mm. to 64 × 48 × 31 mm., with an average mean diameter of 58 mm. The edge/circumference ratios are 20, 24 and 37 per cent.

Polyhedrons (4 specimens)

All four examples are made from quartz or quartzite and each has three or more sharp, bifacially flaked edges. The length/breadth/thickness measurements range from 99 × 74 × 69 mm. to 63 × 59 × 43 mm., with an average mean diameter of 68 mm.

Discoids (9 specimens)

Five examples are made from quartz or quartzite and four from lava. In all the specimens the whole or the greater part of the circumference has been bifacially flaked. The edges are jagged and the extent of utilisation varies from heavy battering to light chipping. With one exception,

these tools are very crude. The largest specimen, made of lava, appears to be unfinished and is undercut on one side by deep step flaking, beneath a massive lump on the upper face. The length/breadth/thickness measurements range from 105 × 87 × 62 mm. to 45 × 39 × 34 mm., and the mean diameters vary from 84 to 33 mm., with an average of 57 mm.

Spheroids (10 specimens)

With the exception of one lava example, the series is made from quartz or quartzite. The majority of the specimens are faceted, with the projecting ridges only partially reduced by battering. One side is often more smoothly rounded than the opposite. A few examples are slightly oblong. The length/breadth/thickness measurements range from 103 × 101 × 81 mm. to 45 × 36 × 34 mm., with an average of 78 × 72 × 66 mm., and the mean diameters vary from 98 to 32 mm., with an average of 72 mm.

Subspheroids (25 specimens)

With the exception of two lava specimens, these tools are made from quartz or quartzite. They resemble the spheroids but are less symmetrical and include a number that are more massive than any found in Bed I. The length/breadth/ thickness measurements range from 104 × 108 × 94 mm. to 33 × 30 × 30 mm., with an average of 69 × 66 × 55 mm., and the mean diameters vary from 102 to 31 mm., with an average of 63 mm.

Modified battered nodules and blocks (14 specimens)

One example is of horneblende gneiss, similar to the variety found at Kelogi, and the balance are of quartz or quartzite. They consist of sub-angular blocks and other fragments with a minimum of shaping while the edges show varying degrees of utilisation. The mean diameters vary from 79 to 33 mm., with an average of 59 mm.

Scrapers, light-duty (13 specimens)

This series includes five small square-ended scrapers made on chert flakes, trimmed transversely across the tips that also show some chipping on the lateral edges. The balance, also made from chert, are round-ended. In a number of examples the working edges are relatively narrow, resembling those of nosed scrapers. The length/ breadth measurements range from 43 × 23 mm. to 19 × 21 mm., with an average of 33 × 27 mm. (Fig. 55, nos. 1–12.)

Awls (4 specimens)

These consist of chert flakes in which sharp points have been made by means of a notch on either side; in two examples the points are at the tips and in two on one lateral edge. Length/breadth measurements vary from 53 × 40 mm. to 29 × 25 mm., with an average of 45 × 32 mm. (Fig. 55, nos. 13–16.)

Sundry tools (6 specimens)

These consist of irregular-shaped chert nodules with one or more working edges, either pointed or straight. They are too formless to assign to any particular tool category, but probably represent small chopping tools. The length/

112

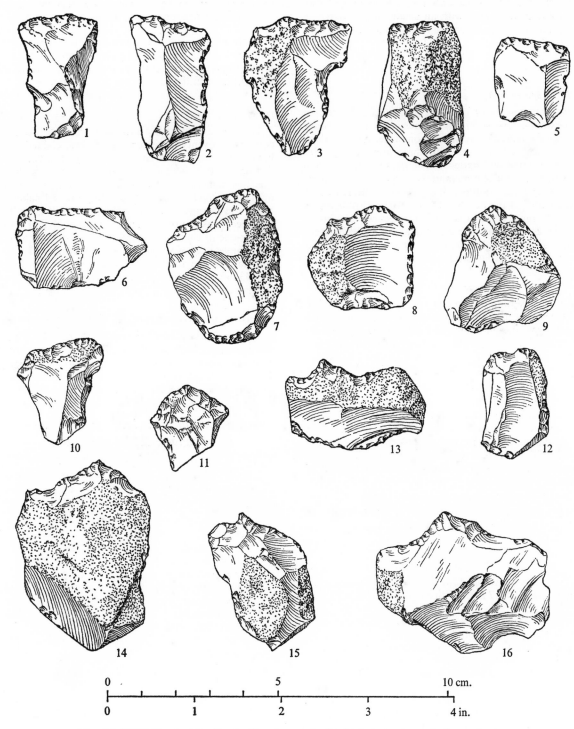

Fig. 55. FLK North. The Sandy Conglomerate. Light-duty tools made from chert.
(1) to (12) scrapers; (13) to (16) awls.

breadth/thickness measurements range from 68 × 62 × 31 mm. to 46 × 33 × 23 mm., with an average of 54 × 46 × 31 mm., and the mean diameters vary from 53 to 34 mm., with an average of 43 mm.

UTILISED MATERIAL

'Anvils' (2 specimens)

Both examples are of lava and show additional use as hammerstones. One specimen is unusual in that it bears an artificially pecked depression on one face. It consists of a subspherical cobblestone with three areas of the circumference pitted and battered. The depression measures approximately 35 × 24 mm. and is 5 mm. deep, with a somewhat irregular outline, not so clearly defined as in the pitted 'anvil' from Levels 1/2. (109 × 102 × 71 mm. Mean diameter 94 mm.) (Pl. 18.) The second specimen consists of an oblong cobblestone with one end artificially truncated. One lateral edge is also damaged by use. (113 × 92 × 65 mm. Mean diameter 90 mm.)

Hammerstones (11 specimens)

With the exception of two quartz or quartzite examples, these consist of lava cobblestones showing pitting and bruising. Two specimens are more extensively battered on one face than on the opposite and may be broken spheroids which were subsequently re-utilised. The mean diameters range from 85 to 35 mm., with an average of 72 mm.

Cobblestones (14 specimens)

These specimens are all of lava and include a number that are broken. They show a minimum amount of chipping or crude flaking but no recognisable working edge, or the type of utilisation seen on hammerstones. The mean diameters range from 86 to 46 mm., with an average of 63 mm.

Light-duty flakes and other fragments (36 specimens)

With straight edges (8 specimens). These consist of three quartz or quartzite and five chert flakes with utilisation on edges that are approximately straight. The utilisation is usually in the form of light chipping and may be on one or both faces. The length/breadth measurements range from 56 × 55 mm. to 30 × 17 mm., with an average of 42 × 29 mm.

With concave edges (9 specimens). There are three quartz or quartzite flakes and six of chert, with notches on one or more edges. These are generally chipped from one direction only, usually from the primary flake surface. The length/breadth measurements range from 61 × 40 mm. to 20 × 19 mm., with an average of 37 × 25 mm. The notches vary in width and depth from 15 × 4·5 mm. to 13 × 2·5 mm., with an average of 16 × 2·9 mm.

With convex edges (12 specimens). There are two quartz or quartzite and ten chert specimens. They consist of flakes and other fragments with chipping on rounded edges. The chipping is usually from one direction only, either from the upper or the lower surface. The length/breadth measure-ments range from 55 × 24 mm. to 22 × 20 mm., with an average of 33 × 28 mm.

There are, in addition, seven chert flakes with indeterminate chipping and blunting on the edges. The average length/breadth measurements for the whole series of thirty-six light-duty utilised flakes are 36 × 27 mm.

DEBITAGE

There is an unusually low proportion of *débitage*. It consists of twenty-three complete flakes, eighteen broken flakes and chips and twenty core fragments. The fact that sieving was not carried out may be in part responsible for this low figure, but it cannot be entirely so, since the number of small tools and light-duty utilised flakes is not below the average for the same level at HWK East. Thirty-five specimens are of quartz or quartzite, five of lava and twenty-one of chert. The length/breadth measurements for the complete flakes vary from 97 × 83 mm. to 30 × 24 mm. with an average for both end- and side-struck flakes of 48 × 43 mm. The bulbs of percussion and the angles of the striking platforms fall within the usual ranges.

UNMODIFIED COBBLESTONES, NODULES AND BLOCKS

Twenty-one lava cobbles were recovered, for which the average mean diameter is 66 mm., together with three quartz or quartzite blocks and two lava nodules. Because of the nature of the deposit, it is not possible to determine whether these are manuports or are of natural origin.

Analysis of the industry from the sandy conglomerate at FLK North

	Nos.	%
Tools	110	47·0
Utilised material	63	26·9
Débitage	61	26·1
	234	
Tools		
Side choppers	22	20·0
End choppers	3	2·7
Polyhedrons	4	3·6
Discoids	9	8·2
Spheroids	10	9·1
Subspheroids	25	22·7
Modified battered nodules and blocks	14	12·7
Scrapers, light-duty	13	11·8
Awls	4	3·6
Sundry tools	6	5·4
	110	
Utilised material		
'Anvils'	2	3·2
Hammerstones	11	17·5
Cobblestones	14	22·2
Light-duty flakes and other fragments	36	57·1
	63	

Débitage	Nos.	%
Whole flakes	23	37·7
Broken flakes and chips	18	29·5
Core fragments	20	32·8
	61	

3. MNK, THE SKULL SITE (MARY NICOL KORONGO)

Archaeological number (71)   Geologic locality 88

Excavations at MNK were carried out in both the lower and upper parts of Middle Bed II, namely at the Skull Site where the remains of hominids 13, 14 and 15 were found, and at the Main Occupation Site, which is at a higher level. The two sites are approximately 60 ft. distant from one another, the Skull Site being in the lower part of the gully, to the right of the footpath that leads up to the Main Site, see Fig. 3 (in pocket), and Figs. 56, 57.

The general information concerning the MNK gully and the sequence of deposits in Bed II is given here, followed by the description of the Skull Site. The description of the Main Occupation Site will be found in the next chapter, which deals with the upper part of Middle Bed II.

The MNK gully lies on the right bank of the Side Gorge, opposite FC and approximately 0·8 of a mile upstream from the confluence with the Main Gorge. The greater part of Beds II, III and IV is visible, as far down as the Marker Tuff I^F at the top of Bed I, although, in the upper part of the gully, a small section of Bed II is not exposed. The Marker Tuff I^F can also be seen in a small cliff upstream of the MNK gully, where it occurs 10–12 ft. below the chert horizon.

During 1935 two fragments of a human skull (H. 2) were found by the writer on the lower part of the erosion slopes of Bed IVa at the head of the gully (see chapter VII). In the same area the greater part of the skeleton of an elephant and a horizon containing many bivalve Mollusca were exposed by erosion in Bed III.

The upper part of the gully is transected by a fault with a downthrow to the south-east. Numerout cracks and fissues, together with minor displacements related to this fault, can be seen at MNK, where the beds have also become tilted to the south-east in certain areas.

Excavations in Bed II were begun in March 1963, following the discovery the previous year of parts of well-preserved horn cores of *Strepsiceros grandis*, together with choppers and other artefacts eroding from Bed II on the eastern side of the gully. These occurred at a height of approximately 40 ft. above the base of Bed II, which reaches a maximum thickness of 80 ft. in this area.

The sequence of deposits in the lower 50 ft. of Bed II, as exposed in the gully and in the excavated trenches, is as follows, from the top downwards (see Fig. 57):

(*a*) Re-worked tuffs, exposed to a thickness of 10 ft., having localised patches of clay and grey sand at the base and often reddened in the upper part. The main occupation levels in Bed II occur within the lower 4 ft. of this tuff.

(*b*) Approximately 3 ft. of hard grey tuff, containing coarse pumice particles in the lower part. The upper surface is irregular, and had become eroded prior to the deposition of the overlying tuff.

(*c*) 3 ft. of clay.

(*d*) 4 ft. of re-worked tuffs containing thin gravel seams, usually partly reddened. Probably basaltic.

(*e*) An irregular layer of limestone, 9 in. thick.

(*f*) Approximately 13 ft. of re-worked tuff, clayey-tuff and clay. Artefacts and parts of Hominids 13 and 15 were found in the upper part of these beds.

(*g*) A nodular limestone band, approximately 1 ft. thick.

(*h*) 2 ft. of tuff.

(*i*) Two horizontal bands of white chert nodules approximately 9 in. apart.

(*j*) A fine-grained tuff, varying locally from 1½ to 3½ ft. in thickness also has rootlet holes.

(*k*) A level with scattered nodules of yellow chert.

(*l*) 1 ft. of clay.

(*m*) 10–12 ft. of clayey tuff with root casts.

(*n*) The marker Tuff I^F at the base of Bed II.

The hominid remains from the Skull Site were found after the excavations at the Main Occupa-

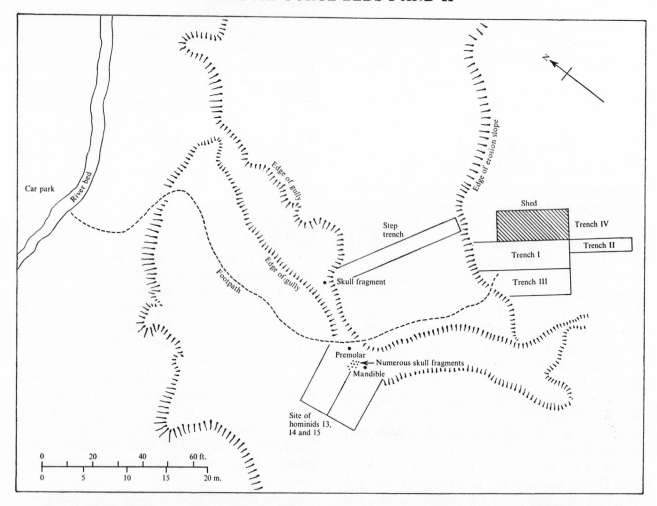

Fig. 56. MNK. Sketch plan of the gully, showing the positions of the Skull Site and the Main Occupation Site.

tion Site had been completed (see chapter VII). Two fragments of H. 13 were found *in situ*, as well as the three teeth that represent H. 15. The few cranial fragments of H. 14 were found on the surface. The remains were associated with an industry that appears to be Oldowan. Side choppers are particularly common, but spheroids, subspheroids and modified battered nodules, together with light-duty tools, all of which are characteristic of the Developed Oldowan, are either missing or very scarce.

In order to explore the *in situ* deposits, and ascertain, if possible, the horizon from which the hominid remains had been eroded, two parallel trenches were cut into the slope to the west of the footpath above the highest point where the

hominid fragments had lain on the surface. Each trench was 12 ft. wide and aligned approximately north/south. Relatively little overburden was present.

At the Skull Site, the uppermost horizon encountered after the hillwash had been removed consisted of a grey, sandy, re-worked tuff, of which a maximum thickness of $4\frac{1}{2}$ ft. was recorded. This yielded the three teeth of H. 15. Beneath the tuff there occurred a clay horizon approximately 6 ft. thick, in which the two fragments of H. 13 were found *in situ*. The upper surface of the clay was uneven, and the topmost few inches had become altered and crumbly in texture, indicating a weathered surface. A trial pit dug down to a lower level, after the horizon of H. 13 had been identified,

116

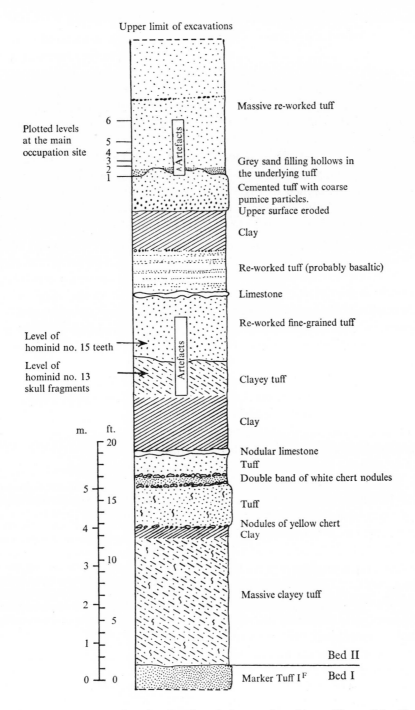

Upper limit of excavations

Plotted levels
at the main
occupation site

6
5
4
3
2
1

Massive re-worked tuff

Grey sand filling hollows in
the underlying tuff
Cemented tuff with coarse
pumice particles.
Upper surface eroded

Clay

Re-worked tuff (probably basaltic)

Limestone

Re-worked fine-grained tuff

Level of
hominid no. 15 teeth

Level of
hominid no. 13
skull fragments

Clayey tuff

Clay

m.   ft.

20

Nodular limestone
Tuff
Double band of white chert nodules

15

Tuff

Nodules of yellow chert
Clay

10

Massive clayey tuff

Bed II

Marker Tuff I F   Bed I

Fig. 57. MNK. Composite section showing the relative stratigraphic positions of the Skull Site
and the Main Occupation Site.

117

revealed an irregular horizontal layer of limestone at the base of the clay. This was underlain by 1–1½ ft. of tuff which rested on the highest of the chert beds.

A step trench was also dug on the opposite (eastern) side of the gully, from the lowest point of the excavations at the Main Occupation Site, down to the uppermost chert bed. A sequence of deposits identical to that on the western side of the gully was revealed, and it was possible to determine the relationship of the hominid horizons to the Main Occupation Site. Reference to Fig. 57 will show that the two *in situ* skull fragments of H. 13 occurred at a height of 8 ft. above the chert and 24 ft. above the base of Bed II, while the lower part of the main occupation horizon is about 17 ft. higher.

Some faunal remains and artefacts were found in association with the skull fragments, at a depth of approx. 9 in. from the top of the clay at the Skull Site. Many of the bones from this level are encrusted with lime, similar to that which coated the mandible of H. 13 that was found on the surface. The majority of the bones are broken, and they appear to represent the usual debris found on occupation sites. (Fig. 58). The upper surface of the clay also yielded artefacts and faunal remains. In addition, a number of bone fragments and artefacts were found scattered sparsely through the clay to a depth of 18 in. Large numbers of unusually small bone fragments, many less than 5 mm. in length, were also recovered when the clay was washed. (The size of these fragments may be assessed from the fact that a total of over 14,000 weighs under 15 lb.).

The faunal remains are discussed in chapter IX, but it may be noted here that a number of fossilised fragments of snail shell were found, belonging to a large land snail, as well as the usual mammalian and avian bones; it seems that at this site snails formed an additional article of diet.

The sandy tuff above this level, in which the three teeth of H. 15 were found, yielded relatively few fossil bones or artefacts. The few that did occur, moreover, were not on any particular horizon but distributed throughout the deposit.

THE LEVEL OF H. 13

The industry associated with H. 13 appears to stand closer to the Oldowan, as represented by the assemblages from immediately above and below the marker Tuff I^F, than to the Developed Oldowan from other sites at a comparable stratigraphic horizon in Bed II. The closest analogy is to be seen in the assemblages from FLK North, Levels 1–2, and from Level 1 at HWK East. This applies to the varieties of tool types and their relative proportions as well as to the form of raw materials employed—which may be in part responsible for the similarities (73·2 per cent of the heavy-duty tools is of lava, whereas at the Main Occupation Site at MNK 77·0 per cent is of quartz or quartzite.

Although the series is not large, there is a wide variety of choppers. Side choppers are the most specimens are all represented. Spheroids, subspheroids, modified battered nodules and blocks are poorly represented: of these three groups there is a total of only six subspheroids, whereas at the Main Site these three allied tool types amount to almost half the tools. Bifaces, burins and awls do not occur.

TOOLS

Side choppers (14 specimens)

Twelve examples are made on lava cobblestones and two on quartz blocks. Three show hammerstone type of utilisation on the butt ends. There are four unifacial specimens in which the flakes are struck from the cortex surface. The flake scars are relatively shallow and the working edges even, although they vary from straight to curved. Chipped utilisation is usually present and one specimen also shows two crushed indentations measuring 26×4·5 and 23×2 mm. respectively. Among the bifacial choppers there are three with wide, curved working edges. The utilisation has been particularly severe in these specimens and has resulted in the edges being shattered. There are also two choppers with sharp and jagged bifacially flaked working edges which are virtually straight. The first specimen shows some utilisation on a second short edge, 22 mm. long. Among the side choppers with hammerstone utilisation on the butt ends, there is one quartz specimen with a wide, curved and relatively even working edge, formed by large shallow flake scars on either face. The butt and both lateral edges have been considerably battered. In the second specimen, which is slightly rolled, the working edge is uneven and has been blunted and damaged by use. The butt end is heavily battered and cracked. (Fig. 59, nos. 1–4, 7.)

The length/breadth/thickness measurements range from

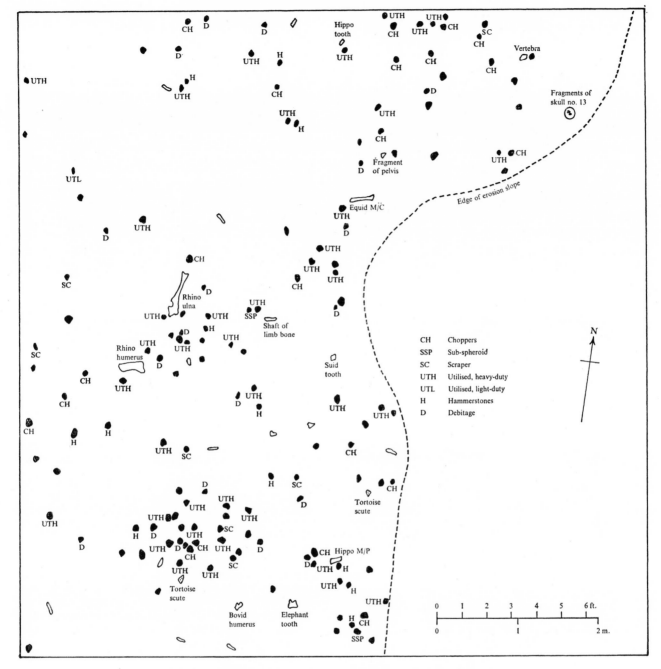

Fig. 58. MNK Skull Site. Plan of remains on the level of H. 13.

84 × 90 × 63 mm. to 64 × 75 × 50 mm., with an average mean diameter of 70 mm. The edge/circumference ratios vary from 69 to 21 per cent with an average of 39 per cent.

End choppers (*7 specimens*)

These are made exclusively from lava cobblestones. Five are bifacial with jagged working edges, showing chipped utilisation on either face. Two are unifacial and in both of these the edges are relatively straight; one is sharp and fresh, whilst the second is blunted by use.

The length/breadth/thickness measurements range from 94 × 64 × 66 mm. to 67 × 57 × 55 mm., with an average of 78 × 61 × 55 mm., and the mean diameters vary from 74 to 59 mm., with an average of 65 mm. The average edge/circumference ratio is 24 per cent. (Fig. 59, nos. 5, 6 and 8.)

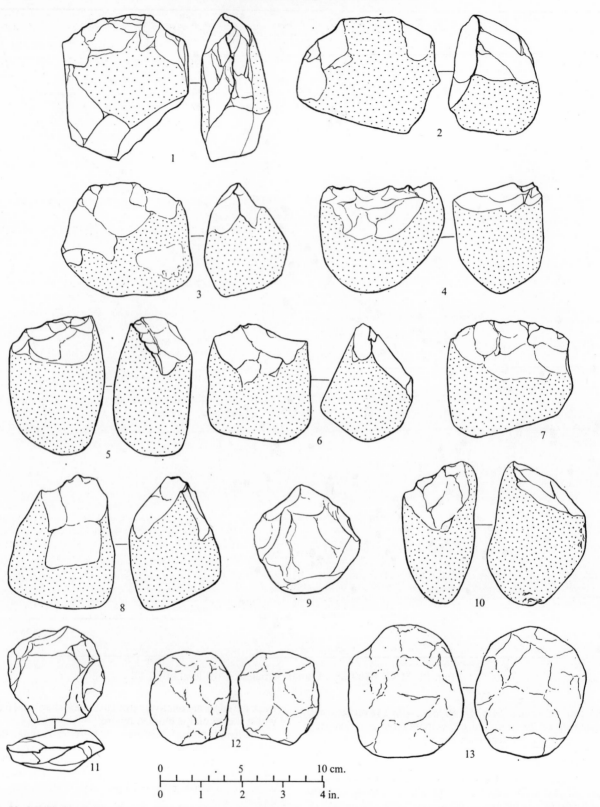

Fig. 59. MNK Skull Site. Level of H. 13. Diagrams of choppers, a discoid and two subspheroids: (1) to (3) bifacial side choppers; (4) and (5) unifacial side and end choppers; (6) bifacial end chopper; (7) and (8) bifacial side and end choppers; (9) pointed chopper; (10) chisel-edged chopper; (11) discoid; (12) and (13) subspheroids.

Two-edged choppers (3 specimens)

Two examples are made from lava cobblestones with cortex surface remaining at either end. One is of quartz. The lateral edges have been crudely flaked on either face, to form uneven, jagged working edges. Chipped utilisation and blunting is evident.

The measurements are 95 × 78 × 60 mm., 78 × 70 × 60 mm. and 85 × 63 × 60 mm., and the average mean diameter is 71 mm.

Pointed chopper (1 specimen)

This specimen is made from a lava cobblestone and is discoidal in general form. It is slightly rolled. The butt consists of cortex surface and the working edge is bifacially flaked with a number of plunging scars. The tip is pointed. The measurements are 64 × 64 × 50 mm., and the mean diameter 58 mm. (Fig. 59, no. 9.)

Chisel-edged chopper (1 specimen)

This is made from a lava cobblestone. It is narrow-edged, with unifacial flaking of the working edge, opposed to the cortex surface. The edge is sharp and fresh, with only slight utilisation. The butt end is pointed, battered and pitted. (83 × 59 × 43 mm. Mean diameter 61 mm. Edge/circumference ratio 19 per cent.) (Fig. 59, no. 10.)

Polyhedrons (2 specimens)

One example is made from lava and one from quartz. Both exhibit a number of short intersecting edges which are in fresh, sharp condition. Slight chipped utilisation is evident. (Measurements: 63 × 56 × 48 mm., and 61 × 56 × 45 mm. Mean diameters 55 mm., and 89 mm.)

Discoids (2 specimens)

These consist of a flat lava specimen and a miniature example made of quartz. Both are well finished and symmetrical. (Measurements: 58 × 57 × 24 mm., and 26 × 28 × 17 mm.) (Fig. 59, no. 11.)

Subspheroids (6 specimens)

Two examples are of lava and the remainder of quartz or quartzite. All six are angular, with the ridges and projections only partially reduced by battering. The mean diameters range from 86 to 37 mm., with an average of 56 mm. (Fig. 59, nos. 12, 13.)

Scrapers, heavy-duty (5 specimens)

These consist of:

(*a*) An irregular-shaped fragment of horneblende gneiss, with flat upper and lower faces, steeply trimmed round the edge which is extensively blunted by use. The flake scars are large and the edge is uneven. (80 × 69 mm.)

(*b*) Three high-backed specimens made on lava cobblestones. Cortex surface is retained on the butts, and on the greater part of the dorsal surfaces. The working edges are markedly curved and are steeply flaked from one or two flat negative flake scars on the under-surface. The edges are chipped and blunted by use. The measurements are 66 × 45 mm., 93 × 83 mm. and 70 × 59 mm.

(*c*) A block of quartzite with two steeply trimmed working edges on one side. Chipped utilisation is evident. (58 × 55 mm.)

The average length/breadth measurements for the five specimens are 73 × 62 mm.

Scrapers, light-duty (4 specimens)

There is one discoidal specimen made on part of a quartz flake which has been steeply trimmed on the greater part of the circumference. (37 × 27 mm.) A second example is made on an end-struck lava flake, trimmed transversely across the tip to a relatively straight working edge. The trimming also extends along part of both lateral edges and there is a utilised notch on one side. (48 × 32 mm.)

There are also two hollow scrapers. One (39 × 34 mm.) is a broken lava flake with two notches, side by side, on one lateral edge. Both notches are steeply flaked and in one the edge has been subsequently crushed. The notches measure 49 × 4·5 mm. and 13 × 3·5 mm., respectively. The second is a broken quartz flake with a notch 18 mm. wide and 4·5 mm. deep on one lateral edge. (45 × 39 mm.)

UTILISED MATERIAL

'Anvils' (3 specimens)

One example is made from lava. It is high-backed, with a flat, circular base, heavily utilised on the circumference. (84 × 85 × 83 mm.) The remaining two specimens are made from quartz blocks with flat upper and lower surfaces, extensively battered and chipped round the edges. The mean diameters are 78, 72 and 71 mm.

Hammerstones (15 specimens)

These consist of the usual waterworn cobbles, bruised and pitted on the extremities and on other projecting areas. One example is of quartz or quartzite and the balance of lava. The mean diameters range from 79 mm. to 54 mm., with an average of 61 mm.

Cobblestones (43 specimens)

These are waterworn lava cobbles, broken and damaged by use. The mean diameters range from 80 to 30 mm., with an average of 61 mm.

Nodules and blocks (11 specimens)

These generally lack evidence of artificial shaping, but show some chipping and blunting of the edges. Two are of horneblende gneiss, six of quartz or quartzite and the balance of lava. The mean diameters range from 84 to 51 mm., with an average of 61 mm.

Light-duty flakes and other fragments (4 specimens)

Two broken flakes and two core fragments of quartz show utilisation on the edges. The average measurements are 31 × 29 mm.

DEBITAGE

The *débitage* amounts to 568 specimens and consists of thirty-one complete flakes, three re-sharpening flakes with longitudinal dorsal crests, 484 broken flakes and chips and fifty core fragments. Eight of the complete flakes are of lava, although this material represents only 9·7 per cent of the total.

The majority of the flakes are end-struck (twenty-five) and all are divergent. The length/breadth measurements in millimetres for the complete flakes are as follows:

	Range	Average
Lava		
End-struck	60 × 38 to 35 × 20	48 × 35
Side-struck	17 × 26 (1 specimen)	—
Quartz/quartzite		
End-struck	63 × 50 to 23 × 19	36 × 31
Side-struck	43 × 60 to 22 × 31	28 × 35

The bulbs of percussion are variable and analysis of this small series will not be given. The angles of the striking platforms in the six measurable lava flakes are within the range of 110–129°. In the quartz/quartzite series seven specimens are between 90° and 109° and four between 110° and 129°.

The re-sharpening flakes are of quartzite. One is broken in half, the two fragments being found some distance apart. (64 × 52 mm. and 57 × 57 mm.)

MANUPORTS (*67 specimens*)

In view of the fact that this assemblage was found in a fine-grained clay the series of sixty-seven unmodified lava cobblestones must be regarded as manuports. Twenty-three are broken, possibly by human agency, although there is no evidence of utilisation other than simple fractures.

Analysis of the industry from the level of H. 13 at MNK

	Nos.	%
Tools	45	6·5
Utilised material	76	11·0
Débitage	568	82·4
	689	
Tools		
Side choppers	14	31·1
End choppers	7	15·6
Two-edged choppers	3	6·7
Pointed chopper	1	2·2
Chisel-edged chopper	1	2·2
Polyhedrons	2	4·4
Discoids	2	4·4
Subspheroids	6	13·3
Scrapers, heavy-duty	5	11·1
Scrapers, light-duty	4	8·9
	45	

Utilised material	Nos.	%
'Anvils'	3	4·0
Hammerstones	15	19·7
Cobblestones	43	56·6
Nodules and blocks	11	14·4
Light-duty flakes and other fragments	4	5·2
	76	
Débitage		
Whole flakes	31	5·4
Re-sharpening flakes	3	0·5
Broken flakes and chips	484	85·2
Core fragments	50	8·8
	568	

THE LEVEL OF H. 15

It is not possible to assess the nature of the industry associated with the teeth of H. 15 owing to the very limited material available for study. The total number of artefacts amounts to only 145 specimens: seven tools, four utilised pieces, 134 *débitage*, and nine unmodified cobbles.

TOOLS

End choppers (3 specimens)

Two examples are made from lava cobblestones and one from a weathered lava nodule. In the latter the working edge is jagged and sharp, with a minimum of bifacial flaking. The butt end consists of natural weathered surface and there is only slight chipped utilisation on the working edge. One of the specimens made from a cobblestone shows unifacial flaking of the working edge, with cortex surface on the opposite face. The edge is relatively straight and even, with only slight utilisation. The second example is very crude and may be unfinished. One face is flat and bears a single negative flake scar, from which the opposite face has been steeply trimmed.

The length/breadth/thickness measurements range from 65 × 61 × 53 mm. to 87 × 80 × 59 mm., and the mean diameters vary from 59 mm. to 75 mm., with an average of 65 mm. The average edge/circumference ratio is 25 per cent.

Two-edged chopper (1 specimen)

This specimen is made on a lava cobblestone and has two working edges at right angles to one another. One is bifacially flaked and the second is trimmed on one face only from the cortex surface. Both edges are chipped and blunted by use. Lengths 80 and 82 mm. respectively. Length/breadth/thickness 91 × 75 × 65 mm., mean diameter 77 mm.

Scraper (1 specimen)

This consists of a quartzite flake, steeply trimmed at the tip and along one lateral edge to a narrow nosed scraper. (40 × 21 mm.)

Burins (2 specimens)

These consist of two angle burins. They are made from fine-grained quartzite and quartz respectively. The quartzite specimen is trimmed across the tip and has only a single burin spall removed from one side. The working edge is 3 mm. wide and is blunted by use, having a 'frosted' appearance. The quartz specimen is broken transversely across the working end and shows a number of small burin scars on one lateral edge, struck from the broken surface. Width of chisel-edge: 4 mm. Measurements: 29 × 22 mm. and 43 × 16 mm. respectively.

UTILISED MATERIAL, DEBITAGE AND MANUPORTS

The utilised material consists of one lava cobblestone with slight shattering, together with three flakes with chipping and blunting on the edges.

In the *débitage* there are seven whole flakes, 120 broken flakes and chips and seven core fragments. Four specimens are of lava and the balance of quartz or quartzite. The average length/breadth measurements for the complete flakes are 28 × 25 mm.

The manuports consist of nine unmodified lava cobblestones, four of which are broken.

Analysis

	Nos.	%
Tools	7	4·8
Utilised material	4	2·7
Débitage	134	92·4
	145	

CHAPTER V

THE UPPER PART OF MIDDLE BED II

Site EF–HR, The Main Occupation Site at MNK.
Sites FC West and FC. Site SHK

1. SITE EF–HR (EVELYN FUCHS–HANS RECK)

Archaeological number (23)   Geologic locality 12

This site was first found and recorded by Sir Evelyn Fuchs and the late Professor Hans Reck on the same day, during the 1931 expedition to Olduvai, and was designated by their joint initials. It is situated on the north side of the Gorge, approximately 0·8 mile upstream from the Third Fault. It lies between the aeolian member of Bed II and Tuff II^c and is therefore slightly higher in the sequence than the MNK Skull Site, but lower than FC West and the Main Occupation Site at MNK.

Excavations at EF–HR were undertaken for a period of one month from mid-September to mid-October 1963. In the first instance two parallel trenches, each 4 ft. wide and 11 ft. apart, were cut into the slope in the area where flakes and tools were seen eroding. The intervening area was also subsequently dug, the total then exposed being 19 by 22 ft. Artefacts were found to be particularly plentiful to the south and the excavations were later extended 9 ft. in this area.

Reference to Fig. 1 will show that the implementiferous horizon occurred at a height of 4–5 ft. above the upper of two substantial layers of limestone included in the upper part of the Aeolian Tuff in this area. In places the upper limestone is overlain by a deposit of clay, but elsewhere, where the clay has been cut out, it is overlain by a coarse gravel containing some implements. The section exposed by excavation revealed a channel which cut down through this gravel and also through the tuffs which overlay it, to the level of the underlying clay (Fig. 60, Section). Most of the artefacts were concentrated at the junction of the gravels with the clay.[1]

The specimens are generally unabraded and it seems likely that they originally lay on the surface of the clay and that a few were caught up in the lower part of the gravel. The majority occurred in two areas on the higher parts of the clay surface, separated by an oblong gravel-filled depression or channel, 2–2½ ft. deep. This was aligned east/west with the eastern end truncated by present-day erosion, whilst the western end was not exposed. It is therefore impossible to state whether the channel continued for some distance or was purely a local phenomenon. The available evidence, however, indicates that the site represents a small temporary camp on either side of a shallow water course.

The industry is unique among those from sites excavated in Bed II, although it is similar to the industries from DK East and Elephant Korongo, two sites which are also situated in the eastern part of the Gorge but have not yet been explored. It represents an early Acheulean industry in which 53·8 per cent of the tools are bifaces. Burins, awls and *outils écaillés* are not present, while light-duty scrapers, which are common in every known Developed Oldowan assemblage, amount to only 3·3 per cent. Most of the waste flakes are typical 'handaxe' flakes and exhibit characters not found in any Developed Oldowan series. The bulbs of percussion are wide and well marked, often extending across the entire width of the flakes. A marked lip on the primary flake surface beneath

---

[1] The exact positions of the tools could not be plotted owing to a freak rainstorm which displaced most of the specimens after they had been uncovered and before the plan had been drawn.

124

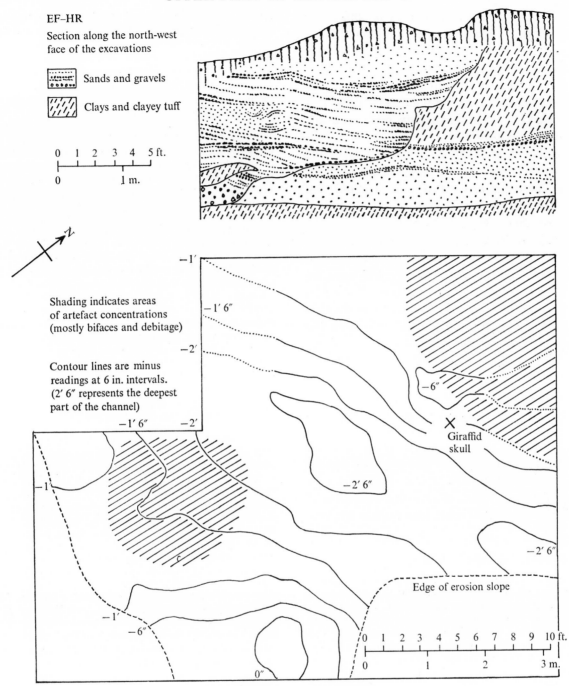

EF–HR

Section along the north-west
face of the excavations

:::::::: Sands and gravels

///// Clays and clayey tuff

0 1 2 3 4 5 ft.

0 1 m.

Shading indicates areas
of artefact concentrations
(mostly bifaces and debitage)

Contour lines are minus
readings at 6 in. intervals.
(2′ 6″ represents the deepest
part of the channel)

X
Giraffid
skull

−1′

−1′ 6″

−2′

−1′ 6″   −2′

−1′

−6″

−2′ 6″

−2′ 6″

−6″

Edge of erosion slope

−1′

−6″

0″

0 1 2 3 4 5 6 7 8 9 10 ft.

0 1 2 3 m.

Fig. 60. EF–HR. Section and plan.

the edge of the striking platform is also a characteristic feature. Side- and end-struck flakes occur in almost equal proportions and the average overall size of the lava flakes exceeds that of any in Developed Oldowan assemblage.

The most common form of biface is an irregular ovate. One specimen is double-pointed, others have flat butts and some are trihedral. Oblong and heavy-duty picks and a single example of a well-made cleaver also occur. The type of flaking is bold and most of the tools have been shaped by means of a minimum of well-directed flakes.

125

Step-flaking, which usually occurs on bifaces in the Developed Oldowan, is not common. Many of the bifaces are made on large flakes struck from boulders or large cobbles with a minimum of secondary flaking on the primary surface. The tips often lack retouch and the points are formed by the intersection of two flake scars, giving rise to a triangular cross-section.

A small number of very heavily rolled flakes and other artefacts was found scattered through the gravels. These specimens are in an entirely different physical condition from the rest of the assemblage and have therefore not been included in the analysis. In order to augment the series available for description, however, it has been considered justifiable to include artefacts collected from the surface on the slope immediately beneath the site, since they are in an identical state of preservation and are typologically indistinguishable from the *in situ* specimens. Furthermore, no additional implementiferous levels from which they might have been derived are known to occur in the vicinity.

Fossil bones were scarce and generally in a fragmentary condition, with the exception of a complete and well-preserved cranium of *Giraffa jumae* which was found lying palate upwards on the northern bank of the channel. No further parts of the skeleton were present. It is difficult to account for the presence of an isolated cranium of this size by any means other than human agency.

TOOLS

Side choppers (11 specimens; 7 in situ, 4 surface)

These are all made on lava cobblestones, with cortex surface retained at the butt ends. With the exception of one unifacial specimen they are bifacial, with multiple scars on either side of the working edges. These are jagged and have generally been chipped and blunted by use. The length/breadth/thickness measurements range from $93 \times 96 \times 66$ mm. to $57 \times 78 \times 34$ mm., with an average of $74 \times 84 \times 49$ mm., and the mean diameters vary from 85 to 56 mm., with an average of 69 mm. The edge/circumference ratios vary from 50 to 32 per cent, with an average of 38 per cent.

End choppers (3 specimens; 1 in situ, 2 surface)

One is unifacial, with the trimming scars struck from the cortex surface, and two are bifacial, with multiple scars on either face and sharp, jagged cutting edges. All three are made from lava cobblestones. The length/breadth/thickness measurements range from $110 \times 107 \times 68$ mm. to $69 \times 61 \times$

30 mm., with an average of $99 \times 82 \times 58$ mm. The mean diameters range from 95 to 53 mm., with an average of 79 mm. The average edge/circumference ratio is 30 per cent.

Bifaces (49 specimens)

These consist of thirty-six complete, six unfinished and seven broken specimens (Figs. 61–68).

Irregular ovates (21 specimens; 17 in situ, 4 surface). Four examples are made of quartz and the balance of lava. They are mostly on flakes and are flat on the lower face with a minimum of trimming, usually just sufficient to trim off the bulb. Only five are biconvex in cross-section, with an equal amount of flaking on the upper and lower faces. In some examples the trimming extends along part of one or both lateral edges, but seldom as far as the tip. They are usually chisel-ended. In the series made on flakes it is possible to identify five as side-struck and one as end-struck. Cortex surface is to be seen on the dorsal aspect in seven of these specimens, suggesting that they were struck from lava bounders or large cobbles. In one example the cortex surface extends round the butt as in choppers, but in the remainder the entire circumference is flaked to a cutting edge. The flaking is normally bold, with relatively large scars. Step-flaking is rare. In many specimens the tips and the anterior parts are trihedral in cross-section with a longitudinal dorsal ridge formed by the intersection of the trimming scars on either edge. The edges are generally sharp with chipped utilisation rather than blunting or battering. (Figs. 61, no. 5 and 62, no. 2.)

Double-pointed biface (1 specimen, in situ). This is the largest biface in the series. It is also remarkably symmetrical and consists of a large side-struck lava flake with cortex surface remaining on the greater part of the dorsal aspect. The bulb has been trimmed away, but the primary flake surface is otherwise not retouched. One extremity and the greater part of both lateral edges have been evenly trimmed. The median part of one edge also shows a number of broad denticulations for 110 mm. The trimmed extremity is more sharply pointed than the opposite end, which is relatively thin and broadly spatulate. (Fig. 63.)

Flat-butted bifaces (7 specimens; 6 in situ, 1 surface). These consist of three quartz and four lava specimens, in which the butt ends are formed by a flat vertical surface, either transverse or oblique to the length of the implement. In two examples this surface has been roughly flaked, but in the remainder it consists of an untrimmed natural fracture. All the complete specimens have sharply pointed tips and are relatively broad at the butt ends; they tend to be triangular in outline, although they vary considerably in length. Only one is biconvex in cross-section; in the remainder the under-surfaces are flat, with a minimum of trimming scars. In this group, as in the ovates, the tips are generally trihedral in cross-section, with a median longitudinal dorsal ridge. Two examples are chisel-ended, (Fig. 61, nos. 3 and 4.)

The average number of trimming scars on the above twenty-nine specimens is 9·5.

126

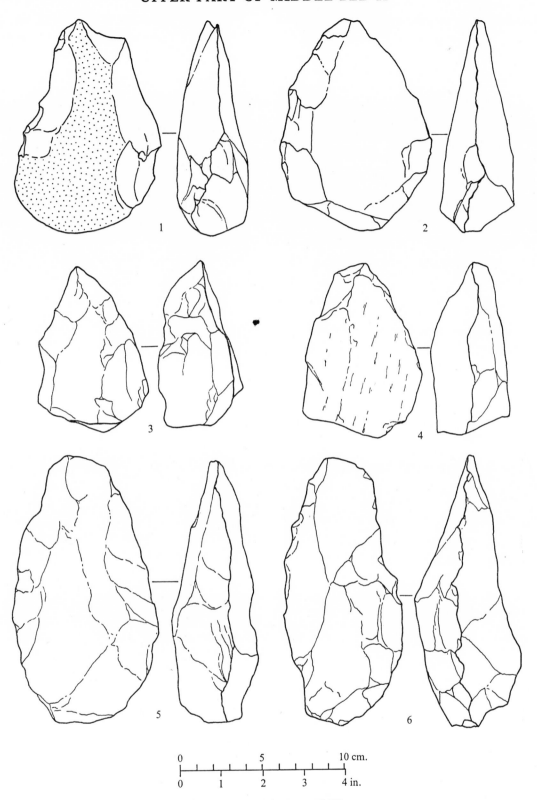

Fig. 61. EF–HR. Diagrams of bifaces.

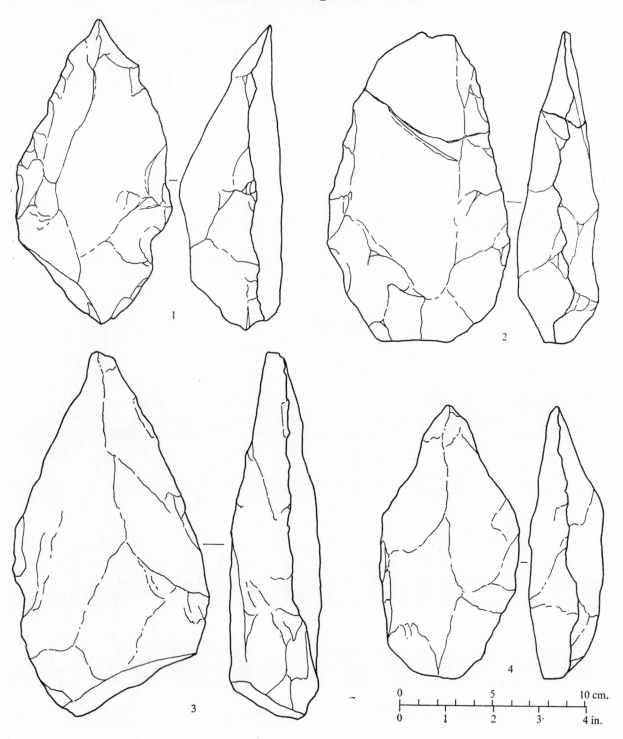

Fig. 62. EF–HR. Diagrams of bifaces.

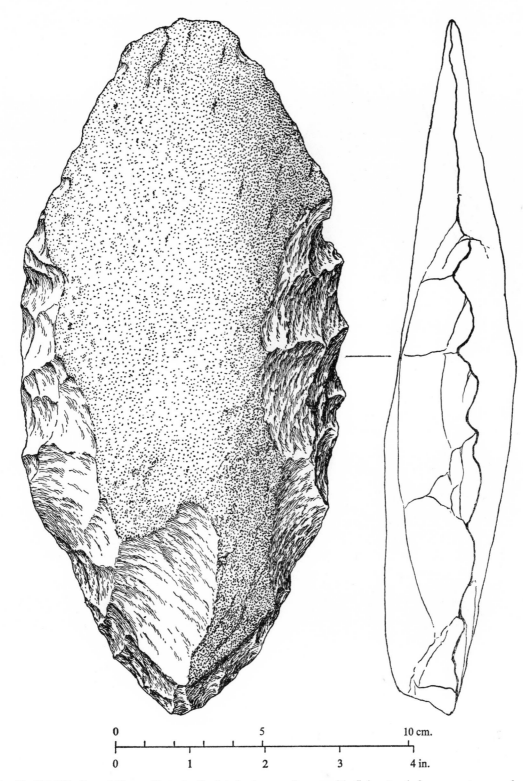

0   5   10 cm.

0   1   2   3   4 in.

Fig. 63. EF–HR. Lava biface with a denticulated edge, made on a side flake struck from a waterworn boulder.

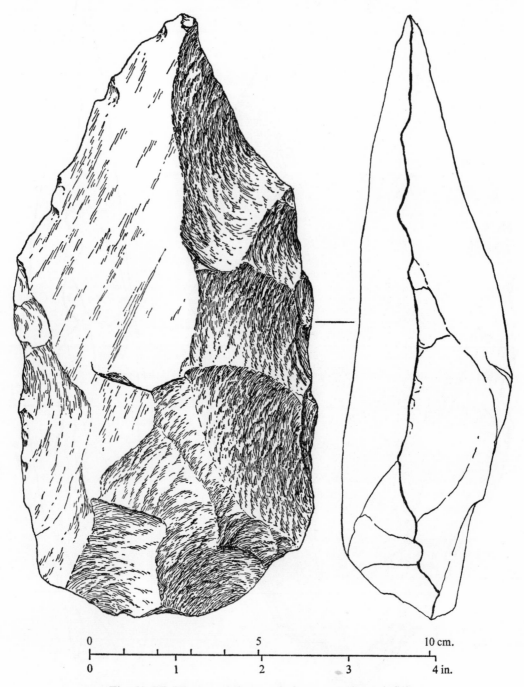

Fig. 64. EF–HR. Lava biface made from an end-struck flake.

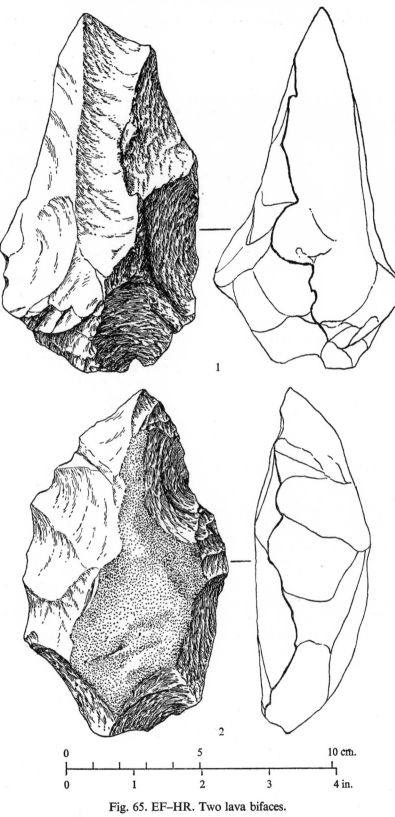

1

2

0   5   10 cm.

0   1   2   3   4 in.

Fig. 65. EF–HR. Two lava bifaces.

Measurements for the thirty-six complete specimens of bifaces, Site EF–HR

	Length/breadth/thickness (mm.)	Mean diameter (%)	Breadth/ length ratio (%)	Thickness/ length ratio (%)	Totals
Irregular ovates					
Range	178 × 108 × 45 to 123 × 76 × 34	110–51	94–41	39–22	21
Average	142 × 83 × 42	89	58	30	
Flat-based biface					
Range	195 × 105 × 50 to 97 × 74 × 48	116–72	89–53	51–36	7
Average	123 × 81 × 50	83	68	42	
Double-pointed biface	232 × 112 × 44	129	48	18	1
Cleaver	144 × 86 × 41	90	59	28	1
Oblong picks					
Range	162 × 72 × 62 to 132 × 71 × 65	198–88	53–42	49–31	5
Average	168 × 72 × 57	82	49	39	
Heavy-duty picks	117 × 90 × 91	99	76	77	1
Total					36

Cleaver (1 specimen, in situ). This is a particularly well-finished and symmetrical specimen, made on a side-struck lava flake. The transverse working edge is straight and the bulb of percussion on the primary flake surface has been entirely trimmed away from the reverse direction to the trimming on the opposite lateral edge, resulting in a parallelogram cross-section. The specimen has particularly sharp edges, slightly chipped by use, but not blunted. (Fig. 66, no. 1.)

Oblong picks (5 specimens; 4 in situ, 1 surface). One example is of quartz and four are of lava. These tools are oblong, generally with steeply flaked, somewhat massive butts. Two specimens are flat on the under surface and have been made on end-struck flakes, although the bulb has been trimmed away. The remaining three are biconvex in cross-section, with relatively steep trimming on both lateral edges and at the butt ends. The edges are sharp and somewhat jagged with virtually no fine trimming. In one specimen the tip is sharply pointed, but in the remainder the tips are either blunt or have a straight, oblique edge, resembling narrow cleavers (Fig. 67).

Heavy-duty pick (1 specimen in situ). The butt end consists of cortex surface. One face is relatively flat, whilst the opposite face has been steeply trimmed from both edges. These are particularly jagged. The tip appears to have been broken off during use.

Unfinished bifaces (6 specimens; 4 in situ, 2 surface). These consist of three large flakes (two end-struck and one side-struck), together with three cores, all of which have been roughly blocked out in the form of bifaces. Two are of quartz and four of lava.

Broken bifaces (7 specimens; 6 in situ, 1 surface). The broken bifaces consist of three well-made tips, one small example

in which only the tip is missing and three butt ends, one of which has been re-trimmed after fracture. Six are of lava and the seventh of quartz. The present measurements are as follows: tip ends range from 104 × 113 × 50 mm. to 74 × 84 × 44 mm., with an average of 92 × 95 × 47 mm. Butt ends range from 86 × 90 × 48 mm. to 71 × 80 × 57 mm., with an average of 75 × 75 × 44 mm. The example with the broken tip measures 72 × 57 × 34 mm.

Polyhedrons (5 specimens; 2 in situ, 3 surface)

With the exception of one rolled example these are in fresh condition with sharp, bifacially flaked and intersecting working edges. The mean diameters range from 94 to 54 mm., with an average of 73 mm.

Discoids (8 specimens; 3 in situ, 5 surface)

Two examples are of quartz and the balance of lava. With the exception of two, which are plano-convex in cross-section, these discoids are relatively thick and markedly convex on both faces. In one diminutive quartz specimen the edge is regular and even, but in the remainder the edges are bifacially flaked and jagged. The general form is somewhat irregular and the tools are only approximately discoidal. The length/breadth/thickness measurements range from 101 × 97 × 63 mm. to 40 × 32 × 22 mm., with an average of 70 × 65 × 43 mm., and the mean diameters range from 87 to 31 mm., with an average of 59 mm.

Spheroids (2 specimens, in situ)

Both specimens are made of quartz. The surfaces are considerably battered, with the projecting ridges greatly reduced, but neither example is sufficiently symmetrical or well-rounded to class as a stone ball. (65 × 59 × 47 mm. and 41 × 38 × 36 mm.)

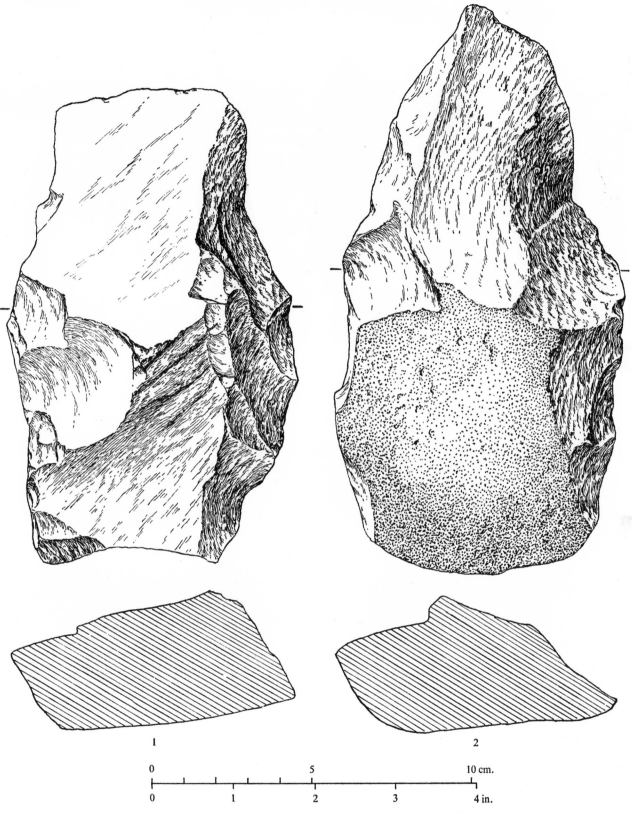

Fig. 66. EF–HR. A cleaver and a biface, both made on lava flakes.

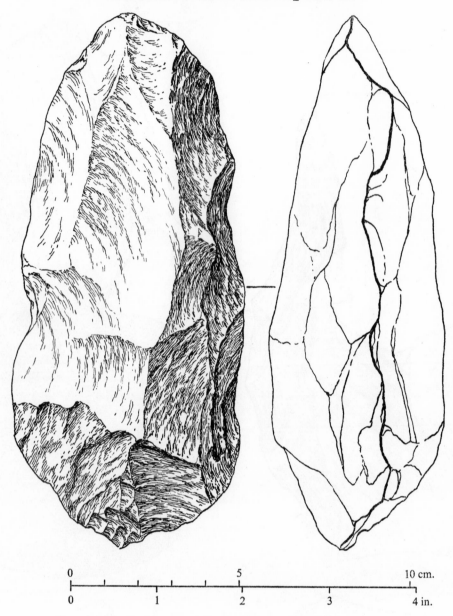

0 ⊢ ⊢ ⊢ ⊢ 5 ⊢ ⊢ ⊢ ⊢ 10 cm.

0 ⊢ 1 ⊢ 2 ⊢ 3 ⊢ 4 in.

Fig. 67. EF–HR. Oblong pick made from lava.

Subspheroids (7 specimens: 4 in situ, 3 surface)

Five examples are of quartz or quartzite, one of pegmatite and one of lava. They are spherical in general form, but somewhat asymmetrical and sub-angular, with relatively sharp projecting ridges. The length/breadth/thickness measurements range from $101 \times 92 \times 76$ mm. to $32 \times 30 \times 22$ mm., with an average of $64 \times 60 \times 49$ mm., and the mean diameters vary from 89 to 28 mm., with an average of 58 mm.

Scrapers, heavy-duty (3 specimens; 2 in situ, 1 surface)

In two specimens, made on lava cobbles, the working edges are rounded and steeply flaked from a flat under-surface. The third specimen is a hollow scraper made on an angular fragment of quartz with a relatively large chipped notch, 27 mm. wide and 7 mm. deep on one edge. The length/breadth measurements range from 103×77 mm. to 66×54 mm., with an average of 84×62 mm.

Scrapers, light-duty (3 specimens; 2 in situ, 1 surface)

These consist of a broken quartz flake (29×35 mm.) steeply trimmed along one lateral edge, which is slightly curved and two lava flakes. In one of these (26×34 mm.) the upper margin of the striking platform has been trimmed into a scraping edge, whilst the second (49×46 mm.)

134

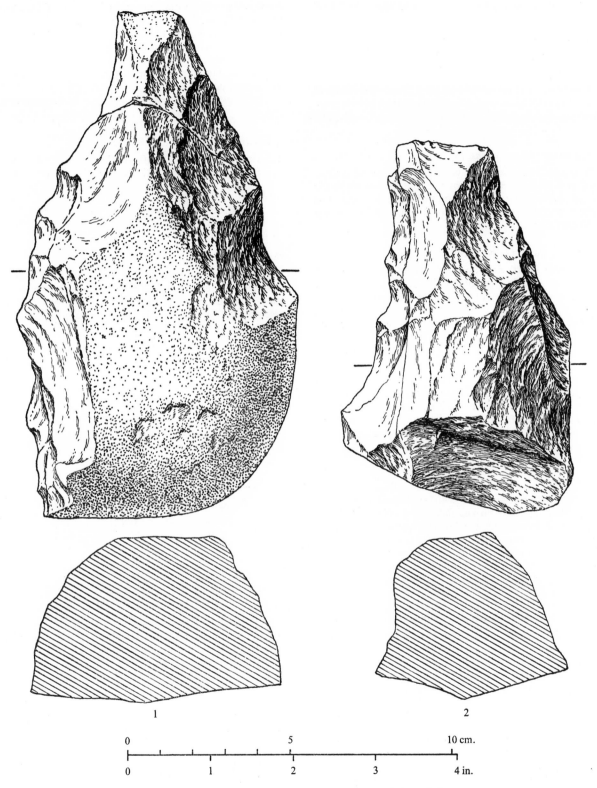

1

2

0   5   10 cm.

0   1   2   3   4 in.

Fig. 68. EF–HR. Two bifaces made on end-struck lava flakes.

shows irregular flaking round the top and along the lateral edges.

UTILISED MATERIAL

Hammerstones (4 specimens, in situ)

These consist of two quartz and two lava cobblestones in which the extremities and other parts of the exterior show battering and bruising. The mean diameters range from 82 to 45 mm., with an average of 64 mm.

Cobblestones (10 specimens, in situ)

Nine lava and one quartz cobblestones have been shattered and flaked or chipped by use, but do not show the pitting and bruising characteristics of hammerstones. The mean diameters range from 103 to 49 mm., with an average of 60 mm.

Heavy-duty flakes (2 specimens)

An oblong quartz flake and a triangular fragment of lava exhibit some chipping and flaking along the edges. (Measurements: 125 × 71 mm. and 80 × 63 mm.)

Light-duty flakes and other fragments (10 specimens; 6 in situ, 4 surface)

Three specimens are of quartz, six of lava and one of chert. They include whole and broken flakes as well as core fragments. There are four specimens with chipping on relatively straight edges, two with notches, two with convex utilised edges and two with slight chipping on two edges. The length/breadth measurements range from 90 × 56 mm. to 27 × 26 mm., with an average of 54 × 37 mm.

DEBITAGE

The total *débitage* amounts to 405 specimens, comprising 147 whole flakes, 209 broken flakes and chips and forty-nine core fragments. Of the 328 specimens found *in situ* seventy-seven were on the surface. 65·5 per cent are of lava, 33·5 per cent of quartz and quartzite, and 0·9 per cent of chert (four small pieces of broken flakes). In the complete flakes the figure for lava is somewhat higher and amounts to 78·2 per cent.

Complete flakes (147 specimens; 91 in situ, 56 surface)

Thirty-two are of quartz and 115 of lava. The series includes a small number of large flakes which may have been intended for making bifaces, although they have not been trimmed; they are generally side-struck, measure over 150 mm. in length and have pointed tips. An unusually large proportion of flakes is side-struck (46 per cent), a very much higher figure than in any Developed Oldowan assemblage.

The bulbs of percussion are also generally more pronounced, not only in the degree of swelling but also in lateral expansion. In many flakes the entire primary surface is markedly convex at the bulbar end, with the bulb extending across the whole width of the flake and not confined to the median areas as is usual in Developed Oldowan flakes. Another characteristic feature is a distinct lip beneath the edge of the striking platform where it abuts on to the primary flake surface. The striking platforms are relatively wide and the lip extends across the entire width of the flake but is more pronounced on either side than in the central part.

The length/breadth measurements in millimetres are as follows:

Lava	Range	Average
End-struck	110 × 101 to 21 × 17	64 × 45
Side-struck	103 × 175 to 30 × 40	48 × 64
Quartz/quartzite		
End-struck	96 × 65 to 27 × 19	58 × 39
Side-struck	96 × 113 to 32 × 37	55 × 71

Bulbs of percussion

Very few bulbs of percussion are scarred or shattered and triangular flakes with reduced platforms situated at one apex, such as commonly occur in Developed Oldowan assemblages, are exceedingly rare. The bulbs of percussion can be subdivided as follows:

	Lava	Quartz
Marked	67·8 %	56·2 %
Slight	25·2 %	37·5 %
Negative	2·6 %	3·1 %
Shattered	3·4 %	3·1 %
Double	0·9 %	—
Totals	115	32
	147	

Angles of striking platforms

Angle	Lava	Quartz
70– 89°	0·9 %	—
90–109°	29·2 %	50·0 %
110–129°	68·0 %	50·0 %
130° +	1·8 %	—
Totals	106	24
	130	

(Many pebbles and some cobblestones occurred in the gravel overlying the occupation level, but there was no indication that these had been introduced by human agency.)

Analysis of the Industry from EF–HR

	Nos.	%
Tools	91	17·4
Utilised material	26	5·0
Débitage	405	77·6
	522	

Tools	Nos.	%
Side choppers	11	12·1
End choppers	3	3·3
Bifaces, including broken and unfinished	49	53·8
Polyhedrons	5	5·5
Discoids	8	8·8
Spheroids	2	2·2
Subspheroids	7	7·7
Scrapers, heavy-duty	3	3·3
Scrapers, light-duty	3	3·3
	91	
Utilised material		
Hammerstones	4	15·4
Cobblestones	10	38·5
Heavy-duty flakes	2	7·6
Light-duty flakes and other fragments	10	38·4
	26	
Débitage		
Whole flakes	147	36·3
Broken flakes and chips	209	51·6
Core fragments	49	12·0
	405	

2. SITE MNK. THE MAIN OCCUPATION SITE

The general description of the MNK gully and of the sequence of deposits in the area has been given in the preceding chapter in connection with the MNK Skull Site. It should be noted, however, that the Main Occupation Site described below was 17 ft. higher in the sequence than the Skull Site.

THE EXCAVATIONS

Three parallel trenches were cut into the slope, in a north-east/south-west direction, in the region where artefacts and fossil bones had been noted on the surface. An extension from the first trench, 6 ft. wide and 25 ft. long, was later made to the south-east, in order to explore what appeared to be a depression in the occupation level. This, however, proved to have been caused by subsequent earth movements connected with the nearby fault and was of no archaeological significance. The combined width of the trenches north-west/south-east amounted to 33 ft. and the length of each trench, as demarcated, was 30 ft., but the area of undisturbed deposit remaining intact depended on the extent of erosion to the north-east.

Reference to Fig. 57 will show that the occupation remains were found throughout a thickness of approximately 4½ ft., in the lower part of a fine-grained re-worked tuff. With the exception of the basal horizon, where the artefacts, fossil bones and manuports lay on the eroded surface of an underlying hard grey tuff, the remains did not occur on any recognisable 'surfaces', but were dispersed throughout the deposit, although they were more concentrated at certain levels. The distribution of remains at these levels was recorded and the plans are shown in Figs. 69–74. It must be stressed, however, that each plotted level represents objects found throughout a depth of several inches and not on a single clearly defined occupation surface.

A small number of bone fragments and a few of the heavy-duty tools are abraded, indicating some movement by water action, although there is no apparent grading according to size and the specimens were not orientated in any particular direction. It seems likely, therefore, that the remains were found more or less in the position in which they were left when the site was abandoned. A possible interpretation of their occurrence throughout the depth of 4½ ft. may be that this site was reoccupied on successive occasions, at sufficiently long intervals for vegetation and soil to have accumulated over previous occupation surfaces.

This explanation would also account for the unusually large number of unmodified cobblestones found at all levels with the artefacts. These must be considered to have been introduced by human agency since they are of a size which could only be transported naturally by torrential water action for which there is no evidence. If, however, stones and other remains became covered over between successive periods of occupation, it would have been necessary to bring in fresh supplies of cobblestones each time the site was reoccupied, since such stones appear to have been an essential element at all living sites of the period.

Remains on the two lower levels included a number of bone splinters standing vertically, which appeared to have been placed in position artificially (Fig. 69). No particular type of wear or utilisation could be detected on the extremities, although

137

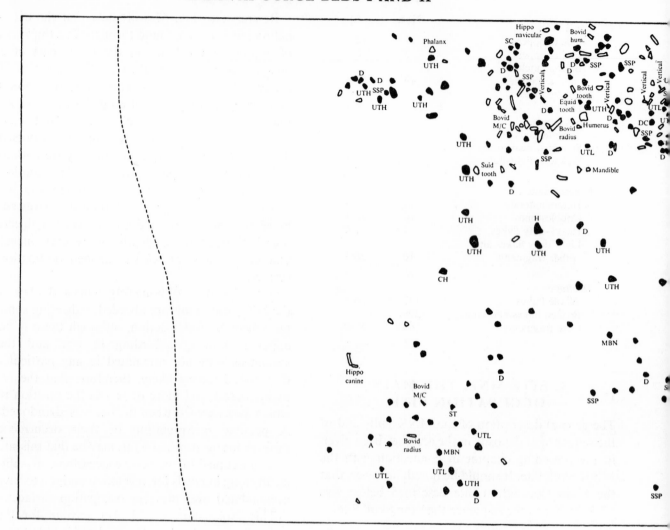

the upper ends of two specimens were slightly chipped.

The lowest occupation level in the last trench to be excavated (Trench IV) has been preserved for the benefit of visitors. A plan of this area is not included, owing to the difficulty of correctly identifying artefacts or bones whilst they are still embedded in the deposit.[1]

[1] The undesirability of detaching artefacts from their matrix when they occur on a 'floor' which is intended to be preserved for exhibition has been demonstrated at Olorgesailie, where Acheulean bifaces were lifted from a land surface for cleaning and inspection and were unconsciously replaced in careful alignment. This was subsequently thought to be authentic and regarded as evidence that the material had been aligned by water action.

THE INDUSTRY

Analysis of the industry from this occupation site has led to the entire assemblage being considered as a single cultural stage. At the time of excavation the material from the lower grey tuff was treated separately, but it appears to be so similar to the assemblage from the overlying re-worked tuff that a distinction does not seem to be valid.

The industry is crude. With the exception of a few bifaces, it is clearly not far removed from the Oldowan, although the choppers compare un-favourably with those from the upper levels of

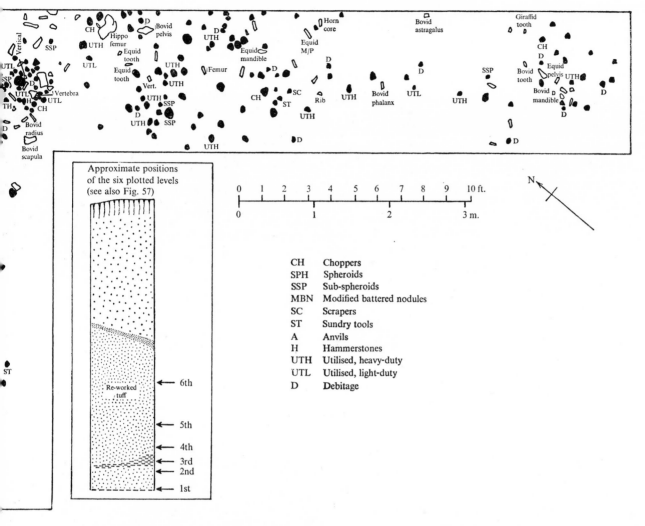

Fig. 69. MNK Main Occupation Site. Plan of remains on the 6th level (approx. 1 ft. 6 in. above the 5th level).

Bed I, both in technique and in variety of types. A higher proportion of the industry is made from quartz and quartzite than any hitherto described, (91.0 per cent of the total assemblage). Horneblende gneiss, although not common, occurs more frequently at this site than in earlier assemblages. Some pieces are identical to the gneiss found at the Kelogi inselberg, 4½ miles distant to the west.

Some fragments of the bones of larger mammals show unmistakable evidence of chipping and flaking. These are described in chapter VIII, together with the other worked and utilised bones.

Side choppers are relatively common, but small, light-duty specimens are rare. Other forms of choppers are also scarce, with eighteen end, seven two-edged and two chisel-edged examples. Discoids are well represented and they include a number of light-duty specimens. With one exception, the cutting edges extend round the whole circumference. Polyhedrons are rare but include a particularly large specimen. The bifaces include a crude heavy-duty pick and a cleaver, together with one well-made, double-pointed handaxe of unusually large size. The whole series of complete and broken bifaces amounts to only 2 per cent of the tools.

139

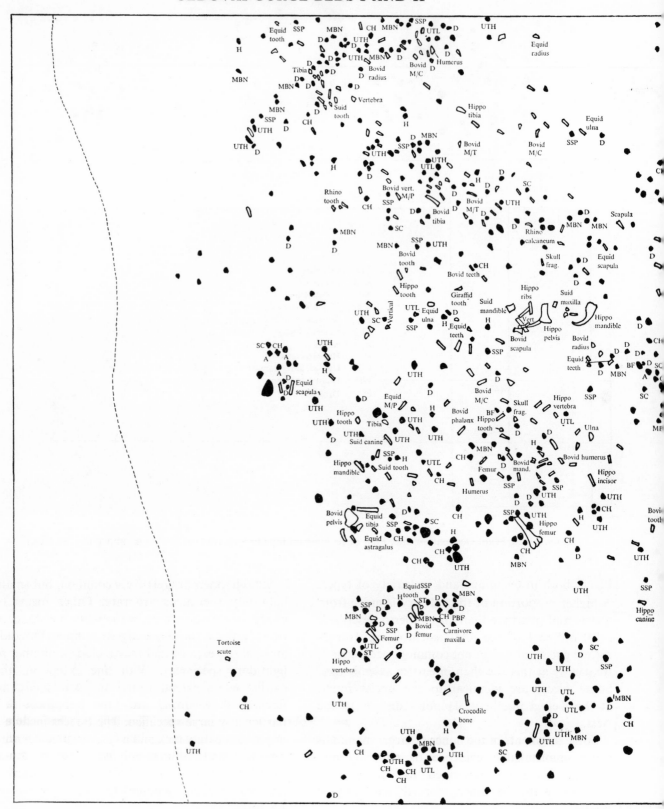

140

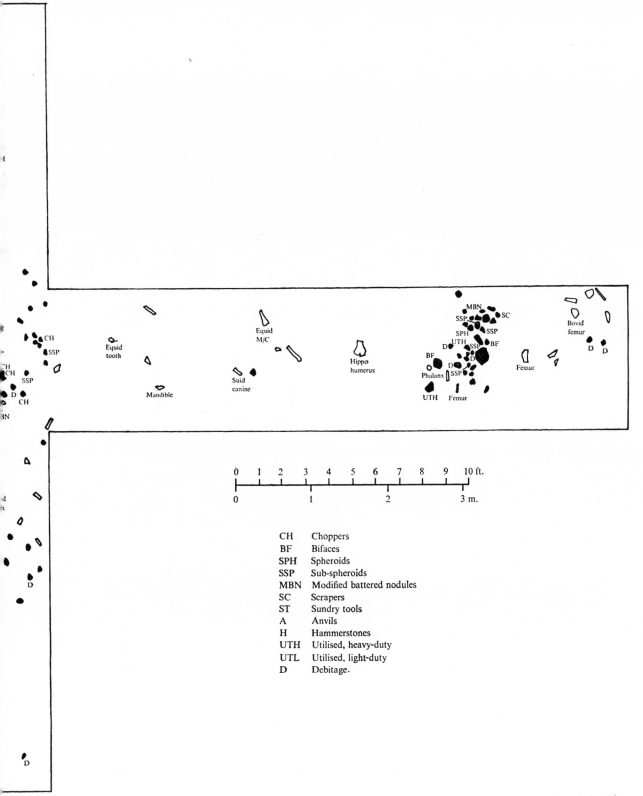

CH   Choppers
BF   Bifaces
SPH   Spheroids
SSP   Sub-spheroids
MBN   Modified battered nodules
SC   Scrapers
ST   Sundry tools
A   Anvils
H   Hammerstones
UTH   Utilised, heavy-duty
UTL   Utilised, light-duty
D   Debitage.

Fig. 70. MNK Main Occupation Site. Plan of remains on the 5th level (approx. 10 in. above the 4th level.)

141

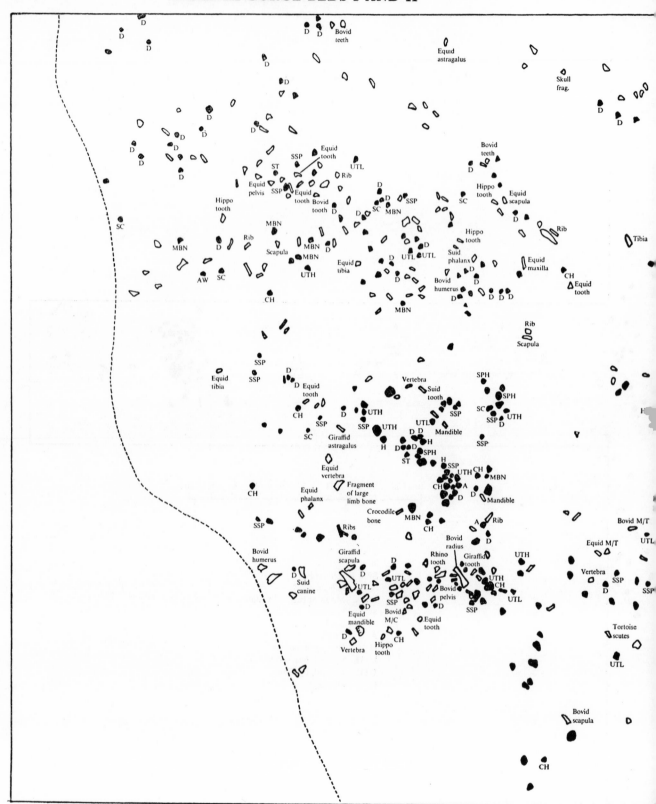

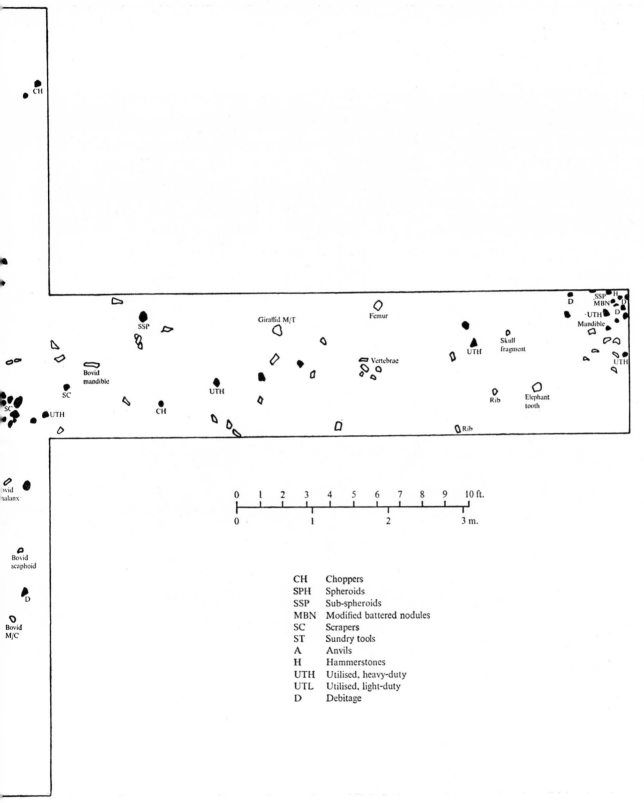

CH   Choppers
SPH   Spheroids
SSP   Sub-spheroids
MBN   Modified battered nodules
SC   Scrapers
ST   Sundry tools
A   Anvils
H   Hammerstones
UTH   Utilised, heavy-duty
UTL   Utilised, light-duty
D   Debitage

Fig. 71. MNK Main Occupation Site. Plan of remains on the 4th level (approx. 8 in. above the 3rd level).

143

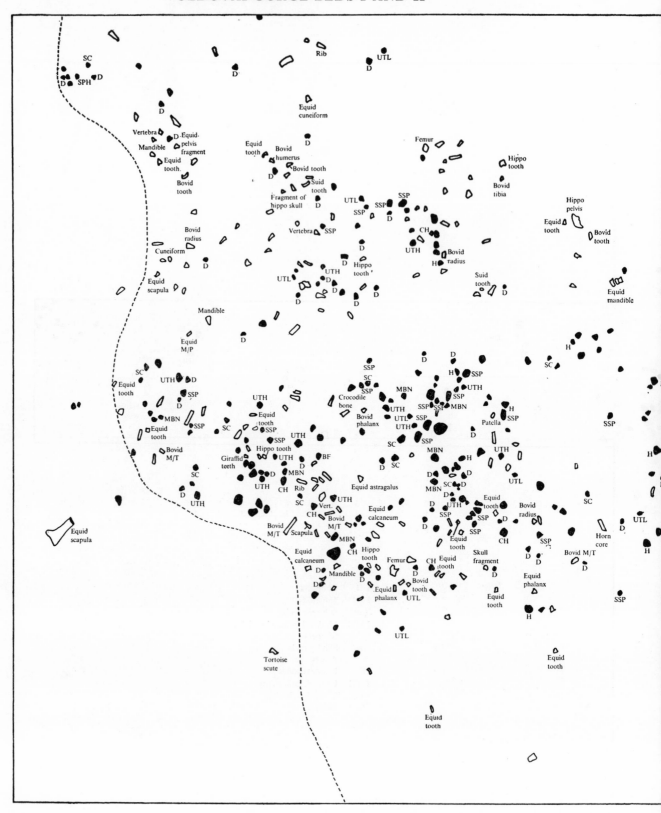

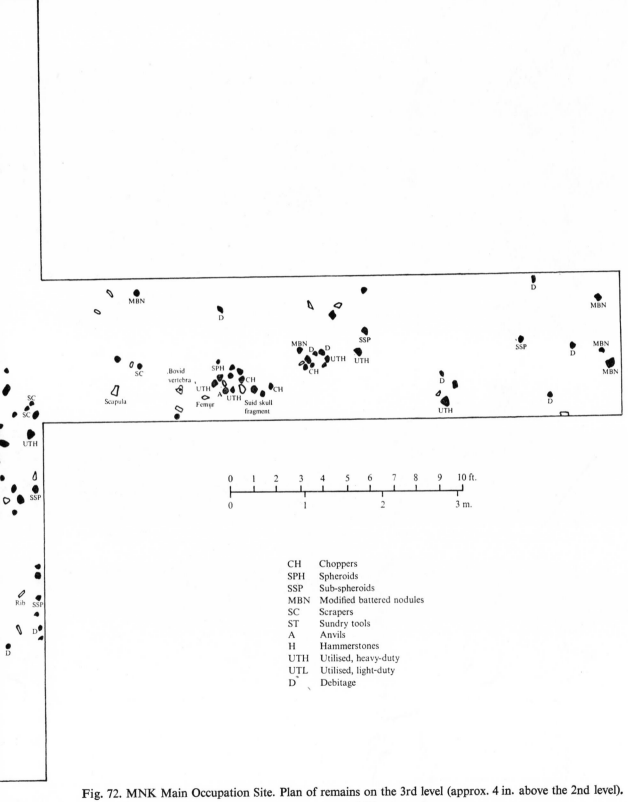

CH   Choppers
SPH   Spheroids
SSP   Sub-spheroids
MBN   Modified battered nodules
SC   Scrapers
ST   Sundry tools
A   Anvils
H   Hammerstones
UTH   Utilised, heavy-duty
UTL   Utilised, light-duty
D   Debitage

Fig. 72. MNK Main Occupation Site. Plan of remains on the 3rd level (approx. 4 in. above the 2nd level).

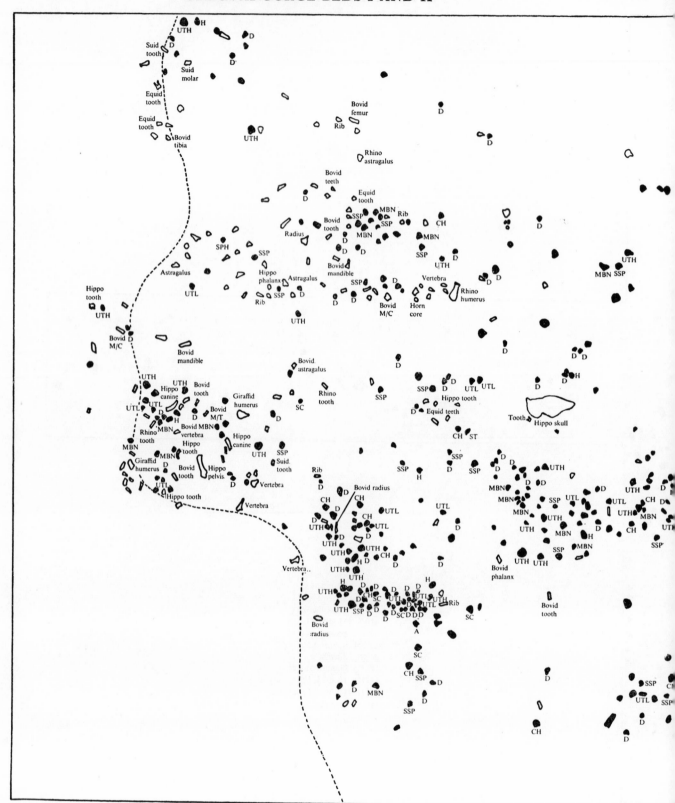

146

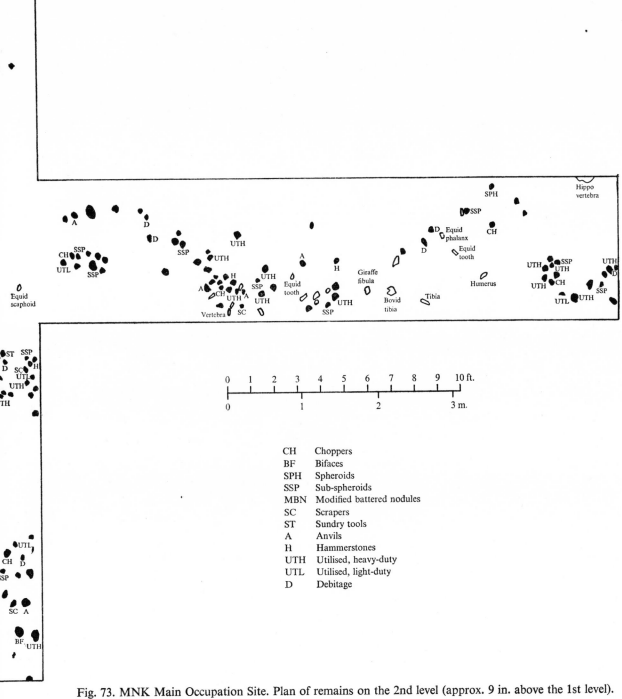

CH   Choppers
BF   Bifaces
SPH   Spheroids
SSP   Sub-spheroids
MBN   Modified battered nodules
SC   Scrapers
ST   Sundry tools
A   Anvils
H   Hammerstones
UTH   Utilised, heavy-duty
UTL   Utilised, light-duty
D   Debitage

Fig. 73. MNK Main Occupation Site. Plan of remains on the 2nd level (approx. 9 in. above the 1st level).

IO-2

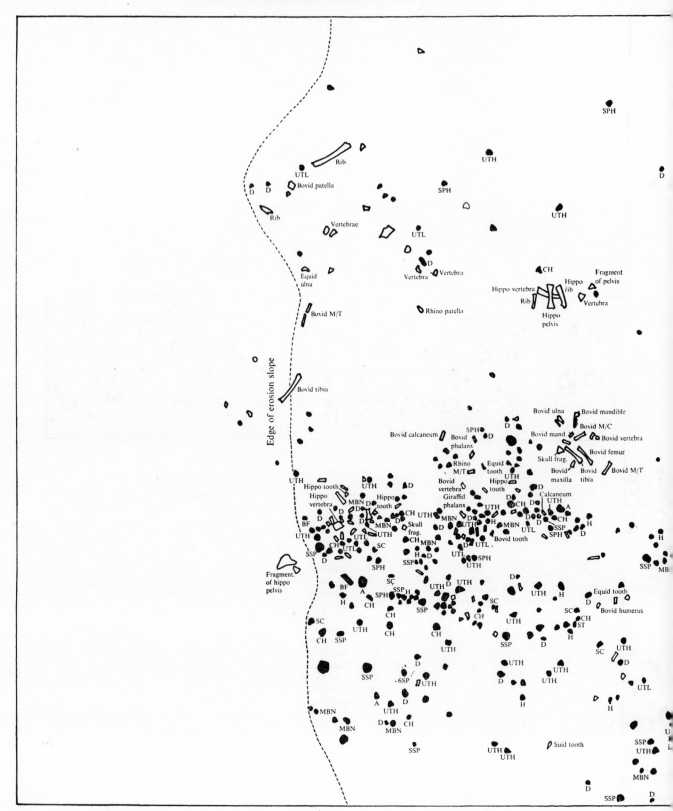

148

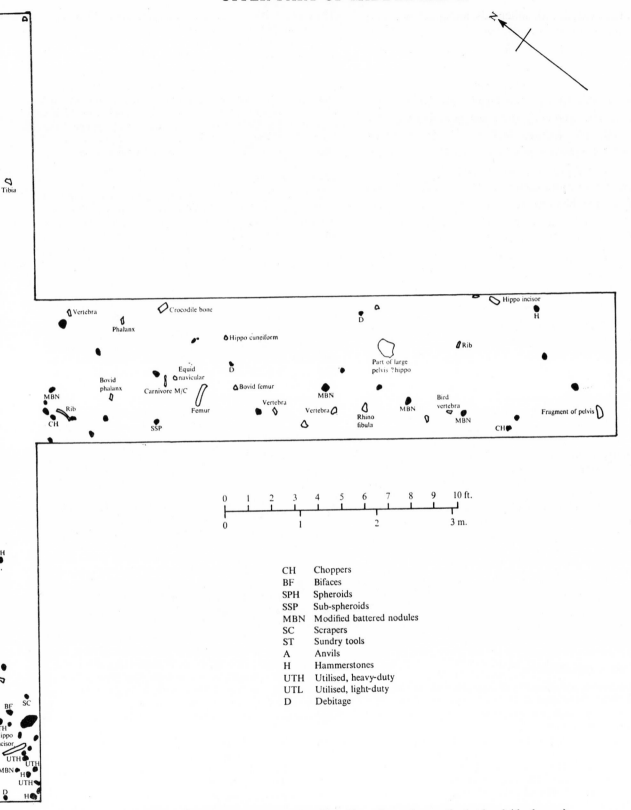

CH   Choppers
BF   Bifaces
SPH   Spheroids
SSP   Sub-spheroids
MBN   Modified battered nodules
SC   Scrapers
ST   Sundry tools
A   Anvils
H   Hammerstones
UTH   Utilised, heavy-duty
UTL   Utilised, light-duty
D   Debitage

Fig. 74. MNK Main Occupation Site. Plan of remains on the 1st level (the lowest).

On the other hand, spheroids, subspheroids and modified battered nodules together represent almost 50 per cent. Symmetrical stone balls do not occur. Among the angular, subspherical specimens are twelve massive examples in which the average weight is 6 lb. 10 oz., the largest weighing 14 lb. Both heavy- and light-duty scrapers are well represented, the former including a number of particularly massive specimens. In the light-duty series end scrapers are scarce and short, stumpy specimens are more common. It is noticeable that very few have been made from tabular quartzite, a material which was extensively used for making scrapers at other sites. The remaining tools consist of one poorly made burin and eight small pointed flake tools or awls.

The usual utilised material is represented with the addition of a few particularly symmetrical and well-made circular anvils of a type not found at lower levels.

TOOLS

Side choppers (69 specimens)

Forty examples are made of quartz and quartzite, one of horneblende gneiss and the balance of lava. They are mostly made on cobblestones, both of lava and of quartz and quartzite. Six specimens are unifacial; seven show multiple flaking on one face, opposed to a single scar on the obverse. The working edges are generally jagged. In a few specimens over 50 per cent of the circumference has been trimmed. Chipping and blunting due to utilisation are generally present, together with a number of crushed indentations. Five specimens exhibit hammerstone utilisation on the butt ends. There are seven very heavily rolled examples which appear to be derived. The length/breadth/thickness measurements range from $94 \times 123 \times 85$ mm. to $35 \times 37 \times 26$ mm., with an average of $65 \times 75 \times 57$ mm., and the mean diameters vary between 100 and 32 mm., with an average of 64 mm. The edge/circumference ratios vary from 71 to 21 per cent, with an average of 41 per cent.

End choppers (18 specimens)

Five examples are of quartz or quartzite and the balance of lava. With the exception of two quartz specimens, the whole series is made on cobblestones. There are three unusually large, crude examples, one of which weighs 5 lb. Three are unifacial. Particularly heavy utilisation is present on a number of specimens and one has been further used as an anvil. The length/breadth/thickness measurements range from $143 \times 120 \times 93$ mm. to $60 \times 54 \times 38$ mm., with an average of $86 \times 63 \times 50$ mm., and the mean diameters vary from 118 to 35 mm., with an average of 65 mm.

The edge/circumference ratios vary from 48 to 15 per cent, with an average of 26 per cent.

Two-edged choppers (7 specimens)

Five examples are of lava and two of quartz. Six are bilateral, with a bifacially flaked working edge on either side. In the seventh the edges are at right angles, situated at one end and on one side. One specimen is heavily rolled. The length/breadth/thickness measurements range from $120 \times 74 \times 51$ mm. to $61 \times 51 \times 31$ mm., with an average of $86 \times 63 \times 50$ mm. The average mean diameter is 65 mm.

Chisel-edged choppers (2 specimens)

These are made from a lava cobblestone and a fragment of fine-grained quartzite respectively. Both examples are oblong, with working edges at right-angles to the upper and lower surfaces. The trimming is bifacial and the edges measure 33 and 40 mm. in length. (Measurements: $102 \times 76 \times 40$ mm. and $87 \times 50 \times 43$ mm.)

Bifaces (9 specimens, including 3 broken and 1 unfinished)

The bifaces from this level and those from FC West are the earliest found in association with a Developed Oldowan industry, they occur at approximately the same stratigraphic horizon as the early Acheulean site of EF–HR. The tools in the series from MNK are large and well-made. Miniature, light-duty bifaces, such as occur in the later phases of the Developed Oldowan, are not represented. The nine specimens may be described as follows:

(*a*) A stumpy specimen, with a broken tip made from lava. The whole circumference is bifacially flaked with many plunging scars. The edge is sinuous and noticeably more blunted by use on one lateral edge than on the other.

(*b*) A short, stumpy specimen made from lava. Both extremities are relatively broad and curved. The edge is jagged with some bifacial chipping, probably caused by utilisation. The flake scars are relatively large and shallow, although the specimen is thick in cross-section. (Fig. 75.)

(*c*) A large lava specimen weighing $6\frac{1}{2}$ lb. and pointed at both ends. The edge is sinuous and is bifacially flaked round the whole circumference. There is a small area of flat weathered surface in the central part of both the upper and lower faces, indicating that the tool was probably made from a tabular piece of raw material. The flake scars at the tip are large and shallow, whilst a proportion of those on the lateral edges are stepped. Chipped utilisation is present, but is much less pronounced at the tip than on the sides, where it also includes an indentation 23 mm. wide and 5 mm. deep, chipped from one face only. (Pl. 20.)

(*d*) A cleaver made from quartzite. One face is formed by a natural cleavage surface with a longitudinal ridge running down the centre. One lateral edge consists of the intersection of this surface with a second flat surface, which may be a natural fracture or part of a large truncated flake scar. The opposite edge is bifacially trimmed and the trimming extends round the butt. The tip is wide. It is now broken and damaged by use, but was probably straight and oblique when complete. (Fig. 76.)

(*e*) A heavy-duty pick made from lava. This resembles an unusually large, crude biface of 'Chellean' type. The butt is

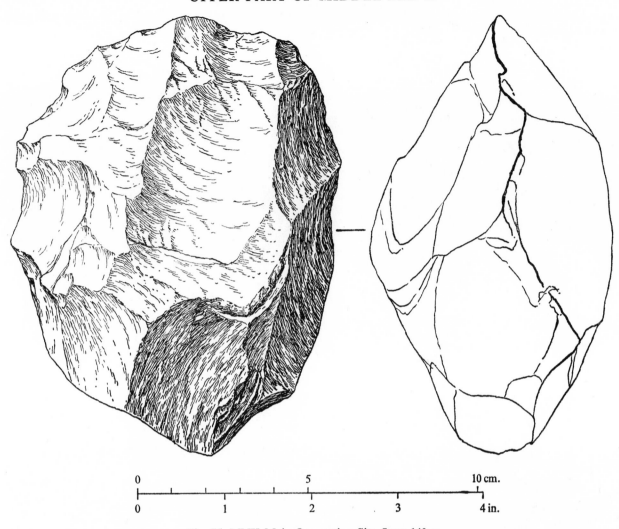

0   5   10 cm.

0   1   2   3   4 in.

Fig. 75. MNK Main Occupation Site. Lava biface.

wide, thick and massive; the width exceeds the length and the tool tapers rapidly to a rounded, blunt point. The edge is even and relatively straight at the tip, but somewhat jagged on the lateral edges.

The broken and unfinished bifaces consist of the following:

(i) The tip end of a large quartz biface, which appears to have been comparable in size to (a). It is made of particularly coarse-grained material and the flake scars are difficult to determine precisely, but they appear to be shallow and relatively large. There is no step-flaking. The edge is even and virtually straight, but considerably chipped and blunted by use. The tool has been broken obliquely and there is some evidence of utilisation on the fractured surface. (Present length/breadth/thickness: 130 × 127 × 64 mm.)

(ii) A sharply pointed tip, broken obliquely. The under-surface is flat and the lateral edges are steeply trimmed. Made of lava. (Present measurements: 75 × 35 × 23 mm.)

(iii) A butt end made of quartzite, with flat upper and lower faces. (Present measurements: 36 × 88 × 30 mm.)

(iv) A side-struck lava flake with a longitudinal dorsal ridge on one face. There is a minimum of flaking on the lateral edges, and it appears to represent an unfinished biface. (142 × 101 × 49 mm.)

The following are the measurements for the five complete specimens:

	Length/breadth/thickness (mm.)	Mean diameter (mm.)	Breadth/length ratio (%)	Thickness/length ratio (%)
(a)	118 × 97 × 64	93	82	54
(b)	126 × 95 × 68	96	75	53
(c)	297 × 144 × 68	169	48	22
(d)	210 × 116 × 72	132	55	34
(e)	124 × 126 × 103	117	100	83

151

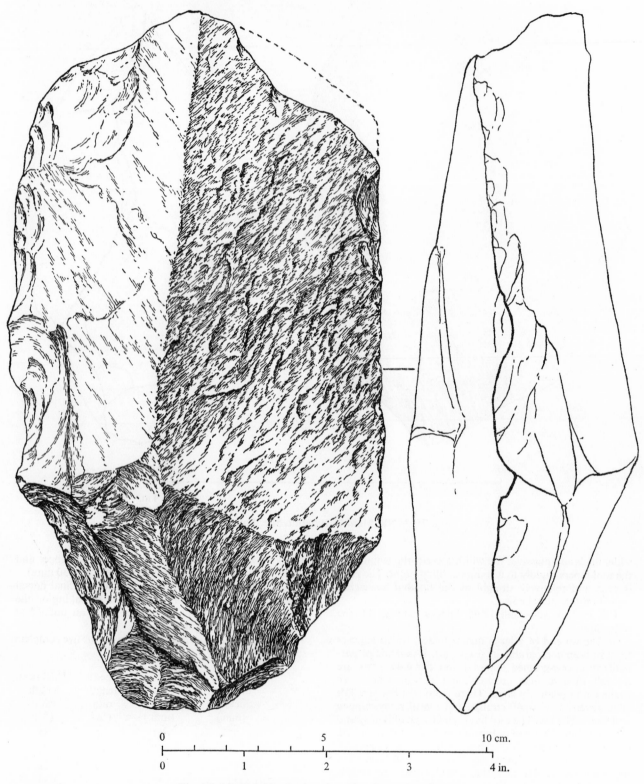

Fig. 76. MNK Main Occupation Site. Quartzite cleaver.

Polyhedrons (9 specimens)

Three are made from lava and the balance from quartz or quartzite. There are two particularly massive specimens, one of which weighs 5 lb. The whole series is angular, with markedly projecting sharp edges. The mean diameters range from 111 to 52 mm., with an average of 74 mm.

Discoids (19 specimens)

Eight examples are made from lava and eleven from quartz or quartzite. Several are high-backed, either biconvex in cross-section or plano-convex with one face relatively flat. The edges are generally jagged, with bifacial radial trimming that extends round the whole circumference. Utilisation is usually present and one example is heavily rolled. Four diminutive quartz specimens, in which the average mean diameter is 26 mm., are included in the series. The length/breadth/thickness measurements range from $108 \times 92 \times 68$ mm. to $28 \times 27 \times 15$ mm., with an average of $68 \times 62 \times 46$ mm. The average mean diameter is 58 mm.

Spheroids (16 specimens)

The whole series is made from quartz or quartzite. Although true stone balls do not occur, the surfaces of most of the specimens have been extensively battered and the projecting parts greatly reduced. There is considerable variation in size and weight within this series. The mean diameters range from 84 to 25 mm., with an average of 59 mm.

Sub-spheroids (143 specimens)

Most of these tools are made of quartz or quartzite, but the series also includes two of gneiss, eight of lava and one of pegmatite. Twelve massive specimens are included, of which the largest weighs $14\frac{1}{2}$ lb. (Pl. 21.) The mean diameter for the whole series ranges from 169 to 23 mm., with an average of 62 mm.

Modified battered nodules and blocks (63 specimens)

These consist of angular and sub-angular blocks and nodules with a minimum of flaking but with battering and blunting on the edges. Quartz and quartzite specimens predominate but there are also one of pegmatite, two of quartzo-feldspathic gneiss, two of horneblende gneiss and two of lava. The mean diameters range from 110 to 30 mm., with an average of 58 mm.

Scrapers, heavy-duty (24 specimens)

The heavy-duty scrapers are generally crude; they are mostly made of quartz or quartzite, but there are also three of lava and one of gneiss. The working edges are variable, but tend to be curved rather than straight. The series may be described as follows:

(*a*) In seven specimens made on slabs of tabular quartz the working edges are steeply trimmed and generally even, although in one example there are four crushed notches with intervening projections which appear to have been caused by use. Utilisation is usually evident and is particularly heavy on two specimens. In one quadrilateral specimen trimming is present on two lateral edges which meet to form a convergent scraper. These seven examples range in size from 108×85 mm. to 62×81 mm. and the lengths of the working edges from 120 to 80 mm.

(*b*) The two side scrapers are made on flakes which have been trimmed on one lateral edge. One is approximately discoidal, although trimming occurs on only part of the circumference. It is in sharp, fresh condition. The second is on an end-struck flake and shows more extensive use. The length/breadth measurements are 68×66 mm. and 62×60 mm. respectively. The lengths of the working edges are 63 mm. and 90 mm.

(*c*) Two examples are made on quartzite cobbles. In one there is a single large negative flake scar on the undersurface, from which the edge has been steeply trimmed to form a large-nosed scraper. (67×70 mm. Length of edge 95 mm.) The second specimen has been trimmed to a short and almost straight working edge from the cortex under surface. (75×93 mm. Length of edge 55 mm.)

(*d*) Four crude specimens which may be unfinished but appear more likely to have been damaged through unusually heavy use. Two are made of quartz or quartzite, one of horneblende gneiss and one is of a lava cobblestone. The working edges are very uneven and exhibit large irregular flake scars. The length/breadth measurements range from 78×105 mm. to 67×94 mm., and the length of the working edges varies from 127 to 96 mm.

(*e*) Three specimens made on parts of quartzite and lava cobblestones. The working edges are straight or only very slightly curved and have been trimmed from a natural flat surface on the underside. Length/breadth measurements vary from 85×58 mm. to 66×96 mm. and the length of the working edges range from 72 to 43 mm.

(*f*) Two double-edged specimens. Both have two steeply-trimmed and heavily utilised working edges situated on the upper and lower faces respectively. The length/breadth measurements are 71×94 mm. and 62×72 mm. and the lengths of the working edges are 96 and 103 mm., and 80 and 70 mm.

(*g*) Three further specimens may be described as follows:

(i) A high-backed discoidal quartz scraper, steeply trimmed round the whole circumference. The undersurface consists of a flat cleavage plane. (81×75 mm.)

(ii) A massive quartzite specimen, roughly circular in shape, weighing 4 lb. 3 oz. The under-surface is flat and the greater part of the circumference has been trimmed. (131×123 mm. Length of edge 338 mm.)

(iii) A high-backed quartzite specimen with almost vertical trimming that forms a large nosed scraper. The edge is considerably blunted by use. (66×57 mm. Length of edge 87 mm.)

The average length/breadth measurements for the entire series of twenty-three heavy-duty scrapers are 77×82 mm. and the average length of the working edges is 99 mm.

Scrapers, light-duty (59 specimens)

With the exception of one side and one hollow scraper made of lava, the whole series is of quartz or quartzite. It includes small discoidal and triangular specimens trimmed on the entire circumference, side scrapers, end scrapers, double-edged scrapers, a single hollow scraper and two nosed scrapers. Specimens made on fragments of tabular material, which are common at other sites, are relatively scarce at this level where almost equal proportions are made on flakes or on irregular-shaped core fragments.

End scrapers (9 specimens). Seven are made on flakes and two on pieces of tabular material. The working edges vary from straight to convex and are even or slightly jagged. The measurements range from 56 × 49 mm. to 30 × 24 mm., with an average of 45 × 42 mm.

Discoidal scrapers (16 specimens). These tools are steeply trimmed round the circumference but are usually not quite symmetrical. The smallest example measures 19 mm. in diameter. The measurements range from 53 × 44 mm. to 19 × 18 mm.

Side scrapers (25 specimens). This series is made partly on flakes and partly on core fragments. The edges are generally curved and the retouch is usually fine and regular. One example is trimmed on two edges. The measurements range from 49 × 60 mm. to 22 × 29 mm.

Doubled-edged scrapers (4 specimens) These tools are similar to the two heavy-duty double-edged scrapers. The working edges are evenly curved with steep retouch, but in one example the edges are slightly jagged. The length/breadth measurements range from 56 × 43 mm. to 44 × 41 mm.

There are also two nosed scrapers with narrow, rounded working edges (46 × 38 mm. and 40 × 37 mm.), two triangular perimetal scrapers (36 × 22 mm. and 38 × 24 mm.) and one hollow scraper on an end-struck flake that has been trimmed transversely at the tip into a notch 27 mm. wide and 1·5 mm. deep.

The average length/breadth measurements for the entire series of light-duty scrapers are 34 × 33 mm.

Awls (7 specimens)

These consist of quartz flakes trimmed at the tips to small, sharp points. In some specimens the points are formed by a trimmed notch on either side and in others by straight convergent retouched edges. Utilisation is present at the points on both the upper and lower faces. The length/breadth measurements range from 67 × 49 mm. to 28 × 33 mm., with an average of 48 × 42 mm.

Sundry tools (3 specimens)

One consists of a tongue-shaped piece of lava, 60 mm. long and 47 mm. wide, boldly flaked over both faces. The butt is formed by a vertical cleavage plane. The second specimen is made from quartz. It is roughly oval in shape and has been trimmed along parts of the circumference. (98 × 82 × 40 mm.) The third consists of a large quartz flake which has been trimmed at the tip to a sharp point. (97 × 89 mm.)

UTILISED MATERIAL

'Anvils' (24 specimens)

Eighteen examples are of quartz or quartzite, five of lava and one of quartzo-feldspathic gneiss. Seven circular specimens are flaked vertically on the circumference, with utilised edges on both the upper and lower faces. In several specimens incipient cones of percussion can also be seen on these surfaces. There is also an irregular block of quartzite that shows utilisation on all the edges, but this may have been imported as raw material. It weighs 17½ lb. and measures 214 × 158 × 155 mm. The remaining specimens are somewhat irregular in form, but all have edges approximating right angles which show battered utilisation. The mean diameters range from 175 to 48 mm., with an average of 89 mm.

Hammerstones (64 specimens)

These consist of rounded, waterworn stones with pitting and bruising on projecting parts of the exterior. Fourteen specimens are of quartz or quartzite, one of horneblende gneiss (similar to that which occurs at the Kelogi inselberg) and forty-nine of lava. The mean diameters range from 103 to 47 mm., with an average of 65 mm.

Cobblestones (136 specimens)

These specimens show evidence of utilisation in the form of crude flaking and shattering, but not the pitting characteristic of hammerstones. Five examples are of quartz or quartzite, one of horneblende gneiss (of the Kelogi variety) and the balance of lava. The mean diameters range from 121 to 35 mm., with an average of 72 mm.

Nodules and blocks (9 specimens)

These consist of angular blocks with some chipping and blunting on the edges. Three are of quartz, one of horneblende gneiss and five of lava.

The mean diameters range from 101 to 36 mm., with an average of 67 mm.

Light-duty flakes and other fragments (139 specimens)

With straight edges (26 specimens). These are of quartz or quartzite, with the exception of one broken lava flake. The utilisation occurs mostly on whole or broken flakes, but there are also five small core fragments in which one or more edges are chipped and blunted. Many of the flakes are larger than those from Oldowan assemblages. The chipping on the edges is usually fine, but a few examples occur in which coarse, irregular chips have been removed. The length/breadth measurements range from 74 to 37 mm. to 27 × 27 mm., with an average of 47 × 35 mm.

With concave edges (44 specimens). This series is entirely of quartz and quartzite. Most of the specimens are whole or broken flakes, but there are also eight irregular-shaped core fragments with notches. In three examples the edges of the notches have been crushed and are now quite blunt. The length/breadth measurements range from 71 × 56 mm. to 23 × 21 mm., with an average of 38 × 30 mm. The notches vary in width from 22 to 7 mm. and in depth from 3·5 to 1·5 mm., with an average of 14 × 2·2 mm.

With convex edges (27 specimens). All except one are of quartz or quartzite. The series consists mostly of whole or broken flakes in which the tip, or one lateral edge, has been utilised. A few specimens show chipping on both faces. The length/breadth measurements range from 76 × 49 mm. to 27 × 24 mm., with an average of 43 × 35 mm.

Miscellaneous (42 specimens). These specimens show some irregular chipping and blunting on one or more edges. There is one flake of lava and the remainder is of quartz or quartzite. The length/breadth measurements range from 65 × 35 mm. to 28 × 21 mm., with an average of 43 × 35 mm.

DEBITAGE

The total number of unmodified flakes and fragments amounts to 3,579, of which only 226 are complete flakes. As usual, by far the largest category consists of broken flakes and chips, which total 2,901. There are, in addition, 449 core fragments and three re-sharpening flakes. Amongst the complete flakes divergent specimens greatly outnumber any other type. Lava is particularly scarce and amounts to only 5·9 per cent of the total, although in the complete flakes it is more common and represents 12·2 per cent. End-struck flakes are the most numerous and amount to 77·2 per cent. The length/breadth measurements in millimetres for the 226 complete flakes are as follows:

Lava	Range	Average
End-struck	105 × 80 to 31 × 20	64 × 44
Side-struck	50 × 69 to 26 × 35	30 × 26
Quartz/quartzite		
End-struck	110 × 61 to 24 × 21	45 × 35
Side-struck	90 × 91 to 16 × 31	36 × 46

Bulbs of percussion

The bulbs of percussion are variable but are well developed on the whole, particularly in the lava flakes. They can be subdivided as follows:

	Lava	Quartz/quartzite
Marked	61·9 %	55·7 %
Slight	33·3 %	35·9 %
Negative	4·8 %	1·2 %
Shattered	—	7·2 %
Totals	27	194
		221

Angles of striking platforms

It is possible to measure the angles of the striking platforms in 141 flakes, as follows:

	Lava	Quartz/quartzite
70–89°	—	5·0 %
90–109°	10·0 %	55·3 %
110–129°	85·0 %	38·0 %
130°	5·0 %	1·6 %
Totals	20	121
		141

The three re-sharpening flakes are of quartz or quartzite. They exhibit longitudinal dorsal ridges.

MANUPORTS

Cobblestones (668 whole and 162 broken specimens)

These are mainly of lava with a few quartz and quartzite specimens. The rolled condition of some of the bone fragments and a few of the artefacts indicates that some degree of water action took place at this site. There is, however, no suggestion of fast-flowing torrential water such as would have been required to transport the large number of cobblestones. These specimens are therefore regarded as probably artificially introduced. In a random sample of thirty specimens the mean diameter is 51 mm.

Nodules and blocks (86 specimens)

These include some irregular-shaped lava nodules, but the majority consists of angular blocks and slabs of quartz and quartzite. There are also a few examples of horneblende gneiss. In a random sample of thirty specimens the mean diameter is 51 mm.

Analysis of the industry from the main occupation Site at MNK

	Nos.	%
Tools	448	10·2
Utilised material	372	8·4
Débitage	3579	81·3
	4399	
Tools		
Side choppers	69	15·4
End choppers	18	4·0
Two-edged choppers	7	1·6
Chisel-edged choppers	2	0·4
Bifaces, including broken and unfinished	9	2·0
Polyhedrons	9	2·0
Discoids	19	4·2
Spheroids	16	3·5
Subspheroids	143	32·0
Modified battered nodules and blocks	63	14·1
Scrapers, heavy-duty	24	5·3
Scrapers, light-duty	59	13·2
Awls	7	1·6
Sundry tools	3	0·7
	448	
Utilised material		
'Anvils'	24	6·4
Hammerstones	64	17·2
Cobblestones	136	36·5
Nodules and blocks	9	2·4
Light-duty flakes and other fragments	139	37·4
	372	

Débitage	Nos.	%
Whole flakes	226	6·3
Re-sharpening flakes	3	0·1
Broken flakes and chips	2901	81·0
Core fragments	449	12·5
	3579	

3. SITES FC WEST AND FC
(Fuch's Cliff)

Archaeological numbers (62) and (63)

Geologic locality 89

The exposures of Bed II at FC and the extension of the site to the west have been known for many years to be particularly rich in artefacts and faunal material. The sites lie on the left bank of the Side Gorge 1 mile above the point where it joins the Main Gorge. The main exposures at FC are on the right of the track which leads down into the Gorge and across to MNK on the opposite side, where the same beds are exposed. FC West is immediately upstream of the main site, but cannot be seen from the track on account of a projecting bluff.

During 1961 a trial trench was started at FC by L. S. B. Leakey. This proved unsatisfactory and was later abandoned. No further work was carried out until 1963, when a second trial trench was begun in the upper part of Bed II. This was also discontinued since it proved disappointing in regard to both the sections exposed and the amount of cultural and faunal material obtained.

SITE FC WEST

At this site a trial trench 10 ft. wide was dug, in a series of steps, from beneath Bed III to the lowest exposed horizon in Bed II, which proved to be the chert bed. The total depth amounted to approximately 50 ft. (Fig. 3, in pocket).

The deposits exposed in this trench will not be described in detail since they are characteristic of the sequence in this area (see p. 115). In brief, the following succession was noted: the 14 ft. of deposits lying above the chert bed consisted of tuffs and clays and included a horizon of alternating grey and reddish-brown tuffs which can be traced over a considerable distance in this area

(Tuff II^B). A thin gravel bed, not more than a few inches thick, also occurs within this horizon, at a height of 11 ft. above the chert. No artefacts or faunal remains were found in these deposits, although a particularly rich occupation level occurred immediately above, on the surface of a clay. This yielded over 1,900 specimens from an area of 170 sq.ft. The occupation level was overlain by 1½–3 ft. of re-worked tuff which also yielded a considerable number of scattered artefacts and bone fragments, including a well-made biface and part of a hominid molar tooth. The upper surface of this deposit had been deeply eroded prior to the deposition of the overlying beds.

The cultural material from these two levels is described separately, but since there are no apparent differences between the two assemblages and since the two levels are contiguous, the material has been pooled for the final analysis.

Scattered artefacts and a few fossil bones and teeth were found in five higher levels, as follows:

(*a*) Tuff II^D, which is here 4 ft. thick and lies 42 ft. above the chert bed, yielded one quartz flake and one bone splinter.

(*b*) A fine-grained buff-white tuff, 5 ft. thick and 32 ft. above the chert, yielded a bovid metatarsal, fibula and phalanx, a suid astragalus, a damaged equid terminal phalanx and four indeterminate bone fragments.

(*c*) A clayey tuff, 4 ft. thick and 26 ft. above the chert bed, yielded seven flakes, an equid canine and two foot bones, two suid foot bones and one bone splinter.

(*d*) A fine-grained sandy tuff, 3 ft. thick and 21 ft. above the chert level, yielded nine artefacts, three equid phalanges and one splint bone, a suid ulna, part of a bovid basi-occipital, an astragalus, part of a tibia and part of a metacarpal, together with seven indeterminate bone fragments and a coprolite.

(*e*) A consolidated, fine sand 1 ft. thick and 20 ft. above the chert, yielded nine quartz and quartzite artefacts, including a small chopper, part of a suid canine, part of an equid acetabulum, a bovid incisor and two terminal phalanges, a tortoise scute, the centrum of a large vertebra and two bone splinters.

The proportions of tools, utilised material and *débitage* from the occupation floor and re-worked tuff stand very close, as do the percentages of the various tool forms. The choppers from both levels are on the whole less well made than in the Oldowan from Upper Bed I, although a proportion of the side choppers have wider and more even working edges with some secondary trimming. Side choppers are, as usual, the most common form and account for 13·0 per cent of the tools. Quartz and quartzite specimens outnumber those of lava and a relatively high proportion has battering on the butt ends. There are three whole and parts of five broken bifaces. They are not highly finished and are typical of what was formerly termed the 'Chellean'. Two quartz examples are made on fragments of tabular material and are similar to the series recovered from the Lower Occupation Floor at TK, which is within a few feet of the top of Bed II. Spheroids, subspheroids and modified battered nodules are the most numerous group of tools and amount to 50 per cent of the total. Heavy-duty scrapers are more common than light-duty specimens although at other sites the latter are usually more numerous. The *débitage* includes a number of flakes which are considerably larger than any known from Oldowan sites.

THE OCCUPATION FLOOR

The cultural and faunal material from this level was exceptionally concentrated and occurred at a density of 27·6 specimens per cu.ft. It was confined to the surface of the clay and to within a few inches of the top, unlike the material from the overlying tuff, where fossil bones and artefacts were scattered throughout the whole depth of the deposit. Mammalian bones were well preserved, but were relatively scarce and amounted to only 7·5 per cent of the total occupation debris, while artefacts represented 75·8 per cent and natural cobblestones 16·1 per cent.

Although there are no heavily rolled artefacts or bones, a proportion of both is either weathered or abraded to some extent and is not in the mint-fresh condition usually seen in material on Bed I

living floors. It seems possible that here, in common with the majority of Bed II sites, there had been some displacement of the material by water action, although it had clearly not been transported for any considerable distance.

Remains were particularly concentrated in two areas (see Fig. 77). The larger of the two areas was oblong, measuring 8 × 11 ft., and lay in the southern part of the trench. One end, however, had been damaged by erosion and the north/south diameter may originally have been somewhat greater. The second dense concentration of remains occurred within a roughly circular area, approximately 6 ft. in diameter. It lay to the north, with a relatively barren zone, 2 or 3 ft. wide, between the two.

The total number of artefacts from this level amounts to 1,184, of which 73·1 per cent is *débitage*. In common with the series from the overlying re-worked tuff, the number of tools exceeds that of utilised specimens, with 16·0 per cent in contrast to 10·9 per cent. Quartz and quartzite were used predominantly as raw materials and account for 70·4 per cent of the tools and 84·1 per cent of the total assemblage. Choppers of various forms amount to 22·4 per cent whilst light-duty tools are unusually scarce. No complete bifaces were found, but five broken specimens indicate that they were present, although exceedingly rare, as at the MNK Main Occupation Site. In addition to the artefacts there are 251 unmodified cobblestones and blocks. With some minor variations, mainly in the proportion of certain groups of artefacts, the assemblage does not differ to any appreciable extent from the contemporary material from the MNK Main Occupation Site.

TOOLS

Side choppers (28 specimens)

Fifteen examples are made of quartz or quartzite and the balance of lava, generally on cobblestones. In ten of the quartz and quartzite specimens the butt ends show pitting and bruising which appear to have been caused subsequent to the manufacture of the tools. Two examples, however, are clearly made on broken hammerstones. Eight are bifacially flaked. One has been extensively damaged by use and has a shattered and blunted working edge. Three are in fresh condition and the balance show only slight damage. In three examples that are made on relatively flat

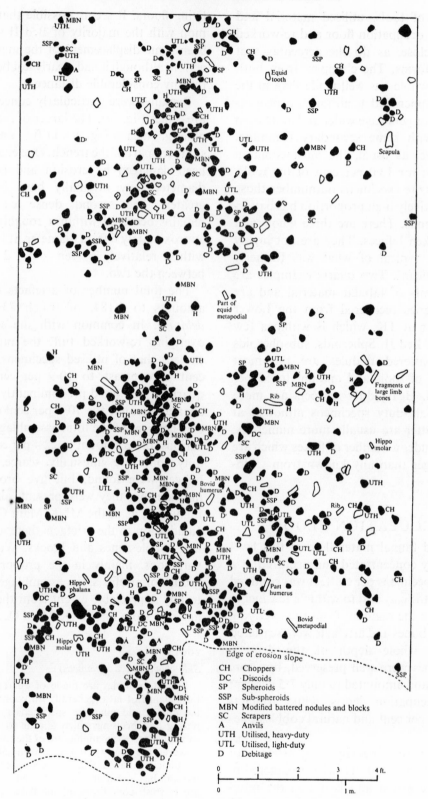

Fig. 77. FC West. Plan of remains on the Occupation Floor.

158

cobblestones the working edges are wide and curved, with some secondary flaking, so that they are less jagged than usual. Three lava choppers are particularly crude, with steep, irregular flaking on the working edges and a number of plunging scars. There is also a subspherical specimen resembling a core, in which bold, flat flakes have been removed from one face, struck from a single negative scar on the obserse. The length/breadth/thickness measurements range from 122 × 135 × 73 mm. to 31 × 43 × 29 mm., with an average of 57 × 67 × 43 mm., and the mean diameters vary from 110 to 34 mm., with an average of 55 mm. The average edge/circumference ratio is 41 per cent.

End choppers (17 specimens)

Thirteen examples are of lava and four of quartz or quartzite. In four specimens the butt ends have been used as hammerstones. The whole series is bifacially flaked, but includes some examples with particularly jagged working edges and others with secondary trimming which has rendered the edges considerably more even. Utilisation is variable. The length/breadth/thickness measurements range from 119 × 97 × 58 mm. to 59 × 47 × 39 mm., with an average of 80 × 64 × 50 mm., and the mean diameters vary from 92 to 48 mm., with an average of 64 mm. The average edge/circumference ratio is 29 per cent.

Pointed choppers (3 specimens)

These consist of three lava side choppers with well-defined median points on the working edges. The edges are bifacially flaked. In two specimens the points are made by means of a bold, deeply indented flake scar on either side and in the third by a number of small trimming scars. The length/breadth/thickness measurements range from 82 × 90 × 62 mm. to 48 × 77 × 33 mm., with an average of 66 × 64 × 45 mm., and the mean diameters vary from 78 to 52 mm., with an average of 65 mm. The average edge/circumference ratio is 49 per cent.

Chisel-edged chopper (1 specimen)

A relatively large oblong lava cobblestone has had three flakes removed at one end forming an edge 46 mm. wide which is at right angles to the upper and lower faces of the tool. The butt end is extensively battered. (114 × 82 × 80 mm.)

Bifaces (5 broken specimens)

(a) The median part and butt end of a large biface made on a slab of tabular quartzite. One lateral edge is trimmed from one direction only, whilst the opposite edge is bifacially flaked. The edges are even to sinuous and considerably blunted by use. (Present measurements: 122 × 10 × 59 mm.)

(b) Two butt ends of quartz specimens. (Present measurements: 64 × 97 × 33 mm. and 54 × 59 × 34 mm.)

(c) A small quartz specimen in which the tip is broken. It resembles a miniature handaxe and is flaked over both faces, with a sinuous edge on the whole circumference. (47 × 36 × 24 mm. Mean diameter 35 mm.)

(d) A second quartz specimen with a broken tip. The under-surface is flat and only flaked on part of the circumference, whilst the upper face is steeply trimmed all round, although the central area is flat. The butt end is rounded and damaged. (70 × 56 × 38 mm. Mean diameter 51 mm.)

Polyhedrons (4 specimens)

Three examples are of lava and one of quartz. Three specimens have one edge extending round the whole circumference, as in discoids. There are also a number of shorter, subsidiary cutting edges, all of which are in particularly sharp condition. The measurements range from 84 × 80 × 59 mm. to 66 × 56 × 41 mm. The average mean diameter is 63 mm.

Discoids (4 specimens)

Three examples are of quartz and one of lava. The latter is unusually flat and thin whilst the quartz specimens are thick in cross-section. One is symmetrical and particularly well-made. The mean diameters range from 53 to 34 mm.

Spheroids (10 specimens)

All the spheroids in this series are made of quartz or quartzite. They are symmetrical and well finished. They are generally battered over the whole or the greater part of the surface, but three of the smaller examples are faceted. These are almost exactly uniform in size and weigh 87, 85 and 98 grams respectively. The mean diameters range from 94 to 39 mm., with an average of 56 mm.

Subspheroids (38 specimens)

These tools are generally more angular than the spheroids. Thirty-two examples are of quartz and quartzite, four of lava, one of quartzo-feldspathic gneiss and one of horneblende gneiss. The mean diameters range from 76 to 26 mm., with an average of 55 mm.

Modified battered nodules and blocks (53 specimens)

These specimens vary greatly in shape and size, but have a minimum degree of flaking and also battered utilisation. Forty-two examples are of quartz and quartzite, seven of lava, two of quartzo-feldspathic gneiss and two of horneblende gneiss (cf. Kelogi variety). The mean diameters range from 95 to 22 mm., with an average of 47 mm.

Scrapers, heavy-duty (11 specimens)

Nine specimens have curved and steeply trimmed working edges; two are double-edged. Four examples are made on parts of lava cobbles and five on blocks of quartz or quartzite. The lengths of the working edges vary from 125 to 33 mm., with an average of 79 mm., and the length/breadth measurements range from 114 × 98 mm. to 48 × 65 mm., with an average of 77 × 65 mm. There are also two heavy-duty hollow scrapers. One is an oblong sickle-shaped fragment of lava, with a trimmed notch 38 mm. wide and 7 mm. deep on the concave edge. The second specimen, made of quartzite, is triangular, with the under-surface and one edge formed by natural cleavage planes. Both the remaining edges are trimmed along their entire lengths and there is a blunt point at their intersection, formed by a notch on either side. There is also a third and longer notch towards the butt. The measurements of the three notches are 58 × 8, 27 × 3 and 12 × 2·5 mm.

159

Scrapers, light-duty (9 specimens)

With the exception of one atypical example with a broad, transverse edge, these scrapers are made on core fragments, generally on pieces of tabular quartz or quartzite. Discoidal specimens, trimmed round the greater part of the circumference and sometimes slightly denticulated are the most common form. End scrapers are not represented. The length/breadth measurements range from 68 × 50 mm. to 29 × 25 mm., with an average of 40 × 34 mm.

Burin (1 specimen)

This is a well-made quartz example. The chisel edge is 13 mm. wide and trimmed by means of a single longitudinal scar extending the length of the tool on one side and with multiple scars on the opposite side. The butt end is relatively thin and shows scaled utilisation, similar to that of *outils écaillés*. (45 × 24 mm.)

Awls (2 specimens)

There are two quartz flakes trimmed bilaterally at the tips to sharp points. In one specimen there is additional chipping on the under surface, possibly due to use. The measurements are 43 × 37 mm. and 40 × 33 mm. respectively.

Sundry tools (3 specimens)

There are three bifacially flaked tools, made from quartz, which cannot be included in any of the usual categories. Two specimens resemble miniature ovates, but are too small to be classed as such. The measurements are 42 × 35 mm. and 38 × 37 mm. respectively. The third specimen is an oblong, pointed tool, steeply trimmed along both lateral edges and with a longitudinal dorsal crest. The undersurface is flat, but has been partly trimmed along the edges. (78 × 53 mm.)

UTILISED MATERIAL

'Anvils' (7 specimens)

These consist of cuboid and circular blocks of quartz and quartzite, with extensive battering on right-angled edges. One spherical specimen is double-edged. The mean diameters range from 124 to 49 mm. with an average of 77 mm.

Hammerstones (23 specimens)

This is a series of cobblestones exhibiting pitting and bruising on the extremities and on other projecting areas. Nineteen examples are of lava, three of quartz or quartzite and one of pegmatite. The mean diameters range from 85 to 37 mm., with an average of 60 mm.

Cobblestones (58 specimens)

These consist of fifty-seven lava cobblestones and one of quartz on which there is some evidence of utilisation, either shattering or crude flaking. The mean diameters range from 87 to 42 mm., with an average of 63 mm.

Light-duty flakes and other fragments (39 specimens)

With straight edges. These consist of six quartz flakes with relatively straight edges, chipped and blunted by use.

With concave edges. Two flakes and eight sundry fragments of quartz and quartzite exhibit chipped or crushed notches on the edges. The chipping is from one direction only and varies from small 'nibbling' in shallow notches to deeper and usually steeper flaking in the larger specimens. The notches vary in size from 35 × 3·5 mm. to 18 × 1·5 mm., with an average of 15 × 2·7 mm.

With convex edges. These consist of eleven broken quartz and quartzite flakes and other fragments with chipping and blunting on edges that are convex and generally thick-set. The chipping is usually intermittent.

Miscellaneous. A further twelve specimens, mainly of quartz, but including one of lava and one of quartzite, show some utilisation of the edges, but to a lesser extent than in the foregoing categories.

The overall measurements for the whole series of utilised flakes range from 100 × 62 mm. to 27 × 21 mm., with an average of 46 × 39 mm.

DEBITAGE

The total of unmodified flakes and other fragments amounts to 868 specimens, of which ninety-nine are whole flakes. Of the total, 94·0 per cent are of quartz or quartzite. Broken flakes and chips are the most numerous, with 607 specimens.

A rectangular block of brown chert, from which a number of flakes has been struck, was also found at this level. It measures 110 × 87 mm. and is the only chert artefact in the assemblage. The type of chert is quite unlike the variety found in Bed II.

The overall size of both the whole and broken flakes is generally greater than in Oldowan assemblages, particularly for the lava specimens. Among these are ten flakes of a size greatly exceeding any known from Oldowan sites. Most of the flakes are divergent, but a few convergent and parallel-sided specimens also occur. There are, in addition, three quartz re-sharpening flakes with longitudinal dorsal ridges. These measure 67 × 45 mm., 66 × 42 mm. and 55 × 30 mm. respectively. The length/breadth measurements in millimetres for the complete flakes are as follows:

Lava	Range	Average
End-struck	108 × 66 to 23 × 22	62 × 47
Side-struck	73 × 86 to 33 × 36	44 × 33
Quartz/quartzite		
End-struck	105 × 64 to 21 × 17	45 × 34
Side-struck	59 × 71 to 24 × 27	37 × 43

Bulbs of percussion

The bulbs of percussion in the lava specimens tend to be more pronounced than in those of quartz or quartzite.

160

There are two examples with twin bulbs. The series may be subdivided as follows:

	Lava	Quartz/ quartzite
Marked	51·8 %	37·4 %
Slight	37·0 %	41·6 %
Flat	7·4 %	19·3 %
Double	3·7 %	1·6 %
Totals	27	62
		89

Angles of striking platforms

In the lava flakes striking platforms with angles between 110° and 129° predominate, but in the quartz and quartzite specimens lower angles tend to be rather more numerous, as follows:

	Lava	Quartz/ quartzite
70–89°	—	2·3 %
90–109°	35·2 %	51·1 %
110–129°	64·7 %	46·5 %
Totals	17	43
		60

UNMODIFIED COBBLESTONES, NODULES AND BLOCKS (251 SPECIMENS)

199 lava cobblestones and fifty-two nodules or blocks of various materials were associated with the artefacts. In view of the possibility of some disturbance by water action at this level, it cannot be stated with certainty whether they were introduced by natural or artificial means, although it is likely that a proportion, at least, were brought to the site by man.

Sample measurements give mean diameters ranging from 84 to 48 mm., with an average of 55 mm. Among the nodules and blocks, quartz and quartzite, pegmatite and horneblende gneiss (cf. Kelogi variety) are all represented. The mean diameters for these range from 88 to 26 mm., with an average of 50 mm.

THE RE-WORKED TUFF OVERLYING THE OCCUPATION FLOOR

As previously noted, the finds from this level were scattered through the deposit without any appreciable concentration, although they were slightly more numerous at a height of 6 in. to 1 ft. above the base than at any other level.

The proportions of artefacts, fossil bones and unmodified cobblestones stand close to those of the underlying occupation level, faunal remains being unusually scarce in both contexts, although the existing bones are well preserved. The finds in this deposit were plotted as they were uncovered, but since it is clear that they were not on any particular horizon, the plans are not reproduced.

TOOLS

Side choppers (*8 specimens*)

Three examples are of lava, four of quartz or quartzite and one of horneblende gneiss similar to the variety which occurs at Kelogi. The working edges are generally wide and curved, with bifacial flaking. The lava specimens are made on cobblestones, but in the three made of quartz the butt ends consist of flat vertical surfaces which have been battered round the edges. The length/breadth/thickness measurements range from 70 × 106 × 70 mm. to 50 × 58 × 48 mm., with an average of 56 × 74 × 49 mm., and the mean diameters vary from 82 to 48 mm., with an average of 59 mm. The average edge/circumference ratio is 46 per cent.

End choppers (*2 specimens*)

One example is made of pegmatite and one of lava. The latter is rolled and made on an oblong cobblestone with a minimum of bifacial flaking at one end. The edge is chipped by use. The pegmatite specimen has a virtually straight and even working edge, also chipped by use. It is in particularly sharp, fresh condition. The length/breadth/thickness measurements are 98 × 83 × 66 mm. and 54 × 48 × 33 mm. respectively, with mean diameters of 82 and 46 mm. The edge/circumference ratios are 18 and 23 per cent.

Two-edged choppers (*2 specimens*)

There are two oblong quartz specimens with jagged, bifacially flaked working edges on either side. Measurements: 121 × 99 × 68 mm. and 77 × 65 × 61 mm.

Chisel-edged chopper (*1 specimen*)

There is a single unifacial specimen made on a lava cobble. It is slightly rolled. The working edge is 40 mm. long, blunted and chipped by use and has been flaked from the cortex surface. (77 × 76 × 66 mm.)

Bifaces (*3 specimens*)

(*a*) A rather crude asymmetrical specimen made of lava. One lateral edge is relatively straight, whilst the other projects in a 'shoulder' near the butt end. Both ends are bluntly pointed. The flaking includes several plunging scars. The edge is sinuous and shows only slight utilisation. (Fig. 78.)

(*b*) This specimen is made on a tabular piece of quartzite. The lateral edges are trimmed from opposite directions and the cross-section is approximately a parallelogram. The butt is rounded and a broad chisel edge, 44 mm. wide, is

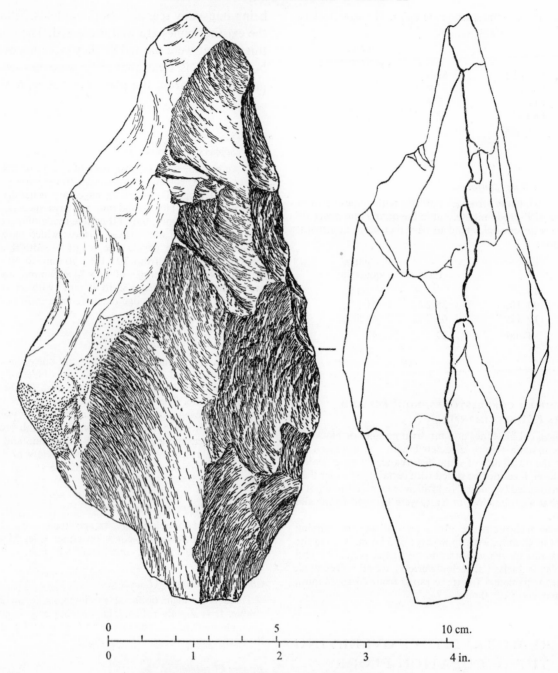

Fig. 78. FC West. Lava biface from the re-worked tuff.

present at the tip. The edges are blunted and crushed by utilisation.

(c) A crude stumpy specimen, made from horneblende gneiss, with a longitudinal ridge on one face. Only a minimum of flaking is present and the tip appears to have been broken. The butt end is thick and has been considerably battered. The measurements for these three specimens are as follows:

	Length/ breadth/ thickness (mm.)	Mean diameter (mm.)	Breadth/ length ratio (%)	Thickness/ length ratio (%)
(a)	168 × 90 × 59	105	53	35
(b)	174 × 99 × 54	109	56	31
(c)	113 × 76 × 62	83	31	54

162

Polyhedrons (2 specimens)

These consist of an angular quartz specimen with three relatively long, intersecting edges and a weathered example made from lava. Measurements: 67 × 56 × 53 mm. and 95 × 81 × 65 mm.

Discoids (4 specimens)

These are all made from quartz. They are symmetrical and the edges are bifacially flaked on the whole circumference. The length/breadth/thickness measurements range from 57 × 51 × 28 mm. to 39 × 38 × 19 mm., with an average of 47 × 45 × 29 mm. The average mean diameter is 40 mm.

Spheroids (6 specimens)

These tools are all made from quartz or quartzite. Two examples have been smoothly rounded on the exterior and four are faceted. The mean diameters range from 67 to 27 mm., with an average of 44 mm.

Subspheroids (16 specimens)

Two examples are of lava and the balance of quartz or quartzite. They are similar in every respect to subspheroids described from other levels. The mean diameters range from 96 to 23 mm., with an average of 59 mm.

Modified battered nodules and blocks (15 specimens)

With the exception of one example made from horneblende gneiss the whole series is of quartz or quartzite. These tools consist of sub-angular fragments, showing a minimum of flaking and utilisation of the edges. The mean diameters range from 61 to 33 mm., with an average of 45 mm.

Scrapers, heavy-duty (12 specimens)

Two examples are made on lava cobblestones, one on a lava flake, one on a quartz cobblestone and the balance on fragments of quartz and quartzite, some of which are tabular. The working edges are rounded and in some specimens they are evenly curved, while in others there are slight projections at the intersections of the flake scars. The trimming is steep and has been carried out from flat under-surfaces. The working edges vary in length from 155 to 45 mm., and the overall length/breadth measurements range from 104 × 82 mm. to 46 × 44 mm., with an average of 68 × 62 mm. There are also two hollow scrapers made on fragments of tabular quartz that have been trimmed along one edge to well-defined notches measuring 27 × 6 mm. and 32 × 5·5 mm. respectively. The length/breadth measurements are 64 × 51 mm. and 95 × 74 mm.

Scrapers, light-duty (9 specimens)

These tools are made of quartz or quartzite. They are all thick-set and stumpy. One is discoidal and is trimmed round the entire circumference; a second is a crude end-scraper. The remaining seven are too atypical to fit into any of the recognised categories. The length/breadth measurements range from 51 × 39 mm. to 27 × 25 mm. with an average of 36 × 34 mm.

Burin (1 specimen)

This consists of an angle burin made on a quartz flake. A single longitudinal flake has been removed from one lateral edge and the opposite side is trimmed from the under-surface into a shallow notch. The working edge is 5 mm. wide. (40 × 30 mm.)

Sundry tools (6 specimens)

(*a*) There are three small oblong tools, flaked over both faces, with evenly trimmed cutting edges on the circumference. They resemble, in miniature, the 'core axes' of the Lupemban. The measurements are 44 × 33 × 27 mm., 56 × 38 × 26 mm. and 40 × 31 × 22 mm. Mean diameters 38, 40 and 31 mm.

(*b*) Two quartz flakes are trimmed to points at the tips, but are not sufficiently sharp to be termed awls. In one specimen the trimming extends across the tip, forming a miniature nosed scraper. The measurements are 35 × 17 mm. and 38 × 42 mm. respectively.

(*c*) An oblong fragment of quartz has been trimmed along both lateral edges at one end to form a relatively thin, spatulate tip which appears to have been subsequently broken. The butt is relatively thick and consists of natural cleavage planes. (76 × 52 × 28 mm.)

UTILISED MATERIAL

'Anvils' (2 specimens)

These consist of a cuboid block and a circular fragment of quartzite with vertical sides. Both specimens exhibit typical utilisation on the edges and some preparatory flaking. The measurements are 93 × 78 × 60 mm. (mean diameter 77 mm.) and 68 × 60 × 53 mm. (mean diameter 60 mm.).

Hammerstones (8 specimens)

These consist of rounded lava cobbles with pitting and bruising on various parts of the exterior. The mean diameters range from 82 to 50 mm., with an average of 66 mm.

Cobblestones (22 specimens)

A series of lava cobblestones that have been shattered or chipped by use, but do not show the utilisation characteristic of hammerstones. The mean diameters range from 119 to 47 mm., with an average of 66 mm.

Light-duty flakes and other fragments (22 specimens)

Small utilised flakes are relatively scarce at this level and the greater part of the series consists of angular fragments of quartz and quartzite. Notched specimens are the most numerous.

With straight edges (1 specimen). This is an oblong quartz flake with chipping along one lateral edge.

With concave edges (13 specimens). The series consists of four flakes and other sundry fragments, all of quartz or quartzite, in which there is a chipped notch on one edge. These vary in width and depth from 27 × 3·5 mm. to 6 × 1·5 mm., with an average of 17 × 2·3 mm.

Analysis of the industries from the occupation floor and the re-worked tuff at FC West

	Occupation floor		Re-worked tuff		Total	
	Nos.	%	Nos.	%	Nos.	%
Tools	189	16·0	87	12·9	274	14·0
Utilised material	127	10·7	54	8·0	181	9·2
Débitage	868	73·3	532	79·0	1,500	76·7
	1,184		673		1,955	
Tools						
Side choppers	28	14·8	8	9·2	36	13·0
End choppers	17	9·0	2	2·3	19	6·9
Two-edged choppers	—	—	2	2·3	2	0·7
Pointed choppers	3	1·6	—	—	3	1·1
Chisel-edged choppers	1	0·5	1	1·1	2	0·7
Bifaces, including broken	5	2·6	3	3·4	8	2·9
Polyhedrons	4	2·1	2	2·3	6	2·2
Discoids	4	2·1	4	4·6	8	3·0
Spheroids	10	5·3	6	6·9	16	5·8
Subspheroids	38	20·1	16	18·4	54	19·6
Modified battered nodules and blocks	53	28·0	15	17·2	68	24·6
Scrapers, heavy-duty	11	5·8	12	13·8	23	8·3
Scrapers, light-duty	9	4·7	9	10·3	18	6·5
Burins	1	0·5	1	1·1	2	0·7
Awls	2	1·0	—	—	2	0·7
Sundry tools	3	1·6	6	6·9	9	3·3
	189		87		276	
Utilised material						
'Anvils'	7	5·5	2	3·7	9	5·0
Hammerstones	23	18·1	8	14·8	31	17·1
Cobblestones	58	45·7	22	40·7	80	44·1
Light-duty flakes and other fragments	39	30·7	22	40·7	61	33·7
	127		54		181	
Débitage						
Whole flakes	99	11·4	39	7·3	138	9·8
Re-sharpening flakes	3	0·3	1	0·2	4	0·3
Broken flakes and chips	607	70·0	417	78·3	1,024	73·1
Core fragments	159	18·3	75	14·1	234	16·7
	868		532		1,400	

With convex edges (*4 specimens*). These are all of quartz and the utilisation varies from fine 'nibbling' to irregular coarse chipping.

Miscellaneous (*4 specimens*). An additional four quartz specimens show a minimum of chipping on parts of the edges.

The average length/breadth measurements for the series of twenty-two specimens are 42 × 33 mm.

DEBITAGE

The unmodified flakes, broken flakes, chips and core fragments amount to 532 specimens of which 97·4 per cent are of quartz and quartzite. In common with the series from the underlying occupation level, the overall size of the whole and broken flakes tends to be greater than in

Oldowan assemblages. There is one re-sharpening flake with a longitudinal dorsal ridge. Most of the thirty-nine complete flakes are divergent (twenty-seven specimens); 57·5 per cent are end-struck.

The length/breadth measurements in millimetres for the series are as follows:

	Range	Average
Lava		
End-struck	85 × 74 to 52 × 40	66 × 51
Side-struck	52 × 81 to 53 × 72	53 × 72
Quartz/quartzite		
End-struck	84 × 70 to 26 × 20	50 × 41
Side-struck	53 × 65 to 20 × 23	34 × 42

The bulbs of percussion are variable and there is no appreciable difference between the lava and quartz or quartzite flakes. Considering both groups jointly, equal numbers have well-marked or slight bulbs, with only a very few flat or negative examples. In all the lava and thirteen of the quartz flakes the angles of the striking platforms are between 110° and 129°, while in a further twelve quartz flakes they are between 90° and 109°.

UNMODIFIED COBBLESTONES, NODULES AND BLOCKS (107 SPECIMENS)

101 lava cobbles and six nodules or blocks of quartz, quartzite and gneiss were recovered from this level. They bear no evidence of utilisation but were probably introduced by human agency. A sample of the lava cobbles gives an average mean diameter of 63 mm.

SITE FC

The small collection of artefacts from the second Trial Trench at this site was obtained from the upper levels of Bed II, at a considerably higher level than that of the assemblage described from FC West. The specimens occurred as scattered finds within tuffs and clays and were not at any definable level. They consist of the following: three side choppers, one discoid, two bifaces, one spheroid, five subspheroids, eight modified battered nodules, two heavy-duty hollow scrapers, five sundry tools, one hammerstone, eighteen light-duty utilised flakes, 124 unmodified flakes and other fragments and twelve unmodified lava cobblestones.

All the tools and the majority of the utilised and unmodified flakes are of quartz or quartzite.

The tools include two bifaces which are both made on pieces of tabular quartzite; they may be briefly described as follows:

(a) This is made on a slab 42 mm. thick with the central areas of both the upper and lower faces consisting of natural cleavage surfaces. Both lateral edges are steeply trimmed and both extremities are pointed.

(b) In this specimen only one face retains the natural cleavage surface, the opposite face being flaked all over. The form is an elongate ovate and the edge is bifacially flaked on the entire circumference. The measurements for the two specimens are as follows:

	Length/ breadth/ thickness (mm.)	Mean diameter (mm.)	Breadth/ length ratio (%)	Thickness/ length ratio (%)
(a)	119 × 71 × 42	77	59	35
(b)	145 × 86 × 63	98	59	43

4. SITE SHK (Sam Howard Korongo)

Archaeological number (68)   Geologic locality 92

The SHK gully lies on the right bank of the Side Gorge, 1·4 miles above the confluence. The main site lies on the west side of the gully, at the point where it debouches into the valley of the Side Gorge. The subsidiary site, known as the Annexe, is about 100 yards further up the gully and is also on the south side.

The site is named after Mr S. Howard who first noted that it was unusually rich in artefacts and faunal material when he visited Olduvai with the 1935 expedition. During the following years various fossils and stone tools were collected at SHK as they became exposed by erosion, but no digging was undertaken until 1953. Among the more important fossils from the site are the remains of a herd of small antelopes (*Phenocotragus recki*), which were discovered in 1935. A well-preserved skull of *Hippopotamus gorgops*, now in the British Museum of Natural History, was also found during the same year, at a higher level in Bed II. An exceptionally fine tusk of *Elephas recki* was found subsequently in the same horizon that had yielded the antelope remains.

The exposures on the west side of the SHK gully, in the immediate vicinity of the Main Site, are limited to the upper part of Bed II and Bed III. A more complete sequence is exposed on the eastern side, extending from the top of Bed II down to Tuff I^F, at the top of Bed I, including the chert horizon. Marker Tuff II^D is also visible at a height of approximately 62 ft. above the base of Bed II. It can be traced eastwards, down the Side Gorge, through SC and FC to MNK.

The sequence of implementiferous and fossil-bearing deposits at the Annexe and the Main Site is as follows:

	Annexe	Main Site
(a)	2½ ft. of tuff, resembling Tuff II^D	8 ft. of tuffs and clayey tuffs
(b)	An occupation level on the surface of the underlying clay	Conglomerate filling a channel 2½ ft. deep
(c)	Chestnut brown clay; base not exposed. The top is at a height of approximately 32 ft. above the base of Bed II	Chestnut brown clay (as at the Annexe)

165

The lowest exposed deposit of brown clay is indistinguishable at the two sites. At the Annexe a rich occupation level occurred on the surface of the clay, overlain by a tuff which also contained a small number of scattered fossil bones and artefacts. This tuff strongly resembles Tuff II^D which occurs at site BK. The resemblance led, for a time, to the two sites being considered contemporaneous, but mineralogic analysis carried out by R. L. Hay has shown that the tuff overlying the occupation surface at SHK Annexe is distinct from Tuff II^D, which is at a higher level.

During 1953 a small trench was dug at the main SHK site, followed in 1955 by some further digging which lasted for a period of two weeks. During 1957 more extensive excavations of approximately one month's duration were carried out at the Main Site and at the Annexe. At that time, however, owing to the fact that only very limited financial resources were available, it was not possible to excavate on the systematic basis undertaken from 1960 onwards. Only a minimum number of African staff could be maintained and sieving was not always carried out. The material from this excavation therefore necessarily lacks a proportion of the smaller elements and cannot be analysed as accurately as is possible when an entire assemblage is available. A brief description of the artefacts from this site was given by L. S. B. Leakey at the Pan African Congress, in 1955. (Leakey, L. S. B., 1957).

THE OCCUPATION LEVEL AT THE ANNEXE

The concentration of occupation debris on the surface of the clay occurred within a limited area, not exceeding 15 × 10 ft. Quantities of small bone splinters were found, in addition to some more intact faunal remains and artefacts. The conditions suggest that this site represents a living surface where the debris had remained undisturbed by water action or other causes. Rolled artefacts do not occur. The assemblage as a whole appears very similar to that from the conglomerate and may be approximately contemporaneous.

THE CHANNEL CONGLOMERATE AT THE MAIN SITE

The channel measured approximately 2½–3 ft. in depth and 5–6 ft. in width and was orientated in a general north/south direction. It cut through the lower part of the tuffaceous clays in which the remains of antelopes and the tusk of *Elephas recki* had been found, down to the surface of the underlying brown clay. The filling consisted of a coarse conglomerate, almost entirely composed of artefacts and bone fragments, the proportion of unmodified cobblestones being no higher than that found on many living floors where there had been no water action. Most of the artefacts and bone fragments are in fresh condition, or show only very slight abrasion, but a few specimens, generally of the larger tools, are considerably rolled. Among the choppers the rolled specimens amount to 10 per cent of the total.

THE TUFF ABOVE THE CHANNEL AT THE MAIN SITE

This deposit contained both coarse- and fine-grained tuffs. Artefacts and faunal remains were not concentrated at any particular level, but were generally found in the coarser beds. Some specimens are rolled. The proportion of waste material is unusually low, but in other respects the assemblage closely resembles those from the Annexe and the channel conglomerate. Besides the antelope remains and elephant tusk this deposit yielded the largest known anvil, a subspherical block of quartzite weighing 72 lb. It was found in close association with the elephant tusk.

THE INDUSTRY

The cultural assemblages from the three levels at SHK were, in the first place, classified and analysed separately since they are derived from three distinct stratigraphic horizons. It became evident, however, that all three assemblages were essentially alike in respect of the relative proportion of the various tool categories, typology and size. The material was therefore pooled and treated as representing a single cultural stage.

166

Analysis of the utilised material and *débitage* has not been possible owing to the fact that all cobblestones, whether utilised or otherwise, were discarded at the site, together with a large proportion of the *débitage*.

Subspheroids are the most common tool form, followed by choppers, which include side, two-edged, end and pointed forms. Side choppers greatly exceed any other variety. Approximately 50 per cent are made on cobbles and 50 per cent on blocks of quartz and quartzite. Bifaces amount to 7·4 per cent of the tools. They are generally crude and poorly made. Some small scrapers, burins, awls, *outils écaillés* and laterally trimmed flakes also occur, but are not common.

TOOLS

Side choppers (124 specimens)

Seventy-one examples are of quartz and quartzite, two of horneblende gneiss, one of pegmatite and fifty of lava. With the exception of three unifacial examples, in which one side of the working edge consists of cortex surface, the whole series exhibits multiple, bifacial flaking. The side choppers can be divided into those made on cobbles and those made on angular blocks.

Side choppers made on cobblestones (63 specimens). These consist of classic side choppers such as are found throughout the Oldowan and Developed Oldowan. The butt ends are formed by well-rounded natural cortex surface and the working edges are jagged, with bifacial flaking and scars that are generally deeply indented. Chipping and blunting of the edges, resulting from utilisation, is usually present. In the majority the working edges are relatively wide and curved, but there are also a few examples in which the edges are less jagged and relatively straight. The quartz and quartzite specimens tend to be more asymmetrical than those made from lava, owing to the greater irregularity in the shape of the cobbles. Twelve specimens exhibit hammerstone type of utilisation on the butts. The length/breadth/thickness measurements range from $105 \times 138 \times 85$ mm. to $34 \times 41 \times 25$ mm., with an average of $71 \times 80 \times 54$ mm., and the mean diameters vary from 109 to 33 mm., with an average of 69 mm. The edge/circumference ratios vary from 68 to 26 per cent, with an average of 46 per cent.

Side choppers made on blocks (61 specimens). This series of choppers may be further subdivided into two groups. In the first the butt ends are rounded and the cross-sections are generally biconvex. The tools are made on blocks or cores which are flaked over the greater part of the surface. The working edges are bifacially flaked and generally jagged, although in a few specimens, which have been subjected to particularly heavy utilisation, the projections on the edges have been knocked off. One particularly massive specimen also shows crushed areas on both lateral edges.

The specimens in the second group conform very closely in type although they vary considerably in size. The butt ends and the upper and lower faces are generally flat, the butts being formed either by a vertical cleavage plane or by a negative flake scar. In the majority the upper and lower edges of the butts have been chipped and blunted, perhaps in order to facilitate handling. The working edges are curved and jagged and some specimens also show chipping and blunting on the edges. Fifteen examples bear hammerstone utilisation on the butt ends. The length/breadth/thickness measurements range from $129 \times 139 \times 108$ mm. to $27 \times 31 \times 22$ mm. with an average of $59 \times 73 \times 47$ mm., and the mean diameters vary from 125 to 26 mm., with an average of 60 mm. The edge/circumference ratios vary from 74 to 25 per cent with an average of 51 per cent.

In general, the cobble-choppers tend to be larger than those made on blocks, the average mean diameter for the former being 51 mm., in contrast to 46 mm. for the latter. Although the average lengths of the edges in the two groups are virtually identical (112 mm. and 113 mm. respectively), the average edge/circumference ratio in the cobble-choppers is lower than in those made on blocks, the ratios being 46 and 51 per cent respectively.

End choppers (21 specimens)

These are mostly made on cobblestones: nine examples are of quartz and the balance of lava. Except for two unifacial specimens the series is bifacial with multiple flaking on both sides of the working edges. Chipping and blunting from utilisation are generally present and in two of the examples made on cobblestones there is additional utilisation in the form of pitting and bruising of the butts. The length/breadth/thickness measurements range from $126 \times 95 \times 64$ mm. to $41 \times 36 \times 24$ mm., with an average of $90 \times 74 \times 55$ mm., and the mean diameters vary from 98 to 37 mm., with an average of 74 mm. The edge/circumference ratios vary from 34 to 21 per cent., with an average of 26 per cent.

Two-edged choppers (21 specimens)

Thirteen examples are made from quartz and quartzite and eight from lava. In these choppers the two working edges are variously situated, unlike those of earlier assemblages in which the working edges generally occur on either lateral edge. The relative positions are as follows: (*a*) on opposite ends (two examples), (*b*) on opposite lateral edges (nine examples), (*c*) on one lateral edge and one extremity (nine examples), (*d*) on both edges of a vertical surface (one example).

The lava specimens are made on cobblestones and the quartz/quartzite series on irregular blocks. The edges are jagged, with multiple bifacial flaking, and most have been chipped and blunted by use. The length/breadth/thickness measurements range from $115 \times 91 \times 57$ mm. to $45 \times 43 \times 28$ mm., with an average of $82 \times 67 \times 55$ mm., and the mean diameters vary from 87 to 38 mm., with an average of 68 mm.

Pointed chopper (1 specimen)

This is made on a lava cobblestone. The butt consists of rounded cortex surface and the working edge is trimmed by means of relatively flat flaking on the under surface and two large, deeply indented scars on the upper face. These are almost vertical and intersect to form a well-defined point. (78 × 88 × 43 mm. The edge/circumference ratio is 52 per cent.)

Unfinished and broken choppers (2 specimens)

In addition to the series described above, there is one lava specimen, which appears to be unfinished, and one of quartz, split down the centre.

Bifaces (68 specimens)

Thirty examples are made from quartz or quartzite, one from horneblende gneiss and the balance from lava. There are twenty-three medium-size bifaces of various forms, two double-pointed, one subtriangular, one cleaver, two oblong picks, one heavy duty pick, ten large end-struck quartz flakes with minimal trimming, six unfinished specimens, eight butt-ends (four of which have been retrimmed after fracture), three tip ends and two examples in which the tips only are missing.

The group of twenty-three medium-size bifaces includes one well-made example that is both better-finished and larger than the rest of the series which are generally crude and often asymmetrical although they can be broadly termed irregular ovates. The cutting edges usually extend round the whole circumference, and the trimming is steep with many plunging scars. There are some broad, relatively short specimens and others that are elongate, with thick, massive butts: the tips are either pointed or spatulate. The degree of utilisation is variable, but it is most pronounced on the largest biface in which it has resulted in complete blunting of both lateral edges.

Among the diminutive series made from quartz there is one specimen that resembles a M.S.A. bifacial point. It measures 38 × 32 mm. and is elliptical in cross-section, both faces being trimmed by means of flat, even scars. The remaining examples include small irregular ovates and pointed, square-butted specimens.

One of the double-pointed bifaces is made on an end-struck lava flake with the platform oblique to the long axis of the tool. The primary surface has been trimmed along one lateral edge and there is relatively steep trimming on the dorsal surface round the whole edge, with the exception of the striking platform. This specimen is considerably rolled. The second example, also made of lava, is bifacially flaked round the whole circumference and is sharply pointed at both ends.

The single example of a cleaver is made from coarse-grained lava. The edges at either side and at the butt end are bifacially trimmed and sharp. The butt is thick and rounded and the lateral edges converge slightly towards the cutting edge. This is formed by a single oblique transverse scar on either face and is chipped and damaged by use.

The triangular biface consists of a diminutive, sharply pointed specimen trimmed on the circumference, but with a straight transverse edge at the butt end. This forms a sharp angle on either side, where it abuts on to the lateral edges.

The two oblong picks are parallel-sided and superficially resemble the 'core axes' of the Lupemban. The larger of the two is approximately trihedral in cross-section. Both extremities are blunt and the lateral edges are particularly jagged and uneven. The second specimen is considerably smaller but otherwise very similar. One end is blunt and rounded and the opposite end appears to have been broken.

The heavy-duty pick is a massive, crude tool in which the thickness exceeds the width. The cross-section is quadrilateral. Both extremities are pointed and exhibit relatively fine retouch, indicating that this is a finished tool although it resembles a crude rough-out.

The ten large quartz flakes are all end-struck and generally trihedral in cross-section, having a longitudinal ridge on the dorsal aspect and also some trimming of the edges on this face. Some chipping and blunting of the edges is present and it is evident that the tools were used in their present form.

One of the unfinished bifaces consists of a large lava flake with cortex surface on the dorsal aspect, indicating that it was detached from a large waterworn cobble or a boulder. It is trimmed only at the tip. In two further specimens it is possible to detect cracks and partially detached flakes, suggesting that the material was found to be faulty.

Polyhedrons (21 specimens)

Six examples are made from quartz and the others from lava. These tools are very similar to the polyhedrons described from Bed I and other sites in Bed II. They are angular, with three or more well-defined cutting edges which are bifacially flaked and usually intersecting. Chipped utilisation and slight blunting is normally present, but there is no extensive battering of the edges, such as occurs on subspheroids. Nine of the specimens are made on cobblestones. The length/breadth/thickness measurements range from 142 × 107 × 88 mm. to 59 × 44 × 39 mm., and the mean diameters vary from 112 to 40 mm., with an average of 75 mm.

Discoids (62 specimens)

Fifty-two examples are of quartz and quartzite, one of horneblende gneiss and nine of lava. There is considerable variation in general form within this series (some examples are almost circular, others are oblong and a few are sub-angular) but each specimen exhibits a bifacially flaked working edge on the circumference, generally showing utilisation. There is also considerable variation in the cross-sections. Some specimens are relatively flat on both the upper and lower faces, others are markedly biconvex and some are plano-convex. Twelve examples are rolled. The mean diameters range from 94 to 24 mm., with an average of 50 mm.

Spheroids (60 specimens)

With the exception of one lava specimen, these are made from quartz or quartzite. They consist mostly of well-founded stone balls, battered smooth over the whole exterior, but a few faceted examples also occur, together with some in which the projecting ridges have been only partially reduced by battering. The mean diameters range from 105 to 28 mm., with an average of 62 mm.

Measurements for the forty-nine complete specimens of bifaces, Site SHK

	Length/breadth/thickness (mm.)	Mean diameter (mm.)	Breadth/ length ratio (%)	Thickness/ length ratio (%)	Totals
Irregular ovates					
Range	198 × 106 × 57 to 65 × 47 × 28	120–46	94–50	57–23 }	23
Average	109 × 74 × 44	77	70	42	
Diminutive series					
Range	60 × 42 × 22 to 38 × 32 × 14	48–28	84–63	71–36 }	9
Average	51 × 39 × 23	37	75	45	
Double-pointed bifaces					
Range	185 × 92 × 39 to 152 × 80 × 86	106–105	52–49	56–21 }	2
Average	168 × 86 × 62	105	50	38	
Cleaver	113 × 82 × 59	84	72	48	1
Subtriangular biface	81 × 64 × 39	61	79	48	1
Oblong picks					
Range	131 × 60 × 45 to 75 × 40 × 31	75–48	53–45	41–34 }	2
Average	103 × 50 × 28	61	49	37	
Heavy-duty pick	147 × 86 × 93	108	58	63	1
Flakes with minimal trimming					
Range	164 × 105 × 51 to 110 × 71 × 48	106–76	87–48	57–31 }	10
Average	139 × 80 × 50	93	64	39	
Total					49

Subspheroids (258 specimens)

244 examples are made from quartz and quartzite, one from welded tuff, twelve from lava and one from pegmatite. These tools are less symmetrical and more angular than the spheroids, but projecting ridges have been largely reduced by battering. The mean diameters range from 129 to 23 mm., with an average of 59 mm.

Modified battered nodules and blocks (115 specimens)

These consist of angular fragments of quartz and quartzite with evidence of artificial shaping and utilisation of the edges, generally in the form of battering and blunting. The mean diameters range from 129 to 21 mm., with an average of 55 mm.

Scrapers, heavy-duty (45 specimens)

Thirty-eight examples are made from quartz and quartzite, one from horneblende gneiss and six from lava. They mostly consist of quartz and quartzite blocks, generally pieces of tabular material, with steeply trimmed working edges and flat upper and lower surfaces formed by natural cleavage planes. The working edges are generally curved, although in a number of side scrapers they are nearly straight. Three examples are made on cobblestones steeply trimmed along one edge, either from the cortex surface or from one or more flat negative scars. Blunting of the working edges is common. When chipped utilisation is present it is usually to be seen only on the upper face.

Some examples show crushed indentations on the edges, measuring up to 17 mm. in width and 3 mm. in depth. The series may be subdivided into end, side, perimetal and discoidal scrapers. One specimen is double-edged, with a working edge at either end. Another, made on a slab of quartzite, is particularly massive and weighs 4 lb. 12 oz. One of the rare specimens made on flakes has a curved working edge at the tip with two crushed indentations, one on either side of a median projection.

The length/breadth measurements in millimetres of the heavy-duty scrapers are as follows:

	Range	Average	Totals
Scrapers			
End	112 × 102 to 53 × 53	77 × 68	20
Side	98 × 108 to 40 × 82	79 × 101	20
Discoidal	84 × 73	—	1
Perimetal	113 × 72 to 53 × 49	74 × 56	4
			45

Scrapers, light-duty (86 specimens)

The light-duty scrapers include a considerable variety of types and the specimens within each group conform closely. Side scrapers are the most numerous, but end, discoidal, nosed, perimetal and hollow scrapers also occur. The series is, on the whole, well made, with even, generally steep retouch, although the edges are sometimes slightly jagged and not smoothly rounded unless they have become blunted by use.

End scrapers (*22 specimens*). One example is made on a thin piece of tabular quartzite and the balance on whole or broken quartz flakes. The working edges are curved and evenly trimmed but vary considerably in width. Four examples, made on cores, are high-backed and resemble small push planes. The series ranges in length and breadth from 58×38 mm. to 26×19 mm., with an average of 40×30 mm.

Side scrapers (*29 specimens*). These are made from quartz and quartzite, with the exception of a single lava specimen. They are variable in form and are made on flakes, high-backed cores or any other fragments which provided a suitable edge. The trimming varies according to the thickness of the specimens and may be either steep or shallow. Working edges are both straight and curved. The length/breadth measurements range from 51×60 mm. to 22×30 mm., with an average of 34×45 mm.

Discoidal scrapers (*15 specimens*). These are trimmed either on the whole or on part of the circumference. With the exception of one lava specimen, they are made from quartz or quartzite. The trimming is generally steep and the edges are often blunted by use. The length/breadth measurements range from 57×57 mm. to 20×20 mm., with an average of 41×39 mm.

Nosed scrapers (*9 specimens*). The whole series is made from quartz or quartzite. The tips are trimmed to a relatively narrow working edge by means of a notch on either side. The length/breadth measurements range from 50×46 mm. to 34×29 mm., with an average of 41×30 mm.

Perimetal scrapers (*9 specimens*). These are all of quartz or quartzite. They are variable in form and may be oblong, triangular or formless but are characterised by trimming on the entire circumference. The length/breadth measurements range from 50×39 mm. to 35×25 mm., with an average of 41×30 mm.

Hollow scrapers (*2 specimens*). Two quartz flakes exhibit relatively deeply indented notches, measuring 8×6 mm. and 19×5 mm. respectively, on one edge.

Burins (*11 specimens*)

These are all made on quartz or quartzite flakes. Angle burins are the most common type but there are also two dihedral specimens. Two of the angle burins are double-ended and also double-edged, with a working edge on either side at both extremities. Seven single-ended examples are made on broken flakes, the burin spalls being struck from either side of the transverse fracture. There is one example of an angle burin with a transverse trimmed notch. The two dihedral specimens are of the usual type with flake scars down either side. Light utilisation is usually evident on the chisel edges.

The length/breadth measurements range from 55×48 mm. to 33×24 mm., with an average of 44×31 mm., and the chisel edges vary in width from 13 to 4 mm., with an average of 7·8 mm.

Awls (*12 specimens*)

This series is made entirely from quartz and quartzite, generally on flakes. A small sharp point is present, either at the tip or on one lateral edge. In the most common type there is a shallow notch on either side of the point, trimmed from the primary flake surface. There are also two specimens in which the notches are trimmed from alternate directions, one with a single notch on one side of the point and another in which the point is formed by the convergence of two straight trimmed edges. In two specimens the points have been broken off during use. The length/breadth measurements range from 67×50 mm. to 20×16 mm., with an average of 37×33 mm.

Outils écaillés (*3 specimens*)

Only three quartz examples are represented in the material now available, but it is likely that further specimens were included amongst the unspecified *débitage* that was discarded, since the presence of these tools was not suspected at the time. The existing specimens are double-ended and entirely typical, with scaled utilisation at either end. One face is slightly hollowed, whilst the opposite face is flat or slightly convex. The length/breadth measurements range from 40×33 mm. to 29×17 mm., with an average of 36×27 mm., and the edge lengths vary from 32 to 12 mm., with an average of 19 mm.

Laterally trimmed flakes (*5 specimens*)

These consist of blunt-tipped quartz flakes, steeply trimmed along both lateral edges. The length/breadth measurements range from 50×29 mm. to 31×22 mm., with an average of 38×26 mm.

UTILISED MATERIAL

'Anvils' (*26 specimens*)

Twenty-four examples are made from quartz or quartzite and two from lava. Almost the entire series has been shaped prior to use. The most usual type is made on a piece of tabular quartzite, approximately circular in shape, with crude vertical flaking on the circumference. The upper and lower faces frequently show traces of blows and incipient cones of percussion, in addition to the utilisation on the circumference. A number of specimens weigh over 14 lb. and the massive subspherical example referred to earlier, weighing 72 lb. measures $340 \times 287 \times 248$ mm., with a mean diameter of 291 mm. In the remainder of the series the mean diameters range from 160 to 60 mm., with an average of 91 mm.

(Hammerstones, together with utilised cobblestones, nodules and blocks cannot be described, since they were discarded.)

Light-duty flakes and other fragments (*123 specimens*)

With the exception of three lava flakes and one of brown chert, the existing series is made from quartz and quartzite. It includes the usual flakes and other fragments with utilisation on the edges, which may be straight,

170

Analysis of the tools from the occupation level, the channel and the tuff at SHK

	Annexe		Channel		Tuff		Totals	
	Nos.	%	Nos.	%	Nos.	%	Nos.	%
Side choppers	23	12·4	86	13·4	15	17·3	124	13·5
End choppers	7	3·8	14	2·2	—	—	21	2·3
Two-edged choppers	4	2·2	13	2·0	4	4·6	21	2·3
Pointed choppers	—	—	1	0·1	—	—	1	0·1
Unfinished and broken choppers	—	—	2	0·3	—	—	2	0·2
Bifaces, including broken and unfinished	9	4·9	49	7·6	10	11·5	68	7·4
Polyhedrons	2	1·1	18	2·8	1	1·1	21	2·3
Discoids	8	4·3	50	7·8	4	4·6	62	6·8
Spheroids	8	4·3	44	6·8	8	9·2	60	6·5
Subspheroids	41	22·2	197	30·6	20	23·0	258	28·2
Modified battered nodules and blocks	20	10·8	86	13·4	9	10·3	115	12·6
Scrapers, heavy-duty	8	4·3	30	4·7	7	8·0	45	5·0
Scrapers, light-duty	42	22·7	40	6·2	4	4·6	86	9·4
Burins	8	4·3	1	0·1	2	2·3	11	1·2
Awls	5	2·7	5	0·8	2	2·3	12	1·3
Outils écaillés	—	—	2	0·3	1	1·1	3	0·3
Laterally trimmed flakes	—	—	5	0·8	—	—	5	0·5
	185		643		87		915	

concave, convex or lacking any particular form (miscellaneous). The numbers and measurements in millimetres of the various groups are as follows:

	Range	Average	Totals
With straight edges	68 × 44 to 30 × 30	46 × 34	20
With concave edges	68 × 64 to 31 × 25	45 × 38	39
With convex edges	66 × 46 to 23 × 22	77 × 58	31
Miscellaneous	54 × 44 to 28 × 23	40 × 36	33
			123

In the concave-edged group the notches vary in size from 21 × 4 mm. to 8 × 1·5 mm., with an average of 16 × 3·3 mm.

DEBITAGE

Since the majority of the *débitage* was discarded, no analysis can be undertaken. A number of complete flakes was retained, however; and it is possible to obtain some information as to the proportion of end- and side-struck flakes, the nature of the bulbs of percussion and the angles of the striking platforms. Analysis of size has not been attempted since only the larger specimens were retained.

The total of waste material now available amounts to 866 specimens, consisting of 449 complete flakes, twenty-seven cores, two re-sharpening flakes, 241 broken flakes and 147 core fragments. A further 2,889 unspecified waste pieces were discarded, bringing the total to 3,755. In the existing series of complete flakes 21 per cent are of lava and nearly all are divergent (93·6 per cent). There are only twenty convergent specimens and eight that are approximately parallel-sided; 28 per cent are side-struck.

Complete flakes (449 specimens)

Marked bulbs of percussion predominate, as follows:

Marked	Slight	Double	Negative	Total
58·2 %	33·8 %	2·2 %	5·8 %	311

The angles of the striking platforms can be measured in 331 specimens, as follows:

70–89°	3·0 %
90–109°	58·3 %
110–129°	38·3 %
130° and over	0·3 %
Total	331

Cores (27 specimens)

A number of cores occurs in this assemblage, although they are not recorded from earlier sites. They are mostly formless and consist mainly of flaked blocks of quartz, quartzite, lava or gneiss, lacking recognisable working edges or evidence of utilisation. A few examples are flat-based and conical, some are cuboid, and there are also some discoidal specimens resembling prepared cores. The mean diameters range from 146 to 27 mm., with an average of 48 mm.

171

CHAPTER VI

UPPER BED II

Sites TK and BK

1. SITE TK (THIONGO KORONGO)

Archaeological number (19)   Geologic Locality 16

The gully known as TK lies on the north side of the Gorge, 0·8 of a mile east of the 1960–4 camp. During the 1931–2 expeditions to Olduvai a number of handaxes made from tabular quartzite were collected from a site near the top of Bed II, on the eastern side of the gully. A further series of handaxes was obtained from Bed IV in a subsidiary gully on the western side, known as Fish Gully owing to the numerous remains of catfish found in association with the tools. This site has since been excavated by Dr J. Waechter, who discovered a number of levels with artefacts within Bed IV*a*.

During 1963 excavations were carried out at the site in Bed II in order to augment the material collected during 1931–2. When the horizon from which the tools were derived had been determined by means of three small trial pits, two trenches approximately 12 ft. apart were cut into the upper part of Bed II. Trench I, which lay to the north, measured 20 ft. north/south and approximately 25 ft. east/west. Trench II was roughly parallel and measured 29 ft. north/south and an average of 15 ft. east/west. (Fig. 80.)

The maximum depth of deposits was reached in Trench I, which was dug down to 13 ft. below the base of Bed III (see Figs. 1 and 79). The following sequence was exposed:

(*a*) The basal part of Bed III.

(*b*) Four feet of tuff and clays interbedded with limestone (such as normally occurs below the base of Bed III).

(*c*) Two and a half feet of tuff, containing scattered artefacts.

(*d*) An occupation floor on the weathered surface of a clay (palaeosol) at the line of contact with the overlying tuff. (This will be referred to as the Upper Occupation Floor.)

(*e*) A tuff containing scattered artefacts, lying between (*d*) and a lower occupation surface. (This will be referred to as the Intermediate Level.)

(*f*) A second occupation floor, similarly on a weathered clay surface, approximately 10 ft. below the base of Bed III. (This will be referred to as the Lower Occupation Floor.)

(*g*) A channel, 3 ft. deep, cut into an underlying tuff; artefacts and bone fragments occurred in the lower part of the filling.

The industries from the five levels at this site stand very close to one another, although there are certain dissimilarities between the material from the Upper and Lower Occupation Floors which cannot be attributed merely to greater abundance of material at the higher level. Most noteworthy is the entire absence of diminutive bifaces on the Lower Occupation Floor, in spite of the fact that this level had proportionately more bifaces. *Outils écaillés*, on the contrary, occur only on the Lower Occupation Floor, although the assemblage from this level is considerably smaller than that from the Upper Floor.

A wide variety of forms is to be found in the series of bifaces. Leaving aside the diminutive specimens which occur only on the Upper Floor, there is still a great diversity in size and morphology, which does not appear to be due solely to different types of raw materials. Spheroids, subspheroids and light-duty scrapers are the most common tools at both the occupation levels. In the utilised material heavy-duty artefacts such as anvils, hammerstones and cobblestones are rela-

172

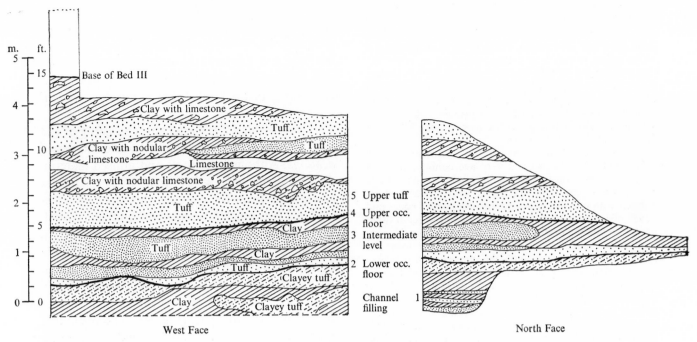

Fig. 79. TK. Sections along the west and north faces of Trench I, showing the two occupation floors and other implementiferous levels.

tively scarce, whereas light-duty flakes are exceedingly common.

This site appears to represent a camping ground which was reoccupied intensively on two occasions and perhaps visited temporarily at the times when the tuffs between the Upper and Lower Floors and above the Upper Floor were being deposited.

THE CHANNEL

This was exposed in Trench I, where part of a steeply sloping bank of what appeared to have been a small stream bed or channel was found in the western part of the trench, running approximately from north to south. It reached a maximum depth of 3 ft. and was filled with clay in the upper part and with alternating bands of sands and silty clays, a few inches thick, in the lower part. Artefacts and faunal remains were comparatively scarce in the upper levels of the filling, but occurred in considerable numbers in the lower levels, together with some broken mammalian bones. Most of the remains were concentrated in two hollows below the eastern bank of the channel. (Pl. 22, Fig. 80 a.)

The area excavated did not extend sufficiently far west for the opposite bank of the channel to be located.

A total of 1,436 artefacts, of which only 1·6 per cent are tools, was recovered from the channel. This is a much lower proportion of tools than has been recorded in any other assemblage at Olduvai and suggests the possibility that waste material was perhaps jettisoned into the stream bed from the adjacent living site.

The most numerous tool categories are light-duty scrapers and awls, with eleven and seven specimens respectively. There are no bifaces and only three choppers. Two of these are side choppers made on lava cobblestones with jagged, bifacially flaked working edges. The third is an end chopper made from an irregular, knobbly lava cobblestone. It is high-backed, with an even, curved working edge. The length/breadth/thickness measurements for the three choppers are 71 × 80 × 47 mm., 58 × 81 × 32 mm. and 86 × 76 × 68 mm., with mean diameters of 66, 57 and 76 mm. The edge/circumference ratios for the two side choppers are 48 and 42 per cent respectively and for the end chopper 38 per cent. The light-duty scrapers comprise three nosed, five side, two end and one hollow scrapers. They are similar in all respects to the series from the higher levels and will not be described in detail. The average length/

173

breadth measurements are 31 × 33 mm. There are also two angle burins made from quartz (34 × 23 mm. and 51 × 30 mm.), each with a trimmed notch at one end from which a single spall has been struck. These spalls extend along the whole length of one lateral edge. The working edges are slightly chipped by use. The awls consist of five broken flakes and two core fragments with fine, sharp points. In two examples the points are chipped from alternate directions and in the remainder from the primary flake surface, with a notch on either side. The average length/breadth measurements are 26 × 35 mm.

With the exception of one small quartz hammerstone (mean diameter 28 mm.) and two lava cobblestones, the utilised material consists of light-duty quartz and quartzite flakes. There are eight specimens with straight edges, thirteen with concave edges, seven with convex edges and eleven miscellaneous. As has been noted in respect of other sites, the chipping on the straight-edged and miscellaneous groups is usually bifacial, whilst it is mainly from the primary flake surface in both the convex- and concave-edged series. The length/breadth measurements for the thirty-nine specimens range from 73 × 69 mm. to 21 × 19 mm., with an average of 35 × 28 mm. The dimensions of the notches in the concave-edged series range from 40 × 3·5 mm. to 4 × 1·5 mm., with an average of 16 × 2·2 mm. This group includes one unusually long triangular core fragment (73 × 69 mm.) in which a relatively thick edge shows a wide shallow notch with scaled utilisation.

The *débitage* amounts to 1,371 specimens, of which only thirty-seven are complete flakes, with 1,106 broken flakes and chips and 228 core fragments. Only 1·1 per cent of the total is made of lava. With the exception of five convergent specimens, all the complete flakes are divergent. Thirty-seven per cent are side-struck. The range in length/breadth for end-struck flakes is from 65 × 46 mm. to 22 × 21 mm., with an average of 40 × 30 mm. Side-struck flakes range from 50 × 56 mm. to 20 × 24 mm., with an average of 30 × 40 mm. Forty-seven per cent of the bulbs of percussion are marked and 36 per cent slight, with the balance shattered. Most of the striking platforms show an angle of between 90° and 109° (69 per cent).

In addition to the artefacts described above the channel filling yielded six unmodified broken lava cobblestones.

Analysis of the industry from the channel

	Nos.	%
Tools	23	1·6
Utilised material	42	2·9
Débitage	1,371	95·4
	1,436	

THE LOWER OCCUPATION FLOOR

This horizon was excavated only in Trench I, because time was limited and very little material was found when a trial pit was dug down to this level in Trench II.

Artefacts and fossil bones were markedly more concentrated in the eastern part of the excavated area where present erosion had also cut into the horizon and exposed the occupation debris. As may be seen from the plan (Fig. 80*b*), the south-east corner of the trench proved virtually barren.

This level yielded 2,153 artefacts, consisting of 123 tools, ninety utilised pieces and 1,940 examples of *débitage*. Although the tools and utilised material do not form such a low percentage as in the assemblage from the channel, they are, nevertheless, in a very much lower proportion than is usual. The remains lay on a single horizon, but no pattern of distribution was evident, with the possible exception of the positions of some bifaces. Six out of the total of fifteen specimens occurred in closely associated pairs, the farthest distance apart of any two being just over 1 ft. (Fig. 80.) The remaining examples occurred as isolated finds. A similar distribution pattern was not found on the Upper Occupation Floor at this site, nor has it been noted elsewhere. Only five side and one end choppers are represented. Two of the former are diminutive specimens, with wide, curved working edges.

TOOLS

Side choppers (5 specimens)

Two examples are of lava and three of quartz. They are all characterised by unusually wide, curved working edges extending round more than half the circumference. The length/breadth/thickness measurements range from 112 × 124 × 73 mm. to 31 × 48 × 31 mm., with an average of 66 × 85 × 49 mm. The average mean diameter is 66 mm.

End chopper (1 specimen)

This is a large, irregular-shaped lava cobblestone with a working edge on a projecting boss. A single flake has been removed from one face and a few shallow parallel flakes from the opposite side. (119 × 118 × 96 mm.) (Mean diameter 107 mm. Edge/circumference ratio 16 per cent.)

Bifaces (15 specimens)

These consist of eight complete specimens, two with the tips missing, three unfinished, a butt end and a tip end. Diminutive specimens such as occur in the Upper Occupation Floor are not represented. Three of the intact specimens are made on pieces of tabular quartz. They include one that is particularly well made and pointed at either end. There are also three thick-set, broad, irregular ovates, one ovate of ordinary proportions and one chisel-ended specimen made from a lava flake.

(*a*) A well-made symmetrical, elongate specimen made from a piece of tabular quartzite. Bifacial trimming of the edge is present at the tip and extends along the entire length of one lateral edge, but the greater part of the opposite edge is trimmed on one face only, with a flat cleavage surface on the opposite side. The edges are, however, evenly curved and considerably blunted, with utilisation mainly on the trimmed face.

(*b*) A double-pointed elongate specimen, also made on a piece of tabular quartzite. The tip is slender, with shallow bifacial flaking, and the edges are sinuous. There are two intersecting cleavage planes at the butt end, forming a chisel-like point. Both upper and lower faces retain part of the natural flat cleavage planes. Blunting and 'frosting' are present intermittently on both lateral edges and to a lesser extent at the tip. (Fig. 81.)

(*c*) A sharply pointed triangular specimen made on a tabular piece of quartzite. The cross-section is a parallelogram and the butt is formed by a vertical transverse fracture which has received only a minimum of flaking. Associated with incomplete specimen (*j*).

(*d*) A chisel-ended biface made from a side-struck lava flake (Fig. 82). The butt is relatively massive and the specimen diminishes gradually in thickness to a thin, slightly spatulate tip, 37 mm. wide. The lateral edge, on which the bulb of the primary flake was originally present, has been bifacially flaked, but on the opposite edge the flaking is from one direction only. Associated with the unfinished biface (*n*).

(*e*) An elongate, asymmetrical beaked specimen, made from quartz, with one lateral edge convex and the opposite edge concave. The point is off-centre and lies towards the concave edge. The butt end is formed by three vertical cleavage planes, one on either side, with a third in the centre.

(*f–h*) Three smaller, rather thick-set quartz or quartzite specimens which might be broadly described as short, stumpy ovates, although one specimen approaches a cordiform. All three specimens appear to be made on end-struck flakes and each has one flat face which shows a minimum of secondary flaking at the butt end. One example has a particularly sharp point with a minimum of trimming.

The measurements for the eight complete bifaces are as follows:

Length/breadth/ thickness (mm.)	Mean diameter (mm.)	Breadth/ length ratio (%)	Thickness/ length ratio (%)
(*a*) 195 × 97 × 55	115	49	28
(*b*) 279 × 124 × 55	152	44	19
(*c*) 154 × 98 × 45	99	63	29
(*d*) 143 × 89 × 50	120	62	34
(*e*) 168 × 80 × 44	97	47	26
(*f*) 110 × 83 × 53	82	75	48
(*g*) 105 × 83 × 48	78	79	45
(*h*) 94 × 90 × 52	78	95	55

Averages

| 156 × 93 × 50 | 103 | 64 | 35 |

Broken specimens

(*i*), (*j*) These consist of two crudely made specimens lacking the tip ends. Both are of quartz. The broken edges at the tips have been chipped and blunted by use, subsequent to the points being broken off. The trimming flakes are irregular and there are a number of plunging scars. Specimen (*i*) was associated with (*l*), the tip end of a quartz biface. Present measurements are 113 × 87 × 66 mm. and 78 × 69 × 42 mm.

(*k*) A butt end made from tabular quartzite. Both upper and lower faces are flat and the edge is trimmed from one direction only. (Present measurements are 71 × 116 × 35 mm.)

(*l*) The tip end of a quartz specimen, flaked over both faces. (Present measurements are 46 × 61 × 30 mm.)

(*m*) This specimen is probably unfinished. It is made from a fine-grained lava and is in mint condition. The edge is usually sharp and jagged, with no evidence of utilisation. The specimen as a whole is asymmetrical. It was found near the chisel-ended lava biface (*d*). (106 × 74 × 30 mm.)

(*n*) A massive slab of tabular quartzite trimmed on one lateral edge, possibly representing the butt end of a large unfinished biface. (150 × 129 × 65 mm.)

(*o*) A fragment of tabular quartzite which has been steeply flaked along one side. One extremity is square. It is possibly an unfinished cleaver. (159 × 64 × 60 mm.)

Polyhedron (1 specimen)

This is a crude, angular example made from lava, with a number of sharp, jagged edges. (110 × 100 × 80 mm.)

Spheroids (3 specimens)

There is one stone ball made from quartzite which is smoothly rounded on the whole surface. The remaining two, made from lava and quartz respectively, are faceted with the projecting ridges only partly reduced by battering, although they are symmetrical and closely matched in size. Mean diameters: 86, 36 and 94 mm respectively.

Subspheroids (28 specimens)

Two examples are made from lava, one from gneiss and the balance from quartz and quartzite. The whole series is less symmetrical and less well made than the preceding category. The mean diameters range from 100 to 27 mm., with an average of 59 mm.

Modified battered nodules and blocks (17 specimens)

With the exception of one specimen made from horneblende gneiss, these tools are from quartz and quartzite. The mean diameters range from 91 to 31 mm., with an average of 50 mm.

Scrapers, heavy-duty (6 specimens)

Massive heavy-duty scrapers, such as those from the Upper Occupation Floor, are not so common at this level where the average size of the specimens is considerably smaller. The series includes two discoidal, one square-ended, two steeply trimmed side scrapers and two hollow scrapers made on flakes. One is of lava and the balance of quartz and quartzite. The length/breadth measurements

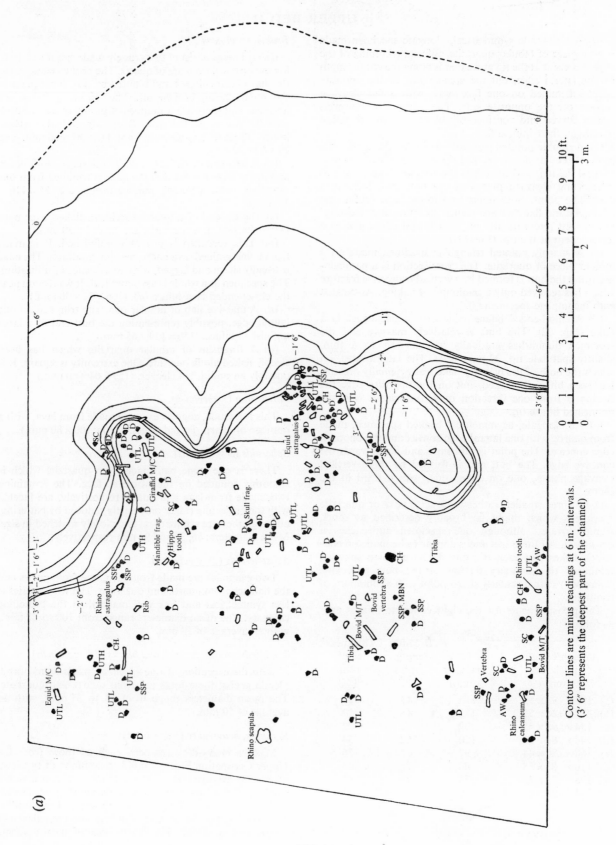

(a)

Contour lines are minus readings at 6 in. intervals.
(3′ 6″ represents the deepest part of the channel)

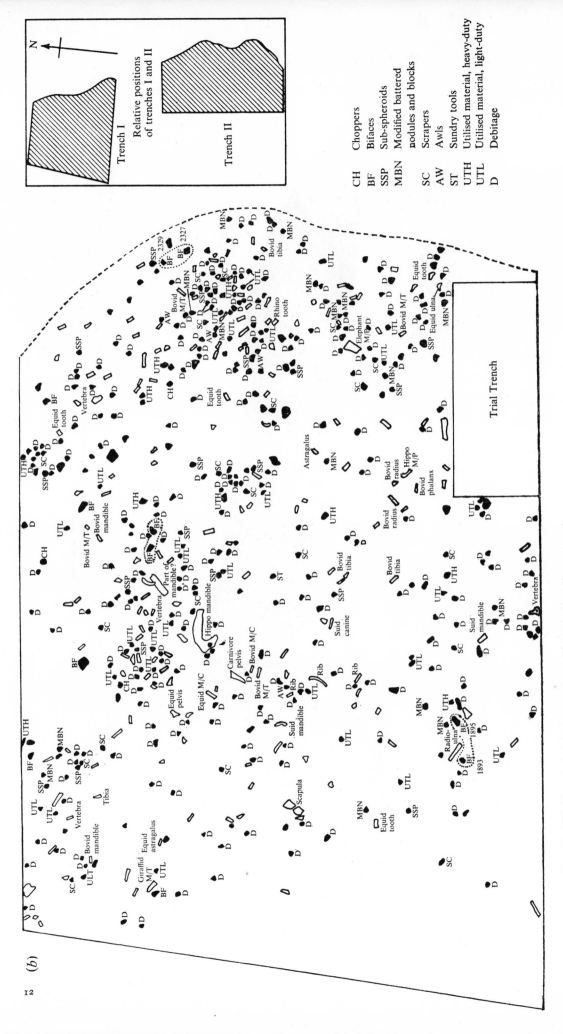

Fig. 80. TK. Trench I: (*a*) above, plan of finds in the Channel and (*b*) below, on the Lower Occupation floor. (The six bifaces found in pairs are shown in (*b*), encircled by dotted lines.)

CH   Choppers
BF   Bifaces
SSP   Sub-spheroids
MBN   Modified battered nodules and blocks
SC   Scrapers
AW   Awls
ST   Sundry tools
UTH   Utilised material, heavy-duty
UTL   Utilised material, light-duty
D   Debitage

Trench I
Relative positions of trenches I and II
Trench II

Trial Trench

(*b*)

12

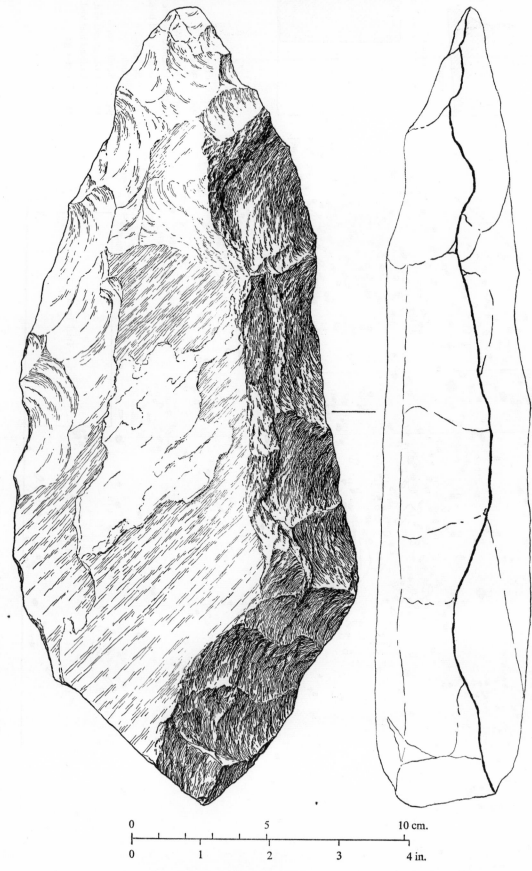

0　　　　　　　5　　　　　　　10 cm.

0　　　1　　　2　　　3　　　4 in.

Fig. 81. TK. Large biface made of tabular quartzite, from the Lower Occupation Floor.

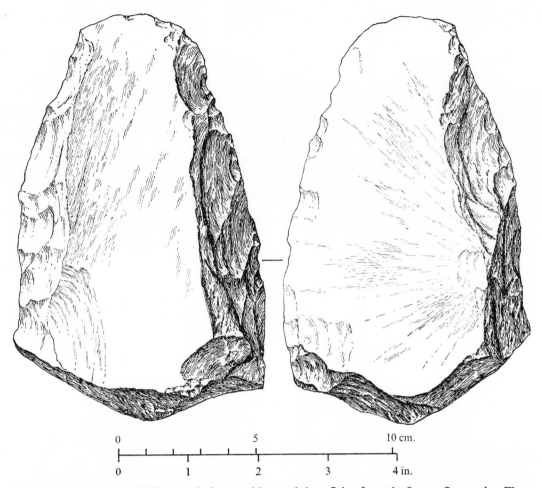

Fig. 82. TK. Chisel-ended biface made from a side-struck lava flake, from the Lower Occupation Floor.

range from 70 × 61 mm. to 62 × 56 mm., with an average of 56 × 74 mm. The notches in the hollow scrapers measure 41 × 4 mm. and 34 × 5 mm. respectively.

Scrapers, light-duty (*25 specimens*)

The whole series is made from quartz and quartzite and includes end, side, discoidal, perimetal, nosed and hollow scrapers.

End scrapers (*6 specimens*). One is made on a fragment of tabular quartzite and the balance on thick flakes. The working edges are curved and are more even than usual. The small projections often present on light-duty scrapers from other sites have generally been trimmed off. The length/breadth measurements range from 63 × 52 mm. to 32 × 20 mm., with an average of 43 × 37 mm. (Fig. 83, nos. 1–3.)

Side scrapers (*3 specimens*). These are made on broken flakes and other fragments, with a working edge along one side, either curved or straight. The trimming is generally steep. (Fig. 83, Nos. 8–10.) The length/breadth measurements range from 38 × 52 mm. to 24 × 29 mm., with an average of 33 × 41 mm.

Discoidal scrapers (*4 specimens*). These are approximately circular but are not necessarily trimmed on the whole circumference. (Fig. 83, nos. 4, 5.) The measurements range from 48 × 44 mm. to 16 × 15 mm., with an average of 27 × 22 mm.

Perimetal scrapers (*2 specimens*). One is subtriangular and the other approximately rectangular. They are steeply trimmed round the whole circumference. (Fig. 83, nos. 6, 7.) The length/breadth measurements are 27 × 27 mm. and 26 × 23 mm.

Nosed scrapers (*3 specimens*). The working edges are rounded, but relatively narrow, with a notch on one or both sides. (Fig. 83, nos. 11–14.) The length/breadth measurements range from 44 × 39 mm. to 37 × 22 mm., with an average of 39 × 32 mm.

Hollow scrapers (*4 specimens*). In two examples there are two notches, one on either lateral edge, together with additional smaller indentations at the tips. (Fig. 83, nos. 15–17.) The length/breadth measurements range from 58 × 55 mm. to 44 × 39 mm., with an average of 48 × 45 mm., and the notches vary from 31 × 4·5 mm. to 17 × 5 mm.

The average length/breadth measurements for the twenty-five light-duty scrapers are 41 × 34 mm.

179

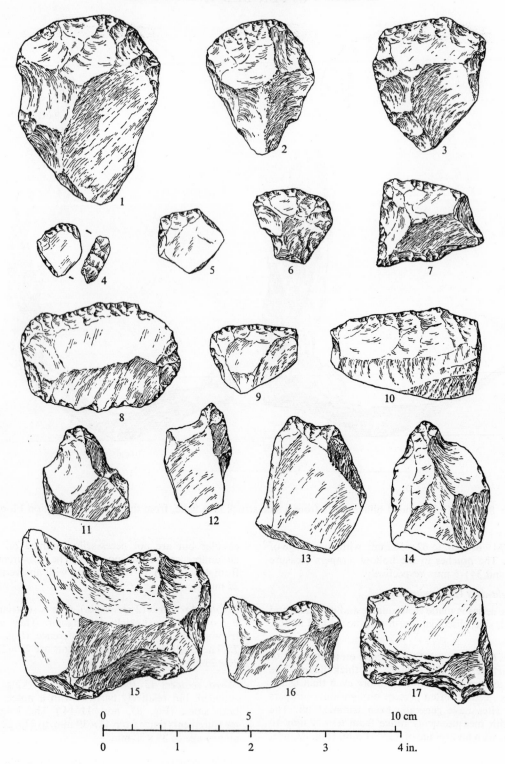

Fig. 83. TK. Light-duty quartz and quartzite scrapers from the Lower Occupation Floor. (1) to (3) end scrapers; (4) and (5) discoidal scrapers; (6) and (7) perimetal scrapers; (8) to (10) side scrapers; (11) to (14) nosed scrapers; (15) to (17) hollow scrapers.

Burins (*8 specimens*)

Three types of burins are represented: angle burins on transverse broken edges (3 specimens), angle burins on transverse trimmed edges (3 specimens) and dihedral burins (2 specimens). All are made from quartz or quartzite. Blunting and chipping on the chisel edges is generally present. In three of the angle burins the utilisation also extends across on to either the upper or the lower face. The series is well made and does not include any of the large and rather crude examples found in earlier assemblages. The overall length/breadth measurements range from 51 × 30 mm. to 23 × 22 mm., with an average of 36 × 23 mm., and the width of the chisel edges varies from 11 to 4 mm., with an average of 7·3 mm. (Fig. 84, nos. 1–5.)

Awls (*8 specimens*)

These consist of quartz and quartzite flakes and other fragments with short, sharp points, formed by a notch on one or both sides of the point. One example is double-pointed. In the majority the notches have been trimmed from the primary flake surface but in two specimens the trimming is from reverse directions. (Fig. 91, nos. 16–20.) The length/breadth measurements range from 58 × 42 mm. to 25 × 25 mm., with an average of 34 × 31 mm.

Outils écaillés (*2 specimens*)

These tools are made of quartz and quartzite respectively and have relatively thin, slightly concave edges on which there is scaled utilisation, usually on both faces. The edges are not so deeply hollowed or so heavily scaled as in a number of similar tools from BK, at a higher level in Bed II. One specimen is double-ended, with typical scaling at either end. (Fig. 84, nos. 6, 7.) The length/breadth measurements are 35 × 38 mm. and 36 × 31 mm.

Laterally trimmed flakes (*4 specimens*)

One quartzite and three quartz flakes are trimmed along the distal parts of both lateral edges to bluntly pointed tips, which are not sharp enough to be classed as awls. (Fig. 84, nos. 9–12.) The length/breadth measurements are 80 × 50 mm., 80 × 55 mm., 55 × 27 mm. and 44 × 29 mm.

UTILISED MATERIAL

'Anvil' (*1 specimen*)

This consists of an oblong slab of quartzite in which the edges of the upper and lower surfaces are shattered and bruised. A vertical ridge on one side is also heavily utilised. (138 × 105 × 90 mm.)

Cobblestones, nodules and blocks (*8 specimens*)

There are three lava cobblestones, three angular blocks of quartz and two pieces of tabular quartzite which all show some evidence of utilisation. The average mean diameter is 67 mm.

Flakes (*2 specimens*)

Two large quartz flakes show some irregular chipping on the edges. (108 × 66 mm. and 79 × 50 mm.)

Light-duty flakes and other fragments (*79 specimens*)

With straight edges (*17 specimens*). The edges are approximately straight, and show either coarse or fine utilisation which is usually present on both faces. The whole series is made of quartz or quartzite.

With concave edges (*28 specimens*). These consist of whole and broken quartz and quartzite flakes with a notch on one edge. The chipping of the notches is fine and is usually present on the dorsal surface only. They vary in width and depth from 51 × 5 mm. to 6 × 1·5 mm., with an average of 15 × 2·1 mm.

With convex edges (*21 specimens*). The edges are rounded and sometimes show steep chipping, resembling that on scrapers, or else shallow 'nibbling'. Utilisation is generally present on the dorsal surface only. The whole series is of quartz or quartzite.

Miscellaneous (*13 specimens*). These are quartz and quartzite flakes and other fragments with some chipping on the edges, but less well defined than in any of the above categories.

The average length/breadth measurements for the seventy-nine light-duty utilised flakes are 37 × 27 mm.

DEBITAGE

The *débitage* from this level amounts to 1,940 specimens, of which eighty-four are complete flakes, 1,608 broken flakes and chips and 248 core fragments. Only 0·1 per cent of the total is of lava, although there is, as usual, a higher proportion of lava among the complete flakes, with 10·6 per cent. There are four convergent and two parallel-sided flakes, the balance being divergent. As in the assemblage from the Upper Occupation Floor, some are triangular in form (sixteen specimens) with a very reduced striking platform at one apex. The length/breadth measurements in millimetres are as follows:

Lava	Range	Average
End-struck	85 × 40 to 23 × 21	59 × 38
Side-struck	51 × 60 to 25 × 33	34 × 42
Quartz/quartzite		
End-struck	123 × 110 to 18 × 17	46 × 34
Side-struck	110 × 112 to 19 × 24	37 × 46

Bulbs of percussion

The bulbs of percussion can be subdivided as follows:

	Lava	Quartz/quartzite
Marked	60 %	56·3 %
Slight	10 %	21·3 %
Double	10 %	1·2 %
Flat	20 %	5·0 %
Shattered	—	16·2 %
Totals	10	82

92

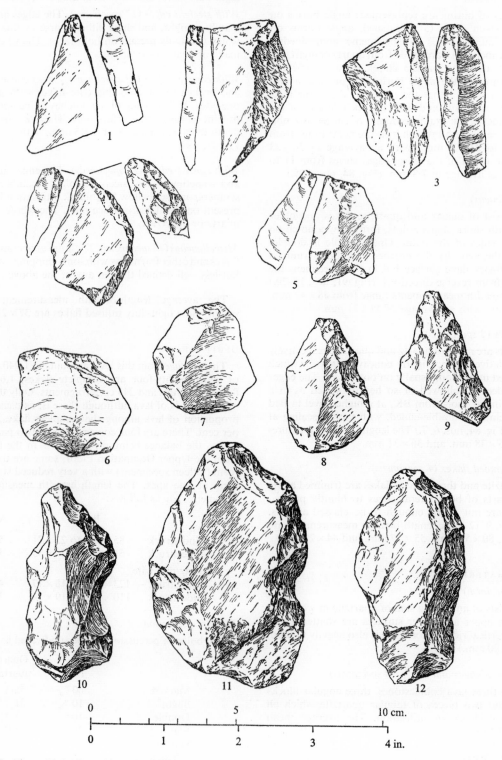

Fig. 84. TK. (1) to (5) burins; (6) and (7) *outils écaillés*; (8) to (12) laterally trimmed flakes. (6) and (10) are made from fine-grained quartzite and the balance from quartz.

It will be seen that marked bulbs are predominant in both the lava and the quartz and quartzite flakes.

Angles of striking platforms

Angles between 90° and 109° predominate in the quartz/quartzite series, whilst the majority of the lava flakes have angles between 110° and 129° as follows:

	Lava	Quartz/quartzite
70–89°	—	—
90–109°	25 %	64·7 %
110–129°	75 %	35·2 %
130°+	—	—
Totals	8	51
	59	

MANUPORTS (21 SPECIMENS)

These consist of eleven lava cobblestones, in which the average mean diameter is 64 mm., and ten blocks of quartz and quartzite with an average mean diameter of 81 mm.

Analysis of the industry from the Lower Floor at TK

	Nos.	%
Tools	123	5·7
Utilised material	87	4·1
Débitage	1,940	90·1
	2,150	
Tools		
Side choppers	5	4·1
End chopper	1	0·8
Bifaces, including broken and unfinished	15	12·2
Polyhedron	1	0·8
Spheroids	3	2·4
Subspheroids	28	22·8
Modified battered nodules and blocks	17	13·8
Scrapers, heavy-duty	6	4·9
Scrapers, light-duty	25	20·3
Burins	8	6·5
Awls	8	6·5
Outils écaillés	2	1·6
Laterally trimmed flakes	4	3·2
	123	
Utilised material		
'Anvil'	1	1·1
Cobblestones	3	3·3
Nodules and blocks	5	5·5
Flakes, heavy-duty	2	2·2
Light-duty flakes and other fragments	79	87·8
	90	

Débitage	Nos.	%
Whole flakes	84	4·3
Broken flakes and chips	1,608	82·9
Core fragments	248	12·7
	1,940	

THE INTERMEDIATE LEVEL BETWEEN THE UPPER AND LOWER OCCUPATION FLOORS

As already noted, this level consisted of a tuff containing a number of scattered artefacts. The deposit varied in thickness from 1 to 2 ft. and the artefacts did not occur on any recognizable horizon, as was the case in the Upper and Lower Occupation Floors. The plan of distribution is therefore not published.

THE INDUSTRY

The assemblage consists of 614 artefacts, of which twenty-nine are tools, forty utilised pieces and 545 débitage. The latter amounts to 88·7 per cent of the total, a slightly lower figure than in either of the underlying levels.

The tools include two side choppers and one end chopper. One of the former consists of an oval lava cobblestone with unusually flat trimming. The working edge is even with little evidence of utilisation. The second specimen, also made on a lava cobblestone, is crude and has only one flake removed from either side. The respective measurements are 66 × 87 × 34 mm. and 83 × 99 × 68 mm., with mean diameters of 62 mm. and 83 mm. The edge/circumference ratios are 74 and 26 per cent. The end chopper is made on a cuboid block of quartz in which one edge has been bifacially flaked to an even, sharp working edge. (72 × 53 × 57 mm. Mean diameter 60 mm. Edge/circumference ratio 27 per cent.)

No finished bifaces occur in this level; there is only a roughly blocked-out example (135 × 136 × 95 mm.) and a large end-struck flake (137 × 92 × 44 mm.) with a minimum of flaking on both faces which may also be an unfinished biface. There is a single well-made discoid. It is of quartz with a sharp, jagged cutting edge on the circumference. (65 × 65 × 48 mm.) Spheroids and subspheroids are represented by a single specimen each. The spheroid is made from quartz and has been battered smooth over the whole exterior. Mean diameter 60 mm. The subspheroid is also of quartz and is faceted, with a mean diameter of 29 mm. Three partly flaked blocks of quartz are crushed and chipped on the edges. The mean diameters are 53, 82 and 72 mm. respectively.

Scrapers are rather more plentiful than any of the foregoing tools, with three heavy-duty and ten light-duty examples. Two of the heavy-duty scrapers are made on tabular fragments of quartz, steeply trimmed along one

183

edge. The third, made from quartz, is discoidal and high-backed. The measurements are 110 × 136 mm., 89 × 76 mm. and 107 × 82 mm. The light-duty series consists of six side, three end and one perimetal scrapers, all of which are made from quartz or quartzite, either on flakes or on fragments of tabular material. The end scrapers are round-ended and the perimetal example subtriangular. The average measurements for the ten specimens are 35 × 34 mm. There is a single burin, consisting of an angle burin made on a quartz flake, transversely fractured at the tip. The working edge is 5 mm. wide and shows some utilisation. (48 × 28 mm.) Four awls complete the series of tools. They are made on quartz flakes with points at the tips, formed by a trimmed notch on either side. In two specimens the notches are trimmed from reverse directions and in two on one face only. The average measurements are 44 × 34 mm.

The heavy-duty utilised material consists of two anvils and two hammerstones. The former are made on an angular piece of quartzite and on a cobblestone, and show extensive battering and crushing on the edges. (117 × 114 × 93 mm. and 100 × 83 × 90 mm.) The hammerstones are both of lava, with mean diameters of 60 mm. and 83 mm. respectively.

There are thirty-six light-duty utilised flakes, comprising six specimens with utilisation on straight edges, seven with notched edges, thirteen with convex edges and ten miscellaneous.

The overall measurements for the thirty-six specimens range from 50 × 43 mm. to 21 × 18 mm., with an average of 32 × 25 mm. In the concave-edged group the notches vary in width and depth from 22 × 3·5 mm. to 9 × 1·5 mm., with an average of 16 × 2·8 mm.

The *débitage* consists of 26 whole flakes, 1 re-sharpening flake, 441 broken flakes and chips and 27 core fragments, amounting to 545 specimens. With the exception of the re-sharpening flake and eighteen broken flakes, which are of lava, the whole series is of quartz and quartzite. All the complete flakes are divergent; seven are side-struck. There are three unusually large and massive flakes measuring over 100 mm. in length. The variations to be seen in the bulbs of percussion and in the angles of the striking platforms fall within the range for the flakes from both the Upper and Lower Occupation Floors. The overall length/breadth measurements for the twenty-six complete flakes range from 170 × 160 mm. to 15 × 13 mm., with an average of 55 × 49 mm. The lava re-sharpening flake has a longitudinal dorsal ridge. (85 × 51 mm.)

Thirteen unmodified lava cobblestones, together with eight blocks of quartz and quartzite and three of horneblende gneiss, were also recovered from this level.

Analysis of the industry from the Intermediate Level at TK

	Nos.	%
Tools	29	4·7
Utilised material	40	6·5
Débitage	545	88·7
	614	

Tools	Nos.	%
Side choppers	2	6·9
End chopper	1	3·4
Bifaces (unfinished)	2	6·9
Discoid	1	3·4
Spheroid	1	3·4
Sub-spheroid	1	3·4
Modified battered nodules and blocks	3	10·4
Scrapers, heavy-duty	3	10·4
Scrapers, light-duty	10	34·5
Burin	1	3·4
Awls	4	13·8
	29	
Utilised material		
'Anvils'	2	5·0
Hammerstone	1	2·5
Cobblestone	1	2·5
Light-duty flakes and other fragments	36	90·0
	40	
Débitage		
Whole flakes	26	4·8
Re-sharpening flake	1	0·1
Broken flakes and chips	441	80·9
Core fragments	77	14·1
	545	

THE UPPER OCCUPATION FLOOR

This horizon yielded the largest number of artefacts since it was excavated in both Trenches I and II. There were also considerable numbers of mammalian bones. These were more plentiful in Trench II than in Trench I, where there was an unusually dense concentration of quartz *débitage*. (Figs. 85, 86). All the material lay at the base of a tuff that rested on an underlying clay. The surface was somewhat uneven but clearly defined and often encrusted with lime.

THE INDUSTRY

There is a total of 5,180 artefacts, of which 88·2 per cent is *débitage*. Tools and utilised material occur in almost equal proportions, with 5·6 and 6·1 per cent respectively. The raw materials are predominantly quartz and quartzite, amounting to 97·4 per cent of the *débitage* and 87·6 per cent of the tools. Light-duty scrapers, spheroids and subspheroids are the most common tools. Bifaces amount to 8·2 per cent and choppers, including side, end and two-edged, to 9·9 per cent of the total.

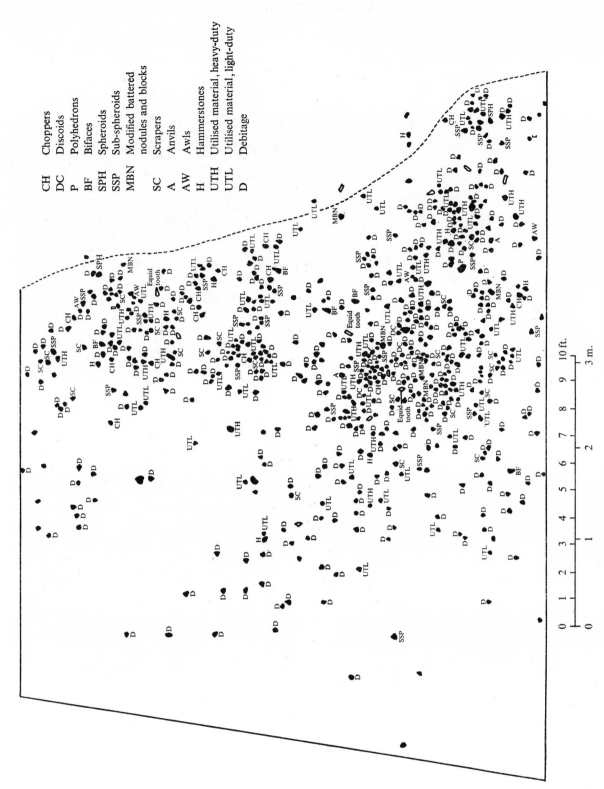

CH   Choppers
DC   Discoids
P   Polyhedrons
BF   Bifaces
SPH   Spheroids
SSP   Sub-spheroids
MBN   Modified battered
      nodules and blocks
SC   Scrapers
A   Anvils
AW   Awls
H   Hammerstones
UTH   Utilised material, heavy-duty
UTL   Utilised material, light-duty
D   Debitage

Fig. 85. TK. Trench I. Plan of finds on the Upper Occupation Floor.

185

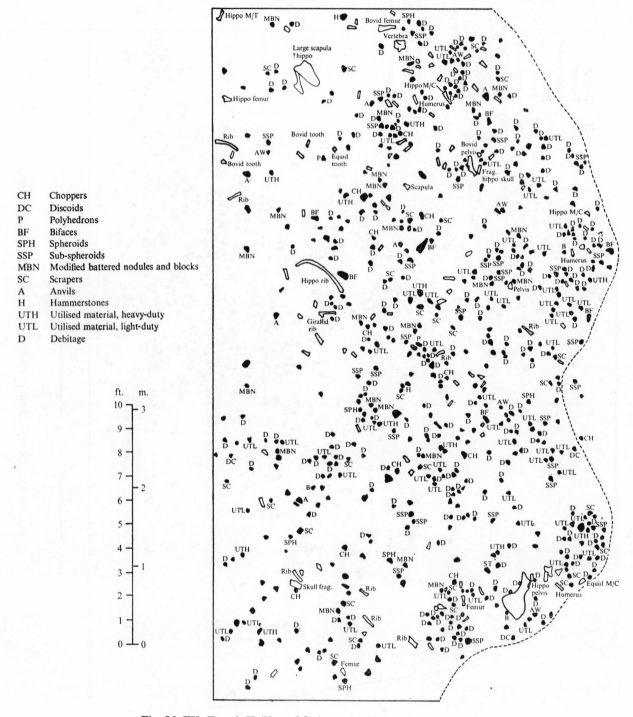

CH — Choppers
DC — Discoids
P — Polyhedrons
BF — Bifaces
SPH — Spheroids
SSP — Sub-spheroids
MBN — Modified battered nodules and blocks
SC — Scrapers
A — Anvils
H — Hammerstones
UTH — Utilised material, heavy-duty
UTL — Utilised material, light-duty
D — Debitage

Fig. 86. TK. Trench II. Plan of finds on the Upper Occupation Floor.

TOOLS

Side choppers (*17 specimens*)

Seven examples are of lava and ten of quartz or quartzite. Two are unifacial. Among the bifacial choppers there are seven with wide, curved working edges in which a large part of the circumference has been trimmed. In three of these specimens there is secondary trimming on the edges which are even and nearly straight. The degree of utilisation varies from heavy blunting and battering to light chipping. A few specimens are in particularly sharp condition. Two exhibit hammerstone type of utilisation on the butt ends. The length/breadth thickness measurements range from $100 \times 108 \times 71$ mm. to $29 \times 37 \times 22$ mm., with an average of $61 \times 76 \times 47$ mm., and the mean diameters vary from 93 to 29 mm., with an average of 61 mm. The edge/circumference ratios vary from 58 to 26 per cent, with an average of 41 per cent.

End choppers (*7 specimens*)

Six examples are made of lava and one of quartz. The series includes two particularly massive specimens with deeply indented trimming scars and exceptionally jagged working edges, as well as five examples in which the edges are trimmed by means of a single scar on one face, opposed to multiple flaking on the obverse. The length/breadth/thickness measurements range from $133 \times 132 \times 106$ mm. to $52 \times 40 \times 33$ mm., with an average of $92 \times 82 \times 80$ mm., and the mean diameters vary from 123 to 41 mm., with an average of 80mm. The average edge/circumference ratio is 30 per cent.

Two-edged choppers (*5 specimens*)

Three examples are made from quartz or quartzite and two from lava. They include: four oblong specimens with blunt ends and bifacial trimming along both lateral edges; a subspherical specimen with working edges on opposite sides; and one unusual trihedral example with one cutting edge extending round the whole circumference and a second on a longitudinal ridge which abuts on to the first at either end. The working edges are all somewhat damaged by use. The length/breadth/thickness measurements range from $92 \times 79 \times 74$ mm. to $74 \times 54 \times 38$ mm., with an average of $81 \times 60 \times 50$ mm., and the mean diameters vary from 81 to 55 mm., with an average of 64 mm.

Bifaces (*24 specimens*)

The collection of bifaces comprises eighteen complete, four broken and one unfinished specimens, together with one heavy-duty pick. The degree of variability in size and technique is considerable and had the specimens not been found in close association on a sealed occupation level, it would be difficult to regard the tools as belonging to a single industry. The series includes large well-made bifaces weighing over 4 lb., together with rather crude diminutive specimens which weigh less than 2 oz. Seventy-two per cent are made from quartz and quartzite, the majority from pieces of tabular material. Many of those made from lava exhibit an area of rounded cortex surface, generally at the butt, indicating that they were made from cobblestones. Only a few specimens are made on flakes and these generally show only minimal flaking on the primary surface. The seventeen complete specimens range in size from $262 \times 106 \times 45$ mm. to $64 \times 27 \times 18$ mm., with an average of $103 \times 64 \times 38$ mm. The breadth/length ratio is also very variable, with a minimum of 40 per cent and a maximum of 98 per cent, the average being 65 per cent.

Irregular ovates are the most common form and include both elongate and broad, stumpy examples. There are several double-pointed bifaces and these also include relatively long, narrow examples and others that are short and broad. One specimen approaches a cordate in form. The series may be described as follows:

(*a*) An elongate specimen made on a slab of quartzite 45 mm. thick (Fig. 87). The butt is formed by two vertical fractures, with a central keel at their intersection. At the tip and extending along approximately one third of the length, the trimming is bifacial; in the median part and towards the butt it is unifacial but carried out from opposite directions on either side, resulting in a parallelogram cross-section. The edge is straight and even, including the area near the tip. This is symmetrically pointed and shaped by means of fine, shallow scars.

(*b*) This specimen is made on a lava cobblestone with part of the cortex surface retained on the butt and on one lateral edge. The butt is bluntly pointed and the tool is not entirely symmetrical, since one lateral edge is more curved than the other. There is a flat area on either face, towards the tip, which is more weathered than the trimming scars, but less so than the cortex surface on the butt, suggesting that an earlier specimen was re-flaked. The edge is straight to sinuous, fresh and sharp, with little damage. The tip is broadly curved and less sharply pointed than in the preceding specimen.

(*c*) An elongate ovate made from coarse-grained lava. It is symmetrical and bifacially trimmed on the entire circumference. Both lateral edges have been subjected to particularly heavy battering and are extensively damaged in the median area. The trimming scars are relatively small and a number of plunging scars also occur, probably caused by the nature of the material.

(*d*) A similar specimen made from a lava cobblestone, in which part of the cortex surface is retained at the butt end. The tip has been broken and the trimming scars are more deeply indented than in (*c*). The edge is irregular and jagged and the tool is generally crude.

(*e*) A short, stumpy biface made on a piece of tabular quartzite 48 mm. thick. The lateral edges are symmetrical and markedly convex, with the widest point in the centre of the tool. The sides converge rapidly at both extremities, which are bluntly pointed. The edge is generally even, bifacially flaked and considerably blunted by use.

(*f*) This specimen resembles a cordate, although the maximum width is situated nearer to the centre than in true cordates. The butt consists of a vertical flaked surface which has been slightly bruised by percussion. The tool is wide relative to its length, with markedly convex lateral edges converging to a small blunt point at the tip. There is a pronounced longitudinal ridge on one face. The edges are sinuous and considerably battered by use.

(*g, h*) Two rather crude specimens made on pieces of tabular quartzite. In one example the tip has been broken.

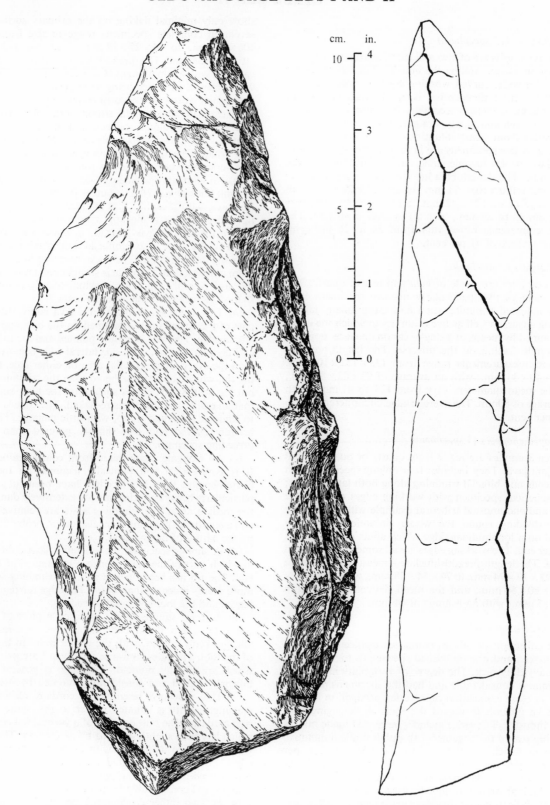

cm. in.

10 — 4

— 3

5 — 2

— 1

0 — 0

Fig. 87. TK. Large biface made of tabular quartzite, from the Upper Occupation Floor.

Both are bifacially trimmed on the circumference, but retain areas of the natural flat cleavage surface in the central part of either one or both faces.

(*i*) A symmetrical and particularly well-finished small biface made on a lava cobblestone. (Fig. 88, no. 4.) Part of the rounded cortex surface forms the butt and the maximum width is at the point where the cortex meets the trimmed area. The lateral edges are virtually straight and converge gradually to the tip. The trimming is regular, with shallow, well-controlled flake scars, resulting in an unusually even edge.

(*j*) This specimen is made on part of a large flake of coarse-grained lava. Only a minimum of trimming is present on the primary flake surface, but the upper face has been trimmed along the greater part of the circumference. Both the tip and the butt are bluntly pointed and the former is damaged by use.

(*k*) A small lava specimen that has clearly been made from faulty material. (Fig. 88, no. 1.) A sizeable lump has remained on one face at the butt end and has been undercut by plunging flake scars, indicating unsuccessful attempts to remove it. The flaking on the opposite face is regular and the specimen is generally symmetrical in outline, with a blunt point at the butt as well as at the tip. The edge is sinuous and shows chipping and blunting from utilisation, indicating that the tool was used in spite of being defective.

(*l–r*) There are also seven diminutive bifaces. Four are of quartz, two of quartzite and one of lava. (Fig. 88, nos. 2, 3, 5.) The average length/breadth measurements for the series are 63 × 39 mm. and the average weight is 67 g. The series includes five double-pointed specimens, one miniature ovate and one example in which the butt is formed by a natural transverse fracture. Two examples appear to be made on flakes and show a minimum of flaking on the primary surface. The remaining specimens are bifacially flaked on the circumference, with edges varying from sinuous to nearly straight. All show blunting and chipping from utilisation. Although two are approximately symmetrical, the flaking is generally irregular and less controlled than on some of the larger examples such as (*a*) and (*i*).

(*s*) A heavy-duty pick made from lava. The butt is rounded and relatively thick and shows some pitting and bruising. The tool tapers rapidly towards the tip, which is formed by the intersection of four almost equilateral planes, three of which consist of negative flake scars, whilst the fourth appears to be a natural cleavage surface. The tip is sharply pointed but has been chipped by use. The butt end is circular in cross-section whilst the median part and the tip are quadrilateral. (94 × 67 × 64 mm.)

The broken bifaces are of quartz and quartzite and consist of two tips and two butt ends. One massive end-struck quartzite flake appears to be an unfinished specimen, possibly a cleaver. There is some bifacial flaking at the distal end, with considerable battering and some plunging scars on one side of the butt, which is relatively thick. (175 × 108 × 68 mm.)

It will be seen from the accompanying table that the seven diminutive specimens are, on the average, approximately half the size of the large and medium-sized bifaces, although the breadth/length and thickness/length ratios are almost identical.

Measurements for the complete bifaces

Length/breadth/ thickness (mm.)	Mean diameter (mm.)	Breadth/ length ratio (%)	Thickness/ length ratio (%)
Large to medium			
(*a*) 262 × 106 × 45	137	40	17
(*b*) 192 × 102 × 74	122	53	38
(*c*) 157 × 87 × 51	98	55	3¾
(*d*) 117 × 90 × 60	89	76	51
(*e*) 86 × 69 × 48	67	80	55
(*f*) 96 × 88 × 64	82	91	66
(*g*) 86 × 61 × 28	58	70	32
(*h*) 96 × 69 × 33	66	71	34
(*i*) 106 × 74 × 32	72	66	37
(*j*) 130 × 74 × 32	78	56	24
(*k*) 84 × 89 × 44	72	58	52
Averages 128 × 83 × 46	85	65	37
Diminutive			
(*l*) 62 × 42 × 33	45	67	53
(*m*) 61 × 51 × 19	43	83	31
(*n*) 65 × 34 × 23	40	52	35
(*o*) 61 × 42 × 28	43	68	45
(*p*) 61 × 60 × 30	50	98	49
(*q*) 74 × 39 × 24	45	52	32
(*r*) 64 × 27 × 18	36	42	28
Averages 64 × 42 × 25	43	66	39

Polyhedrons (3 specimens)

All three examples are made from lava. They are crude and very similar in size and have a number of short, bifacially flaked working edges. The length/breadth/ thickness measurements are 95 × 75 × 69 mm., 94 × 83 × 54 mm. and 88 × 79 × 62 mm., with mean diameters of 79, 77 and 76 mm.

Discoids (9 specimens)

Two examples are made from lava and the balance from quartz and quartzite. The series includes five small, light-duty specimens and one large, crude example that is possibly unfinished. The working edges always extend round the entire circumference and generally exhibit some chipping and blunting. The cross-sections are either plano-convex or biconvex. The length/breadth/thickness measurements range from 136 × 124 × 70 mm. to 34 × 33 × 23 mm., with an average of 60 × 55 × 39 mm., and the mean diameters vary from 110 to 30 mm., with an average of 51 mm.

Spheroids (16 specimens)

Fifteen examples are of quartz or quartzite and one of lava. Two quartzite specimens are of a fine-grained dark purple variety only known from one other site, BK. The series includes five symmetrical stone balls, smoothly rounded over the whole exterior, three faceted examples in which the projecting ridges are relatively sharp and eight specimens in which the projecting areas have been partly

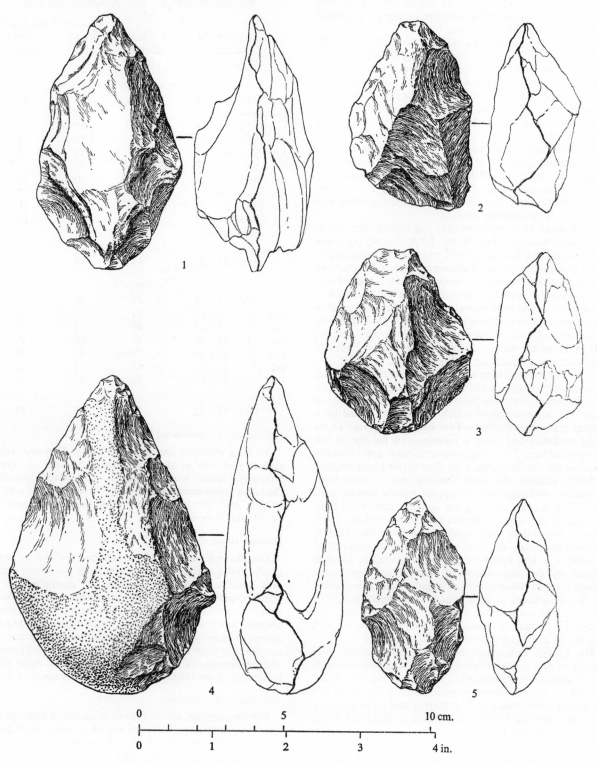

Fig. 88. TK. Small bifaces from the Upper Occupation Floor. (1) and (4) are of lava and the remainder of quartz.

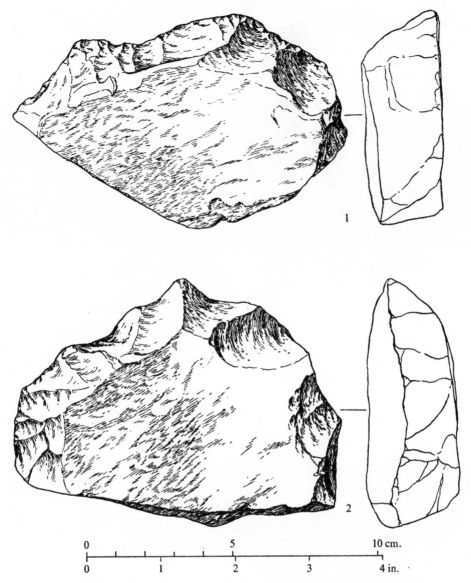

Fig. 89. TK. Two heavy-duty scrapers from the Upper Occupation Floor. Made from quartz.

reduced by battering. The mean diameters range from 99 to 22 mm., with an average of 56 mm.

Subspheroids (60 specimens)

Four examples are made of lava, three of quartzite, one of horneblende gneiss and the balance of quartz. The series consists of the usual asymmetrical subspherical battered tools, intermediate between spheroids and the sub-angular modified battered blocks. One massive specimen weighs 6¾ lb. The mean diameters range from 128 to 28 mm., with an average of 52 mm.

Modified battered nodules and blocks (35 specimens)

The whole series is of quartz or quartzite and consists of sub-angular fragments, including a number of tabular

pieces with extensive battering on the edges. The mean diameters range from 93 to 56 mm., with an average of 58 mm.

Scrapers, heavy-duty (14 specimens)

There are six side scrapers. One example is made on part of a large lava flake which has been broken transversely. The butt end consists of the fractured surface and the working edge extends round the remaining three sides. The flaking is mainly on the upper face, but there are also some scars on the lower face, as in choppers. (83 × 112 mm.) Five examples are made on pieces of tabular quartzite. They have curved and steeply trimmed working edges, generally chipped and damaged by use (Fig. 89, no. 1). The length/breadth measurements range from 114 × 152

191

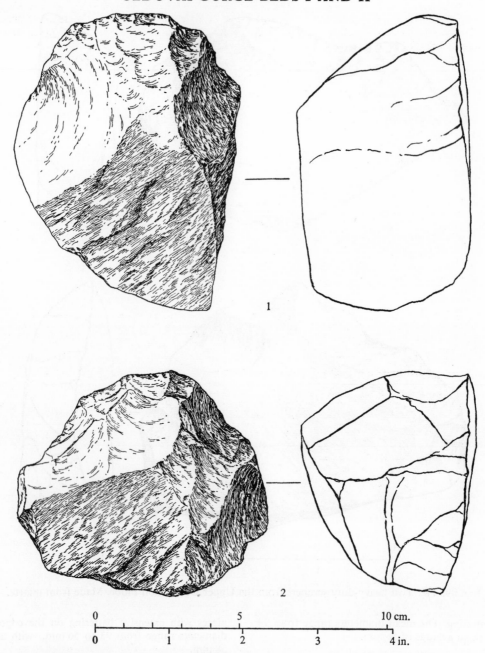

Fig. 90. TK. Two heavy-duty scrapers from the Upper Occupation Floor. Made from tabular quartzite and lava, respectively.

mm. to 54 × 75 mm., with an average of 75 × 106 mm. A discoidal scraper is also made on a slab of tabular quartzite that has been steeply trimmed on virtually the entire circumference, with a number of plunging scars on one side. 69 × 66 mm. The remaining seven specimens consist of: (a) an oblong, irregular-shaped example made from horneblende gneiss, which has been trimmed on the entire circumference and resembles the type described as perimetal in the light-duty series; the under-surface consists of a flat cleavage plane and the radial trimming scars on the

upper face converge to form a high central cone (88 × 120 mm.); (b) a triangular quartzite specimen in which one edge has been steeply trimmed and also chipped by use, the upper and lower faces being flat and the sides vertical (74 × 73 mm.); (c) five high-backed and subdiscoidal examples with a trimmed working edge on only part of the circumference; one is made from lava and the remainder from quartz or quartzite. With the exception of the lava specimen, these scrapers have edges which are evenly rounded and blunted by use (Fig. 90). The length/breadth measurements range from 97 × 74 mm. to 75 × 66 mm., with an average of 83 × 75 mm. The average length/breadth for the thirteen heavy-duty scrapers described above is 78 × 92 mm.

Scrapers, light-duty (77 specimens)

Light-duty scrapers are the most numerous tools in this assemblage and include a number of different types. The most common are side scrapers but end, discoidal and perimetal examples are also well represented. There are three specimens in which two or three types of scraper have been combined in the same tool. The entire series is made from quartz or quartzite.

End scrapers (9 specimens). These are mostly made on flakes that have been trimmed across the tips to slightly irregular working edges, which are generally curved. The length/breadth measurements range from 79 × 55 mm. to 25 × 22 mm., with an average of 40 × 30 mm.

Side scrapers (37 specimens). These include specimens in which the trimming is on the lateral edge of an end-struck flake, on one side of a piece of tabular material, on cores, or on side-struck flakes. The working edges are generally curved but in some examples they are virtually straight. Small notches and projections are usually present, although in some specimens the edges have become rounded from use. The length/breadth measurements range from 55 × 87 mm. to 14 × 22 mm., with an average of 17 × 39 mm.

Discoidal scrapers (9 specimens). All are made from quartz or quartzite. The trimming is generally steep and most of the tools have been retouched on the whole circumference. The measurements range from 48 × 47 mm. to 22 × 20 mm., with an average of 32 × 30 mm.

Perimetal scrapers (10 specimens). These tools vary greatly in shape but the whole series is characterised by the presence of a working edge on the whole or the greater part of the circumference. The trimming is generally steep and the edges are usually blunted by use. The length/breadth range is from 44 × 27 mm. to 29 × 20 mm., with an average of 30 × 20 mm.

Nosed scrapers (6 specimens). The working edges are rounded and narrow relative to the width of the specimens. They are evenly curved, with regular, steep trimming. The length/breadth measurements range from 76 × 63 mm. to 30 × 28 mm., with an average of 41 × 36 mm.

Hollow scrapers (3 specimens). These consist of two flakes and a thin oblong slab of quartzite on which a wide shallow notch has been trimmed along one lateral edge. The trimming has been carried out from one direction only. The notches range in width from 49 to 21 mm. and in depth from 4·5 to 2·5 mm., while the overall size of the specimens varies from 80 × 63 mm. to 45 × 25 mm., with an average of 58 × 39 mm.

Combination scrapers (3 specimens). There are two examples of end and hollow scrapers combined in the same tool and one oblong slab of quartzite on which there is an end, side and hollow scraper. The measurements for the three specimens are: 52 × 47 mm., 43 × 32 mm. and 85 × 66 mm.

Burins (7 specimens)

The burins are made from quartz and quartzite and include the following types:

(*a*) An angle burin on an end-struck flake. A series of longitudinal flakes has been removed from one lateral edge. Some of these flakes have plunged, forming small steps. The transverse edge at the tip appears to consist of a fracture which has been subsequently trimmed. The working edge measures 15 mm. in width and has a median projection formed by the intersection of two spalls. (63 × 39 mm.)

(*b*) A small specimen in which the spalls have been struck from an oblique transverse fracture. The working edge is 5 mm. wide and has been blunted and heavily used, causing damage to the lower surface in addition to blunting of the edge itself. (34 × 18 mm.)

(*c*) This is made on a triangular fragment of tabular quartzite 17 mm. thick. Parts of both lateral edges appear to be natural fractures and trimming scars are present only at the tip. Utilisation has resulted in blunting and 'frosting' of the working edge, which is 8 mm. wide. (57 × 32 mm.)

(*d*) A specimen with multiple spalls removed from both sides of the working edge. This has been entirely blunted and is also chipped by use. (43 × 28 mm.)

(*e*) This is made on an oblong fragment of quartzite with flat upper and lower faces. It is 18 mm. thick at the working end and tapers to 11 mm. at the butt. One lateral edge consists mainly of a fractured surface, with trimming only at the tip, whilst the opposite edge is formed by multiple longitudinal scars. The working edge is 16 mm. wide and is entirely blunted by use. (58 × 27 mm.)

(*f*) This is made on a piece of tabular quartzite 25 mm. thick. The burin edge is 17 mm. wide, sharp and fresh, with little evidence of utilisation. Fresh trimming scars are present on one lateral edge, but the scars on the other side, struck from the upper and lower faces, are considerably more weathered and possibly antedate the manufacture of the tool. (63 × 43 mm.)

(*g*) A small triangular specimen with a narrow working edge only 4 mm. wide, slightly chipped by use. Longitudinal trimming scars are present on one lateral edge. The opposite edge is damaged, but appears to consist of a natural fracture. (28 × 32 mm.)

The average length/breadth measurements for the series of seven specimens are 49 × 31 mm. and the average width of the working edges is 10 mm.

Awls (15 specimens)

These tools are all of quartz and quartzite and the majority is made on flakes, with the points at the tips, although there are a few examples with points on one lateral edge. As in the series from other sites, the points have been made by three clearly recognisable techniques: a notch trimmed on either side (the most usual form), a notch trimmed on one side only, and by means of bilateral trimming converging to the point.

In general the notches have been flaked from the primary flake surface, but in two examples they are from alternate directions. When not damaged by use the points are sharp, somewhat stumpy and triangular in cross-section. In one specimen there are two points on opposite edges of the flake. The length/breadth measurements range from 58 × 44 mm. to 24 × 29 mm., with an average of 36 × 33 mm. (Fig. 91, nos. 1–15.)

Laterally trimmed flakes (3 specimens)

These tools are oblong and high-backed, with dorsal ridges. Two examples are of quartz and one of fine-grained quartzite. They are steeply flaked on both lateral edges and also at one or both extremities, which are obtusely pointed. In two examples there are pronounced indentations on the lateral edges, formed by exceptionally deep flake scars and subsequent utilisation. The lower faces consist of the primary flake surfaces. The measurements of the three specimens are 71 × 38 × 26 mm., 65 × 31 × 22 mm. and 40 × 21 × 17 mm.

UTILISED MATERIAL

'Anvils' (8 specimens)

There is evidence of some preliminary flaking and preparation prior to utilisation in the majority of these specimens. Two examples are circular with a utilised edge on the circumference of a flat surface. Small bruised areas, indicating points of impact, are usually present on the upper and lower surfaces and in one example twenty-one such points of impact can be seen. The series is made from quartz and quartzite, mostly from pieces of relatively thick tabular quartzite in which use has been made of the natural flat surfaces. The mean diameters range from 101 to 53 mm., with an average of 78 mm.

Hammerstones (15 specimens)

These consist of waterworn cobblestones which have been pitted and bruised at the extremities. Eleven are of lava and four of quartz or quartzite. The mean diameters range from 84 to 34 mm., with an average of 66 mm.

Cobblestones (22 specimens)

These also consist of lava cobblestones similar to the hammerstones, but the type of utilisation is in the form of shattering and crude flaking suggestive of heavy and forceful impact. The mean diameters range from 91 to 42 mm., with an average of 68 mm.

Nodules and blocks (15 specimens)

These specimens consist of tabular fragments of quartzite and two pieces of lava, in which there is no evidence of shaping but in which the edges are chipped or otherwise damaged by use. The mean diameters range from 121 to 40 mm., with an average of 60 mm.

Heavy-duty flakes (3 specimens)

Parts of two large quartzite flakes and one of quartz are heavily chipped and damaged on the lateral edges. They range in length/breadth from 125 × 113 mm. to 85 × 72 mm.

Light-duty flakes and other fragments (252 specimens)

With straight edges (57 specimens). These consist of whole or broken flakes, core fragments and tabular pieces of quartzite in which one or more approximately straight edges show chipping and blunting from use. Although utilisation may be present on any convenient edge, it occurs mainly on the lateral edges of flakes. It varies from small, regular chipping to larger and more uneven scars, which have resulted in roughly denticulated edges. The length/breadth measurements range from 70 × 71 mm. to 18 × 18 mm., with an average of 29 × 29 mm.

With concave edges (47 specimens). This group consists of flakes and other fragments in which there is a utilised notch on one or possibly two edges. Occasionally there is additional utilisation on other edges. The edges of the notches are crushed rather than chipped and this is usually only evident on one face. With the exception of one lava and one quartzite specimen, the series is of quartz. The overall measurements range from 66 × 45 mm. to 20 × 18 mm., with an average of 34 × 27 mm. The notches vary in width from 32 mm. to 7 mm., with an average of 15 mm., and in depth from 5·5 mm. to 0·5 mm., with an average of 2·3 mm.

With convex edges (95 specimens). With the exception of one lava flake and two of quartzite, the series is of quartz. The type of chipping corresponds closely with that seen on the straight-edged specimens. Whole and broken flakes predominate but there is also a number of core fragments and two pieces of tabular quartz. The length/breadth measurements range from 71 × 48 mm. to 22 × 21 mm., with an average of 37 × 30 mm.

Miscellaneous (53 specimens). These consist of quartz flakes and other fragments with less well-defined areas of utilisation than those in the foregoing series. A degree of chipping or blunting is usually present on more than one edge. Core fragments are proportionately more numerous and tabular quartz is not represented. The length/breadth measurements range from 74 × 61 mm. to 21 × 19 mm., with an average of 51 × 29 mm.

DEBITAGE

The *débitage* amounts to 4,573 specimens, of which 183 are complete flakes, 3509 broken flakes and chips and 881 core fragments. Twenty-one per cent of the whole flakes are of lava, although lava represents only 2·6 per cent of the total. Side-struck flakes are more numerous in this assemblage than is usual and amount to 38 per cent; thirteen are of lava and fifty-five of quartz and quartzite. A proportion of the latter is triangular, with a greatly reduced striking platform. Most of the flakes are divergent, but there are four lava and fourteen quartz and quartzite

194

Fig. 91. TK. Awls from the Upper and Lower Occupation Floor. Made of quartz or quartzite.

examples that are convergent. The length/breadth measurements in millimetres for the series of 183 complete flakes are as follows:

Lava	Range	Average
End-struck	102 × 67 to 38 × 27	51 × 39
Side-struck	46 × 62 to 24 × 26	33 × 41
Quartz/quartzite		
End-struck	93 × 88 to 23 × 15	44 × 32
Side-struck	80 × 93 to 19 × 24	37 × 45

Bulbs of percussion

The bulbs of percussion are again more pronounced in the lava flakes than in those of quartz and quartzite, as follows:

	Lava	Quartz/quartzite
Marked	74·2 %	47·2 %
Slight	12·9 %	30·9 %
Double	6·4 %	—
Flat	3·2 %	6·5 %
Shattered	3·2 %	15·4 %
Totals	31	145
	176	

Angles of striking platforms

	Lava	Quartz/quartzite
70–89°	—	6·2 %
90–109°	33·3 %	65·6 %
110–129°	66·6 %	27·0 %
130°	—	1·0 %
Totals	21	96
	117	

It will be seen that the angles of the striking platforms are generally lower in the quartz and quartzite series than in that of lava.

MANUPORTS (139 SPECIMENS)

These consist of sixty-eight complete and forty-one broken cobblestones. One is of welded tuff, six of quartz or quartzite and the balance of lava. There are also thirty angular blocks, two of which are of horneblende gneiss and the balance of quartz and quartzite. The average mean diameter for the cobblestones is 61 mm. and for the blocks 65 mm.

Analysis of the industry from the Upper Floor at TK

	Nos.	%
Tools	292	5·6
Utilised material	315	6·1
Débitage	4,573	88·2
	5,180	

Tools	Nos.	%
Side choppers	17	5·8
End choppers	7	2·4
Two-edged choppers	5	1·7
Bifaces, including broken and unfinished	24	8·2
Polyhedrons	3	1·0
Discoids	9	3·1
Spheroids	16	5·5
Subspheroids	60	20·5
Modified battered nodules and blocks	35	12·0
Scrapers, heavy-duty	14	4·8
Scrapers, light-duty	77	26·4
Burins	7	2·5
Awls	15	5·1
Laterally trimmed flakes	3	1·0
	292	

Utilised material		
'Anvils'	8	2·5
Hammerstones	15	4·8
Cobblestones	22	7·0
Nodules and blocks	15	4·8
Heavy-duty flakes	3	0·9
Light-duty flakes and other fragments	252	80·0
	315	

Débitage		
Whole flakes	183	4·0
Broken flakes and chips	3,509	76·7
Core fragments	881	19·2
	4,573	

THE TUFF ABOVE THE UPPER OCCUPATION FLOOR

This tuff, which was approximately 2½ ft. thick, yielded a number of artefacts and a few small fragments of mammalian bones. These were diffused throughout the deposit in a similar manner to the remains in the tuff between the Upper and Lower Occupation Floors.

THE INDUSTRY

This series of artefacts consists of only twenty-three tools, fifty-three utilised pieces and 657 *débitage*. The tools are indistinguishable from those found in the underlying levels and will be described only briefly. They consist of the following:

(*a*) A small end chopper made on a quartzite pebble. The working edge is sharp and jagged, but trimmed from one direction only. (47 × 40 × 26 mm. Edge/circumference ratio 30 per cent.)

(b) A small discoid made from coarse-grained quartzite, with a working edge on the entire circumference. (34 × 33 × 23 mm.)

(c) A spheroid, battered on the whole exterior, although projecting ridges have been only partly reduced. (50 × 47 × 38 mm.)

(d) Seven subspheroids. These are generally angular, but show a degree of battering on the projecting parts. The mean diameters range from 42 to 24 mm., with an average of 34 mm.

(e) Light-duty scrapers. There are eleven examples, including two nosed, four side, two that are approximately discoidal, two perimetal and one end scrapers. The average length/breadth measurements for the series are 33 × 26 mm.

(f) Two small flakes with trimming on the dorsal aspect of both lateral edges. (23 × 20 mm. and 31 × 27 mm.)

There is only one utilised heavy-duty block of quartzite, although light-duty flakes are unusually plentiful. They amount to fifty-two, comprising nine with utilisation on approximately straight edges, twenty-three with concave or notched edges, twelve with convex edges and eight miscellaneous examples. The average length/breadth measurements for the fifty-two specimens are 34 × 27 mm.

The *débitage* consists of thirty-eight complete flakes, 462 broken flakes and chips and 157 core fragments. With the exception of six complete and seven broken lava flakes, the entire series is of quartz and quartzite. All the complete flakes are divergent, twelve are side-struck (30 per cent). The average length/breadth measurements are: end-struck 36 × 28 mm., side-struck 32 × 39 mm.

Analysis of the industry from the tuff above the Upper Floor at TK

	Nos.	%
Tools	23	3·1
Utilised material	53	7·2
Débitage	657	89·6
	733	
Tools		
Side-chopper	1	4·3
Discoid	1	4·3
Spheroid	1	4·3
Subspheroids	7	30·5
Scrapers, light-duty	11	47·8
Laterally trimmed flakes	2	8·7
	23	
Utilised material		
Block	1	1·9
Light-duty flakes and other fragments	52	98·1
	53	
Débitage		
Whole flakes	38	5·8
Broken flakes and chips	462	70·3
Core fragments	157	23·9
	657	

Analysis of the combined industries from the five levels at TK

	Nos.	%
Tools	490	4·8
Utilised material	540	5·3
Débitage	9,086	89·8
	10,116	
Tools		
Side choppers	27	5·5
End choppers	10	2·0
Two-edged choppers	5	1·0
Bifaces, including broken and unfinished	41	8·4
Polyhedrons	4	0·8
Discoids	11	2·2
Spheroids	21	4·3
Subspheroids	96	19·6
Modified battered nodules and blocks	55	11·2
Scrapers, heavy-duty	23	4·7
Scrapers, light-duty	134	27·3
Burins	18	3·7
Awls	34	6·9
Outils écaillés	2	0·4
Laterally trimmed flakes	9	1·8
	490	
Utilised material		
'Anvils'	11	2·0
Hammerstones	17	3·1
Cobblestones	28	5·2
Nodules and blocks	21	3·9
Heavy-duty flakes	5	0·9
Light-duty flakes and other fragments	458	84·8
	540	
Débitage		
Whole flakes	368	4·0
Re-sharpening flake	1	0·01
Broken flakes and chips	7,126	78·4
Core fragments	1,591	17·5
	9,086	

2. SITE BK (BELL'S KORONGO)

Archaeological number (66)   Geologic locality 94

The gullies known as BK are situated on the right bank of the Side Gorge, approximately 2 miles above the confluence of the two gorges. The area was first recorded as being particularly rich in fossil bones during 1935 and the gullies were named after Mr G. T. Bell, who was then attached to the Olduvai expedition in order to collect birds on behalf of the British Museum of Natural History. Among the earliest finds at this site was a

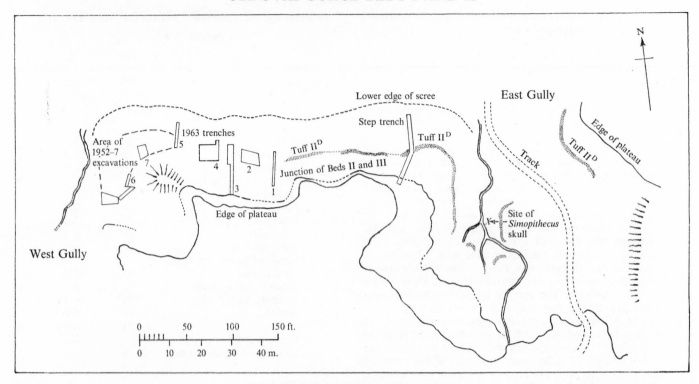

Fig. 92. BK. Sketch map of the site.

particularly fine pair of horn cores of *Pelorovis oldowayensis* and parts of *Libytherium* 'antlers'.

The site consists of two erosion gullies linked by a short cliff which runs parallel to the river course (Fig. 92). Beds II, III and IV are exposed in the two gullies and also in the intervening cliff, although Bed IV has been largely denuded. Fossil bones and artefacts may be found on the surface of Bed II in both gullies, with unusually rich concentrations in certain localities; notably on the scree of Bed II at the mouth of the western gully, where the first excavations were undertaken, and at approximately the same level on both sides of the eastern gully. It was, in fact, from this second area that the skull of a *Simopithecus* bearing a depressed fracture, which is described in chapter VIII, was obtained in 1955.

The maximum exposed thickness of Bed II at BK is approximately 30 ft., not including the lower levels, which are nowhere visible and which were not located when a trial pit was sunk 12 ft. below the lowest point of the exposures.

Although the principal site was first described as representing 'a low level in Bed II', the detailed study of the stratigraphy which has now been carried out indicates clearly that it lies high in Bed II and that, in fact, it represents the highest known occupation site in Bed II, approximately 25 ft. higher in the sequence than Site SHK. The original misconception of the stratigraphic position was in large part due to erroneous identification of Tuff II^D with a tuff that occurs at the base of Bed II at HWK and elsewhere, to which it bears a strong superficial resemblance.

Prior to 1963 work was carried out at this site for short periods during 1952, 1953, 1955 and 1957. Shortage of funds precluded long visits to the Gorge and necessitated more hurried digging than was desirable. During 1957, however, two months were spent at the site and excavations were also carried out at SHK, approximately half a mile down the Gorge from BK. During the four successive seasons an area approximately 100 ft. long and 20–30 ft. wide was eventually dug. This yielded very rich cultural and faunal assemblages, including large numbers of horn cores of the giant

198

bovid *Pelorovis oldowayensis* and numerous remains of Suidae. Two hominid teeth of australopithecine type were also found during 1955.

During the earlier excavations the site was interpreted as representing a camping place of early man adjacent to a river channel or swamp, in which the majority of the remains of *Pelorovis* were found (Pl. 23). The detailed stratigraphy was by no means clear, however, and in 1963 it was decided that further excavations should be undertaken. A series of trenches was therefore dug along the cliff face between the two gullies, from the area of the original excavations eastwards to a point where Tuff II^D is exposed, in order to ascertain the relationship of the implementiferous and fossil-bearing levels to this marker tuff (Fig. 93). It soon became apparent that not only the clay in which the *Pelorovis* remains had been found but also the whole series of tuffs, clays, silts, sands and gravels in which artefacts and fossils occurred represented the filling of an old river channel which could be seen to cut out Tuff II^D in the most easterly of the trial cuttings. Evidence of cross-bedding indicates the probability that the river flowed in a general south-west/north-east direction, with a maximum depth of the channel in the excavated area of 8½ ft. The western bank of the old channel could not be identified and appears to have been destroyed by the present gully. However, substantial blocks of Tuff II^D, which may be seen in the face of one of the earlier trenches, indicate that it was probably not far distant from the most westerly point of the excavations. The distance between the eastern and western limits of the channel, as exposed by excavation, is approximately 400 ft., but since the line of trenches is diagonal to the inferred direction of the channel the transverse measurement must have been considerably less (Fig. 93).

Attempts to establish a sequence within the channel proved impossible owing to the extent of cross-bedding. The whole deposit has therefore been considered as a single unit. It varies from coarse sand and gravel, with occasional ferruginised bands, to fine silts and clays. The cultural material has likewise been regarded as belonging to a single industrial phase.

A few of the artefacts and bones from the coarser horizons are rolled, but these form a negligible proportion of the whole and it is clear that the occupation debris had not been transported far enough for it to become abraded: probably only from a camp site on the bank of the river.

The more complete remains of *Pelorovis oldowayensis*, of which parts of twenty-four individuals were recovered, were found in the clay filling of a channel which seems to represent a swamp or quiet backwater adjoining the main river. In the case of one virtually complete skeleton, which was mainly articulated, the limb bones were found standing vertically in the clay, at a lower level than the trunk and head, indicating that the animal had almost certainly died in a standing position after having become engulfed in the mud. Choppers and other tools, including one biface, were found close by, and the suggestion put forward some years ago by L. S. B. Leakey that the animals had been driven into the swamp by early man and then slaughtered, seems likely to be correct.

THE INDUSTRY

The industry from this site was originally described as 'Chellean' (Leakey, L. S. B., 1957). It is now referred to the Developed Oldowan B.

In the following description the total assemblage from all the excavations has been considered, but for the final analysis only the 1963 material has been considered, since this is known to represent a total assemblage which can be compared on an equal basis with material from other sites excavated since 1960. For the analysis of raw materials, however, all the available material has been considered.

Subspheroids are the most numerous tools in this assemblage and amount to 24·4 per cent of the 1963 material. They are followed by light-duty scrapers (14·6 per cent) and modified battered nodules and blocks (12·9 per cent). Side choppers constitute only 8·9 per cent and other types of choppers are both scarce and generally poorly made, but they include a number of diminutive specimens. Awls and *outils écaillés* are more

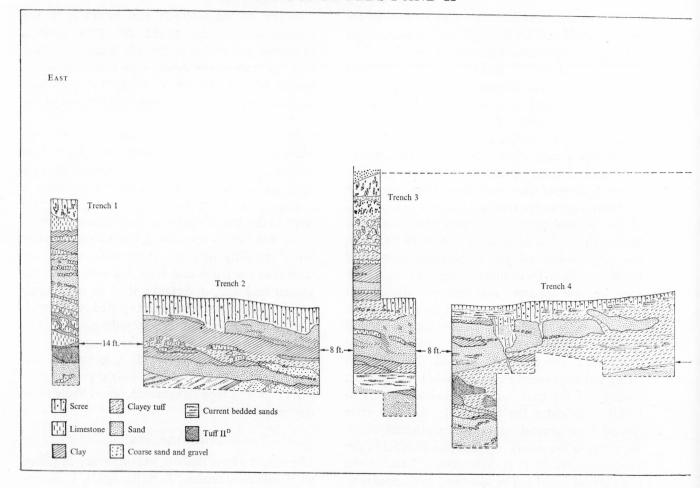

EAST

Trench 1

Trench 2

Trench 3

Trench 4

←—— 14 ft. ——→ ←— 8 ft.— ←— 8 ft.—

Scree   Clayey tuff   Current bedded sands

Limestone   Sand   Tuff II^D

Clay   Coarse sand and gravel

plentiful than in any of the earlier assemblages, with 6·2 and 5·1 per cent respectively. Quartz and quartzite were extensively used for all types of tools, including choppers, of which only 13 per cent are of lava.

TOOLS

Side choppers (164 specimens)

The side choppers here, as at SHK, can be divided conveniently into those made on rounded cobbles and those made on angular blocks. A proportion of the former has also served as hammerstones. Nine examples are rolled.

Side choppers made on cobblestones (72 specimens). Twenty-three examples are made from quartz and quartzite and the balance from lava. In the majority the working edges are trimmed by means of multiple bifacial flaking, but there are also four unifacial examples in which the edges are

flaked on one face only, with cortex on the opposite face. In a further four examples there is multiple flaking on one face, opposed to a single negative scar on the obverse. The edges in these eight specimens are noticeably more even than in the bifacial series with multiple flaking. Chipping and blunting due to utilisation are generally present. The length/breadth/thickness measurements for these choppers range from 111 × 122 × 69 mm. to 25 × 34 × 21 mm., with an average of 60 × 73 × 47 mm., and the mean diameters vary from 100 to 26 mm., the average being 59 mm. The edge/circumference ratio varies from 76 to 21 per cent, with an average of 41 per cent. (Fig. 94, nos. 13–17.)

Side choppers made on blocks (92 specimens). One example is made of horneblende gneiss, one of lava and the balance of quartz and quartzite. With the exception of two unifacial specimens, the working edges have been prepared by means of multiple bifacial flaking. The edges are generally jagged, as in the cobble-choppers, but there are also a number of examples with wide, curved edges which are relatively even, the projecting points between inter-

200

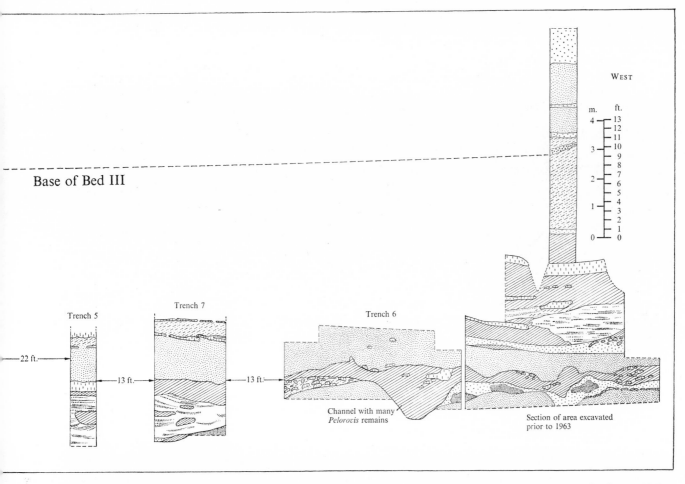

West

m. ft.

Base of Bed III

Trench 5

Trench 7

Trench 6

22 ft.

13 ft.

13 ft.

Channel with many
Pelorovis remains

Section of area excavated
prior to 1963

Fig. 93. BK. Sections exposed in the southern faces of Trenches 1 to 7 and in part of the area excavated prior to 1963.

secting flake scars having been removed by secondary retouch. In the majority of specimens the butt ends are formed by a transverse vertical fracture or a negative flake scar, trimmed and battered on the upper and lower edges. The length/breadth/thickness measurements range from 103 × 96 × 72 mm. to 24 × 32 × 16 mm., with an average of 49 × 57 × 40 mm., and the mean diameters vary from 90 to 27 mm., with an average of 48 mm. The edge/circumference ratios vary from 71 to 25 per cent, with an average of 48 per cent. (Fig. 94, nos. 1–12.)

The average edge/circumference ratio for these choppers is thus 7 per cent higher than for those made on cobblestones, the figures being 41 and 48 per cent respectively. The overall size, however, is considerably greater, with an average mean diameter for the cobble-choppers of 59 mm. in contrast to 48 mm. for those made on blocks.

End choppers (*27 specimens*)

Fourteen examples are made of quartz and quartzite, one of hornblende gneiss, one of quartzo-feldspathic gneiss and the balance of lava. Three specimens are uni-

facial, with the flakes struck from cortex surface. Four others have one large flake scar on one face, from which multiple flakes have been struck on the obverse. There is only one example which shows hammerstone utilisation. In the bifacial specimens with multiple flaking the edges are mainly sharp and jagged but also show some chipping and blunting due to use. Eighteen examples are made on rounded cobblestones and these, as with side choppers, are slightly larger in overall size than those made on blocks, although the edge/circumference ratios are considerably lower, owing to the working edges being narrow in proportion to the width of the specimens. The average mean diameter for the cobblestone series is 65 mm. and for the series made on blocks 55 mm. There is no appreciable difference in the relative length of the working edges to the circumferences in the two series. The length/breadth/ thickness measurements range from 127 × 75 × 71 mm. to 43 × 28 × 24 mm., with an average of 73 × 58 × 49 mm., and the mean diameters vary from 98 to 31 mm., with an average of 60 mm. The edge/circumference ratios vary from 50 to 19 per cent, with an average of 31 per cent. (Fig. 95, nos. 1–3.)

201

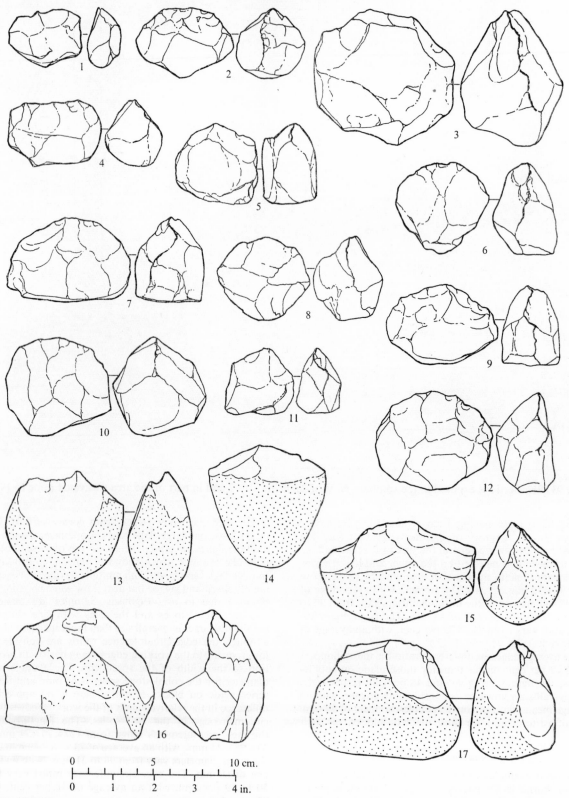

Fig. 94. BK. Diagrams of side choppers. (1) to (12) are made of quartz or quartzite blocks and (13) to (17) on lava cobbles.

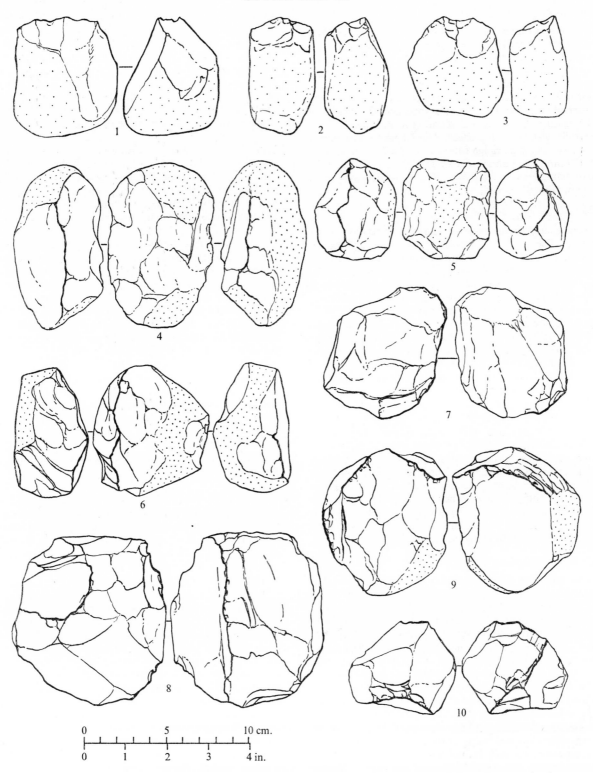

Fig. 95. BK. Diagrams of choppers and polyhedrons. (1) to (3) end choppers; (4) and (5) two-edged choppers; (6) to (10) polyhedrons.

Two-edged choppers (29 specimens)

Thirteen examples are made from quartz or quartzite and sixteen from lava. Three are rolled. The working edges are generally bifacially flaked and are usually situated on either lateral edge. In five examples, however, the working edges are on one lateral edge and at one end. Two of these lie at right angles, as in chisel-edged choppers. The general form is variable and most of the lava specimens are made on cobblestones. Chipping and blunting from utilisation are generally visible on the edges. The length/breadth/thickness measurements range from $116 \times 87 \times 73$ mm. to $44 \times 37 \times 29$ mm., with an average of $75 \times 60 \times 50$ mm., and the mean diameters vary from 94 to 36 mm., with an average of 61 mm. (Fig. 95, nos. 4, 5.)

Chisel-edged choppers (10 specimens)

Four examples are made of quartz or quartzite and six of lava. The working edges are proportionately shorter than in either the side or end choppers and lie at right angles to the upper and lower faces. They have usually been trimmed by means of multiple bifacial flaking but in three examples there is a single negative scar on one face, opposed to multiple scars on the opposite face. Two specimens are rolled and three have been used as hammerstones. The length/breadth/thickness measurements range from $103 \times 84 \times 72$ mm. to $44 \times 45 \times 30$ mm., with an average of $76 \times 73 \times 51$ mm.. and the mean diameters vary from 83 to 39 mm. with an average of 65 mm. The average edge/circumference ratio is 16 per cent.

Pointed choppers (2 specimens)

Both examples are made from quartz. The undersurfaces are flat and consist of single negative flake scars while the upper surfaces are steeply trimmed. A sharp median point is present on both specimens. The points are formed by a single negative scar on either side. The edges are slightly chipped by use. The measurements for the two specimens are as follows: length/breadth/thickness $48 \times 65 \times 36$ mm. and $65 \times 56 \times 50$ mm. Mean diameters 45 mm. and 57 mm. Edge/circumference ratios 41 and 49 per cent.

Bifaces (80 specimens)

The series of bifaces includes a high proportion of diminutive quartz and quartzite specimens similar to those described from the Upper Occupation Floor at TK. Only two examples are rolled. Even at this site there is a complete absence of 'wood technique' flaking and the trimming scars are generally deeply indented and often plunging. The series is crude on the whole and, apart from a small number of the better-finished specimens (mostly ovates), there is such individual variation that classification is difficult. It is possible, however, to subdivide the collection as follows: ovates and irregular ovates, diminutive bifaces of various forms, medium-size bifaces of various forms, trihedral specimens, oblong picks, a single cleaver and a single heavy-duty pick (Fig. 101). The broken specimens include tip and butt ends and also median parts with butt ends, lacking the tips.

Ovates and irregular ovates (11 specimens). This series is made entirely from lava and includes five elongate specimens with slender points that are the most symmetrical and highly finished bifaces from the site. Two of these are made from end-struck flakes. There is also a crude specimen, larger than the average ($175 \times 113 \times 63$ mm.), made almost entirely by means of step-flaking (Fig. 99), together with five small bifaces for which the average length/breadth/thickness measurements are $89 \times 59 \times 30$ mm. These are less symmetrical and less well-made than the larger specimens.

Trihedral bifaces (3 specimens). All three examples are made on side-struck lava flakes. The primary flake surfaces have received a minimum of trimming and there is a longitudinal ridge on the dorsal aspect. The points are relatively sharp and in two examples the dorsal crest rises at the butt end to form a heel. (Fig. 96, nos. 6, 7; Fig. 100, no. 8.)

Diminutive bifaces, various (29 specimens). All these specimens are made from quartz or quartzite. They are generally stumpy and thick in cross-section. None exceeds 50 mm. in mean diameter. The whole series is crude and there is a considerable variety of forms: some resemble miniature ovates, others are bluntly pointed at both ends and others pointed at the tips with square butts. There are also a few subtriangular examples. The average mean diameter for the series is 39 mm. (Fig. 100, nos. 1–6.)

Medium-sized bifaces, various (11 specimens). Three examples are of lava and the balance of quartz and quartzite. There is the same variation in form as in the diminutive series. In both groups this variability appears to be due to crude workmanship rather than to deliberate shaping. Two specimens are made on end-struck flakes and the balance on cores. The average mean diameter for this group is 58 mm.

Cleaver (1 specimen). This consists of a quadrilateral side-struck lava flake. The striking platform extends along the greater part of one lateral edge and has been crudely trimmed. Apart from some minor chipping at the edges, caused by use, there is no further retouch. The material is coarse-grained and faulty, resulting in marked irregularities on the primary flake surface. (Fig. 96, no. 1.)

Oblong picks (9 specimens). Five examples are made from quartz and quartzite and four from lava. With the exception of one lava specimen which is biconvex in cross-section, these tools are steeply flaked along both lateral edges on the upper face from a flat under-surface. In four examples the lateral trimming does not meet along the centre line and the cross-section is quadrilateral, with a central flat area on the dorsal aspect. In the remaining specimens the under-surfaces are flat and there is a longitudinal dorsal crest at the points and for part of the length, resulting in a triangular cross-section. Four examples are made on flakes. In two examples, made from lava, the butt ends consist of vertical fractures which project upwards forming a heel. The points are generally sharp with relatively fine retouch along both edges. The flaking is otherwise minimal and crude. (Fig. 96, nos. 8 to 10 and Fig. 100, no. 7.)

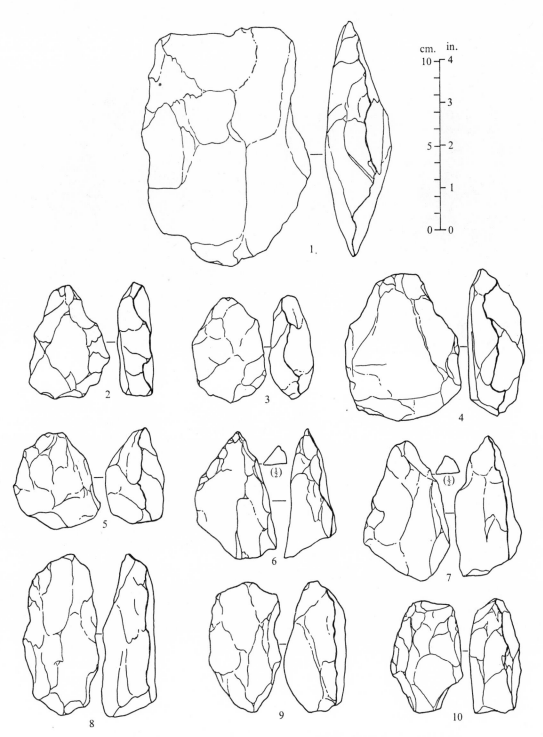

Fig. 96. BK. Diagrams of (1) a cleaver, (2) to (7) bifaces; (8) to (10) oblong picks.
(Nos. 6 and 7 are trihedral specimens.)

205

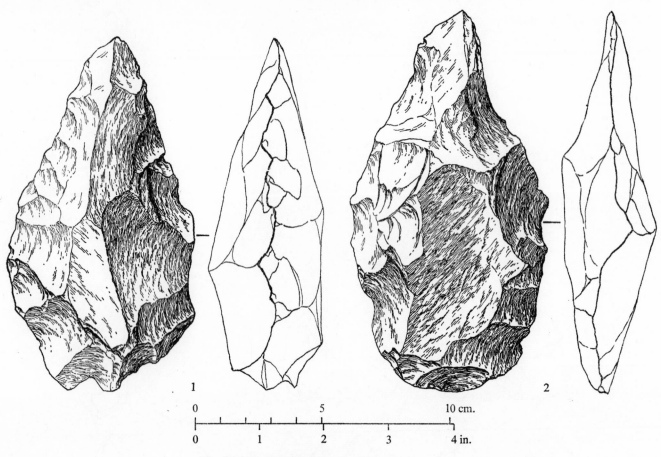

Fig. 97. BK. Two irregular ovates made from lava.

The complete bifaces

	Length/breadth/ thickness (mm.)	Mean diameter (mm.)	Breadth/ length/ ratio (%)	Thickness/ length ratio (%)	Totals
Ovates and irregular ovates					
Range	175 × 113 × 63 to 81 × 56 × 26	110–52	69–49	39–22	11
Average	121 × 71 × 37	72	61	31	
Trihedral bifaces					
Range	120 × 70 × 43 to 80 × 44 × 31	77–51	59–35	44–35	3
Average	95 × 55 × 37	62	57	39	
Diminutive bifaces					
Range	61 × 51 × 37 to 44 × 28 × 13	49–28	97–66	64–31	29
Average	52 × 40 × 25	39	77	49	
Medium-sized bifaces					
Range	90 × 68 × 54 to 69 × 44 × 35	70–49	96–60	60–28	11
Average	80 × 60 × 38	58	74	48	
Cleaver	145 × 97 × 37	93	66	25	1
Oblong picks					
Range	94 × 58 × 41 to 58 × 38 × 31	64–38	75–46	62–31	9
Average	75 × 45 × 34	51	60	47	
Heavy-duty pick	125 × 103 × 71	99	83	56	1
Total					65

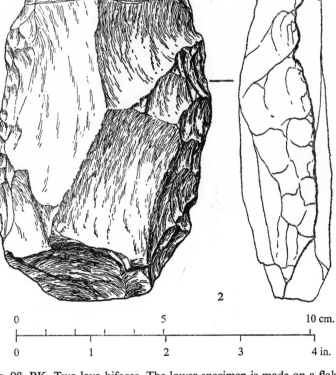

0				5				10 cm.

0	1	2	3	4 in.

Fig. 98. BK. Two lava bifaces. The lower specimen is made on a flake.

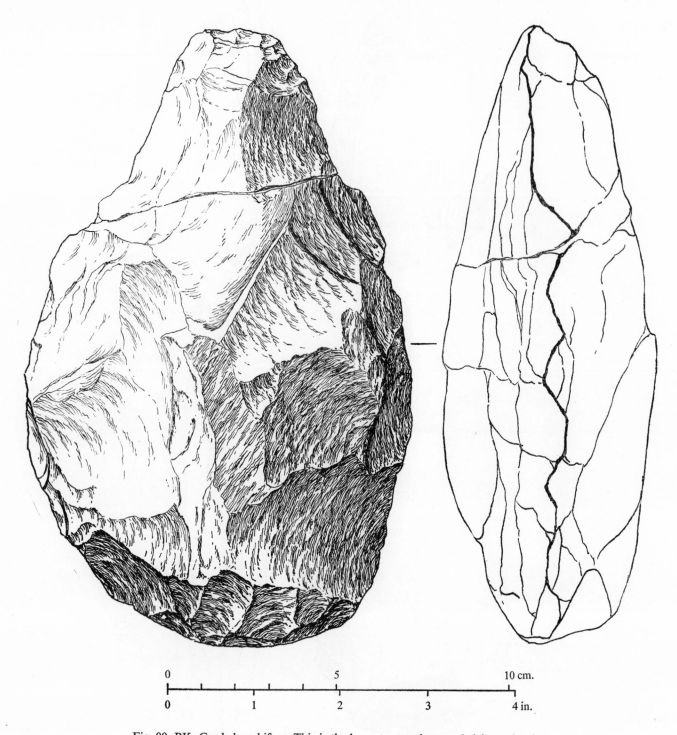

Fig. 99. BK. Crude lava biface. This is the largest example recorded from the site.

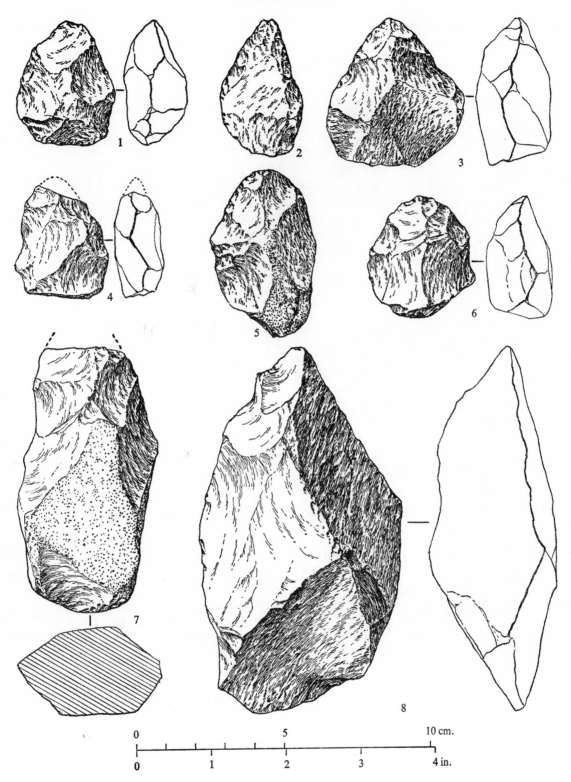

Fig. 100. BK. Bifaces. (1) to (6) diminutive quartz specimens; (7) oblong pick with broken tip, made from lava: (8) crude trihedral specimen made on a lava flake.

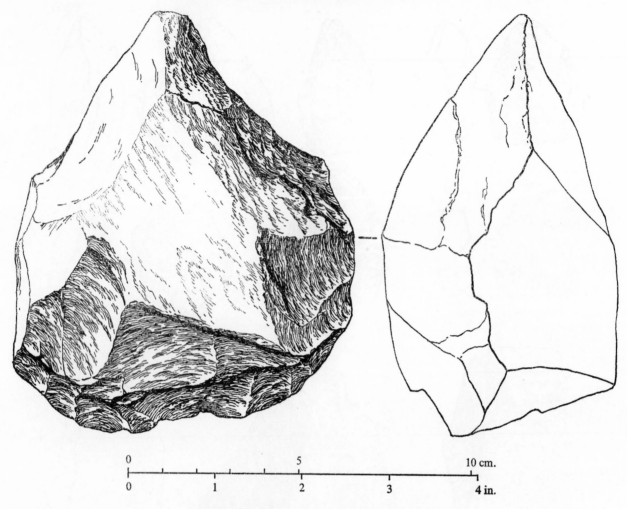

Fig. 101. BK. Heavy-duty pick made from gneiss.

Heavy-duty pick (*1 specimen*). This tool is made from gneiss. The butt is thick and massive and the under-surface flat, with a minimum of flaking. The tool tapers rapidly to a sharp point which is formed by a single deeply indented flake scar on either side. (Fig. 101.)

Broken and unfinished bifaces (*13 specimens*). These consist of six bifacially flaked points, broken transversely, all of which are of quartz or quartzite, one butt end, four crude specimens lacking the tips, and two crudely flaked examples which are probably unfinished.

Polyhedrons (*40 specimens*)

Nineteen examples are of quartz or quartzite and the balance of lava. Six of the latter exhibit areas of smooth cortex surface, indicating that they were made from cobbles. In the majority there are three principal edges with the addition of one or more that are shorter and subsidiary. Most of the series is in sharp, fresh condition and utilisation has resulted in chipping rather than blunting of the

edges. Three specimens are rolled. The mean diameters range from 107 to 32 mm., with an average of 64 mm. (Fig. 95, nos. 6–10.)

Discoids (*106 specimens*)

Eighteen examples are of lava, five of gneiss (including one similar to the variety found at Kelogi), one of pegmatite and the balance of quartz and quartzite. Eight specimens are rolled. The series includes both crude, irregular-shaped examples and others that are well-made and symmetrical. Most of these tools are biconvex in cross-section but they are generally more markedly convex on one face than the other. Thirteen specimens are plano-convex, with flat under-surfaces and relatively high backs. The whole series shows radial bifacial flaking. The edges are jagged as in choppers, with a minimum of secondary chipping, except in four small specimens which are elliptical in cross-section and have been finely trimmed on the circumference. In fifty examples the flaking extends round the entire circumference. The edge/circumference ratio for

210

the whole series is 97·5 per cent. One specimen is made on a large, thick flake which has been trimmed on the greater part of the circumference although the bulb has been retained. Another specimen is unusually well made and symmetrical, with regular and evenly spaced radial trimming scars and a series of crushed notches on the circumference, forming a denticulated edge. The mean diameters range from 108 to 20 mm., with an average of 52 mm. (Fig. 102.)

Spheroids (60 specimens)

Six examples are made from gneiss, eleven from lava and the balance from quartz and quartzite. The series includes both battered and faceted specimens. There are also four examples of symmetrical stone balls, smoothly rounded over the whole exterior. The mean diameters range from 114 to 31 mm., with an average of 69 mm. (Pl. 24.)

Subspheroids (386 specimens)

Eleven examples are made from gneiss, four of which are similar to the variety found at Kelogi, thirty from lava and the balance from quartz and quartzite. The tools in this series are spherical in general form, but somewhat irregular. Ridges and projecting parts have usually been reduced by battering, but a few of the specimens are sharply angular. The mean diameters range from 119 to 22 mm., with an average of 52 mm. Unusually large, heavy examples, such as were found at MNK and SHK, are not represented. (Pl. 25.)

Modified battered nodules and blocks (189 specimens)

Eight specimens are made from horneblende gneiss, four from quartzo-feldspathic gneiss, two from lava and the balance from quartz and quartzite. These tools do not conform to any particular shape, but are characterised by battering and blunting on edges and projections. The mean diameters range from 86 to 24 mm., with an average of 51 mm.

Scrapers, heavy duty (64 specimens)

Eight examples are made from lava, six from horneblende gneiss, five from quartzo-feldspathic gneiss and forty-five from quartz or quartzite. Ten are made on cobblestones and seven on pieces of tabular quartz. Most of the specimens are high-backed with flat under-surfaces, usually consisting of a natural cleavage plane but sometimes of a negative flake scar or cortex surface. The working edges are generally rounded but are not evenly curved and often exhibit small pointed projections as well as crushed indentations. The trimming is steep and the edges are often blunted and chipped by use on the upper face. Additional utilisation is sometimes visible on other parts of the tools. Three examples are rolled. Twenty-six examples are made on sub-angular blocks of no particular form, but with steep trimming along one or more edges. Seventeen are side scrapers, three of which are double-edged. Thirteen are discoidal and six perimetal. There are also four hollow scrapers, two of which occur in combination tools. The side scrapers are of the usual form, with convex or nearly straight working edges. In the double-edged examples the edges are trimmed from reverse directions. The discoidal and perimetal varieties conform closely in type to those described previously: the former are roughly circular but are trimmed on only part of the circumference, whilst the latter are trimmed all round but vary greatly in shape. They include some triangular specimens. The two hollow scrapers that are combined with other tools are described below. A further two examples consist of a broken quartz flake with a single chipped indentation on one edge, measuring 23 mm. in width and 4 mm. in depth, and part of a lava cobblestone with two chipped and crushed indentations on one edge, 65 mm. apart and separated by a marked projection. These notches measure 47 × 11 mm. and 21 × 4 mm. respectively.

There are also three combination scrapers. These consist of: (*a*) a side scraper with hollow scraper, (*b*) an end chopper with hollow scraper and (*c*) an end chopper with scraper. The first specimen, made on a fragment of tabular quartzite measuring 91 × 72 × 27 mm., has an uneven scraping edge 122 mm. long on one side, together with an unusually deep chipped indentation, 31 × 9·5 mm., at one end. In the combined end chopper and hollow scraper there is a jagged, bifacially flaked and curved chopper edge 94 mm. long at one extremity, together with an indentation 23 mm. wide and 5 mm. deep on one lateral edge. In the third specimen, made from horneblende gneiss, there is a rounded scraping edge, measuring 88 mm. in length, steeply trimmed from a flat under-surface at one extremity, combined with a jagged bifacially flaked chopper edge at the opposite end. (73 × 72 × 61 mm.)

The following are the measurements in millimetres of the heavy-duty scrapers:

	Range	Average	Totals
Formless	97 × 84 to 52 × 60	69 × 68	26
Side	71 × 95 to 49 × 58	58 × 86	17
Discoidal	84 × 78 to 51 × 44	61 × 59	13
Perimetal	93 × 77 to 66 × 50	71 × 56	6
Hollow	147 × 87 to 82 × 59	114 × 73	2
Total			64

Scrapers, light-duty (215 specimens)

Light-duty scrapers are well represented and comprise end, side, discoidal, nosed, perimetal and hollow varieties. Side scrapers are by far the most numerous, with ninety-eight examples. Four specimens are rolled.

End scrapers (41 specimens). With the exception of two lava specimens, these tools are made from quartz or quartzite. They are mostly on flakes, although the bulbar extremity has usually been either trimmed away or broken off. Additional trimming is often present on one or both lateral edges. Approximately round-ended specimens predominate, although the edges are not symmetrical or evenly curved. Other examples are also round-ended but have a small projection or spur either in the centre or at one side of the working edge. The remainder are square-ended. The trimming is generally steep and the edges show both blunting and chipping from utilisation. One specimen is rolled. The length/breadth measurements range from 63 × 48 mm. to 25 × 24 mm., with an average of 40 × 32 mm. (Fig. 103, nos. 1–5.)

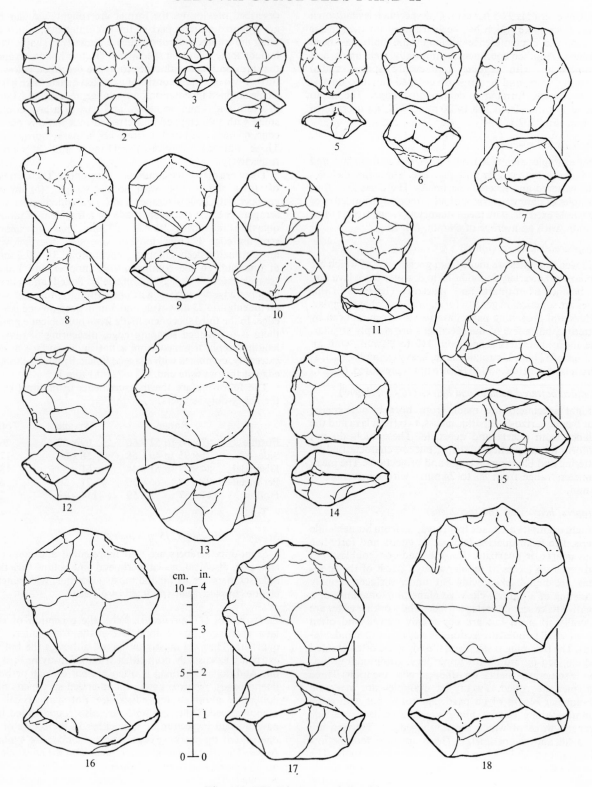

Fig. 102. BK. Diagrams of discoids.

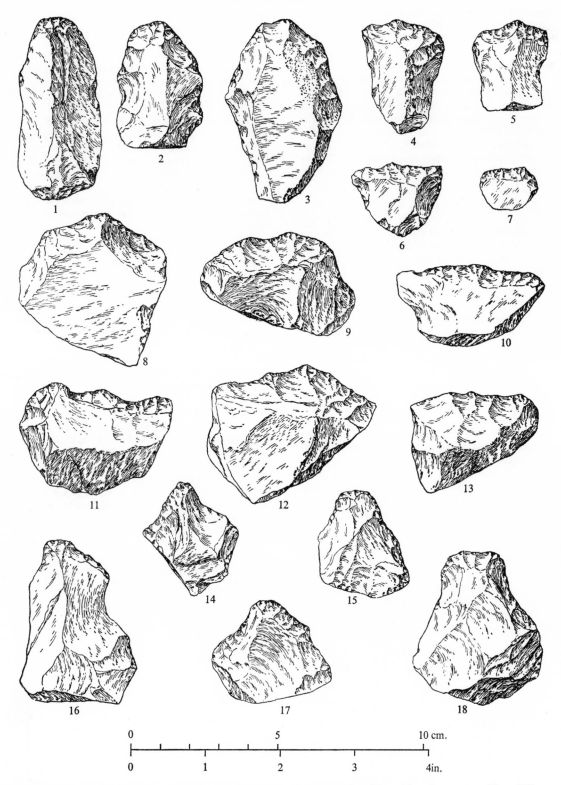

Fig. 103. BK. Light-duty scrapers made from quartz or quartzite. (1) to (5) end scrapers; (6) to (13) side scrapers; (14) to (18) nosed scrapers.

Side scrapers (*98 specimens, including 2 broken*). This series is made from quartz or quartzite, with the exception of one pegmatite specimen. The majority is made on core fragments or parts of flakes, with only a negligible proportion on pieces of tabular quartzite. Most of the specimens have curved working edges and some also show a small projection or spur similar to those noted on a number of the end scrapers. In the remainder the edges are essentially straight, although they show minor irregularities. The trimming is generally steeper than on the end scrapers and a higher proportion is made on cores. Four specimens are rolled. The length/breadth measurements range from 47 × 57 mm. to 18 × 25 mm., with an average of 28 × 40 mm. (Fig. 103, nos. 6–13.)

Discoidal scrapers (*16 specimens*). These tools are all made from quartz or quartzite. They are approximately discoidal, although they are not entirely symmetrical and are usually trimmed on only part of the circumference. The measurements range from 53 × 52 mm. to 19 × 18 mm., with an average of 32 × 32 mm. (Fig. 104, nos. 9–12.)

Nosed scrapers (*28 specimens*). This group is made entirely of quartz or quartzite. The tools are of the usual type, with a median projection on the working edge, generally flanked on either side by a trimmed notch. The trimming is usually steep and often extends along part of the lateral edges. The length/breadth measurements range from 60 × 39 mm. to 27 × 18 mm., with an average of 34 × 33 mm. (Fig. 103, nos. 14–18.)

Perimetal scrapers (*20 specimens*). The whole series is made from quartz or quartzite. Although the bulbs of percussion have been trimmed off in every case, the tools usually appear to have been made on flakes. In three small examples the working edges are trimmed partly from the primary flake surface and partly from the dorsal face, i.e. from reverse directions. The edges are generally blunted and chipped by use. The length/breadth measurements range from 62 × 43 mm. to 24 × 22 mm., with an average of 36 × 30 mm. (Fig. 104, nos. 1–8.)

Hollow scrapers (*12 specimens*). These are all made from quartz or quartzite. They consist of flakes and core fragments with well-defined indentations which appear to have been flaked deliberately. One specimen shows two notches, one on either lateral edge. Two examples are rolled. The length/breadth measurements range from 23 × 5 mm. to 15 × 2·5 mm., with an average of 20 × 3·6 mm. (Fig. 104, nos. 13–17.)

Scraper combination tools (*6 specimens*). All these specimens are made from quartz. They consist of an awl + scraper, a side chopper + scraper, a burin + scraper, an *outil écaillé* + scraper and two end + side scrapers. The awl + scraper is slightly rolled; it measures 66 × 50 mm. and has a steeply trimmed trihedral point at one end, opposed to a scraping edge, which is also steeply trimmed and considerably blunted by use. In the second specimen a small bifacial side chopper is combined with a steeply flaked side scraper on the opposite edge. (40 × 41 mm.) In the third specimen there is a dihedral burin at one end, with a working edge 11 mm. wide and a rounded scraping edge on the opposite

end. (42 × 36 mm.) The fourth specimen consists of a small broken quartz flake which has been trimmed to a shallow scraping edge along one side and has also been used as an *outil écaillé* at one end where it shows typical scaling on both faces. (30 × 20 mm.) The end + side scrapers measure 49 × 33 mm. and 30 × 22 mm. respectively.

Burins (*32 specimens*)

The whole series is made from quartz or quartzite. Twenty-three of the specimens were obtained during the 1963 excavations, although the amount of material from that season is considerably less than from the previous years. It seems probable, therefore, that a number of burins was overlooked among discarded waste during the earlier seasons, since the occurrence of these tools was not suspected and shortage of water prohibited washing the specimens.

Three types of burin are represented, namely dihedral (thirteen specimens), angle burins on broken transverse edges (ten specimens) and angle burins on trimmed transverse edges (eight specimens). There is also a single double-ended angle burin. The working edges are generally sharp, although they show chipped utilisation. The 'frosted' appearance often seen on the edges of other tools is not present.

In the majority of the dihedral specimens there is a single scar on either side of the working edge, whilst the angle burins on broken edges usually exhibit a single longitudinal scar on one lateral edge. In this group the transverse edge may be either at right angles or oblique. When the transverse edges are trimmed, they are usually slightly concave and worked from the primary flake surface. In one example the spall scars extend round on to the under-surface, as in *burins plans*. The length/breadth measurements for the series of thirty-two specimens range from 56 × 55 mm. to 27 × 19 mm., with an average of 35 × 25 mm. The average lengths of the chisel edges in each group are somewhat variable: dihedral, 7·1 mm.; angle burins on broken edges, 5·9 mm.; angle burins on trimmed edges, 8·8 mm. The only double-ended specimen measures 34 × 19 mm. Two spalls have been removed on one lateral edge, from opposite ends, one of which is trimmed and the other formed by the natural cortex surface. The lengths of the two working edges are 7 and 5 mm. respectively. (Fig. 105.)

Awls (*71 specimens*)

With the exception of one rolled chert specimen, the series is made from quartz or quartzite. Only twenty specimens were obtained from excavations prior to 1963, suggesting that a number were accidentally discarded as in the case of burins. These tools are generally made on flakes with small sharp points formed by means of trimmed notches on either side. They are mostly trimmed only on the upper or dorsal aspect but in a few examples the notches are flaked from both the upper and lower faces, in reverse directions. The points are generally situated at the distal ends of the flakes but in a few examples they are present on one lateral edge. Some have been broken across the tip. Three specimens are double-pointed. The length/breadth measurements range from 56 × 47 mm. to 25 × 14 mm., with an average of 34 × 28 mm. (Fig. 106.)

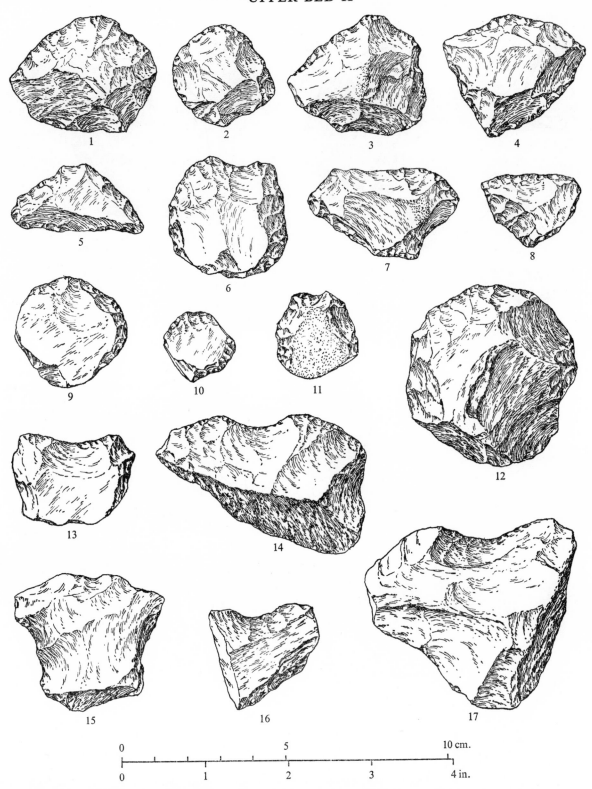

Fig. 104. BK. Light-duty scrapers made from quartz or quartzite. (1) to (8) perimetal scrapers; (9) to (12) discoidal scrapers; (13) to (17) hollow scrapers.

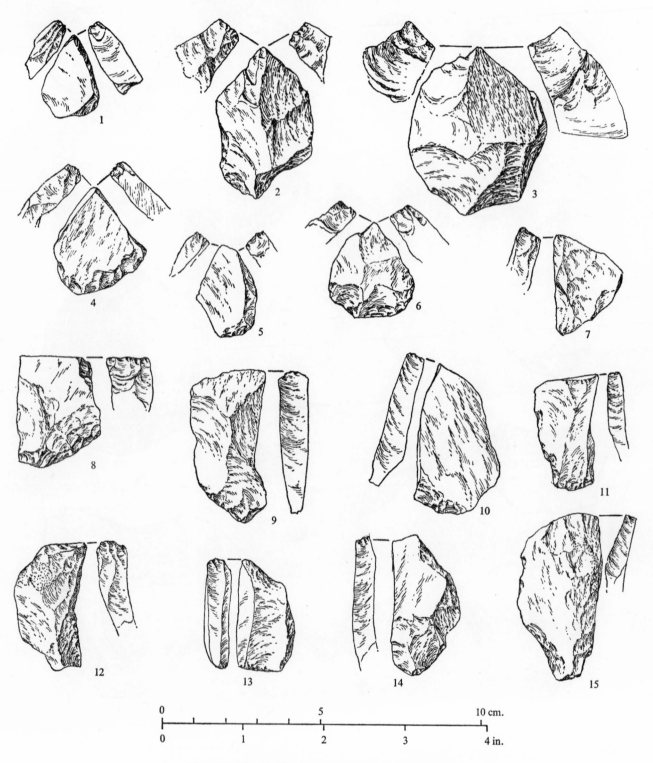

Fig. 105. BK. Burins made from quartz or quartzite.

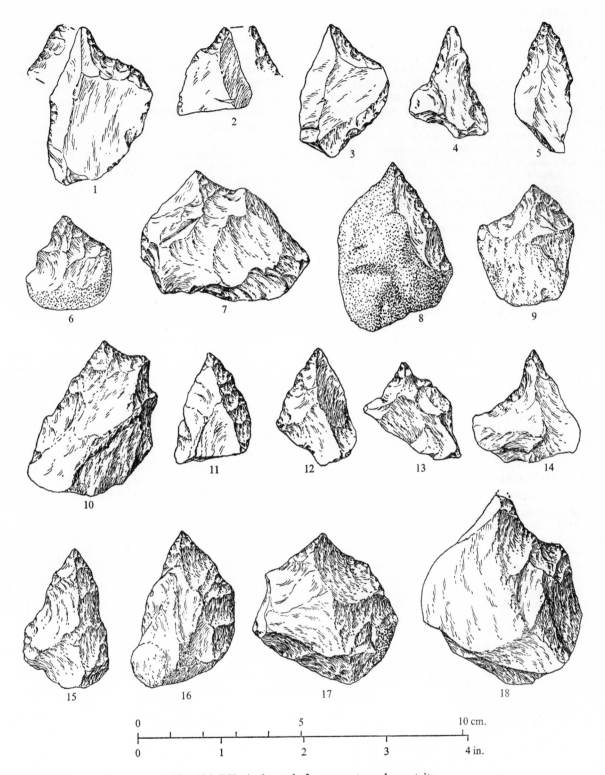

Fig. 106. BK. Awls made from quartz and quartzite.

Outils écaillés (59 specimens)

The whole series is made from quartz or quartzite, generally on parts of flakes or core fragments. As in the case of burins and awls, the fact that thirty-seven of these tools were obtained in 1963, as against a total of twenty-two for all the previous excavations, indicates that a proportion was inadvertently discarded in the earlier years. Double-ended specimens are the most numerous, with thirty-five examples. The scaled working edges are generally blunted and 'frosted'. They are usually only slightly concave or nearly straight, but in twenty examples they have been worn into a marked hollow on one face. Scaling may be present on one or both faces, but is usually more pronounced on one side. In a few of the double-ended specimens the two edges lie at right angles to one another.

The length/breadth measurements range from 65 × 30 mm. to 21 × 17 mm., with an average of 31 × 25 mm., and the lengths of the working edges vary from 29 to 5 mm., with an average of 14 mm. (Fig. 107.)

Laterally trimmed flakes (42 specimens)

These consist of one lava flake and forty-one of quartz or quartzite, in which one or both lateral edges have been retouched. The retouch is usually present on the dorsal face, but in the single lava specimen it is on the lower face only; it varies from steep to shallow. The flakes are variable in form and do not appear to have been trimmed to any particular shape. The tips may be broad, rounded or pointed. Two pointed specimens are trihedral in cross-section. The length/breadth measurements range from 100 × 67 mm. to 30 × 18 mm., with an average of 46 × 31 mm. (Fig. 108.)

UTILISED MATERIAL

'Anvils' (23 specimens)

Three examples are of lava and the remainder of quartz or quartzite. The series includes two pitted specimens, a form of anvil which is rare in the Oldowan and Developed Oldowan. Both examples consist of lava cobbles and exhibit well-defined depressions. The larger of the two specimens measures 107 × 90 × 73 mm. and has an irregular depression 31 × 20 mm. in diameter and 7 mm. deep on one face, which is otherwise flat. The interior of the depression is rough, without any suggestion of abrasive wear. There is a noticeable difference in colouration between the surface of the cobble and the interior of the depression, which appear to have penetrated beyond the weathered crust. In the second specimen there are two circular depressions, one on either face of a small discoidal cobblestone of vesicular lava which measures 56 × 52 × 35 mm. Both depressions are pitted and rough on the interior and measure 23 × 22 mm. and 22 × 24 mm. in diameter, with depths of 6 mm. and 5 mm. respectively.

Most of the remaining anvils consist of circular or cuboid blocks of tabular quartz in which either one or both faces are natural flat cleavage planes. They have been extensively battered on the circumference and also show small circular crushed areas, indicating the points of impact. All the specimens have been artificially shaped prior to use. One example is broken vertically. There is considerable variation in size, from massive specimens weighing up to 4 lb. to diminutive examples of only 3 or 4 oz. The mean diameters range from 103 to 31 mm., with an average of 67 mm.

Hammerstones (43 specimens)

These consist entirely of waterworn cobblestones which have been pitted and battered by use. Nine examples are of quartz, one of hornblende gneiss and the balance of lava. The mean diameters range from 92 to 40 mm., with an average of 62 mm.

Cobblestones (129 specimens)

Twenty-two examples are of quartz or quartzite, three of hornblende gneiss, one of welded tuff and the balance of lava. The type of use has resulted in shattering and cracking rather than the pitting and battering seen on the hammerstones. The mean diameters range from 107 to 28 mm., with an average of 67 mm.

Nodules and blocks (43 specimens)

Thirteen examples are of hornblende gneiss, two of lava and the balance of quartz and quartzite. They consist of irregular angular blocks which have not been artificially shaped but which bear some chipping and blunting on the edges. The mean diameters range from 107 to 40 mm., with an average of 73 mm.

Light-duty utilised flakes and other fragments (452 specimens)

In common with other light-duty material, the number of these specimens recovered in 1963 exceeds that for previous years. Except for one lava flake and one fragment of hornblende gneiss, the entire series is made from quartz and quartzite.

With straight edges (94 specimens). Twenty-nine specimens were recovered prior to 1963 and sixty-five during 1963. The average length/breadth measurements for the 1963 series are 32 × 24 mm., in contrast to 40 × 28 mm. for the material collected previously, a difference of 8 mm. in length and 4 mm. in width. The range in size for the 1963 series is from 77 × 55 mm. to 26 × 19 mm.

With concave edges (147 specimens). Sixty-two examples were recovered prior to 1963 and eighty-five during the excavations that year. The chipping of the notches is generally fine, but a few specimens show coarse and uneven wear. There are four examples with double notches and two with multiple indentations forming denticulated edges. In the 1963 series the length/breadth measurements range from 58 × 42 mm. to 23 × 23 mm., with an average of 37 × 27 mm. The notches range in size from 22 × 3·5 mm. to 10 × 1·5 mm. Measurements of the notches on the series collected prior to 1963 stand very close, but the length/breadth measurements again exceed those for the 1963 series.

218

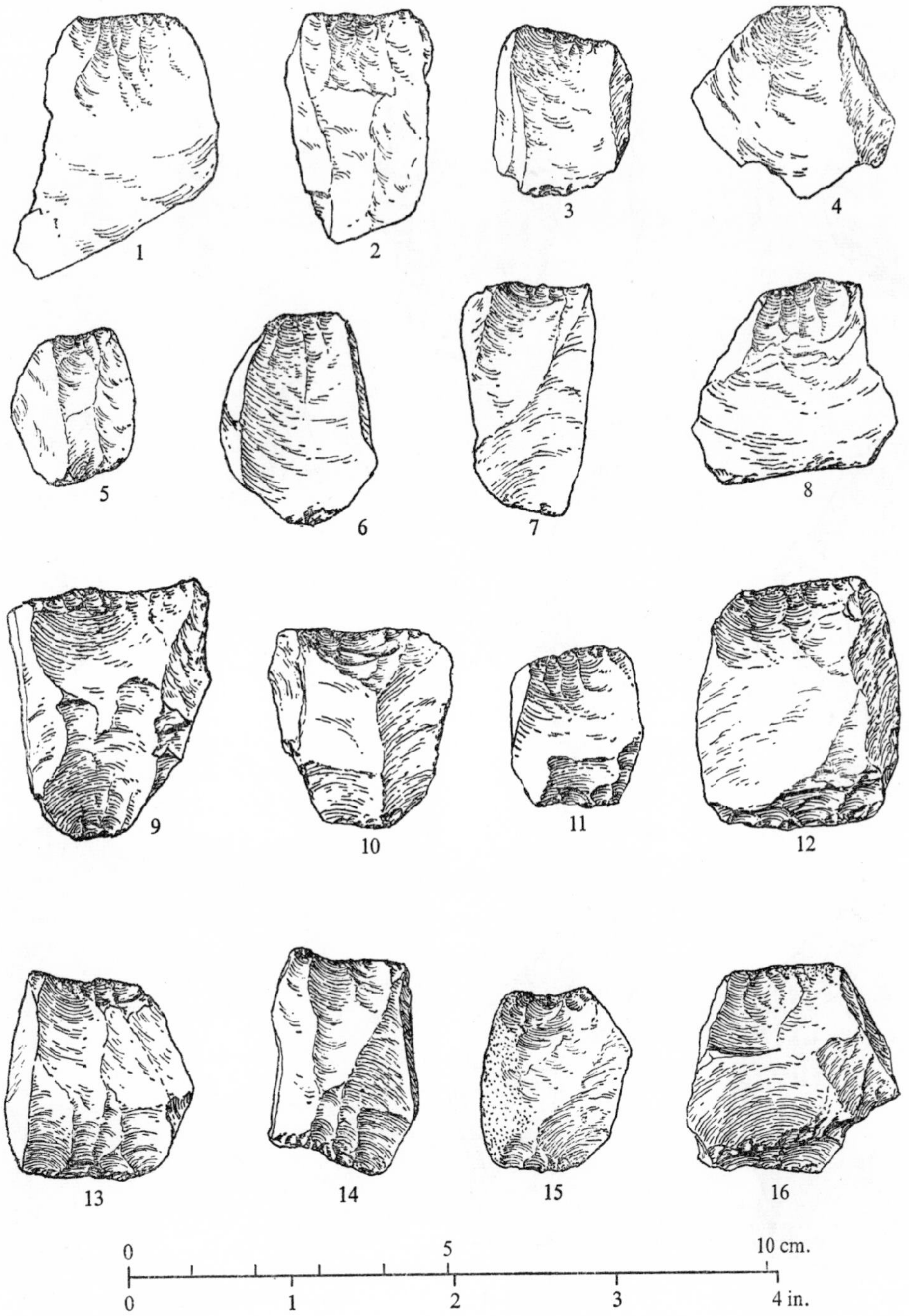

Fig. 107. BK. *Outils écaillés* made from quartz and quartzite. (1) to (8) single-ended; (9) to (16) double-ended.

With convex edges (*134 specimens*). In this group the edges are chipped on both sides and have sometimes become quite blunt. The length/breadth measurements for the 1963 series range from 57 × 49 mm. to 20 × 18 mm., with an average of 33 × 24 mm., a lower figure than for the series collected previously.

Miscellaneous (*77 specimens*). These consist of a variety of whole and broken flakes and other fragments with some traces of utilisation on the edges. The length/breadth measurements range from 57 × 49 mm. to 20 × 18 mm., with an average of 33 × 24 mm. (These figures refer to the 1963 material.)

219

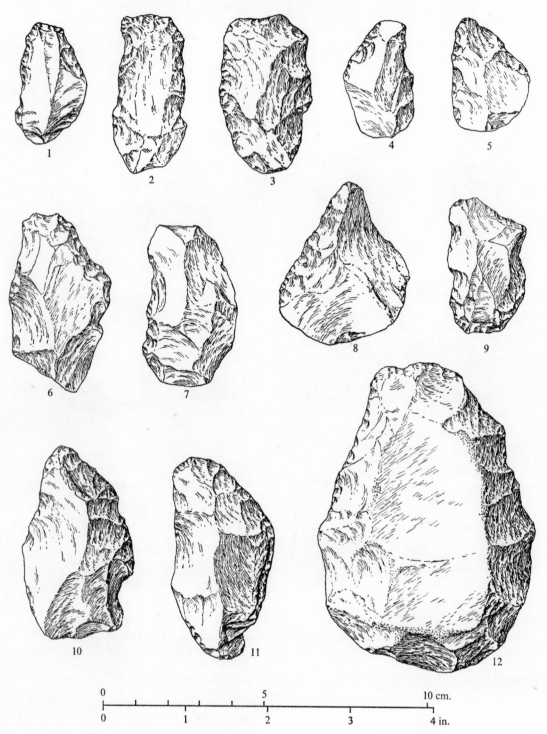

Fig. 108. BK. Laterally trimmed flakes made from quartz and quartzite.

Total débitage

	Whole flakes	Re-sharpening flakes	Broken flakes and chips	Core fragments	Cores	Unspecified waste (discarded)
Prior to 1963						
Lava	75	1	34	13	1	
Quartz/quartzite	337	5	840	244	3	
Gneiss	—	—	—	2	—	4,615
Feldspar	—	—	—	—	—	
Chert	—	—	—	1	—	
1963						
Lava	100	1	127	7	2	
Quartz/quartzite	552	4	4,268	608	6	
Gneiss	—	—	7	1	1	
Feldspar	—	—	1	2	—	
Chert	—	—	—	—	—	
Totals	1,064	11	5,277	878	13	4,615

DEBITAGE

The total *débitage* from all the excavations amounts to 11,858 specimens. (See above table).

In the following description of the *débitage* only the material obtained from the 1963 excavations has been measured and analysed, since the waste material from the earlier excavations now available for study is incomplete.

Whole flakes

Most of the 652 complete flakes from the 1963 excavations are made from quartz; 15·3 per cent are of lava and a small number are of fine-grained quartzite. The flakes are generally irregular and divergent, although there are a few examples that are convergent, with the maximum breadth at the striking platform. End-struck flakes are the commonest form, although side-struck flakes are more numerous than in earlier assemblages from Bed II. They represent 32 per cent of the lava and 27·4 per cent of the quartz/quartzite series. Several of both the end- and side-struck flakes are triangular in shape, of the type noted at SHK, with a greatly reduced striking platform at one point. The length/breadth measurements in millimetres are as follows:

Lava	Range	Average
End-struck	99 × 71 to 25 × 16	49 × 37
Side-struck	80 × 112 to 25 × 28	40 × 51
Quartz/quartzite		
End-struck	82 × 62 to 20 × 13	39 × 29
Side-struck	41 × 44 to 17 × 14	29 × 42

Bulbs of percussion

The bulbs of percussion are generally well marked, although in a proportion of specimens, particularly in the triangular quartz flakes with reduced platforms, they are sometimes shattered. They can be studied in 596 examples, with the following results:

	Lava	Quartz/quartzite
Marked	60·0 %	55·9 %
Slight	29·5 %	31·3 %
Double	5·2 %	10·8 %
Negative	5·2 %	2·0 %
Totals	95	501
		596

Angles of striking platforms

The angles of the striking platforms are proportionately higher in the lava flakes than in the quartz and quartzite specimens. The measurements are as follows:

	Lava	Quartz/quartzite
70–89°	1·2 %	3·3 %
90–109°	36·2 %	59·8 %
110–129°	62·5 %	36·6 %
130°	—	0·3 %
Totals	80	363
		443

Re-sharpening flakes (5 specimens)

One example is made from lava and four from quartz or quartzite. All show a longitudinal dorsal crest. The length/breadth measurements range from 81 × 47 mm. to 43 × 23 mm., with an average of 59 × 35 mm.

Cores (9 specimens)

These consist of formless blocks from which flakes have been struck. They show no evidence of utilisation.

Analysis of the industry from BK obtained in 1963

	Nos.	%
Tools	721	10·6
Utilised material	393	5·7
Débitage	5,687	83·6
	6,801	

Tools		
Side choppers	64	8·9
End choppers	16	2·2
Two-edged choppers	15	2·1
Chisel-edged choppers	6	0·8
Bifaces	38	5·3
Polyhedrons	8	1·1
Discoids	33	4·6
Spheroids	23	3·2
Subspheroids	176	24·4
Modified battered nodules and blocks	93	12·9
Scrapers, heavy-duty	18	2·5
Scrapers, light-duty	105	14·6
Burins	23	3·2
Awls	45	6·2
Outils écaillés	37	5·1
Laterally trimmed flakes	20	2·8
Sundry tool	1	0·1
	721	

	Nos.	%
Utilised material		
'Anvils'	4	1·0
Hammerstones	18	4·6
Cobblestones	83	21·1
Nodules and blocks	25	6·3
Light-duty flakes and other fragments	263	67·0
	393	

Débitage		
Whole flakes	652	11·5
Re-sharpening flakes	5	0·1
Cores	9	0·1
Broken flakes and chips	4,403	77·4
Core fragments	618	10·9
	5,687	

UNMODIFIED COBBLES, NODULES AND BLOCKS

These consist of 394 lava cobbles, pebbles and nodules, seventeen fragments of quartz and quartzite, seven of hornblende gneiss (five of which appear to be identical to the variety found at the Kelogi inselberg) and one small piece of feldspar.

222

PART II

CHAPTER VII

THE DISCOVERIES OF HOMINID REMAINS

In this chapter the facts relating to the discoveries of the various hominid remains from Olduvai have been recorded. Whenever possible, the name of the finder, the stratigraphic horizon, the nature of any associated industry and the factors which led to the discoveries have been given. Parts of no fewer than thirty-three individuals have been found since 1913 when the late Professor H. Reck discovered the complete skeleton buried into the upper part of Bed II, which, for a time, was considered to be of Middle Pleistocene age. For convenience, the hominid specimens have been designated by the letter H. with Arabic numerals, in order to avoid possible confusion with the geological sequence in which the beds are designated by Roman numerals. It will be seen that the greater number of the discoveries was accidental, although once a hominid site had been identified by finding a surface specimen the material was usually substantially augmented by excavation. Three specimens were found as a result of deliberate search for hominid remains: H. 5 from FLK, H. 12 from VEK and H 16 from FLK, Maiko Gully; found respectively by the writer, Margaret Leakey and M. Mutumbo (who also found H. 11). The balance was discovered either in the course of general prospecting or as a result of excavation.

In many respects this chapter would have been appropriate in a later volume in which P. V. Tobias will describe further hominid remains discovered since the cranium of *Australopithecus boisei*. It has been considered preferable, however, to publish it in the present volume, since this includes the correlated sections by R. L. Hay, to which the stratigraphic positions of the remains can be referred, together with accounts of excavations at the various sites and the descriptions of any associated industries.

H. 1, SITE (26a) RK (RECK'S KORONGO), GEOLOGIC LOCALITY 9

The skeleton referred to as H. 1 (and also as 'Reck's man') does not strictly concern the present publication, since it consisted of an intrusive burial, post-dating the primary Olduvai sequence. The skeleton was found by Professor H. Reck during 1913 on his first expedition to Olduvai. It was excavated from deposits in a gully on the northern side of the Gorge, on the north side of the Third Fault. At the time of the discovery it was considered to be contemporaneous with Bed II and was the subject of a prolonged controversy before being finally accepted as an intrusive burial. The skeleton had been buried in a contracted position in a grave dug into the top of Bed II and was overlain by a deposit containing minerals that are found in Bed V. There were no associated grave goods. Had there been, the ensuing controversy might never have arisen. The skull is of *Homo sapiens* type and resembles those of the Kenya Capsian from Gamble's Cave II and Naivasha Railway Rockshelter in Kenya. A living site with a microlithic industry dated about 10,000 B.P. is known to exist within a short distance of the Olduvai burial and it is possible that the two are associated. (It has been stated in various publications that the incisors had been filed, but this appears to be incorrect, the unusual appearance being due to particularly uneven wear.)

References: Foster Cooper (1932); Gieseler and Mollison (1929); Leakey, L. S. B. (1931, 1935); Leakey, Hopwood and Reck (1931); Leakey, Reck, Boswell and Hopwood (1933); Reck 1914*a*, *b*); Vaufrey (1933); Weinert (1939).

H. 2, SITE (71*d*) MNK (MARY NICOL KORONGO), GEOLOGIC LOCALITY 88

Two cranial vault fragments, belonging to a particularly thick skull, were found by the writer in 1935 near the head of the MNK gully where Beds III and IV are exposed (see chapter IV). The gully lies on the right bank of the southern branch of the Gorge and has since yielded further hominid material from Bed II (H. 13, 14, 15). The fragments of H. 2 were found on the surface of the lowest horizon of Bed IV*a* and are in a similar physical condition to numerous mammalian bones derived from this level. Artefacts are also relatively plentiful in the same locality and include bifaces of Acheulean facies. These two fragments compare closely in thickness with H. 9 from Upper Bed II and with H. 12, also from Bed IV*a*, both of which probably represent *Homo erectus*.

References: Leakey, M. D. (1965); Oakley (1964*b*); Tobias (1965*d*).

H. 3, SITE (66) BK (BELL'S KORONGO), GEOLOGIC LOCALITY 94

One molar tooth and one canine were found at this site during excavations carried out by L. S. B. Leakey in 1955. The teeth were obtained from the upper part of the BK channel which cuts into Tuff II^D (see chapter VI). The channel also yielded large numbers of Developed Oldowan B artefacts and well-preserved fossils, belonging to the latest known occupation level in Bed II. At the time when the teeth were discovered, however, the level was considered to be in Lower Bed II and the associated industry was therefore assigned to Stage 1 of the 'Chellean' as defined in 1951. It is, however, entirely characteristic of the Developed Oldowan.

In the first publication announcing the discovery of the teeth L. S. B. Leakey claimed that the molar represented a second left lower deciduous molar. This view was not shared by Robinson, von Koenigswald and others, who preferred to regard it as either a permanent or a deciduous upper molar of australopithecine character.

References: Dahlberg (1960); Leakey (1958*a, b*, 1963, 1965*a, b*); Robinson (1960*a*); Tobias (1965*a, b*); von Koenigswald (1960).

H. 4, SITE (24*a*) MK (MACINNES KORONGO), GEOLOGIC LOCALITY 11

At the end of June 1959, three weeks prior to the discovery of the 'Zinjanthropus' skull, our senior African assistant, H. Mukiri, found a worn hominid molar tooth embedded in a small block of consolidated tuff while he was searching the Bed I exposures at the MK site. When the matrix was subsequently removed this proved to be a lower third molar still in place in a fragment of mandible. The specimen has since been made a paratype for *Homo habilis*.

The site MK is situated on the left bank of the Gorge, half a mile downstream from DK. The tooth was found in a small gully approximately 50 yards west of the main MK gully where the Bed I exposures have been known for many years to be particularly rich in fossil material and where the first crocodile and fish remains ever found in Bed I were collected in 1931. This horizon is in Lower Bed I, beneath Tuff I^B, and corresponds to the clays above the occupation surface at DK (Pl. 26). It is the only level at MK where any appreciable numbers of fossil bones or artefacts occur, although the series of steep-sided gullies, which collectively form the site, cut through the entire sequence from the basalt at the base of the upper member of Bed I to Bed IV.

Following the discovery of the tooth by H. Mukiri, a trial trench was excavated in Bed I and this yielded parts of two further hominid teeth *in situ*, besides a number of crocodile remains and some broken mammalian bones, most of which were considerably rolled. The teeth were recovered from an uneven stratum of coarse-grained tuff (identical to the matrix adhering to the original tooth) which lay immediately beneath Tuff I^B. No artefacts were found in association, although they are known from the adjacent main gully where they appear to be eroding from a lower level, possibly corresponding to the occupation floor at DK.

226

References: Leakey (1963, 1965*a*, *b*); Leakey, Evernden and Curtis (1961); Leakey, Tobias and Napier (1964); Tobias (1965*a*, *b*, *d*, 1966*a*); Tobias and von Koenigswald (1964).

H. 5 AND 6, SITE (41*a*) FLK (FRIDA LEAKEY KORONGO), GEOLOGIC LOCALITY 45

H. 5

The circumstances attending the discovery of the cranium of *Australopithecus* (*Zinjanthropus*) *boisei* have already been described in previous publications, but it seems desirable that an account should also be published in the present volume, in order that this record of hominid discoveries at Olduvai should be as complete as possible.

Part of the cranium was first observed by the writer on 17 July 1959, whilst searching the Bed I deposits in the FLK gullies (Pl. 27). It was largely obscured by scree, but a small part of the right mastoid region had become exposed by erosion. Although the morphology of the bone was suggestively hominid, it was so massive and so permeated with air cells that it was not until a premolar had been exposed that the find could be positively identified. Since Mr Des Bartlett, of Armand Denis Productions Ltd, was due to arrive in camp the following day, the skull was left in position for twenty-four hours, after being protected by a pile of stones, so that Mr Bartlett might make a complete photographic record of its uncovering and removal. Plate 28 shows the position of the skull when partially uncovered. It had been considerably broken by earth pressure, although all the fragments lay close together, within an area of about 14 × 10 in. Some damage had also been caused by weathering on the parts exposed by erosion, notably on the anterior part of the parietal bones and on the adjoining area of the frontal, where a small part of the skull is missing. It is otherwise virtually complete, including the dentition, except for small areas of the face where the bone is particularly thin.

The cranium was partly embedded in silty clay and was overlain by a hard yellowish-white tuff, about 9 in. thick. Excavation established that the tuff was unquestionably *in situ*, since the deposit continued horizontally, without break, into the main Bed I sequence. Any possibility that the skull had slumped down from a higher level was thus ruled out. The stratigraphic position proved to be approximately mid-way in Bed I, 20 ft. below the marker Tuff I[F] and approximately the same distance above the basalt.

During 1959 a small excavation was carried out at the site of the discovery and this yielded numbers of broken animal bones, some micro-faunal remains and a series of artefacts, all lying near the skull and at the same level. More extensive excavations undertaken the following year revealed that this area represented a marginal part of an occupation floor on which there were many hundreds of broken animal bones and artefacts typical of the Oldowan. A description of the occupation floor and industry is given in chapter II.

References: Kurth (1960); Leakey (1959, 1960*b*, *c*, 1962, 1963, 1965*a*, *b*); Leakey, Evernden and Curtis (1961); Robinson (1960*b*, 1963); Tobias (1963, 1965*a*, *b*, *d*, 1967*a*).

H. 6

The remains attributed to this individual consist of six vault fragments of a very thin skull, an upper molar and a lower premolar. They were found during 1959 and 1960 in the course of sieving the surface soil from the slope immediately below the '*Zinjanthropus*' site, and are assumed to be from that level. They have been assigned to *Homo habilis*.

A tibia and a fibula (Pl. 28) found on the occupation floor were at first considered to be associated with the cranium of '*Zinjanthropus*'. The detailed morphological studies which have been carried out on these two bones and on the foot bones from FLK NNI have revealed such close compatibility between the limb bones and the calcaneum and astragalus from the latter site that it now seems more likely that they should be associated with *Homo habilis* (H. 6) rather than with '*Zinjanthropus*' (H. 5).

References: Davis, Day and Napier (1964); Leakey (1960*d*, 1962, 1963, 1964, 1965*a*); Leakey, Tobias and Napier (1964); Tobias (1965*a*, *b*, *f*, 1966*a*); Tobias and von Koenigswald (1964).

H. 7 AND 8, SITE (38*b*) FLK NN (FLK NORTH-NORTH), GEOLOGIC LOCALITY 45

The first discovery of any importance at this site was part of the mandible of a small species of sabre-toothed feline which was found on the surface of the Bed I slopes by J. H. E. Leakey during 1960. Subsequent sieving for further machairodont material unexpectedly brought to light the first hominid tooth and a terminal phalanx. A trial trench dug into the deposits revealed that the hominid remains had been derived from an occupation floor on a palaeosol which was on the surface of a clay immediately overlying Tuff I^B. The '*Zinjanthropus*' horizon could also be identified and occurred approximately 1½ ft. higher in the sequence. The position of the hominid remains was thus intermediate between that of H. 4 from MK (which was beneath Tuff I^B) and that of H. 5 from FLK. The remains of both H. 7 and H. 8 were widely scattered over the occupation surface (see Fig. 20) and were also in a very fragmentary condition. They also exhibit tooth marks, indicating that they had been damaged by scavengers. Most of the remains were found by J. H. E. Leakey with the exception of the foot bones of H. 8, which were uncovered by the writer.

H. 7

This consists of parts of a juvenile individual which has now been made the Type of *Homo habilis*. It is represented by the following bones:

(*a*) A mandible with partial dentition (3rd molar not yet erupted), the lower border is damaged and the greater parts of both ascending rami are missing (Pl. 29).

(*b*) The left parietal, almost complete (Pl. 30).

(*c*) Parts of the right parietal; the anterior region is missing and the existing part is made up from a number of small fragments found separately.

(*d*) A fragment of the occipital bone.

(*e*) Fragments of both the right and left petrous bones.

(*f*) Sundry small skull fragments.

(*g*) Twenty-one bones of the hand, including the trapezium, scaphoid and a number of phalanges.

All the parts listed above were found *in situ*. One upper molar, a terminal phalanx and a broken capitate bone, found on the surface, probably also belong to this individual.

References: Holloway (1965, 1966); Leakey (1960*d*, 1961*a*, *b*, 1962, 1963, 1964, 1965*a*, *b*); Leakey, Evernden and Curtis (1961); Leakey, Tobias and Napier (1964); Napier (1962*a*, *b*, 1963, 1964*a*, *b*); Oakley and Campbell (1964); Robinson (1965, 1966); Tobias (1964*a*, *b*, 1965*a–f*, 1966*a*, *b*); Tobias and von Koenigswald (1964).

H. 8

This is an adult individual, possibly female, represented by the following parts:

(*a*) Twelve associated foot bones, comprising the astragalus, calcaneum, cuboid and navicular, cuneiforms 1, 2 and 3, the proximal ends and most of the shafts of all five metatarsals (Pl. 31).

(*b*) The proximal ends of one metacarpal and three finger phalanges.

(*c*) The shaft of a radius.

(*d*) A clavicle, complete except for the extremities, which are damaged (Pl. 31).

All the above were found *in situ*, but a broken permanent molar found on the surface probably also belongs to H. 8.

Both the right parietal of H. 7 and the astragalus of H. 8 exhibit the tooth marks referred to earlier. There are four roughly parallel grooves 4–5 mm. wide on the parietal, above the asterion, while on the astragalus there is a series of puncture tooth marks, the largest of which measures 6 × 4 mm. These clearly represent the tooth marks of a fair-sized carnivore, but it is doubtful whether a hyaena was responsible, since the bones are so

228

slender that they would almost certainly have been totally destroyed if they had been gnawed by one of these animals.

It may be noted—although it may not be of any particular significance—that the almost complete left parietal of H. 7 exhibits a crushed area, 7 × 5·5 mm. in diameter, situated almost centrally, in which the bone has become pulverised and from which there are a number of radiating cracks. When discovered, the whole bone was crushed flat (Pl. 30). It has never been taken apart, but it was necessary to dissolve partially the preservative in the matrix filling the cracks in order to restore the original curve. The fact that the cracks radiate from a central point may be due entirely to natural causes, resulting from earth pressure being greatest on the most convex part of the bone, but it is also possible that they may have been caused by a blow.

The hand and foot bones have been studied by J. R. Napier, who states that they bear strong resemblances to those both of modern man and of a juvenile gorilla. The terminal phalanx of the thumb is broad and well developed, indicating that a precision grip of the human type was possible, although not developed to the extent found in modern man. The foot bones have been studied by J. R. Napier and M. H. Day. They report that the metatarsal of the big toe was parallel to the other four metatarsals, indicating that the big toe was not divergent as in apes, but lay parallel as in present-day man. The foot is also well-arched and is considered to indicate a 'bipedal plantigrade propulsive gait'.

The description of the site and industry is given in chapter II, but it may be stated briefly that the industry associated with H. 7 and 8 appears to be typical of the Oldowan and that conditions at the living site, taken in conjunction with various faunal elements, indicate that it was situated near the lake or close to a swamp.

References: Davis, Day and Napier (1964); Day and Wood (1968); Leakey (1960*d*, 1963, 1965*a*); Leakey, Tobias and Napier (1964); Tobias (1965*a–d, f*).

H. 9, SITE (64) LLK (LOUIS LEAKEY KORONGO), GEOLOGIC LOCALITY 46

This consists of the greater part of the calvaria of a particularly thick skull with massive supra-orbital ridges. It is attributed to *Homo erectus* and was found by L. S. B. Leakey on 2 December 1960, when visiting exposures in company with R. Pickering of the Tanzania Geological Survey. Most of the pieces were found on the surface, lying close together in the centre of a small gully in which only Beds III, IV and the upper part of II are exposed. The gully is situated on the left bank of the Side Gorge, a short distance above the point where it joins the Main Gorge.

No parts were found *in situ*, but a considerable amount of matrix adhered to the base of the skull and this proved to be identical to a re-worked tuff 7–8 ft. thick, which occurs just above the level where the main skull fragments were found. The lower part of this tuff lies at a depth of 10–12 ft. below the base of Bed III. Excavations were carried out in this deposit over an area of approximately 32 × 24 ft., but only two quartz side choppers, six utilised cobblestones and forty-four quartz flakes and other fragments were found. Fish remains were relatively common but there were only a few fragmentary mammalian bones. Sieving of the surface soil lower down the gully, however, yielded a number of further fragments of the skull which could be fitted on to the original pieces. One lay at a distance of 80 ft.

This skull, unfortunately, became known as 'Chellean Man' before the cultural sequence in Bed II had been systematically explored. It occurred at a level where Developed Oldowan has now been found and which is considerably higher stratigraphically than the lower Acheulean site of EF–HR. Since the few utilised stones and flakes found in the re-worked tuff are not in any way diagnostic, it is impossible to associate this specimen of *Homo erectus* definitely with either cultural stream. (Remains of *H. erectus* have since been found in Bed IV associated with the Acheulean.)

References: Heberer (1963); Kurth (1965); Leakey (1961*a*, 1963, 1965*a*, 1966); Tobias (1965*a, d, f*).

H. 10, SITE (40*b*), FLK (NORTH), GEOLOGIC LOCALITY 45

This individual is represented only by the terminal phalanx of the right big toe. The bone was found in 1961 by J. Mutaba on the occupation floor of Level 5 at FLK North, where it was associated with an Oldowan industry and many broken mammalian bones. This level is approximately 3½ ft. below the marker Tuff I^F at the top of Bed I. (A description of the site will be found in chapter III.)

The bone is particularly well preserved and has been described by M. H. Day and J. R. Napier, who have compared it with hallucial phalanges of modern man (including Bushman), chimpanzees and gorillas and also with the Neanderthal phalanges from Skhul and Kiik-Koba. The Olduvai specimen is considered by these authors to show great resemblance to that of modern man, although its morphology is not precisely matched by any of the compared material. They state however, that 'the Olduvai toe bone belonged to an upright, bipedal hominid possessing a plantigrade propulsive gait' and also point out that a comparable type of gait had already been postulated for the *Homo habilis* foot recovered from a lower level in Bed I, at FLK NN.

References: Day (1967); Day and Napier (1966); Leakey (1966); Tobias (1965*a, d*).

H. 11, SITE (22), DK (DOUGLAS LEAKEY KORONGO), GEOLOGIC LOCALITY 13

This consists of the greater part of the left half of a palate and maxillary arch from which the crowns of all the teeth have been lost. It was found on 11 April 1962 by M. Mutumbo, who discovered it in the stream bed at the bottom of a gully near the DK excavations. It is thus impossible to assign the specimen to any stratigraphic level, although the condition of the bone, which bears a pinkish tinge, is similar to that seen in fossil bones from a conglomerate at the head of the DK gully belonging to the lower Ndutu Beds (formerly included in Bed V).

Reference: Tobias (1965*d*).

H. 12, SITE (45*b*) VEK (VIVIAN EVELYN KORONGO), GEOLOGIC LOCALITY 86

This consists of the greater part of the occipital and both parietals, parts of the left and right temporals, including the left mastoid process, part of the right supra-orbital ridge and the left half of the palate and maxillary arch from which all the crowns of the teeth have been lost.

Remains of this skull were discovered by Margaret Leakey on 2 June 1962. She first noted a number of small, weathered fragments of remarkable thickness which were lying on the eroded slope of Bed III, on the west side of the gully known as VEK. The fragments proved to have washed down from Bed IV*a* and had undoubtedly lain on the surface for a considerable length of time. Many showed fresh breaks and had been chipped round the edges by the trampling of Masai cattle. An extensive search for further fragments was undertaken. This involved scraping off the surface soil from the slope on which the original specimens had been found and putting it through sieves. When the work came to a close, all the surface soil had been removed from an area 300 ft. long and 40 ft. wide. A number of widely scattered fragments were recovered, the left temporal being at a distance of 190 ft. from the palate. The latter was found on the slope just below the Marker Tuff IV^A and was still encrusted with a gritty matrix. A trial trench 20 ft. long was also dug into the undisturbed deposits of Bed IV, but no further hominid remains came to light.

Although no parts of this skull were found *in situ*, it can safely be assumed to belong to Bed IV*a* on the basis of the matrix adhering to the palate. It probably can be attributed to *Homo erectus*.

References: Leakey and Leakey (1964); Tobias (1965*d*).

H. 13, 14 AND 15, SITE (71a AND b) MNK (MARY NICOL KORONGO), GEOLOGIC LOCALITY 88

Hominid remains were discovered at this site on 22 October 1963, after the excavation of the Main Occupation Site in Bed II had been completed and when the protecting shed over part of the excavations was being built. The discovery was accidental and entirely due to the excellent powers of observation of N. Mbuika who, in fact, was one of the less experienced workmen. He and several other men had been set to collect small stones for mixing into concrete. They chose to collect them by hand into portable containers, in preference to shovelling gravel from the stream bed into barrows. When picking up stones near the footpath, about 60 ft. distant from the excavated site, N. Mbuika observed a tooth which had been lying beneath the stones. He recognised it as being of interest and left it in position, after carefully covering it over with a little pile of stones. He reported the discovery to L. S. B. Leakey on the following day. When the tooth was examined, it was immediately recognisable as a well-preserved hominid premolar. Several fragments of a very thin skull were also noted, lying on the slope within a few feet of the tooth, partly obscured by grass and scrub (Pl. 32).

The area was then marked out and the vegetation removed, after which the loose soil on the slope was carefully scraped off and subsequently washed through sieves with $\frac{1}{16}$ in. mesh. The mandible, two pieces of maxilla, parts of both temporal bones and several other fragments came to light almost immediately, whilst many small fragments were recovered when the soil was washed. It was noticeable that a proportion of the fragments, particularly of the mandible, was encrusted with small spherical lime concretions. A line of similar concretions could be discerned in the undisturbed deposit above the slope from which the skull parts had been recovered, providing an indication as to the horizon from which they had come. When excavations were carried out later, it was confirmed that this was the horizon of H. 13, since two small pieces of the right parietal were

found *in situ*, one of which fitted on to the fragments found on the slope.

When the loose soil above the footpath had been cleared away, the silt and rubble filling the gully below the site was removed down to the point where it drains into the stream bed of the Side Gorge, a distance of 80 ft. But, although many fragments of bone which had washed down from the main MNK occupation site and from the higher levels were recovered, only four small pieces of hominid skull were found, two of which fitted H. 13. These lay at a distance of approximately 30 ft. from the other fragments. They occurred in the top few inches of the filling, indicating that the greater part of the accumulated rubble in the gully must have been deposited before the hominid fragments had washed out on to the surface.

When the fragments of H. 13 had been partially fitted together and the other cranial fragments had been examined, it was clear that duplicate parts of two right parietals were present, indicating the existence of at least two individuals. These are represented by the following parts:

H. 13

This consists of a sub-adult skull, probably female, with the third molars coming into wear. It is represented by the greater part of the mandible, including the complete dentition, although the crowns of the incisors are damaged and the left ascending ramus is not preserved; the greater part of the maxillae, represented by two fragments both lacking the anterior portions; the greater part of the occipital; the right parietal and temporal; parts of the left parietal and temporal; together with a few frontal fragments and approximately fifty additional pieces which it has not been possible to fit together.

References: Leakey (1964, 1965b, 1966); Leakey and Leakey (1964); Leakey, Tobias and Napier (1964); Robinson (1965); Tobias (1965a, b, d); Tobias and von Koenigswald (1964).

H. 14

This consists of a very thin skull, apparently juvenile, in which the sutures are entirely unfused.

It is represented by two adjoining fragments of the anterior margin of the right parietal measuring approximately 53 × 41 mm. These include a small section of the sagittal suture. There is also a piece of frontal approximately 43 × 27 mm. and four additional small fragments.

References: Leakey and Leakey (1964); Leakey, Tobias and Napier (1964); Tobias (1965*a, b, d*).

H. 15

This individual is represented by two upper molars and one canine. The teeth are exceedingly robust and show an unusual degree of wear. They were not found in close association; one molar and the canine lay approximately 1 ft. below the top of the tuff in which they occurred, whilst the second molar was 4 ft. distant and 1 ft. deeper in the deposit.

References: Leakey and Leakey (1964); Tobias (1965*a, b, d*); Tobias and von Koenigswald (1964).

The stratigraphic positions of the remains of H. 13, 14 and 15 are discussed in chapter IV but may be briefly summarised as follows: no parts of H. 14 were found *in situ*, but two parietal fragments of H. 13, which could be fitted on to the pieces found on the surface, were recovered from a clay horizon 24 ft. above the base of Bed II. The three teeth of H. 15 were found *in situ* in a tuff approximately 2½ ft. higher in the sequence. Faunal remains and artefacts were found at both horizons. The tools associated with H.13 appear to be typical of the Oldowan, but the series found at the level of H. 15 is too scanty for its affinities to be determined.

H. 16 AND 17, SITE (43) FLK (MAIKO GULLY), GEOLOGIC LOCALITY 45

H. 16

Remains of H. 16 were found by M. Mutumbo on 30 November 1963. Although a complete skull is represented, including parts of the face and mandible, it was in a deplorable condition when discovered, since it had been reduced to innumerable small fragments by the trampling of cattle. Leaving aside the larger fragments which have been pieced together, forming the vault, there are a further 1,500 fragments of bone and of teeth, many smaller than a grain of rice, which it has been impossible to assemble. It is unusual for fossil bones to become broken to this extent, even when they have been exposed on the surface for a considerable time; the condition of H. 6 is due to the fact that the fragments were washed down on to the line of a cattle track leading to a watering point in the Gorge (Pl. 33).

Most of the pieces were found scattered over the surface of Tuff I^F in a small gully now named Maiko Gully, after the discoverer of the skull. The tuff is considerably harder than the overlying deposits and forms a flat shelf traversed by the cattle track. It is overlain by the coarse-grained grey tuff noted at FLK North and HWK East. This, in turn, is overlain by a clay which appears to be the equivalent of the clay with root casts at FLK North and of Level 2 and HWK East.

During 1963, when the skull was found, no attempt was made to dig the *in situ* deposits, although the surface soil and the silt in the gully below the site of the discovery was sieved. When work was resumed at Olduvai in 1968 trenches were dug into the lower 7 ft. of the Bed II deposits. Three further teeth of H. 16 were found *in situ* at the base of the clay with root casts, at a height of 2 ft. above marker Tuff I^F. Two premolars were also found on the surface, where they had become exposed by erosion since the close of the previous season.

References: Leakey (1965*b*, 1966); Leakey and Leakey (1964); Leakey, Tobias and Napier (1964); Tobias (1965*a, b, d*); Tobias and von Koenigswald (1964).

H. 17

This consists only of a small fragment of a deciduous molar, found in the stream bed of Maiko Gully when the soil was sieved during the search for parts of H. 16. The stratigraphic position is unknown.

232

H. 18, SITE (42) FLK WEST, GEOLOGIC LOCALITY 45

This consists of a second phalanx of the hand. It was found on the surface of Bed II, below Tuff II^C by K. Kimeu during 1969.

H. 19, SITE (62b) FC WEST (FUCH'S CLIFF), GEOLOGIC LOCALITY 89

This individual is represented only by part of one tooth. It consists of approximately half a very worn molar and was obtained from the re-worked tuff above the occupation level at FC West, at a height of approximately 15 ft. above the base of Bed II, where it was associated with a Developed Oldowan B industry. The tooth was not identified during the excavations, but was recognised as being hominid by Dr. E. Tchernov in the Centre for Prehistory, Nairobi, when sorting through fragmentary material recovered during sieving.

H. 20, SITE (46c) (HENRIETTA WILFRIDA KORONGO, HWK HEAD OF GULLY), GEOLOGIC LOCALITY 44

This consists of a fragment of the proximal end of a large left femur. The head is missing and both the greater and lesser trochanters are damaged. The specimen was found during 1959 on the surface, either on the lower slopes of Bed II or on the upper part of Bed I. It was not recognised as being hominid until 1968, when surface material from Olduvai was being indexed in the Centre for

Prehistory, Nairobi. (Field Catalogue No. 1959/ HWK 399.)

Reference: M. H. Day (1969).

With the exception of the Upper Palaeolithic skeleton, H. 1, believed to be in Munich, the two fragments representing H. 2, now in the British Museum of Natural History, London and the post-cranial material being studied by Dr Michael Day, the entire series of hominid remains is in East Africa. The cranium of *Australopithecus* (*Zinjanthropus*) *boisei* has already been returned to Tanzania and is housed in the National Museum, Dar es Salaam. The remainder of the collection is at present at the National Centre for Prehistory and Palaeontology, Nairobi, but will also be transferred to Tanzania when the specimens have been described.

NOTE

Since this chapter was written a number of additional hominid remains have been found at Olduvai. Space does not permit a detailed description of these finds, but they have been listed in the table overleaf where essential data are briefly recorded.

H. 24, a crushed cranium from Lower Bed I at DK East, can be attributed to *Homo habilis* and promises to contribute important additional information regarding this taxon, particularly in respect of cranial capacity.

Remains from Bed IV*a* include half a mandible and an extremely robust innominate bone and femur shaft that were found in close association with an Acheulean industry at site WK. The latter are from the same stratigraphic level that yielded H. 12 and can be assigned to *H. erectus*.

Table 2. *List of hominid remains found at Olduvai Gorge*

Specimen nos.	Date of discovery	Locality	Stratigraphic position	Finder and circumstances of discovery	Parts found	Taxonomic status	Associated industry
H. 1	1913	RK	Intrusive burial in Bed II	H. Reck, during exploration	Complete skeleton	*H. sapiens*	Nil
H. 2	1935	MNK	Surface, base of Bed IV*a*	M. D. Leakey, during exploration	Two fragments of cranial vault	cf. *H. erectus*	*Inferred* Acheulean
H. 3	1955	BK	*In situ*, Upper Bed II	During excavation	One canine, one molar	*A. boisei*	Developed Oldowan B
H. 4	1959	MK	*In situ*, Lower Bed I, and surface	H. Mukiri during exploration	One molar in socket, two broken teeth	*H. habilis*	*Inferred* Oldowan
H. 5	1959	FLK	*In situ*, Middle Bed I	M. D. Leakey, during exploration	Almost complete cranium	*A. boisei*	Oldowan
H. 6	1959–60	FLK	Surface, *inferred* Middle Bed I	During excavation	Two teeth and some skull fragments	*H. habilis*	*Inferred* Oldowan
H. 7	1960	FLK NN	*In situ*, Middle Bed I	J. H. E. Leakey, during excavation	Mandible, parietals, hand bones, etc.	Type of *H. habilis*	Oldowan
H. 8	1960	FLK NN	*In situ*, Middle Bed I	J. H. E. and M. D. Leakey, during excavation	Foot and hand bones, clavicle, etc.	*H. habilis*	Oldowan
H. 9	1960	LLK	Surface, Upper Bed II	L. S. B. Leakey, during exploration	Calvaria	*H. erectus*	Nil
H. 10	1961	FLK North	*In situ*, Upper Bed I	J. Mutaba, during excavation	Terminal phalanx of big toe	?	Oldowan
H. 11	1962	DK	Surface, possibly from Ndutu Beds	M. Mutumbo, during exploration	Palate and maxillary arch	*Homo* sp.	Nil
H. 12	1962	VEK	Surface, Bed IV*a*	D. M. Leakey, during exploration	Palate, maxillary arch and cranial fragments	*H. erectus*?	*Inferred* Acheulean
H. 13	1963	MNK, Skull Site	*In situ*, Lower Middle Bed II, 5 ft. above chert horizon	N. Mbuika	Mandible, maxilla and cranial fragments	*H. habilis*	Oldowan
H. 14	1963	MNK, Skull Site	Surface, *inferred* same horizon as H. 13	During excavation	Cranial vault fragments	?	*Inferred* Oldowan
H. 15	1963	MNK, Skull Site	*In situ*, Lower Middle Bed II, above level of H. 13	During excavation	One canine, two molars	*Homo* sp.	Indeterminate
H. 16	1963	FLK, Maiko Gully	*In situ*, base of Bed II	M. Mutumbo, during exploration	Many skull fragments and upper and lower dentition	cf. *Australopithecus*	*Inferred* Oldowan
H. 17	1963	FLK, Maiko Gully	Surface	During excavation	Part deciduous molar	?	Nil
H. 18	1969	FLK	Surface Bed II, 10 ft. above the base	K. Kimeu	Phalanx of the hand	?	?
H. 19	1963	FC West	*In situ*, Middle Bed II, 15 ft. above chert horizon	During excavation	Part worn molar	?	Developed Oldowan B
H. 20	1959	HWK Head of Gully	Surface, *inferred* Lower Bed II	Surface collecting	Fragment of left femur	*A. boisei*?	Nil
H. 21	1968	FLK North	Surface, in gully	P. Nzube, during exploration	Small, unworn upper left M^1	*H. habilis*	Nil
H. 22	1968	Side Gorge between VEK and MNK	Surface, indeterminate gravel	M. Mwoka, during exploration	Right half of mandible with P_3–M_2	cf. *H. erectus*	Nil
H. 23	1968	FLK	*In situ*, Bed IV*b*	E. Kandini, during exploration	Part mandible with left M_1, M_2, P_4	Indeterminate	Acheulean
H. 24	1968	DK East	Surface, Lower Bed I	P. Nzube, during exploration	Crushed cranium	*H. habilis*	Inferred Oldowan
H. 25	1968	Geologic Locality 54	Surface Bed IV*a*	P. Nzube, during exploration	Frag. left parietal in region of asterion	Indeterminate	Inferred Acheulean
H. 26	1969	FLK West	Surface, Upper Bed I (probably ex lower Bed II)	E. Kandini, during exploration	Large, unworn lower right M_3	*A. boisei*?	Nil
H. 27	1969	HWK	Surface, upper Bed I	B. Musomba, during exploration	Unworn lower right M_3	*H. habilis*	Nil
H. 28	1970	WK	*In situ*, Bed IV*a*	During excavation	Shaft of femur and left innominate bone	*H. erectus*	Acheulean
H. 29	1969	JK West	*In situ*, Beds III and IV*a*	During excavation	Fragment of molar	Indeterminate	Acheulean
H. 30	1969	Maiko Gully	Surface, Lower Bed II	M. Mutala and E. Kandini, during exploration	Parts deciduous and germ dentitions	Indeterminate	*Inferred* Oldowan
H. 31	1969	HWK East	Surface, Upper Bed I	M. Mutala, during exploration	Broken molar	Indeterminate	Nil
H. 32	1969	MNK	Surface, Middle Bed II	P. Nzube, during exploration	Broken molar	Indeterminate	Nil
H. 33	1969	FLK NN	Surface, Bed I	P. Nzube, during exploration	Vault fragments of very thin skull	Indeterminate	Nil
H. 34	1962	JK West	*In situ*, Beds III and IV*a*	M. Kleindienst, during excavation	Slender femur and part of tibia shaft	*Homo* sp.	Acheulean

CHAPTER VIII

MAMMALIAN BONES FROM BEDS I AND II WITH EVIDENCE OF HOMINID MODIFICATION

At the time of writing there is, as yet, no general agreement regarding the extent to which bone was worked and used in Lower and Middle Pleistocene times. It is evident that more basic research on the effect of artificial fracture and use of bone, as distinct from damage caused by natural means, is required before bone debris from early living sites can be satisfactorily interpreted. C. K. Brain has already made a valuable contribution in this direction with his analysis of goat bones from Hottentot middens (Brain, 1967a). This will be discussed in chapter X.

It is probable that the majority of the broken mammalian bones found on living sites in Beds I and II at Olduvai merely represents food debris. Some may also have been further broken by carnivores after the sites were abandoned. There is, however, a relatively small number which appear to have been artificially flaked and abraded. Other bone fragments are often chipped and may also have been used, but this cannot be determined with any certainty.

Bones that are here regarded as having been broken and flaked by artificial means are mainly parts of massive limb bones such as those of elephant, giraffe or *Libytherium*. Some bones of Equidae and Bovidae, as well as a few hippopotamus and suid canines, also appear to have been chipped by use.

Artificially shaped bones are more common in Upper Bed II and in the upper part of Middle Bed II than in the earlier levels. Bed I has so far yielded only five specimens.

BED I

These consist of the following:

(i) Part of an equid first rib showing evidence of polishing and smoothing at the fractured end. It was found in Level 3 at FLK NN amongst a group of tortoise scutes. There is an oblique fracture of the shaft of the rib, towards the proximal end, which runs transversely from the lower to the upper margin. One edge of the fracture is abraded and smooth, showing that the bone was used after it had been broken. An area of the upper margin of the rib, adjacent to the abraded point, also shows polishing. Comparison with an unaltered modern equid first rib shows that there is a natural, smooth-surfaced, shallow notch in this area, which has been further smoothed and polished in the fossil specimen. The butt end is slightly chipped, but shows the spongy texture to be found at the articulation with the sternum, indicating that it has not been extensively damaged. Length 127 mm., greatest width (at the butt end) 27 mm. Length of fractured surface with abraded edges 33 mm. (Pl. 34.)

(ii) and (iii) Two further specimens were obtained from Levels 1–2 at FLK North (Pl. 35). The first consists of the distal half of a bovid metacarpal of about the same size as that of a wildebeeste. The articular end is entirely sharp and fresh, but the tip of the fractured shaft is extensively abraded. The bone measures 151 mm. in length and 43 mm in maximum width (at the articular end). It has been fractured approximately in mid-shaft and a longitudinal splinter, almost as long as the existing part of the shaft, has been detached from one side. Several longitudinal cracks parallel to this fracture can also be seen. The edges of the fracture are worn smooth at the tip, but are sharp and fresh towards the butt. Several flakes have been removed and the tip; the point is formed by a broken surface on one side and a flake scar on the opposite side, so that the point is chisel-like. The whole of this area is abraded. A fragment of the splinter broken from the shaft was found approximately 2 ft. distant. It measures 54 mm. in length and fits exactly on to the fractured surface.

The second specimen consists of a shaft splinter from a bovid radius, again of approximately the same size as that of a wildebeeste. It measures 156 mm. in length and 22 mm. in maximum width. Both ends are pointed, but only one, which is somewhat spatulate, shows abrasion. There are longitudinal fractures on either side and also on the inner surface of the bone, so that the original thickness has been somewhat reduced; the point is 9 mm. wide and 4·5 mm. thick, whereas the thickness of the undamaged bone in the adjacent parts of the shaft is in the region of 7 mm. The degree of wear is not so great as in the previous specimen; it extends for a distance of 25 mm. on one side and for rather less on the opposite side.

(iv) and (v) The two flaked fragments of limb bones from DK are similar in size, measuring 120 and 125 mm. respectively. They are comparable in thickness to limb bones of hippopotamus. Both are roughly triangular in shape, with one pointed and one straight end. In one specimen the pointed end exhibits a number of flake scars on the convex side as well as subsequent chipping and blunting. In the second specimen one long flake has been removed from the pointed end but more intensive chipping and blunting is present on the opposite straight end.

BED II

A minimum of 105 specimens from Bed II exhibit modification. They consist of:

(1) Parts of long bones with articular ends in which the ends of the broken shafts show flaking and wear. In massive bones, such as those of rhinoceros, hippopotamus, giraffe or *Libytherium*, the articular ends are usually split longitudinally.

(2) Scapulae in which the borders of the blades and the spines are chipped and damaged.

(3) Massive bones, generally of elephant, such as an axis, a patella, a footbone and the broken condyles of long bones in which the surfaces have been battered and pitted.

(4) Fragments of long bone shafts (generally of massive bones) with flaking and chipping along the edges, either on the sides or at the tips. Some examples are pointed at the extremities and others are spatulate.

(5) Hippopotamus canines and incisors with chipping at the tips and suid canines with similar damage at both ends, together with flakes of hippopotamus ivory (rare).

(6) Bifacially flaked fragments.

(7) Crania and limb bones with depressed fractures.

(1) PARTS OF LONG BONES WITH ARTICULAR ENDS

These include distal ends of humeri, distal ends of tibiae, proximal and distal ends of metapodials and proximal ends of radii. Femora and ulnae are not represented.

(a) *Humeri, distal parts* (14 specimens)

These range in size from a complete distal end of a *Libytherium* humerus, 198 mm. long and 173 mm. wide, to one of a medium-sized bovid, 52 mm. long and 58 mm. wide. Five specimens are of *Libytherium*, one of giraffe, three of bovids, three of large equids, one of rhinoceros and one of hippopotamus. The articular ends are complete in eight examples, but in six of the massive specimens, belonging to *Libytherium*, rhinoceros or hippopotamus, they have been split longitudinally so that only part of the median epicondyle remains. The fractures of the shafts are variable, but they are usually jagged, with chipping on both the inner and outer surfaces. In six examples the fractures are pointed, with a number of flake scars on the exterior surface running from the tip towards the articular ends. A proportion of these specimens appears to represent the ends of bones in which the shafts were shattered to extract the marrow and which have been subsequently utilised, but others, including the pointed series and those split longitudinally, seem to have been expressly shaped. (Fig. 110, no. 3.)

(b) *Tibiae, distal parts* (7 specimens)

Three equid and two large bovid tibiae have been fractured approximately in mid-shaft. They are remarkably similar in appearance, with sharply pointed fractures formed by distinct flake scars. They vary in length from 221 to 112 mm. A hippopotamus tibia has also been flaked to a point. It measures 153 mm. in length and has been broken nearer to the end than the bovid and equid tibiae.

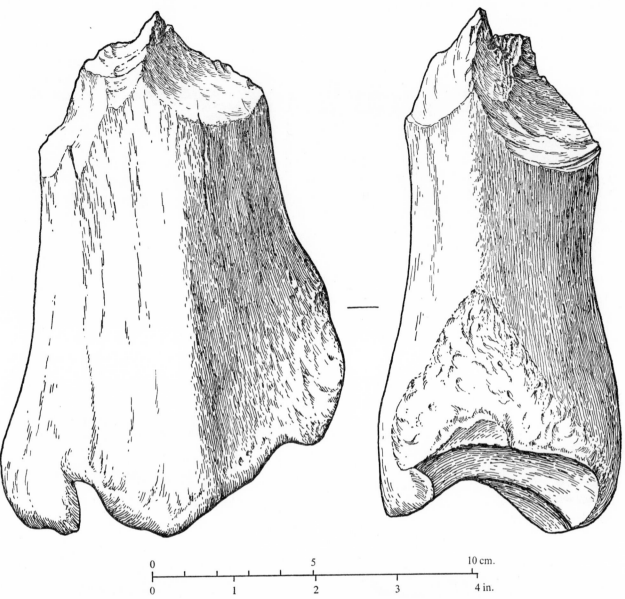

Fig. 109. The distal end of a hippopotamus tibia in which the broken shaft has been bifacially flaked to a point. From FLK II.

A further bovid specimen has also been broken closer to the articular end and has a broad, curved fracture, extensively chipped and blunted by use. (Figs. 109, 110, nos. 1, 2.)

(c) Radii, proximal parts (2 specimens)

One example consists of the proximal end of a giraffid radius, split longitudinally, with a burin-like point at the tip of the fractured shaft and at right angles to the inner and outer surfaces. It measures 12 mm. in width and is chipped by use on both sides. (Length 93 mm.)

The second fragment consists of the complete proximal end of an equid radius, broken close to the articular end. The fracture is transverse and the edge has been extensively chipped on the outer surface. (Length 57 mm.)

(d) Metapodials, distal parts (3 specimens)

Two bovid metacarpals have been broken 3-4 in. from the articular ends and are chipped on the edges of the fractured shafts. (Lengths 102 and 93 mm. respectively.) There is also an equid metapodial which has been split longitudinally, forming a long slender point that is chipped along the edges and at the tip. (Length 156 mm.)

237

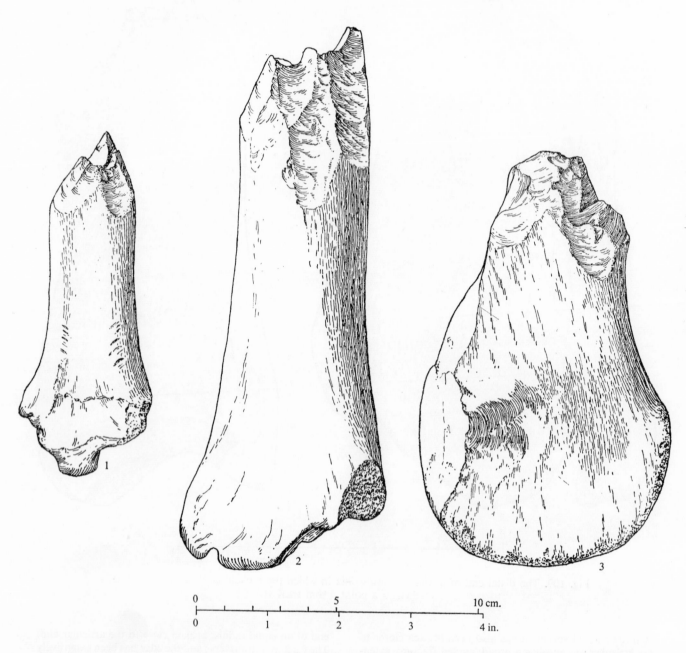

Fig. 110. (1) and (2) Distal ends of a bovid and an equid tibia. The broken shafts have been flaked to points. From MNK, Main Occupation Site and FLK II, respectively. (3) The distal end of a *Libytherium* humerus, split longitudinally. The broken shaft has been extensively battered. From MNK, Main Occupation Site.

(e) Metapodials, proximal parts (2 specimens)

A giraffid metatarsal has been broken approximately 4 in. from the proximal end. Part of the fractured edge is convex and has been chipped and battered by use. The edge of the articular surface has also been damaged and flaked on part of the circumference. This specimen is slightly rolled. (Length 112 mm.) The second example is the proximal end of a medium-sized bovid metatarsal, split longitudinally. The fracture of the shaft is pointed and it is chipped along the edges. (Length 89 mm.)

(2) SCAPULAE (15 SPECIMENS)

It is noticeable that most of the utilised scapulae belong to the larger animals. There are two of rhinoceros, one of hippopotamus, six of giraffids (two of which are probably *Libytherium*), three of large equids and three of large bovids. In the majority the glenoid cavity and part of the blade are preserved, but in three specimens both extremities are missing and only the median parts of the blades and spines are present. Four of the giraffid specimens are, however, much more complete. Almost the whole bone is preserved, although the edges of the blades and the ends of the spines are chipped and flaked.

In both the rhinoceros scapulae the blades have been broken off less than 11 in. from the glenoid cavities. The edges are extensively damaged and the coracoid processes have been almost entirely broken off. In one specimen the circumference of the glenoid cavity has also been damaged. (Lengths: 227 and 275 mm. respectively.) The hippopotamus scapula shows similar wear, including chipping on the rim of the glenoid cavity, but a larger part of the bone is preserved than in the preceding specimens. The spine is virtually intact, although the edges of the blade have been largely chipped off. (Length 330 mm.)

The extent and type of wear evident on the four nearly complete giraffid scapulae are almost identical. The ends of the blades and lateral edges are chipped. In three specimens the chipping begins at a distance of approximately 9–11 in. from the glenoid cavity, whilst in the fourth the wear is confined to the end of the blade. The greater parts of the spines are undamaged but in each case a single flake has been removed from the utilised ends. The rims of the glenoid cavities are also chipped. (Lengths: 670, 560, 580 and 535 mm. respectively.)

In two additional giraffid scapulae both ends of the bones have been broken off and only the median parts of the blades and the base of the spines are preserved. These appear to have been subjected to particularly heavy use and are more extensively damaged than any others in the series. Numerous large flakes have been removed from the various edges, including one 140 mm. long. Most of the spine has also been flaked off in one example and a shallow notch 130 mm. long has been chipped out near one end, possibly to serve as a hand hold. (Lengths: 390 and 370 mm.) (Pl. 37.)

An unusually large equid scapula has similarly had both ends removed and has been chipped round the whole circumference of the blade. A number of large shallow flakes has also been removed from one extremity and part of the spine is damaged. (Length 330 mm.)

In the six medium-sized scapulae belonging to large bovids and equids the blades have also been broken off and the remaining parts chipped along the edges, including the spines. The largest of these measures 270 mm. in length and the smallest 140 mm., the average length for the six specimens being 201 mm.

One further scapula of indeterminate species, but of approximately the size of a small giraffid, has been broken only a short distance from the glenoid cavity and exhibits oblique longitudinal flake scars on one face. (Length 109 mm.)

(3) VARIOUS BONES WITH BATTERED UTILISATION (8 SPECIMENS)

These consist of a variety of bones, generally massive, with pitting and battering on the surface. They appear to have served as anvils and comprise the following:

(*a*) An elephant axis. This has been extensively damaged over the greater part of the exterior. The transverse processes and the spine have been broken off and the surface of the bone, particularly in the region of the odontoid process, has been almost entirely removed, exposing the inner spongy tissue. (Pl. 38.)

(*b*) A cervical vertebra of a very large bovid, possibly *Pelorovis*, in which the anterior articular surface and the

239

edges of the posterior surface have been battered and chipped, again exposing the spongy tissue.

(c) An elephant foot bone. One surface shows the same type of utilisation as (a) and (b), but the pitting has penetrated even deeper.

(d) An elephant patella. The articular surface shows a number of indentations, the largest being 7 mm. in diameter.

(e) A large bovid astragalus with pitting on the convex anterior articular surface over an area 24 × 21 mm. The pitting consists of a number of overlapping triangular-shaped indentations which have penetrated several milli-metres into the bone.

(f) Three fragments of the condyles of massive limb bones, probably the proximal ends of femora or humeri, comparable in size to those of an elephant, with battering, pitting, grooving and scratching on the articular surfaces. In one example the surface has been crushed inwards over an area 37 × 23 mm. The length/breadth measurements are 160 × 114 mm., 130 × 109 mm. and 129 × 117 mm.

(4) SHAFT FRAGMENTS OF LONG BONES

These usually consist of splinters of massive limb bones, commonly of the same thickness as those of elephant, *Libytherium*, giraffe, hippopo-tamus and rhinoceros, although a few fragments of large and medium-sized bovid and equid bones are also included.

(a) *With pointed extremities (6 specimens)*

In three examples the points are burin-like, lying at right angles to the inner and outer surfaces of the bones. They vary in width from 8 to 14 mm. and have been formed by longitudinal flakes struck from the tips. In two specimens the edges are heavily chipped and blunted by use, but in a third they are sharp and only slightly chipped. The point in the fourth example has been made by a number of multi-directional flake scars and there is also fine chipping at the tip. The two remaining specimens have flaked points which have been subsequently abraded and worn smooth, in a similar way to the three utilised bones from FLK NN and FLK North. The series of six specimens varies in length and breadth from 96 × 53 mm. to 212 × 84 mm., with an average of 146 × 61 mm. (Fig. 113, No. 3.)

(b) *With spatulate extremities (11 specimens)*

The fractures are broad and curved and have been chipped along the edges, generally more extensively on the exterior surface. In the largest specimen, which is 284 mm. long, both ends have spatulate fractures which have been flaked and chipped and also worn smooth. The series varies in length and breadth from 284 × 89 mm. to 60 × 33 mm., with an average of 140 × 64 mm. (Fig. 111.)

(c) *Miscellaneous (25 specimens)*

This series includes six fragments of particularly massive bones, probably of elephant, fifteen of approximately the

thickness of those of giraffe, rhinoceros or hippopotamus and four similar to those of an equid or large bovid. There is considerable variation in the size and form of these fragments and also in the nature of the chipping and flaking of the edges. The two largest specimens consist of pieces of elephant long bones. One has been split longi-tudinally down the centre and has bluntly pointed extremities with flakes removed from both the inner and outer surfaces. It measures 330 mm. in length and now weighs 6 lb. (Fig. 112, no. 1.) The second specimen is a flat plate also derived from a massive bone, possibly an elephant scapula or pelvis. It has been extensively flaked at one end and to a lesser degree on the lateral edges, whilst the opposite end has been blunted and worn smooth (Fig. 114). It measures 275 mm. in length, 166 mm. in maximum width and is 33–20 mm. thick.

Among the remaining specimens are five splinters in which one lateral edge has been extensively flaked, recalling side scrapers (Fig. 113, nos. 2 and 4). In another there is a transverse fracture at one end which has been steeply flaked. In a few specimens the utilised end is gouge-shaped. Otherwise, as stated above, the series consists of miscellaneous fragments with chipping, flaking or other forms of wear on one or more edges. The size variation is from 330 × 132 mm. to 72 × 33 mm., with an average of 122 × 65 mm.

(5) HIPPOPOTAMUS CANINES AND INCISORS, SUID CANINES AND FLAKES OF HIPPOPOTAMUS IVORY

(a) *Hippopotamus canines and incisors (7 specimens)*

There are five lower canines and two incisors in which the tips are considerably damaged by use. In the canines the utilisation is usually present on the outer aspect of the teeth and on the edges of the wear facet. It extends on to the lingual aspect in only one specimen. The damaged areas are in fresh, sharp condition, in contrast to the smooth surface of other parts of the teeth, including the wear facets. Two specimens from the MNK Main Site, which were found close to one another and which are probably from the same animal, appear to have been extracted from the mandible intact. They measure 220 and 225 mm. in length respectively. The remaining specimens are broken short of the roots. One is part of a massive tooth with a diameter of 72 mm. (Fig. 116.)

In the two central incisors, which are very different in size, the tips are damaged on the whole circumference. In the larger specimen the tip is still pointed, owing to the conical formation of the tooth, although the outer layers of ivory have been chipped away, whilst in the small example the tip has been broken off. Both these teeth are nearly intact and measure 350 and 206 mm. in length respectively. (Pl. 40.)

(b) *Suid canines (2 specimens)*

A nearly complete canine of *Afrochoerus* has been chipped at the tip, where one flake 53 mm. long has also been removed. The root end is also damaged. It is battered

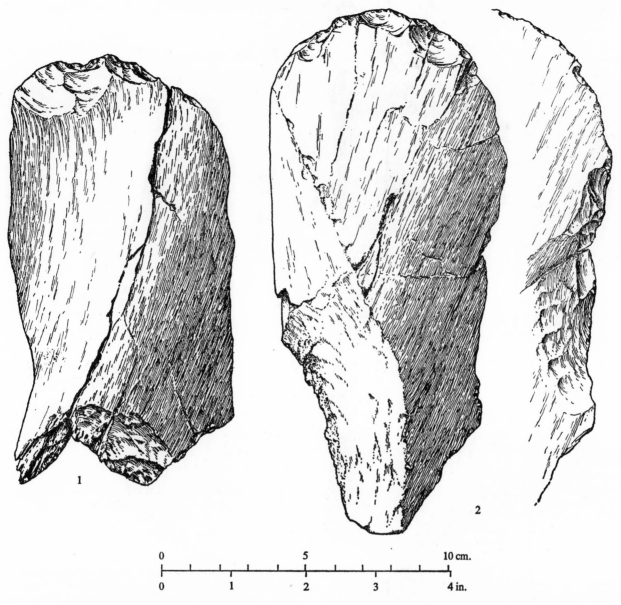

Fig. 111. Parts of shafts of massive limb bones with utilisation on rounded edges. The right-hand specimen has also been chipped on the inner surface of one lateral edge. From BK.

round the circumference, where parts of the outer surface have been flaked off. (Length 470 mm., maximum diameter 59 mm.)

The root end of another, more massive canine shows similar but more marked utilisation. (Length 181 mm., maximum diameter 73 mm.)

(c) Flakes (2 specimens)

The first specimen was obtained from SHK during 1957, from the re-worked tuff above the channel conglomerate.

It is virtually complete and consists of a flake, 145 mm. long and 76 mm. wide, struck from part of a large hippopotamus canine. The tooth appears first to have been broken transversely and the fractured surface then used as a striking platform for detaching the flake, probably in the manner illustrated in Fig. 115.

The specimen diminishes in thickness towards the tip end and is also slightly splayed, suggesting that it is probably part of the root end. Ridged enamel, typical of hippopotamus canines, is present on the dorsal surface.

241

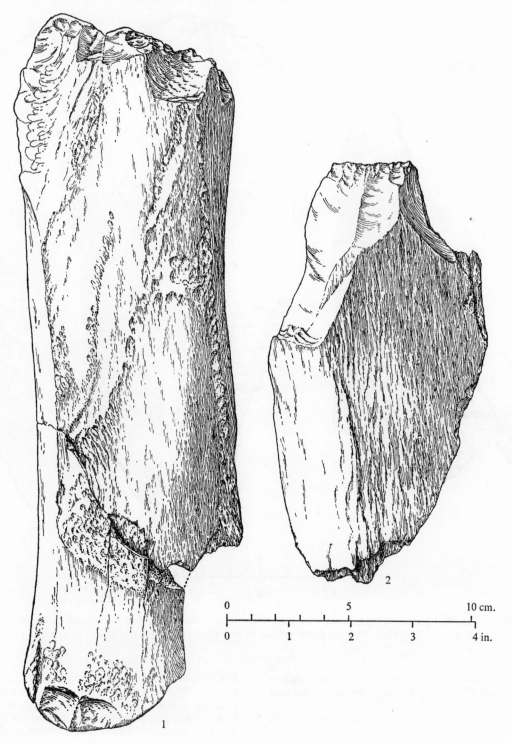

Fig. 112. Fragments of massive limb-bone shafts, chipped and flaked at the extremities. (1) is also abraded at the lower extremity. From BK and HWK East, Level 2, respectively.

242

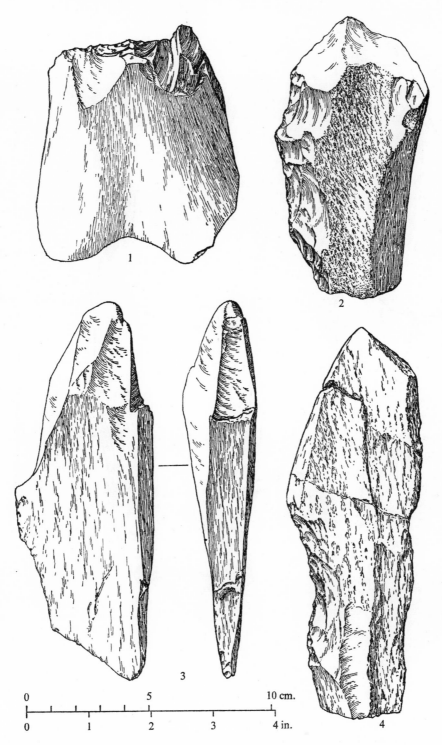

Fig. 113. Parts of limb bone shafts chipped at the ends or along the lateral edges. (3) has been flaked and abraded at the upper end. (1) and (2) from MNK, Main Occupation Level, and (3) and (4) from SHK.

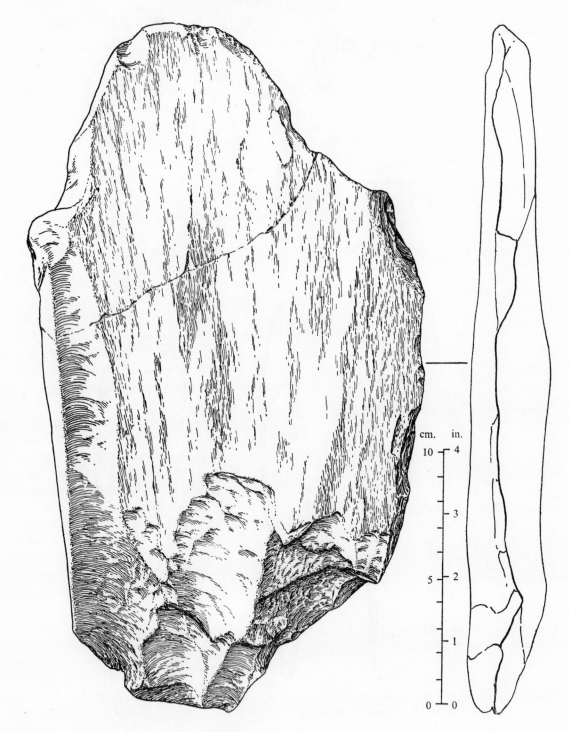

Fig. 114. A thin, flat plate of bone, probably derived from an elephant scapula or pelvis, flaked at the lower end and worn smooth at the upper end. From BK.

244

The striking platform (53 mm. wide and 21 mm. deep) lies obliquely to the long axis. The bulb of percussion is pronounced and well defined. The tool is slightly curved, following the curvature of the tooth, and the distal end is also curved and spoon-shaped, measuring only 3–6 mm. in thickness, in contrast to 21 mm. at the bulbar end. Chipping due to utilisation is evident at the tip and on both lateral edges, particularly on the inner (dentine) surface. (Pl. 39.)

The second specimen consists of a broken flake derived from the tip of a hippopotamus canine. It retains part of the wear facet and this is chipped and damaged along the outer edge, where there is also a crushed indentation 20 mm. wide and 2·5 mm. deep. (Length/breadth 90 × 44 mm.)

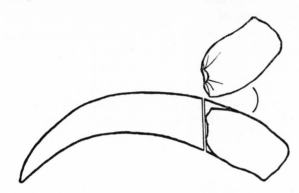

Fig. 115. Suggested method by which the flake of hippopotamus ivory shown in Plate 39 was detached.

(6) BIFACIALLY FLAKED BONE FRAGMENT

A fragment of a massive limb bone, probably elephant, has been flaked over the greater part of both faces and closely resembles a biface. One extremity is pointed and the opposite end rounded. It is chipped by use along the edge. The pointed end and part of one lateral edge have exfoliated subsequently and are lighter in colour than the rest of the tool. The measurements are 171 × 82 × 36 mm. (Pl. 40.) This specimen is very similar to one from an Acheulean site in Bed IV*a*, also made from elephant bone and as yet unpublished.

In addition to the bones described above, there are a few with scratches, cuts and grooves. No evidence of utilisation has been observed on tips of horn cores. If horns were used (as seems probable, since many broken examples occur on living floors) they must have been still encased in the horny outer covering, which would have protected the cores from damage.

(7) CRANIA AND LIMB BONES WITH DEPRESSED FRACTURES (7 SPECIMENS)

These consist of three frontlets of the antelope *Parmularius altidens* from FLK North (Bed I), the skull of a female *Simopithecus* from BK East, two metacarpals of *Libytherium* from BK and FC respectively and an equid femur from BK (Bed II).

The three frontlets of *Parmularius altidens* are fractured over the right orbits, below the base of the horn cores (Pl. 41). In one specimen an area of bone, approximately 27 × 18 mm., has been crushed inwards. There are also two radiating cracks, one of which runs upwards and backwards to the base of the horn core. The second crack, which is several millimetres wide, runs across the frontal as far as the middle line. A series of transverse grooves, apparently caused by gnawing, is also present on either side, below the base of each horn core. In the second specimen the fracture is oblong and extends over a rather larger area, with the sunken part of the bone broken into a number of fragments. As in the previous example, there is one crack running backwards from the top of the fracture to the base of the horn core and another across the frontal to the mid-line. The bone fragments within the sunken area have been pushed inwards to a depth of 9 mm. and the area of the fracture measures approximately 44 × 23 mm. The right horn core has also been broken off near the base, with an oblique fracture on the inner side. The third specimen is less well preserved, but appears to have been fractured in a similar manner.

In the skull of the female *Simopithecus* the face has been broken away and there is a depressed fracture on the right side in the area of the coronal suture, about midway between the upper margin of the temporal and the sagittal crest. The bone has been broken into a number of fragments and several have been pushed inwards, over an area of approximately 43 × 28 mm. A number of scratches, some quite deeply incised, are also present in the area of the fracture. The scratches run from the undamaged bone on either side and cross the depressed fragments, which are similarly scratched. It is evident, therefore, that they were made prior to the fracture, which must have been caused by a post-mortem blow. The skull was presumably battered in order to extract the brain, but for some reason the operation was never completed.

The two metapodials of *Libytherium* exhibit depressed fractures of the shafts, where the bone has been broken and a number of fragments smashed inwards, although the blows were not sufficiently powerful to shatter the bones completely.

The equid femur from BK is complete, but there are two areas on the anterior surface, at either end of the shaft, where the bone is cracked and the pieces pushed inwards.

DAMAGE TO BONES BY ANIMALS

A number of other bones has been damaged by animals. There are examples of indented tooth marks, which are generally triangular, of relatively large grooves some of which measure up to 8 mm. in width, and also of small, parallel-running grooves typical of rodent gnawing. (Gnawed grooves can be seen on the skull of H. 13 from MNK and on the astragalus of H. 8 from FLK NN which also shows some indented tooth marks.) A proportion of the limb-bone shaft fragments also show chipping and notches on the edges which resemble hominid damage. Such chipping, however, can be duplicated on many bone fragments known to have been chewed by hyaenas, wild dogs and other large carnivores which can be seen lying on the plains near Olduvai today. The notches appear to have been caused by the penetration of the teeth when the bones were cracked open, in addition to a certain amount of subsequent chipping along the edges when they were chewed.

It is evident from the foregoing notes that the utilised bones from Developed Oldowan sites in Bed II fall into recognisable groups and that some have been shaped prior to use. Many are so well adapted to certain specific purposes that it is tempting to classify them on such a basis. It could be inferred, for instance, that the scapulae were used for digging and shovelling, the sharp splinters of long bones as cutting and scraping tools, the massive bones with pitted surfaces as anvils and the broken long bones as picks, with the articular ends providing a convenient hand-hold. It has been considered best, however, to classify these bones on a morphological basis, grouping them, primarily, according to parts of the skeleton, with subdivisions based on the types of wear or flaking that is present.

A recent examination of the osteodontokeratic material from Makapansgat, made possible by the kindness of Professor R. A. Dart, revealed few resemblances with the modified bones from Olduvai, although there are similarities in the relative numbers of skeletal parts most commonly preserved and also in the various types of fracture (see chapter x).

Most of the forms of utilisation seen on the cannon bones from Makapansgat do not occur at Olduvai and none at all are known from Beds I or II. In Bed IV*a*, however, there are a few bovid cannon bones in which the distal ends have been heavily abraded and in which the cleft between the distal condyles has been enlarged. No examples are known from Olduvai of circular holes, hollowing out of the shafts to form 'scoops' or of the insertion of one bone or horn core within another. Conversely, there appears to be little evidence of flaking among the osteodontokeratic material.

Several cercopithecoid crania from various australopithecine sites bear depressed fractures and in some examples the bone within the fracture is no longer present. This is a feature not found in the four skulls from Olduvai that have been similarly damaged.

The provenance of the modified bones described in this chapter is as shown in the accompanying table.

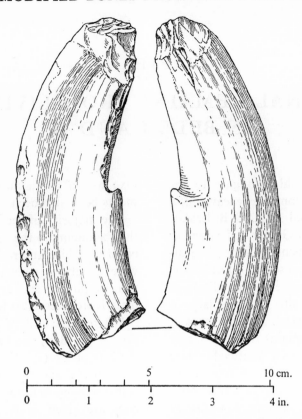

0   5   10 cm.

0   1   2   3   4 in.

Fig. 116. A hippopotamus canine chipped by use at the tip, along one edge of the wear facet and on the outer curve. From FLK II.

Provenance of modified bones from Beds I and II

	BK (Upper Bed II)	SHK (Upper Bed II)	MNK Main Site (Middle Bed II)	FC and FC West (Middle Bed II)	HWK (Lower Bed II)	HWK East, Levels 1–3 (Lower Bed II)	FLK North, Level 1/2 (Upper Bed I)	FLK NN, Level 3 (Middle Bed I)	DK, Level 2 (Lower Bed I)	Totals
1. Parts of long bones with articular ends	9	1	13	2	—	2	1	—	—	28
2. Scapulae	10	2	1	—	1	1	—	—	—	15
3. Various bones, battered	5	1	—	—	—	2	—	—	—	8
4. Shaft fragments of long bones	17	3	19	1	—	1	1	1 (Rib)	2	45
5. Hippopotamus canines and incisors and suid canines	3	1	4	1	—	—	—	—	—	9
6. Bifacially flaked bone fragments	—	—	—	1	—	—	—	—	—	1
7. Skulls and bones with depressed fractures	3	—	—	1	—	—	3	—	—	7
Totals	47	8	37	6	1	6	5	1	2	113

CHAPTER IX

THE FAUNAL REMAINS FROM LIVING SITES
IN BEDS I AND II

Study of the faunal material belonging to the larger mammals obtained from sites excavated in Beds I and II was initiated by L. S. B. Leakey with the help of Mrs Anthea Gentry and a number of assistants. Taxonomic identifications were attempted at first, but these presented considerable difficulties in view of the fragmentary condition of the bones from the living sites and the lack of adequate comparative material. For the present volume, therefore, the remains of the larger mammals and reptiles have been identified merely to within Orders or Families. The former comprise Chelonia, Primates, Carnivora and Proboscidea, whilst the material identifiable to family status includes Crocodylidae, Rhinocerotidae, Equidae, Hippopotamidae, Giraffidae and Bovidae.

The following notes should be regarded merely as a preliminary report, to be amplified when taxonomic identifications and more detailed analyses of the distribution patterns on the living floors have been carried out. For the present, only the relative abundance or scarcity of the principal groups of larger mammals and reptiles has been recorded, together with the common or rare occurrence of certain parts of the skeleton. Since it is clearly impossible to estimate the number of animals represented in any context unless taxonomic identifications have been carried out, no attempt has been made to count the minimum number of individuals. In order to obtain an estimate of the relative abundance of some groups in contrast to others, the number of specimens capable of being allocated to the taxa listed above has been counted and the percentages for the site aggregates noted. Other remains assignable to parts of the skull or skeleton but of unidentified

taxa, as well as the number of indeterminate fragments have also been recorded.

The majority of the faunal material other than that belonging to the larger mammals and reptiles consists of bird and rodent bones. These include a wide variety of genera and species. Remains of fish, amphibia, snakes, small reptiles, bats and insectivores were also found at certain sites.

Whereas the bulk of the fauna from the occupation sites in Beds I and II still awaits identification, the lists of the taxa that have already been determined for these sites and for material previously collected from well-documented stratigraphic horizons are given in Appendix B. These lists are necessarily incomplete, but they are believed to include all the material from Beds I and II for which identifications are available at the time of writing. They have been compiled from preliminary reports published in volume 1 and from various other published and unpublished sources.

Descriptions of certain faunal groups from Olduvai are currently in preparation. Some have been referred to in volume 1, but reports on the Hippopotamidae by Mrs S. C. Savage, on the Suidae by Dr H. B. S. Cooke, on the Rhinocerotidae and Equidae by Dr D. A. Hooijer, the avifauna by Dr P. Brodkorb and on the Crocodylidae by Dr E. Tchernov have been initiated since the publication of volume 1 in 1965.

The fragmentary condition of most of the faunal remains has already been mentioned. The material was obtained almost entirely from living sites and there can be little doubt that it generally represents food debris. Virtually no complete skulls are known and the majority of marrow-containing bones has been broken open. Although direct evidence in the form of tooth marks is not often present, there are indications that the bones on some of the occupation sites were further damaged by scavengers after the sites had been abandoned. Thus, the proportions of ribs and of other parts most easily destroyed by gnawing are usually exceptionally low in relation to the more durable parts of the skeleton.

The relative abundance in which certain parts of the skeleton are preserved on early living sites is discussed in the next chapter. It will be shown that the evidence now available indicates that the seeming imbalance between the different parts of the skeleton which are preserved is in no way incompatible with food debris and that there is no reason to attribute it to hominid selectivity for any other purpose.

Although a detailed analysis of the groups of larger mammals must await taxonomic identification, it can be stated on the basis of this preliminary study that remains of Bovidae are by far the most numerous. A few specimens of diminutive species such as *Nesotragus* (a pygmy antelope) are known, and the large bovid, *Pelorovis oldowayensis*, is relatively abundant in Upper Bed II (Gentry, 1967), but most of the Bovidae represented consist of medium-sized species, ranging from animals the size of a wildebeeste to that of reed buck or bush buck. Gazelles and gazelle-like forms also occur at certain sites (Gentry, 1966). The average percentage of bovid remains in proportion to those of all other large mammals for the sites and levels listed in Table 4 is 48·3 per cent. Equidae and Suidae are the two most common groups following the Bovidae; each amounts to between 8·0 and 10·0 per cent.

Among the Equidae, only *Equus* sp. (cf. *oldowayensis*) has so far been found in Bed I below the level of '*Zinjanthropus*', whereas in Middle and Upper Bed II *Stylohipparion* predominates. The Suidae are represented by a large variety of genera and species, most of which have been described by L. S. B. Leakey in volume 1. It will be seen from Table 4 that the remaining groups of larger mammals are much less well represented than the Bovidae, Equidae and Suidae: the incidence of crocodiles and water tortoises appears to depend largely on the proximity of any particular site to the lake.

BED I
SITE DK

Although the faunal assemblages from the three levels beneath Tuff I^B proved variable in the different areas excavated, crocodile remains greatly outnumber any other group and amount to 65·2 per cent of the total. These consist for the most part of loose teeth, of which there are 4,600. The abundance of teeth in relation to other remains seems to indicate that they were probably shed by living crocodiles rather than that they are remains of crocodiles who had died, when bones and scutes representing more or less complete skeletons might be expected to occur. There is evidence at this site and elsewhere indicating the existence of *Crocodilus* cf. *niloticus* and of a short-snouted variety similar to the present-day West African species *Osteolaemus tetraspis* s. *frontatus*.

Remains of tortoises were also relatively common and account for 16·9 per cent of the total faunal material. Bones and scutes occurred in normal proportions, although they were usually scattered. Among the larger mammals Bovidae predominate, with 12·9 per cent, and Suidae amount to 2·1 per cent, whilst all other taxa are below 1 per cent. These include Primates, Carnivora, Elephantidae, Deinotheriidae, Rhinocerotidae, Equidae, Hippopotamidae and Giraffidae (including *Giraffa*, *Libytherium* and *Okapia*). Bird bones are relatively scarce in all three levels; they include remains of flamingos. Rodent and fish remains are equally scarce, although when the latter occurred they were remarkably well preserved, some fish scales even retaining their transparency.

In Table 3 it will be seen that the figure for identifiable faunal remains is unusually high (81·0 per cent). This is due to the large number of loose crocodile teeth. So far as mammalian remains are concerned the proportion of bones too fragmentary for identification appears to be similar to that found at other occupation sites, but it is interesting to note that among the broken limb-bone shafts there are some massive splinters that can only be proboscidian, two of which, as noted in the previous chapter, appear to have been artificially broken and chipped.

The distribution of crocodile and tortoise remains in Levels 1, 2 and 3 at the different localities that were excavated is somewhat curious in view of the trenches being within 150 yards of one another. In Trench I*c* Level 3, there were no crocodile remains, and only one tortoise scute. No crocodile remains were found at this level in the Trial Trench, but at the main site they amounted to 21·2 per cent of the total and tortoise bones and scutes to 46·3 per cent. Crocodile remains were, on the whole, more abundant in Level 2 than Level 3, but varied from 71·5 per cent in Trench I*b* to 22·9 per cent in the Trial Trench.

The brown clay immediately beneath Tuff I^B (Level 1) was not present in Trenches I*b* and I*c* but occurred at the main excavation and in the Trial Trench. In both these areas crocodile teeth and tortoise remains account for the greater part of the fauna.

SITE FLK NN

It has been shown that the highest occupation surface at this site (Level 1) can be correlated with the level of the '*Zinjanthropus*' floor at FLK, while the lowest (Level 4) corresponds with the deposits beneath Tuff I^B at DK, MK, etc. The intervening levels 2 and 3 are not known to yield artefacts or faunal material at any other site.

Level 4 was excavated only in the lower steps of the Trial Trench and did not yield a quantity of material comparable to that from the overlying levels where a more extensive area was dug. The material is therefore not listed in Tables 3 and 4. Among the 129 specimens recovered from this level 86·6 per cent consist of crocodile teeth, a figure that is even higher than that for DK. Bovidae amount to only 8·3 per cent and Equidae to 2·5 per cent. There are also single specimens belonging to a primate, a suid and a tortoise. Flamingos, ducks and an avocet have been identified among the avifauna.

In considering the faunal material from Level 3, it is necessary to distinguish between the bones of amphibians, birds and small rodents, which were found throughout the deposit, and the broken-up bones of the larger mammals and tortoises, which occurred on the palaeosol surface. These, together with the hominid remains and artefacts, were clearly deposited after the clay had been laid down, whilst the bones of amphibians and other small creatures were probably incorporated during its formation.

Amongst the remains of small creatures which were found throughout the deposit, the number of amphibians including both frogs and toads, is in excess of any other category, even of rodents, which at all other sites are by far the most numerous micro-faunal group. There is a minimum number of eighty-seven amphibians (represented by eighty-seven left tibio-fibulae) in contrast to sixty-six rodents. Moreover, whereas rodents occurred in both Levels 2 and 3 in very similar proportions, no amphibian remains were found in Level 2. It may therefore be assumed that an additional 217 amphibian left tibio-fibulae, which were recovered from sieving the pooled soil of these two levels, were also derived from Level 3. This would bring the total number of Amphibia from Level 3 to approximately 300. Remains of birds, shrews and small rodents are also relatively common and some snake vertebrae, teeth and fangs indicate the existence of a large viperine snake and another similar in size to a python. A few bones of bats, lizards and chameleons also occurred.

The remains on the top and in the upper part of the clay, consisting of the broken-up tortoises and bones of antelopes, suids, carnivores, etc., which were found in association with the artefacts and the hominid remains, appear to represent occupational debris, comparable in scatter-pattern to the remains found on the marginal areas of the '*Zinjanthropus*' floor of FLK and in parts of DK.

In certain areas considerable concentrations of bone splinters and other small unidentifiable bone fragments were found, but the total of larger animals represented is very low, considerably less than the total number of tortoises, of which there is a minimum of seventeen. All the tortoise appear to belong to a single species of hinged tortoise, identified by Dr E. Williams of the Museum of Comparative Anatomy, Harvard, as *Pelusios castaneus*, a species still living in East Africa at the present time. With the exception of one small specimen, found intact with the various parts in position, the remains of the more complete tor-

250

toises were scattered over areas 2–3 ft. in diameter. Careful scrutiny of the carapace and plastron fragments has been carried out, but apart from a very few small indentations, such as could have been caused by a pointed stone, no signs of damage are visible. It seems likely that the shells were not broken open, but fell apart after they had lain in the open for a time.

Among the larger mammals Bovidae are the most common, with 12·2 per cent. Carnivora amount to 3·0 per cent and Suidae to only 1·7 per cent in contrast to over 50·0 per cent in Level 2. Remains of Equidae and Crocodilydae are both under 1·0 per cent, whilst neither Rhinocerotidae nor Hippopotamidae occur.

Level 2 yielded a total of 481 bones and teeth, of which 74·0 per cent are identifiable to taxa. This assemblage is remarkable for the high proportion of Suidae (52·2 per cent) and the absence of arte-facts and tortoise remains, both of which are found in the overlying and underlying levels. A consider-able number of the suid remains are juvenile and include both milk dentitions and bones with unfused epiphyses. Bovidae, Equidae and Carni-vora also occur, together with rodents and birds. Remains of fish consist only of two catfish skulls.

The faunal material from Level 1 comprises 275 specimens, of which 91·3 per cent are identifiable to taxa. Chelonia predominate, with 39 per cent, followed by Bovidae with 33·9 per cent. Suidae amount to 21·5 per cent, while Carnivora, Equidae and Rhinocerotidae are scantily repre-sented. Remains of birds and rodents are rare, although they occur in considerable numbers in Levels 2 and 3. A number of snake vertebrae were found, some of which resemble those of python, as well as a number of teeth and fangs. There were no remains of fish, crocodiles or hippopotami.

Although the majority of fossil bones from this level was poorly preserved, the horn cores and parts of the skull and skeleton of a large antelope described in volume 1 under the name of *Strepsi-ceros maryanus* were in relatively good condition. Indeterminate bone fragments, such as are com-monly found on living floors, were unusually scarce and amounted to only 5·4 per cent of the faunal material.

It may be noted that the bovid material from Levels 1, 2 and 3 consists largely of specimens attributed to *Kobus* sp., which includes the present-day waterbuck and reedbuck, groups of antelopes believed to remain almost constantly near permanent water, thus confirming other lines of evidence which indicate that this site was close to the shore of the lake.

FLK I, THE 'ZINJANTHROPUS' OCCUPATION FLOOR (LEVEL 22)

The distribution of faunal and cultural material on this occupation level has already been described in chapter II and will not be further discussed here.

The collection of 3,510 faunal specimens is mainly composed of small, indeterminate frag-ments derived from the central area of the living floor, where both animal bones and stones were generally broken into very small pieces. There are, in fact, only 1,090 specimens belonging to the larger mammals and reptiles which are capable of identification to taxa or skeletal parts.

Among the larger mammals and reptiles, Bovidae constitute 70·2 per cent of the remains. They include horn cores of *Parmularius altidens*, *Gazella wellsi* and an *Oryx* sp. Chelonia amount to 7·8 per cent, Suidae to 7·4 per cent and Equidae to 6·0 per cent. The latter include both *Equus* sp. and *Stylohipparion*, which is not known from lower levels of Bed I. Primates include parts of two skulls and skeletons of *Galago senegalensis* (described by G. G. Simpson in volume 1 of the Olduvai series) and the upper milk dentition of a cercopithecoid monkey. Giraffidae are represented solely by two halves of a juvenile mandible belonging to *Okapia* sp. There are only fourteen crocodile teeth and one scute.

Remains of fish include three catfish skulls in addition to scattered vertebrae and other frag-ments. Amphibians, birds and rodents occurred in considerable numbers, while chameleons, snakes, shrews and bats are also represented.

Among the four varieties of Mollusca recovered is a species of Urocyclid slug. It is interesting to note that B. Verdcourt (1963) states in his report on the Miocene Mollusca from Rusinga Island that the living species of this slug are only common in evergreen forest where rainfall exceeds 35 in. per year or where damp conditions are maintained by regular mists.

The material from the higher levels at this site has been listed briefly in chapter II. Only two levels, 15 and 13, yielded a sufficient number of faunal remains to justify analysis. In both of these levels, although the total amount of material is much less than in Level 22 and the bones are less broken so that the proportion of identifiable remains is much higher.

Level 15 yielded a total of 259 bone fragments and teeth. Of these 47·5 per cent are identifiable to taxa and 8·9 per cent to parts of the skull or skeleton. Bovidae are the most numerous with 74·0 per cent. Suidae and Equidae amount to 10·5 and 9·0 per cent respectively, whilst Elephantidae and Hippopotamidae are represented by a single specimen each. No remains of tortoises or primates were found.

The total of faunal remains from Level 13 is considerably less, with only 187 specimens. Bovidae are again the most common of the larger mammals, with 58·8 per cent, but Giraffidae, including both *Giraffa* and *Libytherium*, amount to 15·3 per cent. Equidae, consisting only of *Equus* sp. amount to 13 per cent. Tortoises, primates and hippopotami are represented only by single specimens.

SITE FLK NORTH

The five levels excavated within the top 7 ft. of Bed I at this site all proved to be exceedingly rich in faunal remains of large and small mammals, birds, small reptiles, etc. Preliminary reports on the Insectivora, Chiroptera and Rodentia collected during the first season have been published in volume 1.

Among the Bovidae, which greatly outnumber any other group of large mammals in all the occupation levels at this site, *Parmularius altidens* is by far the most common species. *Gazella wellsi* is also well represented, but remains of other taxa are scarce, although there is a considerable variety of different genera (see Appendix B). Carnivora are unusually common, particularly in Levels 3

and 4. They include remains of hyaena, jackal, bat-eared fox, mongoose and a genet.

LEVEL 6

The disposition of the elephant skeleton found in association with a number of artefacts has been described in chapter III. A few bones belonging to a second elephant, some bovid and suid remains and other fragmentary bones also occurred, amounting in all to 614 specimens, of which a minimum of 206 are parts of the elephant. Bovidae amount to 40·4 per cent, Suidae to 14·6 per cent and Carnivora to 1 per cent. The remaining taxa, consisting of Equidae, Giraffidae and Hippopotamidae, are all under 1 per cent. Among the suid remains there is a crushed skull and mandible which has been described and illustrated in volume 1 as the Type of *Ectopotamochoerus dubius*.

LEVEL 5

This level was excavated over a more extensive area than Level 6 and yielded a total of 2,210 faunal specimens, excluding avian and micro-faunal remains. Among the larger mammals and reptiles, Bovidae predominate with 76·5 per cent. They include a frontlet of *Gorgon olduvaiensis* with both horn cores intact. Carnivora are more common than usual in this level and in the overlying levels. They amount to 11·6 per cent, followed by Suidae with 8·1 per cent. Elephantidae and Hippotamidae are poorly represented, while the remains of Crocodylidae, Chelonia, Primates, Equidae, Giraffidae and Deinotheriidae consist of only a few specimens each. Rodent remains were particularly numerous and include a number of different Muridae, *Xerus* sp. and *Heterocephalus* (the naked mole rat). Remains of fish, amphibians, lizards, snakes, birds, shrews and hedgehogs were also recovered.

(Patches of crushed micro-faunal bones that may represent hominid faeces were found at this level. They are described elsewhere, on p. 67.)

LEVEL 4

The total number of specimens from this level attributable to the larger mammals amounts to

929, of which 685 are identifiable to taxa. Only six groups are represented, namely Bovidae (65·3 per cent), Carnivora (21·6 per cent), Suidae (7·0 per cent), Giraffidae (4·4 per cent), Equidae (1·6 per cent), and Hippopotamidae (0·1 per cent). Rodent remains are numerous, although they are less common in relation to the other faunal material than in Level 5. They include a large hare (*Serengetilagus*) and a ground squirrel. Remains of fish, amphibians, lizards, chameleons, snakes, birds, shrews, bats and hedgehogs also occurred.

LEVEL 3

This level yielded 1,254 specimens (excluding avian and micro-faunal remains), of which 803 are identifiable to taxa. As in Level 4, only six groups of large mammals are represented, namely Bovidae (72·1 per cent), Carnivora (14·6 per cent), Suidae (7·6 per cent), Equidae (3·2 per cent), Giraffidae (2·0 per cent) and Rhinocerotidae (0·5 per cent). The additional faunal material consists of the same groups listed for Level 4.

LEVELS 1 AND 2

Faunal material occurred in great abundance in these levels. Remains of the larger mammals were more plentiful than in the lower levels and the whole horizon was particularly rich in remains of amphibians, lizards, chameleons, birds, insectivores, bats and rodents. (Over 14,000 rodents are represented.) These remains usually occurred in concentrated patches, but a proportion were also scattered through the deposit. No articulated skeletons were found, in spite of particularly careful excavation. Mandibles of rodents and other small mammals were relatively common, but skulls and maxillae were scarce—a feature which has been noted elsewhere in connection with micro-faunal remains. It is difficult to account for the vast quantity of micro-fauna at this site, where it occurred in all the Bed I levels that were excavated. If it had been derived from owl pellets,[1] skulls could be expected to be far more plentiful, since

[1] These observations are based on examination of present-day owl pellets collected in Olduvai Gorge.

each pellet usually contains the bones of at least one small animal, including the skull. Equally, the limb bones contained in owl pellets are usually intact, whereas a high proportion of those excavated had been broken. It is possible that small mammals, etc., formed part of the diet of early man, although the mode of occurrence, in small concentrations, is suggestive of accumulations found beneath owl roosts.

Among the remains of larger animals and reptiles, Crocodylidae, Proboscidea and Giraffidae are missing, but there is a slightly wider range of taxa than in the lower levels, although the elements not found in the lower levels are represented only by scant material. The number of bovid remains is proportionately higher than at any other level, amounting to 78·5 per cent. Other groups occur in the following ratios: Carnivora 11·2 per cent, Suidae 6·9 per cent, Equidae 3·0 per cent and Hippopotamidae 0·2 per cent. Remains of Chelonia, Primates and Rhinocerotidae amount to less than 1 per cent each.

BED II

SITE FLK NORTH

At FLK North the clay at the base of Bed II (corresponding to Level 2 at HWK East) yielded a total of 174 bones and teeth, many of which were encrusted with lime. They include two teeth of a juvenile *Deinotherium* and a number of rhinoceros foot bones. Bovid remains are the most numerous, amounting to 67·7 per cent; they include a skull of *Damaliscus angusticornis*. Both *Equus* and *Stylohipparion* occur and four varieties of Mollusca were also found. These are described as freshwater shells, abundant and widespread throughout tropical Africa at the present day, with the exception of one species, *Bulinus truncatus*, which is now known only from north-east Africa. (This species and *B. tropicus* have also been identified from the 'Zinjanthropus' level at FLK.)

The position of the *Deinotherium* skeleton found in a clay horizon 7 ft. above the base of Bed II has been described in chapter III. A number of additional faunal remains was also found at this level, near the *Deinotherium* skeleton. They consist of a crushed hyaena skull, compressed into a thin plate of bone fragments not more than ½ in. thick, part of a suid mandible, the skull and horn cores of *Damaliscus* sp. and sundry bovid remains. (Because only a small number of specimens were recovered from these two levels, the material is not included in Tables 3 and 4.)

No identifiable faunal remains were found in the overlying sandy conglomerate, although this level yielded a number of artefacts.

SITE HWK EAST

The lower levels at this site (Levels 1 and 2) were unusually rich in well-preserved avian remains, including a number of skulls.

In Level 1 the distribution of remains and the proportions of bones belonging to the various faunal groups followed the pattern typical of Oldowan living floors, with 80·9 per cent Bovidae and a variety of other taxa. Level 2, however, was quite dissimilar. A certain number of scattered bones were found throughout the 6½ ft. of clay forming this horizon, but they were more concentrated at two distinct levels. The lower of these contained a high proportion of proboscidian remains, including teeth of both *Elephas* and *Deinotherium*, together with the associated bones of a forefoot and other post-cranial material. There were also some scattered bones and teeth of Bovidae, Equidae, etc., and a complete hippopotamus tibia. The upper horizon contained little besides parts of the skeleton of a rhinoceros, associated with a few artefacts.

In Level 2 crocodile remains amount to 12·9 per cent of the identifiable material of the larger mammals and reptiles, although none were found in either Level 1 or the overlying Levels 3, 4 and 5. Relatively large coprolites, similar in size to those of hyaena and lion, also occurred, together with some snake vertebrae, amphibian and rodent bones and teeth and a fragment of shell belonging to a large gastropod. This level contained only 3·6 per cent of indeterminate bone fragments, a much lower figure than is usual on living floors.

Faunal remains from Levels 3, 4 and 5 (includ-ing the sandy conglomerate) were relatively less plentiful than in Levels 1 or 2 and were markedly more fragmentary. Bovidae and Equidae are the most common families, while the proportion of indeterminate bone fragments (16 per cent) is higher than in Level 2.

THE MNK SKULL SITE

The lower level at this site, in which two fragments of the skull of H. 13 were found, yielded a total of 378 faunal remains, belonging to the larger mammals and reptiles, 216 of which are identifiable to taxa. Tortoise fragments are the most numerous and amount to 76·7 per cent. Bovidae constitute only 13·4 per cent and other taxa are considerably lower. They include Crocodilia (3·7 per cent), Suidae (2·7 per cent), Hippopotamidae (1·3 per cent) and Elephantidae, Equidae, Rhinocerotidae, all of which amount to less than 1 per cent. A few fragments of ostrich eggshell, some rodent bones and teeth and about thirty bird bones were also found.

The presence of numerous small fragments of shell belonging to land snails has been mentioned previously. These are too fragmentary for identification, but it may be noted that they vary in thickness from 0·5 to 1·5 mm. Over 6,000 minute particles of bone were also recovered in the course of washing the deposit through sieves for fragments of hominid material. (Since pieces of comparable size were not recovered from other sites they are not counted in the analysis shown in Table 3.)

The faunal material from the Level of H. 15 is very scarce. The most plentiful remains are of tortoises, as in the lower level. These amount to 69·8 per cent of the identifiable larger mammals and reptiles and consist of forty-four plates and bones, with some additional fragments. Bovidae, Carnivora and Suidae are each represented by only a few specimens. There are also some fish remains, including part of a catfish skull, bones of rodents, amphibians and birds as well as a few small fragments of ostrich eggshell. Small pieces of snail shells were also common, as in Level 2.

MNK MAIN SITE

The total number of faunal specimens from this site amounts to 1,723. Of these an unusually large percentage (50·4 per cent) are indeterminate fragments consisting mainly of splinters from limb bones. (A similarly high proportion of fragments derived from the shafts of limb bones also occurs at BK.) Among the identifiable remains of the larger mammals and reptiles Bovidae amount to 46·0 per cent while both equid and hippopotamus remains are more common than usual, with 21·0 and 12·8 per cent respectively. Specimens belonging to crocodiles and tortoises each amount to approximately 3 per cent.

Rodent and amphibian remains are relatively scarce, but some 609 bird bones were recovered, together with many fish vertebrae and some fragments of catfish skulls.

EF–HR

The faunal remains recovered from this Acheulean site amount to only thirty-four specimens and are not listed in Tables 3 and 4. They include the complete cranium of *Giraffa jumae* referred to in Chapter v, some bovid remains and two distinct equids, as well as single specimens belonging to a carnivore, a rhinoceros, a suid and a tortoise.

SITE FC WEST

The Occupation Floor at this site yielded only 127 faunal remains, a figure that is very low in comparison to the number of artefacts. Among the identifiable large mammals and reptiles, Bovidae and Equidae are represented in equal proportion (31 per cent). Hippopotamidae amount to 12·1 per cent and Crocodylidae to 13·8 per cent. Suidae and Chelonia are represented by only three specimens each. There is also a small fragment of an elephant molar.

Faunal remains from the re-worked tuff overlying the Occupation Floor were rather more numerous and amount to 254 specimens, although only ninety-one of these can be identified to the larger mammals and reptiles. Bovidae are the most common group, with 51·6 per cent, whilst Equidae and Hippopotamidae occur in equal proportions (18·7 per cent). There are only a few specimens belonging to Giraffidae, Suidae and Chelonia. Some fish and avian remains also occurred.

(A list of the known taxa from SHK is given in Appendix B but no analysis of the faunal material has been undertaken since a total assemblage is not available.)

SITE TK

Faunal remains were scarce in proportion to the artefacts at all the five levels excavated at this site. The highest figure is for the Lower Occupation Floor (6·3 per cent), while the average figure for the five excavated levels is only 4 per cent of the total number of objects recovered. In view of the small size of the assemblages from the various levels, all the material has been pooled.

Bovidae are the most common group, with 45·6 per cent. Equidae reach the highest recorded figure with 28 per cent and include *Equus* sp. and *Stylohipparion*. Suidae amount to 10·7 per cent and Hippopotamidae (including one nearly complete mandible) to 7·4 per cent. Giraffidae include both *Giraffa* sp. and *Libytherium*. Reptiles are represented by only one snake vertebra, comparable in size to that of a python.

SITE BK

The analysis of faunal remains from this site is confined to specimens recovered during the 1963 excavation. A great deal of material was obtained during previous years and the identified genera and species in these collections are listed in Appendix B.

As previously noted, the site yielded many remains of *Pelorovis oldowayensis*. These have been the subject of a report by A. W. Gentry (1967), who is of the opinion that *Pelorovis* should be included among the Bovidae, in spite of the original diagnosis. He also considers that specimens previously described as *Bularchus arok* from PLK II and other sites at Olduvai are merely a sexual variation of *Pelorovis*.

Remains of both *Equus* sp. and *Stylohipparion* occur in considerable numbers. (The discovery of a complete cranium of *Stylohipparion* in 1963 revealed that the anterior dentitions previously assigned to *Eurygnathohippus* belong in fact to *Stylohipparion*.)

During the 1963 excavations 2,957 faunal remains were recovered. A considerable proportion of these (53·9 per cent) consists of unidentifiable fragments of limb-bone shafts such as occurred at MNK (Main Site). Among the specimens identifiable to the larger mammals and reptiles 53·2 per cent are of Bovidae, including at least ten distinct genera. The Suidae are also strongly represented and include six different genera. Among the Giraffidae there are a few specimens belonging to *Giraffa* sp. and one molar

tooth of *Okapia* sp., but by far the greatest number of specimens are of *Libytherium*. These include broken 'antlers', upper and lower dentitions and broken limb bones, some of which show evidence of utilisation on the fractured edges.

Hippopotamus remains have been assigned mainly to *H. gorgops*, but a few specimens, including part of a mandible, appear to belong to a pygmy species that was recognized among the material at the National Centre for Prehistory and Palaeontology, Nairobi, by Mrs S. C. Savage. Both *Ceratotherium simum* and *Diceros bicornis* are present, although the former (the White Rhinoceros) is more common. Remains of small mammals, reptiles and amphibians are relatively scarce, although bird bones occur in some quantity and pieces of ostrich eggshell were unusually plentiful.

Table 3. *Proportions of identifiable and indeterminate remains of the larger mammals and reptiles from excavated sites in Beds I and II*

Sites	Identifiable to taxa		Identifiable to skeletal parts		Indeterminate fragments	
	Nos.	%	Nos.	%	Nos.	%
BK	988	33·4	375	12·7	1,594	53·9
TK, all levels	215	46·8	83	18·1	161	35·1
FC West						
Tuff	91	35·8	12	4·7	151	59·4
Floor	58	45·7	14	11·0	55	43·3
MNK Main Site	677	39·3	177	10·3	869	50·4
MNK Skull Site, level of H. 13	216	57·1	27	7·1	135	35·7
HWK E						
Levels 3, 4, 5	214	79·5	12	4·5	43	16·0
Level 2	541	85·7	67	10·6	23	3·6
Level 1	319	75·1	58	13·6	48	11·3
FLK North						
Levels 1–2	1,721	52·2	297	9·0	1,276	38·7
Level 3	803	64·0	130	10·4	321	25·6
Level 4	685	70·6	42	5·1	202	24·3
Level 5	1,054	47·7	117	5·3	1,039	47·0
Level 6	478	77·8	51	8·3	85	13·8
FLK						
Level 13	124	66·3	21	11·2	42	22·4
Level 15	123	47·5	23	8·9	113	43·6
'Zinjanthropus' Level	675	19·2	415	11·8	2,420	68·9
FLK NN						
Level 1	251	91·3	9	3·3	15	5·4
Level 2	356	74·0	85	17·6	40	8·3
Level 3	1,893	87·7	146	6·7	119	5·5
DK, all levels	8,085	81·0	445	4·4	1,454	14·6

Table 4. *Faunal remains from excavated sites in Beds I and II. Proportions of whole and broken bones and teeth, etc., of the larger mammals and reptiles identifiable to taxa*

Site	Chelonia		Croco-dylidae		Primates		Carnivora		Probo-scidea		Equidae		Rhino-cerotidae		Suidae		Hippo-potamidae		Giraf-fidae		Bovidae	
	Nos.	%	Nos.	%	Nos.	%	Nos.	%	Nos.	%	Nos.	%	Nos.	%	Nos.	%	Nos.	%	Nos.	%	Nos.	%
BK	24	2·4	26	2·6	16	1·6	9	0·9	7	0·7	178	18·0	19	1·9	89	9·0	20	2·0	74	7·5	526	53·2
TK, all levels	—	—	—	—	—	—	2	0·9	1	0·4	60	28·0	8	3·7	23	10·7	16	7·4	7	3·2	98	45·6
FC West, Tuff	2	2·2	—	—	—	—	—	—	—	—	17	18·7	—	—	6	6·6	17	18·7	2	2·2	47	51·6
FC West, Floor	3	5·2	8	13·8	—	—	—	—	1	1·7	18	31·0	—	—	3	5·2	7	12·1	—	—	18	31·0
MNK																						
Main Site	19	2·8	21	3·1	2	0·3	9	1·3	2	0·3	142	21·0	10	1·5	53	7·8	87	12·8	21	3·1	311	46·0
Skull Site Level of H. 13	66	76·8	8	3·7	—	—	—	—	1	0·5	2	0·9	1	0·5	6	2·8	3	1·4	—	—	29	13·4
HWK E																						
Levels 3, 4, 5	3	1·4	—	—	—	—	9	4·2	—	—	18	8·4	4	1·9	6	2·8	7	3·3	4	1·9	163	76·1
Level 2	18	3·3	70	12·9	—	—	7	1·3	64	11·8	14	2·6	29	5·4	33	6·1	7	1·3	5	0·9	294	54·3
Level 1	2	0·6	—	—	—	—	2	0·6	6	1·9	25	7·8	—	—	16	5·0	2	0·6	8	2·5	258	80·9
FLK North																						
Levels 1–2	1	0·05	—	—	1	0·05	193	11·2	—	—	52	3·0	1	0·05	118	6·9	4	0·2	—	—	1,351	78·5
Level 3	—	—	—	—	—	—	117	14·6	—	—	26	3·2	4	0·5	61	7·6	16	2·0	—	—	579	72·1
Level 4	—	—	—	—	—	—	148	21·6	—	—	11	1·6	—	—	48	7·0	1	0·1	30	4·4	447	65·3
Level 5	9	0·8	1	0·1	2	0·2	122	11·6	1	0·1	19	1·8	—	—	85	8·1	1	0·1	8	0·7	806	76·5
Level 6	—	—	—	—	—	—	5	1·0	206	43·1	2	0·4	—	—	70	14·6	1	0·2	1	0·2	193	40·4
FLK																						
Level 13	1	0·8	—	—	1	0·8	2	1·6	—	—	16	13·0	—	—	11	8·8	1	0·8	19	15·3	73	58·8
Level 15	—	—	—	—	—	—	1	0·8	1	0·8	11	9·0	—	—	13	10·5	1	0·8	5	4·0	91	74·0
'Zinjanthropus' Level	53	7·8	14	2·1	30	4·4	12	1·8	—	—	40	6·0	—	—	50	7·4	—	—	2	0·2	474	70·2
FLK NN,																						
Level 1	98	39·0	—	—	—	—	4	1·6	—	—	8	3·2	2	0·8	54	21·5	—	—	—	—	85	33·9
Level 2	—	—	—	—	—	—	7	2·0	—	—	19	5·3	—	—	186	52·2	—	—	—	—	144	40·4
Level 3	1,549	81·8	14	0·7	—	—	56	3·0	—	—	10	0·5	—	—	32	1·7	—	—	—	—	232	12·2
DK, all levels	1,370	16·9	5,274	65·2	62	0·8	34	0·4	20	0·3	42	0·5	17	0·2	167	2·1	34	0·4	19	0·2	1,046	12·9

CHAPTER X

SUMMARY AND DISCUSSION

R. L. Hay has reviewed the evidence for potassium–argon dating of the Olduvai deposits in his section on the stratigraphy of Beds I and II and it is only necessary to mention here the two most important dates that have been obtained by this means, both of which are now generally accepted. These are 1·9 million years for the basalt at the base of the Upper Member of Bed I and 1·75 million years for Tuff I^B which overlies DK and other sites at the same stratigraphic horizon. A date of 1·7 million years for Tuff I^F at the top of Bed I is probably acceptable and compatible with paleomagnetic evidence. No acceptable date has been obtained for Bed II.

(1) THE OCCUPATION SITES

The sites excavated in Beds I and II can be subdivided into four groups, as follows:

(*a*) *Living floors*, in which the occupation debris is found on a palaeosol or old land surface with a vertical distribution of only a few inches (0·3 ft.).

(*b*) *Butchering or kill sites*, where artefacts are associated with the skeleton of a large mammal or with a group of smaller mammals.

(*c*) *Sites with diffused material*, where artefacts and faunal remains are found throughout a considerable thickness of clay or fine-grained tuff.

(*d*) *River or stream channel sites*, where occupation debris has become incorporated in the filling of a former river or stream channel.

Sites where artefacts are sparsely scattered on a former surface or palaeosol are also known, but none has been excavated.

Ten of the occupation levels that have been described consist of living floors, namely DK Level 3, FLK NN Levels 1 and 3, FLK the '*Zinjanthropus*' Level, HWK East Level 1, EF–HR, the Floor at FC West, the Annexe site at SHK and the

Upper and Lower Floors at TK. Two kill sites were found at FLK North, in the upper part of Bed I and the lower part of Bed II respectively. Levels of clay or fine-grained tuffs with diffused artefacts and faunal remains were uncovered at DK Levels 1 and 2, FLK NN Level 2, FLK Levels 7 and 10 to 21, FLK North Levels 1–5, HWK East Level 2, the MNK Skull and Main Sites, the reworked tuff at FC West, the tuff above the channel at SHK and the Upper and Intermediate tuffs at TK. Stream channel occurrences were found at SHK, TK and BK.

Debris on most of the living floors and at the butchering sites is unweathered and shows no evidence of orientation by running water. Material from the clays and fine-grained tuffs is also generally unweathered, but some of the artefacts and faunal remains from the river channels have been abraded. This is particularly evident in the material from the channel at SHK and from the coarser parts of the channel filling at BK.

The geological and faunal evidence now available[1] indicate that the occupation sites in Beds I and II were situated close to water, either by the lake shore or by rivers and streams. In Bed I sites DK and FLK NN were almost certainly near the margin of the lake. This is indicated by the presence of many crocodile and fish remains, bones of aquatic birds, reed casts and fossil rhizomes resembling those of papyrus. The occurrence of flamingo bones at FLK NN and at DK, at a level beneath Tuff I^B suggests that the lake water was alkaline in these areas and contained the microorganisms on which flamingos subsist.

At TK the Lower Occupation Floor was adjacent to a stream channel in which the filling was entirely fine-grained, consisting of clays and

---

[1] Attempts to recover pollen grains from deposits in Beds I and II have so far proved unsuccessful.

silts. This probably represents a small stagnant stream similar perhaps to the larger clay-filled channel at BK which lies close to the main channel and where many remains of *Pelorovis* and other large mammals were found.

Re-worked concentrations of occupation debris occurred in stream-channel deposits at SHK and BK, but are unknown in Bed I. At BK large quantities of artefacts and faunal debris became incorporated in the filling of a river channel as much as 8 ft. deep and of considerable width. It seems likely that at this site and at SHK the living sites were situated on the banks of the rivers and that the debris was swept into the channels by flood waters or by a shifting of the channel. Only a small percentage of the specimens is rolled and it is evident that most of the material came to rest before it had travelled far enough to become abraded.

A re-worked tuff and sandy conglomerate which reaches a thickness of 2 ft. in certain areas and which lies 10–15 ft. above the base of Bed II contains an exceptionally high concentration of artefacts over a wide area. It extends north-west from KK as far as FLK NN, a distance of 0·6 mile. The deposit is characterised by the presence of chert artefacts in addition to those of lava and quartz. This bed appears to represent a gravel sheet laid down during the period of erosion that followed the onset of faulting in Bed II.

The usual mode of occurrence of Oldowan and Developed Oldowan occupation sites on palaeosols or in clays or fine-grained tuffs is in contrast to the conditions at many Acheulean sites, where the material is often found in sands as, for example, at Olorgesailie, Isimila, Kariandusi, etc., and even the Acheulean sites in Bed IV*a* at Olduvai itself. (The artefacts at the early Acheulean site of EF–HR in Bed II, however, were found on a clay surface.) This presumably indicates a somewhat different environment for the Oldowan and Developed Oldowan and the Acheulean living sites, but the implications are difficult to interpret. It has been suggested that the habitation sites in sandy hollows at Olorgesailie might represent camping places in dry river beds, where it would be possible to dig for water (Isaac, 1966). This explanation is possible,

but the danger of the camps being swept away by sudden floods is an objection to this theory. By analogy with the Olduvai sites, it seems more likely that the Acheulean sites may have been situated on the banks of rivers or streams and that the debris was swept into the channels, as appears to have been the case at SHK and BK.

There is, unfortunately, no means either of assessing the length of time during which any camp site was occupied or of estimating the number of resident hominids. Some light may be thrown on this problem when the study of Bushman sites now being undertaken by De Vore, Lee and Yellen has been completed, since the Bushmen are undoubtedly one of the nearest modern parallels to the early hunter-gatherers of Africa.

On the basis of Bushman economy it seems likely that the groups of early hominids were never very large, but comprised a sufficient number of active males to form hunting bands and to protect the females and young in case of attack. Hunting and fishing were unquestionably practised in view of the remains found on the living floors, but it is probable that scavenging from predator kills was also a method of obtaining meat. Judging by the habits of present-day hunter-gatherers it seems likely that the major part of the diet consisted of plant foods, with the addition of small mammals and reptiles, snails, grubs and insects.

The evidence of the small concentrations of crushed microfaunal bones from FLK North is not conclusive, but it is quite possible that they represent the residue of hominid faeces. If this is the case, then small mammals, lizards, chameleons and small birds were eaten—apparently whole—by the contemporary hominids. Somewhat surprisingly, fragments of snail shell have so far only been found at one locality, the MNK Skull Site, where snails almost certainly formed an article of diet.

The density of remains on the Oldowan and Developed Oldowan living floors varies greatly (see Table 5). The highest concentration was at FC West, where remains on the living floor occurred at a density of 27·6 objects per cu.ft. The remains on the Upper and Lower Occupation Floors at TK were also densely concentrated, with

21·9 and 17·4 objects per cu.ft. respectively. The lowest figure for a living floor was at Level 1, FLK NN where there were only 0·4 objects per cu.ft.

Table 5. *Density of finds at the principal occupation sites in Beds I and II*

Site	Depth of deposit (ft.)	Density of finds (per cu.ft.)
BK	5·0 (av.)	1·6
TK		
Upper Floor	0·3	21·9
Lower Floor	0·3	17·4
FC West		
Tuff	2·4	2·3
Floor	0·3	27·6
MNK Main Site	4·5	1·5
EF–HR (Floor)	0·3	3·9
MNK Skull Site, Level of H. 13	2·0	1·3
HWK East		
Levels 3–5	5·25	5·8
Level 2	6·75	0·4
Level 1 (Floor)	0·3	2·4
FLK North		
Levels 1–2	1·75	2·4
Level 3	0·5	2·8
Level 4	0·9	1·4
Level 5	1·5	1·4
Level 6	1·75	1·1
FLK 'Zinjanthropus'		
Floor	0·3	6·5
FLK NN		
Level 1 (Floor)	0·3	0·4
Level 2	0·8	0·3
Level 3 (Floor)	0·3	3·3
DK		
Level 1	1·75	0·3
Level 2	2·25	0·7
Level 3 (Floor)	0·3	1·7

There is a marked rise in the number of artefacts in proportion to faunal remains in Middle and Upper Bed II where at all recorded sites they exceed 50·0 per cent of the total remains, in contrast to Bed I, where the highest figure is 40·6 per cent on the 'Zinjanthropus' floor at FLK (see Table 6). This may be due in part to greater facility in toolmaking and greater accessibility of raw material or to the fact that remains of large mammals such as hippopotamus, *Libytherium*, giraffe and rhinoceros are more common at sites in Middle and Upper Bed II than in Lower Bed II or Bed I. It is evident that any group of hominids would require fewer such animals in order to subsist than would be the case if they relied mainly on antelopes and smaller game. The accumulation of bones at the living sites would thus be much less, particularly if the meat were generally removed from the carcass where the animal was killed, as is the usual custom today. Equids are also more common in Upper Bed II than in Lower Bed II or Bed I. This may be partly due to selective hunting by the hominid population, but the increase is more likely to have been caused by the change in ecology that followed the earth movements in Bed II. The Bed I lake was largely drained and areas that had previously been under water or marshes became open grassland.

Examination of the distribution of cultural and faunal remains on the occupation sites, shows that only in the case of living floors on palaeosols can any patterns of possible significance be detected. In so far as the re-worked tuffs are concerned, where repeated accumulations of debris occur throughout a considerable thickness of deposit, the position is not clear, although the most likely explanation appears to be that these sites were reoccupied on successive occasions.

The pattern of distribution on the 'Zinjanthropus' living floor at FLK is undoubtedly the most complete that was uncovered. The oblong central area of densely concentrated and very fragmentary remains was surrounded by a relatively barren zone, particularly to the south and east, beyond which debris again became more plentiful and consisted of more complete material than in the central area. It has been suggested in discussion that the central living area may have been enclosed, at least to the south and east, by a thorn fence or windbreak, which would correspond with the barren zone, while objects found on the outside might have been thrown out over the fence by the occupants of the camp.

Two adjacent circular areas containing concentrated artefacts and faunal remains were also

SUMMARY AND DISCUSSION

Table 6. *Proportions of faunal remains, artefacts and manuports at living sites in Beds I and II*
(excluding micro-vertebrate and avian remains)

Site	Faunal remains		Artefacts		Manuports	
	No.	%	No.	%	No.	%
BK	2,957	29·1	6,801	66·8	419	4·1
TK						
Upper Floor	230	4·2	5,180	93·3	139	2·5
Lower Floor	147	6·3	2,153	92·8	21	0·9
Channel	43	2·9	1,436	96·7	6	0·4
FC West						
Tuff	254	24·6	673	65·0	107	10·3
Floor	127	8·1	1,184	75·8	251	16·1
MNK Main Site	1,723	24·5	4,399	62·5	916	13·0
EF–HR	34	6·2	522	93·8	—	—
MNK Skull Site, Level of H. 13	378	33·3	689	60·7	67	6·0
HWK E						
Levels 3–5	269	7·8	1,989	57·8	1,184	34·4
Level 2	631	65·4	313	32·4	21	2·2
Level 1	425	57·3	154	20·7	163	22·0
FLK North						
Levels 1, 2	3,294	69·9	1,205	25·6	210	4·5
Level 3	1,254	85·5	171	11·8	39	2·7
Level 4	929	91·7	67	6·6	17	1·7
Level 5	2,210	92·5	151	6·3	29	1·2
Level 6	614	82·5	123	16·5	7	1·0
FLK						
Level 13	187	91·9	11	8·1	—	—
Level 15	259	93·2	9	6·8	—	—
'Zinjanthropus' level	3,510	57·8	2,470	40·6	96	1·6
FLK NN						
Level 1	275	89·0	16	5·2	18	5·8
Level 2	481	100·0	—	—	—	—
Level 3	2,158	96·8	48	2·2	24	1·0
DK all levels	9,984	89·3	1,198	10·7	—	—

uncovered in the uppermost occupation level at FLK North. At FC West, in Middle Bed II, a living floor occurred on a clay palaeosol similar to those in Bed I. Here, again, the artefacts and faunal remains were concentrated within two roughly circular areas, lying close together and reminiscent of the pattern uncovered at FLK North. At TK, however, although the debris on both the Upper and Lower Occupation Floors occurred on palaeosols and was confined to limited areas, there was no discernible pattern in the distribution. It is perhaps significant that the faunal remains and a proportion of the artefacts

from this site are weathered, indicating that they were exposed on the surface longer than usual before being buried and so were possibly displaced from their original positions.

It is probable that the stone circle at DK formed the base of a rough windbreak or simple shelter. The two factors that are most suggestive of an artificial structure are the small heaps of piled-up stones that form part of the circle and the fact that occupation debris did not occur in comparable density within the circle and in the surrounding area.

The stone circle and the distribution patterns of the debris on the three living floors described above, where little or no disturbance appears to have taken place after the camps were abandoned, suggest that some form of crude shelter was probably constructed at Oldowan and Developed Oldowan living sites. This may well have been no more than a protective thorn fence, but the existence of some factor affecting the horizontal diffusion of debris on the living floors is indicated.

Some information concerning the methods by which animals were hunted and killed has come to light at certain sites. The discovery of skeletons of an elephant, a *Deinotherium* and remains of *Pelorovis oldowayensis* embedded in clay and associated with numbers of stone tools suggests that these animals may have been deliberately driven into swamps by the early hominids. The possibility that they became engulfed accidentally cannot be ruled out entirely, but the repeated discovery of large animals that appear to have died under identical conditions is suggestive of hominid activity. Remains of two herds of antelopes, similarly embedded in clay, have also been found: one in Bed II at SHK and the second in Bed IV*a* at the Fifth Fault.

The depressed fractures on the three frontlets of *Parmularius altidens* from FLK North can be taken to indicate that the animals were killed by means of a blow, delivered at close quarters, since the fractures are accurately placed above the orbits, on the most vulnerable part of the skull.

Although there is no direct evidence that spheroids were used as bolas, no alternative explanation has yet been put forward to account for the numbers of these tools and for the fact that many have been carefully and accurately shaped. If they were intended to be used merely as missiles, with little chance of recovery, it seems unlikely that so much time and care would have been spent on their manufacture. (Possible methods by which spheroids were used are discussed on page 266.)

(2) THE LITHIC INDUSTRIES

Before summarising the evidence concerning the industries of Beds I and II that has come to light in the course of the 1960–3 excavations, it is desirable to clarify the relationship of the cultural sequence published in 1951 with the results of the present work.

At the time when the first volume on Olduvai was being prepared there was a general tendency to follow the late Abbé Breuil in subdividing the Acheulean and indeed the majority of Stone Age lithic industries into a whole series of evolutionary stages and phases, basing the subdivisions largely on typology of selected specimens and not on entire assemblages. This tendency undoubtedly led to the division of the cultural material from Olduvai collected during the 1930 and 1931 expeditions into eleven stages of the Acheulean or 'Chelles-Acheul', in addition to the Oldowan or 'Pre-Chellean' from Bed I.

A certain amount of selectivity in the specimens studied was inevitable, since the conditions under which the earlier expeditions to Olduvai were forced to work made it impossible to undertake the type of large-scale systematic excavations that were carried out later. There was thus no opportunity to recover a total assemblage from any site and the overall picture published in 1951 was based entirely on specimens observed *in situ* and material obtained from small exploratory excavations.

In the 1951 publication particular emphasis was laid on the new elements appearing in successive levels. Owing to the fact that these mainly consisted of various bifaces, they were perhaps given undue prominence, although it was clearly stated that choppers and other tools also occurred throughout the sequence.

The Oldowan from Bed I must be considered first. It has now been confirmed that no bifaces occur at this level, while the existence of 'small rough scrapers' and utilized flakes, whose presence was indicated in 1930–1, has also been fully established. These were among material originally found *in situ* in Bed I, but at the time it was not considered justifiable to claim that they were typical of an Oldowan assemblage.

The choppers that are described and illustrated appear to be typical specimens with the exception of one made from chert, which it is now known can only have been obtained from the chert-bearing levels in the lower part of Middle Bed II. (It appears that these horizons were originally included in Bed I, L. S. B. Leakey, personal communication.)

Among the specimens selected to illustrate the new element characterising Stage 1 of the cultural sequence were several that are typical of what have now been termed 'proto-bifaces' which are found most commonly in Upper Bed I and Lower Bed II. There are another three bifaces illustrated for this stage that appear to be too highly evolved on the basis of present knowledge and it is possible that their provenance was not correctly identified. The sites from which the series of illustrated specimens were obtained are not specifically mentioned, but the horizon is described as being 'at the junction of Bed II, as well as the lowest level of Bed II proper'. (This would, in fact, correspond to Levels 1 and 2 and HWK East.)

The tools described as typical of Stage 2 of the cultural sequence consist of massive pick-like specimens with heavy butts, usually triangular in cross-section. They are reported to have been found, usually singly, at a number of different localities 10–15 ft. above the base of Bed II. There is, however, some doubt as to their exact stratigraphic position and also as to whether all the specimens attributed to this stage are in fact contemporaneous. No similar tools have been found at this level during recent years and L. S. B. Leakey now considers that this stage may not be distinct.

On a stratigraphic basis, Stage 3 appears to correspond to the main site at MNK and to FC West, where bifaces similar to those illustrated were found during the 1960–3 excavations. They form such a small percentage of the tools at both sites, however, that the industry has now been termed Developed Oldowan B rather than Acheulean, for which a substantial proportion of bifaces is considered by the writer to be an essential criterion.

It has not been possible to determine the horizon at which tools attributed to Stage 4 were found. They are described as occurring on an average 10 ft. below the junction of Beds II and III and were obtained from a number of different sites, including FLK, FLK South, HWK and CK. When they were collected it was not realised that the upper part of Bed II varied considerably in thickness at different localities, so that the figure of 10 ft. below the junction with Bed III does not necessarily everywhere refer to the same level. For example, the marker Tuff II^c, which lies only 3 ft. below the junction of Beds II and III at CK, is approximately 25 ft. below the junction at HWK. It seems probable, therefore, that the tools attributed to this stage are not all from the same horizon, although they are from the upper part of Bed II.

Tools of Stage 5 are described as coming from the junction of Beds II and III. They were considered to be somewhat more evolved than those of Stage 4, with some evidence of cylinder-hammer technique. TK is referred to as one of the sites where this stage is represented and a large biface made from tabular quartz is figured from this site. Excavations at TK during 1963 yielded a number of similar specimens which were found on a living floor 10 ft. below the junction of Beds II and III. In common with the industry formerly described as Stage 3, this assemblage contained only a negligible proportion of bifaces with a very much stronger Oldowan element and has, therefore, been referred to the Developed Oldowan B industry.

A number of the specimens from sites in the eastern part of the Gorge appear to be more evolved and were attributed to stage 6. They are believed to have come from Bed III.

The raw materials employed for making artefacts have been discussed by R. L. Hay in his section on the Geologic Background of Beds I and II and need only be briefly referred to here.[1] Except in the lower part of Bed II, when chert became available for a time, the artefacts are made almost exclusively from fine-grained lavas, quartz and to a lesser extent from quartzite (see Table 7). In Bed I, with the exception of the 'Zinjanthropus' level at FLK I, 80–94 per cent of all the heavy-duty tools such as choppers, polyhedrons, discoids, spheroids, etc., are made from lava, while in Middle and Upper Bed II quartz and quartzite are the most common material. The increase in the use of these materials

[1] Fieldwork carried out in conjunction with R. L. Hay during 1970 has resulted in the identification of the sources of the eight principal types of raw materials used for tool-making in Beds I–IV. Some varieties were transported as far as 8–12 miles to the living sites.

Table 7. *Showing the incidence (as percentages) of the various types of raw materials in the five artefact groups from excavated sites in Beds I and II*

(C = Chert, G = Gneiss, P = Pegmatite, O = Obsidian, M = Migmatite, WT = Welded Tuff.)

	A Choppers, 'proto-bifaces', polyhedrons, discoids, spheroids, sub-spheroids, heavy-duty scrapers			B Light-duty scrapers, burins, awls, laterally trimmed flakes, sundry small tools			C Anvils, hammerstones, utilised cobbles, nodules, and blocks			D Light-duty utilised flakes, etc.			E *Débitage*		
	Lava	Q/zite	Other	Lava	Q/zite	Other	Lava	Q/zite	Other	Lava	Q/zite	Other	Lava	Q/zite	Other
BK	17·5	78·1	4·4 G, P	0·7	98·8	0·5 P, C	65·1	29·4	5·5 G, WT	0·2	99·6	0·2 G	4·2	95·6	0·2 G, P
TK															
Upper Floor	18·9	80·0	1·1 G	—	100·0	—	55·6	44·4	—	0·8	99·2	—	2·6	97·4	—
Lower Floor	13·2	84·2	2·6 G	—	100·0	—	27·3	72·7	—	—	100·0	—	0·1	99·9	—
SHK, all levels	19·0	80·0	1·0 G, P, WT	0·9	99·1	—	7·7	92·3	—	2·4	96·7	0·8 C	17·5	82·4	0·1 G
FC WEST															
Tuff	16·9	77·5	5·6 G, P	—	100·0	—	93·8	6·2	—	—	100·0	—	2·6	97·4	—
Floor	29·9	67·8	2·3 G	—	100·0	—	86·4	12·5	1·1 P	2·6	97·4	—	5·9	94·0	0·1 C
MNK Main Site	20·3	77·0	2·6 G, P	4·3	95·7	—	81·1	17·2	1·7 G	2·2	97·8	—	2·3	96·6	0·6 G
EF–HR	72·7	26·1	1·1 P	66·7	33·3	—	75·0	25·0	—	60·0	30·0	10·0 C	63·5	35·5	1·0 C
MNK Skull Site	73·2	24·4	2·4 G	50·0	50·0	—	84·7	12·5	2·8 G	—	100·0	—	9·7	90·3	—
FLK North, Sandy Conglomerate	21·8	74·7	3·5 C	—	—	100·0 C	92·6	7·4	—	—	22·2	77·8 C	8·2	57·4	34·4 C
HWK East															
Level 4	27·6	59·0	13·3 C, M	—	7·4	92·6 C	90·0	7·5	2·5 C	1·2	50·0	48·8 C	0·2	71·6	26·4 C
Level 3	35·3	58·0	6·7 C, G	—	18·2	81·8 C	91·4	7·5	1·1 G	4·3	40·0	55·7 C	3·3	69·6	27·1 C
Level 2	31·3	67·2	1·5 C	14·3	28·6	57·1 C	96·3	3·7	—	5·9	70·6	23·5 C	6·1	86·7	7·2 C
Level 1	80·0	20·0	—	100·0	—	—	94·0	4·5	1·5 G	—	100·0	—	45·5	54·5	—
FLK North															
Levels 1/2	82·1	17·2	0·7 G	6·7	93·3	—	74·0	26·0	—	5·9	94·1	—	17·4	82·6	—
Level 3	85·7	14·3	—	—	—	—	76·3	23·7	—	—	100·0	—	15·0	85·0	—
Level 5	83·3	16·7	—	—	—	—	75·9	24·1	—	—	—	—	22·8	77·2	—
FLK, 'Zinj' Level	47·4	50·0	2·6 G	—	100·0	—	82·3	17·7	—	—	100·0	—	3·4	96·5	—
DK all Levels	94·3	5·7	—	64·5	35·5	—	92·6	7·4	—	47·1	52·9	—	64·0	35·8	0·1 C

first evident in Level 2 at HWK East, in Lower Bed II, although there are two sites in the lower part of Middle Bed II where lava predominates, namely the MNK Skull Site and the early Acheulean site of EF–HR.

Quartz and quartzite (and chert when available) are the most usual materials for the light-duty tools, light-duty utilised flakes and *débitage*. DK, however, is an exception, since lava is the predominant material for all the artefacts with the exception of the light-duty utilised flakes. This is also the only known site where the amount of lava *débitage* is sufficient to suggest that the heavy-duty tools may have been made on the spot. At other sites where the majority of heavy-duty tools is of lava the scarcity of lava *débitage* indicates that the tools were made elsewhere, presumably at the sources of the raw materials.

The proportionate occurrences of the various tool types in Oldowan, Developed Oldowan and early Acheulean assemblages in Beds I and II are shown in the histograms of the opposite page (Fig. 117). It will be seen that the predominant tools of the Oldowan are choppers, among which it is possible to distinguish several distinct types. There is also a variety of other heavy- and light-duty tools.

Five types of choppers have been described: side, end, two-edged, pointed and chisel-edged. Unifacial examples are rare and the most common form is a bifacially flaked side chopper.[1] The maximum development of choppers, both in diversity of types and proportionate abundance within an assemblage, is to be found in Upper

[1] Referring the Oldowan choppers, etc., to the *Fiches typologiques africaines*, is of little value at present, since the series so far is only concerned with 'pebble tools' or '*galets aménagés*', whereas the evidence from Olduvai and other sites demonstrates that choppers and other heavy-duty tools were not exclusively made on cobbles, but on whatever material happened to be available. Series 33–64 of the *Fiches* (Biberson, 1967c) does include, however, a number of the types found at Olduvai, namely side and end choppers, discoids, polyhedrons and 'proto-bifaces'. Pointed, chisel-edged and two-edged choppers are not described as yet.

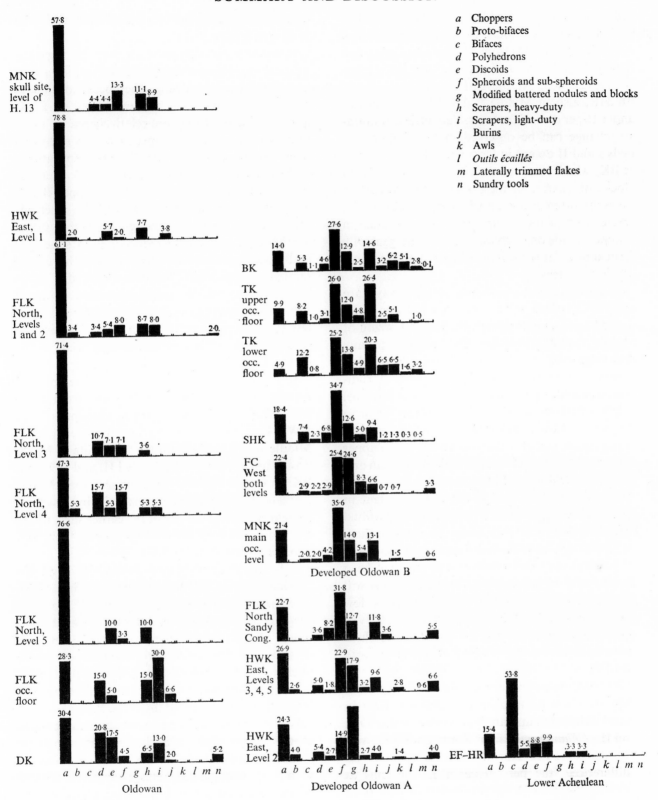

Fig. 117. Histograms of tool percentages in Oldowan, Developed Oldowan A and B and early Acheulean assemblages in Beds I and II.

Bed I and the Lower Bed II, where they amount to 78·7 per cent of the tools. In Developed Oldowan A and B assemblages from Middle and Upper Bed II they do not exceed 35 per cent and fewer types are represented. At the early Acheulean site of EF–HR, also in Middle Bed II, they amount to under 16 per cent of the tools. Very little evolutionary change can be observed in the choppers of Beds I and II except in Upper Bed II, particularly at BK, where many of the choppers are made on blocks of quartz. In these specimens the cutting edges are often evenly curved and extend round a greater part of the circumference than is usual in choppers made on cobbles. The butts are generally formed by a flat vertical face, blunted on the upper and lower edges.

The tools termed 'proto-bifaces' are always rare and are restricted in time span from Upper Bed I to the Sandy Conglomerate, the lowest horizon of Middle Bed II. They do not conform to any particular pattern or technique of manufacture but appear to represent attempts to achieve a rudimentary handaxe by whatever means was possible.

It has been shown that no true bifaces occur in Bed I or in Lower Bed II. In fact, none has been found below Tuff II^B. They occur first in the upper part of Middle Bed II, in both early Acheulean and Developed Oldowan B industries.

The bifaces from Bed II are not consistent in type and exhibit such a degree of individual variation that it is impossible to classify them satisfactorily on the basis of typology. In so far as is possible, the series from each site has been divided into broad groups. The descriptions will not be repeated, but the occurrence of a few cleavers in Bed II, at both Acheulean and Developed Oldowan sites, may be noted, since these tools were previously believed to occur only in Bed IVa.

Polyhedrons are never a common tool type, but they are more plentiful in the Oldowan than in later assemblages and are best represented at DK, on the 'Zinjanthropus' floor at FLK and in Levels 3 and 4 at FLK North. There is virtually no difference in the percentage of polyhedrons at other Oldowan or Developed Oldowan sites, or at the lower Acheulean site of EF–HR, but they become noticeably scarce at Developed Oldowan B sites in Upper Bed II.

Spheroids and subspheroids must be regarded as tools of considerable significance in the various assemblages under review. They occur at all sites and at all levels with the exception of FLK, although in Bed I they are relatively scarce and a total of only twenty-four specimens was recovered from the four excavated sites. The first appearance of symmetrical stone balls, smoothed over the entire surface, is at FLK North in Upper Bed I. They are always rare, however, and the spheroids are generally faceted, although projecting ridges are battered and partly reduced. Both spheroids and the less symmetrical specimens that have been termed subspheroids become markedly more numerous in Middle and Upper Bed II at all Developed Oldowan B sites, where they are never less than 20 per cent of the tools and where the range in size is also more extensive than in the earlier assemblages.

In Fig. 118 the range in weight has been plotted for the spheroids and subspheroids from three sites. They consist of seventeen specimens from HWK East, Levels 3, 4 and 5 (in the lower part of Middle Bed II), 159 from the Main Site at MNK (in the upper part of Middle Bed II) and 199 from BK (in Upper Bed II). It will be seen that there is a greater number of specimens weighing less than 4 oz. at BK than at either of the earlier sites, where the most common weight is between 4 oz. and 1 lb. The earliest series from HWK East, Levels 3–5, is also noticeably more limited in range. No specimens from this site exceed 3 lb. in weight, whereas in both the later series a few examples weigh considerably more. Although any interpretation of the use to which these tools were put must be largely speculative, they appear more likely to have served as some form of missile than any other purpose. Their use as bolas stones has been strongly supported by L. S. B. Leakey and may well be correct. Experiments by R. E. Leakey in this connection have shown that a pair of spheroids, each attached to a piece of cord about a yard long, entangle more effectively round upright posts than does a group of three; a pair is also easier to aim accurately.

266

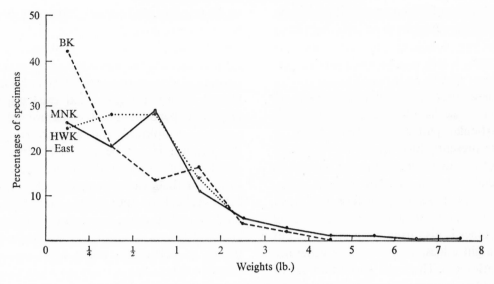

Fig. 118. Graph to show the weights of spheroids and subspheroids from three sites: HWK East Levels 3, 4, 5; MNK Main Occupation Site; and BK.

The fact that spheroids are rare in Bed I but occur in relatively large numbers in Bed II probably reflects an important change in the tool requirements, which may possibly have been the introduction of missiles as hunting weapons.

The artefacts that have been termed 'modified battered nodules and blocks' are also numerous at Developed Oldowan sites. Unlike the utilised nodules and blocks of the Oldowan, they show some degree of flaking and shaping in addition to extensive battering. The amorphous appearance of the whole group at first suggests reject material, but this does not seem to be consistent with the evidence of utilisation.

The scrapers from the Oldowan, the Developed Oldowan and the early Acheulean fall into two groups, namely heavy-duty and light-duty, with virtually no borderline cases. Certain heavy-duty scrapers would probably be termed 'push planes' by some workers, but since they are morphologically identical to specimens in the light-duty group, except for size, the term 'scraper' has been preferred. Heavy-duty scrapers are usually less numerous than light-duty specimens. Side scrapers are the most common form in both groups. A number of different types of light-duty scrapers are well represented at all Developed Oldowan B sites in Upper Bed II. They are also numerous on

the 'Zinjanthropus' living floor, where they constitute the highest percentage of any of the six tool categories represented, even exceeding choppers. Although burins are not common in any assemblage, they occur at the majority of Oldowan and Developed Oldowan sites and also at the early Acheulean site of EF–HR. They are most numerous at TK and include a variety of angle burins that would not be out of place in an Upper Palaeolithic industry. The small retouched points that have been termed 'awls' have not been found at any Oldowan site. They occur first in Lower Bed II, at HWK East, Level 2, where they are made exclusively of chert. They are rare in Middle Bed II but become comparatively common in Upper Bed II at TK and BK and exceed the number of burins at these two sites. A few *outils écaillés* are known from SHK, but they only occur in any quantity in Upper Bed II, at BK and on the Lower Occupation Floor at TK. They are made exclusively from quartz and quartzite and both single- and double-ended examples are present.

There remains only one further group of light-duty tools to be mentioned, namely laterally trimmed flakes. These occur for the first time in Level 2 at HWK East, in common with the awls. They are always relatively scarce but are more common at SHK, TK and BK than at any other sites.

267

The various forms of utilised material require no comment with the exception of the light-duty flakes. These are common at nearly all sites throughout Beds I and II and are made almost exclusively from quartz and quartzite, except for the levels where chert was available. There is no indication that these flakes were made to accord with any particular pattern, but three types of utilisation are present which appear to be related to the form of the edge, suggesting the possibility of some specialisation in use. On rounded edges the chipping is usually seen on one face only, as in scrapers. Similarly, on notched edges, the chipping within the notches is also usually on one face. On relatively straight edges, however, it is generally present on both faces. There are also a number of flakes and other fragments with haphazard chipping.

Evidence of utilisation is usually present on the working edges of choppers and other heavy-duty tools. It varies from light chipping to extensive battering which has completely blunted the edges. Some specimens also exhibit small, deeply indented crushed notches, which appear to have been caused by a grinding action against a hard substance.

The greater part of the *débitage* from the occupation sites in Beds I and II consists of broken flakes and chips. Complete flakes are relatively scarce and only the ten levels listed below have yielded a sufficient number for analysis to be of any significance. End-struck flakes are invariably more numerous than side-struck, particularly in the nine Oldowan and Developed Oldowan assemblages where, on the average, they amount to 68 per cent. Side-struck flakes are proportionately more common at the early Acheulean site of EF–HR, where only 54 per cent are end-struck.

Although the dimensions and the angles of the striking platforms of the *débitage* flakes have been recorded, the variations that exist appear to be largely dependent on the nature of the raw materials employed and are probably of little significance. It can be stated, however, that the average figure for the angles of the striking platforms for the lava flakes tends to be higher in the early Acheulean and Developed Oldowan series than in the Oldowan. The average size for both the lava and quartz side-struck flakes is also greater in the early Acheulean, but a few unusually large end-struck lava flakes from the Main site at MNK exceed those from EF–HR. The average size of the quartz series, however, is less. Attention has been drawn to the quartz flakes from Oldowan and Developed Oldowan assemblages in which the striking platforms are reduced to a minimum and consist merely of a point of impact. These contrast very strongly with many of the early Acheulean lava flakes in which the striking platforms—and even the bulbs of percussion—extend across almost the whole width of the flakes. A few similar specimens occur in Developed Oldowan B assemblages. They appear to be typical roughing-out flakes derived from the manufacture of bifaces.

It seems likely that a proportion, at least, of the sharp flakes among the *débitage* may have served as small tools, possibly for cutting meat or other soft substances that would leave no evidence of use on the edges. That they are not merely waste material is indicated by the occurrence of large numbers of such flakes, nearly always made of quartz and quartzite, at sites where the majority of heavy-duty tools is of lava and where the number of quartz and quartzite core tools is insufficient to account for the number of flakes.

An interesting present-day example of unretouched flakes used as cutting tools has recently been recorded in South-West Africa and may be mentioned briefly. An expedition from the State Museum, Windhoek, discovered two stone-using groups of the Ova Tjimba people who not only make choppers for breaking open bones and for

Sites	Total no. of complete flakes	End-struck flakes (%)
BK (1963)	652	72·0
TK		
Upper Floor	183	62·0
Lower Floor	84	68·1
SHK	449	72·0
FC West, Floor	99	71·0
MNK Main site	226	77·2
EF–HR	147	54·0
HWK East, Level 3	88	73·0
FLK North, Levels 1, 2	178	62·6
FLK, the '*Zinjanthropus*' level	258	68·5
DK	242	67·0

other heavy work, but also employ simple flakes, un-retouched and un-hafted, for cutting and skinning (McCalman and Grobbelaar, 1965).

The question as to whether certain specimens should be described as cores is largely subjective; but if the term 'core' is intended to imply a simple nucleus which was put to no further use after flakes had been struck from it, then, in the writer's opinion, it is inapplicable to any of the material from Beds I and II, with the possible exception of a few specimens from SHK and BK. It is true, however, that the majority of choppers, polyhedrons, discoids and bifaces, as well as many of the heavy-duty scrapers, are in fact made on 'cores', but this is tacitly implied in the descriptions of any tools that are made on cobbles or blocks of raw material, as distinct from flakes.

In concluding this review of the lithic material from Oldowan and Developed Oldowan Sites the grooved and pecked phonolite cobble found in Upper Bed I at FLK North must be mentioned. This stone has unquestionably been artificially shaped, but it seems unlikely that it could have served as a tool or for any practical purpose. It is conceivable that a parallel exists in the quartzite cobble found at Makapansgat (Dart, 1959) in which natural weathering has simulated the carving of two sets of hominid—or more strictly primate—features on parts of the surface. The resemblance to primate faces is immediately obvious in this specimen, although it is entirely natural, whereas in the case of the Olduvai stone a great deal of imagination is required in order to see any pattern or significance in the form. With oblique lighting, however, there is a suggestion of an elongate, baboon-like muzzle with faint indications of a mouth and nostrils. By what is probably no more than a coincidence, the pecked groove on the Olduvai stone is reproduced on the Makapansgat specimen by a similar but natural groove and in both specimens the positions of the grooves correspond to what would be the base of the hair line if an anthropomorphic interpretation is considered. This is open to question, but nevertheless the occurrence of such stones at hominid sites in such remote periods is of considerable interest.

Before considering industries that may be analogous to the Developed Oldowan and early Acheulean of Bed II, the grounds for differentiating these two industrial complexes must be stated. The Developed Oldowan appears to represent an uninterrupted local continuation from the Oldowan, in which the same tool forms persist, with the addition of some new elements and an increase in others that were rare in the Oldowan. These are notably bifaces, various small flake tools, spheroids and subspheroids. There was thus an overall increase in the tool kit. This is clearly demonstrated by the fact that, while the average number of tool types for seven Oldowan levels in Bed I and the base of Bed II amounts to only six, the average figure has risen to over ten for nine Developed Oldowan levels in Bed II. The enlargement of the tool kit is already evident in the industries of the lower part of Middle Bed II (Developed Oldowan A), although this horizon lacks bifaces. Up to and including this level there is no suggestion whatever of duality in the known lithic assemblages which are remarkably constant in character, in spite of minor differences in the proportionate representation of certain tool types.

In Middle Bed II, however, the first unquestionable bifaces appear, including a few cleavers as well as handaxes. At some sites they occur in sufficiently large numbers (over 50 per cent of the tools) for the term 'Acheulean' to be applied without hesitation to the industry. (The term 'early or lower Acheulean' as used here denotes those stages that were previously termed 'Chellean' or 'Abbevillian'.) At other sites bifaces occur in small numbers (an average of 6 per cent of the tools) in assemblages that are otherwise wholly Developed Oldowan in character.

No bifacial tools that could be considered intermediate between the 'proto-bifaces' of Upper Bed I and the true bifaces of Middle Bed II have come to light. This is not necessarily significant, since it is doubtful if the evidence for such a transition would be preserved. The possibility cannot be overlooked, however, that the Acheulean was intrusive to the area, as indeed *Homo erectus* appears to have been.

While there will be general agreement in applying the term 'Acheulean' to those industries con-

269

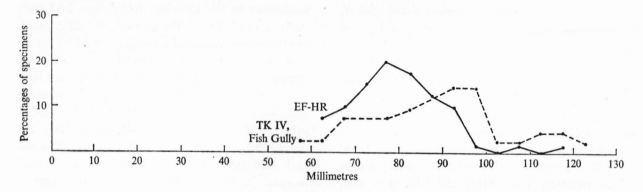

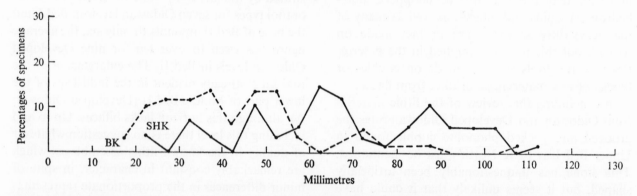

Fig. 119. Graphs showing the mean diameters of Acheulean bifaces from EF–HR and TK IV Fish Gully and of Developed Oldowan bifaces from SHK and BK.

taining 50 per cent or more bifaces, it may be argued that the term should also be applied to the contemporary assemblages where a low percentage of bifaces is found in an industry otherwise characteristic of the Developed Oldowan. This is perhaps a matter of opinion, but it does not appear reasonable to the writer to consider bifaces or any other single tool as an all-important index fossil to the exclusion of the predominant elements of an industry. For the present, the proposal put forward by M. R. Kleindienst (1962) that there should be not less than 40–60 per cent of bifaces if an industry is to be classed as Acheulean seems acceptable, although a more specific diagnosis would be of advantage, but this will only become possible when detailed analysis of a substantial number of assemblages from sealed horizons has been carried out.

In addition to the overall dissimilarity of the early Acheulean and the Developed Oldowan B industrial complexes, there is a marked difference in the nature of the bifaces. This is not so much in typology, since there is too great a degree of individual variation for valid typological classification, but in size, morphology and method of manufacture. The contrast in size, breadth/length and thickness/length ratios is shown in the accompanying graphs (Figs. 119–121). In Fig. 119 the mean diameters of bifaces from EF–HR and from an Acheulean assemblage in Bed IVa (TK, Fish Gully) are shown, together with those of the bifaces from BK and SHK—the only two Developed Oldowan sites to yield a sufficient number of specimens for statistical purposes.[1] It will be seen that in both the Acheulean groups the curves are regular and follow a similar pattern, although the Bed IV series tends to be slightly larger than that from Bed II. In the Developed Oldowan groups, however, the curves are entirely haphazard and suggest

[1] The series from Bed IV is predominantly of quartz and that from EF–HR predominantly of lava. Both materials are almost equally represented at BK and SHK.

270

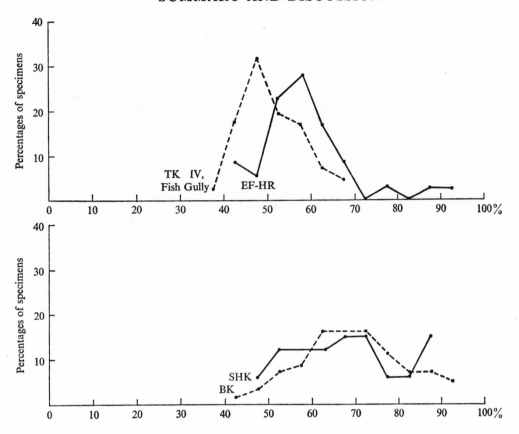

Fig. 120. Breadth/length ratios of Acheulean bifaces from EF–HR and TK IV, Fish Gully, and of Developed Oldowan bifaces from SHK and BK.

that the size of the tools depended largely on whatever piece of raw material happened to be available. About half the specimens, however, are smaller than any in the Acheulean series.

The breadth/length ratios for the Bed IV Acheulean bifaces follow a simple curve, the maximum number of specimens having a ratio of between 40 and 50 per cent. The series is more restricted in range than the Early Acheulean, which includes a number of specimens that are wider.

The thickness/length ratios of the Bed IV bifaces show an entirely even curve in the lower range, corresponding closely to that of the early Acheulean, although the latter includes a number of thicker specimens. In the Developed Oldowan the curve for SHK is remarkably even, but the ratio for the maximum number of specimens lies between 40 and 55 per cent, a higher average than for either of the Acheulean groups.

There is also a considerable difference in the numbers of trimming flake scars on the bifaces from the early Acheulean and Developed Oldowan industries. Omitting quartz specimens, in which it is virtually impossible to count the number of flake scars accurately, the average for the early Acheulean series is 9·7, for the SHK series 18, and for the BK series 16·5.

Although the number of bifaces recovered from other Developed Oldowan sites is too small to permit statistical analysis, the few specimens from the Main site at MNK and from the Lower Floor at TK conform more closely in size and morphology to the early Acheulean than to Developed Oldowan series from BK, SHK and the Upper Occupation Floor at TK. This is an anomaly which cannot be explained for the present, although there are several possible interpretations.

271

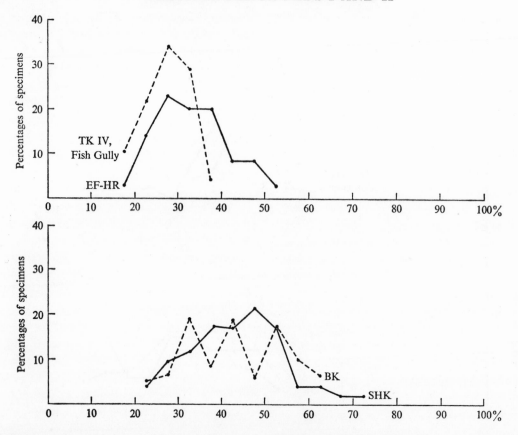

Fig. 121. Thickness/length ratios of Acheulean bifaces from EF–HR and TK IV, Fish Gully and of Developed Oldowan bifaces from SHK and BK.

It has been suggested that the industries termed here Developed Oldowan might in fact belong within the Acheulean and that their dissimilarity from the classic Acheulean might be due to different environment or ecology. An alternative interpretation put forward is that they might reflect a form of activity different from that at sites where bifaces are the predominant tools. While both hypotheses are possible, the evidence at Olduvai does not lend support to either since Acheulean and Developed Oldowan assemblages have been found under what appear to be identical environmental conditions. Furthermore, although the period of habitation certainly varied at each site, the usual criteria for living sites are always present i.e. tools, *débitage*, utilised lithic material and also a variety of broken animal bones.

Consideration of all the factors, therefore, would seem to indicate that the two dissimilar industrial complexes of Middle and Upper Bed II should be interpreted, for the present, as representing two distinct cultural traditions, perhaps made by two different groups of hominids. The position will almost certainly be clarified by further field work, but the existence of two contemporary cultural streams does not seem in any way impossible, particularly when it is known that *Homo erectus*, *Homo habilis* and a robust australopithecine all existed at Olduvai during Bed II times. Two of these, at least, must supposedly have been toolmakers and it would be surprising if their industries proved to be identical. If *Homo habilis* is accepted as the maker of the Oldowan—and in view of the cumulative evidence, this seems to be an inescapable conclusion—then it would be reasonable to assume that he was also responsible for the Developed Oldowan. Although both *Homo habilis* and the Oldowan had long existed in the area, there is as yet little to suggest the existence of antecedents either for the Acheulean or for *Homo erectus*. It is tempting therefore to link the two, but since the calvaria from LLK was not associated with any industry, this interpretation remains hypothetical for the present.

When analogies for the industries of Beds I and II at Olduvai are sought elsewhere in Africa the lack of total assemblages that can be used for comparative purposes proves a serious handicap. For the Oldowan itself, as represented in Bed I and the base of Bed II, it is doubtful whether any comparable assemblages exist. Choppers, 'pebble tools' or '*galets aménagés*' are widely known and some are certainly from early contexts. But since it has been amply demonstrated at Olduvai that these tools form only one element of the Oldowan, although admittedly the most obvious and the most abundant, it is of little value to consider them alone. This is especially true when it is realised that they are a tool form which has persisted from the Villafranchian until the present day. (McCalman and Grobbelaar, 1965, and M. D. Leakey, 1966*b*.)

P. Biberson has, in fact, separated the Moroccan 'Pebble culture' into three stages: a lower, middle and upper (Biberson, 1961). Only about 100 specimens are known for the earliest phase and these are said to consist largely of unifacial choppers. Many of the tools attributed to this stage have been included on the grounds that they are the most heavily rolled specimens in assemblages from raised beaches, which also contain moderately rolled and fresh groups. The site of Tardiguet-er-Rahla, however, appears to be promising from the point of view of obtaining more material under good stratigraphic conditions. It has yielded a stage of the 'Pebble Culture' considered to be Middle Villafranchian in age (Biberson, 1967*b*).

The succeeding stage, for which a great deal more material is known, is dated as Upper Villafranchian. There is a greater variety in the forms of the choppers and many are bifacial. Polyhedrons also occur. The specimens illustrated from this stage undoubtedly resemble some from Olduvai, but unfortunately no tools other than choppers and polyhedrons are described. Several

sites in the neighbourhood of Casablanca are said to be exceedingly rich in artefacts of this stage and would certainly also repay fuller investigation.

In the last stage of the Moroccan 'Pebble Culture', recovered from the basal '*poudingue*' at the Sidi Abderrahman Extension quarry, choppers continue to occur, but a number of the figured specimens resemble crude bifaces. They approach true bifaces more closely than do the Oldowan tools that have been termed 'proto-bifaces'. Biberson questions whether this stage might not be more correctly included in the beginning of the Acheulean. This, in fact, appears to be the case. (Biberson, 1961).

Undoubtedly the closest analogies to the Developed Oldowan B industrial complex from Olduvai is to be found in the collections of artefacts from Swartkrans and from the West Pit, Sterkfontein, both of which I have been able to examine personally during recent visits to South Africa through the kindness of Dr C. K. Brain and Mr Alun Hughes. Since work is now in progress at these sites, the collections will undoubtedly be augmented within the near future, but even in the somewhat limited series now available, the resemblances are very striking, both in the tool types represented and in their proportionate occurrence. (M. D. Leakey, 1970*b*).

My classification of the Sterkfontein material differs in certain respects from the description published by R. Mason (1962*a*), mainly in that most of the specimens which he regarded as cores I would class either as choppers or polyhedrons. These, in my view, are the two most common tool types. Mason also considers that the scarcity of bifaces and lack of flakes indicates that the assemblage is incomplete. The bifaces, however, occur in almost the same proportions as to those in the Developed Oldowan. As regards the lack of flakes, it is now generally known that flakes derived from the manufacture of heavy-duty tools are lacking or very scarce at most early living sites, where the tools appear to have been introduced in a finished or half-finished state.

An aspect of the lithic material from the australopithecine caves that has received little attention so far is the number of small sharp-edged chert fragments which occur in the breccia alongside the orthodox tools and the faunal remains. Many of these have been chipped on the edge and it is possible that they are the equivalent of the small quartz flakes from Oldowan and Developed Oldowan sites which appear to represent small cutting tools. Unfortunately, the type of chert found in the dolomite formation of the Transvaal does not flake with a conchoidal fracture and there appears to be no sure means of determining whether these fragments were artificially fractured. When the position of material in the undisturbed breccia comes to be recorded, the distribution of the chert in relation to the heavy-duty tools may prove informative.

Although the lithic material from the australopithecine caves stands closest to the Developed Oldowan at present, the site at 'Ubeidiya in Israel may well provide even closer parallels when it is more fully explored. This site was similarly situated near the shore of a fluctuating lake, so that a number of successive occupation levels were buried rapidly enough for the debris to be preserved in place, as was the case at many of the Olduvai sites. The artefacts from 'Ubeidiya can be divided into two main groups. The earliest was named by the late Professor M. Stekelis the 'Israel Variant of the Oldowan' (Stekelis, 1966). It contains choppers of several types, polyhedrons, spheroids and cuboids, but few bifaces. The second group contains a high proportion of bifaces as well as some choppers and a few polyhedrons. Although this site was first claimed to be of Villafranchian age, the faunal material as well as the nature of the stone industries indicate that it is more likely to be early Middle Pleistocene and therefore approximately contemporary with the lower part of Middle Bed II at Olduvai.

Yet a third site that may provide a parallel with the Oldowan or Developed Oldowan is Melka Kontouré in Ethiopia. This site lies in the Awash valley, approximately 50 km. from Addis Ababa, and was found by G. Dekker in 1963. It consists of a series of sedimentary deposits within a former lake basin (Chavaillon and Taieb, 1968). The deposits reach a known thickness of 40 m. and are predominantly lacustrine, consisting of tuffs, clays,

and sands. Three distinct levels containing occupation debris are known. The industry from the highest level appears to be an Acheulean of fairly advanced facies, but the lowest level has so far yielded only choppers, polyhedrons, spheroids, etc. (Chavaillon, 1967). Excavations now being carried out will certainly yield a larger series of specimens than is available at present and make it possible to determine more precisely the nature of this industry. The dating also remains to be established satisfactorily.

The Acheulean assemblages from two sites at Peninj, on the western side of Lake Natron, bear a strong resemblance to the early Acheulean from Olduvai, as has been pointed out by G. L. Isaac (1965). The Peninj series, however, contains a higher proportion of cleavers and none of the specimens appears to be so highly finished as a few from EF–HR. Both at Peninj and at Olduvai the tools have been shaped by means of a minimum of well-directed flakes and the average number of 9·7 flake scars per specimen is identical in both series. The Peninj sites are within 50 miles of Olduvai and on the evidence of the geology and the faunal remains they appear to be approximately contemporary with Middle Bed II.

The industries from two sites in South Africa, Kliplaatdrif and Three Rivers, both of which are in the Transvaal, do not seem unlike the Acheulean of Bed II, Olduvai, judged on the basis of the published description (Mason, 1962b). Comparison of both these assemblages is made difficult by the fact that the method of classification is not the same as that used for the Olduvai material. For example, specimens that would have been classed as choppers by the writer are listed as cores, in spite of evident utilisation. The bifaces appear to be very similar to the East African series, with minimal, bold flaking; it is interesting to note that Mason comments that they have rarely had more than ten flakes removed, as in the series from Olduvai and Peninj.

There are also resemblances with the early Acheulean of North Africa, particularly in some of the bifaces from the Sidi Abderrahman quarry near Casablanca. Although the whole collection from this site was originally lumped together and

274

described as 'Clacto-Abbevillian' by Neuville and Ruhlmann (1941), Biberson considers that it is probably a mixed series containing material of different ages. He has divided it into three groups, on the basis of *état physique*. In the most heavily rolled series, choppers and faceted spheroids are said to predominate, but in both the slightly rolled and fresh series bifaces are the most common tool type. They include a series of trihedral specimens which appear very similar to those from the East African early Acheulean sites, characterised by a triangular cross-section near the tip, although the general form of the tools is variable. This resemblance, however, may well be coincidental, since the Moroccan specimens are made on large flakes struck from boulders as was the case at EF–HR, Olduvai. It is also noticeable that all the specimens illustrated for this stage exhibit the minimal bold flaking that appears to be characteristic of the early Acheulean bifaces from East and South Africa that have been referred to here.

(3) THE MODIFIED BONES

The series of utilised and flaked mammalian bones that has been described in chapter VIII indicates that bones were sometimes used as tools and that occasionally parts of massive bones were employed as a substitute for stone in tool-making. The presence of relatively large flake scars and the splitting of the articular ends of *Libytherium* limb bones and others of comparable size are the factors which indicate most clearly that these bones have been modified by human agency. Certain types of flaking can undoubtedly be caused by carnivores who are also capable of splitting fair-sized limb bones, including the extremities. But even those of present-day giraffe are seldom split right through and these do not compare in robustness with the bones of *Libytherium*. It would also be impossible for animals to detach flakes 10 cm. long, or more, in the course of chewing; percussion would be required. Smaller flakes are, however, frequently removed by gnawing and a series of such flakes often simulates a 'utilised' edge. Other forms of apparent utilisation brought about by natural means can also be deceptive. Brain (1967*b*) has

shown that partial weathering in a dry climate and subsequent movement in sand, such as can be caused by the trampling of animals, can simulate artificial polishing and abrasion.

The occurrence of flaked fragments of bone has been recognised at the Acheulean site of Ambrona in Spain, a butchering site where the remains are principally of elephants (Biberson, 1964). But there are no records of any unquestionable specimens from the East African Acheulean sites of Olorgesailie, Kariandusi and Isimila, although examples are known in the Acheulean of Bed IV*a* at Olduvai itself. These include a large biface made from a fragment of elephant bone.

As regards the 'Bone and Antler Industry' from Chou Kou Tien (Breuil, 1939), the illustrated specimens, with few exceptions, appear to represent food debris rather than bones that have been shaped or utilised. But without examination of the original specimens it is impossible to form a satisfactory estimation.

Further detailed analysis of human and carnivore food debris, such as that carried out by Brain on the Hottentot goat remains, should provide data by which it will be possible to determine whether bones from occupation sites have been artificially shaped as tools, utilised, or are merely debris. For the present it is evident that great caution is needed before accepting as artefacts bones with apparent hominid modification. In general, the presence of flaking appears to be the surest criterion, but certain forms of abrasion, such as that on the bone point from the West Pit, Sterkfontein and on the metapodials from Makapansgat, must also be considered artificial.

(4) THE FAUNAL REMAINS FROM THE LIVING SITES

The disproportionate preservation of certain parts of the skull and skeleton among the faunal remains on prehistoric living sites has long been a puzzling feature and has never been satisfactorily explained in the past. It has often been attributed to deliberate selection of certain parts of the animals by the hominid populations and has also been cited as lending support to the authenticity of

Table 8. *Faunal remains from excavated sites in Beds I and II*

Percentages of the various parts of the skull and skeleton of the larger mammals. (Reptiles are not included)

	BK II	TK, Upper Floor	TK, Lower Floor	FC West Tuff	FC West, Floor	MNK II Main Site	MNK Skull Site, Level of H.13	HWK East, Levels 3–5	HWK East, Level 2	HWK East, Level 1	FLK North, Levels 1–2	FLK North, Level 3	FLK North, Level 4	FLK North, Level 5	FLK North, Level 6	FLK I, Level 13	FLK I, Level 15	FLK I, 'Zinj.' level	FLK NN, Level 1	FLK NN, Level 2	FLK NN, Level 3	DK I, Level 1	DK I, Level 2	DK I, Level 3
Crania	0.1	—	—	—	—	0.1	—	—	—	—	—	0.3	0.3	0.3	0.2	—	—	0.1	1.2	0.4	0.2	—	—	—
Cranial fragments	5.3	5.3	—	4.0	5.0	3.3	10.0	1.3	4.1	2.1	3.1	4.9	1.7	2.5	2.1	2.1	1.4	4.0	1.2	0.7	8.4	5.3	8.3	7.0
Horn Cores	1.4	1.5	—	3.0	—	1.0	—	0.4	2.0	2.7	1.2	2.3	0.7	2.2	0.6	4.9	1.4	0.4	1.8	0.7	0.2	1.0	1.5	0.9
Maxillae	0.6	—	—	—	—	0.5	1.4	0.4	1.5	1.9	0.5	1.0	0.3	0.5	0.6	2.8	—	0.5	1.8	0.9	2.5	1.0	0.7	0.9
Mandibles	5.2	1.5	4.8	1.0	—	3.1	—	2.2	2.2	2.9	3.2	4.5	4.7	2.9	2.6	7.0	6.2	10.6	6.2	4.4	4.8	2.6	4.7	3.8
Isolated teeth	28.0	51.5	39.0	62.3	41.0	40.6	33.7	41.4	42.2	22.7	15.4	17.2	21.0	24.2	26.8	18.2	18.5	19.5	43.2	19.2	14.7	35.3	32.7	31.7
Vertebrae	7.1	0.8	4.8	1.0	3.3	6.5	4.3	8.5	9.5	10.4	7.8	8.0	8.0	4.3	16.8	11.9	4.1	8.7	14.2	3.9	18.1	10.0	6.3	8.0
Ribs	12.1	12.1	3.8	—	5.0	4.7	8.6	1.8	5.6	8.8	10.1	6.8	1.2	3.1	16.6	3.5	9.6	22.8	2.5	18.2	16.8	11.1	6.7	9.4
Scapulae	2.1	1.5	1.9	—	1.6	2.5	1.4	3.6	0.5	1.3	2.7	1.3	1.2	1.7	1.3	3.5	3.4	2.1	1.2	2.4	2.3	2.1	1.8	1.3
Pelves	2.0	4.5	2.9	2.0	1.6	1.9	1.4	0.8	1.5	2.9	3.4	4.5	1.8	2.2	1.5	2.1	0.6	2.2	3.1	1.2	1.4	1.0	1.8	1.4
Humeri — Complete	—	—	—	—	—	—	—	—	0.2	0.5	0.2	—	—	0.2	0.6	—	—	0.1	—	0.2	—	—	0.1	0.3
Humeri — Proximal	0.2	—	—	1.0	—	0.1	1.4	—	0.2	—	—	0.4	0.3	—	—	0.7	—	0.6	—	0.2	—	0.2	0.5	0.2
Humeri — Distal	2.4	1.5	0.9	1.0	1.6	1.3	1.4	1.3	0.8	2.9	2.1	3.4	2.2	1.6	1.5	5.5	2.7	1.7	2.5	2.9	1.5	—	1.9	2.4
Radii — Complete	0.2	—	—	—	—	0.1	—	—	0.3	1.1	0.4	0.3	0.1	0.4	0.7	0.7	—	0.2	—	1.2	—	—	0.5	0.2
Radii — Proximal	1.1	0.8	0.9	—	1.6	1.2	—	1.3	0.5	1.6	1.8	1.1	1.2	1.0	0.6	2.8	2.7	1.6	1.8	1.7	1.5	0.5	1.1	0.6
Radii — Distal	0.5	—	0.9	1.0	—	0.8	—	1.3	0.7	1.6	1.0	0.5	0.8	0.3	0.7	—	1.4	0.4	—	—	0.6	0.5	1.1	0.6
Ulnae — Complete	0.2	—	—	—	—	0.1	1.4	—	0.3	0.8	0.3	—	0.1	—	0.4	0.7	—	—	—	0.2	—	—	0.1	0.2
Ulnae — Proximal	1.4	—	0.9	—	—	1.1	1.4	0.4	—	1.9	2.0	1.7	1.0	1.5	1.3	0.7	2.0	1.3	0.6	1.7	2.1	0.5	1.1	0.6
Ulnae — Distal	—	—	—	—	—	0.9	—	—	—	—	0.1	—	—	—	—	—	—	0.2	—	0.2	—	—	0.2	0.6
Metacarpals — Complete	0.6	1.5	—	—	—	0.6	—	—	1.2	2.1	1.1	1.0	0.8	1.3	1.3	0.7	2.0	0.2	1.2	2.7	0.6	—	1.0	0.2
Metacarpals — Proximal	1.0	0.8	1.9	—	—	1.0	1.4	1.7	0.8	0.5	1.1	1.6	0.6	1.0	0.4	2.8	3.4	0.9	1.8	0.4	1.0	0.5	0.5	1.1
Metacarpals — Distal	0.4	—	—	2.0	—	0.2	4.3	1.7	0.2	—	0.8	0.9	1.0	0.3	0.6	—	—	0.5	—	—	—	—	0.3	0.6
Femora — Complete	0.2	—	—	—	—	0.3	—	—	—	—	0.1	—	—	—	0.6	—	—	0.1	1.2	—	0.6	—	0.1	0.6
Femora — Proximal	0.5	—	—	—	—	0.3	—	0.8	0.2	0.8	0.8	0.9	0.8	0.8	—	—	—	—	0.5	0.6	—	0.5	0.3	0.5
Femora — Distal	0.5	2.3	—	—	—	0.2	—	0.4	0.2	0.5	1.2	1.1	1.0	1.1	0.6	1.4	0.7	0.7	—	0.2	—	1.0	0.6	1.1
Tibiae — Complete	0.2	—	—	—	—	0.3	—	0.4	0.2	0.8	0.3	—	—	0.2	0.7	—	0.7	0.2	0.6	0.2	0.2	—	0.1	0.8
Tibiae — Proximal	0.5	—	0.9	—	—	0.2	—	—	0.3	—	0.8	0.8	0.4	0.4	0.2	2.8	1.4	1.4	—	0.9	0.2	—	0.2	0.6
Tibiae — Distal	2.0	—	—	—	1.6	1.1	—	2.2	0.8	2.9	3.2	2.4	0.6	2.0	0.4	4.2	6.2	0.4	0.6	0.9	0.8	—	2.1	0.9
Metatarsals — Complete	0.5	0.8	0.9	—	—	0.6	—	0.7	0.8	1.0	1.1	0.4	1.2	1.5	—	2.0	0.5	3.7	0.9	—	—	—	0.3	0.9
Metatarsals — Proximal	1.4	—	0.9	—	1.6	1.5	1.4	1.3	0.3	3.4	2.4	0.8	1.7	1.6	0.2	1.4	4.1	1.1	1.2	1.7	0.4	1.6	0.7	0.9
Metatarsals — Distal	0.6	—	1.9	1.0	1.6	0.1	—	0.8	0.5	0.3	1.1	0.4	0.4	0.5	0.6	—	—	1.0	—	—	—	1.0	0.4	0.6
Metapodials, indet.	1.4	—	3.8	3.0	11.5	2.2	7.1	1.3	1.7	1.1	1.9	0.9	2.2	3.4	0.4	1.4	0.7	0.3	1.2	0.4	0.2	1.0	2.5	3.5
Podials, patellae, fibulae, sesamoids	12.6	9.1	16.2	14.8	14.7	16.0	12.8	20.6	24.5	13.6	21.6	24.2	39.8	32.7	16.1	4.9	13.0	[12.6	3.7	23.9	14.1	22.6	19.6	15.9
Limb-bone shafts	7.4	4.5	12.4	3.0	8.2	4.1	—	2.2	4.7	6.9	6.5	5.8	4.5	4.4	1.5	13.3	11.6	2.5	2.5	5.9	6.1	—	1.1	1.8
No. of specimens listed from each site or level	1,313	132	105	101	61	854	70	223	520	375	2,018	933	727	1,161	529	144	146	1,023	162	401	476	190	1,084	628

the 'Osteodontokeratic culture'. The analysis of goat remains from Hottentot middens by Brain (1967a) has shown, however, that those parts of the skeleton most commonly preserved. The distal end of the humerus, proximal ends of the radius and ulna and the distal end of the tibia are the parts with the most resistance to chewing and gnawing; those that have, in fact, the greatest durability. He attributes this partly to the morphology of these bones and partly to the early fusion of the epiphyses.[1]

Brain states that as goats are the main source of

[1] A study of baboon remains from leopard lairs in caves on Mount Suswa, Kenya, by J. W. Simons and others (1966) has shown that the parts usually destroyed by chewing are the proximal ends of the humeri, the blades of scapulae, both ends of radii, the end of the olecranon process, the heads of femora and the proximal ends of tibias. Foot-bones and patellae are also said to be rarely preserved.

wealth in the Hottentot economy; they are highly prized, so that when one is killed for meat no edible parts are wasted. The usual procedure is for the heads to be boiled after the horns have been chopped off. The limb bones are smashed with a stone in order to obtain the marrow. When the villagers have eaten everything possible, the bones are thrown to the dogs, which are described as being of about the size of a jackal. There is thus a combination of human and scavenger activity similar to conditions at early living sites where hyaenas and other scavengers are known to have gnawed the bones discarded by the hominid population.

The various proportions of the preserved parts of bovid limb bones from Olduvai and Mapakansgat and of goats from Hottentot middens are shown in Table 9. It will be seen that all three collections stand very close as regards the bones of the foreleg, particularly the humerus, radius and ulna. In the metacarpals, however, proximal ends outnumber distal ends at Olduvai and among the goat remains, but at Makapansgat they are not as numerous as the distal ends. As regards the hind leg, parts of the tibia are represented similarly in all three collections, but in the goat remains the proximal ends of the femur are more common than the distal. At Olduvai and at Makapansgat this position is reversed. The proportions of the proximal and distal ends of the metatarsal follow the same pattern as that for the metacarpal: the proximal ends are most numerous at Olduvai and among the goat remains, but at Makapansgat they are scarcer than the distal ends. This is surprising in view of the fact that the proximal ends of both metacarpals and metatarsals should be more resistant than the distal ends, since they fuse before birth, whilst the distal ends are not joined to the shafts until much later—in the case of sheep not until over one year of age (Brain, 1967a). This discrepancy may, perhaps, be due to hominid selectivity, since a proportion of the distal ends of the metacarpals and metatarsals from Makapansgat are indubitably utilised; this is not the case at Olduvai nor, of course, among the goat remains.

It will be seen that the bones of the foreleg are more commonly represented than those of the hind leg. This is because the bones of the elbow joint (that is, the distal ends of the humerus and the proximal ends of the radius and ulna) greatly outnumber any other parts of the leg bones. In each of these bones the commonly preserved extremity is the one in which the epiphysis fuses earliest to the shaft, assuming the order to be the same as in sheep, for which records are available.

A fuller comparison of the Olduvai material with the listed bovid collection from Makapansgat Limeworks and with the entire collection of goat bones is shown in Table 10. The bovid remains from four Olduvai sites —namely DK level 3, FLK North Level 3, MNK Main site and BK— have been pooled. These sites have been selected because they span the whole of Bed II and the upper member of Bed I and therefore provide a representative sample. Both the Olduvai and Hottentot collections amount to approximately 1,500 specimens, whereas the Makapansgat collection is in the region of 3,500 specimens. The range of variation in the percentages of the preserved parts from the four Olduvai sites is also given. It will be seen that in spite of an overall similarity between the three collections there are certain discrepancies. Loose teeth are scarce among the goat material, but constitute the most abundant category at Olduvai and also at Makapansgat. This is probably due to the teeth having weathered out of their sockets in the fossil material. Horn cores and ribs, on the contrary, are abundant in the goat collection, but are not nearly so plentiful at Olduvai or Makapansgat. Phalanges are relatively scarce at Makapansgat and among the goat material, but more numerous at Olduvai.

In spite of these minor differences there are strong resemblances between the three collections, particularly in the parts of limb bones most commonly preserved. It is evident, therefore, that the faunal remains from the Olduvai living sites must be considered to represent food debris, although a certain amount of carnivore activity also took place at some of the sites. This is indicated by the presence of tooth marks, apparently made by large carnivores, that can be seen on a small proportion of the bones. Other bones may also have been broken by carnivores and the fact

277

Table 9. *The proportions of preserved parts of bovid limb bones from four Olduvai sites and the Makapansgat Limeworks compared to those of goats from Hottentot middens*

	Olduvai bovids (sample)		Makapansgat bovids		Hottentot goats	
	Nos.	%	Nos.	%	Nos.	%
Foreleg						
Humerus						
Proximal	4	1·2	33	2·1	—	—
Distal	59	17·5	336	21·9	82	23·1
Radius and ulna						
Proximal	61	18·1	279	18·2	62	17·5
Distal	21	6·2	114	7·4	19	5·3
Metacarpal						
Proximal	38	11·3	129	8·4	24	6·8
Distal	17	5·1	161	10·5	15	4·2
Hind leg						
Femur						
Proximal	11	3·2	28	1·8	18	5·1
Distal	20	6·0	56	3·6	9	2·5
Tibia						
Proximal	14	4·1	64	4·1	13	3·7
Distal	51	15·1	119	7·7	72	20·3
Metatarsal						
Proximal	39	11·6	107	7·0	30	8·4
Distal	2	0·6	110	7·2	11	3·1
Totals	337		1,536		355	
Nos. of foreleg parts and % of total	200	59·3	1,052	68·4	202	57·0
Nos. of hind leg parts and % of total	137	40·7	484	31·6	153	43·0

NOTE. In the published table of bovid remains from Makapansgat only one entry is given for the ulnae. This is assumed to refer to the proximal ends.

that they lack direct evidence of gnawing does not preclude carnivore activity. Tooth marks are seldom obvious on the bones of wildebeeste and zebra that have been killed by predators and are scattered over the Serengeti plains today, although they have often been broken in a manner similar to those from prehistoric living sites. The limb bones are cracked open and the less resistant parts have been chewed off. Skulls and mandibles are often intact, but this would not be the case when hominids were involved. They would almost certainly break open the skulls in order to extract the brains.

(5) TOOL-MAKING

In conclusion, the question of tool-making by the early hominids must be discussed briefly. Before doing so, it should be stated that, in the writer's opinion, evidence for the manufacture of tools by means of using one tool as an instrument to make another is one of the most important criteria in deciding whether any particular taxon had reached the status of man. This stage of tool-making, which marks the beginning of formal tool manufacture, should not be confused with simple modification of objects by means of the hands and teeth, such as is practised by other higher primates. It is true, however, that man's ancestors must

278

Table 10. *To show proportionate occurrence of various cranial and skeletal parts of Bovidae from Olduvai and Makapansgat Limeworks and those of goats from Hottentot middens*

	Olduvai. Pooled material from four sites: BK, MNK Main Site, FLK North (Level 3) and DK I (Level 3)			Makapansgat Limeworks		Goat remains from Hottentot middens	
	Nos.	%	Range at the four sites (%)	Nos.	%	Nos.	%
Skulls							
Horn cores	54	3·8	4·4– 2·2	210	6·0	385	25·3
Cranial fragments	32	2·2	4·8– 1·1	108	3·0	70	4·6
Maxillae	15	1·0	1·3– 0·4	172	4·8	57	3·7
Mandibles	78	5·5	7·9– 4·0	369	10·4	188	12·4
Loose teeth	459	32·5	45·6–19·4	502	14·2	15	1·0
Vertebrae							
Atlas	5	0·3	0·8– 0·2	20	0·6	12	0·8
Axis	11	0·8	1·4– 0·4	25	0·7	14	0·9
Cervical, other	14	1·0	1·9– 0·4	47	1·3	12	0·8
Thoracic	18	1·3	1·7– 0·4	24	0·7	21	1·4
Lumbar	15	1·1	1·7– 0·4	30	0·8	31	2·0
Sacral and caudal	1	0·1	—	17	0·5	1	0·1
Ribs	52	3·7	10·3– 1·9	66	1·9	174	11·4
Scapulae	37	2·6	5·0– 1·1	126	3·6	59	3·8
Innominates	59	4·2	22·3– 1·2	107	3·0	55	3·6
Humeri							
Complete	1	0·1	—	—	—	—	—
Proximal ends	4	0·2	0·4– 0·2	33	0·9	—	—
Distal ends	59	4·2	5·0– 2·4	336	9·5	82	5·4
Radii and Ulnae							
Complete	8	0·8	0·8– 0·6	1	0·03	3	0·2
Proximal ends	51	3·4	4·8– 2·2	279*	7·9	62	4·1
Distal ends	21	1·6	3·6– 0·4	114	3·2	19	1·2
Femora							
Complete	5	0·3	1·1– 0·2	—	—	—	—
Proximal ends	11	0·8	0·9– 0·4	28	0·8	18	1·2
Distal ends	20	1·4	1·9– 0·9	56	1·6	9	0·6
Tibiae							
Complete	8	0·6	1·5– 0·5	—	—	—	—
Proximal ends	14	1·0	1·5– 0·9	64	1·8	13	0·9
Distal ends	51	3·6	4·9– 2·0	119	3·4	72	4·7
Metacarpals							
Complete	10	0·7	1·1– 0·7	4	0·1	8	0·5
Proximal ends	38	2·7	3·2– 2·1	129	3·6	24	1·6
Distal ends	17	1·2	1·7– 1·1	161	4·5	15	1·0
Metatarsals							
Complete	15	1·1	1·6– 1·1	2	0·05	9	0·6
Proximal ends	39	2·7	4·4– 1·5	107	3·0	30	2·0
Distal ends	12	0·8	1·1– 0·4	110	3·1	11	0·7
Astragali	30	2·1	3·6– 0·9	61	1·7	16	1·1
Calcanea	18	1·3	2·2– 0·6	75	2·1	14	0·9
Phalanges	130	9·2	18·6– 2·1	43	1·2	21	1·4
	1,412			3,545		1,520	

* Proximal and distal parts of ulnae are not differentiated. The figure is therefore, assumed to refer to the olecranon processes.

necessarily have passed through this preliminary phase, once they had progressed beyond the random use of sticks or stones. If evidence of tool-making is not counted as a decisive factor for the human status it is difficult to see what alternative can be used for determining at what point it had been reached. Evolutionary changes must have been so gradual that it will never be possible for the threshold to be recognised on the evidence of the fossil bones alone. This would be true even if a far more complete evolutionary sequence of material were available for study: with the scanty and often incomplete material that has survived it is clearly out of the question. An arbitrary definition based on cranial capacity is also of doubtful value, since the significance of cranial capacity is closely linked with stature or body size, of which we have little precise information in respect of early hominids. However, as more and more material becomes available for study it should eventually become possible to recognise the morphological characters that existed when tool-making came into general practice.

The tool-making ability of *Homo habilis* has now been generally accepted. His remains have been found directly associated with Oldowan tools at no less than five sites in Bed I and a sixth site in the lower part of Middle Bed II (H. 13). *Australopithecus boisei* was undoubtedly also present at Olduvai at the same time, but on the evidence now available it seems unlikely that he was responsible for more than tool-using, or possibly for simple modification of objects without employing another instrument for the purpose.

The small, probably female skull, H. 13, is the most recent known occurrence of *H. habilis* at Olduvai. So far, no taxonomically identifiable remains have been found in the upper part of Middle Bed II with the Developed Oldowan, but in Upper Bed II both *Homo erectus* (H. 9) and *Australopithecus* cf. *boisei* (H. 3) are present. If *H. erectus* is accepted as the probable maker of the Acheulean, as is now generally thought to be the case, his remains may also be expected to come to light in the upper part of Middle Bed II where the Acheulean first occurs. No identifiable hominid remains other than the robust australopithecine teeth of H. 3 have yet been found directly associated with the Developed Oldowan industry, so that at present we have no indication as to who the maker may have been.

The hominid remains so far recovered from Bed IV consist of an incomplete, small cranium (H. 12), two particularly thick vault fragments (H. 2), the right half of a mandible (H. 22), and an associated femur shaft and innominate bone found on an Acheulean living site during 1970 (H. 28). All these specimens appear to belong to *Homo* cf. *erectus* and, so far as is known, are from the upper part of Bed IV *a*. A small, slender femur and part of a tibia shaft (H. 34) that do not appear to be morphologically compatible with the remains provisionally attributed to *Homo erectus* were discovered in 1962 at a lower stratigraphic level within Beds III–IV *a*.

Recent discoveries of hominid fossils on the eastern side of Lake Rudolf in north Kenya and in the Omo basin, southern Ethiopia, have established the existence of two distinct taxa at a period considerably earlier than Bed I, Olduvai. These consist of a robust australopithecine that stands close to *A. boisei* and *A. robustus* although the degree of robustness is even more pronounced than in the later species. The second taxon is more lightly built. It seems likely to be linked with the artefacts found in the Koobi Fora area of East Rudolf, in a tuff dated at approximately 2·6 million years (M. D. Leakey, 1970*a*) and may, perhaps, prove to be allied to *Homo habilis*.

The position in South Africa concerning the early tool-makers of the Transvaal caves has remained obscure for many years, in spite of the wealth of hominid fossils and the discovery of tools at both Sterkfontein and Swartkrans that bear such close resemblances to those of the Developed Oldowan from Middle Bed II (M. D. Leakey, 1970*b*). The question of whether *Homo erectus* or *Australopithecus* was responsible for these tools has been discussed at length by various authors (Robinson, 1962; Mason, 1962*a*; Tobias, 1965*b*, Oakley, 1968; *et al.*). Arguments in favour of one or other taxon (or both) being tool-makers continued to be largely hypothetical until 1969 when several cranial fragments from Swartkrans, including part of a palate that had formerly been ascribed to *Telanthropus capensis* and later to

Homo erectus were fitted together by R. J. Clarke (Clarke and Howell, 1970). The assembled pieces leave little doubt that the specimen belonged to the genus *homo* although not necessarily to *Homo erectus*; it may, in fact, possibly represent the South African counterpart of the East African *Homo habilis*.

The affinities of the robust australopithecine from South Africa to *A. boisei* and even to the more massive specimens from East Rudolf and the Omo basin are unquestionable. All clearly belong to the same lineage with only minor variations. But the question of whether or not *Australopithecus africanus* is represented in East Africa is by no means clear. It has been suggested by some authorities that *Homo habilis* should be regarded as the East African counterpart of *A. africanus*: that he was an australopithecine who had reached a more advanced stage of development than *A. africanus* and had consequently become capable of organised tool-making. Recent discoveries in East Africa, particularly at East Rudolf, do not support this view. They suggest, further, that the validity of *A. africanus* as a taxon distinct from *A. robustus* may be doubtful. The possibility that *A. robustus* and *A. africanus* represent the male and female of a single species deserves serious consideration. The nearly complete cranium from Bed I, Olduvai discovered in 1968, in which the facial region is preserved as well as the greater part of the vault and the base of the skull, indicate that *Homo habilis* differed significantly from *A. africanus* in a number of features generally regarded as critical in assessing the status of fossil hominids.

The wealth of hominid material that has been obtained in East Africa during the last decade—ranging in time from the Plio/Pleistocene through the Lower and Middle Pleistocene—should provide answers to many of the problems related to human evolution and the early tool-makers, once it has been fully studied.

APPENDIX A

LIST OF THE RECORDED SITES IN OLDUVAI GORGE

(S) refers to surface material. Beds III–IV*a* refers to areas where these beds are not divisible. *Inferred* indicates assumed stratigraphic position or cultural status. A map of the Gorge appears on pp. xx–xxi

Site no.	Geologic locality	Name	Stratigraphic Position	Nature of finds	Industry	Date recorded	Dates excavated
			MAIN GORGE, NORTH SIDE				
(1)	71	Not named	Bed I: approx. 4 ft. below Tuff I^A	Faunal remains only, including teeth of Suidae and *Elephas*	Nil	1962	—
(2)	74	Hoopoe Gully	Beds III–IV*a*: 22–24 ft. above base	Fragmentary faunal remains	Nil	1960	—
(3)	77	Kar. K	Beds III–IV*a*: near base	Artefacts, faunal remains and buffalo skull		1962	—
(4)	79	Not named	Beds III–IV*a*: (S)	Artefacts		1962	—
(5)*a*	80	RHC	Beds III–IV*a*: quartz sand, 40 ft. below base of IV*b*	Bifaces, etc.		1962	—
(5)*b*	80	RHC	Bed II: exact horizon uncertain (S)	Bifaces, etc.	Acheulean	1931	—
(6)	—	Not named	Beds III–IV*a*: base (S)	Bifaces and faunal remains		1931	—
(7)	—	Not named	? Horizon uncertain (S)	Artefacts and faunal remains		1931	—
(8)	83	Vth Fault K	Beds III–IV*a*: 18 ft. below base of IV*b*	Remains of approx. 13 antelope skulls and skeletons	Indeterminate	1962	1962
(9)	84	Kestrel K	Beds III–IV*a*: exact horizon uncertain	A few artefacts including bifaces	Acheulean	1931	—
(10)	—	Handaxe C	Beds III–IV*a*: exact horizon uncertain	Bifaces, etc.	Acheulean	1962	—
(11)	—	Rhino K	Beds III–IV*a*: exact horizon uncertain	Part skull and mandible of rhinoceros (*Ceratotherium simum*), also bifaces	Acheulean	1962	1962
(12)*a*	25	FK East	Beds III–IV*a*: near base	Bifaces and faunal remains	Acheulean	1931	—
(12)*b*	25	FK West	Beds III–IV*a*: near base (S)	Buffalo skull	Nil	1962	—
(13)	24	HK	Secondary context of recent date	Hand-axes, cleavers and other tools as well as some fossil bones	Acheulean	1931	1931
(14)	—	Dal. K	Beds III–IV*a*: exact horizon uncertain (S)	Scattered faunal remains	Nil	1962	—

APPENDIX A (*cont.*)

Site no.	Geologic locality	Name	Stratigraphic Position	Nature of finds	Industry	Date recorded	Dates excavated
			MAIN GORGE, NORTH SIDE (*cont.*)				
(15)	23	PLK	Bed II: uppermost level	Occupation site with artefacts and cat fish remains. Horn cores of *Pelorovis* also found in 1935	Indeterminate	1935	1961, 1963
(16)	—	Not named	Beds III–IV*a*: exact horizon uncertain	Bifaces, etc.	Acheulean	1962	—
(17)*a*	—	MJTK	Bed I: clay beneath Tuff I^F	Micro-vertebrate remains	Nil	1962	1962
(17)*b*	—	MJTK	Bed II: exact horizon uncertain (S)	Part skull and horn cores of *Gorgon* sp.	Nil	1962	—
(18)*a*	18	TK, Fish Gully	Beds III–IV*a*: conglomerate 8 ft. above base	Scattered bifaces and faunal remains	Acheulean	1931	—
(18)*b*	18	TK, Fish Gully	Beds III–IV*a*: approx. 26 ft. higher than *a*	Bifaces, etc., and faunal remains	Acheulean	1931	1962
(18)*c**	18	TK, Fish Gully	Beds III–IV*a*: approx. 20 ft. higher than *b*	Occupation site with many fish remains	Acheulean	1931	1962
(18)*d*	18	TK, Fish Gully	Beds III–IV*a*: approx. 4 ft. higher than *c*	Occupation site, similar to *c*	Acheulean	1931	1962
(18)*e*	18	TK, Fish Gully	Beds III–IV*a*: approx. 4 ft. below IV*b*	Type specimen of *Xenocephalus robustus*, a few artefacts	Indeterminate	1931	1962
(19)*a*	16	TK, Channel	Bed II: 13 ft. below base of Bed III	Channel containing debris from adjacent living floor	Indeterminate	1931	1931, 1963
(19)*b*	16	TK, Lower Floor	Bed II: 10 ft. below base of Bed III	Occupation floor	Developed Oldowan B	1931	1931, 1963
(19)*c*	16	TK, Indeterminate Tuff	Bed II: tuff overlying *b*	Scattered artefacts and faunal remains	Indeterminate	1931	1931, 1963
(19)*d*	16	TK, Upper Floor	Bed II: 7 ft. below base of Bed III and overlying *c*	Occupation floor	Developed Oldowan B	1931	1931, 1963
(19)*e*	16	TK, Upper Tuff	Bed II: tuff overlying *d*	Scattered artefacts and bone fragments	Indeterminate	1931	1931, 1963
(20)*a*	14	JK 1 and 2	Bed III	Occupation site	Indeterminate	1931	1961–2
(20)*b*	14	JK 1 and 2	Bed III–IV*a*: 9 ft. above base	Occupation site, also type specimen of *Damaliscus niro*	Acheulean	1931	1931, 1961–2
(20)*c*	14	JK 1 and 2	Beds III, IV exact horizon uncertain	Occupation site Remains of H. 34	Acheulean	1931	1931
(21)	14	JK	Bed I: below Tuff I^B (S)	Scattered artefacts and faunal remains	*Inferred* Oldowan	1962	—
(22)	13	DK	Bed I: below Tuff I^B	Occupation site and stone circle	Oldowan	1931	1962, 1963
(23)*a*	12	EF–HR	Bed II: 8½ ft. above Tuff II^A	Occupation site, also type specimen of *Giraffa jumae*	Early Acheulean	1931	1931, 1963

* The artefacts at this level have since been proved to be in a disturbed context of recent origin.

APPENDIX A (cont.)

Site no.	Geologic locality	Name	Stratigraphic Position	Nature of finds	Industry	Date recorded	Dates excavated
			MAIN GORGE, NORTH SIDE (cont.)				
(23)b	12	EF–HR	Bed IVa: exact horizon uncertain	Bifaces, etc., and faunal remains	Acheulean	1931	—
(24)a	11	MK	Bed I: below Tuff Iᴮ (cf. DK, etc.)	Teeth of Hominid 4 and fragmentary faunal material	Nil	1959	1960, 1961
(24)b	11	MK	Bed I: below Tuff Iᴮ	Faunal remains and some artefacts	Oldowan	1931	—
(24)c	11	MK	Bed IVa: sandy horizon, approx. middle of bed	Bifaces, etc.	Acheulean	1931–2	—
(25)a	10	LK	Bed I: below Tuff Iᴮ (S)	Artefacts and faunal remains	Oldowan	1931	—
(25)b	10	LK	Bed IVa: reddened horizon above basal sand of IVa	Bifaces, etc., and type specimen of *Taurotragus arkelli*	Acheulean	1931–2	—
(26)a	9	RK	? Horizon uncertain, but higher than Bed IVb	Human burial, probably Upper Palaeolithic (H. 1)	Nil	1913	1913
(26)b	9	RK	Bed II: upper part	Type specimen of *Strepsiceros grandis*	Nil	1931	—
(27)a	7	CK	Bed II: conglomerate 24 ft. above the aeolian member of Bed II (S)	Bifaces and faunal remains including type specimen of *Libytherium olduvaiensis*	Early Acheulean	1931–2	—
(27)b	7	CK	Bed IVa, base	Occupation site with bifaces, etc.	Acheulean	1931–2	1931–2
(27)c	7	CK	Bed IVa: sandy horizon 15 ft. above base	Occupation site with bifaces, etc.	Acheulean	1931–2	1931–2
(28)	—	'Capsian' Site	On floor of Gorge, overlain by Naisiusiu Beds	Occupation site with microlithic industry	Late Upper Palaeolithic	1931	1931
(29)	4	Not named	Bed IVa: lower part	Type specimen of *Simopithecus leakeyi* and other faunal remains	Nil	1931	—
(30)	3	Kit. K	Bed II: upper part	Horn core of *Beatragus antiquus*	Nil	1962	—
			MAIN GORGE, SOUTH SIDE (WEST END)				
(31)	64	Not named	Bed II: approx. 4 ft. from base (S)	Scattered artefacts	Indeterminate	1962	—
(32)	61	Not named	Bed II: base (S)	Artefacts and fragmentary faunal remains	Indeterminate	1962	—
(33)	53	MLK West	Beds III–IVa: approx. 20 ft. above base	Primate skull, cf. *Colobus* sp.	Nil	1962	1963
(34)	52	MLK East	Beds III–IVa: base	Occupation site with bifaces, etc.	Early Acheulean	1952	1955
(35)	49	Not named	Beds III–IVa: basal part of beds (S)	Bifaces, etc.	Acheulean	1962	—
(36)	—	Bos K	Beds III–IVa: exact horizon uncertain	Artefacts and buffalo skull	*Inferred Acheulean*	1962	—

APPENDIX A (*cont.*)

Site no.	Geologic locality	Name	Stratigraphic Position	Nature of finds	Industry	Date recorded	Dates excavated
			MAIN GORGE, SOUTH SIDE (*cont.*)				
(37)	48	Croc. K	Beds III–IV*a*: exact horizon uncertain	Artefacts and faunal remains including skull of crocodile	*Inferred* Acheulean	1962	—
(38)*a*	45	FLK NN, Level 4	Bed I: clay beneath Tuff I^B	Many avian and crocodile remains	*Inferred* Oldowan	1960	1960
(38)*b*	45	FLK NN, Level 3	Bed I: clay overlying Tuff I^B	Occupation site and remains of Hominids 7 and 8, also type specimen of *Potamochoerus intermedius*	Oldowan	1960	1960, 1961, 1962
(38)*c*	45	FLK NN, Level 2	Bed I: tuff above Level 3	Faunal remains only	Nil	1960	1960, 1961, 1962
(38)*d*	45	FLK NN, Level 1	Bed I: clay overlying Level 2 (corresponds to the '*Zinjanthropus*' level at FLK I)	Artefacts and faunal remains	Oldowan	1960	1960, 1961, 1962
(39)	—	FLK, Ostrich Site	? Horizon uncertain, either Bed I or II	Partial skeleton of an ostrich, some artefacts and other faunal material	Indeterminate	1959	1959, 1960
(40)*a*	45	FLK North, Level 6	Bed I: clay approx. 5 ft. beneath Tuff I^F	Butchering site: artefacts scattered round the skeleton of an elephant	Oldowan	1960	1962
(40)*b*	45	FLK North, Level 5	Bed I: clay approx. 3½ ft. beneath Tuff I^F	Occupation floor, also phalanx of Hominid 10 and type specimen of *Ectopotamochoerus dubius*	Oldowan	1960	1960–2
(40)*c*	45	FLK North, Level 4	Bed I: overlying Level 5	Occupation floor	Oldowan	1960	1962
(40)*d*	45	FLK North, Level 3	Bed I: 1½–2 ft. below Tuff I	Occupation floor	Oldowan	1960	1962
(40)*e*	45	FLK North, Levels 1, 2	Bed I: immediately below Tuff I^F	Occupation floor	Oldowan	1960	1962
(40)*f*	45	FLK North	Bed II: clay above Tuff I^F	Scattered artefacts and faunal remains	Oldowan	1960	1962
(40)*g*	45	FLK North	Bed II: 6–7 ft. above Tuff I^F	Butchering site: artefacts scattered round the skeleton of a *Deinotherium*	*Inferred* Oldowan	1960	1962
(40)*h*	45	FLK North	Bed II: sandy conglomerate 10 ft. above Tuff I^F (cf. 48*c*)	Artefacts, including some made from chert	Developed Oldowan	1960	1962
(41)*a*	45	FLK, the '*Zinjanthropus*' Level (22)	Bed I: a palaeosol 20 ft. below Tuff I^F	Extensive occupation floor with skull of '*Zinjanthropus*' and two limb bones of H. 6, also type specimen of *Promesochoerus mukiri*	Oldowan	1931–2	1931, 1959, 1960, 1961, 1962

285

Site no.	Geologic locality	Name	Stratigraphic Position	Nature of finds	Industry	Date recorded	Dates excavated
			MAIN GORGE, SOUTH SIDE (*cont.*)				
(41)*b*	45	FLK, Level 21	Bed I: tuff overlying *a*	Faunal remains only	Nil	1960	1960
(41)*c*	45	FLK, Level 17	Bed I: approx. 17½ ft. below Tuff I^F	A few artefacts only	Indeterminate	1960	1960
(41)*d*	45	FLK, Level 16	Bed I: clay approx. 17 ft. below Tuff I^F	A few broken fossil bones	Nil	1960	1960
(41)*e*	45	FLK, Level 15	Bed I: clayey tuff approx. 13 ft. below Tuff I^F	Scattered artefacts and faunal remains	Indeterminate	1960	1960, 1961, 1962
(41)*f*	45	FLK, Level 13	Bed I: clayey tuff approx. 12 ft. below Tuff I^F	Some artefacts and a number of faunal remains	Indeterminate	1960	1960, 1961, 1962
(41)*g*	45	FLK, Level 12	Bed I: tuff overlying *f*	A few crushed mammalian bones embedded in limestone nodules	Nil	1960	1960, 1961, 1962
(41)*h*	45	FLK, Level 11	Bed I: tuff and clay 9–10 ft. below Tuff I^F	A few faunal remains only	Nil	1960	1960, 1961, 1962
(41)*i*	45	FLK, Level 10	Bed I: coarse tuff overlying *h*	Some faunal remains and artefacts	Indeterminate	1960	1960, 1961, 1962
(41)*j*	45	FLK, Level 7	Bed I: clay, 5–6 ft. below Tuff I^F	A few faunal remains	Nil	1960	1960, 1961, 1962
(42)	45	FLK (west of 40)	Bed II: Tuff II^C and overlying clay	Occupation site	Developed Oldowan B	1931–2	1931, 1960, 1963
(43)	45	FLK, Maiko Gully	Bed II: base	Hominids H. 16 and H. 30	Oldowan	1963	—
(44)*a*	45	FLK South	Bed II: the sandy conglomerate corresponding to 40*h* and 48*c*	Artefacts and faunal remains	Developed Oldowan A	1931	—
(44)*b*	45	FLK South	Bed II: upper part	Bifaces and other artefacts	Indeterminate	1931	—
(45)*a*	86	VEK, north side of gully	Bed II: exact horizon uncertain	Bifaces and other artefacts	Indeterminate	1931	—
(45)*b*	86	VEK, north side of gully	Bed IV*a*: above Marker Tuff IV^A	Parts of the skull of Hominid 12	*Inferred* Acheulean	1962–3	1962, 1963
(45)*c*	86	VEK, north side of gully	Bed IV*a*: base	Bifaces and other artefacts	Acheulean	1931	—
(46)*a*	44	HWK, mouth of gully	Bed I: upper part	Type specimen of *Parmularius altidens*	Nil	1931	1931
(46)*b*	44	HWK, mouth of gully	Bed II: clay overlying Tuff I^F	Artefacts and faunal remains, including *Deinotherium* skeleton	*Inferred* Oldowan	1931	1931
(46)*c*	44	HWK, head of gully	Bed II: clay overlying Tuff I^F	Partial skeleton of *Giraffa gracilis* and other faunal remains. Hominid femur fragment (H. 20) from surface	Oldowan	1959	1959

APPENDIX A (*cont.*)

Site no.	Geologic locality	Name	Stratigraphic Position	Nature of finds	Industry	Date recorded	Dates excavated
			MAIN GORGE, SOUTH SIDE (*cont.*)				
(46)*d*	44	HWK, Castle	Bed IV*a*: base	Bifaces, etc., and faunal remains, including Type specimen of *Parmularius rugosus*	Acheulean	1931	1931
(47)	44	HEB/G	Bed IV*a*	Occupation floor	Acheulean	1962	1962
(48)*a*	43	HWK East, Level 1	Bed II: surface of clay overlying Tuff I^F	Occupation floor	Oldowan	1931	1962, 1963
(48)*b*	43	HWK East, Level 2	Bed II: clay approx. 5 ft. above Tuff I^F. (Corresponds to *f* at at site 40)	Faunal remains and artefacts	Oldowan or Developed Oldowan A	1931	1962, 1963
(48)*c*	43	HWK East, Levels 3, 4, 5	Bed II: re-worked tuffs and a sandy conglomerate 8–10 ft. above Tuff I^F (corresponds to level 40*h* and level 44*a*)	Artefacts and some faunal remains	Developed Oldowan A	1931	1962, 1963
(49)	42	KK	Bed II, level corresponding to 48*c*, etc.	Many artefacts and faunal remains	*Inferred* Developed Oldowan A	1959	—
(50)	40	MCK	Bed II: tuff immediately below Tuff II^D (S)	Partial skeleton and mandible of *Simopithecus* sp.	Nil	1962	1962
(51)*a*	38, 39	Long K	Bed II: various levels (S)	Scattered artefacts and faunal remains at various localities	Indeterminate	1931–2	—
(51)*b*	38, 39	Long K	Bed IV*a*: various levels (S)	As for *a* above	*Inferred* Acheulean	1931–2	—
(52)	36	WK	Bed IV*a*:	Bifaces, and H. 28	Acheulean	1931	1970
(53)*a*	—	PDK	Bed I: clay underlying Tuff I^B (corresponds to MK, DK, etc.)	Skull and two incomplete skeletons of *Hippopotamus gorgops*	Nil	1959	1959, 1960
(53)*b*	—	PDK	Bed IV*a*: in channels cutting through Tuff IV^A	Bifaces, etc. and faunal remains on living sites	Acheulean with pitted anvils	1970	1970
(53)*c*	—	PDK	Bed IV*a*: below Tuff IV^A	Bifaces, cleavers, etc.	Acheulean	1970	1970
(54)	—	THC	Bed I: clay beneath Tuff I^B (S) (corresponds to MK, DK, etc.)	Foot bones of *Ancylotherium* cf. *henigi* and other faunal remains	Nil	1931	—
(55)	32	Elephant K	Bed II: conglomerate above Tuff II^A (S) (possibly corresponds to EF–HR)	Bifaces, etc., and faunal remains	*Inferred* Early Acheulean	1931	1931
			SIDE GORGE, NORTH SIDE				
(56)	97	NGC	Bed IV*a* (S)	Bifaces, etc.	Acheulean	1935	—
(57)*a*	96	CMK	Bed IV*a*: basal part (S)	Faunal remains, bifaces and other artefacts	Acheulean	1935	—

APPENDIX A (*cont.*)

Site no.	Geologic locality	Name	Stratigraphic Position	Nature of finds	Industry	Date recorded	Dates excavated
			SIDE GORGE, NORTH SIDE (*cont.*)				
(57)*b*	96	CMK	Bed IV*a*: sandy level a few feet below IV*b* (S)	Bifaces, faunal remains	Acheulean	1935	—
(58)	95	GTC	Bed IV*a*: basal part	Bifaces, etc., and faunal remains	Acheulean	1935	—
(59)	—	MRC	Lower Ndutu: conglomerate overlying Bed IV*a*	Mandible of *Simopithecus* sp. and sundry other faunal remains	Nil	1935	1960
(60)	—	SC	Bed II: Tuff II^D (S)	Artefacts with some bifaces and faunal remains, including type specimen of *Alcelaphus howardi*	*Inferred* Developed Oldowan B	1935	—
(61)	—	GRC	Bed IV*a*: exact horizon uncertain	Bifaces, etc., and faunal remains	Acheulean	1935	—
(62)*a*	89	FC West, Floor	Bed II: 14 ft. above chert horizon	Occupation floor	Developed Oldowan B	1931	1963
(62)*b*	89	FC West, Tuff	Bed II: overlying *a*	Artefacts, faunal remains and broken hominid tooth (H. 19)	Developed Oldowan B	1931	1963
(63*a*)	89	FC	Bed II: various levels	Artefacts and faunal remains	Indeterminate	1931	1963
(63)*b*	89	FC	Bed IV*a*: basal part	Artefacts and faunal remains, including skeleton of python	Indeterminate	1931	1962
(64)	46	LLK	Bed II: tuff, 10–12 ft. below base of Bed III	Calvaria of *Homo erectus* (H. 9)	Nil	1960	1961, 1962
			SIDE GORGE, SOUTH SIDE				
(65)	—	GC	Bed IV*a*: basal part (S)	Bifaces, etc., and faunal remains	Acheulean	1935	—
(66)	94	BK	Bed II: channel cutting into Tuff II^D	Large numbers of artefacts, faunal remains and two hominid teeth (H. 3). Abundant fauna includes Type specimens of *Damaliscus antiquus, Mesochoerus olduvaiensis, Orthostonyx brachyops, Afrochoerus nicoli* and *Notochoerus compactus*	Developed Oldowan B	1935	1952–7, 1963
(67)	93	DC	Bed II: upper part	Faunal remains, including elephant tusk and mandible	Nil	1931	—
(68)*a*	92	SHK West, Annexe	Bed II: approx. 32 ft. above base	Occupation floor	Developed Oldowan B	1935	1957
(68)*b*	92	SHK West, Main Site	Bed II: conglomerate in channel cutting into *a*	Artefacts and faunal remains	Developed Oldowan B	—	1957

APPENDIX A (*cont.*)

Site no.	Geologic locality	Name	Stratigraphic Position	Nature of finds	Industry	Date recorded	Dates excavated
			SIDE GORGE, SOUTH SIDE (*cont.*)				
(68)*c*	92	SHK West, Main Site	Bed II: tuff, overlying *a* and *b*	Artefacts and many faunal remains, including herd of antelopes (*Phenacotragus recki*)	Developed Oldowan B	—	1957
(69)	92	SHK East	Bed II: various levels (S)	Artefacts and faunal remains	Indeterminate	1935	1957
(70)*a*	—	SWK	Bed II: upper part	Artefacts and faunal remains	Indeterminate	1935	—
(70)*b*	—	SWK	Bed IV*a*: exact horizon uncertain	Bifaces and faunal remains	Acheulean	1935	—
(71)*a*	88	MNK, Skull Site,	Bed II: clay, 24 ft. above base	Artefacts, faunal remains and fragments of Hominid 13	Oldowan	1963	1963
(71)*b*	88	MNK, Skull Site,	Bed II: re-worked tuff, overlying *a*	Teeth of Hominid 15 and a few artefacts	Indeterminate	1963	1963
(71)*c*	88	MNK, Main Occupation Site	Bed II: re-worked tuff, 40 ft. above base	Occupation site	Developed Oldowan B	1962	1963
(71)*d*	88	MNK	Bed IV*a*: basal part (S)	Bifaces etc., faunal remains and fragments of Hominid 2	Acheulean	1935	—
(72)	—	PEK	Bed I: exact horizon uncertain (S)	Faunal remains, including elephant foot bones	Nil	1960	—

LIST OF IDENTIFIED FAUNAL REMAINS FROM KNOWN STRATIGRAPHIC HORIZONS IN BEDS I AND II

by Margaret Leakey

(For divisions of Beds I and II see Table I. L refers to levels in excavations)

Order	Family	Genus	Species	Bed I (Upper Member)			Bed II		
				Lower	Middle	Upper	Lower	Middle	Upper
Pulmonata	Limnaeidae	*Lymnea*	*natalensis*	—	—	—	FLK Maiko Gully	—	—
		Bulinus	*tropicus*	—	FLK, '*Zinj.*' level	—	FLK Maiko Gully	—	—
		Bulinus	aff. *truncatus*	—	FLK, '*Zinj.*' level	—	—	—	—
	Testacellidae	*Streptostele*	sp.	—	FLK, '*Zinj.*' level	—	—	—	—
	Urocyclidae	Indet.		DK	FLK, '*Zinj.*' level	—	—	—	—
	Stenogyridae	*Homorus*	sp.	—	—	FLK N, L/4	—	—	—
Eumellibranchiata	Cyrenidae	*Corbicula*	*africana*	—	—	—	—	SHK	—
?	?	*Anisus*	*natalensis*	—	—	—	FLK Maiko Gully	—	—
Gastropoda	Indet	—	—	—	—	—	HWK E, L/2	MNK. Skull Site	—
Ostariophysi	Clariidae	*Clarias*	sp.	DK, L/1, 2	FLK, '*Zinj.*' level; FLK NN, L/2, 3	—	—	FC W, reworked tuff; MNK, both sites; SHK	BK
Acanthopterygii	Cichlidae	*Tilapia*	sp.	DK	FLK NN, L/2, 3	—	—	MNK, Main Site; ?SHK	?BK
		Indet.	—	—	FLK, '*Zinj.*' level; FLK NN, L/3	—	—	—	—
Anura	Pipidae	*Xenopus*	sp.	DK, L/1	FLK, '*Zinj.*' level; FLK NN, L/2–3	FLK N, L/2,3 5, 6	—	—	—
		Indet.	—	DK, L/1	FLK NN, L/2–3	FLK, all levels	—	—	—
	Bufonidae	*Bufo*	sp.	—	—	FLK N, L/1, 2, 3, 5, 6	—	—	—
		Indet.	—	—	FLK, '*Zinj.*' level; FLK NN, L/2–3	FLK N, L/1, 2, 3, 4, 6	—	—	—
	Ranidae	*Rana*	sp.	—	FLK NN, L/2–3, 3	FLK N, L/2, 3	—	—	—
		Ptychadena	sp.	—	FLK NN, L/2–3	FLK N, L/1, 1–3, 5, 6	—	—	—
		Indet.	—	DK L/1, 2	FLK, '*Zinj.*' level	FLK N, L/1, 3	—	—	—
	Indet.		—	—	—	—	HWK E, L/2	MNK, both sites	BK
Chelonia	Pelomedusidae	*Pelusios*	*castaneus*	—	FLK NN, L/1, 3	—	—	—	—
	Indet.		—	DK, all levels	FLK, '*Zinj.*' level	FLK N, L/1, 2, 5	FLK N HWK E, all levels	FC W, both levels; MNK, both sites; EF–HR	BK

APPENDIX B (*cont.*)

Order	Family	Genus	Species	Bed I (Upper Member)			Bed II		
				Lower	Middle	Upper	Lower	Middle	Upper
Crocodilia	Crocodylidae	*Crocodylus*	*niloticus*	DK, all levels	FLK, 'Zinj.' level; FLK NN, L/3	FLK N, L/1, 2, 5	FLK N HWK E, L/2	MNK. both sites; FC W, Floor	BK
		Crocodylus	sp. nov.	DK, all levels	—	—	HWK E, L/1, 2	FC W, Floor	—
		Crocodylus	sp.	MK, PDK, FLK NN L/4	FLK, 'Zinj.' level	FLK N, L/5	HWK E, L/1, 2	FC W, Floor; FLK, II; MNK, both sites	BK
Squamata	Agamidae	Indet.		—	—	FLK, 'Zinj.' level; FLK NN, L/2–3	—	—	—
	Chamaeleontidae	Indet.		—	—	FLK, 'Zinj.' level; FLK NN, L/2–3	FLK N, all levels	—	—	—
	Scincidae	Indet.		—	—	FLK, 'Zinj.' level; FLK NN, L/3	FLK N, all levels	—	—	—
	Boidae	*Python*	sp.	DK, all levels	FLK, 'Zinj.' level; FLK NN, L/1, 2–3, 3	FLK N, L/6	HWK E, L/2–5	—	TK, Upper Floor
		Indet.		DK, L/1, 2	FLK, 'Zinj.' level; FLK NN, L/2–3, 5	—	—	—	—
	Colubridae	Indet.		DK, all levels	FLK, 'Zinj.' level; FLK NN, L/2–3, 3, 4	FLK N, all levels	—	—	BK
	Elapidae	*Naja*	sp.	DK, all levels	FLK NN, L/2, 3	—	—	—	—
		Indet.		DK, L/2	FLK NN, L/2–3	FLK N, L/1	—	—	—
	Viperidae	*Bitis*	sp.	DK, all levels	FLK, 'Zinj.' level; FLK NN, L/2–3, 3	FLK N, L/2, 3 4, 5, 6	—	—	BK
		Bitis	*nasicornis*	—	FLK NN, L/2–3	—	—	—	—
		Indet.		DK, L/1, 3	—	—	—	—	—
Struthioniformes*	Struthionidae	*Struthio*	sp.	DK, L/1, 2	FLK, 'Zinj.' level FLK NN, L/3	—	HWK E, L/1	FC W, reworked tuff; MNK, Skull Site; SHK	BK
Ciconiiformes	Phoenicopteridae	Indet.		DK, all levels FLK NN, L/4	—	—	—	—	—
Insectivora	Erinaceidae	*Erinaceus*	cf. *major*	—	—	FLK N, L/3, 4, 5	—	—	—
	Macroscelididae	*Nasilio*	sp.	—	—	FLK N, L/1–5	—	—	—
		? *Elephantulus* Indet.	sp.	—	—	FLK N, L/1–5	—	—	—
				—	FLK, 'Zinj.' level; FLK NN, L/2, 3	—	—	—	—
		Indet.		—	—	FLK, 'Zinj'. level	—	HWK E, L/2	—	BK
	Soricidae	*Myosorex*	cf. *robinsoni*	—	FLK NN, L/2, 3	FLK N, all levels	—	—	—
		Crocidura	cf. *hindei*	—	FLK NN, L/1, 3	FLK N, L/3, 4, 5	—	—	—
		Suncus	sp.	—	—	FLK N, L/1–5	—	—	—
		Suncus	cf. *lixus*	—	FLK NN, L/1, 2, 3	—	—	—	—
		Suncus	cf. *orangiae*	—	FLK, 'Zinj.' level	FLK N, all levels	—	—	—
Chiroptera	Megadermidae	Indet.		—	—	—	FLK N, L/2. 3	—	—
	Vespertilionidae	Indet.		—	—	FLK NN, L/3	FLK N, 1–3	—	—	—

* No determinations of the avifauna are available other than for ostrich and flamingos.

APPENDIX B (cont.)

Order	Family	Genus	Species	Bed I (Upper Member) Lower	Bed I (Upper Member) Middle	Bed I (Upper Member) Upper	Bed II Lower	Bed II Middle	Bed II Upper
Primates	Lorisidae	Galago	senegalensis	—	FLK, 'Zinj.' level	—	—	—	—
		Galago	sp.	DK, L/2	—	—	—	—	—
	Cerco-pithecidae	Simopithecus	cf. oswaldi	DK	FLK NN, L/3	—	—	SHK E and W MNK,	BK E and W, MRC, DC, MCK BK
		cf. Cercocebus	sp.		—	—	—	—	
		Papio	sp.	DK, L/2, 3	FLK NN, L/2 or 3	—	—	—	—
	Indet.	—	—	—	—	—	HWK E, L/1–2	—	—
Rodentia	Cricetidae	Tatera	sp.	—	FLK, 'Zinj.' level; FLK NN, L/1, 2, 3	FLK N, all levels	—	—	—
	Muridae	Otomys	kempi	—	FLK, 'Zinj.' level; FLK NN, L/1, 2, 3	FLK N, all levels	—	—	—
		Gerbillus	sp.	—	—	FLK N, all levels	—	—	—
		Saccostomus	sp.	—	FLK, 'Zinj.' level	FLK N, all levels	—	—	—
		cf. Grammomys	sp.	—	FLK NN, L/3	—	—	—	—
		cf. Steatomys	sp.	—	FLK, 'Zinj.' level; FLK NN, L/1, 2, 3	FLK N, all levels	—	—	—
		Dendromys	sp.	—	FLK NN, L/3	FLK N, all levels	—	—	—
		Various	—	—	FLK, 'Zinj.' level FLK NN, L/1, 2, 3	FLK N, all levels	—	—	—
	Sciuridae	Xerus	sp.	—	—	FLK N, all levels	—	—	—
	Pedetidae	Pedetes	sp.	—	—	FLK N, L/1	—	—	—
	Hystricidae	Hystrix	sp.	DK, L/2	FLK, 'Zinj.' level; FLK NN, L/1	FLK N, L/1, 6	—	—	—
	Bathyergidae	Heterocephalus	sp.	—	—	FLK N, L/3, 4, 5, 6	HWK E, L/2	MNK, both sites	—
Lagomorpha	Leporidae	Serengetilagus	sp.	—	FLK, 'Zinj.' level	FLK N, L/1–3, 4, 5	—	—	—
Carnivora	Canidae	Thos	mesomelas	DK, 1/2	FLK 'Zinj.' level	FLK N, L/3	—	—	—
		Otocyon	recki	—	FLK NN, L/3	FLK N, L/3, 4	—	—	—
		Indet.	—	—	FLK NN, L/2–3	—	—	MNK, both sites	TK, Upper and lower Floors
	Mustelidae	Lutra	sp.	MK	—	—	—	—	—
	Viverridae	Herpestes	sp.	DK, L/3	—	FLK N, L/3, 4	—	—	—
		cf. Myonax	sanguineus	—	FLK NN, L/3	—	—	—	—
		Mungos	sp.	—	FLK NN, L/2	FLK N, L/4	—	—	—
		Mungos	dietrichi	—	—	FLK N, L/4	—	—	—
		Herpestinae indet.	—	—	—	FLK N, L/1	—	—	—
		Genetta	sp.	—	FLK NN, L/2–3	FLK N, L/4	—	—	—
		Pseudocivettictis	ingens	—	FLK NN, L/3	—	—	—	—
		indet.	—	—	—	—	FLK N	SHK ?	—
	Hyaenidae	Crocuta	sp.	DK, L/3	FLK, 'Zinj.' level, L/16	—	—	—	—
		Crocuta	aff. ultra	DK	FLK, 'Zinj.' level	FLK N, L/4	—	—	BK
		Crocuta	crocuta	—	—	FLK N, L/1	—	—	—
	Felidae	Felis	cf. serval	—	—	—	—	SHK	—
		Panthera	cf. tigris	—	—	—	—	—	BK
		Panthera	sp.	—	—	—	—	—	BK
		cf. Acinonyx	sp.	—	—	—	HWK	—	—
		indet.	—	DK, L/2	—	FLK N, L/1	FLK N	—	—
		Machairodontinae indet.	—	DK, L/2	FLK NN, L/2 or 3	—	FLK N	SHK ?	—

APPENDIX B (*cont.*)

Order	Family	Genus	Species	Bed I (Upper Member)			Bed II		
				Lower	Middle	Upper	Lower	Middle	Upper
Proboscidea	Deinotheriidae	*Deinotherium*	cf. *bozasi*	DK, L/2, 3	—	FLK N, L/5	HWK E, L/2 FLK N;	—	—
	Elephantidae	*Elephas*	*recki* (early form)	DK, L/1, 2; MK	? FLK, upper levels	FLK N, L/5, 6	FLK N; HWK E, L/1, 2	—	—
		Elephas	*recki* (evolved form)	—	—	—	—	MNK, both sites; SHK, FC W, Floor	BK; TK, Lower Floor; DC
Hyracoidea	Procavidae	Indet.	—	DK, surface	—	—	—	—	—
Perissodactyla	Equidae	*Equus*	cf. *oldowayensis*	DK, L/2, 3	FLK NN, L/1–3, FLK, 'Zinj.' and upper levels	FLK N, all levels	FLK N, HWK E, L/1, 2	MNK, both sites; SHK; EF–HR; FC W, HWK E, L/3–5	BK; TK, all levels; DC
		Stylohipparion	sp.	—	FLK, 'Zinj.' level	FLK N, all levels	FLK N; HWK E, L/1–2	MNK, both sites; SHK; FC W, HWK E, L/3–5	BK; TK, all levels; DC
	Chalicotheriidae	*Ancylotherium*	cf. *hennigi*	THC	—	—	—	—	—
	Rhinocerotidae	*Ceratotherium*	*simum*	DK, all levels	FLK NN, L/1	FLK N, L/1–2, 3	FLK N; HWK E, L/2	SHK; MNK, both sites; EF–HR; FC W, HWK E, L/3–5	BK; TK, all levels
		Diceros	*bicornis*	—	—	—	—	MNK, Main Site	BK
Artiodactyla	Suidae	*Mesochoerus*	*heseloni*	—	—	—	—	—	TK, Lower Floor
		Mesochoerus	*olduvaiensis*	—	—	—	HWK E, L/1	MNK, both sites; SHK	BK; TK, Upper and Lower Floors; DC; SWK
		Potamochoerus	*majus*	—	—	—	—	—	BK
		Potamochoerus	*intermedius*	DK, L/2, 3	FLK NN, L/3	—	—	—	—
		Promesochoerus	*mukiri*	DK, L/2, 3	FLK, 'Zinj.' level; FLK NN, L/2	FLK N, L/1	—	—	—
		Ectopotamochoerus	*dubius*	DK, L/2, ?3	FLK, 'Zinj.' and upper levels	FLK N, L/6	—	—	—
		Pronotochoerus	cf. *jacksoni*	DK, L/2	—	—	—	—	—
		Notochoerus	*euilus*	—	—	FLK N, L/1–3	—	—	—
		Notochoerus	*compactus*	—	—	—	—	SHK	BK
		Notochoerus	sp.	DK, L/2	FLK, 'Zinj.' level	—	HWK E, L/2	MNK	—
		Tapinochoerus	*meadowsi*	—	—	—	—	MNK, Main Site; SHK	BK
		Tapinochoerus	sp.	—	FLK, 'Zinj.' level	—	—	—	TK, Lower Floor
		Afrochoerus	*nicoli*	—	—	—	—	SHK	BK; DC; MLK
		Orthostonyx	*brachyops*	—	—	—	—	MNK, Main Site; SHK	BK
		indet.	—	—	—	—	FLK N,	EF–HR; FC W, both levels	—
	Hippopotamidae	*Hippopotamus*	*gorgops*	DK, all levels PDK	FLK, upper levels	FLK N, L/1–2, 4, 5, 6	FLK N; HWK E, L/1, 2	MNK, both sites; FC W, HWK E, L/3–5	BK; TK, all levels
		Hippopotamus	sp.	—	—	—	—	—	BK
	Giraffidae	*Giraffa*	*jumae*	—	FLK, upper levels	—	—	EF–HR	—
		Giraffa	*gracilis*	—	—	—	HWK	—	—
		Giraffa	sp.	DK, L/2, 3	—	FLK N, L/1–3, 4, 6	HWK E, L/1	MNK, Main Site; HWK E, L/3	BK; TK, Lower Floor
		Okapia	sp.	DK, L/3	FLK, upper levels	FLK N, L/3	—	—	BK
		Libytherium	*olduvaiensis*	DK, L/2, 3	?FLK, upper levels	FLK N, L/1–3	FLK N; HWK E, L/1, 2	FC W, reworked tuff; MNK, Main Site; SHK; HWK E, L/3, 4	BK; TK, Channel
	Bovidae	*Strepsiceros*	*maryanus*	DK	FLK NN, L/1–3; FLK, 'Zinj.' and upper levels	FLK N, all levels	HWK E L/1, 2	—	—

APPENDIX B (*cont.*)

Order	Family	Genus	Species	Bed I (Upper Member)			Bed II		
				Lower	Middle	Upper	Lower	Middle	Upper
Artiodactyla	Bovidae	*Strepsicercos*	*grandis*	—	—	—	—	MNK, Main Site; SHK	BK
		Strepsicerotini	indet.	DK	FLK, 'Zinj.' level	—	—	SHK	—
		Pelorovis	*oldowayensis*	—	—	—	—	HWK E, L/5; MNK, Main Site; SHK	BK, PLK
		Bovini (small)	indet.	DK	FLK, 'Zinj.' level	FLK N, L/1–3, 6	HWK E, L/1, 2	MNK, Main Site; SHK	BK, TK
		Kobus	*sigmoidalis*	—	FLK NN, L/1–3, FLK 'Zinj.' and upper levels	—	—	—	
		Kobus	sp.	DK	FLK NN, L/2, 3	FLK N, L/3, 4, 5	HWK E, L/1, 2; FLK N	MNK, Main Site; FC; SHK	BK, GTC
		Redunca	sp.	—	—	FLK N, L/4	—	—	—
		Hippotragus	*gigas*	DK	FLK NN, L/1; FLK, L/13	—	—	FLK	BK, TK
		Oryx	sp.	—	FLK, 'Zinj.' level	—	—	—	—
		Hippotragini	indet.	—	FLK NN, L/1, 2	FLK N, all levels	HWK E, L/2	MNK, Main Site	—
		Parmularius	*altidens*	DK	FLK 'Zinj.' and upper levels	FLK N, all levels	—	—	—
		Xenocephalus	sp.	DK	—	—	HWK E, L/1	MNK, Main Site; SHK	BK
		Beatragus	*antiquus*	—	—	FLK N, L/3	—	Kit K	—
		Gorgon	*olduvaiensis*	—	—	FLK N, L/5	—	SHK	BK
		Aepyceros	sp.	—	—	—	—	—	BK
		Damaliscus	*angusticornis*	—	—	—	FLK N, Rootlet Clay	FLK, SHK	—
		Damaliscus	*niro*	—	—	—	—	SHK	BK
		Alcelaphini	indet.	DK	FLK NN, L/1–3; FLK, 'Zinj.' and upper levels	—	HWK E, L/1, 2	HWK E (above L/5)	BK
		Neotragini	indet.	—	—	FLK N, L/5	—	—	—
		Gazella	*wellsi*	DK	FLK NN, L/1–3; FLK, 'Zinj.' and upper levels	FLK N, all levels	HWK E, L/1	—	—
		Phenacotragus	*recki*	—	—	—	—	SHK	BK
		Gazella	sp.	—	—	—	—	FC; SHK	BK
		Antilopini	indet.	DK	—	—	FLK N	MNK, Main Site; FC	BK, TK
		Pultiphagonides	*africanus*	—	—	—	—	MNK, Main Site; SHK	BK
		Tribe indet.	sp. nov.	—	—	FLK N, L/5, 6	—	—	—

294

REFERENCES

Alimen, M. H. (1962). *Les origines de l'homme.* Paris: Fayard.

Alimen, M. H. and Chavaillon, J. (1962). Position stratigraphique et évolution de la Pebble Culture au Sahara nord-occidental. In *Actes du IVe Congrès Panafricain de Préhistoire et de l'Etude du Quaternaire* (ed. G. Mortelmans and J. Nenquin), vol. III, pp. 3–26. Tervuren.

Arambourg, C. (1960). L'hominien fossile d'Oldoway. *Bull. Soc. Préh. Fr.* **57**, no. 3–4.

Bailloud, G. (1965). Les gisements paléolithiques de Melka Kontouré, Addis Ababa. *Cahiers de l'Institut Ethiopien d'Archéologie*, vol. I.

Balout, L. (1965). *Préhistoire de l'Afrique du Nord.* Paris: Arts et Métiers graphiques.

Balout, L. (1967). Procédés d'analyse et questions de terminologie dans l'étude des ensembles industriels du Paléolithique inférieur en Afrique du Nord. In *Background to Evolution in Africa* (ed. W. W. Bishop and J. D. Clark) pp. 701–35, Chicago University Press.

Biberson, P. (1961). *Le Paléolithique inférieur du Maroc atlantique.* Rabat: Pub. Services des Antiquités du Maroc, Fasc. 17.

Biberson, P. (1964). Notes sur deux stations Acheuléens de chasseurs d'éléphants de la vieille Castille. *Monografias Inst. de Preh. y Arch.*, vol. VI.

Biberson, P. (1967a). Stratigraphical details of the Quaternary of north-west Africa. In *Background to Evolution in Africa* (ed. W. W. Bishop and J. D. Clark), pp. 359–64. Chicago University Press.

Biberson, P. (1967b). Some aspects of the Lower Palaeolithic of north-west Africa. In *Background to Evolution in Africa.* (ed. W. W. Bishop and J. D. Clark), pp. 447–75. Chicago University Press.

Biberson, P. (1967c). Galets aménagés du Maghreb et du Sahara, *Fiches typologiques africaines.* Paris: Muséum National d'Histoire Naturelle.

Boné, E. L., S.J. (1964). *Homo habilis*, nouveau venu de la Paléoanthropologie, Louvain, *Nouv. Rev. Théol.* **86**, 619–32.

Bout, P. (1960). *Le Villafranchien du Velay, et du bassin hydrographique moyen et supérieur de l'Allier.* Le Puy: Imp. Jeanne d'Arc.

Brain, C. K. (1958). The Transvaal ape-man-bearing cave deposits. *Transvaal Museum Mem.*, no. 11. Pretoria.

Brain, C. K. (1967a). Hottentot food remains and their bearing on the interpretation of fossil bone assemblages, Windhoek, *Sci. Papers of the Namib Desert Research Station*, no. 32.

Brain, C. K. (1967b). Bone weathering and the problem of bone pseudo-tools. *S. Afr. J. Sci.* **63**, no. 3, 97.

Breuil, H. (1939). Bone and antler industry of the Choukoutien *Sinanthropus site. Pal. Sin.*, New Series, D, no. 6.

Broom, R. and Robinson, J. T. (1949). Thumb of the Swartkrans ape-man. *Nature, Lond.* **164**, 841–2.

Campbell, B. G. (1964). Just another man-ape? *Discovery* **25**, 6, 37–8.

Canby, C. (ed.). (1961). *The Epic of Man.* New York: Time–Life Inc.

Chavaillon, H. (1967). La préhistoire éthiopienne à Melka Kontouré. *Archeologia* **19**, 56–63.

Chavaillon, J. and Taieb, M. (1968). Stratigraphie du Quaternaire de Melka Kontouré (vallée de l'Aouache, Ethiopie): premiers résultats, *C. R. Acad. Sci.* **266**, 1210–12.

Clark, J. D. (1962). The Kalambo Falls prehistoric site: an interim report. In *Actes du IVe Congrès Panafricain de Préhistoire et de l'Etude du Quaternaire*, (ed. G. Mortelmans and J. Nenquin), vol. III, pp. 195–201, Tervuren.

Clark, Sir W. le Gros (1964). The evolution of man. *Discovery* **25**, 6, 32–3.

Clark, Sir W. le Gros (1967). *Man-Apes or Ape-Men?* New York: Holt, Rinehart and Winston.

Clarke, R. J. and Howell, F. C. (1970). More evidence of an advanced hominid at Swartkrans, *Nature, Lond.* **225**, 1219–22.

Cole, S. (1963). *The Prehistory of East Africa.* New York: Macmillan.

Coon, C. S. (1963). *The Origin of Races.* New York: Alfred Knopf.

Cornwall, I. W. and Howard, Maitland M. (1960). *The Making of Man.* London: Phoenix House.

Cox, A. (1969). Geomagnetic reversals. *Science N.Y.* **163**, 237–44.

Curtis, G. H. (1965). Potassium–argon dates for the early Villafranchian of France. *Trans. Am. Geophys. Un.* **46**, 178.

Curtis, G. H. (1967). Notes on some Miocene to Pleistocene potassium–argon results. In *Background to Evolution in Africa* (ed. W. W. Bishop and J. D. Clark), pp. 365–9. Chicago University Press.

Curtis, G. H. and Evernden, J. F. (1962). Age of basalt underlying Bed I at Olduvai, *Nature, Lond.* **194**, 611.

Dahlberg, A. (1960). The Olduvai giant hominid tooth. *Nature, Lond.* **188**, 962.

Dart, R. A. (1957a). The Makapansgat Australopithecine Osteodontokeratic culture. In *Proc. 3rd Pan-African Congress on Prehistory* (ed. J. D. Clark and S. Cole), pp. 161–71. London: Chatto and Windus.

Dart, R. A. (1957b). The Osteodontokeratic culture of *Prometheus africanus*, Pretoria, *Transvaal Museum Mem.*, no. 10.

Dart, R. A. (1959). How human were the South African man-apes? *South African Panorama*, November pp. 18–21.

Davis, P. R., Day, M. H. and Napier, J. R. (1964). Hominid fossils from Bed I, Olduvai Gorge, Tanganyika. *Nature, Lond.* **201**, 967–70.

Day, M. H. (1965). *Guide to Fossil Man.* London: Cassell.

Day, M. H. (1967). Olduvai Hominid 10: a multivariate analysis. *Nature, Lond.* **215**, 323–4.

Day, M. H. (1969). Femoral fragment of a robust australopithecine from Olduvai Gorge, Tanzania. *Nature, Lond.* **221**, 230–3.

Day, M. H. and Napier, J. R. (1966). A hominid toe bone from Olduvai Gorge, Tanzania. *Nature, Lond.* **211**, 929–30.

Day, M. H. and Wood, B. A. (1968). Functional affinities of the Olduvai Hominid 8 talus. *Man* (London), **3**, no. 3, 440–55.

Evernden, J. F. and Curtis, G. H. (1965). Potassium–argon dating of late Cenozoic rocks in East Africa and Italy. *Current Anthropology* **6**, 343–85.

Fleischer, R. L. *et al.* (1965). Fission track dating of Bed I, Olduvai Gorge. *Science, N.Y.* **148**, 72–4.

Foster Cooper, C. (1932). The Oldoway human skeleton. *Nature, Lond,* **192**, 312.

Gentry, A. W. (1966). Fossil Antilopini of East Africa. *Bull. Br. Mus. Nat. Hist.* **12**, no. 2.

Gentry, A. W. (1967). *Pelorovis oldowayensis* Reck, an extinct bovid from East Africa. *Bull. Br. Mus. Nat. Hist.* **14**, no. 7.

Gieseler, W. and Mollison, Th. (1929). Untersuchungen über den Oldoway Fund. *Verh. Ges. phys. Anthrop.* **3**.

Grommé, C. S. and Hay, R. L. (1971). Geomagnetic polarity epochs: age and duration of the Olduvai normal polarity event. In *Earth and Planetary Science Letters*, **10**, 179–85.

Hay, R. L. (1963 *a*). Stratigraphy of Bed I through IV, Olduvai Gorge, Tanganyika. *Science, N.Y.* **139**, 829–33.

Hay, R. L. (1963 *b*). Zeolitic weathering in Olduvai Gorge, Tanganyika. *Bull. Geol. Soc. Am.* **74**, 1281–6.

Hay, R. L. (1965). Comments on paper by Evernden and Curtis. *Current Anthropology* **6**, 367, 381–3.

Hay, R. L. (1966). Zeolites and zeolitic reactions in sedimentary rocks. *Special paper, Geol. Soc. Am.* **85**, 130.

Hay, R. L. (1967). Revised stratigraphy of Olduvai Gorge. In *Background to Evolution in Africa* (ed. W. W. Bishop and J. D. Clark), pp. 221–8. Chicago University Press.

Hay, R. L. (1968). Chert and its sodium-silicate precursors in sodium-carbonate lakes in East Africa. *Contr. Mineral. Petrol.* **17**, 255–74.

Heberer, G. (1963). Über einen neuen Archanthropinen Typus aus der Oldoway-Schlucht. *Z. Morph. Anthr.* **53**, 171–7.

Holloway, R. L., Jun. (1965). Cranial capacity of the hominine from Olduvai Bed I. *Nature, Lond.* **208**, 205–6.

Holloway, R. L., Jun. (1966). Cranial capacity of the Olduvai Bed I hominine. *Nature, Lond.* **210**, 1108–9.

Howell, F. Clark (1965). *Early Man.* New York: Time–Life International (Nederland) N.V.

Howell, F. C. (1968). Omo Research Expedition. *Nature, Lond.* **219**, 567–72.

Howell, F. C. and Clark, J. D. (1963). Acheulean hunter-gatherers of sub-Saharan Africa. In *African Ecology and Human Evolution* (ed. F. Clark Howell and F. Bourlière), pp. 458–533. Viking Fund Pub. 36. Chicago: Aldine Publishing Co.

Howell, F. Clark, Cole, Glen H. and Kleindienst, M. R. (1962). Isimila, an Acheulean occupation site in the Iringa Highlands, Southern Province, Tanganyika. In *Actes du IVe Congrès Panafricain de Préhistoire et de l'Etude du Quaternaire* (ed. G. Mortelmans and J. Nenquin), vol. III, pp. 43–80. Tervuren.

Isaac, G. Ll. (1965). The stratigraphy of the Peninj beds and the provenance of the Natron australopithecine mandible. *Quaternaria* **7**, 101–30.

Isaac, G. Ll. (1966). New evidence from Olorgesailie relating to the character of Acheulean occupation sites. In *Actes del V Congreso Panafricano de Prehistoria y de estudio del Cuaternario* (ed. L. D. Cuscoy), vol. 6, II, pp. 135–45. Pub. Mus. Arg. Santa Cruz de Tenerife.

Isaac, G. Ll. (1967). The stratigraphy of the Peninj group—early Middle Pleistocene formations west of Lake Natron, Tanzania. In *Background to Evolution in Africa* (ed. W. W. Bishop and J. D. Clark), pp. 229–57. Chicago University Press.

Keith, Sir A. (1925). *The Antiquity of Man.* London: Williams and Norgate.

Kleindienst, M. R. (1962). Components of the East African Acheulean assemblage: an analytical approach. In *Actes du IVe Congrès Panafricain de Préhistoire et de l'Etude du Quaternaire* (ed. G. Mortelmans and J. Nenquin) vol. III, p. 81–111. Tervuren.

Kleindienst, M. R. (1967). Questions of terminology in regard to the study of Stone Age industries in eastern Africa: 'Cultural Stratigraphic Units'. In *Background to Evolution in Africa* (ed. W. W. Bishop and J. D. Clark), pp. 821–59. Chicago University Press.

Koenigswald, G. H. R. von (1960). Remarks on a fossil human molar from Olduvai, East Africa. *Proc. K. Ned. Akad. Wet.* series B, no. 1, pp. 20–5.

Koenigswald, G. H. R. von, Gentner, W. and Lippolt, H. J. (1961). Age of basalt flow at Olduvai, East Africa. *Nature, Lond.* **192**, 720–1.

Kurth, G. (1960). *Zinjanthropus boisei* aus dem Unterpleistozan von Oldoway, Ostafrika. *Sond. der Naturwiss.* **12**, 265–74.

Kurth, G. (1965). Die (En) Homininen. *Menschliche Abstammungslehre*, pp. 357–425. Stuttgart: Gustav Fischer Verlag.

Leakey, L. S. B. (1928). The Oldoway skull. *Nature, Lond.* **121**, 499.

Leakey, L. S. B. (1931). *The Stone Age Cultures of Kenya Colony.* Cambridge University Press.

Leakey, L. S. B. (1935). *The Stone Age Races of Kenya.* Oxford University Press.

Leakey, L. S. B. (1951). *Olduvai Gorge.* Cambridge University Press.

Leakey, L. S. B. (1957). Preliminary report on a Chellean 1 living site at BK II, Olduvai. In *Proc. 3rd Pan-African Congress on Prehistory* (ed. J. D. Clark and S. Cole), pp. 217–18. London: Chatto and Windus.

296

Leakey, L. S. B. (1958a). A giant child among the giant animals at Olduvai? *Illust. Lond. News*, pp. 1103–6.

Leakey, L. S. B. (1958b). Recent discoveries at Olduvai Gorge, Tanganyika. *Nature, Lond.* **181**, 1099–103.

Leakey, L. S. B. (1958c). Some East African Pleistocene Suidae. *Fossil Mammals of Africa*, no. 14. London: Mus. Nat. Hist.

Leakey, L. S. B. (1959). A new fossil skull from Olduvai. *Nature, Lond.* **184**, 491–3.

Leakey, L. S. B. (1960a). An alternative interpretation of the supposed giant deciduous hominid tooth from Olduvai. *Nature, Lond.* **185**, 408.

Leakey, L. S. B. (1960b). The discovery of *Zinjanthropus boisei. Current Anthropology* **1**, 76–7.

Leakey, L. S. B. (1960c). The affinities of the new Olduvai australopithecine. (Reply to J. T. Robinson.) *Nature, Lond.* **186**, 458.

Leakey, L. S. B. (1960d). Recent discoveries at Olduvai Gorge. *Nature, Lond.* **188**, 1050–2.

Leakey, L. S. B. (1961a). New finds at Olduvai Gorge. *Nature, Lond.* **189**, 649–50.

Leakey, L. S. B. (1961b). The juvenile mandible from Olduvai. *Nature, Lond.* **191**, 417–18.

Leakey, L. S. B. (1961c). *Progress and Evolution of Man in Africa*. London: Oxford University Press.

Leakey, L. S. B. (1962). The Olduvai discoveries. *Antiquity* **36**, 119.

Leakey, L. S. B. (1963). East African fossil Hominoidea and the classification within this super-family. In *Classification and Human Evolution* (ed. S. L. Washburn), pp. 32–49. Viking Fund Pub. 37. Chicago: Aldine Publ. Co.

Leakey, L. S. B. (1964). The evolution of man. *Discovery* **25**, 8, 48–50.

Leakey, L. S. B. (1965a). *Olduvai Gorge* 1951–1961. Vol. 1. *Fauna and Background*. Cambridge University Press.

Leakey, L. S. B. (1965b). Facts instead of dogmas on man's origins. In *The Origin of Man* (ed. P. De Vore), pp. 3–19. Chicago.

Leakey, L. S. B. (1966). *Homo habilis, Homo erectus* and the australopithecines. *Nature, Lond.* **209**, 1279–81.

Leakey, L. S. B., Curtis, G. H., Evernden, J. F. and Koenigswald, G. H. R. von (1962). Age of basalt underlying Bed I, Olduvai. *Nature, Lond.* **194**, 610–12.

Leakey, L. S. B., Evernden, J. F. and Curtis, G. H. (1961). Age of Bed I, Olduvai. *Nature, Lond.* **191**, 478–9.

Leakey, L. S. B., Hopwood, A. T. and Reck, H. (1931). Age of the Oldoway bone beds, Tanganyika. *Nature, Lond.* **128**, 724.

Leakey, L. S. B. and Leakey, M. D. (1964). Recent discoveries of fossil hominids in Tanganyika: at Olduvai and near Lake Natron. *Nature, Lond.* **202**, 5–7.

Leakey, L. S. B., Protsch, R. and Berger, R. (1968). Age of Bed V, Olduvai Gorge, Tanzania. *Science, N.Y.* **162**, 559–60.

Leakey, L. S. B., Reck, H., Boswell, P. G. H. and Hopwood, A. T. (1933). The Oldoway human skeleton. *Nature, Lond.* **131**, 397.

Leakey, L. S. B., Tobias, P. V. and Napier, J. R. (1964). A new species of the genus *Homo* from Olduvai Gorge, *Nature, Lond.* **202**, 7–9.

Leakey, M. D. (1965). Descriptive list of the named localities in Olduvai Gorge. Appendix 2 in *Olduvai Gorge* 1951–1961, vol. 1, by L. S. B. Leakey. Cambridge University Press.

Leakey, M. D. (1966a). A review of the Oldowan culture from Olduvai Gorge, Tanzania. *Nature, Lond.* **210**, 462–6.

Leakey, M. D. (1966b). Primitive artefacts from the Kanapoi Valley. *Nature, Lond.* **212**, 579–81.

Leakey, M. D. (1967). Preliminary survey of the cultural material from Beds I and II, Olduvai Gorge, Tanzania. In *Background to Evolution in Africa* (ed. W. W. Bishop and J. D. Clark), pp. 417–446. Chicago University Press.

Leakey, M. D. (1970). Stone artefacts from Swartkrans. *Nature, Lond.* **225**, 1222–25.

Leakey, M. D. (1970a). Early artefacts from the Koobi Fora Area. *Nature, Lond.* **226**, 228–30.

MacCalman, H. R. and Grobbelaar, B. J. (1965). Preliminary report of two stone-working Ova Tjimba groups in the northern Kaokoveld of S. W. Africa. *Cimbebasia*, **13**.

Mason, R. J. (1962a). Australopithecines and artefacts at Sterkfontein, Part II. *S. Afr. Arch. Bull.* **17**, no. 66, 109–25.

Mason, R. J. (1962b). *The Prehistory of the Transvaal*. Johannesburg: Witwatersrand University Press.

Napier, J. R. (1962a). Fossil hand bones from Olduvai Gorge. *Nature, Lond.* **196**, 409–11.

Napier, J. R. (1962b). The evolution of the hand. *Scient. Am.* **207**, 56–62.

Napier, J. R. (1963). The locomotor functions of hominids. In *Classification and Human Evolution* (ed. S. L. Washburn), pp. 183–4. Viking Fund Pub. 37. Chicago: Aldine Publ. Co.

Napier, J. R. (1964a). Profile of early man at Olduvai. *New Scient.* **386**, 86–9.

Napier, J. R. (1964b). Five steps to Man. *Discovery* **25**, (6), 34–6.

Napier, J. R. and Weiner, J. R. (1961). Olduvai Gorge and human origins. *Antiquity* **36**, 41–7.

Neuville, R. and Ruhlmann, A. (1941). *La Place du paléolithique ancien dans le Quaternaire marocain*. Inst. des Hautes-Etudes marocaines, vol. VIII. Casablanca.

Oakley, K. P. (1964a). The evolution of man. *Discovery* **25**, 8, 49.

Oakley, K. P. (1964b). *Frameworks for Dating Fossil Man*. London: Weidenfeld and Nicholson.

Oakley, K. P. (1968). The earliest tool-makers. *Sond. aus Evolution und Hominisation*. Stuttgart: Gustav Fischer Verlag.

Oakley, K. P. and Campbell, B. G. (1964). Newly described Olduvai hominid. *Nature, Lond.* **202**, 732.

Oakley, K. P. and Campbell, B. G. (1967). *Catalogue of Fossil Hominids. Part I. Africa*. London: Br. Mus. Nat. Hist.

Pickering, R. (1958). Oldoinyo Ogol, Serengeti Plain, East. *Geol. Surv. Tanganyika*. Quarter degree sheet, 12 S.W.

Pickering, R. (1960a). Moru, Serengeti Plain, West. *Geol. Surv. Tanganyika*. Quarter degree sheet, 37.

Pickering, R. (1960*b*). A preliminary note on the Quaternary geology of Tanganyika. *Proc. C.C.T.A. Joint Ctee. Geol., Leopoldville*, 1958.

Pickering, R. (1964). Endulen. *Geol. Surv. Tanzania.* Quarter degree sheet, 52.

Pickering, R. (in the Press). *A Contribution to the Geology of the Olduvai Gorge.* Report RP/23. Geological Survey of Tanzania.

Reck, H. (1914*a*). Erste vorläufige Mitteilung über den Fund eines fossilen Menschenskelets aus Zentralafrika. *Sond. aus den Sitzungsberichten der Gesellschaft naturforschender Freunde*, no. 3. Berlin.

Reck, H. (1914*b*). Zweite vorläufige Mitteilung über fossile Tier- und Menschenfunde aus Oldoway in Zentralafrika. *Sond. aus den Sitzungsberichten der Gesellschaft naturforschender Freunde*, no. 7. Berlin.

Reck, H. (1951). A preliminary survey of the tectonics and stratigraphy of Olduvai. In *Olduvai Gorge* (by L. S. B. Leakey), pp. 5–19. Cambridge University Press.

Robinson, J. T. (1960*a*). An alternative interpretation of the supposed giant deciduous hominid tooth from Olduvai. *Nature, Lond.* **185**, 407–8.

Robinson, J. T. (1960*b*). The affinities of the new Olduvai australopithecine. *Nature, Lond.* **186**, 456.

Robinson, J. T. (1962). Australopithecines and artefacts at Sterkfontein. *S. Afr. Arch. Bull.* **17**, 87–107.

Robinson, J. T. (1963). Adaptive radiation in the australopithecines and the origin of Man. In *African Ecology and Human Evolution* (ed. F. Clark Howell and F. Bourliere), pp. 397–405. Viking Fund Pub. 36. Chicago: Aldine Publ. Co.

Robinson, J. T. (1965). *Homo habilis* and the australopithecines. *Nature, Lond.* **205**, 121–4.

Robinson, J. T. (1966). Comment on: The distinctiveness of *Homo habilis* (by P. V. Tobias). *Nature, Lond.* **209**, 957–60.

Robinson, J. T. and Mason, R. J. (1957). Occurrence of stone artefacts with *Australopithecus* at Sterkfontein. *Nature, Lond.* **180**, 521–4.

Savage, D.E. and Curtis, G. H. (1970). The Villafranchian stage-age and its radiometric dating. In *Geological Society of America Special Paper* 124 (ed. Orville Bandy).

Silberbauer, G. B. (1965). *Bushman Survey.* Mafeking: Bechuanaland Press.

Simons, J. W., *et al.* (1966). The presence of leopard and a study of the food debris in the leopard lairs of the Mount Suswa caves, Kenya. *Bull. Cave Explor. Group of E. Africa*, vol. I.

Stekelis, M. (1966). *Archaeological Excavations at Ubeidiya*, 1960–1963. Jerusalem: The Israel Academy of Sciences and Humanities.

Tobias, P. V. (1963). Cranial capacity of *Zinjanthropus* and other australopithecines. *Nature, Lond.* **197**, 743–6.

Tobias, P. V. (1964*a*). The Olduvai Bed I hominine with special reference to its cranial capacity. *Nature, Lond.* **202**, 3–4.

Tobias, P. V. (1964*b*). The evolution of man. *Discovery* **25**, 49–50.

Tobias, P. V. (1965*a*). Early man in East Africa. *Science, N.Y.* **149**, 22–3.

Tobias, P. V. (1965*b*). *Australopithecus, Homo habilis,* tool-using and tool-making. *S. Afr. Arch. Bull.* **20**, 167–92.

Tobias, P. V. (1965*c*). *Homo habilis*, pp. 252–5. Britannica Book of the Year.

Tobias, P. V. (1965*d*). New discoveries in Tanganyika, their bearing on hominid evolution. *Current Anthropology* **6**, 391–9, 406–11.

Tobias, P. V. (1965*e*). Comment on: Cranial capacity of the hominine from Olduvai Bed I (by R. L. Holloway). *Nature, Lond.* **208**, 206.

Tobias, P. V. (1965*f*). *Homo habilis:* last missing link in hominine phylogeny? In *Homenaje a Juan Comas en su 65 aniversario* (ed. S. Genoves), vol. II, pp. 377–90. Mexico City.

Tobias, P. V. (1966*a*). The distinctiveness of *Homo habilis. Nature, Lond.* **209**, 953–7.

Tobias, P. V. (1966*b*). Cranial capacity of the Olduvai Bed I hominine (reply to R. L. Holloway). *Nature, Lond.* **210**, 1109–10.

Tobias, P. V. (1967*a*). *Olduvai Gorge.* Vol. 2. *The Cranium of* Australopithecus (Zinjanthropus) boisei. Cambridge University Press.

Tobias, P. V. (1967*b*). Cultural hominization among the earliest African Pleistocene hominids. *Proc. Prehist. Soc.* **33**, 367–76.

Tobias, P. V. and Koenigswald, G. H. R. von (1964). A comparison between the Olduvai hominines and those of Java and some implications for hominid phylogeny. *Nature, Lond.* **204**, 515–18.

Vaufrey, R. (1933). Nouvelles précisions sur l'âge de l'homme d'Oldoway. *L'Anthropologie* **43**, 431.

Verdcourt, B. (1963). The Miocene non-marine mollusca of Rusinga Island, Lake Victoria, and other localities in Kenya. *Sond. Palaeontographica* **121**, Stuttgart.

PLATES

1. **DK**. Tuff I[B] (above the ranging pole) and the deposits beneath. One of the narrow channels cutting into the tuff below the occupation surface can also be seen.

2. **DK.** The circle of lava blocks. The ranging poles mark the limit of the Trial Trench which destroyed part of the circle.

3. A rough shelter of branches and grass with stones supporting the bases of the branches, made by the Okombambi people of South West Africa, for comparison with the stone circle at DK. (Photograph reproduced by kind permission of MacCalman and Grobbelaar.)

4. DK. Polyhedrons made from lava.

5. FLK NN. General view of the site from the north-west, during the early part of the excavations.

6. FLK NN. Section through the deposits exposed in the south-west face of Trench VI. The occupation Levels 1 and 3 can be seen, with the tuff of Level 2 intervening. The deposit of fawn-coloured tuff is on the left, unconformable to the tuffs and clays of Bed I. It includes a channel with gravel in the base of the filling.

7. **FLK.** Excavations in progress during 1960. The concrete plinth in the foreground marks the position of the '*Zinjan-thropus*' cranium and the two ranging poles the positions of the hominid tibia and fibula.

8. FLK. Part of the occupation floor at the '*Zinjanthropus*' level, showing bone splinters, flakes and horn cores of *Parmularius altidens*.

9. FLK. Close-up view of bone fragments and flakes on part of the occupation floor.

10. FLK. The mandible of an equid lying on the occupation floor, showing the damage to the lower margin.

11. **FLK North.** General view of the excavation during 1960, seen from the north-west. The Marker Tuff I^F at the top of Bed I can be seen above the stacked sand bags. The level in Bed II which yielded the skeleton of a *Deinotherium* lies just below the line of white limestone.

Rootlet
clay

Grey
tuff

Marker
tuff I^F

Levels
1

2

3

4

5

12. **FLK North.** Section exposed in the south-east face of the excavation, showing the five occupation levels, the marker Tuff I^F, the coarse-grained grey tuff and the rootlet clay in lower Bed II.

13. FLK North. The elephant skeleton in Level 6. The mandible and a tooth can be seen on the right.

14. FLK North. Broken bones, artefacts and manuports on the occupation floor of Level 1.

15. FLK North. A group of mammalian bones on the occupation floor of Level 1. One equid and two bovid metapodials, the distal end of a humerus, a radius and an ulna can be distinguished.

16. FLK North. Spheroids and subspheroids made from lava.

cm.   in.

10 — 4

— 3

5 — 2

— 1

0 — 0

17. FLK North. Two pitted anvils. The top specimen is from the chert-bearing Sandy
Conglomerate in the lower part of Bed II, and the second is from Level 1 in Bed I.

0   5 cm.

0   1   2 in.

18. FLK North. A grooved and pecked stone. The row of pecked marks can be seen on the left,
near the bottom of the stone.

19. HWK East, Level 3. Spheroids and subspheroids. With the exception of two lava specimens, shown at either end of the top row, all are of quartz or quartzite.

cm.   in.

10 ⊢ 4

3

5 ⊢ 2

1

0 ⊢ 0

20. MNK, Main Occupation Level. A large lava biface measuring 297 mm. in length and weighing 6½ lb.

```
0                    5              10 cm.
├──┼──┼──┼──┼──┼──┼──┼──┼──┤
0·         1         2         3       4 in.
```

21. MNK, Main Occupation Level. A large quartzite subspheroid weighing $14\frac{1}{2}$ lb.

22. TK. The channel adjacent to the Lower Occupation Floor after the removal of the silty filling. Broken mammalian bones and artefacts can be seen on the bottom of the channel. A bovid cannon bone is lying against the side.

23. BK. Part of the clay-filled channel which yielded many remains of large mammals, including *Pelorovis oldowayensis*.

24. BK. Spheroids.

0   5   10   15 cm.

0   1   2   3   4   5   6 in.

25. BK. Subspheroids.

26. MK. Dr Matthew Stirling of the National Geographic Society points to the level beneath Tuff I^B where the teeth of H.4 were found.

27. FLK. July 1959. The writer indicating the position of the skull of H. 5, *Australopithecus* (*Zinjanthropus*) *boisei*, before removal. (Photograph by Des Bartlett.)

28. FLK. Top: the hominid fibula *in situ*. Below: removing the matrix from the palate of '*Zinjanthropus*'. The left temporal can be seen below and to the right of the teeth. (Lower photograph by Des Bartlett.)

29. FLK NN. The mandible of H. 7 *in situ*, lying teeth downwards. Note the damage on the lower margin.

30. FLK NN. The left parietal of H. 7 lying *in situ* at the base of a 6 in. ruler. The hard white tuff of Level 2 can be seen above the parietal, overlain by the clay of Level 1.

34. FLK NN. The utilised equid rib from Level 3.

33. FLK Maiko Gully. M. Mutumbo is standing at the site where he found the broken skull of H. 16. Tuff I^F can be seen on the left, horizontally bedded. The clay from which the skull had eroded is behind M. Mutumbo, approximately at knee height.

32. MNK Skull Site. The site where H. 13, 14 and 15 were found, shortly after the discovery.

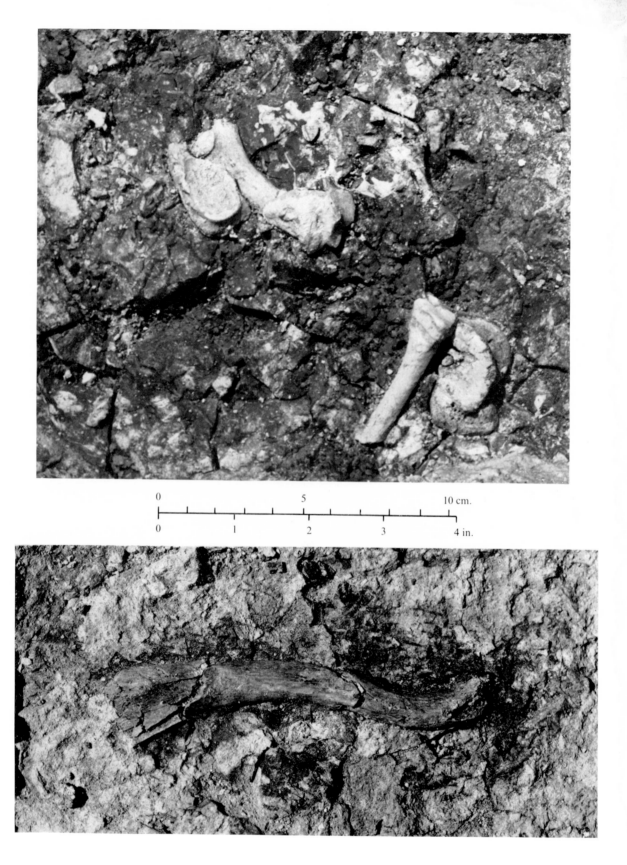

31. FLK NN. The foot bones of H. 8 *in situ*. Two metatarsals can be seen, together with the astragalus (bottom right) and navicular (top left) lying next to one of the metatarsals. Below: The clavicle of H. 8 *in situ*.

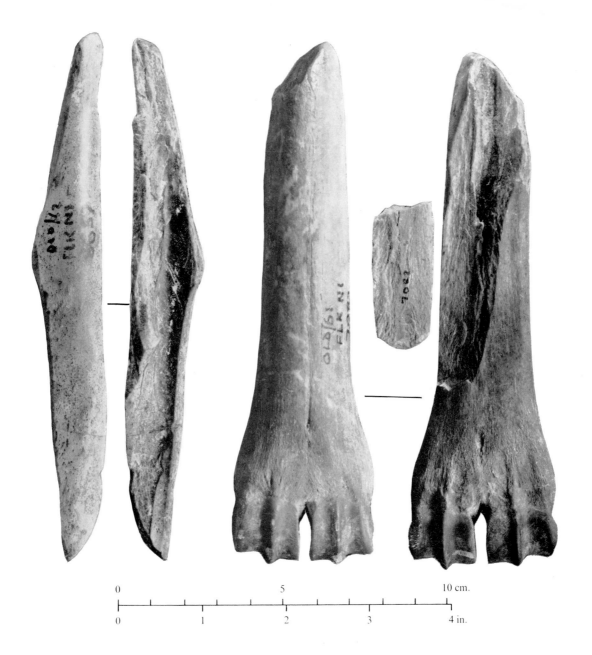

0   5   10 cm.

0   1   2   3   4 in.

35. FLK North. Two utilised bones. The abrasion at the tips can be seen most clearly on the inner aspects of the bones. The fragment fitting on to the shaft of the cannon bone on the right is also shown.

36. Parts of long bones with flaking and chipping at the ends of the broken shafts. From sites in Middle and Upper Bed II (Photograph by R. I. M. Campbell.)

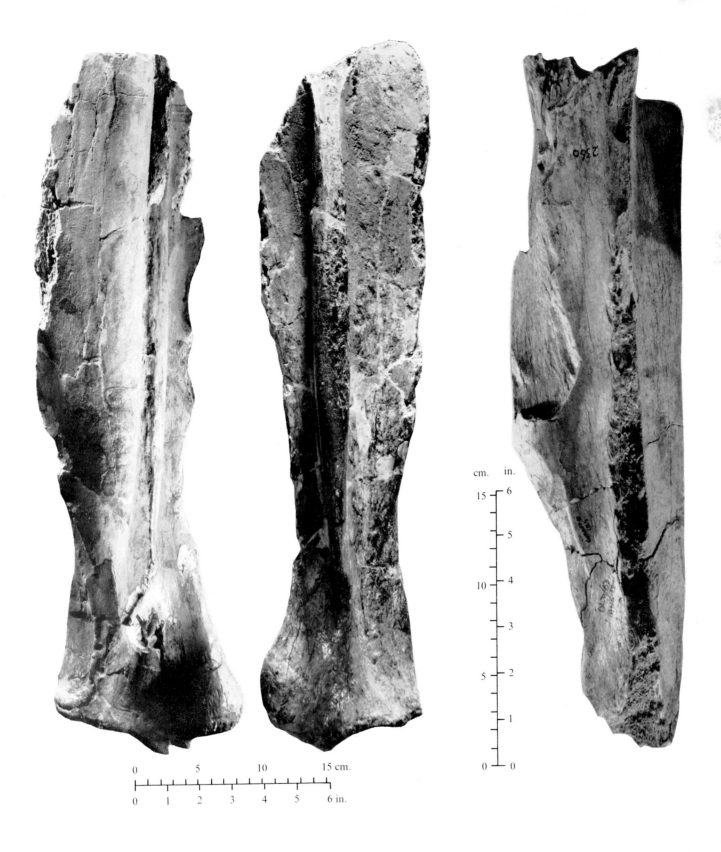

cm.   in.

15 — — 6

     — — 5

10 — — 4

     — — 3

 5 — — 2

     — — 1

 0 — — 0

0   5   10   15 cm.

0   1   2   3   4   5   6 in.

37. Giraffid scapulae damaged by use. Note the flaking on the right-hand specimen. The two specimens on the left are from SHK and that on the right from the Main Site at MNK. (Photograph by R. I. M. Campbell.)

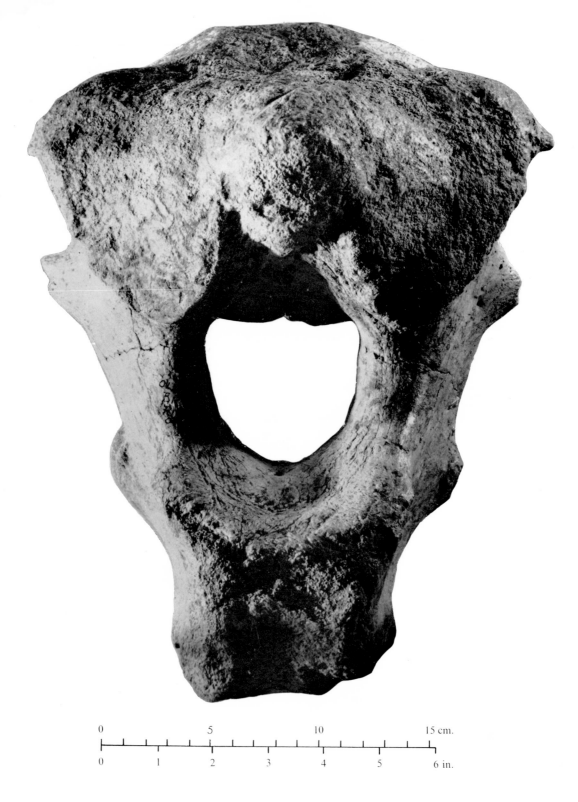

0   5   10   15 cm.

0   1   2   3   4   5   6 in.

38. BK. An elephant axis in which the surface has been extensively damaged, possibly as a result of use as an anvil. (Photograph by R. I. M. Campbell.)

```
0                    5                    10 cm.

0          1          2          3          4 in.
```

39. **SHK**. Utilised flake of hippopotamus ivory. Note the striking platforms and bulb of percussion seen in left-hand view.

40. Two hippopotamus incisors damaged by use at the tips and an artefact resembling a biface made from a fragment of a very massive bone. The incisors are from the Main Site at MNK and the specimen on the right is from FC. (Photograph by R. I. M. Campbell.)

41. FLK North. Two frontlets with horn cores of the antelope *Parmularius altidens*, showing depressed fractures over the right orbits. In the second specimen the right horn core has also been broken off.

INDEX

Acanthopterygii, 290

Acheulean industry, 2, 262; sites of, 3, 259, 282–9; at EF–HR, 124, 264, 265, 266, 268; intrusive to Olduvai area, 269; bifaces of, compared with Developed Oldowan, 270, 271, 272; artefacts of, at sites other than Olduvai Gorge, 274–5

Acinonyx, 292

Aeolian Tuff Member, of Bed II, *see* tuffs, II A

Aepyceros sp., 294

Afrochoerus, modified teeth of, 240–1

A. nicoli, 288, 293

Agamidae, 291

Alcelaphus howardi, 288

Ambrona, Spain, Acheulean butchering site at, 275

amphibian remains, 290; FLK NN, 42, 43, 250; FLK, 251; FLK N, 253; HWK East, 254; MNK, 254, 255

Ancylotherium hennigi, 21, 287, 293

angles of striking platforms on *débitage* flakes, 268; FLK, 58, 66, 68, 72, 83; HWK East, 106, 108; EF–HR, 136; MNK, 155; FC West, 161, 165; SHK, 171; TK, 174, 183, 196; BK, 221

Anisus, 290

antelope remains: FLK NN, 42, 43; FLK, 50, 60; FLK N, 71; SHK, 165, 166

Antilopini, 294

Anura, 290

anvils, 7, Pl. 17; DK, 37; FLK, 53, 58, 59; FLK N, 64, 66, 68, 72, 81, 84, 86, 99, 114; HWK East, 104, 107, 109, 110; MNK, 121, 122, 150, 154, 155; FC West, 160, 163, 164; SHK, 166, 170; TK, 172, 181, 183, 184, 194, 196, 197; BK, 218, 222

Arambourg, Prof. C., 49

artefacts, 16–17; water-rolled, 87, 96, 110, 126; percentage of, in finds at different sites, 261

Artiodactyla, 293–4

australopithecine caves, Transvaal, 273, 274, 280

Australopithecus africanus, 280, 281

A. boisei, 280; *see also* '*Zinjanthropus*'

A. robustus, 280, 281

awls, 7; percentage of, at different sites, 264, 267; HWK East, 95, 102, 107, 109, 111; FLK N, 112, 113, 114; MNK, 150, 154, 155; FC West, 160, 164; SHK, 167, 170, 171; TK, 173, 174, 181, 183, 184, 193–4, 195, 196, 197; BK, 199, 214, 217, 222

baboons, bones of, in leopard lairs, 276 n

Balbal Depression, 10

balls, stone, 9, 110

Bartlett, Des, xix, 48, 227

basalt: flows, 10; Member of Bed I, 10, 15; tools of, 17; nodules and blocks of, 37, 47, 51, 83; hummocks, 21, 86; age of, 258

basement rock, tools of, 17, 18

Bathyergidae, 292

bats, remains of, 250, 251, 252–3, 291

Beatragus antiquus, 284, 294

Bedacryl, 43, 85

Bell, G. T., 197

Biberson, P., 273, 275

bifaces, 2, 5, 265, 269–70, 272, Pl. 20; term replaces 'hand axes', 3, 172; of elephant bone, 245, 275; none from Bed I, 262; comparison of Acheulean and Developed Oldowan, 270, 271, 272; EF–HR, 124, 125–32, 133, 135, 137; MNK, 139, 150–1, 155; FC West, 157, 159, 161–2, 164; FC, 165; SHK, 167, 168, 169, 171; TK, 172, 174–5, 178, 179, 180, 184, 187–9, 190, 196, 197; BK, 204, 205, 207, 208, 209, 222; at sites other than Olduvai Gorge, 273–5

bird remains: FLK NN, 39, 40, 42, 43, 250, 251; FLK, 58, 251; FLK N, 67, 253; HWK East, 88, 254; MNK, 118, 254, 255; DK, 249; FC West, 255

Bitis, 291

BK (Bell's Korongo) site, 1, 3, 197–222, 259; map, 198; sections, 200–1; Pls. 23, 24; hominid remains at (H. 3), 3, 226, 234, 280; modified bones at, 198, 242, 244, 245, 246, 247; faunal remains at, 255–6; density of finds at, 260; percentages of different finds at, 261; tools at, (materials) 264, (types) 265, 266, 267, 268; Developed Oldowan bifaces at, 270, 271, 272

Blanchard, G., xix

blocks, *see* nodules and blocks

Boidae, 291

bones: tooth-marks of scavenging animals on, 43, 50, 246, 277–8; in concretionary nodules, 61, 67, 259; altered by stomach acids, 61, 68–9; fragments of, 118; modified mammalian, 235–47, 275; splinters of, standing vertically, 137–8; *see also under groups of animals*

bovid remains, 248, 257, 293–4, Pls. 15, 22; modified bones, 235–6, 237, 238, 239, 240, 246; comparison of, from Olduvai, Makapansgat, and goats from Hottentot middens, 277, 278, 279; FLK NN, 39, 40, 250, 251; FLK, 50, 58, 60, 251, 252; FC West, 156, 255; DK, 249; FLK N, 251, 252, 253, 254; HWK East, 254; MNK, 254; EF–HR, 255; BK, 255, 256

Bovini, 294

Brain, Dr C. K., 235, 273, 275, 276

Breuil, Abbé, 262, 275

British Museum of Natural History, London, 165, 197, 233

Brock, Dr A., 15

buffalo skull, 284

Bufo, 290

Bufonidae, 290

Bularchus arok (sexual variation of *Pelorovis*), 255

Bulinus, 253, 290

Burg Wartenstein Symposium, 3

burins, 1, 7; percentage of, at different sites, 265, 267; DK, 23, 34, 36, 48; FLK, 48, 53, 58; HWK East, 92, 93; MNK, 123, 150; FC West, 160, 163, 164; SHK, 167, 170, 171; TK, 174, 181, 182, 183, 184, 193, 196, 197; BK, 214, 216, 222

Bushman sites, 259

butchering sites, 258; FLK N, 61, 64, 258, 285; Ambrona, 275

butt-end scrapers, 102, 103, 111

Calcrete, 10

Campbell, R. I. M., xix

Canidae, 292

Capsian: artefacts (Upper Kenya), 10; living site, near RK, 225, 284; skulls (Kenya), 225

carbon-14 dating, 10

carnivore remains, 257, 292; DK, 249; FLK NN, 250, 251; FLK N, 252–3; MNK, 254; EF–HR, 255

carnivores: bones regurgitated by, 61, 69 n; dung of, 67, 68

cat, sabre-toothed, 228

cat-fish remains, 43, 172

Centre for Prehistory and Palaeontology, Nairobi, 233, 256

Ceratotherium simum, 256, 282, 293

Cercopithecidae, 292

Cercocebus, 292

Chalicotheriidae, 292

chameleon remains, 67, 250, 251

Chamaeleontidae, 291

channels: at DK, 23; FLK NN, 40; FLK, 49; HWK E, 89, 90; EF–HR, 124, 125; SHK, 166, 259; TK, 173–4, 176, 258–9; BK, 199, 259

Chavaillon, J., 274

Chelles–Acheul industry, 262, 269

Chellean industry, 150, 157, 199, 226

Chelonia, 251, 252–3, 255, 257, 290